ANDREW CARNEGIE

ANDREW CARNEGIE

DAVID NASAW

THE PENGUIN PRESS

NEW YORK

2006

THE PENGUIN PRESS
Published by the Penguin Group
Penguin Group (USA) Inc., 375 Hudson Street, New York, New York 10014, U.S.A. · Penguin Group
(Canada), 90 Eglinton Avenue East, Suite 700, Toronto, Ontario, Canada M4P 2Y3 (a division of
Pearson Penguin Canada Inc.) · Penguin Books Ltd, 80 Strand, London WC2R oRL, England ·
Penguin Ireland, 25 St. Stephen's Green, Dublin 2, Ireland (a division of Penguin Books Ltd) ·
Penguin Books Australia Ltd, 250 Camberwell Road, Camberwell, Victoria 3124, Australia (a division of
Pearson Australia Group Pty Ltd) · Penguin Books India Pvt Ltd, 11 Community Centre, Panchsheel
Park, New Delhi–110 017, India · Penguin Group (NZ), Cnr Airborne and Rosedale Roads, Albany,
Auckland 1310, New Zealand (a division of Pearson New Zealand Ltd) · Penguin Books (South
Africa) (Pty) Ltd, 24 Sturdee Avenue, Rosebank, Johannesburg 2196, South Africa

Penguin Books Ltd, Registered Offices:
80 Strand, London WC2R oRL

First published in 2006 by The Penguin Press,
a member of Penguin Group (USA) Inc.

Copyright © David Nasaw, 2006
All rights reserved

Library of Congress Cataloging in Publication Data

Nasaw, David.
Andrew Carnegie / David Nasaw.
p.   cm.
Includes bibliographical references and index.
ISBN 1-59420-104-8
1. Carnegie, Andrew, 1835–1919.   2. Industrialists—United States—Biography.
3. Philanthropists—United States—Biography.   I. Title.
CT275.C3N37 2006   2006044840

Printed in the United States of America
1   3   5   7   9   10   8   6   4   2

Designed by Marysarah Quinn

CONTENTS

INTRODUCTION

W E THOUGHT WE KNEW HIM, but we didn't. And that was how he wished it.

He wore high-heeled boots and a top hat to disguise his lack of size. And he talked and wrote volumes in an effort to construct a life that stood taller than his own.

His biographers have taken as their framework the account he provided in his memoirs. But the *Autobiography of Andrew Carnegie*, written and rewritten over decades, then rearranged and rewritten again by an editor chosen by his wife, Louise, offers only a partial account of selected incidents. There are errors of omission, errors of chronology, and attempts, by author or editor, to mislead. My account of Carnegie's life leaves out several of the familiar stories told in the *Autobiography* and retold by his biographers, because I could not independently confirm their validity.

Carnegie's first biographer, Burton J. Hendrick, was specially chosen by Louise Carnegie to write her husband's life. Hendrick was paid as a Carnegie employee; he received no royalties for his work and agreed that should his biography not be to Mrs. Carnegie's liking, it would not be published. Carnegie's next major biographer, Joseph Wall, added an enormous amount to the story of Carnegie's success as a steelmaker, but he lacked the sources to veer off the path set by the *Autobiography* and by Hendrick.

In the half century since Wall began his research, new archival sources have been opened and electronic finding aids have made it possible to locate previously unavailable ones. The raw material out of which this biography is fashioned was discovered in public and university archives, government documents, and privately held family papers in England, Scotland, Wales, and the United States. It includes material on the Carnegie family's arrival in Dunfermline, unpublished oral histories taken in Scotland by Burton Hendrick, the first drafts of Carnegie's memoirs, his

Civil War tax returns, unpublished manuscripts and travel diaries, his multi-year correspondence with his future wife and their prenuptial agreement, and letters and telegrams not previously available to and from every American president from Benjamin Harrison to Woodrow Wilson, Kaiser Wilhelm II, William Ewart Gladstone and several other British prime ministers, Herbert Spencer, Matthew Arnold, Samuel Clemens, two generations of Morgans and Rockefellers, and Henry Clay Frick.

Andrew Carnegie was a critical agent in the triumph of industrial capitalism in the decades surrounding the turn of the twentieth century. That much is undeniable. But the source materials I have uncovered do not support the telling of a heroic narrative of an industrialist who brought sanity and rationality to an immature capitalism plagued by runaway competition, ruthless speculation, and insider corruption. Nor do they support the recitation of another muckraking exposé of Gilded Age criminality. The history of industrial consolidation and incorporation is too complex to be encapsulated in Whiggish narratives of progress or post-Edenic tales of declension, decline, and fall.

Carnegie survived and triumphed in an environment rife with cronyism and corruption. Much of the capital invested in his iron and steel companies was derived from business activities that might be today, but were not at the time, regarded as immoral or illegal. He differed from his contemporary Gilded Age industrial barons not in the means with which he accumulated his fortune, but in the success he achieved and the ends to which he put it. Long before his reputation as a friend of the workingman was destroyed by events at Homestead, he had determined to give away his fortune. He did so not out of shame or guilt or religious motives nor to atone for any sins he might have committed as an employer of men. He was simply, he explained, returning his fortune to the larger community where it rightfully belonged. He urged his fellow millionaires to do the same.

Andrew Carnegie's decision to give away all he earned set him apart from his contemporaries. It also, paradoxically, encouraged him to be even more ruthless a businessman and capitalist. Recognizing that the more money he earned, the more he would have to give away, he pushed his partners and his employees relentlessly forward in the pursuit of larger and larger profits, crushed the workingmen's unions he had once praised, increased the steelworkers' workday from eight to twelve hours, and drove down wages.

Carnegie was born in Dunfermline, Scotland, in 1835, the eldest son of a failed linen weaver and an entrepreneurially minded mother who kept shop and took in work from local shoemakers to put food on the table. At age thirteen, after no more than a year or two of formal schooling, young Andrew set sail with mother, father, and younger brother for America. Poor though the Carnegies were, they were supported by his mother's extended family and by the Scottish emigrants who had preceded them to America and Allegheny City, across the Monongahela River from Pittsburgh. Andra, as he was called, was put to work as a bobbin boy at a cotton mill, but after less than a year in the mill, found work as a telegraph messenger, taught himself Morse code, and was hired as private telegraph operator and secretary to Thomas A. Scott, the Pittsburgh division superintendent of the Pennsylvania Railroad. For the next twelve years or so, he would work for the railroad. At age thirty, Carnegie resigned his position to go into business for himself with his former bosses, Tom Scott and J. Edgar Thomson, the president of the Pennsylvania Railroad. Together, they organized a series of companies—with Scott and Thomson as secret partners—that were awarded insider contracts to supply the Pennsylvania Railroad with raw materials and build its iron bridges. By his early thirties, Carnegie had, with help and investment capital from his friends, accumulated his first fortune—in Pennsylvanian oil wells, iron manufacturing, bridge building, and bond trading.

His business career was, to this point, not unlike that of other ambitious English-speaking immigrants who made their fortunes by being in the right place at the right time. In the early 1870s, he moved away from the source of his income, Pittsburgh, to New York City. He would continue to oversee his iron and bridge companies from his hotel suite in New York—which he shared with his mother. Day-to-day decision making was delegated to a succession of partners, including his brother Tom, Henry Clay Frick, and Charlie Schwab. He seldom attended board meetings and visited Pittsburgh only three or four times a year.

For the next thirty years, his workday was confined to a few hours in the morning—and an occasional luncheon or dinner—but he accomplished as much in these hours as most men do in a week, and was proud of it. Although he professed to have made the move to New York for business reasons, there were more important considerations behind his decision to live a day's journey by train from his manufactories. He was thrilled with his success as a businessman and capitalist, but far from satisfied. He wanted more from life—and would spend the rest of his days in pursuit of it.

His ultimate goal was to establish himself as a man of letters, as well known and respected for his writing and intellect as for his ability to make money. He had as a child and young man read widely and memorized large portions of Robert Burns's poetry and Shakespeare's plays. In New York and London, he continued his self-education. He befriended some of the English-speaking world's most renowned men of letters, among them Herbert Spencer, Matthew Arnold, Richard Watson Gilder, editor of the *Century* magazine, and Sam Clemens; published regularly in respected journals of opinion on both sides of the Atlantic; wrote two well-received travelogues and a best-selling book entitled *Triumphant Democracy,* and with his "Gospel of Wealth" essays established himself as the moral philosopher of industrial capitalism. He spent half of each year in Britain, delegating to himself the role of cultural and political liaison between what he referred to as the two branches of the English-speaking race. He became the confidant of Republican presidents and secretaries of state and Liberal prime ministers and cabinet members, and inserted himself into the domestic and foreign affairs of the United States and Great Britain.

Meanwhile, his fortune grew and grew. Every major business decision he made appeared, in retrospect, to have been the right one. He was the first Pittsburgh iron manufacturer to move into steel, then the first steelmaker to diversify production from steel rails to structural shapes. To his partners' dismay, he plowed most of the companies' profits back into the business, integrating horizontally and vertically, modernizing, expanding, and securing steady cheap supplies of raw materials by buying a majority interest in the H. C. Frick coke works and leasing Rockefeller's iron ore mines in the Mesabi Range at a huge discount. By 1901, when he sold his interest in Carnegie Steel to J. P. Morgan, he was arguably the richest man in the world.

On retirement, he accelerated his giving to communities for library buildings and church organs so that parishioners could be introduced to classical music. He also set up a number of charitable trusts, each charged with a specific task: free tuition for Scottish university students; pensions for American college professors; a scientific research institution in Washington, D.C.; a library, music hall, art gallery, and natural history museum in Pittsburgh; a Hero Fund for civilians; a "peace endowment." Only as he approached his later seventies did he realize that, with his payout from selling Carnegie Steel at 5 percent a year on more than $200 million, he was running out of time to give away his fortune. Disheartened that he would fail at the most important task he had taken on—to wisely give back to the community the millions he had accumulated—he established the Carnegie Corporation to receive and disperse whatever was left behind when he died.

He had entered retirement intending to devote all his time and efforts to his philanthropy. But his last years were consumed with another cause: world peace. Arguing against his own self-interest—Carnegie Steel made millions manufacturing steel armor plate for the U.S. Navy—he campaigned for naval disarmament, then an international court, a league of peace, and treaties of arbitration between the nations of Europe and the United States. With considerable rhetorical power, he opposed American intervention in the Philippines and the British war with the Boer Republics in South Africa. As the European nations, followed closely by the United States, entered into an escalating naval arms race, he inserted himself into the diplomatic mix as an insider with access to the White House and Westminster. He would spend the rest of his days as an outspoken "apostle of peace," commuting back and forth between his homes in New York and Scotland and the world's capitals. Only at age eighty, in the second year of the Great War, did he recognize that his efforts had been in vain. He spent his last years in silence, isolated from his friends, unable to return to his home in Scotland, his optimism shattered.

A Scotsman in America, an American in Britain, businessman, capitalist, steelmaker, author, philanthropist, peace activist, pamphleteer, son, husband, and father, Carnegie wore his many hats well. He was in his long life seldom at a loss for words, never fearful of taking on a new role or task, and never less than passionate about whatever he happened to be engaged in at the moment.

The biographer is often asked at the conclusion of his project whether he has grown to like or dislike his subject. The answer of course is both.

But the question is misplaced. This biographer's greatest fear was not that he might come to admire or disapprove of his subject, but that he might end up enervated by years of research into another man's life and times. That was, fortunately, never the case. The highest praise I can offer Andrew Carnegie is to profess that, after these many years of research and writing, I find him one of the most fascinating men I have encountered, a man who was many things in his long life, but never boring.

ONE

Dunfermline, 1835–1848

H E WAS BORN in the upstairs room of a tiny gray stone weaver's cottage in Dunfermline, Scotland, to Margaret Carnegie, the daughter of Tom Morrison, the town's outspoken radical, and William Carnegie, a handloom weaver of fine damasks. He would be called Andrew, following the Scottish custom of naming the firstborn son after the father's father. Mag Carnegie, unable to afford a midwife, had called on her pregnant girlhood friend Ailie Fargee for assistance. A few months later, when Ailie's time came, Mag was there to minister to the birth of Ailie's son, Richard.[1]

The stone cottage in which Andra, as the child was known, was born (and which has been preserved as the Andrew Carnegie Birthplace Museum) was impossibly tiny, with two stories and two rooms. The bottom floor was occupied almost entirely by Will Carnegie's loom. The top story served as kitchen, dining room, and living quarters. It was all but dominated by the family's bed. Looking at the cottage today, one wonders how two adults and a child could have lived there.

Carnegie's birthplace, Dunfermline (the accent is on the second syllable, with a broad, lingering vowel sound), is situated about fourteen miles north of Edinburgh and forty miles east of Glasgow. It was already, in 1835, an epicenter of the social upheaval that we refer to today as the Industrial Revolution. "Beloved Dunfermline" was also, as Carnegie recalled in his *Autobiography*, a glorious place to grow up in, a town rich in history, the ancient capital of the Scottish nation. It was to Dunfermline that Malcolm Canmore had returned in the year 1057 after seventeen years of exile to take back the throne from the usurper Macbeth. Malcolm built himself a castle on a mound of earth at the foot of a small river that provided the future town with a reminder of its past and a name that would stay with it forever. "Dunfermline," a word of Celtic origin, is a composite term, meaning "castle" (dun) that "commands or watches over" (faire) a "pond" (linne) or "stream" (loin). In 1070, four years after William the Conqueror, Duke of Normandy, defeated the English army and made himself king, Malcolm married Margaret, one of the Saxon royal family who sought exile in Scotland. It was Queen, later Saint, Margaret who was instrumental in establishing an ecclesiastical center where once only a fort had stood and bringing what was regarded as a modicum of English civilization to the rough northern land. Malcolm and Margaret ruled Scotland from Dunfermline and were buried there, as in later years were successors to the Scottish throne.

By 1835, the only remnants of Dunfermline's past glories were the ruins of Malcolm's Tower and the Abbey, but they loomed large over the horizon. In 1818, while clearing away the earth in order to build a new church on the site of the old, workmen came upon an ancient vault, seven and a half feet in length, within which was a very large body, about six feet long, encased in lead. After laborious examinations of the site and the vault and body, it was determined beyond any reasonable doubt that the body was that of Robert the Bruce, the heroic king who had defeated the English army at Bannockburn in 1314 and restored Scottish sovereignty.

"Fortunate in my ancestors," Carnegie would later lecture his readers in his *Autobiography,*

> I was supremely so in my birthplace. Where one is born is very important, for different surroundings and traditions appeal to and stimulate different latent tendencies in the child. Ruskin truly observes that every bright boy in Edinburgh is influenced by the sight of the Castle. So is the child of Dunfermline, by its noble Abbey. . . . The ruins of the great monastery and of the Palace where Kings were born still stand. . . . The tomb of The Bruce is in the center of the Abbey, Saint Margaret's tomb is near, and many of the "royal folk" lie sleeping close around. . . . All is still redolent of the mighty past when Dunfermline was both nationally and religiously the capital of Scotland. The child privileged to develop amid such surroundings absorbs poetry and romance with the air he breathes, assimilates history and tradition as he gazes around. These become to him his real world in childhood—the ideal is the ever-present real. The actual has yet to come when, later in life, he is launched into the workday world of stern reality.[2]

Carnegie's reflections are testimony to his realization that the portrait of Dunfermline he offered in his *Autobiography* was a partial one, more ideal than real. Dunfermline was a glorious place to grow up, but only if one was able to close one's eyes to the misery and dislocation that the Industrial Revolution was going to visit upon it, to look past the poverty and the fear that enveloped the town's weavers as their livelihoods were taken from them.

Dunfermline at Andra's birth was a rather prosperous town, with a population that had more than doubled since the turn of the century. Dozens of well-built stone weavers' cottages like the Carnegies' were situated on the streets and alleyways that sloped down from the High Street, where the town's shops and its three banks stood. The town council had begun, in recent years, to spruce up the place. Outside stairways that had obstructed street traffic were ordered removed; new streetlamps installed; public wells more carefully "attended to"; and the streets paved with newly hewn stones and washed regularly, though not enough to clear away the pools of rotting "fluid garbage" that lingered after every rain. The major industry was, as it had been for generations, fine linen weaving.[3]

The weavers spent the daylight hours at their looms, which, too heavy to go anywhere else, took up the ground floors of their stone cottages. The Carnegies had been weavers for as long as anyone could remember. Weaving —of cottons, woolens, silks, and linens—was by far the largest employment in Scotland and Great Britain in the first decades of the nineteenth century. Having destroyed the East India textile industry by import restrictions, and monopolized the Latin American trade during the Napoleonic Wars, the British were now selling their textiles in every major market in the world. During the eighteenth and early nineteenth centuries, landless migrants from the Scottish Lowlands, from the Highlands, and from Ireland streamed into the towns, villages, and cities of southern Scotland, many of them to take up the weaving trade. The number of handloom weavers more than tripled between 1780 and 1820.[4]

The elites of the trade were the "fine" or "fancy" weavers of silk and linen. To weave cotton yarn into coarse cloth suitable for shirts and shawls required a minimum of skill; to weave delicate threads into ornately decorated tablecloths and napkins took experience, dexterity, and a not inconsiderable degree of hand and arm strength. The handloom weavers of Dunfermline who worked only with the finest of damask linens were, as might have been expected, both proud and protective of their craft. Every weaver in town could recite the recent history of the trade: how James Blake, feigning idiocy, had crawled under a damask loom in Edinburgh to learn the secrets of its construction, memorized what he saw there, and returned to Dunfermline to build his own; how John Wilson of Bridge Street had introduced the flying shuttle, which made it possible for one man to work a loom by himself without need of helpers to position the shuttle; how in 1825 Alexander Robertson and Messrs R. and J. Kerr had imported the Jacquard machine, invented by Monsieur Jacquard, a weaver of Lyons. Before the invention of the Jacquard machine, the linen weavers had had to laboriously refit their looms for each new design. The machines now reduced the preparation time from five or six weeks to a day or less.[5]

The Carnegies arrived in the Dunfermline area in the mid-eighteenth century. Andrew, the eleventh Earl of Elgin, whose land the Carnegies leased on arriving in the south, believes that they had been forced to flee their home in the northeast, in the Dundee area, after the unsuccessful 1745 uprising led by the Stuart pretender, Prince Charles. The English confiscated the estates of rebel landowners, forcing many of their tenants, like the Carnegies, to seek refuge farther south.

The name Carnegie appears for the first time in Dunfermline registers in 1759 with the baptism of Elizabeth, the daughter of James Carnegie. The Carnegies were, at the time, located in Pattiesmuir, a tiny village that was part of Lord Elgin's Broomhall estates, just outside the royal burgh of Dunfermline. That the Carnegies were weavers we know from the Broomhall "Particular Household Expenses," kept by Lady Elgin, who noted payments of two pounds in May 1768 and fourteen shillings in January 1769 to "Carnegies for working the coarse web." A 1771 map of the Elgin lands shows that the Carnegies leased a tiny plot with a garden in the village and a small field just beyond.[6]

James's eldest son, Andrew, who all his life would be known as "Daft Andrew," was born in 1769. Like his father, he set up his loom in Pattiesmuir, just outside Dunfermline, perhaps to avoid having to join the burgh's weavers' guild, pay its dues, and abide by its regulations. "Daft Andrew," from whom his grandson of the same name claimed to have inherited the "sunny disposition" that rose-colored his own past, was, according to a local historian writing in 1916, "a 'brainy' man who read and thought for himself" and gathered about him the radical-minded weavers of the town.

They called the public house they met in their "college," and "Daft Andrew," who may have spent more time there than anyone else, the "professor." Whether because he was fonder of drink than of his loom or because he spent more time at the "college of Pattiesmuir" than at his cottage workshop, "Daft Andrew" fell heavily into debt to his landlords. An entry in the Estate Record Book of Thomas, seventh Earl of Elgin, who was himself deeply in debt after his costly transplant of the Parthenon marbles from the Acropolis to London, notes that Andrew Carnegie's "arrears of house rent" of £34. 10s. had been written off as "doubtful and desperate debts" because Carnegie was "very poor and unable to pay anything."[7]

Andrew's son William, the third generation of Lowland weavers, was born in Pattiesmuir in 1804, but, on coming of age, left the family holdings and relocated to Dunfermline proper, where in the 1820s there was plenty of work, even for those who did not belong to the guild. By 1834, William was doing so well at his loom that he was able to marry Margaret Morrison of Dunfermline. Mag was taller than her husband, with "a fine dignified carriage; dark in complexion, with black eyes and 'wee hands and feet,'" one Dunfermline neighbor remembered. William was a little, fair-haired man, handsome in his way, but not terribly imposing. Their first child, Andra, who was born a year after their marriage, would take after the Carnegies in looks—he too was small and fair-haired—but had the Morrisons' fiery temperament.[8]

The standard rise-and-fall narrative of the Dunfermline weavers attributes their downfall to the coming of power looms and manufactories; but because of the delicacy of their fabric and designs, the linen weavers were protected from industrialization far longer than those who worked with wool or cotton. Through the 1820s and 1830s, they profited from an American export market that remained strong because tariffs on linen were lower (America had no linen weavers to protect) than those on other textiles. In 1833, the Dunfermline weavers reaped the whirlwind when the Americans removed all tariffs on "bleached and unbleached linens, table linen, linen napkins, and linen cambrics," precisely those products that were exported from Dunfermline. With the tariff removed, the price of fancy linens declined and demand soared. Fine damask table covers, cloths, and napkins—imported from Germany, Ireland, and Scotland—became a mark of distinction and refinement in urban American middle-class homes from Charleston to Providence. The total value of linen goods imported into the United States rose from $2.5 million in 1830 to $6.1 million in 1835, the year of Andrew's birth.[9]

By 1836, when Andra was a year old, more than half of the fine linens produced in Dunfermline were being shipped to America. Two grand estuaries, the Clyde and the Forth, connected by canals and newly improved roads, linked Dunfermline to the port of Glasgow, which was closer to the New World than competing European ports. Will Carnegie was able to expand his workshop, add a few new looms, and move his wife, young Andra, his workshop, and his associates into more spacious quarters in a larger cottage on Edgar Street in Reid's Park.[10]

The Morrisons, Andra's relatives on his mother's side, were like the Carnegies artisans and political radicals, but that was as far as the similarities went. In 1927, after Carnegie's death, the authorized biographer selected by Mrs. Louise Carnegie, Burton Hendrick, interviewed townsfolk and relatives who had either known or were the children of parents who had known the Carnegies and Morrisons. Much of what he discovered was kept out of his biography, so as not to embarrass the family. The marriage of the Morrison and Carnegie clans was not, it appeared, one made in heaven. The Morrisons looked down upon the Carnegies as too poor, uneducated, and ill-mannered a family for their daughter to marry into; the Carnegies, for their part, according to Andra's cousin Ann Alexander, thought the Morrisons "a 'queer lot' . . . who never went to church and did not believe in God." Worse yet, Mag's brother Tom not only bragged of his disbelief but mocked the solemnity of the Sabbath by tending his garden on Sundays.[11]

Thomas Morrison the elder, the head of the family and Andra's maternal grandfather, a cobbler by trade and an agitator by calling, was not only the leading political orator, writer, organizer, and activist in Dunfermline, but a trusted associate of William Cobbett, the widely known English radical journalist, who published Morrison's articles in his *Political Register*. Morrison was an uncompromising advocate of universal suffrage, an outspoken foe of aristocratic privilege, a supporter of a ten-hour law for factory workers, an enemy of the Established Church, and a proponent of land nationalization and the division of the large aristocratic estates among those who worked them. Morrison rode through the environs of Dunfermline preaching his gospel in open-air meetings to all who would listen. He also "scribbled" columns in the local newspapers, particularly the

Glasgow Free Press, and in 1833 he started up his own Dunfermline radical newspaper, *The Precursor,* "devoted to the interests of the Tradesmen and Mechanics in particular," which regrettably lasted but three months and three issues.

The residents of Dunfermline, as well as those of the adjoining shires, were represented in the 1830s in the House of Commons by a Whig aristocrat, Lord Dalmeny, whose only qualification for his position, Thomas Morrison believed, was his aristocratic birth. The Reform Bill of 1832 had expanded the franchise to include the urban middle classes, but not the workingmen of Dunfermline. Throughout Britain, the size of the electorate rose from about 6 percent to 12 percent. Scotland, which had been miserably underrepresented in the Commons, got eight additional seats, a step in the right direction. The reforms did not, of course, go nearly far enough. The tiny size of the electorate and the fact that members of Parliament were unpaid made it difficult to turn out men like Dalmeny and replace them with representatives in tune with the needs of the urban working classes.

The reforms of 1832 energized radicals like Tom Morrison, who believed them insufficient, but a beginning toward a representative government. In December 1834, either during or just after Lord Dalmeny's election, Morrison advised him in a widely circulated open letter, to "remain at home." Dalmeny, Morrison insisted, had no business attempting to represent the people of Dunfermline: first, because he was a lord—and the interests of the people and the aristocracy were "different, nay opposite"; second, because he was too young and inexperienced; and third, perhaps most important of all, because "Nature" had not bestowed on him the talents to be a legislator.

> Now, my Lord, if hereditary legislation is to be continued, and if you want to learn the art, I will tell you how to acquire it, that is, if you have the capacity. First, you must read and study, reason and reflect. Then you must mix in society, with the people of all grades, and in every condition of life. . . . Make yourself acquainted with the producing part of the community, with those who till the land, build the houses, make the clothes—who in short, support you in luxury and themselves in life: learn their wishes, their wants, and various conditions . . . Should your Lordship think, as you probably will, that I have not written in a style sufficiently respectful,

I assure you I do not wish to give unnecessary pain; but I have a duty to perform to my townsmen and country men, which must not be compromised. You may hear from me again.[12]

Dalmeny did hear from him again. In fact, Thomas Morrison continued to send him unsolicited "advice" until the day Morrison died. His son Tom, Andra's uncle, known as Bailie (i.e., alderman) after his election to the Dunfermline municipal council, was every bit the political agitator his father had been—and more so. With his gnarled black walking stick, a bushy black beard, and long frock coat, Bailie Morrison commanded attention at every public gathering even before he opened his mouth to hurl his snarling, piercing "Hear, Hear" at the speaker on the podium. The result of his heckling was inevitably that all eyes turned to him and he was escorted to the platform, walking stick in hand, to awaken the crowd with his radical preachings against the Established Church, the intellectually and morally stunted aristocracy, and the corruption of a political system that allowed a tiny minority to elect Lord Dalmeny to represent the working people of Dunfermline.

Young Andra knew and admired his grandfather and Uncle Bailie Morrison from a distance. They were far too busy to spend much time with the boy. With his father at work at the loom and his mother assisting him, keeping house and, in hard times, earning extra money by binding shoes and running her own "sweetie" shop, Andra was left to his own devices from the moment he was old enough to open the door of the family cottage. Much of his free time was spent with his uncle George Lauder, who had married Mag Morrison's older sister, Seaton, and his son, George Jr., known to the family as Dod. Lauder, who owned a small grocery, had Sundays and evenings free. He took his son and nephew on long walks around the Abbey, told them stories from Scottish history, recited lines from Robert Burns, and scared poor Andra half to death with his ghost tales.[13]

Will Carnegie at age thirty-one, when Andra was born, was doing rather well for himself—as were the other linen weavers of Dunfermline. The American export market was absorbing all the fine tablecloths and napkins they could produce and the manufacturer-merchants who controlled the transatlantic trade had no option but to rely on them, as the linen they wove was too delicate and their Jacquard designs too elaborate to put onto power looms. With the prosperity of the mid-1830s had come an influx of new weavers to Dunfermline, including a large number of men from the cotton trade, but as long as the American market remained strong, there was enough work to go around.

And then, with no warning, calamity struck. The Panic of 1837 in the United States drained American coffers of gold, the medium of international exchange. Credit evaporated, banks failed, wages fell, and unemployment soared. As in any economic downturn, it was the luxuries—like linen tablecloths and napkins imported from Scotland—that were sacrificed first. To sustain their rates of profit in the wake of a diminishing export market, the manufacturer-merchants who put out the work to the handloom weavers and sold their finished products reduced piece rates. The weavers throughout the district went on strike, but only in Dunfermline was there open violence. The objects of the strikers' wrath were the journeymen weavers, who continued to take in work at reduced rates.[14]

By September 1837, the local papers were reporting that over a thousand Dunfermline handloom weavers were out of work or out on strike, an unemployment rate of close to 40 percent. To make matters worse, the town was plagued by a series of epidemics— typhus, measles, and influenza— which were no doubt exacerbated by malnutrition. Ebenezer Henderson, a chronicler of life in Dunfermline, noted that in 1837 alone, there had been "493 interments in the Abbey Churchyard," an increase of 187 over the previous year.[15]

Because Scotland was exempt from the provisions of the British Poor Laws, there were no funds available to provide assistance to the destitute. In Glasgow and Paisley, the spinners' and weavers' associations petitioned Parliament for relief. Parliament declined to take any action, but appointed a Royal Commission to investigate the conditions of the weavers. The cotton spinners struck their mills, swearing not to return until paid a living wage. The government's response was to arrest the strike leaders. They were found guilty of "illegal conspiracy to keep up wages" and instigating "disturbances," and were sentenced to seven years' banishment to an overseas penal colony.[16]

Was it any wonder that a year later, the spinners and weavers of Glasgow and Paisley, along with those in Dunfermline, enthusiastically joined the campaign for a People's Charter? The political reforms called for by the People's Charter—universal male suffrage, secret ballots, annual parliaments, equal electoral districts, no property qualifications for candidates, and the payment of members of Parliament—would not automatically resolve the crises faced by Scotland's weavers and spinners, but they were a necessary first step. The plan devised by the Birmingham radicals who initiated the Chartist campaign was to send delegates through the British Isles to solicit support for the charter and signatures on a massive petition to be submitted to Parliament. In southern Scotland, the delegates were greeted by mass demonstrations everywhere they traveled and thousands of signatures were gathered. A committee was established in Dunfermline, with Will Carnegie and Thomas Morrison among its founding members. On July 7, 1838, Will Carnegie published a letter in the *Edinburgh Monthly Democrat and Total Abstinence Advocate,* proudly announcing that the "Working Men's Association of Dunfermline,"* the local Chartist organization, had collected 6,106 signatures on the petition they were dispatching to Birmingham. "The work goes on gloriously here. Some of our friends have gone to the surrounding towns and villages, and I am happy to state they were most enthusiastically received, and their labors crowned with the most cheering success. . . . Indeed, we flatter ourselves, were all the country as the 'Western district of fife,' the advocates of misrule and corruption would soon have to give place to a better order of things." Will Carnegie signed the letter on behalf of the Working Men's Association, prefixing his signature with a line from Robert Burns: " 'It's coming' yet for a' that,' etc."[17]

In late 1838, a modest upturn in trade and a compromise between the manufacturers and weavers on piece rates brought a degree of normalcy back to Dunfermline. The promise of future profits prompted renewed interest and new investment in power looms. According to Ebenezer Henderson, the major event of 1838 was the arrival of a "Mr. R. Robertson, manufacturer," and the construction of the "Baldridge Works . . . for the weaving of table linen, etc., by steam power." Though Robertson's manufactory did not succeed, there was no guarantee that the handloom linen weavers would be as fortunate the next time. The forward march of the power looms appeared almost inexorable. In 1813, there had been no more than 1,500 of them in all of Scotland; by 1829, there were 10,000; by 1845, nearly 22,300.[18]

The heady optimism of 1838—when thousands gathered in Glasgow and elsewhere to cheer on the coming of the People's Charter—gave way

---

*I have not included redundant information in the notes when the source of a citation is found in the text.

to a gritty, determined realism. The charter would not be easily won or soon won, but the fight was too important to give up. By the spring of 1839, there were close to 130 Chartist associations in Scotland, all of them gathering signatures for the petition. In June 1839, the National Petition for a People's Charter was submitted to Parliament and promptly rejected by an overwhelming vote. Chartist leaders in England and Scotland, including those in Dunfermline, regrouped and dispatched agitator-orators to tour again, eliciting support for what they hoped would be an even larger petition drive in the near future. New Chartist newspapers, friendly societies, and churches were established, new conventions planned.

The supporters of the charter recognized full well that the political reforms they demanded were not going to usher in the workers' millennium. But they had enough faith in representative government to believe that, once given the vote, the working males of Great Britain would set in motion a process of change that would eliminate the corruption, the privileges, and the downright stupidity that characterized the unreformed parliamentary government. The charter was not only, as Friedrich Engels put it in 1844, a "means to further ends. 'Political power our means, social happiness our end,' is now the clearly formulated war cry of the Chartists." It was also the vehicle with which the working class would secure the vote for itself. And the vote, as Edward Thompson reminds us, was for the Chartists "a symbol whose importance it is difficult for us" who have grown disillusioned with our two-party systems to understand. "It implied, first *égalité*: equality of citizenship, personal dignity, worth. . . . The claim for the vote implied also further claims: a new way of reaching out by the working people for *social control* over their conditions of life and labour."[19]

Young Andra, at five and six years of age, was a precocious witness to the events transpiring in the adult world. One imagines a small, blond-haired child with a huge forehead, always underfoot, always questioning. "These were times of intense political excitement," he recalled of his childhood in his *Autobiography*, "and there were frequently seen throughout the entire town, for a short time after the midday meal, small groups of men with their aprons girt about them discussing affairs of state. . . . I was often attracted, small as I was, to these circles and was an earnest listener to the conversation, which was wholly one-sided. The generally accepted conclusion was that there must be a change. Clubs were formed among the townsfolk, and the London newspapers were subscribed for. The leading editorials were read every evening to the people, strangely enough, from one of the pulpits of the town." Because the Scottish Chartists were "moral force" men, opposed to violent protest or protest that might grow violent, there was no reason to bar Andra or any other children from the open-air meetings that were the major form of Chartist education and agitation. "These political meetings were of frequent occurrence, and, as might be expected, I was as deeply interested as any of the family and attended many. One of my uncles or my father was generally to be heard."[20]

Though there is considerable evidence of his uncles' involvement in the upheavals of the 1840s, there is little to support Carnegie's contention that his father was also a Chartist leader. Will Carnegie, unlike the Morrisons, was a quiet, reserved, soft-spoken man, more a "trailer" than a leader, or so Carnegie would much later in life confide to his friend Hew Morrison (not a relation).[21]

In early 1840, in the midst of the campaign for the People's Charter, Anne Carnegie was born. Unlike her robust, bubbly brother, Anne was a sickly child who required a great deal of care. She would not live to see her second birthday.

There is curiously no mention of his sister in the *Autobiography* or in any of Carnegie's writings. She is also missing from the biographies written during Carnegie's lifetime and from Burton J. Hendrick's two-volume authorized biography, published in 1932. In telling the story of his childhood, Andra could find no room for Anne, as to write of her death would have obligated him to write of the heartache that death must have caused him and his mother, Margaret. His mother was his heroine, a larger-than-life figure he hoped his readers would come to admire as much as he did. It was Mag who held the family together through the hard times, Mag who put food on the table, Mag who made up for her husband's incapacity as breadwinner and head of household, Mag who in the end made the decision to relocate to the New World. Carnegie dared not imagine a situation, like the death of a child, that might have been too much even for his mother. And so, he banished it from consciousness. Anne Carnegie's descent into oblivion is, in the end, rather brutal testimony to her brother's capacity to brush aside the tragic aspects of his early life in Dunfermline.

The fancy linen weavers' greatest fears were for the future and for their children. Dunfermline was and had always been a one-industry town. The power looms had already conquered cotton production. Linen was surely next. What would happen when there was no more work to give out to the handloom weavers? How would the next generation of townsfolk support themselves? There were coal mines on the outskirts, but these were no place for the children of weavers to make a living. The other trades were open only to the sons of artisans already practicing them.

The Scots had always been a highly mobile people, and now—from 1830 onward—they stepped up the pace. The migration from Scotland exceeded that from England and Wales. More than two million Scots would depart the British Isles between 1830 and 1914. Most traveled from Glasgow, by steamship, across the Atlantic to Canada and the United States. The majority were landless, with nothing but their labor to sell, but because Scotland had in the early nineteenth century become the home of myriad small manufacturing concerns—textiles and metalworking, in particular— they had acquired artisanal skills that were transferable elsewhere.[22]

One of Andra's uncles and his twin aunts had, with their families, joined the stream of Scottish emigrants to America in the early 1840s. Mag Carnegie had hoped to follow them to America, but was dissuaded from doing so by her sister Anne, who wrote in October 1840, soon after arriving in Allegheny City, Pennsylvania, that "things being in such an unsettled condition in this country at present, it would be the height of folly to advise . . . you . . . to venture out this season at any rate, as it is very difficult for one to get employment of any kind, and more particularly weaving which is scarcely carried on here . . . The thought therefore that William may be idle etc. renders us all very uneasy but if affairs were once settled again, I would not hesitate to recommend you to come."

Unlike Dunfermline, where one grew up in a trade and continued to work at it come what may, Allegheny City was wide open. When times were good—as sister Annie hoped they would soon be again—there was plenty of work for newcomers, whether or not they had undergone apprenticeships or had any skills at all. "It is easy to get into situations here of different sorts, although you may know nothing at all of the work to be done, the people here stick at nothing,—just set to, and drive on the best way you can; many of them will be at two or three different occupations in a very short time. Thomas [her husband] for instance knew as little of his present trade as you do now, when he went to the factory, & he gets along wonderfully." Still Anne felt obligated, in a letter that carefully alternated good news with bad, to inform her sister that "the worst thing [about Thomas's new position] is, that it is very dirty work and he gets no <u>cash</u>—just orders on stores for all his wages, which is a very unpleasant way of going to work indeed, but it is carried on to an amazing extent in this place . . . but this state of affairs cannot continue long—as in fact change seems to be a striking characteristic of everything here."[23]

Though Mag agreed with her sister that with the United States still in the snares of the 1837 Panic, it was no time to emigrate, she was becoming increasingly desperate about the future. While her husband had been able to put food on the table during good times, he was buffeted more than most by the cyclical downturns that ripped through town with increasing frequency. The hidden truth uncovered by Burton Hendrick during his 1927 research trip to Scotland but artfully disguised in his biography was that Will Carnegie was, as ninety-one-year-old William Macgregor put it, "a decent chap . . . but no hard worker. . . . He was regular in his habits, a gude churchman, and as moral a gentleman as one could wish—but he didna love to work. Would idle away his time even when he had a web. Was reading and such, much given to foolishness." Everyone Hendrick interviewed on that trip had much the same thing to say about Will Carnegie. Mrs. Clanachan, whose parents lived in the same house as the Carnegies, reported that Mag Carnegie had had to take up binding shoes for her brother Tom because "Willie Carnegie was not contributing greatly to the family support. . . . He simply did not like to work,—much rather read the newspaper. He was nae bad a mon," but not very diligent a weaver. The members of the Morrison family were even more scathing in their commentaries on Mag's husband, whom they identified as "shiftless," "aimless," "no earth-shaker," "a weakling," a man who "lacked industry, thrift and go-aheadness—also intelligence."[24]

By the 1840s, Mag had taken over the role as chief family breadwinner. She put bread on the table, first, by taking in work from her brother Tom, the cobbler, then by setting up her own "sweetie" shop in the front room of the family's cottage. The specialty of Mag's shop was something called potted meat, which a neighbor later described as "a confection largely composed of the miscellaneous contents of a pig's head . . . made into little balls." Mag also sold cabbages, leeks, and carrots she procured from local farmers.[25]

Andra, now ten, made himself as useful as he could, both to his mother and to his uncle George Lauder. He ran errands, kept accounts, at times may have stood behind the counter. What is most interesting about his childhood work is that it was done for his mother and his uncle, not his father. Andra was, it was clear, the first in a long line of Carnegies who was not going to be raised to the loom.[26]

Margaret Carnegie thought again about leaving Scotland in 1842, but was dissuaded as she had been two years before by a letter from her sister. America was, Aunt Aitkin wrote from Allegheny City, still in the throes of the banking crisis that had led to a dearth of hard currency. "You can scarcely form any idea of the state of money matters in this country for some time past; indeed I may say ever since we came, things have been getting worse and worse in as much, that at present, you cannot get a dollar changed unless by taking more than the half in merchandise. . . . It seems as if the country was entirely drained of gold silver and copper. . . . I would not advise any person to come out at present who can get a lively hood at home, as trade is very dull here, indeed many who are both able & willing to work find it impossible to get employment." Now might not be the time to emigrate, she warned, but that did not mean that the Carnegies would be better off staying indefinitely in Dunfermline. "Still, with all this, America is not to be compared with the old country; as there are very few but can get enough to eat and to spare. As a day's work can procure nearly as much as serve a family for a week, especially if they would be content to live as they do at home,—which is far from being the case, for the people here go for good living."[27]

At the age of eight, Andra had begun attending school. Although he implies in his *Autobiography* that it had been his decision to put off school until then, eight, in fact, was the age at which most Scottish boys entered the classroom. There were numerous schools in Dunfermline in the early 1840s, thirty-three of them to be exact, almost half endowed or supported by the kirk (church) or the municipality. Andra was sent to one of the "adventure" schools, so called because they were started up and supported "entirely on the teachers' own adventure."[28]

Every school in the town charged tuition. Only paupers were admitted gratis, but the stigma attached to charity was such that few parents or children accepted it. The best schools—those with the most qualified rectors and masters, relatively commodious accommodations for the scholars, and the largest teaching staffs—were the Burgh or Grammar School and the Commercial School, but they charged higher tuition than the Carnegies could afford. Andra was enrolled instead in the Rolland School on Priory Lane, where the fee was two shillings a quarter, paid in weekly installments, less than half that charged at the better schools.

In his *Autobiography*, Carnegie lavishes only superlatives on the Rolland School and its principal and teacher, Mr. Martin. The more we know about this school—and its dour headmaster, Robert Martin—the more striking such a glowing tribute becomes. According to the Reverend Peter Chalmers, author of *Historical and Statistical Account of Dunfermline*, published in 1844, the year Andra entered the Rolland School, there were "between 180 and 190 children taught, almost all of the working and poorer classes." The school had been established by a local philanthropist "for the education of the poor of the parish," but because the money was not invested wisely—or perhaps at all—the endowment was quickly depleted. With no funding from the bequest, the municipality, or the kirk, Martin could not afford an assistant and taught all the students by himself in one classroom, employing the Lancastrian or factory school method of rote learning.

The Lancastrian system, invented and advertised by Mr. Joseph Lancaster, an English Quaker, had been designed to bring the blessings of civilization to the children of the poor by importing into the classroom the efficiency of the factory. Poor children, he believed, required, above all else, training in discipline, decorum, and decency. They also needed to learn their letters, their sums, and their catechism; any attempt to awaken other faculties would be gratuitous or worse, a needless distraction.

The Lancastrian school young Andra attended was, like all the others, designed for maximum efficiency. It was housed in a one-room schoolhouse, with a tiny fireplace near the front door that barely removed the chill. Martin's desk was on an elevated podium. On it sat his "lum," or satin high hat, and his "tawse," a leather strap he employed regularly on those he found sleeping or slovenly or just stupid. The classroom was arrayed in "forms," rows of stiff-backed benches on which the scholars sat, ranged in order of age and accomplishment. Each form was ruled by an older student who acted as form monitor or dictator. Martin, whom his daughter later described as "tall, though stoop-shouldered," provided the monitors with words or sums which they dictated to their forms, each member of which was expected to copy the dictation on his or her slate and/or recite it in unison to the "dictator." While the instruction proceeded on the floor below, Martin watched from his perch, on the ready to hurl his tawse at a recalcitrant scholar, who was bidden to retrieve it, return it to the podium, and receive a lash across his hands.[29]

The sole activities in class were memorization and recitation. Fortunately, young Andra excelled in both, and never had to be punished. Andra stood out from his classmates not only for his prodigious memory skills but for his exemption from catechism lessons. While every other student had to recite daily from the 107 questions and answers in the Shorter Catechism, his father and his uncle George Lauder, neither of whom were members of the Established or the Protesting Presbyterian Church, arranged for their boys to be excused.

EVERY MORNING before leaving for school, Andra was delegated to fetch water for the household from the town reservoir on Moodie Street. This was no simple task in Dunfermline, where the "old wives" of the town had instituted their own queuing system for filling their cans and pails in the morning. Every evening, they would reserve their places in line by putting their cans in a row in front of the well. Young Andra refused to abide by the system. Instead of waiting in line behind the ladies, he pushed his way to the front so as not to be late for school. "I would not be put down even by these venerable old dames. I earned the reputation of being 'an awfu' laddie.' In this way I probably developed the strain of argumentativeness, or perhaps combativeness, which has always remained with me." Carnegie's admission to having been "an awfu' laddie" was confirmed by a distant relative who recalled, in her 1927 interview with Burton Hendrick, that young Andra had indeed been "somewhat impudent as a boy. . . . He would follow older people and mimicked them and even made ungentlemanly remarks."[30]

Andra might not have gotten along with the "old dames" at the well or with the boys who teased him for being Martin's pet at school, but he was for the most part, as William Macgregor remembered, "a very nice boy—white haired—and . . . liked by the other boys. . . . But he was very keen; Even then we knew there waur somethin' in him."[31]

THE SCOTLAND THAT Andra Carnegie grew up in was, as he himself tells us in his *Autobiography*, "in a state of violent disturbance in matters theological as well as political." Organized religion played a much larger role in everyday life in nineteenth-century Scotland—and the United States—than it does today. The Morrisons and Carnegies were among the distinct minority in Dunfermline that avoided attending or supporting any church whatsoever. Mag Carnegie inherited her opposition to the Established Presbyterian Church from her father, who had criticized it—and its teachings—in print only a few years before Andra was born. In an article ostensibly about education, written as a letter to William Cobbett and published in his *Political Register*, Thomas Morrison, Sr., bitterly registered his objections to "flogging out of very young children" answers to the 107 questions in the Shorter Catechism that each Scottish Presbyterian child was supposed to learn. "'Tidings of Damnation'; 'The wrath and curse of God'; all the 'miseries of this life'; death itself; and the pains 'of hell for ever'!! Such are the subjects upon which infantile imagination is exercised. Oh! I remember as I do the events of yesterday, the sleepless nights, the horrific dreams of an awful devil and tremendous hell awakened by the task of memorizing catechism answers."[32]

What was unique about the Morrisons was not that they were opponents of the Established Presbyterian Church, but that they stayed equally distant from its rival, the Scottish Free Church. They were as close to practicing atheists as anyone in mid-nineteenth-century Scotland. Though by disposition Will Carnegie was more inclined to submit to the discipline of an organized church, he too, after marrying into the Morrison family, became an opponent of the Calvinist rigidities to which the Scottish church was returning in the 1840s: he left the Presbyterians while Andra was a boy.

Mag and her brother Tom, like their father, had nothing to do with any church, established or free. Her sisters, however, gravitated from the Presbyterians into Dunfermline's—and later Allegheny City's—tiny Swedenborgian community and brought Will Carnegie along with them into the Church of the New Jerusalem. The Swedenborgians were everything the

Scottish Presbyterians were not: tolerant, unitarian, and committed to establishing communication with worlds hereafter. "Dear William," wrote Mag's sister Anne Aitkin from Allegheny City in October 1844 to her brother-in-law in Dunfermline, after he had converted to the Swedenborgians, "How are you getting on now? What church do you attend, I hope you still continue to read and receive the heavenly Doctrines revealed by our illuminate scribe [Emanuel Swedenborg]. . . . Does Margaret take any interest in religion? And how does the new Church society get along in Dunfermline? Are you a member? Our small society is still moving along with her face eastward, but as yet our advancement is slow, owing to the density of resisting mediums, which retards her progress, but her course is still onward."[33]

Will Carnegie found little solace for his real-world problems in the Swedenborgian church. In 1842, another nail had been hammered into the linen weavers' coffin when the U.S. Congress, reacting belatedly to the economic downturn that had begun five years earlier, raised the rates on tariffs and removed linen and many other products from the "free list." Inevitably, as prices on imported linens rose, demand fell, and with it both piece rates and the amount of work available. The younger weavers migrated to Paisley and to Glasgow where there was work available in the factories; the older ones economized as best they could and waited for better times to return.[34]

By 1843, when Andra was seven and his new brother Tom one year old, Parliament responded to the weavers' and spinners' requests for assistance by establishing a Royal Commission to investigate the conditions of the poor in Scotland. Assistant commissioners were dispatched to every corner of the nation, questionnaires in hand. They arrived in Dunfermline in February 1844 and interviewed a leading manufacturer, the Reverend Peter Chalmers, the "surgeon to the poor," the convenor of the "poorhouse committee," and a few others. Conditions in Dunfermline, they were told, had deteriorated so rapidly that the local authorities had raised a voluntary subscription to erect a poorhouse on the town green to shelter paupers, orphans, and lunatics. The consensus of those interviewed by the commissioners was that the poorhouse had vastly improved conditions in town. No one of course asked the poor what they thought, but the "surgeon to the poor" reported that he was quite "satisfied with the mode in which" the paupers were cared for at the poorhouse. "He has found no inconvenience from having some insane persons in the house. The orphans in the house are sufficiently accommodated with beds in an apartment by themselves, separate from the adults." There were, he admitted, a great many paupers in town who had chosen not to enter the poorhouse or had been prohibited from doing so because there were limited beds available. But the surgeon was satisfied that those paupers who remained on the outside were sufficiently sheltered from the "effects of the weather," and did not suffer from wind or rain "coming into their homes." Regrettably, their cottages were often "deficient in point of furniture and of fuel," their bedding was "wretched," and "there is a want of clothing amongst them," but such poverty was almost always due to their "intemperate habits." As for the vagrants who pockmarked the streets of other towns, Dunfermline had none. "It is the custom," reported Erskine Beveridge, one of the town leaders, "to give vagrants a night's lodging and a ticket for a certain allowance of bread, and to pass them on next day." Thus were the streets cleared of human refuse not otherwise confined to the poorhouse.[35]

The weavers were not eligible even for the meager relief—a bed and a few meals—offered those sheltered by the poorhouse. Relief for the able-bodied unemployed, town and church authorities agreed, was a deterrent to their ever finding work. The problem with the weavers who remained in town, unemployed, rather than looking elsewhere for work, was that they were unwilling to accept the rates the manufacturers were constrained to pay them. Both the Reverend Chalmers and James Hunt, Esquire, of Pittencrieff, reported that one of the town's leading manufacturers had "pledged himself to employ every weaver in the place at present out of work till the end of April or May next, at a reduction of twenty-five per cent on the rate of wages at present paid." But the weavers had turned down the offer, fearing that it was a stalking horse for the manufacturers, who planned to reduce wages 25 percent across the board with or without the workmen's agreement.[36]

The handloom weavers of Scotland, once the elite of artisans, had fallen so far in status—and compensation—that they were now, for purposes of the commissioners' survey of "weekly wages," included with the "lowest class of labourer" instead of with other artisans. In West Fife, which included Dunfermline and the towns and villages surrounding it, the average weekly wage for the weavers had fallen to 6 shillings, compared to 13.5 for masons and 12.6 for wrights, and this was before the 25 percent wage reduction that the manufacturers were calling for in early 1844.[37]

It was the beginning of the end for the Carnegies. Over and over again, the same ghastly events were being played out. The market for fine damask linen goods would tighten; the manufacturers would reduce rates; the weavers would go on strike; the leading manufacturers would meet with the weavers and establish "rates," only to have the agreements fall apart when renegade manufacturers refused to abide by those rates and put out work to journeymen who agreed to work for less than their peers. There was little work at any wage for linen weavers during 1844; 1845 was worse yet. "We cannot detail the shame and disasters of this year," wrote Daniel Thomson in his 1903 history of the Weavers' Incorporation of Dunfermline; 1845 was "a hideous nightmare." In the summer of 1846, flooding submerged hundreds of shops and looms. Then came the disastrous winter of 1847–48, "the worst in living memory."[38]

In later years, Carnegie would claim that it was the arrival of the power loom that had brought disaster to the family; but the bitter truth is that Will Carnegie and the handloom weavers of Dunfermline were ruined long before. By the mid-1840s, they were entirely beholden to the manufacturer-merchants who supplied them with orders and raw materials, and when they were finished at their looms, took their cloth away, had it dyed, finished, transported to Glasgow, and sold in America. As trade declined and orders fell, the value of the looms upon which the weavers worked and the skills with which they wove were worth less and less. By 1846, there were only about 60,000 handloom weavers remaining in the British Isles, compared to 200,000–225,000 ten years earlier. In Scotland, the numbers fell from almost 85,000 in 1840 to less than 25,000 ten years later.[39]

"I began to learn what poverty meant," Carnegie later recalled of these years. "Dreadful days came when my father took the last of his [finished woven] webs to the great manufacturer, and I saw my mother anxiously awaiting his return to know whether a new web was to be obtained or that a period of idleness was upon us. It was burnt into my heart then that my father, though neither 'abject, mean, nor vile,' as Burns has it, had nevertheless to

> 'Beg a brother of the earth
> To give him leave to toil'"

In an *Autobiography* that is resolutely upbeat, almost perversely so, the two paragraphs in which young Andra describes his father's defeat stand out. As if he were constitutionally unable to continue in this vein, he pauses in mid-paragraph and then deftly changes the subject from his tragic father to his heroic mother: "We were not, however, reduced to anything like poverty compared with many of our neighbors. I do not know to what lengths of privation my mother would not have gone that she might see her two boys wearing large white collars, and trimly dressed."[40]

If the present was dark, the future looked even worse. In his entry for the year 1847, Ebenezer Henderson reported that a Mr. Scott had established "The Dunfermline Steam-Power Weaving Factory" in an abandoned building on Pitmuir Street. Though Scott's venture would ultimately prove "unsuccessful," the opening of the steam factory caused such a stir in town that Henderson saw fit to highlight it as the event of the year.[41]

This was the "turning point" in Will Carnegie's career as a weaver, his son recalled in an article he wrote in 1899. "One evening I heard my father tell my mother that steam looms were coming into the trade and bothering him. This steam machinery, he said, was best handled in big factories, which made it bad for the independent master weavers. . . . Not very long afterwards—it was in 1847—he came in one day from delivering some finished damask, looked at me quizzically, and said: 'Andy, I have no more work.'"[42]

Even Mag found it difficult to put bread on the table through the depression of 1847–48. In starving times, with the linen weavers out of work, there was little pocket money to spare for sweets and "'peerie,' a kind of treacle beer, of non-alcoholic character," her best-selling items. Her husband was a broken man, too old to take up a new trade, unable to earn anything at the old one. All Will Carnegie had ever known was weaving—and he had been moderately successful at it. But what would he do now to support his family? Always a quiet, almost withdrawn and retiring little man, he retreated into a stunned silence. Mag's fear was not so much for Will, who had given up, but for her two boys, whose lives and livelihood stood before them. What would they do in a one-industry town that had lost its industry? The only solution was for her to follow the route of her brother and twin sisters and "pack the whole crowd off to Ameriky." She expressed her determination in a well-known Scotch saying: "'Either make a spoon or spoil a horn'"—that is, she would risk the whole family fortunes on a single throw. She would break the Carnegies or make them.[43]

The problem was finding the funds to finance their trip to America. Will had sold his looms, which had fetched little. The Carnegies owned nothing else of value: no furniture, no family keepsakes, no property. Mag's brother Bailie Morrison, the cobbler and radical, might have been able to pay for the trip, but he was against their leaving. Uncle George Lauder, whom his relatives would later claim helped out, had nothing to spare. The only one with money to lend—and enough faith in Mag to do so—was her childhood friend Ailie Fargee (Ella Ferguson), with whom she had grown up, courted, and, as young marrieds, shared a two-family cottage. The women were so close, they had even presided at one another's deliveries. Like Mag, Ailie was married to a weaver, but one who, even in the most dire times, was able to find work. Also like Mag, Ailie earned money on her own, by selling bread, but with her husband gainfully employed, she had been able to put aside her earnings. She now offered to loan Mag twenty pounds, which made it possible for her to plan her escape.[44]

TWO

To America, 1848–1855

A T AGE TWELVE, there is nothing quite as exciting as a long journey—especially when one doesn't know how long it will be. Aside from a brief trip to Edinburgh to see the Queen, Andra had never ventured outside the town limits. This only lent more drama to the journey. Though travel was, in the mid-nineteenth century, a decidedly uncomfortable and, for the most part, unpleasant activity, especially for those who had to book the cheapest accommodations available, for Andra Carnegie, it was great adventure. He was a remarkably good traveler, immune to travel sickness. This quality would stand him well later in life, when he became a regular transatlantic passenger—for business and pleasure.

The Carnegies' trip from Dunfermline to Allegheny City had been well plotted and followed the path taken by other Lowland emigrants, Mag's brother and twin sisters among them. Unlike the hundreds of thousands of Irish men, women, and children who crossed the ocean to escape the famine, or the German republicans and radicals who were forced into exile after the political defeats of 1848, the Carnegies did not have to travel far to their port city or wait long for their ship. They set off from Dunfermline in July 1848, traveling south along the railway tracks built by the fifth Lord Elgin to move coal and linens to Charlestown Harbor on the Firth of Forth. Though the first leg of the trip was by "rail," the passenger omnibus the Carnegies traveled on was pulled by horses, not a locomotive. Andra would no doubt have chosen to sit on top, holding on to the railing, but he was not given that choice. He was bundled inside the coach with the rest of the family. From Charlestown Harbor, the family was shuttled into a small boat and rowed across the Firth of Forth to the steamer that would take them to the port of Glasgow.

The steamer trip down the Clyde to Broomielaw, Glasgow's port, took all day. The next morning, the family set sail on the *Wiscasset*, which Carnegie describes in his *Autobiography* as an "800-ton sailing ship." He exaggerates. The *Wiscasset* was in fact a 380-ton, eighteen-year-old Maine whaler, which only the year before had been transporting whale oil and whalebone for a Sag Harbor whaling firm.[1]

The traffic in human cargo, much of it from Ireland, via Liverpool, had by the late 1840s expanded to the point where sailing ships of every variety, even retired whalers like the *Wiscasset*, were being refitted to serve the emigrant trade. Few of these ships had been built to carry passengers. The *Wiscasset* had been leased or bought by Taylor & Merrill of 77 South Street in lower Manhattan, who had started their own transatlantic line in 1842 and evidently added the *Wiscasset* in 1848. Although most of the Taylor & Merrill ships sailed from Liverpool, the *Wiscasset* set sail from Glasgow in early July (not May 17, as Carnegie wrote in his *Autobiography* and his biographers have repeated) and was forty-two days at sea (not fifty as Carnegie recounted). One hundred forty-four passengers, including the Carnegies, traveled in steerage; nine in the cabin; and unidentified "merchandise" in the hold.[2]

Fortunately for historians, Congress in 1818 had demanded that all ships landing in the United States deliver a manifest of all passengers taken on board with names, ages, occupations, and the ports they sailed from. Most of the adult men who traveled on the *Wiscasset* were listed as skilled artisans: weavers, clerks, dressmakers, masons, shoemakers, printers, and engineers. The majority were accompanied by their wives and children. Because Scottish immigrants traveled without any official documents, they were free to change their age in any direction they chose. Will, who was forty-four gave his age as forty (younger men were more likely to get jobs); Mag, who was thirty-eight, claimed to be thirty-four. Andra, who was four months shy of his thirteenth birthday but no taller than a ten-year-old, was nonetheless listed as fifteen. Only Tom's correct age was given: he was four.[3]

Andra tells us in his *Autobiography* that he had a fine time at sea and it is likely that he did. All his life, people would remark on his remarkably sunny disposition, his broad smile, and nonstop, good-natured chatter. Life was an open-ended adventure for the boy, as it would be for the man. After getting over the initial shock of leaving his hometown, he quickly acclimated himself to his new role as world traveler. Andra may have enjoyed the passage to America, but it is difficult to believe that anyone else in the family did; surely not his mother, who had to devote most of her waking hours to feeding, clothing, and keeping her family free from disease. Beginning in 1842 British ships had been required to carry provisions for their passengers (earlier passengers had provided their own food), but the ships' stores carried only bread and biscuit, which quickly got stale or waterlogged; rotted potatoes; some sugar and molasses; perhaps a bit of beef or pork. Fresh water was stored in wooden casks that seldom kept it very fresh, and doled out in drips and drops. During daylight hours, when the weather was good, passengers were allowed to wander the decks. Most of the time, they were confined below in cramped quarters, with negligible ventilation and no privacy. Though reformers tried to segregate men and women, they failed. The emigrants, most of whom traveled in families, preferred to stay together and sleep alongside one another on wooden shelves built into the hold. The worst part of the trip—aside perhaps from the foul air, dreadful food, and fetid water—must have been the tedium. For those who remained healthy, there was nothing to do and little to see except the endless expanse of ocean below and sky above.

The Carnegies' passage was relatively uneventful and mercifully short—there seems to have been no ship fever, cholera, or typhus, no fires on board, no squalls to send the ship off course and delay their arrival. But forty-two days and nights on board a converted whaler—with one garrulous twelve-year-old and one toddler—could not have been a very pleasant experience for anyone save that twelve-year-old. Young Andra had already developed a talent for befriending and attaching himself to adults in positions of power. It stood him in great stead on this journey. He made himself useful to the sailors, became their mascot and helper, and "in consequence . . . was invited by the sailors to participate on Sundays, in the one delicacy of the sailors' mess, plum duff [a sort of pudding]."[4]

The four Carnegies arrived in New York Harbor in the midst of one of the largest immigrations this—or any other country—has ever seen. The Irish Potato Famine had become progressively more serious through the late 1840s. In 1848, upwards of 200,000 men, women, and children crossed the Irish Sea to Liverpool, a port made prosperous by the slave trade, where they boarded ships for America and Canada. The largest number of them were bound for New York City. On Monday, August 14, the same day that the *Wiscasset* with its passengers from Glasgow entered the port of New York, so did three ships from Liverpool: the *Boston*, with 216 passengers; the *Ocean Queen*, with 316; the *Mersey*, with 18; and the *William Carson*, from Dublin with 139 on board.[5]

The *Wiscasset*, like every other ship entering the port, picked up a pilot boat at Sandy Hook and then as it entered the Narrows was boarded by New York health officials, who speedily inspected the passengers, sending those obviously and seriously ill to the Marine Hospital at Tompkinsville on Staten Island. In 1848, there was still no central point of disembarkation for the immigrants, no Castle Garden or Ellis Island. Some ships discharged their passengers instead at East River piers; others along the Hudson River; a few in New Jersey. Wherever they landed, they were greeted by an army of fast-talking ne'er-do-wells poised to rob them of any currency that might remain on their persons. Peddlers, hucksters, newsies, and hawkers offered them food and information in whatever native language they happened to speak, while nattily dressed "runners" festooned with smiles grabbed at their luggage and directed them to boardinghouses or tried to sell them passage—at a bargain—to their final destinations.

The Carnegies were, at this point in their travels, more fortunate than most. Like the majority of Scottish emigrants, Will and Mag Carnegie were literate, had marketable skills, spoke, read, and wrote English, and had contacts with landsmen and family who were already established in America. Mag had arranged for the family to camp overnight with a childhood friend, Euphemia Douglas, who had, like her, married a weaver, John Sloane. The Sloane boys, John and Willie, would later follow their father into the carpet trade, but on the retail end, as the proprietors of W. & J. Sloane Company.[6]

The Carnegies were not, as most of the new immigrants were, ignorant peasants adrift in a strange, new world. They knew where they were going, if not quite how to get there. Their destination was Allegheny City, where Mag's sisters and their families lived, and where the Carnegies would be supported until Will found work. Allegheny City lay west of New York City. The most direct route would have been south, by coastal steamer or sailing packet, to Philadelphia and then about 400 miles west to Pittsburgh, across the Allegheny River from Allegheny City, but that would have involved crossing the Allegheny Mountains by horse-drawn wagon. The Carnegies were advised to take a more roundabout but cheaper water

route, north on the Hudson to Albany, west along the Erie Canal to Buffalo, southwest across Lake Erie to Cleveland, then south and east by canal
boat and railroad to Allegheny City.

The first leg of their trip, up the Hudson to Albany, was the shortest,
less than twelve hours. The Hudson River, as Domingo Faustino
Sarmiento, an Argentine who traveled to and through America in 1847,
had written the year before, had already become "the center of life in the
United States poetically, historically, and commercially. . . . Its waters are
always so literally covered by boats that there are traffic jams, as in the
streets of the great cities. The steamboats cross each other's paths like
shooting stars, and tugboats tow a veritable carnival of barges whose keels
sent out a tide before them. . . . The passenger steamboats on American
rivers are like two-story floating houses, with flat roofs and covered
porches." During his trip north, Sarmiento had been captivated by the
landscapes: the "perpendicular wall of rock cliffs" at the Palisades, then the
"villages, cities, orchards, hills, and forests" as the steamer proceeded up
the river, past "occasional ruins" and the "living monument at West Point."
The Hudson, he declared—and he was not the only one to do so—
"competes with the Rhine in beauty and has no rival, except in China, for
the volume of its traffic."[7]

Arriving in Albany, the Carnegies had several choices. They could
travel by railroad the entire 360 miles to Buffalo for about three cents a
mile. When the roadway was clear, the weather good, and the engines running well, the trip took from fifteen to twenty-four hours. The alternative
that the Carnegies chose was the canal boat, which cost much less but
took far longer, a full four or five days. Dragged along the Erie Canal by
horses for much of the route, the canal boats drifted through forests and
swamps, farmlands and wilderness, up and down locks, all at the very
leisurely—sometimes maddeningly monotonous—pace of three to four
miles an hour. There were stops along the way so that passengers could buy
staples and fresh produce to take on board for their meals. Below decks,
where the passengers spent all of their nights and a good part of every day,
lay three cramped, connected compartments, the middle one stowed with
freight, the rear fitted with kitchens to prepare food and tables to eat it on,
the front serving as sitting room by day and dormitory at night. The most
distressing aspect of travel on the canal, for many European travelers, was
the promiscuous mixing of passengers below decks. James Lumsden, a

Scotsman from Glasgow who had traveled this route in 1843, had been quite distressed to discover that he would have to share quarters with an assemblage of rough-and-ready, unwashed, and unkempt Americans. "Such a motley crew has seldom been seen. In taking notice of this mode of conveyance, it is merely to guard my countrymen from traveling much by canal in the States."[8]

At Buffalo, the Carnegies disembarked from the canal boat to board yet another steamer (their third), this one bound for Cleveland along the shores of Lake Erie. From Cleveland, it was back into a succession of canal and riverboats which carried them south to Akron, then southeast to Beaver, Pennsylvania, twenty miles from Allegheny City, where they discovered that the steamboat they had expected to board for the last leg of their trip—on the Ohio River to Allegheny City—was nowhere to be seen. They had no choice but to wait out the night on the wharfboat that ferried passengers to the steamer.

It was mid-September now—they had left Dunfermline in July—and the four Carnegies were temporarily marooned on the swampy edge of the Ohio River. "This was our first introduction to the mosquito in all its ferocity. My mother suffered so severely that in the morning she could hardly see. We were all frightful sights, but I do not remember that even the stinging misery of that night kept me from sleeping soundly. I could always sleep." The next morning, Will, Margaret, Andy, and Tom boarded the Ohio River steamer for the final leg of their marathon journey.[9]

ALLEGHENY CITY was at the time a separate city from Pittsburgh. Anthony Trollope, who visited it in 1861–62, considered this to be yet another sign of American obtuseness: "Pittsburgh and Allegheny . . . regard themselves as places apart; but they are in effect one and the same city. They live under the same blanket of soot, which is woven by the joint efforts of the two places." Like Charles Dickens and, it appears, every other foreign visitor, Trollope could not resist comparing Pittsburgh to a city back home. These comparisons were never flattering—to either city. "Pittsburgh is the Merthyr-Tydvil [a nightmare of an industrial town near Cardiff in South Wales] of Pennsylvania," Trollope reported, "or perhaps I should better describe it as an amalgamation of Swansea, Merthyr-Tydvil, and South Shields. It is without exception the blackest place which I ever saw. The three English towns which I have named are very dirty, but all their combined soot and grease and dinginess do not equal that of Pittsburgh." Alexander Mackey, who had visited in 1846–47, just before the arrival of the Carnegies, noted that Pittsburgh's residents referred to their city as the "Sheffield of the West" to call attention to the quality and variety of its manufactures. Mackey thought the comparison apt, but for a different reason: "In one thing, [Pittsburgh] certainly resembles Sheffield—in the dingy and sickly character of the vegetation in its immediate vicinity; the fresh green leaf and the delicate flower being begrimed, ere they have fully unfolded themselves, by the smoke and soot with which the whole atmosphere is impregnated."[10]

Like its sister cities across the Atlantic, Pittsburgh was first and foremost a manufacturing town. By the 1840s, Pittsburgh's glass factories and iron foundries were supplying settlers on the western frontier with bottles, pots and pans, kettles, stoves, grates, tools, and utensils; its nail factories were turning out hundreds of tons of cut and wrought-iron nails; its rolling mills were converting pig iron into iron bars, which were then rolled and molded into a variety of shapes. All of this manufacturing left its mark—in the air and on the ground. The machine shops, foundries, mills, boiler yards, and factories spewed tons of ash, soot, and smoke into the air, almost all of which fell to earth on the cities below, leaving a film of dust in the lungs of the inhabitants, on the roofs of their homes, in the streets, on the rivers and canals.[11]

After a joyous family reunion, probably at the wharves where their steamer docked, the four Carnegies followed their relatives to what would become their new home at 336 Rebecca Street.* Mag's twin sisters Annie (Aunt Aitkin) and Kitty and their husbands had prospered in the decade they had lived in the New World. Annie's husband, who had died a few years before the Carnegies arrived, had left her with a share of the Rebecca Street property, which she owned with Kitty and Kitty's husband, Thomas Hogan. Thomas was, by 1848, employed as a clerk in a crockery shop and, by the time of the 1850 census, would be worth at least $1,000. The Hogans lived with their four children, aged one to fourteen, in the house at the front of the lot at 336 Rebecca. In the rear, off an alley, was a smaller cot-

---

*Carnegie's birthplace in Dunfermline has been preserved, but his first home in America was torn down in the 1960s to make room for Three Rivers Stadium.

tage, the ground floor of which was occupied by Thomas Hogan's older brother, Andrew, a weaver. There were two small rooms upstairs.[12]

The Carnegies/Morrisons/Hogans/Aitkins were one big extended family, with branches in Allegheny City and Dunfermline. The four Carnegies, the latest addition to the chain migration, were invited to move into the rooms on the second floor of the cottage in the back of the lot, rent-free, until they were able to pay their way.

Allegheny City was not, in 1848, the most pleasant place on earth to pitch one's tent. In addition to the soot and grime on the ground and the black smoke in the sky, the city suffered from almost annual flooding. "We have had a flood this year," Andra reported almost matter-of-factly to his Dunfermline cousins in the spring of 1852. "Every season when the snow melts on the mountains the Rivers raise very high but they have not been so high for 20 years before. It rained for 3 weeks almost constantly and both rivers rose at once. It was up to the ceiling in our house and for 2 days we had to live upstairs and sail about in rafts and skiffs. It was a great time. The lower part of Allegheny was all flooded. It caused great destruction of property."[13]

Had the streets been paved, such floods would not have caused as much distress as they did. But Allegheny City was growing too fast for its infrastructure to keep pace. During the 1840s alone, its population doubled, from 10,000 to 21,262. (Pittsburgh's grew at roughly the same pace.) There was no municipal water system in Allegheny City until 1848, no gas lines and consequently no street lighting until 1853, no underground sewers, no sanitation system. Dogs, rats, and hogs roamed the streets, even after the early 1850s when, according to a local historian, Leland Baldwin, "the attacks of savage porkers upon children . . . finally stirred the authorities to take some measures to enforce the long-standing law against hogs running free. A pound was set up and a reward of one dollar was paid for each hog brought in, much to the delight of the street urchins, who found it an entrancing mode of earning pocket money."[14]

A good part of the year, especially in the spring flood season, the streets overflowed with storm water, wastes, and sewage, which seeped into the yards and front rooms. Disease coursed through the city, striking down the youngest and the oldest. There were cholera epidemics in 1849, 1850, 1854, and 1855.[15]

The Carnegies had not expected to find paradise in Allegheny City.

For all its Old World charms, Dunfermline too had had its epidemics, its scavenging rodents, muddy streets, and clean water shortages. The reason why the Hogans and the Aitkins and the Carnegies and thousands like them had come to the United States in general, and the Pittsburgh area in particular, had less to do with health, hygiene, or the physical environment than with an abundance of well-paid jobs. In this respect, Pittsburgh and Allegheny City were everything that Dunfermline was not: their markets for manufactured goods were expanding rapidly, their economies were diversified, and there were no craft restrictions on the employment of skilled artisans.

Divided from the eastern seaboard by the Allegheny Mountains and linked to the west by the Ohio River, Pittsburgh and Allegheny City prospered as the nation's population moved west. The "bottoms," which had been formed along the banks of the rivers by centuries of flooding and erosion, were perfect locations for large manufactories. Better yet, goods manufactured on either bank of the Allegheny and Monongahela Rivers could be transported cheaply and quickly via canal and river to Cincinnati, Louisville, St. Louis, New Orleans, and to hundreds of small towns and settlements in the West at much less than it cost eastern manufacturers to ship their products around or across the Allegheny Mountains. As a local real estate firm proclaimed in 1845, the geographic advantages of Pittsburgh made it a "perfect place for manufacturing."[16]

These were not the only comparative advantages bestowed by geography on greater Pittsburgh's manufacturers. Western Pennsylvania and the Ohio River valley were rich with grain, livestock, and produce. More important for its burgeoning manufacturers, there was abundant and easily accessible timber in the hills, one of the world's largest soft coal seams in the ground below, and iron ore close by.

By the 1840s, Allegheny City had begun to exploit its natural advantages. The city's largest employers were its five cotton mills, which enjoyed their best year ever in 1847. Although cotton was one of the few raw materials not found in the region, steamboats could transport it north, upstream, as cheaply as finished goods could be moved south and west, with the current. By 1850, Allegheny City's cotton mills were consuming 15,000 bales of cotton a year, which they converted into yarns, sheeting, and batting worth almost $1.5 million.[17]

The Carnegies relocated to Allegheny City because Will Carnegie could not support his family in Dunfermline. His wife, Mag, hoped he would have better luck in the New World. He did not. Either because he was "shiftless," "aimless," and a "weakling," or, more likely, because, at age forty-four, he was not prepared to start over again, he delayed looking for wage work as long as he could. Beguiled, perhaps, by his good luck at finding living quarters on the second floor of a weaver's cottage, he bided his time until the weaver who lived there moved out. He then rented his loom and "began making tablecloths," much as he had in Dunfermline. He met with the same lack of success. Unable to find any dealer willing to sell his products, he had to resort to peddling his wares door to door, still without much success.[18]

Mag Carnegie had no choice now but to continue in the role of chief family breadwinner. Thousands of miles across the Atlantic, in a fairy-tale coincidence, she discovered that one of her neighbors, Harry Phipps, was a master shoemaker from Shropshire, with binding to give out. For her labors, which she could do at home while watching over her two sons, she received four dollars a week.

Mag's four dollars a week was all that the family earned. Will continued to weave tablecloths he could not sell. The family survived only through the kindness of Aunt Aitkin, who allowed them to continue to live rent free in the cottage off the alleyway.

Andra turned thirteen in November and, though small for his age (as he would be at every age), Mag reluctantly conceded that he had to be sent out to work. She delayed as long as possible, no doubt because the prospects for an undersized, unskilled thirteen-year-old who spoke with a heavy Scottish accent were not promising.

Still, the family was desperate. A temporary solution was found when Andra and his father were offered positions at the Anchor Cotton Mills, owned by Mr. Blackstock, a Scotsman. Blackstock and his fellow cotton mill owners were, at the time, in dire need of new hands. The previous July, a new state law had taken effect, mandating a ten-hour day, sixty-hour week, and prohibiting the employment of children under twelve. Though the mill owners agreed not to hire any mill girls under age twelve, they refused to abide by the ten-hour provision and demanded that all factory hands who wished to keep their jobs sign special contracts, allowed under the new law, agreeing to a twelve-hour day. When the vast majority of the workers refused, the owners shut down operation. On July 31, the first of the cotton mills was reopened—but only to those who signed the special contracts giving up their rights to a ten-hour day. At 5:00 A.M., when the gates swung open, a crowd of mostly young girls assembled outside the mill to hoot, howl, and pelt the returning "scabs" with "stones, eggs, potatoes, and mud." The scene got uglier when the owner ordered a foreman to shoot a stream of hot steam into the yard where the protesters were gathered. A few of the girls were scalded and the crowd, enraged, stormed the mill, breaking windows and vandalizing machinery. The response of the Allegheny City Select and Common Councils was to allocate $1,000 for the arrest and conviction of the rioters. Ten days later, the owners of three mills, including Blackstock's, opened their gates, but again only to those who agreed to work a twelve-hour day. Through the fall and into the winter, while sixteen protesters, five of whom were girls, were brought to trial for violating antiriot statutes, the mill owners hired scabs to replace those who refused to sign twelve-hour contracts.[19]

Short of laborers, Mr. Blackstock offered Will and Andra jobs at his Anchor Cotton Mills. Needless to say, they had to sign special contracts agreeing to work a twelve-hour day. To get to the mills by five, father and son rose in the middle of the night and had breakfast "by candle light." The Anchor Mills were more than a mile away—a long walk in the bitterly cold Pittsburgh winter. As a bobbin boy, Andra spent his twelve-hour workday, with a short break for breakfast and forty minutes for dinner, running up and down the aisles exchanging fresh bobbins for used ones. "The hours hung heavily upon me and in the work itself I took no pleasure."[20]

A short time after they began work at the mills, Will quit to return to his loom on the ground floor of the Carnegie cottage on Rebecca Street.* With her husband having failed again as a breadwinner, Mag had to find additional work. On Saturdays, she took off time from binding shoes and running the household to help out her widowed sister, who had opened a small grocery store.

The only ray of hope for the Carnegies was their oldest son, whose earning potential as a teenager was already superior to his mother's and his father's. There was something about the lad that inspired older Scottish

---

*There is a listing for a "Carnegie, William, weaver, Rebecca Street" in *Woodward & Rowland's Allegheny Directory for the Year 1852.*

men, to entrust him with responsibilities he was not quite ready for. The Carnegies had relocated to an American manufacturing city filled with enterprising, upward-rising Scotsmen, ready and able to help out young landsmen. Andra's stint as a bobbin boy for Mr. Blackstock had barely begun when another Scottish expatriate manufacturer, John Hay, offered him a position for two dollars a week, almost double his wages. Hay owned a workshop at the corner of Lacock Street and Race Alley in which he and his four "hands" turned out the bobbins that, with the recent boom in cotton manufacturing, were in greater demand than ever.[21]

Andra's new job was to fire the boiler in the basement with wooden chips and tend the engine that turned the nine lathes in the workshop. When Hay, however, discovered that Andra had a fine "hand" and was good with figures, he moved him out of the basement and entrusted him with the bill-keeping. Regrettably, Hay's workshop was too small to employ a full-time bookkeeper, so Andra had to fill in most of his workday with work less frightening but every bit as distasteful as tending the boiler: bathing every newly turned bobbin in vats of crude Pennsylvania petroleum. "Not all the resolution I could muster, or all the indignation I felt at my own weakness, prevented my stomach from behaving in a most perverse way. I never succeeded in overcoming the nausea produced by the smell of the oil."[22]

Andra's experience as a bobbin boy, boiler attendant, and soaker of bobbins in vats of oil was sufficient to convince him that to prosper at business he would have to move off the factory floor into the backroom offices. He set his sights on becoming a full-time bookkeeper. Those plans were put on hold when, after less than a year with John Hay, he was presented with another opportunity by yet another Scotsman. His uncle Hogan regularly played draughts (or checkers as it was known in the United States) with David Brooks, the manager of the Pittsburgh office of the Atlantic & Ohio Telegraph Company, also known as the O'Rielly Telegraph Company, after its founder, Henry O'Rielly.* When, one evening over the draughts board, Brooks asked "if he knew where a good boy could be found to act as messenger," his uncle mentioned Andra's name and volunteered to inquire whether his parents would let him take the job. It paid $2.50 a week, 25 percent more than he was getting from Mr. Hay. Andra

---

*He had perversely changed the usual spelling of the family name as a young man.

"was wild with delight" at the thought of getting away from his vats of oil and his mother agreed that he should take the job. Only Will Carnegie was opposed. The new position—as messenger boy—would "prove too much for me, he said; I was too young and too small. For the two dollars and a half per week offered it was evident that a much larger boy was expected. Late at night I might be required to run out into the country with a telegram, and there would be dangers to encounter. Upon the whole my father said that it was best that I should remain where I was."[23]

In the end, mother and son prevailed. Will agreed to let Andy interview for the position, but, still worried about the undersized thirteen-year-old, accompanied him across the St. Clair Street Bridge, a wooden structure that would soon be replaced by John Roebling's Sixth Street Bridge, into Pittsburgh. The O'Rielly telegraph office was at 100 Fourth Avenue, where PPG Place (Pittsburgh Plate Glass) stands today. A century and a half ago, this location, adjacent to Market Square, was at the geographic and business center of Pittsburgh, the perfect location to establish a telegraph office.

Like all thirteen-year-olds, especially newly arrived immigrants, Andy, as he would now be known, was mortified by the presence of his father, who could be identified from a block away as a man of the Old World. On arriving in America, the boy's accent had, like his father's, been broad enough to mark him immediately as a "Scotchie." But he worked hard to make it go away. After less than four years in America, he recalled in a letter to his uncle Lauder how John Sloane had, on his visit to Allegheny City, laughed aloud because Andy could "not say *sow crae* as broad as he says it. I tried it over and over but could not do it." Andy hastened to reassure his uncle that while his accent was disappearing, he was no less a Scotsman. "Although I cannot say *sow crae* as broad as I once could, I can read about Wallace, Bruce and Burns with as much enthusiasm as ever, and feel proud of being a son of Old Caledonia and I like to tell people when they ask 'Are you native born?' [They would not have asked had his accent remained.] 'No, sir, I am a Scotchman,' and I feel as proud I am sure as ever Romans did when it was their boast to say, 'I am a Roman citizen.'"[24]

For his interview for the telegraph messenger position, Andy wanted to appear as American as possible. David Brooks who managed the Pittsburgh office was a Scotsman, and his immediate superior, James Reid, the company's general superintendent, was not only Scots but from Dunfermline; but Andy was convinced that he "could make a smarter showing if alone with Mr. Brooks than if my good old Scotch father were present, perhaps to smile at my airs." He not only left his father out on the street to wait for him, but he must have intimated to Reid that his father had died. Reid would later refer, in his 1879 history of the telegraph industry, to having hired the "little lad named Andrew Carnegie, who, with his widowed mother, had lately arrived from Scotland, his native land."[25]

Dressed in his one white linen shirt and his "blue round-about," a short, tightly fitted blue jacket, Andy Carnegie made enough of an impression to counter his lack of size and experience with the Pittsburgh streets. He was offered the position and volunteered to begin at once. He had, with the help of his landsmen, landed in the right place at the right time. Pittsburgh, the gateway to the West, was destined to be a central hub in the network of telegraph poles that were beginning to connect the nation. The first telegraph line had been completed five years earlier, in 1844, when Samuel F. B. Morse, with $30,000 in federal funding, connected Washington to Baltimore. Morse and his partners had expected to get funding to build additional lines from the federal government, but their experience securing their first $30,000 had been so debilitating that they gave up entirely on the public sector and turned to private capital to fund their new telegraph lines. Henry O'Rielly secured the franchise and agreed to raise the capital to string telegraph poles from east to west. His plan was to extend one line from Buffalo to Chicago, the other across the Alleghenies from Philadelphia through Pittsburgh, to St. Louis, and then north to Chicago, and south to New Orleans.

Although customers were scarce and the first telegraph lines were continually breaking (or being broken by bands of boys who took great joy in throwing stones at the glass insulators that glistened in the sunlight), O'Rielly and the handful of entrepreneurs who believed in the future of telegraphy raised sufficient capital to extend their lines mile by mile. By late 1846, they had also connected Boston to Washington, via New York City and Philadelphia; New York City to Buffalo, through Albany; and in late December, Philadelphia to Pittsburgh, via Lancaster and Harrisburg. By August 1847, O'Rielly had linked Pittsburgh and Cleveland, through Canton and Akron, and Pittsburgh and Cincinnati via Columbus and Dayton. By the end of the year, his oak posts and insulated copper wires reached all the way to St. Louis. As Colonel John P. Glass, one of the managers of the Pittsburgh office, wrote in triumph, the St. Louis connection resulted in an immediate increase of 15–20 percent in the number of messages sent and received in Pittsburgh. "The western offices having to communicate with the East through us, this will be the Great Distributing Post Office of the Western lines."[26]

Andy Carnegie was assigned to deliver telegrams with news from the "Eastern line": shipping reports from Europe transported across the Atlantic by steamer; stock prices from New York City; commercial news from Philadelphia and Baltimore; political news from Washington and the state capital in Harrisburg. Here was the perfect position for an ambitious, affable young man. Every day brought him face-to-face with Pittsburgh's top businessmen and politicians. With no telephones and intracity transportation rudimentary, the boys on foot provided the only link between Pittsburgh and the eastern seaboard and between local businessmen and their families and offices. The boy who delivered his messages without delay and offered to deliver return messages on his way back to the office was noticed and remembered.

It was not easy being a messenger boy in Pittsburgh or in any city whose streets did not cross at right angles in a New York City–style grid. Andy's greatest fear was that he would not be able to find the offices he was supposed to deliver messages to. "So I started in and learned all the addresses by heart, up one side of Wood Street and down the other. Then I learned the other business streets in the same way." After memorizing the street map, he learned the names—and faces—of the city's businessmen so that, should he manage to meet one in the street, he could say hello and, in those rare but magical moments when he had a telegram, deliver it on the spot.[27]

Andy Carnegie wasted no time making his mark. On November 2, 1849, three weeks shy of his fourteenth birthday, his name appeared in the newspaper for the first time, on page three of the *Pittsburgh Daily Gazette:* "A Prize—A messenger boy of the name of Andrew Carnegie employed by the O'Reilly [sic] Telegraph Company, yesterday found a draft for the amount of five hundred dollars. Like an honest little fellow, he promptly made known the fact, and deposited the paper in good hands where it waits identification."

The "honest little fellow," in truth, had not had much of a chance to be dishonest. A draft for five hundred dollars was worth nothing until converted into currency and it would have been difficult for Andy—or anyone in his family—to get this done. While Andy Carnegie might not have deserved praise for his honesty, he should certainly be saluted for his skills as a self-promoter. Sheer luck might have put the draft into his hand in the first place, but it took pluck and the right contacts to get the story into the paper. For the next few weeks at least, Andy would be known everywhere, at home and on the streets of the Pittsburgh business district, as that "honest little fellow" who had returned the five-hundred-dollar draft. The boy had a talent for publicity, one that would stand him in good stead all his life.

The turnover in the telegraph office was considerable and Andy quickly became one of the senior boys. His partner delivering telegrams from the "Eastern line" was David McCargo, also the son of a Scottish immigrant, who would become and remain one of his dear friends. Soon after Davy's arrival, Robert Pitcairn, who, like Andy, was "not only Scotch, but Scotch-born" got a job at O'Rielly's. The boys were among the fortunate few. Instead of being sequestered from dawn to dusk in airless factories and dust-filled mills, messengers spent their days out-of-doors; while their peers lived under the harsh supervision of often brutal foremen, messengers were left on their own to deliver their messages. "A messenger boy in those days," Carnegie recalled in his *Autobiography*, "had many pleasures. There were wholesale fruit stores, where a pocketful of apples was sometimes to be had for the prompt deliver of a message; bakers' and confectioners' shops, where sweet cakes were sometimes given to him." And there was the Pittsburgh theater, which in return for free telegraphic service, admitted the operators—and sometimes the messengers—for free. Andy quickly learned the tricks of the trade, such as withholding messages for the theater until curtain time, in the hope that the theater manager would invite the messenger to "slip upstairs to the second tier" to see that evening's performance, perhaps Fanny Kemble performing Shakespeare or the singer Jenny Lind, who Carnegie thought "the strangest woman I ever heard."[28]

The O'Rielly office occupied two floors. The operators worked on the second floor; the public did its business on the first. Because Andy was eager to please—and got along well with adults—he was occasionally asked by Colonel Glass, the downstairs manager, to watch the office. Again, as in Mr. Martin's school in Dunfermline, Andy was singled out for special treatment and, in doing so, incurred the dislike of his companions. "At that time I was not popular with the other boys, who resented my exemption from part of my legitimate work." At fourteen, Andy Carnegie, it appeared, was also something of a prig, which set him apart from his comrades. He did not enjoy roughhousing or sexually charged banter or dirty stories of any kind. One of the boys he worked alongside, Tom David, declared years later that he had always thought Andy was "religiously inclined." Why else, David reasoned, would he recoil so from "salacious stories"? Though already the family breadwinner, Andy remained very much a mama's boy, afraid of misbehaving lest his mother think less of him. His Sunday school classmate William Macgregor had noticed this years before in Dunfermline, when he observed that Andra "never kicked up rumpuses," like the other boys, perhaps because he was too "much under the control of his mother."[29]

Andy Carnegie, David also recalled, was already hell-bent on improving himself. Every Monday morning, he would stop by Tom's table to tell him about the debate by mail he was carrying on with his Scottish cousin about slavery. "The whole trend of your mind," Tom remembered in a later letter to Carnegie, "seemed to be towards big things—Indeed I recall that your efforts to do the pranks of the average boy struck me at the time as being almost grotesque. You would not follow the fashions in dress, because, I supposed you believed it to be evidence of a little mind."[30]

Andy had given up his plans to become a bookkeeper. His new business goal was to graduate from telegraph messenger to operator. "The click of the telegraph instruments fascinated me," he wrote in an 1899 article. "I tried to understand it, by listening, by going to the office early and playing with the key. Mr. Reid finally agreed to help me to learn."

One morning, before the office had officially opened for business, while Andy was sweeping up, he "heard the Pittsburgh call given with vigor." Instead of ignoring it—and waiting for the regular operators to take the message—he answered the call and "let the slip run." In those days, the messages were imprinted—in Morse code—with dots and dashes on slips of paper. As each message was received, the operator called it out to a "copyist," who translated it into English, then summoned a boy to deliver it. Andy, informed that the call was a "death message" from Philadelphia, took it down himself, translated it, and delivered it. He then returned to the office, where he "waited anxiously for Mr. Brooks to come in." Rather than scolding him for meddling, as Carnegie had feared, Brooks complimented him—with the warning to be careful in the future not to make any mistakes in transcribing messages.[31]

Andy began filling in when the operator on duty was absent. Possessed of what he later referred to as "a sensitive ear for sound," he taught himself to take messages by ear, instead of waiting to transcribe the printed slips as was the common practice. "This," he recalled in an 1896 article for *Youth's Companion,* "brought me into notice." In June 1851, no more than about eighteen months after he had taken the messenger job, he was sent to Greensburg, Pennsylvania, halfway between Pittsburgh and Johnstown, to replace the regular operator who had to be absent for two weeks. Aside from nearly getting himself electrocuted by venturing "too near the key" during a lightning storm, Andy performed admirably at Greensburg and returned to Pittsburgh "surrounded with something like a halo, so far as the other boys were concerned." As he proudly wrote his cousin Dod (George Lauder, Jr.'s, nickname) in Dunfermline, "I have got past delivering messages now and have got to operating. I am to have four dollars a week and a good prospect of soon getting more." He was still about five months shy of his sixteenth birthday.[32]

IN 1851, in celebration perhaps of his newfound status in the world or perhaps on the occasion of his birthday, Andy and his little brother Tom posed for formal portraits in the studio of R. M. Cargo on Federal Street. Andy's arm is loosely extended around the shoulder of his brother who, as befits a seven- or eight-year old, looks at the camera with a quizzical smirk in one photo, a frown in the other. Andy is dressed formally in a long double-breasted black frock coat (which he had probably borrowed for the photograph), a white shirt, collar, and bow tie, all a few sizes too large for him. In an attempt to look worldly-wise, he stares straight at the camera with a gaze that appears almost mournful. His head is abnormally large and heart-shaped, with small, narrow eyes, a puggish nose, tightly closed mouth, and a high broad forehead, topped by neatly brushed blond hair, parted on the left, with a slight pompadour effect.

Although he displays little joy or warmth in the photograph, Andy was mighty pleased with himself and his new position. "I still continue to like my business and intend to continue at it," he wrote his uncle in May 1852. "I have very easy times and I may say I have no master, for the operators in the office are very nice men and never say a cross word, at least very seldom." While he confessed that he sometimes thought he "would like to be back in Dunfermline," he was "sure" that it was "far better for me that I came here. If I had been in Dunfermline working at the loom it is very likely I would have been a poor weaver all my days, but here I can surely do something better than that, if I don't it will be my own fault, for anyone can get along in this Country. I intend going to night school this fall to learn something more and after that I will try and teach myself some other branches."[33]

To be a man of the world, he had to read more. This much he knew. But where was he going to come by reading material? The "wants of the family," he recalled in his *Autobiography*, left him with no "money to spend on books." And as his uncle Aitkin had complained in one of his first letters after arriving in Allegheny City in 1840, while almost everything a man could hope to buy was cheaper in the States, reading matter was not. "Would you believe that I was charged a sixpence and on one occasion a 1/- [one pound] a week for the reading of a pretty large volume—and that to be a regular subscriber of an ordinary library I would require to pay 75 cents (halfpence) per month $6 dollars per year. . . . There is no possibility of getting papers or periodicals to read here for a small sum—most of the people being in the habit of purchasing them for their own use. This has been to me a great deprivation. I really find that books here are as dear as in the old country everything considered."

Uncle Aitkin hoped to remedy this flaw in American cultural life—and make a profit at it—by starting up his own lending library. "I am now convinced that for any one to keep a library and to give works out at a cheaper rate would pay very well & I think I will be engaged in this business in a short time,—after I make a little money by lecturing etc." Regrettably—for Uncle Aitkin and for Allegheny City's starved readers—he never got around to setting up his business.[34]

A decade later, Colonel James Anderson, a successful Allegheny City manufacturer, established the city's first quasi-public library. Unlike Uncle Aitkin, his purposes were philanthropic, not commercial. Every Saturday afternoon, he invited the city's apprentices and working boys to visit his private library and, if they chose, borrow a book for the week. The response was so overwhelming that Anderson felt obliged both to expand his holdings and to offer his library to the city, stipulating only that the Allegheny City Select and Common Councils find rooms to house the collection and hire a part-time librarian to maintain it. The councils agreed in principle, but not in practice, and the new institution "languished and was finally closed," only to be rescued—temporarily—by the Young Men's Christian Association (YMCA). It was then incorporated by a group of local businessmen who tried to make it self-sufficient by charging users an annual two-dollar fee. In the spirit of Anderson's original bequest, working boys needed to present only their guardians' or parents' "surety" to be allowed to borrow books for free. For a few short years, the library was housed on Federal and Diamond Streets in Allegheny City and opened Tuesday through Saturday evenings. But when it again ran short of funds, sometime in 1853, neither the city councils nor the YMCA nor the businessmen who had incorporated it were willing to bail it out. In an attempt to keep the institution alive, it was moved to the home of librarian Robert Donaldson at 611 Diamond Street. To increase revenues, the two-dollar annual fee was reinstated for working boys like Andy Carnegie who were not formally bound by letters of apprenticeship.[35]

Out of self interest, combined with a sense of moral outrage, Andy protested the fee in a May 9, 1853, letter to the editor of the *Pittsburgh Dispatch*, which he pointedly signed: "a working boy though not bound." Firmly, but without any hint of youthful aggression, he prefaced his protest by praising the *Dispatch*'s editor and, by implication, its readers. "Believing that you take a deep interest in whatever tends to elevate, instruct and improve the youth of this country I am induced to call your attention to the following." He then proceeded, with a literary flourish, to ridicule the library's intention to charge a fee. The library had, he informed the *Dispatch*'s readers, "been in successful operation for over a year scattering precious seeds among us. . . . But its means of doing good have recently been greatly circumscribed by new directors who refuse to allow any boy who is not learning a trade & bound for a stated time to become a member. I rather think that the new directors have misunderstood the generous donor's intentions. It can hardly be thought he meant to exclude boys employed in stores merely because they are not bound."

The letter prompted an immediate response by the librarian who, signing his letter "X.Y.Z.," corrected "working boy" by noting, rather contemptuously, that had he "applied to the right place, which is the Library, he would have obtained correct information"—namely, that the library had been founded in 1849, not 1848 as Andy had claimed in his letter, and that the founder, Colonel Anderson, did not "bequeath" any money but had instead "made a present of about 2000 vols. to the city of Allegheny." The directors, X.Y.Z. claimed, had in the past admitted "working boys" who were not apprentices, but could no longer afford to do so.

Andy was not deterred by minor corrections. In a second letter to the editor, "working boy" acknowledged his "mistakes" but reiterated his claim that the "managers" of the Anderson Library, in restricting boys not bound, had "certainly misunderstood the generous donor's intentions." Unwilling to continue a never-ending literary duel, the librarians had no choice but to capitulate. Three days after Andy's second letter, a notice appeared on the editorial page of the *Dispatch*: "A 'Working Boy' will confer a favor by calling at our office." Andy was invited back to the library and permitted to borrow one book a week, as he had been doing, without having to pay a fee.[36]

The story of Andy Carnegie defeating the villainous adults played well in his *Autobiography* and the biographies that drew from it, but there is another side to the tale which we should not neglect. The Anderson Library was not a free public library, funded by the city, but a subscription library, which relied in great part on the support of its patrons.* Although "working boys" should, as he had argued, have been allowed to borrow books without paying the two-dollar subscription fee, Andy Carnegie, six months from his eighteenth birthday, was hardly a "working boy." He held a man's job and received a man's pay of twenty-five dollars a month. Was it unreasonable for the librarians to ask him to contribute a two-dollar annual subscription fee to keep the library from having to close its doors for the third time in its young history?

Andy thought so. With a talent for cloaking self-interest in larger humanitarian concerns, he made a premature case for free public libraries. As a descendant of generations of self-taught Carnegie and Morrison males,

---

*There were, indeed, no public libraries in Pittsburgh or Allegheny City, as the *Pittsburgh Post* complained bitterly in an 1853 editorial.

Andy took his own self-education seriously. He wanted to read widely because that was what a man and citizen did, whether artisan or mechanic, clerk or merchant, Scottish or American. Book learning was a means toward, and a sign of, moral distinction. His early tastes had been shaped by his uncle Lauder, who raised him on the Scottish poets, Robert Burns, Robert Tannahill, James Hogg, Robert Fergusson, and Allan Ramsay, and on the novels and histories of Sir Walter Scott. In Allegheny City, he became a devotee of well-written, national histories, the longer the better: William H. Prescott's *A History of the Conquest of Mexico;* Thomas Macaulay's four-volume *History of England;* and his special favorite, George Bancroft's ten-volume *A History of the United States.* He devoured the artfully crafted, though somewhat pedantic, literary essays of Charles Lamb and Thomas Macaulay and buried himself in scientific studies like Mary Somerville's *On the Connection of the Physical Sciences.*[37]

Much of his reading in Allegheny City was devoted to learning about his new country. From the moment the *Wiscasset* docked in New York Harbor, Andy had become an American patriot. To buttress his arguments for American supremacy, he scoured the Pittsburgh papers, the *New York Daily Tribune* (which he read in the telegraph office), and history books borrowed from the Anderson Library.

Scottish radicals like the Morrisons made use of the American example to criticize Her Majesty's government, but, as Andy discovered via the mail he received from his uncle Lauder and his cousin Dod in Dunfermline, it was one thing to criticize the lack of democracy in Britain from within Scotland, quite another to do it from foreign shores. "Naig" (as his cousin had called him from boyhood, and as he signed his letters to Dunfermline) harped constantly in his letters on American superiority in politics, technology, marine navigation, railroad building, even in temperance legislation, which began to grate on his Scottish relatives. After reading one too many paragraphs celebrating democracy in the New World, Dod retaliated with his own brand of rhetorical fury.* How could Andy possibly speak with such passion and eloquence of American institutions and American liberties in the face of "the Monster Iniquity," slavery? Rather than God's gift to freedom-loving people, the United States, because of

---

*Regrettably, Dod's letter to Carnegie has been lost. We know of its contents only from Andrew's response.

slavery, should be despised, not celebrated, as "the most tyrannical [country] in the world." Dod challenged his cousin to a transoceanic written debate comparing the British and American forms of government.

"Dod's letter put me in an awful way," Andy wrote his uncle Lauder, perhaps because there was little he could say in reply. "I could hardly forbear from writing him the same hour his came to hand but I concluded (after I had filled three or four sheets in reply) to read some authorities upon the subject before 'proceeding to business.' I have the characteristics of 'our folks' rather 'strongly developed' . . . and am of course therefore a great, or rather small, dabbler in politics, and the proposition pleases me first rate. It will no doubt be beneficial to both of us to examine into the systems of Government by which we are ruled and it will prompt us to read and reflect on what perhaps we would never had done without that stimulant. I have therefore accepted Dod's challenge."[38]

The letters that followed, written when Andy was the age of today's high school seniors, read like the work of an accomplished scholar, albeit with a dash of boyish enthusiasm. Though he had left school at twelve, he had grown up in a family of radical political pamphleteers and speechmakers and learned, perhaps from their example, how to construct complex arguments and marshal evidence to support them. His analyses were powerful, his documentation thorough, his prose style distinctive and persuasive.[39]

Andy made his case for the superiority of American institutions in an almost breathless, celebratory prose that borrowed a great deal—in style and content—from George Bancroft's ode to Jacksonian democracy. Because, in the United States, "government is founded upon justice and our creed is that the will of the people is the source, their happiness, the end of all legitimate government," there was no need to employ the "wretched props" and "contrivances" Her Majesty's government required. "Our army consists of a few thousand men employed in protecting our frontiers from Indian depredations. Our police force is insignificant. Allegheny City for instance with a population of 22,000 has but four." Following the formula he would later employ in *Triumphant Democracy,* he assembled a wealth of statistical evidence to prove that democracy worked. "We have now in the National Treasury nearly $22,000,000"; annual government receipts exceeded expenditures; populations were increasing everywhere; American commerce was already "second in the world and is rapidly taking the first position." From Pittsburgh alone, fifty-two steamers a year were being launched, some over 1,000 tons. "We publish 2800 papers and magazines, 350 of which are dailies, number of copies printed annually estimated at 422,600,000. . . . Our railroads extend 13,000 miles. . . . Our telegraphs embrace 21,000 miles. . . . We have about $550,000,000 invested in manufactures. Every business yields a fair remuneration. Pauperism is almost unknown." In reply to the argument that government by itself had "little to do with this state of affairs," Andy called his cousin's attention to Canada: "Where are her railroads, telegraphs and canals? We have given to the world a Washington, a Franklin, a Fulton, a Morse. What has Canada ever produced?"[40]

In September 1854, Andy returned to battle, this time to compare the manner in which Great Britain and America selected their "sovereigns." Sounding much like his great-uncle had in attacking Lord Dalmeny, he skewered the British system in which "we see a person called Sovereign, exalted to the head of Government, not for any great service done to the state, not for any extraordinary virtue possessed, not because of any superhuman endowment, not for any towering ability or sir, not because the mighty voice of a free people calls him . . . but all for the mere accident of birth—an idea utterly at war with freedoms sentiment that all men are created equal."[41]

While his relatives in Scotland had fought—and failed—to get their charter or their reform bills written into law, "we" in America, Andy reminded them, "have the charter which you have been fighting for for years as the panacea for all Britain's woes, the bulwark of the people." In America, political reform, once achieved, had been translated directly into economic opportunity, as the Chartists back home had hoped it would. That is why so many English, Scots, Irish, and Welsh workingmen, "tax ridden and oppressed in their own country," had chosen "to seek a home in the new." Here they found "no Royal Family (increasing with fearful rapidity) to squander their hard made earnings, no aristocracy to support, no established church with its enormous sinecures . . . no primogeniture and entail to curse the land and stop improvements in the soil," no backbreaking taxes, no "merciless [hereditary] landlords."[42]

The cousins' debate ranged wide and far over several years. In February 1854, Naig was called upon to explain why America had not "come forward as France and England have" to defend Turkey and the "sacred right of nations" against the Russian usurper in the Crimean War. Carnegie's response bristled with sarcasm. "Oh! Dod! Dod! That's capital. Great Britain come forward? Why she has brought upon herself the contempt of honest men throughout the world for her course on this very question." Castigating the British for intervening in the Russian-Turkish conflict, Andy proclaimed that America's position in world affairs was guided by George Washington's admonition, "'Friendship with all, entangling alliances with none.'" Because America's "great mission" was to serve forever as a "pioneer of liberty," it dared not compromise its purity of purpose or its security by military adventurism, no matter how enlightened the cause might appear. "Our path, Dod, is plain, we will let Europe manage its own affairs while we take care of the American continent. Let those ruling by divine right fight and quarrel about successions and protectorates while we clear the forests and build school houses, preparing homes for the hard working bees forced to leave the old hive."[43]

If, on questions of politics, Andy was dead certain in his beliefs, in theology—a matter as critically debated among his circle of friends and relatives—he was still finding his way. His father, soon after arriving in Allegheny City, followed his sister-in-law into the tiny Swedenborgian church, known formally as the New Jerusalem Society of the City of Pittsburgh and Its Vicinity. Bobby Pitcairn, Andy's friend and fellow telegraph messenger, was a member of the congregation, as was Bobby's father. By May 1852, Andy was as well. (His mother and brother would remain apostate on matters Swedenborgian.) "Our Meeting House," he wrote his uncle Lauder, "is the story above our Office. I have just come down into the Office from Sunday School. We have a nice school. I take great interest in it and am a young Swedenborgian. Do you still read the Works?"[44]

Andy may have ended up "a young Swedenborgian" because, once landed in Allegheny City, he had to be something, and it was easier to follow his father and aunt into the society than to look elsewhere. It is difficult to underestimate the place of religion—and churchgoing—in mid-nineteenth-century America. Every foreign visitor—no matter where he or she had come from—felt obligated to remark on the American propensity for establishing churches and visiting them on Sundays. "There is no country in the world," Alexis de Tocqueville observed during his travels in the 1830s, "where the Christian religion retains a greater influence over the souls of men than in America." Thirty years later, Anthony Trollope described the same phenomenon, albeit with a touch of irony. "A man here is expected to belong to some church, and is not, I think, well looked on if he profess that he belongs to none. He may be a Swedenborgian, a Quaker, a Muggletonian:—anything will do. But it is expected of him that he shall place himself under some flag, and do his share in supporting the flag to which he belongs."[45]

Swedenborgianism, an older European-based variant of spiritualism, had been embraced not only by Andy's father and aunts but by New England intellectuals like Henry James, Sr., and the Transcendentalists. It remained nonetheless a marginal sect in the United States and in Scotland. The "texts" on which it was founded had been written a century before by Emanuel Swedenborg, a Swedish nobleman, scientist, and inventor, who, in many, many published volumes, recorded visions revealed to him in which "heaven was opened," and he was visited by Jesus Christ during Easter weekend in 1745 while Swedenborg was having dinner in a London inn. After telling Swedenborg that he was eating too much, Jesus returned later that night to reveal the spiritual meaning of the scriptures. The Lord Jesus was not the only source of revelation for Swedenborg. He also talked—rather often, it appeared— to a variety of spirits and to the heavenly angels—in their own language, which, he reported, was unlike any earthly language, as it relied predominantly on the vowels "u" and "o," lacked hard consonants, and was spoken "like a gentle stream, soft and virtually unbroken."[46]

Andy paid little heed to the more bizarre elements of the Swedenborgian creed. He may have temporarily embraced the sect because it was, in many ways, the antithesis of the Scottish Presbyterianism that his relatives and he—found so abhorrent. It was a gentle religion, with no infant damnation, no authoritarian ministers, and lots of wonderful music. Andy found in the society a tolerance, gentleness, and openness to discussion, which he cherished. He came into contact there with men like David McCandless, a fellow Scotsman, successful merchant, and years later, one of his business partners in the steel business.

The Swedenborgians nourished Andy's intellectual appetites and literary aspirations. Among his papers in the Library of Congress is a handwritten essay in pencil, entitled "Home," dated July 2, 1854, and another, also in pencil, marked "Dewdrops," the name of the society's magazine. In the latter, Andy argued, quite persuasively, that in the campaign against war, "one of the most important points to be gained is to render war and its instruments abhorrent to the young." Apparently, a Swedenborgian publication had paid tribute to a military hero or battle, and Andy took exception to this, as he would for the rest of his life. "If each one was educated to look upon those machines made expressly for the destruction of their fellow men—with the same horror that they behold the scaffold and the Guillotine—if they could be seen only in the museums as relics of a barbarous age instead of their likeness being paraded in our religious newspapers, how long would such scenes as that recently enacted . . . take place to shake our belief in man's possessing anything in common with his God." The sentences go on too long, the constructions are a bit unwieldy, but the energy and power of the prose is impressive, especially for an unschooled eighteen-year-old.[47]

Never one content to remain merely a member of the congregation, Andy was elected "librarian" of the society in November 1855, and reelected in 1856 and 1857. He was also an enthusiastic member of the choir, though he had difficulty holding a tune and a less than stellar singing voice. "The leader, Mr. Koethen, I have reason to believe, often pardoned the discords I produced in the choir because of my enthusiasm in the cause."[48]

Andy remained a member of the society for several years, leaving it only when he moved to Altoona in 1858. It served as a safe social haven, from which he could venture forth to explore theological questions with his friends from Allegheny City. "The mysteries of life and death, the here and the hereafter," he tells us, were matters of pressing interest among the young men of his "inner circle." Though he and the friends of this "inner circle"—a group of like-minded immigrant boys about his age and, like him, smart, ambitious, and inexhaustible—all worked five days a week and a half day on Saturday, they had organized themselves into a quasi-formal debating society that met in Henry Phipps's cobbler's shop. Phipps's older son, John, was a charter member of the group; his younger boy, Harry, hung around at the edges. The senior member, Thomas Miller, got to sit on the leather seat of old man Phipps's cobbling bench. The boys organized debates on religion and politics, teased one another about their "best girls," went skating on the Allegheny River, and visited Colonel Anderson's library.[49]

One of the chief topics for discussion was how to reconcile received religion with democracy. Charles G. Finney, a central figure in the Second Great Awakening that had blazed through western New York in the late 1820s and 1830s, had argued passionately and articulately against accepting doctrine solely "on the ground of authority. If I tried to accept those doctrines as mere dogmas, I could not do it. I could not be honest in doing it; I could not respect myself in doing it." The young men of Andy's inner circle believed, with Finney, that reason, not authority, had to be their guide in matters of the spirit and the soul. "This 'doing of a thing' because our grandfathers did it I can assure you is not an 'American Institution,'" Andy wrote Dod in August 1853. "We have little veneration for those rules and principles rendered sacred by the seal of the 'Ancients' whether in Church or State."[50]

As Andy left behind the family cottage at Allegheny City for Pittsburgh and the O'Rielly telegraph office every morning, Will Carnegie remained alone on Rebecca Street, working at his loom in the ground-floor workshop. In a letter to his cousin Dod in Dunfermline in June 1851, Naig reported cheerfully on his father's work: "Father has been working a linen web for a lady these two weeks past and has got along first rate with it, he is also working some linen cloths for himself. He thinks he can make more on them than on cotton ones. He is the same as when he left, not a bit of difference in him."[51]

It was easier to weave the cloths than to find buyers for them. In the spring of 1852, when Andy was sixteen and on temporary assignment to the telegraph office in Steubenville, Ohio, seventy miles downstream from Pittsburgh, he learned that his father would be stopping over on his way "to Wheeling and Cincinnati to sell the table cloths he had woven. I waited for the boat which did not arrive till late in the evening," he wrote in his *Autobiography*, "and went down to meet him. I remember how deeply affected I was on finding that instead of taking a cabin passage, he had resolved not to pay the price, but to go down the river as a deck passenger, I was indignant that one of so fine a nature should be compelled to travel thus." Greeting his father, Andy joked that before long Will and Margaret Carnegie would be riding in their own carriage, paid for, he implied, by their successful son. At this, his father, "usually shy, reserved, and keenly sensitive," lost his self-control, a rare occurrence, and "murmured slowly" that he was proud of his son. "The voice trembled and he seemed ashamed of himself for saying so much. The tear had to be wiped from his eye, I fondly noticed, as he bade me good-night and told me to run back to my office. . . . My father was one of the most lovable of men, beloved of his companions, deeply religious . . . not much of a man of the world, but a man all over for heaven."52

William Carnegie spent the last three years of his life working at his loom in an increasingly desultory fashion, reading the newspapers, and, like his son, taking increasing pride in American democracy and know-how. "Father said this morning," Andy wrote Uncle Lauder in the spring of 1852, "to be sure and tell you that the greatest Reform of the age has just taken place here." He was referring to the Homestead Act, which passed the House of Representatives that year, but would not become the law of the land for another ten years. "He does not take very much interest in politics here [compared to British politics]," Andy confessed to his uncle, "but that Land Reform has really excited him, he is in great glee about it." A year later, in another letter to Uncle Lauder, Andrew wrote that "Father is in good health and has about $70 of cloth which he intends to sell as soon as the good weather sets in. His letter is not yet commenced but he promises fair yet to write soon—in the meantime he sends you all his very best respects. He is highly delighted with the Caloric Ship [the latest example of American know-how] just now and looks forward to the time when Steam will be among the things that were—You will see that it has stood the test nobly it went to Norfolk by sea from New York and encountered a hard storm. The machinery worked regularly all the time—It will soon visit your shores, another monument of American genius."53

In October 1855, Will Carnegie died. We don't know the cause of death. He was fifty-one years of age; his eldest son almost twenty.

In his *Autobiography,* Carnegie reports Will Carnegie's death as having occurred three and a half years earlier, just after their distressing encounter at Steubenville. Why, we are left to wonder, did the son prematurely kill off his father? Had he simply misremembered the date of his death? Or, as is more likely, had he already, at age sixteen, given up any hope that his father might play a meaningful role in his life?

It was perhaps easier, in the end, to rhetorically kill his father than to try to come to terms with his life. Will Carnegie haunts the pages of the *Autobiography,* but as a spectral, almost disembodied figure, not as a caring, active father. Carnegie rarely, if ever, referred to him in other writings or in conversation, not because he was ashamed of his father, but because he never quite figured out what to make of the man. Carnegie was close to his uncle, with whom he would carry on a lifelong conversation about history and literature and politics. He adored his mother and would share living quarters with her as long as she lived. But his father was never an important part of his life.[54]

THREE

Upward Bound, 1853–1859

TIME WAS MONEY. The sooner American bankers, merchants, manufacturers, and government officials got information—on crops, commodity prices, currencies, etc.—the sooner they could act on it, and with fewer risks. Along the eastern seaboard, turnpikes, canals, steamers, and railroads had reduced the time it took to get the news from Washington to Boston from eighteen days in 1790 to less than three in 1841. The telegraph had then made news transmission instantaneous.

There was unfortunately no way to lay railroad tracks or string telegraph poles across the Atlantic. The Cunard steamships had reduced travel time from six weeks to two. Enterprising news merchants met the vessels in Halifax, Nova Scotia, offloaded the European newspapers, and shipped them via express steamer and pony express to Boston. One ingenious businessman who was later hired by the Associated Press sped the process along by transcribing the news onto thin strips of tissue paper and flying it to Boston via African carrier pigeon. In November 1849, about six months after Andy began delivering messages at O'Rielly's, the carrier pigeons were retired as the final telegraph poles were strung, connecting Halifax to Boston via Calais, New Brunswick, and Portland, Maine.[1]

In Pittsburgh, the editors of the six daily papers formed a pool to receive and distribute transmissions from Halifax. "The taking of successive 'steamer news'" for the pool quickly became "one of the most notable" duties entrusted to telegraph operators—and one of the most difficult. Each message had to traverse several different telegraph lines on the long route to Pittsburgh. An electrical storm anywhere along the line could—and usually did—result in partial transmissions. When stymied by a partial transmission, most operators asked their counterparts at the other end of the line to start again; Andy guessed at the missing letters or words and, to his delight, discovered that he was almost always right. He became so adept at transcribing the messages from Halifax that the "steamer news" was soon assigned to him. There were several perks associated, including the dollar-a-week bonus the reporters paid him to make copies of every dispatch from Halifax. "I was working for myself now, on an independent contract, doing something beyond my task. That [dollar] a week I considered my own. It did not go to the family support. It was my first capital."[2]

The little white-haired boy with the faintest of Scottish accents had rather quickly become the most-sought-after operator in the company. Among those who asked for him when he had a message to receive or deliver was Thomas A. Scott of the Pennsylvania Railroad. The railroad had been organized in 1846 by Philadelphia businessmen, concerned that unless they inserted their city into the east-west railroad grid, it would be eclipsed by Baltimore to the south, as it had by New York City to the north. In the fall of 1850, the first stretch of track was completed along the 137-mile corridor from Harrisburg to the foothills of the Alleghenies. Because the Pennsylvania had not yet bridged the mountains with tracks, it connected at Hollidaysburg with the state-operated Allegheny Portage Railroad, which transported passengers across the mountains in "land carriages" hauled up five ascending inclined planes by locomotives, horses, and stationary engines, and then let down another five carefully tethered to those same stationary engines.

J. Edgar Thomson, the Pennsylvania's chief engineer and soon to be its president, hired Tom Scott to manage the station in Hollidaysburg. Scott, a handsome, genial young man, born in Pennsylvania of Scots-Irish parents, had worked as a toll collector and chief clerk for the state's railroad/canal system and as a shipping agent for a freighting and commission firm. He knew the transportation business well and was, like the man who hired him, a hard worker, a native-born Pennsylvanian, and self-educated. Scott's ascent through the ranks of the Pennsylvania Railroad hierarchy was as rapid as Andy's had been at O'Rielly Telegraph. Within a year of his appointment as station manager at Hollidaysburg, he was dispatched to Pittsburgh in anticipation of the completion of the western division of the railroad. In December 1852, when the Pennsylvania tracks reached Pittsburgh, Scott was named the western division's first superintendent. He was twenty-nine years old.

As division superintendent, Scott was in charge of everything that moved between Altoona and Pittsburgh. Because Thomson had not yet raised enough capital to build a second track, Scott had to juggle eastbound and westbound trains along a single track. When the weather was good and the trains ran on time, there was little danger of accident or delay; but when snow covered the tracks or rain flooded them or engines broke down or there were difficulties loading freight or passengers, delay was inevitable and collisions all too likely. The standard procedure on one-track railways, which Scott followed along his western division, was to designate one train as "superior" and give it the right-of-way. If, for one reason or another, the "superior" was delayed, every other train on the line was ordered to pull onto the nearest siding and wait until it passed. If, after an hour of sitting on the siding, the superior train did not show up, the waiting train was allowed to proceed slowly to the next siding, with a flagman walking in front. Though these procedures made accidents less likely, they led to pyramiding delays for every train in the system.[3]

In Great Britain, railroads relied on the telegraph to locate the whereabouts of delayed trains; in America, most railroad executives distrusted the technology and the operators. Scott and Thomson were different. In the spring of 1853, they began putting up telegraph poles along the tracks from Philadelphia to Pittsburgh. Until their own line was in operation, Scott arranged with the O'Rielly office to use its lines and hired Andy Carnegie as his personal operator, for the grand sum of thirty-five dollars a month.[4]

"The Teleg. Co.," Andy wrote Uncle Lauder after accepting his new job, "would have increased my salary to $400 per year if I had remained there but we all thought that the new situation held out better prospects for the future." As long as he stayed at O'Rielly's, he would be "an employee, and the highest station I could reasonably expect to attain to was Manager of an office with seven or eight hundred a year." That was not enough.[5]

For an immigrant lad of seventeen, Andy Carnegie made an astute business decision by shifting his allegiance from O'Rielly's to the Pennsylvania Railroad. The telegraph business in western Pennsylvania was highly unstable, beset by technical problems, undercapitalization, and intense competition. The Pennsylvania Railroad, on the other hand, was entering a period of steady and unparalleled expansion. Gross receipts would increase from under $2 million in 1852, the year Andy began work for the railroad, to $5,285,300 in 1858; profits from $617,025.87 to $2,163,445.64.[6]

"I am liking [my new position] far better than the old one," Andy confided to his uncle a month after he had begun work at the railroad. "Instead of having to stay every night till 10 or 11 o'clock I am done every night at six—which is a great advantage. . . . [Mr. Scott] is having an office fixed up for his own use and I am to be along with him in it and help him. I have met with very few men that I like so well in this country—and I am sure we will agree very well."[7]

Andy acted not only as Scott's telegraph operator but as his secretary and chief assistant. Their office was located at the Outer Depot, a twenty-acre complex north of the downtown commercial area. Andy and Tom Scott worked out of a small room nestled within the larger complex of offices and rooms set aside for conductors, brakemen, and firemen. Instead of isolating himself from his new companions, as his mother might have preferred, Andy, seventeen and full grown but as curious and garrulous as ever, may have joined them in some of their after-hours pursuits. As he confessed in coded language in his Autobiography, "I ate, necessarily, of the fruit of the tree of knowledge of good and evil for the first time."[8]

Andy's early career on the railroad replicated his first days as a telegraph operator. He ingratiated himself with supervisors, learned as much about the industry as possible, and did more than was expected of him.

Executives of large railroads that spanned thousands of miles of track and operated hundreds of individual stations had no choice but to decentralize authority. Division superintendents like Tom Scott were princes of their realms, with "general charge of all employees" within their regions and responsibility for assuring "that they perform the duties assigned them." Train crews, station managers, and the skilled and unskilled laborers who worked on the tracks and in the yards could be reprimanded, disciplined, fined, suspended, or fired by Scott, with no recourse or appeal to higher authority.[9]

Written rules decreed how freight was to be loaded, passengers boarded, coaches scrubbed, brakes operated, engines fired, fares collected, and delays and accidents reported. "Propriety and manners were also a subject of regulations," according to Walter Licht, author of *Working for the Railroad*. Conductors, ticket agents, and station managers had to dress appropriately, speak clearly, and refrain from the use of alcohol or tobacco. To make sure that discipline was maintained in the absence of supervisors, workers were encouraged to spy on one another and warned that they would be disciplined if they did not report "misconduct or negligence."[10]

This system of management worked only to the extent that all power remained lodged in the company, with no unions interceding on behalf of aggrieved workers. The Brotherhood of Locomotive Engineers, the first effective trade union organization among railroad workers, would not come into being until the mid-1860s. As late as 1873, Herbert Gutman has written, "most railroad workers were without unions of any kind." Any hint of agitation, attempt at organization, or protest was met with swift disciplinary action.[11]

Carnegie, son of a weaver and nephew of activists, was quickly socialized into the authoritarian ways of railway management. Although he made a great deal of his Chartist ancestors in his *Autobiography* and in later writings and speeches, he had, in crossing the Atlantic, effectively severed his ties with them and their movement. Chartist agitators, political protest, and activist union leaders had a different and more necessary role to play in undemocratic Britain than they did in republican America. Andy Carnegie, as he approached the age of twenty, though very much a Chartist and a radical in Scottish affairs, was every bit the company man in Pittsburgh. He tied himself to Tom Scott's coattails and never let go. Whatever Scott wanted, Andy took care of it.

The Pittsburgh business community had never entirely accepted the Pennsylvania Railroad or trusted the Philadelphia bankers and merchants who dominated its board of directors. One of Scott's chief tasks was serving as plenipotentiary to Pittsburgh and removing obstacles placed in the railroad's path in the attempt to enlarge its terminal facilities. To help out his boss, Andy wrote an anonymous article for the *Pittsburgh Journal*, praising the new railroad and criticizing the business community and the people of Pittsburgh for not being more supportive. "The pen," he noted in his *Autobiography*, "was getting to be a weapon with me."[12]

Though he had no experience working on a train or in a station like the railroad's other managers, Andy's dedication to boss and company was formally rewarded when Scott requested and was given permission to leave his assistant in charge of the division while he traveled away from the office "for a week or two." Andy's two weeks as prince regent were uneventful until a ballast train suffered a minor accident. Though ballast trains carried only stones, Andy was infuriated by what he considered "the inexcusable negligence" of the crew. "That this accident should occur was gall and wormwood to me." Without asking permission from anyone in Philadelphia, Andy "held a court martial, examined those concerned, dismissed peremptorily the chief offender, and suspended two others for their share in the catastrophe." When Scott returned, he proposed to investigate the accident on his own. Andy explained "that all had been settled" and the guilty punished. Though he had by this time decided he had been too peremptory and "severe" in his punishment, he did not want Scott to intervene and was grateful when he refused to hear the men's appeals. In the end, Andy's punishments stood. One man lost his job and two others were suspended without pay.[13]

Andy Carnegie was, we can see, learning a great deal from superiors like Tom Scott about managing an organization. But the most critical lesson he took away from his tenure at the Pennsylvania Railroad had to do not with running a corporation but with exploiting his position to enhance his personal finances.

By 1855 or so, Andy and his mother had paid off the family's debts to Ailie Fargee and become the owners of the Rebecca Street lot and the two houses on it. The property, as Andy proudly wrote his uncle, was worth close to $700 when he bought it from Aunt and Uncle Hogan, but because repairs were needed after a recent flood, he got it for only $550, payable over two years.[14]

The Carnegies were by no means prosperous. Mag was still binding shoes, and her income, combined with Andy's forty-dollar salary at the railroad, was enough to pay off what they owed on the house and to keep Tom out of the workforce and in public school. And then, in October 1855, as Carnegie wrote in his *Autobiography*, "Fortunatus knocked at our door, Mr. Scott asked me if I had five hundred dollars. If so, he wished to make an investment for me." Scott offered Andy the opportunity to buy ten shares of Adams Express, a privately traded company, which, like its chief competitors, Wells Fargo and American Express, expedited the movement of documents, securities, and parcels from city to city. Six months earlier, in March 1855, the Pennsylvania Railroad had given Adams Express an exclusive contract to use its rails to transport its packages between Philadelphia and Pittsburgh.[15]

The timing of Scott's offer suggests that the shares he offered Andy had been made available to railroad officers as part of a quid pro quo for the contract Adams Express had just received. As Scott's telegraph operator, Andy was privy to every communication that his boss sent or received. It would have made sense for Scott to include him in on the spoils.

Because Andy didn't have the cash to buy the stock himself, Scott loaned him the $500 he needed. When, six months later, Scott's note came due, Andy borrowed the money to pay back his boss, and then arranged, through his mother, to mortgage off their newly acquired property in Allegheny City to cover the costs of the second loan. In the end, with the help of his mother, he acquired the stock and the guaranteed ten-dollar monthly dividend check that came with it.[16]

Andy's reaction to getting his first dividend check, as recorded in his *Autobiography* and elsewhere, was euphoric, as it should have been: he was getting a guaranteed 24 percent interest on his investment. "I shall remember that check as long as I live . . . It gave me the first penny of revenue from capital—something that I had not worked for with the sweat of my brow. 'Eureka!' I cried. 'Here's the goose that lays the golden eggs.'" Before cashing the check, he showed it to his friends at their Sunday afternoon gathering. "The effect produced . . . was overwhelming. None of them had imagined such an investment possibility." They were all amazed, he would later write in an article in *Youth's Companion*, by the magical properties of investment capital. "How money could make money, how, without any attention from me, this mysterious golden visitor should come, led to much speculation upon the part of the young fellows, and I was for the first time hailed as a 'capitalist.'"[17]

Carnegie's excitement is quite revealing. It is difficult to imagine his Scottish uncles receiving such a check without hesitating a moment to inquire whether they were, in taking money they had not worked for, doing the right thing. Where, they might have asked, did such money come from? Were dividends like the rents that landlords collected—without working—because they owned the land on which others toiled? Andy asked no such questions. He accepted the codes of capitalist behavior without a moment's pause. Upon arriving on American shores, he had abandoned the moral economy of his Scottish forefathers for the political economy of his new employers. He was a citizen of a brave new world now. The Adams Express dividend checks were only the beginning.

While working for Tom Scott, Andy Carnegie continued with his self-education. He had neither the money nor the time to attend school. Instead, he read as much as he could, wrote letters, position papers, and articles for the Swedenborgian journals, and sought out situations in which he could sharpen his writing and debating skills. It was an article of faith for him and his friends that learning to read, write, and argue would make them better citizens, men, and earners.

After several years of debates among themselves on matters theological and political, the Allegheny City boys moved out of old man Phipps's cobbler shop and into the more rarefied districts of the "Webster Literary Society" in Pittsburgh, which in 1856 was housed in the "third story room of the Vigilant engine house on Third Street at a rental of Three dollars a month."[18]

Following the example of Daniel Webster, whose name they had taken for their club, the young men debated issues of constitutional history and political theory. Their debates were much more formal than the Allegheny City boys had been used to, with adversaries referring to one another as "sir" and "honorable friend," and proceeding in a decorous parliamentary style. Andy took radical positions on several political questions, arguing for the affirmative in "Should the judiciary be elected by the people?" Among his papers at the Library of Congress is a lengthy manuscript on this subject, written on long blue, lined paper in black pen, and then copied again, in very neat handwriting, with several lines carefully crossed out.[19]

Carnegie was a great storyteller. One of his best stories, which he told in *Triumphant Democracy*, published in 1886, concerned his second investment: in the stock of the Woodruff Sleeping Car Company. In 1858 or 1859, while traveling on a Pennsylvania Railroad train, Andy was approached by T T Woodruff, "a tall, spare, farmer-looking kind of man [who] drew from a green bag . . . a small model of a sleeping berth for railway cars." On returning to Pittsburgh, Andy showed the model to Tom Scott. Scott and his boss, J. Edgar Thomson, were so impressed by Woodruff's invention that they offered him a contract to place at least two of his sleeping cars on the Pennsylvania Railroad line as soon as he could build them. In recognition of his role, Andy was offered an interest in the Woodruff Sleeping Car Company. He borrowed money from a local banker to pay for it and was richly rewarded with monthly dividends that were large enough to pay back his loan—and leave him something beside.[20]

It is a charming story, the kind nineteenth-century autobiographies and biographies specialized in, about a "good" boy who, through a combination of luck and pluck, succeeds in making his fortune. Other young men might have dismissed the "farmer-looking" stranger in the train, but Andy did not because he was respectful of his elders and astute enough to recognize the commercial potential of Woodruff's invention. The only problem with the story is that it wasn't true. The first person to dispute it was T. T. Woodruff himself, who, in a letter to Carnegie after the publication of *Triumphant Democracy*, contradicted every element. Carnegie wrote back, explaining that he had never intended to write a full history of the sleeping car company, but only mentioned it in passing.[21]

The truth was that Woodruff, as he reminded Carnegie, was in 1858 a successful inventor who had already secured contracts for his sleeping car with several railroads, including the Pennsylvania. Andy Carnegie's role in the deal was considerably less grand than he had represented it. He had never been a principal in the negotiations, but functioned instead as a sort of "bagman." "One of the conditions of the said agreement was that a certain specified interest [in the Woodruff Sleeping Car Company] should be held by another person, and represented (as the talk ran) by a boy then in the superintendent's office at Altoona." In other words, before Thomson and Scott signed an agreement with Woodruff, they wanted a kickback in the form of partial ownership of the company. To disguise their stake, they requested that their stock be put in Andy Carnegie's name. For his troubles, Andy was given a few shares for himself.[22]

Capitalizing on insider information to invest in companies that were about to be enriched by lucrative contracts was standard operating procedure for railroad executives. Indeed, J. Edgar Thomson, according to his biographer James Ward, only invested in projects he had inside information about: "Usually he knew at least one person in the business who would feed him the needed intelligence. . . . Even when he entered a risky speculation, it was only after much aforethought and with reliable inside information."[23]

Until the Crédit Mobilier scandal of 1873, there was no clear consensus that it was morally wrong or illegal for railroad presidents and superintendents to invest in the companies that did their construction work or that bought and sold real estate adjacent to new railroad lines. Only after the findings of a committee of the House of Representatives that the owners of the Union Pacific Railroad had pocketed between $33 and $50 million from Crédit Mobilier, which they owned and to which they had contracted construction work for their railroad at highly inflated prices, did such private deals receive much public scrutiny.[24]

By the time Carnegie wrote about his deal with Woodruff, what had once been commonplace had come to be regarded as scandalous, if not criminal. It is no wonder that he felt compelled to invent a story to account for how he made his first "considerable sum."

Andy Carnegie was growing up fast. In January 1858,[*] Tom Scott was promoted to general superintendent and took his young-looking, diminutive twenty-two-year-old assistant with him to Altoona. Although relocating meant leaving behind family and friends, Carnegie didn't hesitate to follow his boss and mentor. "This breaking up of associations in Pittsburgh was a sore trial, but nothing could be allowed to interfere for a moment with my business career."[25]

Altoona a decade before had not even existed; but by the time Scott and Carnegie arrived, it had ballooned into a small industrial village of nearly 3,500, almost all of them railroad employees. Located in a valley in the geographical center of the state, the town was dominated by the railroad's huge roundhouses, engine shops, repair shops, a smithy, and the foundry where new locomotives were built. There were a few general stores, some churches, a school, several lodging houses, and one good hotel—Logan House—where Andrew stayed with Scott, until Scott, a widower, was able to send for his children and his niece Rebecca Stewart to look after his family.

Marooned more than 100 miles from home, without family or friends, Andrew found himself spending a great deal of time at the Scotts' residence with Rebecca Stewart. "Life at Altoona," he tells us, "was made more agreeable for me through Mr. Scott's niece." Introducing Miss Stewart to the readers of his *Autobiography,* Carnegie informs us that she "played the part of elder sister . . . to perfection," but it is difficult not to read more into their relationship. "We were much together, often driving in the afternoons through the woods." Was he romantically interested in his boss's niece? Perhaps, but he may have been too shy to declare himself to a woman who was a few years older and much wiser in the ways of the world than he was.[26]

---

[*]In his *Autobiography,* Carnegie erroneously dates the change to 1856.

"Beck" Stewart would be the first of several older women who took Andy Carnegie into their homes and taught him the manners he sorely lacked. Dinner at the Scott household, with silver cream pitchers and other domestic luxuries, was quite different than it had been at the Carnegie home in Allegheny City.[27]

Out of guilt or need or some combination of each, Andy sent for his mother and brother Tom about the time that Rebecca Stewart arrived in Altoona. The family's Allegheny City property was sold in March 1858 and the proceeds used to buy a large house in Altoona, sufficiently far from the smoke and grit of the railway yards in the valley. To mark his own rise in the business world, Andy hired a servant for the household. His mother refused at first to let a stranger into their home, preferring to take care of her two boys by herself, but she soon relented. For the rest of her and her son's life, their households would be filled with servants.[28]

Andy was delighted to be able to take care of his mother. Nothing was too good for the woman who had kept the family together through the bad times in Dunfermline and Allegheny City. She had, almost literally, been the financial support of her boys since they were born. Now, after twenty years as a breadwinner, she could enjoy a life of leisure.

Carnegie worked for six and a half years alongside Tom Scott, first in Pittsburgh, then in Altoona. It was the perfect apprenticeship for a young businessman. American railroads, the Pennsylvania perhaps foremost among them, were the first complex business enterprises to employ the principles of accounting to keep track of their far-flung operations. The Pennsylvania, according to Alfred Chandler, was maintaining 144 different sets of accounting records by 1857. Almost manically detailed data were compiled, month by month, station by station, division by division on every category of expenditure, from "advertising" to "wood, labor preparing." Division superintendents kept separate records on each locomotive engine, with information on its builders, the date it went into service, its size, weight (loaded and unloaded), miles run with different types of equipment, total cost, cost per 100 miles for repairs, fuel, and fluid, oil, waste, and tallow. They recorded how many passengers entered and left each station each month, where they were bound, and whether they were traveling locally or transferring to another railway. They noted, again station by station, and month by month, the gross tonnage and the revenues generated from over one hundred specific articles of freight from "agricultural implements" to "wool and woolen yarn."[29]

Later in life, Scott would be better known for his political skills, but he was, like his mentor Thomson, a master of cost accounting. Together, the two men steadily cut unit costs and increased revenues by investing in capital improvements—new and larger locomotives, better braking systems, improved tracks, new bridges. Instead of running several smaller trains along the same route, they ran fewer but longer trains with larger locomotives and freight cars. To minimize delays—a major factor in escalating costs—they erected their own telegraph lines, built a second track and extended sidings alongside the first one, and kept roadways, tunnels, bridges, and crossings in good repair.

Carnegie watched, listened, learned. Nothing was lost on the young man. With an exceptional memory and a head for figures, he made the most of his apprenticeship and within a brief time was acting more as Scott's deputy than his assistant. Tom Scott had proven to be so good at his job that when Pennsylvania Railroad vice president William Foster died unexpectedly of an infected carbuncle, Scott was named his successor.

Carnegie was distraught at the notion that he would be left behind in Altoona to work for Scott's replacement. But in the reorganization that followed, he was promoted: to superintendent of the Pittsburgh division. He was only twenty-four years old, but he knew the railway business as well as anyone else and was trusted by Scott and Thomson to do their bidding and keep their secrets. Not least among his attributes was his total confidence in his ability to get his job done: "I was at an age when I thought I could manage anything."[30]

FOUR

War and Riches, 1860–1865

T HE 1860 *Directory of Pittsburgh and Allegheny Cities* lists Andrew Carnegie as "Superintendent of the Western Division of the Pennsylvania Railroad," with an office at the Outer Depot and a residence at 10 Hancock, Pittsburgh. Now twenty-five and head of the Carnegie household, he was still probably no more than five feet tall, smaller than his younger brother and mother, though with a barrel chest and a huge head that slightly compensated for his tiny size.

Upon leaving Altoona, the Carnegies had decided not to return to Allegheny City, but to settle across the Allegheny River in a rather upscale Pittsburgh neighborhood. They didn't last there very long. Hancock, soon to be named Eighth Street, appeared genteel enough and housed a great many religious institutions and schools, including the Female College, the Hebrew Church, and the Christ Methodist Church, but it was too close to the mills to afford much protection from a dense covering of smog in the air and soot on the ground. "The smoke permeated and penetrated everything. If you placed your hand on the balustrade of the stair it came away black; if you washed face and hands they were as dirty as ever in an hour. The soot gathered in the hair and irritated the skin . . . life was more or less miserable."[1]

Since there was no way to remove the soot and grime, Carnegie, on the recommendation of David Stewart, a freight manager at the Pennsylvania Railroad and the brother of Rebecca Stewart, removed his family instead to the section of Homewood known today as Point Breeze, a wooded suburb about eight miles from downtown. The air was relatively clean, the sky almost smokeless, there was abundant greenery and undeveloped acreage, and the Carnegie property was a short carriage ride from the

East Liberty railway station. Andy and Tom, who was now his older brother's secretary and telegrapher, could take the 6:03 morning train from East Liberty, which arrived in Pittsburgh at 6:30 A.M., and return home on the 6:25 P.M. or the nine o'clock train. There was an 11:00 P.M. milk train for occasions when the boys went to the theater—as often as not with their mother.[2]

After a lifetime spent in the grime of Dunfermline and Allegheny City, the family had fallen in love with the countryside in their year and a half in Altoona. Homewood was almost as pastoral. With its hills and meadows and high sky, the landscape was more like Scotland than anything the Carnegies had encountered in the New World. Their house was situated within the exclusive suburban community that had been carved out of the estate of Judge William Wilkins, one of the region's wealthiest and most powerful individuals. "With this change to the country," Carnegie recalled, still with a bit of wonder at his rapid social ascension, "came a whole host of new acquaintances. Many of the wealthy families of the district had their residences in this delightful suburb. It was, so to speak, the aristocratic quarter." Among the Carnegies' new neighbors were Judge Wilkins and his wife, who was the daughter of George W. Dallas, a former vice president of the United States; Leila Addison, an "Edinburgh lady" who had been educated abroad; and William Coleman, a rich, successful, and well-respected local businessman.[3]

Carnegie, who had until now spent most of his hours outside the workplace in the company of Scottish workingmen and their families, had entered a social setting for which he was quite unprepared. He sought out, as he had earlier in Altoona in the person of Rebecca Stewart, older women to serve as his tutors, the most important of whom was Leila Addison, who, he thought, took him on as a project because he was Scottish. Miss Addison, who was also Scottish, corrected his speech, his manners, his behavior, and his dress: "Great heavy boots, loose collar, and general roughness of attire were then peculiar to the West and in our circle considered manly. Anything that could be labeled foppish was looked upon with contempt." He learned from Miss Addison and Mrs. Wilkins that, no matter how important manly dress might be at the workplace—especially for a tiny man who still looked like a boy—the opposite was the case in the drawing room. There, it was a sin against society to dress carelessly or make any gross display of manly roughness.[4]

. . .

AS WESTERN DIVISION SUPERINTENDENT, Andy was on duty twenty-four hours a day. Responsible for all traffic between the Alleghenies and Pittsburgh, he had a telegraph connection extended from the East Liberty station to his home so that he could stay in constant touch with his office. He drove the men who worked for him relentlessly, day and night, to clear tracks of wrecks, to repair broken rails, to keep the road in proper repair. If he could survive with little or no sleep over long stretches, so should they. "I was probably the most inconsiderate superintendent that ever was entrusted with the management of a great property, for, never knowing fatigue myself . . . I overworked the men and was not careful enough in considering the limits of human endurance." There is the slightest hint of regret coupled with resignation here. Carnegie did not enjoy directly supervising his workingmen. He was, he recognized, too impatient, too lacking in sympathy to establish any sort of rapport with the men who worked for him. This was not a moral failing but an operational one. To work men to the ultimate, one had to understand their limits. Carnegie didn't—and hence got less out of them than he should have. Though he would subsequently employ hundreds of thousands of workingmen, he would never again put himself in the position where he was responsible for supervising any of them.[5]

The day after Carnegie's appointment took effect, on December 1, 1859, some 200 miles from Pittsburgh, John Brown was hanged for murder, conspiracy to incite slave rebellion, and treason against the State of Virginia. Brown had failed in his attempt to incite a slave rebellion, but his eloquence in defending his actions had won him—and the cause of abolition—sufficient sympathy in the North to thoroughly frighten southern slaveholders and politicians and persuade them that there was little possibility of compromise over the future of slavery. Within the year, Abraham Lincoln would be elected president and South Carolina would begin the exodus of southern states from the Union.

The South's secession set Carnegie "all aflame for the flag." He had always been "a strong anti-slavery partisan." When his cousin Dod in Dunfermline criticized the Kansas–Nebraska Act of 1854 for repealing the Missouri Compromise and laying the way open for the organization of Kansas as a slave state, Carnegie responded that no one could "hate the measure more than I do." He predicted that the northerners who had voted for the measure would be consigned to "infamy" by the "just indignation of an insulted and betrayed people."[6]

The founding of the Republican Party offered him a way to transmute his antipathy for slavery into support for the politicians who had pledged to oppose its spread. He organized a club among the employees at the Outer Depot to subscribe to the *New York Weekly Tribune*, edited by Horace Greeley, the nation's most outspoken Republican, and wrote short notes to the paper, one of which was published. By late 1855, he had become, he wrote Dod, "an enthusiastic & ultra abolitionist," who regarded slavery as "the greatest evil in the world" and promised to use "whatever influence I may acquire . . . to overthrow it. . . . In short I am a Republican & believe in our Noble declaration 'that all Men are born free & equal.'"[7]

In March 1861, Abraham Lincoln was inaugurated in Washington, D.C. Five weeks later, at four-thirty in the morning of April 12, Fort Sumter and its American flag in Charleston Harbor were fired on by Confederate troops. The undermanned federal garrison surrendered the following day. "No sooner had the news of the surrender at Fort Sumter been confirmed," wrote Erasmus Wilson in his 1898 *Standard History of Pittsburg*, "than the whole community was up in arms. Preparations were made on the 15th to enroll and equip a large volunteer force in the cities and suburbs in response to the call for 75,000 men by the President. No such popular uprising had ever been seen here before." At an open meeting at the City Hall, Judge Wilkins, a lifelong Democrat, called on the 4,000 to 5,000 people assembled to bury all distinctions of party "in an ocean of patriotism" and unite behind the president. A Committee of Public Safety, headed by Wilkins, was organized to oversee the defense of the city, "keep a sharp lookout for traitors," and supervise the recruitment of the volunteers Lincoln had requested.[8]

On April 17, two days after Lincoln issued the call for 75,000 volunteers, his secretary of war, Simon Cameron of Pennsylvania, asked his friend and fellow railroad executive J. Edgar Thomson to arrange transportation for them to Washington. Thomson dispatched Tom Scott to Harrisburg "to assist in the movement of troops from all parts of the State to the camps at the Capital of Pennsylvania, which troops were there to be organized and equipped, and forwarded thence to the National Capital."[9]

The major weapons arsenal in Pennsylvania and, indeed, in the entire mid-Atlantic region, was the Allegheny Arsenal, located in Pittsburgh on Penn Avenue, less than a mile and a half from the Outer Depot where Carnegie had his office. Carnegie was enlisted by Thomson and Scott to supervise the transportation to Harrisburg of arms and armaments from the arsenal and volunteers from Camp Wilkins, the temporary encampment for volunteers. From April 19 on, he was in regular telegraphic communication with Scott in Harrisburg. Rather than attempting to communicate directly with the arsenal on what might be less than secure telegraph lines, Scott and military commanders in Harrisburg used Carnegie's office in the Outer Depot. On April 20, Scott telegraphed Carnegie with an order from a Major Porter in Harrisburg to "forward the ammunition by fast train tonight." Carnegie delivered the message himself to the arsenal commander, then telegraphed back to Scott that the materiel had been "loaded onto wagons and driven to the rail yards. . . . Will all be ready to go . . . without fail." In the same telegram, Carnegie informed Scott that Governor William Dennison, Jr., of Ohio had telegraphed to arrange transportation to Harrisburg for Ohio troops that had arrived in Pittsburgh the day before. "Eleven hundred of them have just gone to the City Hall intending to remain the night. I have sent down and will see how soon we can get them off perhaps not till morning."[10]

Transporting soldiers and armaments along the Pennsylvania Railroad tracks the 170 miles to Harrisburg was the easy part; moving them the next 70 miles to Baltimore and then the final 40 miles to Washington was much more difficult. Only one railroad—the Washington Branch of the Baltimore & Ohio (B&O)—linked Baltimore and Washington, and by a single track. Should that single track be blockaded or ripped up or the bridges into Baltimore destroyed, the nation's capital would become isolated from the North. And that is what happened on April 19.

About 1,800 volunteers of the Sixth Massachusetts Regiment had arrived in Baltimore, bound for Washington. The citizens of Baltimore, the fourth largest city in the nation in 1860, were divided between support for the secessionists, neutrality, and adherence to the Union. The mayor was a lukewarm unionist; the police chief a secessionist; the business community split between those whose trade was with the North and those whose commercial ties were to the South. The city was, as Allan Nevins puts it, "a powder tub ready for a match" when the Massachusetts volunteers arrived at the President Street station en route to Washington.[11]

Baltimore had no central railway station. Each railroad operated its own terminal. The Philadelphia, Wilmington & Baltimore line which connected the city to the North had its depot on President Street; the Washington Branch of the B&O had its across town on Camden Street. There were no train tracks linking the two stations. The Massachusetts volunteers, upon arriving at the President Street depot, had to evacuate their railroad cars and march in formation across town to Camden Street to board the trains that would take them into Washington. They had proceeded only a short distance when they were, as their colonel reported to Washington, "furiously attacked by a shower of missiles, which came faster as they advanced." The soldiers, still in formation, accelerated their pace, which only angered the mob. Shots were fired at the soldiers—and returned.[12]

The president of the B&O, though a strong unionist himself, reluctantly informed Secretary of War Cameron's representatives that, given the situation in Baltimore, he could not transport any more northern soldiers through the city. The Baltimore police commissioners were even more concerned with the threat of disorder on the streets. Convening on the evening of the riot, they concluded, without dissent, that they would permit no more soldiers to march through their city. The railroad bridges that connected Baltimore to the North were burned, the telegraph lines cut.[13]

It is difficult to imagine the shock that the events in Baltimore sent through the North. Until Baltimore was pacified, Washington would remain isolated from the rest of the North—and from the troops and ammunition required to protect it from invasion. Almost every telegram from Carnegie to Scott asked for news of Baltimore. But there was no good news.[14]

Secretary of War Cameron and J. Edgar Thomson had no choice now but to find another route to the nation's capital for the eight hundred Massachusetts volunteers under General Benjamin F. Butler marooned in Philadelphia and the thousands more assembling there and in Harrisburg. Cameron favored sending troops to Baltimore to forcibly open the city; but Lincoln would not allow this, as he did not want to antagonize Maryland's citizens to the point where they would join the Confederacy. Thomson came up with a better solution: Baltimore could be bypassed entirely if troops were transported south from Philadelphia to Perryville at the mouth of the Susquehanna River and then ferried—on Pennsylvania

Railroad—owned or leased steamers—through Chesapeake Bay to Annapolis, Maryland, where there were railway connections to Washington.

The most dangerous segment of the route around Baltimore was the final one, the stretch of tracks from Annapolis to Washington, which had to be protected from Confederate sabotage. In his *Autobiography*, Carnegie dons the hero's mantle and tells us that it was he—and the "corps of assistants" he brought with him from Pittsburgh—who secured this stretch of track. In the course of doing so, he was slightly injured, receiving "a gash in my cheek which bled profusely. In this condition I entered the city of Washington with the first troops, so that with the exception of one or two soldiers, wounded a few days previously in passing through the streets of Baltimore, I can justly claim that I 'shed my blood for my country' among the first of its defenders. I gloried in being useful to the land that had done so much for me."[15]

There is no irony intended here. He intended to equate his gash—acquired when a telegraph wire snapped up to smite him—with the wounds suffered by the Union soldiers in arms. As a little man and a foreigner, Carnegie needed to establish his credentials as man and patriot—and what better way to do so than by inventing a story of Civil War heroism?

Carnegie's story, though accepted at face value by his biographers,* doesn't bear scrutiny. He might indeed have suffered a gash in the cheek, but not at the time and under the circumstances he so vividly describes in his *Autobiography*. Carnegie was, in fact, still in Pittsburgh on April 25, when General Butler, a Massachusetts lawyer and politician with no military experience but enough self-confidence to bluff his way through, reopened the tracks from Annapolis to Washington and sent his Massachusetts Sixth and a regiment from New York on their way to the capital. Butler had among his troops a number of railroad men. His soldiers, not Carnegie's crew, repaired the track from Annapolis to Washington and were the first to enter the beleaguered city.

---

* The only source for this story, except for Carnegie, is David Homer Bates, *Lincoln in the Telegraph Office*, published in 1907. Bates tells the same story as Carnegie, but inadvertently qualifies its value as primary evidence by writing that his "account of Mr. Carnegie's work . . . was prepared after a recent interview with him, and has received his indorsement"—Bates, *Lincoln in the Telegraph Office* (New York: Century Co., 1907), 20.

Once the route from Philadelphia to Washington via Annapolis was opened, the troops from Harrisburg could be safely transported south. Scott, his presence no longer required in Harrisburg, left for Washington on April 25. Later that week, Carnegie left Pittsburgh for Annapolis. Though his eventual destination was Washington, where he had been asked to serve as Scott's assistant, he spent the first few weeks of May in Annapolis, making sure that the road to Washington stayed open. Toward the middle of the month, he moved on to Washington.[16]

He and Scott were still employees of the Pennsylvania Railroad and received their salaries—and instructions—from J. Edgar Thomson in Philadelphia. From his perch in the War Department, Scott, first as a colonel of the District of Columbia militia and then as assistant secretary of war, served his two masters well. He made sure that troops, arms, armaments, coal, grain, and livestock were transported over the Pennsylvania system and that the railroad was well paid for the service.[17]

The arrival of the Massachusetts and New York volunteers in Washington on April 25 put an end to Lincoln's immediate fears of invasion. By May, there were troops of varied uniforms quartered throughout the city, in every government building, at the Georgetown Seminary, and in tents on Franklin Square and Meridian Hill. The task entrusted to Scott and his assistant Carnegie was to move them south through the city and across the Potomac into Virginia, where the rebels lay waiting.[18]

Before the war, Congress, determined to prevent Washington from becoming just another marketplace, had forbidden the laying of tracks through the city and over the Long Bridge that spanned the Potomac. In peacetime, this meant only an inconvenience to passengers who took horse-drawn omnibuses from the B&O station in the city to the Long Bridge and then crossed it either by foot, wagon, or ferry. In wartime, a better way had to be found to move troops, horses, armaments, and supplies across the Potomac into Virginia.

Andy Carnegie and the Pennsylvania Railroad men he had brought with him laid tracks across the city and over the Long Bridge. By late May, the path through Washington and over the Potomac had been prepared for the troops and the tons of equipment they required for their march south. Carnegie crossed the Potomac with the army and set up headquarters in Alexandria, where he was put in charge of rebuilding, reinforcing, and extending the telegraph and rail lines from Washington to Alexandria and from Alexandria southwest along the route the northern troops would travel.

On July 16, the Union troops began their march on Manassas Junction—and its critically important rail crossing, which lay just across Bull Run, a slow-moving stream clotted with trees. While the troops slogged their way on foot with fifty-pound packs, Secretary of War Cameron, whose visit to the battlefield, Carnegie thought, "would have an excellent effect upon the troops and the country," took the train to Fairfax and then rode the rest of the way on horses Carnegie transported (also by train) from the Treasury Building stables in Washington.[19]

On the morning of July 22, Union troops forded Bull Run Creek, and finding little resistance, pushed back the Confederate lines, cheered on by reporters, congressmen, and assorted civilian sightseers with picnic baskets who had taken the day trip from Washington to watch the battle through binoculars. From Pittsburgh, Tom Carnegie telegrammed his brother asking for "reliable information" about the battle: "Great excitement here this morning. All anxious to hear the news."[20]

The early news was good. But in mid-afternoon, backed by fresh reinforcements, the rebels broke through the Union lines. Instead of retreating in orderly fashion, the raw, inexperienced, ill-trained ninety-day northern recruits tumbled over one another—and the civilians who urged them back to battle—dashed madly across the Bull Run, discarding their packs and weapons along the way, and then raced north and east to the railroad tracks that led into Alexandria and, they hoped, safety.

Trying to put the best possible spin on the disaster, Carnegie telegraphed a dispatch to the *Pittsburgh Chronicle* that was published the same day, under the heading, "From the Seat of War." Union troops had been "forced to retire," he admitted, but all was not lost. They were re-forming their lines "at Alexandria, and will attack the enemy again shortly."[21]

Carnegie convinced himself—as he hoped to convince others, including his friend W. H. Holmes in Pittsburgh—that the defeat at Bull Run had been a "blessing in disguise. We shall now begin in earnest. Knowing our foes, the necessary means will be applied to ensure their overthrow." He was "delighted," he told Holmes, that he was in the thick of things. "How gratifying to lie down at night & think By George you are of some use in sustaining a great cause."[22]

To Tom, Andy explained by telegram that the Union troops had been defeated only after they had become "utterly exhausted and a fresh army attacked." Washington was "perfectly safe—fortifications fully manned with fresh troops. Rebels have made no demonstrations looking to an advance. Their loss fully equals ours."[23]

His major tasks—laying track through Washington, opening the Long Bridge and the ferry services across the Potomac, and setting up rail and telegraph lines in northern Virginia—having been completed, Carnegie returned to Pittsburgh and the Pennsylvania Railroad in late August, after four months in Washington. He was a Republican loyalist, an opponent of slavery, a foe of secession, and committed to fighting the war to conclusion. But he was not willing to absent himself indefinitely from job, family, and his developing business interests, which were, by the summer of 1861, already quite extensive. There was no need for him to remain in Washington. The war department had begun to replace civilians with military men in the management of communications and transportation for the Union armies. Unlike several of his colleagues at the Pennsylvania Railroad, including Tom Scott and Bobby Pitcairn, Carnegie would play no further part in the Civil War. He was not a professional soldier, had no military training, and no desire to remain in government service. He could best serve his nation—and himself—by keeping the trains running smoothly in and through Pittsburgh. Besides, he had several investments of his own that needed looking to.

He now held stock in two express companies, as well as Western Union, two horsecar companies, at least two coal companies, an oil company, the Freedom Iron Company near Lewistown, Pennsylvania, and the Woodruff Sleeping Car Company. These investments were paying handsome dividends, dividends which Carnegie was anxious to reinvest in new projects. Unwilling to wait until the war was won, Carnegie dedicated himself to extending his own economic empire.[24]

Though he still looked like a youth of sixteen, he had learned to dress, walk, and talk the part of the businessman. To cover up that boyish face, he had grown a beard—or tried to. An 1861 photograph taken in Philadelphia shows him with a rather wispy affair crawling around the outskirts of his face, barely touching his chin; his lip is bare. Skimpy as it was, the beard served its purpose. Staring straight at the camera, wearing a long frock coat, vest, and tie, his head slightly tilted forward, his gaze as solemn as a preacher's at a funeral, Andrew Carnegie was a portrait of self-assurance and competence.

In the past he had looked to his partners, Scott and Thomson, to include him in their investments. But from this point on, he intended to scout out his own opportunities. There was risk involved in proceeding on his own, but that could be minimized, if not eliminated entirely, by following the rules of the game he had learned from his mentors: Only invest in companies you have investigated yourself; only invest in companies about which you have insider knowledge; only invest in companies that sell goods or services for which demand is growing; never invest as an individual, but always with a group of trusted associates who together will own a controlling or dominant interest in the company.

Carnegie had all his life found a way to attach himself to older people who could be of use to him—and he to them. On arriving in Homewood, he had worked his charm on his wealthy neighbors, including William Coleman, whose daughter Lucy would later marry Tom Carnegie. Coleman had already made two fortunes—in iron manufacturing and coal mining—and was on his way to a third in oil drilling. For a businessman like Coleman, Carnegie was a valuable friend. He was division superintendent of the Pennsylvania Railroad, had money to invest and, more important, access to other sources of capital. It was surely not a secret to Coleman that Carnegie was part of an informal investment pool with Scott, Thomson, and several prominent businessmen in Philadelphia.

In 1861, Coleman purchased a parcel of land on Oil Creek in Venango County, not far from where Edwin Drake had drilled the first American oil well two years earlier. Drake's success in getting the oil out of the ground had set in motion a frenzy of real estate speculation up and down what had become known as Oil Creek, a tributary of the Allegheny River that extended northward about fifteen miles from Franklin, Pennsylvania, to Titusville.[25]

That there was oil in the ground was no secret; it was everywhere in the region, contaminating water wells and seeping out from underground sources to deposit a thin, viscous, bluish coating on the creek. Unfortunately, except for local tribes of Native Americans, who used the oil as a medicine and to waterproof canoes, and a few imaginative patent medicine dealers, no one had found any real use for the substance. Only in the late

1850s did a number of enterprising businessmen, with the help of chemists, discover that it was possible to distill Pennsylvania crude rock oil into a cleanly burning illuminant. Pennsylvania crude was more plentiful, cheaper, and burned more efficiently than whale oil (which was getting scarce and expensive as the species was killed off), lard oil (produced from pork fat), or coal oil (which smelled dreadfully as it burned). The excitement in the oil regions was all-consuming and would continue for the next decade. Every day there were new sightings made, new contracts written, new fortunes imagined. The *Pittsburgh Daily Commercial,* the city's business paper, ran a regular front-page section which it entitled "El Dorado."

William Coleman was one of the more respectable businessmen to join the first wave of prospectors. While most of the prospectors who decamped along Oil Creek had only enough money to lease the farms they drilled on, Coleman in 1859 bought the 500-acre Story farm in the center of Oil Creek for about $40,000. In May 1861, while Carnegie was in Washington, Coleman organized the Columbia Oil Company, which he invited his young neighbor to invest in upon his return from Washington. Carnegie was intrigued, but before putting down money, asked Coleman to take him on a tour of the oil region.

Though Oil Creek was about 100 miles due north of Pittsburgh, there were, as yet, no direct or indirect—rail connections. Coleman and Carnegie boarded an Allegheny River steamer for Franklin, Pennsylvania. At Franklin, the two men either transferred to a horse-drawn wagon or, more likely, boarded a flatboat that was pulled upstream by horses to the Story farm. The region was pockmarked by crude wooden prospector shanties which dotted the shoreline. Alongside the shanties rose the wooden derricks each prospector hoped would bring black gold out of the earth. A considerable number of these derricks—and shanties—had been abandoned; others had been singed or burned down by the oil fires that were endemic in the region. "What surprised me was the good humor which prevailed everywhere. It was a vast picnic, full of amusing incidents. Everybody was in high glee; fortunes were supposedly within reach; everything was booming."[26]

It was one thing to get the oil from the ground, another to get it to Pittsburgh to be refined and distributed. Following the path of the lumbermen who had mined the Oil Creek valley of its second most valuable resource, timber, the oilmen damned the creek at each of the several sources that fed into it from the north. Twice a week, they opened the floodgates, releasing the dammed water in a floodtide that floated hundreds of flat-bottom boats, some loaded with barrels, others with loose oil, south to Franklin, where it was loaded onto steamers bound for Pittsburgh. The flat-bottom boats leaked to begin with, and leaked even more as they were hurled along in the floodtide, crashing into one another and the shoreline, and taking on more water, which displaced more oil. The waste was appalling—probably two thirds of the oil pumped from the ground—but no one seemed to mind, as the supply appeared inexhaustible.

Carnegie, having satisfied himself that there was oil in the ground and a way to ship it to Pittsburgh, agreed to invest in Coleman's oil company. While other prospectors fantasized only about the liquid gold that lay deep in the ground, Coleman and Carnegie believed that in the not too distant future the wells would run dry. To prepare for that day and turn it to their advantage, Coleman proposed—and Carnegie agreed—to construct a man-made lake, pump the oil from their wells into it, and leave it there until the supply dwindled and prices rose. Coleman and Carnegie waited for the region to run out of oil while their lake leaked thousands of barrels daily. Unable to find any efficient way to store the oil, they had to sell it on the open market.

It was the right decision. By June 1863, the Columbia Oil Company had made so much money it was able to pay investors a dividend of 30 percent. In August and September, it paid additional dividends of 25 percent each; in October, 50 percent. In the first six months of 1864, another 160 percent. Carnegie was suddenly a very rich man.[27]

He was, as he would be for the rest of his life, generous in spreading his newfound wealth. He sold some of his stock in Columbia Oil to his old Allegheny City friend Tom Miller; he also shipped barrels of oil to Scotland to set up Cousin Dod in the "oil trade." When Dod was unable to sell enough barrels to pay for the initial shipment, Naig assured him that he "was in no hurry for funds" and would wait as long as he had to for Dod to make a go of it.[28]

The tens of thousands of dollars Carnegie earned in the four years he held the Columbia Oil stock were quickly reinvested in other projects. As oil was found in other places—in Duck Creek in 1864 and Pithole Creek in 1865—Carnegie investigated and invested in new oil companies.

The Civil War had unleashed productive forces that, properly harnessed, were going to yield millions to those aggressive enough to take the reins. Once the war was over—and the North had won, as Carnegie was convinced it would—trade could be expected to expand in every direction, especially west following the route of the settlers who were going to occupy the 2.5 million acres opened to cultivation with passage of the Homestead Act in 1862.

There had been discussion, for more than a decade, of building a Pacific railroad across the plains and the mountains all the way to California. In the summer of 1862, President Lincoln signed legislation authorizing two new companies to construct that road with federal subsidies. The Union Pacific would lay track westward and the Central Pacific eastward until the two met somewhere between Omaha and Sacramento. Neither the Pennsylvania Railroad nor any of the eastern railroads participated in building the new transcontinental railroad, though every one of them expected to profit from increased east-west traffic when it was completed.

Carnegie knew too much about the industry to invest directly in railroad stocks. It was less risky—and in the long run far more lucrative—to put his money in companies that had sweetheart contracts with the roads to supply coal, wood, and iron; to build their bridges; grade their crossings; manufacture their rails; and manufacture their rolling stock, locomotives, and specialized freight, passenger, and sleeping cars.

His investments in oil had paid off handsomely enough for him to contemplate going into business for himself. In doing so, he fully intended to capitalize on his position within the Pennsylvania Railroad and his contacts with its two leading executives, Thomson and Scott. He would supply the railroad with whatever was required—and make a profit doing so.

As the man in charge of keeping rail traffic moving in western Pennsylvania, Carnegie had an intimate understanding of the damage the railroad's infrastructure had suffered in the course of the war. Heavy traffic in materiel and soldiers and reduced expenditures on maintenance had created a near-crisis situation. One of the flashpoints was the wooden structures that bridged city streets and rivers, lakes, streams, creeks, and valleys. None of these had been built to last or to support the heavy loads being transported in wartime. Several had been damaged by fire started by sparks emitted from crossing trains; dozens were literally rotting away. These wooden bridges would all eventually have to be replaced by iron ones that were fireproof and capable of bearing heavier loads.

In 1862, Carnegie invited Jacob Linville, the Pennsylvania's chief bridge engineer, and John Piper and Aaron Shiffler, also engineers, to join him, Scott, and Thomson in organizing a new company to build iron railroad bridges in Pittsburgh. The new company, Piper & Shiffler, was a fine example of nineteenth-century crony capitalism. Carnegie would oversee operations and finances from Pittsburgh. Scott and Thomson, who remained silent partners in the enterprise, would make sure the new company received lucrative contracts for iron bridges from the Pennsylvania and its affiliated companies. As he had become the modus operandi of their investment partnership, Carnegie held Scott's stock in his own name. Thomson's shares were put in his wife's name. Linville's participation in the company was also kept secret as, with Scott and Thomson, he remained an employee of the railroad.[29]

Carnegie was active in other "start-ups" as well, so many in fact that not even he could keep track of them. When it came time to write his *Autobiography* in 1903, he had to contact his old friend, Tom Miller, to ask him to go over his records. Miller responded with a detailed account of their joint investments, which included the Citizen's Passenger Railway, the Birmingham Passenger [horsecar] Railroad, the Pennsylvania Coal Company, two oil companies, the Third National Bank in Pittsburgh, Pittsburgh Grain Elevator, Western Union, and something called the Library Hill Company. "So you see Andy," Miller concluded. "You were in a lot of things in those active years" of 1860–65.[30]

In the spring of 1862, some nine months after he had returned to Pittsburgh to take up his post as division superintendent, Carnegie requested and was granted a leave of absence from the railroad so that he could take a three-month holiday in Scotland. "I can scarcely believe my senses," he wrote Cousin Dod in May 1862, "and yet I'm sure I have just been notified that our Company grants me three months leave of absence to date from July first. Hurrah! Three cheers for this! There is nothing on earth I would ask in preference to what has just been given me. The exuberance of my joy I find is tempered by a deep feeling of thankfulness for the privilege vouchsafed—it seems so much in advance of my deserts. I hope I may be enabled to make good use of the blessing."[31]

He had dreamed of returning to visit Dunfermline for the fourteen years he had lived in Pittsburgh. Now, his pockets filled with oil money, he was able to finance that dream. It was time to celebrate, show off his good fortune, and reward his mother for all that she had done to make her boy a success in the New World.

On June 28, 1862, as the Army of Northern Virginia, commanded by Robert E. Lee, and the Army of the Potomac, led by George McClellan, collided just outside of Richmond, Virginia, in what would become known as the Seven Days' Battle, with 30,000 killed or wounded, Andrew Carnegie, with his mother and Tom Miller, boarded the steamship *Etna* for the two-week trip to Liverpool. From Liverpool, they took the train north to Scotland and Dunfermline. Carnegie evinced no hesitation at all in leaving his country at this critical moment. He had done his part in the war and done it well. As his presence was no longer required in Pittsburgh, which was, for the moment at least, safely behind Union lines, there was no earthly reason for him to stay behind. He needed a vacation and, having been granted one, sailed away without the slightest regret. His first responsibilities were to his family, particularly his mother, whom he now brought back to Dunfermline in triumph. She had left in disgrace as a poor man's wife; she returned as a rich man's mother.

Their first glimpse of Dunfermline brought tears to his mother's eyes and this alone made the trip worthwhile. They stayed with the Lauders in their cramped living quarters on top of the High Street shop. Like every adult returning to a childhood home, Carnegie was astounded at how "everything seemed so small, compared with what I had imagined." Dunfermline, so grand in memory, had shrunk in size and importance, as had its shops, its parks, its houses, and its people. "Here was a city of the Lilliputians. . . . Everything was there in miniature." His relatives were "exceedingly kind, but they found it impossible to understand how far he had already climbed in the New World." His dear old Auntie Charlotte, for one, could think of nothing grander for a man than to "keep a shop in the High Street," which she hoped would be Andrew's goal now that he had put some money aside. The visit ended disastrously, with Carnegie taken ill, we don't know with what.[32]

When he was well enough to travel again, he went down to London, where he stayed with his mother and Tom Miller in the luxurious Grosvenor Hotel and visited the Crystal Palace. "Its thirteen acres filled with whatever this world has to show of Art and Invention. You have there the most wonderful of everything," he wrote his brother Tom, left behind in Pittsburgh to look after the family's business holdings. "I take it that Monsieur Carnegie has the office matters all in tip top order, and a prodigious balance in the safe, the result of some brilliant financiering."[33]

AT TWENTY-SIX, Carnegie set himself a pattern he would follow for the rest of his life: declaring a vacation, disappearing from the workplace, and leaving his partners to look after his affairs. He had enough money now to travel whenever he chose. His dividend checks arrived whether he was in Pittsburgh or Scotland, at work or at leisure. Had he relied on his salary, he might have been more hesitant to take time off, but the $2,400 he received annually from the Pennsylvania Railroad constituted only about 5 percent of his annual income.

Later in life, when Carnegie was called upon to advise young men on how to succeed in business, he never suggested that unceasing hard work was a prerequisite for acquiring wealth. Though born a Scotsman, he was not a Calvinist in any sense of the word. He did not regard hard work as a virtue in itself. Nor did he believe that the accumulation of wealth was a sign of his "election" or a just reward for past diligence. The piling up of wealth signified nothing in itself, except that one had been in the right place at the right time, avoided a variety of moral vices, and wisely concentrated one's energies and talents.

Although Carnegie had, from infancy on, nurtured an abiding dislike for the landed aristocracies of the Old World, it was this status—and lifestyle—that he now aspired to. "I am determined," he declared to his cousin Dod, "to expand as my means do." His ultimate goal was to accumulate enough money to "own a noble place in the country, cultivate the rarest flowers, the best breeds of cattle, own a magnificent lot of horses and be distinguished for taking the deepest interest in all those about my place." He wanted, in short, to be "a British gentleman," but one with a social conscience, "who labors diligently to educate and improve the condition of his dependents." This was, as yet, the sum total of his philanthropic impulses; but then again, he was still in his mid-twenties and captivated by his newfound wealth.[34]

Carnegie had decided to leave business while still in the prime of life, enter politics, and, as he explained to his cousin, dedicate himself to "laboring to correct some ancient abuse—to curtail the privileges of the few and increase those of the many." He might stay in America or, then again, he might invest his New World dollars in an Old World estate. "I sometimes think I would like to return to Scotland and try the character [of the British gentleman] myself, but that cold chilly summer we had was enough to disgust one."[35]

By October, the Carnegies were reunited in Homewood and Andy was back at work at the Outer Depot. While the family had been vacationing in Dunfermline, the rebels had seized the initiative. In early July, northern troops under General McClellan had been turned back from Richmond. By August, Robert E. Lee and "Stonewall" Jackson had taken the offensive, moved north, and won a decisive victory at the Second Battle of Bull Run in northern Virginia.

During the summer of 1862, Lincoln had called on the states to recruit 300,000 soldiers for three year terms. Putting muscle behind the president's request, Congress passed a law defining all able-bodied men between the ages of eighteen and forty-five as eligible for militia service and authorizing the president to call state militia into active duty. The states were required—by federal law—to fill their quotas, by all means necessary, including a draft. In August, the War Department asked for an additional 300,000 recruits for a nine-month term.

Carnegie, twenty-seven years old and an able-bodied young man, was likely to be drafted when Pennsylvania ran out of recruits to fill its allotment. Although it was recognized that railroad men were vital to the war effort, the new federal laws provided no exemptions for them. Tom Scott, recently returned to Pennsylvania after retiring as assistant secretary of war, wrote Secretary of War Edwin Stanton pleading with him to provide a blanket exemption for railroad employees. He knew, from firsthand experience in Washington, that the railroads were indispensable to the Union war effort and that experienced train crews and executives were at a premium. A draft of executives, engineers, brakemen, or even unskilled yard hands would make it more difficult to move troops and supplies. It would also force up wages and compel some of the lines now moving troops, like the Pennsylvania, to curtail other services. Stanton, bombarded by similar requests for exemptions from other railroad executives, revised his policy to formally exclude telegraph operators and engineers. He would not, he notified Scott by telegraph, grant blanket exemptions for other railroad employees, but he would make sure that those "whose services were found to be indispensable to the railroad" would, if drafted, be discharged immediately.[36]

This informal understanding protected Carnegie from the draft, but it also provided him with an incentive to keep his position at the railroad at a time when he was making far more money from his outside business activities. In 1863, as Robert E. Lee's augmented Army of Northern Virginia moved northward into Pennsylvania, threatening Pittsburgh, the city's leading businessmen, Carnegie probably among them, met at the Monongahela House on June 12 to plan their defense against J.E.B. Stuart's Confederate cavalry, which they expected momentarily. It was agreed to suspend all business activity and put every able-bodied man to work digging trenches and erecting redoubts around the perimeter of city.[37]

"You will see by the newspapers that Pittsburg is busy fortifying," he wrote Dod on June 21; "6800 men (volunteers) have been at work all week, we will not quit till the city is surrounded by formidable works and then we are secure from rebel raids." To those in Scotland who had doubted the North's resolve—and resources—he proudly pointed to the "30,000 volunteers armed and equipped [who had been] called together in less than 3 days." There was no question, in Carnegie's mind, but that the North was going "to emerge triumphant, and slavery to go down," if only because its cause was just. "A week or a month more or less makes no difference."[38]

As the war approached its fourth year, with no immediate end in sight, and with new recruitments and reenlistments dwindling, Lincoln was compelled to conscript 500,000 men in February 1864 and 200,000 more in mid-March. Carnegie's name was called. Not even his position at the railroad was going to gain him an exemption or immediate discharge, so dire were the Union's manpower needs. On receiving his draft notice, Carnegie contacted H. M. Butler, a Pittsburgh draft broker, who found a recent immigrant from Ireland named John Lindew who, for $850, was willing to report for duty in Carnegie's place. On July 19, 1864, Lindew having fulfilled his promise (unlike many other "substitutes" who took their money and ran), Carnegie received his "Certificate of Non-Liability" exempting him from the draft until July 1867.[39]

There is no evidence that Carnegie felt any shame at sending another man off to war in his place. This was the common practice. A large number of the men of his generation who would later be referred to as "robber barons," including Philip Armour, Jay Cooke, J. P. Morgan, George Pullman, Jay Gould, Jim Fisk, Collis P. Huntington, and John D. Rockefeller, spent the war, as he did, making money by providing the Union armies with fuel, uniforms, shoes, rifles, ammunition, provisions, transportation, and financing.

TOWARD THE END OF 1863, Carnegie jotted down his assets and investments on "Superintendent's Office, Pittsburgh Division, Pennsylvania Rail Road Company" letterhead. There are fifteen separate entries on this "Income 1863" list, with a bottom-line total of $47,860.67 (nearly $8.5 million today)." Almost 45 percent of that income came from his Columbia Oil investment; 50 percent from investments in companies that had large contracts with the Pennsylvania Railroad.[40]

Carnegie was not the only enterprising young man who was striking it rich in Pittsburgh. His friends Tom Miller and Henry Phipps, the son and namesake of the shoemaker who had given Margaret Carnegie shoe-binding work fifteen years earlier, were also taking advantage of the wartime boom. Miller, a slightly sinister-looking young man with a goatee and full mustache, worked as a purchasing agent for the Pittsburgh, Fort Wayne & Chicago Railroad. Miller bought axles for railroad cars from the Kloman brothers, Anton and Andrew—two Prussian black-

---

*There is no foolproof scheme of comparing the economic power of individual incomes in years past to today. Historians have traditionally used the Consumer Price Index (CPI) to compare the worth of dollars in times past with today. Unfortunately, the CPI, while accounting for inflation over time, cannot measure the economic power of dollars, based on the size of the total economy. Using data supplied by EH.Net and Professor Samuel H. Williamson, I have chosen to use either the nominal Gross Domestic Product (GDP) per capita or the relative share of the GDP as the measures I apply to compare the values of incomes. This is, though imperfect, the best way, I believe, to account in today's dollars, for the economic power of individual incomes in the past. For the worth of incomes prior to 1890, I use the nominal GDP per capita; after 1890, as the economy begins to grow enormously in size, I use the relative share of GDP as my measure. As the most recent figures available for this purpose are the 2004 GDP figures, it is these I use for comparison. For further information on these measures, please see Samuel H. Williamson, "What Is the Relative Value?" *Economic History Services,* December 14, 2005: http://www.eh.net/hmit/compare/.

smiths who operated a forge in Millvale, just east of Allegheny City. Sometime in 1859, the Klomans, in need of $1,600 to buy a second trip-hammer to expand their business, offered Miller a one-third interest in the firm in return for the money. Unwilling to invest money in his own name in a company he did business with for the railroad, Miller asked Henry Phipps to join him in the investment and register Miller's stock in his name.

Henry—or Harry, as he was known to his friends and family—was the younger brother of John Phipps, a member of Carnegie's "inner circle" who had died after falling from his horse. Four years younger than Carnegie and Miller, Harry still lived in his father's house at 338 Rebecca Street, and commuted across the river to his job as a bookkeeper in Pittsburgh. Though only in his early twenties, Harry Phipps was already a bit stoop-shouldered, with the world-weary look and neatly trimmed beard and mustache of a much older bookkeeper. He was a small man, like Carnegie, and a very quiet one, probably the most reticent of any of the men Carnegie would work with. Phipps never spoke out of turn or with much expression, but he knew precisely what he was doing and was impossible to intimidate or ignore. He agreed to take half of Miller's investment for himself, hold Miller's shares in his name, and keep the books for the Kloman brothers.

The coming of war and Pittsburgh's critical position as the home of the Allegheny Arsenal, a major supplier of weaponry for the Union armies, led to a wholesale expansion of business for the Klomans—and profits for their young partners. By late 1861, the firm was working to capacity forging gun carriages which, when completed, were floated across the river to the arsenal. Even with their second trip-hammer, the Klomans had more government orders than they could fill. They leased additional land across the river in Pittsburgh, within walking distance of the arsenal, and constructed a new mill, the Iron City Forge, to manufacture "wrought iron, plates, bars and nails" on government contract.[41]

Miller had originally wanted to enlist Carnegie as a partner in the new ironworks, but Andrew Kloman, the younger and more dominant of the brothers, feared that Carnegie was too aggressive a businessman and would quickly take over the enterprise. Kloman was an innovative blacksmith and iron forger, but excessively mistrustful of his partners. Soon after the incorporation of the new firm, he ousted his brother Anton, who he feared was getting "careless." Miller bought Anton's shares, which gave him and Harry Phipps majority ownership in the foundry. Andrew Kloman, in an attempt to regain control of his own firm, demanded that Phipps sell him his share of the company. When Phipps refused, Kloman switched course and demanded that Miller relinquish his share. Phipps sided with Kloman. Miller, who had brought Phipps into the business, was furious, but outnumbered. The former friends, barely on speaking terms now, could agree on only one thing: that they needed an outside mediator and that Carnegie, whom they both knew from childhood, was the best man for the job.[42]

Carnegie agreed to mediate, convinced that he could charm the three partners into agreement. But not even his considerable powers of persuasion were enough. The rancor between Miller, Kloman, and Phipps grew to the point where Carnegie recognized that reconciliation was impossible. Tom Miller was Carnegie's oldest and dearest friend, the man who had accompanied him and his mother to Dunfermline, and then helped to nurse him back to health when he took ill there. But Miller was, as Carnegie later noted, an Irishman with a temper. Carnegie reluctantly recommended that Miller remove himself from the management of the firm, absent himself from the mill, reduce his ownership stake from four ninths to a sixth, and sign an agreement stipulating that Kloman and Phipps could, with sixty days' notice, compel him to "retire from the firm" and sell back his stock.

Kloman and Phipps agreed at once to the proposal. There remained one obstacle. Harry Phipps, who was to have a one-third share in the reorganized company, to be known as Kloman & Phipps, had to come up with $10,000, which he didn't have. Into the breach stepped Tom Carnegie, who bought part of Phipps's share with money borrowed from his brother.

While suffering through the impossible task of negotiating an agreement, Carnegie had picked up a great deal of insider information about the iron business in wartime, enough to convince him to finance his brother's entry into Kloman & Phipps. When soon afterward, Tom Miller, no longer a partner in Kloman & Phipps, suggested that he and Carnegie go into the iron business on their own, Carnegie agreed and put up the money for the new firm.

In the spring of 1864, Miller and Carnegie leased a five-acre plot of land, four blocks from the Kloman & Phipps Iron City Forge, organized the Cyclops Iron Company, and began construction of a state-of-the-art rolling mill. In his *Autobiography*, Carnegie claims that he joined with Miller because he was convinced that his friend had been "unfairly treated" by Phipps and Kloman. And that is no doubt true. But there is more to the story, as there always was with Carnegie. With Tom Carnegie as his Trojan Horse inside Kloman & Phipps and Harry Phipps in his debt, Andrew may have been looking ahead to the inevitable merger of his new firm with the one four blocks away.[43]

As war was still going on in 1864 and government contracts for iron goods were as lucrative as ever, the iron business was enjoying an unprecedented boom. Kloman & Phipps had its best year ever. Once the war was over, there would be a period of readjustment, followed immediately by a new building boom. New rails would be laid, new locomotives built, new bridges built. And they would be built of iron.

Kloman & Phipps fought the competition from Cyclops Iron for about six months before suing for peace. Miller was reluctant to enter into combination with his former partners, who had so recently ousted him, but Carnegie convinced him that the deal was worth making. In May 1865, the merger was completed. The new company was called the Union Iron Mills. Its president was Andrew Carnegie, its vice president Tom Carnegie; Kloman was named superintendent.

FIVE

Branching Out, 1865–1866

ALMOST THIRTY, Andrew Carnegie was the principal shareholder in several thriving companies, a partner in several more, and a force in local business circles, well known and respected for his acumen and his access to capital. He paid taxes on an income of $17,500 in 1864, with an additional $1 tax for his one-horse carriage. A year later, his income had risen to $38,735 ($5.6 million today), on which he paid a tax of $3,655. Again, he was charged an additional $1 tax for his carriage, $2 for his gold watch, and $4 for his pianoforte.[1]

Since William Carnegie's death ten years earlier, everything had gone right for the family. Tom, though only twenty-two, was an accomplished telegraph operator and apprentice capitalist. Mag now presided over her own country estate. And Andrew Carnegie was one of Pittsburgh's wealthiest young capitalists.

There is a price to be paid for achieving so much, so soon, and Carnegie, at thirty, was beginning to pay it. Driven as he had been from an early age to make himself the family breadwinner, he had never had the leisure to contemplate a life devoted to anything else. Only now did he allow himself the luxury of wondering whether there was not something missing.

On New Year's Day 1865, a month after his twenty-ninth birthday, Carnegie had written to remind Tom Scott of a promise he had earlier made. Carnegie had, "for many personal reasons," decided that the position as American consul to Glasgow "would be a very desirable one for me. . . . It is the only enterprise before me just now into which I could best throw my whole energy." Scott agreed to contact Simon Cameron on Carnegie's behalf to ask if he could arrange for a consular appointment.

His "young friend Carnegie," he informed Cameron, "retires from Railway life 1st April next—having struck oil, in large quantities [he is] now financially independent and intends to spend a few years in Europe—being one of Scotland's boys he has a strong desire to go there in some official capacity."[2]

Carnegie was ready for a change of scenery—and occupation. As he approached thirty, his lack of education and cultivation concerned him more than ever. He had never been to any of the European capitals and knew nothing about classical architecture or Renaissance painting or the other subjects required of a man of learning.

In April 1865, as the Civil War came to an end with General Robert E. Lee's surrender to General Ulysses S. Grant at Appomattox, Carnegie formally resigned his position with the Pennsylvania Railroad, set his personal business affairs in order, gave his brother Tom instructions on how to look after the family's investments, and said good-bye to his mother. Having had no response to his request for a consular position, he made up his mind to leave Pittsburgh anyway on a yearlong trip to Britain and Europe, where he hoped to acquire some of the cultural capital he so sorely lacked.

He recruited Harry Phipps and a new acquaintance, John Vandevort, a neighbor in Homewood, to accompany him. He chose his companions carefully. Phipps and Vandevort ("Vandy") were friends but not his equals, intellectually or financially. Both were four years younger than he and considerably poorer. Phipps was now an officer at the Union Iron Mills, where he had made a handsome living during the Civil War. Vandy had acquired the funds he needed for the trip by investing, with Carnegie, in the Columbia Oil Company.[3]

On May 17, 1865, Andy, Vandy, and Harry—"the boys," as they would refer to themselves—having paid $132 each for first-class cabin tickets, boarded the *Scotia*, the newest, fastest (it held the transatlantic record), and most luxurious ship in the Cunard Line. Phipps was seasick the entire trip, a source of amusement to his friends. Carnegie suffered not at all. He played chess like a "champion," visited with old friends from Pittsburgh and new ones he met on board, got "badly tanned" and "weather beaten," and quickly recovered in the open air from the "slight cold" he had contracted in New York. "An ocean voyage," he wrote his mother and brother from shipboard, "is good fun for me and I think we might do as the Duncans [who had also sailed on the *Scotia*]—have a summer estate in Scotland and go over every season to enjoy it. How does the idea strike the two members of the Carnegie firm at Homewood? If approved, how many acres shall we have? Will Pittencrief [sic], or Pitreavie [the grandest country estates in Dunfermline], answer?"[4]

The *Scotia* landed in Liverpool in early June; Carnegie took a quick side trip by himself to Dunfermline to see his relatives. The evening before he left Dunfermline, he stayed up all night singing Scottish songs and telling stories with Uncle Lauder and family friends. "It was wondrous strange," Carnegie wrote home, "to be surrounded with old men who were our father's boon companions. In America we are an entirely new family, and outside of Aunts Aitkin and Hogan [his mother's sisters] we have no relatives nor associations. Here we have a local history extending to the third generation, and many a one speaks kindly of our ancestors." Reunited with Phipps and Vandy and joined by John Franks, a distant relative of Phipps, "the boys" were to begin their walking tour of England the next morning. "We have our knapsacks, gum coats, canes, etc. and by our next week we will be able to report progress. We go into the campaign with strong hearts, and as far as tested, very strong legs, but we will not boast until we can go our twenty miles per day. . . . I continue to have excellent health, am wearing the very heaviest underclothing and taking good care not to catch cold in the evenings, which are generally cool, notwithstanding that the days are quite warm."[5]

The walking tour had barely commenced when the boys decided to take a detour back to London for the triennial Handel Festival at the Crystal Palace. Carnegie was overwhelmed at the spectacle of four thousand musicians performing the *Israel in Egypt* oratorio. The next six weeks were spent hiking through England, Wales, Ireland, and Scotland, interspersed with stays at the nation's most "fashionable watering places" in Leamington Spa, Bath, Bristol, and Brighton, and a few side trips "to see some rail mills."[6]

Carnegie had taken this year off to enrich his mind as well as to reinvigorate his body and soak up as much European culture as was possible in twelve months. Off the trails, Andy, Vandy, John, and Harry stayed in reputable hotels, ate in good restaurants, spent their days sightseeing, and their evenings in Europe's grandest theaters, concert halls, and opera houses. In Paris, they "imitated the Parisians, in sitting down at the tables in the boulevards, sipping our lemonade"; in Mannheim, they drank a bottle of Johannesberg while they groaned at "Andy's joke of 'having taken a bit at Worms and liking the Diet.'" They bought tulips and hyacinths in Holland, toured a diamond manufactory in Amsterdam, acted out the trial of Othello in the Doges' Palace, spent Christmas Day at St. Peter's, ascended the Tower in Pisa, and visited Vesuvius in the early morning mist. They were, in short, Americans on the Grand Tour.[7]

Sundays were devoted to "literary labours." Vandy, John Franks, and Carnegie kept travel diaries in the form of long letters: Vandy to his brother, John to his sister, Carnegie to his mother. While his companions, however, were satisfied with writing to their families, Carnegie, according to John Franks, devoted part of each Sunday "communicating his constant experiences to the Editor of the *Pittsburgh Commercial*." Carnegie had literary ambitions and was attempting to break into print by publishing travel letters in the newspapers. Writers as celebrated as Margaret Fuller, Bayard Taylor, Henry Adams, and Mark Twain had done the same, though their correspondence had been commissioned before they left.[8]

The boys got along famously. "John acts as treasurer and does finely," Carnegie informed his mother. "Harry attends to outside matters generally, and I play gentleman at present. However I am trying to be careful to make a show of doing something." He was joking, of course. His friends found it difficult to keep up with him. He had to visit every museum, take in every concert, opera, and theatrical event.[9]

"He is full of liveliness fun and frolic," John Franks wrote his sister from Frankfurt. "It is extremely difficult to keep him within reasonable bounds, to restrain him within the limits of moderately orderly behavior, he is so continually mischievous and so exuberantly joyous." Nothing pleased Carnegie more than throwing himself headfirst into conversation—with friends, strangers, shipmates, the people at the adjoining table in the café. The boys argued incessantly, though good-naturedly, Franks reported, "upon most questions, social, political, etc., Andy brimming first upon one side, then upon the other, with admirable impartiality, and possibly to keep the balance even." He had an opinion on everything: the national character of the Germans and French, the merits of Raphael versus Rubens, religion and war, architecture and music, female labor. Whenever there was some disagreement, as, for instance, on why there were so many flags flying from so many houses in Coblentz, Andy not only offered his opinion but backed it up with a wager, on this occasion a pair of gloves. He reveled in excess: his conversation was endless, his letters too long, his spending uncontrolled. The boys tried to rein him in and, when they could not, teased him mercilessly about his "practice of paying high prices for articles which could easily be bought for about fifty percent less. We continually remind him that the price is his measure of quality."[10]

A year was a long time to be absent from home and family. Carnegie begged his brother to write him weekly and his mother to write him as often as she could. When she did not, he sent her lighthearted reminders: "You promised to write me a letter, old girl. Now set about it and see what you can do in that line. I haven't got such a memento and would prize it highly, I assure you."[11]

In response to one letter from his brother describing a family gathering at Homewood, Andy assured Tom and his mother that he derived "more happiness hearing of a pleasant evening spent there with our friends than you can have in being part of the company, for it brings back the old times . . . I pity the poor wretch who hasn't a home to which his best thoughts and warmest affections can always be turned, and now that I am so far from you, it is the old story—'distance lends enchantment to the view' with a very lavish hand indeed."[12]

From thousands of miles away, he demanded news of the improvements Tom and his mother were making to the family home. A true country estate requires a name and Andrew, from afar, tried out a few on his brother. For a time, he referred to their residence as the "Fairview Estate," then settled on "Fairfield," which he and his brother agreed was a better name.[13]

Although he had been deterred by the high price of gold from "buying many things upon the Continent," including a fancy music box and some pictures he had had his eye on, Andy hoped that Tom and his mother would, in his absence, do all they could "to add still further to the attractions of our home." From Dorchester in the west of England, he wrote Tom to suggest that he "get the necessary straw targets, bows and arrows, etc. for a fancy archery arrangement on our place. If you can't get them in the East, let me know and I will bring over a set. You don't know how nice this sport is! I think it will add another attraction to the Fairview Estate."[14]

Carnegie was, he confessed, a "home bird," but he was, at the same time, in no hurry to start his own home—with his own family. All around him, men of his age and younger were marrying and starting their own families. In Homestead, his brother Tom, eight years younger than he was, was already preparing for his marriage to Lucy Coleman. The boys in Europe constituted themselves into a "Committee on Matrimony," which, according to John Franks, spent hour after hour "passing in review . . . the beauties of Pittsburgh and neighborhood and discussing their various charms, physical, mental and metallic, having especial reference to the latter." Andy, Tom, and Vandy had already picked out future brides, though Franks confided to his sister that it was "possible the Ladies in question may have something to say upon the matter before it is finally decided."[15]

Who, if anyone, Carnegie had in mind is impossible to ascertain. Some of the early biographies offer unsubstantiated rumors that he had, in his twenties, been interested in Ann Dike Riddle, reportedly one of the most beautiful girls in Pittsburgh and the daughter of Samuel Riddle, the publisher of the *Pittsburgh Gazette,* but that she had been wooed away from him by Tom Scott. According to Scott family legend, Andy had asked his friend and mentor to look after Miss Riddle, who was taking the train, unchaperoned, to Philadelphia. Scott did so and, in 1865, the same year Carnegie resigned from the railroad and escaped to Europe, Ann Dike Riddle became the second Mrs. Scott.[16]

Carnegie's only mention of Riddle is in an 1899 article, in which he declares that he had done his widowed mentor a "good turn" by arranging for him to escort "one of the sweetest girls in Pittsburg. . . . Well the trip was made as I planned it, and eventually Colonel Scott and Miss Riddle were married. She was a charming girl and made him a good wife."[17]

What is, for our purposes, as interesting as the story itself is the fact that it outlived him. Everyone who has written about Carnegie has tried to find evidence of his romantic involvements as a young man. There may have been some, but it appears most likely that Andy Carnegie was, in his twenties, thirties, and forties, too occupied with business to tie himself down to a wife and family.

It is also possible that he felt self-conscious about his looks and his size. During the 1865 tour of Europe, he wrote his mother—who, like all mothers, worried about her boy's health—that his was now robust, and cited as evidence the fact that he had gained weight and was now "7 stone, 11 lbs, in all 109 lbs." It is difficult to imagine a thirty-year-old man, in good health and of medium frame, weighing 109 pounds and standing more than five feet tall.[18]

There remains one more reason—and a compelling one—for his reluctance to marry: the possibility that his relationship to his mother precluded his bringing another woman into his home. As Carnegie matured from boy to youth to man, his admiration for his mother increased. He was now, at age thirty, no longer a worshipful child, but he adored his mother more than ever, considered her among his best friends, and spent more time in her company than with anyone else. She fretted about his health; he teased her about her weight. He greeted her every morning with "jokes before breakfast"; she refused to pay attention to anything he had to say until she had "her cup of tea." He marveled at her skill at whist and euchre, respected her business savvy, and was delighted that she was now willing to travel widely, by herself, to visit her relatives in the Midwest and her son in Washington.

In Dunfermline, in September 1865, he spent an evening with relatives exchanging stories about her. "Uncle and Aunty Morrison cannot get over laughing at the extent and frequency of your travels," he wrote her from Dunfermline. "When they hear of you starting off for six or seven hundred miles [on a visit to a relative in Iowa], it confounds them completely . . . Although considerably impressed while at home with the belief that Mother isn't any of the ordinary kind of mortals, it is only when I come here and we sit up till midnight going over old times that I fancy Tom and I have a 'raal born genius' for a maternal prototype. . . . Uncle says, 'When Mag just makes up her mind to it, there is no difficulty whatever.'"[19]

Carnegie did not ignore business entirely on his trip abroad. The boys arranged for their mail to be held for them at specially designated locations in each city, so Carnegie could receive written reports from Tom on the state of their business interests. He expected a great deal of Tom and his business partners at home while he was abroad. In mid-June, barely a month after he had left, Carnegie implored his brother to do more to "pull up and develop the Union Iron Mills [and to] arrange the locomotive matter as proposed." He wanted to know about the "Brick concern," congratulated his brother for going to Chicago to look after "their supply agents," and advised him that the bill from the Adams Express Company was correct and had to be paid.[20]

"The Carnegie family, my boy, are destined always to be poor," he wrote Tom later that summer or in the early fall, after receiving from him a statement of accounts, "but I am poorer than I expected if $8000 in debt. We must work like sailors to get sail taken in." He directed Tom to sell some of the shares in an iron company, at least half their "locomotive stock," one third of their investment in real estate, their Pioneer Coal stock, and, if Tom could sell above "par," some Union Telegraph and Lochiel Iron stock. "Few things, my boy, hold on to. C.T. [Central Transportation Company, which had absorbed the Woodruff sleeping car company], and Adams, UIM [Union Iron Mills] and Keystone Bridge, and Freedom Iron. They are pets, family treasures which I cannot part with."[21]

The Carnegie family had, through Andrew's efforts, accumulated capital that Tom hoped would be safely put away or used to meet the obligations his brother had entered into. His older brother, however, had no intention of playing it safe. The only way to make money was to invest it; the only question was where.

Carnegie had become more and more interested in the iron business since being brought in to mediate the Kloman, Phipps, and Miller controversy and ending up as part owner of the Union Iron Mills. While abroad, he made several side trips—by himself or with his companions—to inspect iron mills in Wales, England, Scotland, Germany, and France. When Vandy, Harry, and John Franks left Paris for Switzerland, Andy returned to England to visit more factories and forges. On their tour of Saxony, he persuaded the three of them to visit Rurort, "where . . . for purposes of business [Andy] wished to stay, there being large iron works in the neighborhood."[22]

In July of 1865, with Dod (who had been trained as a mechanical engineer at Glasgow University) as his guide, he visited an iron mill that was rolling rails strengthened by steel facings. The weld between the iron and the steel, which had been made according to a newly conceived process invented by an Englishman, Thomas Dodd, was, Carnegie wrote Tom in Pittsburgh, tight enough "to defy separation." Carnegie planned to investigate further, though he reassured his brother that he was not ready to spend any money. "I have sufficient faith only to be interested. You need not fear, therefore, that I shall invest largely for the American right, but I intend to watch practical results."[23]

After assuring his brother in late July that he had no intention of buying the American rights to the Dodd process, Carnegie returned to London in September to negotiate the deal. Instead of apologizing for throwing the family into a rather speculative enterprise, Carnegie bragged about his bargaining skills. "Have had to exercise every whit of my business ability to convince these gentlemen that it was far better to give our party their patents without any cash down than to get £5,000 gold from others, but I have succeeded, and feel repaid for the three weeks I have lost for Switzerland."[24]

"I have two or three days to spend here in England," he wrote his mother, "trying to arrange for some valuable patents, and will be in London next week, a place which takes my fancy above all others. I wish I knew the ropes and points in business affairs in London as well as I do in the Iron City. I would certainly try to persuade the family to come there and try it for a while at least. Nothing like being at headquarters, and all other places are villages compared to London. How would you like to try a residence near Hyde Park, eh? Or if Tom <u>will</u> insist on getting married (a very proper thing to do), he might run the machines in America and I do the foreign business. Seriously, however, I am quite taken with London and would like to spend a year or two there."[25]

The news from home was favorable. As John Franks reported to his sister on November 12, the Pittsburgh boys were "elated by glorious news in their letters of continued advances in prices, of stocks advancing, of their mills doing double turns, of large orders pouring in, of new patents pending, and of still greater success in the future."[26]

Still, Carnegie was concerned that he was overextended. From Dresden, in mid-November, he half jokingly apologized to his brother for placing his—and the family's—finances in jeopardy. "Your finances are reputed far from healthy," he had written Tom. "But how can they ever be otherwise? It was never intended. One of the firm, at least, was made to be forever head and ears in debt and to crowd full sail, despising to bury in the ground any of the talents (silver talents, I mean) which might reach his coffers, or to lie long under the suspicion of having at the bank even a moderate balance upon the right side of the ledger." Carnegie had fantasized that "a whole year's absence from opening up new enterprises . . . while the funds remained in charge of a super man, might possibly afford him, upon his return, a new sensation," that of being solvent. But that was not going to happen. Attempting to cajole Tom out of his understandable anger by making light of the situation, Carnegie suggested that he enlist Tom Miller to compose "a 'jolly dog' song on the subject beginning: 'For a borrower he is, and a borrower he'll be.'"[27]

CARNEGIE RETURNED to Pittsburgh in the spring of 1866. The soldiers were gone now, the city quieter. Compared to the year before, the streets were deserted; so too the hotels, theaters, and pothouses (taverns) that had done so lively a trade in wartime. The wharves and railroad stations no longer bustled with the comings and goings of wounded veterans, raw recruits, and the volunteers who cared for them, then sent them on their way. The federal contracts that had so generously fueled the expansion of the city's manufactories, especially its ironworks, were no more. But they had increased the nation's industrial capacity. More coal was being mined, more pig iron produced, more goods and people moved from east to west. The increased business activity had not been distributed equally. The big concerns—like the Pennsylvania Railroad and Western Union, in which Carnegie owned stock—had grown fatter on government contracts; the marginal companies, without access to federal funds, had suffered and died.

And there remained the smoke, the stench, the dust, and the dirt. Pittsburgh had not gotten any cleaner. Conditions only worsened as the factories that polluted the air multiplied one upon another. The city was prospering, the smoke a perverse indicator of manufacturing vitality. On December 16, 1865, an editorial writer in the *Pittsburgh Daily Commercial* looking forward to the coming year could not "refrain from expressing the belief that a glorious future is opening for Pittsburgh. Blessed with almost unexampled prosperity, rich beyond measure in most of the natural elements of solid character and sure growth, the heart of an unequaled mineral region, with an industrious and unostentatious population, the present prosperity of Pittsburgh and the glorious future before her" were guaranteed.

The propeller pulling the local and national economies forward was the railroad. Railroad construction, which had slowed with the downturn of 1857–60 and then virtually halted during the war years, was resumed. The American economy would be transformed in the second half of the century as the expansion of the railroads—and their organization into coherent east-west and north-south transportation networks—made possible a national market. By lowering the costs of transportation, the railroads lowered the final price of goods and produce, which led to a surge in national and international trade. Everything from Texas steers to Nebraska corn to Massachusetts boots and Pennsylvania glass could now efficiently and effectively be produced in one location and sold in another, thousands of miles distant.

As the railroads laid track across the nation—25,000 miles between 1865 and 1871 and another 50,000 between 1871 and 1881—their capacity to devour first iron, then steel for rails, engines, wheels, and bridges provided the impetus behind the spectacular growth of that basic industry. Already by the 1860s, half the iron rolled in the country was being bought by the railroads; by 1880, three quarters of the nation's steel would be used to manufacture rails. Iron- and steelmaking establishments that had remained far less advanced than those in Europe through the 1860s took off in the post–Civil War period. Eight hundred and fifty thousand tons of iron and steel were rolled in 1870; 3.3 million in 1880; 10.6 million in 1900.[28]

Unlike the California gold rush of the early 1850s or the Pennsylvania oil boom a half decade later, the railroad mania reached across the nation, touching small and large businesses, brokers, bankers, bond traders, real estate operatives, builders, landowners, manufacturers, merchants, politicians, and financiers in every region, every state and territory. Henry Adams, on his return to the United States in 1868 after a hiatus of seven years, was astonished at the way the railroads had captured the imagination of his and Carnegie's generation. "From the moment that railways were introduced, life took on extravagance." The "task" of railroad building was "so big as to need the energies of a generation, for it required all the new machinery to be created—capital, banks, mines, furnaces, shops, power-houses, technical knowledge, mechanical population, together with a steady remodeling of social and political habits, ideas, and institutions to fit the new scale and suit the new conditions. The generation between 1865 and 1895 was already mortgaged to the railways, and no one knew it better than the generation itself."[29]

Andrew Carnegie was only two years older than Henry Adams and, like him, very much a part of the generation that was "mortgaged to the railways." He had resigned from the Pennsylvania Railroad just before his thirtieth birthday not because he intended to sever his relationships with his business partners, Thomson and Scott, but because by removing himself from day-to-day responsibilities to the railroad, he would be freed to exploit his business connections with it.

Carnegie returned from England with what he thought was the exclusive franchise to apply the special technology Thomas Dodd had invented to coat iron rails with a steel facing that would vastly increase their strength and durability. His intention was to enter into a business agreement with Thomson, similar to his bridge-building and sleeping car company arrangements. Thomson would get an ownership interest in the "Dodd process," and Carnegie's company would get the contracts to manufacture steel-faced rails for the Pennsylvania Railroad.

It was common knowledge that tons of rails would be needed in the postwar period. Through the 1850s, railroad executives had raced one another to extend track into new regions, with little attention paid to the quality of their rails. Track was expected to stay in place only long enough to win government subsidies and provide evidence to investors that the roads were actually being built. British iron makers had catered to the American predilection for cheap rails by producing an inferior grade for export at bargain prices. To sweeten the deal, they financed the purchase of these cheap rails with loans. American iron makers, who could not produce rails as cheaply and were in no position to offer credit, had a difficult time meeting the British competition.

During the Civil War, the American railroad system, burdened by heavier than usual loads of freight, soldiers, and war materiel, began to fall apart. With credit tight and the investment market for private securities nearly closed, the railroad companies had tried to put off repairs and new purchases until the war was over. But when cheap brittle rails cracked, bent, split, flaked, or were ripped apart by sabotage, they had to be replaced. Unable to import cheap rails from England during the war or afford the more expensive domestic product, purchasing agents bought "used" rails that had been re-rolled out of scrap iron. But the re-rolled iron rails, which cost half the price of new ones, did not last long. Nor did the newly rolled American ones, most of which were made of iron inferior even to the cheapest British grades.

J. Edgar Thomson had become so distressed at the need for constant repairs and replacements that in 1863 he purchased 150 tons of steel rails from Britain at almost twice the price of iron rails. Thomson installed the new rails in the Altoona and Pittsburgh yards where traffic was heaviest. The new rails did not hold, but Thomson, unwilling to give up as yet, imported another batch of steel rails. The second batch worked better. Thomson, convinced that steel was the future for rails, purchased the essential patent rights and, in June 1865, laid plans to erect a steel rail mill in Steelton, a suburb of Harrisburg, Pennsylvania.[30]

Carnegie, who was at the time on his yearlong European tour, did not participate in the organization of the new steel company. When he returned, however, he organized his own company to secure the rights to the Dodd process for strengthening iron rails by coating them with steel facings. Thomson agreed to appropriate $20,000 of Pennsylvania Railroad funds to test the new technology.

On March 12, 1867, Thomson wrote to tell Carnegie that his Dodd-processed rails had failed their first test: "treatment under the hammer. . . . You may as well abandon the Patent—It will not do if this Rail is a sample." Three days later, Thomson wrote Carnegie again, this time marking his letter with a handwritten "Private" in the top left-hand corner and "a word to the wise" penned in just below. Carnegie had apparently asked Thomson for more time—and/or money—to continue his experiments. Thomson replied that the experiments his engineers had made had so "impaired my confidence in this process that I don't feel at liberty to increase our order for these Rails."[31]

Instead of giving up, Carnegie pushed forward, hawking his new steel-faced iron rails to other railroad presidents, attempting to get a new contract with Thomson, and reorganizing the Freedom Iron Company in Lewistown, Pennsylvania, in which he was a major investor, into Freedom Iron and Steel. In the spring of 1867, he succeeded, despite Thomson's misgivings, in getting the approval to manufacture and deliver a second 500-ton batch of steel-faced rails. The new rails fared as poorly as the old ones. There would be no further contracts forthcoming from the Pennsylvania Railroad or any other railroad.[32]

Carnegie tried to bluff his way through. When his contacts in England recommended that he purchase the American rights to a better process for facing iron rails with steel, this one invented by a Mr. Webb, Carnegie retooled his mill for the new process. He was fooled a second time. Not only was the Webb process as impractical as the Dodd, but there was, as there had been with the Dodd process, confusion as to who held the American patent rights. Within a year, the company Carnegie had organized to produce the new steel-faced rails was out of business.

There was a larger problem here, one that his brother had anticipated. Andrew Carnegie had been so successful with previous investments that he had begun to believe his judgment infallible. Instead of conserving his capital, as Tom Carnegie had hoped, Andrew had decided to invest it as rapidly as he acquired it. In February 1865, even before he gambled on the Dodd and Webb steel-facing processes, he had advanced money to two local businessmen, William W. Grier and R. H. Boyd, to secure the patent for and construct two prototypes of a coal-mining machine. Unfortunately, there was no way of proving the machine's worth without a trial and no coal company was prepared to interrupt mining activities to set one up.[33]

The result of this string of failures is evident in the income tax assessment rolls. In 1865, Carnegie declared an income of $38,750; a year later, his income fell by nearly half, to $20,940.[34]

These early failures did not deter him from investing in other start-up companies and technologies, but he would in future be a bit more careful before committing his capital. In March 1869, Tom Scott solicited his advice about investing in the rights to a new "Chrome Steel process." Carnegie replied that his "advice (which don't cost anything if of no value) would be to have nothing to do with this or any other great change in the manufacture of steel or iron. . . . I know at least six inventors who have the secret all are so anxiously awaiting. . . . That there is to be a great change in the manufacture of iron and steel some of these years is probable, but exactly what form it is to take no one knows. I would advise you to steer clear of the whole thing. One will win, but many lose and you and I not being practical men would very likely be among the more numerous class. At least we would wager at very long odds. There are many enterprises where we can go in even."[35]

CARNEGIE'S GREATEST SUCCESS was the Union Iron Mills, in which he had increased his stake to 39 percent by buying out Tom Miller. Through the 1860s and early 1870s, the Union Iron Mills' major source of revenue was its contracts with another Carnegie company, Piper & Shiffler (and its successor, Keystone Bridge), to supply iron parts for railroad bridges for the Pennsylvania Railroad. Carnegie and his silent partners, Thomson and Scott, made money on both ends of the deal. They profited from the contract between the railroad and the bridge company; then profited again when the bridge company purchased its iron from their iron mill.

Thomson, the president of the Pennsylvania Railroad (whose Keystone shares were held in his wife's name), made sure not only that Keystone was awarded Pennsylvania Railroad contracts, but that it was guaranteed a healthy profit on each of them. When inflation threatened to reduce the bridge company's profits for erecting a single-span iron railway bridge across the Ohio River at Steubenville, Thomson, acting on behalf of the railroad which had commissioned the bridge, renegotiated the contract to allow "an extra sum to secure us from loss," as Carnegie wrote in his *Autobiography*. "A great and good man was Edgar Thomson, a close bargainer for the Pennsylvania Railroad, but ever mindful of the fact that the spirit of the law was above the letter." What Carnegie didn't mention was that in sweetening the deal for the bridge company, Thomson was taking money from the railroad's stockholders to give it to a privately held company in which he held stock.[36]

In 1868, Thomson increased his investment in Keystone Bridge and directed his chief engineer to have all remaining wooden bridges on the Pennsylvania replaced by iron ones. Scott also remained a very active, though silent partner in the bridge company. When, in the spring of 1869, Carnegie got word that Cornelius Vanderbilt intended to build a "new bridge across the Hudson at Albany," he wrote Scott asking for "a letter of introduction—making reference to the Keystone Bridge Co., and its bridges in such terms as the facts may seem to you to warrant."[37]

The connection between Keystone and the Pennsylvania was no secret, though few were privy to the fact that Thomson and Scott were investors. When, in the fall of 1868, the young Washington A. Roebling, future builder of the Brooklyn Bridge, visited Keystone, he described the company in a letter to his father as "the direct offspring of the Penna. RR." The bridge builders who ran the operation had "all learned their trade there, and their numerous foremen have all been employed there for some time; and at present they still do all the Bridge work for the Pa. RR." Roebling was impressed with the scale of the operation. "They have work enough at present for a year to come; they have never less than 20 to 25 bridges on hand at once; last fall they had 44 under way at once." Roebling was struck by the connection between Keystone and "the Union iron works next door" from which the bridge company got its iron. "Each party is interested in the other's business. That alone gives them an advantage as they have both the quality and the supply of the iron fully under their control." After being shown around the bridge works, Roebling visited the iron mills, where he met "the two brothers Carnegie, former supts. on Penna. R.R.," whom he found to be "very pleasant people." He was more impressed by the remarkable state of the "labor saving machinery" employed at both shops, which he described in exhaustive detail.[38]

Ten years later, when it came time to build their own masterpiece in Brooklyn, the Roeblings would contract with Keystone Bridge in Pittsburgh for their iron anchor bars.[39]

SIX

A Man of Energy, 1867–1868

THE HISTORIAN Howard Mumford Jones characterized the half century between the end of the Civil War and the onset of the Great War as "the age of energy." Energy, he reminds us, has many meanings. "It may refer to force or vigor in style," or to the exercise of power, movement, agency, change, or propulsion in the physical sense.[1]

Carnegie, who was thirty at the dawn of the "age of energy," embodied it in every one of these meanings. A self-contained dynamo, he was in continual motion himself and served as a motive force setting off waves of activity wherever he set his mark. This was what capitalists did. And it was as a capitalist that he now defined himself.

The postwar years were a heady time for men like Carnegie. As peace returned to the nation, the forces of industrial capitalism were let loose to work their magic. The eastern railroad magnates, having consolidated and integrated dozens of short-haul, local roads into four or five east-west "through" networks, were poised now to extend these networks from the Mississippi, where they terminated, all the way to the Pacific. Each of these east-west trunk lines would require dozens of feeder lines. No city or town wanted to be left out of the web of tracks that threaded its way across the nation from east to west and north to south.

There was little rhyme or reason in much of the construction. Many of the new roads were built to connect as yet unpopulated areas in the prairie states. Others were built along well-served routes. Had there been some central organizing authority or less capital or better places to invest it, the building process might have proceeded more efficiently. But in the postwar period, as eastern merchants whose capital had once funded the cotton trade turned to investment banking, as reserve funds flowed into New York City banks from the hinterland, as capital was freed up with the refunding of the Union's war debts, and the federal government showered cash subsidies and land grants (convertible into cash or credit) on the roads, the incentives to invest in a new national railway network were too great to resist.

In later years Carnegie would insist that he had never traded or manipulated or speculated in stocks, but had made his money from manufacturing iron and steel products. His *Autobiography* backs up his assertions, but only by carefully editing out a critical period in his business career. From 1866, when he returned from his yearlong tour of Europe, to 1872, when he entered the steel business, Carnegie would accumulate the fortune that was later reinvested in his steel mills by doing precisely what he would later condemn: buying and selling shares in companies whose assets he knew were worth far less than the value of their stock.

In 1864, Thomson and Scott, with their Philadelphia investment partners, had entered the transatlantic sweepstakes by taking control of a small Kansas railroad, the Union Pacific, Eastern Division.* Although the UPED cost the Pennsylvania Railroad and Thomson's investment partners $1 million, the price was cheap considering the possible gains. The federal government had granted the railroad 500,000 acres of land for completing its first forty miles of track, with more to come if the railroad could beat its rivals in the race to lay track west.[2]

Carnegie did not invest in the UPED. He had neither the cash nor the interest in tagging along as a junior partner in an enterprise he was not going to control. There were other ways to make money from the new railroads. Those who knew where the track was going and where stations and railyards would be located could make fortunes by buying property cheaply and selling it at a premium when news of the route was disclosed.

"I think this railroad will make me a small fortune yet," George Noble, the division superintendent of the UPED in Wyandotte, Kansas, wrote Carnegie in late 1866, proposing that the two work together. "Of course I don't expect to make such a one as you have made and will make, but I will be satisfied with a much less one. If I can buy land . . . cheap, I will do so

---

*Though the names were similar, the Union Pacific, Eastern Division, was not connected to the Union Pacific.

and draw on you for the money taking an Equal interest with you." Carnegie forwarded "four hundred dollars to be invested in land in Kansas for our mutual benefit." That $400 bought 38 of the 960 acres in what would become the city of Ellsworth, Kansas. "We own 1/25th of the whole," Noble wrote Carnegie. "It is thought that this will be a large city. There is quite an excitement about it already. . . . A large hotel is going up now and it is thought there will be 2000 inhabitants there by the first of August. I think we can make a little money out of it and can't lose much you know." Two months later, on May 8, 1867, Ellsworth was formally established. By June, it had a population of 2,000, not much less than its population today, but Carnegie and Noble's $400 investment was already worth $1,000. "It will go perhaps to $2000," Noble wrote his partner on May 28: "then I think I will sell."[3]

Carnegie was doing nothing out of the ordinary or illegal by taking advantage of his connections to make a quick profit from buying and selling real estate or securities. Insider trading in securities would not, in fact, be outlawed until 1934 with the passage of the Securities and Exchange Act.

In the years following his resignation from the railroad, Carnegie continued to make money in partnerships with Thomson and Scott. In April 1867, he organized the Keystone Telegraph Company, took much of the stock for himself, and distributed the remainder to Scott and Thomson. Though Keystone Telegraph's stock was valued at $50,000, its only assets were a contract from Thomson which gave it the right, for an annual fee of four dollars a mile, to string two wires along the Pennsylvania Railroad's telegraph poles. Within six months—before a single wire had been strung on a single telephone pole—Carnegie sold Keystone Telegraph to the Pacific & Atlantic (P&A) Telegraph Company, a small Pittsburgh firm that needed a telegraphic connection to Philadelphia. He received in payment 6,000 shares of Pacific & Atlantic stock, valued at $150,000, and the contract to string the wires from Pittsburgh to Philadelphia, for which he was to be paid three dollars in stock for every dollar expended for construction costs.[4]

After making a similar deal in 1871 to string telegraph wires along a route Tom Scott controlled between St. Louis and Indianapolis, Carnegie secured enough stock to take control of the P&A. In 1873, he traded up again and exchanged his, Scott's, and Thomson's shares in the P&A for shares in the much more valuable Western Union company.[5]

If ever there were a textbook case of how to wheel and deal one's way to fortune, this was it. Carnegie created a company with no assets, added value to it by making deals with his partners Thomson and Scott, and then, after a series of negotiations and exchanges, transmogrified stock worth no more than the paper on which it was engraved into shares of Western Union that he would hold and collect dividends on for the rest of his life. This was crony capitalism at its most basic. And there were no laws on the books to stop it, no Securities and Exchange Commission to regulate it. Anyone with the money to print stock certificates and the political influence to get an act of incorporation through a state legislature could play the game.

AT THE SAME TIME that he was organizing his Keystone Telegraph Company, Carnegie reentered the sleeping car business, another industry poised to ride the postwar railway boom. By 1867, the Central Transportation Company (CTC), the successor to the Woodruff sleeping car company, had secured contracts to run its cars not only on Pennsylvania Railroad trains but along most of the major routes in the mid-Atlantic states. Its only competition came from George Pullman's company, which was dominant in the Middle West.

Early in 1867, the Union Pacific announced that it was ready to award the sleeping car franchise for its transcontinental trains. The Union Pacific contract promised to be an enormously lucrative one. While sleeping cars were a luxury that could be forgone on shorter journeys, they were a necessity for transcontinental trips lasting several days to a week.

In the competition for this contract, Pullman's company had a giant head start. A brilliant manufacturer and master publicist with a flair for the spectacular, George Mortimer Pullman was by the mid-1860s building sleeping cars that were sturdier, quieter, and much more luxurious than the CTC's. "The car runs so smoothly," reported a *New York Times* special correspondent on the way to Council Bluffs, Iowa, "that the motion of the water in a tumbler is hardly perceptible. The hangings and upholstery are simply sumptuous; no other word will describe them. Each car contains thirty-two double berths, and it is no exaggeration to say that one may sleep in them nearly as comfortably and quietly as it is possible to do in a hotel or at home."[6]

To make sure that everyone knew how "sumptuous" his cars were, Pullman courted the press, politicians, and railroad executives. In October 1866, when the Union Pacific (UP) reached the 100th meridian, its directors, with Pullman's help, planned a celebration, complete with a simulated "Sioux" raid, a buffalo hunt, and a closing banquet with fresh-killed game, champagne, speeches, fireworks, and a band concert. To transport the assembled guests—and journalists—from Omaha over the newly laid track, Pullman volunteered four of his "palace Sleeping Cars" at no charge, thereby endearing himself to the UP officers who could, despite appearance, ill afford the celebration they were sponsoring.[7]

Recognizing Pullman's genius and drive, Carnegie was prepared to do whatever was necessary to fold his old firm into the expanding Pullman empire. Pullman, for his part, was a shrewd enough businessman to recognize that it would cost more to fight Carnegie than to accommodate him. The CTC already held several patents on which Pullman had infringed in building his cars. Needing all the capital he could raise for expansion, Pullman did not want to be pulled into a lengthy battle in the courts. While he now controlled the midwestern market for sleeping cars—and was making inroads in the South—he was locked out of the lucrative Pennsylvania Railroad franchises. Suspicious though he might have been of Carnegie, he knew that behind the little man from Pittsburgh stood Thomson, Scott, and lots of capital.

Pullman did not make things easy for Carnegie. A self-made businessman brimming with aggressive, almost ruthless self-confidence, he shared too much in common with Carnegie not to be wary of his advances. Had Carnegie not been a master suitor, the marriage of minds—and businesses—would never have happened.

Carnegie worked out the projections for future costs, revenues, and profits in pencil on brown pieces of scrap paper. When he was satisfied with the numbers, he drafted a proposal for the new partnership. There was no response from Pullman. Six weeks later, in late May 1867, Carnegie wrote again. The members of the CTC board, Carnegie warned, were convinced that they were going to win a huge judgment against Pullman for infringing on their patents. Pullman had two choices: He could lose in court or he could agree to consolidate his interests with those of the CTC.[8]

It would take many months before Carnegie hammered out a mutually acceptable agreement between the CTC stockholders, Pullman, and the Union Pacific officials, who now demanded that UP be made a partner in any company chartered to attach sleeping cars to its trains. In the end, Carnegie got what he wanted: a large ownership stake in a sleeping car company run by George Pullman.[9]

Carnegie, having become Pullman's partner, did everything he could for the new company. In March 1872, he wrote Thomson recommending that he invest his own—and the Pennsylvania Railroad's—money in Pullman stock. "It is important for the Pennsylvania Railroad to be the largest railroad interest in a concern which influences to so great an extent the first class passenger travel of this country. . . . I should know Mr. Pullman by this time & his mode of conducting business. You can rely upon him & upon the satisfactory condition of his enterprise & I am as sure as I can be of anything you will scarcely number, among all your strategic investments, one which will be regarded hereafter with more favor than that I now take the responsibility of recommending."[10]

Thomson and Scott made large purchases of Pullman stock, then arranged a series of sweetheart deals with the company so overly generous that an "investigating committee" appointed by the Pennsylvania Railroad's stockholders in 1874 indirectly condemned them for making such a disadvantageous deal and recommended to the stockholders that, in future, the railroad's "officials and employees . . . be entirely free from any interest [in] private transporters" like the Pullman Palace Car, which did business with the Pennsylvania. "There is a tendency in such companies to verge too far in looking after their own interests, and there may be an inclination to infringe upon the interests of your Company."[11]

THERE WAS NO END to the business opportunities that were opening up as the nation and its railroads moved west. For a time it looked as if Carnegie were attempting to take advantage of every one of them. The only constant in his business adventures was the umbilical cord that connected him to Thomson, Scott, and the Pennsylvania Railroad.

As owner of Keystone Bridge and principal partner in the Union Iron Mills, which supplied that bridge company with its iron, he was perfectly positioned to take advantage of the business opportunities opened by the legislation President Andrew Johnson signed in July 1866 authorizing the construction of seven bridges across the Mississippi River and one across the Missouri River at Kansas City.[12]

Carnegie refashioned himself into a traveling salesman for Keystone Bridge, hawking his wares to local boosters, bankers, promoters, and politicians up and down the Mississippi, Missouri, and Ohio Rivers who hoped to cash in on the railroading boom by siting bridges in their cities. Carnegie had done no business west of Pittsburgh, but in partnership with Thomson and Scott, who controlled the largest rail network in the East and access to considerable capital, he became a formidable competitor for new bridge contracts.

Bridge building was not a business for the faint of heart or risk-averse. Competing firms had to bid low to get the jobs, but not so low that the bridges they built would not be strong enough to withstand the increasingly weightier loads they had to bear. Structures and supports had to be stress-tested before, during, and after fabrication; piers and supports had to be deep enough to withstand the highest tides and the weight of the debris they carried with them. While structural security was a prime consideration in letting contracts, it was not the only one. Town fathers, embarked on multimillion-dollar projects, expected that their bridges would not only be sturdy enough for the heaviest locomotives and the longest freight trains, but monumental and magnificent-looking.

Securing the contract to build the bridge was only the first—and often the easiest—step in the process. With all the goodwill in the world, the local bridge-building committees were ill equipped to secure the requisite capital to begin construction. To guarantee that there would be funds to pay Keystone Bridge, the Union Iron Mills, and his partners and subcontractors, Carnegie had to raise capital himself by selling bridge bonds and stocks. But before he could do this, he had to get commitments from the railroads to pay tolls to use the proposed bridges, arrange for terminals and freight yards to be built, secure rights-of-way, purchase the needed land, and design the approachways. He then had to write up the prospectuses.

In a few instances, the local committees were able to do some of this advance work, but as often as not, the ultimate responsibilities fell on Carnegie. From 1866 until 1872, when he began to shift his focus to steel manufacturing, he was on the road almost continuously, shuttling back and forth to New York and Philadelphia to meet with investors and railroad executives; to Pittsburgh to consult with his engineers and iron makers; and up and down the Mississippi to meet with local committees, railroad executives, and the contractors on the job.

He spent more time in St. Louis than anywhere else, for it was here that the nation's most ambitious Mississippi River railroad bridge was being built. St. Louis, the largest city in the Midwest and fourth largest in the nation (third if Brooklyn and New York City are counted as one, which they were not in 1870), was an obvious choice for a bridge and one of the sites authorized by the 1866 legislation.

Tom Scott had in 1867 been elected a director of the company chartered to build the bridge, in the hope that he would direct Pennsylvania Railroad traffic to St. Louis. Because Scott had his own road to run—or rather, several of them—he brought in Carnegie to make sure that the bridge got built. Carnegie was enthusiastic about the project. In January 1870, he forwarded to Scott $150,000 worth of stock in the bridge company and predicted that "within five years it will be worth double."[13]

Captain James Buchanan Eads of St. Louis, the chairman of the local bridge committee, named himself chief engineer. Vain, arrogant, and self-confident, Eads both fascinated and infuriated Carnegie, who was forced to work with him on design, contracting, construction, and financing. "I don't know what new fangled notion he may try next," Carnegie wrote Scott during one series of exasperating negotiations with Eads. "He seems unable to adopt anything that has been proved to be good, while anything new & untried captures his senses."[14]

The St. Louis Bridge contract was only one of several that Carnegie was working on simultaneously. In November 1867, he won the contract to build the iron superstructure for the pivot drawbridge over the Missouri River at Kansas City. Keystone Bridge was also awarded the contracts to erect bridges over the Mississippi at Dubuque and 150 miles to the south, at Keokuk, Iowa.[15]

AS CARNEGIE spent most of his time on the road, commuting back and forth between New York, Philadelphia, Pittsburgh, and towns and cities along the Mississippi and Missouri where he was building bridges, he had no need of a permanent residence of his own. The family's Homewood estate had been taken over by Tom and his wife, Lucy. Margaret Carnegie lived with them. When in Pittsburgh, Andrew boarded at the Union Depot Hotel, adjacent to Union Station. In New York City, where he spent more time than ever making deals and selling bonds, he stayed at the St. Nicholas Hotel.

In December 1868, at the St. Nicholas Hotel for a meeting with Thomson, Carnegie, who the month before had celebrated his thirty-third birthday, sat down with his stub-nosed pencil and a scrap of paper to take stock of his life—and his finances. He tallied his current assets and income and then wrote himself a memo. His net worth, he discovered, was about $400,000 (close to $75 million today); his annual income in dividends over $50,000. If he carefully managed his assets over the next two years—and stopped taking fliers on new investments—he would, he estimated, be able to guarantee this level of income in the future. He resolved: "Beyond this never earn—make no effort to increase fortune, but spend the surplus each year for benevolent purposes. Cast aside business forever except for others." He had already sacrificed too much to the pursuit of wealth. Like other men, he realized that he had to "have an idol," a god or goal to reach for. Until now, this "idol" had been "the amassing of wealth," which was, he recognized, "one of the worst species of idolatry. No idol more debasing than the worship of money." Having chosen his goal, he had been almost single minded in its pursuit, unwavering, undeterred, inexorable in his movement forward. "Whatever I engage in I must push inordinately," discarding all cares and concerns that might detour him. "To continue much longer overwhelmed by business cares and with most of my thoughts wholly upon the way to make more money in the shortest time, must degrade me beyond hope of permanent recovery."

There was no self-pity here, no regrets. He was thinking only of the future. Three years earlier, he had contemplated retiring to Europe to pursue his own education, but he had spent only a year abroad. He had, since then, multiplied his fortune many times, but he had not proceeded very far in acquiring the cosmopolitan polish he lacked. He did not want to spend what remained of his life making stock deals and chasing bridge contracts. He was ready now to put aside moneymaking and choose a way of life "which will be the most elevating in its character." He would devote the next two years to making money, while spending his "afternoons in securing instruction, and in reading systematically." He would "resign business at Thirty Five," then "settle in Oxford & get a thorough education making the acquaintance of literary men." This, he estimated, would take him about "three years active work," during which he would "pay especial attention to speaking in public." At age forty, he would take up his new life in earnest and "settle then in London & purchase a controlling interest in some newspaper or live review & give the general management of it attention, taking a part in public matters especially those connected with education & improvement of the poorer classes."[16]

There are many fascinating elements in this memo. One that stands out is the absence of any mention of a future wife or family. Carnegie was still not ready to contemplate getting married. It is possible that, absent the self-education he planned to pursue, he did not think himself an eligible suitor yet.

Another remarkable aspect about this note—and the life plan outlined in it—is the absence of any external motivating force. Carnegie had decided to "resign business" not because anyone had asked him to, not because he had pangs of guilt or shame, not because he had a religious-inspired calling to pursue. He was changing his life because he wanted to—and had the resources to—and because he did not consider the amassing of dollars an end in itself.

His pencil-written note was never, it appears, shared with family or friends. There is no mention of it in the *Autobiography* or any of his writings, nor is it included in the papers that were later donated to the Library of Congress. But he held on to it for the rest of his life, and after his death, his wife included it with material she left to the New York Public Library.

Carnegie would not retire at age thirty-five or forty-five or fifty-five; he would never acquire an Oxford education, or settle in London. But he would, in his own way, try to live the rest of his life according to the principles he set down in December 1868.

SEVEN

"Mr. Carnegie Is Now 35 Years of Age, and Is Said to Be Worth One Million of Dollars," 1870–1872

ON MARCH 9, 1870, Carnegie set sail for Liverpool on the *Russia*, the Cunard Line's first propeller-driven steamship. It now took eight days to sail the Atlantic, instead of forty-two as it had twenty-two years earlier when he first crossed the ocean.

Arriving in London, Carnegie made his way to 22 Old Broad Street, the office of Junius Spencer Morgan, to request an appointment. He had been preceded by a fulsome letter of introduction by Thomson, who was already well known to Morgan.[1]

Junius Morgan, American by birth and upbringing, had moved to London in 1854 to become the partner of George Peabody, the most successful American banker in the city. A tall man, with a prosperous middle and a serious mien, Morgan was by 1870 the senior member in his own firm, J. S. Morgan & Company, and a not always silent partner and majority investor in his son Pierpont's firm, Dabney, Morgan & Co. Carnegie, who had not yet met Junius, had become acquainted with his son Pierpont two years earlier when they crossed the Atlantic together.

Carnegie had come calling with the prospectus for the St. Louis Bridge bonds that he had written in New York, polished on board ship, and had printed as soon as he landed. Though Morgan wrote his son's firm in Philadelphia that he found it quite "novel" to buy "a mortgage bond upon a *Bridge*," he was prepared to move forward, probably because Carnegie had priced the issue so low that Morgan would have no trouble reselling it at a considerable profit. Before finalizing the agreement, he asked that adjustments be made in the wording of the bonds. As it would take at least three weeks to get approval of these changes from St. Louis, he suggested that Carnegie, who had planned to vacation later in Dunfermline, had "better go now." Carnegie, fearful that Morgan might in three weeks' time change his mind, sent the proposed changes to his partners via the transatlantic cable. When, the next morning, he received a return cable approving the changes, he had his deal.[2]

The young and now successful bond trader spent the rest of the week in London helping Morgan resell the bonds by telling whoever would listen—principally the financial editors of the London papers—that the Erie Railroad scandals of the late 1860s, in which Cornelius Vanderbilt, Jim Fisk, Jay Gould, and Daniel Drew had gambled with the lives and fortunes of investors by driving up, down, and sideways the price of stock in the Erie, had been a once in a lifetime aberration. There was, Carnegie insisted, no connection whatsoever between his rock-solid bridge bonds and the water-soaked railroad stock. The Erie Railroad was a state-chartered corporation; the St. Louis Bridge, on the other hand, was a "National Post Road," over which "the Supreme Court had direct jurisdiction."[3]

Carnegie was making it up. The U.S. Supreme Court had no jurisdiction whatsoever over the St. Louis Bridge Company, its stock and bonds, and he should have known this. Still, in the interests of the larger truth—that the St. Louis bonds were sounder than Erie Railway stock—he had no hesitation about misleading London's financial writers and investors.

Carnegie's skill as a courtier acquired over the years in his interactions with employers and mentors served him well in London, as did his diminutive, non-threatening size, his irrepressible charm, and his grasp of financial details. He had again worked his magic with a man old enough to be his father. Having written the prospectus with Morgan in mind, he was able to respond immediately to any objections offered. The fact that he and J. Edgar Thomson were already invested in the St. Louis project and would suffer financially should it fail must also have carried some weight with Morgan.

CARNEGIE's successful bond-selling venture in London convinced him that he was suited for the world of high finance. With enviable foresight, he had chosen the perfect moment to enter international bond trading.

Bond trading was then as now, an extraordinarily lucrative line of work for those who were neither risk-averse, risk-happy, nor weak-hearted. It was, in short, the ideal profession for thirty-five-year-old Andrew Carnegie. Although later in life he would profess that he had never speculated on stocks or bonds, that was clearly far from the case. He was through much of his thirties boldly trading in equities and debt, including some highly speculative bridge bonds.

The successful bond salesman had to play many parts and play them well. This posed no problem to Carnegie, who had been trying on new roles since childhood. To sell bonds for bridges that had not yet been built, he acted the part of the gentleman-banker whose word was as good as gold; calculated as a trained bookkeeper would the interests, commissions, and exchange rates for every eventuality; researched and wrote persuasive prospectuses; and sold his wares with the gusto of the Yankee peddler and the enthusiasm of the loyal town booster.

New York had, in the years following the Civil War, become the financial center of the New World, and Carnegie found himself spending more and more time there doing deals. In 1869, he leased a room for himself at 64 Madison Avenue near Twenty-seventh Street and opened an office at 19 Broad Street in the heart of the Wall Street district. The following year, he hired a personal secretary, Gardner McCandless, the son of David McCandless, a future Carnegie partner. Gardner, or "Gardie," as Carnegie called him, kept track of financial transactions and correspondence and forwarded messages to Carnegie when he was out of the office, which was most of the time.[4]

In 1870, after his bond-selling trip to London, Carnegie decided to take up permanent residence in New York. His mother Margaret decided at this time to leave behind Tom and Lucy, their three children, and the family home in Homewood to move to New York. Margaret no doubt wanted to be useful—and with Lucy now looking after Tom, perhaps believed she could do more good taking care of her older unmarried son. A woman of sixty, in excellent health, she may also have welcomed the excitement of reestablishing herself in a new city.

Andrew, for his part, welcomed his mother. The idea of a grown businessman sharing a hotel suite with his mother was not as bizarre in 1870 as it might appear today. As Howard P. Chudacoff has noted in *The Age of the Bachelor,* the number and proportion of unmarried men in urban communities increased markedly in the last third of the nineteenth century, and a large number of the older, more financially secure bachelors lived with one or more parents.[5]

Living with his mother made perfect sense to Carnegie. Her presence converted his hotel suite into a home. It also gave him a base from which to explore all that the city had to offer wealthy bachelors: theaters, opera houses, salons, concert halls, social clubs, and, perhaps, less respectable places of amusement.

Andrew and Margaret Carnegie made for a strange pair. Neither was particularly attractive, but where the son radiated charm, warmth, and gentility, the mother projected an austere solemnity. Like her son, she had a broad, flat face, but with tiny eyes and a turned-down mouth. The photographs show a glum woman, old beyond her years, who never smiled. Andrew, on the contrary, looked younger than his years. At thirty-five, he sported a mustache to go with his full, bushy beard. His forehead was high to begin with and he parted his sandy-colored hair in such a way as to make it look higher. The effect was to make the huge head sitting directly on broad shoulders with no neck visible appear even larger. He had put on enough weight to fill out the boyish frame into that of a middle-aged man. His blue eyes still sparkled.

CARNEGIE had been thinking about leaving Pittsburgh for some time— and not entirely for business reasons. The problem with Pittsburgh was not that it lacked contacts or opportunities for the ambitious businessman, but that that was all there was. The city was home to hundreds of factories, foundries, potteries, rolling mills, machinery works, and oil refineries, a few distinguished-looking cast-iron office buildings downtown, and very little else. There were no fine hotels, no first-class opera company, no symphony society, no respectable theater, and no men's social club until the Duquesne Club was founded in 1873.

Wealthy citizens, like Carnegie and his neighbors in Homewood, amused themselves in the privacy of their parlors where they gathered to play cards and charades. While such entertainments might once have been sufficient for Andrew, they were so no longer. Having traveled to London and Paris and spent a great deal of time in New York and Philadelphia, Carnegie could no longer close his eyes to the reality that

Pittsburgh was just too small, too provincial, too uncultured and unculti-
vated for him.

There was no question but that he and his mother would, on relocating
to New York City, take a suite of rooms in one of the city's grand hotels. It
made no sense to set up housekeeping in a private residence when they
could live in luxury, with all services provided. Though still frowned upon
by the older New York families as not entirely respectable, luxury hotels
had become the favored residence of the newly enriched. The grand residential hotel was an American invention, so vitally and peculiarly American that Anthony Trollope devoted an entire chapter to it in *North
America,* the record of his 1861–62 travels in the New World. "They are always built on a plan which to a European seems to be most unnecessarily
extravagant in space." He was disturbed only by the dismal quality of the
food served in the cavernous hotel dining rooms: "I never yet made a single comfortable meal at an American hotel. . . . If need be I can eat food
that is disagreeable to my palate, and make no complaint. But I hold it to
be compatible with the principles of an advanced Christianity to prefer
food that is palatable. I never could get any of that kind at an American
hotel."[6]

Carnegie might have decided to lease his rooms in any one of dozens
of luxury hotels. He chose the St. Nicholas, the grandest, most luxurious,
and most public of them all. The Carnegies took one of the "family suites,"
with spacious parlors for Margaret and her son, large bedchambers, adjoining dressing rooms, and luxuriously outfitted private baths.

The St. Nicholas Hotel was the preferred New York residence—and
office—for the nation's leading railway executives, including Scott and
Thomson, who favored it for its location at Spring Street and Broadway, in
the heart of the city's amusement, shopping, and commercial sex district.
Wallack's Theatre, which Carnegie frequented, was on the next block;
there were dozens of exclusive and expensive retail shops close by, including Tiffany's (regularly patronized by Carnegie), Brooks Brothers cloth-
iers, Lord & Taylor's dry-goods establishment, Crouch & Fitzgerald.[7]

The side streets off Broadway housed numerous high-class, protected
houses of prostitution. Whether Carnegie ever frequented them we do not
know, but if he did not occasionally do so, he would have been somewhat
of an anomaly among the city's wealthy bachelor businessmen.[8]

The hotel offered amenities as yet unheard of in private homes. For ladies, there were several "parlors," including a 24- by 50-foot room on the second floor with "gold-colored brocade satin damask window curtains, interwoven with bouquets of flowers." For the gentlemen, there was more: "The city's most fashionable barber, Phalon, rented the store just to the right of the main entrance. . . . The lobby alone included a post office that sold stamps and stationery; a bookstall with newspapers, books and magazines; a travel agent who had tickets for any means of conveyance to almost anywhere in the world." There was, as well, a beautifully outfitted "Gentlemen's Drawing Room and Reading Room," a billiard room, and a bar room with its own "Telegraph Office, with operators in constant attendance by whom messages are transmitted to any point with as much certainty and dispatch as from the general offices of the different telegraph companies." Like the city's other grand hotels, the St. Nicholas was run according to the American plan, with three meals, each with several sittings, offered in the massive dining room on the second floor.[9]

Straight down Broadway was New York's burgeoning financial center. Commuters, packed tightly, thirty or more at a time, rode in carriages pulled along rails by teams of two to four aged, overworked horses. There were smaller, more private omnibuses, drawn by two horses, which, not stuck on rails, could dart in and out of traffic. Carnegie probably used private hackney carriages, the preferred mode of transportation for men who could afford them.

By early 1870, Carnegie had moved his New York business office about a quarter mile west from 19 Broad Street to a larger suite of rooms at 57 Broadway. A half block from the Stock Exchange, the new office was almost directly adjacent to the Adams Express Building and just up the block from 26 Broadway, where John D. Rockefeller would, in a decade's time, build his nine-story corporate headquarters.

Carnegie's office served also as New York headquarters for the Union Iron Mills, Carnegie & Associate, an investment company he had set up with J. Edgar Thomson, several railroads with which he did business, and the Iowa Contracting Company that he had organized to build a feeder railroad into Keokuk, Iowa. In 1872, business had picked up to the point where Carnegie hired DeWitt Loomis as bookkeeper and general assistant. Harry Phipps, who kept the books of Carnegie's Pittsburgh companies, had recommended Loomis for the singularly complicated job, pointing out that "Your books are more difficult to keep than those of an ordinary firm—owing to the different interests that you manage."[10]

By the fall of 1870, Carnegie had become enough of a presence in the business community to be featured on the front cover of the November 19, 1870, *Railroad Gazette,* the premier trade journal of the rail industry. The *Gazette* was not in the practice of running anyone's portrait on its front page. The issues preceding this one had led with articles on "Improved Sliding Door Fixtures," "Ferris & Miles Patent Steam Hammer," and "M. N. Forney's Improved Tank Locomotive."

The article, which was written by J. T. Reid, who had been Carnegie's first employer at O'Rielly Telegraph, was congratulatory, but surprisingly short on information. It recounted how Carnegie, though "very small and spare," had as a boy impressed his potential employers at the telegraph office with a "cheerful, fixed look about his eyes which said very clearly, 'If you employ me I will do my duty.'" At the Pennsylvania Railroad he had become "an object of universal confidence and respect . . . Mr. Carnegie is now 35 years of age, and is said to be worth one million of dollars. He carries with him the same unostentatious manner and the same self-poise and confidence which marked him as a boy."

"Andy, as we call him," was described in adulatory terms taken directly from the success manuals written for would-be businessmen. He was "prompt, correct and faithful," with "steady, industrious habits," "a cautious and well poised brain," a "cheerful, hopeful, or rather confident, element," and a "steady, earnest unfaltering will." He was also public-spirited, "liberal in his charities," and fond of books.[11]

That Carnegie was the subject of this front-page profile is testimony to his growing reputation in the railway industry, not as a builder but as a financial middleman. The only reference to his current business dealings appears at the end of the second to last paragraph when we are told that Carnegie has recently returned from a successful bond-selling trip to London.

One year after the completion of the first transcontinental railroad, there were railroads, bridges, towns, and cities waiting to be built; and a young army of entrepreneurs eager to organize the labor, resources, and capital needed to get the job done. At the center of the enterprise were the bond traders, Carnegie among them. Federal and state governments contributed some funds, but the bulk of the capital needed to move forward had to be raised privately.

The process for raising capital was simplicity itself. The railroads, including those that existed only on paper, secured government charters and then issued bonds, the proceeds of which they dispensed to "improvement companies," which were contracted to build the roads. The system was designed to facilitate and disguise waste and corruption. The men who chartered the new railroads and issued stock in them did not expect to make much profit from the freight or passenger tolls that might come their way once their roads were built. They made their fortunes instead by skimming money—lots of it—from the construction phase of the project. Because the same group of men owned stock in the railroad and the "improvement company," it was easy enough, far too easy in fact, for them to overpay themselves at every phase of the construction process. It would later be estimated that the directors of the Union Pacific had funneled to themselves, through the Crédit Mobilier, $30 to $50 million, which had been allocated for construction purposes but wound up in their pockets.

Tom Scott, who in the early 1870s pushed the Pennsylvania Railroad's network westward, followed the standard financing practices of the time and established improvement companies similar to the Union Pacific's Crédit Mobilier to do the construction work for new railroads. In 1870 alone, he incorporated three new improvement companies. In 1871, he added at least nine more. Obscuring the fact that these companies were paper entities controlled entirely by the railroad directors, he gave them grandiose names: Overland, Empire, Domain, South, Madison, Continental, Occidental, and Central, among others.[12]

The end result of this kind of financing was failure for the railroads, though not for their directors. The more money skimmed from construction funds, the less remained to complete the projects in time for them to begin to pay off bondholders. It was the rare railroad that did not suffer at least one failure, bankruptcy, and reorganization. Gerald Berk estimates that in the 1870s alone, railroads accounting for "over 30 percent of domestic mileage . . . failed and fell into court ordered receivership."[13]

In late 1870, it was the Union Pacific's turn. Never adequately capitalized, the railroad approached bankruptcy when President Ulysses S.

Grant's attorney general ruled that it had to repay the interest on its bonded debt. The news that the railroad was liable for the interest on hundreds of thousands of dollars in loans forced the price of securities "down almost out of sight," as Cornelius Bushnell, one the chief directors, later testified before a congressional committee, "and we had not the money on hand to pay the interest on our First Mortgage bonds, due on the first of January."[14]

Carnegie was approached to see if he could arrange a loan from the Pennsylvania Railroad. He did so in return for shares of Union Pacific stock which he and his partners were to hold until their $600,000 loan was repaid. On New Year's Eve 1871, he wrote to tell Scott that he had secured an "irrevocable Power of Attorney" for these shares and could buy enough additional stock to give him and his partners "an absolute majority" and control of the railroad. "There is a fortune for us connected with the management of this property if attended to—as well as enhanced reputation— Our aid is so essential that we can make a good bargain. . . . This would only be the beginning." With the control of the Union Pacific would come control over the Omaha Bridge which the railroad had contracted to build.[15]

The $600,000 loan solved the UP's short-term cash flow problems. Its more serious long-term capital shortage was alleviated when Congress passed a special bill on February 26, 1871, authorizing the railroad to issue a new series of first-mortgage bonds for the construction of the Omaha Bridge. The timing of the legislation—weeks after Scott and Thomson had taken control of the railroad—was far too suspicious to avoid notice. Scott was later questioned about, but denied having knowledge of funds having been "used directly or indirectly with members of Congress to secure the passage" of the legislation.[16]

Ten days after the legislation was passed, the UP directors met formally in Boston to ratify the takeover of the railroad by the "Pennsylvania interests." Scott was named president; Carnegie, Thomson, and George Pullman were elected to the board of directors.[17]

Two weeks later, on March 22, Carnegie sailed to London with a satchel full of Union Pacific–backed Omaha Bridge bonds to sell. Just before sailing, he authorized his New York broker, Morton, Bliss & Co., to sell the UP stock that was locked away in his vaults as collateral for the loan. The rescue of the railroad had dramatically forced up the price of the stock to the point where he could not resist cashing it in. When the UP directors and stockholders discovered that the "Pennsylvania interests" had, within two weeks of being elected to the board, sold their stock in the company—at a considerable profit—their suspicions were confirmed that Scott, Thomson, et al. were not interested in rescuing the railroad, but in turning a quick profit by manipulating its stock. The three were voted off the railroad board.

Carnegie blamed Scott for the debacle, claiming that it had been his decision to sell the stock; but that was not the case. The order to sell had come directly from Carnegie. It was, in retrospect, a wise decision. The UP was a losing proposition in the short term and Scott and Carnegie had no interest in any other term. As romantic as its quest had been—and remains even today—the first transcontinental railroad was not a profit-making enterprise. Its income, though growing, was not and would never be sufficient to pay off the interest on its bond issues. While "through traffic from the Pacific coast" had picked up, there was growing competition from other transcontinentals. "As for the future of the road," the *Railroad Gazette* noted on March 16, 1872, "it is not very certain."

CARNEGIE would spend ten of the next eighteen months overseas, selling bridge and railroad bonds. He took easily to his new trade. The rhythm of the work was far different than that he had become accustomed to. The traders he dealt with kept reasonable business hours. There was research to do before and after the meetings, a great deal of prospectus writing, tinkering with the numbers, and communications back and forth via transatlantic cable, but this still left plenty of free time to enjoy life in London, Paris, Frankfurt, and other European financial centers.

In May 1871, just as he was settling in, he was unexpectedly called back to New York by a telegram from Gardie McCandless, his private secretary. Scott and Thomson required his presence as soon as possible because, as McCandless put it in his telegraph, the Keokuk Bridge business was "not going smoothly." The railroads which had agreed to run traffic over the bridge were threatening to cancel their contracts, because the bridge had not been completed on schedule. Thomson and Scott were worried that the entire enterprise—and their large investments in it—would come crashing down. They needed Carnegie to put things right again.[18]

Carnegie booked passage on the next ship to New York and took the train from there to Keokuk, where he assured the concerned parties that their bridge would soon be ready and this was no time to cancel their contracts. He worked the same magic in St. Louis, where bridge construction was also falling further and further behind schedule. His greatest difficulties were in his hometown, Pittsburgh, where a virtual war had broken out between his two companies, Keystone Bridge and Union Iron.

While he was absent in Europe, Keystone had purchased new machinery to manufacture iron links, "the evident intention being to take from the Union Iron Mills this branch of their business." This Carnegie could not permit. Any savings Keystone might gain by manufacturing its own links in its own plant would come at great loss to Union Iron, which had been tooled to make structural parts for Keystone. Carnegie tried diplomacy at first to convince the Keystone officers to reverse course. "You [Keystone Bridge and Union Iron] are not competitors; on the contrary you are necessary to each other. The true policy is to work together. Each has its special business and happily both have been too successful to render it necessary for one to interfere with the other . . . I beg most respectfully to protest and to ask at your hands and of that of your associates, a careful reconsideration of the questions involved. Let me ask you to consider whether the profits to be made by entering into competition with a friendly interest, are sufficient to counterbalance the weightier considerations connected therewith. . . . As a Director in your Company, I might also protest as in my judgment it is as unwise as unfair, as it is unnecessary and uncalled for, that we should attack our neighbor in this manner."[19]

When diplomacy failed, Carnegie took the gloves off. In mid-August, he wrote Jacob Linville, the president of Keystone, that he, his brother, Harry Phipps, and the other officers of Union Iron had "unanimously decided that we were prepared to undergo any pecuniary sacrifice to protect our property." Carnegie notified Linville that he and his partners were resigning from the board of directors and applying "for an injunction against you and if defeated there we propose to have a settlement of accounts with Keystone C. and let her seek elsewhere what we have hitherto supplied her. Our Mills can run half time if necessary, that we can stand . . . but one thing we can't and won't do, no set of men shall attempt to render any part of our property useless and succeed, if we can help it. The Keystone Bridge Company never took so dear a step as this will prove, I think."[20]

Linville and the Keystone officers, upon receiving Carnegie's letter, backed down.

At some point during the summer of 1871, while shuttling back and forth to Keokuk, St. Louis, and Pittsburgh, Carnegie was visited in his New York office by Colonel William Phillips, the president of the Allegheny Valley Railroad. Phillips was in need of a quarter million dollars, but had been unable to raise it by selling Allegheny Valley Railroad bonds, which were payable in dollars, not in gold as the London bankers preferred. Carnegie recommended that Phillips swap his "dollar" bonds for "gold" bonds held by J. Edgar Thomson in the Pennsylvania Railroad treasury. Carnegie did the numbers and arranged the bond swap. All he asked of Phillips in return was the commission to sell the gold bonds Phillips received. To sweeten the deal for Thomson, he offered to share with him the profits he expected to make from selling Phillips's bonds.[21]

On August 16, 1871, with a fresh supply of bonds, including issues from Tom Scott, who needed financing for new roads in the West, Carnegie returned to Europe. His first priority was to gain access to Baring Brothers, the oldest merchant bank in London.

From Queenstown, off the coast of Ireland, Carnegie cabled Baring Brothers requesting an appointment. Upon arriving in London, he settled in the Langham Hotel on Portland Place and awaited the summons to the Baring Brothers office on Bartholomew Lane. He didn't have to wait long. On August 28, he received the note he was waiting for: "Messrs. Baring Brothers and Co. present their compliments to Mr. Andrew Carnegie and as he requests will be happy to give him an interview at 12 o'clock on Tuesday, the 29th, inst."[22]

The next day, Carnegie presented his formal letter of introduction from Morton & Rose, his London brokers: "The bearer of this, Mr. Andrew Carnegie of Pittsburgh in the US has asked us for a letter of introduction to you and we have pleasure in complying with his request. He brought letters to us from our New York friends and was accredited to us as a gentleman of high character, who is connected with important Railway & Iron interests in the United States. He is a leading Director of the Union Pacific Railway Co. & is well known to our friends in New York."[23]

The interview went well, but the Barings in the end declined to buy, Carnegie claimed in a letter to Thomson, because the German chancellor, Otto von Bismarck, had impounded millions of dollars of pounds sterling, leaving the firm temporarily cash-poor. The likely reason for the Barings' decision to pass on the bonds was that Carnegie had priced them too high.[24]

Carnegie turned to J. S. Morgan & Co., and sold the same bonds "at a reduced price as compared with that agreed to by the Barings." The price was, indeed, so reduced that Junius Morgan offered to buy not only all the bonds Carnegie had in hand, but $2 million more still held by the Pennsylvania Railroad. Carnegie arranged the sale, by cable, with Thomson in Philadelphia. Morgan then organized a syndicate to resell the bonds and offered both Drexel & Co., the Philadelphia firm to which his son was now attached, and Carnegie a 25 percent interest in profits from the resale.[25]

Probably because the deal had been consummated so quickly and Carnegie, in his estimation, had done little more than send a cable, Thomson refused to pay his commission. Carnegie was incensed at being treated like a Pennsylvania Railroad employee or messenger boy instead of a bond salesman, but kept his calm. "I am not extravagant in my views," he wrote Thomson, almost apologetically, "having learned through many years in your service, that the Officers of the Great Corporation are paid only about one half of the value of their services in cash, and the other half in the honor which is conferred upon them, by being connected with so great an institution. I would therefore propose that you settle with me upon the usual basis; give me one half of the ordinary two and a half per cent Commission allowed for such negotiations, and the other half I am very sure I shall feel fully compensated for, in the undoubted honor conferred upon my by having been entrusted by you with such an important mission. To receive nothing but honor would not be agreeable."[26]

We don't know whether Carnegie ever got his commission. It didn't much matter. He came away from Europe demonstrating that he could sell securities to London's private bankers. In the past, J. Edgar Thomson had marketed the Pennsylvania's bonds by himself. Carnegie now offered him unsolicited advice on how he should in future proceed.[27]

He was extraordinarily confident for a man so new to the bond-trading business. As a bond trader, Carnegie was honest, but not too honest to turn down mutually beneficial partnerships, such as those Morgan had offered him. And he had a surfeit of that elusive quality called character. "Character," as Richard White has written, was not, for Gilded Age financiers, "synonymous with honesty; it had as much or more to do with honor, dependability, forcefulness, and strength." A man of character was one who made things happen, who carried through on his promises, who acted when others might procrastinate. As the *Railroad Gazette* had declared in its front-page profile: "What he takes hold of he carries through without fear of miscarriage. This cheerful, hopeful, or rather confident, element in him is quite marked. His mind seems instinctively to take hold of the right thing in the right way, and to move it to fruition by a steady, earnest unfaltering will."[28]

In his communications with London bankers, Carnegie unfailingly called attention to his knowledge of the railroads and his personal relationships with the men who ran them. "I find myself keenly regretting my failure to bring your house & our great Pennsylvania Railroad Co., into business relations with each other," he wrote Baring Brothers soon after the collapse of the negotiations for the P&E bonds. "The PRR Co. has control of the Transportation of the very heart of this Continent. Even its leased lines as a whole, will, this year, show a direct cash profit. Small, it is true, but certain to increase rapidly, year by year, as the West grows in population & wealth . . . Perhaps Mr. Thomson may entrust me with some of his loans in the future and I may succeed in my wish to do the business through your house."[29]

In a letter to Junius Morgan written at the same time, he argued that it was he, and he alone, who had convinced Thomson and the Pennsylvania Railroad directors to agree to Morgan's terms. "I had to plead the fact that what you undertook would go through to satisfy some of our friends here. . . . They will share my faith next time."[30]

MUCH OF CARNEGIE'S energies as a bond seller were spent raising money for Tom Scott, who had been named president of the Pennsylvania Company, the fully owned subsidiary of the Pennsylvania Railroad which controlled routes west of Pittsburgh. Scott had discovered that it was far more lucrative—and exciting—to build new railroads than to manage those up and running. He was a master promoter, a genius at securing the charters needed; cajoling local businessmen to invest, and incorporating improvement companies to do the construction work.

While Scott served as the public face of the new roads, Carnegie hovered in the background, doing the preliminary accounting work, writing up the prospectuses, floating the bond issues which provided the affiliated improvement companies with construction funds, and preparing for and contesting the inevitable suits brought by disgruntled bondholders. It is doubtful that either man truly believed that the new railroads, when built, would carry enough traffic to earn back their construction costs. A great number of them were along lightly traveled routes, which, like the Gilman, Springfield & Clinton Railroad in Illinois, connected small cities that did little business with one another. The roads were being built because money could be made building them. Carnegie profited from the commissions on the bond sales; Scott from diverting funds earmarked for construction into the hands of the select number of investors, himself included, who were directors of both the railroad and the improvement companies.[31]

To raise money for roads not yet built and probably not really needed, Carnegie and Scott trafficked in what Richard White refers to as "the utilitarian fictions of capitalism." Together, they constructed "plausible fictions" about the railroads, the passengers and freight that would ride them, the tolls that would be collected, the villages that would grow into towns and the towns into cities, creating new populations, products, and commerce.[32]

Carnegie, a consummate optimist, took naturally to the task. He was the classic Yankee promoter, the boomer, the salesman, the purveyor of success tales writ large, but he was also a self-trained professional who knew how to construct prospectuses for bankers, who had heard it all before. Before he approached Junius Morgan with a new offering of first-mortgage bonds for the Mansfield, Coldwater & Lake Michigan Railroad, he wrote Tom Scott from London to request "general data about the route, its objects, location, towns & cities it passes through, and all features contributing to impress capitalists with its importance." When Morgan declined to make an offer, Carnegie returned to the drawing board and gathered still more material to make a new and better case for the Mansfield bonds.[33]

In March 1872, he asked the railroad's president to secure "a strong letter from the Governor of your State, saying all he can about the enterprise, its importance, rich land to be developed and certainty to pay, etc., anything on official paper, and his signature attested by the Secretary of Commonwealth under Seal, etc." A week later, he drafted the governor's letter of support by himself, as well as additional endorsements to be signed by Thomson, Scott, and John Sherman, the senator from Ohio. Sherman's letter, he recommended, should be "on official Senate Chamber paper" and should emphasize that because the senator's "place of residence" was Mansfield, "all of [the] managers of the line are personally known to me. They are men of the highest character and responsibility; in whose representations, full reliance may be placed."[34]

On March 16, he signed separate agreements with Drexel Morgan in New York and Drexel & Company in Philadelphia to act as their agent and partner in Europe. The following month, he set sail for an extended bond-selling campaign, this time accompanied by his mother, her traveling companion, Miss Robinson, and Eddie McCandless, Gardie's brother, who had been brought along to look after the ladies and act as Carnegie's traveling secretary.[35]

Their first stop was Frankfurt, Germany. The London markets were saturated with American railroad securities and Junius Morgan had suggested that Carnegie take his bond issues to the Morgan correspondent firm, Sulzbach Brothers. Carnegie, as always, had no trouble ingratiating himself with his new clients, whom he visited several times during his six months in Europe. He was assisted by his mother who, dour as she might appear, got along famously with the Sulzbach women.[36]

The Sulzbachs, though cordial, were highly suspicious of American securities and had dozens of questions about the details of Carnegie's prospectus for the Davenport & St. Paul Railroad bonds. Why, they wanted to know, were the directors of the railroad also directors of the construction company? Why wouldn't Thomson and Scott guarantee, on behalf of the Pennsylvania Railroad, that the line would be completed? Why were the meetings of the executive committee of the Davenport & St. Paul Railroad Company held in New York City instead of Davenport?[37]

The spring and summer of 1872 were not the best of times to sell American securities in London or Frankfurt. The financial markets were in a state of prolonged hibernation, awaiting news of the settlement of the British-American dispute over what had come to be known as the *Alabama* claims.

In July 1862, with British sentiment for the Confederacy at its apogee, the *Alabama*, a steam-powered, wooden-hulled sloop, left England, ostensibly for a trial run. Transformed in the Azores into a Confederate man-of-war, the vessel spent the rest of the Civil War roaming the North Atlantic and inflicting substantial damage on merchant ships doing business with the Union. The American government, led by Ambassador Charles Francis Adams in London, demanded reparations from the British for what it claimed—rightly—was a hostile act of government-assisted piracy.

Adams, who was ambassador to Great Britain until 1868, failed to secure a settlement. In 1869, after his departure, an agreement was reached, but rejected by the U.S. Senate for being too favorable to the British. The conflict between the United States and Britain had now consumed the better part of seven years. President Grant, frightened by the saber rattling of his Democratic opponents, demanded that his secretary of state, Hamilton Fish, reach an agreement before the 1872 presidential election. Fish enlisted the services of bankers on both sides of the ocean, including a number of the men Carnegie did business with, such as Anthony Drexel of Philadelphia, Levi Morton of New York, and John Rose, the Scotsman who was Morton's partner in London. In the spring of 1871, the British and American governments agreed to submit the question of monetary claims to impartial arbitration in Geneva, Switzerland.

Carnegie, like other businessmen with transatlantic interests, paid close attention to the negotiations. In February 1872, he wrote a long letter to Horace Porter, President Grant's executive secretary. Fearful that Grant might accede to those who demanded that the British pay not only the "direct" cost of the wartime damage but the "indirect" costs as well, Carnegie urged the president not to ask the Geneva arbiters for outsized reparations. To protect the president from political repercussions, Carnegie proposed his own convoluted compromise plan. Indulging in the grandiose flattery that would later become his trademark, he suggested to Porter that Grant could secure himself a place in history alongside President Lincoln if he accepted the scenario Carnegie had laid out for him.

"Lincoln is to stand in History, when all other of his acts shall have been forgot, as the Emancipator of Four Millions of his fellow men. Grant may secure equal prominence among the very few essentially great characters of the world's history if he succeeds . . . in being the first who leads nations to substitute for the barbarous appeal to the sword, the device of peaceful arbitration."[38]

In his letter to Porter, Carnegie intimated that he was in close touch with London insiders. He made the same sort of claims to Baring Brothers, to whom he confided that he had been present when "the president met some of his friends in Philadelphia," and, based on that meeting, he was "very happy to be able to say that the policy of binding England & American together, in the closest bonds of friendship, has no stronger supporter than General Grant & this fact should not be lost sight of by your Government." Carnegie asked the Barings to warn the British government that Grant "should not be pressed too far, otherwise, we may have a much less friendly administration in power."[39]

The negotiations in Geneva over a monetary settlement dragged on into May and June. The longer they took, the more frightened the capital markets became. None of the major financial houses, including Sulzbach Brothers in Frankfurt, was willing to buy or sell securities until it was known if a settlement was going to be reached, how much the British would be obliged to hand over to the Americans, and what effect the transfer of millions of pounds sterling would have on the price of gold.

Carnegie, after his exploratory visit with the Sulzbachs, had no choice but to take a European vacation. He spent a day in Brussels sightseeing with his mother and Miss Robinson; enjoyed an "elegant dinner" with Mr. Jones, the American ambassador; then took off for Antwerp and London to try to do some business. He met up again with his mother and the full entourage in Paris and crossed the Channel with them in mid-May. "It is too uncertain for me to predict however as to what Mr. A.C.'s movement will be," Eddie wrote his brother from London on May 12, "as the state of the *Alabama* case prevents his doing much."[40]

Carnegie decided to remain in London with his mother and Mrs. Robinson "until the *Alabama* is definitely decided—& we see how matters look." His letters to Gardie in New York suggest that he was not terribly upset at being forced into taking an indefinite vacation. "We find room somehow or other at all the interesting shows. . . . Miss Robinson turns out just splendid. Mother & she are perfectly jolly the whole time except when I suggest that we may have to return ere long—This quiets them."[41]

The Carnegies' stopover in London turned into an extended vacation. Late in the summer, the arbitrators in Geneva decided on a British liability of £3.25 million, a vast sum, but one which Prime Minister Gladstone's government agreed to pay. Carnegie was able now to return to work and conclude the negotiations with Sulzbach Brothers and other bankers in

Amsterdam, Antwerp, Brussels, Paris, and London that he had initiated earlier in the spring.

IT IS IMPOSSIBLE to discount the importance of this 1872 bond-selling trip for Carnegie. The market instability caused by the *Alabama* affair had forced on him an extended period of leisure in which he had tasted the fruits of semiretirement and found them quite exhilarating. Although he had not yet celebrated his thirty-seventh birthday, Carnegie would never again return to a full-time work schedule.

His experience in Europe that spring and summer also had a profound effect on the development of the peace program that Carnegie would spend the final decades of his life promulgating. It was not, as he would learn in 1872, "actual war itself which the world in our day has most to dread. . . . It is the ever-present danger of war, which hangs over the world like a pall, which we have to dispel." There had been no war between Great Britain and America over the *Alabama* claims, but the strained relationship made it difficult to do business and gave unscrupulous politicians, like Senator Charles Sumner, a platform for their warmongering.[42]

Disputes between nations were inevitable, but some way short of bloodshed had to be found to settle them. The willingness of both the British and American governments to submit their claims to impartial arbitration in Geneva had been an important step forward. For the rest of his life, Carnegie would refer to the settlement of the *Alabama* claims case in Geneva as an exemplary moment in international diplomacy and Anglo-American relations, where reason and common sense had peaceably solved a long-festering conflict.[43]

IN HIS *Autobiography* and his other lectures and writings, Carnegie devotes very little space to his years as a bond salesman. Burton Hendrick ignores this period of his life entirely, as if he had jumped directly from working for the railroad to manufacturing iron and steel.

Carnegie avoided mention of his bond trading not because he had performed any criminal acts, but because he was loath to call attention to some morally if not legally questionable deals. Carnegie was sued countless times during his years as a trader by bondholders like the Sulzbach Brothers, who claimed that he had made false statements about the issues he was selling, and bond issuers who claimed that he had pocketed profits that belonged to them. In 1874, to cite but one example, he was sued by a Springfield businessman, Dr. Samuel H. Melvin, who had been one of the organizers of the railroad connecting Gilman with Clinton and Springfield, Illinois. Melvin charged that Carnegie and the Morton brokerage firms in New York and London had colluded four years earlier to cheat local stockholders of $400,000. Carnegie, the suit claimed, sold the Gilman railroad bonds to the Morton firms at less than market value. The Morton firms then resold them at a huge profit, which they divided with Carnegie and his partner, Tom Scott.[44]

The charges, which would wend their way through the courts for years before they were dismissed, were true. In December 1871, Morton & Rose in London, in a letter marked "Confidential," confirmed that Carnegie and Scott would divide one quarter of any profit the firm made from reselling the Gilman railroad bonds. In March 1872, Carnegie received a check for $29,244.94 (over $6 million today), covering his and Scott's share of Morton & Rose's profits.[45]

AS A BOND TRADER, Carnegie was obliged to make promises he could not keep. The prospectus he had written for the St. Louis Bridge bonds he sold to Junius Morgan had, for example, promised that within eighteen months, by December 1871, the bridge would be earning revenues from toll-paying traffic. But this goal, Carnegie knew, was not going to be met. The insurmountable problem was Captain Eads's insistence that the bridge arches be built of steel even though the only steel then available was expensive, brittle, difficult to work with, and impossible to secure in large quantities. "I wish the Captain's genius could devise some plan in which Iron could be used," Carnegie wrote William McPherson, a company director and fellow Scotsman whom he considered an ally, in October 1870. "We would then be independent. . . . You may think self interest comes in here as we Manufacture Iron but if so you are simply wrong. I have a much deeper interest at stake in rendering St. Louis Bridge a success."[46]

By late 1871, with Eads still in control of design and construction,

Carnegie had had enough. He began selling his stock in the bridge company—and offered to do the same for Scott and Thomson. "As we are partners in this St. Louis affair, I think I should offer to take care of your interests as of my own. . . . I am disgusted with the affair, throughout."[47]

Only in his correspondence with Junius Morgan did Carnegie continue to boost the St. Louis Bridge as an income-generating project. In September 1872, he predicted that the bridge would be open for traffic by the summer of 1873, then, as that date approached, promised that it would be done by the end of 1873. Morgan, his frustration barely disguised, wrote back in May of 1873 that he and his partners were "glad to hear there is some prospect of the St. Louis Bridge being ready for traffic during the present year. We have been told the same story the last three years; we shall therefore not encourage too strong hopes of the accomplishment of what we have been so long anxiously waiting for."[48]

It would take another year before Keystone completed work on the St. Louis Bridge's superstructure. On May 23, 1874, the bridge was opened to pedestrian traffic. Some 25,000 people paid ten cents apiece to walk across the upper deck and then, because the work on the east embankment had still not been completed, turn around and walk back. In June, the lower deck for railway traffic was finally completed. On July 2, as crowds cheered from the shore below, an elephant was led across the lower railway deck. The belief was that if the bridge were unsafe, the elephant would sense it and turn around. When the elephant strolled the length of the bridge without hesitation, the bridge was tested again and found satisfactory by fourteen locomotives, averaging 40 tons each.[49]

The St. Louis Bridge over the Mississippi would succeed for a time as a tourist attraction, but fail as a business venture. By the time it was completed, the major east-west railroads had made other arrangements to cross the Mississippi. With few toll-paying rail customers, the St. Louis Bridge Company quickly defaulted on its loans. In April 1875, the company declared bankruptcy and surrendered its assets to two receivers, one of them Pierpont Morgan, Junius's son. The Morgans held on to the bridge company for three more years, then reorganized it in August 1878. Under the reorganization plan, the bondholders, including Morgan and his associates, were fully protected. Stockholders were not. The stock which Carnegie and his associates had so wisely sold years earlier was now worthless.[50]

Though the St. Louis company had gone rather quickly into default, Carnegie, his associates, and the Morgans had made their profits and moved on. Timing was everything in railroad and bridge financing. Each time there was a delay in completing the project or a cost overrun, new monies had to be borrowed to pay off old loans. Private bankers, like the Morgans, were happy to lend such money, for short terms and at inflated rates. Delayed projects—and almost all of them were delayed—led to pyramiding debts for railroads and bridge companies and pyramiding profits for bankers and middlemen like Carnegie who arranged short-term loans to back up long-term bonds.

The failure of the St. Louis Bridge project had no effect on the Morgans' perception of the business acumen of the little man who had sold them the bridge bonds in 1870. They remained on good terms with Carnegie and continued to buy his bond issues. What counted in the end was not the ultimate success or failure of the railroad or bridge, but whether the investors made a reasonable amount on their investments. And the Morgans had.

EIGHT

"All My Eggs in One Basket,"
1872–1875

CARNEGIE RESIGNED from the railroad because he wanted to be his own man; but without capital to float large issues on his own, he remained dependent on the Morgans, the Drexels, and the Morton firms to form the syndicates, market the issues, and handle the always complicated exchanges from gold to pounds to dollars and vice versa. Had his responsibilities to others ended with the sale of the bonds, he might have been more content. But as the chief and often the only liaison between European bankers and American railroad, bridge, and construction companies, he was on constant call. It was he, and he alone, who was required to know precisely what was going on at all times. Were the roads the bonds were supposed to fund being built on schedule? If there were delays—which there always were—what was causing them? How soon could tolls be collected and interest payments made?

THE CARNEGIE ENTOURAGE returned to New York in September 1872 after an absence of almost five months abroad. Andrew and Mag hoped that Tom and his wife Lucy would be at the pier to greet them, but the Tom Carnegies were reluctant to interrupt their holiday at Cresson, an exclusive mountain resort in the Alleghenies. And so the day after their arrival, Mag and Andy were back on the road again, this time via the Pennsylvania Railroad to Cresson, to visit Tom and his family.[1]

Carnegie spent much of the fall with his mother in Cresson, with side trips to Pittsburgh for business. He could board the express in the morning and arrive in Pittsburgh four and a half hours later, in early afternoon. Though a resident of New York City, his monies were invested almost entirely in Pittsburgh firms. He held two-fifths interest in Carnegie, Kloman & Co. (Union Iron Mills), one-fifth in Keystone Bridge, stock in several western Pennsylvania railroads and manufacturers, and a two-fifths interest in a new furnace company named Lucy, in honor of Tom's wife.[2]

Unlike their competitors, the Carnegies and Harry Phipps were newcomers to the iron business. Andrew Kloman was the only partner who had any experience in the trade, but as a mechanic, not a manufacturer. Carnegie was convinced that the fact that he had begun work for the railroads, rather than in the iron industry served him well. He was astonished by the laxity with which the iron barons kept their books. "I was greatly surprised to find that the cost of each of the various [production] processes was unknown." He instructed Harry Phipps to set up the kinds of cost-accounting procedures that were already in place at the railroads. "I insisted upon such a system of weighing and accounting . . . as would enable us to know what our cost was for each process and especially what each man was doing, who saved material, who wasted it, and who produced the best results." Phipps sent his monthly accounts to Carnegie's New York office, where the absentee partner examined them line by line. "By the aid of many clerks and the introduction of weighing scales at various points in the mill, we began to know not only what every department was doing, but what each one of the many men working at the furnaces was doing."[3]

As his Pittsburgh firms expanded in size and profitability, Carnegie extended his oversight. He was not an engineer and had no technical training, but he enjoyed an insider's understanding of the mechanical arts and the iron trades and was a shrewd judge of talent. His initial success in iron manufacture and bridge building had come, in large part—and he recognized this—because he had partnered with engineers Jacob Linville and John Piper at Keystone Bridge; a brilliantly innovative mechanic, Andrew Kloman, at Union Iron Mills; and two solid businessmen, his brother Tom and Harry Phipps, who oversaw his Pittsburgh operations.

William Abbott, who knew both Carnegies from their early days at the Pittsburgh iron mills, thought Andrew a genius, but regarded Tom as the "better business man." Tom, Abbott told Burton Hendrick, "was solid, shrewd, farseeing, absolutely honest and dependable." The two brothers had very different notions about business. Andrew was the ambitious one, filled with new ideas; Tom "was content with a good, prosperous, safe business and cared nothing for expansion. He disapproved of Andrew's skyrocketing tendencies, regarded him as a plunger and a dangerous leader. Tom wanted earnings in the shape of dividends, whereas Andrew insisted on using them for expansion." There were other differences as well. While Andrew sought out publicity, Tom ran away from it. He was silent, retiring, "not a mixer in society, was tongue-tied at dinner parties and social gatherings." As a child and young man at the dinner table, Tom would "disappear from the family circle—into an upper room," away from his talkative brother. Like his older brother, Tom Carnegie was remarkably efficient and known for his ability to accomplish a day's work in a morning. He got along well with his subordinates and was well liked by the workingmen. His fatal flaw was his drinking. According to Abbott, he would leave the office for lunch and drink all afternoon, seldom returning to work before four o'clock.

Harry Phipps, on the contrary, never seemed to leave the office. An extraordinary bookkeeper, he spent his days watching over costs and seeking out new efficiencies. "He was a cheese-parer in every direction," Abbott recalled, "making economies that would never occur to anyone else." Like the Carnegie brothers, he was a tiny little man.[4]

While Tom and Harry Phipps watched over the business, kept costs down and orders up, Carnegie supplied, from a distance, a businessman's sense of the directions in which the market was moving and how to capitalize on them. He also organized and directed the firms' early ventures into marketing, publicity, and advertising. The sales pamphlets and illustrated catalogues for Keystone were among the most polished in the industry, with beautifully designed wood engravings of bridges and detailed tabular summaries of the firms' past accomplishments. In the mid-1870s, after Linville invented what he called the "Rivetless Post," Carnegie suggested that the company place "advertizements [sic] in every journal devoted to the mechanical, engineering & architectural arts. . . . Some one should read a paper upon it before the Engineers—your Franklin Institute should know about it—indeed I should, within ten days, have so advertised it as to render it almost impossible that any man of intelligence should be ignorant of the fact that an important step had been taken by us in the use of wrought iron columns. Excuse me for dwelling upon the immense importance of publicity & of printers ink—It is a department in which I believe you have permitted our most formidable rivals . . . to distance you." Carnegie sketched for Linville the kind of "short well-displayed advertisement" he had in mind and cautioned him to "go to work & get up some handsome lithographs, add below a few words explanatory of their merits [and] don't mix up this new Post advertisement with anything else—It should stand alone as a specialty."[5]

In early 1874, Carnegie learned that Calvert Vaux, the architect commissioned to design the "Centennial Palace" at the 1876 Philadelphia Exposition, had decided to construct it of wood instead of iron. He fired off a letter to an acquaintance, J. Lowber Welsh, whose father was president of the exposition's board of finance. Making his case for an iron structure, Carnegie argued that it would demonstrate American progress in the "arts, manufactures, and products of the soil and mine," the theme of the exposition. He also conjured up images of the fire that might destroy the exposition should the "palace" be constructed of wood. "If our great Centennial Palace is to be only a modern tinder box how will foreign exhibitors be affected—can any one be induced to risk valuable articles in such a structure? The risk of fire during the two years it will be under construction will be even greater than while it is occupied—a spark may render any exhibition at all impossible." To save the centennial palace from potential conflagration, Carnegie offered to build it of iron for $4.5 million, only $1.75 million more than it would cost in wood. He closed his letter with a veiled threat to go public with his concerns—about safety, sparks, and fire damage—if the commissioners declined his offer. The notion that "Pennsylvania and especially Philadelphia" might hold its exposition in a wooden building "fairly amazes me—perhaps I am too partial to iron as an iron manfr. Still we shall see how the country takes the idea."[6]

The commissioners took Carnegie's advice and constructed the main building's skeleton of iron. They did not, however, award Carnegie the contracts for the ironwork on the main exposition buildings. The only contract Keystone Bridge was given was for the iron skeleton for the smaller horticultural building.[7]

To guarantee his companies' products a prominent place at the exposition, Carnegie had himself appointed to the "committee of seven" that the American Iron and Steel Association organized to oversee the display of iron ores and goods. When the exposition opened on May 10, 1876, with President Grant presiding, the "Carnegie Brothers & Company" displays were so well placed "along the southern portion of the Main Building" that J. S. Ingram noted in his guidebook, *The Centennial Exposition, Described and Illustrated,* that they were among the few that "prominently attracted our notice." Though it is unlikely that the general public flocked to see Carnegie's "rolled wrought-iron coupling" or the model of his Lucy furnace, contractors who bought and sold iron products certainly did.[8]

CARNEGIE HAD RETURNED from Europe in the fall of 1872 with money in his purse from his bond sales, which, as a good capitalist, he felt obliged to invest. The Pennsylvania oil business was already being colonized by Rockefeller of Cleveland and was, in any case, too speculative for Carnegie. He knew better than to invest in overpriced railroad stock. His coal-mining investments were paying a reasonable dividend, but not enough to encourage him to invest more. His iron furnace, iron mills, and bridge-building company were sufficiently capitalized at present and doing well.

A less adventurous capitalist might have bided his time and hoarded his money or made incremental investments in familiar firms. But Carnegie was convinced that there were fortunes to be made manufacturing stronger, more durable rails, of steel. In 1870, the Republicans, now in control of the presidency and the Congress, turned the business environment upside down with the imposition of a $28-a-ton tariff on imported steel. The door was opened wide for American steel manufacturers. At a stroke of the pen, the British steel mills lost their competitive advantage. The iron and steel tariff would remain in place, in one form or another, for the next thirty years—as long, that is, as Carnegie remained in the steel business. It became the centerpiece of Republican policy and, with the Republicans the dominant party in Washington, a cornerstone of national economic policy. The passage of the 1870 tariff was, Carnegie later claimed, the single most important event in prompting him to enter the steel business.[9]

Carnegie had kept abreast of the latest iron- and steelmaking technologies since the mid-1860s. No trip to Europe had been complete without a pilgrimage to iron and steel foundries and discussions with the manufacturers. While waiting for the settlement of the *Alabama* case in the summer of 1872, he had traveled to Sheffield to tour Henry Bessemer's steel plant and marvel at his new furnaces.[10]

Bessemer had invented a process for making a less brittle, stronger iron product that he first called malleable iron, then changed the name to Bessemer steel. Because Bessemer steel was cooked in large batches in giant converters, it could be produced more efficiently, with much less labor, than the wrought iron which was currently being manufactured in small ovens in the Pittsburgh mills.

The technological advances pioneered by Bessemer in England, combined with the new protective tariff, induced several American manufacturers to move into the steel business. By 1872, there were eight steel manufactories in the country, including Pennsylvania Steel in Steelton and Cambria Iron in Johnstown, Pennsylvania. Curiously enough, while Pittsburgh was the home of a large number of iron mills, there were as yet no steel manufactories in the city.

Carnegie's partner in the oil business, William Coleman, who had experience in the iron industry, began scouting the nation's Bessemer steel plants to see for himself whether it made sense to invest in the new technology. He was intrigued by what he saw, especially in Harrisburg, Johnstown, and Troy, New York, and began rounding up partners to invest in a steel rail mill in Pittsburgh. By the time Carnegie returned from his bond-selling European tour to Pittsburgh in mid-September 1872, Coleman had contracted with Alexander Holley to design the new plant. Holley, who had graduated from Brown University, was, at age forty, the foremost steel engineer in the nation. He had already played the lead role in designing steel mills at Troy, Cambria, and Steelton. There was no one better qualified or with more experience. Having secured Holley's services, Coleman took out an option on a site in Turtle Creek Valley at Braddock's Field, so named because it was on this spot that General Edward Braddock had been defeated in the French and Indian War in 1755.[11]

It was an ideal site for a new steel plant. The two major ingredients in manufacturing steel were coke (made by cooking bituminous coal until the gas has been expelled) and iron ore low in phosphorous (high-phosphorous ores did not work well in Bessemer furnaces). The best coal for coking was found in the Connellsville region, fifty miles southeast of Pittsburgh. Quality iron ore came from the Lake Superior iron mines, which were considerably farther but, via lake steamer and rail, closer to Braddock than to any other steel mill. The Baltimore & Ohio tracks ran through the center of the site; the Pennsylvania Railroad tracks ran along the northern border; the Monongahela River, still a major highway, flowed along the southern edge. The city of Pittsburgh was barely twelve miles away.

Carnegie was one of the first to join with Coleman in the new venture. The steel manufactory was organized as a separate partnership, with no legal ties to any of Carnegie's other Pittsburgh firms. On November 5, 1872, Carnegie signed both the lease for the Braddock site and the "Articles of Co-Partnership." Coleman and Carnegie chose for their partners men of wealth and reputation. David McCandless, vice president of the Exchange National Bank, agreed to invest $100,000 for ten shares of stock. Coleman took ten for himself. Carnegie, the principal stockholder, subscribed for twenty-five. The other partners—John Scott (who was not related to Tom), a railroad vice president and bank president; David Stewart, Carnegie's partner in Pittsburgh Locomotive and Tom Scott's nephew; and Phipps, Tom Carnegie, and Andrew Kloman—purchased five shares each. As was standard operating procedure, the stockholders were expected to pay for their shares on a monthly basis. The new firm was named Carnegie, McCandless, and Company, in recognition of Carnegie's oversized financial contribution and McCandless's reputation. Everyone but Carnegie lived and worked in Pittsburgh.[12]

The fall of 1872 marks the beginning of a new chapter in Carnegie's life. Burton Hendrick describes the moment with operatic overkill: "The change that came over the man in this, his thirty-seventh year, resembled the religious experience known as conversion, and like that experience it came as the exaltation of a single moment. A mind that had lived in apparent darkness was illumined by a sudden flash of light. . . . The dazzling brilliance of a Bessemer converter . . . in the twinkling of an eye, transformed Andrew Carnegie into a new man."[13]

Hendrick may be forgiven for substituting metaphor for analysis in attempting to explain how Carnegie, the businessman who had so many balls in the air, could in the space of only a few years let almost all of them fall to earth so that he could focus his attention—and his capital—on the steel business. Carnegie, returning from Europe in September 1872, was no Saul on the road to Damascus. There had been no blinding revelation, no moment of exaltation, no sudden conversion from iron to steel. Carnegie had no intention of concentrating either his capital or his attention on the steel business. At the same time that he became a partner in the new steel rail mill, he was selling bonds for several bridge and rail concerns, negotiating the merger of Pacific & Atlantic Telegraph Company with Western Union, overseeing the completion of the long-delayed St. Louis Bridge project, opening discussions to build a bridge over the Hudson River at Poughkeepsie, attempting to secure control of the rail lines that connected the proposed Poughkeepsie bridge to New England, and purchasing, with William Coleman, a new coal company in western Pennsylvania, Kier Coal & Works.[14]

The only business activity he backed away from was active bond trading, and that decision was dictated by market conditions. It was becoming increasingly difficult to market bonds in Europe because of the glut of securities on the market. In January 1873, some sixty days after he had signed the co-partnership agreement for the Braddock steel mill, the Sulzbachs informed him that they had been unable to sell the bonds "for which we have contracted with you." By the spring, the situation had deteriorated to the point that Morgan suggested Carnegie put off his already planned bond-selling trip. "Our market is at the moment over-supplied with American securities and we do not think you could accomplish anything by coming now. On the continent it is still worse, as they have as a rule a more stringent money market and have also suffered largely by investments in second or third class American Railroad Bonds, so that we doubt if they would touch anything at this moment."[15]

To scare up commissions for new bond issues would have meant another round of travel—to Iowa and Missouri and Kansas and Illinois, where new roads and bridges were being built. In previous years, Carnegie might have been prepared to take to the road again and live out of his satchel for days on end, cajoling railroad purchasing agents, chambers of commerce, and self-appointed men of affairs who had decided to establish themselves and their cities by building bridges across the Mississippi or Missouri. But he had lost his taste for this sort of wheeling and dealing, especially in a down market. It made more sense to invest his money in Pittsburgh and to oversee the new business from his home in New York.

IT REMAINED for the partners to agree on a name for their steelworks. Carnegie, thinking strategically as always, suggested they name it after the nation's most respected railroad executive, J. Edgar Thomson, in the expectation that the name would provide the works—and the rails it produced—

with an instant reputation for reliability. The name might also lure other investors to the project and help secure contracts for steel rails. Thomson himself might even invest.

In late October, Carnegie wrote to ask Thomson for permission to use his name. The letter is an early masterpiece of manipulative flattery of the sort that Carnegie would employ for the rest of his life in conversing with the rich and powerful. He and his partners, he reported to Thomson, had grappled with the question of

> what to call the Works . . . until "Edgar Thomson" was suggested & carried by acclamation. "Just the very thing," was the unanimous expression. . . . We are all quite satisfied that Pittsburgh is the best present location in the Country for the Manfr. of Steel Rails & we hope to give the "Edgar Thomson" brand a place alongside of the "John Brown" Rails [the premium imported English product at the time]. If we felt that calling our Works after you were an honor conferred upon you we could readily offer reasons why you deserve it, but as we all sincerely feel that the honor will be entirely upon our side in being permitted to do so, we have nothing to say except to assure you that there is not one of our party who is not delighted that an opportunity has arisen through which expression can be given, however feebly, to the regard they honestly entertain for your exalted character & career.
>
> With sincere respect, I am always
>
> Your Obt. Servt.
>
> Andrew Carnegie[16]

In mid-November, Thomson granted Carnegie permission to "use the name you suggest, if the names you sent me [the partners] are individually liable for its success and as I have no doubt will look after its management—I have no funds at present to invest, having been drained by the Texas & California [Scott's new railroad]—and Sanborne's Mexican project [a highly speculative railroad enterprise]."[17]

Carnegie also tried to enlist Tom Scott to invest in the new steelworks, but Scott was even more "drained" of capital than Thomson. In the end, he agreed to purchase some stock—we don't know how much—but, like Thomson, did not want to be listed as a partner. He asked that his shares be registered in his secretary's name, not his own. "Mr. Scott was alarmed at danger of becoming a partner," Carnegie wrote one of his Pittsburgh associates, "& I relieved him of that. I only hope he will never be involved in anything worse."[18]

The partners didn't really need Thomson's or Scott's money. While they expected to be awarded Pennsylvania Railroad contracts for their rails, they did not intend to operate as a subsidiary of one railroad. The intent behind the decision to build the new steel mill adjacent to the B&O tracks and on the Monongahela River was unmistakable. Carnegie, who had made his fortune by playing the game of crony capitalism, was signaling to Thomson that he would play that game no longer. The Edgar Thomson steelworks would sell its wares to the highest bidders—for the highest price—and transport its raw materials and finished goods on the roads that offered the best rates. It would be captive to neither Thomson nor his Pennsylvania Railroad.[19]

In later years, Carnegie's enemies would claim that one of the sources of his early success was the "special concessions" on freight rates his companies received from the Pennsylvania Railroad. Carnegie denied that the Pennsylvania gave him any preferential treatment. He claimed on the contrary that the railroad discriminated against him and his companies. "I was fighting the Pennsylvania Railroad all the time." Having broken faith with the company, he courted trouble. In the years to come, he would have to fight every inch of the way to get reasonable freight rates from Thomson's successors.[20]

The first priority was hiring a general manager for E.T. (as Carnegie would in future refer to the steelworks at Braddock). Carnegie was looking for a "business man" as shrewd and calculating as he was. The "business man," as such, was a relatively new arrival—so new, in fact, that it would not become a single word for a few decades to come. Prior to the 1880s, men in business were identified by industry or function. There were railroad superintendents and presidents, iron manufacturers, merchants, financiers, and so on, but no "businessmen" such as Carnegie was looking for with skill sets readily transferable from one sector to another.[21]

Carnegie's choice for general manager was Daniel Morrell, the "aristocratic" Philadelphian who in the mid-1850s had been brought in to reorganize the Cambria ironworks near Johnstown. Morrell had stayed on as manager and a principal owner, and in 1871 he oversaw the conversion to steel production. Carnegie was so convinced of Morrell's worth that he

agreed to pay him the annual salary of $20,000 that he demanded, an un-
usually high amount in 1872, with no doubt an additional offer of equity in
the company. Carnegie's partners were opposed to bringing in Morrell—
at such a high price—and offended that their New York partner had acted
on his own in opening negotiations with him. They agreed, nonetheless,
to "stand up loyally for whatever you have done if the thing is settled between you."[22]

In the end, Morrell refused the position. Carnegie and his Pittsburgh
associates offered it next to William Shinn, a vice president at the Allegheny Valley Railroad who came highly recommended by McCandless
and by John Scott, president of the railroad. Shinn was a tough manager,
a disciplined accountant, and an ambitious businessman. Though self-
contained, solemn, and introverted, he was not shy about offering his
opinions, even when they conflicted with Carnegie's own. This too was a
plus. Carnegie was confident enough in his own judgment not to require
affirmation from his subordinates. Carnegie worried only about Shinn's
loyalties, as he refused to resign his vice presidency at the Allegheny Valley
Railroad after agreeing to take on the new position at E.T.[23]

Because neither Shinn nor any of the partners had experience in steelmaking, it was imperative that they hire—as general superintendent—
someone who had. The Union Iron Mills and the Lucy furnace had proved
so successful because, while Phipps and Tom Carnegie ran the business,
Andrew Kloman served as general superintendent. What Carnegie needed
was someone like Kloman with the capacity to oversee men at work. He
found those qualities—and much more—in Captain William Jones (the
title was an honorary Civil War one). Although Carnegie, who adored telling
stories about workingmen who had risen through his ranks to become millionaires, claimed that Jones had come to work for him as a "two-dollar-a-
day mechanic," that was far from the case. The son of a dissenting Welsh
minister, Jones had risen to the rank of chief assistant to the general superintendent at Cambria before resigning his position. Alexander Holley
hired Jones to assist him in designing and building E.T., and when construction was completed, recommended him for plant superintendent.
Like Carnegie, the captain was tiny, always on the move, and spoke with a
slight accent (Welsh, not Scottish). Until he was killed in a furnace explosion in 1889, Jones oversaw the day-to-day operation of the steelworks,

invented and patented a large number of labor-saving improvements, and supervised the skilled workforce.[24]

ONE OF CARNEGIE'S many gifts as a businessman was his capacity to generate enthusiasm for his projects—in partners, potential customers, and the public at large. Carnegie was not a "dour Scotsman," or a cold, calculating capitalist, but a little man brimming with excitement for whatever business he was engaged in at that moment. He was, in the early 1870s, consumed by excitement about steel rails, as he had earlier been about sleeping cars and iron bridges. By applying the same cost-accounting procedures he had employed in his other Pittsburgh firms and constructing the most efficient plant in the nation, Carnegie was confident that he would be able to undersell the domestic market for steel rails. With a $28-a-ton tariff slapped onto their products, British manufacturers would never be able to compete. In a letter written in mid-December to the Sulzbach Brothers in Frankfurt, he sounded like a child with a new toy: "I have been very busy with my Iron business. We are building a Works to manufacture one hundred tons Steel Rails per day, in addition to our present Mills for Iron, etc., so you see, in this fast Country one can't stand still."[25]

He was so energized by the new project that in early November, six months before ground was even broken for the mill, he was already contracting for the low-phosphorous iron ore required to manufacture steel through the Bessemer process. In New York, he met with Samuel Tilden, the future Democratic nominee for president and, at the time, a partner in a firm that owned mines in the Marquette district of Michigan. Carnegie contracted for 10,000 tons of Tilden's "first class 'New York mine' speculum ore," which he believed, combined with western Pennsylvania "fuel" (i.e., Connellsville coke), would yield high-quality "Bessemer Pig Metal." He invited Tilden and/or his agents to visit his Pittsburgh furnace during the smelting "and follow the product until it appears as a steel rail, as we trust it will."[26]

As excited as he might have been by his new business venture, Carnegie had no intention of overseeing it from Pittsburgh. He worked in spurts now, and spent as much time away from the office as in it. In February 1873, five months after his return from Europe, he abandoned his partners in Pittsburgh and his office in New York for a two-month rail and riverboat excursion to New Orleans and Jacksonville, Florida. He was accompanied by his mother; Miss Robinson, her traveling companion; his niece Retta; his partners Coleman and McCandless; Uncle George Lauder, who was visiting from Dunfermline; Sol Schoyer, one of his lawyers; and all of the wives. Carnegie was the perfect travel guide. There was never a dull moment on a Carnegie excursion. During their stay in Jacksonville, where the hotels were "all filled and a great deal of gayety [was] going on," the party enjoyed "several dances."[27]

Carnegie returned to New York via Washington and Philadelphia in early spring, stayed a few weeks, and then, when the weather turned warm, relocated with his mother, a small entourage of servants, their carriage, and a horse or two, to Cresson in the Alleghenies.

Accessible only by the railroad, hours from smoky Pittsburgh and far enough from an almost equally polluted Altoona, Cresson offered Philadelphia and Pittsburgh businessmen, railroad executives, and politicians aesthetic and hygienic relief from putrid city air and threats of cholera, typhus, and tuberculosis. The first building on the site had been a sanitarium because the springs there were believed to have healing powers. There was hiking, hunting, and fishing, well-groomed paths for carriages and horseback riders, and a boardwalk for pedestrians. Most of the vacationers stayed in the Mountain House, a luxury resort hotel; the privileged few, like the Carnegies, rented private cottages for the season.[28]

In 1873, Andrew and his mother spent the entire season at Cresson. Tom and Lucy joined them there for a few days; Uncle Lauder and his wife for two weeks. The family took its meals in the Mountain House dining room and slept in Cottage D, a four-room wooden cabin. The total cost for the summer was $1046.40, including $50 per week per person for board, an additional $9 for wine, 30 cents for postage and paper, $27 for six crates of peaches, $10 for fires, $1 for laundry, and $52 for livery charges.[29]

Carnegie, the good-natured paterfamilias, organized amusements, took family and friends for horseback or carriage rides, hunting, and fishing, and, after dinner at Mountain House, chose, rehearsed, directed, and starred in the evening's amateur theatrical, led his guests in songs and storytelling, or organized rounds of whist.

With the Pennsylvania Railroad tracks a short carriage ride away, no need went unmet. When supplies were required, Carnegie wrote or telegrammed his private secretary in New York. On August 7, 1873, he asked Gardie McCandless to "please send another case champagne—same as last—also claret—likewise three packs cards." He told Gardie that he was already looking forward to the following summer, when he planned to build his own cottage and invite Gardie with his wife and daughter to visit. If Gardie's wife "should happen just accidentally to have a delightful friend (say Miss Waller for instance) to accompany her, why we could manage her too, I mean we could manage to provide for her."[30]

Carnegie was, it appeared, as he approached age forty, beginning to advertise his availability as an eligible bachelor. Cresson was the perfect place to entertain female guests. But as comfortable as Carnegie was at Cresson, he never stayed there—or for that matter, anywhere—for long stretches of time. In July, he left on the train bound for Pittsburgh and then continued on to Marquette, Wisconsin, to oversee the first shipment of iron ore from Tilden's mine to the Lucy furnace. For any other businessman, a trip to the iron mines of Wisconsin would not have afforded much time for pleasure, but Carnegie was a master at making the best of any situation. "It is quite cold—light overcoat is indispensable," he wrote Gardie on July 9 from the North-Western Hotel in Marquette. "This is the place for avoiding summer heat sure. I am having a splendid time of it—fishing and boating. My complexion may be classed as 'rosey.' I am awfully sun burnt of course. We have quite a number of Pittsburghers at the Hotel."[31]

He returned to Cresson in late summer and remained there with his mother through early autumn. On September 17, he again took the train west to Pittsburgh, to spend a week "getting all matters right" before returning to New York City "for the season. . . . All well," he reported to Gardie, "but all sorry to leave the Mountains. It is warm this morning even here." He suggested that Gardie plan his own vacation: "I think you should take a week or two in Philadelphia for a change with Mrs. McC & the baby. You could do so nicely when I return."[32]

Gardie was not to get that "week or two" for quite some time.

THE DAY AFTER Carnegie posted his letter, his idyllic summer came to a halt with the receipt of a telegram announcing the bankruptcy of Jay Cooke & Co., one of the nation's most respected bankers. The failure came as a shock not only to Carnegie but to the rest of the nation's businessmen. If the house of Cooke could fall, was any firm safe?

The repercussions were immediate. Carnegie was kept abreast of the deteriorating situation by telegrams received at the nearby rail station. Like all financial panics, the signs had been there to see—but no one bothered to look until it was too late. Businesses had been failing and banks hiking their interest rates since the spring. Jay Cooke, who had in 1869 been overtaken by the transcontinental madness, found it difficult, then impossible, to borrow what he needed to complete construction of his Northern Pacific Railroad. When he ran out of his own and his investors' money, he reached into his banking clients' accounts and "borrowed" until there was nothing left. He attempted to sell Northern Pacific bonds at a deep discount, but there were no takers. With his railroad only partially built and his own, his investors', and his company's coffers empty, he had no choice but to declare bankruptcy on September 18, 1873.

The failure of Jay Cooke & Co. set off a round robin of bank and business failures. Stocks tumbled, out-of-town banks took back the reserves they had parked in New York City, causing New York banks to call in their old loans and raise the rates on new ones. The sell-off of securities was so panic-driven that the New York Stock Exchange closed its doors on September 20—and stayed closed for ten days. The railroads, which survived on credit, were instantly crippled. The effect on Pittsburgh's manufacturing firms, including Carnegie's, was immediate because the railroads with which they did so much business no longer had money to pay their bills. Banks were no use in the crisis. Those that remained open suspended payments. In October, customers who tried to withdraw their deposits from the Mellon Bank in Pittsburgh were sent away with Judge Mellon's promise that they would get their money eventually, but not now.[33]

The Panic of 1873 spun Carnegie's business life in a new direction. Until this point, he had been able to juggle many balls in the air and add new ones from time to time. Suddenly, he had to cease all new investments and concentrate his energies on keeping his existing businesses intact and protecting his investment in E.T. To raise money to meet his payrolls, he sold stock in a variety of businesses, including the Pullman Company. He also paid exorbitant rates for short-term loans.

"We are all right for ten days or two weeks," he wrote Gardie on

October 24 from Pittsburgh, where he had relocated to manage the crisis. "I think we can go through all right. I find nobody is paying anything [either past-due bills or interest on outstanding loans] but we have gone paying right along. We can ease up that way if we are forced to do it. We have now no loans outside of Pittsburgh and we can manage them."[34]

Through the fall, as the crisis deepened, Carnegie tried to keep his spirits up, until the strain became too much even for him. Marooned in Pittsburgh, where he was staying with his brother until the situation stabilized and he could return to New York, he took sick late in October and was "confined to the house." "I have never suffered so much in my life & am still very weak," he wrote Gardie on November 8.[35]

By mid-November, he convinced himself that he and his companies had weathered the immediate storm. "We are now all right for a while at least. I shall hope our Banks can squeeze through. You know they haven't suspended. . . . So far Pittsburg comes out splendidly." He sent his mother ahead to New York and wrote to ask Gardie to look in on her. He was, he confided, feeling better, but still had to be careful. "Glad to see you are selling Pullman [stock] so well—We need money but are not just bare. Business awful as a general thing & the order of the day." He then listed the Pittsburgh businesses which had recently failed.[36]

With the railroads, the Carnegie firms' major customers, still unable to pay their bills, he and his partners had no choice but to borrow money from the local banks. His partners had solid reputations in the Pittsburgh business community; Carnegie did not. "Up to this time," he admitted in his *Autobiography,* "I had the reputation in business of being a bold, fearless, and perhaps a somewhat reckless young man. . . . Although still young, I had been handling millions. My own career was thought by the elderly ones of Pittsburgh to have been rather more brilliant than substantial. . . . My supply of Scotch caution never has been small; but I was apparently something of a dare-devil now and then to the manufacturing fathers of Pittsburgh. They were old and I was young, which made all the difference."[37]

Carnegie was able to convince the bankers that, appearances notwithstanding, he was not a speculator and owed no money to anyone. On the strength of his and his partners' business statements, the endorsement of William Coleman, and the expectation that the "bills receivable" from the railroads would one day actually be received, the banks agreed to lend his companies what they needed to survive.

His strategy of investing everything he earned paid off in the end. By the fall of 1873, when the panic struck, he had accumulated a healthy portfolio of stocks and bonds which, even when liquidated at a loss, provided the capital required to keep the Union Iron Mills, the Lucy furnace, and Keystone Bridge companies afloat. Still, the shortage of investment capital that was both cause and consequence of the Panic of 1873 forced him to temporarily halt construction of his new steel mill, sell off almost all his holdings in other industries, and cease investing in new ventures. He had survived the worst of times without defaulting on his loans or having to declare any of his firms bankrupt. The panic surely could not last forever, and when it was over, he would pick up where he had left off. In a December 1873 letter he assured Junius Morgan that "we are steadily outgrowing the foolish panic here—It is most a fright—& the spring will see things prosperous again—but we must drive slower."[38]

CARNEGIE was among the fortunate few to weather the Panic of '73 without significant losses. Tom Scott, who as the years passed had become more adventurous than his former pupil, was not so fortunate. Like Jay Cooke, he had been stricken by the transcontinental madness and had poured his energies and resources—and those of his friends and associates—into building a new railroad along the southern borders of the nation, from New Orleans through Texas to California. Carnegie would later claim that he had urged Scott not to proceed with the project, but in his first reference to Scott's new railroad, in February 1872, he recommended only that Scott not name it the "Texas Pacific Railroad. Names are great things, and Texas is not comprehensive enough for a through route. Southern Pacific is far batter, and should be adopted exclusively." Scott met him halfway and changed the name to the "Texas and Pacific ."[39]

Scott offered Carnegie one of forty $250,000 shares in the construction company he had organized to build his new railroad and asked him to inquire whether Morgan and Sulzbach Brothers were interested in buying shares for themselves or putting together a syndicate to market the bonds in Europe. Carnegie, who had subscribed for one $250,000 share, and J. Edgar Thomson, who had subscribed for two, had both been led to believe that Scott would "call" on them for only 10 percent of the stock price. But Scott was desperate for capital.[40]

In July 1873, while Carnegie remained behind in the United States having been warned by Junius Morgan that the market for American securities was all but dead, Scott traveled to London and the Continent to try to sell his Texas & Pacific bonds. He failed. In August, desperate for funds, and having exhausted the resources of his associates, Scott asked Thomson to loan him marketable securities from the Pennsylvania Railroad treasury. On August 18, a month before the panic, the Pennsylvania Railroad board approved Scott's request and received, as security, $4 million in T&P construction bonds.[41]

The fall of Jay Cooke & Co. and the bank failures that followed made it impossible for Scott to secure the additional short-term loans he needed to keep his project alive. He remained in Europe through the autumn, trying but failing to raise cash by selling the Pennsylvania Railroad securities Thomson had loaned him. By late October, his Texas & Pacific railroad and construction companies were more than $7 million in debt. Having exhausted all other possibilities, Scott called on his investors, Thomson and Carnegie among them, to put up more cash. Thomson, who was personally liable for the half million in stock purchased in his own name and professionally responsible for the debts incurred by the Pennsylvania Railroad, pressured Carnegie to give Scott what he asked for. "I think that you should tax your friends, if you have not the means yourself, to meet your calls for the Texas Concern," he wrote Carnegie. "The scheme itself was good enough, but it has been most woefully mismanaged financially, Scott having acted upon his faith in his guiding star, instead of sound discretion. But Scott should be carried until his return, and you of all others should lend your helping hand where you run no risk—if you cannot go further."[42]

Carnegie came up with the money. But further than this he would not go. In November, another note for $300,000 fell due, and the Texas & Pacific, with no resources to meet the payments, began its final slide into bankruptcy.

On January 12, 1874, Carnegie received a telegram from Scott in Philadelphia: "Please come over tomorrow Monday on 12:30 train and meet me at my house at 4 p.m. If you cannot come over at that time, come over later in the day so I can see you at my house between 10 and 11 p.m. I shall be out early in the evening. Important—please answer."[43]

Scott asked Carnegie to endorse some of the outstanding notes. By endorsing the notes, Carnegie would have made himself liable to repay them if the T&P defaulted. He refused to do so. This, he tells us, "marked another step in the total business separation which had to come between Mr. Scott and myself. It gave more pain than all the financial trials to which I had been subjected up to that time. It was not long after this meeting that the disaster came and the country was startled by the failure of those whom it had regarded as its strongest men. I fear Mr. Scott's premature death can measurably be attributed to the humiliation which he had to bear."[44]

Carnegie exaggerates both the magnitude of Scott's tragedy and his responsibility for it. Scott remained in control of the Texas & Pacific until a month before his death, when he sold his holdings to Jay Gould for a reported $2.4 million ($425 million today). He died in the spring of 1881, at age fifty-seven, not a remarkably young age by nineteenth-century standards. On his death, he left an estate which the newspapers claimed was worth not "less than $17,000,000."[45]

Until his dying day, Scott remained in touch with Carnegie and collaborated with him on several business deals. In December 1874, less than twelve months after Carnegie had refused to bail him out, Scott arranged the loan (no doubt through the Pennsylvania Railroad, of which he was then president) that made it possible to complete construction at E.T. Carnegie repaid this favor on several occasions. In May 1876, to mention just one, he used his good offices to broker an agreement with Collis P. Huntington, who was at the time racing with Scott to complete a southern transcontinental railroad. When, after long delays, Scott was finally ready to lay tracks through Texas, Carnegie was among the first to bid for the steel contract.[46]

Though they continued to do business together, the breach between them was never entirely healed. And this greatly bothered Carnegie. He prided himself on his loyalty to friends—and his generosity—and could not forgive himself for not finding a way to help out Scott in his time of trouble. In January 1879, traveling in Singapore, Carnegie learned from "a line in a New York paper, picked up here . . . the terrible news" that Scott had "been stricken with paralysis and taken abroad. All our miserable differences vanish in a moment—I only reproach myself that they ever existed," he wrote in a long handwritten letter so heartfelt that Scott uncharacteristically kept it until his death. "This blow reveals there lay deeper in my heart a chord which still bound me to you in memory of a thousand kindnesses for which I am your debtor—I wish I were near you. . . . If you are not so ill as I fear, & return to work, we can remain apart—If you are still ill & in Europe, I wish to go to you as I pass but in either event rest assured for the future I have nothing but kind thoughts & kind words for you & of you."[47]

In his *Autobiography*, Carnegie tells his story of the break with Scott in rather mawkish detail not simply because he was sorry for what he had done, but to emphasize that by the early 1870s he was his own man, beholden to and linked with no one else, certainly not a speculator like Thomas Scott. He preferred to be remembered as the stolid capitalist and manufacturer who put his friend's life at risk rather than endorse his bad debts. This would be a recurrent theme in Carnegie's later accounts of his business career. He insisted in language that borrowed its moralistic tone from generations of success manual authors, from Benjamin Franklin to Samuel Smiley, that a man's reputation was the most valuable of all assets and should be kept inviolate, and that he himself had never strayed from the path of righteousness, had never speculated, cheated, lied, or deceived. To solidify his moral standing as a businessman, Carnegie elevated his decision not to endorse Scott's notes into a general business principle. In "The Road to Business Success: A Talk to Young Men," a lecture delivered to the Curry Commercial College in Pittsburgh in 1885, he identified three dangers that lay in the path of success for the young businessman: "I beseech you, avoid liquor, speculation, and indorsement." The first two could be found in most success manuals. But the final one was Carnegie's own. "The third and last danger against which I shall warn you is one which has wrecked many a fair craft which started well and gave promise of a prosperous voyage. It is the perilous habit of indorsing—all the more dangerous, inasmuch as it assails one generally in the garb of friendship." He repeated his warnings against the dangers of "indorsement" in a later article, "How to Win Fortune," and again in his *Autobiography*.[48]

CARNEGIE and his mother rode out the financial storms of 1873–74 in New York, a full day's journey from his Pittsburgh firms. Celebrating their good fortune perhaps, they changed their residence in 1874 from the luxurious but dated St. Nicholas to the even more luxurious Windsor Hotel on Forty-sixth Street and Fifth Avenue. Unlike the St. Nicholas, the Windsor was "removed from the bustling business centres" and had been designed as a "family residence," offering large suites with multiple bedrooms, each with its own bathroom and fireplace. The hotel's main dining room was on the second floor; there were smaller dining rooms "for the accommodation of late diners or private parties"; and two children's dining rooms, "one for those attended by white servants and the other for such as have colored servants waiting on them." The servants' quarters were carefully sequestered from the rest of the hotel, in the basement. For the convenience of businessmen, the main floor had a newsstand, a telegraph office, and an elaborately designed barbershop.[49]

"The world and his wife came to the Windsor, and I met them both," James Bridge, who became Carnegie's assistant in the 1880s, wrote of his time with Carnegie at the Windsor. The Carnegies had their regular table in the main dinning room, as did most of the permanent guests. Leland Stanford's table was close to the Carnegies'. George Pullman and wife, who stayed at the Windsor when in New York City, always came by to "exchange greetings with Carnegie and shake his mother's hand." George Westinghouse, a business acquaintance from Pittsburgh whom Carnegie had tried to help when he was struggling to patent and make money for his air brake, spent winters at the hotel with "his somewhat eccentric wife . . . her blonde hair 'bobbed' and prettily curled," and their boy, "dressed in velvet and lace like Lord Fauntleroy." Jay Gould, who lived at 578 Fifth Avenue at Forty-sixth Street, stopped by to read the newspapers and talk business in the lobby with his broker and railroad colleagues. The editor and writer Frank A. Munsey lived at the Windsor, as did Josh Billings, the humorist and lecturer, who was one of Carnegie's favorite authors.[50]

Carnegie was, it appears, spending more time now with women of a marriageable age: at the theater, at dinner, and riding in the park. As he approached forty, he may have been considering—but only considering—the possibility of marriage. Sprinkled through his correspondence are lighthearted references to women, including Miss Waller and a certain Miss Wright, whose name first appeared in a letter written to Gardie from London in May 1872. Although the city was "overflowing—such a jam . . . we might even squeeze a small one, say Miss Wright, into a place if only we had her here." A year later, he was still asking after Miss Wright. "I trust Miss Wright is now well—you don't say—and that I shall see her next week."[51]

He was acquiring something of a reputation as not only a *bon vivant* but a ladies' man, or at least a man who enjoyed being around young ladies. In February 1874, when Mrs. E. D. Loomis of Cincinnati, the mother of DeWitt, his bookkeeper, heard that he was planning an excursion by rail to Yosemite and San Francisco, she wrote to suggest he might take a friend of hers with him. "I have just returned from spending an evening with my charming friend Mrs. D. Murphy, and when I told her I heard you were going to get up a party this summer for a trip to the Yosemite Valley, she exclaimed 'O,' I wonder if he won't invite us to chaperone his young ladies, supposing of course you are to be the Napoleon of the party, and that party to be composed of young and pretty girls." There was "not the most remote probability," Mrs. Loomis assured Carnegie, of her accepting any invitation to accompany the party, but she wanted him to know that he "could not have a greater acquisition to it in the form of an agreeable and fascinating woman than Carrie Murphy."[52]

One of the singular advantages of the Windsor was its proximity to the park and its nine miles of carefully groomed carriage trails. Carnegie was seldom as happy as when he was on horseback, sitting high in the saddle, boots polished to a shine, cap pitched at a jaunty angle, looking down on every man and woman standing. Carnegie, the most sociable of people, seldom rode alone. Several "young ladies," he admitted in his *Autobiography*, were on his list of riding companions. Among them were his future wife, Louise Whitfield; Mary Clark of Hartford, a friend of the family; the Shakespearean actress Ellen Terry; and a few women whose names we cannot identify.[53]

Carnegie put a great deal of money into his horses and carriages. They not only provided him and other gentlemen of his era with an acceptable way to spend an afternoon with a proper woman; they were, in the last decades of the nineteenth century, an essential element in everyday life. It is difficult in the twenty-first century to comprehend the vital importance of horses to the metropolis—or the variety of vehicles they pulled behind them: delivery carts, wagons, and wagonettes; hearses; sleighs; lightweight buggies and buckboards; hansom cabs, broughams, phaetons, omnibuses, stagecoaches, and personal carriages. From Fourth to Sixth Avenues and along the side streets in the Forties and Fifties, within walking distance of the Windsor Hotel, were hundreds of storefront establishments catering to the horse-and-coaching set. Carnegie patronized dozens of them, including several saddle, harness, and bridle and carriage makers; horseshoeing establishments; tailors and importers of ladies' riding habits. His horses were stabled at 58 West Forty-third Street.[54]

He was always in the market for a good horse. In February 1882, a P. Tobin of the Philadelphia Riding Club Stable wrote to tell him that he had found a "five year old Kentucky horse, brown color, highly bred and very stylish," to match the one Carnegie had purchased in May 1881. Tobin, knowing that Carnegie, unlike his fellow millionaires, was less interested in racing or breeding his thoroughbreds than in riding with lady friends in the park, assured his customer that the Kentucky horse, though "very spirited," was easily handled. "I will give him to my most timid lady customer without any hesitation or advice as to how she will handle him. He has a slight quarter crack, but I will hold myself responsible that it will never amount to anything and would not be noticed. I will keep this horse for you until I hear from you and I hope you will try and come over and see him in action."[55]

Carnegie treated his horses as if they were family. He sent them to be cared for in New Jersey when he traveled and had them shipped—along with his carriages—to Cresson for the summer in private railway cars, courtesy of the Pennsylvania Railroad. The price for transportation from New York via ferry to Jersey City and then Cresson in June 1880: "four horses, 16,000 lbs @43 cents per hundred: $68.80 . . . and transportation free for one man. Two carriages on flat car, 20,000 lbs @23 cents pr. 100: $46."[56]

CARNEGIE had moved to New York City because it was becoming the "literary" as well as the "financial" capital of the New World. He had promised himself in late 1868 that he would, as soon as practicable— probably in two years—"settle in Oxford & get a thorough education making the acquaintance of literary men." Though he had chosen New York rather than Oxford, he was dedicated to fulfilling the rest of the bargain he had made with himself.[57]

As in the past, he chose as his tutor and cicerone an older woman, Madame Anna Botta, the sixty-year-old wife of a professor of Italian literature, who had for more than a quarter century presided over New York's most distinguished literary salon. From the 1840s and 1850s, celebrated writers, actors, and politicians who passed through New York stopped at Madame Botta's parlor to pay their respects and engage in the elevated conversation she presided over. At her salons, one might encounter the actresses Fanny Kemble, Lydia Sigourney, or Adelaide Ristori; Senators Henry Clay and Daniel Webster; writers Bayard Taylor and Margaret Fuller; editor and poet William Cullen Bryant, and Edgar Allan Poe. As Madame Botta outlived her guests, they were replaced by a new generation of writers and editors, including Henry Ward Beecher, Richard Watson Gilder, Julia Ward Howe, Charles Dudley Warner, Robert Ingersoll, and Andrew White, the president of Cornell. "The position of the Bottas in the literary and artistic world," Carnegie later wrote admiringly, "enabled them to draw together not only the best-known people of this country, but to a degree greater than any, as far as I know, the most distinguished visitors from abroad, beyond the ranks of mere title or fashion. No home, I think, in all the land compared with theirs in the number and character of its foreign visitors." Carnegie had sought admission to this salon in large part because it was short on "millionaires and fashionables" but replete with "the literary, musical, professional, and artistic celebrities—the leading ministers, physicians, painters, musicians, and actors, and especially the coming man or coming woman in these branches." He wanted to be judged—and accepted—as a man of culture, not just another millionaire recently moved to the great metropolis.[58]

Unlike the ill-spoken, ill-educated, and crudely dressed provincial businessmen who drove Edith Wharton's New York social elites to distraction, Carnegie had impeccable manners (learned earlier in Pittsburgh's drawing rooms), could quote lines from Burns and Shakespeare appropriate to any occasion, had traveled widely, and was a great storyteller. He made no apologies for being a businessman or a Scotsman, but integrated these attributes into his own complexly exotic persona. Approaching age forty, he had become slightly portly. His white beard and graying hair were finely trimmed; his three-piece suits well tailored; his lack of stature compensated by perfect posture. Intellectually curious, he had an appetite for new ideas. Though he could—and often did—dominate the conversation, when in the company of people whose intellects he admired he restrained himself, listening with rapt attention and good humor, before he contributed his opinions.

As MUCH AS he might have preferred to dedicate his full time and energy to securing a privileged position within New York's literary circles, Carnegie could not afford to ignore Pittsburgh entirely. He was not independently wealthy and had no large stocks of cash or rent-paying real estate to rely on. The largest part of his fortune, indeed almost all of it, was tied up in his Pittsburgh iron and bridge firms and the plot of land where construction had begun, but been halted, on the Edgar Thomson steel rail mill.

In 1874, Carnegie had planned on taking his mother and a large group of friends on a railroad excursion west when the weather got warm; but William Coleman, the senior partner at Edgar Thomson whom he had invited along, suggested they postpone their vacation and try instead to raise money in Europe to complete construction of their steel mill.[59]

Coleman recommended that Carnegie ask Alexander Holley, the plant's designer, to accompany him to Europe. When Holley learned that Carnegie was prepared to offer him $2,500 plus expenses, he accepted the invitation. "I shall be prepared to devote the necessary time—say from four to six weeks, (besides voyages)—to your service, in explaining E.T. advantages to capitalists, etc., and in visiting the various steel works and getting hold of all such drawings and information as may be of value to the Company."[60]

The trip to Europe turned out to be more vacation than work for both of them, and for John Scott, another partner whom Carnegie brought along at his expense. As Holley wrote his father from London in August, the "money-raising part" of the business trip abroad was "abandoned" when Carnegie discovered that his Pittsburgh associates could secure better terms at home than he could abroad. By the time Carnegie returned to the United States in the fall, construction had started up again.[61]

It was not the best of times for iron and steel manufacturers whose major customers were the railroads. In December 1874, just as E.T. began turning out its rails, Carnegie took the train to Philadelphia for an emergency meeting of the American Iron and Steel Association. With demand for finished iron and steel products drastically reduced, a committee of furnace owners had determined that the only way out of a spiraling price war was for them all to voluntarily limit their output. After a heated discussion, a resolution mandating that the furnace owners reduce production to one-half capacity was passed, with the proviso that it would not go into effect until two thirds of the furnace owners signed it.[62]

Two months later, the American Iron and Steel Association held its regular annual convention in Philadelphia, which Carnegie also attended. Again, the delegates were greeted with a somber report on the state of the industry. "The decline in the world's demand for iron which commenced in 1873," they were told, if they didn't already know it, "has continued during 1874, and, with the decline in demand there has ensued a resulting fall in prices. . . . It has been most severely felt in the United States."[63]

In Pittsburgh, the iron manufacturers responded to the fall in prices and profits by cutting the wage rates of the puddlers, who cooked the raw pig iron in their ovens, stirring, heating, and watching over it until it became wrought iron. The puddlers were paid by the ton according to a preestablished "sliding scale." When the price of iron went up, so did the rates the puddlers were paid on every ton; when the price went down, so did the rates, but never below a negotiated minimum. Though Carnegie would later intimate that the notion of the sliding scale had been his, the idea had first been broached by the Sons of Vulcan, the puddlers' union, in their 1865 negotiations with Pittsburgh's iron manufacturers. In 1867, the manufacturers had abandoned the scale, but the iron workers went on strike and stayed out until it was reinstituted.

Now, in November 1874, after seven years of peace and stability, the iron manufacturers gave thirty days' notice that they were going to terminate the existing scale and substitute, in its place, one with a lower minimum. When the Vulcans refused to accept the new scale, the iron manufacturers, including Carnegie's Union Iron Mills, locked out their puddlers. The lockout continued in force through the spring, ending only in April 1875, when the iron manufacturers, who were losing contracts to firms outside Pittsburgh, "officially capitulated" and invited the puddlers back to work at their old rates.[64]

The Sons of Vulcan won their battle but not without great difficulty. It had not been easy to convince other skilled workers to stay off the job to protect the puddlers' wage rates. As soon as the lockout was called off, they reached out to the unions that represented the other skilled metalworkers. In 1876, the Sons of Vulcan joined the other metalworkers' unions in the new and stronger Amalgamated Association of Iron and Steel Workers.

In the end, both labor and management suffered from the extended lockout: the workers lost months of wages; the manufacturers, contracts for new work. The Amalgamated, which was born of the crisis, committed itself, from this point on, to doing everything possible to avert future lockouts and strikes. The iron manufacturers, for their part, recognized that they had little choice now but find a way to work with the new union, which was too strong to ignore, but, fortunately, too conservatively led to pose any enormous problem, at least for the moment.

Carnegie remained in New York City during the winter and early spring of 1874–75, leaving his partners in Pittsburgh to manage the crisis, which they did, by following in lockstep with the other iron manufacturers. There is no indication that he had strong opinions as yet about the unions or their sliding wage scale.

NINE

Driving the Bandwagon, 1875–1878

GEORGE THURSTON, who published one of the many centennial histories of Pittsburgh that appeared in 1876, was near ecstatic in his
description of the new Edgar Thomson steel mill at Braddock. "These
works, standing . . . on the very area of a famous frontier battle, are a striking illustration of the conquests of trade, the progress of civilization, and
yet more so of the progress and growth of Pittsburgh. No grander monument to the growth of the nation, the progress of the city, or the triumph
of American manufactures and of American mechanics, could well be
built, than this complete and comprehensive steel works."[1]

Everything about the works was designed to perfection. The first
American steel manufacturers had had to squeeze their converters into
functioning iron mills. Alexander Holley was given a bare plot of land, 106
acres in size, equal to one hundred football fields or sixty-six New York
City–sized blocks. He laid out the transportation grids first and then
placed the sheds, structures, and yards accordingly. As he later explained in
Engineering, he designed the Edgar Thomson steelworks "not with a view
of making the buildings artistically parallel with the existing roads or with
each other, but of laying down convenient railroads with easy curves; the
buildings were made to fit the transportation." The tracks that led to the
two buildings in which coal was burned were elevated so that the coal
could be delivered in railroad cars straight from the mines and dumped,
without need for laborers to offload it, "directly upon the floors."[2]

E.T. was supplied with pig iron by rail from the Lucy furnaces (a second furnace had been constructed in 1877) in Lawrenceville, eleven
miles away. On arriving at the steel mill, the pig iron, now solidified, was

Making Bessemer Steel

re-melted in a 107- by 44-foot cupola house. The molten iron was then poured with two 12-ton tilting ladles into 6-ton, egg-shaped converting vessels, heated by coke and mounted on axles. Blasts of air were shot into the vessels—and through the iron—at high pressure. The air stoked the fire and burned away the carbon and other impurities, which exited the top of the vessel in an avalanche of white flames and sparks. At this signal, a small amount of Spiegel, an iron compound with a high percentage of manganese and carbon, was added to the mix, "carburizing" the purified iron and converting it into steel. The vessel was then tipped onto its side, pouring white-hot liquid steel into a casting ladle, which conveyed it to the molds.

The explosion of flame and sparks from the top of the converter, followed almost immediately by the flow of molten steel, was both exhilarating and intimidating to those who witnessed it. In *The Jungle,* Upton Sinclair's fictional character Jurgis Rudkus, after applying for a job at a Chicago steel mill, is taken on a tour of the "domelike building, the size of a big theater," that housed the Bessemer converter. There before him were

three giant caldrons, big enough for all the devils of hell to brew their broth in, full of something white and blinding, bubbling and splashing, roaring as if volcanoes were blowing through it—one had to shout to be heard in the place. Liquid fire would leap from these caldrons and scatter like bombs below—and men were working there, seeming careless, so that Jurgis caught his breath with fright. . . . And suddenly, without an instant's warning, one of the giant kettles began to tilt and topple, flinging out a jet of hissing, roaring flame. Jurgis shrank back appalled, for he thought it was an accident; there fell a pillar of white flame, dazzling as the sun, swishing like a huge tree falling in the forest. A torrent of sparks swept all the way across the building, overwhelming everything, hiding it from sight; and then Jurgis looked through the fingers of his hands, and saw pouring out of the caldron a cascade of living, leaping fire, white with a whiteness not of earth, scorching the eyeballs. Incandescent rainbows shone above it, blue, red, and golden lights played about it; but the stream itself was white, ineffable. Out of regions of wonder it streamed, the very river of life; and the soul leaped up at the sight of it, fled back upon it, swift and resistless, back into far-off lands, where beauty and terror dwell.[3]

The steel that flowed out of the furnace was hardened into molds or shaped into multiton ingots, then loaded on railway cars and transported along internal narrow-gauge track to the 380-foot-long rail mill, the largest and perhaps most imposing structure on the lot. Here the ingots were successively rolled into smaller and smaller shapes, until they left the finishing end of the mill as rails. Finally, they were loaded into their own containers and transported on another internal low-level wide-gauge railway to the B&O and the Pennsylvania Railroad tracks for shipment to their destinations.

"Our competitors in steel," Carnegie noted in his *Autobiography,* "were at first disposed to ignore us. Knowing the difficulties they had in starting their own steel works, they could not believe we would be ready to deliver rails for another year, and declined to recognize us as competitors. . . . We sent our agent through the country with instructions to take orders at the best prices he could obtain; and before our competitors knew it, we had obtained a large number—quite sufficient to justify us in making a start."[4]

In his telling of the tale, Carnegie presents the Edgar Thomson steelworks as the underdog, the new kid on the block who must prove himself. He describes the challenges he and his associates encountered during the Panic of 1873 and gives us thumbnail descriptions of key partners. He also pays special tribute to Captain Jones, and then, almost as a postscript, concludes that success was inevitable. "So perfect was the machinery, so admirable the plans, so skillful were the men selected by Captain Jones, and so great a manager was he himself, that our success was phenomenal."[5]

What he does not do, either in his *Autobiography* or any of his other writings, is take credit for the triumph at Braddock. He did not claim that he, as an individual, had been responsible for the success of the venture. Nor, for that matter, did he believe any of his fellow millionaires had accumulated their fortunes because of their particular virtues or talents. On the contrary, as he explained in an article published in 1906 in the *North American Review,* in "the commercial and industrial age in which we live . . . wealth has been produced as if by magic, and fallen largely to the captains of industry, greatly to their own surprise." Attempting to divine the root cause behind the "difference in wealth" that marked this age, Carnegie found it not in "labour, nor skill. No, nor superior ability, sagacity, nor enterprise, nor greater public service. The *community* created the millionaire's wealth. While he slept it grew as fast as when he was awake."[6]

To illustrate his point, Carnegie offered his readers the story of a millionaire who had made his fortune in Pittsburgh. Although he did not ex-
plicitly identify himself as that millionaire, there was no mistaking the
autobiographical character of the narrative. The first and most significant
step in the future steelmaker's rise to success was a fortuitous accident.
Through no foresight on his part, he had been "so fortunate as to settle in
Pittsburgh when it had just been discovered that some of the coalfields, of
which it is the centre, produced a coking-coal admirably adapted for iron-
ore smelting. . . . Everything indicated that here indeed was the future
iron city, where steel could be produced more cheaply than in any other location in the world. Naturally, his attention was turned in this direction.
He wooed the genius of the place. This was not anything extraordinarily
clever. It was in the air. He is entitled to credit for having abiding faith in
the future of his country and of steel, and for risking with his young companions not only all he had, which was little or nothing, but all they could
induce timid bankers to lend from time to time." The key to their success
was the rapidly growing domestic population which demanded their products. "Without new populous communities far and near, no millionairedom
was possible for them. The increasing population was always the important factor in their success."[7]

What Carnegie was trying to say was that his success was due, in large
part, to his luck in being in the right place, Pittsburgh, at the right time,
the last decades of the nineteenth century, when the nation and its railway
networks were expanding westward. Most of his biographers have assumed that Carnegie succeeded as a steelmaker primarily because he ruthlessly undersold his competition, stole their orders, forced them out of
business, and established a monopoly. This explanation presupposes that
the steel manufacturers competed with one another on price, which was
seldom the case. On the contrary, they allocated market shares among
themselves, based on productive capacity. Because Carnegie was always
among the largest producers, he got the largest share of the market. The
key to his success was the scale of his operation and his insistence on producing more each year than he had the year before.

The railroads, their major customers, did not encourage price competition among the steelmakers, but did what they could to make sure each of
them succeeded. "Railroads and steel mills were not," as Thomas J. Misa
has argued in *A Nation of Steel*, "atomistic actors meeting in a classical free

market." With considerable capital invested in the steel companies, the railroads had an incentive to make sure the mills made a decent profit selling their rails. Any reduction in steel company profits would diminish the value of their investments. There was another reason why the railroads were committed to securing the financial health of the steel companies: the steel producers were well on their way to becoming the railroads' largest freight customers. The higher their profits, the more steel they would produce; the more steel they produced, the greater the shipping charges they would pay the railroads to transport finished rails and coal, coke, iron ore, and limestone.[8]

Rail prices were usually determined not in free market competition, but by gentlemanly negotiations among the steel companies and between them and the railroads. The nation's ten steel manufacturers were a cozy little group. With few exceptions, their plants were designed and constructed by Alexander Holley, with whom they still consulted. They shared the same basic patents and had organized themselves as the Bessemer Association, which divided royalties on those patents and licensed (or, more often, refused to license) new plants to use the patents. As the holder of the critical patents needed to produce Bessemer steel, the association was able to block the construction of new steel mills, thereby guaranteeing its members a healthy profit.[9]

On June 1, 1875, three weeks before the plant was scheduled to go on line, Carnegie asked Shinn to get in touch with Tom Scott and request permission to bid on the following year's Pennsylvania Railroad order. "Unless Mr. Scott can aid us here I fear before we get a chance Pennsylvania Steel and Cambria will be quietly arranged with for the 500 tons steel required. I think you should address a communication asking permission to offer for them and Mr. Scott should see to it. . . . [P.S.] The harder we fight for this the sooner our friends will agree to our sharing of offers especially if Mr. Scott is going to offer the proposed resolution."[10]

The quietly assured tone of the letter is indicative of Carnegie's confidence that, with Tom Scott behind him, his competitors would have no choice but to cooperate with him. No one wanted a bidding war. Carnegie was a known quantity in Pittsburgh and a familiar of presidents Daniel Morrell of Cambria (whom he had tried to hire at E.T.) and Samuel Felton, the former railroad president who now ran Pennsylvania Steel.

Cambria and Pennsylvania Steel, founding members of the Bessemer Association, were owned in part by the Pennsylvania Railroad, delivered most of their rails to it, and cooperated with one another—and the railroad—on production quotas and price schedules. One June 10, 1875, Daniel Morrell invited William Shinn to the meeting in Philadelphia at which the firms divided up the market. It made perfect sense for Cambria Iron and Pennsylvania Steel to include the Edgar Thomson works in their informal cartel, as they could not, by themselves, meet the Pennsylvania Railroad's demand for new steel rails. In the end, E.T. ended up with a share of the rail order equal to that of the other Pennsylvania steel mills.[11]

With this order guaranteed, E.T. had no problem turning a profit from the very first day. After eight months of production, Carnegie, in a letter to Shinn, was already extolling the profitability of the new mill: "It is a grand concern, and sure to make us all a fortune. With you at the helm, and my pulling an oar outside, we are bound to put it at the head of rail making concerns. . . . Where is there such a business." Carnegie estimated profits of, on average, $40,000 for each $100,000 in stock, or a 40 percent return on investment. "Some years we shall do far better, but as an average it is not too sanguine."[12]

Carnegie then set out to establish a working relationship with its chief rival, the Baltimore & Ohio. John Garrett, the B&O president, had delayed switching to steel because, his railroads having suffered severe service disruptions and financial setbacks during and immediately after the Civil War, he could not afford them.[13]

Carnegie, knowing that the tariff had raised the price of steel imports so drastically that Garrett would have to switch to domestically produced steel, had cleverly sited his new plant on the B&O tracks. In November 1875, he called on Mr. Garrett personally on a Saturday morning to discuss the possibility of selling steel rails to the B&O. He followed up with a note to William Keyser, the B&O's second vice president in charge of purchasing. The B&O would, he estimated, require up to 7,000 tons of new steel rails in the year to come. Carnegie asked for "a small order now to prevent the stoppage of our works during the winter months." It was, he argued, in the railroad's interest to keep E.T. open and prosperous as the steel company was shipping its coke and other raw materials to Pittsburgh on B&O trains. Should E.T. be forced to stop production for lack of orders, the B&O would forfeit considerable freight charges it might otherwise collect.[14]

Knowing that the B&O was short of cash, Carnegie offered to take "car wheels and old axles" (which he would then melt down and reuse elsewhere) in exchange for steel rails. If the B&O preferred to pay cash, he would sell the rails outright for $66 a ton. Garrett chose neither option, but instead declared that he was going to convert the rail mill he had erected at Cumberland, Maryland, from iron to steel and produce his own rails. Carnegie volunteered to give him an estimate of how much the conversion would cost. His figures must have been persuasive because Garrett dropped the idea and, after failing to incite a bidding war between Pennsylvania Steel and E.T., divided his order between them.[15]

"Shinn bossed the show; McCandless lent it dignity and standing; Phipps took in the pennies at the gate and kept the pay-roll down; Tom Carnegie kept everybody in a good humor . . . Andy looked after the advertising and drove the band wagon!" So reported an Edgar Thomson insider to James Bridge, Carnegie's former secretary who, after a falling out, wrote a rather unflattering, but not entirely inaccurate *Inside History of the Carnegie Steel Company*.[16]

Carnegie appointed himself chief salesman for Edgar Thomson. In mid-December 1874, months before the works went on line, he wrote Shinn to tell him that he had "been thinking that this office [at 57 Broadway] might try to represent the concern & do its best to obtain orders. No commission received. The Company might pay part of cost, rent, stationery, clerks etc. We should want more room than we now have—but there will be time enough to talk over this. Meanwhile we should not lose a day in informing the railroads [that E.T. was prepared to take orders]."[17]

He was a master booster and salesman for steel rails, as he had earlier been for iron bridges. Even James Bridge, his harshest critic, was moved to admiration by his skill. "The part at first selected by Andrew Carnegie for himself was the development of outside trade and the procurement of orders. Here he displayed an originality so marked that it amounted to genius. Endowed with a ready wit, an excellent memory for stories, and a natural gift for reciting them, he became a social favorite in New York and Washington, and never missed a chance to make a useful acquaintance. His mental alertness, ready speech, and enthusiastic temperament made him a delightful addition to a dinner party; and many an unconscious hostess, opening her doors to the little Scotchman from Pittsburgh, has also paved the way to a sale of railroad material."[18]

It was difficult not to like the little man built like a pony, with broad shoulders and a white mane. "Carnegie's sunny personality radiated warmth and light," Bridge recalled. "He loved to find his own joy of living reflected by those about him. He was the most consistently happy man I ever knew."[19]

Carnegie's charm was not a come-on or a performance intended to solicit or win business contacts. Good conversation was, for him, not a means to an end but an end in itself. He was as proud of his gift of gab as he was of his business acumen. With an easy, open smile, he was easy to befriend. If some among those befriended might later prove helpful in his business, he would have been a fool not to follow through. Andrew Carnegie and his steel business were one entity. It only made sense that personal friends would become company friends—and vice versa.

He approached his colleagues from the railroad industry, like Sidney Dillon at the Union Pacific and Collis Huntington at the Central Pacific, "as brother capitalists." Without preamble or excuse, he asked that they "give me a preference" should they be in the market for steel. Those he had helped out in years past were reminded that he had done them a favor and asked for a favor in return. "It was," he added, "good business for them to do it," as his steel was the best—and cheapest—product on the market.[20]

Years later, testifying before a House of Representatives investigating committee, Carnegie took issue with those who believed that huge corporations would always outperform partnerships. Carnegie Steel, though incorporated by the state of Pennsylvania, was administered not as a corporation but as an old-fashioned partnership, with "the partners managing their own business." The firm was an extension of their persons. If it failed, they failed. If it succeeded, they succeeded. Partners were there for the duration and could be trusted to follow through on their promises. The railroad presidents he dealt with knew that he stood behind his products and, trusting him, trusted his steel.[21]

THE MID-1870S were not an auspicious time to throw more steel rails onto the domestic market. By the fall of 1875, when the first rails were rolled at Edgar Thomson, the depression that followed the panic was at its height—and the iron and steel business at its nadir. The railroads had virtually stopped buying new rails; those that absolutely needed them had no cash, but were instead offering securities and/or notes. Carnegie, anticipating that he might have to accept railroad securities instead of currency for his rails, wrote to Junius Morgan in August 1875, the week before the works opened: "Our ET steel works start this week—shall make 40,000 tons steel rails per annum." He inquired whether Morgan would buy the "good railroad paper" he expected to acquire as payment for his rails.[22]

Having secured his first orders from the Pennsylvania Railroad, Carnegie used that bit of information to win contracts with its affiliates. He wrote Franklin B. Gowen, president of the Philadelphia & Reading, on Christmas Eve 1875, to remind him of his earlier "promise to try a lot of our steel rails. . . . We have just been awarded 5,000 tons by the Pennsylvania Railroad—should like very much indeed to have you test our rails in comparison with others upon your line—Prices at all times equal to the most favorable." Similar letters were sent to dozens of other railway presidents. As Carnegie asked only for a trial for his new rails—and promised to undersell his competitors—it was difficult to turn him down. Few did.[23]

CARNEGIE quickly catapulted himself into the lead position among the Edgar Thomson partners. His critics, James Bridge chief among them, charged that he gained majority control of the company by ruthlessly shoving aside his partners and extorting their shares. That was not the case. Each of the partners had pledged to pay for his interest in the company on the installment plan. When, following the Panic of 1873, they had trouble doing so, Carnegie bought them out. "That is what gave me my leading interest in this steel business. . . . I had to buy so many of them out during the panic that I became the controlling" partner.[24]

Among the partners who sold their shares to Carnegie was William Coleman, who had been the principal force behind the company's founding. Coleman had asked Carnegie for a loan so that he could hold on to his E.T. shares, but Carnegie, short of cash, offered instead to buy Coleman's ten shares in the steel company, pay him 6 percent annual interest on his $100,000 investment over the next five years, and return the principal in

years six, seven, and eight. Coleman tried to get a "better bargain," but after six months of negotiations—and consultations with Tom Carnegie—
he accepted Carnegie's terms.[25]

In 1879, Carnegie, traveling in Shanghai, received word that William
Coleman had died. In a lengthy paragraph, one of the few to be excised
from his travel journal when it was published by Scribner's four years later,
Carnegie converted Coleman's death into a personal tragedy: for him. "I
could not realize for a time that I was to miss upon my return one of my
oldest, best, and dearest friends—one who had been a friend in boyhood to
me, when the aid of such a man counted for so much. Why did I not appreciate him sufficiently while he lived? But we never do. The finest characteristics of our friends seem only to shine with the brightest luster when
we are denied their presence on earth."[26]

THOUGH EDGAR THOMSON had gone on line in a depressed business
climate, Carnegie did not let this slow him down. On the contrary, he appeared almost to glory in the adverse conditions. Other entrepreneurs
might have reduced output until the market was stronger, but Carnegie
pushed Shinn to keep the new plant operating seven days a week, twenty-
four hours a day.

Steel rail prices fluctuated wildly through the 1870s and early 1880s. In
1873, the railroads could afford and were paying up to $120 a ton. By the fall
of 1875, when E.T. rolled its first rails, the price at which the railroads were
willing to buy them had fallen to $66. By December 1876, it was down to
$52; a year later, to $42.[27]

Where his competitors, in bad times, reduced production, cut shifts,
and laid off workers rather than accept orders at low prices, Carnegie insisted that E.T. take whatever orders it could get, no matter what the price,
in order to keep the plant running and the workforce intact. The key to
success was pumping up volume and not worrying about the profit margin
per unit. "You know my views," he wrote Shinn that December, only
months after the first rails had been rolled, "fill the works at a small margin of profit—get our rails upon the leading lines next year. The year after,
take my word for it, you will make profit enough." "Don't be greedy," he
warned Shinn the following month, "'small profits & large sales' in golden
letters above your desk is respectfully recommended."[28]

Carnegie's tactics made little sense to his competitors and several of his partners. "The Cambria people," Shinn wrote back in December 1875, "are becoming very bitter against us for making, as they claim, unnecessary concessions in prices, so early in the season, each reduction fixing the market at a price which will be still further reduced at the next sale. Our Board are very apprehensive of bad effects from this policy, and while I know your view of our policy is, to fill up at any price not involving loss, I feel it my duty to advise you that the managers are of the opinion that it would be better to make less tonnage at a fair profit."[29]

Carnegie's response was that he was willing to cooperate with his competitors, but not if it meant restricting production in his mills. If Cambria and Pennsylvania Steel agreed to fix prices for rails in the West, as they were already doing in the East, Carnegie would be prepared to enter into an agreement with them. But until that happened, it was every company for itself.[30]

By early 1877, Carnegie had gotten his way. Daniel Morrell at Cambria recognized the folly of trying to compete with the Carnegie juggernaut and agreed to enter into a variety of pooling and price agreements with his new rival. The two companies divided orders, purchased and transported iron ores from the Great Lakes together, and in May agreed to "appoint joint Agents" to solicit new orders for rails in the West.[31]

THOUGH HE HAD inserted himself into most major areas of decision making, Carnegie rarely visited Pittsburgh. He seldom attended board or executive committee meetings and took no administrative title or position in his new steel company. He and his partners knew from the very beginning that there would be limited face-to-face communications between them. New York City was just too far away from Braddock.

It takes ninety minutes today to fly from New York to Pittsburgh and another thirty minutes to drive from the airport to Braddock. In the mid-1870s, the trip took fifteen hours. Travelers to Pittsburgh began their journey at the Cortlandt Street pier on the North River, as it was then known, where they boarded the ferry for Jersey City. The "Fast Line" train departed at 9:30 A.M. and arrived in Philadelphia at 12:20 P.M., where passengers boarded the express to Pittsburgh. The first stop after Philadelphia was Harrisburg, where the train stopped at about four for a quick dinner break. There was a second stop at Altoona around eight o'clock. If the weather was good, the track clear, and there were no delays, the train reached Pittsburgh sometime after midnight. The trip to Braddock took another half hour.[32]

Carnegie relied heavily on the telegraph to communicate with Pittsburgh. Telegrams offered instant communication, but they were unreliable for many business purposes. The cost was prohibitive, the telegrams were delivered in ungainly and almost unreadable formats, and there was no guarantee of privacy. To protect themselves from eavesdropping operators, businesses developed elaborate cipher books. Large corporations had their own printed and distributed to key personnel. Smaller ones bought blank cipher books and filled in the words and phrases they were most likely to use in their messages.

The black leatherbound book marked "1878" found in Carnegie's papers at the Library of Congress is an example of the self-made code book. Each page has two columns: on the left, an alphabetized series of words, some real, some invented; on the right, the Edgar Thomson code. In coding or decoding telegrams, Carnegie, or more likely Gardie, scrolled down the left-hand column. "Abaft" meant "Have received letter of 1st"; "Avenge" was "We are awaiting reply to telegram of"; "Laugh"—"Delivered at Boston Massachusetts by rail"; "slow"—"Bank of Pittsburgh"; "spray"— "Cambria Iron Company." By 1896, the company was publishing its own "Private Code for Use of the Carnegie Steel Company, Limited, and its Partners and Agents" with both columns preprinted. The 1896 cipher book was 192 pages long, with sixty to seventy entries on each page.[33]

The primary vehicles of communication between Carnegie and his partners and managers were the detailed cost sheets delivered monthly by U.S. mail to his office at 57 Broadway, then marked up and sent back to Pittsburgh, often with lengthy memos attached. Every month he was sent, on his request, a statement of the costs per ton for raw materials, labor, maintenance, repairs. A quick learner, with a head for figures and a prodigious memory, he kept track of everything: the price of limestone, the amount of coke used to smelt a ton of pig iron, the length of time a cast-iron mold should last before wearing out, the number of tons of steel ingots produced per heat in the furnaces. He was preoccupied with getting the lowest possible costs—on limestone, coal, coke, ores, freight rates, and labor. "Carnegie never wanted to know the profits," Charles Schwab remarked much later to publisher Clarence Barron. "He always wanted to know the cost."[34]

When Carnegie discovered an item that cost more than he thought it should have, he asked for an explanation. If the explanation were not forthcoming or insufficiently enlightening, he followed up with a rebuke and a warning to pay more attention in the future. One of the advantages of being at a distance from Pittsburgh and dealing with numbers on a cost sheet was that Carnegie was spared face-to-face confrontations with flesh-and-blood supervisors who might not be pulling their weight and laborers whose wage rates were going to be reduced. Since leaving the railroad, he had purposefully constructed a life that kept him away from men with shovels. He had no taste for the daily grind of superintending a workforce, no desire to run roughshod over people.

Surprisingly, given later developments, Carnegie paid little attention to his workers, their attempts at unionization, or their pay scales through most of the 1870s. He had, as far as we can tell, no input into his partners' decision in late 1874 to join the other iron mill owners in locking out their puddlers. His letters to Pittsburgh were more likely to touch on the price of limestone, the quality of iron ore, the availability of coke, the costs of freight shipments. Labor was, for him, simply another item in his cost sheet, one that was being efficiently controlled by his on-site managers.

At E.T., he relied on Captain Jones to get the most out of his large and growing workforce. Both men supported the industrywide "sliding scales" that had determined wage rates in the metal trades since 1865. Skilled labor, Carnegie believed, was entitled to share capital's prosperity in good times, but only if it agreed to share its sacrifices in slack times. Friction between capital and labor would be eliminated forever, he would later explain in a 1886 *Forum* article, if both sides could agree to "a plan by which the men will receive high wages when their employers are receiving high prices for the product, and hence are making large profits; and, *per contra*, when the employers are receiving low prices for product, and therefore small if any profits, the men will receive low wages."[35]

In theory, the "sliding" wage scale appeared fair; in practice, it had worked rather well in the metal trades. But there was a fatal flaw in the scheme. While capital and labor could with comparative ease agree on how to share the wealth in good times, there was no consensus on how to share sacrifices in bad times. When markets soured, prices fell, and profit margins dipped, capitalists might rein in personal and corporate spending, but their sacrifices seldom endangered their own or their families' well-being. Wage workers, on the contrary, no matter how skilled they might be, existed at the margins of prosperity. To ask them to accept cuts in wages that would reduce their take-home pay to less than they needed to feed, clothe, and keep their families warm in winter was far different from asking capitalists to accept smaller profit margins. The workers, of course, recognized this and built into the sliding scale a minimum wage rate.

Captain Jones expected Carnegie to pay the Edgar Thomson skilled steelworkers well so that he, Jones, could work them hard. Just as Carnegie did not stint on buying the highest-grade ore, so should he not hesitate to employ the highest-grade workforce. Years later, testifying before a congressional committee, Carnegie parroted almost verbatim Jones's message to him: "You have got to pay men in this country the wages you can get the best men for. Labor is a commodity like anything else. . . . It pays to get the best men and pay the highest wages for labor. . . . Fewer men do your work, and you are getting honest, respectable, sober men."[36]

Jones's and Carnegie's commitment to decent wages was commendable. Still, there is no gainsaying the inevitable callousness that resulted from their looking at labor in the abstract as just another commodity, one of many "inputs" in their production system. "Had an unfortunate accident this morning," Jones informed Carnegie in March 1877. "Rope on cupola hoist broke and cage fell catching the Hoist Boy in the act of crossing under, crushing him to a jelly. It was caused by the boy's carelessness, and disobedience of order and the poor fellow paid the penalty with his life. Delayed Works slightly. Damage slight."[37]

Let it suffice that the "poor fellow" is not given a name and is held accountable for his own death. In the end, what appears to matter most for Jones and Carnegie is that the accident only "slightly" slowed down production and that the "damage" was minimal.

Even in extolling the work habits of their workers, the captain and Carnegie seldom referred to them as individuals. When, in March 1878, Carnegie pushed Jones to speed up production to meet new orders, the captain, demurring, reminded him of a recent horse race in Louisville: "You noted that they did not rush the horses on the first mile, but aimed at a gait that would give a good four mile average . . . now in conclusion you let me handle this nag in this race, I think I will keep her on the track, and may keep her nose in front. I think at the end of this year I will have her ahead, and when we stop to rub down, you will find her in excellent condition."[38]

Though Carnegie would, in later years, profess himself a supporter of organized labor, neither he nor his unacknowledged mentor, Jones, believed in collective bargaining. They did not intend to give their steelworkers the same control over the pace and rhythm of work that the puddlers exercised in the iron mills. Nor did they believe they had to.

The technologies of iron- and steelmaking were radically different. Unlike steel, which was cooked in huge converters, iron had to be "puddled" manually by highly skilled artisans, who stirred the molten mass with an iron rod inserted through a hole in the furnace door. The puddlers worked in two-man teams, spelling one another just before exhaustion set in. They were their own supervisors. Only they knew how long each "heat" was going to take, when it was time to pour off the molten metal, and when it was time to take a break. By custom—codified by union rules—the puddlers ran five heats a day, which generally took about ten hours to complete. On Saturday, they devoted a half day to repairing equipment and cleaning out the furnaces; on Sunday, they rested.

As long as the puddlers remained at the center of the production process, there was no way to expand output other than by building more furnaces and hiring more puddlers. One of the great advantages of the Bessemer process—at least from the point of view of the employers—was that it eliminated the puddlers and their control over the workplace. In the Bessemer converters, the "stirring" of the molten metal was not done by puddlers wielding iron rods, but by air blasts, which could be regulated by "managers." This meant that the pace of work could be sped up as fast as the technology would allow. While the puddlers managed only five heats a day or twenty-five a week, Carnegie's Bessemer furnaces, operating twenty-four hours a day, seven days a week, could run more than one hundred heats.

Because they employed no puddlers and their mill was located in Braddock, just beyond the Pittsburgh city limits, Carnegie and his partners were able to detour around the Amalgamated Association of Iron and Steel Workers which represented the skilled metalworkers in Pittsburgh. Edgar Thomson rolled its first mills as a non-union shop. Its owners were determined that it remain as such. In November 1876, barely a year after the works had begun operations, Carnegie and Jones shut down operations for routine maintenance and repairs. There was nothing out of the ordinary in such a shutdown, especially of a steel plant which, unlike the iron mills, operated twenty-four hours a day, seven days a week. Workers were accustomed to being sent on hiatus—without pay—while machinery was overhauled. In December, five weeks after the shutdown, Captain Jones announced that the works were going to reopen, but only to those workers who agreed to sign an "ironclad" agreement to "join *no* Union and quit all you belong to," modeled on the one Daniel Morrell had instituted at Cambria. Jones simultaneously announced that the Edgar Thomson mills would henceforth pay the same wage rate that the non-union workers at Cambria were receiving. When some of Carnegie's men refused to sign the agreements, they were barred for life from returning to the site.[39]

HAVING EXPELLED the Amalgamated from the E.T. works, Carnegie and Jones were better prepared than most employers, certainly better prepared than the railroads, to weather the storms that swept through Pittsburgh—and the nation—in July 1877, when the trainmen went on strike. Like the iron industry, the railroads had been hit hard by the Panic of 1873 and had reacted by cutting wages. Three and a half years later, their profit rates still endangered, as much from financial malfeasance as the lingering effects of the panic, the railroads instituted a second round of wholesale wage reductions. On May 24, 1877, Tom Scott announced that all Pennsylvania Railroad employees who earned more than a dollar a day would be cut 10 percent on June 1.

As the engineers were the most highly paid, the least readily replaced, and the best organized of the trainmen, their actions were carefully monitored in the days that followed Scott's announcement. If they went out on strike, the rest of the railroad's employees would certainly follow.

Though Carnegie had not worked for the railroad for more than a decade, he felt obligated to intervene. A prolonged railroad strike would have a devastating effect on the local economy and on the companies, like his own, which relied on the railroad for orders. On May 29, the day before he was to sail for Liverpool for his summer vacation and two days before the Pennsylvania Railroad's wage cut was to take effect, Carnegie wrote a personal letter to more than a dozen engineers, offering unsolicited advice:

"I am not interested any more in the Pennsylvania Railroad, either pecuniarily or officially; but I do profess to have a lasting interest in its welfare and in the welfare of the men, like yourself, with whom I was associated for many of the best years of my life and I wish to express to you my opinion, as a friend, that, taking into consideration all the circumstances, the Engineers should acquiesce in the reduction as proposed. These are trying times and the country must now bear the penalty of past inflation, and no class can escape contributing its share." The railroad, Carnegie insisted, had "dealt fairly with their employees" and had "not been unwilling to share their prosperity with them." It was now the employees' obligation to reciprocate and accept the wage cut. If they decided to "refuse to serve for reduced compensation," Carnegie warned, they would not "carry public opinion" with them.[40]

While Carnegie was in the mid-Atlantic on his way to Liverpool, a grievance committee of engineers and firemen representing the local brotherhoods met with Tom Scott in Philadelphia to discuss the rate reduction. Following the meeting, the committee agreed to accept the cut. It appeared that the railroads would have their way.

Early in July, Captain Jones closed down the steelworks for repairs and to "put in some additional machinery." The new machinery worked "admirably," he wanted Carnegie to know, and "gives us complete control of rail from rolls to hot bed, and also allows us to dispense with services of two men and two boys, saving us at least $100 per month on wages, and as the machine did not cost of $100 you will see that it is a very good investment. We are running Works under tight rein."[41]

Five days after Jones's letter, less than 200 miles away in Martinsburg, West Virginia, firemen and brakemen working for the Baltimore & Ohio Railroad, upon being informed that their wages were being reduced by 10 percent, walked off their jobs. The West Virginia militia, deployed to keep rail traffic moving, joined the strikers instead. The strike quickly spread to other railroads and other cities, including Pittsburgh, where by July 20 it encompassed even the reluctant engineers who six weeks earlier had accepted the wage reduction.

When the Pittsburgh militia refused to disperse the strikers who had gathered at the railroad yards, six hundred militiamen from Philadelphia were dispatched to protect railroad property and end the strike. They arrived on Saturday, July 22, and that same day fired into a crowd of

unarmed, unemployed, and angry trainmen and civilians at the Outer Depot on Twenty-eighth Street. The crowd, incensed and terrified by the
gunfire—and the sight of twenty fallen comrades—surged forward to repulse the soldiers. They moved on to attack Pennsylvania Railroad property, destroying more than a hundred locomotives, two thousand railway
cars, and almost every building in the yard.

And then there was quiet, an eerie silence suffused by the acrid smell of
smoke. Having wreaked their vengeance on the Pennsylvania Railroad, the
crowds retreated. There were reports that mill workers in the city and the
adjoining suburbs were preparing to join the railroaders in what some
hoped—and others feared—might be the beginning of a general strike.
Many workers, including those from the tubeworks at McKeesport and
Carnegie's steel mill at Braddock, expressed their solidarity with the railroad men by leaving their jobs on July 24 and parading in their support.
They did not, however, go out on strike.

The events of July 1877 pushed local labor leaders to step up their organizing at the workplace and to enter the political arena through the
newly established Greenback Labor Party. But they did not appear to have
any long-term effects at Edgar Thomson or the other Pittsburgh iron and
steel mills. Though Carnegie and the manufacturers had been frightened
by the specter of a general strike, they concluded, in the end, that the cause
of the uprising had been the railroads' intransigence and the local authorities' incompetence. Carnegie and his partners would continue to work
with the Amalgamated in the iron mills where it was well established, but
do everything they could to prevent it from establishing a beachhead at
Edgar Thomson.[42]

Confident that he had nothing to fear from organized labor, Carnegie, in
May 1878 from his safe haven in New York City, suggested to Captain Jones
that as steel prices hovered around $40, an all-time low, it might be neces-
sary to reduce wages across the board. Jones "earnestly" implored him to

leave good enough alone. Don't think of any further reductions. Our men
are working hard and faithfully, believing that hard pan has been reached.
Let them once get the notion in their heads that wages are to be further
reduced and we will lose heavily. I am or have promised rewards, if we accomplish certain output. It looks as if what I am aiming at will be accomplished. So of all things, don't think of reducing wages. Now mark what I

tell you. Our labor is the cheapest in the country. Our men have "Esprit de corps," and our cost of maintenance is way under that of any other works. Low wages does not always imply cheap labor. Good wages and good workmen I know to be the cheapest labor. Our men are taking good care of our property and are pulling with us so heartily that I even can't dream of again attacking them.[43]

Carnegie—recognizing that Captain Jones knew better than he how hard his workingmen could be pushed—acquiesced. Wage rates would not be cut in 1878.

TEN

Round the World, 1878–1881

When A.B. Farquhar, a Pennsylvania businessman, mentioned to Carnegie that he was always sure to be in his office by "seven in the morning," Carnegie remarked laughingly:

"'You must be a lazy man if it takes you ten hours to do a day's work.'

"'What I do,' he said, 'is to get good men, and I never give them orders. My directions seldom go beyond suggestions. Here in the morning I get reports from them. Within an hour I have disposed of everything, sent out all of my suggestions, the day's work is done, and I am ready to go out and enjoy myself.'"[1]

What was most remarkable about Carnegie's newfound success as a capitalist was how little it required of him. At each stage of his business career from bobbin boy to steelmaker, he had worked less and earned more. Since moving to New York City, in his middle thirties, and settling into a state of semiretirement, his income had increased exponentially. Carnegie had no delusions at all about the virtues of hard work. He avoided the topic of "diligence" in his lectures, speeches, and articles on "how to succeed in business." On the contrary, he took great pride in his own rather idiosyncratic work habits. He had become, as Farquhar noted in his memoir, an "absentee landlord." With an eerie similarity to the English landed gentry he so despised, Carnegie had established a residence in the city, a day's journey from the land that provided his succor, and left his estates in the hands of superintendents.

With his partners watching over the business in Pittsburgh, Carnegie could devote more of his time and energy to self-education, literary and cultural pursuits, and his nascent career as a philanthropist. Contrary to a common, but quite mistaken notion, Carnegie began giving away his money long before he retired. Although he did not, like his contemporary John D. Rockefeller, regard philanthropy as a "religious duty" and had not, as Rockefeller had, donated 6 percent of his first paycheck to charity, he was by age forty giving away significant sums of money.[2]

Carnegie's first formal benefactions were to Dunfermline, to which he donated £5,000 in 1874 for a combination recreation and health club, to be known as the Carnegie baths. The centerpiece of the facility was the 70- by 30-foot swimming "pond," with a smaller pond in another part of the building and separate "Turkish, sitz, vapour, and plunge baths." Carnegie placed control of the baths in the hands of a group of local trustees, chosen by him.

The baths were formally dedicated, in his presence, in the summer of 1877 in a grand event, fully covered in the local papers. The provost opened the proceedings by toasting Carnegie. He was followed by "Mr. Wilson, Chairman of the Associated Swimming Clubs of Scotland [who] then pointed out, in a very forcible manner, the importance of swimming as a branch of science and as a means of promoting sanitary reform—giving some excellent illustrations of the same." After members of the Swimming Clubs had demonstrated the standard strokes, as well as "ornamental swimming; plunging, touching, and turning; diving, sculling, floating, and spinning," some of the local gentlemen, "including one clergyman and several members of Town Council—had a swim in the pond." Carnegie closed the proceedings with a short speech. He hoped the baths would be used "and would lead to good results, more especially among the working classes. If such was the effect, he would, he was sure, be amply repaid, and he wished the Council to take the baths as an evidence of the deep and abiding interest he had always had, and ever would have in the prosperity of his native town."[3]

WITH MORE free time and money in his pocket, Carnegie was able to indulge himself in his favorite pastime: reading and in preparing himself for the literary career that had long been his dream. In childhood, he had had to rely on the kindness of others for reading material. A rich man now, he could indulge himself in buying and subscribing to books and journals. In 1880 alone, he purchased subscriptions from Brentano's Literary Emporium at 39 Union Square for dozens of American and British literary and political journals, including *Harper's* and *Harper's Weekly*, *St. Nicholas*, *Leslie's*, *The Nation*, *Bullinger's Monitor Guide*, *Blackwood's Magazine*, *Contemporary Reviews*, *Fortnightly*, *Nineteenth Century*, *North American Review*, *Punch* (of London), and the *Scottish American Journal*. He was a subscriber as well to New York's most solidly conservative and Republican Party newspapers, the *New York Times* and the *Evening Post*, and to a number of trade journals, including *Railway World* and *Railway Gazette*, *American Manufacturers*, and *Iron Age*.[4]

Reading was not a solitary occupation for Carnegie. He was too sociable, in fact, to do anything by himself. As a teenager in the United States, he had read American history and political theory to prepare for his debate with his cousin and uncle in Dunfermline, then organized informal reading and discussion groups with his Allegheny City friends, and joined a larger Pittsburgh debating society. As a young man, he had dived into the literature of Swedenborgianism in the company of his aunts and his father.

Much of what he read, he committed to memory. When, in 1878, he took his trip "round the world," he left his books of Burns poetry behind because, he claimed, he had memorized so much he no longer needed to refer to the text. "No, no Robin, no need of taking you in my trunk; I have you in my heart." He took with him instead the thirteen-volume set of Shakespeare that his mother gave him as a going-away present.[5]

In the travel diary which he later published, he cited hundreds of lines from Burns and Shakespeare, and dozens more from Tennyson, Byron, Cowper, Sterne, Milton, Arnold, Macaulay, Thackeray, and Wordsworth, as well as a Scottish clergyman, Norman Macleod; the German poet Friedrich Schiller; the German-born Oxford professor and translator Max Müller; and a number of American writers, including Twain, Bryant, Emerson, Bayard Taylor, and Bret Harte.

Carnegie's talent for memorization did not wane as he grew older. Richard Gilder, his poet-friend, toured Canada with him in 1906, and reported in a letter home that he was receiving "a liberal education. A.C. is truly a 'great' man, i.e. a man of enormous faculty and a great imagination." Gilder couldn't recall ever having met anyone with "such a range of poetical quotation . . . (not so much *range* as numerous quotations from Shakespeare, Burns, Byron, etc.)."[6]

Carnegie recycled literary citations into his conversation, his letters, and his publications. Armed with a working memory of lines from the great poets, historians, novelists—from contemporary plays, ancient philosophers, and the latest articles in the leading journals—he could enter any room and engage anyone in conversation. College presidents, theologians, philosophers, university professors, industrialists, or politicians: Carnegie declaimed before them all, and with such good cheer that seldom did anyone complain of his being pompous or pretentious. He memorized and recited poetry because he loved the sound of the words—and of his own voice. He was a literary name-dropper, but a rather sophisticated one. Most of his citations were close to perfect.

Carnegie recognized at an early age how useful his talent for recitation might be. In the Carnegie Papers at the Library of Congress, there is a two-page, unrevised transcript he dictated for his *Autobiography,* but never published. Recalling the officials he worked with at the Pennsylvania Railroad, he confessed that he could not "at the moment think of one who could be called a Reading Man." This gave him a comparative advantage, which he exploited to the fullest. "I think that my influence grew more from [my ability to provide] apt quotations than anything else . . . Some times I suspected they passed as original. This was delicious. One case in point. President Thomson of the Pennsylvania Railroad had risked his private fortune to complete the railroad to Chicago." When Thomson's plans were disrupted by Jay Gould, who had surreptitiously offered an exorbitant sum to lease one of the roads Thomson required to complete his through route, Carnegie advised him to swallow his pride, recognize that he had been successfully blackmailed, and offer to lease the road for the same terms Gould had proposed.

> After giving my views of the immense advantages certain to flow from one united railroad interest from the Seaboard to Chicago the needed quotation came to mind and I wound up with, "And thus, Mr. Thomson, you will 'pluck from the nettle danger, the flower safety.'"
>
> "What's that, Andy? What's that?" I hear the very tones of his voice. I repeated it. Great point also to be called "Andy" by the formal President, so reserved to others. Such are the things that tell.
>
> . . . My subsequent intimacy with him and calls to Philadelphia upon

occasions may be largely attributed, I think, to that apt quotation and perhaps some others, hitting the nail on the head and clinching it, as Shakespeare does.

In this unpublished fragment from a draft of his *Autobiography,* he
warned the young men he hoped would read and profit from his teachings
not to confine their reading to books that had a practical application to
their work. "Nothing will bring promotion—and better still, usefulness
and happiness, than culture giving you general knowledge beyond the
depths of those with whom you may have to deal. Knowledge of the gems
of literature at call find a ready and profitable market in the industrial
world. They sell high among men of affairs as I found with my small stock
of knowledge."[7]

For some time now, Carnegie had been contemplating a second
career—or vocation—as a writer. He had first begun writing letters to the
editor of the *New York Tribune* in the 1850s, had sent a firsthand report of
the Battle of Bull Run to the *Pittsburgh Chronicle* in 1861, composed a series of travel letters for publication during his 1865–66 European tour, and
in November 1867 wrote Major William Blackwood II, the current editor
of *Blackwood's Magazine,* in Edinburgh, to complain about coverage of
American matters and offer his services as writer or contributing editor.[8]

To become a published author, he required a subject to write about and
the free time to do it. A trip "round the world" would furnish both. He had
been contemplating such a trip since 1873, but had had to postpone it, most
recently, because of the illness of his friend and traveling companion, John
Vandervort (Vandy).[9]

On October 12, 1878, he bid farewell to William Shinn, the E.T. general superintendent, sent off his "last business note for about a year" to Edward Y. Townsend, the president of Cambria Iron, and made the first entry
in the travel diary of his trip around the world.[10]

"Bang! click! the desk closes, the key turns and goodbye for a year to
my wards—that goodly cluster over which I have watched with parental
solicitude for many a day; their several cribs full of records and labeled
Union Iron Mills, Lucy Furnaces, Keystone Bridge Works, Union Forge,
Cokevale Works, and the last, but not least, that infant Hercules the Edgar
Thomson Steel Rail Works—good lusty bairns all, and well calculated to
survive in the struggle for existence—great things are expected of them in

the future, but for the present I bid them farewell; I'm off for a holiday, and the rise and fall of iron and steel 'affecteth me not.'"[11]

The first stop was Pittsburgh, where he met up with Vandy. The two had hoped to take a leisurely train ride across the country, but upon learning that their ship was to leave four days earlier than scheduled, they secured seats on specially chartered Pennsylvania Railroad cars straight through from Pittsburgh to St. Louis to Council Bluffs, Nebraska, where they boarded a Northern Pacific train of three Pullman cars bound for Ogden. At Ogden, they changed trains again, onto the Central Pacific line to Sacramento, then southwest to San Francisco.[12]

The day before he sailed for Japan, Carnegie cabled his private secretary in New York with final instructions: "Send my foreign papers to Lucy after you read them. You will not subscribe for any that run out. Remember to duplicate my Christmas gifts on this side. You needn't send any to Scotland as I shall be there."[13]

IN THE three decades since Carnegie's first ocean voyage, the world had grown considerably smaller. His ultimate destination, "the East," was halfway round the world, but not so far that he couldn't be reached in an emergency. Underwater cables, linked to landlines, connected North America to Europe, via Newfoundland; Europe to Egypt, via Malta and Sicily; Egypt to Bombay, via Aden; India to Penang and Singapore; Singapore to Hong Kong and Shanghai on the mainland.[14]

Though Carnegie considered himself a fearless traveler, he had no intention of departing from the well-worn paths of other round-the-world travelers or visiting locations out of reach of a telegraph office. He and Vandy would stay in large cities with a significant Western presence, sleep in the best hotels, eat in restaurants that catered to Westerners, and travel back and forth across the China Sea on European-managed steamers and ferries.

Vandy was the perfect traveling companion, amused, not annoyed, by his friend's gregariousness, boundless energy, and mild eccentricities. In his own travel diary, Vandy recalls how on Christmas Day, 1878, in Hong Kong, after enduring a sleepless night because of the mosquitoes and suffering from a cold he had carried with him from Canton, he was roused from a very "uncomfortable morning" by Carnegie bounding into the room to wish him a Merry Christmas and present him with "a pair of Japanese shirt studs and sleeve buttons." Though he would much have preferred to stay in for the day, Carnegie persuaded him to "take a stroll though the upper portion of the Chinese town. AC, having the gong fever badly insisted on going into every junk shop we passed and trying their gongs—tried several but they did not come up to his idea of sound so did not invest—did not wonder as he had already purchased some 10 in Canton. Almost every thing he takes a notion for he goes for them wholesale."[15]

Vandy's travel diary was—like the man—understated and squeezed into two tiny notebooks. Carnegie's was much grander, written into a sturdy full-size notebook, with a brown marbled cover. On returning to the States, Vandy put away his notebooks; Carnegie had his transcribed, edited, privately printed, and widely distributed.

There was, he knew, no better way to break into print. Travelogues required neither plotting nor characters, presented no organizational problems, and could be written in the first person. There were dozens of models to draw upon, from Washington Irving to James Fenimore Cooper to Henry Wadsworth Longfellow, Nathaniel Hawthorne, Bayard Taylor, and, most recently, Mark Twain. As William Stowe has noted in *Going Abroad: European Travel in Nineteenth-Century American Culture,* the traveling class was also a reading and a writing class. "By 1875 so many people were sending accounts of their travels to newspapers that the guidebook author M. F. Sweetser saw fit to warn his readers that 'among the thousands of our people who visit Europe every summer, many scores are afflicted by the *cacoethes scribendi.*'"*[16]

Carnegie's account of his trip is readable, though filled with clumsy stylistic flourishes, extended asides, and intrusive citations from Burns and Shakespeare. His sentences are lengthy but, while not particularly well crafted, never lose their way. The little man without much formal schooling could not resist displaying his learning to the folks back home. In the first five or so pages of what is ostensibly a record of his trip, he expatiates on the human need to fulfill "early dreams," America's newfound supremacy in raising and training "trotters," the future of the American export trade in beef, how Bret Harte's work deteriorated when he relocated to the east coast from the west, a comparison between "fresh California grapes" and the "hot-house grapes of England," and the future of Ameri-

---

Cacoethes scribendi, translated best into an itch or mania for writing, has been attributed, among others, to Juvenal, Addison, and Oliver Wendell Holmes, Sr.

can winemaking—all this before he boards ship. In the edition published by Scribner's in 1884, Carnegie subjects his extended audience in the first sixty pages alone to miniature essays on Buddhism, Chinese immigration, American missionaries and Chinese converts to Christianity, Japanese decorative arts, Queen Victoria's lavish and expensive lifestyle, and Japanese currency inflation.

What saves readers from drowning in tedium is the narrator's sprightly conversational tone, his self-deprecating humor, and his remarkable powers of observation. There is lots of information on local workers and wage scales, much of it apparently garnered from Vandy's travel diary. In China, tradesmen earned fifteen cents a day and received a rice ration worth another six to eights cents. In the coffee plantations of Ceylon, men were paid eighteen cents a day, women fourteen cents. In India, "railroad laborers and coolies of all kinds receive only four rupees per month . . . these are worth just now forty cents each . . . Upon this a man has to exist. Is it any wonder that the masses are constantly upon the verge of starvation?"[17]

We are, as we proceed with Carnegie across Asia, left with renewed admiration for this little adventurer in his pith helmet. He is never dismissive, condescending, or prey to simplistic racial stereotyping. He constantly warns his readers that despite appearances, Japanese, Chinese, and Indians are all the product of old and established civilizations and religions that deserve respect. At a moment in U.S. history when few, indeed, had kind words to say about the Chinese, Carnegie dissents from the prevailing wisdom. "Let us not forget that our ancestors were using their fingers—barbarians that they were—when the Chinese had risen, centuries before, to the refinement of these [chop]sticks, for the fork is only about three hundred years old." He dismissed the agitation against the Chinese in California as little more than "the usual prejudice of the ignorant races next to them in the social scale."[18]

Wherever he traveled, Carnegie took it on himself to investigate and write about the status of women. In Shanghai, he took note of "the almost total absence of young ladies [at] a very good amateur theatrical performance" in which "Shanghai society was present in force, and in full evening dress." He then segued into a long commentary on "the marriage customs of the East." Directly addressing "my lady friends," he described the sad plight of women in China and Japan who were forced to cede their separate individualities. Only if and when the married woman gave birth to a manchild was she "invested with a halo of sanctity which secures rank and reverence from all. . . . The older she becomes the more she is reverenced as being nearer to heaven, dearer to the gods." Robbed of all distinguishing characteristics, Chinese women were—for Carnegie and, he ventured, for Chinese men as well—indistinguishable. "They are as like as peas, and one may as well marry one as another." Husbands in China might never know "the joys of love," he continued, but neither would they suffer "the anxieties pertaining to that super-sensitive condition," for the wife, once chosen, was not selected to be the man's "constant companion. . . . The position of woman, would seem, therefore, to be almost entirely different from what it is with us: in youth she is nothing there, in old age everything; with us it is the opposite. The 'just mean' between the two would probably yield better results than either."[19]

At the conclusion of his travelogue, Carnegie returned again to the subject of matrimony, evidence that he was, though thousands of miles away from home, thinking about his own future as a husband. The East, he wrote, lacked two of the "most important elements" that made life worth living in the West. There was no day of rest, no Sunday, to break up the workweek; and there was a decided

> want of intelligent and refined women as the companion of man. . . . It has been a strange experience to me to be for several months without the society of some of this class of women—sometimes many weeks without even speaking to one, and often a whole week without even seeing the face of an educated woman. And, bachelor as I am, let me confess what a miserable, dark, dreary, and insipid life this would be without their constant companionship! This brings everything that is good in its train, everything that is bright and elevating. . . . To see a wealthy Chinaman driving along in his carriage alone was pitiable. His efforts had been successful, but for what? There was no joy in his world. The very soul of European civilization, its crown and special glory, lies in the elevation of woman to her present position (she will rise even higher yet with the coming years), and this favor she has repaid a thousand-fold by making herself the fountain of all that is best in man. In life, without her there is nothing.

Carnegie attributed even the absence of music—"Not an opera nor a concert—not even a hand-organ. Scarcely a sweet sound in all our journey"—

to the absence of women from social life. "Were women there as with us, wouldn't music spring forth also!"[20]

These remarks might be read as a public admission that Carnegie was ready to marry and determined not to settle, as he feared Chinese men did, for a wife who was any less of an "individual" than he was or one with whom he would be unable to fully experience the "joys of love." There can be no doubt that Carnegie's admiration for his mother had had a profound influence on his thinking about women. Like all the Morrison women, Meg had been every bit as capable as her husband when it came to providing for her family. But that she had had to supplant her husband as bread-winner was not, in the end, healthy for her or her family. It would have been far better for all had Will Carnegie been able to put food on the table, leaving his wife to run the household, raise the children, and bring sweet-ness and light into the home as Carnegie hoped his wife would.

CARNEGIE concluded his year abroad in Dunfermline, where he met up with his mother before sailing to New York. Two years earlier, he had ded-icated the private baths and recreation center. Now, with his mother beside him, he offered the city a second grant, this one for a library and reading room to be built above the indoor "ponds." Unlike the first grant, this one was conditional on the town corporation agreeing to support the library, once it was built.

The Library Act of 1850, which had been extended to Scotland in 1855, provided town corporations with the authority to levy a small tax on local rate payers for such a purpose, but the Dunfermline councilors were evenly divided on whether or not to do so. Carnegie privately offered the town an additional £5,000, "conditioned upon acceptance of the Library act." As he wrote his uncle Lauder in December, he would withdraw the offer if there was any "contest over the question—It must be generally—say universally approved or not submitted at all." In February 1880, Carnegie's proposal was accepted at a public meeting in Dunfermline.[21]

CARNEGIE and his mother returned to New York City in the early sum-mer of 1879, then boarded the train for Cresson, where he intended to put the finishing touches on his travel diary. To help him in the process, he hired, as his personal editor, John Denison Champlin, a writer and editor who was currently employed by the publisher Henry Holt. Champlin, writing on Henry Holt letterhead, returned the first thirty-one pages of the manuscript on July 7, 1879, with a note to Gardie McCandless. "You will see by the marks that I have been obliged to score it pretty badly. If Mr. Carnegie is very particular to have it correct, I think it would be well for me to see another proof of these pages after my corrections have been made. . . . Please suggest to Mr. Carnegie that the opening sentence is a little confused, the pronouns being in both the third and second persons. . . . I have endeavored to preserve his language all through, and to make the sentences according to his marks; but if I had carte blanche in the matter, I should not make the sentences quite so long in some places, as they are apt to be a little involved at times."[22]

Notes on a Trip Round the World was published in the fall of 1879 (the later Charles Scribner's edition was revised and published under the title *Round the World*). Bound in red leather and professionally edited by Champlin, the book was designed to present Andrew Carnegie in a new light. It was sent to hundreds of people, including distant family members; new and old friends from Dunfermline, Allegheny City, St. Louis, Chicago, and New York; business associates; unmarried women; and the men of letters whose attention Carnegie was most interested in. He received, in return, dozens of personal notes, postal cards, and letters of acknowledgment. Uncle Lauder in Dunfermline congratulated him on the abundant citations from Robert Burns. His old friend Holmes, with whom he had worked as a messenger boy in Pittsburgh, reported that he had been surprised by Carnegie's "literary style." Robert Ingersoll, lawyer, politician, lecturer, and freethinker, whom Carnegie had befriended in New York City, thanked his "dear friend" for the book, which he had read "with great interest. It is filled with joy and . . . above all is natural." Anthony Drexel claimed that he had read the travelogue in a single sitting. Collis Huntington told Carnegie that he too had read it "from end to end," which for him was remarkable since he had "not read a book for years except my ledger, and I did not intend to read yours, but when I began it I could not lay it down." Carnegie also received warm notes of congratulation from several dozen women.

Lidie Laughlin of Pittsburgh, the thirty-year-old daughter of steel magnate James Laughlin, a founder of Jones & Laughlin, thanked Carnegie for his "delightful looking book," which she had not yet read. "I expect [it] to be very entertaining, spicy, and instructive. I thank you very much for remembering me. It is very good of you to give your friends the benefit of your travels. We shall be very glad to have you call and see us when you are in Pittsburgh." Lydia Harper, the twenty-four-year-old daughter of a Pittsburgh bank president, was every bit as congratulatory. Bertha Harton, in a mildly flirtatious note, marked "At Home Sunday" in the upper-left-hand corner, addressed her note to "My good friend. A long time ago you asked me to tell you 'six things' that pleased me in your book, and now after closing it for the second time I realize how impossible it would be for me to select only 'six' out of dozens that delighted me. In this book you have shown yourself the many in one. No one 'ideal' man could have written such a book. The eye of artist and poet, the head of the statistician and the statesman; the common sense of a practical man, and the heart of one who loves his fellow men, are all clearly defined, each holding his own place, never clashing with each other." Fanny Richardson, a twenty-nine-year-old teacher, was quite enthusiastic, as was Laurie Faulkner, who suggested that Carnegie "take a short journey (not around the world) from the Windsor to 345 Fifth Avenue some Tuesday evening and give us a personal outline of the 'great journey.'" Jennie Johns from Pittsburgh, who would later be invited to accompany Carnegie on a coaching trip in Britain in 1881, thanked him for the book and for the "pretty shawl" he had also sent her.[23]

Although it is never easy to read between the lines of formal notes written by unmarried women, there is no mistaking the coquettish tone in a large number of them. Had Carnegie somehow authorized such behavior by giving these women the impression that he was, at age forty-five, prepared to take a bride? It appears he had. The year before, his Dunfermline relatives had come to the conclusion that he had, in fact, already married—without telling them to whom. "We have all been much exercised about his marriage," his uncle, George Lauder, wrote to a friend. "Today we have looked over the papers to see if there is any mention, but no."[24]

Carnegie had somehow signaled to his family in Dunfermline and to the women he corresponded with in America that he was ready to get married. An undated newspaper article, probably from the mid-1880s, found among his papers, describes a visit to Cresson by a reporter who was "denied the pleasure of an interview with Mr. Carnegie, not because he is not approachable to a news gatherer but for the fact that he is, I am told, almost continually SURROUNDED BY LADIES while at Cresson. It was, however, our privilege to pass him on the road . . . a slight rain falling at the time. He was almost hidden by the umbrella which he was striving to hold over two pretty girls that were clinging to each arm. We had given about the last dollar we had for a buggy to do this trip in, while the man who owned the whole country thereabouts was footing it in the rain, with his companions laughing and talking like a boy and girl just out of school."[25]

It was soon after his return from his round-the-world trip that Carnegie became reacquainted with the woman he would eventually marry: Louise Whitfield.* He had met Louise years before on a New Year's Day call with his friend Alexander King, a Scotsman who had prospered in the thread business. King was a friend of Louise's father, John Whitfield, a partner in a house that specialized in notions, fancy dress materials, and imported French and English white goods. The Whitfields, an old and respected though not particularly wealthy New York family, lived in their own house on Forty-eighth Street, between Fifth and Sixth avenues.

Having been initiated into the custom of making New Year's Day calls, Carnegie, in the years to come, returned several times to the Whitfield home. He paid little notice during these holiday calls to Louise, the oldest daughter, a well-schooled, well-groomed young lady who had done all the things young women were supposed to do to prepare them for marriage. She had toured Europe with her family at age sixteen, was educated at Henrietta B. Haines's School in Gramercy Park, learned French from Mademoiselle de Janon, Miss Haines's partner in the school, learned to sing and play the piano, and "came out," though informally, at eighteen at a private party in the Whitfield parlor in December 1875.

That same year, her mother, Fannie, was taken ill—she would be an invalid for the rest of her life—and Louise took over the household. While

---

*Louise Whitfield kept a diary all her life, which forms the basis—with interviews—of the biography written by Burton Hendrick and his collaborator, Daniel Henderson. Because I was unable to locate any of Louise's personal papers, I have had to rely on the Hendrick and Henderson biography for most of what follows. It is entitled *Louise Whitfield Carnegie: The Life of Mrs. Andrew Carnegie*, and was published by Hastings House in 1950.

the servants did most of the household work, Louise knew enough about cooking, baking, dusting, and polishing silver to supervise them. When, in 1878, her father died, Louise took on the added responsibility for raising her four-year-old brother, Henry (Harry), and her sister, Estelle (Stella), who was a few years younger than she was, but quite frail and "delicate," like their mother.

On New Year's Day 1880, Carnegie, who had turned forty-four in November, walked the two blocks north from the Windsor Hotel and round the corner to call on the Whitfields. This time he took special notice of Louise. Though never a beauty, Louise Whitfield had grown into a rather attractive young lady, slender, with brown hair, blue eyes, and a perfect complexion. She was taller than Andrew, but not by much. Louise already had a full supply of callers and suitors, but perhaps because of her mother's illness, her father's death, and her family responsibilities, she had paid little attention to any of them.

Carnegie was interested enough to make a subsequent call, perhaps with his mother, and ask Mrs. Whitfield if he might take her oldest daughter, who was an accomplished equestrienne, riding in Central Park. Once Mrs. Whitfield's permission was secured, Andrew began to call on a regular basis to ask Louise to go riding with him. He would send his valet in the morning with a note to alert her that he was going to call that afternoon. If she did not reply at once, he would appear at her door to escort her to the stable.[26]

Carnegie, who was only two years younger than Louise's father would have been, appeared at first a most unlikely suitor for the twenty-three-year-old woman. He was tiny, white-bearded, devoted to and living with his mother, and growing stouter by the day. But she was enchanted nonetheless. "The courtship," according to Louise's biographers, who had access to diaries that have subsequently been lost, "began over a book," *The Light of Asia,* Edwin Arnold's narrative prose poem about the life and teachings of Buddha. Carnegie had become captivated by the story of Prince Siddhartha, its pacifist message, and the comparisons Arnold drew between the teachings of Buddha and Christ. Carnegie, as the story goes, bought a copy of the book for Louise and the two spent many hours reading it to one another. It became a talisman of their relationship. Louise later told her biographers that she carried the book with her always. On their wedding day, Andrew would give Louise a first edition: on the flyleaf, he acknowledged that the book was "the first gift I ever gave to my wife, then the young lady Louise Whitfield . . . Reading and quoting it at times to her, I first discovered she had a mind and heart above, and beyond, those of others of her own age."[27]

Carnegie and Louise went riding often that spring of 1880, then separated with the warm weather, Carnegie to Cresson, Louise with her mother and siblings to the Catskills and then on to her aunt and uncle's farm in Oyster Bay, New York. In the fall, they renewed their friendship. On New Year's Day 1881, he sent her flowers with a note on his calling card: "Happy New Year, To My Fair Equestrienne 1881." By early 1881, their mothers had also become acquainted with one another. On February 7, Louise noted in her diary that Mrs. Carnegie had come to take "mama and Harry and Stella to drive and Mr. C. came for me to ride. Splendid time." Three days later, Carnegie and his mother took Louise and her mother "to Booth's to see Salvini in 'Macbeth.' Had a splendid time." Soon afterwards, Margaret Carnegie introduced Louise to Tom's wife, Lucy, who was visiting New York. In March, Andrew left a calling card for Mrs. Whitfield requesting permission for Louise "to go with us to the races at 12:20 today."[28]

By the spring of 1881, Andrew and Louise, with their mothers' acquiescence, if not approval, had been seeing one another for almost fifteen months. All that was missing was some declaration of a desire to marry. But Carnegie said nothing. He was apparently not ready yet to settle down or attach himself to anyone other than his mother, who demanded very little of him. He had his steelworks in Pittsburgh to watch over, albeit from a distance; his literary career, which was just beginning to blossom; and extensive travel plans.

In February, while spending more and more time with Louise, Carnegie began to lay plans for an 800-mile "coaching" excursion through Great Britain.* His guests were to include Davey McCargo, his friend and fellow messenger boy from Allegheny City; his partner Harry Phipps; his secretary, Gardie McCandless; and Alexander King and his wife, Aggie. His old friend Vandy could not come along, but Vandy's brother Benjie

---

*There are two versions of Carnegie's account of this trip. The first, privately printed in 1882, was entitled *Our Coaching Trip;* the second, published by Charles Scribner's Sons in 1883, was entitled *An American Four-in-Hand in Britain.*

took his place. Alice French of Davenport, Iowa, a family friend (and future published author) accepted his invitation. So did Jennie Johns, the woman Carnegie referred to in the published version of his travelogue as the "Prima Donna." Jennie received her invitation on Valentine's Day, which, according to Carnegie, "caused her young heart to flutter. What a pretty reply came! . . . 'I am the happiest girl alive.'"[29]

Andrew wanted Louise to join the party and may have invited the Kings, old family friends of the Whitfields, with this in mind. He intended to formally request Mrs. Whitfield's permission, but asked Louise "to speak to Mama" first. In her diary, Louise recorded Mama's answer: "She says I cannot possibly go. So unhappy." A few days later came a second entry in the diary on the same subject: "I cannot become reconciled to my disappointment. Mr. C. has invited me to go on his . . . trip, but Mother says it is not proper for me to go."[30]

Carnegie tried one last time to secure Mrs. Whitfield's permission. There were other single women going on the coaching trip and several suitable chaperones, including the Kings. But instead of going to Mrs. Whitfield himself, he dispatched his mother with a formal invitation. He should have known better than to trust Mag Carnegie with such an errand. After issuing the invitation, she "pointed out the inconveniences of such an expedition for a girl of 23. 'If she was my daughter' said the old lady, 'I wouldna let her go.'" Though it was, in the end, Mrs. Whitfield who made the final decision, Louise never forgave her future mother-in-law for interfering.[31]

The truth—as Louise would later explain to Burton Hendrick—was that Mag Carnegie had decided on her own that Louise was too young and frivolous to make a suitable match for her son. "She would not have objected to Andrew's marrying, provided he had selected someone nearer his own age, and one whom [she] regarded as more sedate. In fact she had herself picked out a wife—Mary Clark," a Hartford woman, who was a friend of Mag and of Lucy Carnegie. We know little about Mary, other than that she was one of Carnegie's Central Park riding companions and had traveled with Mag to Pittsburgh in 1884 and lost her trunk, which Carnegie was delegated to find. She was also close enough to the family for David Stewart to include her when he sent his "regards" to Andrew and his mother in 1884. Decades later, after Mag's death and his own marriage, Carnegie provided Mary Clark with a pension of $4,800 a year. Because he did not want her to know the source, he forwarded her funds to Lucy Carnegie to distribute to her. Only in 1913 did Mary discover where her pension came from. From that point until her death soon afterwards, Carnegie paid her directly.[32]

Louise was distraught at the thought of being left behind in New York and worried that this might be the end of their courtship. "I am so unhappy about the trip. I want to go so much and yet I see it is impossible," she wrote in her diary on April 16. On April 18, she consented to go riding with Carnegie; then, on April 27, she sent word, via a household servant, that she would not "ride this afternoon." The thought of riding with him in the park, then saying good-bye as Carnegie prepared to sail to England, may have been too much for her. By May 7, she had changed her mind and went riding again, all the way to Morrisania in the Bronx. When Carnegie invited her to attend a concert with him that evening, she refused.[33]

On May 31, the night before his departure, Carnegie addressed an envelope to Miss Whitfield, with a pressed clover blossom, a carnation, a red rose, and an invitation to a farewell dinner at the Windsor Hotel. Louise preserved the envelope and its contents as a reminder of the trip that would not be—and the man who had left her behind. The dinner was everything she had feared. Mag Carnegie presided; several of the traveling party were in attendance; the major topic of conversation was the trip to come: "Was very sorry I went," Louise recorded the next day, "but did not know how to get out of it."[34]

Louise spent the summer with her mother in the Catskills and at Oyster Bay instead of traveling through England and Scotland with Carnegie and his guests. She did not hear from Carnegie for more than a month. When he wrote, he seemed oblivious to the pain he was causing. "Well, my dear Friend," he wrote from the Queens Hotel in Reading, "I have waited until I could tell you whether the 'Gay Charioteers' were a success or not, and now I can say that no estimate of the pleasure derivable from coaching which I made was half high enough. . . . Our party are so enthusiastic, so happy, so good, that it does seem almost too much like paradise. . . . Not one mishap, nor an ache, nor a pain so far. Our luncheons by the way side are just idealistic. . . . It is all I pictured it, and more. . . . Not one shower of rain so far." He closed with an apology for not having properly said good-bye. "I was so sorry at reaching the Parlor only a few minutes after you had left; please excuse me. I was detained. Kindest regards to Mamma.

May you enjoy your summer!" Almost as postscript or afterthought, he added beneath his signature: "Please let me hear from you, care J. S. Morgan & Co. London."[35]

CARNEGIE'S ACCOUNT of his coaching trip presents him as he wanted to be regarded now: a carefree man of leisure, not a grim businessman; a sporting man and writer; a loyal son and generous friend; the jolliest, yet most gentlemanly, of ladies' men. Although he did not acknowledge it in his book, he paid everyone's expenses and made all the decisions on the itinerary. This was his trip, from beginning to end.

The party sailed on a luxury liner, the *Bothnia*, on June 1. In his letter to the Cunard agents confirming the reservations for eleven adults, a nurse, and three children (the children were not going on the coaching trip), he requested that his party be given "the end seats at the table opposite the Captain's." The "eldest child is not five yet, so I presume you will take them and nurse as one adult."[36]

On June 11 the ship landed at Liverpool and the Carnegie entourage was greeted "by kind friends on the quay." George Pullman and his wife, who had sailed with the party, placed a private railway car at everyone's disposal for the trip into London. "We began our traveling upon the other side under unexpectedly favorable conditions."[37]

Carnegie and his guests spent six days in London at the Westminster Hotel, observed the House of Commons in session, "heard a performance of the 'Messiah' in [the] Albert Hall," and visited prominent friends for lunch. They then took the train to Brighton, where they met their coach and horses; Perry, their coachman; and Joe, their footman. As there was no space on the coach for their trunks, they were to be "forwarded every week to the point where we are to spend the succeeding Sunday, so that every Saturday evening we replenish our wardrobe, and at the Sunday dinner appear in full dress."[38]

The party stayed at the finest inns and the most luxurious hotels. "Several people of note in the neighborhood dropped into the inn, as a rule, to see the American coaching party, whose arrival in the village had made as great a stir as if it were the advance show-wagon of Barnum's menagerie." Every morning, before they departed, usually at nine-thirty, Alice French saw to it that the "two coaching hampers, very complete affairs" they had purchased in London, were "filled . . . with the best the country could afford." They took their luncheon in the open air, "near an inn" where the horses could be watered. The luncheon place having been chosen the night before, all that was left was to select the finest "piece of the velvety lawn" upon which to lay the "armfuls of rugs" they carried with them. When Joe and Perry had laid the rugs, they departed briefly to put up the horses and fetch "mugs of foaming ale, bottles of Devonshire cider, lemonade, and pitchers of fresh creamy milk" to accompany the lunch. Then the party returned to their coach to complete their journey to the next town. If overtaken by thirst along the way, they would stop again at a local inn for ale and refreshments. When they came upon a particularly gorgeous brook or field of flowers, they would leave the carriage for a stroll.[39]

In her diary of the trip, Alice French noted that when the party "crossed the border" into Scotland, they left the carriage and "walked to site of old blacksmith shop," where they met an "intelligent small boy. . . . Mr. C. gave him some money & a card with his address bidding him learn Burns & Scott and become a mechanic & he would give him a place." On yet another walk, this one in Sanquhar, with only Carnegie and Gardie McCandless along, they engaged "a trio of hedge cutters" in conversation, who informed them, among other things, that "America's a deal soight better place than this."[40]

Arriving at twilight at the inn where they would spend the night, Gardie McCandless, deputized as "general manager" for the trip, "examined the rooms and assigned them; Joe and Perry handed over the bags to the servants; the party went direct to their general sitting-room, and, in a few minutes were taken to their rooms, where all was ready for them. The two American flags were placed upon the mantel of the sitting-room, in which there was always a piano, and we sat down to dinner a happy band." As darkness does not fall in northern England and Scotland until late in the summer night, the "Gay Charioteers" (as Carnegie referred to the group) had several hours after dinner to tour the location, after which they returned to their sitting room for "an hour of musical entertainment." As Gardie saw to all the arrangements, Carnegie's only function, as he acknowledged in his travelogue, was to reign as "king in a constitutional monarchy." Like Queen Victoria, he was not "allowed to do anything." This, he was delighted to report, left him plenty of time to serve as "scribe."[41]

Throughout his book, Carnegie takes time out from his observations of the landscape and the people he meets to remind the reader of the importance of leisure. "Your always busy man accomplishes little; the great doer is he who has plenty of leisure . . . Moral: Don't worry yourself over work, hold yourself in reserve, and sure as fate, 'it will all come right in the wash.'" Speaking to his own situation, that of a man retired in the prime of his career, Carnegie indulged in an orgy of self-congratulation. It was the height of foolishness, he had found, to delay gratification and put off retirement until one was too old to enjoy it. "Sound wisdom that school-boy displayed who did not 'believe in putting away from tomorrow the cake he could eat-to-day.' . . . Among the saddest of all spectacles to me is that of an elderly man occupying his last years grasping for more dollars." Americans, Carnegie declared, were of all the world's peoples the most victimized by a work ethic gone mad. Two years earlier, he recalled, he and Vandy, on returning from their trip round the world, had observed to one another "that the Americans were the saddest-looking race we had seen. Life is so terribly earnest here. Ambition spurs us all on, from him who handles the spade to him who employs thousands. We know no rest. . . . In this world we must learn not to lay up our treasures, but to enjoy them day by day as we travel the path we never return to." Americans, Carnegie was convinced, worked harder than was necessary and much harder than the British. "No toilers, rich or poor, like the Americans!" he remarked, ignoring the fact that it was manufacturers like him who set the work hours and that just eighteen months earlier Captain Jones, with his approval, had threatened havoc on local clergymen who suggested that the steelworks be shuttered on Sundays.[42]

There is something charmingly subversive in Carnegie's attempt to disrupt the American success narrative by preaching the virtues of idleness, leisure, and immediate gratification. From Cotton Mather to Benjamin Franklin to the McGuffey Readers and biographies of great Americans, the point had been hammered home to American boys that industry, diligence, perseverance, frugality, and sobriety were godly and pragmatic virtues without which no man could succeed. Carnegie, however, instead of praising Americans for their work ethic, disparaged their efforts as inhuman and counterproductive. "I hope Americans will find some day more time for play, like their wiser brethren upon the other side."[43]

Though Carnegie paints himself into the center of every scene in his travelogue, his mother is usually by his side. In the published work he referred to her, only half ironically, as "Queen Dowager, Head of the Clan (no Salic Law in our family)." She was given the place of honor atop the coach alongside Perry, with the right to choose who would sit next to her until she discovered there was more fun to be had elsewhere and had her seat moved inside so that she could, for the rest of the journey, be guaranteed "an audience of no less than six for her stories and old ballads. Her tongue went from morning till night, if I do say it, and her end of the coach was always in for its share of any frolic stirring."[44]

The highlight of the tour was the entry into Dunfermline on July 27. Carnegie had asked his mother to lay the "Memorial Stone of the Free Library" and she had been practicing her speech, teased along by her son, who worried aloud that it would be a long one, knowing that it would not. The town had declared a holiday to welcome its benefactor and his mother. Carnegie, Alice French wrote in her journal, appeared uneasy at having "to play the part of a popular hero even for a day." He would soon get used to the role. As the cheers rumbled through the streets of Dunfermline and the Abbey bells tolled in his honor, he was able to find strength, as he later put it, "in the knowledge that the spark which had set fire to their hearts was the Queen Dowager's return and her share in the day's proceedings. Grand woman, she has deserved all that was done in her honor on that." Excised from the published edition of the book was the observation that followed: "What she has done for her two boys is incredible . . . what she has done for herself is more incredible still, for she is the centre from which radiates, in small as in great things, the clear rays of unimpeachable truth and honor. Mother's statements from 'I shall be glad to see you,' uttered to an acquaintance, up to the most serious things of life, fall as if preceded with 'Thus saith the Lord,' for they are always true."[45]

Another telling passage excised from the Scribner's edition, no doubt by Carnegie, concerned Provost Mathieson's remarks at the banquet honoring the Carnegies in Dunfermline. Having already heaped abundant praise on him, the provost remarked that "the only flaw in Mr. Carnegie's character is that he wanted a wife. (Laughter and cheers.) I attribute that very much to the fact of his having a mother. (Laughter.) His mother has taken good care over him, and has showed that she does not want to hand him over to the tender mercies of some half-cousin, or any of the half-dozen young ladies who are with him today. (Laughter.)"[46]

In these two passages—and the fact that they were among the very few cut from the travelogue when it was published commercially—we can see that Carnegie was of two minds about his mother's indomitable presence. To claim that she had taught herself to speak with the authority of "the Lord" and that others looked upon her as Andrew's surrogate wife was to acknowledge the reach of her influence and the double-edged effect it had had on his life. No matter how hard he might try to escape her pull, he was inevitably and irresistibly lured back within her orbit. The privately published edition of *Our Coaching Trip* was dedicated, as perhaps it should have been, to "My Brother and trusty associates who toiled at home that I might realize the happiest dream of my life." The dedication in the Scribner edition read: "To My Favorite Heroine, My Mother."

THE "Gay Charioteers" were back in New York by August 24, nearly two months after they had departed. Carnegie was by now convinced that the pen would be his path to influence and fame (fortune he already had). "If any man wants *bona fide* substantial power and influence in this world, he must handle the pen—that's flat. Truly, it is a nobler weapon than the sword, and a much nobler one than the tongue, both of which have nearly had their day."[47]

Carnegie spent more time revising and polishing the manuscript than he had his round-the-world travelogue. *Our Coaching Trip* was published privately in March 1882. Two years later, Charles Scribner's Sons brought out a commercial edition entitled *An American Four-in-Hand in Britain*.

Carnegie peppered the published work with political commentary. Thirty years earlier, he had debated his cousin Dod on whether the British or American political system was more conducive to human happiness and progress. He now returned to the subject. While his praise of American republicanism was, if anything, more effusive than it had ever been, he was far less harsh on the British system of governance than he had been as an eighteen-year-old. America was as yet, he had to admit, the only home for men who long "not only to be free but to be equal. . . . But England will soon march forward: she is not going to rest behind very long. . . . England is at work in earnest, and what she does, she does well. I prophesy that young England will give young America a hard race for supremacy."[48]

Carnegie had appointed himself ambassador extraordinaire from each nation to the other, a role he believed he was uniquely qualified to take on. "The man who knows from personal experience the leading characteristics of the people upon both sides of the ferry is invariably a warm and sincere friend. The two peoples have only to become acquainted to become enthusiastic over each other's qualities." It would be his task from this point until the end of his life to make them better acquainted.[49]

ELEVEN

Making a Name, 1881–1883

BEGINNING IN 1880, with a report of his gift to Dunfermline, the name of Andrew Carnegie began to appear with some regularity in the newspapers. When Ferdinand-Marie de Lesseps, the builder of the Panama Canal, was fêted at a banquet at Delmonico's, Carnegie was listed as one of the two hundred dignitaries who subscribed and attended. His name appeared again in December 1880 as one of "a party of about 25 gentlemen, representing some of the largest business houses in New-York," who accompanied former President Grant on a ceremonial visit to Paterson, New Jersey. Three months later, he was part of another "notable gathering in Delmonico's" that raised $300,000 for a future New York World's Fair. Carnegie's pledge of $5,000 was among the most generous donations listed. Carnegie closed out the year by contributing $1,000 to the Manhattan Eye and Ear Hospital and by sponsoring a roast turkey, vegetables, pies, and ice cream Christmas dinner for 250 homeless boys at the East Side Boys' Lodging House and school. "At the close of the festival the boys were presented with warm flannel shirts and shoes. . . . Special prizes were given to boys who had punctually attended night school during the past two months."[1]

He continued to spend a good deal of time with Louise. On returning to New York after his tour, Carnegie had attempted to resume the relationship as if there had been no jarring interruption and Louise had permitted him to do so. She accepted his invitations to the races at Jerome Park and to go riding. Side by side, they rode through Central Park, and sometimes farther north on Bloomingdale Road (now Broadway above Fifty-ninth Street) into northern Manhattan, or via the High Bridge into the Bronx. In the evenings, they read together in her parlor, and, with her mother along, sat in his private box at the theater. In the spring, they were both guests, along with his mother, at a wedding reception at 574 Fifth Avenue. On New Year's Day, he addressed his calling card, as he had the year before, to "My Fair Equestrienne," but added: "And many such to follow" after the "Happy New Year" greeting.[2]

He seldom visited Pittsburgh anymore, though he kept in touch with his partners by telegram and post. Carnegie's business had suffered not at all from his lengthy absences, in large part because every other partner remained active. When William Shinn resigned as general superintendent in 1879, he declared his intention to retain his stock in the firm. Carnegie informed him that he had to give up his ownership stake. There were to be no absentee partners at E.T. All, except for Carnegie himself, were expected to work full time for the company. "Surely you don't want your colleagues to do all the work & you sit down only to share ingloriously in their triumphs. No, no, if you go, go. Sell out & try another party. We want no drones in the E.T. if we can help it."[3]

With Shinn's departure, preceded by David McCandless's death, Tom Carnegie assumed a larger role in the management of the company, as did Harry Phipps. Neither was, perhaps, as important to the overall operation of the steel mill as Captain Bill Jones: When in the fall of 1880, Jones asked the Carnegie brothers for more money "to provide for the rainy day," he was told by Andrew "to say what you want & don't put it low either." Jones refrained from naming a salary, but informed Carnegie that he knew it "to be a fact that Bethlehem Co. are now paying their Gen Supt. $15,000 per annum, and formerly paid him $20,000. I am egotist enough to say that I can walk right around him on all points connected with a Work of this kind." Though we don't know what the final offer was, it was enough to keep Jones in Carnegie's employ for the rest of his life.[4]

By the early 1880s, the E.T. works had exploded in revenues and profitability to the point where it dwarfed the other Carnegie properties. Railroad construction nationwide, which had shrunk to less than 2,400 miles a year during the 1870s, ballooned to 6,700 miles in 1880, 9,800 in 1881, and 11,569 in 1882. Concurrent with the boom came the abrupt and irreversible shift from iron to steel rails. In 1871, only 5 percent of rails manufactured domestically were made of steel; by 1875, when Edgar Thomson came on line, that percentage had increased to 37 percent; by 1879, to 62 percent; and by 1883, to 95 percent.[5]

When, in later years, Carnegie argued that it was the "community," not the "individual," who was the source of all wealth, he was doing so from experience. He and his partners had not created the conditions for the boom in railroad construction that made them so miraculously wealthy in the early 1880s. But they rode the boom as expertly and more effortlessly than they had the depression that preceded it. Receipts, which had languished through the mid-1870s, pyramided as steel prices stabilized, while production costs decreased with the addition of new labor-saving machinery. Profits at the Carnegie companies exploded from half a million dollars in 1879 to over $2 million in 1882, tracking rather precisely the increase in new track laid.[6]

As E.T. grew in size and profits, Tom Carnegie and Harry Phipps found themselves devoting more time to the steel concern and much less to the Lucy furnaces and the Union Iron Mills. To give both men a larger ownership stake in the steel company commensurate with their added responsibilities, Tom requested and Andrew agreed to consolidate all their enterprises into a new corporation, Carnegie Brothers & Company, Ltd. The new firm, which was organized on April 1, 1881, was as closely held as the old ones had been. Carnegie, who had entered the steel business with a 37 percent interest in E.T. and then bought out several of his partners' shares, ended up after the consolidation with 54.5 percent of the stock in the new company. Tom Carnegie and Harry Phipps emerged with 17.6 percent each in stock; David Stewart, John Scott, and Gardie McCandless with smaller shares; John Vandevort received 1 percent; and Cousin Dod, who had recently emigrated, 0.6 percent.[7]

IN 1881, the year Carnegie Brothers was organized, Tom Carnegie and Harry Phipps entered into an agreement with the man who would within less than a decade succeed them both as Carnegie's chief lieutenant. Faced with the mounting problem of securing a steady, expandable, and relatively inexpensive supply of high-grade coke for their new blast furnaces at Edgar Thomson and the Lucy furnaces in Lawrenceville, Phipps and Tom Carnegie approached Henry Clay Frick, the owner of a large and growing empire of coke fields and ovens.

Frick, at the time in his early thirties, had entered the coke business ten years earlier, in 1871. With money borrowed from relatives and investors, including his friend Thomas Mellon, the son of the Pittsburgh banker, Frick steadily expanded his operation. By 1880, the H. C. Frick Coke Company controlled about 150 acres of land and operated fifty beehive coke ovens, each about 11 to 12 feet in diameter, 6 to 7 feet high, in which bituminous coal was cooked into coke. As the need for coke to feed Pittsburgh's furnaces expanded, so did the business. By early 1882, his company operated over one thousand ovens at nine different coke works, all in the Connellsville region.[8]

Frick, the native-born son of German and Swiss ancestors who had emigrated to the United States in the late eighteenth century, was, like Carnegie, a little man and a self-made millionaire. He was fourteen years younger than Carnegie, but looked younger still. In 1880, he had still not grown a full beard, but sported a walrus-like mustache. He rarely smiled or joked, but seemed to glower instead. He most certainly did not sing or tell stories at the dinner table, like his future partner.

The deal that Tom Carnegie offered Frick was beneficial for both the coke and the steel companies. Frick needed new capital to expand his holdings—which the Carnegies supplied—in return for a regular and inexpensive supply of high-grade coke. The Carnegies purchased a little more than 11 percent of H. C. Frick Coke Company stock. Two years later, they would increase their stake to 50 percent; by 1888, Andrew Carnegie and Carnegie Steel would own 74 percent of the stock in the Frick company; Frick only 21 percent.[9]

The deal was sealed with a toast at the Windsor Hotel. Frick and his bride, Adelaide Childs, the daughter of Pittsburgh businessman Asa Childs, had come to New York to celebrate their honeymoon in December 1881 and accepted Carnegie's invitation to a formal dinner with him and his mother. After dinner, Andrew raised a glass to salute his new partner in the coke business.

Wildly exaggerating the extent of his investment in Frick's company, Carnegie immediately wrote Robert Garrett, vice president of the Baltimore & Ohio Railroad, to brag about the "purchase of one half of Frick & Co.'s coke works. This with our own ovens makes us by far the largest manfr. of the article." The route from Connellsville to Pittsburgh on which Frick's coke would travel was served by both the B&O and the Pennsylvania Railroad. Carnegie threatened Garrett that if the B&O did not lower its rates to match the Pennsylvania's, he would ship the vast quantities of

H. C. Frick coke he now controlled exclusively by the Pennsylvania Railroad.[10]

IN EARLY 1881, Carnegie made his first American library gift, for a reading room at the Edgar Thomson works at Braddock. The idea to fund a library for his steelworkers had come from Captain Jones. Jones had been engaged in a dispute with local clergymen or, as he referred to them, "our bigoted and sanctimonious cusses," who demanded that he shut down the steelworks for the Sabbath. He responded by threatening the clergymen that if they even tried to "interfere with these works, I will retaliate by promptly discharging any workman who belongs to their Churches and thereby get rid of the poorest and most worthless portion of our employees. If they don't want to work when I want them, I shall take good care that they don't work when they want to."[11]

In April 1880, Jones was approached by a Reverend C. DeLong of the United Brethren Church in Braddock, who, instead of berating him for not observing the Sabbath, asked for assistance "in procuring a library for use of the Sunday School connected with his church." Jones offered to do what he could to assist the reverend, explaining to Carnegie that the minister was "full of faith, but minus money. I told him I knew a gentleman in New York that possessed D——d little faith, but had lots of money, and was liberal in matters of this kind."[12]

Carnegie had not attended any church for years. The last one he had been in was the Swedenborgian chapel in Pittsburgh, which he had left behind when he moved to Altoona. He had no desire to help out any denominational church, even one with a reverend who came recommended by Captain Jones. Still, he was intrigued by the idea of opening a reading room for his steelworkers at Braddock. "I fully approve of the Library idea," Jones wrote in November 1880, in response to Carnegie's proposal to set aside space at the steel mill for a library, "but think we can wait awhile until we get all the main improvements completed about the Works." In January 1881, Carnegie forwarded to Jones "by Adams Express" an encyclopedia "for the Library at the Works." The following spring, according to a local history of Braddock, Carnegie announced "his purpose of establishing a free library at Braddock for the benefit of his workmen."[13]

In establishing a library or reading room for his workmen, Carnegie

was anticipating what would, in the early twentieth century, be characterized as corporate "welfare work." According to the labor historian Daniel
Nelson, "libraries, restaurants, club houses, and other social or recreational
facilities," built and paid for by employers, "appeared in increasing numbers after 1875." In 1879, two years before the E.T. library was established,
the Philadelphia manufacturers who owned Cambria Iron built a library
for their employees in Johnstown (which Carnegie, after the flood of 1889,
would help rebuild). Such efforts were, Nelson insists, "seldom purely philanthropic gestures. Employers who financed libraries . . . looked upon
their expenditures as investments in a more efficient as well as a more conservative working class."[14]

In November 1881, a year after deciding to fund a reading room at
E.T.,* Carnegie, in a letter to Mayor Robert W. Lyon of Pittsburgh, offered to build a public library for Pittsburgh. He attached the same conditions to this gift as he had to his Dunfermline benefaction. "I beg to offer
to the City of Pittsburgh a Free Library upon which I will expend Two
hundred & fifty thousand dollars if the City will accept it when completed
and agree for its proper use and maintenance not less than Fifteen thousand dollars per year. I have named the lowest sum required properly to
carry out the work in view."[15]

The grant for the Pittsburgh public library was turned down by the
Pittsburgh City Councils. Because there was no law in Pennsylvania similar to the British Library Act, the city officials believed they lacked the authority to apply public monies for the use of a public library. Carnegie
would not make another such offer for a public library until 1886. He
would instead, over the next five years, donate additional monies for his library at E.T. and build two more "reading rooms" for his employees at the
Union Iron Mills and Keystone Bridge works.[16]

E.T.'s MONOPOLY on steel production in the Pittsburgh region did not
last long. As orders rolled in for steel instead of iron rails—and profits increased—the owners of the city's most successful iron mills gathered together to organize their own cooperative venture in steelmaking, the

_____

*The magnificent Carnegie library and social center at Braddock, with swimming pool, public baths,
bowling alleys, art gallery, gymnasium, and billiard hall, was constructed in 1889.

Pittsburgh Bessemer Steel Company, and buy a plot of land at Homestead, Pennsylvania, a mile west of Braddock on the other side of the river. In August 1881, Pittsburgh Bessemer rolled its first rails at Homestead.

William Clark, the owner of the Solar Iron Works, was named general manager of the new steel plant. Clark believed that because the plant was located outside the city he could, with impunity, defy the union and set wage rates below the going rate. The skilled workers—who performed much the same work at Homestead, heating, reheating, rolling, molding, and shaping structural steel, as they had in Pittsburgh—retaliated with slowdowns, shutdowns, and walkouts. On January 1, 1882, in a pigheaded attempt to eliminate future conflicts with labor at Homestead, William Clark decreed that all skilled employees sign ironclad contracts that pledged them never to strike, never to join the Amalgamated Association of Iron and Steel Workers, and to resign if they were already members. When a majority of workers refused to sign, Clark shut down the mill and recruited scabs to replace them. The Amalgamated responded by organizing its own defense forces to prevent any scabs from entering Homestead and taking union jobs. By March 1882, after two months of battles, the mill remained closed. With the company beginning to default on outstanding orders and unable to take new ones, Clark admitted defeat, agreed to the union's demands, resigned his position, and left Homestead forever.[17]

The Amalgamated's success at the Pittsburgh Bessemer plant at Homestead emboldened it to try again to organize Carnegie's mill across the river. Captain Jones believed he had matters well under control. "I now feel sure that the Union will not get a foothold here," he wrote Carnegie in February. "I will ask the Company to agree to loan such good men as I may select, say from $600 to $800 this year to assist them in building homes. This is an effective plan to keep out the Union. Every good man that wants to build, encourage. You should calculate on a reasonable investment in that direction. Give them the money on fair interest. Another thing I merely suggest to you is to erect a decent Hotel. No one here has the enterprise. It is badly needed. Give this a thought."[18]

Jones badly underestimated the attraction of the Amalgamated for the skilled workers at Edgar Thomson. His and Carnegie's attempt to buy off the skilled metalworkers with a reading room and the offer of cheap mortgages for selected favorites was not going to persuade them to remain nonunion forever. In April, days after its victory at Homestead and no doubt energized by it, the Amalgamated proudly announced that it had orga-nized a lodge at the E.T. works. The captain's response was to resign his position. He had always, he claimed, gone out of his way to look after "his" workers, to make sure they were well paid and protected; he had even re-duced their workday from the twelve hours that had been standard in the iron mills to eight hours at E.T. How dare they betray his trust and confi-dence by joining the Amalgamated?[19]

Carnegie, at the time in Cresson completing the revisions on *Our Coaching Trip,* took the train into Pittsburgh to persuade Jones to stay on the job. Carnegie's experience at the Union Iron Mills had convinced him that it was possible to do business with the Amalgamated. For the past six or seven years, ever since the 1874–75 lockout of the puddlers had been set-tled, he and his partners at the Union Iron Mills had gotten on well with the Amalgamated leaders, whom Carnegie regarded as thoroughly profes-sional and, more important, quite conservative. To assure Jones that this was the case, he arranged for him to meet some of the Amalgamated offi-cers. As William Martin, one of the officials at the meeting, would later re-port, Carnegie, after introducing Jones, "stated the 'important business.' It was nothing more nor less than that Mr. Jones had conceived the idea that the Amalgamated Association was going to greatly interfere at Braddock; that it was the intention to bring wages up . . . etc., and he had sent for us so as to have an understanding. He (Carnegie) believed the Amalgamated Association was a good institution, it was highly spoken of by the man-agers" at the Pittsburgh iron mills. The union officials assured Jones "in plain English that he need have no fears. Whatever was done by the Amal-gamated Association at Braddock the firm would be consulted, and the question would be discussed pro and con, etc. . . . The interview did not last fifteen minutes, but on the strength of it the Amalgamated Associa-tion was recognized at Braddock."[20]

Carnegie's intervention won him the immediate respect of the Amal-gamated and a reputation as a friend of labor. Edgar Thomson became the only steelworks in the state to permit a union within its gates. That spring, when the Pittsburgh iron puddlers, following on the success of the Home-stead workers, demanded a higher wage scale, the Carnegie-owned Union Iron Mills alone among the thirty-six iron rolling mills in Pittsburgh agreed to their demands.[21]

Carnegie's acceptance of the Amalgamated's terms in his Pittsburgh iron mills—and his acquiescence at the organization of a new lodge at Edgar Thomson—must have infuriated his competitors. It certainly frightened Captain Jones, who feared that such accommodation would be interpreted as a sign of weakness. In November 1882, as Jones opened negotiations with the Amalgamated for a new contract in which he was going to demand a reduction in wage rates to match a fall in the price of steel rails, he warned Carnegie to stand tough: "There is one thing I wish to urge on you, that is, if necessary to enforce a proper reduction, we must fight. Don't let us make, or ask for anything we are not prepared to force. The time has arrived for positive action, and when we say to these men, that we ask for a 20% reduction that we mean it, and mean to have it. Avoid a fight if possible, but if we have to fight, let us fight for something tangible."[22]

The E.T. workers accepted the wage reduction, hoping perhaps that increased output would compensate for the decreased rates, and frightened that the alternative to accepting a wage cut was to lose their jobs entirely. "We are still getting along finely," the "special correspondent" at Edgar Thomson reported in the *National Labor Tribune* on March 31 and then repeated, in almost the same words, on April 14 and April 28.[23]

THE FALL in rail prices, which Jones and Carnegie insisted necessitated a decrease in wage rates, occurred in the autumn of 1882. Carnegie's partners proposed that Edgar Thomson cease bidding on new contracts until prices went back up. Carnegie was enraged. With his characteristic exaggeration and doomsday prophecies, he declared that his partners were putting the steelworks at risk by inviting Chicago and St. Louis mills to take away work that belonged to them.

> And all for what, the hope (a wild one) that by some unprobable change in affairs we may net a dollar or two more per ton . . . I wash my hands now of all responsibility. I show you a large profit & what is far more important looking at lasting results—a safe & steady business for our works and I enter my protest against this new doctrine of taking risks . . . I say it would pay us better to run full for almost nothing than to act in this way & give our competitors work to which they are not entitled when our respective costs are considered. I hope if any one has reasons to urge against this

policy he will be good enough to try to formulate them in writing, the effort I believe will soon convince him that he has but a vague and unreasonable hope that a miracle will come to relieve him."[24]

Carnegie, who did most of his business by post, had honed his letter-writing style to a sharp edge. In his private correspondence, he was warm and delightfully witty; in his business letters—to partners and competitors alike—he was tough, imperious, often verging on the abusive. To avoid the disastrous consequences of pricing wars, the Pennsylvania steel firms met every year in Philadelphia to set minimum prices for their products. When in the spring of 1882 Carnegie was informed that Edward Townsend, of Cambria Iron, had secretly accepted a large contract by bidding $5 a ton under the minimum price he had previously agreed upon, Carnegie was incensed and demanded, by letter, that Townsend divide the order with the Edgar Thomson steelworks.

Carnegie's letter was a small masterpiece of controlled invective. He charged Townsend not only with breaking a business agreement but with betraying the trust of a longtime colleague who had done nothing to deserve such treatment. "Consider it all over & try to think whether you have done to your colleague as you would like to be done by." He hoped that Townsend would accept his proposal to divide the order. If he did not, Carnegie asked that the matter be submitted to arbitration.[25]

More comfortable negotiating in person, Townsend suggested the dispute could be quickly resolved in a face-to-face meeting. Carnegie refused to back down. "I have always been glad to talk over matters with you . . . but feeling that I have reason to consider myself unfairly dealt with by you for the first time in all our transactions, I do not think any good can come from verbal communications until I am told by an unprejudiced arbiter that I am mistaken. While trying to advance our mutual interests by holding up the prices of Rails here to figures approved by you [intimating that he could have undersold Townsend had he wished to], I little expected to be stabbed in the back by the hand whose duty it was to co-operate with me."[26]

Townsend responded briefly and to the point that he was "surprised and pained" by Carnegie's angry eloquence, believed his language had been "unwarranted," and begged him to "withdraw such offensive expressions" so that they could rationally discuss their differences. Carnegie backed off and agreed to withdraw his charges, and Townsend agreed to split the new contract fifty-fifty. Neither man wanted to damage a mutually beneficial pooling agreement and enter into needless price competition.[27]

CARNEGIE'S COURTSHIP of Louise remained active through the early 1880s, but was continually interrupted—not by Louise, who never ventured far from home and seemed keen to accept his invitations, but by Carnegie, who like a hyperactive child could not remain in one place for long.

In the fall of 1882, after his spring and summer vacation in Britain and his fall retreat to the cottage at Cresson, he arranged to take a group of Scottish friends on an all-expenses paid railroad tour of the West. Once again, Louise was left behind.

The party of eighteen traveled by train to Chicago, where they boarded the "special car" of Alexander Mitchell, the Scottish expatriate president of the Milwaukee & St. Paul Railroad. "The conductor said his instructions were to go where we wished, stop and start on any train desired, and when we were done with him he was to return with his car to Milwaukee. We spent days in that car, visited St. Paul in the North, and Davenport in the West, and did not traverse one mile of line which that Scotch boy had not built." Their return route took them through Grafton, Virginia, Baltimore, Washington, D.C., Philadelphia, and then back to New York. The trip cost Carnegie more than $6,000.[28]

He returned to New York—and Louise—in mid-November 1882, having been absent since June. He had taken a bit of a risk in abandoning her for such a stretch. Louise was not married and Andrew Carnegie was not her only suitor, a fact he often joked about, perhaps to ward off his own anxiety.

"Am off tomorrow eve for Pittsburgh," he wrote on the envelope in which he enclosed his 1883 New Year's Day calling card. "Do you think you could stand an hour's drive this P.M.? I'll be over this eve if you are home. Are you to be, or are you off with some young swell?"

"My dear L.W.," read another such penciled note. "You are such a belle nowadays, one has to ask when you are at home? Tonight, or tomorrow night—when is it? . . . You were pretty at Mrs. Whitney's. Many said so— all thought so, and so did Yours, [signed] A.C."[29]

Louise, who turned twenty-five in the spring of 1882, was a bit old to be unmarried by the standards of the day, but so was Andrew, now approaching his fiftieth birthday. With each passing year, his bachelor status was becoming more and more of an anomaly. While nearly 20 percent of New York's male population aged 35–44 was unmarried, according to 1890 figures compiled by Howard Chudacoff, the percentage of bachelors in Andrew's age cohort, 45–64, was just half that.[30]

Louise and Andrew had been seeing one another for more than two years, but there was still no sign from Andrew that he might be considering marriage. All around her, Louise's friends were getting engaged or married. From London, that June, Carnegie wrote to tell Louise that he had met her friend, "Miss Taylor," on the ship crossing the Atlantic and that she had "promised to ride with me in New York. She is very nice, I think, but as she is engaged you need not think you are going to be let off in any way from your duties as my Chief Equestrienne. I don't think Engaged Ladies very desirable companions." The note, addressed, as always, "Well, My Dear Friend," was signed: "Sincerely, your friend always."[31]

Through the winter season of 1883, the two continued to see one another and write notes back and forth like teenagers. "Enjoyed the eve with Aggie and Alex," Carnegie wrote her early in 1883, after an evening spent with their mutual friends, the Kings. "Mary Clark was along. It wasn't anything like as nice as Saturday—not to be compared at all, at all! I think I'll not try another girl. No use; shall go back to you."[32]

That spring, for the fourth consecutive year since they had begun seeing one another, Andrew left New York and Louise for Britain. While he was socializing with men like Prime Minister Gladstone, *Fortnightly Review* editor John Morley, Matthew Arnold, and Herbert Spencer, Louise spent the summer at Tremper House in Phoenicia, a Catskills resort, and then in Oyster Bay, with her mother, her sister Stella, and brother Harry, now nine. Her communications with her "friend" in Europe were warmer and more intimate than ever.

"Oh, how glad your letter made me!" she wrote in July, after receiving a letter from London. "For I was really afraid this year you would forget all about writing. But you didn't forget after all, and so made a certain individual very happy. I carried it off all by myself, to the loveliest little nook in the woods, and had such a good time reading of all your gay doings. What a delightful time you must be having in the society of such congenial people! But I hope you won't get to like them too well!" Her friend was adding fame to his fortune, and though she worried that this might make her less attractive in his eyes, she was delighted for him nonetheless. "Rumors are constantly reaching us of the stir you are creating, and on this side everybody is talking about your book. . . . We are all very proud of you, and love to think that you are our friend." She was enjoying her summer in the Catskills, but missed him and their long rides on horseback.

> The drives are very fine, and I am looking forward to some nice rides, but I am afraid that will depend upon whether any nice gentlemen come here, whom I shall have confidence enough in to ask to escort me. . . . As pleasant as the summer is, the fall is pleasanter, when we are all gathered together in NY once more, and I almost hope that Scotland may not be quite so kind as usual, in order that you may hasten your return home. . . . I only received your letter four days ago, and here I am answering it right away. Am I not good? But how can I help it, when you are always so good to me? . . . Au revoir, mon ami. May all your undertaking prosper! May you make hosts of friends, but may you never forget your stay-at-home friend, too, who misses you sadly.[33]

When, two weeks later, Edwin Arnold, their favorite author, gave Carnegie the manuscript of *The Light of Asia*, Louise wrote to say that she rejoiced with him "in the possession of your treasure. How much you must prize it, and yet how much more must you value the friendship that prompted such a gift—from such a man! May I hope to have a glimpse of it some time in the Fall? . . . Need I say how glad I shall be to welcome you home once more? I think not, for you must know it already. . . . So now, Good night, my friend. . . . Hoping your voyage may be a pleasant and speedy one, and that you may return safe and sound."[34]

Carnegie returned safe and sound to New York a few weeks later, but instead of visiting Louise in Oyster Bay, he traveled to Cresson where his mother was staying. In mid-September, he returned to New York to be greeted by a "welcome home" letter from Louise: "Would that I might accompany this little note, and be in reality the first one to greet you on your return to America, but rest assured, in thought I am certainly with you. Well you see we are still at Oyster Bay, but by the time this reaches you, we shall be on our way home too. . . . It is good of you to say you will come to see me so soon; I do so hope nothing will prevent your coming. . . . Thank you so much for your nice letters—and for the many and kind thoughts you have for me. They have been a great happiness to me. But I am forgetting that I am to see you soon, or, rather, I cannot realize that it can be true. I hope you are well, and that these storms we have had have not reached you on the ocean. Au revoir, then, until we meet face to face." As a postscript, she added that she had "just this minute" received his last letter from Cresson "and its contents fill me with delight. Has your previous knowledge of me taught you no better than to imagine my friendship a 'slight and passing one.' We shall indeed see, My Friend. This past week has seemed like a year. Will Monday never come?"[35]

When the two dear friends met again, Carnegie—according to Louise's biographers—finally declared his love for Louise and his intention to marry her. She fainted. Carnegie returned by train to Cresson and sent roses. Louise telegrammed, then wrote her "dearest one" to thank him and apologize for having fainted. "I am feeling more like myself this morning . . . I am of a very nervous temperament anyway, and although perfectly strong and well, cannot stand much excitement, which accounts for my suddenly breaking down as I did the other day. I hope I did not frighten you very much. . . . I am looking nicely now, and as soon as I can get a little more used to my new happiness I shall be all right. You know they say a sudden joy affects like grief or pain—so you will bear with me, dear, for my heart, small and insignificant as it is, is yours and yours alone." The note was signed: "Very lovingly yours, Louise."[36]

Whatever had been decided between the two, their lives did not appreciably change. Margaret Carnegie, now in her seventies, was not well and required more looking after than ever. Her son was not about to introduce a new person into the household, especially one his mother did not believe he should marry. Louise and Carnegie went their own ways when they returned to New York City for the winter season. They saw each other regularly, but not much more than in previous years.

TWELVE

Mr. Spencer and Mr. Arnold, 1882–1884

WITH THE PUBLICATION of *An American Four-in-Hand in Britain*, which was well reviewed and enjoyed good sales, Carnegie moved a step closer to his goal of being as well known as a writer and intellectual as he was as a businessman. He was elected a member of the Nineteenth Century Club in early 1883. The club, founded by Courtlandt Palmer, whom Carnegie had met at Madame Botta's salon, was, the *New York Times* reported on January 10, "a new departure in polite society . . . The idea was to have a radical club, 'not too radical,'" according to Palmer, "'but just radical enough.'"

Palmer, though a professed freethinker and radical, was every inch an old New York gentleman. He held the meetings of the club in his Gramercy Park residence, "his wife receiving as if at any private *soirée,* and the guests appearing in evening dress." In a lecture later published in London, Palmer acknowledged that, in an effort "to preclude the intrusion of bores and bigots into the discussion," he invited "none but speakers of known capacity and courtesy." When his guests were seated—and the ladies escorted to their places by a special committee enlisted for this task—Palmer introduced the main speaker, who lectured for an hour. After a five-minute recess, Palmer returned to introduce the "disputants," who were given an hour to comment on the lecture. The speaker then returned for a fifteen-minute rebuttal. "At the conclusion of the formal exercises adjournment to the dining room for light refreshments became the order of the evening, and after an additional hour thus spent amid good cheer and general conversation the gathering would disperse."[1]

Palmer invited the nation's best-known men of letters to speak to his club: President Charles Eliot Norton of Harvard and the Reverend Dr. James McCosh, president of Princeton (then known as the University of New Jersey), spoke on "The Place Religions Should Have in a College"; the Reverend Noah Porter, ex-president of Yale, on "Evolution"; Dr. Oliver Wendell Holmes on "Emerson"; Henry George on "the Irish Question"; Julia Ward Howe on "Woman Suffrage"; Elizabeth Cady Stanton on "the Influence of Christianity upon Womanhood"; and Thomas Wentworth Higginson on "The Aristocracy of the Dollar." It was during this last address that Carnegie made his debut as a speaker, having been invited by Palmer to be one of the disputants. "This was," Carnegie recalled in his *Autobiography*, "my introduction to a New York audience."[2]

With the self-assurance of a man born into his wealth, Higginson had spent an hour criticizing the new "aristocracy of the dollar" for its poor manners, selfishness, and lack of self-respect. Carnegie, who, with the evening's other disputants, had been given a copy of the lecture in advance, turned his attention to the "aristocracy of birth," which Higginson appeared to hold as his ideal. The Old World's kings, princes, dukes, and lords, he explained with a barbed humor that would have made his Scottish uncles proud, had never been known for their manners, intelligence, fecundity, or good looks. "Let any visitor see the House of Lords when it is filled, which will only be for one of two reasons, either when the lords can, in the character of national legislators, legislate for themselves, or when they can reject a measure beneficial to the masses. Upon such an occasion one would really think, as he watches the peers pass, or rather hobble in, that every reformatory, asylum, or home for incurables in Britain, had been asked to send up to Westminster fair specimens of its inmates. The peers are not a fine-looking body of men."[3]

As for the United States, Carnegie denied the existence of any such thing as an "aristocracy of the dollar." In no American city, certainly not Boston, Philadelphia, or New York, did men of wealth "hold front rank in the circles of our recognized best." If there was an American aristocracy, Carnegie asserted, it was an "aristocracy of intellect," not "an aristocracy of the dollar."[4]

Carnegie thought so much of his response to Higginson that he had it privately printed in pamphlet form, with the subtitle "My First Speech in New York Somewhere in the Early Eighties." This was the beginning of a lifelong practice of spending his own money to have his speeches and articles reprinted in pamphlet form.

Having proved himself a witty and provocative respondent, Carnegie was invited back several times. When, early in 1884, the subject of debate at the club was "the objects and limits of science," he took the rather radical position—even for this group—of dismissing religion as playing any role in the governance of mankind. His remarks were cited in the February 21 *New York Times* and picked up by several other papers.

Simultaneously with making his mark in New York, Carnegie was forging his way into London's intellectual circles. In February 1882, he made his debut in print in the most prestigious of English journals, the *Fortnightly Review,* founded in 1865 by Anthony Trollope, and edited from 1866 on by John Morley. On returning to New York from his 1881 coaching trip in England, a British friend suggested he write an "account [of] what your dozen of Americans guests thought of us." His observations were precisely of the sort that John Morley was delighted to publish in the *Fortnightly Review,* which had, under his leadership, become the leading Liberal journal of opinion. His friends, Carnegie observed, had been astounded to discover that the British "people were in a ferment, satisfied with nothing, but agitating for drastic changes in almost every institution." The only solution to the dissatisfaction in Britain was thoroughgoing reform of church, state, and society, precisely what Liberals like Morley were already agitating for.[5]

Morley, though the same age and height as Carnegie, had little else in common with him other than politics. He was intrigued, nonetheless, by the Scottish American millionaire. The two men began at once a conversation that would last the rest of Carnegie's life. Morley introduced him round London's literary and Liberal circles. It was through Morley's good graces that Carnegie, in 1882, met both Prime Minister Gladstone and the man who would become his intellectual hero, Herbert Spencer.

Spencer was, at the time, the English-speaking world's best-known and best-selling philosopher. He published his first book, *Social Statics,* in 1851, and from that point on issued a steady stream of closely argued but remarkably readable articles and books on what he called his "synthetic philosophy," an all-encompassing philosophical system, based loosely on recent findings in biology and psychology. By the 1860s, Spencer's work had begun appearing in the United States, due largely to the efforts of his chief disciple, Edward Livingston Youmans. The American philosopher and historian John Fiske read Spencer for the first time in 1862 while a student at Harvard. "My soul is on fire," he wrote to his mother. Carl Schurz, the future senator from Ohio, read Spencer's *Social Statics* in his Civil War tent "by the light of a tallow-candle." The *Atlantic Monthly*, in 1864, proclaimed Spencer "a power in the world," and especially in America, "for here sooner than elsewhere the mass feel as utility what a few recognize as truth."[6]

"In the three decades after the Civil War," Richard Hofstadter has written, "it was impossible to be active in any field of intellectual work without mastering Spencer." Even Mrs. Lightfoot Lee, the heroine of Henry Adams's novel *Democracy* (1880), had talked of him "for an entire evening with a very literary transcendental commission-merchant."[7]

Spencer was tall, gaunt, and balding. He looked a bit like a villain from a Dickens novel—and acted like one. He had little use for well-wishers, critics, journalists, waiters, cabmen, or new acquaintances; he seldom engaged in conversation since he believed talk "fatigued him and diminished his power for work"; he dined alone, when possible, and when not possible, put on specially designed ear-pads to blot out frivolous chatter; he seldom made jokes, but had opinions to offer on everything.[8]

Spencer's friends and admirers invited him to visit the United States, but the English philosopher had, with age, grown increasingly insomniac, hypochondriacal, and resistant to any change that might interfere with his work. Having successfully survived a trip to Egypt the year before and wanting very much to see North America before he died, which he considered a possibility at any moment, he finally consented to tour the continent in the summer of 1882. His oldest friend, Edward Lott, agreed to come along and serve as a "buffer" between him and anyone who dared to approach unbidden. "What he dreaded most," according to his private secretary and later biographer, David Duncan, "was 'the bother of having to see so many people.'" He agreed to attend a public dinner in his honor to be held in New York City, but only because, as he wrote Youmans, "to decline would be awkward; and as I propose to limit myself a good deal in the way of social intercourse and receptions, I must, I conclude, yield to some arrangement which shall replace more detailed entertainments."[9]

The ocean passage was uneventful, except that having secured a berth in the middle of the ship, he was kept awake all night "by the shrieks of the fog-whistle, which was just over my head." He was clearly in no mood to converse with voluble Scottish-born American industrialists; but Carnegie, having determined to make his acquaintance, was irresistible. He had booked passage on Spencer's ship, and approached the philosopher while they were on the tender at Liverpool that ferried passengers and provisions to the ocean liner and handed him a letter of introduction from John Morley. He then arranged to be seated at Spencer's table, where, Spencer recalled in his autobiography, he "pressed me to visit him at Cresson, a place on the Alleghenies . . . used as a summer refuge by over-heated Americans. I eventually yielded to the pressure."[10]

Spencer, who wrote in some detail about his visit to America, had little to say of his trip to Pittsburgh and Cresson, and none of it positive. Though he had resolved to stop only at hotels so as to avoid having to engage in unnecessary conversation and take too many meals with his hosts, "the repulsiveness of Pittsburgh" induced him to accept an invitation to stay overnight with Thomas Carnegie in Homewood. After a whirlwind tour of the Edgar Thomson steel mill, he and Mr. Lott were transported east to Cresson "by special carriage, which to my great comfort contained a sleeping compartment." They stayed only a day at Carnegie's cottage before setting out on their travels again, this time to Harrisburg, which Spencer found a "not-very-interesting town," then to Washington, where "the waiters, negro and half-caste, were considerably surprised by my disregard of their dictations" and he was considerably annoyed at the "passion of the Americans for iced water." Then on to Baltimore, where he spent five days at the Montebello residence of John Garrett, the president of the B&O.[11]

The highlight of the tour, at least for Spencer's American admirers, was the special dinner held in his honor at Delmonico's in New York, which was reported at length in the next morning's newspapers. Spencer, obsessed with the fear that he might break down entirely, begged William M. Evarts, the former secretary of state who presided over the event and sat next to him, "to limit his conversation with me as much as possible, and to expect very meager responses."[12]

The guests who honored Spencer that evening included prominent men from business, politics, the arts, and the academy. Carnegie, though he was not one of the official organizers, attended, as did journalists E. L. Godkin and Charles A. Dana; the industrialist Cyrus Field; current and future U.S. senators Carl Schurz, Chauncey Depew, and Elihu Root; New York City Mayor—and former iron maker—Abram Hewitt; Congressman Perry Belmont; Albert Bierstadt, the artist; Charles Francis Adams, Henry's father and former ambassador to Great Britain; sociologists William Graham Sumner and Lester Ward; and two of the country's most influential preachers, Henry Ward Beecher and Lyman Abbott.[13]

Spencer's trip marks the beginning of Carnegie's infatuation or obsession with the English philosopher. For the rest of Spencer's life (despite his fears, he would live to the ripe old age of eighty-three), Carnegie referred to him in his writings and lectures, sought him out when he visited London, and showered him with letters and gifts, including a grand piano. Spencer replied to every letter and every gift, but insisted that he was too busy or too ill for a visit. On January 11, 1883, in response to a letter from Carnegie hoping to see him that summer in London, Spencer wrote, almost warmly, that he indeed recalled Mr. Carnegie. Although he encouraged Carnegie to "look me up forthwith after your arrival," he held out only a small hope that they might get together. "A journey to Queen's Gardens [Spencer's home] may prove bootless; for I am very apt to be out. If in the morning I am able to work, I am away from the house at my study; and in the afternoon I usually go into town. But the Athenaeum Club is my constant haunt in the later part of the day; and you are almost certain to find me there after 4 or 5 o'clock."[14]

A year later, Carnegie wrote again: "The Cable tells us you are about to sail for Australia—That this is necessary for your recovery. This is sad news for me and I must write and express my feelings—I have lived much with you since we met—Have read your works and have that satisfaction in life which comes only from the informed mind.—In one great department I have learnt from you my teacher. I rejoice that you are about to take a long sea voyage but do go on a sailing ship—I wish I were to be your Companion. . . . Perhaps you will come home this way—How many would be glad if you did so. . . . It fills the mouth to say Bon Voyage, My Master, I wish we shall meet ere long." Above the signature and salutation, Carnegie had written: "to you reverence."[15]

Carnegie was only slightly exaggerating when he claimed in the *Autobiography* that it was only with Spencer's help that he finally "got rid of theology and the supernatural [and] found the truth of evolution." Having discarded the basic tenets of Calvinist orthodoxy—the doctrines of original sin and infant damnation—and then left the Swedenborgians, he tried hard as a young man to hold on to some kernel of religious belief. He wanted desperately to believe that there was some moral order to the universe, but refused to put his faith in a divine being whose existence and omnipotence he found entirely unreasonable. "At this period of my life I was all at sea. No creed, no system, reached me. All was chaos. I had outgrown the old and had found no substitute." Why did some individuals and societies succeed, while others failed? Was there any connection between good deeds on earth, material rewards, and eternal salvation? Was there an afterlife? The law of evolution provided a systematic way of answering such questions and explaining, without recourse to the supernatural, the "sublime truth of the upward ascent of man." It provided a scientific basis for a belief in human progress.[16]

Spencer's synthetic philosophy was founded on the proposition that continuous motion and change were constants in nature and history. Molecules evolved into complex organisms; nebulae into planets; microscopic intrauterine germs into human bodies; families into tribes; and tribes into complex societies. With increasing heterogeneity came enhanced integration. Complex organisms succeeded simple ones, disorganization and anarchy gave way to organization and coordination. Primitive societies were, for example, ruled haphazardly by solitary chieftains; advanced civilized societies were coordinated more effectively by a series "of regulative classes—governmental, administrative, military, ecclesiastical, legal, etc." The apogee of human achievement was industrial society, with its complex division of labor among individuals, towns, regions, nations, and continents; its "commercial process by which a million's worth of commodities is distributed daily"; its varieties of multiform national governments, each "aided by its subordinate local governments and their officers, down to the police in the streets."[17]

What counted most for Carnegie was not simply that Spencer had decreed that evolutionary progress was inevitable and industrial society an improvement on its forbears, but that this progress was moral as well as material. There was, for Spencer, a discernable order to the course of human events and the structure of human societies, study of which would reveal the existence of moral laws that were "like the other laws of the universe—sure, inflexible, ever active, and having no exceptions." Societies that obeyed these moral laws would prosper; those that disregarded them were doomed to failure. The social edifice that lacks "*rectitude* in its component parts [and] is not built on *upright* principles . . . will assuredly tumble to pieces. As well might we seek to light a fire with ice, feed cattle on stones, hang our hats on cobwebs, or otherwise disregard the physical laws of the world, as go contrary to its equally imperative ethical laws."

"The enslavement of the negroes serves for a good example." Acting from the precepts of a political economy that did not coincide with moral laws, the slave masters had sought for themselves "a mine of wealth" by replacing free with slave labor. "Their golden visions have been far from realized however. Slave countries are comparatively poverty-stricken all over the world. . . . West-Indian history has been a history of distress and complainings. . . . The southern states of America are far behind their northern neighbors in prosperity."[18]

The natural world and human society were governed by "beneficent necessity." Turning Thomas Malthus on his head even more radically than Darwin would seven years later, Spencer argued in 1852 that population growth led not to accelerating destitution, but to "greater production of the necessities of life." "From the beginning pressure of population has been the proximate cause of progress. . . . It forced men into the social state; made social organization inevitable; and had developed the social sentiments . . . it is daily pressing us into closer contact and more mutually dependent relationships."[19]

As societies grow in size, they become more heterogeneous, more differentiated, more specialized, more social, more cooperative, more integrated, and ever more capable of adapting to new situations.

> Progress, therefore, is not an accident, but a necessity. Instead of civilization being artificial, it is a part of nature; all of a piece with the development of the embryo or the unfolding of a flower. . . . As surely as the same creature assumes the different forms of cart-house and race-horse, according as its habits demand strength or speed; as surely as a blacksmith's arm grows large, and the skin of a labourer's hand thick . . . so surely must the human faculties be moulded into complete fitness for the social state; so surely must the things we call evil and immorality disappear; so surely must man become perfect.[20]

Spencer offered Carnegie and his generation an intellectual foundation for their optimism, their sense that history was a record of forward progress, by arguing that material progress went hand-in-hand with moral progress, that industrialization was a higher state of civilization than that which had preceded it, and that the future would be even rosier than the present. In his *Autobiography*, Carnegie recalled that after reading Spencer, "'All is well since all grows better' became my motto, my true source of comfort. Man was not created with an instinct for his own degradation, but from the lower he had risen to the higher forms. Nor is there any conceivable end to his march to perfection. His face is turned to the light; he stands in the sun and looks upward." Henry Adams, born in February 1838 a little more than two years after Carnegie, spoke for their generation when he wrote in his own autobiography, that "for the young men whose lives were cast in the generation between 1867 and 1900, Law should be Evolution from lower to higher, aggregation of the atom in the mass, concentration of multiplicity in unity, compulsion of anarchy in order."[21]

Whether they read Spencer for themselves, as Carnegie had, or absorbed his teachings secondhand, his evolutionary philosophy provided the Gilded Age multimillionaires with a framework for rationalizing and justifying their outsized material success. In the Spencerian universe, Carnegie and his fellow millionaires were agents of progress who were contributing to the forward march of history into the industrial epoch. Carnegie was not exaggerating when he proclaimed himself a disciple of Spencer and referred to him, in almost idolatrous terms, as his master, his teacher, one of "our greatest benefactors," and the "great thinker of our age."[22]

SPENCER WAS THE prize specimen in Carnegie's collection of writers and intellectuals. His next conquest, Matthew Arnold, was every bit as impressive. Carnegie met Arnold at a June 1883 dinner party in London given by Dolly Thompson, the wife of the owner of the *Pall Mall Gazette*, the evening newspaper that John Morley had edited since leaving the *Fortnightly Review* the year before. Carnegie invited Arnold to dine with him. Arnold graciously accepted: "Would Tuesday in next week suit you? If so, I will dine with you on that day with great pleasure, whether in hotel, palace, or cottage."[23]

If Herbert Spencer was the English-speaking world's greatest living philosopher, Matthew Arnold was surely its best-known man of letters. Poet, cultural critic, social commentator, and, most recently, the author of several books on the Bible and modern Protestantism, Arnold had become so well known that, when he finally consented to undertake a lecture tour of the United States, he was represented by Richard D'Oyly Carte, Gilbert and Sullivan's producer and the manager-owner of the Savoy Theatre, and Major James B. Pond, America's premier lecture agent and promoter.

When Carnegie discovered that Arnold was contemplating a lecture tour of the States, largely to pay off debts incurred in sending his son to Oxford (from which he was asked to leave without a degree) and to Australia (where he failed to make his fortune), he volunteered his services as host. His offer was accepted.[24]

In late October 1883, Arnold, with his wife and daughter, arrived in New York. "We expected a two or three hours wait with our baggage, but Mr. Carnegie met us with his Secretary, took all trouble off our hands, and bore us away up to the Windsor Hotel in a carriage," Arnold wrote his sister. He was something of a celebrity in London, but never envisaged the fanfare with which he was greeted in New York. "The blaring publicity of this place is beyond all that I have an idea of," he wrote on arrival. "My managers are anxious I should not refuse to see people—the press people above all . . . but there are so many of them that from 8½ a.m. to 10 p.m. the knocking at one's door and the bringing in of cards is incessant. . . . The interviewers have made life terrible." It would have been far worse had not Carnegie had his secretary reserve "a parlor and two bed rooms" for the Arnolds at the Windsor Hotel and arrange for them to be seated at his table for dinner.[25]

Carnegie, having invited the Arnolds to be his guests at the Windsor, intended to make the most of their presence. On October 30, Andrew and his mother hosted a reception for them at the Windsor Hotel. When Mrs. Youmans, whom Carnegie had met with her husband during Spencer's tour, asked how she should dress for the affair, she was told by his secretary that "Mr. Carnegie says he supposes most of the guests will come in full dress on Saturday evening, but thinks the ladies know best."[26]

The *New York Times,* on October 28, listed among the guests whom Mr. Carnegie had presented to Mr. Arnold, E. L. Godkin, editor of *The Nation* and the *Evening Post;* the industrialist Cyrus Field; Mr. and Mrs. August Belmont; Leopold Damrosch, conductor of the Oratorio Society and New York Symphony Society; and a smattering of churchmen, including Rabbi Gottheil of Temple Emmanuel and the Hindu reformer, Babu

Protap Chundr Mozoomdar. The Astors and the Vanderbilts had been invited but stayed away. They did not, in general, patronize newly arrived industrialists who lived in hotels.[27]

On November 4, the week after the event, the *New York Times* ran a second item, a satire about a "'reception' at a public house by a rich ironmaster."

"'Who the deuce is Mr. Andrew Carnegie?' asked a character named Mahlstick,* disdainfully, holding out at arm's length an invitation card. 'And why should he invite me to meet Matthew Arnold, whom he possibly does not know? And if I go to meet, to be introduced to, Mr. Matthew Arnold, who is to introduce me to Andrew Carnegie?'"

"In this free-and-easy land it is the privilege of every man to consider himself acquainted with every other man whose acquaintance is temporarily desirable," the *Times* columnist answered. "If people who are in society or who hope to be—with money—invite nobody to their parties but those whom they know they might fare hardly at times."

Three days later, Andrew and his mother accompanied the Arnolds to Chickering Hall for Arnold's first lecture. The 1,250-seat theater had been completely sold out—at one dollar a ticket. Unfortunately, Arnold, who had never before lectured to so many in so large a hall, was inaudible beyond the first few rows. In this age before electricity, microphones, or amplification of any sort, it took a special kind of voice—and training—to project into a large auditorium. The only sounds echoing through Chickering Hall that evening were audience members screaming at Arnold to speak louder and, when he did not, making their way to the exit. When the Arnolds and Carnegies returned to their hotel, Andrew warned his friend that to succeed as a lecturer he had to place himself under the tutelage of an elocutionist.[28]

From this point on, the Arnolds and the Carnegies would remain great friends, and visit one another whenever they had the chance. Carnegie's attraction to Arnold was genuine—and vice versa. Arnold, the Oxford-educated son of the headmaster of Rugby, like Carnegie, the unschooled son of a Dunfermline handloom weaver, had an omnivorous intellectual curiosity, and was a brilliant conversationalist. Both men respected American

---

*The name was borrowed from the collapsible cane that artists used as a walking stick when strolling the city's streets and to prop up their hands while painting.

political institutions; feared and abhorred the Philistine insularity of the English-speaking middle classes; were sympathetic to and curious about non-Western cultures and religions; regarded much of organized religion as "clap-trap"; disdained British aristocracy for its inbred dullness; adored the poetry of Robert Burns; and believed fervently that literature, art, and culture "mattered," especially in "the mechanical and material civilization" they inhabited. For Carnegie, who sought to improve his mind wherever he might be, Arnold was the ideal companion, teacher, and friend. Carnegie would deeply grieve the premature death of his "dear, good and great friend" in 1888.[29]

THIRTEEN

"The Star-spangled Scotchman," 1884

CARNEGIE AND Louise Whitfield had, by the fall of 1883, entered into an informal engagement. They were committed to marriage, but had set no date and they had made no announcements. Carnegie was waiting for his mother to regain her health so that he could break the news of his engagement to her, or conversely, though he would not have put it so bluntly, he was waiting for her to die. She did neither and the engagement remained in a strange sort of limbo.

Carnegie tried to include Louise in his activities, but because their engagement remained secret, there were limits placed on the frequency with which they could meet. Louise remained at Carnegie's mercy, never knowing when or if he was going to call, or where he would be the following week. She was not invited to the reception for Matthew Arnold, though she did, with her mother, hear one of his New York lectures. She was excluded from the Nineteenth Century Club meetings until Carnegie in April 1884 asked his secretary to request that Courtlandt Palmer add her name to the guest list. As single women did not go out, even to lectures, by themselves—and as he could not escort Louise without inviting talk—he asked that the Reverend and Mrs. Eaton also be added to the list so that they could accompany Louise to meetings.[1]

While the relationship with Louise remained chaste and, except when they were on horseback, chaperoned, there were other women whom Carnegie visited unchaperoned. On March 30, 1883, to cite but one example, he received a specially delivered message at the Windsor from Charles Mackie, his private secretary—"Telegram from Everett House signed

Carrie reads: 'please call this afternoon between four and six, am alone.'" Four months later, in August 1883, a Miss Vincent wrote asking Mackie to call on her at once. Mackie, who may or may not have visited her as she requested, responded a week later that he was "unable to assist you in any way and . . . you will therefore have to wait till Mr. Carnegie's return. As requested, I will treat your letter as confidential." We unfortunately don't know who either Carrie or Miss Vincent were, but the way the messages from them were handled suggests that there was something about the relationships that had to remain hidden.[2]

The months following their informal engagement were not easy ones for Louise or Andrew. Each, it appeared, harbored significant doubts about marriage. The fragments from Louise's diary that are cited by her authorized biographers demonstrate her mounting ambivalence about leaving her mother and younger siblings. Had Carnegie been willing to settle down at once, Louise's decision might have been an easier one. But Carnegie showed no inclination, even at age fifty, to give up his wandering ways or spend more than half the year in New York. Louise, for her part, was not sure she wanted to be away from her family for extended periods.

In late April 1884, as Carnegie prepared to leave as usual for England and Scotland for the warm weather months, Louise "took the last sad step" and broke off their engagement. They would continue to see one another in New York City, and, when separated by an ocean, to correspond. But talk of marriage was put on hold, indefinitely, perhaps permanently.

Carnegie wrote Louise from Britain that June—as he did each June—describing in detail his adventures, expressing his hope that her summer was going to turn out to be "a happy one," and giving her avuncular advice about good literature. He was off on yet another coaching trip, this one studded with celebrities, as he gleefully informed her. William Black, who had acquired a transatlantic reputation for his widely read fictional account of a coaching journey, was along for the ride, as was Matthew Arnold and his daughters, and "Mr. Edwin A. Abbey, who illustrates for *Harper's*. How delightful it all has been!" The prime minister was unable to join them, but had sent along a son and daughter instead. Edwin Arnold, Louise and Andrew's favorite author, joined the party for part of the way, as did John Champlin, his editor (who would publish his own book-length account of the coaching tour), and Samuel Storey, a radical MP.[3]

The tour was a grand success, Carnegie, "bronzed and tanned by wind and weather," enthusiastically reported in an interview with the *Pall Mall Gazette* on his return to London. "'If I were not an ironmaster, I would be a gypsy,' said Mr. Carnegie, although he added *sotto voce* that 'a small reserve at one's bankers' would be pleasant to fall back upon.'"[4]

The coaching party included "three American girls—a very pretty colony they formed: one of them with a picturesque hat, whose sweep of brim and feathers ferociously set the wrong way formed one of the most conspicuous objects in our subsequent travels." Black did not mention Carnegie by name in his *Harper's New Monthly Magazine* article, but described his host as "a shrewd and able Scotchman, who went to America a good many years ago, and achieved a fair enough competence there, which he modestly attributes, not to his own brains and business capacity, but to the excellence of republican institutions, toward which he is proportionately and warmly grateful. . . . The Star-spangled Scotchman, as we have got to calling him, is abundant and even eager with all his information, and hath a pretty gift of eloquence, moreover; so that through the agency of his eulogies and paeans and grateful hymns of praise we have come to construct in our imagination a very fine America indeed—a land of purity and peace, of sweetness and light, of incorruptibility and harmonious aim, where the office-seeker is not, and the Wall Street lion and lamb lie down together, and Tammany Hall is but a dream of the envious foreigner."[5]

Carnegie was, truth be told, becoming a bit insufferable on the subject of the backwardness of British social and political institutions. Unable to remain on the sidelines in what he considered to be the ongoing battle between feudalism and democracy in Great Britain, he had, the year before, put his money where his mouth had always been and invested in a newspaper syndicate with the North Country radical MP, journalist, and publisher Samuel Storey. It had always been Carnegie's dream to own a newspaper—he had mentioned it in his 1868 note to himself. Now, with Storey's assistance, he had become part owner of nearly twenty of them, an informal chain extending from Newcastle, Storey's constituency, through Birmingham, the center of radical agitation, to London.

Carnegie had entered the newspaper business because he thought he could make money at the same time as he promoted the republican cause in Britain. His notion was that by importing a bit of American dazzle to the still rather staid English weekly, he could increase circulation, reduce costs, and attract a new constituency of workingmen to his newspapers— and the "radical" program.

In aligning himself with Storey, Carnegie had taken a perch on the far left wing of the Liberal Party. The centerpiece of the radical agenda in Britain in 1883 was the extension of the franchise. The Reform Act of 1867 had more than doubled the electorate and given the vote to male heads of households, but it had not extended the vote to all men, regardless of income, status in the household, or location. Carnegie hoped that this issue would be the central focus of his weeklies. "I believe in the triumph of the Radical element," he wrote Storey on January 3, 1883, at the beginning of their partnership. "The extended franchise is the lever we need to accomplish our ends, ergo:—Go for that; other things can wait. I hope you are to be found in the front charging solidly for that one thing—extended franchise." Though he was not a newspaper man and acknowledged as much, Carnegie offered suggestions on every aspect of the business. The London *Echo,* their prize possession, was, he feared, "not well printed. Seems to me that white paper would eventually make it more popular. Nothing should be omitted to give it circulation." Carnegie was convinced that success was assured. He planned, in fact, to shift his full attention from steel to newspapers, as soon as he could. "I am going out of business," he confessed to Samuel Storey, "but it takes a little more time than I bargained for—that's all. Then I want more papers, so look about you for another at Portsmouth. I'll have ready cash some day you know!"[6]

As might have been expected, the entry of a Scottish-American ironmaster into the still rather closed world of English journalism was not warmly received by either the newspaper or the political establishment. His and Storey's objective was, his critics charged, nothing more than a "gigantic conspiracy to 'nobble' the press." (The term was usually applied to racehorses. To nobble a racehorse was to drug it; the word also referred to stealing, swindling, and cheating.) Readers of the Storey-Carnegie papers were warned that they were not going to get honest Liberal opinions, but rather "a mere reprint of instruction from headquarters in Birmingham or London, or from the writing-room of a prosperous ironmonger living in Pittsburg, Penn."[7]

To his British critics, Carnegie embodied the worst of Yankee traits. He was brash, loud, overbearing, self-righteous, and contemptuous of ancient British institutions. Having made clear his disdain for the monarchy, he had now taken to expressing his contempt for a Parliament that refused to take up the question of political reform. Asked by an American reporter who visited him at Cresson whether it was true that he "wished to stand for Parliament," he responded that he would not "care much to enter Parliament even if I were a British citizen. The press is the true source of power in Britain, as in America. The time of Parliament is consumed discussing trifling affairs. . . . Members of Parliament sit merely to carry out the plans dictated by the press, the true exponent of the wishes of the people." He could exercise more power over the course of British affairs as a press lord than as a member of Commons.[8]

Carnegie's ungentlemanly habit of speaking his mind to reporters about what he unfailingly referred to as Britain's "antiquated institutions and abuses" did not sit well even with those who agreed with his agenda. The next year, upon applying for membership in the Reform Club, he would get twenty blackballs, more than enough for rejection. "I am afraid he will be annoyed," Matthew Arnold wrote his daughter, "as an active political club, like the Reform, is just the sort of place he would enjoy."[9]

Despite Carnegie's enthusiasm and the rapidity with which he bought newspapers and tried to organize them into a syndicate, the business never took off. His Pittsburgh enterprises had succeeded because he had carefully chosen competent business partners he could trust. Samuel Storey was more an agitator than a businessman and unwilling to dedicate himself to presiding over Carnegie's newspaper trust. (He was also the only Carnegie partner who was a tall man. All the rest of them—Phipps, Tom Carnegie, Frick—were almost as small as he was.) Without a Phipps or Captain Jones or Tom to watch over it, Carnegie's newspaper venture never had a chance. By 1885, he was ready to declare the experiment a failure and sell his shares in the business.

His British critics had charged that he had become a press baron because he intended to enter British politics. And, indeed, he had begun to think along these lines. He came by such aspirations naturally: his uncles Morrison had been successful local politicians. Why should he not follow in their footsteps?

Throughout the early 1880s, he made contacts and formed friendships with leading Liberals, including the party's grand old man, William Ewarts Gladstone, and Lord Rosebery, the dashing, rich, and eloquent young Scottish lord whom everyone was sure would one day ascend to the prime minister's office. Carnegie's need to be always in the company of the wise and powerful was overwhelming. He cared little for the size of a man's pocketbook, much more for the quality of his mind and the extent of his political influence. He was drawn to Rosebery, as he had been to Morley and would be to Gladstone, because he was both learned and influential. Rosebery's family estates were in Edinburgh and Carnegie invited him to attend the opening of his Dunfermline library, which Rosebery declined, with regret. In August 1883, learning that Rosebery planned to visit America, he offered his services as tour guide, as he had to Herbert Spencer and Matthew Arnold.

> The question is how can I be of service to you and lady Rosebery upon the other side. I do not know your plans, but if you can give me a week or so of your time, I should like to take a special [private railway] car and show Pennsylvania to you. Eastern Pennsylvania you have the . . . anthracite deposits and colleries—our own Western Pennsylvania, the natural oil wells, our iron, Coal, Steel Rail mills and at Pittsburgh the dirtiest place on earth. I think you and Lady Rosebery could really spend a novel week in the [private railway] car, we take a cook . . . and can either sleep in it, or go to Hotels when there are to be had. If you know how great the pleasure would be to me if I can give you a pleasure. One thing I should guarantee to keep you to yourselves and not bore you with uninteresting people. If we kept to the car we should avoid all occasion for Company.

At the end of their Pennsylvania tour, Carnegie hoped Lord and Lady Rosebery would accompany him to Cresson, where he would put them up at the nearby Mountain House.[10]

They accepted his invitation. Their tour was a success. Rosebery and Carnegie got along so famously that Rosebery offered to put Carnegie up for the seat in Commons from Edinburgh. Carnegie was intrigued, but had to say no. "Referring to the Edinburgh idea," he wrote Rosebery, "much as this stirs my ambition I must still decide that it will not do to enter upon it until I see more clearly the result of matters in America. I may have to give attention to affairs for a year, and besides all this you know I must be governed by my mother's condition—she has no one but me. Please let matters rest for the present—I am greatly indebted for the interest you take in the matter, and perhaps ere the necessity arises for deciding I may be free to act."[11]

Six months later, when he was again invited to stand for Commons from Edinburgh, he responded as he had to Rosebery that, while flattered by the invitation, he was "compelled . . . to say, that as at present situated, I am not yet prepared to enter public life and devote myself wholly to the advocacy, and support of those radical reforms which I have so much at heart. If, however, it ever happens, in some future day, that, after a full and frank exposition of my political convictions, before the advanced Liberals, they select me as their stand-bearer [sic], and elect me, then I shall have found the one position which I would not exchange for any other upon Earth, for believe me, I should much rather rise, in the House of Commons, to speak in Edinburgh's name for some great reform than to play at 'King of Great Britain.'"[12]

It was through Morley and Rosebery that Carnegie came into closer contact with Prime Minister Gladstone. Carnegie, given to a sort of hero worship, was smitten at their first meeting.

No two men could have been more dissimilar. Gladstone, the son of a wealthy Tory manufacturer, had been educated at Eton and Christ Church, Oxford. Carnegie, the son of an impoverished linen weaver, had ended his formal eduaction at the age of twelve. Carnegie was small, barrel-chested, with a full mane of white hair and white beard; Gladstone was tall, gaunt, bald, and clean-shaven. He was also somber, pious, a devout Christian, and an outspoken critic of Herbert Spencer. Like all Carnegie's new friends, he was an enthusiastic conversationalist who could talk at breakfast, luncheon, and far into the night on any subject. Gladstone brilliantly gave voice to Carnegie's still nascent political views. He was for Home Rule in Ireland, tolerance for religious and national minorities inside and outside Great Britain, international arbitration, and, as far as any prime minister might be, a fierce opponent of British chauvinism and militarism.

Gladstone's influence over his younger Scots-American admirer extended beyond the political realm to the ethical. Carnegie did not regard being a millionaire as a particular badge of honor, but neither had he been ashamed of his status—until, that is, he listened to Gladstone, in one of his thundering lecture sermons, excoriate what he regarded as a new and decidedly inferior species of American millionaire. In January 1885, Carnegie wrote Gladstone from the Windsor Hotel enclosing with his letter £200 for Gladstone's "two charities." He then made the rather startling confession that "after this year, I expect never to make or rather save another dollar. . . . I remember well Mr. Gladstone's words anent our American millionaires. 'The desire to hoard' (said he, shaking that finger of his)—is the lowest form of intellectual degradation." Carnegie reported to Gladstone that when he told Herbert Spencer about their exchanges, Spencer remarked that "'Mr. G. should have said "Moral" degradation, the motive is moral.' Well," Carnegie concluded, "whichever it is, I intend to avoid it."[13]

This letter was written almost four and a half years before the publication of the "Gospel of Wealth" essays, in which Carnegie pledged to give away his fortune and urged other millionaires to do the same.

The sons of fathers with resources, Gladstone, Morley, and Arnold disdained those who devoted their lives to accumulation. From this point on, Carnegie would dedicate himself, as they had done, to public service and higher literary pursuits. He would not run from the opportunity to make money, but neither would he let it absorb the larger part of his energies. On April 27, 1884, he made his first headlines as a philanthropist when he donated $50,000 for the building and equipping of teaching laboratories for medical students at Bellevue Hospital. The *New York Times* article announcing the gift singled him out as "one of those, too few in number, who, like the late Peter Cooper, desired to enjoy in their life-time the good which they do to others."

The following March, in 1885, Carnegie was the key speaker at the Bellevue Hospital Medical College graduation at the Metropolitan Opera House. "When he stepped to the front of the stage," the *New York Times* reported, "the entire graduating class rose and gave him three sonorous cheers." Carnegie's speech to the graduates was the first in a series he would give over the next several decades on similar occasions. He began by indirectly calling attention to himself in telling the graduates how fortunate they were to have been born without fortunes. Being born poor—he would emphasize in this speech and countless more to follow—was a virtue, not a deficit, as it forced the young man to be self-sufficient at an early age. "You should be grateful to a kind Providence for fathers who have not burdened you with riches. . . . By bequeathing the necessity to work the poor man leaves a richer heritage to his son than the millionaire can possibly give.

Poverty at the beginning of life is a positive blessing." He then congratulated them on their choice of profession and urged them to extend their reach from the "bodily ailments" to the "subtler realm of mind" and prepare themselves to be "the sage counselor, the confidential friend and physician to the moral and mental faculties as well as to the body."[14]

CARNEGIE had planned to spend the summer of 1884 in England and Scotland; but, worried about his mother's failing health, he returned to the United States in mid-July. "Yes, My Friend," he wrote Louise upon arriving at Cresson,

> I am upon this side and the receipt of your bright letter this morning has made me happier than anything that has occurred since my arrival here. . . . Did you see Miss Arnold [Matthew's daughter] is engaged to a New York lawyer? Her younger sister is the cleverer, but she isn't pretty. Too bad clever young ladies are rarely beautiful. There are exceptions; I think of one. I spent a night at the Windsor—walked past your home to see it all closed, but boasting a . . . new awning over the door. Not a soul in town I knew, or cared to see that night, except I did want to find you, and you were gone, too. Just as well—better, no doubt, I said, and walked back to the Hotel. I have avoided the sad point till the last. Mother is not doing well. She was better for a few days, but this week there seems to be a relapse. She hasn't been out of bed for two days, and I have the heart taken out of me whenever I fail to keep that subject out of mind. Your letter this morning gave me a respite, and I was bright and happy for a while. I hope you will write to me now and then.[15]

Their letters that summer were warm and flirtatious. A few months' separation may have convinced both that they had been hasty in ending their courtship. They tried to imagine a life together, each desirous of but reluctant to make a commitment.

"Sometimes it is the best discipline to compel one's self not to give way and write," Andrew wrote her later in the summer.

> I have been trying it. Dangerous ground, this, for me. I wish you were here, many a time. . . . We drive or ride every day. It is hot this P.M. and we four

drive at five. Why doesn't Mother write you, and why couldn't you come if she did? I ask, but this is absurd. You have your duties to keep you with your Mother always. Pity it is not different, for I'm sure you would enjoy Cresson. So sorry you are anxious to return to town. I am just the reverse. The mountains for me! Still, I must be in NY about September 1st or a little later, and that the pretty housekeeper [Louise] will be at 35 W. 48th does make the prospect less deplorable. Mother goes to Tom's September 15th from here, and I'll be alone in NY for a time. Until your circle returns, perhaps you will take pity upon me and tell me I can visit you often and be welcome. . . . [Mother] sends regards to you and says Mrs. Whitfield is so fortunate in having a good, kind capable daughter. I think so, too, and we both conclude by saying kind things about you, and I see you, oh, how clearly, in all your grace and beauty![16]

Louise and Carnegie returned to New York in the fall, not quite knowing what to expect. Their first few meetings were awkward. Instead of running into his arms and professing that she truly loved him, Louise confessed her fears about married life. Carnegie, upset with himself for anticipating that the doubts she had harbored in the spring would have vanished by the fall, was unable to comfort her as she needed to be comforted. With his own anxieties about marriage fully present, he was incapable of making hers go away. Frightened now that an attractive younger woman could never truly love a strange-looking, pear-shaped man, several inches shorter and twenty years older, he gave up and called off any attempt at reconciliation.

"Excuse me tonight. I am not in the right mood to see you," he wrote that autumn, in what he expected would be their last communication for some time.

Twice you have longed for me when absent. Twice my presence has brought you only dead sea fruit. No further proof necessary to prove we are only made to be friends. I know this now quite as well as you do, or better, and accept it, but a little more time should elapse before we start anew as friends. I shall be away and so busy next week. Upon my return I shall call and begin a friend's part. By that time you will feel a sense of relief and be free and happy. Believe me, when the man comes whom alone you should marry, your nature will thaw and burst into flame. You never can be more than friend to me, as you know. Don't try.

P.S. We cannot say the true word to each other. I refuse to believe it when you are close beside me. You can't bear to say plainly what you feel. You have been good and honest and brave enough to do so several times, but how painful to you! There is no justification for annoying you so. In my heart I understand. I write these words as the only means of conveying the truth.[17]

In a painfully eloquent letter, Louise forcefully denied that Carnegie's presence in her life had "brought me only dead sea fruit," as he had so bitterly claimed. "One thing I do know, that your presence has made me glow with life and happiness as nothing else has ever done before." Further than this she was not prepared to venture. She had tried to be honest with him and confess her apprehensions about married life, but that had gotten them nowhere, as each partner's doubts, once articulated, only reinforced the other's. She would not take the blame for their failed courtship, nor would she allow him to define their future. She had given him the opportunity to wash away her hesitancies, but he had failed.

"You tell me doubts are natural," she almost berated him,

—and the minute a doubt comes, (which was only a foolish, morbid fear arising from reading something I did not understand, and which I relied upon you to explain away), instead of letting me lean on your better understanding, you magnify the doubt and we are both landed in the ditch again.

I do not wish to marry. I am far too happy as I am to wish to enter upon the cares and responsibilities of married life without being fully assured that my choice is the right one—you know this as well as I—I only want you to know that I understand what you mean by "not trying."

Neither do I want you to be my friend on my account. I care too much for you to enjoy a friendship on unequal terms, but I have felt lately that you were more truly my friend than ever before. You have lost confidence in me—I do not wonder at it. I knew it must be so. All right, I'll bear it calmly, and maybe some day we will understand it all. At any rate it has done me good, and I am a better woman for having known you.[18]

Louise had written on a Sunday evening. The next morning, she dispatched another note to Carnegie. "I really thought you would come last evening. Not that you would painfully pull yourself into the right mood and come, but that relying on your true affection and friendship for me, it would give you pleasure to come. . . . I am contented with whatever lot falls to me—but I will not be misjudged. My nature is very slow, but facts cannot be disputed, and I don't care who knows that the serene happiness of the past two months has been caused by your presence."[19]

Louise was at her wits' end. Not only had Andrew not called, but she had learned (we don't know from whom) that he had invited the famed actress Ellen Terry, who was starring in *Much Ado About Nothing*, to go riding with him. Carnegie acknowledged as much, but insisted that the engagement had been canceled because the actress was "ill and can't drive this PM. I only asked her in a desire to get someone out of the ordinary. You had to be banished somehow. Now will you go with me at half past two, and let us have a talk? Perhaps this is all wrong, but I do so wish to talk with you."[20]

Carnegie sent the note to the Whitfield residence, via John, his valet, with the instructions to "Get Reply." Louise agreed to see him. They met that afternoon. By the time they had parted, the doubts, hesitancies, and anxieties had magically lifted, and their engagement was renewed. The next morning, Carnegie left on his business trip, sped along by the kind of letter from Louise he had always dreamed of receiving: "The peace and glory of this day surpasses anything I have ever known" Louise had written. "I have reached the haven at least—the calm after the storm. I am so glad you feel this, too. How dreadful it must have been for you before! But that time is all over now."[21]

Their letters over the next few days were near ecstatic, their relief palpable that they had now, after almost five years, vanquished all doubts and fully committed themselves to one another. Carnegie, the industrialist, man of letters, and man of the world, was almost beside himself with happiness.

"Well my Dear One," he wrote from Pittsburgh on November 21,

Is it really true that you are at last sure as the rock, that your destiny has come? I can scarcely rest in this assurance. I read and re-read it and tremble lest it isn't certain for all time. But it will come so and must be so, I say to myself; she is slow to yield, but sure and steadfast. Oh, my beloved one, I shall be so tender, so true to you and keep you from all harm, and more than that, make your life broad and deep and fruitful; only trust in me. . . .

I shall see you Monday eve, take you to my heart, and you will nestle there more closely than ever, will you not, Darling? I am so happy you are happy. I am content, rested, happy, sure, and look into the future with you as the most glorious possible. It is all right, Darling, with you in the nest at home. Your mate will ever long to fly to that home and live with you forever and ever.[22]

The next day's letter was even more joyful. He had never imagined that Louise would feel for him the same love—and physical attraction—he had always felt for her. But it had happened, at last.

You now begin to feel what I have told you. The right feeling for the Man, when it comes, drives all else into comparative insignificance. It is the mainspring of our life. I was right—you will not be cold any more, but glowing, and the heat comes from the sacred fire which comes to man and woman when the two meet and combine into one greater life. I, too, am happy, and seek silence like you. Awe stricken, somewhat, with the splendor of the picture presented to my gaze. Your lovely being! And all Mine! Just think of it! That I may prove worthy of you, Louise, is my prayer. Your favor, presence, counsel, love will do everything for me.[23]

Louise's letters were rather subdued in comparison: "Have just received your note. How good of you to think of me in your hurry! Your flying around the country in this way doesn't seem quite so dreadful to me when I know where you are, and that you have time to give me a thought. Don't rush around too rapidly. You do enough to kill two ordinary men. Remember you are mortal, and that you have given me the right to be interested in the welfare of this mortal." She was preparing herself, as best she could, for their future together, trying with all her being to banish any doubts she might still have harbored. "I have made an important discovery: there is nothing like interesting work to drive morbid fears and ghosts out of one's head. I never was made to be a fine lady and sit with folded hands and be waited on. I must work—with head and hands and heart—all three— in order to be happy, and in you I have a glorious exemplification of that fact."[24]

As committed as Louise and Andrew were to marriage, there remained two insurmountable obstacles in their way: their mothers, both elderly, both infirm, both excessively devoted to and dependent on their eldest child. Had there been only one surviving mother, she could easily have been folded into a new household. But it was impossible to imagine a situation in which the four could cohabit peacefully under the same roof. Though neither Louise nor Andrew acknowledged it in writing, both understood that their wedding plans would probably have to be put off until one or the other of the mothers passed away.

Louise told her mother about their engagement and reported back to Andrew that Mrs. Whitfield had approved. "She is so unselfish and so happy, too." Carnegie said nothing to his mother.[25]

FOURTEEN

Booms and Busts, 1883–1885

WITH SUCCESS following success at Edgar Thomson, Carnegie became more confident, as the years passed, in his and his partners' capacity to navigate the unruly seas of an ever-changing market. The ups and downs of the business cycle were inescapable facts of life in nineteenth-century America—and he accepted this. While he had no doubt but that the American economy would proceed in an upward spiral over the long term, he was well aware that cyclical depressions were always just around the corner. The wise businessman was the one who prepared for bust in boom times, and vice versa.

The laying of new track, which had proceeded at record levels in 1881 and 1882, slowed in 1883 and 1884 and hit its low for the decade in 1885. Because the business downturn, though relatively minor, came unexpectedly in the midst of a period of rapid expansion, hundreds of companies which had gone deeply into debt in the expectation that the boom would continue failed. Between 1883 and 1886, twenty-two national banks collapsed. In Pittsburgh, several of the largest iron manufacturers went bankrupt.[1]

The Pittsburgh Bessemer Steel Company, which had never quite gotten back on track after the disastrous strike of early 1882, did not survive the recession. Its owners, unable to meet their obligations to creditors, sold their Homestead plant to Carnegie and his partners. Anticipating that the market for steel rails, though strong, would have to slacken eventually, Carnegie decided to retool the Homestead mills to produce steel plates and structural shapes. He was, again, a step ahead of the business curve. Over the next seven years, from 1883 to 1890, while rail production would increase by 61.7 percent, the manufacture of structural steel products would expand by 807.8 percent.[2]

The price of steel rails continued to decline through the autumn of 1883, leading to demands by some manufacturers for drastic wage cuts. Carnegie alone, it appeared, had no intention of provoking a strike among his workers. He had established a reputation as a friend of labor and it had stood him well. While competing Pittsburgh firms had had to close down—in 1879 and 1882—because of wage disputes, he had kept his furnaces and mills running full. In 1879, the Union Iron Mills had been among the first firms to settle with the boilers and reopen their plant after a brief lockout. In 1882, Carnegie and his partners had again broken ranks with their fellow manufacturers and agreed to the wage rates demanded by the Amalgamated. "Carnegie Brothers," the *New York Times* reported on June 1, 1882, "give as a reason for signing that they are crowded with orders which must be filled at all hazards."[3]

In the long and short runs, especially when business was good, it made more sense, Carnegie and his partners had decided, to give the unions what they wanted than risk a lockout or strike and the resultant loss of orders. "We have unions in Pittsburgh," Carnegie explained to the reporter from the *New York Tribune* in a September 24, 1883, interview "but no mill east of us will tolerate them. We have always held that in this free country our men have a right to belong to any union they please. And up to the present hour our relations with the trades-unions have been satisfactory. I believe the trades-union is of great benefit to the men, and it has certainly developed many more able men. As a rule, the more intelligent labor is the less difficult it is to deal with it, if capital only asks for what is fair and just." Carnegie reported that two of the country's twelve steel mills had had to stop production because of "disputes with their men," but prophesied that such would never be the case at his works because he understood, where his competitors did not, that "labor is all that the working man has to sell, and he cannot be expected to take kindly to reductions of wages, even, when such are necessary in order that he may have any work at all. I think the wages paid at the mills on the seaboard of the United States to-day are about as low as men can be expected to take." Asked if he thought his workers would strike, Carnegie confidently predicted they would not. "The situation is much too serious. Unless the market improves our men will readily see that it is a question of work at some price or no work at all. They will therefore be ready to meet any reasonable demand made by their employers."

Carnegie, as was his practice, was basing his predictions of labor peace on very little firsthand evidence. His belief that there would not be "any trouble" at his mills and that the workers would accept a new contract with moderate wage cuts was wishful thinking. Or at least Captain Jones and Tom Carnegie believed so. "I feel that our men should readily agree to a reduction," Jones wrote Carnegie on November 2, "but for fear they might kick I feel like cautioning you to be ready for such an emergency."[4]

Tom Carnegie agreed with Jones. The situation in Pittsburgh was, he feared, grim and growing grimmer. On November 8, 1883, six weeks after his brother's interview, Tom was quoted in a front-page *New York Times* article as predicting that if prices for rails did not soon stabilize, he would "have to close his works and throw 5,000 men out of employment." Andrew disagreed, though not in print. He remained convinced that the company could ride out the storm without layoffs by running full and selling rails at whatever price the market would bear.

Carnegie, realizing that some sort of wage reduction would be necessary, called a special meeting of his partners "to consider the labor question intelligently" and asked Captain Jones to prepare, in advance of the meeting, a statement of:

1st COLUMN	Present number of men employed in the various branches
2nd	Number which Captain Jones thinks sufficient
3rd	Compensation per ton
4th	Compensation thought sufficient
5th	Saving in number of men
6th	Saving in Dollars[5]

On December 4, Carnegie took the train to Pittsburgh to meet with his partners and Jones. They agreed to reduce wage rates by 13 percent for skilled workers when the current annual contract expired on December 31. On Saturday, December 11, two weeks before Christmas, the Amalgamated lodges and the Knights of Labor assemblies convened to consider the firm's offer. "After much animated discussion," the *National Labor Tribune* reported on December 12, "the proposition was accepted." There was little sentiment for a strike just before Christmas.

The Pittsburgh newspapers, including the *National Labor Tribune*, hailed the peaceable resolution of the conflict as a hopeful sign of things to come. "It is pleasing to know that the affairs at the Edgar Thomson mill have been arranged so that the works will continue in operation," the *NLT* editorialized, "though the cut in wages is pretty heavy and about the same percentage as the cut in the price of rails. However there is a good deal gained in the method by which the amicable arrangement was reached. Time was—and it was not long ago—when wages reductions were made arbitrarily. No reason was volunteered, and none given if asked. . . . Now this is all changed. . . . The Edgar Thomson management offered to show by undoubted figures [the ones Carnegie had asked Jones to assemble], giving recent operations, that at $35 [a ton for steel rails] the old wages could not be paid. . . . All that is needed to reconcile whatever conflict there is between capital and labor is a fair article of justice on both sides." This hopeful, congratulatory editorial on the front page of the *NLT* represented the views of the Amalgamated leadership. On page four, which was devoted to news from the lodges, the local correspondent from the Edgar Thomson mills at Braddock reminded readers that the steelworks had now reduced wages five years in succession and would continue to do so—until all skilled workers joined and supported the union.

Carnegie Brothers, after reducing wages at Edgar Thomson by an average of 13 percent, moved on to reduce them at their new plant at Homestead by 17 percent. Once again, the *National Labor Tribune* refused to criticize the company. "Several conferences were held and the matter was finally adjusted in a compromise. We are glad this trouble is settled for another year. It is the best that could be done under existing circumstances," the paper editorialized on January 19, 1884.

A week later, on January 26, the *NLT* ran another positive item about Carnegie, still considering him a friend of labor. "At the reading room of the Union Iron mills . . . can be found a very interesting volume by the senior partner, Mr. Andrew Carnegie, entitled *American Four-in-Hand.* It is dedicated to the employees in the following language by the author: 'No copy of my book has gone forth from me with such heartfelt, cordial good wishes as this I send to the reading room of our own employees of the Union Iron mills. I hail this movement upon the part of our men as the dawn of a better day, when labor will share *directly* in the profits of capital.' Mr. Carnegie," the article concluded, "has always had a warm place in the hearts of his employees; and such sentiments as the above will tend to still further cement the harmony that exists between that gentleman and his workman."

Rather than castigating Carnegie for reducing wages, the editors of the *National Labor Tribune* applauded his open management style, in large part perhaps because it stood in such vivid contrast to the almost monarchical posture of other Pittsburgh manufacturers. Instead of issuing decrees, Carnegie explained the rationale behind his actions. He claimed to be in the same boat as his employees, a creature dependent on market forces, unable to resist the inexorable downward movement of prices and costs.

Carnegie did not adopt this stance because it allowed him to evade responsibility for his actions, which it did, nor because it was a handy negotiating tactic, which it was, but because it accorded with the tenets of Spencerian evolution in which he had become a true believer. His success as a businessman, he believed, depended on his adherence to the laws of the marketplace, which, because they were embedded in a larger evolutionary schema, were as moral as they were inexorable. The path of evolutionary progress he was following would be strewn with hardships and sacrifice; but these were unavoidable in the short term if mankind was going to benefit over the long term. It was unfortunate that American steelworkers had to work for declining wages; it was unfortunate, as well, that there was no safety net to catch the unemployed, the maimed, and the unemployable. But it would have been sheer folly to interfere with the workings of what Spencer had termed "beneficent necessity" by violating the laws of the marketplace and paying workers more—in wages or benefits—than was called for.

"It seems hard that an unskillfulness which with all his efforts he cannot overcome, should entail hunger upon the artisan," Herbert Spencer had written, almost as if he were advising Carnegie not to give in to the demands of employees. "It seems hard that a labourer incapacitated by sickness from competing with his stronger fellows, should have to bear the resulting privations. It seems hard that widows and orphans should be left to struggle for life or death. Nevertheless, when regarded not separately, but in connection with the interests of universal humanity, these harsh fatalities are seen to be full of the highest beneficence."[6]

Carnegie and his workers were caught in what Spencer called an "unhappy. . . . state of transition" to a new age of industrialization. Their moral responsibility was not to flee or complain about it, but to understand and adapt. "The process *must* be undergone, and the sufferings *must* be endured. No power on earth, no cunningly-devised laws of statements, no world-rectifying schemes of the humane, no communist panaceas, no reforms that men ever did broach or ever will broach, can diminish them one jot. . . . Every attempt at mitigation . . . eventuates in exacerbation of it."[7]

It is entirely possible that Carnegie would have reduced the wages of his employees had he never encountered Spencer or read *Social Statics*. He did not need Spencer to teach him how to be a capitalist. He had done quite well before he read him. Where Spencer was indispensable was in providing Carnegie with a moral imperative for his actions.

Carnegie's success as a businessman, writer, and speaker owed a great deal to his ability to associate his own interests with those of his employees and the larger public. His reading of Spencer had reinforced his growing faith that he and his fellow industrialists were agents of progress. This belief in the righteousness of his pursuits fueled his outrage at those who got in his way, which was the way of progress and prosperity.

From the mid-1880s, the chief villain was his old employer, the Pennsylvania Railroad, which controlled much of the freight traffic in and out of Pittsburgh. When, in early 1884, the Pennsylvania raised the rates for shipping coke to the Edgar Thomson works, Carnegie exploded with indignation. He would accept the increase in rates, he wrote Frank Thomson, the railroad's vice president, in a "personal and confidential letter," but only if the same increase were levied on the coke traffic of every other steel manufacturer. This was not going to happen—and he knew it. The Pennsylvania was charging him higher prices to ship his coke to Pittsburgh because there was no freight to move in the opposite direction. To cover the costs of moving empty cars back to Connellsville, it had raised the freight rates to Pittsburgh. With a stranglehold on three quarters of the coke traffic to Pittsburgh and no real competition, the Pennsylvania could charge whatever it chose to.

While Carnegie fully understood the business logic behind the Pennsylvania's "discriminatory" practices, he cried foul nonetheless and threatened to wreak havoc if the railroad did not do right by his and other Pittsburgh firms. "We do not agree to be singled out & discriminated against," he wrote Thomson. "Every manfr. in Pittsburgh & in the West will rise in indignation. It is infamous & I give you due notice you can't impose upon us." Though he added that he did not mean "this as a threatening notice," it was clearly intended as such. Carnegie warned that his next appeal would be "to Mr. Roberts [the railroad's president], failing here, we appeal to the Directors, failing here, we send a circular to every shareholder & failing here we make our appeal to the great public whose opinion no corporation these days can successfully withstand."[8]

As it became apparent that his threats were falling on deaf ears, Carnegie broadened the field of those he spoke for to include the "hundreds of poor men" who worked in western Pennsylvania's coal mines and coke furnaces and who, he claimed, awaited the decision of the railroad on rate rollbacks, "for on that depends whether they are to be permanently displaced or not." When the Pennsylvania official in charge of setting the rates requested a personal meeting, Carnegie turned him down. "It is not my business to meet you and other gentlemen you name. We want you to decide . . . now. . . . It is barbarous for you to keep these poor people idle in uncertainty."[9]

It was in vain. The Pennsylvania executives knew that Carnegie had no choice but to transport coke on their tracks and that he would pay whatever he had to for the privilege. There was no alternative route to and from southern Pennsylvania. But that was about to change. Carnegie's New York City neighbor William Henry Vanderbilt, a chief stockholder in the New York Central, had decided to invest $5 million to build a competing railroad, the South Pennsylvania, from Philadelphia to Pittsburgh, through the southern coke regions, to retaliate for what he believed was the Pennsylvania's intention to build a competing road, the West Shore, between New York City and Buffalo.[10]

In February 1894, Carnegie wrote Hamilton Twombly, a Vanderbilt in-law, and promised to raise $2 million as soon as Vanderbilt pledged his $5 million. As in the old days when he had doubled and tripled his interests by taking on multiple roles in new companies, Carnegie demanded, as a condition for his investment, that his iron and steel companies be granted a "preference" in bidding on the contracts for steel rails and iron bridges. He also requested that he be given the commission to sell the new company's bonds in Europe. "I believe I can sell the whole issue of these bonds in Europe and if you will get me the right to sell the syndicate bonds . . . I will go to London at my own expense and undertake the sale of the whole $20 million of bonds."[11]

As the railroad giants moved forward with their plans to invade their rivals' territories, investors, fearing the inevitable rate wars that would result from competition on two of the most profitable routes in the nation, sent the price of railroad stocks and bonds lower. Pierpont Morgan, with the value of his and his father Junius's sizable holdings in New York Central stock declining steadily, decided to intervene.

In July 1885, Morgan boarded his yacht, the *Corsair*, in New York Harbor, with Chauncey Depew, the president of the New York Central, alongside him, then crossed the Hudson to Jersey City to pick up George Roberts, president of the Pennsylvania Railroad, and Frank Thomson, his vice president. During a nine-hour cruise north from Jersey City to Garrison, south to Sandy Hook, then north and south again, they hammered out a deal. The Morgan interests would buy the West Shore Railroad from the Pennsylvania and a majority interest in the South Pennsylvania from Vanderbilt. They would then lease the West Shore to the New York Central and sell the South Pennsylvania to the Pennsylvania, thereby solidifying each road's monopoly in its home state.[12]

The *Corsair* compact had an immediate impact on the price of railroad securities and on Morgan's reputation as banker and power broker. The major losers were the Pittsburgh manufacturers who had invested in the South Pennsylvania Railroad, which, though almost 60 percent completed, was to be turned over to the Pennsylvania and surely scuttled.

Carnegie was in Europe at the time and not a party to the negotiations. No one quite knew where he stood or what he would do on his return. Vanderbilt had promised to sell his stock in the South Pennsylvania. Would Carnegie follow his lead? Or would he join those who were attempting to maintain the South Pennsylvania as a viable alternative to the Pennsylvania?

George Roberts sent an emissary to Tom Carnegie, who was vacationing at Cresson, with a promise to pay the Carnegies "cost and interest" if they would turn over all their stock in the South Pennsylvania. Tom contacted Andrew, who agreed to sell his stock, knowing that by his action he was sounding the death knell of the South Pennsylvania. Nothing, apparently, was put in writing. Questioned by a *New York Times* reporter in late

August as to what he was going to do, Carnegie uncharacteristically but politely refused to comment.[13]

In September, the Pennsylvania legislature, under increasing pressure from Pittsburgh manufacturers, sought and received an "antitrust" injunction preventing the Pennsylvania from buying up its potential rival's stock. Work on the South Pennsylvania had, in the meantime, ceased while the injunction wound its way through the courts.

Carnegie said nothing about his own arrangement with the Pennsylvania Railroad. It would have been impolitic, to put it mildly, for him to have made public his conclusion that, in this instance at least, it made more sense to ally himself with the Pennsylvania than to fight it. "My partners and myself have no desire to enter into a dispute with your Company," he wrote President Roberts. "On the contrary, all our interests tend to strengthen the desire which we have to co-operate harmoniously with it. I think our interests should be made mutual, therefore I prefer to stand upon the fact that your Company promised us cost and interest for our investment, if we used it so as to give you control of the South Penn. There is no legal obstacle to prevent the Company from paying us what it agreed to pay. It is simply a matter of dollars, and the PRR is quite able, and should be quite willing, to fulfill its honorable obligations to us."[14]

FIFTEEN

The "Millionaire Socialist," 1885–1886

"AMILLIONAIRE SOCIALIST. MR. ANDREW CARNEGIE PROCLAIMS IN FAVOR OF SOCIALISTIC DOCTRINES." So read the headline of the January 2, 1885 front-page story in the *New York Times*, occasioned by Carnegie's remarks "in favor of Socialism" at the December meeting of the Nineteenth Century Club. One of the guests at that meeting was John Swinton, the publisher of a rather obscure radical weekly named *Swinton's*. Swinton invited Carnegie to sit for an interview and again he spoke positively of socialism.

Carnegie's name had been appearing with some regularity in the papers, not in this context, but as a guest of honor at prominent weddings, a pallbearer at funerals, speaker at dinners given by the St. Andrew's Society and the New York City Burns Society, and a donor to cultural and medical organizations—he was on the board of directors of the Oratorio Society, the American School of Opera, and the Bellevue Hospital Medical College, and a dues-paying member of the Choral Club, the Gentlemen's Glee Club, and the Symphonic Society. Although he had not been elected to the city's most prestigious men's clubs—the Knickerbocker, the Calumet, the Metropolitan, or the New York Yacht Club—he was a member in good standing of the Republican Union League Club, once the home of bankers and merchants, which had begun accepting millionaire manufacturers as members.[1]

His pronouncements on socialism had to have come as a shock to those who knew him in New York as a wealthy Pittsburgh iron maker. It was impossible to imagine his contemporaries in business or finance—Rockefeller, Morgan, Vanderbilt, Gould—speaking out as he had. "The open confession of Socialism of Mr. Andrew Carnegie, who is at the head of the most extensive iron and steel manufacturing plants in America," the *National Labor Tribune* wrote in its lead story on January 10, 1885, "is serving for 'a nine days' wonder' for press and public."

In a series of interviews, later published in the *New York Times*, the *New York Tribune*, the *Pittsburgh Leader*, and elsewhere, Carnegie expanded on his surprisingly radical views. Asked about inherited wealth, he replied in almost the same words he would use four years later in his "Gospel of Wealth" essays. "I believe the day is coming when a man who leaves more than a million at his death, except for public uses, will be regarded as not having properly administered that for which he was only the trust." Asked about the labor situation in the iron and steel industries, he delivered what sounded very much like a rationale for a strike. "Labor is all that the working man has to sell, and he cannot be expected to take kindly to reductions of wages, even when such are necessary in order that he may have any work at all."[2]

In the January 2 interview with a *New York Times* reporter, he declared plainly that "to an evolutionist and a student of history it is plain that workingmen must rise in the future as they have in the past. Once they were all serfs, and just as sure as they have obtained the advantages they possess to-day just so sure are they to improve still further."

"But are you a Socialist?" the reporter asked.

Carnegie did not answer directly. "I believe socialism is the grandest theory ever presented, and I am sure some day it will rule the world. Then we will have obtained the millennium. . . . That is the state we are drifting into. Then men will be content to work for the general welfare and share their riches with their neighbors."

"'Are you prepared now to divide your wealth' [he] was asked, and Mr. Carnegie smiled. 'No, not at present, but I do not spend much on myself. I give away every year seven or eight times as much as I spend for personal comforts and pleasures. Working people have my full sympathy, and I always extend a helping hand. I am a workingman and in my young days worked in a cotton mill and ran an engine. . . . Speaking of the present position of the workingman, I believe co-operation is his hope.'"

The reporter, still hoping to trap Carnegie, pushed forward with what he must have hoped would be the *coup de grâce*.

"Still, Mr. Carnegie, you have closed down the Edgar Thomson Works, and some people will wonder how you can hold such principles and throw your employees into idleness." (The reporter was referring to the fact that Carnegie and his partners had closed down the mill at Christmastime and announced that they would not reopen it until the workers agreed to a substantial wage reduction.)

"The workmen are to blame for that," Carnegie answered.

"In what respect?" answered the reporter, thoroughly disoriented.

"They allow other Bessemer mills to work at less wages than we pay. There is the Pennsylvania Steel Mill at Harrisburg, where they can make and sell steel rails at $27 a ton. We cannot do it, and must close rather than manufacture rails to sell at less than cost."

Carnegie had neatly turned the situation upside down and pinned the labor difficulties in his Pittsburgh plants squarely on the shoulders of the unionized workmen who had "allowed" competing steel manufacturers to pay their men less than they were paid. He closed the interview by delivering his own *coup de grâce*, affirming his support for the steelworkers' union and challenging it to organize the competition. "I am a firm friend of the Amalgamated Association, and no one ever heard of my having trouble with them."

It was one thing to speak well of socialism before what John Swinton had described as a "select audience of full-dress millionaires of both sexes" at the Nineteenth Century Club; it was another to repeat those views and then declare oneself a "firm friend" of the Amalgamated in interviews with the daily newspapers.

Carnegie never bothered to explain what he meant by socialism. The *National Labor Tribune* in Pittsburgh claimed, on his behalf, that his ideas were not associated with "Herr [Johann] Most's destructive [anarchist] theories," but closer to the "socialism described by Fourier and his kind." Carnegie was not advocating violence or a political overthrow of the state. He was arguing instead for workers' control and ownership of workshops and factories, but in the future, not now.

Try as the editors of the *National Labor Tribune* might, neither they nor anyone else could account for the startling disconnect between what he was saying to the press in New York and what his company was doing in Pittsburgh. "The working people in and about Pittsburgh for the past two days," the *New York Times* reported on January 4, "have been trying their best to reconcile the Socialistic views expressed by Mr. Andrew Carnegie with the practices enforced in the industrial establishments in which he is the leading spirit." One possible explanation was that the demands for large wage reductions had come from his Pittsburgh partners and that Carnegie was trying to minimize or eliminate them. The *National Labor Tribune,* the voice of the Amalgamated Association in Pittsburgh, continued to give him the benefit of the doubt in this regard. "He has been sufficiently practical in his radicalism and fair in his dealings hitherto, to be entitled to have his present acts and expressions regarded generously. He has, perhaps, been as unselfish as can be expected of human nature, and decidedly much more so than wealthy men in similar positions usually are, but the workingmen who wait for relief from the unselfishness which Mr. Carnegie's socialism implies, may as well start out with intent to wait until that epoch he referred to—the millennium."[3]

The *NLT* had not been nearly as charitable to Tom Carnegie three weeks earlier when, citing a *Pittsburgh Times* article, it informed its readers that the younger Carnegie brother had joined with a group of American and European yachtsmen to build a "winter rendezvous and club . . . on Cumberland Island, Georgia. The club house will cost about $50,000" ($10 million today). The *NLT* remarked sarcastically that no one had yet ascertained "whether it is the intention of that gentleman . . . to have the men pay, through reductions in their wages, part or all of the $50,000 club house."[4]

In past years, the Amalgamated had approved contracts with provisions for wage reductions. What was different now was that Carnegie and his partners at Edgar Thomson had decided not only to cut wage rates, but to increase the workday from eight to twelve hours, thereby eliminating an entire shift of workingmen. In the heating furnaces where labor-saving machinery was going to be introduced, twelve men would be kept on to do the work formerly assigned to sixty-three; fifty-one jobs would be cut on the rail mill train; sixty-two chargers and helpers eliminated at the blooming and rail mills. In all, it was estimated that more than three hundred jobs or close to 20 percent of the total skilled workforce would be let go. "Where these men are to find other employment in times like the present is a conundrum," the *NLT* concluded on February 7, 1885.

Captain Jones, who had been charged with finding a way to reduce labor costs, was worried, as he was every year when it came time to negotiate a new agreement, that Carnegie lacked the backbone to follow through. "I fully agree with you that we must get cost down," he wrote Carnegie in December 1884. "Now stick to that & no lowering of the flag. If we can't get down to hard pan now, we are done for. . . . We certainly must cut close in our rates for next year, and all we have to do is keep a stiff upper lip."[5]

Jones recognized that while the Amalgamated might be willing to accept another round of wage rate reductions, it was not going to allow the workday to be increased to twelve hours—and a shift of workers eliminated—without a fight. There was probably no issue on which factory owners and workers were in greater disagreement than on the number of hours that should make up a working day. That issue had arisen in the 1830s and 1840s when gas lighting was introduced, making it possible to extend the workday beyond daylight hours. From the 1850s on, the eight-hour day was at the top of the list of demands made by workingmen's organizations. Shortening the workday from ten or twelve hours to eight would, it was argued, create jobs for more workers and exert upward pressure on wages. But more important, it would make it possible for workingmen to live as humans rather than as beasts of burden. "To know 'nothing but work, eat and sleep,' was to strip a man of his humanity, to make him 'little better than a horse,'" Daniel Rodgers quotes a Pennsylvania workingman as arguing. How could a man improve himself, spend time with his family, read the newspaper, become a worthy citizen, if he was forced to work twelve hours a day?[6]

Captain Jones had closed down the plant for maintenance and the installation of new machinery in mid-December of 1884, as he did most years. But this time, he waited until February to reopen it, and then only to those who agreed to work for twelve hours a day and accept a reduced rate per ton. There was talk of a strike, but no more than talk. After a six-week unpaid furlough, it would have been very difficult to organize one. The men returned to work on the company's terms. The Amalgamated leaders, having failed to protect the skilled workers from the worst of all fates—the return of the twelve-hour day—disbanded their lodges at Edgar Thomson, leaving behind a few poorly organized Knights of Labor assemblies.

With hundreds of workers displaced and those who remained working twelve-hour shifts, the *NLT* reported that the reopened mill seethed with palpable discontent. Upon returning to the job and "hearing the company's terms, one man quit at once . . . and there are dozens of other good men who will only remain until the winter is over," before looking for other work. Many of those who had wanted to strike had decided not to because they lived in houses purchased with company mortgages; they were "compelled to accept lower wages, and perhaps go to work as 'non-union' men, rather than sacrifice their little homes."[7]

The installation of the twelve-hour workday had a profound effect on the workforce, turning once proud artisans into animals, too debilitated by exhaustion to live like men. In *Out of This Furnace*, his 1941 novel about three generations of Slovak steelworkers, Thomas Bell, who grew up in Braddock, described the daily routine of one workman, Kracha, who

> worked from six to six, seven days a week, one week on day turn, one week on night. . . . At the end of each day-turn week came the long turn of twenty-four hours, when he went into the mill Sunday morning at six and worked continuously until Monday morning. Then home to wash, eat and sleep until five that afternoon, when he got up and returned to the mill to begin his night-turn week. The long turn was bad but this first night turn coming on its heels was worse. Tempers flared easily; men fought over a shovel or a look and it was fatally easy to be careless, to blunder. . . . Night-turn weeks were periods of mental fog; he went back and forth to the mill in half a daze which lasted until the end of his turn Sunday morning, when he was given twenty-four hours to himself. Sometimes he went to early mass; other times he went directly home and rolled in bed. When he rose late that afternoon there was little time to do anything. Usually he got drunk. Only whisky could pierce the shell of his weariness, warm him, make him think well of himself and his world again.[8]

The slump in steel rail demand and prices that the Carnegie brothers and Captain Jones claimed had compelled them to increase the workday to twelve hours and eliminate a shift of workers did not last forever. By the winter of 1885–86, steel rail prices were up almost 40 percent, to $35 a ton. "Mr. Andrew Carnegie, of the great rail manufacturing firm of Carnegie Brothers, of Pittsburgh . . . talked freely regarding the cheerful outlook for the coming year," the *New York Times* reported on January 4, 1886. Asked if, with the rise in steel prices, his firm was going to increase wage rates, he gleefully answered in the affirmative. "We announced an increase of 10 per cent. to our skilled workmen before they asked for it. The new scale of wages, I have just been informed by telegraph, has been accepted by all our employees in the rail mills."[9]

A master at putting the best possible spin on any story, Carnegie neglected to add that while the employees in the rail mills had accepted his offer of a pay increase, the blast furnace men had threatened to walk out if the workday was not reduced to eight hours. When Captain Jones declined to even discuss the possibility, they went out on strike. Without a steady supply of pig iron from the furnaces, production was crippled. Jones had only two choices: to accede to the furnace men's demands and return the plant to three turns, or try to replace them with scabs. He chose the latter course, a decision that immediately backfired when the men in the other departments at Edgar Thomson refused, as the *NLT* reported on January 16, "to work the metal turned out by the workmen who took the places of those on strike. The spirit of unionism is not yet dead at Braddock." Jones, still refusing to negotiate, shut down the plant, hoping that the workers would, as in previous years, return to work. But they did not. By early April, with steel prices still high and orders going unfilled, he had no choice but to reinstitute the eight-hour day.[10]

"The entire force employed at the Edgar Thomson steel works," the *NLT* reported on April 3, "went to work on the three-turn system this week. Three turns of eight hours each will now be the rule in the rolling, blooming and converting mills, and as a result, three hundred additional workmen will find full employment. So much for the glorious eight-hour system."

What is most significant about these annual skirmishes over wage reductions and the extended workday was Carnegie's absence from the field of battle. Though he consulted with and approved every step Jones took, it was the captain, not Carnegie, who was held responsible for instituting the twelve-hour day during the slump in 1885 and then refusing to negotiate a return to eight hours in the boom that followed in 1886.

The skilled workers and day laborers who had suffered through a succession of wage cuts in the mid-1880s did not have their wages restored with the return of high prices to the steel business. Only at the Keystone Bridge works, which had suffered perhaps the largest wage reduction of any Carnegie company in January 1885, did the revival of business bring with it a tangible, unexpected benefit. In October of that year, the *Pittsburgh Commercial* reported in a story picked up by the *New York Times* that

"Mr. Andrew Carnegie had made a magnificent present to the workmen at the Keystone Bridge Works. . . . It is a house and a lot worth $25,000 or $30,000 to be used as a public library and meeting place for the men, and a cash donation of $1,000 toward buying books for the library. The gift was a complete surprise to the employees." That same month, Carnegie also donated $50,000 for a new public library at Braddock to replace the workers' reading room he had earlier funded.[11]

IT WAS IN 1885 that Andrew Carnegie embarked on a new writing project in New York City. He had, so he tells us in his *Autobiography*, often marveled at "how little the best-informed foreigner, or even Briton, knew of America, and how distorted that little was. It was prodigious what these eminent Englishmen did not then know about the Republic." He intended to remedy that deficiency by providing them with an easily digestible compendium of information culled from the 1880 census and *Scribner's Statistical Atlas*—to be entitled *Triumphant Democracy*. It would be organized, analyzed, and interpreted to demonstrate the superiority of republican institutions to monarchical ones.[12]

His new book, he knew, would so clearly manifest his allegiances to the republic that he would never be able to go "home" again as anything but a dyed-in-the-wool American. His disillusion with British governance, institutions, and imperial ambitions had been exacerbated in late 1884 by Prime Minister Gladstone's decision to send the British army into the Sudan to rescue General Charles Gordon, who was under siege in Khartoum. Carnegie was adamantly opposed to such military interventions, as he made clear whenever given the opportunity. Buttressing his antiwar and anticolonial instincts with the logic of Spencerian evolution, Carnegie believed that civilization was evolving from monarchic militarism to republican pacifism. Wars—especially colonial ones—were caused by the reckless, at times savage adventurism of "strong military classes" that were bred by and supportive of monarchical institutions.[13]

In March 1885, answering a request that he stand for election to the House of Commons, this time at Birmingham, he insisted that were he to do so, he would have to denounce "as infamous" the campaign against Sudan. Burton Hendrick claims that Carnegie's differences with Gladstone and the Liberals on foreign policy, real as they were, had little to do with his ultimate decision not to take a hand in British politics. The real reason he did not stand for Parliament was that he was "not a British subject, but an American citizen."[14]

Hendrick got the story exactly backwards. Carnegie was not barred from serving in the House of Commons because he was a U.S. citizen. On the contrary, he became an American citizen in the spring of 1885 only after abandoning any thought of becoming a British MP. The timing of his application for citizenship is significant. On Thursday, May 28, 1885, just before leaving for Cresson to work on his new book, Carnegie formally filed for citizenship. It was granted, as of August 26, by the District Court of the United States for the Southern District of New York. Andrew Carnegie was at the time six months shy of his fiftieth birthday and committed now to the land of *Triumphant Democracy*.[15]

"*ROUND THE WORLD* and then *American Four-in-Hand*," Carnegie recalled in his *Autobiography*, "gave me not the slightest effort, but the preparation of *Triumphant Democracy* was altogether another matter. It required steady, laborious work. Figures had to be examined and arranged, but as I went forward the study became fascinating. For some months I seemed to have my head filled with statistics."[16]

He was assisted by James Bridge, Herbert Spencer's former assistant, who had arrived in New York in the fall of 1884. As instructed by Spencer, Bridge had presented himself—with a letter of introduction—to E. L. Youmans, Spencer's chief disciple in the New World and the editor of *Popular Science Monthly*. Youmans, who had no work for Bridge, suggested that he call on Andrew Carnegie, which he did. "Mr. Carnegie received me and my Spencer letter with a characteristic burst of friendliness," Bridge wrote later. "I was just the man he was looking for, he said; he was about to write a history of the material development of the United States during the preceding fifty years, and I was to go forthwith to Mr. John Denison Champlin, at Scribners in Broadway near Grace Church, who would take me to the Astor Library in Lafayette Place, and show me just what researches I should make for use in the forthcoming book—not yet started! It was like a fairy story, for I was to fix my own salary!"[17]

For Carnegie, who adored everything about the writing life except the solitude, the appearance of Bridge was a godsend. With Bridge at his side, the task of writing a full-length book became much more pleasant. Carnegie wrote in pencil "with a pad on his lap while seated with one leg tucked under him." When he finished a passage he was especially proud of, "he read it aloud with sparkling eyes and declamatory voice." If Bridge found fault, they debated the issue; Carnegie won most of the arguments.[18]

Abandoning Louise in New York yet again, Carnegie decamped to Cresson in the spring of 1885 with Bridge, his mother, and their entourage of servants—coachman, groom, maid, cook, and nurse for Mrs. Carnegie. The Carnegies now lived in the spacious cottage that he had built for himself and his mother a decade earlier. Carnegie had at the time complained about the price of construction to his friend George Bitner, a Pittsburgh builder. Bitner looked at the bills and reminded him that his cottage cost more than his neighbors', including the one built by the Chalfant family, because it was much larger and more ornate. "The foundation is higher and the building is five feet deeper and two feet higher." Carnegie had insisted on a "stucco cornice in all the first floor . . . two more mullion windows to the floor, with veranda and canopy, inside shutters . . . four rooms on second floor. You have more and better washstands, and your painting on first floor is all zinc finish."[19]

The wooden cottage was not a typical millionaire's summer mansion. It lacked central heating, cooking facilities, a dining room, servant's quarters, and anything resembling a ballroom, but it was comfortable and large enough for Andrew and his mother and quite grand by Cresson standards. Guests were put up in the nearby hotel.

Carnegie intended to spend the spring at Cresson, completing his book, and looking after his mother, who remained ill.

Bridge, having worked for the dour Mr. Spencer, was astounded by his new boss's wit and sparkle. The cottage was filled that spring and summer with guests whom Carnegie entertained when he was not working on his book. "Carnegie gave a flat contradiction to the silly saying that Scotchmen are devoid of humor," Bridge wrote. "With him life itself was a jest and a jewel, and every one of its many facets sparkled into ripples of light and laughter. Once while absorbed in the study of Scribners' chart of the industrial progress of the United States . . . I was startled as a book came hurtling through the air, striking the wall above my head."

"'Let's leave these statistics—these dry bones, and get out into the sunshine.'

"A moment later Carnegie had joyously herded everybody . . . on to the porch and away into the woods."

When one of Carnegie's guests—a distinguished lawyer soon to become a railway president—"essayed to climb a tree" and failed, he challenged Bridge to "attempt the feat, offering to buy me a new suit of clothes if I spoiled those I was wearing. But Carnegie vetoed the contest, declaring he could not risk the neck of his literary assistant until *Triumphant Democracy* was finished and in the printers' hands!"[20]

Carnegie and Bridge worked during the day, with time out for "rides over the mountains [and] tramps along the trails." At night, in front of the fireplace, they sang Scottish ballads, conversed, and quipped, Carnegie always leading the way with anecdotes about the famous men and women he had met, or recitations, from memory, of lines from Burns or scenes from Shakespeare, his voice changing "as he passed from one character to another." "Mr. Carnegie was the mainspring of all our activities, as he was the fascinating center of every circle he entered." If he was actively pining for Louise, it wasn't apparent to Bridge.[21]

Carnegie shared the spotlight with one person only, his mother. Although in appearance she was every bit as dour as Mr. Spencer, she too, Bridge discovered, had a rather remarkable sense of humor, a strangely majestic bearing, and a regal sense of entitlement. "The old lady," Bridge recalled, "came into the library at Cresson one day when we were both busy, and began asking trivial questions while she fumbled the papers on the table. Andrew was visibly disturbed, but he carefully concealed it from her. After a while the old lady started for the door, saying as she went: 'Well, Andree, I'll go now. I only came in to bother ye.' 'But mother,' he replied, 'you didn't succeed'; and placing his arm about her poor old shoulders, he led her gently out of the room."[22]

Carnegie had expected to remain at Cresson all summer. Margaret, he feared, was too ill to be left alone. Louise was summering with her family at the Stags Head Inn in the Catskills. They had both—she less happily than he—accepted the fact that they would be separated for at least four months. In late June, Carnegie wrote to inform Louise of a sudden change in plans. He was going to sail to England with Mr. and Mrs. Phipps and his cousin, Dod. "Mother really asked me to go," he explained to Louise. "I had not thought of doing so, but really, Mother is better . . . and really my newspaper business demands my presence for a week or two in London. Then two weeks in Scotland is all I have." He would return on August 22 "and see you very soon thereafter. I shall think of you every day and every night and hope you are so happy, but at times feeling that someone absent would be so welcome."[23]

Louise was shocked by the sudden turn of events. "It was rather of a thunderbolt," she wrote back, "but I am glad, oh, so glad for your sake, that you are going! It will do you a world of good in every way." She thanked him for sending along the copy of the address he had just delivered at the Curry Commercial College in Pittsburgh and reminded him that he had promised to send a photograph. "I do really want it so much, and I feel you are so much further away in England than at Cresson. I shall follow you every step of the way."[24]

Try as she might, Louise could not help but feel abandoned by Andrew's sudden departure, and deceived as well. He had left New York early that year so that he could care for his mother and complete his book; but at the first opportunity, he had flitted away to England and his English friends who, it appeared, were more important to him than anything else, herself included. His letters from England only confirmed her fears that he preferred the company of London society to hers.

"Here we are in the whirl," he wrote from the Metropole Hotel in London on July 23. "My parlor overlooks the Thames and the pretty gardens on the Embankment. . . . Rather lonely some mornings, at breakfast in my room alone, but I like it in some ways. So quiet (bachelordom has its advantages). Miss Mother much in such big rooms. Wish a certain young, beautiful lady were only here to brighten them up with her smiles and silvery laugh, but she is having fine hours with many admirers, no doubt, and a photograph." Totally oblivious to the effect his letter might have had on Louise, left behind in the Catskills, Carnegie went on to list all the celebrities he had visited and who had visited him, the dinners held in his honor, the great men clamoring for his attention. "Can't tell you my numerous visits, but of course, I have been at Gladstones', Lord Rosebery's, Morley's, etc. A great dinner to me at Colin Hunter's, R.A.* Miss

---

*Colin Hunter was a well-known painter; the R.A. stands for Royal Academy.

Mary Anderson [one of Britain's most renowned actresses] there . . . didn't get home last night at all, for it was early morning. I spent last Sunday with the Howards, Clapham Hall, and next I go to the Arnolds. Of course, Mr. Arnold and Herbert Spencer have been with me here to lunch, etc. . . . Made a speech at the Arbitration League yesterday before a lot of well-known people. Success! Got the cheers. Have declined to speak as a partisan several times: won't mix in public politics." He was on his way to Scotland to scout out future country homes for the two of them. "Half of Scotland said to be for sale. I am deluged with plans of Estates which I am supposed to be likely to buy. Am going to have a peep at one of two while north—but truly, you should be along to select."[25]

Carnegie returned to New York City in late August, but spent only a few days there before taking the train to Cresson, where he would remain through September and October, working with Bridge on his book, with his mother, feeling better now, in the next room.

Separated from Louise, he was revisited again by doubts about the wisdom of marriage and required almost daily reassurances that she truly, unconditionally loved him. He received, instead, distant, lukewarm, almost coldly indifferent letters. Louise was plainly angry with him for staying away so long. The summer had come to an end, and everyone, it appeared, had returned to town except Andrew. Hurt by his absence, but unwilling to make any demands or suggest that he should return to her, Louise expressed her melancholy with a studied aloofness. Carnegie, reading her letters as carefully as any scholar ever examined any text, felt the coldness—and was frightened, as he should have been. Instead of laying the matter to rest by returning to her in New York, he remained in Cresson and responded in kind. When Louise remarked that his letters had become "indifferent," he acknowledged that this was truly the case, but blamed her for it.

"You are right in some degree about [the] indifferent letter the last time I wrote," he wrote her from Cresson in mid-September,

> for truly I have been feeling while abroad that your letters proved to me that my absence made but little difference to you. They told me of your external acts, your jaunts and all that—but ah, Louise, they told not of any longing, any loneliness! Cold and formal, they felt, and I went back to the state of doubt. No use, no use. "You are only a friend, and can be naught else." Why deceive yourself longer? Stop, and allow so nice a woman to

find what she cannot be happy without—one who will stir the depths that lie there yet unfathomed. Your letters were less affectionate than those of even two years ago—far less so. You are so true a woman that you dissemble not—you cannot. Well do I know that every letter is a truthful embodiment of your real feelings—even the address means much from you. You are truth itself—clear as crystal—and I'm certain this year you have felt I was less essential to your life than you did. Is this not so? You never spoke of my visiting you in any of your letters. I could not resist the feeling that absence had this summer proved to you that you only liked me up to a certain point, and were perfectly reconciled to have "good times" with others, and hoped and expected to have them. I have not met any one—nor are my feelings changed except as the result of the seeming hopelessness of ever gaining your whole heart.[26]

Louise responded at once. "What a silly goose you are!" The problem between them was that he was so "high minded and honorable," he could not understand her "littleness." She confessed to him, for the first time apparently, "the truth of the summer": she had felt abandoned, betrayed, and troubled by her future husband's need to be always elsewhere, surrounded by the fine and mighty, while she, Louise Whitfield, was left by herself at a family resort in the Catskills. "When you went abroad, I wrote to you, trying to be as cheerful as possible, for the lonelier I felt, the more I tried not to show it. A young lady at [Gilbertsville, where she was staying] also had friends on the 'Etruria' [the ship on which Carnegie returned], and we both looked for letters. Hers came, mine did not, and my heart turned to stone. Your letters also spoke only of external acts—to be sure you wished me with you. Who wouldn't wish their friends with them when they are happy? But I said, 'How long would he stay with <u>me here</u>, in this dreary place?' That is the test."

Having sufficiently chastised him for his thoughtlessness, Louise assured Carnegie that she had no intention of breaking off their engagement a second time. She was no longer the silly girl she had been; the doubts of the past two years were vanquished. "The old life has no longer any charms for me, and the 'good times' with others are thoroughly revolting to me. You have made yourself thoroughly essential to my life—my highest and best life, but to keep me in that belief I must be assured by actions, more than by words, although I want those, too—that I am equally essential to yours. I know I have done nothing but check and repulse you, but until you tell me plainly that you have met some one you care for more than you do me, I shall cling to you, for, Andrew, I do love you, and my only chance of happiness in life is in being with you and making you happy." Louise knew her man well and had found a reservoir of strength to draw on. She had toyed with his affections—but only a bit, and only to punish him for his inattentions. "I like to have you get discouraged a little, for that shows me you do need me a little,—that gives me something to do, and to keep in a healthy state of mind I must have action."[27]

Carnegie thanked her for her "welcome letter," but he needed more from her. His insecurities were legion. It is difficult to reconcile our portrait of the self-confident industrialist and author with the frightened little man who, unable to believe anyone could truly love him as he was, demanded constant reassurance. He feared, he wrote Louise, that he was still "not clear out of doubt yet." His love for her was so strong it should have made her "joyously happy" and swept away all other sentiments. He implicitly criticized her again for being "cold" and unable to love him the way she should have. Exercising his authority as the man in the relationship—both older and wiser than she could ever be—he lectured her on the nature of "true love. . . . Even to the coldest temperaments it brings warmth and a glow of rosy joy. I have tried to produce that, and my failure seems sure, but I'll be at your side some evening next week and we shall see."[28]

Louise, perhaps moved, if only in part, by pity for the little man who needed so much from her, now gave him what he wanted. "Yes, dear," she wrote him on October 2, "I am <u>yours, yours, all yours,</u> for you have thrown the mantle of your great love around me, and I am no more cold and trembling, but warm and strong."[29]

Her love letter, which parroted back to him what he so wanted to hear, was tonic to the troubled man's soul. "Well, My Own Sweet Darling, you have written me a true love letter. The fountain has burst and flows at last. And you are truly warm and strong and now know that all I have told you real love was, is true, and more than true. I am so happy." Unable any longer to sustain the emotional level of their previous letters, he reverted to more mundane chatter, informing her that his mother "keeps well . . . but has her ups and downs," and that he had "sent today for Boxes, Symphony and Oratorio meetings—also have Box for Popular Concerts. Then there's the Grand German Opera (you remember Die Walkure). We shall have happy days in New York, <u>My Own</u>, and our lives shall shadow forth what is to be some day."[30]

Strangely, he did not follow up his letters with a visit to New York. There was his book to finish in Cresson and business in Pittsburgh. "I gave our Rail Mill men [at Braddock] fifty thousands dollars Friday, for Library, etc. Hurrah! . . . I have been so busy. We have consolidated some of our Works and Interests into one [Carnegie, Phipps, & Co.], and this has taken my time and thoughts. A new firm organized, but I have had quiet moments and always the hour before sleep your lovely form and voice and oh! Such a lovely rippling smile come dancing in upon me to give me such exquisite happiness."[31]

Carnegie battled his demons and insecurities in silence. He was a master at compartmentalizing his life, building barriers between Carnegie the lovesick suitor, Carnegie the powerful industrialist, and Carnegie the man of letters, disciple of Herbert Spencer, and confidant of Matthew Arnold. His distress at the ups and downs of his courtship was kept secret from everyone, lest word leak to his mother, now seventy-five, who he hoped would live her last years in peace instead of anguish at her son having chosen the wrong wife. He suffered quietly and alone, and kept busy, impossibly busy.

Carnegie dedicated himself anew to his self-appointed role as ambassador extraordinaire from the New World to the Old. While he had, through much of the 1880s, paid more attention to Westminster than to Washington, he had not neglected to cultivate connections with the nation's most powerful Republicans. His closest acquaintance in Washington was probably James G. Blaine of Maine, who had run for the presidency in 1880 only to withdraw at the last moment in favor of James Garfield. Garfield repaid the favor when he was elected by naming Blaine his secretary of state.[32]

Carnegie and Blaine dined together often in New York and Washington. Carnegie enjoyed the fact that Blaine, arguably the most powerful Republican in the nation, was interested in him. Blaine, for his part, was intrigued by Carnegie, who was not only a witty conversationalist but a wealthy Republican and a political power in Pennsylvania. Carnegie may also have been a source of investment advice for Blaine, who, it was later remarked by no less an authority than the *Dictionary of American Biography*, had become "wealthy without any visible means of income."[33]

Blaine had been a candidate for the Republican nomination twice before finally securing it in 1884. Writing to Morley in October, Carnegie was full of enthusiasm for what he hoped would be a new stage in Anglo-American relations. "The dawn has come, phantoms must depart. I think Blaine will be elected. You [will] have a new Minister from Washington, I know this . . . next Minister will be in sympathy with you and Chamberlain. I am to have a voice in his selection. Blaine is an . . . admirer of England."[34]

Carnegie was determined to use his connections at the highest level of the Liberal Party in Britain and the Republican in America to bring the two nations into greater harmony. When, in the spring of 1885, Gladstone paid tribute to George Washington in a speech in Parliament, Carnegie wrote to say that he was having Tiffany's in New York cut and fashion a walking stick for Gladstone from a honey locust which George Washington had planted at Mount Vernon. "By and by it will reach you. I hope that you will be long spared to use it, and that you will like to carry it with you, and that it will serve to turn your thoughts at times to your 'kin beyond the sea'—to this giant child of dear old England . . . The present 'Uncrowned king' of the Motherland leaning upon a staff from a tree planted by the first 'uncrowned King' of the Childland suggests strange thoughts."[35]

Ten weeks later, Carnegie, now in London, wrote Gladstone again. Since his offer of the walking stick, Gladstone had resigned as prime minister and retired to his country estate. Carnegie, ever adaptable, found a way to take advantage of Gladstone's defeat to carry forward his own plans. Carnegie entreated him to "take this rare opportunity to visit your Kin beyond the Sea. Come with me early in August." The Carnegies and Gladstones would together cross the ocean in one of the "immense new Cunarders" and travel by "special car to Niagara, Chicago, Cincinnati, Pittsburgh, Washington, etc. . . . It can be done in about a month. You would return early in October, at furthest, having rendered to the two Nations a great political service. In their union lies the truest hope for the progress of the World—they have taught the world Arbitration. . . . I write this that it may demand your grave <u>conscientious</u> consideration, depend upon it, Mr. Gladstone, you can in no other way so greatly serve man as in doing what I here suggest."[36]

From this point on, Carnegie would continue to shower Gladstone with suggestions as to how he might best serve Britain by adopting American political institutions. Whatever the problem, it could, Carnegie believed, be solved by following the American example. When Gladstone took up the cause of Irish Home Rule, which was to result in his greatest political defeat, Carnegie suggested that he "refer to the rights of States in the American Union as being the proper position for Ireland. Such a measure will strengthen the bonds of union between Ireland and Great Britain; for America has proved through the federal system that the present self-government of the parts produces the strongest government of the whole."[37]

It was, of course, enormously presumptuous of the fifty-one-year-old Scottish-American industrialist to be telling the seventy-seven-year-old prime minister how he might solve the Irish problem. But Carnegie proceeded to offer his unsolicited advice nonetheless.

Triumphant Democracy, its writing delayed by Carnegie's trip to England in the summer of 1885, was completed in the late fall and published by Scribner's the following spring. In gratitude for the assistance of James Bridge and John Champlin, Carnegie assigned them his royalties and warmly acknowledged their help—and that of *Scribner's Statistical Atlas*—in his preface. Though some would later question whether Carnegie, without formal education of any sort, could have been the author of the book that bore his name, it should have been apparent to anyone who read *Triumphant Democracy* that it could only have been written by the "Star-spangled Scotchman." No one else dared write with such exuberance, such unbridled optimism, and so many superlatives.

Like his intellectual hero and model, Herbert Spencer, Carnegie began with his conclusion—that America had triumphed materially, culturally, and socially because of its republican institutions—and then assembled evidence to support it. Thomas Huxley's comment on Spencer that "if he ever wrote a tragedy, its plot would be the slaying of a beautiful deduction by an ugly fact" could just as easily have been applied to Carnegie.[38]

From first page to last, the volume was suffused with a sunny optimism that drove its more critical readers to distraction. In Carnegie's land of milk and honey, there were no social, ethnic, racial, or class conflicts: no ethnic discrimination, no battles over racial supremacy in the South, no political corruption in the northern cities, no challenges from the under-classes at the polls or in the workplaces, no unionists, no anarchists, no strikes, no agrarian agitation. The new nation had suffered growing pains, but was now materially prosperous, socially mature, and politically stable. Even the infamously corrupt Tweed Ring existed no more. "The leader," Carnegie proudly reported, "was required to surrender his property, imprisoned in the penitentiary, and died there. Others fled abroad and lived in hiding. . . . Since then the city government has been comparatively pure."[39]

In his tribute to his new nation and its "Triumphant Democracy," Carnegie concentrated his attention on America's ties to its motherland. Four fifths of Americans, he insisted, without providing any statistical evidence, were British in "ancestry. The other fifth is principally German." The German contribution to the American racial mixture was special cause for celebration. The "generally diffused love of music which characterizes America" came from the Germans, for "there is in the German a part of his nature 'touched to fine issues.'"[40]

Unlike many of his contemporaries, Carnegie was neither prejudiced against nor fearful of any of the new European immigrants. In his weighty corpus of private correspondence, letters to the editor, articles, essays, speeches, and books, there are few, if any ethnic slurs, anti-Semitic anecdotes, or caustically disapproving comments on "Romanists," Celts, "Hunkies," or Slavs. For him, there were no ungovernable races, no peoples who could not benefit from becoming full members of the American republic.

Carnegie was so eager to establish American supremacy at every level—political, social, cultural, and moral—that he overlooked any evidence that might get in the way of his conclusions. This tendency was most striking in his discussion of "our fellow-citizens of African descent." The problem of the Negro in America had been solved by emancipation, he maintained. "Grave apprehensions were entertained that freedom suddenly granted to these poor slaves would be abused. . . . It was asserted that the negro would not work save under the lash of the overseer." Nothing, he reported, could have been further from the truth. More cotton was being produced after emancipation, and at less cost. "Under the reign of freedom the material resources of the South have increased faster than ever before." Here was empirical evidence that the Negro problem had been solved.[41]

Combining a positivist belief that empirical evidence revealed the un-varnished truth of existence with Spencer's faith in evolutionary progress, Carnegie assembled statistics—most of them from the 1880 census—to demonstrate that the United States had succeeded Britain as the greatest nation in the world. America had the highest literacy rate, the most read-ers and writers, the greatest numbers of newspapers, more libraries, more books, and more tons of paper used for printing than Britain or any other nation. It spent more on education, was more generous to its soldiers and sailors and widows and orphans, had the fewest paupers, the best public credit rating, and the lowest national debt. Its women were "the most in-telligent, entertaining and most agreeable in the world"; its opera houses and theaters, because newer, were "much superior to those in Europe"; its major periodicals, *Harper's* magazine and the *Century*, "surpassed anything before known in the history of periodical literature" in editing, printing, and engraving. There were still areas in which the Americans were behind the British. English choirs were better, the voices smoother, the enuncia-tion perfect. The American voice was "thin to begin with—the effect of climate, I fear—and to this is added the abominable practice of slurring over or cutting off troublesome syllables." Americans were also behind Eu-ropeans in "history and allegory" painting, though their equals in portrai-ture and their superiors in landscape.[42]

The monarchy, Carnegie argued, was at the root of Britain's failure to keep pace with America. "Monarchical institutions emasculate even edu-cated men, and the ignorant masses in greater degree." British commoners suffered twice: from the loss of privileges that noble birth conferred and from the inferiority complex that accompanied the absence of those privi-leges. The British class system further debilitated the nation by placing at the pinnacle of state and society "people who are exempt from honest la-bor and despise it." In Britain, "the dignity of labor has not only no place but . . . is actually looked down upon!" The result was that British workers drank more, worked fewer hours, took more holidays, and were less well paid and less honored than their American counterparts.[43]

THOUGH THE BOOK was a ham-handed assault on all that was British, Carnegie expected to find an appreciative audience in England and Scot-land. In March 1886, he dispatched Bridge to London, armed "with advance sheets of the book." "I think, we should deluge Britain with *T.D.*," he wrote Bridge from Cresson in April. "Suppose we let radical clubs, reading rooms and coffee rooms know that copies will be sent (free or cheap edition) upon application. I would send copy of first edition to every library, reading room, &c, free—cheap edition for any who apply. Perhaps it would be best if you engage some young radical to attend to disposing of cheap edition in various towns & give him discretion to distribute gratis to every club, &c, &c . . . Do put *T.D.* into hands of people—want 25,000 copies at least to go there."[44]

Carnegie had written his book as an activist and reformer, in the expectation that on studying it, the British would see the folly of retaining their monarchical institutions and the Americans the wisdom of honoring their republican ones. He had imagined, quite incorrectly as it turned out, that his British Liberal and radical comrades would applaud his effort. They did not. Even his closest friend in London, John Morley, who had joined the Gladstone government in early 1886 as Irish secretary, found too many of Carnegie's passages "a trifle too republican for a middle aged monarchist like me: I mean too <u>aggressively</u> republican."[45]

The man whose opinion he valued most in the world, Herbert Spencer, was even more pointed in his critique of Carnegie's "political thesis." While agreeing that the United States was in the vanguard of civilization and had accomplished wonderful things in its brief existence as a nation, Spencer faulted Carnegie for attributing such triumphs to the influence of republican institutions. "A large part, if not the greater part, of what you ascribe to democracy," he wrote Carnegie on May 18, "is, it seems to me, simply the result of social growth in a region furnishing abundant space and material for it, and which would have gone on in a substantially similar way under another form of government." Having demolished Carnegie's central thesis, Spencer went on to criticize his assumption that material prosperity was

favorable to human life. Absorbed by his activities, and spurred on by his unrestricted ambitions, the American is, to my thinking, a less happy being than the inhabitant of a country where the possibilities of success are very much smaller; and where in the immense majority of cases, each has to be content with that hum-drum career in which circumstances have placed him, and, abandoning hopes of any great advance, is led to make the best of what satisfactions in life fall to his share. I believe on the whole that he gets more pleasure out of life than the successful American, and that his children inherit greater capacities for enjoyment. Great as may be hereafter the advantages of the enormous progress America makes, I hold that the existing generations of Americans, and those to come for a long time hence, are and will be essentially sacrificed.[46]

American friends were more generous, though they too were bothered by his overexuberant optimism. George Pullman, whose views of the American workingman were not nearly as benign as Carnegie's, believed that the publication of *Triumphant Democracy* had been "very timely," because "owing to the excesses of our turbulent population, so many are uttering doubts just now as to whether democracy has been a triumph in America." Henry George, from the opposite end of the political spectrum, found the book "extremely interesting and very suggestive, although, as it seems to me, you have given only one side of the picture, ignoring the shadows. To my mind, however, these come, not from too much, but from too little democracy."[47]

Carnegie retained the private letters and the published reviews, negative as well as positive. What mattered most was that he be taken seriously as a thinker and author. On these grounds alone, *Triumphant Democracy* was a triumph. It was widely reviewed and commented on, for the most part favorably in the American press, critically in the British. Andrew Carnegie had at age fifty-one achieved a reputation as a man of letters; his name and work were now recognized on two continents.

SIXTEEN

Things Fall Apart, 1886–1887

HAVING FOUND an audience for his books and articles, Carnegie turned them out with regularity now. His voice and perspective were unique—and he knew this. No other American businessman dared offer his thoughts to the public and none, had he done so, would have been able to present them so clearly. His range of expertise was breathtaking. There were few subjects on which he was not willing to give his views. He offered his solution to the "Irish Question" in a letter to the Irish League of Pittsburgh published in the *New York Times* on September 30, 1885. In January 1886, he published an article on British reform legislation in the *North American Review*. But his specialty, the subject on which he wrote and spoke most now, was labor-management relations.

His tone was neither preachy nor didactic; his prose forceful but not bullying; his suggestions often modest; his outlook always optimistic. He instructed his readers, as a good Spencerian should, that current political and social problems could only be understood within the context of larger evolutionary patterns. Labor, as he explained patiently in "An Employer's View of the Labor Question," published in *Forum* in early 1886, had been engaged in an ongoing struggle "during the past three hundred years, first against authority and then against capital." The "permanent relations to each other of labor and capital" were still evolving and this was bound to produce some friction. Carnegie took it upon himself to suggest how that friction might be reduced.[1]

As in his comments the year before in praise of socialism, he commended workers' cooperatives as the solution to labor-capital conflicts, while making it clear that he did not believe workingmen were at present capable of running their own establishments. Proposals that differences between labor and management be settled by arbitration were, he thought, on "firmer ground." He agreed, on this point, with the Knights of Labor, who at their first general assembly in Reading, Pennsylvania, in 1878, had called, as he did, for the "substitution of arbitration for strikes." If manufacturers were going to arbitrate their differences with their workingmen, it was critical that the workingmen be responsibly represented. Carnegie was, on the whole, quite supportive of both the Knights of Labor and the Amalgamated, which he claimed were led by responsible, conservative unionists. It was high time, he maintained, abruptly breaking ranks with his fellow manufacturers, that employers recognized the right of their employees to join labor organizations. "The right of the workingmen to combine and to form trades-unions is no less sacred than the right of the manufacturer to enter into associations and conferences with his fellows, and it must sooner or later be conceded."

Carnegie's position on trades unions was not, he insisted, derived from abstract political principles, but from his own experience as an employer. In all his pro-union pronouncements from this period, he never mentioned his Chartist forbears or the fact that his uncles and his father had been strike leaders in Dunfermline in the 1840s. What happened in the past on the other side of the ocean had no bearing on the present. Lockouts and strikes were to be avoided because they were bad for business— and bad for the workingmen. The pragmatic business leader navigated around them by cementing a cordial relationship with responsible union leaders. "My experience has been that trades-unions, upon the whole, are beneficial both to labor and to capital. They certainly educate the workingmen, and give them a truer conception of the relations of capital and labor than they could otherwise form."[2]

An article by a millionaire industrialist in favor of labor unions and co-operatives was such an anomaly it was bound to get attention—and it did. "An Employer's View" was excerpted in several newspapers. At the meeting of the Baptist Social Union at Delmonico's on April 1, Deacon William Richardson, in opening the discussion on "Strikes, Their Causes and How They May Be Prevented," read aloud from it. The editors of the *National Labor Tribune* who, since the institution of the twelve-hour day at Edgar Thomson in 1885, had begun to take a more critical view of Carnegie's pronouncements, devoted a full editorial to his article. Referring to Carnegie's aside that America lacked a "retired class of men of affairs" to serve as arbitrators in labor diputes because "our vile practice is to keep on accumulating more dollars until we die," the editors suggested that Carnegie "take the initiative in stopping this 'vile practice' . . . by giving to charity, or to your present employees, *all* of your interests in your large manufacturing establishments! . . . To do as we suggest would be practicing what you preach. Set an example. . . . Do this, Mr. Carnegie, and we will argue in favor of your being a proper person to become 'arbitrator.' Fail in this, Mr. Carnegie, and we will oppose you as arbitrator on the ground that you are not competent to distinguish the difference between enough and a feast."[3]

CARNEGIE had written his *Forum* article in the midst of another busy winter season. New York was a concertgoer's paradise, with two dueling maestros, Leopold Damrosch and Theodore Thomas; three symphony orchestras (the two major ones: the New York Symphony Society, to whose board Carnegie had been elected in 1885, and the New York Philharmonic Society, would not merge until 1928); and two grand opera companies, at the Academy of Music downtown and the newly built Metropolitan Opera House uptown. Carnegie went out nearly every evening.

During the day, when the weather was suitable, he went riding with Louise or attended the races at Jerome Park. He kept up this pace until early March, when, claiming total exhaustion, he fled south to Dungeness, his brother's estate on Cumberland Island off the coast of Florida.

It didn't take long for him to regain his strength. "One week since we arrived here, and now I am to report progress. I am truly much better," he reassured Louise. "Have got rid of that half suffocated feeling which troubled me in the city, and am much stronger than I was. I walk a great deal, a little at a time. The yacht is my delight."[4]

He remained in Dungeness, cared after by his sister-in-law Lucy, whom he adored, through the rest of the month. Then, after a week in Pittsburgh, he retired to Cresson for the remainder of the spring and summer. Again this year, because of his mother's steadily failing health, he had decided to give up his trip abroad. Unwilling any longer to remain separated from Louise for months at a time or to break the news to his mother that he planned to marry her, Carnegie resorted to subterfuge to get Louise to Cresson. Alexander King, the Scottish manufacturer who had introduced Carnegie to the Whitfield family, had leased a cottage just ten minutes up the hill. Carnegie arranged for King and his wife Aggie to invite Louise and her mother and younger sister to their cottage. Mrs. Whitfield, having been told of her daughter's engagement, had no objections. Margaret Carnegie, having taken to her bed, was too ill to object.

Carnegie's major project that summer was to design a baronial house for himself. At age fifty, poised on the threshold of marriage (though it was a broad threshold not easily crossed), he had decided that it was now time to own a home of his own. All his life, he had lived either in his mother's home or in leased rooms. He bought five hundred acres from the corporation that owned and operated the Cresson resort and then, with the assistance of Frederick Law Olmsted, the landscape architect who had designed Central Park with Calvert Vaux, sited his future "castle" at the crest of the mountain. Matthew Arnold, who visited Cresson in July, was much taken with its "unfailing spring of water" and absence of mosquitoes. Still, he wrote his sister, he thought the "Scotch baronial house" that Carnegie was planning to build on his newly purchased mountainside better suited for Scotland than Pennsylvania.[5]

Carnegie spent the spring, summer, and early fall of 1886 in the protective cocoon of the cottage while the outside world was being rocked by an unprecedented wave of labor disturbances, political protests, work stoppages, and strikes "Eighteen-eighty-six," as the historian Jeremy Brecher puts it, "was a year of tumult. . . . The number of strikers in 1886 tripled compared with the average for the previous five years, and the number of establishments struck nearly quadrupled." Membership in the Knights of Labor, the nation's leading workingmen's organization, grew from 111,395 in July of 1885 to 729,677 a year later.[6]

Carnegie had predicted in his *Forum* article a future of labor peace and harmony. On the date his article appeared in print, April 1, 1886, the workers on Tom Scott's Texas & Pacific Railroad, now owned by Jay Gould, went on strike, the beginning of a massive walkout against the roads in Gould's southwestern railway system. Then, on May Day, in response to the call for a general strike for the eight-hour day, thousands of workers in industrial cities across the nation left their jobs. Two days later, at a rally at Chicago, a dynamite bomb ripped through Haymarket Square, killing a police officer and igniting a riot that resulted in several civilians and policemen dead and scores wounded. The police arrested hundreds of labor activists and anarchists. Within eighteen months, four of those accused of conspiracy in the bombing would be hanged; a fifth would take his own life in prison.

The events of May 1886 brought out of the shadows the specter of the "general strike" that had arisen briefly in 1877. The 1886 strikes for the eight-hour day were, if anything, more widespread and long-lasting. There were loosely coordinated rallies and work stoppages in dozens of cities across the country, from Troy, New York, to Pittsburgh, Baltimore, Grand Rapids, St. Louis, and Milwaukee. Carnegie, surveying the situation from his sanctuary in Cresson, found the hysteria of the business classes more alarming than the protests themselves. Capital had "been frightened almost into panic," he wrote in a follow-up article entitled "Results of the Labor Struggle" and published in August in *Forum,* "and many leaders of public opinion seemed to lose self-command. . . . Our magazines, reviews, and newspapers have been filled with plans involving radical changes considered necessary . . . for the restoration of proper relations between capital and labor." Carnegie took it upon himself to set the record straight, to talk sense to his fellow businessmen, to put the present strife within a larger evolutionary scheme. There had been strikes, and many of them, but the republic and its institutions were not in danger; there was no need to confine "the suffrage . . . to the educated" or hold "the masses . . . in stricter bonds." While acknowledging that a quarter million men had left their jobs to protest for the eight-hour day, Carnegie insisted that the "eruption was not, in itself, a very serious matter, either in its extent or in its consequences," as that quarter million was but a fraction of the "more than twenty millions of workers who earn their bread by the sweat of their brow."[7]

Workingmen were, he declared, becoming more intelligent; union leaders more conservative. The sporadic violence that had marked recent labor disputes was unfortunate and had been rightly condemned. But it was important that the larger public, while condemning violence, also "give due consideration to the terrible temptation to which the working-man on a strike is sometimes subjected. To expect that one dependent upon his daily wage for the necessaries of life will stand by peaceably and see a new man employed in his stead, is to expect much. . . . The employer of labor will find it much more to his interest, wherever possible, to allow his works to remain idle and await the result of a dispute, than to employ the class of men that can be induced to take the place of other men who have stopped work."[8]

Carnegie had taken upon himself the mantle of impartial observer and wise man. He was above the fray, interested not in promoting the interests of either labor or management, but in getting them both to see that they had no choice but to work together. His innate optimism, reinforced by his reading of Spencer, convinced him that the current battles of labor and management would soon be consigned to the dustbin of history. In the meantime, he counseled caution and conciliation on both sides.

It is doubtful that anyone was listening. The manufacturers considered him something of a renegade—and not entirely reliable. The labor leaders, for their part, put little stock in his words, but looked instead to his actions as an employer. Still, they could not help but be impressed by the fact that he had, in his August article, come out strongly against hiring "scabs" to replace workingmen on strike.

THROUGH most of the summer of 1886, Andrew Carnegie wrote about the labor situation, cared for his ailing mother, entertained the visiting Arnold family, made plans for his "Scotch baronial house," consulted with Allegheny City officials on his gift of a library and concert hall, finished his second *Forum* article, prepared for Louise's visit to Cresson, and conferred regularly with his Pittsburgh partners. On July 21, he collapsed from exhaustion again and summoned his personal doctor, Fred Dennis, from New York City to Cresson. "Had a relapse," he wrote Louise, who was in Oyster Bay with her family. "Only allowed milk, no solid food. Dr. Dennis and assistant arrived today. Dr. D. says disease will develop in few days but attack will be mild, since every symptom is favorable. His assistant remains. Mother poorly, of course. . . . Don't be alarmed, but do not expect to hear for few days."[9]

The following day, he wrote again, preoccupied in his weakened state with his still precarious relationship to his secret fiancée.

I have not written to you because it seems you and I have duties which keep us apart. Our parents are better, and I have known what you said recently was true. To leave your mother—"You could not think of it"—nor could I leave mine. You seemed interested a little in other suitors, just a little, I thought, and probably some one might arise who would come into your household and make not only you happy but your mother and family also. This would be the ideal way. Therefore I have stood away back, as it were, and resolved that it was best to let you alone and free, but now when I hear [that you will be in Cresson on] the 29th I thrill with gladness and await your coming, even if I do not see that we can go beyond our present relations at present. . . . Mother <u>seems</u> really better; it is miraculous. I trust yours is also better. Everything does hang upon our Mothers with both of us. Our duty is the same—to stick to them to the last. I feel this every day.[10]

Louise arrived, as promised, on July 29, and, though she stayed at the King cottage with her mother and sister, she and Andrew were able to spend a good deal of time together. Her diaries, as her biographers report, told "of joyful happenings: 'AC walked home with me in the starlight. . . . Andrew brought me home all alone—took long lovely walk. Such wonderful happiness.' The day before she left for the city was 'the happiest day of my life.'"[11]

The Whitfields returned to New York in September. Andrew wrote to tell Louise that Harry Phipps had thought her wonderful and pretty. But she's engaged, Carnegie responded, not saying to whom. No matter, said Phipps, pursue her anyway.

Three days later, Carnegie wrote again, this time with bad news. His brother had been taken ill. "Was thought dying, but is now better, but very weak. I am so concerned about him and especially about Lucy and the children."[12]

On October 3, Andrew reported that Tom was feeling better. He then returned to his favorite theme, his feelings for Louise. "Your last love letter was best of all," he wrote, and then, employing an erotic analogy probably never used before or since, he told her that she was "like Pittsburgh Iron—it is very hard to heat at first, but once hot, it is very, very hot indeed, and retains its heat extraordinarily! So it will be with you, Darling." He was, he gleefully informed her, on his way north. He had a meeting in Philadelphia on Tuesday morning and would, he hoped, reach New York that evening. He tantalizingly hinted that he might lease a house on Forty-eighth Street. "I dislike Hotels so much. What near neighbors we would be! Not near enough, though, but that's soon to be all right."[13]

Because Margaret was too ill to be moved, Carnegie did not take the train north to New York after his meeting in Philadelphia, but returned to Cresson. "I had a chill last night, and am now in bed, and the doctor attending me," he wrote Louise on October 16. "He says it's the old malarial touch got at the Windsor, and I'll be all right soon. Don't be alarmed. Nothing serious—sure!"[14]

The doctor was wrong: Carnegie had contracted typhoid fever. Only hours after writing Louise, he lapsed into a near coma and was put to bed in the room at the top of the stairs, adjoining his mother's. A local doctor and nurse were called in at once and Dr. Dennis was summoned again from New York. In Pittsburgh, on almost the same day Carnegie was stricken with typhoid, his brother Tom left his office early with what he thought was a minor cold. Thomas Carnegie died of pneumonia a few days later.[15]

Carnegie's cousin Dod, who was now a full partner in the Pittsburgh firms, took the train east to Cresson with Harry Phipps and Andrew's friend John Walker to break the news of Tom's death. James Bridge, who had remained in Cresson all summer and fall, was asked to prepare Carnegie for his visitors.

"George Lauder [Dod] has come up from Pittsburgh," I said, "and Tom is very sick."

"What's the matter with him?" asked Andrew.

"He has got pneumonia."

"Then he'll never get over it! That's the end of Tom! Oh this life, this life!" And with that he threw up his hands and turned his face to the wall. Nothing more was said, and I tip-toed out of the room.[16]

Tom's early death had come as no surprise to his brother or their partners. He had been a heavy drinker all his life— and suffered for it. Margaret was not told of the death of her younger son. Andrew himself, according to Dr. Dennis, had a relapse upon hearing the news. With both Andrew and his mother critically ill, the cottage was turned into a hospital. Dr. Dennis and his chief assistant, Dr. Jasper Garmany, spent their days and nights there, assisted by a full staff of nurses. The fireplaces were stoked to the maximum and rugs hung against the windows to keep out the cold. Built as a summer vacation home, the cottage had no central heating.[17]

James Bridge took on the role of press secretary, communicating by telegraph with both Louise and the New York City and Pittsburgh newspapers, which reported almost daily on Carnegie's illness, often on their front pages. In late October, Charles Mackie forwarded to Cousin Dod in Pittsburgh Carnegie's securities, collaterals, notes, bills, and everything else in his vault, including "Life Membership Certificates, letters of thanks, Resolutions, etc." The expectation was that Carnegie would not survive the winter.[18]

Margaret Carnegie died on the morning of November 10. Andrew remained critically ill in the next room. The news of his mother's death was kept from him. James Bridge and Dr. Dennis directed that her casket be lowered out the window of her bedroom. It was then placed on the back of a horse-drawn wagon, driven down the hill to the train station, and put on a train for Pittsburgh, where Margaret would be buried alongside her son Tom.

For the next two weeks, Carnegie remained nearly comatose, so weak he was unable to move and barely able to take nourishment. Louise remained in touch, but did not visit, perhaps because she was afraid to see Carnegie in such a weakened state or because, still not officially engaged, it would not have been proper for her to travel south to be with him.

On November 24, Carnegie raised his head, conversed briefly with Dr. Dennis, then picked up his pencil to write Louise:

> It is six weeks since the last word was written and that was to you as I was passing into the darkness. Today as I see the great light once more my first word is to you. . . . I shall get to NY soon, stay with Dr. Dennis, but here comes one last separation—I have to go to the South of France, so say the doctors, and if I do, and attend to getting strength, my health will be more robust than ever. Whether you can come to me soon, and let us be quietly married there, or whether I must return for you, we shall see soon. I shall see few in NY—but daily and hourly, almost, we must be together. Louise, I am now wholly yours—all gone but you. Oh, dear one, be careful of your health.[19]

On November 29, he wrote again to tell Louise that he had decided the best place to recuperate was in England, with cousin Dod Lauder and a personal physician to watch over him. He asked her to meet him in Liverpool, where they would be "quietly married. . . . Then you and your maid, I and [my valet] John (for I take him along) go off on a driving tour. . . . They will not be in our way at all. Don't interpose any objections,

Beloved—let me have this to ponder over at night when I am wakeful. It's my Dream."[20]

After so many years of silence, Louise was desperate to tell her friends about her marriage plans. Carnegie urged her not to. "Darling, there is only one reason why the whole world should not know of our happiness. It would not seem in good taste to announce it so soon [after Margaret's death] . . . Therefore I hope the public will not get hold of it. Tell one, tell all, Louise. . . . In the Spring, when you sail [for Liverpool] with your maid and in charge of some friend, then of course all will be understood by our friends, and it will take a week to spread. By that time we shall be united forever. I feel just as you do; we must have plans. Well, Angel Mine, were I to return for you [and get married in N.Y.] I must have many business questions presented, and a great hubbub would ensue. I could scarcely get away for some time." He did not want them to begin life together in the glare of New York celebrity. Better that they marry and honeymoon in England, away from friends, business acquaintances, and reporters. "Then, Darling the quietness that would surround our union, so appropriate after recent events, and the months that would ensue before our return to New York life, would, as I see it, enable us to begin life together so much sooner without violating the proprieties. Think all this over, my Love."[21]

Louise considered his suggestions—and rejected them. She would not, she wrote her betrothed, slink away to England in secret to be married. "Darling, as long as my Mother lives, I never can leave her house but as your wife."[22]

Carnegie agreed reluctantly. They would be married in New York in the spring, after he had returned from Europe, fully recuperated. In the meantime, he intended to take over the Whitfield finances so that neither Louise nor her mother would ever again have to worry about money. "What a blessing we are laden with dollars. They are of some good. Yes, you and I have dollars plenty, so Mother [Mrs. Whitfield] is all right, and all her family. Your troubles, brave love, are mine also, only I smile at the business part." Having written every day, Carnegie apologized for having let a few days go by without a letter. "I have been so busy with partners one day, and two days with Mr. Maravetz [his lawyer] on my will, that when done I could not write." Though still quite weak, he had begun to transact business again.[23]

There was much to be done. The first item on the agenda was finding a way to provide for Lucy Carnegie and her children by cashing in Tom's one-sixth interest in the business. Andrew agreed to buy Tom's stock for himself and pay Lucy for it over an extended period of time.

More pressing was the question of succession. Tom had been a critically important part of the Carnegie Brothers management team, perhaps the most important part. Phipps agreed to succeed him as chairman of the board, but this, it was tacitly agreed, was but a stopgap measure. As good as he had been as treasurer and senior partner, Harry Phipps had neither the talent nor the inclination to run the company.

Since Andrew's recovery, Phipps had been working with company lawyers on a plan to protect the company—and the remaining partners' investments—should Carnegie be taken ill again. As Andrew owned more than 50 percent of the stock and Tom another 16 percent, had they died together they would have taken the company with them; there would have been no way for the surviving partners to buy up their stock.

Phipps proposed that the partners protect themselves from such an eventuality by signing an "ironclad" agreement—"ironclad" being the accepted nomenclature for agreements that, once signed, could not be broken—which stipulated that should any partner leave the firm, by death or any other means, that partner's interest could be bought back by the company at the "value of the interest, as it shall appear to be on the books." Because the so-called book value was far below the market value of the shares, the "ironclad" agreement guaranteed that, in future, the company would be able to purchase the stock of deceased members at discounted prices.

Unlike capitalists who overvalued their holdings, Carnegie and his partners purposefully undervalued theirs on their books. "They prided themselves on keeping everything down," Carnegie's lawyer explained in 1912 to the congressional committee investigating U.S. Steel for possible antitrust violations because it was, "nobody else's business but their own, and they kept depreciating the values. Having no stock to sell, or anything like that, to the public, and no credit to keep up in the public eye, they prided themselves on going to the other extreme."[24]

Phipps's "ironclad" agreement not only provided that a deceased partner's stock could be bought back at the discounted "book value," but gave the remaining partners plenty of time to do so—a full fifteen years in the case of Carnegie's 50 percent share of the company. There was a second part to the agreement. Phipps proposed that at any time in the future, for any cause whatsoever or no cause at all, three quarters of the stockholders, if they held among them three quarters of the stock, could force any of the partners to leave the company and sell back his interest at "book value." Since Carnegie held 50 percent of the stock, no ejection could take place unless he agreed to it. He was the only partner so protected.[25]

"The year 1886 ended in deep gloom for me," Carnegie wrote in his *Autobiography*. It was the year in which he said good-bye to his mother and brother—and to Cresson, which had been his favorite place on earth. He gave up plans to build his castle and abandoned the cottage that had been his and his mother's second home for more than a decade. The year 1886 was also a year of new beginnings, one in which he invited Louise Whitfield to be his partner in marriage, and Henry Clay Frick to join him in the steel business.[26]

CARNEGIE'S RELATIONS with Frick were nearly as complicated as were his relations with Louise Whitfield. Frick had invited Carnegie and his partners to invest in the H. C. Frick Coke Company in 1881 because he needed capital for expansion. When, in August 1883, he suggested that the coke company that bore his name acquire two new properties, Carnegie, by this time the company's largest stockholder, demurred. Frick responded with anger and no little contempt for the steelmaker who had presumed to tell him how to manage his coke business. "I am free to say, I do not like the tone of your letter," he wrote Carnegie directly. "Outside of my desire to follow and accept your views as the largest stockholder in our Company, I have great admiration for your acknowledged abilities and your general good judgment, and would much prefer to defer to your views but in the matter of the values of the properties in question & the propriety of increasing our stock I will have to differ with you & think the future will bear me out."[27]

In 1886, when the Connellsville coke workers threatened to strike if the previous year's wage cuts were not restored and irregularities in weighing their product remedied, Carnegie and Frick found themselves on opposite sides of the bargaining table. Frick, looking after the interests of his coke companies, which supplied not only Pittsburgh but Illinois Steel in Chicago with fuel, was willing to risk a lockout or strike to keep wage rates down. Carnegie and his steel partners, with large orders to fill, could not afford any work stoppage.

Carnegie believed a wage increase in the coke fields was inevitable and suggested that Frick try one more time to reach an agreement. "Naig says make best terms, but make them" as soon as possible, Phipps asked Lauder in Pittsburgh to instruct Frick. When it became apparent that no such agreement was possible, Carnegie wrote Frick directly to caution him that if he chose to break the strike, the "fee for protection should be overwhelming. It will never do to let the discontented beat your protective forces."[28]

Frick, in the end, did as Carnegie suggested and settled with the striking coke workers by raising their wage rates. Then, having done his bit to keep the steel furnaces fueled, Frick asked for stock in the steel company and offered to pay for it with stock in his coke company. Carnegie bluntly advised him that to exchange shares in his own company for Carnegie's "would be the mistake of your life. Your career must be identified with the Frick Coke Co." Because he, Carnegie, had found it unbearable working for concerns he did not found, own, and control, he could not imagine Frick doing so. "You never could become the Creator of CB and Co. Twenty years from now you might be a large owner in it, perhaps the principal, still the concern would not be your work and you could not be proud of it." He suggested that Frick use whatever capital he had or could raise to increase his stake in the company that bore his name. The letter was signed: "Your friend, Andrew Carnegie," with a postscript: "File this for future reference. AC."[29]

Frick let the matter drop. Eight months later, with the landscape altered irremediably by Tom Carnegie's death, the partnership plan was reintroduced. Carnegie, recognizing that he needed to replace his brother with a man with executive talents and knowledge of the coke industry, offered Frick a 2 percent share in Carnegie Brothers, with no down payment. The full cost of Frick's stock—plus interest—would be deducted, over time, from his share of the profits. It was a wise move for both men. Frick would turn out to be the ablest executive ever to work for Carnegie—and he would grow immensely rich and powerful doing so.[30]

BY DECEMBER, Carnegie was well enough to travel. His doctors agreed to let him return to New York, but only on the condition that he stay at Dr.

Dennis's home at 542 Madison Avenue. He was taken north in a private railway car dispatched to Cresson by his childhood friend, Bobby Pitcairn, and arrived in New York on December 12, so exhausted from the trip that his reunion with Louise had to be delayed for five full days. From mid-December on, Louise visited Carnegie regularly. On one of these visits, he presented her with an engagement ring from Tiffany which she hid away and wore only when alone in her room.[31]

He decided not to recuperate in England or the South of France, as originally planned, but at Dungeness. Space was booked for him and Dr. Garmany on a steamer bound for Florida.

The enforced separation from Louise was painful to both, but flew by rapidly. Andrew was doted over by Lucy, whom he adored, and surrounded by her children. They spent their days fishing and going on walks; their evening at whist. Louise, left behind as always in her mother's house, had plenty to occupy her time. Andrew had charged her with arranging their wedding, hiring a personal maid, and having the dressmaker prepare a new wardrobe. Their engagement remained a secret, though news was starting to leak out; how, neither of them quite knew. Andrew had told no one, not even Lucy. When Louise expressed her concern that she might somehow have betrayed their secret, Andrew reassured her. "It matters little, my Darling, although it is preferable that we escape talk, and especially the newspapers. So don't put yourself too much about—let your friends suspect and talk as they will. You do what is comfortable for yourself."[32]

They were to be married when he returned to New York in April and escape immediately to England for their honeymoon. Andrew, still worried about his health and frightened lest too much activity tire his bride, suggested that they disembark in Southampton rather than Liverpool, and go directly to their honeymoon retreat at Bonchurch on the Isle of Wight. After some time together—accompanied only by his valet John and her maid—they could travel "north and see our friends in London." Louise agreed entirely. "So delightful to avoid friends until we feel just like seeing them. You always do think of the very nicest way of doing things, and I do love you so, you angel."[33]

Alone in New York, with no one to confide in or seek assistance from, Louise was spending a good deal of her waking hours worrying. "Nothing short of perfection as I see it, will satisfy me," she wrote Andrew on March 12, "so of course everything becomes vitally important, but I know I sometimes carry this too far, only I do like everything perfect." Her latest concern was finding a way to let her friends and acquaintances know about their marriage. As they planned to be married in the Whitfield home before no more than twenty-five to thirty guests, with no parties or receptions planned, there would be no way to notify anyone of their marriage before the newspaper notices appeared. The only solution was to send out announcements in advance, timed to reach their friends at the very moment they sailed to England. But there were complications here, too. It would take time to design, order, and print the announcements, and if they did so too far in advance of the event, they risked having news of their wedding leaked to the press.[34]

Andrew tried to reassure Louise. She needn't worry about the announcements. They could wait until he returned to New York City, the week before the wedding, and order them from Tiffany. But what of the outer envelopes in which the invitations would have to be placed? Louise asked next. They had to be ordered early, as it would take hours to hand-address them all. Andrew replied that Louise could buy them in advance at any stationers in the city and address them herself. That, Louise responded, would never do, because if she bought the outer envelopes at a stationers, they would not match the inner envelopes from Tiffany. "I cannot pick up envelopes anywhere, and make them do."[35]

Andrew finally agreed that they would have to order the outer envelopes from Tiffany as well.

AT THE SAME TIME she was planning their wedding, Louise was looking for a place for them to live. Her heart was set on the house owned by the California railroad magnate Collis Huntington, on Fifty-first Street off Fifth Avenue, just three blocks from her mother's home. Huntington's second wife, Arabella, had convinced him to buy and modernize the town house—they had even installed a new Otis elevator—but no sooner had the renovations been completed than Arabella decided the house was too modest for her tastes and prevailed upon her husband to build a more luxurious and ostentatious one on the avenue.

Though a grand house by any standards, the Carnegies' new home would be dwarfed by the mansions just to the east along Fifth. William Henry Vanderbilt's twin palaces occupied the entire block front on the west side of Fifth Avenue, from Fifty-first to Fifty-second Streets. Vanderbilt's son, William Kissam Vanderbilt, had built his own French Renaissance mansion across the street. Farther north on Fifty-seventh and Fifth sat the mansion of William Kissam's older brother, Cornelius Vanderbilt II, this one also in the style of the French Renaissance—but more restrained and classical. Across Fifty-seventh Street, Collis Huntington, having sold the Fifty-first Street house which Arabella found wanting, constructed a city château that was so oversized, even by New York standards, that it took up five 25-foot lots. The house the Huntingtons sold the Carnegie newlyweds had been squeezed into one 50-foot double lot.[36]

Though Arabella Huntington might not have thought much of the address or the town house at 5 West Fifty-first Street, the future Mrs. Carnegie was charmed by it. The Carnegies, rich as they might be, were not going to live like other Gilded Age millionaires in French Renaissance châteaux on Fifth Avenue. Louise found the house—which was twice the size of her mother's—the perfect one in which to begin life as Mrs. Andrew Carnegie. "To me it is the most attractive in every way," she wrote Andrew. "It would seem almost impossible to find a house already built with so many advantages—large yet unobtrusive, and such a choice location." Carnegie contacted Huntington and reported to Louise that he thought the property could be bought for what it had cost Huntington, $170,000 plus the $10,000 Huntington had spent on improvements. "We shall decide, angel, when we meet and confer. Must have a fireproof, sunny home, love, but whether this is the one, or not, is the question."[37]

Carnegie was still a bit patronizing toward his much younger fiancée, but he was learning to trust her. He began discussing business with her, because he wanted her to understand the full extent of his fortune. The steel business was booming. "We never did a business as now. Tremendous boom. I'll surprise you with some figures when we meet. Millions for us, my Love, to spend for the good of our fellows. Isn't it just glorious?" Louise wrote back at once to congratulate him. "I am so glad everything is so flourishing, so you will have no anxiety in your absence. Your partners, too, will be more contented, and bear your absence better."[38]

Less afraid now of being overwhelmed by her future husband's celebrity, Louise took pride in his growing renown as a philanthropist and peace activist who had taken a strong stand against British military intervention in the Sudan. Carnegie had decided to devote his life to a higher calling. And she loved him for it. "I certainly feel more in harmony with all the world after having been in communion with you, my Prince of Peace. I say this reverently, dear, for truly that is what you are to me, and I am so glad the world knows you as the Great Peacemaker." "What ideal lives we shall lead, giving all our best efforts to high and noble ends, while the drudgery of life is attended to by others. Without high ideals, it would be enervating and sinful. <u>With them,</u> it is glorious, and you are my prince among men, my own love."[39]

If Louise, for her part, had once worried that she was too plain a girl for so fine a man, those anxieties were starting to dissipate. She began to envision now, perhaps for the first time, a role for herself as the great man's adviser and partner. Carnegie encouraged her in this. When she wrote from New York about attending a musicale, he responded that they were his "weakness" as well. "If you will get the best musicales in NY at our house, then take first prize—Model Helpmeet. Won't we cultivate real talent, and push it forward! Indeed we shall. We can develop it when found. Money, my dear, money to spend on its education, that's the essential, and bless the Lord, we have it."[40]

AFTER TWO MONTHS of recuperation, Carnegie was ready to return to New York. On the way north, he stopped over in Pittsburgh to meet with his partners. He was back in full health and vigor and prepared to assume his role as chief spokesman and salesman for his Pittsburgh firms. There was much to do—and only a week set aside for it all. "Am writing now with four of my partners talking away," he wrote Louise from Pittsburgh on April 1. "I'm supposed to be listening, and to give my views. I fear I'm not deeply interested. 'Trifles, my dear, trifles.'"[41]

The following day he wrote Collis Huntington from Pittsburgh. Huntington, he had learned, had become discontented with Carnegie Brothers operations while Carnegie was indisposed. He wanted Huntington to know that his "people" in Pittsburgh "say the man of all our customers they have tried to do the most for is yourself, postponing rails when you asked postponement, hurrying up when you asked them to hasten, and in every way showing you that they were determined to place you under such obligations to us that you would never think of buying a rail from any other concern. . . . I hope, by the time this reaches you, you will be in your natural good humor, and satisfied that at all times, and under all circumstances, your alliance with us is under 'the most favored nation clause.' Let us know what we can do for you and it shall be done." In a postscript, he added that he was ready now, having had a "hurried look at" Huntington's house on Fifty-first Street, to make a bid and "would give you cost for it, which you told me was $170,000, adding to this the amount you have expended upon it."[42]

On April 4, with only eight days left until their wedding day, Carnegie realized that he had run out of time and wrote Louise to put off their wedding for ten days. He was, he explained, due in court on April 12 and couldn't get a postponement. Two days later, he wrote again, this time to tell her that the court case had "assumed a new phase and it probably will be arbitrated." It was by now too late to return to their original wedding date of April 12. They would be married instead on April 22 and leave for their honeymoon the next day. To reassure Louise that he was not, no matter how much it might appear, trying to escape his vows, he reassured her with every letter that he loved and missed her more than ever. The delay was torture for him. He could not concentrate on business. "I write now in office with talk, talk, talk all around," he declared on April 6. "You see how busy I'm kept." And the very next day, "I snatch a few minutes to write you because, my Love, I can't help it. Must turn to you . . . and after I have, as it were, kissed you tenderly, I can return to Steel and Iron."[43]

A week later, he was back in New York, attending a reading by Walt Whitman at Madison Square Theatre in honor of the anniversary of President Lincoln's death. It was the last such gala that he would attend alone.

SEVENTEEN

A Wedding and a Honeymoon, 1887

ANDREW AND LOUISE were wed at the Whitfield house at 24 West Forty-eighth Streeth at a little past 8:00 P.M. on Friday, April 22, ten days late, and seven years after they had begun courting. The wedding, which took everyone by surprise, was reported the next morning on the front page of the *New York Times*. It was performed by the Whitfields' minister, Reverend Charles Eaton, pastor of the Church of the Divine Paternity, a Universalist church. There were no bridesmaids and no best man. Louise's mother gave her daughter away. Carnegie wore a "four-button black cutaway coat [and] dark-colored trousers." Louise "was very plainly attired in a tailor-made gray camel's hair traveling dress, heavily braided." Among the guests were Carnegie's literary assistant James Bridge, his private secretary Charles Mackie, and his lawyer and doctors; Alex and Aggie King; his niece, Margaret Carnegie; Mrs. Vandervort, the mother of John Vandevort, his oldest friend and traveling companion; and his partners, David Stewart, Harry Phipps, and Cousin Dod. Immediately after the ceremony and a "simple collation" in the dining room, the "happy pair" were "driven direct to the Bremen steamer pier in Hoboken," where they boarded the steamship *Fulda*, accompanied only by his valet and her maid. They spent their first night as husband and wife on board ship, and the following morning, at 6:00 A.M., set sail for Southampton.[1]

On Sunday, the *New York Times,* in its review of the week's society weddings, commented that the "town [was] still wondering why the wealthy and popular bachelor should have chosen Friday as his wedding day [and] why the bride consented to the choice." A moment's thought would have provided the answers. They were married on Friday night because their ship left on Saturday morning. This was the only way Andrew could protect himself and his bride from reporters and well-wishers. He was still not fully recovered and did not want to risk his health more than he had to.

Colonel William d'Alton Mann, owner, editor, and writer of *Town Topics,* New York's gossip paper for the well-connected, was more amused than distressed by the couple's unconventional nuptials and rapid exit. "Mr. Andrew Carnegie made short work of his marriage. He refused to admit its approach to the papers till he was forced to, and he got married and left the country between dinner and breakfast times. This is quick work for even so energetic a man as the head of the great Edgar Thomson Steel Works. . . . Mrs. Carnegie looked rather rattled during the ceremony, and no wonder. To be telegraphed from maidenhood to matrimony at such a rate would upset any girl." Mann, who admired Carnegie and shared his Republican allegiances, added that he believed the couple would "do a great deal of entertaining when they settle here for good. Both Mr. and Mrs. Carnegie are companionable people, though neither is given to the lighter vanities of life. There has not been as congenial a match in NY for a long time as theirs."[2]

Just moments before they exchanged their vows, Andrew and Louise repaired to the second-floor sitting room of the Whitfield house to sign their prenuptial "marriage agreement." In return for an annual income of $20,000 (more than $3 million today), Louise gave up her rights to her husband's estate.

The prenuptial began by stipulating the obvious: that "the said Andrew Carnegie is possessed of a very large amount of property, both real and personal, within the state of Pennsylvania and elsewhere, and said Louise Whitfield is fully advised as to the amount and value of said property, and of the rights which would accrues to her under the laws of New York, Pennsylvania and other States in case she should survive said Andrew Carnegie." It then proceeded to declare that "Said Andrew Carnegie desires and intends to devote the bulk of his estate to charitable and educational purposes, and said Louise Whitfield sympathizes and agrees with him in said desire, and fully approves of said intention."[3]

Louise was not coerced into surrendering her rights to the Carnegie estate. She knew precisely what she was doing. Her husband was going to give away his fortune during his lifetime and she was going to help him.

The April 22, 1887, prenuptial agreement provides evidence that Andrew Carnegie, a full two years before the publication of his "Gospel of Wealth" essays, five years before the violence at his Homestead steelworks, and fourteen years before his official retirement, had already decided to give away his fortune. This flies in the face of claims that Carnegie became a philanthropist to rescue his tarnished reputation and pay penance for the lives lost at Homestead in the course of the 1892 lockout and strike. On the day the prenuptial agreement was signed, Andrew Carnegie had not the slightest reason to be concerned about his future reputation. Peace reigned at his iron mills and steelworks; he was well liked and well regarded, he thought, by his employees, to whom he had donated reading rooms, mortgages, and cheap coal. He had, as he reported to Louise, been "cheered" several times by his workmen on his return to Pittsburgh after his illness. He enjoyed, in short, the clearest of consciences when on April 22, 1887, he signed the marriage settlement with Louise that stipulated that he planned to give away his fortune.[4]

LOUISE AND ANDREW departed for their honeymoon with joy and trepidation. A honeymoon photograph, taken at Bonchurch on the Isle of Wight, shows two stiff, rather unhappy-looking people: Carnegie sitting, hat in one hand, cane in the other; Louise, looking more like grandchild than wife, standing in her traveling dress, not particularly attractive, but not unattractive either, her jaw squared, her expression blank. (Because of their height difference, they were seldom photographed standing together.) In this picture, both stare straight ahead at the photographer, barely acknowledging one another's presence.

Their glum expressions may have had more to do with the formal requirements of photographic portraiture than with their moods. Carnegie had arranged their honeymoon with the same care that he took when planning his summer vacations. The honeymooners went directly by ferry from Southampton to Bonchurch, where he engaged rooms in a beautiful old hotel surrounded by miles of wildflowers. Louise's letters home paint a picture of a woman fully satisfied that she has made the right choice in marrying her longtime suitor. She was, she assured her mother on a regular basis, enjoying the perfect honeymoon. "You should see us at our meals in our cozy parlor," Louise wrote, "with grate fire burning, bright flowers everywhere and such a glorious view of the sea from our windows. We can sit at table and look out to sea at the ships crossing to France. This morning after breakfast we took a lovely walk, first around the grounds of the hotel, which are beautiful beyond description." A few days later, she wrote again. "We have been walking and driving and having such a wonderful time. This morning we sat for a long time on the cliffs, overlooking the sea; the air so warm and genial, we seem to drink in health at every breath."[5]

After a week to themselves, the honeymooners were visited by Carnegie's favorite relative, Uncle Lauder, and his daughter Maggie. Louise had worried about this moment, but soon discovered that she had nothing to fear. Andrew's Scots relatives were as charming as he was—and delighted that he had finally taken a bride. "Uncle Lauder is most cordial and Maggie Lauder is so very pleasant. They brought me a pretty ecru plaid shawl with a sweet note from 'Aunt Lauder,' and I felt at home with them at once." Uncle Lauder had been scouting country houses for the newlyweds. It was decided that they would move into Kilgraston House in Perthshire after a short tour of England and a few weeks in London at the Metropole Hotel, the perfect spot from which to watch the royal procession marking Queen Victoria's Jubilee. Carnegie had refused to subscribe to the Queen Victoria Jubilee fund in America because "as an American citizen and republican he [feared he] would stultify himself were he to celebrate the reign of any hereditary ruler." That did not mean, however, that he was averse to watching the festivities from his hotel window with his bride.[6]

Carnegie would have preferred to spend much more of the spring and summer in London, showing off Louise to his many friends and admirers, but, as he wrote Lord Rosebery, while his "recovery from typhoid has been rapid," he remained "under Doctor's orders not to try doing London Society." He had instead leased Kilgraston House for the season. "You will probably be in demand for speeches near us [Rosebery was standing for election] and in that case I do hope Lady Rosebery and you will pay us a visit, and 'do' the district with us. I wish you both to know my wife. I have indeed been fortunate."[7]

Louise knew her husband was rather well known and extraordinarily sociable, but not even she, who had kept such careful track of his comings and goings over the past several years, could have guessed at the extent of his fame. "Have met more celebrities than I can count," she wrote her mother on June 10 from the Metropole, "the poet Robert Browning, and Edwin Arnold, writer John Morley—and spent the day with Lord and Lady Rosebery at their place at Mentmore. Sunday we spent with the novelist William Black." On June 13, William Gladstone, almost a year to the day after he had dissolved Parliament following a crushing defeat on Irish home rule, came calling with his wife. As Gladstone recounted in his diary entry, "Mr. Carnegie offered me as a Loan 'any sum' needful to place me in a state of abundance, without interest, repayable at my death, if my estate would bear it; if not, then to be cancelled altogether. Such was my construction of his offer: so large, & so entirely disinterested. Of course, with gratitude, I declined it altogether. But I tried to turn him a little towards the election fund. He said he should consider it disgraceful to die a rich man. His income is £370,000 p[ounds]. ann[um]," equivalent in today's dollars to more than $37.5 million.[8]

When Gladstone refused to accept his offer of a loan, Carnegie took another tack and suggested that he boost his income by writing a book. To avail himself of the protection of American copyright laws, Gladstone would have to write at least part of his book in the United States. "You might honor us by coming direct to our house, & return soon as you pleased. We should keep you as free from interruption as possible." Carnegie asked for a small favor in return. He was traveling with the Blaine family and hoped to bring together the senator, who expected to run again for the presidency in 1888, with Gladstone, who Carnegie hoped would in time return to Downing Street (as he indeed did, in 1892). "When you and [Senator Blaine] are next in power I expect a treaty to be made between the two Countries agreeing to arbitration. What a service for you to make War impossible between English speaking men. It is coming."[9]

Gladstone thanked Carnegie for his suggestions, and then, apologetically and rather obliquely, asked for a contribution to what remained of the party. The disastrous split over Home Rule had cost the party the recent election and Gladstone his position as prime minister. Gladstone explained that he had given £700 to the party, but feared that that would not be nearly enough to hold the Liberals together until the next election. Carnegie responded immediately with a letter and a check. "I send my contribution to you direct. It is so largely a personal admiration for your own self that prompts me to contribute at this time (I mean when a General election is not soon) that I wish you to have the disposal of enclosed."

Carnegie wanted Gladstone to use £700 to reimburse himself for his contribution, then turn the remainder over to Mr. Morley to dispose of. He then offered Gladstone his own ideas as to how the prime minister might revivify his dormant party. He promised, in a future letter, to "work up my idea about Workingmen Candidates," to whom he pledged to "contribute . . . when necessary."[10]

The following year, and on several occasions after that, the Carnegies would visit the Gladstones in London, and at their family estate at Hawarden in Wales. Louise was as taken with the couple as her husband was. In what Gladstone's biographer, Roy Jenkins, has described as Catherine Gladstone's passionate "engagement with the success and wellbeing of her husband," Louise found a model on which to fashion her own relation to her husband. In 1888, after their visit to Hawarden, she would write Mrs. Gladstone to thank her for her hospitality and apologize for the poor quality of the fruit that had preceded her note as a gift. "We feel that we are a better man & woman for this glimpse of your sweet home life, & wherever you go & whatever you do, we shall always follow in spirit with even greater interest than ever before."[11]

Louise was in the midst of learning what it meant to be the wife of a great man surrounded by other great men. "Well, Mother Mine, we are in the whirl, nothing but a rush and bang all the while. I begin to experience the realities of life now and oh! . . . I am not a bit homesick, but I begin to realize how much a man wants and how important it is for a woman not to have any wants or wishes of her own."[12]

From London, after a few more stops at country estates and at Wolverhampton, where Carnegie still owned a newspaper, they were off to Edinburgh, where on July 9, they laid the memorial foundation stone for the new Carnegie library and were publicly fêted by the city's officials. "Our reception exceeded anything I ever experienced (ever saw given to a private individual) or could ever imagine," Louise wrote her mother. "It equaled the receptions given to our Presidents. . . . It is all right enough for Andrew but imagine me, who three months ago was not known. . . . I had to bow right and left in response to the cheers with which we were greeted from thousands who lined the streets. Every window was crowded to the fifth and sixth stories and American flags displayed everywhere."[13]

Carnegie took great delight in traveling with Louise. In his speech in the Edinburgh council chambers, he joyfully informed his audience that

Mrs. Carnegie was, "like all converts . . . beginning to out-Herod her husband in her love and devotion to Scotland. There is no tartan she sees that she does not want to wear. . . . Ladies and gentlemen, believe me that my wife is as thoroughly Scotch already as I am myself, and I leave it to your imagination to say what she will become when she lives here as long as I have had the pleasure of living among you."[14]

The Edinburgh festivities were marred only by an unfortunate incident over Senator Blaine, reported fully in the New York papers. Senator James G. Blaine, with his wife Harriet, and their two daughters, had been with the Carnegies almost from the moment he arrived in London—and would travel and stay with them for most of the next three months. He had been invited to the Edinburgh festivities, along with Senator Eugene Pryor Hale of Maine, but when the two of them arrived thirty minutes late and without tickets, they were turned away by the janitor guarding the door of the Edinburgh Council Hall. Carnegie was initially furious at everyone involved, including the Lord Provost, but when informed of the circumstances, apologized. The next day, at another gathering in honor of the Carnegies, Blaine was able to give the speech he had prepared for Edinburgh.[15]

From Edinburgh, the Carnegies and Blaines were driven to Kilgraston near Perth. Unlike the houses where the Carnegies would spend succeeding summers, Kilgraston did not have the wild, forbidding feel of a Highland estate. Instead of densely wooded, rugged crags and peaks, the hills in Perthshire were gentle and rolling, the fields well kept and mowed. The house itself was described by Senator Blaine as "quite literally a 'castle,'—a great stone structure, one hundred and ten feet in length by seventy-five in width, with an innumerable array of rooms of all possible description. There are fifteen or sixteen spare chambers after the family are all accommodated." It was in the style of a Palladian English country house, in red stone, situated on gently rising ground, with, as Louise described it to her mother, perfectly manicured lawns, gardens, riding paths, "lovely shady walks," a trout stream, and berry patches of "black, white and red currants, gooseberries—huge ones such as Scotland is famous for, raspberries—and such strawberries." The bedrooms, with dressing rooms attached, were on the second floor; a large entry hall, parlors, and drawing rooms on the first; the servants' quarters and kitchens in the basement. Despite its eighteenth-century-style architecture, Kilgraston was replete with the most modern amenities, having been rebuilt almost from the ground up in 1880. Louise was enchanted, as Carnegie hoped she would be.[16]

Worried that his bride would not be comfortable running a large establishment—with dozens of guests—Carnegie had asked Uncle Lauder and his daughter Maggie to engage a butler, coachman, and housekeeper. The housekeeper brought with her a full complement of valets, ladies' maids, housemaids, two full-time cooks, and a kitchen staff. She turned out to be such a "treasure" that (as Matthew Arnold reported to his sister after his visit to Kilgraston), the Carnegies decided to bring her back to New York in the fall—with six members of her staff—"to start Mrs. Carnegie in her new house." The estate was also served by "gillies," gameskeepers, and a full complement of grooms and stable boys to look after the horses. Because Louise had fallen in love with the sound of the bagpipes, Carnegie hired a piper. "He plays every morning on the lawn to waken us," Louise informed her mother, "and to summon us to dinner and during dinner. It is most thrilling, I can assure you, to hear the Scotch reels, laments, etc. How you would enjoy it."[17]

Matthew Arnold, when he visited in mid-September, was given a "bedroom with an excellent dressing room, both looking south over the park to the Ochil Mountains." The house, "a fine one in red stone," was "very comfortable; at dinner was champagne, a menu, and all you could wish." The guests were served by the staff of nineteen, though "Carnegie will not stand *footmen*, so we are waited on by the Butler and a parlour-maid."[18]

Mrs. Blaine was astounded at the ease with which her old friend had assumed his new roles as husband, head of household, and host to the visiting multitudes. "Andrew Carnegie may be little," she wrote her son Emmons from Kilgraston, "but his hoard and heart are great, and he is a happy bridegroom, and rejoiceth as a bridegroom to have his happiness sure, so that we are enjoying, as only pilgrims and sojourners at hotels can enjoy, this oasis of home life, and day and night I bless the Providence which has set the solitary in families and moved them to hospitality."[19]

Carnegie refused to let his guests excuse themselves from each day's festivities. When Senator Blaine objected to taking the carriage to a town thirty-five miles away that was honoring Carnegie and Louise, he was allowed to "go by train, though he had to give his word to coach back" the next day. "Our most generous and hospitable host," Mrs. Blaine confided in a letter to a friend, "is very peremptory." Still, she conceded in a letter to her son that the Carnegie holiday regimen was having a beneficent effect on all his guests. "Your Father is getting so much benefit from the open air, in which he spends the entire day, and think, how long the days are in this latitude. . . . He has discarded woolen socks and gaiters, and one overcoat, and is getting really a color. Also he has danced the Haymaker, which is our Virginia Reel, on the lawn, and has played skittles. We breakfast every morning at nine, and as Mr. Carnegie will not sit down to the table without him, he gets up in good season, a great advantage over that long and enervating lying in bed which at home, he so much indulged in."[20]

Carnegie had always been sociable, but never on such a grand scale. His friend John Hay, the future ambassador to London and secretary of state, visited that summer. In a letter to Henry Adams in Washington, he described his visit "to Andy Carnegie in Perthshire, who is keeping his honeymoon—having just married a pretty girl—in the sensiblest manner imaginable, by never allowing an opportunity for an hour's *tête-à-tête* from one week's end to another. The house is thronged with visitors—sixteen when we came away,—we merely stayed three days, the others were there for a fortnight. . . . Carnegie likes it so well he is going to do it every summer, and is looking at all the great estates in the Country with a view of renting or purchasing."[21]

"Mrs. Carnegie poured coffee this morning for sixteen," Mrs. Blaine wrote her friend on July 18. "Our hostess, Mrs. [Courtlandt] Palmer . . . and young Palmer [aged sixteen] have gone into Perth—for what? To buy a piano, so our autocrat of the breakfast, dinner, and lunch table has decreed. Young Palmer is a musical genius, and this old 'grand,' belonging to the effete nobility, whose purse is light, suddenly found itself condemned last night . . . and it was ordered that its successor should be installed in office before the evening of another day. Hence Perth, which is four miles off."[22]

There was much music making at Kilgraston. Walter Damrosch, the son of Leopold, the founder and conductor of the Oratorio Society and the New York Symphony Society Orchestra, had sailed with the Carnegies across the Atlantic and been invited by Andrew to visit them at Kilgraston. Each night, after dinner, he entertained the guests at the piano. Over a period of several evenings, he performed and discussed Wagner's "Nibelungen Trilogy" (which we today know as the *Ring* cycle) and Beethoven's Fifth Symphony.[23]

"Carnegie," Damrosch wrote his brother Frank on August 5, "is a strange man full of contradictions, of great and good ideas and small conceits, but I consider myself lucky that he is my friend."[24]

To prove to his friend Lord Rosebery that American orchestras were every bit as good as English ones, Carnegie was thinking about sponsoring a European tour by the New York Philharmonic, conducted by Theodore Thomas. Damrosch, who had succeeded his father as conductor of the rival New York Symphony, convinced Carnegie to send him and his orchestra instead. "I think I have got Carnegie to support me in a tour to England with the Orchestra," he wrote Frank from Kilgraston. "He was going to send Thomas, not that he thought Thomas a good conductor but that his orchestra was the best. I've nipped that in the bud and yesterday after starting on a coaching tour he promised me to back us . . . Carnegie will be all right if he is worked carefully by some of our directors. . . . He will do a great deal for us. Wait and see. . . . If you can arrange to have a reporter to meet me on the steamer I could get up an interesting interview about this summer without of course breathing a word about Carnegie and his plans . . . I am having a glorious time, but getting too fat."[25]

Carnegie had always been a remarkable conversationalist, but now, at the head of his table, he blossomed as a host as well. "In conversation, Mr. Carnegie is cheerful and child-like," observed one visitor to Kilgraston; "he can guide discussion of the topics of the moment—whether they relate to men or events—without making speeches, or repelling the youngest or most diffident of the company; and he has another and a rarer gift—the gift of expressing himself without reticence upon keenly controverted subjects, and that too without giving cause of offence to any one." He spoke with "complete conviction," but without the authoritarianism of the know-it-all, never lost his temper, never raised his voice in anger, and never allowed any discussion, on any subject, to become too acrimonious. He also led his guests in song, dance, card and parlor games, and every variety of wholesome entertainment. "In company Mr. Carnegie indulges in music and delights in humorous stories," another of his guests observed, "and when solicited by his friends he sings a good song, or gives a recitation with dramatic effect."[26]

Louise was always at her husband's side: at the breakfast table, where she poured coffee for their guests; at the dinner table; in the parlor; or outside in the gardens. Although she had no responsibilities for housekeeping, meal preparation, or supervising the help, there were several occasions, she wrote her mother, in which she found herself "in tight places, but I wriggle out of them and the ladies all compliment me on my management." Her major difficulty was in keeping up with the guests. There were far too many of them and no surcease from their constant comings and goings. "Well, our house is now full," she wrote her mother on July 17. "I really have no actual care, but it oppresses me to have so many people around." She had been plunged into an entirely new life—Andrew's—and was finding it a bit difficult to adjust. Sundays were her loneliest days. "I miss the old sweet routine and the great change in my life comes over me more then than at any other time. . . . It all seems so very sudden; there has been no growth, no gradual transition. I seem to be leading two lives—outwardly I am the mature married woman, while inwardly I am trying to reconcile the old and the new life. I get awfully blue sometimes but I know it is very wrong to indulge in this feeling." Louise's discomforts at her new station in life were more than compensated by her growing affection for her husband. "Andrew and I are growing more and more together every day. We snatch so many happy moments together and he is so much more thoughtful in little things than he was before we were married. He takes keen delight in all my pleasures and is so thoughtful of my welfare. You need have no anxiety, Mother; I have a husband who knows how to take good care of me."[27]

Released from the care of doctors, Carnegie did not behave like a fifty-two-year-old man recovering from typhoid fever. He spun in perpetual motion all summer, as did his wife and those who fell within his orbit. From Lord Provosts to members of town councils to workingmen's associations to Liberal Party enclaves, everyone, it appeared, wanted to greet and honor the Scottish-American millionaire and his American wife. In early September, with Louise at his side, Andrew delivered his speech at Stirling. They continued on to Glasgow, where he addressed the Glasgow Junior Labor Association at St. Andrew's Hall on the subject of "Home Rule in America," and then drove to the Grangemouth Town Hall to personally mark the opening of a newly built Carnegie free library. Reveling in his newfound celebrity as "something of a public man," he accompanied Louise to the Grangemouth Dockyard Company for the christening of a Mexican steamer, the *Tabasqueño*. At the luncheon following the launch, Carnegie delivered his second speech of the day on, among other topics, land tenure, the Corn Laws, and the necessity for the British to emulate the Americans and "cease primogeniture, entails, and settlements."[28]

Carnegie seized every occasion to get into print. His remarks in Grangemouth were recorded and published alongside his Glasgow and Stirling speeches in the *Dunfermline Saturday Press,* then reprinted by him in pamphlet form for distribution to friends, family, admirers, and his libraries and reading rooms. Years later, Margaret Barclay Wilson collected his published pamphlets and donated them to the Carnegie Library in Pittsburgh. They fill five bound volumes.

Regardless of the occasion, Carnegie's message was the same: he praised American republicanism, advocated Irish Home Rule, and denigrated the British monarchy, the House of Lords, and the aristocracy. Like his uncles in Dunfermline, whom he was proud to emulate, he had become a bit of a rabble-rouser. Colonel Mann of *Town Topics* noted in his December 15, 1887, issue that Carnegie's "freedom of speech" had gotten him into some trouble "across the water while he was on his wedding tour last summer." Invited to speak before a rather distinguished audience in Dunfermline, Carnegie had insulted many of them with "a most disloyal speech, viewed from a British standpoint," in which he criticized the Queen, her court, and the royal family, for being worthless drains on Britain's treasury. Mann claimed that an old friend of Mr. Carnegie's had remarked at the time that he was afraid that "the democratic bee is going to buzz Andrew clean out of his head before he gets through. Ever since he began to print his ideas he has grown fonder and fonder of forcing them on people, and he shows no discretion in doing it, either." Carnegie so outraged respectable British opinion that a "sort of black list has been set up in England against Mr. Carnegie's 'Triumphant Democracy.' This ought to make it one of the most popular political publications of the day."[29]

As their honeymoon holiday passed into autumn, husband and wife grew closer together still. The more Louise came to know her husband, the more she admired and loved him—and the more she was astounded by his little kindnesses and his doting attention on her. "I believe he becomes dearer to me every day of our lives," Louise confided to her mother. "Of course this big life is not altogether one I would choose [but] as long as Andrew and I are so thoroughly united I never can be otherwise than the happiest woman alive. No one, not even you, can begin to imagine the sweetness of that man's disposition." "Yes, Mother, it is a go," she wrote on yet another occasion, "as Andrew says: 'Happily married—two words fraught with the deepest meaning in the world.'"[30]

As happy as Louise was, Andrew was happier yet. All his worries had evaporated into thin air. Louise loved Scotland and had agreed that they should have a Scottish home and spend every summer in it. She had taken to his Dunfermline relatives and British friends—and they to her. Even Uncle Lauder, who could be grumpy, found her "a lovable lady" and "a jewel in your crown. I have taken her to my heart as a member of the family and every one of us has done the same," he wrote Carnegie after Louise's visit to the Lauder home.[31]

Carnegie had found what he had so long been looking for, without quite knowing it: a wife who loved, honored, and admired him, and who did not seem to mind that he was old and white-haired and growing more gnomelike by the day. With Louise, he could have a home of his own and a fixed center in the whirlwind that was his life. And this, he realized, was what had been missing.

On his return to New York from their extended honeymoon, he wrote his friend Vandy and invited him to New York to meet his wife: "Ah Jackie I've got the treasure—only trouble is all my friends like her so much better than they do me—Scotland England America, all in love with Louise. We have a fire proof house double lot. . . . quiet and sunny . . . Am very well, a Leetle stout—but mean to work it off soon riding. . . . Do come East and see us all, spend time with us here—you will dote on Louise, everybody does. . . . Foolish, poor old batch [bachelor] I'm sorry for you."[32]

EIGHTEEN

The Pinkertons and "Braddock's Battlefield," 1887–1888

WHILE THE Carnegies were honeymooning in Britain, Frick was again confronting striking coke workers in Connellsville.

The strike wave of 1886 had not been an evolutionary aberration, as Carnegie had predicted, but a harbinger of things to come. The Knights of Labor, having proved their mettle and emerged victorious in their strikes against the Gould railroads in the Southwest, enlisted hundreds of thousands of new laborers across the country, including Pennsylvania coal miners and coke workers. In the spring of 1887, the Connellsville workers who tended the ovens in which the coal was converted to coke threatened to go out on strike for a second year in a row if their wage rates were not raised when their contracts expired. The coke operators, led by Frick, agreed to submit the matter to arbitration. When the arbitrators' decision was handed down, it was accepted by the employers and by the national unions, but not by the local lodges, who called for a strike. Frick, along with the other coke operators, was determined to break the strike, but Harry Phipps and John Walker, the presidents of Carnegie's steel mills at Braddock and Homestead, ordered him to come to terms with the strikers at once.

Frick did as they demanded—he really had no choice as Carnegie and his partners owned the majority of the shares in his coke company—then offered his letter of resignation. "Having temporized with our employes and made concession after concession to satisfy them and largely in your interest [i.e., the interests of the steel companies], and against the interest and judgment of all other coke producers . . . I think that, cost what it may, we should . . . not start our works until our employes resume work at the old wages, but inasmuch as you have large interests depending on our works being operated I do not feel like standing in the way of you managing the property as your judgment and interests dictate."[1]

Frick hoped and expected that Carnegie, on being apprised of the situation in the coke fields, would support his decision to break the strike. He was wrong. Carnegie sided with Phipps and Walker and accused Frick of not doing enough to ensure peace and full production in the coke fields. "Please don't mislead me second time," Carnegie warned him by cable from Scotland, referring to the year before when coke production had been temporarily stalled by a strike. "Remember suffered enough last time. Make no mistake now. No stoppage tolerated. Reply."[2]

Six days later, on June 7, Frick officially resigned his position at H. C. Frick Coke and lodged his "serious protest" against "so manifest a prostitution of the Coke Company's interests in order to promote your steel interests." The board accepted his resignation, without comment, and replaced him as president with Harry Phipps. The strike was settled—and coke continued to flow into the Edgar Thomson and Homestead steelworks.[3]

The following month, Frick left Pittsburgh for a European vacation. Arriving in London, he found a letter from Carnegie welcoming him "to Britain's Isle" and inviting him to spend a week at Kilgraston. There was no mention of Frick's resignation or his "serious protest" at the steelmakers' interference. "It's superb—Come and see what one gets in Scotland these summer days," Carnegie wrote. "Blaine the happiest man you ever saw. Let me hear your movements. Can take you all in any time." Frick, probably put out at Carnegie's decision not to back him against Phipps and Walker, declined the invitation. Refusing to take no for an answer, Carnegie issued a second invitation in early September. "H.P. [Harry Phipps] tells me you can spare a few days about 19th to visit us. Come ahead. Shall be so glad to have Mrs. Frick and her sister and yourself and any others of your party. We hope you will find Scotland in fine trim but we can't expect July weather in September, so don't expect it to be always dry. . . . We sail *Fulda* 9th October. Can't you come with us. Splendid ship & Captain."[4]

Frick accepted Carnegie's second invitation. There is no written record of what the two men talked about at Kilgraston, but whatever the content of their conversations, Carnegie succeeded in assuaging Frick's anger and convincing him to take up again his post at H. C. Frick Coke. Carnegie had decided that the young man from the coke fields, as impetuous as he might be when it came to breaking strikes, was too valuable a resource to be let go.

Frick returned to Pittsburgh in October and the following month was reelected president of the company that bore his name.

THE CARNEGIES sailed back to the United States a few weeks after the Fricks. From Scotland, Carnegie had written to alert his New York City neighbor and now Secretary of the Navy William Whitney that he would be accompanying a deputation of British MPs and members of Workingmen's Councils to Washington. The delegation hoped to meet with President Grover Cleveland to discuss a treaty of arbitration between Britain and the United States. The response from Washington was positive, and on October 31, Andrew Carnegie and the British representatives gathered in the White House library at four o'clock. "The President," the *New York Times* reported the next day, "who had been busily employed up to the time of the arrival of the deputation, laid aside his work and greeted Mr. Andrew Carnegie cordially as he advanced with the visitors arranged in a wide semicircle." Carnegie formally introduced the delegates, who gave brief speeches. Cleveland then responded with a speech of his own in favor of an Anglo-American arbitration treaty. In his *Autobiography*, Carnegie claims that he was so stirred by the event that "from that day the abolition of war grew in importance with me until it finally overshadowed all other issues."[5]

In December, Carnegie addressed the Nineteenth Century Club on "Triumphant Democracy." After being introduced by Courtlandt Palmer, Carnegie recapitulated the argument of his book, that America was the land of progress and that conditions were steadily improving for working people. He then veered abruptly away from his encomium to American virtues to attack those who did not agree with him. "You will find many men even in America who cannot see the glories of the sun. They notice but the spots. They are the kind who would find that in Paradise the halos do not fit the heads." Immigration, sectarianism, and intemperance were not going to bring down the glorious American republic, as the pessimists feared. Nor was socialism a threat to future peace and prosperity. "It did not begin here, but it may find its end here. It breeds under old forms of government, under loyalism, under monarchies. In the land of triumphant democracy it withers and dies. It received its lesson at Chicago. . . . If you want to live in this country you must be quiet citizens or quiet corpses. That you may understand this we have hanged a few of your fellows, and if you don't observe that intimation we will hang more of you."

Those who preached socialism and anarchism were not workingmen, he told his rich and pampered audience, dressed in their tuxedos and ball gowns, nor did they represent working people. They "talk and rant, but won't work except with their mouths. Instead of seeking work they seek gloomy halls, where they rant about wage-slavery and the wrongs of property. They are mostly foreigners, and the scum and dregs of the native population, the idle ne'er-do-well and dissipated. They are men whom the honest workmen of the country turn their backs upon. . . . During the late war in this country expression was given to the popular sentiment in regard to any one who attempted to pull down the United States flag in the words, 'Shoot him on the spot.' And if any one attempts to establish anarchy in this country, the cry again will be, 'Shoot him on the spot.'"

Concluding what appeared to be prepared remarks, Carnegie changed direction again and quoted from "a letter by the club's President, Courtlandt Palmer, to a meeting of Anarchists, in which Mr. Palmer encouraged them and said that the souls of the Chicago Anarchists [who had been hanged] would go marching on for the good and glory of workmen just as John Brown's soul went marching on for the emancipation of slaves." According to Carnegie, Palmer, a sympathizer of Henry George, the founder of the single-tax movement and a recent New York City mayoral candidate, had declared that it was unjust for landlords to collect rent on property they had not improved. "If Mr. Palmer, who does not believe in rent, did not take rent to-day from the property which he did nothing to create he would be a beggar. The unearned increment surrounds him like a halo. I think when Mr. Palmer next addresses a meeting of Anarchists he would better tell them how to reconcile practice and theory." Carnegie proceeded to attack Palmer for claiming that American workingmen were exploited. Had Palmer studied the census, as Carnegie had, he would have learned that the opposite was the case. "There is no sober workman in this country who, under present conditions, cannot earn his living, teach his children, and save a competence. Bring the man here who can prove that true workingmen—not mouth workingmen—are not satisfied with the condition of things. Show us a true organization of labor that wants Socialism."[6]

Carnegie's *ad hominem* attack on Palmer was widely covered in New York and in Pittsburgh. The *New York Times* reported on the address on December 7 and then ran two additional articles on the 9th, one giving Carnegie the opportunity to defend his actions, the second a "Society Topics of the Week" account of "the first unpleasant incident in the history of the Nineteenth Century Club. . . . Whatever may be Mr. Courtlandt Palmer's attitude towards the Socialistic problems of the day it is felt by the members of the club that Mr. Carnegie's attack upon him was, to say the least, incorrect from the standpoint of etiquette and refinement, and it has produced much feeling in the club, which it is not probable Mr. Carnegie will be again invited to address."

Carnegie, for his part, dismissed talk of a quarrel with Palmer. He had mentioned Courtlandt Palmer in his address, he told the *Times,* because Palmer was "the foremost and most influential assailant of the existing relations between capital and labor, and, as such, I honored him by attacking his views and combating them. . . . He made a very vigorous attack upon my class and called them very hard names. I tried to show that he was mistaken."

When the Nineteenth Century Club reconvened two weeks later, Courtlandt Palmer announced that Mr. Carnegie had resigned. Palmer had initially accepted Carnegie's resignation but now regretted it. "Mr. Carnegie is made of too good stuff for us to lose him. He had been too valuable, energetic, faithful, earnest, and progressive for us to permit him to go. His fear was that if he remained his presence would create a division in the club." Palmer asked the members present to join him in requesting Carnegie to remain a member.[7]

The last word on the subject was delivered, as it so often was, by Colonel Mann of *Town Topics,* who, like Carnegie, could not abide armchair socialists. "In many years of experience with the small tempests in the social teapot in New York," Mann wrote on December 14,

I have never encountered a more amusing one than Mr. Andrew Carnegie succeeded in brewing at the Nineteenth Century Club last week. Not that Mr. Courtlandt Palmer did not deserve a scoring for his Anarchistic bid for the notoriety he is so fond of, but it still was rather unconventional that he should have got his dressing-down in the club he counts among his personal property. . . . As for Mr. Carnegie's speech, though one may question his taste in delivering it as he did, one cannot question its soundness. Mr. Carnegie is a very hard-headed, sensible man. He is not a hypocrite, either. His democracy is a study, not a fad, and no matter how many millions he may be worth he need not rely on them to obtain him consideration. Besides, he earned his millions himself, and if this has made him a trifle self-assertive, his egotism is not that of a Josiah Bounderby [the self-righteous villain in Dickens's *Hard Times*], a mere gaseous inflation from the crucible in which his gold is cooked.

Mann, who was a rock-solid conservative, had clearly enjoyed Carnegie's attack on Palmer's armchair socialism. But he may have been in the minority in praising him as he did. The truth was that Carnegie was becoming more and more of an anomaly in polite New York society. He had already made himself something of a pariah by coming out so strongly in favor of workingmen's associations. He had then done the unpardonable and attacked a friend publicly and viciously. No one knew quite what he was going to do next.

THE CONNELLSVILLE coke strike that Carnegie had forced Frick to settle in 1887 was the beginning, not the end, of a cycle of labor disputes that would rip through the Carnegie firms for the next five years, ending only with the Homestead lockout of 1892. While earlier Carnegie had stood pretty much on the sidelines and allowed Captain Jones and his brother Tom to set labor policy in Pittsburgh, he now felt obligated to show his fellow manufacturers the path to industrial harmony. He had publicly and in print in his 1886 *Forum* articles laid out his plan to restore labor peace through the use of arbitration and the sliding scale. What better way to demonstrate the wisdom of his plan than to put it into operation at his Pittsburgh steel mills.

In analyzing past labor conflicts, Carnegie had found that employer intransigence and insensitivity were the precipitating causes. Because he believed himself infinitely smarter than his fellow industrialists, he was confident that he could avoid the errors they had made. There were, he recognized, hotheads in every group of employees, including his own, who, aided and abetted by "foreign anarchists" and armchair socialists, would attempt to provoke trouble. But he counted on the union leaders he had worked with in the past, and never ceased to praise publicly—most notably William Weihe of the Amalgamated Association of Iron and Steel Workers and Terence Powderly of the Knights of Labor—to listen to reason (his) and outargue, shout down, or shut out the "ignorant demagogues" who regarded "capital as the natural enemy of labor" and tried their best to "embitter the relations between employer and employed." That this approach—relying on leaders to control their rank-and-file—had failed in Connellsville where the local lodges had refused the arbitration package agreed to by the national unions seemed not to deter him.[8]

Having committed his ideas to paper, Carnegie prepared to put them into practice—at his Edgar Thomson works at Braddock. On December 16, 1887, weeks before the existing labor contract was due to expire, notices were posted at the gates of Edgar Thomson announcing that the works would be shut down the next day for "annual repairs." On December 28, the Knights of Labor presented its wage demands for the new contract to Captain Bill Jones. (The Amalgamated, having disbanded its lodges two years earlier, was no longer a presence at Edgar Thomson.) Jones had no response—for the moment.

In New York City, Carnegie outlined the firm's position in an interview with the *New York Times* on January 26, 1888. Because both steel rail and pig iron prices were down by 20 percent, it was "only fair to ask the men to submit to a 20 percent reduction in wages." However, he intended to request only a 10 percent wage cut. "If this were not satisfactory to the employes . . . his firm would not only be willing but anxious to submit the matter to arbitration." He did not expect the men to refuse arbitration or go on strike, as this would be "contrary to the fundamental laws of the Knights of Labor, to which organization the men belong to a great extent."

On February 8, Captain Jones summoned the Knights of Labor "conference committee" to the company offices in Pittsburgh and formally presented his firm's proposal for a 10 percent cut in wages. The men rejected the wage offer, but agreed to submit it to arbitration on the condition that any settlement reached be in effect for six months only, to July 1, and that from this point on, the annual contract expiration date be, as at Homestead, July 1, not January 1. The Knights leadership knew that it would be easier to organize a strike, should one ever be necessary, in the summer, when gardens could supply strikers with food and there was no need to purchase fuel for home heating. They were also persuaded that with rail prices depressed they would be better off negotiating a short-term agreement and waiting six months before signing a new contract.

To this point, there was nothing out of the ordinary about the negotiating process or timetable. That the Knights had turned down Jones's initial offer, and he theirs, was not in itself cause for alarm. Nor was the fact that the mills remained closed and the workers locked out during a slack period with few new orders coming in. (Only the furnace departments remained in operation, as was customary during shutdowns.)

Jones and Carnegie had expected that the Knights leadership and the rank-and-file would, after a few months of being locked out, accept the new wage offer. But they did not. In late February, with the lockout still in effect, Carnegie visited Chicago with Louise, then stopped over in Pittsburgh on his way back to New York. On arriving at the Hotel Duquesne, Carnegie was taken to the company's headquarters on Fifth Avenue, where, according to the newspapers, he remained in consultation with his partners for several hours. The Knights of Labor officials who had been waiting for negotiations to resume interpreted his visit as a signal that he had decided to intervene. "Andrew May Settle It. . . . Employes Expect Good Results" read the headline of a *Pittsburgh Press* article announcing his arrival in Pittsburgh. "The employes at the Edgar Thomson Steel Works have a high regard for Andrew Carnegie," a Knights official explained to a reporter. "He fully understands the men, and they have full confidence in him. He has settled difficulties there before by simply calling a meeting of the employes and discussing the points at issue in a business-like way."[9]

Carnegie did not take the train to Braddock to meet with the locked-out Edgar Thomson workers or the Knights of Labor leaders. He returned instead to New York, but not before issuing what the newspapers referred to as the "startling statement" that Pittsburgh steel was in grave danger of being driven out of markets in the Midwest and Northwest "by Chicago manufacturers" who paid their workers less than he paid his. His comments, broadcast the next day on the front page of the *New York Times* and in the Pittsburgh papers, "created a sensation." It was assumed that he was laying the groundwork for his wage cut proposal by intimating, none too subtly, that if his workers didn't accept reductions, he might move his plant to a location with lower labor costs.[10]

Carnegie was not simply crying wolf about the competition from Chicago. He had looked into the future—and hadn't much liked what he saw. Pittsburgh was rapidly losing its locational advantage to Chicago, which was nearer to the western states where the majority of new track was being laid, and to the Lake Superior region, the largest source of high-grade iron ore. In 1880, 53 percent of the nation's iron ore had come from New York, New Jersey, and Pennsylvania, with less than 24 percent from the states bordering Lake Superior. Ten years later, the situation was reversed: less than 20 percent of ore was produced in the three mid-Atlantic states, with more than 56 percent shipped from Minnesota, Michigan, and Wisconsin. By 1895, the Lake Superior region would supply almost two thirds of the nation's iron ores; the mid-Atlantic states, less than 10 percent.[11]

Carnegie had poured millions of dollars into the Edgar Thomson steel mills. He was prepared to do whatever he had to to protect this investment from the new competition posed by the Chicago steel mills. While he couldn't undo the locational advantage the Chicago firms enjoyed, he could eliminate their advantage in labor costs.

From the safe haven of the library at his new home on Fifty-first Street, Carnegie had been studying the detailed records assembled by Captain Jones at Edgar Thomson and discovered that his labor costs were higher than those paid for comparable work in Chicago's steel mills. The only solution to the competition, he quickly determined, was to both cut the wage rates he paid his skilled workers and increase the length of their workday to twelve hours, as was standard practice in Chicago.

Having decided to give away his fortune—and confirmed as much in his prenuptial agreement—Carnegie was ruthlessly single-minded in his determination to keep his steel company competitive. It was of vital importance, he believed, that Edgar Thomson survive and prosper, not because this would further enrich him and his partners—he had already accumulated more money than he could ever spend—but because a successful steel mill would benefit the larger community, first by providing employment to thousands, then by generating profits which would be given back to the community on his retirement. With a self-righteousness

born of self-confidence in what appeared to him to be his historic role in a
larger evolutionary drama, Carengie felt fully justified in demanding whatever sacrifices were necessary from his workingmen to keep Edgar Thomson afloat and profitable.

IN MID-MARCH, in the third month of the lockout, the Knights leadership, hoping to restart negotiations and still confident that Carnegie was
more sympathetic to their plight than Captain Jones, dispatched a three-
man conference committee to New York City. Carnegie welcomed the delegation to the Windsor Hotel, where he wined, dined, and lectured them
on the steel business, freight rates, rail prices, and the competition from
Chicago. He then presented what he claimed was the solution to all their
problems: a new "cooperative," profit-sharing, sliding-scale plan, which
would obviate forever the need for strikes or lockouts. Under his sliding
scale, wages would be adjusted every month according to the price that
steel rails had fetched the month before. When the price of rails went up,
so would wages; when it fell, wages would fall accordingly.[12]

The daily newspapers, informed, probably by Carnegie, of his grand
new plan, outdid themselves with praise. The *New York Times* devoted two
front-page articles to "Mr. Carnegie's New Plan. A Surprise In Store For
His Striking Workmen." The *Pittsburgh Press* praised "Carnegie's Big Surprise." B. T. Stewart, one of the Knights delegates who had traveled to
New York City, commended Carnegie for talking "fair." Stewart, the papers reported, did not think there would be trouble reaching a settlement.
Only the *National Labor Tribune* refrained from commenting until "all the
points of the proposition shall be at hand."[13]

The outstanding question, which only the *NLT* even hinted at, was
why Carnegie had jettisoned the proposal Captain Jones had made and
come up with an entirely new wage plan. The answer was that he had decided that Jones's proposal did not go far enough toward eliminating the
advantage he believed his Chicago competitors enjoyed. His "sliding-
scale" plan, despite the rosy rhetoric with which he presented it, was intended to establish a new precedent for cutting labor costs by adjusting
them to steel prices, which Carnegie knew were bound to fall in the future,
as they had in the past. More important, Carnegie had decided that at the
same time that he instituted his new sliding scale, he was going to in-

crease the length of the workday for skilled workers from eight to twelve hours.

After their day of talks at the Windsor Hotel, Andrew Carnegie sent the three delegates back to Pittsburgh with copies of the April 1886 article in *Forum* in which he had first outlined his ideas for a sliding-scale wage plan. He said nothing to them about his intention to increase the workday. Instead, he promised them that he would put his current views "into a letter and transmit it to the Executive Board."[14]

On March 28, the executive board of District Assembly 3 of the Knights of Labor met in a special evening meeting to read Carnegie's letter aloud and discuss it. The letter described the new sliding scale in broad generalities. "I wish our men and ourselves to become practically partners by paying them upon a monthly sliding scale based upon the price received for rails during the month preceding." After referring to competition provided by the Chicago mills, Carnegie let loose his first bombshell: "It follows that we must do as our competitors do, viz., run two turns [of twelve hours each] where and when they do so." If that were not enough to jolt the Knights delegates out of their mistaken belief that Carnegie was going to offer them a better agreement than the one Jones had put on the table, reading on, they discovered that Carnegie insisted that the new labor contract be made binding not for a year, as was normal in the trade, or for the six months the Knights had asked for in February, but for a full three years. The extended time period was necessary, he claimed, "to give the sliding scale a fair trial." He added that he wanted every worker in the plant to sign the new contract "individually and for himself." Recognizing, of course, that by demanding this he was at the stroke of his pen eliminating the Knights as the bargaining agent at Edgar Thomson, he slyly added that he "had no objection to any committee signing also, as a committee." His ultimate intention to restrict, if not remove the Knights' influence at the works was indicated in the statement that "of course our managers would select such men as they desired to serve under them." The change from three to two shifts was going to result in the layoff of hundreds of skilled workers in every department. Carnegie was making it clear that the union was to have no role of any sort in determining who stayed and who was discharged.[15]

On Thursday, March 29, the executive committee presented Carnegie's letter at an open meeting of the four Knights of Labor lodges at Edgar Thomson. The meeting was attended by some two thousand steelworkers.

"Carnegie is Answered. His Proposition Falls Very Flat," read the headline in the *Pittsburgh Press* the next morning. The *Pittsburgh Times* reported that the steelworkers had been "surprised" by the proposal. Though they were "generally pleased with the document as opening a means of settlement," they refused to vote it up or down, as Carnegie had demanded. Instead, they authorized the selection of a committee of nineteen, each member representing one of the departments at E.T., to "confer on the proposition," discuss it with Mr. Carnegie, and make it clear to him that they "did not favor a return to the 12-hour turn."[16]

The following Tuesday, April 3, the Committee of Nineteen, having met all weekend, sent an almost fawning letter to Andrew Carnegie, Esq., who had returned to Pittsburgh in the interim. "There is evidently a misunderstanding between the firm and the men," the committee wrote, "and we believe that if we could have a full and free conference with you that the relations between us might be improved. . . . We are somewhat restless under the fear that you are not in possession of all the facts in connection with the unfortunate condition of things. We want to assure you that there is no disposition on our part to interfere with the management of your works, and yet, while the force of circumstances compels us to labor, we are men of like passions with yourself, having interests dear to us involved in the price of our labor, and we are ready to be corrected if we are wrong. Therefore we hope you will concede to us this conference." The letter went on to assure Carnegie that the committee—and the men they represented—agreed with the "fundamental principles underlying your proposition to pay us on a sliding scale." Should their conference not result in a settlement, the Knights agreed to "submit what we disagree on to arbitration." Carnegie granted the men their meeting on Wednesday morning at the Monongahela House. Then, "after congratulating them on the tone of the letter, he politely told them his proposition was his ultimatum and they would have to accept it as written."[17]

Though he had insisted that he was not going to negotiate on the terms of the new contract, no one quite believed him. Rumors surfaced daily that he had agreed to meet with the Knights in Pittsburgh or New York City or had delegated Captain Jones or his cousin George Lauder to reopen negotiations in Pittsburgh. A local Catholic priest, the Reverend Father Hickey, offered at his own expense to lead a new delegation to New York City. Only when Carnegie informed Father Hickey by telegram that he had finished talking and would not meet with any more committees did the citizens of Braddock begin to take him at his word. "Won't Confer Again. Carnegies Say They Have Had Enough of Committees," the *Pittsburgh Press* reported in a front-page headline on April 17.

The people of Braddock, Pennsylvania, prepared for what they were now sure was going to be a long lockout. The largest grocer in town closed its doors; several more cut off credit for Edgar Thomson workers. Captain Jones called in the "minor bosses" to oil the machinery, put the rollers in tallow, and otherwise prepare the works for a lengthy period of inactivity. The skilled steelworkers who were able to find work elsewhere did so. The Knights concentrated on holding their members together; they held weekly rallies at the skating rink and tried to raise strike funds from the District Assembly, the national union, and other labor organizations. They also did their best to reach out to the skilled workers and unskilled Eastern Europeans who did not belong to the union.[18]

In mid-April, Father Hickey thrust himself into the headlines again by assuming what he called "a protectorate of the non-union men." He declared that he was going to hold a referendum at the local parochial school at which all Edgar Thomson workers would be asked to vote on whether to return to work. The Knights boycotted the referendum. In the end, fewer than 500 of the 4,500 E.T. workers cast ballots.[19]

Carnegie and Jones did not act until it became clear that Hickey's referendum was going nowhere. And then they made their move.

On Thursday, April 19, Jones arrived unannounced on the 12:45 train from Pittsburgh. On the way to the steelworks from the station, he stopped his carriage and "spying the boss bricklayer ordered him to get his men ready for work Monday. The effect of this order," the *Pittsburgh Times* reported the next morning, "was electrical. At every corner groups of men congregated, wondering what was in the wind. They were not long kept in waiting for the mill policemen appeared on the street, hunted up the bosses in the various departments and informed them that Captain Jones wished to see them at the works immediately." When they arrived, Jones told them that the works would be opened on Monday and that they should round up their men. Joe Wolf, the boss of the "Hungarians"—the generic term applied erroneously to the unskilled Eastern European day laborers—was also directed to bring in his men. "The general feeling at Braddock," the *Pittsburgh Times* reported, "was one of intense, suppressed

excitement. It was seen that the crisis had come, and trouble is feared."
Asked if he intended to reopen the works as non-union, Captain Jones
parried the question by claiming that Carnegie Brothers did not "discrim-
inate against any one because of race, creed, or organization. We have
posted our terms and anyone who desires can sign. The choice of positions
goes of course to those who sign first. I do not anticipate any trouble from
the Knights and certainly hope there will be none. But I shall start the
works by hook or crook and there are laws in the country, which as the
largest taxpayer in the borough, we have a right to invoke for our protection." The implication was clear. If the Knights leadership did not order its
members to return to work at once, Jones would fill their jobs with outsiders. "Among the Knights of Labor faction," the *Pittsburgh Times* reported, "the news was received in grim silence and the feeling that the
conflict between them and the firm had now begun."[20]

Jones insisted to reporters that he was in charge, but acknowledged that
he had met with Carnegie in New York a few days earlier, and, on his return to Pittsburgh, received final instructions by telegram.

On Sunday morning, April 22, three days after Jones had announced
that he was reopening the rail mill, the people of Braddock awoke to discover that shortly past midnight, a small army of Pinkertons had arrived
and now stood guard over the Edgar Thomson steelworks in preparation
for Monday's reopening. The Pinkertons had by 1888 established a well-
deserved reputation as strikebreakers. The so-called Detective Agency had
been founded by Allan Pinkerton, a Scotsman who had emigrated in 1842,
just six years before Carnegie. Pinkerton at first provided guards for banks
and businesses, then expanded his operation to guarding railroads against
robberies. Beginning in 1866, the agency began providing armies of paid
strikebreakers to coal companies and manufacturers who had the means to
hire them. Because the Pinkertons had no ties to the communities they
were sent into, they could and did act with brutal efficiency in protecting private property and breaking strikes. Their arrival was a signal that
company owners were willing to use any violent means necessary to get
their way.

"Braddock's Battlefield. Warlike Character Around the Edgar Thomson" read the headline in the *Pittsburgh Press* on Monday, April 23, the first
day of the Pinkertons' occupation. "When the residents of Braddock and
Bessemer's [the area immediately surrounding the works] woke yesterday

morning and strolled out towards the works they found them in charge of strangers, all armed, gloomy and determined," the *Pittsburgh Times* reported that same day. "One or two of the more curious walked toward the mill only to be halted in true military fashion. . . . At first only a few of the people of Braddock had encountered the guards in the gray of the morning, but these quickly returned to the town and in a few minutes the whole population was out of bed and shortly after hundreds were swarming around the guards. . . . The first feeling was one of curiosity," which soon gave way to anger and fear. "Fully convinced finally of the purpose of the armed men, the Braddock people fell back and every individual began a discussion of the new phase of things. The more prominent of the Knights of Labor were insistent and outspoken in their denunciations, and they found eager and ready listeners. Their wives and children, and even persons who were not personally interested in the matter of a resumption, joined in the talk, and there was all morning a fever of suppressed excitement." The Braddock police were bewildered, but Allegheny County Sheriff Alexander McCandless quickly deputized fifty new men to patrol on the outside of the works and establish a barrier between the town and the Pinkertons. Captain Jones explained that he had hired the men only as a precaution and had decided to house them in a barracks inside the yards, rather than in the town proper, where they might not be welcome.[21]

Jones took full credit for the decision to bring the Pinkertons to Edgar Thomson, though it is inconceivable that he could have made such a decision without at least tacit agreement from Carnegie, with whom he was in direct contact. Testifying in 1912 before the congressional committee investigating U.S. Steel for antitrust violations, Carnegie declared that "Pinkerton guards were never employed except when I was away in Europe" in 1892. When confronted with testimony to the contrary, he asserted that if Pinkertons had indeed been engaged at Edgar Thomson, it had been "without my knowledge. I never heard of it until now, as far as I remember. We would have no use for Pinkertons."[22]

It is clear from the available evidence that Carnegie, who had in the past declared that he would never bring in substitutes to replace his workers, had changed his mind. His mills had been shut down for almost four months; he could not afford to keep them closed any longer. The market for steel rails, which had been almost dormant in early 1888, had come alive again, the *National Labor Tribune* reported on April 21 and reaffirmed on

April 28. If the Knights refused to return to work on his terms, which he was convinced were fair, he would replace them with men who would. And if that necessitated armed protection for substitute workers, he would provide it.[23]

Jones's demand that the men return to work and the introduction of the Pinkertons transformed a peaceful lockout into a potentially violent strike. The works having been secured by the Pinkertons inside the gates—and the sheriff's deputies outside—Jones and Carnegie could now bring in substitute workers on the B&O tracks that ran through the works. While insisting that he would rather have his old men back than introduce new workers, Jones admitted to the reporters that he had received dozens of job applications. The company was already refitting a number of old houses in the yards "for those men who are brought from other places," the *Pittsburgh Times* reported on April 25.[24]

In its lead editorial on Monday morning, April 23, the *Pittsburgh Press*, like most of the local papers, expressed shock and dismay at Carnegie's decision to bring in the Pinkertons. "It seems, as our recollection serves us, that Mr. Carnegie was quite emphatic, yet now we find him turning the Edgar Thomson into an arsenal instead of a library, and garrisoning the works with extra police, special deputy sheriffs and Pinkerton detectives in order to effect a resumption of the works by force if force should be necessary." Carnegie, the editorial concluded, had every right to run his works as he pleased, but not to lie to his workers about his intentions. "The men may be expected to regard his statements and addresses to them with extreme caution in the future." There was no response from Carnegie, nor would there ever be to criticisms of his bringing in the Pinkertons.

The Knights continued to talk tough to whomever would listen and insist that the introduction of the Pinkertons had only solidified the resolve of their members to fight on. But they recognized now that there was no way they could prevent Carnegie from reopening the steelworks with non-union men from Braddock and scabs from elsewhere. Their only hope was that Carnegie would invite them back to the bargaining table. Carnegie himself, in an interview with a reporter from the *Pittsburgh Dispatch*, insisted that he was finished negotiating. "Carnegie's Crusher" read the *Pittsburgh Press* headline on April 28, 1888. "Effect of His Last Statements on Men At Braddock. Depression Exerted By Realization of the Fact That The Steel Works Will Start."[25]

On the first Friday evening after the Pinkerton invasion, the unskilled laborers—almost all Eastern European immigrants who though not members of the Knights had stayed away from the plant in large numbers until now—held a giant rally with their wives and children at the corner of Thirteenth and Washington. Their spokesmen announced, in several languages, that while the "Hungarians" had no love for Carnegie or his new wage scales, they needed work and would give the Knights until Monday to reach a settlement. If no progress had been made by then, they would return to Edgar Thomson.[26]

On Monday morning, large numbers of "Hungarians," joined by a significant number of skilled workers, went back to work. On Tuesday, Wednesday, and Thursday, other skilled workers, fearful that if they did not return at once they would lose their jobs to scabs, left their homes at daybreak, their lunch pails in hand, and walked silently past the lines of picketing strikers, who jeered them as they entered the gates of the plant. Once inside, safely through the cordons of strikers, police, and Pinkertons, the returning workers were forced to sign Carnegie's labor agreement before they were allowed to take their places among the strangers who had replaced their striking companions. Ten days after the arrival of the Pinkertons, enough skilled and unskilled workers, including a few members of the Knights' Committee of Nineteen, had returned to Edgar Thomson to permit Captain Jones to start up production.[27]

The question now was no longer if the Knights would call off their strike, but when. In its May 5 issue, the *Commoner & American Glass Worker*, the local Knights' newspaper, admitted that the strike was still on, but near defeat because "those buzzards of labor, the Hungarians, were flocking to Braddock daily." Carnegie's "real object," the Knights charged, was "to crush the union. . . . Should not this condition of affairs stamp Carnegie with his true colors? Hypocritical protestations of love and regard for his workmen will not stand when compared with the facts."[28]

The Knights called off the strike a few days later, and then, having given up their only bargaining card, "called upon Capt. W. R. Jones in order, if possible, to effect a settlement." Having lost all else, they meekly requested that Carnegie and Jones not ban the union from Edgar Thomson, that grievance committees be recognized, that jobs be found in other Carnegie mills for workers who were going to lose theirs in the switch from three eight-hour to two twelve-hour shifts, and that a general amnesty be provided. Jones replied that he was not authorized to grant any demand regarding the future of the Knights at Braddock, but that he would do his best to "obviate" the most disagreeable features of the new contract.[29]

The week the strike ended and the Pinkertons left, Carnegie's name appeared again in the Pittsburgh papers, this time for donating $5,000 to the Exposition Society, which proposed to build a grand new music hall in Pittsburgh. On May 15, when Carnegie arrived in Pittsburgh to meet with his partners, as he did every spring before leaving for Europe, Edgar Thomson was back in operation. In the switch from three to two shifts, hundreds of jobs had been lost. Those who had been fortunate enough to keep their jobs had agreed, over their signatures, to abide by the terms of the new three-year contract, accept a sliding scale with no minimum rate, work a twelve-hour day, take whatever position the company offered them, and pledge themselves as "men and citizens [to] abide by and obey the rules and regulations" posted at the Carnegie steelworks and furnaces.[30]

Twenty-four years later, in 1912, seventy-seven-year-old Andrew Carnegie, testifying before the U.S. Steel congressional investigating committee, insisted that the Edgar Thomson workers had freely and of their own accord signed the sliding-scale agreement he had offered them. "It is astonishing what you can do for workmen when you get their confidence. I have never had any trouble with them."[31]

From this point on, Edgar Thomson would be run as a non-union shop. Carnegie and Jones would no longer bargain with union committees about grievances, wage rates, work rules, or transferring or firing recalcitrant workers. In crushing the Knights, Carnegie had won himself at least two and a half years of labor peace at Edgar Thomson and made it clear to the Amalgamated at Homestead that he could bust that union, too, if it offered resistance to his plans.

What, in the final analysis, is perhaps most astounding about the Edgar Thomson strike of 1888 is its virtual erasure from history. The New York press reported on Carnegie's wondrous, inventive sliding-scale plan when he introduced it, but ignored what went on when he tried to force it on his workforce. Many of Carnegie's biographers have overlooked the story entirely. Had more attention been paid to what happened at Edgar Thomson in 1888, there would have been less surprise at what transpired at Homestead in the summer of 1892.

NINETEEN

Friends in High Places,
1888–1889

I T WAS to be Louise's first coaching trip. As had become his custom, Carnegie had assembled an illustrous collection for the occasion. Joining the Carnegies in their four-in-hand were Senator Blaine, still the most well-known Republican in the land, with his wife and her cousin, the author Gail Dodge. The coaching party, which also included Walter Damrosch and Louise's friend and pastor, Dr. Eaton, departed from the Metropole Hotel in London on June 7, 1888. Lord Rosebery and John Morley were there to see them off, as were "hundreds of slightly astonished Englishmen and women" who watched from the sidewalk as the men, in their tall white hats, and the women in their traveling costumes—Louise's was blue serge—were escorted to the coach. Carnegie, also in a serge suit, with a red rose in his buttonhole, took his place alongside his wife, and they were off on a six-week coaching trip to Cluny castle in the Scottish Highlands, where they were to spend their second summer as husband and wife, once again with the Blaines as houseguests.[1]

As the coaching party made its way through Britain, the Republicans gathered in Chicago to nominate a candidate to run against Grover Cleveland in November. Blaine, the plumed knight from Maine and the only Republican to have been defeated in a presidential election in thirty years, had insisted he was not a candidate, but no one, including his supporters, quite believed him. For the next twenty days, as the Republicans debated and then chose their nominee, Carnegie's coach was trailed by reporters. "New York newspaper reporters have followed us from place to place by rail, horseback and tricycle," Walter Damrosch wrote his brother, Frank. Carnegie appointed himself the senator's unofficial press secretary. "Our host," Harriet Blaine wrote to her son James, "is not a man to turn a deaf ear to a reporter's appeal."[2]

On June 23, at the ruins of Linlithgow Castle, the four reporters who were trailing the party presented Blaine with the telegram announcing Benjamin Harrison's nomination. Blaine, according to Walter Damrosch, "bade a friendly good-by to the four young sleuth-hounds . . . and we continued our journey farther north until we arrived at Mr. Carnegie's home, Cluny Castle, on the evening of July 3."[3]

Carnegie had rented Cluny from the Macpherson clan, which, like other ancient Scottish clans, had fallen on hard times and been forced to lease its ancestral home in the Grampian Hills. The estate comprised 11,600 acres of mountain, valley, forest, and moorland in the Cairngorm mountain area in the southeast section of the Highlands along the River Spey. Because of the heavy and almost constant rainfall, the vegetation in this area of the Highlands is extraordinarily lush from spring through fall. The fields of heath give the area an almost purple look, enlivened by yellow gorse and broom, pink and purple rhododendron, wild lupine, and bluebells, overhung by low-lying clouds and a dark mottled-blue sky. Heather-colored hills sparkled in the near distance, with mountains rising up behind them, craggy, forlorn, and forbidding. For Carnegie, who had in *An American Four-in-Hand in Britain*, described landing a big fish as a "more thrilling sensation" than "making a hundred thousand," the estate, crisscrossed by streams, burns, and rivers, with several magnificent lochs for fishing, was paradise.[4]

Carnegie's American guests were enchanted by the landscape, but put off by the weather. "It rains at Cluny every day and at all hours. . . . And it is so cold," Harriet Blaine wrote her son Walker. "When we go out driving we bundle up, as we do in Augusta [Maine] only in winter." Mrs. Blaine, who enjoyed carriage drives, was also distressed to find that there were but three serviceable roads in the vicinity: "Mr. Carnegie has a coach, a landau, a closed carriage, two wagonettes, saddles and saddle horses, and baggage traps of all kinds, ten horses at least, but it is like the equipage of a railway with no tracks, there are no drives." Still, despite the cold and the rain and the absence of drives, Harriet, the senator, and their two daughters, one of whom was to marry Walter Damrosch, enjoyed themselves. "The walks about the castle are fascinating, wild, running by the mountain torrents up hill and down, sheep everywhere and a loneliness which may be felt," Mrs. Blaine told Walker. "Then the hospitality is immense, and I must not forget the long days, which reduce candle light to a minimum, for we leave the dinner table at nine and lights at ten seem an impertinence, only Damrosch, who plays Wagner music every evening, needs candles to make out his operas."[5]

Cluny was not, like Kilgraston, a castle, but a large turreted house of white granite with a slate roof. There were several bedrooms on the second floor, and drawing, dining, and sitting rooms downstairs. Each room had a fireplace, fueled by peat, which was abundant in the Highlands. "The house itself is not so large or beautiful as Kilgraston," Walter wrote his brother Frank, "but very comfortable and imposing surrounded by gardens and park land with a splendid trout stream running over the rocks down the hill and a fine loch a few miles distant. We are eight miles from the railroad. . . . The staff of servants is very large."[6]

"We are all in love with Cluny already," Louise wrote her mother soon after arriving. It would remain, for her, the favorite of all the Carnegie houses. "Such walks, such drives, such romantic little nooks! Imagine the most beautiful mountain brooks, one each side of the Park, with rustic bridges, beautiful waterfalls, plenty of shade trees and shrubs and all surrounded by high rocky mountains with not a tree on them—nothing but rocks and heather—and you have some idea of it all." Whereas Kilgraston had been rather like a large hotel run by the servants, Louise found Cluny "much more homelike and I just revel in it. From my little sitting room, steps lead right to the lawn, and Andrew's business room opens from my sitting room; so we slip from each other's rooms and out to the lawn with the greatest ease. . . . The lawn is like velvet and the flowers bloom continually. They have no end of gardeners about the place, and they keep it in beautiful order." Andrew and Louise went hiking and horseback riding— with a groom along for the longer rides "to attend to us if we want stirrups altered, etc."[7]

The daily routine was much like the one Carnegie had established at Kilgraston the summer before. Carnegie, Louise, and their guests were awakened at 8:00 A.M. by the piper who circled the house. Everyone ate breakfast together (often yesterday's catch, "rolled in oatmeal flour and deliciously fried"). After the meal, Carnegie retired to his rooms to read, write, and answer correspondence, leaving his guests to their own devices. They reassembled for luncheon. Carnegie organized and led his guests on the afternoon's activities and excursions. A full-dress dinner was held at 7:00 P.M., with the guests led to table by the piper. After dinner, there was music, dancing on the lawn—Highland flings and Virginia reels—group singing, and more conversation, often about politics.[8]

If earlier in life Carnegie had been a good listener, especially in the company of politicians and writers, that trait had by now almost entirely vanished. Possessed of an astonishing gift of gab, he had, with age and success, let it run away with him, often to the delight, occasionally to the dismay of his dinner companions and houseguests. Fishing, hiking, picnicking, in his carriage or on horseback, at table or on the lawn outside, he always had something to say.

"The Laird of Cluny was earnest and emphatic in conversation, and not always too respectful of the opinions of his guests," Louise's biographers reported of Carnegie in his middle fifties. "Mrs. Carnegie was vigilant and tactful in averting or softening little social crises. . . . Occasionally Carnegie, at the height of one of his most enthusiastic outbursts, would catch a glimpse of his wife, preening the front of her dress. 'Oh!' he would exclaim, 'Lou thinks I'm talking too much,' and quiet down. Another signal was the scarcely perceptible switch of her skirt—which Carnegie, however, would see and understand."[9]

Walter Damrosch had hoped to return to Britain that summer with an orchestra of his own, sponsored by Carnegie. Though this had not happened, he had been invited to spend his second summer with the Carnegies and was determined to make the most of it.

Carnegie was now president of two of New York's major musical organizations, the Oratorio Society and the Symphony Society, neither of which had a permanent home. Damrosch suggested that Carnegie build a new concert hall for these and New York's other choral and symphonic societies. Carnegie declined. "Mr. Carnegie," as Damrosch explained a half century later, "insisted that if he built the hall, it would have to be a business enterprise." The young conductor was not discouraged. "Tell [Morris] Reno [manager of the Symphony Society and the Oratorio Society]," he wrote Frank in August, "not to worry about the rent for the S.S. and O.S. We are all right and as soon as Carnegie can afford it we will have a hall of our own. Steel rails are rather low now but the time will come."[10]

. . .

THE CARNEGIES returned to New York in October 1888 at the height of what had become the most hotly contested political campaign in years. The Republicans were trying to unseat Grover Cleveland, the first Democrat elected president since James Buchanan in 1856.

Andrew Carnegie had always been a Republican. He had been attracted to the party as a young man because of its antislavery platform and Abraham Lincoln. He had grown more attached to it because of its support for high tariffs and hard money. Through good times and bad, protected tariffs on imported steel rails had kept the domestic steel business strong—and the steelmakers, a major force in Pennsylvania politics, had responded by doing all they could to reelect pro-tariff Republicans. Three weeks before the 1884 elections, Carnegie had written his partners in Pittsburgh that "Bethlehem, Penna. Steel Co., Cambria, and Lackawanna I & C [Iron & Coal] have each given $5,000 to the Republican National Committee and we have been asked to give the same amount which I think is only fair."[11]

Despite the manufacturers' contributions, Cleveland had defeated Blaine in the election of 1884. The protected manufacturers were frightened at the prospect of a shift of power in Washington, but they need not have been. Though a Democrat, Cleveland was not a champion of tariff reform. In October 1887, Carnegie declared that Cleveland's first-term administration had been "highly creditable. . . . I for one will shed no tears if Mr. Cleveland is re-elected."[12]

Six weeks later, on December 6, in his annual message to Congress, Cleveland changed course and declared himself an advocate for substantive tariff reductions and an opponent of the "trusts," which, he claimed, were strangling competition. Cleveland had decided to fight the 1888 elections on the issue of tariff reform. In their effort to hammer home the message that protected tariffs stole from poor consumers to enrich wealthy industrialists, the Democrats pointed directly at Andrew Carnegie as the prime beneficiary of a Republican economic policy that redistributed wealth from West to East and from labor to capital. Carnegie, a Scotsman and rich beyond imagination, was an easy target, especially in Pennsylvania. Cartoonists had a field day with the little man with the big head, usually picturing him in some sort of kilt or Scottish headdress, though he had never in his life worn either. The fact that Carnegie had in the spring of 1888 been engaged in battle with the workers at Edgar Thomson gave the Pennsylvania Democrats added ammunition. So too did the charges, launched first by Congressman William Lawrence Scott of Pennsylvania, that Carnegie was not an American citizen.

In an open letter, reprinted on page one of the *New York Times*, Carnegie answered the charges, though a bit indirectly. He claimed that he had confronted Congressman Scott at a meeting of the House Ways and Means Committee in Washington. "I said to Mr. Scott: 'You have been making speeches around the country saying that I would not consent to become an American citizen and that I was a foreigner profiting by the high tariff.'" According to Carnegie, Scott replied "that he had made that statement under a misapprehension, and he now knew it was not true. He had read 'Triumphant Democracy' and knew that I was an intensely patriotic American."[13]

Other Democrats kept up the barrage through the spring and the summer of 1888. Not a week passed during the campaign without some reference to Carnegie and his millions, the workers he was exploiting, and his

PUCK SUGGESTS A SUITABLE TABLEAU FOR THE PROCESSION IN HONOR OF
THE UNCROWNED KING OF THE G.O.P.

extended and luxurious Scottish vacations. Carnegie tried to counter the attacks by leaking to the press the news that the workers at Edgar Thomson, under his new three-year sliding scale, earned more in August 1888 than they would have under the wage rates originally proposed by the Knights of Labor. That much was true, but only because, as the *National Labor Tribune* noted, they were working twelve hours a day instead of eight.[14]

On his return to the United States in October, Carnegie invited reporters to his library at 5 West Fifty-first Street. The next morning, the text of his interview was published in the *New York Times* and, on page one of the *New York Tribune*, under a headline almost as long as the article: "A CHAT WITH MR. CARNEGIE—DISPOSING OF SEVERAL CAMPAIGN LIES—NO STEEL TRUST IN THIS COUNTRY—TRUSTS FLOURISH UNDER FREE TRADE—HOW HIS OWN BUSINESS WILL BE AFFECTED BY THE ELECTION OF HARRISON—A PLEASANT COACHING TRIP DESCRIBED."

Carnegie began the interview with a monologue on the joys of coach riding in Scotland. When he had finished, the reporter from the *Tribune* asked the first question.

"You have recently been much talked of in certain quarters in connection with steel rail monopolies and such affairs. A good deal has been said about trusts during the campaign. Have you any objection to speaking on this subject?"

Carnegie did not. The public, he explained, had no reason to fear trusts. Competition was the lifeblood of the new industrial age and would, in the end, bring any trust to ruin. "There is no possibility of maintaining a trust. It is bound to go to pieces sooner or later, and generally to involve in ruin those foolish enough to embark in it." The more successful a trust was in raising prices, the more likely it was that those high prices would encourage competitors to enter the industry and sell similar goods at lower prices. "When you find me trying to organize a steel rail trust, set it down that softening of the brain has surely begun." As to the reports that he—and other steel manufacturers—were making "unusual profits," he asserted that "nothing could be more groundless. . . . The rail business is good about one year in five, and then for four years manufacturers are fortunate who pay their interest accounts. Competition is terribly severe."[15]

Carnegie's denial that he belonged to a formal steel trust was technically true. The steelmakers had not established a formal trust in the same way that Rockefeller had with Standard Oil. But they had set up a number of informal pools, which set prices and divided markets for rails, beams, wire nails, steel billets, axles, channels, and angles. The differences between formal trusts, with centralized boards, stock certificates, and dividends, and the informal pools, which were non-binding on any of the participants, were significant. Their purposes—to control, if not eliminate competition— were identical.

BENJAMIN HARRISON, the Republican candidate for president in 1888, was something of an unknown quantity. Blaine and Carnegie were not, and they bore the brunt of the Democrats' attack in Pennsylvania in the months preceding the November election.

The Republicans, the Democrats charged—and rightly—were the party of protectionism, of tariffs which enriched manufacturers like Andrew Carnegie. "After a long sojourn with the nabobs of Europe, and a full month's indulgence at Cluny Castle," the *National Labor Tribune* wrote on October 6, James Blaine

> comes home arrayed in English clothes and shod in English leather, and, like a great horny-handed toiler, begins to talk about the blessings of protection and the comforts of the poor people of this country compared with those of Europe. Mr. Blaine says nothing about his host, Mr. Carnegie, or about the system that makes it possible for him to live abroad in regal style and maintain an expensive, lordly castle in a foreign country, three thousand miles away from his place of business. Plain people who hear these matters discussed, and who have read about Mr. Blaine's coaching tour abroad, and who are asked to vote to continue the conditions that have given Cluny Castle an international reputation, are reading and thinking, and the more they read and think the better they are satisfied that this protection Mr. Blaine talks so glibly about is a fraud and only protects such men as Mr. Carnegie, while the producers and workers get nothing but the protection afforded by Pinkerton's police. . . . Shame on the protection that permits one man to live on the fat of the earth wrung from the sweat and toil of three thousand.[16]

Two weeks later, the *New York Times* published a list of Pittsburgh millionaires—there were one hundred of them, forty-nine of whom were or had been "beneficiaries of the present protective tariff system." At the top of the list was Andrew Carnegie, whose wealth was estimated at $20 million (about $3.5 billion today). Further down came Henry Phipps, Jr., at $5 million and H. C. Frick at $1 million.[17]

Carnegie did not dispute his inclusion in this list. He focused instead on the more damaging charge being made that he was not an American citizen. On October 24, months after the accusations had first been leveled in public, the *New York Times* published a front-page article which it claimed settled "the question of Andrew Carnegie's citizenship," citing his assertion that he had become a citizen three years earlier but had mislaid his naturalization papers. A court document attesting to Carnegie's having become a citizen on May 28, 1885, was appended to the article.[18]

Carnegie had delayed so long in furnishing proof of his citizenship, not because he had mislaid his papers, but because he did not want to admit that he had not applied for citizenship until 1885, when he was fifty. When the charges first surfaced, he asked his lawyers in Pittsburgh, one of whom was the highly connected Republican Philander Knox, who would later serve as senator from Pennsylvania, attorney general, and secretary of state, to find out whether his having worked for the War Department in 1861 or 1862 and taken "the oath of office, which is one of allegiance," had made him a citizen. He also directed his lawyers to search for any records that might demonstrate that his father had been naturalized—or applied for naturalization. Had William Carnegie become a citizen before he died, his minor son would have been one as well. His attorneys informed him that his service in the War Department did not make him a citizen and that there were no records that his father had ever been naturalized or declared his "intention" to be naturalized.[19]

Carnegie asked them to look again for his father's application for citizenship. On November 8, 1888, his lawyers wrote back that they had again found no record of his father's ever having filed a "declaration of intent" to become a citizen. They had, however, located Jared Brush, the court clerk who would have received such a declaration had it been filed in 1854. Brush had, at their request, signed a "duplicate" of what he now claimed was the "declaration of intent" he had accepted from William Carnegie thirty-four years earlier.

At the time he signed the document, Brush was no longer a court clerk. He had left decades earlier, gone into politics, served as mayor of

Pittsburgh, and then gone into business. The 1880 census listed him as an "iron manufacturer." When asked to help out Mr. Carnegie, a fellow Republican and iron maker, he no doubt agreed to do so by signing his name. To protect himself legally, Brush clearly wrote "duplicate" in red ink on the left-hand margin of the document he signed. That notation was afterwards erased from the "declaration of intent" which Carnegie held on to during his lifetime and later deposited with his papers at the Library of Congress.*[20]

BENJAMIN HARRISON was elected president of the United States in November 1888, though he lost the popular vote to Grover Cleveland. Carnegie telegraphed his congratulations from New York: "First for the continued prosperity of the Republic. Second for your personal merits, I tender you my heartfelt congratulations upon being called to the foremost position in all this world."[21]

The changing of the guard in Washington occurred at the same time as a similar transfer of power in Pittsburgh. Harry Phipps, who had reluctantly assumed the chairmanship of Carnegie Brothers on Tom's death, resigned in October 1888 and was replaced by David Stewart, one of the original partners. When Stewart died almost immediately after assuming the post, he was replaced by Henry Clay Frick.

Even before his formal appointment, Frick had begun to serve as Carnegie's chief lieutenant in Pittsburgh. One of his primary tasks, in the fall of 1888, was to get from the Pennsylvania Railroad the money it had owed Carnegie since 1885, when it agreed to buy his shares in the South Pennsylvania Railroad. Carnegie, having reluctantly decided that there was no way to fight the Pennsylvania's monopoly on freight traffic to and from Connellsville, was "most anxious," as he wrote Frick in September, "to get

---

*The original document, on which "duplicate" is clearly written, was sequestered in a safe at the Home Trust Company in Hoboken, New Jersey, a private bank Carnegie established in 1901 to administer his trust funds and serve as the executor of his will. Only when the building in which the papers were stored was demolished in 1998 was this document, along with Carnegie's 1888 correspondence with his lawyers, discovered by the contractor and, with the assistance of Kenneth Miller and Vartan Gregorian, purchased by Columbia University. All documents regarding William Carnegie's naturalization are in series IX, box 8, folder 10, CCNY; for a copy of the "Declaration of Intent," without the "duplicate" notation, see vol. 1, ACLC.

into closest alliance with PRR. It is worth all the other RRs to us put together. . . . We could do much for PRR. . . . My policy is to keep to our own business [i.e., making steel, not building railroads]—work loyally with Mr. Roberts [the Pennsylvania's president]—do all we can to advance PRR. . . . We should all agree to put [the money originally invested in South Pennsylvania stock] into its shares and hold it as a permanent investment—I would take a million of its stock."[22]

When Roberts refused to pay Carnegie full price for his stock but offered him 60 percent, without interest, Carnegie threatened to sue the railroad for making the deal in the first place. Roberts, Carnegie insisted, had, by offering to buy his stock in the South Pennsylvania, circumvented the court order prohibiting the Pennsylvania from swallowing up the South Pennsylvania, a potential competitor. "I have not the slightest doubt but that the Penn. Railroad Co. has rendered itself liable to every South Penn stockholder," he wrote Frick on February 2, 1889. "The Courts of Pennsylvania will be indignant at the Penn. Railroad officials evading the spirit of their decisions. . . . You know that I have been right in several legal matters," he assured Frick. "Believe me, I am right in this, that we now have the Penn. Railroad in a position where it must settle in full with us. I know the men to summon and the questions to ask. Roberts and Thomson are nearer to going to jail to-day than they ever yet have been." He added, as postscript, "Keep this to ourselves for present."[23]

Frick counseled caution. He was wary of entering into battle with the state's most powerful corporation. Carnegie refused to back down. "Frank Thomson [PR vice president] can be convicted of contempt of court and so can Mr. G. R. Roberts—that is quite clear. Now if they will [agree to pay us, even in installments] we can let matters go. . . . Mr. Roberts cannot expect us to be cheated."[24]

In the spring of 1889, Carnegie made good his threats. In a series of speeches at the Franklin Institute of Philadelphia, the Pennsylvania state legislature in Harrisburg, and at the dedication of his new library at Braddock, he publicly accused the Pennsylvania Railroad of crimes against the people of Pennsylvania, particularly those who lived in the western sections of the state. Few knew that his anger had been stoked by the Pennsylvania Railroad's refusal to pay him in full for his South Pennsylvania stock. Carnegie claimed, instead, that he was speaking out against the behemoth only because the exorbitant rates it charged for shipping raw

materials to Pittsburgh impeded the state's "commercial growth" and men-
aced "her future prosperity." While other cities, Chicago in particular, benefited from cheaper freight rates for shipping raw materials to their
factories and finished goods to their customers, Pittsburgh was being
squeezed by the Pennsylvania Railroad. It was not only the manufacturers
who were being injured by the extortionate rates; jobs were being lost. Positioning himself as spokesperson and representative of "the great army of
labor" whose livelihood was imperiled by the Pennsylvania Railroad, and
using language as provocative as that employed by the armchair socialists
and foreign anarchists he had so recently castigated, Carnegie reminded
his listeners that during the Civil War Pittsburgh's workers had taken to
the streets to prevent guns from being shipped south. "They did this in the
interest of the nation. Are they to be forced into a similar protest against
the Pennsylvania Railroad Company carrying supplies past Pittsburgh furnaces to furnaces in other states upon terms they refuse us?" To eliminate
the threat of violence, which he himself had called into being, Carnegie
asked the Pennsylvania legislature to regulate the railroads by passing a
"state Commerce law similar in its scope to the Interstate Commerce law,"
approved by Congress in 1887.[25]

His language was bombastic and incendiary, and that was intentional.
He wanted to draw headlines again, this time as Pittsburgh's knight in
shining armor, riding to its rescue against the evil villain. Savvy as he was,
however, he could not control what was written about him. The stories in
the Pittsburgh papers that praised Carnegie for his attack on the Pennsylvania Railroad reminded readers of the rumors that he had earlier plotted
to block the completion of the South Pennsylvania Railroad.[26]

AT THE SAME TIME that Carnegie was blasting the Pennsylvania Railroad for being unfair to Pittsburgh, he was extolling its virtues in letters to
his British friends. He was immensely proud of the fact that American
railroads were outstripping the British in the luxuries they offered their
passengers. "I am traveling homeward from Pittsburgh to New York at rate
of forty miles an hour upon the Pennsylvania Limited, which runs daily
between New York and Chicago, a distance of 1000 miles, without
change," he wrote William Gladstone in February 1890.

The cars are connected by a covered passage-way, so that we can pass from end to end of the train. The train has a Dining car, its tables beautifully ornamented with flowers, excellent meals provided, fresh cooked on the train, a Ladies' Maid who waits on the ladies, men servants, all the latest daily and weekly papers, bath rooms for ladies and gentlemen, a barber shop, an excellent library, special telegrams of public interest are received as we proceed; but the latest addition is the Official Stenographer to whom I am now dictating. All of these are free of charge. Passengers can thus write home and business men can clear up their correspondence. We happen to have on board to-day a Clergyman who has dictated the heads of his Sunday sermon. . . . You have received thousands of letters, but none written, I venture to say, under such circumstances.[27]

IN THE MIDST of his public battle with the Pennsylvania Railroad, Carnegie returned to Braddock in March 1889 to dedicate his new library. The dedication ceremonies were held at the largest venue in town, "Leighton's rink," which the year before had been the site of the Knights of Labor rallies against him.[28]

Carnegie refused to apologize for the Pinkertons or the breaking of the strike or the institution of the twelve-hour day and the new sliding scale. On the contrary, his address was a full-throated paean to himself and the gifts he had bestowed on Braddock and his Edgar Thomson employees. He had funded their cooperative stores and beneficial societies, invested their money in his savings banks, offered them reasonable mortgages, and built a library for their use. The sliding scale had established a new era of peace and harmony and motivated him and his partners to do even more for the workingmen of Braddock. "Never before have my partners and myself taken such pride, such interest, such satisfaction in our business as this year, when, having adopted the sliding scale, we walk through these mills knowing that instead of Labor and Capital standing face to face, jealous and distrustful of each other, we and our workmen are now practically partners, sharing in the present depression of prices together, but also bound to share in the advance of prices which must come sooner or later. This common interest has changed the feelings of my partners and myself to our workmen. You are no longer only employees, you are also sharers with us in the profits of our business, and, sooner than return to the old plan by which Capital and Labor were antagonized, and we had to quarrel every year upon the subject of wages, I would retire from business altogether." The effect of the sliding scale upon management, he continued, had been nothing less than transformative. "It made us feel that we were prepared to make any sacrifice necessary to give steady employment to you who were now shoulder to shoulder with us. . . . The firm could probably make more money just now, in depressed times, by manufacturing less, but where would labor be with work perhaps only half the year? . . . If we had not made a partnership with our workmen, we might have considered the proposition [of closing down until prices rose for rails]. Having them with us in the struggle we reject it, and will continue to run our works to their capacity."

He took enormous pride in having provided "steady employment" for his workers, but he also rejoiced in the fact that under the sliding scale their "aggregate wages" were higher than they had been. "You have to work harder, no doubt," he conceded, acknowledging that the workday had been extended, but he assured his listeners—without any hint of irony—"that in these times the owners of the concern have to work harder also."

Carnegie was, he claimed, a "fellow workman" himself. The more he made such a claim—and he would make it repeatedly in the years to come—the more he came to believe it. He was no idle landlord or coupon clipper who lived on dividends, but an active partner—a worker—in the steel mill. The fact that he now "worked" out of his library in New York and was usually finished after a few hours in the morning did not, in his mind, disqualify him:

I resent the idea that because the interest of the firm compelled me to remove to New York and attend to a special department, I am to lose my rank as a worker with you in the business. . . . Let it always be understood that we are workers together, and although I no longer work with my hands, as I am proud to say I once did, yet when I pass through the works I object to the airs which the men at the lathes or the blooming mill, the converting works, or blast furnaces seem to put on as I pass along. I am just as much entitled to the proud appellation of "workingman" as any of you, and I hope you will remember this hereafter and treat me with proper respect as one of the great guild of those who labor and perform a use in the community, and who upon that basis alone founds his claim to live in comfort.

He objected also to those who considered him "no longer a Pittsburgher." He had "put all my eggs in one basket, right here in Western Pennsylvania. I may be ranging the earth, but my heart must be directed to the home of my youth, and my thoughts to the prosperity of those industries in which I have not been afraid to invest, and am not now afraid to let my capital remain. When Pittsburgh sinks, I sink with it, and when Pittsburgh swims, I shall swim with it."

If the steelworkers of Braddock and Homestead, most of whom were already on a twelve-hour day, wanted to blame someone for their situation, they should look not to him but to themselves and their unions. "The real enemy of labor is labor, not capital." Carnegie could not be expected to unilaterally reduce the workday at his plants to eight hours when his competitors enjoyed the advantage of twelve-hour shifts. The unions, having failed to do their job and compel his competitors to institute the eight-hour day, had no choice now but to attempt to reduce the workday "by slow degrees through State laws." Until that occurred, he counseled the workingmen to make the best of their lot. "Even, as at present, if workmen used well the time they have at their disposal they will soon rise to higher positions. You need not work twelve hours very long; most of us have worked more hours than twelve in our youth." With astounding insensitivity to the demands that a twelve-hour workday made on a man's body and soul, Carnegie admonished the Edgar Thomson workingmen not to "forget the importance of amusements. . . . It is a great mistake to think that the man who works all the time wins in the race. Have your amusements. Learn to play a good game of whist or a good game of drafts, or a good game of billiards. Become interested in baseball or cricket, or horses, anything that will give you innocent enjoyment and relieve you from the usual strain. There is not anything better than a good laugh."

Well aware that his words were going to appear in the newspapers the next morning and be reprinted and circulated in pamphlet form (paid for by him), Carnegie seized the opportunity to issue a rather brazen challenge to his employees at Homestead. He read aloud a "letter . . . from a Homestead man" who asked when Carnegie was going "to do something for Homestead," and then launched into an attack on the Amalgamated Association, which, he claimed, stood in the way of his instituting his sliding-scale plan. Only when the skilled workers at Homestead, like those at Edgar Thomson, agreed with him that a new wage rate structure had to be instituted to protect the interests of capital and guarantee steady employment would he welcome them as partners and build them a new library. "As a friend of labor, I advise them to accept the sliding scale and be done with labor disputes." He did not have to mention what would happen if they did not. The Homestead workers and the Amalgamated were already well aware of how, with the assistance of the Pinkertons, he had broken the strike—and the union—at Edgar Thomson.[29]

TWENTY

The Gospels of Andrew Carnegie, 1889–1892

A T THE BRADDOCK LIBRARY dedication in the spring of 1889, Carnegie announced his decision "to withdraw more and more from business. My intention is to devote less and less of my time to it."[1]

Like the grandfather retired to his rocking chair, he wanted to spend his remaining days dispensing advice to whoever would listen. He was embarking on his most productive period as a writer. Between the spring of 1888, when he broke the Edgar Thomson strike, and late 1891, he published articles in leading literary journals on the major issues of the day: trusts, tariffs, monopoly regulation, the gold standard, wealth and poverty. Because he believed fervently that he was not writing propaganda, he became a superb propagandist for industrial capitalism and the Republican Party that protected it through high tariffs, maintenance of the gold standard, and the provision of the minimum antitrust regulation necessary to keep working-class and agrarian dissidents at bay.

In his pronouncements on questions of capital and labor, Carnegie claimed for himself the disinterested status of a social philosopher who looked beyond present-day fads and fancies to "the great laws of the economic world, [which] like all laws affecting society . . . alone remain unchanged. . . . Whenever consolidations, or watered stocks, or syndicates, or Trusts endeavor to circumvent these, it always has been found that after the collision there is nothing left of the panaceas, while the great laws continue to grind out their irresistible consequences as before."[2]

Carnegie presented his arguments within the framework he had borrowed from Herbert Spencer. Larger evolutionary laws governed the workings of the domestic economy in its transition into and beyond industrialization. The proper role of government was to remain on the sidelines and let these laws work their magic. Carnegie repeatedly invoked the "laws" of wages and profits, competition, consolidation, aggregation, supply and demand, and accumulation of wealth to justify his business practices. He was not alone in doing so. Answering critics who suggested that there was something unnatural, even criminal about the extraordinary "increase in the value of [Standard Oil's] possessions," John D. Rockefeller claimed in his 1909 "memoirs" that "it was all done through the natural law of trade development." Jay Gould, asked in 1885 by a Senate investigating committee if he believed a "general national law" was needed to regulate railroad rates, responded that they were already regulated by "the laws of supply and demand, production, and consumption."[3]

While fully understanding the value of protective tariffs, Carnegie was enough of a pragmatist to understand that periodic revision of the rates was necessary, as was some regulation of the railways and trusts. Gestures had to be made, crumbs offered the angry masses to protect the larger capitalist edifice. He endorsed the Interstate Commerce Commission, established in 1887, and recommended that Pennsylvania establish its own railway commission.

Only when it came to the gold standard did he and his fellow captains of industry oppose any compromises. Those who held large amounts of capital, no matter how accumulated, did not want the value of that capital diluted by inflation, as it would be were additional dollars coined of silver. The more dollars in circulation, the less each one would be worth. As critical, the nation's bankers, merchants, manufacturers, and railroad directors feared that European financial houses would not purchase American stocks and bonds unless they were fully backed by and convertible to gold.

When, in 1890, Congress passed the Sherman Silver Purchase Act, which mandated that the Treasury buy and coin 4.5 million ounces of silver, businessmen outside the western silver states were outraged at what they regarded as blatant political interference in economic affairs. The fact that Republicans had voted for the bill was particularly disheartening. "The idea of reintroducing silver currency" was, for J. P. Morgan, as his biographer Jean Strouse has noted, "about as welcome as a biblical plague."[4]

Carnegie, who had taken on himself the task of educating the public on economic matters, sat down at once to write a primer on the gold standard, "The ABC of Money," which was published in the *North American Review* in June 1891. He relied, as always, on the evolutionary theories he had adapted from Herbert Spencer to make his case. There were, he explained, two metals currently in use in "civilized countries" as standards of value: silver and gold. Less advanced nations like the South American republics and Japan had adopted and retained the cheaper metal, silver, as their standard. The United States, like "the principal nations of Europe . . . being further advanced and having much greater business transactions, found the necessity for using as a standard a more valuable metal than silver, and gold was adopted." To facilitate commerce between gold standard and silver standard nations, it had been agreed to value 15½ ounces of silver as the equivalent of 1 ounce of gold. "Everything went well under this arrangement for a long time. The more advanced nations were upon a gold basis, the less advanced nations upon a silver basis, and both were equally well served." As more silver was mined, however, it lost its fixed value relative to gold. The British government had, as a consequence, wisely disposed of its holdings in silver; but American politicians, under the sway of the "silver power," had required their government to continue to buy and coin silver, even as it declined in value. This meddling in the evolutionary process, Carnegie argued, threatened the prosperity of the nation. No country could long endure with two standards, just as no people could salute two flags. Because silver was worth less than gold, individuals, companies, and nations would pay for American goods in silver; employers, given the choice, would also pay their workers in the cheaper currency. The immediate losers would be the nation's farmers and wage earners, who would receive a debased currency for their crops and their labor.[5]

Reaffirming his credentials as a disinterested public servant, Carnegie concluded his primer by claiming that the protection of the gold standard was, for him, even more important than the maintenance of the protective tariff. "In the next presidential campaign, if I have to vote for a man in favour of silver and protection, or for a man in favour of the gold standard and free trade, I shall vote and work for the latter, because my judgment tells me that even the tariff is not half so important for the good of the country as the maintenance of the highest standard for the money of the people."[6]

CARNEGIE's most provocative and best-known article dates from this period. Originally entitled "Wealth," it was published in the *North American*

Review in June 1889 and subsequently republished in the British *Pall Mall Gazette* as the "Gospel of Wealth," a title Carnegie adopted as his own.

The "Gospel of Wealth" was a primer on the workings of the political economy and an advice manual for millionaires. It was also a self-conscious attempt on Carnegie's part to understand why so much wealth was accumulating in so few hands and why he, the son of a Dunfermline weaver and an ex-bobbin boy from Allegheny City, had become so fabulously wealthy.

Had he been a man of faith, as was his contemporary John D. Rockefeller, he might have attributed his material success to divine providence. But Carnegie could not accept the notion of a supreme being who randomly blessed some with riches on earth and everlasting joy in heaven while condemning others at infancy to eternal damnation. He also put no credence in the chief tenet of the nineteenth-century success manuals, that success was the fruit of hard work. How could he base his right to his millions on the hard work he had expended in earning them when he had, from his mid-thirties on, devoted but a few hours to business every morning? Diligence was obviously not a prerequisite for material success. On the contrary, Carnegie took great pride in his state of semiretirement and urged others to follow his example.

It was clear to him, as he would explain in a 1906 *North American Review* article entitled "Gospel of Wealth II," that wealth was "not chiefly the product of the individual under present conditions, but largely the joint product of the community." No man could possibly earn millions by his own exertions. He illustrated this point by conjuring up the stories of four representative millionaires who had made their fortunes in railroads in New York, iron and steel in Pittsburgh, meatpacking in Chicago, and mining in Montana. Though he did not name names, it was clear that the railroad millionaires were Vanderbilts; that he himself was the model for the iron and steel magnate; Philip Armour or Gustavus Swift for the meatpacking king; and William A. Clark for the Montana miner. In each case, the wealth that found its way into the hands of the individual had been created by the larger community. The railroad stocks of the first millionaire would have remained worthless had the communities his railroads served not soared in population. "Floating on a tidal wave of swelling prosperity, caused by the increased traffic of rapidly increasing communities, he soon becomes a multi-millionaire."

Similarly with the iron and steel manufacturer and his partners. "Their venture was made profitable by the demand for their products . . . from the expanding population engaged in settling a new continent." The same could be said of the meatpacker: the growth in his business, profits, and fortunes was "based solely upon the wants of the population." The fourth millionaire, the Montana miner, "did not create his wealth; he only dug it out of the mine as the demands of the people gave value to the previously worthless stones."[7]

The word "millionaire," which had barely existed a few decades earlier, had entered the American lexicon. From the mid-1870s onward, American newspapers would be glutted with stories of the newly wealthy, their comings and goings, mansions and fêtes, European excursions and Newport holidays. "This is an age of great fortunes," the *New York Times* exclaimed in 1882. "Never before in the history of the Republic have there been so many men who are very rich." And "very rich" today, as the *New York Times* instructed its readers, was quantitatively different from "very rich" in any other era of the nation's history. "One who might have been 'very rich' in 1842 would not be accounted rich at all, with the same fortune, in 1882." The *Spectator of London,* in an article reprinted in the *New York Times* in November, marveled at "the evidence forthcoming from America that fortunes may be accumulated on a scale of which Englishmen have little conception." While the English were pleased to earn 4 percent on their investments, Americans were satisfied with nothing less than "three times to ten times that rate."[8]

It was these facts of modern life that Carnegie felt obliged to make sense of in his "Gospel of Wealth" articles. "The conditions of human life have not only been changed, but revolutionized, within the past few hundred years. In former days there was little difference between the dwelling, dress, food, and environment of the chief and those of his retainers. . . . The contrast between the palace of the millionaire and the cottage of the laborer with us today measures the change which has come with civilization." Others, including Carnegie's former friend Courtlandt Palmer, and Henry George, who had run for and come close to being elected mayor of New York City in 1886, believed that this growing gap between wealth and poverty was a social problem to be solved. Carnegie "welcomed [it] as highly beneficial. It is well, nay, essential for the progress of the [human] race that the houses of some should be homes for all that is highest and best in literature and the arts, and for all the refinements of civilization, rather than none should be so. Much better this great irregularity than universal squalor."[9]

Carnegie made no excuses for conditions he had not brought into being. Like everyone else, he was a creature of long-term evolutionary processes, albeit a very fortunate one.

The historical changes Carnegie described which had led to this gap between rich and poor were "inevitable," governed by "laws" that were immutable. There was no reversing the transition from the household or workshop mode of manufacture, which fostered "social equality" but had resulted in "crude articles at high prices," to the present industrial system, which generated social inequalities but produced goods in such abundance and so cheaply that the poor could now "enjoy what the rich could not before afford." The new industrial age with its huge business establishments required for its leaders men with a "talent for organization and management." Because such men were in short supply, they had to be highly recompensed, often with partnership stakes. As they increased the capital of the business organizations they administered, so too did their own capital holdings increase. "It is a law . . . that men possessed of this peculiar talent for affairs, under the free play of economic forces must, of necessity, soon be in receipt of more revenue that can be judiciously expended upon themselves." And this was for the best. "Not evil, but good, has come to the race from the accumulation of wealth by those who have had the ability and energy to produce it."[10]

There was, for Carnegie, no turning back the clock of history. The only question worth asking was: "What is the proper mode of administering wealth after the laws upon which civilization is founded have thrown it into the hands of the few?" The answers could be deduced from the work of Herbert Spencer. If, as Spencer claimed, a "beneficent necessity" governed the workings of human history, then it followed that there was an evolutionary purpose behind the accumulation of great wealth in the hands of the few. Just as the "laws upon which civilization is founded" had decreed that wealth fall into the hands of those with the rare but essential "talent for organization and management," so too did they decree that these same men should administer this wealth on behalf of the larger community. "This, then, is held to be the duty of the man of wealth: To consider all surplus revenues which come to him simply as trust funds, which he is called upon to administer . . . in the manner which, in his judgment, is best calculated to produce the most beneficial results for the community." The millionaire's wealth was not his to spend, but his to wisely give away. "Rich men should be thankful for one inestimable boon. They have it in their power during their lives to busy themselves in organizing benefactions from which the masses of their fellows will derive lasting advantage, and thus dignify their own lives."[11]

Like much of Carnegie's writings from this period, his "Gospel of Wealth" articles are suffused by a barely disguised anger. His confidence in the wisdom of his preachings was beginning to spill over into abuse of those who disagreed with him and those who did not behave as he thought they should.

In these articles, he criticized utopian thinkers with unembarrassed zealotry. "Our duty is with what is practicable now—with the next step possible in our day and generation. It is criminal to waste our energies in endeavoring to uproot, when all we can profitably accomplish is to bend the universal tree of humanity a little in the direction most favorable to the production of good fruit under existing circumstances." Carnegie reserved his greatest scorn not for his ideological and political opponents, but for the men of his own class, who, not having foreseen what he was going to propose, had not followed his as yet unwritten precepts for administering their wealth. He began by assailing those who left "great fortunes to their children. If this is done from affection, is it not misguided affection? Observation teaches that, generally speaking, it is not well for the children that they should be so burdened. . . . Looking at the usual result of enormous sums conferred upon legatees, the thoughtful man [i.e., Andrew Carnegie] must shortly say, 'I would as soon leave to my son a curse as the almighty dollar,' and admit to himself that it is not the welfare of the children, but family pride, which inspires these legacies." As he and Louise did not at the time have any children and none appeared to be on the way, these were not difficult statements for him to make.[12]

The man of wealth who left his fortune for others to administer after his death was only slightly less deserving of rebuke. "In many cases the bequests are so used as to become only monuments of his folly. It is well to remember that it requires the exercise of not less ability than that which acquired it, to use wealth so as to be really beneficial to the community."

The rich man who abjured the responsibility that came with his wealth—of wisely administering it for the good of the community—did that community a grave disservice. "The memories of such cannot be held in grateful remembrance, for there is no grace in their gifts." To prevent the bestowal of vain and foolish legacies, Carnegie advocated the steepest possible inheritance taxes. "By taxing estates heavily at death the State marks its condemnation of the selfish millionaire's unworthy life."[13]

Having condemned as misguided, vain, and selfish most of his fellow millionaires for not giving away their money during their lifetimes, Carnegie turned his rage toward those who did give it away, but indiscriminately and unwisely. Sounding much like Ebenezer Scrooge, he poured forth a torrent of abuse at the rich man who "gratified his own feelings [and] saved himself from annoyance" by giving alms to the unworthy. "It were better for mankind that the millions of the rich were thrown into the sea than so spent as to encourage the slothful, the drunken, the unworthy. . . . Neither the individual nor the race is improved by almsgiving. . . . He is the only true reformer who is as careful and as anxious not to aid the unworthy as is to aid the worthy, and, perhaps, even more so, for in almsgiving more injury is probably done by rewarding vice than by relieving virtue."[14]

He concluded by damning yet again the millionaires who died with their fortunes intact. "The day is not far distant when the man who dies leaving behind him millions of available wealth . . . will pass away 'unwept, unhonored, and unsung,' no matter to what uses he leaves the dross which he cannot take with him. Of such as these the public verdict will then be; 'The man who dies thus rich dies disgraced.'"[15]

Carnegie was immensely proud of his new article. So was Louise, who forwarded a copy directly to Gladstone. "We think we have found the true path," Louise wrote the prime minister, in language a bit more theocratic than Carnegie might have used. "It is the one we meant to tread—if it commends itself to you we shall be so happy. Hoping you will find time to read it—With every good wish for your prolonged health and happiness, in all of which you know my husband most heartily joins me."[16]

The article created such a stir that the editor of the *North American Review* asked Carnegie to write a follow-up piece with recommendations on how the wealthy might spend their fortunes to benefit the larger community. That piece, entitled "The Best Fields for Philanthropy," was published in December 1889. Carnegie suggested that the rich dedicate their surplus wealth to founding or funding schools and colleges, libraries, hospitals, public parks, concert halls, public baths, church buildings, or other institutions as they saw fit. "The only point required by the gospel of wealth is that the surplus which accrues from time to time in the hands of a man should be administered by him in his own lifetime for that purpose which is seen by him, as trustee, to be best for the good of the people."[17]

By fashioning Spencer's evolutionary philosophy into a high-minded, scientific apologia for capital accumulation, Carnegie had both persuaded himself and his fellow multimillionaires of the moral worthiness of their enterprises and offered them a doctrine with which they could do battle with their enemies. The gospel of wealth provided an ideological antidote to socialist, anarchist, Communist, agrarian, single-taxer, and labor protests against the unequal distribution of wealth by arguing that the common good was best served by allowing men like himself to accumulate and retain huge fortunes. The more wealth that landed in wise hands, the more that could be given away—wisely—by the retired capitalist acting "as trustee and agent for his poorer brethren, bringing to their service his superior wisdom, experience, and ability to administer, doing for them better than they would or could do for themselves."[18]

In November 1890, the *Nineteenth Century* focused the attention of the British public on Carnegie's article by publishing a lengthy review by William Gladstone. "It seems like a dream," Carnegie wrote Gladstone upon receiving a copy of the review, "that you who was to the little Scotch Lad, something beyond human—should be attracted by anything he has promulgated & that he should really know you in the flesh."[19]

Gladstone's review was positive, but tempered. He disagreed with Carnegie most strongly on the question of inherited wealth, which he found "a good and not an evil thing," as the "hereditary transmission of wealth and position" was often conjoined "with the calls of occupation and of responsibility." Gladstone also dissented from Carnegie's call for the rich to divest themselves in their lifetimes of their entire surplus wealth. Charity was a good thing and the donor, Gladstone argued, should be free to decide how much of his fortune he was going to give away. He proposed the organization of a voluntary association, each member of which would pledge, on his "bond of honour," to give a portion of his annual income to charity.[20]

In qualifying Carnegie's demand that the rich give away their entire fortunes, Gladstone was dismissing the larger point which Carnegie, leaning heavily on Spencer, was attempting to make. The wealthy, Carnegie insisted, were merely "trustees" for their communities, with no individual right to the money they held in trust. In his letter to Gladstone, Carnegie asked if he and Mrs. Carnegie could "be enrolled as Members [of the voluntary association]—I presume we who hold that all surplus should be bestowed may nevertheless be eligible as Members of a Society, or Brotherhood, which asks that its adherents only bestow a part—the greater should include the less." In the rebuttal he wrote for the March 1891 issue of the *Nineteenth Century,* Carnegie ignored Gladstone's "association of givers," focusing instead on the prime minister's defense of inherited wealth. Poverty, he claimed, not wealth, was the "only school capable of producing the supremely great, the genius." Inherited wealth robbed the inheritors of their self-respect and blocked the "fittest" from advancing. No society could reach its highest potential if it gave the rich an advantage over the poor in attaining positions of leadership and responsibility.[21]

The month after Gladstone's review, the *Nineteenth Century* continued the debate by publishing three more reviews of Carnegie's "Gospel," the most damning by the Reverend Hugh Price Hughes, a Methodist bishop. Hughes believed Carnegie to be "personally a most estimable and generous man . . . entirely worthy of Mr. Gladstone's hearty praise. But when I contemplate him as the representative of a particular class of millionaires, I am forced to say, with all personal respect, and without holding him in the least responsible for his unfortunate circumstances, that he is an anti-Christian phenomenon, a social monstrosity, and a grave political peril." Carnegie's gospel was based on the premise that the accumulation of wealth in the hands of the few was both "natural" and salutary. Hughes argued, to the contrary, that millionaires were "the unnatural product of artificial social regulations [like the protective tariff]. . . . Millionaires at one end of the scale involved paupers at the other end, and even so excellent a man as Mr. Carnegie is too dear at that price."[22]

Carnegie counterattacked vigorously in his rebuttal, published in the *Nineteenth Century* in March 1891. Millionaires were good for society, he declared unambiguously, as they created the wealth that made its way, disproportionately of course, into everyone's pocket. The industrial era had not witnessed growing impoverishment of the masses; on the contrary, "poverty, want and pauperism are rapidly diminishing quantities." Work-ingmen, whether employed "at the shipyards of Glasgow, the iron and steel mills of Sheffield, the coal-mines of the Midlands, or at industrial estab-lishments generally," were receiving "much greater compensations for their services than they ever did." The greater the number of millionaires in any society, the better the "condition of the masses." There was far more abject poverty in China or Japan or India, where there were no millionaires, than in Russia, where there were one or two, Germany, where there were two or three, or England, where there were more than on the entire Continent combined. Millionaires were in greatest abundance in the United States, where, Carnegie declared, "the skilled artisan . . . receives more than twice as much as the artisan of Britain." Here was proof positive that the "masses" benefited from economic and political systems that encouraged rather than fettered the accumulation of millions in the hands of the few.[23]

Bishop Hughes had attacked the millionaire as "anti-Christian," but had not John Wesley, the founder of Methodism, admonished his flock to "gain all you can by honest industry," and if, after providing for "your wife, your children, your servants and others who pertain to your household," you ac-cumulate an "overplus, do good to them that are of the household of faith. If there be still an overplus, do good to all men"? Far from being "anti-Christian," Carnegie declared with no false modesty that his "gospel of wealth seems founded" on Wesley's sermon. "Indeed, had I known of its ex-istence before writing upon the subject, I should certainly have quoted it."[24]

Developing and forcefully articulating an argument that big business would make use of for the next century, Carnegie declared that millionaire industrialists were community benefactors because they provided "steady employment to thousands, at wages not lower than others pay . . . and steady employment is, after all, the one indispensable requisite for the wel-fare and the progress of the people." There was nothing unique in this ar-gument: Rockefeller would make it in his *Random Reminiscences of Men and Events,* as would dozens of other rich men, but none as forcefully as Carnegie. For he was the only one who argued that the millionaire bene-fited his community twice: once in making his fortune and providing employment and cheaper goods in doing so; and then again by wisely dis-tributing the fortune he had earned.[25]

Having answered his critics, Carnegie dismissed them—and their arguments—and took to preaching his gospel whenever he could. "There is scarcely a day," he proudly wrote Gladstone in March 1892, "I do not have an opportunity to expound the doctrine."[26]

CARNEGIE, having now publicly declared that he would give away his fortune, set to work doing so. He began in Pittsburgh.

In 1881, he had offered the city $250,000 to build a public library, with the stipulation that the city provide funds for books, maintenance, and staffing. Because there would not, until 1887, be a law in Pennsylvania like the one in Britain giving municipalities the right to levy taxes for such purposes, the Pittsburgh city officials turned down his request. In December 1889, only days after the publication of his second "Gospel of Wealth" article, the Pittsburgh City Council dispatched a committee to ask Carnegie whether he might be willing to renew his offer of funding for a library. Carnegie answered that he was not only willing, but intended to increase the size of the donation from $250,000 to $1 million: $700,000 for a central library, with $300,000 for branch libraries. His conditions were relatively few: he wanted decisions on siting and construction of the buildings and control of the library put into the hands of commissioners, the majority of whom he would name. He also demanded that the city allocate an annual $40,000 for maintenance of the library.[27]

The obvious location for the new library would have been in the triangle of land between the rivers where the majority of Pittsburgh's working people still lived and worked; but Carnegie had no intention of squeezing his new library into a densely populated business district or a run-down working-class neighborhood. His sights were set instead on the fashionable suburbs in the East End, which had been annexed in 1868.

Frick involved himself in the site selection, as he did in all Carnegie's projects. On February 28, 1890, only four days after Pittsburgh had formally accepted Carnegie's offer, Frick wrote "regarding site for Library; it is a most important question." He suggested that Carnegie consider a piece of land in the East End owned by Bobby Pitcairn, now a major Pennsylvania Railroad executive. Frick warned Carnegie, however, that should they select Pitcairn's land on the East End "or any other site near to it, it would raise a tremendous howl at first, but I believe would be eventually indorsed by every one."[28]

As it became known that Carnegie's library might be built on the East

End, probably in the Oakland area, the "howl" reached a crescendo, with angry letters in the newspapers, and a protest to Carnegie from the Central Trades Council that the library should be built in the "heart of the city," where it could "confer the greatest good on the greatest number." Carnegie, anticipating such battles, had prepared for them by establishing a library commission, well insulated from political pressure.[29]

There were many reasons why it made sense to build the library in Oakland, which Carnegie believed would soon be the residential center of the city, connected by horsecar and trolley with downtown. The year before, Mary Schenley, one of the city's largest landowners, had donated 300 acres for a park. Carnegie hoped to get her to donate land adjacent to what would become Schenley Park for his library. In July 1890, Carnegie paid Mrs. Schenley a visit—she lived in England—thanked her for her generous gift to Pittsburgh, and laid out his proposals for a library. On July 9, he wrote his former business associate James Scott, now the president of the library board and chair of the building committee, to suggest that he approach Mrs. Schenley about donating an additional 100 acres for the library. "The best way to present the matter to her, in case she has not already acted, is to show that the ground in question is absolutely necessary to make the Park she has given available. And that being established, I think she will give it upon the same terms as she did the other one-hundred acres."[30]

The following October, the land for the library was secured—on 19, not 100 acres, purchased from Mary Schenley. The national competition to design the new library building, with space for a music hall, natural history museum, and art gallery, was, so the architectural historian Franklin Toker tells us, "the most heralded contest in American architecture up to that time [with] 102 entries and 1,300 drawings from 96 architects in 28 cities." The commission was eventually given to the firm of Longfellow, Alden & Harlow, whose principals had ties to Stanford White and H. H. Richardson. The design selected was in the Beaux-Arts monumental style that American architects and city builders had become so fond of in the years leading up to the Chicago Exposition of 1893. The Carnegie Library of Pittsburgh was to have everything a grand building should: mass, height (two decorative towers on either side of the Music Hall), late Gothic windows, a red-tiled roof, elaborate surface decorations, a curved exterior in front—where the Music Hall would be located. The library proper would be housed in a classically symmetrical building with an almost square foot-print; the art gallery and museum would be placed, in rectangular-shaped wings, along each side.[31]

This was to be Carnegie's gift to the city—and to himself—and he wanted it to be perfect. In March 1891, he notified James Scott that he intended "to spend a whole week, if necessary, in Pittsburgh, if you can stand me so long," to help with the planning.[32]

Fearing that the smoke which permeated Pittsburgh might do damage to a granite exterior, Carnegie suggested that his library be constructed of brick, which was cheaper and more durable. "The more I think upon the subject, the more I am inclined to believe that brick of a proper shade will make a far richer and finer effect than granite under the smoky conditions which will exist. Of course I am willing to give the extra one-hundred thousands dollars if necessary to make a creditable building, but as I feel at present, I am not willing to pay extra for granite; on the contrary I think it would be better to pay a little more for brick." In the end, Carnegie was prevailed upon to donate the additional $100,000 needed for the stone exterior.[33]

The Music Hall, which was probably modeled after Charles Garnier's opera house in Paris, occupied the front of the building. It was—and is—a marvel all its own, with remarkable acoustics. "You will not have as perfect a hall as we have in the Music Hall here," Carnegie wrote James Scott from New York in late 1893, "but as you will have the best hall in Pittsburgh, people will think it perfect, and it will only be when you honor us with a visit to New York, and sit in our Music Hall that you may then feel that perfection is not to be found anywhere else, but we shall try to console you in other ways."[34]

CARNEGIE had been extraordinarily generous in providing Allegheny City, Braddock, and Pittsburgh with first-class music halls attached to his public libraries. In conversations that extended over several summers, Walter Damrosch made the case for a freestanding music hall in New York to accommodate the city's two symphony orchestras and the Oratorio Society. The Metropolitan Opera House at Thirty-ninth Street was barely suitable for opera, and totally unfitted for orchestral music, as was the aging Academy of Music on Fourteenth Street. The other major recital halls were in the showrooms of the city's major piano manufacturers, Steinway Hall on Fourteenth Street and Chickering Hall on Eighteenth Street.

Carnegie, an habitué of all of these halls, did have to be convinced of the need for an all-purpose "music hall," but he declined to donate any money for one. His "admiration for music in its simpler forms," Damrosch wrote in his memoirs, "never crystallized into as great a conviction regarding its importance in life as that he had regarding the importance of science or literature, and though always generous in its support, his benefactions never became as great as in other directions. . . . He always insisted that the greatest patronage of music should come from a paying public rather than from private endowment." He donated the money for music halls for Pittsburgh, Allegheny City, and Braddock because he owed these communities something. New York City was a different matter. "He built Carnegie Hall," Damrosch recalled, "but he did not look upon this as a philanthropy, and expected to have the hall support itself and give a fair return upon the capital invested."[35]

In New York, as in Pittsburgh, Carnegie sited his Music Hall in a relatively underpopulated, underused part of the city, "uptown" on Fifty-seventh Street and Seventh Avenue, just south of Dickel's Riding Academy on Seventh Avenue, in an area of stables, coal yards, and vacant lots. He organized a stock company to run the hall, loaned the company the money it needed in return for 90 percent of its stock, put himself and Damrosch on the board, and approved the selection of William Tuthill, a thirty-four-year-old architect who was secretary of the Oratorio Society board and known more for his singing than his buildings.

The Music Hall company purchased several lots and put up three connected buildings. The largest and grandest was the six-story, caramel-colored brick and terra-cotta building with the mansard roof that housed the auditoriums. It did not look much like a concert hall, but could have been mistaken for an ornate bank or office building in the style of the Italian Renaissance. On the main floor was an auditorium which sat around 2,800; beneath it was a recital hall seating about 1,000; on the top floor were the so-called "lodge rooms," which, it was hoped, would be leased at a profit. When that proved impossible, the mansard roof was ripped off and replaced with larger studios that earned a bit more money, but still not enough to make the Music Hall self-sufficient.[36]

The cornerstone for the building was laid in May 1890. A year later, the

"MUSIC HALL, founded by ANDREW CARNEGIE," as it was formally designated by the board of directors, opened with a six-concert festival of orchestral and choral works, presented by the Oratorio Society and the New
York Symphony Society, and conducted by Damrosch.[37]

The draw of the festival was Pyotr Ilich Tchaikovsky, who discovered
upon his arrival that he was, as he wrote to friends in Russia, "on the
whole . . . much more of a big shot here than in Europe." The festival sold
out rapidly, with scalpers cornering the market for the better seats. "Everyone here pampers, honors, and entertains me," Tchaikovsky wrote home.
Still he spent much of his time in New York wishing he were elsewhere.
His letters and diaries are packed with complaints about his full schedule,
the strangers who besieged him at his hotel, the ladies who gaped at him
during intermissions, the bad but abundant meals, and the "coarse" performance of the second-rate pianist engaged to play his concerto. Through
it all, however, he never ceased to be amused by his host, Mr. Carnegie, "a
rich, old man possessing thirty million dollars who resembles [the Russian
playwright] Ostrovsky."[38]

On the Sunday evening, after the conclusion of the festival,
Tchaikovsky was invited to dinner at the Carnegies'. He was astounded to
find that

> this ultra-rich man lives no more luxuriously than others. . . . Carnegie
> [has] remained a modest and simple man, never one to turn his nose up—
> [he] inspires in me unusual warm feelings, probably because he is also
> filled with kindly feelings for me. During the whole evening, he showed
> his love to me in an extraordinarily peculiar way. He clasped my hands,
> shouting that I am the uncrowned but still genuine king of music; em-
> braced me (without kissing—men never kiss here); he stood on tiptoe and
> raised his hands up high to express my greatness; and finally threw all the
> company in delight by imitating my conducting. He did this so seriously,
> so well, and so accurately, that I myself was enraptured. His wife, an ex-
> tremely simple and pretty young lady, also showed her sympathy for me in
> every way. All this was pleasing and somehow embarrassing at the same
> time.[39]

The opening festival was a grand success, but Carnegie's attempt to organize a corporation to operate a self-sustaining music hall was doomed to

failure. In Europe, such halls and orchestras were generously subsidized by the government. Tchaikovsky was quite surprised when he learned that the Music Hall whose opening he was celebrating had been "built from music lovers' money" and that these "same rich lovers of music maintain a permanent orchestra. There is nothing of the kind with us!"[40]

Carnegie had not intended to name the new hall after himself. As he would later explain to Charles Norton Eliot, the president of Harvard, he had wanted to call it "The Music Hall" after Boston's major concert and lecture hall. Unfortunately, the term "music hall" had a different connotation in London, and when the board discovered that foreign artists were turning down invitations because they believed the New York hall was for cheap variety artists, the name was changed. Carnegie insisted to Eliot that he had been in Europe when the name change occurred and had never approved of it.[41]

ANDREW CARNEGIE had achieved no small amount of fame for his philanthropy by the late 1880s, a full decade before his retirement. His biography in the 1887–89 edition of *Appleton's Cyclopedia* noted that he had "devoted large sums of money to benevolent and educational purposes." What was not known was that Carnegie would have given away even more had he been able to. Although his accountants reckoned his net worth in January 1890 as in excess of $14.8 million, more than 90 percent of it was in stocks, bonds, or partnership interests he could not liquidate. His share of Carnegie Brothers and Carnegie, Phipps (which owned the Homestead works) was valued at almost $11 million; his stock and bonds in H. C. Frick Coke at $1.6 million; his Keystone Bridge stock at another $720,000. He retained smaller investments in the newspapers he had purchased in Britain, in a few bridge companies and railroads, including the Texas & Pacific Railway, and in the Columbia Oil Co., which had long ago ceased to be profitable.

His liabilities totaled over $700,000, including $21,000 on the Fifty-first Street house, which was in Louise's name; $429,000 owed to Carnegie Brothers; $13,217 to the Allegheny library; $54,393 to the Edinburgh Carnegie Library; and $146,000 to the "trust accounts" he had set up for dozens of family members, former associates, friends, and colleagues, including John Champlin, Walter Damrosch, Louise's mother, and a mysterious Madame Ximenze. Against these liabilities, he was owed $928,000, including a probably unrecoverable $247,000 he had loaned his cousin Dod and $108,000 loaned to some thirty individuals and small businesses.[42]

We don't know what his annual income was, though Gladstone noted in his diary that in 1887 it was about £370,000, or $1.8 million. Whatever its size, it was eaten up by the expense of maintaining a home and stables in New York City, leasing Cluny in Scotland, and for his coaching trips, winter vacations, gifts, loans, and entertaining and transporting family and friends back and forth across the Atlantic.

Carnegie might have increased his income and made his partners quite happy by authorizing larger distributions of profits, but he was unwilling to do this. So he did the best he could, spending whatever money he had on his libraries, and on more than one occasion making promises without any present means of meeting them.

Early in 1896, after dedicating his Pittsburgh library, he received a request to give money to Cornell University. Carnegie responded at length that he could not do so because he had decided that his "first duty was to [Pittsburgh] the great community to which I owe so much." More important, he didn't have any more money to give away. "You notice in reading the proceedings of the Opening of the Pittsburgh Library [which he had included with his note], I have to spend five millions in and around Pittsburgh. I have yet two millions of that to make, because I have not accumulated a dollar since I gave up daily attention to business. When it is made and spent I shall hope to see clearly the next field which it is my duty to take up. I am happy in being, as it were, a rich poor man largely in debt, as you see. I intend to keep always promised ahead, as one seems then to be in the position of dependence upon Providence, as it were. . . . At present I am in the condition of Mr. Vanderbilt, who once said to me, 'I am invested up to two years ahead.'"[43]

TWENTY-ONE

Surrender at Homestead, 1889–1890

It becomes the duty of the millionaire to increase his revenues. The struggle for more is completely freed from selfish or ambitious taint and becomes a noble pursuit. Then he labors not for self, but for others; not to hoard, but to spend. The more he makes, the more the public gets. His whole life is changed from the moment that he resolves to become a disciple of the gospel of wealth, and henceforth he labors to acquire that he may wisely administer for others' good. His daily labor is a daily virtue.[1]

"THE GOSPEL OF WEALTH" was not simply a defense of capitalism, it was an exhortation to the businessman to work harder to accumulate more profits. The end was all that mattered: the means were not to be questioned. The workingmen at the Edgar Thomson steelworks at Braddock had been the first to bear the brunt of Carnegie's new resolve. Having succeeded in guaranteeing future profitability by dramatically cutting labor costs, Carnegie was ready to do the same at the steel plant he had purchased at Homestead in 1883. He had inherited there a facility with a history of labor militancy, a union contract, several well-organized Amalgamated lodges, and a rail mill that competed with his own at Edgar Thomson. He had, on taking control of the works, curtailed rail production, and, in 1884, built a new mill to manufacture from steel the same kinds of structural shapes—columns, beams, and girders—that had been produced at the Union Iron Mills in Pittsburgh. As the recession of the mid-1880s receded, he and his partners poured more and more money into a massive retooling of the Homestead works. The centerpiece was the construction of a new "universal mill" and a "119 inch plate mill." The "universal mill" rolled gigantic 30-ton steel ingots into slabs, which were then transported to the plate mill, reheated, lifted by cranes onto a 363-foot table, rolled into 119-inch-wide steel plates, then cooled and sliced by hydraulic shears, 29 feet high, weighing 150 tons.[2]

The new mill had been designed to manufacture steel plates thick, wide, and strong enough to serve as armor for American battleships. William Whitney, Carnegie's New York neighbor and former partner in the South Pennsylvania venture, on being appointed secretary of the navy by President Cleveland in 1884, had discovered that no American steelmakers were capable of manufacturing the steel a modern navy required. In 1886, he had suggested that Carnegie enter the armor business.[3]

Carnegie, who spent much of that winter deathly ill at Cresson, replied to Whitney that he was "afraid my illness will interfere with our going into armour. . . . Of course," he added, "we have the largest and best plant and best position to make it, and machinery which we are now about to erect for other purposes our managers assure me would make armour." Having assured Secretary Whitney that his new Homestead plate mill was capable of making the best armor in the country, he then reversed course and argued against producing any.

> To tell the truth I am more than ever opposed to every dollar spent by our Republic upon instruments of any kind destined for destructive purposes. We have no need of any defenses. Nobody wishes to attack us, nor could they injure us much if they did. Our ships of war in various places in the world are so many challenges—chips on our shoulders which we go round the world asking people to do us the favor to knock off. They are bad nurseries for young men of our country. You and I differ about this; but if I were in public life the only issue I would make against your [Democratic] party today is that you are fast transforming a peaceful republic into a warlike power, degrading it to the level of monarchies of the old world. My feeling is that if Carnegie Bros. and Co. cannot earn a living by making instruments of peace they will conclude to starve, rather than make those of war. But of course I will not override the voice of all my partners if they conclude otherwise, even although I hold a majority of the stock. I only give you my individual opinion, and are always, your friend and well wisher."[4]

The eventual decision not to bid on armor contracts was made on purely business grounds. Carnegie was prepared to proceed if his partners thought it best to negotiate the contracts with Whitney. He was relieved when they decided not to submit a bid. "We have decided that our present business increases fast enough and we'll not offer for armour and guns," he wrote Louise a month before their wedding. "I never quite liked the idea of making these barbarous instruments of destruction anyhow. Am quite rejoined that my partners agree to give it up—aren't you?" Louise wrote back that she, too, was "perfectly delighted" that "the Washington business" had been abandoned. "It would be so inconsistent for such an advocate of peace as you are to make horrible guns, even for self-defense. It is so much nicer to let someone else make them."[5]

BY 1888, the plate mill which Carnegie had bragged about to Whitney was up and running, as were four open-hearth furnaces to feed it molten steel. Gigantic as it was (the building which housed it took up several acres), only eight men were required to heat the slabs and another seven to work the rollers and shears. The Homestead works, with their newly installed labor-saving machinery, employed about 1,600 men, two thirds of them unskilled day laborers. There was a clear ethnic division in the workforce as there was at Edgar Thomson and every other steel mill. The skilled workers were native-born or first- or second-generation Germans, Irish, Welsh, or Scotsmen. The unskilled day laborers were almost all Eastern Europeans, mostly Slovak, though they were referred to as "Hungarians," "Huns," and "Hunkies." They were paid by the day for "loading and stocking the furnaces and converters and moving raw and finished materials between the mill and the yard." The men on the stocking crews at the new plate mill earned fourteen cents an hour (about three dollars an hour today in purchasing power).[6]

The retooling of Homestead resulted in increased productivity and labor efficiency. Carnegie, however, remained dissatisfied because the skilled workers earned more than at other plants. This was not, he believed, because they worked any harder, but because the labor-saving machinery he and his partners had installed had increased their productivity and they were paid by the ton. Carnegie wanted to put into operation a wage formula, which would adjust rates downward as improvements pushed worker productivity upward. The union, he knew, would resist any such attempts. Skilled workers, it insisted, were entitled to share fully in the profits that came from their enhanced productivity. Without their labor, there would have been no capital to reinvest and no one to operate the new machinery that capital purchased. The Amalgamated was not opposed to modifying the wage rate structure. But it held fast to its core belief that labor was not a commodity to be bought and sold as cheaply as possible, but a full-fledged partner of capital. The skilled workmen, the Amalgamated argued, were entitled not only to a share of the profits but to a measure of control over the workplace. This Carnegie was not prepared to concede.

Carnegie was committed to doing whatever was necessary to bring down labor costs. Cutting costs protected market share and profit margin, but it also, he was convinced, served the common good. The lower the prices on basic and consumer goods, the greater the portion of the community that might use and enjoy them. Unions that interfered with the natural downward spiral of prices by pushing up costs blocked evolutionary progress. Their power had to be confined or eliminated. They acted on behalf of the particular interests of the men they represented; Andrew Carnegie acted on behalf of the larger community.

THE ANNUAL Amalgamated contracts for iron and steel firms in the Pittsburgh region expired on June 30, 1889. (Only at Edgar Thomson, which the Amalgamated had abandoned to the Knights, did labor contracts expire on December 31.) In years past, the Amalgamated had submitted its terms to the Carnegie firms, as it did to the other steel- and iron makers in Pittsburgh; the manufacturers came back with a counteroffer; and the two sides negotiated a final contract. In 1889, Carnegie instructed his managers and accountants not to wait to hear from the Amalgamated, but instead to design a new sliding-wage scale, such as he had instituted at Edgar Thomson, and present it to the union. The new scale was to be based on the price of steel billets, not pig iron, as was traditional, and structured to take into account the fact that workers at Homestead were turning out more product per shift than their counterparts elsewhere.

While Carnegie and his partners prepared for the June negotiations at Homestead, the Amalgamated was fully occupied at Duquesne, just five miles away, where a new steelworks, Allegheny Bessemer, had been erected. The owners of the new works were determined to run non-union. The result had been a "violent strike," with the owners calling in Pinkertons and policemen to protect their property and the strikers seeking and receiving support from the Amalgamated lodges at Homestead.[7]

Carnegie silently cheered on the new owners in their battle against the Amalgamated. "Upon the whole we shall reap a good deal if Allegheny succeeds," Carnegie wrote Frick in April 1889. It would be difficult for the Amalgamated at Homestead to insist on higher wage rates if a non-union plant just five miles away paid its skilled workers much less.[8]

While rooting for his competitors in their battle with the Amalgamated, Carnegie did all he could to sabotage their efforts to enter the rail business. There were already, to his mind at least, too many steel mills in the country. The best way to destroy the competition was by excluding it from the "rail pool" and then pricing it out of the market. On April 12, less than a month after the first rails had been rolled at Duquesne, Carnegie invited two officers of the Louisville & Nashville Railroad to dine with him and learned from them that Allegheny Bessemer had offered to sell them rails at $26 per ton. The next morning, he telegrammed Frick. "There is but one way for you to do. Put your price at $26 and then go to $25.50 or $25 or lower if necessary. Allegheny can't run regularly unless you let her take more orders . . . now put your figure at $25—take all [orders available]—you bring Allegheny to stop in less than six weeks or so . . . the issue is before you—put Rails where Allegheny can't . . . take $100,000 lost now may prevent years of annoyance."[9]

SEMIRETIRED, living in New York City, a full day's journey from Pittsburgh, and preparing to take his wife on their first tour of the Continent together, Carnegie was not about to take his eyes off his prizes. Almost all his capital was invested in his steel plants and it was from them that he expected to reap the profits he had pledged to administer on behalf of the larger community.

In late April, after consulting with Captain Jones on strategy for the upcoming negotiations with the Amalgamated at Homestead, he wrote William Abbott, one of his young protégés who had risen through the ranks to become chairman of Carnegie, Phipps.* He instructed Abbott to call in the Amalgamated's executive committee for a meeting, submit our proposed scale and say, "If you agree, all right—If not, it is fight to finish. . . . If they don't agree, then our consciences will be easier—We shall have offered _fair_ and agreed not to break with organized labor. . . . Meeting could take place Tuesday 6th or Wednesday 7th. I'll be presentuntil Friday night—Then give them until a certain date to say Yes or No. Of course we must be prepared to say—No means we go ahead anyway."[10]

On Sunday, Carnegie wrote again. He had, he told Abbott, "upon reflection," decided it would "be best for me not to meet" with the Amalgamated's executive committee, "but keep in reserve _if needed later._" He had just learned that Judge Ewing in Pittsburgh had "settled Allegheny strike" and that the Duquesne works would operate as a non-union shop. Abbott could now seize the high moral ground in his negotiations with the Amalgamated. "You can put out your flag and win easily." The executive committee should be told that while Carnegie and his partners would have preferred not to cut wages, they now had no choice if they were to meet the Duquesne competition. Carnegie had been pilloried in the Pittsburgh press the year before because of the lockout at Edgar Thomson. This time he expected to win the battle for public opinion. He was offering his Homestead workers the best possible deal he could, given the existence of a non-union mill just five miles away. "Men can't stand against it—It's so clear, so fair—our money good as any other's money—Labor to blame not Capital."[11]

In early May, Andrew, with Louise and their personal servants, traveled to the Universal Exposition in Paris, which had been organized to mark the centennial of the French Revolution. The French had erected the Eiffel Tower in honor of the exposition and invited the nations of the world to exhibit industrial products, consumer goods, scientific achievements, and artworks. The 1889 Exposition, with the Eiffel Tower as its centerpiece and more than 60,000 exhibits, 1,750 of them from the United States, was the most spectacular world fair held to that point. Carnegie had been appointed a "Commissioner" by the governor of Pennsylvania. "Paris crowded,"

---

*The Carnegie firms in Pittsburgh were organized into two separate companies, each owned by the same group of partners. Carnegie, Phipps owned Homestead; Carnegie Brothers, Edgar Thomson. Abbott was the chairman of the board of Carnegie, Phipps; Frick of Carnegie Brothers.

Carnegie wrote his Pittsburgh partners. "The Exhibition dwarfs every thing ever done of the kind—such magnificence in building & decoration."[12]

On May 31, while Andrew and Louise were visiting the exposition, news reached Paris that the dam at the South Fork Fishing and Hunting Club had collapsed, sweeping away tons of water, debris, railroad cars and tracks, horses, wagons, two-story wooden houses, and drowning survivors down the Little Conemaugh River to Johnstown, destroying the town and killing more than two thousand people. Carnegie, a member of the South Fork Club, knew Johnstown well—it was only fourteen miles from Cresson. "That South Fork calamity," he wrote Frick, "has driven all else out of our thoughts for past few days."[13]

The steel industry was a closely interwoven one: chief executives, salesmen, managers, foremen, and skilled workers knew their counterparts at other plants and consulted with them regularly. The ties between the Cambria mill in Johnstown and Edgar Thomson were particularly tight. Captain Jones had worked at Cambria and, upon leaving for Braddock, had taken with him several department heads. On June 4, Dod wrote to tell Carnegie that Jones, having received "some message from Johnstown," had taken a crew of laborers to the city to help with the rebuilding. "I am staying here [at Edgar Thomson] pretty much all the time—So many of our men have lost relatives that there is some danger of disorganization amongst them, or rather there has been, everything seems now to be pretty well settled down. . . . I do not know when the Captain may come back, but he will no doubt do his duty as he sees it."[14]

Carnegie did what he could to aid the relief effort from Paris. At his suggestion, the American ambassador, Whitelaw Reid, called a meeting of Americans, at which Carnegie introduced resolutions expressing "profound and heartfelt sympathy from the brethren across the Atlantic." Carnegie donated $10,000, and that fall, on his return to the United States, publicly pledged to spend whatever was necessary to rebuild the library. It cost him, in the end, about $55,000 ($1.2 million today).[15]

FROM PARIS and everywhere else he traveled that summer, Carnegie remained in touch with his partners in Pittsburgh. From London, where he and Louise arrived in mid-June, he wrote Frick with news of his recent dinner with "Mr. and Mrs. Gladstone" and then responded to the issues

Frick had cabled about. Regarding matters at Edgar Thomson, he agreed that the man in charge of accounting should be fired. He had been given numerous chances to shape up and had failed each time. "It is as sad a case as I know. Nothing can be done for him I fear." His main concern remained the contract talks at Homestead and the possibility that the men would go out on strike. "Should take this chance to change and get down to least number of men—very important. I have no fear of result at Homestead, will come much sooner than expected—We have right on our side. . . . Don't be alarmed at bluster at Homestead. In their hearts they know that the game is up and that we are forced to ask and get same rates as [Duquesne] on plates [and] Cambria, etc. on other things—This knowledge prevents any earnest fight. They only will make a show of it to scare other manfrs."[16]

Carnegie's letters to Frick were rather avuncular, as if he were trying to curry Frick's favor and establish himself as his business mentor. For all his triumphs in the coke industry, Frick was a relative newcomer in steel. He had been a partner for little more than two and a half years, chairman for only six months. Although Frick would later acquire the reputation for being the more ruthless of the two, Carnegie worried continually that his partner might not have the killer instinct required of a chairman of Carnegie Brothers. From Christiana, Norway (today known as Oslo), he warned Frick to be tough with the Duquesne owners: "I do not believe Allegheny [i.e., Duquesne] will pull through—& do trust you will give no countenance to anything like toleration of that blackmailing concern."*[17]

Having heard nothing to the contrary, Carnegie assumed that all was proceeding as planned in negotiations with the Amalgamated at Homestead. On May 18, Abbott summoned the union leaders to his office and presented them with a wage scale, based on the one in place at the nonunion Allegheny Bessemer works at Duquesne. He informed them, as Carnegie had instructed, that there would be no negotiations. The wage proposal was "an ultimatum." On June 1, all positions at Homestead would be declared vacant. Workers who wanted their jobs back would be required to sign the new agreement, as individuals, as they had at Edgar Thomson.[18]

---

*We don't know why he referred to his rivals as blackmailers. In the heat of battle, he was likely to say such things about competitors.

Carnegie took great stock in the fact that he had broken the union at Edgar Thomson the year before. As he would soon discover, however, there was a world of difference between the two plants. At Edgar Thomson, he had had only the Knights of Labor with which to contend. At Homestead, the Knights were as strong as at Edgar Thomson, and the Amalgamated, which had been a presence at the plant since its opening, stronger still. Worse yet, the two unions cooperated with each other (several workers were members of both) at the workplace and in local politics. Together, they had put union members on the borough council and elected as burgess, or mayor, "Old Beeswax" Charles Taylor, a former English Chartist who had emigrated to the United States six years before Carnegie and who had spent a lifetime in labor politics. There were as well social ties between the skilled and unskilled workers that did not exist at Edgar Thomson. Eastern European immigrants who were Catholics attended the same church, St. Mary Magdalene, as the Irish Catholic skilled workers and union leaders.[19]

The Amalgamated rank-and-file voted in late June to reject Carnegie's proposal. The leadership then reached out to the unskilled common laborers, many of them represented by the Knights of Labor, asked for their support in the event of a strike, and promised, in return, to do all they could to protect their jobs. Instead of waiting for the company to bring in sheriff's deputies and Pinkertons to enforce a lockout and prepare the way for scabs, as it had at E.T. the year before, the Amalgamated appointed an advisory committee and stationed armed guards at "all approaches to the town, allowing no one to enter unless proof was furnished that he was not a black sheep."[20]

The deadline to sign the new agreement came, went, was extended— and still not a single worker put his name to it. On July 1, the company shut the plant and locked out the workers. Notices were posted in the Pittsburgh papers and several employment agencies were recruited to bring in substitute workers. Carnegie cabled his full support from Norway: "I would get hundreds of men [i.e., scab workers], board them around Pittsburgh and then one day put enough in to run Plate Mill sure—next mill in a while, etc., etc. Overwhelming force of Sheriff Officers about—and good quarters inside works [to house the scabs], one weeks run of plate mill decides matters. Of course we have no recourse but to fight it through—am glad of it."[21]

Abbott had already arranged for about one hundred Pinkertons to secure the works and had housed them in Pittsburgh until he needed them.
They arrived armed and dangerous, a vigilante squad of outsiders, available
to do the dirty work companies feared that local officials would be reluctant to take up. On July 10, with the Pinkertons in reserve, Abbott dispatched thirty-one strikebreakers by train to Homestead, accompanied by
Sheriff McCandless, who had stood guard with his deputies between the
Pinkertons and the Knights at Edgar Thomson the year before. The scabs
were greeted by a crowd of some two thousand Homestead men, women,
and children, who blocked the tracks leading to the steelworks. When the
scabs left the train, they were, as the *New York Times* later reported,
"hooted and hissed, jeered and cursed, until they turned and fled the town,
with stones flying all about them." Two days later, Sheriff McCandless returned to Homestead with 125 deputies, intent on securing the works. On
disembarking from the train, his deputies were dispersed, this time by an
even larger crowd, "as if they had been schoolboys."[22]

The Pinkertons waited in Pittsburgh. There was little doubt that, if
called upon, they would be able to open the mill to receive scabs, though
not without violence. "With Pinkerton men guarding the works the hotter
the work the quicker it will be over, at least I hope so," John Walker, Abbott's predecessor as chairman, wrote Frick on July 13. "Hoping to soon
read of the collapse of the strike."[23]

Three days later, the lockout was over; to everyone's surprise, it had
been Chairman Abbott, not the Amalgamated leaders, who blinked first.
Contravening Carnegie's orders, Abbott reopened negotiations with the
Amalgamated and quickly arrived at a settlement. John Fitch, who interviewed hundreds of steelworkers in Pittsburgh in 1907, claimed that Sheriff McCandless had brought the two sides together. Having tried twice to
secure the Homestead works, McCandless realized that a third attempt
would result in considerable bloodshed. The resistance at Homestead encompassed not just the steelworkers but every element of the town: glass-
workers, shopkeepers, local officials, even the clergy. Fighting through it
was not going to be easy.[24]

The telegram announcing the Homestead settlement reached Carnegie
in Berlin early in August. He was distraught that Abbott had negotiated a
settlement with the union, thereby ensuring its continued presence at
Homestead for another three years. "The great objection to the compro-

Andrew and his younger brother, Tom, in 1851, when Andrew was sixteen and his brother Tom ten. The portrait was formally posed and taken in a professional photographer's studio in Allegheny City, Pennsylvania. (*A Carnegie Anthology*, arranged by Margaret Barclay Wilson [New York, privately printed, 1915], abbreviated hereafter as *Anthology*)

Andrew Carnegie, age twenty-five, in a formal photograph taken in 1861 by a Philadelphia photographer. *(Anthology)*

Carnegie, age twenty-six, with his boyhood friend and now business partner, Tom Miller. The photograph was taken during Andrew's triumphant return to Dunfermline with his mother and Tom during the summer of 1862. (ACBM)

Carnegie, age twenty-nine or thirty, flanked by Harry Phipps and John Vandevort (Vandy), his traveling companions on his yearlong tour of Britain and Europe. This is one of the rare photos in which Carnegie allows himself to be photographed standing next to others. (Carnegie Library of Pittsburgh, abbreviated hereafter as CLP)

Carnegie, age thirty-five, with a full beard to add a bit of gravity and maturity to his still-youthful appearance. (ACBM)

A formal posed portrait of Carnegie, age forty-three, and Vandy during their round-the-world trip. The photo was taken in Ceylon in January 1879. (ACBM)

Carnegie, probably in the library of his West Fifty-first Street home, where he and Louise lived from 1887 until they moved into their Ninety-first Street mansion in 1901. *(Anthology)*

A photo from 1892, reportedly of "strikers on the look-out, Homestead Pa." The photo may have been taken during the week following the repulsion of the Pinkertons when the Homestead workers were in control of the town and the plant. It may also have been a staged photo taken later that summer or fall. (LC)

Left, top: A photograph of Carnegie and Henry Clay Frick, taken before the Homestead lockout and strike in July. The notation alongside the photo reads "The Carnegie Party on board the 'Iolanthe' . . . Left N.Y. Feb. 12, 1892. Arrived Pittsburgh, March 23, 1892." Standing next to Carnegie are his sister-in-law, Estelle or Stella, and his wife, Louise. Frick, with cap and full beard, is in the center of the photo. (Courtesy of the Frick Collection/Frick Art Reference Library Archives)

Left, bottom: A group photo taken on the steps at Cluny during the Frick family's visit, probably in 1894. Carnegie occupies the center of the photo. Next to him is Frick's wife, Adelaide, holding their daughter, Helen. On Carnegie's other side is Frick's sister-in-law, Martha Childs. Below him is Childs Frick with his tutor. Frick stands behind Carnegie at the top of the stairs. (Courtesy of the Frick Collection/Frick Art Reference Library Archives)

On July 12, the Pennsylvania State militia took control of Homestead. The caption on this illustration reads "THE FIRST TROOPS IN HOMESTEAD: THE EIGHTEENTH REGIMENT PASSING THE OFFICE AND WORKS OF THE CARNEGIE COMPANY." The illustration, taken from a wood engraving of a drawing by T. de Thulstrup, after a sketch by F. Cresson Schell, appeared in *Harper's Weekly*, on July 23, 1892. (LC)

An 1892 photograph. The caption reads "STATE MILITIA ENTERING HOMESTEAD, PA." The photograph is more likely of the troops participating in a formal drill sometime during their three-month occupation of the plant in the summer and early fall. (LC)

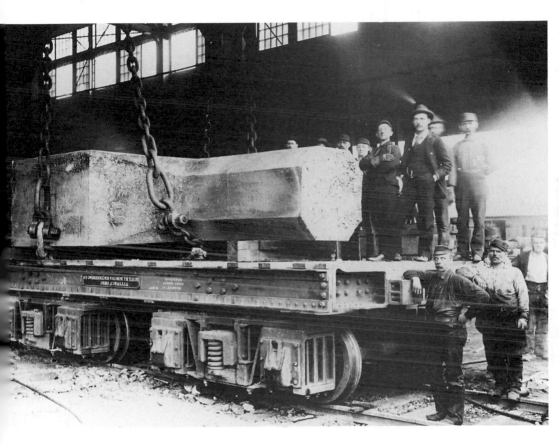

Homestead, 1892–1895: A 90-ton ingot being shipped along the plant's internal railway to the armor department, where it would be rolled into steel plates.

(William J. Gaughan Collection, Archives Service Center, University of Pittsburgh)

Carnegie dictating to James Bertram,
his private secretary, in his library. (CLP)

Carnegie entertaining Rudyard Kipling and Mrs. Joseph H. Choate, the wife of the American ambassador to Britain, on his yacht, *Seabreeze*, in the summer of 1899. The woman between Carnegie and Kipling may be Mrs. Choate; the other two women in the photo are probably Louise and her sister, Stella.

(Carnegie Mellon)

Skibo, 1900, before the extensive alterations that would turn the Gothic mansion
Carnegie had purchased into a veritable castle. (Courtesy of the Carnegie Mellon University
Archives, abbreviated hereafter as Carnegie Mellon)

Skibo, after the new wings were added (Carnegie Mellon)

Skibo gardeners, 1910. (Carnegie Mellon)

Carnegie and his daughter, Margaret,
at Skibo in the early 1900s. (Carnegie Mellon)

mise is of course that it was made under intimidation—our men in other works now know that we will 'confer' with law breakers. . . . I don't like this feature at all. Seems to me a curt refusal to have anything to do with these men would have brought matters right in less time than to you seems possible. Whenever we are compelled to make a stand we shall just have to shut down and <u>wait</u> as at E.T. until part of the men vote to work, then it is easy."[25]

Carnegie had expected that Abbott, with the assistance of sheriff's deputies and Pinkertons if necessary, would secure the works and bring in enough scabs to frighten a majority of the Homestead workers into abandoning the union and returning to work. Those who continued to hold out would be replaced and the union would be broken. By bowing to the pressure exerted by the strikers and the townsmen who supported them, Abbott had handed victory to the Amalgamated. "It's too bad but we must expect three years or so of trouble now," he cabled Frick that same day. "The surrender or conference at Homestead may be right in itself, but the effect at Beaver Falls [a smaller Carnegie-owned steel mill], Coke Works, Keystone is much too great—and not favorable—Must do best we can."[26]

Rather than acknowledging the strength of the ties that bound the workers to their unions, Carnegie attributed the collapse of his union-busting plan to William Abbott's failures as a manager. As Abbott's stock fell, Frick's rose. Anticipating perhaps that Abbott would fail at Homestead and be removed as his only possible rival, Frick acknowledged to Carnegie on July 25 that he was now prepared to make his career in steel. "As I become familiar with the Steel business, it becomes more interesting; always something that can be done to reduce cost; but the business requires close attention, and I will be greatly disappointed if July results are not good. . . . Many other matters should like to write you about, Homestead . . . etc., but we make our cables full, and all those matters can be gone over on your return. The important thing is to neglect nothing here." In a rare display of charm, he jokingly apologized for his curt, unpolished letters, so different from those he received from Carnegie. "I am nothing of a 'literary cuss' any way, which is probably as well, as we have no lacking of it in our concerns. Glad you are enjoying yourself. When I get to be 50 I want to retire and do the same. Kind regards to Mrs. Carnegie."[27]

Carnegie was delighted with Frick's note. "Yours of 25th rec'd just now—very satisfactory indeed. I am so glad the steel business is fascinating you.

It is the greatest of investments in the U.S. in my opinion <u>managed as it can be</u>."[28]

Frick answered as Carnegie had hoped: "I could not and would not remain the official head of any concern that was not well managed. I cannot stand fault-finding and I must feel that I have the entire confidence of the power that put me where I am, in a place I did not seek. With all that, I know that I can manage both Carnegie Brothers and Co. and Frick Coke Co. successfully."[29]

BY EARLY SEPTEMBER, Carnegie could rein in his anger and disappointment with Abbott no longer. In an open letter to his partners, he announced that he had summoned Abbott for a personal interview after receiving a "startling letter" in which Abbott had suggested that the firm should sell the steel plant at Beaver Falls because it was losing money. If Beaver Falls were not turning a profit, Carnegie insisted, it was only because the right man had not been found to manage it. The Carnegie partners were becoming too complacent. In the past, one of them would have volunteered to "reside at Beaver & sleep with that business" until it was turned around. "If we are to admit that . . . anybody else can manage & we can't, let us make up our minds to be driven point by point out of manfg business. . . . We have hitherto been a buying never a selling party & this is no time to sell any works—After a period of depression we are entering one of activity. . . . If Mr. Abbott is ready to admit that Oliver [a possible buyer of the plant] can manage better than he . . . he might as well admit others can manage Union Mills better & prepare to sell these, then Homestead's turn will come next—<u>gentlemen just count me out in this disgraceful roll to ruin</u>. I would blow up every works we have in turn before I would acknowledge that <u>any competitor</u> could beat us—at Beaver Falls or anywhere else." Since receiving Abbott's letter, he claimed he had "been able to think of little else—This is a crisis in our affairs—We must face a serious situation—Mr. Abbott has assured us from time to time that at Beaver Falls we were holding our own. . . . Now he calls upon his partners to make a loss of $300,000. . . . The loss with interest added is about $1000 per working day." Even more upsetting than the monetary loss was the fact that it came as a surprise to the managers who were supposed to be keeping track of the books. "I give you all my views freely—It is evident a new leaf must be turned over. . . . Perhaps you will find me at fault about the remedy & can devise a better policy. So be it. It rests with you. Only don't give me any more surprises. Let us all know month after month promptly where we are going. I can stand losses with you, but object to be deluded."[30]

The following day, Carnegie wrote Frick a personal note confirming that, from this moment on, he would be his number one man in Pittsburgh, with no number two to compete with. "Let me express the relief I feel in knowing that the important departments of our extended business are in the hands of a competent manager. Phipps & I exchanged congratulations upon this point—Now I only want to know how your hands can be strengthened. . . . Good night. Take supreme care of that head of yours. It is wanted. Again expressing my thankfulness that I have found the man. . . . P.S. Abbott made one good point. He said I did the best thing for the concern in getting you—so there's hope for him yet."[31]

On arriving back from Europe in late summer, Carnegie took to the road again, first to Bar Harbor, Maine, for a week with the Blaines, then back to New York City for a few days, before he was in his carriage again and off to the West Side piers for the ferry to New Jersey and the daylong trek to Pittsburgh via Philadelphia, with a stopover in Cresson and a short trip to Johnstown to survey the damage and pledge his support for a new library.

Arriving in Pittsburgh, he met with his partners at their downtown offices and crossed the Allegheny River to check on the progress of his new library and music hall in Allegheny City. At the sight of the new building, the business cares that had preoccupied him were washed away. "If ever there was a sight that makes my eyes glisten it was this gem," he wrote Louise. "A kind of domestic Taj, its tower a pretty clock, so musical in tone too, for it kindly welcomed me as I stood feeling—'Yes, life is worth living when we can all forth such works as this!' . . . The big words Carnegie Free Library just took me into the sweetest reverie and I found myself wishing you were at my side to reap with me the highest reward we can ever receive on earth, the voice of one's inner self, saying secretly, well done!"[32]

Theodore Dreiser, the future novelist, worked in Allegheny City in 1894 as a reporter on the "city hall and police" beat for the *Pittsburgh Dispatch*. He spent many long lunch-hour breaks in Carnegie's library. "What pleased and impressed me most about this institution was its forty or fifty thousand volumes so conveniently arranged that one could walk from stack to stack, looking at the labels above and satisfying one's interest by looking into and nibbling at the various subjects. . . . The place had most comfortable window nooks and chairs between stacks and in alcoves, and in one of these, behind a leaded window which looked out upon the street and the park, I frequently established myself." The library building, "a very handsome affair architecturally," also housed a music hall with "'one of the largest if not the largest' pipe organs in the world." On Sunday, Wednesday, and Saturday afternoons, an organist paid by the city entertained "the public with a free recital. And so capable was he that seats were at a premium and 'standing room only' the rule, unless one arrived far ahead of time." Dreiser, upon moving to Pittsburgh, had become one of Carnegie's most severe critics, and was taken aback by the gifts the tycoon had bestowed on the people of Allegheny City. "This particular manifestation of interest on the part of the public pleased me greatly and somehow qualified, if it did not atone for, in part at least, Mr. Carnegie's indifference to the living welfare of his employees elsewhere."[33]

THE DAY OF Carnegie's visit to the new library began brightly, but ended in mourning. While Carnegie was in Allegheny, Captain Bill Jones was on duty at the Edgar Thomson steelworks. Blast furnace C had been blocked by cinder and he was helping to clear it when the furnace wall gave way, showering flames, hot cinders, ore, and coke on the men below. More than a dozen furnace men were injured. Jones was almost buried by the avalanche of smoldering, half-burnt material that swept him off his feet into the casting pit. He died on Saturday night, two days after the explosion.

He was succeeded by twenty-seven-year-old Charlie Schwab, a handsome lad from Loretto, Pennsylvania, whom Carnegie counted as a protégé. Schwab had worked his way up the Carnegie organization from assistant to surveyor to superintendent of construction for the Edgar Thomson blast furnaces. Two years earlier, on Captain Jones's recommendation, he had been appointed general superintendent at Homestead. He was now recalled from Homestead to Edgar Thomson to replace his mentor.

The death of Jones had a profound—though short-lived—effect on the senior partners. Harry Phipps, who like Carnegie had his fortune tied up in Carnegie Company stock, was increasingly worried that their investments might not be safe. He proposed that he and Carnegie either sell their interests in the Pittsburgh firms or consolidate them into a new trust. Carnegie forwarded Phipps's plans to Frick, though he assured his younger partner that he had done so only "for fun—to show how he is figuring—of course there's nothing in it." Unfortunately for Phipps, who wanted to cash out his investments, the value of his and Carnegie's stock had grown so large that there were few capitalists anywhere who could afford to buy them out. "Parties wouldn't pay my price nor could they give security satisfactory," Carnegie wrote Frick. "The thing is dead anyhow for no combination of various works is possible. . . . I would have nothing to do with Trust—If I went out of business would go out clear & clean & if I stayed in would run with you & our own boys. Good enough for me."[34]

THE STEEL industry continued to rake in huge profits through the 1880s and into the 1890s, due in no small part to the beneficence of the federal government. There was very little *laissez-faire* in nineteenth-century capitalism, no matter what the capitalists might say. The steel industry was doubly dependent on state and national governments for the generous loans and subsidies that fueled railway expansion and rail purchases and the protective tariffs that enabled the manufacturers to keep their prices—and profits—higher than would have been possible had they been compelled to compete with European steelmakers. If, in the beginning, as Carnegie had argued, the tariff had been needed to nurture an infant steel industry, by the mid-1880s that infant had become a strapping, abrasive youth, who kept on growing. Why then, one might inconveniently ask, was there need for a protective tariff? Because, as Carnegie argued in the *North American Review* in July 1890, the steel industry was not yet fully grown and would have to be protected until it was.[35]

On the issue of the tariff—as on few others—Pittsburgh's workingmen were in agreement with Carnegie. They voted Republican in large numbers because the Republicans were the guardians of the protective tariff, and the tariff, they believed, protected their wage rates.

The argument linking the tariff and wages in the manufacturing sector was a compelling one in the industrial states, but nowhere else. As the Democrats took great delight in pointing out, high tariffs led to high prices for all consumers. Through the mid-1880s, a rising tide of outspoken opposition to the tariff, especially in the agrarian states, made unqualified support a significant political liability. Carnegie recognized this of course and supported gradual and moderate downward adjustments in the schedules. What he was unwilling to do was to let the politicians make the final decisions by themselves on an issue so vital to the well-being of the industrial sector. The legislative process in the states and in Washington, he feared—and he was certainly not alone in this—gave too great a voice and vote to the enemies of industrial progress. This distrust of legislatures compelled the steelmakers, individually and through their lobbyist, James Swank, to spend an extraordinary—and increasing—amount of time, effort, and dollars on making their voices heard and their influence count.

The Republican candidate for president, Benjamin Harrison, had been elected in 1888, though he had polled fewer popular votes than his Democratic rival, Grover Cleveland. Cleveland had won a great many of these votes by making tariff reduction the major plank in his platform. Bowing to the inevitable, the Republicans attempted to remove the tariff as a future Democratic campaign issue by sponsoring their own reform legislation. "Tariff work in Washington soon to be done," Carnegie wrote Frick in January 1890. "I'm to see the leaders next week."[36]

Ohio congressman William McKinley was delegated by the Republicans to head up the committee to write new tariff schedules. Carnegie was already on the best of terms with McKinley, having instructed Frick in July 1889 to "write him a private note & send him $5000 from me saying that his speech on silver pleased me so much & I wished to show him he had friends, etc, etc—It is best I don't write direct I think." The McKinley tariff bill, when reported out of committee, proposed only minor adjustments in the iron and steel schedules, thereby virtually guaranteeing that tariff reform would remain a major issue in upcoming political campaigns.[37]

When, in July 1891, William McKinley ran for governor of Ohio, James Campbell, his Democratic opponent, assailed him on the tariff issue. The year before, Campbell reminded voters, the Republicans had guaranteed that the McKinley tariff, by "protecting" the steel industry, would protect the wages of steelworkers. This had not occurred. On the contrary, the Carnegie firms had cut the wages of the Homestead workers. McKinley personally wrote to ask Frick if this was indeed the case. Frick denied it, but provided no data. "We, of course, would prefer that our business should be brought into politics as little as possible."[38]

. . .

FRICK'S POLITICAL connections—and his skill at playing politics—were invaluable to Carnegie on the local level. Almost as deftly as Tom Scott and far more discreetly, Frick had entangled the Carnegie firms in a complicated web of political partnerships, woven of favorable business deals, campaign contributions, and bribes to influential politicians.

These connections came in very handy when, in the winter of 1889–1890, Carnegie tried to secure additional land at Homestead to expand his works. The retooling of the plant—and the construction of the massive new universal and plate mill buildings—had taken up most of the unoccupied land on the site. Fortunately, the property which comprised about 90 acres abutted the 144-acre city poor farm, poor house, and home for the insane. Well-placed bribes had persuaded the Pittsburgh city councils to put the land up for sale and build new facilities for the poor elsewhere. Frick had hired an intermediary, a Mr. McCook, to buy the land, but he had not been able to close the deal.[39]

In January 1890, Frick suggested to Carnegie that, bribery having failed to push the matter along, they try a new approach. "I think we have gone about securing the Poor Farm in the wrong way from the very start. A fair, open offer to the Council, I think, would bring the matter to a conclusion very soon. We are in position to make a much more attractive offer than any other party, and it is rather a dangerous proceeding to allow anybody to use any portion of what we want to pay for the property to bribe officials who claim to control the matter. I want to discuss this fully with you on your next visit here, together with very many other things I can not well write about."[40]

The following week, Frick modified his new approach by suggesting that they seek the assistance of "A. F. Keating, who is a power in councils." Carnegie agreed that this was the best way to proceed. "If Mr. Keating will do us the great favor we may no doubt . . . be in position to show him some day that we stick to our friends."[41]

Unfortunately for Carnegie, Frick, and Keating, the real power in Pittsburgh remained Christopher Magee, the Pittsburgh city boss of whom Lincoln Steffens later wrote that it was his idea "not to corrupt the city government, but to be it, not to hire votes in councils, but to own councilmen." By 1890, nothing much got accomplished in Pittsburgh, certainly nothing that involved city monies or resources or property, without the explicit approval of Boss Magee.[42]

After months of spinning their wheels, Carnegie and Frick dispatched their attorney, Philander Knox, to meet with Magee. "Mr. Knox called on me this afternoon," Frick wrote Carnegie on March 19, "and I think we will now get down to business on the City Farm matter. Magee agrees now to put the matter through, but wants to know our price and just what we will agree to pay him. We have a week in which to give him his figures; in the meantime I shall look carefully into the matter and probably see you."[43]

Carnegie told Knox how much he was willing to pay for the land. Knox and Frick then met with Magee on the Saturday morning before bids were due. Magee had arranged for a dummy bidder—it would not have looked good if the Carnegie firms tendered the only bids—to offer $2,775 per acre for the land and suggested that Carnegie put in a bid for $2,805. When the bids were opened, Frick was surprised to find a third bidder at $2,903. "At present," Frick wrote Carnegie, "it looks as if the Boss has taken us in . . . I may be, and I hope I am, all wrong about Magee, but he has served other people just that way." In the end, Carnegie had to pay Magee his agreed-upon bribe and then shell out more to buy the land from the highest bidder, who had business dealings with the Boss. Even with these off-the-books expenses, the land was a bargain. "I kept several parties from bidding on the farm," Frick proudly informed Carnegie, "who were abundantly able to have purchased it; among others Mellons, who think the farm worthy very much more than $3000.00 per acre" Carnegie had paid for it.[44]

BEGINNING in the spring of 1889, with a Republican back in the White House and his good friend James G. Blaine secretary of state, Carnegie had more occasion than ever to spend time in the nation's capital. On taking office, Blaine had organized a Pan-American Conference between the United States of America and the republics of Central and South America, and appointed Carnegie one of the American delegates.[45]

Carnegie was delighted. When the delegates arrived in Washington for the conference in October 1889, he volunteered his services as tour guide and social secretary, arranged for them to visit Pittsburgh in November, and, in February 1890 hosted a lavish dinner at the Arlington Hotel in

Washington. The *New York Times* reported the event on February 26 in a front-page story, headlined "CARNEGIE'S DAINTY FEAST. THE WHOLE EARTH SEARCHED FOR DELICACIES FOR HIS GUESTS." It "was one of the most elegant affairs of the kind ever given in Washington. . . . The bill of fare consisted of oysters on the shell, clear turtle soup, broiled sole from England, with cold cauliflower; broiled breasts of Spring chickens from Louisiana, with hot asparagus; roasted Spring lamb from Scotland; teal ducks from Currituck Sound, North Carolina, and the usual desserts."

Carnegie was assigned to the committee on patents and trademarks which made its final recommendations in early March 1890. We have no idea how much, if anything, Carnegie contributed to the deliberations. From this point on, however, he would regularly preface his comments and pronouncements on hemispheric relations with the reminder that he knew what he was talking about because he had "sat four months with the representatives of the sixteen South American Republics."[46]

Carnegie spent a great deal of time in Washington that winter lobbying congressmen on the tariff and the secretary of the navy on new contracts for steel armor. In 1886, he and his partners had declined to bid on a contract for steel-plated battleship armor because the terms were not particularly good. Now, three yaers later, they were invited by the new Republican secretary of the navy, Benjamin Tracy, to bid on a much larger contract and agreed to do so. Carnegie was still opposed to naval rearmament on moral and political grounds—and would spend the rest of his life speaking and writing against it, but as a capitalist who had invested millions of dollars in a new plate mill at Homestead—and as the author of the "Gospel of Wealth" essays which had proclaimed that it was the duty of the businessman to make as much money as he could so he would have more to give away on retirement, he was unwilling to turn down the chance to earn millions.

The Harrison administration had, with the enthusiastic support of the Congress, committed itself to building a new generation of steel-armored cruisers to replace the nation's almost laughably outdated fleet of wooden ships. From Washington in March 1890, Carnegie wrote Frick, playfully addressing him as "My dear millionaire." "There's a possible fortune in Navy Dept's attitude toward us—and I am to confer with Secy Tracy next week. So glad we can oblige him by rolling a trial plate with 1% nickel. He will pay us same as he did for one abroad—He wants nothing said about this." Carnegie sent the same message to William Abbott, who, though disgraced, remained nominally in charge of the Homestead facility. "There may be millions for us in armour. To one man should be assigned 'Armour' and he should read up and keep up on the subject."[47]

The legislation authorizing the expenditure of millions of dollars for steel armor required that much of it be made of a nickel-steel alloy. Carnegie opposed the use of nickel, which, in his opinion not only did not strengthen steel, but had to be imported from Canada at considerable cost. He may also have feared that, as no American steelmaker had as yet produced nickel-steel armor, Tracy might, in the end, decide to buy from English firms with experience in manufacturing it.

In a rather transparent attempt to get Tracy to change his mind, Carnegie informed him that he had on his own, as a loyal citizen, examined the "inferior facilities for Armour-plate making" in England and come away convinced that his Pittsburgh works could produce higher-quality pure steel armor than the nickel-steel variety turned out in England. Feigning disinterest in the financial benefits his company would reap should it be permitted to manufacture its steel armor without the nickel added, he asked the secretary to keep his letter secret. "This is strictly a personal letter; is not to go on file in the Department. It is for yourself and Commodore Folger [Tracy's ordnance chief] alone; for as you can well understand, I am a steel manufacturer, and do not wish to antagonize my interests whatever. I thought it my duty, however, to tell you all I know and think upon the subject."[48]

The prospects of government contracts were almost too good to be true. The Homestead mills were already earning a small fortune supplying steel for the first generation of Chicago skyscrapers, a bridge in Brooklyn, and a significant section of New York's elevated railways. Armor production made use of the same open-hearth technologies and could be rolled in the same plate mills. Though the start-up costs were enormous (more than $3.3 million), the potential for profits made the risk worthwhile. "No doubt . . . it can be made the most profitable of all our branches of manufacture, if we go into it thoroughly," Carnegie wrote Frick from Scotland on July 15, 1890. "No make-shifts. It will take a full year to get us fairly started, even with energetic pushing." Concerned that Frick was less than enthusiastic about the project because of the huge cost for retooling, Carnegie wrote him another cheerleading letter in early August: "Armour—No specialty can be had equal to this. Further study of the situation convinces me that we can easily succeed. . . . I think we can average a million per year out of this Dept, with ease—Nobody will follow us."[49]

As loyal Republicans, Carnegie and Frick had anticipated friendly treatment from Washington and were mildly surprised when Secretary Tracy informed William Abbott that the contract for armor he was offering would be less lucrative than the ones his predecessor, William Whitney, had signed with Bethlehem Steel. Frick wrote Carnegie that he had advised "Mr. Abbott to go and see the Secretary, and say to him that we could not accept his offer, nor would we like to accept any offer before your return in October. Ninety days is a very short time, and I take it that the Secretary is a very reasonable man, but this whole matter must be managed with great care, or, as you say, we may get into serious complications with the Government. Mr. Abbott seems to think that one of the reasons the Secretary desires us to furnish Armor at 12½ % less than Bethlehem prices, is in order to do better than his predecessor, Mr. Whitney. I cannot see why he should make capital at our expense. It certainly will be our fault if he does."[50]

Carnegie agreed entirely and telegrammed Secretary Tracy in Washington that while he wanted very much to "help you out with Armour," he could not "risk taking one iota less" than what Bethlehem had received on its contracts. If the secretary was ready to sign off on a contract for "five thousand tons [at the] Bethlehem price, shall order necessary tools and go ahead otherwise must decline. Armour making no child's play."[51]

Tracy agreed to meet Carnegie's terms. On November 20, 1890, the contract for 6,000 tons of nickel-steel armor was signed.

Having invested more than $3 million to retool Homestead, Carnegie hoped to market his armor overseas. He had no expectation of ever winning contracts in Britain, France, or Germany, which had their own steel manufacturers. His objective was the Russian government, which was eager to build a modern navy, but lacked any domestic steel manufacturers. In the summer of 1890, touring Europe with Louise, Carnegie made sure to visit Russia where, in addition to attending choral concerts and meeting Tchaikovsky, he inspected the ships of the new Russian navy, which had been equipped with English-manufactured armor. Determined to wrest the contract from the English, Carnegie enlisted the help of his friend,

Secretary of State James Blaine: "It occurs to me that the great Empire of Russia should no longer plate its war ships with such miserable stuff as I saw there, received from England. . . . I wish we could get a contract to supply the Russian government with such plates as those which have just proved their superiority, and if you can speak to your friend, the Russian Minister upon the subject, I shall be greatly obliged. Russia and ourselves have always been such good friends, that it does seem a pity to have her defrauded upon the vital point of armor for its war ships."[52]

Blaine apparently did as he was asked. In March 1892, Carnegie wrote Frick that he had received "a note from our friend in Washington about the Russian matter, which progresses favorably." In July, he received additional assistance with the Russian contracts from another friend, former Cornell University president Andrew White, who had been selected by Blaine as "envoy extraordinary and minister plenipotentiary at St. Petersburg."[53]

It was not going to be easy to break into the Russian market, which was tightly controlled by the British, but Carnegie, convinced that he could produce steel as tough and as cheap, refused to give up. In April 1894, almost four years after he had first apprised Frick of the potential market for Russian armor, he wrote him again, suggesting that he send someone "to Russia promptly, with note to President White [now ambassador to Russia] who can aid us. An interpreter can easily be provided there, by him. . . . He should then go to Italy on same errand. Unless we get a foreign business our armor plant is certain to be idle for a time. The demands of England for armor are enormous and I do not think her manf's can meet it and do work for Russia and Italy. Here is our time."[54]

Six months later, in the aftermath of the first Sino-Japanese War, in which the Chinese northern fleet lost eight of its twelve warships, Carnegie sought to extend his market further into Asia. "The destruction of the Chinese and Japanese fleets, which is reported," he wrote Frick from Scotland, "will bring both of these nations into the market for armorships, which will be contracted for by English builders. . . . I cannot but feel there is an opening for us to sell armor to builders here. My plan would be to see the leading ship-building people and receive an offer from them for so much armor."[55]

Carnegie's dreams of business expansion always exceeded his grasp. Frick, knowing this, deferred appointing a representative to do business exclusively in Russia and Italy or China and Japan. Bethlehem Steel eventually secured the contract for the Russian armor, but because Carnegie and Bethlehem's president, Robert Linderman, had from the beginning agreed not to compete but to share government contracts, Carnegie felt no embarrassment in asking Linderman to "divide" the Russian order. "There is not much money in the order, but there is a great deal in the armor-making plants working in perfect union. . . . As to the future, we are together, and that is all right, as far as armor is concerned." Though Linderman declined, he agreed to pool subsequent foreign armor contracts.[56]

Having won rather lucrative contracts for armor in Washington, Carnegie began to look longingly at government contracts for guns. He would have preferred—and continued to argue so in print and in person—that the United States and the other nations of the world put away their guns and battleships; as this was not yet the case, he saw no reason why his companies should not secure the profits that came with government contracts. Better that the profits from arms and armor production go to Homestead, to be redistributed to the larger community, than to other firms.

Bethlehem Steel, which had entered the armor and armament business because it could not compete on other steel products, had, by the early 1890s when Carnegie was ready to bid on gun contracts, virtually cornered the American market. "Bethlehem's three and one-half million-contract for guns is a 'stunner,'" Carnegie wrote Frick in August 1891. "With one more tool,—a Boring Mill—we should be ready to compete for next lot." The following month, certainly not by accident, Carnegie reported to Frick that one of his houseguests at Cluny was none other than Commander F. M. Folger, chief ordnance expert and adviser to Secretary of the Navy Tracy. Two weeks later, Carnegie wrote to tell Frick that he had sent Abbott and Dod Lauder off to "visit Krupps and decide upon finishing tools" needed to manufacture guns at Homestead.[57]

Despite Carnegie's continued enthusiasm—and the vastly inflated estimates he offered of the size of the market—the Carnegie firms did not, in the final analysis, go into the armament business in any significant way. Through the mid-1890s, Carnegie would try several times to convince his partners to retool for armament production, but they resisted. In the fall of 1894, having read in the newspapers that Bethlehem and Midvale Steel had submitted a new bid for naval guns, Carnegie sent the clippings and a note to Frick, who forwarded them to Charles Schwab, who was at the time the general manager of the Homestead plant. "I am under the impression that you do not agree with Mr. Carnegie in this," Frick wrote Schwab; "if we could secure a contract such as referred to, it would require a large expenditure to get in shape to take care of the contract. Am I correct in this?"[58]

In the end, Schwab and Frick agreed to disagree with their chief stockholder and mentor and stay out of the gun-forging business. The investment required was too great; the potential rewards far too risky. Homestead would, through the 1890s, turn out millions of dollars worth of steel-plated armor for the U.S. Navy, but it would stay away from armaments on economic grounds, not moral ones.

TWENTY-TWO

"There Will Never Be a Better Time Than Now to Fight It Out," 1890–1891

THE THREE-YEAR sliding-scale wage agreement that had been forced on the Edgar Thomson workforce, with the help of the Pinkertons, in the spring of 1888 was due to expire on December 31, 1890. "Any advance of wages these times is out of the question," Carnegie wrote Frick on December 9, 1890, anticipating that the workers would seek an increase. "It seems to me, now is a good time to tell this to the men. Explain how we are trying to give them work to do by rolling rails for which we do not get paid till next spring." With no union to represent them, Carnegie expected that the men would in the end continue to work at the old wage rates. He was wrong.[1]

On December 30, the day before the old contract was to expire, Frick wrote from Pittsburgh with bad news:

> Blast furnace men, particularly stock fillers have notified Schwab that they will stop work on morning of January 1st unless their hours of labor are reduced to eight; it is a question of hours he says more than wages but of course means the same thing in the end. It is a serious matter to bank [shut down] furnaces* but it looks as if there was no other alternative. Any advance in wages or reduction in hours of labor it seems to me at furnaces is certainly not to be thought of now in view of the depressed condition of

---

*Furnaces, once cooled, were subject to damage and took a considerable amount of time to start up again.

business and gloomy outlook for 1891 and even if trade conditions favored it we could not well entertain a change in the present scale. Managers will meet in an hour to fully discuss it, in the meantime would like to have your views. The matter did not look serious until this morning, and I thought we would get through without troubling you with it at this time. Will have Schwab [general superintendent at Edgar Thomson] and [James] Gayley [head of the furnace department] in at noon. It seems to me we should instruct Mr. Schwab to call the men together and ask them to send a committee to furnace plants of other steel concerns at our expense, particularly eastern ones to investigate for themselves. In meantime the men to continue at work on the present scale. In this way our plant might be kept going until we are ready to stop for repairs and the men by that time brought to realize that business is really very much depressed.[2]

Carnegie had no intention of returning to an eight-hour day at Edgar Thomson for anyone, including the furnace men. The puddlers who worked the ovens at the Union Iron Mills in Pittsburgh endured twelve-hour shifts. Why shouldn't the skilled workers at the Bessemer ovens? The reasons were self-evident to the Bessemer furnace men. Iron puddlers put in a twelve-hour shift, five and a half days a week; because they managed their own furnaces, worked in two-man teams, spelled one another on a regular basis, and took breaks when they needed them, their twelve-hour turn never involved more than ten hours of work a day or fifty a week. The Bessemer blast furnaces, to the contrary, operated continuously twenty-four hours a day, seven days a week, spewing out raw material to be converted into steel and then cut, molded, rolled, and shaped into blooms, ingots, slabs, bars, beams, and the like. The men who tended, stocked, and stoked the ovens worked a full twelve hours a day, seven days a week, with no breaks, no one to spell them.[3]

Frick tried to keep Carnegie out of the loop as the situation spiraled out of control at the Edgar Thomson furnaces. He was intent on taking over full operational management of the Carnegie firms and, for the time being at least, it appeared that that was what Carnegie wanted as well. In December 1890, Louise had been brought down by a severe case of influenza. Carnegie was frightened, as frightened as he had ever been. Every letter to and from Frick referred to her condition.

On New Year's Eve, Carnegie cabled his response to the news of the furnace men's walkout, then followed up with a handwritten letter.

Advance in wages or cost at present time of course impossible. . . . Would have Schwab say to men at a time when we are trying every means to get orders even at a loss . . . when Eastern mills have reduced wages we are asked to increase cost. It is not in our power to do so . . . public sentiment will be with us. [*Pittsburgh*] *Dispatch* might help by a judicious article— saying to labor this is not time to ask advance. Trouble cannot be serious if met vigorously . . . the more all of our men can be told of the position and made to realize the truth the easier the trouble will be over—besides this furnace men should be told boldly that the firm will not be taken by the threat without notice and any man that deserts his post will not be employed again—this is really the strongest and best check you can give— decline to treat with men who threaten such conduct.[4]

Frick wrote back that he didn't think there would be any trouble at the furnaces because the troublemakers were unskilled Eastern Europeans who could be easily replaced. As the work in the steel mills had gotten more dangerous, as the eight-hour day was scrapped for twelve, and the work-week lengthened to eighty-four hours, the English-speaking boys who had once begun their careers in the mills as common laborers, began looking elsewhere for employment. They were replaced by unskilled immigrants who, without savings or language skills, had few alternatives but to work in the mills. The majority of the Eastern Europeans in the Pittsburgh steel mills came from the western parts of the Austro-Hungarian Empire. Most intended to remain only a few years, earning as much money as they could before returning to their villages to pay off mortgages or buy a piece of land. Few got the chance. Wages were higher in America, but so were the costs of living.[5]

The new immigrants kept largely to themselves, lived in boarding-houses with their own people, ate their own foods, drank in their own taverns, read foreign-language newspapers, shopped in stores owned by their landsmen. But they also made accommodation to the new world they now inhabited by learning a bit of the language and joining or cooperating with unions organized and led by English-speaking skilled laborers. They were willing to work long hours for pennies an hour, but when pushed too hard, shoved back.

Even without a union to represent them, the furnace men at Edgar Thomson had decided that they were not going to accede to the firm's ultimatum, even when it came sugarcoated with lengthy explanations as to why wages could not be raised or the workday reduced to eight hours. On New Year's Eve, the first to walk off their jobs rather than accept the new contract, with no reduction in hours or increase in wage rates, were the stockyard fillers, who delivered iron ore, coke, and limestone to the blast furnaces. When Schwab, who lived nearby in company housing, received the message at midnight that the "Hungarian element were organizing at the corner of 13th street, near Wolfe's saloon," he drove to the works in his carriage and, as he reported to Frick in a 3:00 A.M. telegram,

> arrived there about the same time the mob did, there being about 60 in the crowd. They immediately went down to the Stock House and of course after considerable skirmishing managed to chase all the men away from there. They then turned their attention to the men unloading material on trestles and succeeded in cleaning these men out. The crowd was made up largely of drunken fellows with whom you could neither reason, nor induce to leave by any argument and inasmuch as our force at the works was comprised of but a few foremen it was impossible to do anything with them. . . . They went down into the Stock Yard and commenced doing injury to our property by upsetting barrows, etc., when our loyal men . . . made an attack upon them and succeeded in beating them off from the stock house. I do not know that we have gained anything by this, but at this writing, 3 A.M., stock yard is entirely clear.[6]

Schwab hoped things would cool down overnight, and to help the process along, he asked Mr. Wolfe to close his saloon, which he did. It made no difference. On January 1, 1891, an even larger "posse" descended on the furnace department and drove out the few men still working there. Schwab suggested that the Pinkertons be brought in to get the furnaces started up at once. Frick disagreed. He had already dispatched Philander Knox, the company's chief lawyer, "to see the Sheriff and to find out whether the Sheriff will agree to protect our property. Mr. Knox thinks he will; and that if he says he will undertake to do it that it will be done.

Should we get a favorable decision from the Sheriff this will certainly be much better than employing Pinkerton men. . . . In case the Sheriff will not consent to protect our property and the men who are willing to work, we will have to adopt the second method which you propose. This I hope will not be necessary."[7]

Later that day, Frick wrote to tell Carnegie that the sheriff had agreed to intervene, which was a great relief to both of them. Frick was convinced that the matter would now be swiftly settled and the furnaces back at full blast. "This is certainly not anything more than a drunken Hungarian spree, and I do not think can lead to anything else; no reason why it should. . . . A little nerve and patience will certainly bring this matter through all right."[8]

The sheriff, as requested, took the next train from Pittsburgh to Braddock. Schwab met him at the Edgar Thomson plant and then "called together all the workmen who were then at the works [only the furnace department was being struck]; brought them into the office; addressed them, saying it was simply ridiculous for three thousand honest workmen to allow four or five hundred Hungarians to deprive them of work which they so much desired doing. I told them that the Sheriff was here and would swear them in as Deputy Sheriffs."[9]

With the sheriff's approval, Schwab then armed twelve of his best men with "Winchester Rifles (repeating) [and] a large number of other men . . . with small arms and clubs." If the "Huns" attacked again—and Schwab was certain they would—"they will meet with a pretty lively reception as I am determined to drive them out, no matter at what cost or sacrifices. . . . My plan now is, to appeal to the sympathy of the other men, get them to come to work, be sworn in as Deputies." He planned to start up the furnaces right away, "protecting ourselves all the while. . . . If, in this manner, I can get our men to stand right by us, I would much prefer this to getting Pinkerton detectives."[10]

Frick endorsed the strategy but cautioned James Gayley, the superintendent of the furnace department, to "exercise great care as to who you give these revolvers to. They must not be given under any circumstances to any except" those deputized by the sheriff. Frick also alerted Schwab that there was "a rumor that the Huns are arranging in Homestead to go to Braddock tonight in full force. I think it is all idle talk but thought it best to give it to you to be used for what it is worth."[11]

With the sheriff now in place at the head of a small army of armed "deputies," the second battle of Edgar Thomson was won without a shot having to be fired (and without the violent confrontations that might have ensued had the Pinkertons been brought in). The "Hungarians'" threatened attack on the newly deputized sheriffs never materialized. No intruders arrived from Homestead. The furnaces were, within days, again at full blast. With no union to bridge the cultural, language, and economic differences between unskilled "Hungarians" and skilled English-speaking workers, no strike fund, and no way of transmitting their grievances to the larger public, the Edgar Thomson workforce was easily divided and conquered. Carnegie's decision to drive the Knights out of Edgar Thomson in 1889 had been worth all the trouble it had taken.

By late January, the protests at the Edgar Thomson furnaces were a distant memory. The business downturn Frick and Carnegie had expected— and on which they had predicated their refusal to raise wages—never occurred. On the contrary, orders and revenues continued to pour in. "Money is becoming quite easy in Pittsburgh," Frick wrote Carnegie only weeks after crushing the aborted furnace men's strike. "The combined concerns have on hand something over a million and a quarter in cash."[12]

Carnegie was delighted with the news from Pittsburgh, but worried still about his wife's recovery. After another relapse, she appeared to be gathering strength, but slowly. Carnegie had remained at her side through her illness and was getting increasingly restless. "I begin to feel as if I should like to get out of the hospital for a few days," he wrote on January 26, "and see no reason why I can not leave this day week, and spend a few days in Pittsburgh and talk over all the points with you." Two weeks later, still marooned in New York, he wrote Frick that Louise preferred that he not leave "until as she says she gets on solid ground, which means solid food. She tastes an egg today, first morsel and is gaining daily. I'll wait and visit you in a few days."[13]

Carnegie and Frick had solved the labor problem at Edgar Thomson in January, but there was more to come. In February 1891, 10,000 coke workers went on strike in Connellsville against the H. C. Frick Coke Company, in which Carnegie held a majority interest. Frick had anticipated the strike and laid in sufficient supplies of coke for the next several months. By mid-March, however, with no sign of compromise from the strikers, he decided to force a confrontation. "It looks as if the time has about arrived," he wrote Carnegie on March 20, "when we should post up at the coke works the scale of wages we are willing to pay, and make an effort at several of the works to start." As at E.T. in 1888, there would be no negotiations over wage rates. The men would be invited to return to work at the posted wages. If they chose not to work at these rates, they could expect to lose their jobs to the substitute workers the company planned to bring in to replace them.[14]

Carnegie, knowing that there was no immediate need for fresh coke deliveries, suggested that Frick wait a bit before issuing any ultimatums. The longer the men stayed out of work, the hungrier and more desperate they and their families would become, and the easier it would be to break their strike. "To announce terms and try to start ovens is a very serious step to take. It should be postponed until the last day possible, as every day's idleness will render starting easier. I should not think of making a move this month. . . . I do not like the idea of your thrusting it upon them. It would show too clearly your desire to start."[15]

Carnegie agreed with Frick that the unions in the coke regions had to be busted—no matter what it took. The only difference between the two was timing. Carnegie suggested that Frick wait until April or later before forcing any confrontation. Frick and his general manager in the region, Thomas Lynch, wanted to move at once. On March 26, Lynch posted the new wage rates, announced that the coke works would be opened at once, and ordered the men back to work. The Connellsville coke workers responded by organizing themselves into quasi-military units and marching on the coke works, which were defended by private police and sheriff's deputies. Seven strikers were shot dead and dozens injured.

Carnegie, on learning of the events in Connellsville, dashed off a handwritten letter to Frick. The battle had now been joined and Carnegie urged him to fight it to the finish:

> Stand by the scale. Refuse all conference. [Declare that you are] going to run works free from all Labor organizations, etc. Try every means to start and force the Governor to send aid to keep the peace. Seems to me Sheriff can apply to Gvnr saying civil power exhausted "and upon you I throw responsibility." No Governor can stand who declines to take charge and keep the law—and peace. The issue should be clearly made with the Governor. . . . There will never be a better time than now to fight it out. Ad-

vances asked for are obviously ridiculous. Men are in the wrong. . . . You have a great advantage in the men having broken the law—you are entrenched. I believe this is the time to settle matters in the coke region and am willing to stand the cost to the end."[16]

Frick answered that same day that "all parties here feel just as you do, that now is the time to settle all difficulties in the coke regions. . . . Your suggestions as to the policy from now on will have careful consideration. . . . The strike certainly cannot last much longer."[17]

A week later, with Louise now nearly recovered, Carnegie arrived in Pittsburgh on his annual visit prior to sailing for Europe. Asked by reporters about the coke strike, he made a point of explaining that he had "taken no part in the coke question and don't intend to take any. There is a man at the head of the concern who made it, and I don't know anybody in the world who can attend to its affairs as well as Mr. Frick. Besides he is my boss now, and he has only to tell me how I can assist him to secure my support."[18]

Frick's optimistic predictions about a quick end to the strike were entirely off base. As the strike dragged on, Carnegie, frustrated with the lack of progress, couldn't help but gently suggest that had his advice been taken and the confrontation postponed, the men might have been enticed to return to work peacefully. "My idea of beating in a dispute with me is always to shut down and suffer, let them decide by vote when they desire to go to work—say kindly 'all right gentlemen let's hear from you, no quarrel, not the least in the world,' until a majority vote (secret ballot) to go to work— have a good time—when a majority vote to start, start it is. I am satisfied that the Employer or firm who gets the reputation of adhering to that rule never have a prolonged stoppage, or much ill feeling. We did it at E.T. but Abbott failed at Homestead and we have lost ground to recover." It was easier to starve the workers into submission than to do battle with them. The battle having now been engaged, Carnegie insisted that it was necessary "to go ahead to the end."[19]

Frick, with the assistance of the sheriff's deputies, counterattacked in an attempt to resecure the coke works and evict those who lived in company-owned housing. When the sheriff's deputies were driven off by the strikers, Democratic governor Robert Pattison, who had been reluctant to intervene, sent in the state militia to restore order but refused to permanently station troops at the coke works so that scabs could be brought in. Frick arranged instead "for 100 Pinkerton men at Leisenring No. 2," the center of union activity. "Sheriff of Fayette County agreed to deputize them. They will reach here tomorrow morning. . . . With that protection at those works, I think we will be able to get them started, as there are without doubt a large number of men willing to work if properly protected. To-morrow we will begin to evict at a number of places."[20]

On April 21, 1891, Frick cabled Carnegie with the news that he had successfully "landed the hundred Pinkerton men at Leisenring No. 2 about 1:30 to-day, and they were immediately sworn in as deputy sheriffs. A special [train] with fifty Italian miners, secured in the Punxsutawney Region, left here [Pittsburgh] at four o'clock for the same place. I trust with this protection, and this number of men to start with at that works, that we may succeed in running them full before long. We are holding our own at all other places, and gaining a little at some. We must keep at this persistently and patiently, and I am satisfied we will, before many days, get in pretty good shape."[21]

The coke workers were able to hold out for another month, but no longer. On May 20, Frick wrote that production at the coke works was "satisfactorily increasing." On May 27, the strike was called off.[22]

In less than three years, with Captain Jones's and Frick's assistance, Andrew Carnegie had broken strikes—and busted unions—at the Edgar Thomson works at Braddock and at Connellsville. But there remained still more to do before the Carnegie works were freed forever of union interference.

In late June, six months after the furnace men and stock fillers had been beaten back at E.T. and less than a month after the coke strike had been called off, word reached Frick through his network of spies that trouble was brewing at the Duquesne works, which he had purchased for Carnegie six months earlier. The skilled workers who had struggled, unsuccessfully, to organize a union under the old management were at it again. In early July, they quit work and announced that they would not return unless paid according to the wage scale negotiated by the Amalgamated for the iron mills in the Pittsburgh region.[23]

Carnegie had argued in his 1886 articles that it was always preferable to close down a plant than bring in scab workers. But he had discovered, at Edgar Thomson in 1889, that long-term lockouts were too costly to be sustained in boom business periods. Rather than wait indefinitely for workers to return, he had brought in Pinkertons to secure the plant and prepare the way for scab laborers. This was Frick's plan for Duquesne in 1891, with one important distinction: He intended to use the sheriff's office, instead of the Pinkertons, to break the strike.

"The Sheriff will go up on the 10:40 train with ten Deputies," Frick wrote Tommy Morrison, the general manager at Duquesne (and a distant cousin of Carnegie). "I feel satisfied that we can depend upon the Sheriff giving us all the protection we ask for, if needed; at least he has promised our Attorney Mr. Knox that he would do so. . . . We will fight this strike to the end and start the works on exactly the same terms as they were running heretofore. After they are once started we will formulate a sliding scale of our own and insist on every employee signing it. This, however, is a matter that we had better keep to ourselves for the present."[24]

Frick was not content with simply breaking the current strike; he was determined to find and eliminate the organizers. Company spies identified the union men, who were fired at once. "The following named persons," Frick wrote the superintendents at Edgar Thomson and Homestead on July 3, "have been discharged from Duquesne Works. Will you kindly see that they are not employed at Homestead or any other works of Carnegie, Phipps, and Co?" To make sure they would not return to Duquesne, an injunction was taken out against them. "I send you herewith copy of form necessary to be used to get injunctions against the men who are interfering with our operations," Frick wrote Morrison on July 6. "Please read it over carefully and see what it will be necessary to swear to, and whenever you can give the names of the parties acting against us as stated therein we will have no difficulty in getting to Court to enjoin them; Should they then continue to interfere with our employees or with men that want to go to work there will be no difficulty in having them sent to jail."[25]

Carnegie, like Frick, worried less about the strike at the Duquesne works—it would be quickly broken—than on the effect it would have on the Homestead workers. On July 14, Frick assured him there was nothing to worry about. The Homestead workers wanted very much "to see the men at Duquesne organized," but his swift action in breaking the strike would, he thought, "deter the Amalgamated Association from being led into the fight."[26]

He was right. The Amalgamated leadership decided not to support any organizing effort at Duquesne or endorse any sympathy strikes at Homestead or Carnegie's other iron or steel mills. With the sheriff's deputies on site and no support from outside, the Duquesne strike was stillborn. Frick's and, to a lesser degree, Carnegie's close ties with Allegheny County Republican officials were paying off handsomely. The company had only to whistle—and the sheriffs came riding to the rescue. Their support had been indispensable in breaking three separate strikes against Carnegie firms in 1891 alone. If, as Carnegie would later declare in his *Autobiography,* "Labor is usually helpless against capital," it was because capital, at least in Allegheny County, had the state on its side.[27]

IN HENRY CLAY FRICK, Carnegie had found the battlefield lieutenant he required to run his companies. Like Harry Phipps, Frick was a master accountant, with his eye firmly fixed on the bottom line. Like Captain Jones, he was resolutely anti-union and a master strategist in labor disputes. Like Tom Scott, he was politically savvy and politically connected. Carnegie was already relying on him more than he had relied on any of his other partners and managers. In early 1890, as a sign of his increasing faith in Frick's ability, Carnegie notified him that he had decided to spend more time abroad. "Have got Cluny for next year. Sail May 21st . . . We shall probably spend next winter in Italy, chiefly at Rome and not return until following winter and then only for short time. Am now getting all arranged as I planned."[28]

Frick, anticipating Carnegie's retirement, declared his availability to succeed him. "Am now satisfied," he wrote Carnegie in March 1891, "should like to continue my connection . . . but want to be more largely interested, if still agreeable in every respect to you, and satisfactory to all." Carnegie had earlier suggested that if Frick wanted to own a larger share of the steel company, he would sell him some of his own stock. Frick indicated he was now ready to take him up on the proposal.[29]

"I am delighted you think you can now go in and increase your interest," Carnegie responded. "You ought to for there's no business in this world that I know of which will make more money or give your talents greater scope. . . . My hope is you will then concentrate upon this business and make it the greatest ever seen . . . I'll fix it all with you next week or when I go to Pgh."[30]

Over the next year, Carnegie increased Frick's interest in Carnegie, Phipps and Carnegie Brothers to 11 percent, not the 14 percent Frick had requested, but an interest equal to Phipps, and second only to Carnegie himself. Frick was not expected to pay a penny in cash for the securities. Carnegie lent him the money, with the principal and capital to be paid back out of future dividends. He also agreed to Frick's proposal that Carnegie, Phipps, which owned the Homestead plant, and Carnegie Brothers which owned Edgar Thomson and Duquesne, be consolidated into one new company, Carnegie Steel, and that Frick be made chairman of the new company. The consolidation was to take effect on July 1, 1892, not coincidentally the date on which the Homestead labor contract was to expire.

Though Carnegie had done what Frick had asked for, the relationship between the two remained fraught. Carnegie needed more from Frick than the younger man was prepared to give him. Carnegie wanted Frick's loyalty and friendship; he wanted to be appreciated, respected, admired, even loved by the younger man.

Frick worked too hard, played too little, and was in danger of wearing himself out. Like an anxious parent, Carnegie prodded the young man to take better care of himself. "Sorry the grippe has reached you at least," he wrote during the influenza season of January 1890. "If any of you feel the least touch of it do be warned. Go to bed and figure upon ten millions surplus and take a hot whiskey toddy at night. I was well next day after my attack but foolishly went out next day and exposed myself. Walker Blaine's death [James Blaine's son] is a warning to you all. . . . Be careful."[31]

Whereas Carnegie's letters grew warmer, more intimate, and more personal, Frick's remained coldly businesslike. He shared little personal news or gossip and no reports on his health. As his great-granddaughter and biographer would later write, Henry Clay Frick "constructed the fortress of his privacy well: he was taciturn, brusque in his personal relationships, committed virtually nothing of a personal nature to paper, and guarded most of his feelings—although his anger was famous and never forgotten by those who experience it."[32]

Frick was delighted to be Carnegie's business partner, but he had no intention of becoming his confidant or friend, let alone surrogate son. Unlike Carnegie's other partners—young and old—Frick neither idolized Carnegie nor paid special tribute to his business experience and acumen. On the contrary, he considered himself Carnegie's equal, and in some ways his superior.

He too had built a successful business empire from the ground up, become the key figure in a vital industry, and acquired a fortune in doing so. He was young, ambitious, and, as Carnegie had recognized in naming him chairman, the man best suited to be in charge of the Carnegie empire.

Having arranged for Frick to increase his share of the businesses, Carnegie sailed for Britain in May 1891. Frick, as always, kept him informed by letter and coded cable on the progress of their multiple business dealings: in real estate, railroads, coke, iron ore, iron, and steel.

Unbeknownst to anyone, Frick's daughter, Martha, born in August 1885, had swallowed a pin at age two and suffered since then from a series of internal injuries and infections. By the summer of 1891, on the eve of the labor difficulties at the Duquesne mills, she was near death. The doctors, not knowing what ailed her, were unable to offer remedy or hope. Frick decided, as a last resort, that the mountain air and medicinal springs of Cresson might somehow help to heal her. He wired Carnegie in London to apprise him of the situation. "We have had a very sick little girl for two weeks past," he wired Carnegie. "We . . . hope to be able to move her to Cresson some day this week."[33]

Frick spent the month of July commuting back and forth between Cresson, where Martha lay dying, and his office in Pittsburgh, managing Carnegie's business interests, mopping up after the Connellsville strike, and leading the battle against the Duquesne militants. Nowhere in his letters— or at least those that have been left behind—was there a word of complaint or an echo of self-pity or, indeed, any further mention of his daughter's illness. Yet he was close to the breaking point. When Carnegie, sent a document for signature, casually asked for more information before signing, Frick took offense. "It is to be regretted," he wrote Carnegie at Cluny, "that a feeling has been created within you, cautioning you to be more careful in signing papers presented, and that you should think it necessary to exercise more care in the matter. I know nothing that should have engendered that feeling."[34]

Carnegie's response was solicitous. "Yours rec'd," he wrote on July 23, after getting his detailed reports in the post, "all very satisfactory except that you are to be denied your Holiday this year as last—It is really too bad & gives me many twinges of regret—No man can long stand continued pressure such as you work under & I do trust that next year you will feel you can leave business for a long trip." Carnegie had planned to take another of his coaching trips that summer, but now decided against it. "Without you its hardly worth while—We shall reserve it till next year." Toward the bottom of the letter, after a few short, chatty paragraphs on business matters, Carnegie mentioned Martha's illness for the first time: "We have been alarmed about little Martha, hope your decision not to leave home is not owing to her—Where are you for the Summer, Cresson probably—at least your wire was from there—Caught the best basket of Trout Monday last that I ever did—such beauties."[35]

Four days later, he wrote Frick again in much the same tone. "Having a fine summer—I'm fishing every day or two and resting between—In very good trim. . . . Take care of yourself."[36]

As Martha's condition continued to deteriorate, Frick sent for Dr. Garmany, who had helped save Carnegie's life five years earlier. It was too late. Martha died on July 29, 1891, one week short of her sixth birthday.

Frick accepted an invitation from a friend and business partner to move his family to Fishers Island, in Long Island Sound, off the Connecticut coast. Writing his partner on August 14, Carnegie closed a lengthy business letter with a brief reference to Frick's tragedy. "I am glad you have to run backward and forward to Fischer's [sic] Island, which will give you some needed change. Have been thinking that you should take a holiday after the year starts. A trip to Italy for instance, could not fail to keep you interested. . . . I hope you and your family will come with us after January for a trip to Italy. Think it over."[37]

On September 9, having no response from Frick, Carnegie tried again. "Do not work yourself to death, and do arrange to take that trip abroad that I spoke of."[38]

Frick continued to work like a demon. That winter, he moved his family to New York City and commuted regularly to Pittsburgh. His wife was pregnant again and expecting in August, close to the anniversary of Martha's death.

DESPITE his concern for Frick, Carnegie was in a particularly euphoric mood. Louise had fully recovered from her lengthy illness and Cluny was more beautiful and peaceful than ever. He was, he wrote Frick, fishing every day or two "and resting in between." One of his guests that summer was John Champlin, whose passage Carnegie had paid. Carnegie, the most amiable of hosts, assured Champlin that he need not worry about having too much baggage—he would send a van to fetch it at Newtonmore, the nearest train station. "You will need it all—plenty of warm things. . . . send it all here—plenty of room."[39]

Carnegie was right to urge Champlin to bring "warm things." Photos of their picnic excursions that summer of 1891 show everyone bundled head to toe. Carnegie, looking very much like the grandfather of the group, occupies the center of each group photo. Sensitive about his height, Carnegie never allowed himself to be photographed standing, but always sought the higher elevation, the top stair, or arranged for the group to be photographed sitting down. High-heeled boots with thick soles helped a bit, as did the variety of hats, from pith helmets to formal top hats.[40]

Carnegie's otherwise idyllic summer of '91 was marred only by his inability to get much writing done. "It does not seem possible for me to get to work," he wrote Champlin; "really I don't feel able to sit down and apply myself." This was to be a recurrent problem for Carnegie, who had hoped to spend more time writing now that he was semi-officially retired from business.[41]

Always the most self-satisfied of men, Andrew Carnegie was, despite his minor writer's block and his worries about Frick, quite pleased with himself that summer. Never had business been better. The steel firms—Edgar Thomson, Homestead, and the Duquesne works—were, by 1891, the dominant force in the nation's fastest-growing, most significant industrial sector. Carnegie had guessed right in putting his money into steel rails in the mid-1870s and then diversifying into other steel products in the 1880s. In 1880, almost all the steel had been rolled into rails; by 1890, half of it was being used for other products: beams, bars, angles, sheets, rods, pipes, nails, plates, and structural shapes for bridges, buildings, skyscrapers, and ships. His early start in rails, then in structural steel, had put him in a position to profit, as no one else could, from the quarter-century economic boom that began in the mid-1870s. From 1880 to 1890, pig iron production in the United States increased from 4.3 million to 10.3 million net tons and steel production from 1.2 to 4.1 million tons.*[42]

The Carnegie firms were at the forefront of the peculiarly American

---

*These figures include only steel made in Bessemer ovens, not that made in the open-hearth ovens like those Carnegie had installed at Homestead.

system of manufacturing described by Robert W. Hunt, the first historian of steel manufacturing in the United States, as "American push." While the Americans made use of British patents and processes in their mills, they "pushed" their machinery and their workers far harder than the British did. The English industrialist Sir Lowthian Bell, who visited the United States in 1890, was appalled by the "recklessly rapid rate" at which Americans drove their blast furnaces.[43]

Carnegie's hard-driving policies were legendary. Carnegie, Phipps, Captain Jones, Frick, and Charlie Schwab pitted department against department, mill against mill, superintendent against superintendent in an ongoing, never-ending race to increase productivity. The results were evident in the blast furnaces, which year after year dramatically increased their efficiency and productivity. Between 1880 to 1889, Carnegie allocated funds to construct five new furnaces on site to provide additional pig iron for the Edgar Thomson Bessemer converters. Each furnace turned out more pig iron more efficiently than the one preceding it. The one erected in 1889 turned out three and a half times more iron than the original Lucy furnaces, while burning one-third less coke.[44]

The danger inherent in such rapid expansion was that production would outstrip demand. And Carnegie well understood this. To lessen the impact of the cyclical crises of overproduction, Carnegie and his fellow iron and steel manufacturers organized informal "pools" to allocate market share and set minimum prices. Beneficial as these pools might have been in curbing price competition, excessive loyalty to them, Carnegie preached to Frick and his partners, was no virtue. There were times, especially in business downturns, when the pools had to be broken. In January 1892, to cite but one example, Carnegie suggested that Frick consider leaving the beam pool. Although the Carnegie firms were guaranteed 30 percent of the allocation, firms outside the pool were selling below the minimum price and scooping up new business at an alarming rate. "If our business is being cut into by those outside the pool, it would be best to strike vigorously, sweep away all pools, and run awhile until we get the business into fewer hands, just as we have done with rails."[45]

Because the Carnegie firms remained so vitally strong, relatively debt-free, and diversified into many product areas, they could afford to periodically break the pools, lower their prices, expand market share, drive the weaker firms out of business, and then organize new pools, in which they would have a larger share of the market. The strategy of joining, then breaking, then reorganizing the pools was a recipe for continued success, the only downside being that such a policy might be in violation of the 1890 antitrust law that bore Senator John Sherman's name.

The Sherman Antitrust Act forbade "combinations in the form of a trust or otherwise in restraint of trade." Unfortunately, the legislation never made clear what was meant by "restraint of trade," or whether informal pools set up by manufacturers were outlawed "combinations." In 1912, Carnegie told a congressional committee that it had never entered his mind that the steel pools might be illegal. He believed that the antitrust legislation applied not to manufacturers but to railroads. This was indeed the opinion of the Supreme Court in a pivotal 1895 case. It was not until 1898 that the Court would reverse itself and apply the Sherman Antitrust Act to manufacturing concerns.[46]

While Congress and the courts tried to determine what was meant by "combinations" and "restraint of trade," Carnegie proceeded to join and leave the various steel pools at will, without fear that his firms would be indicted for violation of the antitrust laws. At the same time, he did his best to ensure that neither he nor his colleagues in the steel industry incited the politicians to take action against them. Just as he carefully guarded all information about the enormous profits his companies were making, so too did he urge his fellow steelmakers to keep secret the workings of the pools. On July 15, 1890, two weeks after the passage of the Sherman Antitrust Act, Carnegie informed Frick that he had written President Joseph Wharton of Bethlehem Steel, with whom Homestead divided the armor business, "more than once, urging that the allotment farce be stopped, otherwise, that there would be trouble in the Senate. It is so silly to incur public odium, and be classed as a combination controlling product, when there is no truth whatever in the charge. The organization, of course, should be kept together . . . except that the public would not be regaled with statements of allotments every month, which are without the slightest practical bearing upon the acts. I hope you will carry this point." Because the allotment system was informal, non-binding, and did not prescribe the prices the companies had to charge for their rails, it was not, Carnegie insisted, "a combination." Still, he thought it best not to advertise the fact that the largest steel manufacturers met regularly, shared patent information, took orders together, and regarded one another as colleagues rather than competitors.[47]

Carnegie refused to be beholden to anyone and repeatedly turned down suggestions that he might combine or merge with his competitors. When Frick suggested a "closer alliance" between the Carnegie firms and Illinois Steel, Carnegie dismissed the idea out of hand. "We must never think of any consolidation or merging of the concerns, because our property and business is on the rock and invulnerable, and we understand it and can manage it. With the others it is not so."[48]

THOUGH HE TOLD everyone who asked—and many who did not—that he was retired from active business, that was only partly true. He remained tied to Pittsburgh by an umbilical cord as long as the Atlantic cable. Success in business acted on him like an addictive drug. He had always enjoyed the thrill of the game, the competition for profits, the exhilaration of winning an especially lucrative contract. Once he had decided to give away his fortune—and publicly proclaimed as much—he discovered additional reasons to remain a steelmaker. The money he accumulated now—and the much larger sums he intended to add to his fortune in the future—were not for his use, but for the community. The more he earned, the more he could give away, and he was earning more than ever. Profits had increased from under $2 million in 1888 to $3.5 million in 1889 to $5.3 million in 1890. They would, he predicted, climb even higher in the years to come.[49]

The gods were smiling on Carnegie and his partners. Everything appeared to be going their way, even the weather.

"The crops in Europe are evidently, even worse than the authorities care to acknowledge," Carnegie wrote Frick from abroad in 1891. Crop failures in Europe meant higher prices for American wheat, which would, in turn, mean more money for the midwestern states, a fair portion of which was bound to find its way into new construction—of steel rails, steel bridges, and steel structures of every kind. "It is not more than an even chance the sunshine will come," Carnegie gloated to Frick. "If not, our crops will bring higher prices than expected. Of course, the advance in produce and stocks, will soon be reflected in iron and steel, and next spring, I believe, we shall have a boom."[50]

. . .

CARNEGIE went out of his way to solicit interviews and indulge the journalists who appeared at his doorstep. He was immensely proud of all that he had accomplished and wanted the wider public on both sides of the Atlantic to share in his joy. During his 1891 stay at Cluny, the editor of the *Musical Courier,* one of those honored with such an invitation, arrived to find his subject "seated in a very large chair, in a very small study, busily engaged opening letters from a pile. . . . Many of them were begging letters. If wealth brings its pleasures it also brings its trials and one of the greatest trials of the 'Iron King' are these appeals by beggars. . . . Beside Mr. Carnegie was his secretary . . . working away at a typewriter, as if to maintain his employer in bread. Table, covered with books, newspapers, etc., and a fire—and that was all." The journalist, like all visitors encountering Carnegie for the first time, could not get over his tiny stature—and large intellect. "One discovers at once that although comparatively small of body, Mr. Carnegie is mighty of brain. One quickly realizes that he is in the presence of a man of immense force of character, masterful resource, and determination, with an intellect as alert as his body is active."[51]

The publication of *Triumphant Democracy,* followed by his "Gospel of Wealth" essays, had firmly established his credentials as an author and intellectual. Even the president of the United States saw fit to pay him tribute. In the fall of 1891, he shipped President Harrison "a keg of what is said to be best Scotch Whisky in the world" from John Dewar & Sons and received a personally written note acknowledging the gift: "It was very kind of you to think of me as likely to need a 'brace' this winter in dealing with the new Congress." Harrison proceeded to lavish on Carnegie exactly the kind of praise the little Scotsman lived for. "If your Gospel of Wealth should lead you to turn over to unbelievers the large fortune which you have accumulated by your marvelous industry and skill in manufacturing, I think you could earn a living with your pen. I know you will not think me a flatterer when I say that I have been surprised and very greatly pleased to notice how one, who has led so busy a life in trade, could get so large a view of political questions, and the command of so forcible a style."[52]

Carnegie celebrated his fifty-sixth birthday in November 1891, and was, as everyone who visited him felt obliged to remark, in remarkably fine fettle. His marriage was a grand success; his multiple careers as steelmaker, man of letters, public speaker, and philanthropist were thriving; a Republican was in the White House; Frick was at the helm of his Pittsburgh business empire; and Carnegie himself was where he wanted to be—in the public spotlight. There were no clouds on the horizon, only limitless profits to be made and spent for the greater welfare of the greater community.

TWENTY-THREE

The Battle for Homestead, 1892

For two and a half years, Carnegie had been preparing for the summer of 1892 and his next showdown at Homestead. He had tried, but failed, to break the Amalgamated at Homestead in 1889; he expected, with Frick's assistance, to succeed in 1892.

The past years had been profitable ones. Carnegie had made millions of dollars and poured much of it back into retooling the Homestead works. In the spring of 1889, the Homestead workforce had been about 1,600; a year later, it was up to 2,600. By the spring of 1892, with armor manufacture in full swing, almost 4,000 men were employed at the works. Homestead had replaced Edgar Thomson as the most technologically advanced steel mill in the nation. The overhead cranes, rolling tables, hydraulic shears, and gigantic, iron-roofed plate and beam mills were larger than those anywhere else. The open-hearth furnaces routinely turned out 50-ton batches of molten steel (double that of the Bessemer furnaces at Edgar Thomson). The site was grid-ironed with tracks on which materials were pulled through the 100-acre complex by nineteen locomotives. Homestead had its own repair, blacksmith, and carpentry shops; a brick and stone office standing on a hill overlooking the mills; "eight handsome residences" for managers; forty more houses for master workmen; and "a handsome clubhouse for the accommodation of guests and officers."[1]

The town had grown with the works, from a population of about 2,000 in 1880, when the plant opened, to 12,000 in 1892. In 1890, after "Beeswax" Taylor's retirement, "Honest John" McLuckie was elected burgess (the equivalent of mayor), outpolling his three opponents by 811 votes to 5. McLuckie worked in the converting mill, was an active member of the Amalgamated, and had played a role in the defense of the town in 1889.

The 1889 settlement with the company was regarded as a victory for the Amalgamated. The wage rates of most of the skilled workers had been cut, but with increased productivity they were soon bringing home more than they had under previous contracts. Unskilled laborers still earned about fourteen cents an hour. The Amalgamated remained the bargaining agent for all the men on the job. Its 800 dues-paying members, enrolled in eight different lodges, made it the strongest local in the region. Its 24,000 members nationwide made it the largest metalworkers union in the world.[2]

ON JANUARY 30, 1891, Carnegie, studying the previous year's figures on labor costs and productivity, discovered that the former were rising more rapidly than the latter. He now understood, he wrote Frick, why the profits at Homestead were not as high as they should be. He asked for "a thorough investigation of Homestead labor forces. There is certainly $300,000 a year [in labor costs] unaccounted for." Homestead, he feared, had too many workers, and he was paying them far too much.[3]

Frick hired William Martin, a former steelworker, union activist, and editor of the Amalgamated's page in the *National Labor Tribune* to compile an industrywide comparison of Homestead wage rates with national averages. Martin sent out questionnaires to firms across the country, discovered what they were paying each category of skilled workman, then compared tonnage and day rates for these firms with figures for Homestead. His findings confirmed Carnegie's suspicions that skilled workers at Homestead were receiving more than the industry average. Martin was then put to work designing a wage scale for Homestead that was comparable to that of Carnegie's non-union competitors.[4]

The current labor contract was not due to expire until July 1, 1892, but Carnegie was eager to begin work at once. "It has occurred to me," he wrote Frick in December 1891, "that if the labor question could be taken up at Homestead soon, the same months you are spending in negotiating now, might save stoppage in July, when I am certain we shall not wish one day's delay." He suggested that Frick ask his brother-in-law, Otis Childs, a manager at Homestead, to intimate to the Amalgamated leadership that if the skilled workers did not voluntarily agree to wage reductions now, the firm might have to "transfer all the trade . . . from Homestead" to the lower-priced, non-union Duquesne mills. "If Childs and one other, or, perhaps, Childs alone were instructed to take the subject up now, and show that we expected reductions, and that it would be to the interest of the men to give them, perhaps much good would be accomplished. Please think this over."[5]

In January 1892, John Potter, who had replaced William Abbott as general superintendent at Homestead, invited the Amalgamated to submit proposals for a new contract for four of the plant's ten departments. The other six departments, he explained, would operate under the old contract until new machinery was introduced, at which time a new wage rate might be negotiated.

Over the next month, the Amalgamated formulated a wage proposal which differed little from the one signed in 1889. In early February 1892, the union representatives took the train to Pittsburgh to present their proposals to Potter. He rejected them and distributed instead the ones William Martin had worked up. The most striking element in the firm's substitute proposal was a reduction in the minimum rate from $25 to $22 a ton. (The minimum was the rate the company would pay no matter how low the price of a ton of unfinished steel fell.) The company's proposals, Potter insisted, were more than fair as they provided for wage reductions for skilled workers in only four departments, a mere 325 workers out of the 3,800 at Homestead. What Potter didn't call attention to was that the firm reserved the right in the new contract to revise the scale downward for other skilled workers "in the event of the introduction of new methods and appliances." The meeting was adjourned without a date set for another negotiating session.[6]

On April 4, just before he left for Scotland, Carnegie prepared a notice to be posted at Homestead in his absence. The notice, on Carnegie's personal letterhead, declared that as all three Carnegie steel plants were being consolidated into one firm, Carnegie Steel, as of July 1, "there had been forced upon this Firm the question Whether its Works are to be run 'Union' or 'Non-Union.' As the vast majority of employees [all those at E.T. and Duquesne] are Non-Union, the Firm has decided that the minority must give place to the majority. These works therefore, will be necessarily Non-Union after the expiration of the present agreement." Carnegie assured his Homestead employees that they would be treated fairly as non-union workers. "A scale will be arranged which will compare favorably with that at the other works named; that is to say, the Firm intends that the men of Homestead shall make as much as the men at either Duquesne or Edgar Thomson." As further improvements were made at Homestead, Carnegie admitted that jobs might be lost, but he pledged to find work "for desirable employees" at his other plants. He concluded by stating somewhat provocatively, given the contents of the notice, that "this action is not taken in any spirit of hostility to labor organizations."[7]

Carnegie sent his draft to Frick, with a note that "Mr. Potter should roll a large lot of plates ahead, which can be finished, should the works be stopped for a time." Instead of posting the notice, Frick "pigeon-holed" it, according to George Harvey, his authorized biographer, because he was not yet ready to publicly announce that Carnegie Steel was going to be a non-union company. After a face-to-face meeting with Frick in New York City, Carnegie left for Britain on April 13, fully satisfied that Frick would succeed at Homestead without too much difficulty. "I know that you will be sharp now after Homestead costs," he wrote Frick just before sailing, "and I venture to predict that about this time next year, some surprising results will be seen."[8]

When he arrived at Coworth Park, the English country estate in Berkshire County, where he and Louise spent the first part of their holidays (Cluny had no central heating and was not quite fit for habitation until later in the spring), a letter from Frick was waiting for him. "The wage question at Homestead is a most series [sic] one," Frick warned, "and it may become necessary to fight it out this summer. No better time can be selected or expected. We will get ready for a fight immediately. If it be unnecessary, all the better. It may be a stubborn one, but if once gone into, without regard to cost or time, it will be fought to a finish."[9]

On May 4, after consulting with Phipps and Lauder, who were also vacationing in England, Carnegie got back in touch with Frick. He recognized now that his excitement at taking on the Amalgamated had gotten the better of him and that the notice he had asked Frick to post about Homestead going non-union had been needlessly provocative. "You remember I gave you a type-written slip which I suggested you might have to use. It is probable that you will. But I hope you will make this change in it: I did not get it quite right, because I think it said that the firm had to make the decision of 'union' or 'non-Union.' . . . We need not meet that point, and we should not. We simply say that consolidation having taken place, we must introduce the same system in our works; we do not care whether a man belongs to as many Unions or organizations as he chooses, but he must conform to the system in our other works." Carnegie closed by again expressing his faith—and that of his partners—in Frick's leadership. "One thing we are all sure of: No contest will be entered in that will fail. . . . We all approve of anything you do, not stopping short of approval of a contest. We are with you to the end."[10]

There was no doubt in Carnegie's mind that with Frick overseeing day-to-day operations and making necessary tactical adjustments, the strategy that had worked so well at E.T. in 1888 and at Connellsville in 1891 could not help but succeed at Homestead. The firm would make impossible demands. When the union rejected them, the company would cut off negotiations, close the works, lock out the workers, secure the plant with sheriff's deputies and/or Pinkertons, and then, after an indeterminate pause, reopen under armed protection. The workers would be invited to sign individual contracts and return to their jobs; those who refused would be replaced by scabs. "No doubt you will get Homestead right," he reassured Frick on May 23. "You can get anything right with your 'mild persistence.'"[11]

One of the reasons Carnegie was less concerned about a work stoppage at Homestead than he might have been was that 1892 was not turning out to be the banner year he had predicted the summer before. With orders slow and prices slack, the company would not suffer much if it had to shut down Homestead for a few months. "There is altogether too much capacity in every branch, and the turn can come only after a good many works are closed," Carnegie wrote on May 24. "There is no hope of things mending until things get even worse."[12]

Confident that Frick would be able to secure a decent labor contract at Homestead, Carnegie turned his attention to more pressing matters, namely, the reorganization of Carnegie Brothers and Carnegie, Phipps into a new company: Carnegie Steel. Frick, who would emerge as the third major stockholder, was the architect of the reorganization. George (Dod) Lauder, who owned 4 percent of the stock in the two Carnegie firms and would be the fourth-largest stockholder in Carnegie Steel, was prepared to agree to whatever Carnegie wanted. The only holdout was Harry Phipps, who, Carnegie wrote Frick in a long letter on May 13, was "troubled upon several points." Phipps was particularly "afraid of the 'iron clad' agreement," which, Carnegie commented, was "rather curious, inasmuch as he had it prepared. He does not like his own medicine."[13]

Phipps had designed the "ironclad" arrangement in the winter of 1886–87 during Carnegie's convalescence from his near-fatal illness. To enable the firm to buy back the shares of deceased members without bankrupting itself, Phipps had set the "book value" of the company's stock below the market value and stipulated that the firm had to pay only this "book value." The "ironclad"—so named because it was considered unbreakable—further stipulated that at any time, for any reason, an individual partner could be expelled from the firm and required to sell back his shares at "book value," if a combination of three quarters of the partners, holding three quarters of the total stock, requested him to do so. It is not exactly clear what Phipps's objections were to the "ironclad," but he may well have feared giving his partners the right to expel him from the firm at some later date.

Carnegie did his best to persuade Phipps to sign the new agreement. Phipps finally agreed to do so, only to back off again. He was not willing to sign an agreement, he told Carnegie, which gave any number of active partners the right to expel retired members and compel them to sell back their stock to the company at "book value," which was less than market value. Carnegie was inclined to agree with his old friend. "As we never put any one out except for cause it doesn't seem important."[14]

While Carnegie was inclined to let Phipps off the hook, Frick was adamant that every partner, including retired ones like Phipps, sign the new agreement. "It is absolutely necessary, in order to make it binding, that it should be signed by all partners, and it is very important for the interests of every one that such an agreement should be binding." Phipps should have been assured that he would never be thrown out of the company. Because Carnegie owned more than 50 percent of the stock, no combination of partners without him could secure the three-fourths necessary to expel anyone. "No one but yourself can put any one out," Frick assured Carnegie, "that is to say, it requires your vote in order to do so, and certainly Mr. Phipps would not think for a moment that you would join in putting him out. As we all look forward to being retired partners some day, it surely would be short-sighted policy to ever think of trying to put a retired partner out."[15]

Carnegie, in the end, sided with Frick against Phipps. His and Frick's relationship had continued to evolve to the point that when they disagreed, Carnegie was as likely to give in to his junior partner as vice versa.

Carnegie remained very much a force to be reckoned with, but he had reconciled himself to playing more of a subordinate, advisory role than a dominant, supervisory one when it came to matters having to do with the day-to-day operations of his businesses. He had tried, for almost twenty years, to get away from Pittsburgh, but with his money and his ego tied up in his iron and steel plants, had not been able to do so. Now, for the first time, with Frick in charge, he saw an opportunity to concentrate more of his time and energy on his writing and his philanthropy.

The old guard, the men who had built Edgar Thomson from the ground up, were, except for him, dead or retired. The key to the future, he realized, lay in the reorganization of his firms into one concern and Frick's willingness to run it as chief executive officer and chairman of the board. Whatever tools Frick needed Carnegie would supply, even if it meant coaxing his old friend Harry Phipps into doing something he feared. "Of course, Iron Clad is essential to maintenance of our prosperity," Carnegie wrote his "dear Pard" Frick in mid-June. "H. P. sees this now, I asked him to consider how powerless we should be [without the ironclad] in case of another Moore [a former accountant whom Frick had had to let go]; told him about our efforts to get in new blood, etc. . . . He thought we had been too fast giving away interests [to new partners] and I pled guilty, and told him he needn't fear you would blunder in this way,—10 years service probably condition hereafter, etc. . . . He is cranky,—very, in some things, but a dear good heart is his, at bottom. Away from you and all naturally he begins to feel like an outsider. Now his family are leading him into 'Society.' They go to 'Ascot' tomorrow, etc. This new life may interest him and give a happy old age, which I hope for him. He deserves it so well. We must be patient with him,—all will come right."[16]

No matter what the primary topic, the letters back and forth between Frick and Carnegie that spring of 1892 always included some reference to Homestead and its future. "I am not sanguine about Homestead Labor," Carnegie admitted on May 30. He was concerned that Frick at the last minute might, like Abbott before him, agree to negotiate with the Amalgamated. His anxieties were occasioned by his own unarticulated fears that if he were in Frick's place, he might not be able to stand tough. It was easy, he had admitted to Abbott three years earlier, to be "brave" at a distance, far more difficult to do so when one was in the line of fire. He emphasized again how essential it was that the Amalgamated be defeated at Homestead. If it survived, it might well be emboldened to move on to organize Duquesne and Edgar Thomson. If it were stopped at Homestead, it would mark the beginning of a glorious new era for Carnegie Steel in which management would be free to do whatever it thought necessary to cut labor costs and increase productivity.[17]

The problem at Homestead was, he reminded Frick in a June 10 letter, "not only the wages paid, but the number of men required by Amalgamated rules which makes our labor rates so much higher than those in the East." Having informed the union representatives what the company was prepared to pay, Frick must refuse to negotiate, compromise, or arbitrate. "Of course, you will be asked to confer, and I know you will decline all conferences, as you have taken your stand and have nothing more to say. Potter will, no doubt, intimate to the men that refusal . . . means running only as Non-Union. This may cause acceptance, but I do not think so. The chances are, you will have to prepare for a struggle, in which case the notice should go up promptly on the morning of the 25th [of June]. Of course you will win, and win easier than you suppose, owing to the present condition of markets."[18]

Carnegie need not have worried about Frick's resolve. On May 30, Frick took the train to Homestead to meet with John Potter and give him final instructions on the negotiations. Potter was to summon the Amalgamated representatives to a meeting and present them with the company's non-negotiable wage scales. The tonnage rates for the skilled workers in the open-hearth furnaces, the plate mill, and the slabbing mill "would be reduced by 15–18 percent for most workers, and by as much as 35 percent for some." The minimum rate at which the skilled workers would be paid would be reduced from current $25 per ton to $22. To make the terms of the new contract even more unpalatable, Potter was instructed to announce to the union that the new contract would remain in effect until December 31, 1893, instead of June 30, 1893. The union had until June 24 to accept these terms. If it did not do so, the firm would, as it had at Edgar Thomson, bypass the union and ask the workmen to sign the contract as individuals.[19]

There was, of course, no way the Amalgamated could agree to this. On June 4, the *Pittsburgh Post* reported that the firm's ultimatum was "almost certain to be rejected. Developments now indicate that Homestead will be the scene of a great conflict between capital and labor." Among the most dangerous elements of the new contract was the December 31 end date. As William T. Roberts, the chief negotiator for the Amalgamated, explained on July 13, 1892, to a House of Representatives committee investigating conditions at Homestead, the steelworkers feared negotiating a new contract in winter as "the burnt child dreads the fire. We know from past experience— at least, I do—that when winter time comes around and our contract ends in the winter . . . they take that opportunity at that time of the year to starve us into submission. They have done it on every occasion."[20]

Frick and Carnegie, on either side of the Atlantic, prepared for the confrontation they had provoked. The best scenario for the company was that the lockout* would last no longer than a month or two. If that were the case, Frick promised to take up Carnegie on his offer of a vacation in Scotland. "I note you have taken a place in Scotland," Frick remarked in his June 2 letter. "Have no doubt it is a very fine one, and I might take a notion to run over for a short time the latter part of August, say thirty-day trip, if everything should be going all right." Frick was anticipating that by this time his wife, who had become pregnant within weeks of Martha's death the year before, would have delivered her baby and he would be free to leave for a brief vacation.[21]

On June 10, Carnegie asked his cousin Dod, who was in St. Petersburg on armor business, to return to Britain to recruit English and Scottish machinists as possible replacement workers should they be needed at Homestead. "Have wired Lauder to St. Petersburg to come here and get you the men desired. Will, of course, handle very carefully. I do not think anybody but he can do it. No reply from him yet. He may have left Petersburg this morning."[22]

In mid-June, as both sides prepared for the confrontation, Carnegie reminded Frick that he had not forgotten about his "orchestrion"—an elaborate, expensive automatic instrument that Frick had asked Carnegie to purchase for him. Inside the "orchestrion" were a piano, two ranks of organ pipes, a triangle, a cymbal, and some drums. The instrument was operated by changeable perforated paper rolls that contained melodies from

---

*The Homestead events of 1892 can be described as both a lockout and a strike. The lockout came first, when the plant was shut down. But it was transformed into a strike when Frick invited the workers back to the plant—on his terms—and they refused to do so.

opera and the orchestral repertoire. Carnegie wanted to know whether Frick wanted his "finished in light or dark wood." Almost as an aside, he added to a letter filled with other items that "perhaps if Homestead men understand that non-acceptance means Non-Union forever, they will accept."[23]

Frick was, at the time, more concerned with the looming battle at Homestead than with the finish of his orchestrion. "There is really nothing new to report. The indications, however, point to a strike," he reported on June 20. "Regret to say that it does not seem to me that there is any other course open for us. We would better make the fight and be through with it, expensive though it may be. However, a few days may change the outlook."[24]

In a report mailed two days later, Frick informed Carnegie that a committee of non-union mechanics, which claimed to represent one thousand boilermakers, engineers, machinists, pipefitters, carpenters, tinners, painters, riggers, and other mechanics who were paid by the day, had agreed to continue working for three years under the terms of the old contract. The only concession that Potter had made was to agree that the new contract would expire in June, not January. The agreement, Frick thought, was sure to "demoralize the Amalgamated more or less. . . . We will not be trifled with, and are prepared to carry out the policy we have adopted. It may be that we will win without much difficulty, although I am not yet prepared to believe that we will win without a pretty severe struggle, and am not sure, even with the agreement on the part of these men to work, that they will do so, provided we find it necessary to bring in guards. It may be that a very few men, if any, will report for work at first."[25]

While Frick remained doubtful that anything would be settled by late August, Carnegie now appeared almost certain of it. He was delighted to hear that Frick was seriously considering running "over for a month. This would be so wise that I doubt your doing so. . . . Bring a companion along. Choose the one you will most enjoy." Andrew White, the former Cornell president and now ambassador to Russia, planned to visit late in the summer. Carnegie suggested that the two might travel together. In the meantime he was, "getting on well with my book. Will promise not to bore you with it if you come. In Scotland we only play."[26]

On June 23, the day Frick received Carnegie's cheery letter and a week before the Homestead labor contract was to expire, he deviated from

Carnegie's instructions and met with union representatives at 10:00 A.M. at his office in Pittsburgh. The meeting, he reported to Carnegie the next day, had not resulted "in anything. Of course we could have talked all day with them, but made it as brief as possible. . . . They had the impression that Potter got us to consent to changing the minimum to $23.00, but we would make no other changes. . . . We are now preparing for a struggle. . . . It may be, of course, that they will yet propose to accept our ultimatum, but we will have no more conferences with them."[27]

On Saturday, June 25, which was payday at Homestead, Frick, following Carnegie's directive, posted notices at the plant and throughout the town declaring that, the Amalgamated having turned down its final offer, the firm would have nothing more to do with it. Construction was already underway on what would become known as "Fort Frick." The mill was barricaded behind 11-foot-high fences, with portholes just large enough for guns to stick through. On top of the fence were 18 inches of jagged barbed wire. Giant searchlights of 2,000-candlepower each and fire plugs "with an enormous water pressure in each" were erected at the entrances.[28]

There could be only one reason, the *Pittsburgh Post* reported, for the barricades, barbed wire, and searchlights. The company had decided to bring in scabs. "This open preparation for battle has a demoralizing influence upon the men, who have been preparing to conduct a strike, if there be any, peaceably and without violence. They do not relish the red rag of defiance flung right into their faces. . . . The coolest of the men do not deny that there will be grave trouble if the firm attempts to introduce into the mills non-union or scab labor."[29]

The Homestead workers, especially the skilled ones, had an ownership stake in the mills. They were proud to work in the nation's most technologically advanced steel mill—articles in the *National Labor Tribune* were as celebratory as those in the *Iron Age*—but they regarded their right to remain at their jobs as sacrosanct. They would not give up their positions without a fight.

There were other reasons, every bit as significant, why the Amalgamated men could not allow substitute workers to take their places. Homestead was a company town—there were no other jobs available for the men who worked in the plant. Should they lose theirs, they would have to pull up stakes and leave the town and mill they had built.

"The feeling of ownership," Pittsburgh journalist Arthur Burgoyne would write the year after the strike, "had a place in the reasoning of these simple people. Many of them had bought and paid for their homes and were pillars of the borough government. Some were still paying for their dwellings. . . . It was clearly impossible that men of substance, heads of families, solid citizens of a prosperous municipality could be rooted up, as it were, out of the soil in which they were so firmly planted and beaten to earth by the creature of their labor—for without labor, it was argued, capital would be impotent and valueless."[30]

The day the notices were posted, confirming the rumors that the men were being locked out of their jobs and their plant, Frick wrote Robert Pinkerton to reconfirm an earlier arrangement made with him on June 2 to dispatch "300 guards for service at our Homestead mills as a measure of precaution against interference with our plan to start operation of the works on July 6th, 1892." When asked later why he didn't use sheriff's deputies to protect his property, Frick stated plainly that three years earlier the company had called on the sheriff for protection at Homestead, but that the sheriff and his deputies had been outmanned by the strikers. "We did not propose this time to be placed in that position."[31]

On Tuesday, June 28, Frick shut down the plate mill and one of the open-hearth furnaces, locking out the workers two days before their contract expired.

On Wednesday, he shut down the remaining departments at Homestead, completing the lockout. That afternoon, the Amalgamated presented Carnegie and Frick's final offer to 2,800 Homestead steelworkers, skilled and unskilled, at a meeting at the opera house. A motion was made to close the meeting to outsiders and reporters, but it was defeated. The steelworkers had nothing to hide. They were breaking no laws, only exercising their rights as citizens, union members, and workers. It was clear from the barricades being erected around the plant that Frick was preparing for battle. They had no choice but to defend themselves and their jobs. When a union member stepped forward and declared that he had information that three hundred rollers were en route to Homestead from Philadelphia, "there was," the *Pittsburgh Post* reported the next morning, "dead silence, but only for a moment, and then the uproar broke loose. One man yelled: 'Let them come; we'll roll them,' and various other threats were made."

The meeting was adjourned, and the Amalgamated executive committee went into closed session.[32]

Worried about preventing violence, the executive committee elected an "advisory committee" of fifty, with representatives from each of the eight lodges, to coordinate resistance and keep the peace during the lockout. Burgess McLuckie was chosen as a member of the committee; Hugh O'Donnell, a heater at the 119-inch plate mill, was elected its chairman. O'Donnell was a thirty-year-old Irishman, a former newspaperman, a great speaker, and was reported to have the prettiest wife in Homestead. A striking-looking but not handsome man, thin, his hair thick on top and closely cut on the sides, with a full walrus mustache, O'Donnell took immediate charge of the advisory committee. "Special committees were appointed to patrol the river stations and all entrances to the town," Burgoyne wrote. "The patrols were directed to cover their beats night and day and report to the advisory committee. Arrangements were also made to have the river patrolled in skiffs, and the steamboat 'Edna' was secured to aid in this service." The advisory committee, not willing to supplant the local government, but rather to serve as its adjunct, offered to put at Burgess McLuckie's disposal as many men as were needed to keep the peace. "The saloons were visited and the proprietors requested to use special precautions against the promotion of drunkenness and disorderly gatherings, under pain of being required to close their establishments." Determined that the workers would not be the ones to initiate violence, the effigies of Frick and Carnegie that had been strung up all over town were torn down.[33]

On Sunday, July 3, a drizzly, damp day at Homestead, attendance at church was light as the locked-out steelworkers took their positions as pickets and lookouts along the river, the roads, and the railways leading into Homestead. "We do not propose," McLuckie told a *New York World* reporter, "that Andrew Carnegie's representatives shall bulldoze us. We have our homes in this town, we have our churches here, our societies and our cemeteries. We are bound to Homestead by all the ties that men hold dearest and most sacred." The Carnegie companies might have succeeded in importing scab workers into their other plants, but "they never have imported a man into Homestead, and . . . they never will. We shall not permit it. . . . Our people here are hard-working, peaceable, quiet, progressive. There is not a better class of people in any town of this state. . . .

We are asking nothing but our rights, and we will have them if it requires force to get them."[34]

On Monday, which was the Fourth of July, "peace reigned at Homestead," the *Pittsburgh Dispatch* noted, as those steelworkers not on duty as lookouts joined their families for a day of "picnics, excursions, and the shooting of fireworks. . . . The town was alive with rockets and Roman candles. The great works up the river were dark and silent, and the guards of the Amalgamated Association make their rounds and keep their watch."[35]

In Pittsburgh, Frick formally requested the assistance of the Allegheny County sheriff in clearing Amalgamated pickets from the perimeter of the works. He also wrote Robert Pinkerton to finalize plans for the delivery of the detectives: "We have all our arrangements perfected to receive your men at Ashtabula [Ohio], and to conduct them to Bellevue Station, a few miles below this City on the Ohio River, where they will be transferred to two boats and two barges . . . manned with reliable men, and will at once start for our Homestead works, and should arrive there about 3 oclock on the morning of the 6th. The boats are well provisioned, all the uniforms etc. that you have had shipped . . . are on board the boat. There will also be on board the boats the Sheriff's Chief Deputy who will accompany and remain with your men. We have taken all possible precaution to keep the arrangements quiet, but, of course, it is more than likely that we will not be successful in this."[36]

"My time," Frick wrote Carnegie that Fourth of July,

has been very much occupied for several days past looking after all matters pertaining to the Homestead labor trouble. I think we have everything in about as good shape as it could well be.

The workmen seem to be well organized, and have things, so far, very much their own way, that is to say, are guarding every avenue to the works; stopping all who may, or try, to get in the works. This is rather in our favor in view of our arrangements. We have a thorough understanding with the Sheriff. Notice, as per enclosed copy, has been served on him today, and we are having 350 proclamations such as he put up at Duquesne last year, printed for him, which he will, tomorrow, take to Homestead, and distribute and post, at the same time distributing around our works as many Deputy Sheriffs as he can secure.

Tomorrow night, about 11 o'clock, 300 watchmen obtained from Pinkerton, will leave the cars at Bellevue Station on the Fort Wayne Road, and take passage on two barges, and two boats that will be there ready to receive them. They will go at once to Homestead, reaching there, we hope, about three or four o'clock on the morning of the 6th. The barges are well fitted up, and well provisioned, as are also the Boats. The Boats contain the uniforms, the arms, the ammunition, etc.

Potter, with 5 or 6 of his men, will join these guards or watchmen, at Ashtabula tomorrow afternoon at 5 o'clock, and be with them until they land at Homestead. One or two Deputy Sheriffs will go down to Bellevue Station tomorrow evening, and accompany the guards or watchmen, on the boats to Homestead. We expect to land our guards or watchmen in our property at Homestead without much trouble, and this once accomplished we are, we think, in good position.

We have numerous applications from men who are anxious to go to work at Homestead, whom we can, by the use of the boats, deliver from time to time, into the works, where we have everything prepared to receive them and to care for them. Having secured the hearty co-operation of the Sheriff and such watchmen, we think, that we will be able to afford protection to all the men who are willing to work for us. The best information I can get leads me to believe that we have the sympathy of our men at Bessemer [i.e., Edgar Thomson] and at Duquesne, although I get some reports to the contrary. . . .

Homestead seems to be the centre of attraction, and I do not think anything has been left undone towards securing for us a complete victory at that place. Doubtless by the time this reaches you it will be uninteresting, at least I trust so. . . . The new organization [Carnegie Steel, which, as of July 1, 1892, was the corporate owner of all the steel plants] started off without any friction, there is but one fly in our ointment at present, and that is the Homestead trouble. The newspapers, as usual, are inclined towards the enemy, and doubtless will raise a great howl when they discover that we have the audacity to attempt to guard and protect our property. I had the article [Carnegie had earlier urged him to get his side of the story to the newspapers], written by Mr. Weeks [editor of *Iron Age* and a publicist for the steel industry] from data furnished by us to him, reproduced in all of the morning and evening papers of this City, so that I think our position is well defined. We shall, of course, keep within the law, and do nothing that is not entirely legal.

Mailed you a cable to New York to be sent from there tomorrow, giving about as much information as I well could.[37]

The cable would reach Carnegie within hours of transmission; the letter would take ten days to two weeks. Had he found any of this objectionable he could have cabled a response that would have reached Frick in hours. There is no record of any such message having been sent.

It is clear from the matter-of-fact nature of his report that Frick was confident that Carnegie would take no issue with what he had done—or expected to do. They had gone over strategy for breaking the strike in New York and confirmed or amended their plans in numerous letters and cables since then. Carnegie would spend the rest of his life declaring in one form or another that he would have handled the Homestead strikers differently had he been on site. This July 4 letter is evidence that he knew from the very beginning that Frick intended to call in the Pinkertons and had no objections.

On July 5, Sheriff William McCleary of Allegheny County arrived at Homestead by train. At 10:00 A.M., he met with O'Donnell's advisory committee, which offered to provide him with as many men as he thought necessary to preserve the peace and protect company property. The sheriff turned them down and proceeded to the Homestead works on his own. He returned a few hours later to the third floor in the Bost Building, where the advisory committee had its offices. While he confessed to having seen "no signs of disorder any where," he notified the committee that he was obligated nonetheless to send deputies to protect the mill. Later that afternoon, he returned with ten armed deputies, who, getting down from their train, were engulfed by a crowd of townspeople and escorted back to the Bost Building, where the advisory committee suggested that they leave Homestead. The deputies were then marched to the steamer *Edna,* which returned them across the river.[38]

At ten-thirty that evening, the train from Ashtabula, Ohio, with three hundred Pinkertons on board, arrived at Bellevue, where it was met by Homestead's general superintendent John Potter, several of his foremen, and Sheriff McCleary's chief deputy. The Pinkertons boarded two barges, pushed by two tugs, one of which broke down immediately. Inside the barges were uniforms, provisions, ammunition, 300 pistols, and 250 Winchester rifles.

Frick had hoped that by landing the Pinkertons in the middle of the night, they might escape detection by the steelworkers' patrols, but a lookout in Pittsburgh spotted the barges as they passed the "point" where the Ohio River branches into the Allegheny and the Monongahela and sent a warning telegram to Homestead a little after 2:30 A.M. on July 6. The advisory committee, on receiving the telegram, dispatched the *Edna* to intercept the barges. When the *Edna's* captain caught sight of them, he blew the whistle to signal the workers on shore. That set off a further round of whistles, bells, and men on horseback shouting the news of the coming invasion.

A crowd of townspeople, workers, women, and children, many of them armed with revolvers, rifles, and ancient Civil War weapons, upon hearing the alarm, surged toward the riverbank, tearing down the fence that separated the town proper from the works and pushing past it toward the company's pier. Among them were Mother Finch, a white-haired steelworker's widow who ran a Homestead saloon and claimed to have seen forty strikes in her life, and Billy Foy, a middle-aged Englishman who had been head of the local Salvation Army and now worked as a laborer at the mill. As dawn broke, Mother Finch, Billy Foy, the members of the advisory committee, and hundreds of others watched from the pier as the barges, with the Pinkertons on board, were pushed toward land. Hugh O'Donnell worked his way to the front of the crowd, where he pleaded with the Pinkertons to turn back. "We have not damaged any property, and we do not intend to. . . . In the name of God and humanity don't attempt to land! Don't attempt to enter these works by force!" Captain Frederick Heinde of the Pinkertons announced to the crowd on shore that he was not going to abandon his mission. "We were sent here to take possession of this property and to guard it for this company. . . . We don't wish to shed blood, but we are determined to go up there and shall do so. If you men don't withdraw, we will mow every one of you down and enter in spite of you. You had better disperse, for land we will."[39]

As Captain Heinde walked toward the shore, Billy Foy threw himself across the gangplank, a pistol in his hand. Heinde slashed at him with his billy club. Other workers surged forward, including Joseph Sotak, a leader of the Eastern Europeans. Shots rang out. Foy and Captain Heinde fell.

More shots were fired from shore and from the barge. Three steelworkers were killed instantly, including Joseph Sotak, who was hit in the mouth. Dozens were wounded, including O'Donnell, who was grazed in the thumb. The Pinkertons fared only slightly better; several were wounded, one of whom would later die. No one knew who had fired the first shot, but it didn't matter much anymore. The Pinkertons retreated to their barge. O'Donnell tried to take control of the crowd. It was not yet 5:00 A.M.

The tugboat *Little Bill* took the injured Pinkertons to the opposite shore, leaving the Pinkertons on board the barges to fend for themselves. The crowd on shore hastily erected defenses fashioned from scrap iron to protect it from the next round of fire from the Pinkertons' Winchesters. Dozens more townspeople had arrived by now, many armed with weapons, some with skiffs which they took out onto the river, hoping to surround the barges. A 20-pound cannon, a relic of the Civil War, was mounted on the opposite shore and fired. It missed its mark: Shots flew over the barges and landed on shore, killing one of the steelworkers. The advisory committee members and union officials tried to quiet the crowd, but the presence of the dead and wounded among them made that impossible. The crowd wanted revenge, revenge for their losses, revenge against the Pinkertons who had invaded their town.

News of the battle was telegraphed to Pittsburgh, where hundreds of workingmen, some of whom had seen the smoke or heard the gunfire up river, prepared to march on Homestead in support of the steelworkers. They were joined by a small army of reporters and illustrators who would file regular updates throughout the days to come, some of which would make their way, by transatlantic cable, to London and on to Carnegie in Scotland.

At 8:00 A.M., the Pinkertons made another attempt to leave their barges, but were repulsed by gunfire. They fired back. Three more Homestead steelworkers died and several others were wounded. The gunfight continued, with a second Pinkerton killed. The crowd on shore, refusing to obey the advisory committee and retreat, and unable to pierce the shell of the barges and get to the Pinkertons, tried to set the river on fire by launching toward the barges a raft burning with oil-soaked wood. When that failed, they tried again with a burning railroad flatcar, then with explosives and fireworks left over from the Fourth of July. Later that afternoon, several townsfolk, having secured hoses and a hand pump from the fire station, tried to pump oil into the river and set it afire.

In Pittsburgh, the Allegheny County sheriff spent the day holed up in his office with Boss Chris Magee. With the violence showing no signs of abating, the sheriff telegraphed Democratic governor Robert Pattison, requesting that he send the militia. The governor, who owed nothing to Carnegie or Frick, refused, ordering the sheriff to restore order.

As the afternoon wore on, Hugh O'Donnell and William Weihe of the Amalgamated succeeded in convincing the crowd in the mill yard and on the pier to allow the Pinkertons to surrender, leave their boats, and be escorted to the opera house, where they would be held until the sheriff arrived to indict them for murder and take them away for trial. At 5:00 P.M., the Pinkertons hoisted the white flag of surrender. The advisory committee dispatched volunteers to lead them off the barges, over the gang-plank, and up the quarter-mile embankment into the yard. The crowd, incensed at being fired at by the Pinkertons all day and furious at the loss of life on shore, formed itself into a gauntlet, some 600 yards long. As the Pinkertons, easily identified in their blue uniforms, climbed the embankment, they were marched through and pummeled by fists, stones, and wooden clubs. The increasingly bloody procession proceeded through the steelworks and exited the main gate bound for the opera house, where it was met by yet another angry crowd. The newspaper reporters had a field day describing the bloodthirsty women and men who, "frenzied by the long day of fighting and bloodshed," thirsted for revenge. While the Pinkertons "screamed for mercy, they were beaten over the head with clubs and the butt end of rifles. You could almost hear the skulls crack. They were kicked, knocked down and jumped upon. Their clothes were torn from their backs, and when they finally escaped it was with faces of ashen paleness and with the blood in streams rushing down the backs of their heads staining their clothes." So wrote a reporter for the *New York World*. The coverage everywhere was much the same, with images of murderous steelworkers, shrewish wives, and pistol-bearing children assaulting innocent-looking Pinkertons. Though the scene was indeed horrendous to watch and report on, the crowd was not nearly as bloodthirsty as the newspapers described it. While several Homestead workers died in the gunfire that preceded the surrender, no Pinkerton lost his life in the gauntlet.[40]

Harper's Weekly, July 14, 1892.

The sheriff and his deputies arrived after midnight on July 7 to remove the Pinkertons. No arrests were made, no indictments handed down. That same day, the citizens of Homestead buried three of their dead; three more were buried the following day. The Reverend J. J. McIlyar of the First Methodist Episcopal Church presided over the funeral of one of the men, John Morris, a twenty-eight-year-old Welsh immigrant who had been a skilled worker at the mill. McIlyar had no doubt where the blame lay for the dead and wounded of Homestead: "Somebody employed these men, of course. They didn't come without orders. . . . These hired fighters attacked the men of this quiet, peaceful, order-loving community, and the men of Homestead defended themselves. This blessed man lying here; this mortal man, an affectionate husband, sober and industrious, gentlemanly in manner, was killed because a conflict provoked by the Pinkerton clan made it necessary for him and his fellow-workmen to protect their homes and families."[41]

On July 8, the *Pittsburgh Commercial Gazette*, no friend of the steelworkers, reported that the streets of Homestead and the Carnegie works were being patrolled by volunteers of the advisory committee, who had repaired the fences and damage done in the yards the day before. Though the "strikers" were once again "masters of the situation," they exhibited no signs of triumph or exhilaration but waited, fearfully, for the company to attack again. "In all sides of the long tortuous, and at night dangerous-to-tread streets," the reporter noted, "men, women, and children are to be seen sitting on stairs and in doorways. They dread the coming of another assault of armed men on the works. The anxiety of these people is something terrible. They have brothers, fathers, sons among the strikers and they momentarily fear the sounding of the alarm, the crack of Winchesters and the booming cannon that means the death or the wounding of their own loved ones or of neighbors, friends or shopmates of their own bread-winners. . . . A Sunday-like quiet has prevailed here all day and will continue until another attempt is made by the Carnegie company to land men on the mill property."[42]

As the last of the steelworkers were being buried in Homestead, Frick sat for an interview with a handpicked correspondent from the *Philadelphia Press*. If Frick had learned anything from Carnegie, it was the importance of getting out the company's side of the story. The union leaders were masters at this. They had earlier selected a small committee to communicate with the press. Not an hour passed without some member of the Amalgamated press committee paying a visit to Harrigan's ice cream parlor and reading to the reporters who gathered there from a stack of supportive telegrams and letters.

Frick had no intention of pandering to the press or the public, but he had his own constituencies, including but not limited to state and federal officials, with whom he needed to communicate. "The question at issue is a very grave one," he reported in the *Philadelphia Press* interview, which was reprinted in newspapers across the country and in Europe on July 8, 1892. "It is whether the Carnegie Company or the Amalgamated Association should have absolute control of our plant and business at Homestead. We have decided, after numerous fruitless conferences with the Amalgamated officials . . . to operate the plant ourselves. I can say with the greatest emphasis that under no circumstances will we have any further dealings with the Amalgamated Association as an organization." The Amalgamated had broken the law by trespassing on company property and preventing the Pinkertons from landing and protecting the mill, as they had been hired to do. It was now up to the "authorities of Allegheny County" to take back the mill from the union and return it to the control of the company. If the sheriff was unable to accomplish this task, "it is certainly the duty of the governor of the State to see that we are permitted to operate our establishment unmolested. . . . While nobody could regret the occurrences of the last few days more than myself," Frick had no choice but to do his duty, "as the executive head of the Carnegie Company, to protect the interests of the association. We desire to, and will protect our property at all hazards."[43]

On July 8, as his interview appeared on the front pages of newspapers throughout the country, Frick's wife Adelaide gave birth prematurely to a very sick baby boy, Henry Clay Frick, Jr. That same day, Hugh O'Donnell, members of the advisory committee, and elected town leaders boarded the train to Harrisburg in a last-ditch attempt to persuade Governor Pattison not to send in the militia as Frick had demanded. Governor Pattison, who had earlier resisted, could do so no longer. On July 10, he ordered all 8,470 members of the Pennsylvania National Guard to Homestead to "protect all persons [i.e., the owners of the Carnegie works] in their rights [of private property] under the constitution and laws of the State." The troops arrived in the middle of the morning on July 12 and took possession of the plant— and the town—from the advisory committee.

Hundreds of thousands of words were daily being written on the battle of Homestead as the armies of reporters went looking for stories. Preachers, pastors, politicians, steelworkers, union leaders, Pinkerton men, tugboat captains, Homestead officials, sheriff's deputies, self-proclaimed poets, and of course H. C. Frick grabbed their moments in the headlines. One voice was conspicuously silent.

TWENTY-FOUR

Loch Rannoch, the Summer of 1892

O N JULY 6, as the Pinkertons attempted to land at Homestead, Andrew Carnegie was enjoying his favorite pastime, being driven "behind four superb grays in the most elaborate coach that Scotland has ever seen upon its roads." The night before, after dedicating a new Carnegie library in Aberdeen on the east coast of Scotland, he had received a telegram from Frick: "Small plunge, our actions and position there unassailable and will work out satisfactorily." Late that afternoon (morning on the American east coast), as news of the battle of Homestead made its way by cable across the Atlantic, he and Louise were met by reporters at Braemar where they were to spend the night. Carnegie uncharacteristically refused to talk to the reporters. The next morning, the Carnegies' carriage stopped at Pitlochry, where he visited the local cable office and responded to Frick's message: "Cable received. All anxiety gone since you stand firm. Never employ one these rioters. Let grass grow over works. Must not fail now. You will win easily next trial only stand firm law and order wish I could support you in any form."[1]

The Carnegies drove another thirty miles to Kinloch Rannoch, where they left their coach for a noon meal at the Dunalastair Hotel. Approached by a correspondent from the *New York Herald*, Carnegie again had little to say. "The strike is most deplorable, and the news of the disaster, which reached me at Aberdeen, grieved me more than I can tell you. It came on me like a thunderbolt in a clear sky. I must positively decline to enter into any discussion as to the merits or demerits of the case. All I will say is that the strike did not take place in the old Carnegie works, but the difficulty has been entirely in the recently acquired works."[2]

Louise and Andrew's final destination was Rannoch Lodge, in the central Highlands, which they had leased for the season. No sooner had they arrived than a reporter from the Pulitzer papers appeared at the front door to request an interview. He was "received by a dignified English servant in blue livery," who ushered him into a reception room, lined with twenty-eight pairs of antlers. In the center of the room was a table with "two newspapers open and articles in them marked." After a brief wait, "Mr. Carnegie came through the hall with a quick, energetic step and entered the room. The correspondent asked him if he cared to say anything in regard to the troubles at his mills, and Mr. Carnegie in the most contemptuous and insulting manner replied: 'I have nothing whatever to say. I have given up all active control of the business, and I do not care to interfere in any way with the present management's conduct of this affair.'" Asked again if he "did not still exercise a supervision of the affairs of the company," Carnegie repeated himself. "I have nothing whatever to say on that point. The business management is in the hands of those who are fully competent to deal with any question that may arise." He admitted to receiving "several cables and among them several asking my interference with the parties in control."

Still digging, the reporter suggested that Carnegie might "have some opinion in the matter that you are willing to express." "No, sir," Carnegie answered. "I am not willing to express any opinion. The men have chosen their course and I am powerless to change it. The handling of the case on the part of the company has my full approbation and sanction. Further than this I have no disposition to say anything." Carnegie, who had remained standing throughout the interview, left the room.[3]

This interview was carried in newspapers across the country. "MR. CARNEGIE FOUND," read the headline of the *Pittsburgh Leader* story. "A 'LEADER' MAN FOLLOWS HIM TO THE HIGHLANDS OF SCOTLAND. IN A CONTEMPTUOUS AND INSULTING MANNER THE MILLIONAIRE TELLS THE CORRESPONDENT THAT HE IS SATISFIED WITH THE PRESENT MANAGEMENT—HE IS PAYING $10,000 FOR SIX WEEKS' USE OF A SHOOTING LODGE—SERVANTS IN LIVERY."[4]

ANDREW CARNEGIE had chosen to spend the summer of 1892 in one of the more isolated spots in the central Highlands. He had leased the hunting lodge on Loch Rannoch not because it was inaccessible to reporters, as his critics would later charge, but because he needed a degree of isolation so that he could complete the book he had been working on. At the time he rented the lodge in May, he believed that Frick had matters well in hand at Homestead.

He and Louise would have preferred to return to Cluny for the summer, but the Macphersons had decided to make repairs on the estate. Rannoch Lodge was a worthy successor. The house itself was a rather modest stone hunting lodge—though with dozens of rooms, a formal garden courtyard in the rear, and plenty of outbuildings for servants. It was located in one of the lushest and most spectacularly beautiful spots in the central Highlands, on the western edge of Loch Rannoch, close to Rannoch Moor, an endless sea of heather, bog, and stunted trees, so porous and swampy no road could be run through it. (The West Highland Railroad, which stopped at Rannoch station, would not be built until 1894.) On either side of the loch were stands of pine, larch, and birch trees rising over a ground covering of bracken, heather, and blueberries. Directly behind the lodge were mountains, steep and inaccessible, which had for centuries served as hideouts for Scottish nationalists and bandits on the run from the British authorities. The lake and the sky were breathtakingly blue, the fishing superb, and the isolated setting suited to Carnegie's purposes.

Though cut off from much of the world, with the nearest telegraph connection at Struan more than twenty miles away, and the closest train station at Blair Atoll, a few miles further, Carnegie remained in touch with Frick—by cable and post. Letters from Pittsburgh might take anywhere from ten days to two weeks to reach him, but cable messages arrived only hours after they were sent.

On July 11, Frick sent Carnegie a detailed report of the lockout, some newspaper articles, and copies of his correspondence with his lawyers, Robert Pinkerton, and the sheriff's office. "There is no question but what the firing was begun by the strikers," Frick insisted. "All that I have to regret is that our guards did not land, and, between ourselves, think that Potter was to blame. He did not show the nerve I expected he would." Anticipating that Carnegie might blame him for the deaths, injuries, and outpouring of negative publicity, Frick preempted any such criticism.

> Would like to say just here that I had not overlooked the fact that an effort to introduce guards at Homestead so soon might cause trouble, but was just as well satisfied that it would cause trouble if done at any later date,

and we were only letting our property lie idle awaiting the pleasure of one of the worst bodies of men that ever worked in a mill, so concluded it was better to have trouble, if we were to have it, at once. We would so much earlier get our works started and in our own control, and I have not lost any opportunity since the trouble of urging the Sheriff to give us possession of our property, and, as he was unable, to insist that the Governor bring out the military. We finally have succeeded in the latter, and think before long we will be able to resume operations. . . . We will lose no time in resuming operations at Homestead, but it shall be done with the greatest care, selecting the best men, and re-organizing that entire works, so that we do not employ any more men than actually necessary. As you can understand, my time is pretty well taken up, and my letters consequently will have to be as brief as possible. Feel sure, when you become thoroughly acquainted with all of the details that you will be satisfied with every action taken in this lamentable matter.[5]

The next day, Carnegie responded in a lengthy letter in his own handwriting, addressed to "My dear Friend." He was delighted to receive Frick's detailed briefing (which had been cabled to him), but was anxious to learn even more about the situation at Homestead. "All we know here is the repulse of guards, etc.—What your next step is to be cannot tell. If a waiting game I think you might be let alone furnishing armor for Govt. This would give you a nucleus and the works would look alive—quite a point." Carnegie had no objection to Frick's bringing back the Pinkertons to secure the works, provided, that is, that Robert Pinkerton was prepared to fight. "If Pinkerton decides they cannot afford to be beat they can easily win because the striking force will rapidly dwindle—after the excitement many will clear away fearing more trouble." As useful as the Pinkertons might be in the short run, however, Carnegie recognized—as did Frick—that no "private" police force could be as effective as the state in restoring and maintaining the company's rights to its private property. The situation at Homestead was intolerable and would remain so until the strikers had been demoralized, defeated, and demobilized. "Why the Governor will not be compelled to keep order by public sentiment I can't see—seems to me you have only to keep appealing to Sheriff and holding County responsible. No Governor can afford to let a mob conquer."

Carnegie suggested that Frick maintain the lockout for "two or three months," then announce that he was starting up the plant with a new crew of workers, because it would not be possible, "after recent deplorable events," for management and the striking workers to ever again entertain the "pleasant relations" that had once existed at Homestead. "We assume that men will not desire to work for a firm who has in their opinion so treated them as to justify them to attack and kill many men who were employed only to preserve peace and order. Such men must desire to find employers who will treat them better—So be it—The firm recognizes this fully and the Supt. will give every man a certificate according to his merits, which may enable him to find satisfactory employment. Without anger and with deep regret the firm now bids its recent tonnage men— Farewell—Henceforth our paths are separate—we can labor together no more."

It was an excellent plan—on paper. In reality, there was no way to assuage the anger at Homestead, no way that the firm could now, after the loss of lives at the hands of the Pinkertons, claim that it still cared enough for its skilled workers to help them find "satisfactory employment" elsewhere. Carnegie did not want Frick to think he was dictating anything. He needed Frick in place and in control and feared doing anything that might anger him. "Think it all over," he wrote, "anything you do will be right. I only suggest—Am so sorry you have this load to carry just now—but sky will clear rapidly—just as soon as men realize that they must seek work elsewhere, no use waiting—they will melt away like snow in the summer." He agreed entirely with Frick that the works would have to be totally reorganized. "Even our clerks and Asst. Supts. might all be suspended—this would show your resolve—nothing but victory, no matter whether this year or next." As a postscript, he assured Frick that "dollars don't count— let pecuniary considerations go." He then offered one last word of advice: "I hope you are publishing short statement showing the few men affected— their wages and injustice of these payments. Keep the public with you—try short statements."[6]

Carnegie delivered his letter that morning to the nearest post office. When, later in the day, he received word from Pittsburgh that Governor Pattison had decided to send in the militia, he cabled Frick from Struan with his congratulations—and a warning: "Governor's action settles matters. All right now. No compromise." Tough as Frick might be, Carnegie was, at least from a distance, tougher still. There would be no negotiations, no communications, no compromise with the Amalgamated.[7]

THE SUMMER of 1892 was, in every conceivable way, going to be a difficult one for Andrew and Louise. Although the American newspapers, preoccupied with reporting firsthand on the day-to-day drama of life at Homestead, did not devote much space to the absentee owner, the British press, which had never enjoyed being lectured on politics and morals by the expatriate author of *Triumphant Democracy,* seized on the story as a vivid illustration of American backwardness and savagery. The correspondent for the *New York Herald,* the first American newspaper to regularly report European news by cable—and the most adept at it—took notice on July 10 of "the keen delight with which the people of Great Britain view the difficulties at Homestead. . . . The British papers have been uncompromisingly critical of Mr. Carnegie's course." The "atrocities" at Homestead and the unwillingness of the federal government to intervene led the *Daily Telegraph* to suggest "a serious doubt whether after all home rule in American works satisfactorily in practice." *The Times of London* mockingly called attention to Mr. Carnegie's "singular" position. "An avowed champion of trade unions and of organized labour, he now finds himself engaged in an almost ruinous conflict with the representatives of his own views." The London *Echo* headline asked: "WILL MR. CARNEGIE EXPLAIN? Mr. Carnegie is still silent. He continues to drive about Scotland as though nothing had occurred."[8]

The news from Pittsburgh remained rather distressing. There was no sign that the men of Homestead were any closer to accepting the new contract, while their counterparts at Carnegie's other works were threatening to go out on sympathy strikes. Although Frick tried to put the best possible face on events, Carnegie prepared himself for the worst. On July 14, responding to a cable in which Frick had predicted that Homestead "will be running again soon," Carnegie made it clear that he wished he "could share this view. The probability is, that it will not run during this year. We had better make up our minds to this. . . . The Military cannot stay long with you, and after they leave you may find it necessary to announce that the works will not run this year except upon work for the government. . . . Starting a few months sooner or later is nothing compared with starting with the right class of men. The only danger is, that you may be tempted to start too soon. Nothing will cure the disease so thoroughly and give you peace in the future as a long stoppage now. I should be tempted, if in your place, to announce that the works will be closed, government work excepted, for the remainder of the year if the military departs and leaves an excited populace."[9]

Carnegie was worried that Frick, in his desire to start up production and bring in scabs too soon, would make matters worse. Replying to a letter from his cousin Dod on July 17, he confessed that things were not going well. "Matters at home <u>bad</u>, such a fiasco trying to send guards by Boat and then leaving space between River and fences for the men to get opposite landing and fire—still we must keep quiet and do all we can to support Frick and those at seat of war. I have been besieged by interviewers— cables from New York, etc., but have not said one word—silence is best. We shall win of course, but may have to shut down for months—Frick cable yesterday Homestead started slowly—He thinks we'll soon win." The men at the Pittsburgh ironworks and the Beaver Falls mills had gone out on sympathy strikes. "This was uncalled for they had no grievance but we must not bother with them just now—Concentrate everything on Homestead. Win there—then talk to these foolish men—all well."[10]

The company's mobilization of a private army of detectives to battle its own employees, though legal, had been far from popular. The Judiciary Committee of the House of Representatives, responding to outrage across the country, sent investigators to Homestead on July 12 to interview Frick, Sheriff McCleary, Hugh O'Donnell, the captain of the tug that had pushed the Pinkerton barges, and a number of union leaders and advisory committee members. Frick was questioned extensively about the wage dispute that had precipitated the conflict. Why, he was asked, did the tariff not protect the wages of the workingmen, as the Republican supporters of the tariff had promised it would? He replied by denying that he had ever asked the government for the tariff. When Judge William Oates, the committee chairman, asked him directly how much it cost to produce a ton of billets, Frick refused to answer, on the grounds that doing so would disclose privileged information to his competitors.[11]

Four days after the arrival of the congressional investigators, Frick declared the Homestead works open and directed all Carnegie Steel employees who had not taken part in the disturbance to return to the mills. They were given until July 21 to apply for their old positions and sign the new contract, after which their places would be filled by others. Recruitment of substitute workers was already well underway. The one hundred new houses that had been erected within the gates of the plant were, the firm let it be known, for these workers.

Openly advertising for scabs—and building houses for them—was provocative enough. But Frick poured salt into the wounds by publicly demanding that the sheriff indict and arrest dozens of strike leaders, including Hugh O'Donnell and Burgess John McLuckie, on charges of treason and the murder of two men, a Pinkerton and the worker who had been accidentally killed by the cannon fire aimed at the Pinkerton barge. Criticism mounted of his refusal to negotiate with the union, his use of the state militia as cover to bring in substitute workers, and his attempt to stifle dissent by arresting union leaders.

Nonetheless, in his letters to Carnegie in Rannoch, Frick insisted that he had the situation under control. "Looking back over the transactions of this month so far, or previous to that, I cannot see where we have made any serious blunders, or done anything that was not proper and right as between our workmen and ourselves. We certainly had no desire to do anything than what was just and right." He was proceeding, despite criticism in the press, to do whatever he could to "convict all of the men engaged in the riot and in law breaking." He recognized that this was "an uphill job," as politicians would be reluctant in the end to incur the rancor of "the men who have the votes." He was sure of one thing only: "It will all blow over before long, and when we do get started at our several works they will be all non-union, and if we treat the men as we always have done, or desired to do, it certainly will be a long while before we will have any more labor trouble, and we will be in position to secure the best results that will come from close and careful attention to the business."[12]

On Saturday, July 23, exactly one week after Frick reopened the Homestead works and began advertising for scabs, a nervous young man with an accent appeared at his office door in Pittsburgh, sent in his card, and asked for an appointment, claiming that he represented an employment agency ready to supply substitute workers. He was told to return at two o'clock, which he did. Informed that Mr. Frick was still engaged, the man—a twenty-five-year-old self-proclaimed anarchist named Alexander Berkman, who had no connection to anyone in Homestead and no ties to the

Amalgamated or the advisory committee—pushed past the office boy in the anteroom, rushed into the inner office, pulled a revolver out of his pocket, and fired two shots at Frick at very close range. John Leishman, Frick's vice chairman, grabbed Berkman before he was able to get off a third shot. While being wrestled to the ground, Berkman pulled a dagger made out of a file out of his pocket and lunged at Frick, wounding him in the hip, on the right side, and the left leg below the knee. Frick was not a big man, but neither was Berkman. Wounded and bleeding, Frick helped Leishman wrestle Berkman to the ground and hold him there until the clerks, hearing the gunshots, roared into the room. Together, they subdued Berkman before he was able to tear open the explosive mercury capsule in his mouth that would have killed him.

The room filled with police who took Berkman away and doctors who tended to Frick. Before agreeing to go to the hospital, Frick asked that his ailing wife, who had given birth just two weeks earlier, be notified that he had survived the attack. He then cabled identical messages to his mother and Carnegie: "Was shot twice but not dangerously." To Carnegie's telegram, he added two more sentences: "There is no necessity for you to come home. I am still in shape to fight the battle out."[13]

Shaken by Frick's message, Carnegie cabled his next-in-charge, Leishman. "Early anxiety his recovery. . . . Close all works until recovery complete. We regard it as necessary something must be done to save Frick anxiety—his recovery before all." Carnegie's first thought was to return to Homestead and take personal charge; but on receiving the news that Frick would survive, he backed off. "Too glad at your escape to think of anything," Carnegie wired Frick as soon as he could. "Never fear my brave and dear friend my appearing on the scene as long as you are able to direct matters from house and unless partners call. We know too well what is due to you. Am subject to your orders. Louise, Stella [Louise's sister], myself all relieved by cables just received. Be careful to yourself. Be careful of yourself is all we ask."[14]

Frick's trials were only beginning. After being patched together at Mercy Hospital, he was sent to recuperate at Clayton, his Pittsburgh estate, in the room next to that occupied by his bedridden wife, who had barely survived the birth of their premature son. Eleven days after the shooting, Frick's son and namesake died, almost a year to the day after the death of six-year-old Martha. The funeral was held on Thursday, August 4. On

Berkman entering Frick's office, gun in hand,
from *Harper's Weekly*, August 6, 1892.

Friday, Frick awoke, dressed, breakfasted, and took the trolley car to his downtown office, where he sat down to answer his mail.[15]

Carnegie cabled Frick his "hearty congratulations upon your return to the post of duty. Everything is right when you and Mrs. Frick are right. Every other consideration insignificant. You owe it to all your friends to be careful of yourself."[16]

IN THE AFTERMATH of the Frick shooting, the reporters came looking for Carnegie again. The first to find him was from the Associated Press.

"Mr. Carnegie received the correspondent with great courtesy," it was reported on July 27. "He said he had resolutely refused to see any press representative in regard to the Pittsburgh troubles, not because he had not the keenest interest in what was happening there, but because, living as he did, thousands of miles away, he might not fully understand the local situation." The reporter was convinced that Carnegie's "denial of responsibility for the strike trouble was final and that he would not interfere with the administration of the works nor return to America for a long time." As he made ready to depart, Carnegie gave him a written statement to distribute: "I have not attended to business for the past three years, but I have implicit confidence in those who are managing the mills. Further than that I have nothing to say." Reading this account (or any of the others that Carnegie would give to the press or to his friends in the months to come), one would not have known that he had conferred with Frick before he left for Europe in April and remained in touch with him, by cable and post, ever since.[17]

THE YEAR 1892 was a presidential election year. With the two parties evenly matched and Pennsylvania up for grabs, Republican Benjamin Harrison, running for reelection, could ill afford to concede any workingmen's votes to the Democratic challenger, Grover Cleveland. Unfortunately, the events at Homestead did not augur well for the Republicans come November.

Burgess John McLuckie had, from the very beginning, politicized the strike by reminding his constituents that Pittsburgh workingmen had "been persuaded to vote the Republican ticket four years ago in order that our wages might be maintained. As soon as the election was over," however, manufacturers like Carnegie began to cut wages. "You men who voted the Republic ticket voted for high tariff and you get high fences, Pinkerton detectives, thugs and militia!"[18]

It was imperative, local and national Republicans believed, to remove the Homestead issue from the campaign as soon as possible. On July 9, the Pittsburgh papers were reporting, falsely, that Pittsburgh boss Christopher Magee had cabled Carnegie in Scotland, asking him to settle the strike for the good of the party. What Magee had done was to arrange a meeting in Pittsburgh between Republican campaign officials and Hugh O'Donnell. O'Donnell, who feared that with the state militia in place, Frick would have no trouble bringing in enough scabs to break the strike and bust the union, hoped to broker an agreement before it was too late. Though under indictment for murder, he was put on a train to New York City, where he met with Whitelaw Reid, the editor and publisher of the *New York Tribune,* and the Republican nominee for vice president. O'Donnell told Reid that he would settle the strike on the company's terms if the firm would allow the Amalgamated lodges to stay in place. (He didn't tell him that he had no authorization from the advisory committee or the union to do so.) Reid, unable to get Carnegie's address from Frick's office, asked the American consul in London to transmit the cable with O'Donnell's terms to Carnegie in Scotland.[19]

Carnegie did not receive the cable until July 28. While he assumed that Reid was acting on behalf of President Harrison and the Republican Party, he was confused as to how to respond. There had, in the past, been little call on him to make a choice between the Republican Party and his business interests, but this was precisely what Reid was asking of him. If he assented, he would help the party but at the cost of saddling himself with the Amalgamated for another three years. If, on the other hand, he turned down the request to reopen negotiations and recognize the union, the party would suffer in the upcoming elections.

Carnegie's initial response was to welcome Reid's intervention and cable back his preliminary acceptance of O'Donnell's terms. Worried, however, that Frick might take offense and resign if he believed Carnegie was negotiating a settlement on his own, he sent Frick a coded cable, affirming that Frick was to make the final decision. "We have a telegram from *Tribune* Reid through high official London," he cabled. "The proposition is worthy of consideration. Replied 'Nothing can be done. Send H. C. Frick document.' You must decide without delay. Amalgamated Association evidently distressed."[20]

Carnegie also sent telegrams to Dod and Phipps. The following morning, after hearing from them, he cabled Frick again with a quite different message. "After due consideration we have concluded *Tribune* [i.e., Reid's proposal] too old. Probably the proposition is not worthy of consideration. Useful showing distress of Amalgamated Association. Use your own discretion about terms and starting. George Lauder, Henry Phipps, Jr., Andrew Carnegie solid. H. C. Frick forever!"[21]

Reid, meanwhile, had dispatched a ranking member of the Republican National Committee, John Milholland, to meet with Frick in Pittsburgh. Milholland found him "lying in bed when I called, his face and head swathed in bandages." Frick listened as Milholland explained why, for the good of the party, it was important that the Homestead strike be settled at once. Frick then "declared emphatically that he would never consent" to negotiating with the Amalgamated Association, even if asked to do so by President Harrison himself.[22]

Frick was furious with Milholland and Reid, but more so with Carnegie. "I told Mr. Milholland," he wrote Carnegie three weeks after the event, "that I did not think the matter had been placed before you correctly or you never would have entertained, certainly not heartily approve of any proposition to adjust matters with the Amalgamated Association, and that I was surprised you did not avail yourself of the opportunity offered to have emphatically told Mr. Reid and Mr. O'Donnell that you did not propose then, or at any time in the future, to urge your partners here to treat with law-breakers and assassins."[23]

The following week, Frick, still incensed at Carnegie's interference, cabled to tell him that Secretary of War Stephen Elkins and Postmaster-General John Wanamaker wanted to meet with him. Convinced that they had been dispatched by Reid and possibly Harrison to pressure him again to reach a settlement with the Amalgamated, Frick, before they even arrived, asked Carnegie to cable Reid at once "most emphatically . . . that we will never consent to any compromise of any kind . . . I know they think you will interfere sooner or later in their favor."[24]

Carnegie did as he was directed, instructing Reid by cable to "tell [Republican] party no compromise possible." The Amalgamated would, Carnegie added, demand as part of any settlement that newly hired substitute workers be replaced by union stalwarts. This, the firm was honorbound not to do. Two thousand hands were now at work at Homestead and "every one of the twenty-three owners would sink works rather than dismiss one man."[25]

Frick, still seething at the old man's interference, was not yet satisfied. "Frankly, I do not think you sent the proper message to Reid. You should have said emphatically, in my opinion, that we did not propose hereafter, under any circumstances, to deal with the Amalgamated Association."[26]

Carnegie responded that he thought "I had sent a rattling message to Reid, its form is yours and not mine." He reiterated that he had tried to do exactly as Frick had instructed and apologized if he had gotten it wrong. "You have no idea how much in the dark one is up here among the moors, twenty-three miles from a railway station, and a wrong word might easily be said, since I am so ignorant of conditions, and just what you wished to hit at the time and how to hit it."[27]

It turned out that Elkins and Wanamaker had no intention of asking Frick to settle the Homestead strike, as he had feared. They wanted a campaign contribution. Frick met with Wanamaker at Cresson, then, in late October, took the train to New York City to confer with Elkins at the Holland House. Elkins intimated that Carnegie had promised $50,000 to the Republicans, but pledged that he would stand up "for the Carnegie interests," whether or not any contribution was made. Frick offered $25,000 for the general campaign and another $2,500 for Virginia "This pleased him very much," Frick reported to Carnegie, "and he told me that he had had a long talk that night with Secretary [of the Navy] Tracy, who was feeling very friendly towards us, and everything was in good shape." To protect Carnegie Steel from the imputation that the campaign contribution might be seen as a quid pro quo for an armor contract (which in fact it was), Frick paid the $25,000 with an H. C. Frick Coke Co. check and charged it "in a special account against the Carnegie Steel Co. If the election goes Democratic, we would be in a position, if it were necessary, to take the ground that the Steel Company had refused to contribute, owing to having had an armor contract with the Government, but that the Frick Coke Co. had contributed. . . . Think we have done our duty, and hope Mr. Harrison will be re-elected."[28]

As THE WEATHER at Homestead turned colder, more skilled and unskilled men began to drift back to work. Carnegie's major worry now was not the strike—which he knew the men would have to call off eventually—but Frick, who he feared was on the point of breaking down. "I am glad to see from the papers that you took a few days fishing," Carnegie wrote on

August 29. "Go often. Trout fishing has been my refuge during the last two months. I caught eight dozen one day with one fly rod. You should be here, and I hope that Mrs. Frick and you will be with us next summer. With fly-fishing and whist as passions, you will not be badly off for old age when it comes. . . . As for your own behavior, the whole public is at your feet, and I am obliged to paint your history every day; and, of course, you may suspect, I never fail to add 'that is the kind of fellows our firm is made up of—the ablest and best set of men in the world'; all not only partners, but friends."[29]

Responding to an August 19 letter in which Frick had confessed to "a serious problem at Homestead" getting sufficient substitute workers to resume production, Carnegie replied only that he was "not surprised." He had always expected that the "stoppage" would last for at least three or four months. "Nothing but time will give you victory; but this will do it, and we know that we have all the time we want." Indulging again in wishful thinking, as he did whenever his workers did not behave as he thought they should, he blamed the mess at Homestead on the lack of a proper on-site general superintendent. Carnegie had convinced himself that the Homestead workingmen had stood by the union because they had no faith that General Superintendent Potter would look after their interests. He was not able—and would never be able—to face head-on the magnitude of his and Frick's miscalculation about the Homestead workers' loyalty to their union and antipathy to the company. "An exceptional manager there would have mitigated the trouble. . . . Nothing will ever be right at Homestead until a great manager of men takes charge there. . . . Skilled workmen are the race horses, laborers the cart horses; the former have to be driven with a rein although firm, yet gentle. There will never be peace, prosperity or satisfaction at Homestead until the chief men respect and admire their manager. The new manager will win this position in half the time if he be one of our own men, and not a stranger." Frick had hinted that he might bring in a "stranger" to run the mill. Carnegie made it clear that he considered Charles Schwab the best man for the job. Never before had any one man run all the Carnegie steel plants, as Frick had done since July 1 and the organization of Carnegie Steel. For his own sanity and the well-being of the company, he urged Frick again to begin taking time off from work. Carnegie reminded Frick that he'd had the orchestrion shipped to Pittsburgh. He hoped Frick had received it and was finding "some respite from care in its music." He recommended again that Frick take up whist and put together a "whist club to meet at your house, at least once a week." Frick might "induce Mrs. Frick and Miss Childs [Frick's sister-in-law] to take it up. We have been playing here a little recently, and Mrs. Carnegie is going to make a 'No. 1' player. Thanks to you for it was chiefly to please you that she began. . . . I caught a trout yesterday that weighed five pounds one and one-half ounces, had only my light rod, and had to play with him an hour and a quarter up and down the Loch. That's my record."[30]

Troubled and hurt that Frick wrote nothing about his personal life, he tried, with increasing desperation, to assure Frick that he cared for him as a friend as well as a partner. "The most important thing of all: You do not tell me how you are," he wrote on September 20. "Are you as strong as ever? We do not hear from any one but yourself. Please do tell us how you are. Would almost like to hear from an impartial source—Leishman, or Phipps or some one—that you are not overstraining yourself."[31]

Frick's cables and letters remained formal and businesslike, often brusque, sometimes almost reprimanding. He disclosed little about his family, his pain, his suffering, his anxieties. Carnegie tried harder to convince Frick that he cherished his friendship. At the bottom of the last page of his typed business letters, he added long postscripts in pencil, intended not for the typist but for Frick's eyes only "I think many times a day how slender the thread is upon which we depend—your good health—any ordinary man would have broken down ere this—you may not until all is quiet but then you will feel it—I never felt 'nerves' until Louise was out of danger & then I couldn't walk a few squares—Keep before you a grand tour round the world. . . . There is nothing so full of intense interests as a visit to Japan China India. If we don't go home to New York we may take it again and go with you, we four or five, or even six."[32]

Four days later, having heard nothing, he begged again for personal news: "Won't you include in Cables reports about . . . your own health & Mrs. Frick's. Perhaps Mrs. C & I picture you all in much more plight than you are—distance does distort views—Newspapers exaggerate—and our own minds at a great distance imagine."[33]

Carnegie had been on an emotional rollercoaster all summer. His concerns for Frick and for his businesses were so intertwined that he could not tell where one began and the other ended. For his own peace of mind, he needed to know that Frick was well and thriving, that his judgment was as sound as ever, that his personal travails had not affected or diminished his capacity to run Carnegie Steel.

We don't know what Frick wrote in the letter Carnegie opened on September 30, but we can surmise from the tone of Carnegie's response that his younger partner had, perhaps for the first time, mentioned the effects of his infant son's death on himself and his family. Stricken by guilt and shame at being so far distant, geographically and perhaps emotionally, while Frick had been forced to do battle alone, Carnegie tried to empathize with and suffer alongside his younger partner.

"Every now and then," he wrote in pencil, on receiving the letter from Frick,

a flash comes upon your home life and troubles and I feel as if I could sink every mill and mine we own. . . . We then think of you and Mrs. Frick and Mrs. Childs and your Home & could just rush off together to be with you—I wish you would always include in your cables some home news. We have had our trials in all this business—hard enough in some respects harder to bear standing apart in inaction, than if in the midst of the excitement but these melt into nothingness compared to your home agonies. I don't see how you can stand them. If you are like me you will stand until all is quiet and you are out of it and then give way—I have not been so well the past two weeks principally because there is less excitement—and besides fishing is over and then HP [Harry Phipps] has been up for consolation and we have dwelt more upon the crisis—I hope to get my mind somewhat off it, by rushing through Italy etc—fresh sights do much—one of the earliest moves you make should be to take all your family direct to Geneva and bask in Italian scenes. I wish you could join us—You know we are good traveling companions. . . . Business be hanged—Ever your friend. . . . We may go to Italy from London about 15th October but our movements always subject to your wishes.[34]

There was no response, perhaps because Frick still harbored suspicions as to Carnegie's motives in continually inquiring as to his health and suggesting he go on vacation. Frick could not rid himself of the fear that Carnegie might, at any moment, return to Pittsburgh and take personal control, using Frick's mental instability as an excuse for relieving him of responsibility.

Frick's fears were exacerbated when Dod Lauder, no doubt with Carnegie's approval and perhaps at his instigation, cabled from overseas that he "would be glad to come over if he could be of any use in any position whatever." "I wired him not to come at present," Frick wrote Carnegie. "There is a feeling yet that you will in some way interfere to settle this strike question, and Mr. Lauder's coming over now would only give them [the Amalgamated] further hope. There is nothing personal in this matter, so far as I am concerned. I am, so far as I know, only doing what it seems to me to be for the interests of the owners of the property, and if we want to get the full benefit of all that we have gone through, there must be no deviation from the policy we have been pursuing all along. After it is all over, if it is thought somebody else can do better, the position is open for him. I have never sought responsibility, nor, to my knowledge have I ever shirked it."[35]

Carnegie was disturbed at Frick's cavalier dismissal of a senior partner's offer of assistance. Frick seemed too confident in his own judgment and too resistant to seeking advice. "I am very sorry you misinterpret Mr. Lauder volunteering to go to you in this crisis," he wrote at once.

> I feel in my case that to appear on the scene would be construed as a reflection upon you by the men and the public and therefore remained silent and in torment, but we were all ready to take the first steamer should you break down or intimate a wish to have me with you—so we stand today. . . . If I were in your place I would like to have every partner around me and giving me boldly their various views. . . . HP was here and when he read your June letter he said 'Mr. Frick is too touchy. I never could give him my views as I always did give them in the firm.' . . . I know how perplexed you must be and make all due allowance but I do hope you will not write again (if you can possibly help it) about your position being open if it is thought that anyone can do better, etc. etc. . . . We are married—all equal but bound to hear, consider and welcome views even contrary to his own, and if outvoted bound legally to accept them and carry them out. . . . This is a crisis when we should all draw closer together not only as partners, but as friends. I know Lauder and HP wish to be both and cooperate with you, Don't repel them—
>
> One thing more. I have thought what was best for me to do. My judgment says banish the desire to return to New York after election—and do

Italy as you intended. Mrs. C. has never even been in Rome & I have promised to spend a winter doing Italy, Greece etc.—perhaps should run over in the spring, holding myself at all times ready to obey your call, or do anything you think desirable. I wish you would wire what you really think best. I think Spring arrival best when all over and quiet. . . . If Homestead Works could only have disappeared under the ground July 1st how thankful we should all have reason to be. But we must do our duty now. I trust you are not to break down next. If you do I take the post of duty and do the best I can. If the Doctor tells you any signs of overstraining appear, don't let dollars interfere with your taking a round the world trip if necessary let business go to the rear. You have plenty to keep your family upon.[36]

The following week, Carnegie wrote again to warn Frick against attempting to take on too much. "This fight is too much against our Chairman—partakes of personal issue. It is very bad indeed for you—very and also bad for the interests of the firm. . . . There's another point," he continued, "which troubles me on your account—the danger that the public and hence all our men get the impression that it is all Frick—Your influence for good would be permanently impaired—You don't deserve a bad name, but then one is sometimes wrongfully got—Your partners should be as much identified with this struggle as you—think over this counsel. It is from a very wise man as you know and a true friend."[37]

Frick was incensed that Carnegie, after spending a lifetime pushing himself into the limelight, should now accuse his reticent, reluctant junior partner of doing the same. "I am at a little loss to know just why you should express yourself so. . . . I am not naturally inclined to push myself into prominence under any circumstances. . . . I note the counsel you give, but I cannot see wherein I can profit by it, or what action could be taken by me that would change matters in respect to that which you mention." Frick defended himself as well from the implied accusation in Carnegie's letters that he had acted too precipitously in trying to reopen the Homestead plant with Pinkertons, the state militia, private detectives, and a small army of scabs, instead of waiting for the "old men" to return to work. "If we had adopted the policy of sitting down and waiting, we would have still been sitting, waiting, and the fight would yet have to be made, and then we would have been accused of trying to starve our men into submission. This is the way I think. Of course I may be wrong."[38]

Carnegie apologized. "It is all right—I should not have written as I did either but truly I have never had such a trial as during the past four months. Every hour I expected to hear of some catastrophe, such as your health giving away, or nerves rendering my return imperative. Have been on edge as they say. Now I know (or feel, which is the same in effect) that matters are in the best shape you can have them—and that it is only a question of a little time—and calm. We go to Italy and won't return. . . . I think your cross and mine must be the same—for like you I have had to battle all my life with hot blood. I wish I had conquered as completely as you. I am now saintly to a degree, as you know—one thing I am thankful for. Trifles rouse me soonest—in grave situations I really grow philosophic. Maybe if we had learned to swear better in faith we might have experienced relief."[39]

The sad truth, which Carnegie now recognized, was that he needed Frick more than Frick needed him. And that worried him on several counts. He worried that Frick might collapse under the strain of running the company. But he worried as well that Frick might succeed and, in so doing, push the chief stockholder further to the sidelines than he wanted to be.

The two were, as he had put it, bound as if in marriage, but it was not a happy union. Frick believed that he deserved Carnegie's complete and absolute trust, that he had steered the Carnegie companies through good times and bad, steadily increasing productivity and profits. He wanted to be left alone to run Carnegie Steel, as he saw fit. This Carnegie could not allow.

Carnegie was relieved that he had found a manager as capable and tough-minded as Frick, but, as chief stockholder and with more than two decades of experience in the iron and steel industry, he was not about to concede full control of his company to anyone, not even the highly estimable Frick. He was, as well, genuinely worried about the mental stability of his younger partner. Frick had suffered too much at Homestead and from personal tragedies to emerge unscathed. He had become too high-strung, too quick to fly off the handle, and too convinced of his own invincibility. He was beginning to forget that the name of the company he managed was Carnegie Steel, not Frick Steel; it was Carnegie's capital, Carnegie's good sense, and Carnegie's brilliance as a strategist and talent scout that had made it what it was. Though semiretired, Andrew Carnegie, now in his middle fifties, was not ready—and would perhaps never be ready—to recede quietly into the background.

TWENTY-FIVE

Aftermaths, 1892–1894

I n the aftermath of the Homestead lockout and strike, Carnegie kept his silence as the attacks on his probity, his morality, and his sincerity mounted. His English friends tried to cheer him up, but in sending their condolence letters they only heightened his own sense that he had been the victim of a personal tragedy. To William Stead, the editor of the *Review of Reviews* who had written on August 4 asking for an interview, he announced that his lips were "sealed in regard to Homestead, but some day the story may be told. As you can well understand, it is impossible for me to know much about it. I hear of events only two days after they take place. . . . Anything said today would add fuel to the flame, The proper policy to pursue is silence until peace and order are restored."[1]

Stead, as a journalist as well as a friend, wrote back at once. "I think that, while it is difficult for you to know the details about the immediate movement from day to day, you know all about the general question, and I still think that it would conduce to the clearing of the air if you would talk. . . . I am rather uneasy concerning the tendency that there is to run-a-muck at any employer who happens to have a difference with his workmen. I do not think you could have a better opportunity of putting your own views out than what you would have in a good square talk with me." Stead suggested that Carnegie grant him an interview which he would then convert either into "the shape of a Character Sketch or . . . a Special Article."[2]

Carnegie turned him down again, this time sharply. "Homestead and its deplorable troubles should be allowed to rest. It would be absurd for me to write upon events which were as much news to me as to yourself."[3]

He found himself in a difficult position. He was appalled at the loss of life that had occurred when the Pinkertons attempted to land at Homestead, appalled at the resistance the men had put up, and appalled that the lockout and strike had now extended into a third month. But he dared not voice these sentiments for fear that Frick would take offense and resign. Frick had, it was true, followed the overall strategy Carnegie had laid out for him; but he had erred grievously, as Carnegie confided to his cousin Dod in mid-July, in trying to land the Pinkertons by boat, and then erred again by starting up production too soon with scab labor. Frick had won the war but lost too many battles along the way. Had he shown more patience, the same results might have been achieved as they had at Edgar Thomson, without loss of life or the avalanche of negative publicity that was burying Carnegie and his company.

THE LETTER that meant the most to Carnegie arrived in mid-September. Carnegie had written Gladstone a note to congratulate him on his recent electoral victory. Gladstone graciously responded with what amounted almost to a letter of condolence. "I do not forget you have been suffering yourself from anxieties," the prime minister replied on September 19. "I wish I could relieve you from these imputations of journalists, too often rash conceited or censorious, sometimes ill-natured. I wish to do the little, the very little, that is in my power, which is simply to say how sure I am that no one who knows you will be prompted by the unfortunate occurrences across the water (of which manifestly we cannot know the exact merits) to qualify in the slightest degree either his confidence in your generous views or his admiration of the good and great works you have already done."[4]

To Gladstone alone, Carnegie felt obligated to defend himself. In his September 24 letter, Carnegie constructed the first draft of the narrative he would rely on in the years to come to explain what had happened at Homestead in the summer of 1892. The explanation he offered Gladstone was telegraphic in its brevity and its disjunctions, leaping back and forth in short phrases often separated by dashes from Scotland to Homestead— alternately blaming, then absolving Frick and his partners, all the time assigning to himself the role of innocent victim in the evolving tragedy. He insisted that he had been kept out of the loop, that the decisions made at

Homestead had been Frick's alone, that he had played no role in bringing in the Pinkertons or the scab laborers who followed them.

"This is the trial of my life (death's hand excepted)—Such a foolish step* contrary to my ideas—repugnant to every feeling of my nature. Our firm offered all it could offer, even generous terms. Our other men had gratefully accepted them—They went as far as I could have wished but the false step was made in trying to run the Homestead Works with new men. It is a test to which workingmen should not be subjected—It is expecting too much to expect poor men to stand by and see their work taken by others—<u>Their daily bread</u>."

In absolving himself of responsibility, Carnegie took on a new persona, that of the old man in retirement, pushed outside the circle of decision makers, his voice barely audible. He had tried, he insisted to Gladstone, to make his influence felt—he had even "written sketching the plan" of action he wished taken, but "alas too late.—My letter did not reach." (There is no record of or reference to such a letter or cable.) Events spiraled out of control in Pittsburgh. "Feeling had been aroused —Sheriff's aid called in, his Deputies halted—then other Guards sent for <u>with Sheriff's approval</u>, these attacked & then the Military. All this time I heard nothing until days had elapsed. . . . The pain I suffer increases daily. The Works are not worth one drop of human blood, I wish they had sunk. I write to you freely, to no one else have I written so—I must be silent & suffer but after a time I hope to be able to do something to restore good feeling between my young & rather too rash partner & the men over at Homestead."

He concluded by comparing his own sorry state of inaction with that of Gladstone, now returned to office. "I hope you are going to succeed in your great work, but you are to be envied whether you do or not, even failure would be glorious for you are permitted <u>to act</u>. Look at me!—hitherto Master, now condemned to inaction yet knowing the right, and anxious to carry it."

"I have one comfort," he added in a postscript, "self-approval & a second—the support of a wife who is as strong & as wise as she is gentle & devoted—so I shall sail on & let the tempest howl."[5]

Carnegie, though overwrought, was genuinely aggrieved. The Homestead works would survive intact and even prosper, but his proposals for a

---

*We don't know precisely what Carnegie was referring to here. It might have been the landing of the Pinkertons or the decision to bring in scab labor.

partnership between labor and management, based on the sliding scale, had been rejected and his cherished self-portrait as labor's friend and advocate turned to the wall. His days as the workingman's champion now ended, Carnegie struggled to escape becoming labor's scourge. Fortunately for him, Frick was still the primary focus of attention. Carnegie, who was both difficult to reach and reluctant to say anything to reporters, remained a sidebar to the larger Pittsburgh story.

As CARNEGIE had assured Frick, he planned to remain abroad until the strike was settled. In early October, he and Louise relocated to the Metropole Hotel in London. On October 14, Carnegie submitted to an interview with an Associated Press correspondent. He had been, he informed the reporter, "busily engaged all during the Spring and Summer in preparing a new book treating of the industrial problems of the day." He had retired to Scotland to complete the book, but news of "the outbreak at Homestead . . . which had burst upon him like a thunderbolt from a clear sky [was so disturbing] he had been unable to work much [and had] to lay his book aside and resort to the lochs and moors, fishing daily from morning to night." Only now, in mid-October, with, he predicted, the strike coming to an end, was he able to "go to the Continent and work with a fresh and happy mind." Carnegie discussed his forthcoming book at such length that the *New York Times,* which published an account of the interview on its front page, headlined it "CARNEGIE WRITES A BOOK." Carnegie claimed he was a full-time writer now, no longer a businessman. He was writing his new book "from the standpoint of one who had long retired from active business and who had been both an employe and an employer and knew how to sympathize with both." Having previously lectured millionaires on their obligations to society, he wanted now to explain to "the intelligent workman" his place in and responsibilities to the new industrial society. "Improvement," the workingman had to understand, was inevitable, but as "the result of evolution, not revolution." With rather brazen self-confidence, bordering on self-delusion, Carnegie convinced himself that, though an employer of labor and a capitalist, he had transcended any parochial interests and could speak for the larger community. Anticipating that he would, in the long run, succeed at Homestead, as he had at Edgar Thomson, in instituting his sliding scale and establishing a new era of industrial peace and prosperity, he had decided that spring, before the Homestead troubles, to commit to paper his thoughts on the proper relations of labor and capital.[6]

He had finished a first, handwritten draft of chapters on wealth, distribution, cooperation between labor and capital, profit sharing, strikes, and shorter hours while in England. He tried to complete the book at Loch Rannoch, but with no success. It had become apparent to him, though he did not publicly admit it, that his reputation as a wise man in matters of labor and capital relationships had been irremediably tarnished, if not destroyed in the aftermath of the bloody battles with the Pinkertons and the lockout and strike that followed. It was not a propitious moment for Andrew Carnegie to lecture the nation's workingmen on anything. The manuscript was put away; it would never be published.[7]

Carnegie decided instead to bring out a second edition of *Triumphant Democracy*. The new version read much the same as the 1886 edition, though the statistics were updated by research assistants to include the 1890 census figures and some chapters were rearranged. As soon as it was finished, Carnegie began pestering Charles Scribner to rush it into print. "Your note reached me last evening," Scribner wrote him on May 4, 1893, after receiving a hand-delivered message from the author, "and I will do all that I can to hurry the printers. If you consider the very large number of corrections and the irregular way in which the manuscript was delivered to them I do not think they have been slow."[8]

The major difference between the two editions was that Carnegie, in 1893, removed much of the final chapter, "General Reflections," replaced his attack on British institutions with a summary of American accomplishments, then closed with a chapter-length essay, previously published in the *North American Review*, in which he advocated what he called the "reunion" of Great Britain and the United States into a great "federation of the race." Carnegie did not describe how this federation would be governed or what powers would remain with the individual nations and what given to the federation. He acknowledged that his vision of reunification was a bit utopian and he asked his readers to "kindly note" that he had entitled his chapter "A Look Ahead—how far ahead I shall not attempt to guess; nevertheless *it is ahead*, and some time, somehow it is to come to pass. I see it with the eye of faith, the faith of the devotee which carries with it a realizing sense of certain fulfillment."[9]

A Scotsman by birth who was equally at home in Dunfermline, London, and New York, Carnegie paid less attention as the years passed to the political and social differences between Britain and America and more to the similarities between the two branches of what he now unfailingly referred to as "the English-speaking race." It is difficult to know what he meant by this and whether "race," as he used the term, was determined by bloodline, culture, history, or language. Like other nineteenth-century nationalists, he often conflated "race" with "people" and "people" with "nation."

It was, to his mind—and he said so in the new conclusion of *Triumphant Democracy*—an unfortunate accident of history that the American branch of the race had separated itself politically. "Separation," he wrote, putting his own rather idiosyncratic slant on the historical record, "was not contemplated by Washington, Franklin, Adams, Jefferson, Jay, and other leaders. On the contrary, these great men never ceased to proclaim their loyalty to, and their desire to remain part of, Britain, and they disclaimed any idea of separation, which was indeed accepted at last, but only when forced upon them as a sad necessity." It was now, Carnegie proclaimed, after almost 120 years of separation, time to reunite the "nation." As a student of political economy, he feared for the future of Britain, which lacked the population to remain a dominant world power. "Her position is the most artificial of all nations: islands that cannot grow half enough of food to feed her people, but which produce double the amount of manufactured articles they can consume. Such a nation, in order to be secure of her future, must have a market for these surplus articles, and more land from which to draw food for her people." Colonies and distant possessions were not the answer, as it was inevitable that Britain would lose them. And then what? Was Britain destined to become nothing more than an island Belgium?[10]

There was but one possibility for Britain—and that was reunification with its errant English-speaking colonies in North America. He was delighted when a group of Canadian liberals, led by Godwin Smith, organized a "Continental Union League," with offices in Toronto and New York, and an impressive list of American members, including Theodore Roosevelt, John Hay, and Elihu Root. In November 1893, he put his name to a fund-raising letter, soliciting monies to further the cause of a peaceable American annexation of Canada.[11]

. . .

LATE IN October 1892, the Carnegies crossed the Channel to Paris, where they stayed at the Hotel Bristol and dined with the American ambassador. Carnegie was in a buoyantly good mood. Frick had finally agreed to move Schwab to Homestead, which Carnegie publicly applauded in a brief interview with reporters in Paris. "Mr. Carnegie," the *New York Times* reported in a front-page story from Paris on October 22, "said to-day that he was delighted at the return of Mr. Schwab to the management of the Homestead Works, which were most difficult to manage since the company undertook the making of armor." The new appointments at Carnegie Steel, Schwab's among them, "proved that Mr. Frick was one of the foremost managers of men. Mr. Carnegie added: 'If any words from me retain influence with the men at Homestead, I wish to say to them as friends; "All of you for whom Mr. Schwab provides places, take them promptly, for never will you work for a kinder and abler master."'"

The arrival of the sheriff's deputies, followed by the militia, had brought an uneasy peace to Homestead. Under the protection of the militia, Frick had begun, in August, to import scab workers into the mill. By October 15, according to the *Homestead Local News*, there were close to two thousand men employed there, only two hundred of whom had worked in the mill before the strike. This was not nearly enough to resume anything close to full production. Carnegie cautioned Frick to "be patient now" and wait for the strikers to return to their jobs. "Schwab will bring it out all right."[12]

In November, the strike entered its fourth month, with no resolution in sight. Even Frick was astonished at the tenacity of the "old men" who, day after day, refused to return, even as their jobs were being given to scabs. "The firmness with which these strikers hold on is surprising to every one. . . . This strike, of course, will cost us a large sum of money, but we will get it all back in the next two or three years, and, as you know, Homestead has never been well managed, always something going wrong, and a large amount of money has been wasted by poor management. The mills have never been able to turn out the product they should, owing to being held back by the Amalgamated men."[13]

From Paris, the Carnegies traveled south to Florence, then on to Rome and Naples. At every stop along the way, Andrew continued to receive and send cables and letters to Frick in Pittsburgh. Arriving in Milan, he got news of the election returns, which, as expected were not favorable to the Republicans. He seemed not to care that Harrison and Reid had lost the election, nor that he and Frick might have had something to do with the loss.

"Cleveland! Landslide!," he wrote Frick from Italy on November 9. "Well, we have nothing to fear and perhaps it is best. People will now think the Protected Manfrs. will be attended to [i.e., that the new Democratic administration would reform tariffs]—and quit agitating—Cleveland is pretty good fellow." He appeared not overly concerned that the return of the Democrats to power meant the removal from office and influence of the Republicans with whom he had established such cozy relationships. If the Navy wanted to purchase domestic-made steel armor, as Congress had ordered it to do, there were not very many options outside of Bethlehem and Carnegie Steel. Still, there was work to be done in courting the new administration.[14]

On November 18, after four and a half months without paychecks, with the strike funds nearly depleted, and winter approaching, two thousand non-union mechanics and unskilled laborers who had until then stood by the Amalgamated voted to return to work. On Saturday, November 20, the Amalgamated held its regular mass meeting at the Homestead skating rink, after which the leaders convened a special meeting of the five hundred strikers who were union members. The next morning, a vote was formally taken to return to work on the company's terms. The strike was called off.[15]

"Cables received. First happy morning since July," Carnegie cabled Frick from Florence on November 19. "Congratulate all around. Improve works. Go ahead. Clear track." The next day, he followed up with a letter in which he laid out a detailed list of recommendations and commentaries on personnel, prices, production, pools, the tariff, furnaces, the price of ingots at Duquesne, the cost of ore, and the possible effects of Cleveland's election. He concluded by commending Florence to Frick: "It's a marvel—prettiest place we have yet seen—hundreds, yes thousands of villas line hillsides, surrounded with olives and vine—truly exquisite. I hope you are soon to take a long rest and enjoy yourself doing Italy or some new land. It's the thing to do."[16]

On a daily basis now, he congratulated Frick and expressed his relief that the ordeal at Homestead was at an end. "Life worth living again," he cabled from Florence on November 22, then three days later, wrote in a letter: "Now for long years of peace and prosperity. I am now interested in Art matters, until your cable my mind was always running away with me to Pittsburgh." While Frick must have welcomed the congratulatory cables and letters, he could not have been happy with the constant references to Schwab who, Carnegie was convinced, had brought about the final settlement of the strike. "The great compensation for all Homestead trouble and loss is that you have a Manager there at last. Haven't we had a blundering time of it ever since we owned Homestead—just see the difference at Duquesne, you selected the right man and from the first day it is made the most profitable piece of property we own. . . . Mark this, I prophecy Homestead this time next year will show profits worth while—but do get Schwab to become a Homestead man, all over, even if you have to build a palace for him—might send him one from Venice where you can buy for a few thousands dollars— Have bought some things here since your cable which will give you all pleasure."[17]

Carnegie, sensitive to the effects bad publicity might have on a company that was hungry for public contracts and needed tariff protection, hoped that his name—and that of his chief lieutenant—might disappear from the front pages. But that was not to be. In late November, days after the strike was called off, the American newspapers called attention for the first time to the fact that the Carnegie companies in Pittsburgh had, in July, been reorganized into one giant firm, capitalized at $25 million. Though this figure was far below market value for a company that was making between $4 and $5 million a year in profits, it was still a figure of grand proportions. Carnegie, usually only too happy to see his name—and successes—highlighted in the papers, was distressed that this news had leaked out.

"'Twenty-five Millions' makes another roar against capital and looks bad," he wrote Frick on December 2. (As a proportion of the overall economy, $25 million in 1892 is equivalent to almost $15 billion today.) "I wish I had held out for the old fashioned modest five millions. We want 'obscurity' for a long time. Nothing to attract criticism. Pray heaven you are not beginning magnificent 'Carnegie' Building. [There had been plans for some time to build a new office building downtown.] . . . It would give your enemies another handle. Do let that rest. No explanation would avail. . . . Alas, our doings have become of National import and we must move accordingly." The Republicans were, Carnegie noted, beginning to criticize him, claiming that the events at Homestead had cost them the election. While Carnegie declared that he personally didn't "care a cent for this" criticism, he did "see the value of not further enraging even ignorant public sentiment just now."

Now that the press had put Homestead on the map, it would be difficult to remove it. In an age of almost instantaneous cable communication, stories quickly made their way from Pittsburgh to New York to the European papers. "You have no idea how Europe is excited about Homestead, its awful," he complained to Frick. In Naples, where he looked for some respite from the storm of adverse publicity, Carnegie was beset by cable dispatches from Pittsburgh, reprinted in the European newspapers.[18]

Winter was setting in at Homestead and with it increased misery for the jobless and homeless. The strike had been settled, but the thousands of Amalgamated men who did not get back their jobs were left permanently unemployed. "In Homestead there are today 1,800 men," the *Pittsburgh Press* declared, "most of them with families for whom no employment can be found. For many of them the Christmas prospect is an empty cupboard and a cheerless hearth. For many of them there is even now an empty cupboard. . . . The wolf is at the door; innocent children, hard-working mothers, fathers who in the majority of cases simply obeyed higher authorities—all are suffering in the land of plenty."[19]

The suffering was exacerbated by Frick's decision to close down the plant on December 17, only a few weeks after the strike settlement, to "put works in thorough order." Carnegie suggested that the company offer "good men suffering through strike" an advance on "some part future earnings to tide them over stoppage. . . . Will prevent suffering and will show 'heart.'"[20]

Carnegie's initial response to the negative publicity was to keep silent and caution his managers to do the same. Within a month, he had shifted strategy. He was temperamentally unsuited for a passive approach to any problem. Though he still regarded "silence" from him as the best policy for the foreseeable future, he urged his colleagues to take the offensive in the war of public opinion. "The mass of Public Sentiment," he had concluded, though reluctantly, "is not with us about Homestead on the direct issue of re-adjustment of the [wage] scale—people did not understand it, but I observed that Opinion was greatly impressed by the few acts of kindness . . . especially of investing savings of men at high rate of interest—this one feature attracted the most favorable notice. Library came in also." Carnegie Steel would, in future, compensate its employees for lower wages by increasing other benefits. "The partner who can devise a new way by which the Firm can benefit the workmen—improve their surroundings, and make it better for their wives and children, will deserve the medal next year. . . . Nothing can be surer than that immense concerns like ours must show a great many advantages conferred upon the workmen than smaller employers. . . . Carnegie Steel Co., should lead the way. We have to show Non-Unionism better for the men than Unionism. In wages paid, we must be governed by the Market of course, but in things showing thought for the comforts and pleasures of the workmen and their families, we can be our own masters and deal liberally." He closed this pep talk, which he presented in the guise of Christmas greetings, on a personal note. While he had been absent from the scene of battle, he wanted his partners in Pittsburgh to know that he had suffered with them. "Shall see you all early after the New Year, think I'm about ten years older than when with you last. Europe has rung with Homestead, Homestead —until we are all sick of the name. But it is all over now—so once again Happy New Year to all."[21]

On December 27, he thanked Frick "for copies of valuable correspondence, reports, etc. I sent them to Lauder and he to the Squire [Phipps] so all the retired . . . were kept busy. We shall see you sometime next month. Shall try to elude Reporters New York and live a quiet life. We have been both too much before the public for many months, and if ever silence was golden it is now."[22]

CARNEGIE returned to Pittsburgh in late January 1893. In a statement released to the press and published on the front page of the *New York Times* on January 30, he insisted he had "not come to Pittsburgh to rake up, but to try to bury the past, of which I knew nothing. That is beyond recall, it should be banished as a horrid dream." He then made three related points:

(1) He was going to hold on to his stock in Carnegie Steel forever. He had "made his first dollar in Pittsburgh, and I expect to make my last one here." Because he had "hoarded nothing, and shall never accumulate

money," his future security and prosperity, like that of the Homestead workers, depended on the prosperity of the works.

(2) He had the utmost confidence in Mr. Frick. "His four years management stamps him as one of the foremost managers in the world—I would not exchange him for any manager I know. . . . Good workmen or able men, will learn to appreciate Mr. Frick. . . . Violent workmen he does not like, and these will not thrive with him."

(3) He was not now and would never again be in control of the company that bore his name. "I desire now, once for all, to make one point clear. Four years ago I retired from active business; no consideration in the world would induce me to return to it. . . . I believe in retiring and giving younger men a chance. . . . I hope after this statement that the public will understand that the officers of the Carnegie Steel Company, Limited, with Mr. Frick as their head, are not dependent upon me or upon any one, in any way, for their position, and that I have neither power nor disposition to interfere with them in the management of the business; and, further, that I have the most implicit faith in them."

His statement was riddled with contradictions—as majority stockholder he most certainly had a say over who ran the company—but it served its purpose. He had come to Homestead to publicly affirm his support for Frick and to pronounce the tragic events of July over and done with. And that had been accomplished. But try as he might, he could not remove the memory of those events from the collective consciousness. Too many men had been killed and wounded and too many were suffering through a long winter, still without work. For as long as he lived, and longer, Homestead would remain a symbol of all that was wrong with industrial America.

Having declared the incident at an end, he refused to speak of it again.

During the strike, he and Frick had placed an embargo on interviews. Now that the strike was over, they tightened rather than lifted it. When in April of 1893 a reporter infiltrated the Homestead works, John Leishman, Frick's second in command, could only apologize for the breakdown. "While we have done everything possible to prevent articles in regard to our operations etc. from getting into the paper," he wrote Carnegie, "even to the extent of telling the Superintendents to discharge any man that they found retailing our business to the newspapers we do not seem to have been able to stop the nuisance. We are so prominent and the newspapers here so hard up for news that it would be a very hard thing to shut them off entirely, and unless we went to the expense of paying the different papers to keep us out it would not be possible, and even then I am afraid they would make a slip occasionally in order to cater to the working man's vote. Notwithstanding the above discouraging facts will continue our efforts to prevent any newspaper publications."[23]

Five months later, there was another breach in the security wall, this one more serious as journalist Hamlin Garland, accompanied by an illustrator, snuck into the works through a hole in the fence. They published their observations in the June 1894 issue of *McClure's*. There had been portraits of life and work at Homestead prior to this, and there would be many later, but none would resonate with the larger public as Garland's did.

"The town was as squalid and unlovely as could well be imagined, and the people were mainly of the discouraged and sullen type to be found everywhere where labor passes into the brutalizing stage of severity. It had the disorganized and incoherent effect of a town which has feeble public spirit." Garland had secured as a guide "a young man whose life had been passed in Homestead and who was quite familiar with the mills and workmen." Together, the guide, Garland, and the illustrator toured the works from the "finished beam" yard to the converting furnaces and the rolling and finishing mills. "Everywhere were grimy men with sallow and lean faces. The work was of the inhuman sort that hardens and coarsens." There were, Garland observed, no "old men here." Work in the mill "shortens life. . . . The long hours, the strain, and the sudden changes of temperature use a man up. . . . The worst part of the whole business," he was told, was that the work "brutalizes a man. You can't help it. You start in to be a man, but you become more and more a machine, and pleasures are few and far between. It's like any severe labor. It drags you down mentally and morally, just as it does physically. I wouldn't mind it so much if it weren't for the long hours. . . . Twelve hours is too long."[24]

WHAT BOTHERED Carnegie more than the adverse publicity or the name-calling was the recognition that from this moment on, everything he did would be subject to a new level of moral review. Because he had never intended or considered his philanthropy as expiation for his sins as an industrialist, he was surprised, then dismayed, when others did. It was, he believed, grossly unfair—to him and to the recipients of his gifts—to draw connections between the methods by which his money was accumulated and the purposes to which it was donated.

The protests against Carnegie's "tainted money" began with the arrival of the Pinkertons. On July 9, the *Philadelphia Press* had reported that the Window Glass Workers Lodge No. 300 had already inaugurated "a movement . . . that promises to spread. This idea has been rampant since the Homestead outbreak, and to-night found vent at a large meeting of the glass workers. A resolution couched in severe language in its reference to Mr. Carnegie was passed, asking City Councils to repeal the ordinance by which the Carnegie Library gift [to Pittsburgh] was accepted. The resolution stated among other things that the proposed library would only be a monument to Mr. Carnegie, while the men who keep up the library will not derive any benefit from it."[25]

Two days later, a resolution was presented to a special meeting of the Pittsburgh City Councils, calling for rejection of Carnegie's gift. The resolution was blocked by Boss Christopher Magee, who claimed that as the gift had already been accepted, it couldn't be returned. Ever the politician, Magee declared that while he would not defend Carnegie, he could not

FORTY-MILLIONAIRE CARNEGIE IN HIS GREAT DOUBLE ROLE.
AS THE TIGHT-FISTED EMPLOYER HE REDUCES WAGES THAT HE MAY
PLAY PHILANTHROPIST AND GIVE AWAY LIBRARIES, ETC.

imagine how working people would gain anything by giving back the money he had dedicated for a library. "No matter how Mr. Carnegie got this money, he has it. If it belongs to the working people this is a good way of getting it back, and why not take it."[26]

Carnegie received even worse treatment from his former friends in the British labor movement. The British workingmen's organizations that had once competed for his favor, and the pleasure of listening to him lambaste the monarchy and aristocracy, now censured him for sending in the Pinkertons. They too called into question the moral and political advisability of accepting his bequests for libraries. On July 14, 1892, the London Trade Council passed a resolution declaring that it was "to be hoped that in case of any further well-advertised philanthropies on the part of Mr. Carnegie, the workers of the district will show their disapproval in an unmistakable manner." According to a *New York World* correspondent writing from London on July 24, "The general opinion is that Mr. Carnegie will find it quite impossible hereafter to induce towns in Great Britain to accept any of his gifts." The Glasgow Trade Council not only passed a resolution censuring him, but condemned the town council of Ayr, which, after receiving the gift of a public library, had seen fit to honor him.[27]

Instead of responding directly to the workingmen's groups on both sides of the Atlantic, Carnegie wrote an open letter to the Pittsburgh Art Society that was published on December 18, 1892, in the *New York Times* and elsewhere: "I was naturally much grieved at the action of some of the industrial organizations. . . . Whatever was of a personal character I readily understood and passed over, perhaps the more easily because I could not quite see how I deserved it. But the opposition expressed to the library, music hall, and art gallery was a wholly different matter. . . . It was indeed pitiable if the wage earners for whom these were chiefly intended should be permanently prejudiced against them by any shortcomings of the donor, however grievous, for, sadly as he may fail in his efforts to live worthily and do his duty—and no one, alas, knows as well as himself how far he falls short of his own ideal—yet his gifts to Pittsburgh must ever remain stainless and work good continually and never evil." He desired only that "my fellow-workmen (for I have a right to use this title) see that fair play requires them to separate the donor and his many faults from libraries and music halls and art gallery, which have none."

A month later, when the citizens of Mansfield and Chartiers, two small villages east of Homestead, let it be known that they wished to name their new consolidated borough in his honor, Carnegie felt vindicated. "I confess that the whole unexpected action of the people of the Boroughs of Mansfield and Chartiers has quite touched my heart," he wrote one of the men behind the idea. "Coming at this time, it is peculiarly gratifying. Life would not be worth living to me if I felt that the people in and around Pittsburgh did not, at least, in some degree, reciprocate the affection which I have for them; and why should I affect not to value their good opinion, when I consider this as among the chief prizes of life to be won? . . . It is a bold step to christen any place after one still living. That your people have chosen my name, must make me more careful than ever to do nothing that can cause them to lose the confidence evinced that my future life will be such as to place no stain upon it; and although I can never fully deserve the honor they have conferred, I shall hope never wholly to discredit their choice." Five years later, the new borough received its just rewards when Andrew Carnegie donated funds for a Carnegie library in Carnegie, Pennsylvania.[28]

UNABLE TO ERASE the public's memory of Homestead, Carnegie in 1893 redoubled his efforts to dissociate himself from the tragedy. While he could not publicly criticize Frick, he hinted in letters to his friends that he would have handled matters differently.

"I have been in purgatory (if not worse) since July," he wrote his old traveling companion Alice French in February of 1893. "It is terrible. I do not believe in fighting labor, never did, new men are a delusion, employers should <u>shut down</u> when things become intolerable. The whole works are not worth a human life."[29]

He wrote much the same letter to Whitelaw Reid the following month. "This has been the hardest trial I ever had to endure (save when the hand of death has come)—I have been in misery since July, but am reconciled somewhat since I have visited Homestead and gone through all the Works and shaken hands with the chief men." Again he asserted, without equivocation, that things would have turned out differently had he been in charge. "Between ourselves, no manufacturer is wise who attempts to employ new men." The guards had been hired to protect the "old men" who he and his partners were convinced would return to work once the gates were open. But the "workmen were terrorized and dare[d] not appear. Here was the turning point. The works should then have been closed and the firm should have kept on negotiating but never starting until matters were right." He refused to put any blame for the bloodshed and the extended strike on the workingmen. Whatever may have happened, it was not their fault. "No one knew the virtues, the noble traits of the true working man who has not lived with them as I have and there's one consolation in all my sorrow, not one of them but said, Ah Mr. Carnegie if you had only been here it never would have happened." He had much to apologize for in his letter to Reid, who might have been vice president had things turned out differently. "To add to my cup I know the mistake injured my friends, President Harrison and yourself, but I was powerless—after the riot and with Mr. Frick supposed to be dying no step could be taken that would not have complicated matters still more. I was all ready to return by the first steamer, but as my appearance on the scene would have implied Mr. Frick's virtual deposition and he had begged me not to do this, I remained abroad."[30]

Whatever he might imply about Frick's leadership in private, Carnegie refused to second-guess or criticize him in public. He needed him to stay right where he was: in Pittsburgh, as president and chairman of the board of Carnegie Steel. The strike was over, but the labor problems at Homestead persisted. Frick and Schwab had ended up at Homestead with a volatile mixture of scabs and "old men." In May 1893, Schwab notified Frick that he had "decided to take a strong hand [and] investigate every squabble [between former strikers and scabs] whether it occurred in the town, or works, and deal with the guilty parties severely." Union sympathizers who harassed strikebreakers on the job were discharged immediately. When such harassment occurred in the town, Schwab notified the police, who promptly arrested and fined offenders; they were then discharged from the plant. To make sure that Homestead remained non-union, the company would later hire internal spies to report on any organizing activity. In 1894 a new Bureau of Information was organized to coordinate the work of the spies. Potential organizers and troublemakers were let go at once. "My own idea," Schwab wrote Frick in January 1894, "is that if the men hold any meetings or attempt to form any organization, we should be prepared to be fully informed of all that goes on and unhesitatingly discharge any man connected with this movement."[31]

Carnegie was not directly involved in any of this, though Frick and Schwab knew where he stood and acted accordingly. He and Louise had remained overseas until January of 1893, then, after five months in the States, returned to Europe in May and did not move back to New York until November 1893. In February 1894, they sailed again for Europe, en route to Egypt for the winter, England for the spring, and Cluny for summer and fall. Between April 1892 and November 1894, they would spend twenty-six of thirty-one months out of the country.

They were in Europe when, a year after the settlement of the strike, Homestead reentered the headlines once again. In the late summer of 1893, Frick had received a note from an attorney who claimed to represent four men who had documentary evidence of fraud in the armor department. When Frick refused to pay them for the evidence, the four approached Secretary of the Navy Hilary A. Herbert through their attorney and offered him the same material in return for 40 percent of the fines that Carnegie Steel would have to pay if the allegations of fraud proved true. The newly appointed Democratic secretary of the navy, after checking with the U.S. attorney general, offered the informers 25 percent, which they accepted.[32]

The documents the four men provided demonstrated that the superintendents in the armor department had filled in "blowholes," tiny fissures in the steel plates, and secretly re-treated those plates designated by navy inspectors for further testing. The charges were true, but amounted to little. Blowholes were present in all steel plates, did not indicate any weakness in the material, and were routinely plugged to create a smooth surface. And while the superintendents had, indeed, secretly re-treated plates marked for further testing (because the company received a premium for superior work), every one of them was up to standard, including those that had never been re-treated.

Despite the lack of gravity in the charges, the secretary of the navy, in secret and without informing the company, set up a board of inquiry which found Carnegie Steel guilty of fraud. A fine of 15 percent was levied on the total amount the company had received on all its armor contracts. Early in December, Frick was summoned to Washington to meet with Secretary Herbert and told of the board of inquiry's decision and the fine. He appealed the findings directly to President Cleveland.[33]

Carnegie, who was in New York at the time, was outraged by the judgment against his company. On December 17, he took the train to Washington, where, accompanied by his attorney Philander Knox, Frick, and Millard Hunsiker, the firm's armor expert, he met with the secretary of the navy and the president. Later, he put his thoughts in writing in a "confidential & strictly personal" letter to "My dear Mr. Cleveland." On the envelope was written: "This is a personal letter to Mr. Cleveland not to the President & I ask the Secretary to hand it to him unopened. Andrew Carnegie."

Though he did his best to control his anger, it seeped through nonetheless. "We have been accused, tried, found guilty & sentenced without ever having been heard," he wrote Cleveland.

> The vilest criminal has always the right to be heard in his defense. . . . After we had been sentenced we were asked to state our side of the case, not till then—But this is not the worst of it—The so-called Board who should have been our Judges were not allowed to judge. They were <u>instructed practically</u> [by Secretary Herbert], what to find. . . . This is a serious business for us not as to mere money though that is important these times. . . . For three years I have devoted myself to meet the wants of the Country. . . . Spent millions, subordinated every other branch of our business to the Government's needs, succeeded—& then upon the testimony of spies we are charged with irregularities and our men with fraud—I cannot stand this—even at the risk of offending the Secretary, good honest man, but overzealous in this affair, Carnegie Steel must ask to be tried by a Court who will at least visit our Works, <u>listen to explanations upon the ground</u>, & see for themselves before they judge.[34]

Cleveland, unwilling to publicly side with an unpopular Republican contributor and overrule his secretary of the navy, decided nonetheless to reduce the fine to the manageable sum of $140,000. Carnegie accepted the president's compromise, with rather good grace.

"So be it—President compromised—divided amount claimed," Carnegie wrote Frick from the SS *Columbia*, on his way back to Europe. "If this be the last of it the loss is not great." Carnegie worried that this was only the beginning of a string of accusations against the company. "I fear other conspiracies. Carnegie Steel Co. has become the Malakoff [a great stone fortress near Sevastopol that was under constant bombardment during the Crimean War] of the Industrial situation and must bear the first attacks—our competitors escape and yet profit. Its intolerable." The company had no choice but to redouble its efforts to portray itself as a progressive, forward-looking, labor-loving concern. "Our policy should be to strengthen our general position before the Country—Can't hide in a corner and attend quietly to business, as smaller concerns do therefore we should be in advance providing Extra things for our workmen, libraries, etc., etc.—Also pay liberally in case [of] accidents. . . . We cannot fight Trade Unions successfully without repeated losses, except by convincing our men that their best Union is union with their employer. . . . Think over this—prayerfully."[35]

The armor scandal did not go away soon. The House empowered a subcommittee to investigate further, which it did, calling a series of witnesses for hearings that began in the spring and went on for several weeks. Carnegie tried to make light of the new scandal, but that was easier for him, vacationing at the time in Cairo, than for Frick, Schwab, et al., in Pittsburgh. "It had to come out, our enemies—Amalgamated Association—bound to use it," he wrote Frick on March 6, 1894. "The ghost of Homestead is not yet laid." He suggested that Frick should defend himself and the company by blaming the "fraud" on a few "miserable wretches . . . these spies—They could not and did not do the work to our standard and shirked some parts as was discovered." Three weeks later, he wrote again, "Surely this Armor fuss will be the last thing dragging Homestead before the public. I hope so."[36]

CARNEGIE would spend the rest of his life trying to remove the stain of Homestead from his reputation and demonstrate that he had always been a friend of the workingman. In 1912, as he sat down to write his *Autobiography,* he asked his old partner Alexander Peacock to seek out as many former Amalgamated officials and advisory committee members as he could locate and ask if they remembered cabling him for advice in 1892. For years now he had insisted that the majority of Homestead workingmen remained loyal to him and had cabled him at Rannoch in July 1892, "Kind master, tell us what you wish us to do and we shall do it for you." When Peacock wrote back that no one in Pittsburgh had knowledge of such a cable, Carnegie directed him to try again. "It seems to me that rightly managed, those who had part in signing that cablegram would be glad to pass into history as having shown friendly relations between the chief owner and themselves. It might be presented to them in this light, I am sure. Explain fully that what I wish is to leave a record of the past and is not to be published at present. If you were in position to write me a note stating that you had seen certain people who were aware of the message and had told you about it, it would be valuable, next to having their direct evidence; but you would be considered a reliable witness, I am sure, in after years. I should be satisfied with your statement. Shall rest satisfied that you will do the best you can that the truth of history may be vindicated."[37]

Peacock tried and failed again. No cable from the workers to Carnegie was ever found, nor was any Homestead veteran located who would corroborate that one had been sent. None of this prevented Carnegie from quoting in his *Autobiography* from the cable that did not exist.

WHATEVER THE COSTS of the Homestead strike, they proved more than worth it for Carnegie Steel. It is difficult to overstate the long-term effects of management's victory—and the Amalgamated's defeat. In the wake of Homestead, the Amalgamated was virtually driven out of the steel industry. Wage rates were reduced, the twelve-hour shift was instituted in most of the departments that had previously run eight hours, and union rules that had once prescribed occasional breaks were eliminated. Homestead's steelworkers, skilled and unskilled, lost their grievance rights and could, from this point on, be reassigned or discharged at management's will.[38]

The result of breaking the union was, as Carnegie had expected, an unprecedented boom in productivity and profits. While the nationwide depression that began in 1893 would not lift until at least 1897, Carnegie Steel would successfully ride it out, in large part because of Homestead. Between 1893 and 1897, rail production remained stagnant, while the market for steel plates, sheets, and structural shapes, all manufactured at Homestead, grew by 80 percent. By 1897, Carnegie Steel was producing 49 percent of the nation's structural steel. Annual profits, which had fallen to a five-year low of $3 million in 1893, rebounded to $4 million in 1894, $5 in 1895, $6 million in 1896, and $7 million in 1897.[39]

Despite Carnegie's earlier protestations that he regarded his employees as his partners, there was no increase in wages for the workers at Homestead or elsewhere. On the contrary, for the steel industry as a whole, wage rates declined dramatically for skilled workers throughout the 1890s, while holding stable for the unskilled.[40]

THEODORE DREISER visited Homestead in the spring of 1894, soon after his arrival in Pittsburgh. "The battle was already fifteen months past, but the feeling was by no means so," he wrote in *Newspaper Days.* "I did not know then what it was about this town that was so depressing, but I learned afterward, in the six months in which I staid here, that it was a compound of a sense of defeat and sullen despair which was over all. The men had not forgotten." In the hills above the plant were "a few moderately attractive dwellings." There were some "uniform frame houses" on the side streets. But below, in the flats behind the mill where the bulk of the workforce lived, "were cluttered alleys so unsightly and unsanitary as to shock me into the belief that I was once more witnessing the lowest phases of Chicago slum life—the worst I had ever seen." The entire town—the mill, the flats, the side streets, the river below, and the homes on the slopes above—was shrouded in gray smoke, so thick it blotted out the sun.

Two days later, Dreiser took the streetcar to the "east end of Pittsburgh, which was, as I could easily see, the exclusive residence section of the city." As astonished as he had been by the destitution at Homestead—and by the degraded circumstances in which Pittsburgh iron and steelworkers lived in isolated enclaves elsewhere in the city—he was even more dazzled by the wealth on display in and around Oakland. "Here . . . were homes of . . . the most imposing character—huge, verandahed, tree-shaded affairs, with immense lawns, great stone or iron or hedge fences and formal gardens and walks of a most ornate character. . . . The houses here were so very, very noble—vast, roomy, restful, graceful affairs with shaded walks and portly entresols." He passed by the new Phipps Arboretum and Carnegie's "huge and graceful library of white limestone," still under construction. "Truly, never in my life, I think, neither before nor since, either in New York, Chicago or elsewhere, was the vast gap which divides the rich from the poor in America so vividly and forcefully and impressively brought home to me. . . . The poor were so very poor, the rich so rich, and their self-importance was beyond measure."[41]

Carnegie had fled Pittsburgh in the mid-1870s and seldom returned. His absence made it easier for him to ignore the changes that had taken place in the industrial city over the past two decades, as the English-speaking skilled workers who had once manned his iron and steel mills and worked on the railroad were replaced by unskilled day laborers from Southern and Eastern Europe.

The steel magnates had always divided their workforce so as to more easily conquer it. As early as 1875, Captain Jones, in a letter to David McCandless, at the time chairman of the Edgar Thomson steel firm, explained that his "experience has shown that Germans and Irish, Swedes and what I denominate 'Buckwheats'—young American country boys, judiciously mixed, make the most effective and tractable force you can find." In the years that followed, Frick brought in Italian and African-American workers as strikebreakers—and allowed them, in many cases, to keep their jobs after the strikes were settled. After the Homestead strike, there would be a greater and greater reliance on Eastern Europeans, whose primary concern was finding steady work, no matter what it paid. "The one essential," as David Brody has written, "was not wages, working conditions, or living standards, but employment itself."[42]

Carnegie never acknowledged the presence—in larger and larger numbers—of the Eastern Europeans. He also paid no attention, in his speeches or his writings, to the steady increase in the proportion of unskilled common laborers in the steel mills. He preferred to imagine life and work at his plants much as it had been twenty years earlier at the Union Iron Mills and Keystone Bridge, where most of his employees were skilled artisans or on their way to becoming such.

In his mind, there was still abundant opportunity for upward mobility: from manual wage work to foreman to department head to supervisor. He understood—how could he not?—that his laborers were underpaid. But he believed that those who were worthy would quickly transcend that status. They would study and learn—in his own libraries, no doubt—and rise steadily in his employ, much as Charlie Schwab had. He did not ask, as his critics did, how it was possible for a man to improve himself if he was forced to work twelve hours a day, seven days a week, or if his first language was not English, or if he had no connections of kinship, religion, or ethnicity to the bosses above him.

Living in New York, visiting Pittsburgh only occasionally, and then only to stay at the exclusive Duquesne Club or one of the hotels downtown or with Frick at Clayton, Carnegie preferred to make-believe that the world of the Pittsburgh worker was still very much what it had been when he began his climb upward. It was a comforting illusion, one that would sustain him for the rest of his life.

TWENTY-SIX

"Be of Good Cheer—We Will Be Over It Soon," 1893–1895

Less than six months after the surrender of the Amalgamated at Homestead, almost as if it were divine retribution for the sins of the nation's leading steelmaker, the stock market crashed, bringing down with it the broader economy.

There were multiple causes for the crash. As Carnegie had predicted in his 1891 article, "The ABC of Money," the Sherman Silver Purchase Act of 1890 had frightened European investors. The act, which required the U.S. Treasury to purchase and coin millions of ounces of silver bullion, was perceived by bankers as the first step toward a silver standard. Fearful that their American bonds and securities might in future be redeemed in silver instead of gold, European investors began cashing them in. As more gold flowed out of the country and more silver was coined, European concerns were exacerbated and overseas banks accelerated their sell-off of American securities and bonds.

Carnegie, whose bond-trading career had made him acutely sensitive to European fears, wrote the newly elected Democratic president, Grover Cleveland, suggesting that he calm the financial markets by declaring himself in favor of strict adherence to the gold standard. "Until all doubt is put to rest, there is still great danger of the country being drained of its gold. . . . All excitement can be allayed and the crisis safely passed by a simple declaration from you. If I might suggest, somewhat like the following, 'As long as I am President of the United States, the workingman is going to be paid in as good a dollar as the foreign banker is' [i.e., in dollars backed by gold, not silver], I think this would also be good politics. . . . I have spoken to many republicans, and without exception they agree that in standing for sound money . . . you will receive almost the unanimous support of the Republican party." Though Cleveland, having worked for one of the law firms which represented the Morgan interests, understood international finance and the importance of the gold standard, he could not get his party to abandon silver. Through the spring and summer 1893, American gold reserves continued to decline and with them the value of the dollar.[1]

The heart of the American economy—and certainly of the increasingly vital steel and iron sector—remained the railroads. Unable in the spiraling crisis to borrow new money to service their old debts, the weakest among them struggled to stay afloat. "More roads defaulted during the 1890s than at any time in American history," Jean Strouse has written. "A year after the panic, 192 lines operating 40,000 miles of road and capitalized at $2.5 billion had fallen into the hands of receivers." With the failure of the railroads to pay their employees, their creditors, and their suppliers, the economy went into a tailspin. Some 16,000 firms and hundreds of banks closed their doors. "More seriously," as Steve Fraser has written in *Every Man A Speculator*, "thousands were left homeless, tramping the roads searching for work while 20 percent of the labor force could fine none."[2]

The effects of the panic and the depression that followed were felt immediately in the iron and steel industry. The statistics only begin to tell the full story. Pig iron production fell by more than 20 percent from 10.2 million tons in 1892 to under 8 million in 1893; Bessemer steel declined from 4.7 to 3.6 tons; rails almost 27 percent, from 1.74 million tons in 1892 to 1.27 in 1893 and 1.14 million in 1894.[3]

Carnegie was not worried. "Be of good cheer—we will be over it soon," he wrote Frick in late May. The most recent monthly profit statement "took my breath away—Isn't it incredible almost—Am glad you are well & in command—I know you will choke every mill with orders at any price necessary & keep all the Cash you can."[4]

The only immediate casualty, it appeared, would be his Music Hall on Fifty-seventh Street in New York, which had been a losing proposition from the moment it opened. To stay out of bankruptcy, more money would be needed—which Carnegie hoped, but failed, to get in loans from New York banks. In early June 1893, Carnegie asked Frick to try to raise money in Pittsburgh for the Music Hall Company. He promised to endorse the loans himself (i.e., guarantee payment should the Music Hall default) and to make the Music Hall self-supporting by expanding it to include rent-paying "offices and practice studios."[5]

Carnegie miscalculated the breadth and depth of the developing depression. Try as Frick might to hold on to cash, there was simply not enough of it around to keep the Carnegie works running at full blast, especially after the railroads, their biggest customers, struggling to stay out of bankruptcy, stopped paying their bills. As most American banks had ceased giving new loans, Carnegie offered to borrow money from the Bank of Scotland. "We could easily get a million sterling here 5 million dollars if we issued 6% first mtge Gold Bonds. . . . I know how to write the Prospectus and the money would be available at once . . . I shall be anxious to hear just what your plans are and how you feel as to our ability to go on nicely. After a little we shall have money forced upon us of course—but if Congress does not act [on repeal of the Sherman Silver Purchase Act] we shall probably have to wait for money some time. Am glad we have you at the helm for you are the best financier I ever knew. If you get stuck Lord help the rest. . . . I shall be glad to go to you any time [i.e., return from Britain to Pittsburgh] if you feel my presence would be only 'comforting' and no more. There's profitable days before us. If others stop we should take every order at prices which deter their starting."[6]

As the stock market continued to fall, bringing more banks and business down with it, Carnegie, with the bulk of his fortune tied up in his Pittsburgh plants, began to worry a bit. On August 7, Frick wrote to suggest that salaries be cut at once for all Carnegie Steel employees. "No sensible person would expect anything else than that a reduction when made should include everybody." None of his managers, Frick complained, was doing enough to keep costs down. The main culprit was Carnegie's favorite, Charlie Schwab, whom Frick criticized whenever the opportunity arose. "There is no question but what he has great ability, but it is too largely used to make himself popular. He is recklessly extravagant in everything he does for himself or any one else, and I regret to say in many respects unreliable; tells you only that which he thinks will please, without regard to its correctness, and in that way has even misled you. I feel that he has outraged the confidence I have reposed in him in many ways. . . . The management at Homestead [now Schwab's fiefdom] is the embodiment of all that is reckless and extravagant."[7]

"These are anxious days," Carnegie wrote Frick the following day, as if Frick needed any reminders. "I had thought the panic would hold off at least until December meeting of Congress when we should have been prepared for it with $2½ millions more profits, but no amount of capital will enable us to run [un]less paid for our product." Carnegie advised Frick to pay his employees, but no one else. The railroads might threaten to stop carrying Carnegie Steel freight, but they would never follow through as it was their "not paying [for their steel and iron] which render us unable to pay." He had, he told Frick, been to the Bank of Scotland and "showed the Chairman confidentially the two months earnings statement [for the period before the panic broke], which almost knocked him from his chair. I took them away and he promised not one of his Directors would be told." Carnegie and Frick agreed not to provide potential lenders with full financial statements, "as they always ask for earnings and we must not surprise people so. Half million a month is out of all reason." If the size of their profits became public knowledge, it would become impossible to maintain even minimal protective tariffs on their products. Although the financial news from the States was not good, Carnegie remained upbeat. "When [the Bank of Scotland officers] get to know us there will be a splendid pot of money at our disposal all the time, probably will pay us keep door open here as stringency doesn't develop 'contemporaneously' on both sides Atlantic. Congress met yesterday. It ought to clear the skies at once. Stop silver purchases—that's all we need to rebound back to prosperity. Don't fret or take matters too hard—We can't be hurt—It's all coming right."[8]

Congress did repeal the Silver Purchase Act at the end of August, as Carnegie had hoped, but it came too late to halt the damage already done. As the depression deepened, with no sign of a quick recovery, Carnegie was besieged with requests for loans: from Walter Damrosch, who asked for $5,000; from Caroline Vandervort, his friend's wife, who asked for $2,500; from his uncle Lauder, who asked for £100; and from Charles Scribner, who begged him to reimburse the man who had drawn the maps for the latest edition of *Triumphant Democracy*.[9]

Carnegie's business strategy was the one he had followed twenty years earlier: keep production steady by accepting orders at any price. In early

October, he notified Frick that the time had come to leave the rail pool. "I confess I can see nothing so good for us as a 'free hand'" in setting prices. He was willing to lower his prices and profit margin on rails if that was the only way to get the orders he needed to keep his works running. "By this policy we shall keep our men at work." Carnegie had never been entirely happy as a member of the rail pool, especially after Illinois Steel was allocated a greater share than Carnegie Steel. "For my part," he now declared, "I do not wish to play second fiddle in the rail business any longer. I get no sweet dividend out of second fiddle business, and I do know that the way to make more money dividends is to lead. . . . I am sure that The Carnegie Steel Co. can make more dollars, even next year, and certainly in future years, by managing its own business in its own way, free from all understandings with competitors, than by continuing in any combination that possibly can be formed. Now having made my speech, which I trust you will read to all my partners, I take my seat and imagine the loud applause with which my sentiments are greeted."[10]

Carnegie Steel would, in the end, survive the extended depression of the 1890s because, unlike its competitors, it was built to survive market downturns. Since the partners had reinvested so great a portion of their dividends in new machinery, the company could produce rails, beams, plates, and other steel products at costs below its competitors. As important, because capital for internal improvements was generated internally, the firm was not weighed down with debt. In the first six months of the depression, while Illinois Steel, Carnegie's largest rival, posted a huge deficit and thirty-two different steel companies, including Pennsylvania Steel, closed their doors, Carnegie Steel turned a profit of $3 million and increased its share of the market. In 1892, Carnegie Steel had produced 17.8 percent of the nation's steel; by 1893, it had increased its share to 21.5 percent; by 1894, to 25.3 percent.[11]

Though Carnegie had the utmost faith in the long-term trends—for the economy and his company—he worried about the short-term suffering the depression had brought in its wake. "Never such stagnation in business here, as now," he wrote John Morley in mid-December of 1893. "We have resolved that none of our workmen shall suffer—or his family, for food shelter and fuel. . . . I am happy in this—and also in having started a Committee Pittsburgh to adopt same rule as to every Pittsburgh decent workman—Not one shall want except for clothes. I draw the line there. Our own business is so infinitely better than that of others we are thankful, all right with us comparatively."[12]

The committee Carnegie referred to was the Citizens' Relief Committee. He had not organized it himself, as he claimed, but, when solicited by his friend Robert Pitcairn, agreed to contribute "a sum equal to what the citizens of Pittsburgh contribute, dollar for dollar," up to a total of $250,000. The day after Christmas, he wrote to tell Frick of his offer to Pitcairn. With very little free cash of his own to spend, Carnegie had begun relying on Carnegie Steel as a bank from which he drew money as needed, to be repaid out of future dividends. "I couldn't satisfy myself short of the letter written RP today in reply to his. I have no use for money—don't want to die rich—It will never go to a better use than to give work to worthy men in this crisis. I feel better now—hope you approve. Wish Pittsburgh would show itself <u>superbly grand</u> in taking care of its workmen."[13]

Carnegie needed Frick's approval, as only Frick knew whether there was sufficient cash at Carnegie Steel to fund the contribution. Before Frick, however, had had an opportunity to check on this and get back to Carnegie, the letter to Pitcairn appeared in the press. Carnegie feigned surprise at the public disclosure, though he may well have been the one who told the press about his contribution. He instructed Frick to "arrange payments as you think best. . . . Am too sorry this miserable breach of faith has occurred. It teaches us a lesson."[14]

The following day, Carnegie apologized again and thanked Frick for restructuring the gift. "Glad to get your suggestions have wired RP to do as you & he decide—I noted on outside of envelop to him ('consult Frick'). I think it best $1000 per day—my conscience says I must give to Pittsburgh in this crisis. I love the old Smoky City and her people and all my boyhood days return to me and I feel I would give every dollar if necessary for Pittsburgh and her industrious working men." He reassured Frick that there would be no further calls "upon my balance beyond this—Music Hall will take a little cash each month."[15]

Frick, who knew precisely how much Carnegie could afford to spend, seized on the opportunity to ask for something for himself. On December 28, two days after Carnegie offered the Citizens' Relief Committee $250,000, Frick asked that his salary be doubled. He hated being in debt—especially in the midst of a depression when money was tight. He had borrowed from Carnegie to purchase his 11 percent share of Carnegie Steel Co. and owed him $1,696,894.55. Because the value of the coke company shares that secured the loan had increased significantly, there was no longer any chance of default. The loan being almost without risk, he asked Carnegie to lower the interest rate. "I would much prefer to sell my interest at 90 cents on the dollar, and retire from the firm than accept the slightest change unless it came from you freely and cheerfully. I ask only what I would do if our positions were reversed."[16]

Frick had phrased his request in such a way that Carnegie was almost obligated to say yes. But he didn't. He agreed that now that Frick had "mastered the Steel business and made a success," he was worth twice the salary for managing Carnegie Steel that he had earned for managing Carnegie Brothers, which was half its size. He was not, however, going to renegotiate the terms of Frick's personal loan. "Now about interest on loan I cannot at all agree with you—cannot quite understand how you can ask reduction upon a bargain which has made you one million of dollars [Frick's 11 percent interest in Carnegie Steel, for which he had paid not a penny down, had paid him average dividends of $500,000 a year] seems odd— Really I do feel when you look at it in this way you will wish you had never suggested it."[17]

Carnegie read as a veiled threat Frick's rather gratuitous claim that he would rather sell his stock at a loss and retire from the firm than force Carnegie to make a deal he was not comfortable with. But instead of confronting Frick directly, which he dared not do as there was no knowing how the impetuous Mr. Frick might respond, he digressed into a long-winded panegyric on the virtues of putting all one's eggs into one basket and the benefits of a partnership as compared to a corporation. He was, with masterful indirection, reminding Frick that he expected him to concentrate on the steel, not the coke business, and to consult with his partners, as he had neglected to do eighteen months earlier during the Homestead crisis. "I don't believe a man ever lived clever enough to attend to more than one Manfg. Enterprise—Not one—He neglects it to some extent if he has other interests to employ his thoughts. He makes mistakes of omission or commission which he would have avoided had his brains not been scattered." It would, Carnegie conceded, have been preferable to consolidate the Frick Coke Company and the Carnegie Steel Company so that Frick would not have to choose between them, but that was not practicable at this moment. Neither company had the excess capital to purchase the other and Carnegie was not willing to merge them into a publicly owned joint stock corporation. "Don't want anything to do with a corporation as long as I am in business—Partnership is the only thing—no one man can manage well—every one needs the companionships of equals in business to contradict and differ from him—one advises the other . . . I who write you thus have grown gray in the service and speak the words of soberness and wisdom."[18]

There was no response from Frick. Carnegie wrote him a second letter, this one nastier and more peremptory than the first. Carnegie had learned that Harry Phipps, now retired and frightened by the effects of the depression, was considering selling his Carnegie Steel shares at a discount, and that Frick had expressed interest in buying them. Carnegie was furious at the thought that Frick had even considered making such a deal. Carnegie Steel stock was not to be traded for; the partners had signed the ironclad agreement precisely to prevent such deals. When a partner was ready to leave the company, he had no choice but to sell his stock back to the company—at book value. "Don't try to negotiate with H.P. for his interest because he won't negotiate. . . . Bargains from poor men carry no blessing—'The Books' has been our rule why should it be changed? The firm can buy any of his shares with my approval at the Books." Not yet finished berating his junior partner, Carnegie went on to criticize him for not adjusting the book value of the Keystone Bridge properties, as Phipps, fearing his shares were undervalued, had begged him to do. "You promised him to fix it. . . . You do yourself wrong as I see it, to wish to treat your own partners worse than an outsider—I cannot understand this attitude, so foreign to my feelings and I think should be to you. This is good gospel for you my friend—You need a mixture of 'sentiment' to make you the supreme manager nature intended you. Feeling—Imaginations—and Sentiment—these attract the best natures to you and none others are worth attracting."[19]

Carnegie, of course, had no business lecturing Frick. Though his junior partner, Frick was neither a child nor a business neophyte. He was a man of substance, in his mid-forties, a millionaire, and president and chairman of the board of the nation's most profitable steel company. It is true that he had tried to skirt the rules Carnegie had set up, but he did so from the inside.

Frick had to have found it difficult to be on the receiving end of Carnegie's deflating remarks; but rather than say anything in his own defense, he remained silent, biding his time until Carnegie retired.

ANDREW CARNEGIE was as astute a politician as he was a capitalist and political economist. Political change was in the air and it was important to pay attention to it. The election of 1892 had not only resulted in a Democratic conquest of the White House and both houses of Congress, but in the appearance of a new—and, for the eastern manufacturers, even more frightening force in American politics—the People's Party or Populists who, in their first national election, had polled over 1 million votes, or 8.5 percent of the total for their presidential candidate. The Populists had also elected three governors, thirteen congressmen, and two senators.[20]

An optimist at heart, and one who believed fervently that the American capitalist system was just and reasonable, Carnegie expected that those who stood outside the two-party mainstream would eventually troop back in. But to hasten that process, it was necessary to tinker at the edges of the political economy and remove the most obvious traces of corruption, inequity, and injustice.

The Democrats, following the lead of Grover Cleveland in 1888, had identified the protective tariff as the root of all social, political, and economic evils. The growing power of trusts, combinations, and monopolies; the exploitation of the many for the enrichment of the few; the corruption of the governing classes; the prostitution of law and the courts; urban disorder and decay: all was charged, directly or indirectly, to the operation of the protective tariff. Carnegie hoped that if the tariff issue could be taken off the political table, it would become more difficult for politicians to rally support for legislation curbing or regulating the economic power of industrial capitalists.

He was, for this reason, not terribly upset when Cleveland was elected president. While other Republican manufacturers bemoaned the loss of the White House, Andrew Carnegie almost applauded it—and looked forward to the Democratic conquest of the Senate as well—as he believed only the Democrats could reform the tariff and, thereby, remove it from the political agenda. "Shall be sorry if Democrats don't get full control Senate," he had written Frick from Italy in mid-December of 1892. "We can only be rated as honest and not 'Robber Barons' after the Democracy passes the bill [reforming the tariff] that takes the 'Robbery' feature out of the question. They can't attack their own bill by alleging Robbery still exists. No, their action must put down Robbery—one cent per pound for steel doesn't seem to leave much margin, but the public in part believe we have been favored by law. Let the Democrats change these laws."[21]

In December 1893, Carnegie traveled to Washington to lobby for tariff reform. He met with Senator Arthur Gorman of Maryland, the chair of the Democratic caucus, and with his old comrade, Pittsburgh Republican congressman John Dalzell. "Am an authority with both sides on Tariff," he wrote Morley on December 17, "please neither, but still I am pressed to say privately, 'What shall we do?'" He positioned himself as a moderate who believed that the protective tariff on iron and steel had to be lowered, but not precipitously; a Republican who was more than willing to compromise with the new majority party; and a pragmatist who opposed his fellow manufacturers' unyielding opposition to any change in the tariff schedule.[22]

On December 19, the House Ways and Means Committee, chaired by William Wilson of West Virginia, reported out its tariff reform bill. Though the Wilson bill reduced tariffs more than Carnegie thought wise, it was, in his estimation, a reasonable bill, which, with a bit of tinkering, could be made palatable to the nation's manufacturers. On Senator Gorman's suggestion, Carnegie identified what he believed were the lowest possible duties the iron and steel manufacturers would accept on beams, boiler plates, pig iron, hoop iron, rails, tin plate, iron and steel sheets, and wire rods. His greatest fear, at this point, was not that Congress would pass a bill reducing tariff rates on iron and steel products—he could live with this—but that the politicians of both parties in both houses, having taken hold of the tariff issue, would sink their teeth in and never let go.

"The inevitable discussion of the Wilson Bill, if it should continue for six months, is bound to keep the country in turmoil," he wrote Senator Gorman on January 2, 1894. He urged the Republicans to make only the most necessary changes in the schedules and then do all they could to make the Democratic bill a law. "I think manufacturers and Republicans in Congress should see that a reasonable bill passed by the Democratic party would take the tariff out of politics for many years. . . . To secure this desirable result I think manufacturers should be willing to take duties which seem to be lower than necessary. Much better low duties with <u>stability</u> and <u>general approval</u> than high duties subject to attack and deemed unfair by any part of the people." He added, as a postscript, "I wish to see the 'Robber Baron' completely exterminated."[23]

The following day, as he prepared to sail to Europe en route to Alexandria, Carnegie wrote a confidential letter to Whitelaw Reid and enclosed with it a letter to the editor to be published in the next day's *New York Tribune*. "Believe me the manufacturing interests need peace—Wilson Bill is nearly safe <u>and can be made so</u>. There are 8 to 10 Democrats in Senate ready to agree to make necessary modifications <u>provided our people stand by them</u>. . . . Don't fear that passage of satisfactory tariff will enable Democrats to win next election. This is impossible. Trade cannot revive before November or indeed later."[24]

His letter to the editor, which was addressed to his fellow Republicans, repeated these ideas in more decorous language. "What seems most desirable in the interests of manufacturers of the United States is, that a tariff bill should be passed by the Democratic party, and thereby, that the suspicion that even one 'Robber Baron' exits in the broad domain of the Republic, cannot remain in the mind of the most ignorant citizen."[25]

Carnegie had played politics in his own idiosyncratic style: by swooping into the middle of an issue, positioning himself as a moderate power broker, having his say, and then departing in the expectation that his reasoned analysis would carry the day. It didn't. The Wilson bill became the plaything of the politicians, each of whom had his own constituencies to protect. For six months, senators attached amendments to it, in the end transforming it from a template for moderate reform to more of the same. Finally, as Richard Bensel has written, "the House capitulated, adopting the Senate bill without change, 600 amendments and all. Cleveland allowed the bill to become law without his signature." Carnegie was not around for the sorry denouement. He would not, in fact, return to the country until November 1894.[26]

Though he would take credit for the tariff legislation that was finally passed, Carnegie's attempt at bipartisan compromise had failed. Neither the Republicans in Congress nor the manufacturers they represented signed on. Rather than being saluted as a peacemaker and diplomat, he was criticized as a renegade and traitor to his party and his class for supporting tariff reform.

CARNEGIE had at age fifty-eight decided to spend the winter of 1894 touring Egypt, which was all the rage for wealthy Americans and Europeans at the end of the nineteenth century. Before leaving New York, he had, as always, provided Frick with an itinerary, complete with mail and cable addresses. Arriving at Alexandria in early February, he was delighted to find a first "cheering cable" awaiting him. Frick was, as requested, busily scooping the market by accepting orders at prices his competitors could not meet. Carnegie warned him about offering rails on credit to Collis Huntington of the Central Pacific, whom he did not consider "a first class risk. Hope collections from him will be watched. So much for business." He then proceeded to describe his trip in delightful detail and asked Frick to pass on his letter to Dod "and the boys so I needn't write any others." He and Louise were traveling up the Nile and had found "two splendid fellows" from New York. "Rubber whist every night and lots fun—given two dinner parties. . . . Expect reach Cairo about 25th—spend a few days there and about March 18th go to Naples for Amalfi, Sorrento, etc. and be in England about middle April . . . where we shall be glad to receive the Frick household . . . really you ought to take a run over this year— you missed it last summer—maybe Cluny do you more good—come to one or the other—nothing like a trip abroad—'All work and no play' etc." Though Carnegie complained about the grippe—he had become something of a hypochondriac—he and Louise were enjoying their role as pampered tourists.

> We are tanned like Indians by the hot son. Nights and mornings and in the shade always cool and truly the Nile trip is a treat in store for you, only you of all men will be bored by it at first—such beggars, such dust and squalor as I never saw—but the temples are great and the blue sky, green crops always—the banks and the sunsets are all unequaled elsewhere. We take no interest in anything not at least 3000 years B.C. Think of seeing the body of Rameses II—the greatest Conqueror Egypt ever had—buried over 3000 years ago and here he lies in his mummy case in perfect preservation as far as form and features of the face are concerned. . . . Tired but

it is the exercise I need. Mrs. Carnegie is doing it all in her usual thorough manner—deeply impressed with the work done by these people much farther before Christ than we are behind him—can't quite understand it.[27]

For the next nine months, Frick would receive similar letters, filled with good tidings from abroad, a suggestion or two about business, a plea for the Fricks to visit, and a bulletin about his health—"Am really well—slight trace of nasal catarrah remain and I sneeze now and then."[28]

By April, Carnegie was safely settled in at Buckhurst, in Sussex, where he had leased an estate with its own 2,000-acre English park and chapel, equipped with servants, the latest in appliances, and thirty to forty cases of the finest wines, bought from Hedges & Butler on Regent Street. While he still lived rather modestly in New York, at least in comparison with his fellow millionaires, he felt no obligation to do so in England. "Buckhurst appears to be spoiling all of us," he wrote Hew Morrison, his chief lieutenant in Britain. "It is now thought we should have at Cluny a galvanized iron house into which the laundry could be put, so that it might be separated from the house as it is here. As you are a kind of 'Consulting & Supervising Commissioner' for Cluny, would you kindly look into this matter and see what we can get, and the price."[29]

He had asked Morrison to stock some fishing streams at Buckhurst with live trout and was disappointed to find out that it could not be done this late in the season. "Trout cannot be sent by rail in warm weather," Morrison had written on May 31. "They could be sent to Buckhurst in February. The colder the weather the better, the less the deaths by traveling and the more readily do the fish take to new ground." Morrison suggested that instead of shipping dead fish to Britain, Carnegie stock the "Cluny burns and loch," where the fish might survive the colder water. "My idea is that you should put in 500 at once of two-year old trout; so that you may not have to wait long for sport there. You should strictly preserve the streams and loch for your own personal use for two or three years. You could have fishing upon them next season."[30]

From England, Carnegie continued his assault on Frick. "Come over and get a rest to your brain—and if possible come soon so you can all be with us. We shall have no other visitors . . . truly it is worth your while—and you can come later to us in Scotland." Carnegie was in fine shape now, having recovered from a bad cold that had lingered for months. "I am gaining strength and yesterday fished and in afternoon walked and was not fatigued. My only trouble has been 'getting tired.' . . . Haven't worked at anything since I left you. Can't and don't want to. Mean to be idle all this year."[31]

A week later, having heard nothing from Frick about a vacation, Carnegie tried again. "Whatever happens, you take your holiday. No man can stand very long the strains to which you have been unfortunately subjected, unless he takes intervals of rest under changed conditions." In a handwritten postscript, he added: "You don't know the pleasure it will give us to take good care of you all."[32]

Frick, after several more letters, finally consented to bring his family to Cluny—though for a much shorter stay than Carnegie had hoped for. As had become his custom, Carnegie had photographs taken of his guests posed informally on the Cluny front steps. In the center of the frame, Andrew, in his hiking/picnicking outfit with his checkered coat and hat and knee-high boots, sits upright, smiling. At the top of the photo, in the doorway, Frick stands uncomfortably, almost slouching, with a rather grim expression on his face, looking as if he would rather be in Pittsburgh.[33]

CARNEGIE remained in Britain for several months after the Fricks departed, strangely reluctant, it appeared, to step back into the whirlwind. The Pullman workers, many of whom belonged to the American Railway Union (ARU) led by Eugene Debs, had gone out on strike against George Pullman's Chicago works in the spring. After a month off the job—and with no hint of compromise from Pullman—they were joined in a sympathy strike by the ARU men, who refused to handle any trains with Pullman sleeping cars attached. Within days, some 50,000 railroad workers had walked away from the trains, curtailing traffic into and out of Chicago. The strikes were broken only when President Cleveland dispatched troops to get the trains moving again.

From Cluny, Carnegie kept track of events in Chicago, but refused to be disheartened by them. "It is too bad that the country is just out of one great strike [Homestead] to be plunged into another," he wrote Frick in July. "But this will surely be short-lived. The present excited period through which the industrial world is now passing will give place to years of very calm operations. To this you may look forward with confidence. I hope you will not allow any but the most serious occasion to prevent or delay your getting a holiday."[34]

CARNEGIE STEEL continued to be pilloried in the press. Congress held its own investigation and issued a damning report on the armor scandal, which was picked up by the press. Republican Whitelaw Reid led the charge against Frick and Carnegie in an editorial in the *New York Tribune* on August 31, 1894. "In palming off those defective and inadequate armor plates upon the government they were imperiling the lives of thousands of our seamen and jeopardizing the nation's honor and welfare, but they were making money. It is an appalling conclusion. One shrinks from believing a thing so monstrous. And yet there is the record in all its hideous simplicity and clearness."[35]

In previous years, Carnegie would have taken upon himself the role of public defender of Carnegie Steel. But since Homestead, the little man who had once taken such delights in broadcasting his views had become press-shy. He urged Frick to take his place as the company's spokesman. "I note you are averse to newspaper interviews," Carnegie wrote from England in October 1894. "Well, they are easily abused, and in the hands of any but the Master [was he referring, tongue-in-cheek, to himself?], are usually bad, but there are critical exceptions." If Frick was unwilling to represent Carnegie Steel to the press, then Carnegie suggested he hire "a newspaper man." Defending a large corporation was "a great art," one that, he added parenthetically, Francis Lovejoy, the company secretary who had been sending out the press releases, lacked. "If we were a small concern you could easily play ostrich policy, put your nose in the sand and think your body hid, but we are really a national institution." Unfortunately, Carnegie Steel's "overshadowing size" made it a target for public criticism. "This is bad, <u>very</u>, but it is so and should be recognized. . . . In this age every <u>public</u> concern (and we alas are such much to your regret and mine) must carry public sentiment with its action, and to do this it is necessary to acquaint the public with this action as it is, i.e. from our standpoint. Think carefully over this; to be unpopular with the masses (even other than our own employees) is to expose ourselves to injury undeserved. It is not good business policy. If I were Chairman I should myself write an account of all actions," and make sure it was widely distributed.[36]

Frick's failures as a spokesman were more than compensated for by his brilliance as a financier and executive. He was certainly the most talented businessman Carnegie had ever worked with. Carnegie remained extraordinarily pleased with Frick's shepherding of Carnegie Steel, and told him so. Their only area of disagreement concerned Frick's still divided loyalties. Carnegie had, on several occasions, recommended that Frick give all his attention to Carnegie Steel and withdraw from management of H. C. Frick Coke. Frick refused to even consider the possibility.

By January 1895, the two little titans of industry had been entangled with one another and in one another's businesses for a very long time. Unfortunately for Frick, Carnegie held all the cards. He was the chief stockholder not only of Carnegie Steel but of Frick's coke company as well.

The management of H. C. Frick Coke had been a sore point between the two men for more than a decade now. Frick, as founder and president, desired only to be left alone. Carnegie, as chief stockholder, felt obligated to intervene to protect his investment *and* Carnegie Steel's supply of fuel. In July 1894, just before Frick was to visit Cluny, he received an angry letter from Carnegie. Frick was considering entering into a temporary pool agreement with his competitor in coke, William Rainey, much like the ones Carnegie Steel maintained with its competitors in rails and beams. Carnegie was outraged. "You know that this proposed agreement is illegal," he wrote, knowing that if it was illegal, so too were his own pooling agreements. Carnegie demanded that Frick merge his company with Rainey's, as that was the only way to control Rainey, who had for years refused to cooperate on prices or wages. "For my part, I should much rather sacrifice my interest in the concern [H. C. Frick Coke] than be made a plaything for unfair competitors to sport with. As far as my stock is concerned, and also my influence, I give you due notice I will never cease to protest and work against anything but practical consolidation."[37]

The disagreement on how to deal with the renegade coke operator was put on hold when Frick agreed not to do anything until the new year. He had that spring suffered through another disastrously violent coke strike in the Connellsville region and was busy putting back the pieces. Rainey—he and Carnegie agreed during Frick's visit to Cluny—could wait.

In October, just before returning from Scotland, Carnegie brought up the Rainey matter again in a letter to Frick. To facilitate the merger of H. C. Frick Coke with the Rainey firm, Carnegie suggested that it might be necessary to flatter Rainey by suggesting that "one of his sons might make a good Vice President." Frick should consider whether he wanted to act as president of the merged firm or "whether it would not relieve you considerably to let Rainey, or one of his sons Chairman. Anything of that kind should be offered in order to get a start."[38]

ANDREW AND LOUISE returned to the United States in early November, 1894, after ten months abroad. Greeted by reporters as he walked down the gangplank, Carnegie explained that "he had gone abroad to regain his health," the New York Times reported on November 4. "I have not felt so well for years." He answered questions about politics, Tammany Hall, the death of the czar, business conditions in England, and the recently passed tariff bills, before the reporters moved on to interview the actress Lillie Langtry, who had also arrived on the Paris.

Accompanying Andrew and Louise were several barrels of Scotch, 1888 vintage, for distribution to Carnegie Steel's most special friends. Frick cautioned Carnegie that he did not think it "proper at this time to send Secretary [of the Navy] Herbert any," as Carnegie Steel was in the process of submitting bids for new armor contracts. There was no such obvious conflict of interest with Senator Matthew Quay, Republican senator from Pennsylvania and state party boss, who received his own barrel, which Frick assured him would only improve with age if left in the wood. In the meantime, Quay should drink from the gallon drawn from the barrel and bottled separately.[39]

Carnegie wasted no time in making his presence known, which did not greatly please Frick, who had done quite well managing Carnegie Steel in his absence. The first meeting he attended on his return was in New York City with Frick and Bethlehem Steel executives. The Navy had invited bids for millions of dollars of new contracts for steel plate armor and guns for its battleships. Carnegie suggested to the Bethlehem executives that the two companies either divide gun forgings and armor, 50 percent for each, or that Carnegie Steel take over the armor business, leaving armaments contracts to Bethlehem. The companies eventually agreed on the second division.

There was no such agreement on foreign contracts. Carnegie had earlier dispatched his cousin Dod to St. Petersburg, followed by Millard

Hunsiker, his armor expert, to negotiate a secret preemptive agreement for an armor contract with the Russian government. He then sabotaged the effort by leaking the news of the potential contract to the press, thereby alerting Bethlehem to the need to lower its bid.

Frick, who seldom, if ever, criticized Carnegie in public or in private, could not restrain himself in this case. "I was astounded this morning," he wrote Lieutenant C. A. Stone, a Navy officer with whom Carnegie Steel worked closely, "to find that the newspapers had obtained knowledge of Mr. Hunsiker's visit abroad. To my mind, this could only have reached the public through one source (through our leading stockholder), who, it seems, is not able to contain himself at any time or under any conditions. I will have this traced, and ascertain. If it were an employe of this Company, we would have no further use for his services." We don't know if he said anything to Carnegie about his indiscretion, but it is likely he did. And just as likely that Carnegie denied that he had done the company any harm.[40]

Following his New York meetings with Frick and the Bethlehem Steel officers, Andrew and Louise took the train to Pittsburgh, where they stayed with the Fricks at Clayton for ten days.

A Carnegie trip to Pittsburgh resembled nothing so much as a royal visitation. On November 19, the Carnegies, with a party of seventy or eighty, visited the Homestead works. "It might be well," Frick had written Schwab in advance, "if you can spare the time, to come in this afternoon and write out a little programme of what they will see, so it can be distributed among them." From Homestead, the Carnegie party took the train to Braddock, where they were met at the station by General Superintendent James Gayley and taken on a tour of the Carnegie Library. Frick accompanied them wherever they went. "Your letters would have had prompt attention," he apologized to a sales representative in New York, "but for the fact that Mr. Carnegie has been with us for several days past and we have been very busy."[41]

On his return to New York in late November, Carnegie dispatched a warm thank-you note to Frick. A few days later, he was back on a train again, this time to Washington, D.C., to meet with coke company president William Rainey to discuss a merger of his company with H. C. Frick Coke. Frick was neither invited to the meeting nor notified that it was going to take place.[42]

Frick was furious with Carnegie for going behind his back and meeting with Rainey. Rather than confronting Carnegie in person during his visit to New York and dinner with Andrew and Louise in mid-December, Frick waited until he had returned to Pittsburgh and then, in a brief, hand-written letter displaying neither anger nor regret announced his intention to resign from Carnegie Steel.

"Having decided to sever my connection with this association January 1st next, it is but proper you should be at once advised that you may arrange for my successor and the purchase of my interest. The affairs of this association are in splendid shape as you know from examinations made during your recent visit here, in every way better than at any time in the past and the outlook for the future very bright, otherwise I should not think of retiring now." Frick made no mention of the Rainey meeting, but cited personal reasons for his decision. "The past six years have been trying ones to me, and my mind from necessity has been so absorbed in looking after the interests of this great concern, I have had no time for anything else and feel now that I need such a rest as only obtained by almost entire freedom from business cares."[43]

The simple truth was that Frick could no longer tolerate Carnegie's meddling. For ten months now, he had run Carnegie Steel and H. C. Frick Coke while the senior partner and chief stockholder in both companies vacationed abroad. Had Carnegie remained in Britain, all might have been good. But Carnegie, having returned to New York, had signaled that he had no intention of severing his ties to his companies or leaving Frick alone to run his coke company.

Carnegie's response was immediate—and condescending, the exact wrong tone for this situation. "I cannot consider your note for one moment because you will decide upon reflection that it would not be worthy of you to retire without proper notice to your partners and friends. To lay down such a business upon a few days notice would not be fair and therefore I knew you too well to believe you will do it. . . . I have told you of my desire to sell to you and my partners and that I only waited until our affairs were in order when such a proposition could be made without adding to your cares. It is I who should be relieved My Dear Friend not you. . . . You are yet young and should be my successor as chief owner a post I have told you I aimed at your being and left it to you to say when you felt the

Company was ready to take my interest." He added, as a postscript: "You are not well my Friend you are not well. You would never have done me this cruel injustice were you well."[44]

A master of epistolary combat, Carnegie took the initiative in what was now a war of words. Having finished his first letter, he sat down that same day to write another. "I wrote you the minute I had grasped the main point in your letter. I have read it more carefully since and I must say it seems a nicer letter and more worthy of you than at first glance appeared. . . . My Friend, let me now say that what strain you have borne surprises me; that I have insisted on holidays for you perhaps to the point of pressure because I knew (although you didn't apparently) that no brain, no not even yours, and your temperament (the latter as rare as the former) could stand it. Trips to Europe, recreation—hasn't that been my text—not purely because we should thereby have the services of your rare ability, but I can say because I liked you and yours as friends." Carnegie suggested that, instead of resigning, Frick "take a long holiday and go to Egypt." He ended his letter with another melodramatic twist: "As I write your face appears to me as it was the other night when you came to us to dinner. It was worn, you were tired, overstrained, long meetings, vital questions, discussions, had worn you out. I am not alone in seeing recently that just as I was this time last year so now you require just what I did; and if you can only be restored as I have been, to pristine health you will return and smile at matters which now (in your tired state) seem gigantic and annoying. All your partners ask (at least I ask) is that you will be patient and try the cure—not one of them would endanger your health."[45]

Frick's response was as brusque and cold as Carnegie's had been gracious and affectionate. In a second handwritten note, intended only for Carnegie, and therefore not given to the typist, Frick replied that he had "carefully read your note of the 18th. I think I understand what is due between partners and friends and that to a large extent has influenced my action. The decision to retire from the firm was made after the most serious consideration, and I see no reason to recall it."[46]

On December 21, Frick and Carnegie met with the secretary of the navy at the Shoreham Hotel in Washington to discuss future armor contracts. After the meeting, they talked for the first time about Frick's resignation. Carnegie tried to placate Frick by offering to withdraw as chief stockholder and sell his shares in Carnegie Steel to his partners. "I thought he was delighted" with the proposition, Carnegie would later write Harry Phipps.

Back in New York, Carnegie put his plans into writing, the two men's favored form of communication with one another. "My wish is to close my business career fittingly—a splendid close. The opening of the Library [the dedication of the Pittsburgh library was scheduled for October 1895], or rather handing it over to good old Pittsburgh would furnish this." Carnegie proposed to sell his stock in Carnegie Steel to "my dear friends and trusted partners" and receive, in return, twenty- or thirty-year, 6 percent bonds, which he would disperse as gifts "to the various Institutions I have established subject to the revenue coming to me during life. . . . The main point with Mrs. Carnegie and me is the fitting close to my business life. Both set much store upon this ending Oct. . . . I have always intended to hand over my interests to my young partners, and, as you know, I have since my return explained this to you. Assist me then to realize my aim. All of you take the wealth and give me dignified retirement. You will have my blessing, and if I can ever be of service, and am asked advice or my assistance, it will be given—perhaps if I saw something awfully wrong, I might give advice unasked—very likely—the C.S. Co. must always be near to me."[47]

Carnegie's proposal was unacceptable, as he must have known. While it would have guaranteed him a lifetime income—and an immediate infusion of new assets to donate to his various causes—his partners would be left with the burden of paying him 6 percent annual interest on $14 million of first-mortgage bonds, a debt no firm could afford to carry. Frick refused to even discuss the proposal. Having made up his mind to leave the steel company, he was not going to change it. He was exhausted by the strain of running two companies at once, worried that he was not paying enough attention to his own coke company, anxious about the health and mental well-being of his wife and children, concerned about the million dollars or more he owed Carnegie for his Carnegie Steel stock, and furious at Carnegie's pigheaded certitude that he knew better than Frick how to manage the H. C. Frick Coke Company.

Carnegie, for his part, continued to add fuel to the fire. Rather than admit that he had done anything wrong in meeting secretly with Frick's rival, William Rainey, he claimed now that he had done Frick a favor by excluding him from the early negotiations that might not have led anywhere. On December 23, he had written to tell Frick that he was going to meet with Rainey again, accompanied this time by John Walker, a Frick Coke Co. stockholder, but not a director. "The F.C. Co. should be entirely free from any participation in the negotiation," Carnegie wrote. "Now don't object to let Walker and me go ahead and see what can be done. Of course we have no power to conclude anything. . . . Trust your pards and don't know anything just yet. You remember eating of the tree of knowledge was once disastrous. There is nothing to know anyhow—but F.C. Co. should keep aloof—that much is clear to you."[48]

Frick forwarded Carnegie's proposal to Walker and informed hm that he had washed his hands of anything to do with Rainey, Carnegie, or H. C. Frick Coke. "Under no circumstances would I interfere now, or do anything that would look like interfering with what a large stockholder thinks is going to greatly benefit this Company. Let him now work it out his own way. . . . He did not keep his agreement with me, but, leaving my feelings out of the question, he has already done the Frick Coke Company great harm, in my opinion. You will observe he does not send the letter, or a copy of it, received from Rainey. He does not know the man he is dealing with, nor enough about the business, or the affairs of this Company, to negotiate with him if he did."[49]

Two days later, Frick repeated his message—this time in a letter to Carnegie—that any attempt to negotiate with Rainey was bound to fail. "Rest assured, however, I shall do nothing to interfere in the slightest with your program in this matter, much as I deplore the way in which you started about it. Whether you fail or not, I cannot help but think you have placed the Frick Coke Company in a very awkward position indeed. One thing sure, you have added greatly to the merriment of friend Rainey this Holiday season."[50]

When Carnegie at last invited Frick to join him in the merger discussions with Rainey, Frick angrily declined. "You must really get along without me in this negotiation. I thought you had learned there was nothing like starting right, but while the start in this has not been in accordance with my ideas, as you know, yet, let me repeat, I will not in any way hinder nor interfere with your negotiations, and have so written Mr. Walker, and you cannot now afford to lay down and hereafter say it was because I took exception to your way of going about it. That is all I have done, or will do, so you have a clear field. I have had the 'pith' taken out of me times without number, but have seen the thing through without flinching and without sympathy. You now have my sympathy in this, and shall have my support if you evolve something with Rainey that is really to the benefit of the stockholders of Frick Coke Company."[51]

Carnegie, recognizing belatedly that Frick was dead serious about resigning, wrote Phipps a rambling, repetitive letter, imploring him to come to New York as soon as possible.

> None of the firm know the trouble and none shall know it but you and you not till you come and unless it be necessary to tell you. . . . It's not surprising. Frick is not well. He is breaking down and is not of former power. . . . Now this isn't my sole opinion either—but rest may cure him—I hope so—I shall say no more. . . . I am so sorry for Frick. No man could have stood the strain. He ought to have rest. He is not well. Unhappy—overstrained—irritable—all nonsense to talk of his action being caused by our relations for these have never been so thoroughly pleasant. He wishes to sell out, etc., but I shall try to dissuade him and certainly will do nothing till you come and we decide together. He resigned with you once please remember [in 1887, when he was ordered to end the strike at Connellsville] and I had to support you—but this time you will find more serious reasons for him doing so I fear, his health—but now please don't go and talk to anyone about this till you come and see and even not then. I have not told a soul of what happened here—not one and won't not even you till you come down and it is necessary. . . . What rest will do we know not but I hope he will return to us again as he did from your resigning crisis.[52]

What happened next defies explanation. Carnegie forwarded the letter intended for Phipps to Frick in Pittsburgh. It could only have been an accident. He had written Phipps at the same time that he was writing Frick and must have put the wrong letters in the wrong envelopes.

Frick responded on New Year's Day 1895.

"It is high time you should stop this nonsensical talk about me being unwell, overstrained etc.," he wrote Carnegie, "and treat this matter between us in a rational business like way. If you don't I will take such measures as will convince you that I am fully competent to take care of myself in every way. If ever a man penned a sillier lot of nonsense than you did when you wrote that letter to Mr. Phipps—copy of which you sent me, I should as a curiosity like to see it. It is from start to finish untrue and you know it." Frick then quoted back much of what Carnegie had written to Phipps. "Why do you write such stuff? . . . I desired to quietly withdraw, doing as little harm as possible to the interests of others, because I had become tired of your business methods, your absurd newspaper interviews and personal remarks and unwarranted interference in matters you knew nothing about. It has been your custom for years when any of your partners disagreed with you to say they were unwell needed a change, etc. I warn you to carry this no further with me but come forward like a man and purchase my interest, and let us part before it becomes impossible to continue to be friends."[53]

Instead of apologizing or explaining away what he had said—how could he?—Carnegie continued on the offensive. "Of course some mistake has happened about letter to Mr. Phipps," he wrote at once. "Perhaps what I scribbled was not sent to him at all—I probably wrote him a cooler statement—I believe I did. I cannot understand it. . . . What I scribbled I don't know, but still, <u>my friend</u>, I do know you will recognize in it one who likes you and values you." As he proceeded, Carnegie became angrier and angrier at the man he had tried so hard to befriend.

> In the most sacred manner I asked if I might speak as a friend which I said was to be held sacred—you agreed—I did,—and judge my surprise—You disregarded your obligation and told it <u>as a charge</u> I had made about you— I spoke as your best friend and <u>you knew it</u>. Wrong I may be, there may be nothing in it. You may have been yourself during your visit here—so be it—think so if you can but at the same time believe there may be something in it—I am not alone wrong, if wrong—Now I wish to be friends as much as you do. . . . It is simply ridiculous, my dear Mr. Frick, that any full grown man is not to make the acquaintance of Mr. Rainey, or anybody else, without your august permission—really laughable—but I did not do it till you had given approval. No use corresponding any more. You are determined to resign. All right. I am forced to agree that the work of the Carnegie Steel Company and the Frick Coke Company is too much for any man. . . . No one values you more highly as a <u>partner</u>, but as for being Czar and expecting a man shall not differ with you and criticize you, No. Find a slave elsewhere, I can only be a man and a friend.

He signed himself, "Your friend still, Andrew Carnegie."[54]

Five days later, in Pittsburgh, at a special meeting of the board of managers with Carnegie and Lauder in attendance, Frick formally tendered his resignation as chief executive officer of Carnegie Steel. The resignation was accepted at a second meeting a few days later. Carnegie took back 5 percent of Frick's stock, relieving him of the debt he had carried to pay for it, then turned 3 percent over to John Leishman, who succeeded Frick as president. Frick remained in place as chairman of the board.

In the end, what is most remarkable is that after all this turmoil and mutual recrimination, the situation at Carnegie Steel remained much the same. Frick resigned from his position as president of Carnegie Steel in 1895, but he did not leave the firm entirely. On the contrary, he retained his position as chairman of the board of managers and continued to exercise a considerable degree of power. "As you know," Frick wrote Jay Morse at Illinois Steel, on January 11, the day the new arrangements were formally approved, "I have for a long time been anxious to be relieved of a great deal of detail work in connection with the Steel Company, and have at last been able to bring it around pleasantly. I enclose (for your eyes only), and which return after you have read, the changes we have adopted. . . . I shall take the same interest in the concern as I have heretofore done. Mr. Leishman will fill the position of President."[55]

Neither Frick nor Carnegie was willing, in the final resort, to sever their ties with one another. Carnegie could ill afford to lose the talents of so remarkable a businessman as Henry Clay Frick. Frick, for his part, had no choice but to remain an officer of Carnegie Steel, if only to protect his 6 percent share of the company—and his coke company which remained, in all but name, a subsidiary of Carnegie Steel.

TWENTY-SEVEN

Sixty Years Old, 1895–1896

Approaching his sixtieth birthday, Andrew Carnegie looked very much as he had at fifty and would at seventy. His hair and beard were entirely white and closely trimmed; his eyes piercing and alert; his physique that of a man in excellent health.

He had not changed his daily routines in twenty years. He began every morning at his writing desk, with a secretary at his side to take dictation and type up his letters. He regularly shared his unsolicited views on matters of domestic and international affairs with John Morley, William Gladstone, Lord Salisbury, Lord Rosebery, Joseph Chamberlain, Arthur Balfour, and James Bryce in Britain, and with whoever happened to be in the White House or heading up the State Department in Washington. His dear friend James G. Blaine was no longer on the scene as Republican power broker in chief and secretary of state, but Carnegie enjoyed almost equally strong ties with the Republican secretaries of state who succeeded him, including John Foster, John Sherman, John Hay, Elihu Root, and Philander Knox, his former attorney in Pittsburgh.

Beginning in the winter of 1895, much of his letterwriting had to do with the boundary dispute between Britain and Venezuela. For more than fifty years, Venezuela had protested what it considered to be Britain's inclusion of Venezuelan territory in British Guiana; for the past twenty, it had petitioned the United States for assistance in settling the border dispute. Finally, in 1895, Congress, claiming that the Monroe Doctrine authorized it to intervene in the matter, passed a resolution calling on the British government to submit the dispute to impartial international arbitration. President Cleveland directed his secretary of state, Richard Olney, to draft a diplomatic note to the British foreign secretary, reinforcing Congress's call for arbitration. Lord Salisbury, who happened to be both British prime minister and foreign secretary, had ten years earlier declined a similar request for arbitration. This time around, Salisbury again refused arbitration, asserting that Britain did not recognize the applicability of the Monroe Doctrine that Olney had asserted bound the United States to protect Venezuela. President Cleveland's response was to increase the tension by asking for congressional authority to appoint an American commission to determine the rightful boundary between Venezuela and British Guiana, the implication being that when the boundary line was fixed, the American government would recognize it.

Though war with Britain over Venezuela was a preposterous idea at a time when the United States had three warships to Britain's fifty, that did not stop Henry Cabot Lodge and Theodore Roosevelt from arguing that the Monroe Doctrine must be defended at all costs. "'Personally I rather hope the fight will come soon,' Roosevelt wrote Lodge. . . . 'The clamor of the peace faction has convinced me that the country needs a war. Let the fight come if it must; I don't care whether our sea coast cities are bombarded or not; we would take Canada.'"[1]

As rhetoric on both sides escalated, William James at Harvard attempted to insert some reason into the discussion. In letters to the *Crimson*, influential friends, and his congressman, James criticized both President Cleveland's "fearful blunder" and the almost unanimous support his bellicose message had received from press and politicians. Reasoned analysis and discourse, James charged, had given way to frenzied, impulsive, and dangerous threats to international peace—and over a simple border dispute.[2]

Carnegie joined James and others in the "peace faction" that Roosevelt so detested. The border crisis in Venezuela was tailor-made for his intervention, or so he believed. He had influential friends on both sides of the Atlantic, access to major organs of opinion, and an intuitive understanding of public opinion in Britain and the United States. In separate letters to the editors of the *New York Sun* and the *The Times of London,* he pleaded with both sides to listen to reason. He exhorted the British people to pressure their government to accept the American offer of arbitration, while cautioning Americans that the Europeans were in the final stages of their exit from the western hemisphere and, if left alone, would leave peaceably. "Let us recognize the position of these old lands, which so recently possessed the American Continent, and treat them with all the patience and courtesy possible, making their exit as little distressful to them as we can."[3]

When the British government continued to reject calls for arbitration, Carnegie changed his tune and singled out the British for their intransigence. In a lengthy article entitled "The Venezuelan Question," published in February 1896 in the *North American Review,* he accomplished the near-impossible feat of defending British imperialism in theory while criticizing it in practice. He began by acknowledging that "the English-speaking race is the 'boss' race of the world. It can acquire, can colonize, can rule. . . . The action of the race in the old home and in the new in regard to territorial acquisition has . . . been precisely the same. The mother has dominated or acquired almost everything with which she has come in contact and which she coveted, and the son [the United States] has been no discredit to his mother in the same line. It is a root passion, some of us think a prerogative, of our race to acquire territory."[4]

The means by which this territory had been acquired—by both Americans and British—was not always legal or strictly moral, but this was not to be regretted. "The management of the land acquired by our race has been best for the higher interests of humanity. It is an evolution, the fittest driving out the least fit; the best supplanting the inferior; and the interests of civilization rendered the acquisition of the land necessary. It was right and proper that the nomadic Indian should give place to the settled husbandman in the prairies of the East; it is also well that the Maori should fade away, and give place to the intelligent, industrious citizen, a member of our race." Carnegie had no intention of holding Great Britain up "to peculiar opprobrium for playing the wolf to the Venezuelan lamb."[5]

What he objected to was that the British had rejected out of hand McKinley's request that the boundary dispute be submitted to arbitration. For Carnegie, the principle of peaceable arbitration was—and he fully understood the irony here—a cause worth going to war over. He had, he declared in his article, recently resigned as vice president of the Peace Society because he could not its accept its "peace at any price" principles. "Peaceful arbitration is one of the few causes for which it is not only justifiable, but a duty to fight. . . . If ever the industrial, peace-loving Republic has to draw the sword, may it be in vindication of peaceful arbitration, in international disputes, the Christian substitute for barbarous war."[6]

No swords would be drawn. With more serious issues to contend with in Europe, Lord Salisbury backed away from his refusal to arbitrate, and Cleveland and Olney tempered their rhetoric. The crisis environment dissipated almost as rapidly as it had taken shape.

While the subject of arbitration was removed from the public agenda, however, it continued to preoccupy Carnegie, whose goal now was to get the United States and Britain to sign a formal treaty, pledging each nation to submit all future disputes to impartial arbitration. When William Dodge, the president of a new society "formed in the United States to labor for the completion of a general treaty of arbitration between the two branches of our race," asked for his support, Carnegie enthusiastically sent off letters to the influential British politicians he was in contact with, including Balfour, Chamberlain, Gladstone, Rosebery, and Morley, formally introducing them to Mr. Dodge.[7]

From Italy where he, Louise, and Stella vacationed in May and June 1896, and Cluny, where they spent the summer and fall, Carnegie waged his campaign, entreating his friends in high places to exert pressure on Salisbury to publicly declare himself—and the British government—in favor of an arbitration treaty. "Truly this Arbitration [as a substitute] for War," he wrote Gladstone, "seems to me the noblest question of our time & I do wish that you could have put your stamp upon it now." When John Morley published an article in favor of arbitration, Carnegie praised him to the skies. "Never have I a read a stronger article. . . . It is so calm, yet so clear and decided, that it must strongly affect Lord Salisbury. . . . I wish Mr. Gladstone could be induced to support your view. . . . I feel that it is the most important step forward that our race can take in our day."[8]

IN THE AFTERMATH of the Homestead strike, Carnegie had lowered his public profile. In November 1895, within days of celebrating his sixtieth birthday and exactly three years after the Amalgamated had called off its strike, he marked his return to public life by taking the train to Pittsburgh to preside over the opening of his monumental new library.[9]

The dedication was held in the Music Hall portion of the building on November 5. The festivities began just after 8:30 P.M. with the solemn entrance onto the stage of the platform party, each man—and they were all men—bowing to the audience as he entered and took his seat. After a brief invocation by the Episcopal bishop, Carnegie was formally introduced and gave the speech he had that afternoon distributed to the newspapers in time to make the next day's front pages. He began, somewhat defensively, by announcing that he was speaking at the request of the trustees, who desired that he "state the reasons" and the "objects which I had in view" in donating money for the Pittsburgh library. He recapitulated in brilliantly concise and incisive prose the principles he had earlier laid out in his "Gospel of Wealth" articles, defending himself from his critics as he did so.

It was inevitable, he argued, that "surplus wealth must sometimes flow into the hands of the few. . . . To one to whom surplus comes, there come also the questions: What is my duty? What is the best use that can be made of it?" Carnegie had determined early in life that he had no call on this surplus as an individual, but that it had been given him as "a sacred trust, to be administered during life . . . for the best good of my fellow-men." He asked now to be judged by the uses to which he put his money: "the enlightenment and the joys of the mind . . . the things of the spirit . . . all that tends to bring into the lives of the toilers of Pittsburgh sweetness and light." He had built a library to foster a taste for reading, learning, and self-improvement; a museum with plaster casts of the "world's master-pieces of sculpture," so that those who could not travel abroad could enjoy and learn from these rarest, "most interesting and instructive objects"; an art gallery because there was "no surer means of improving the tastes of men . . . than through color and the sense of beauty"; and a Music Hall to spread among the masses of the people "the appreciation and the love of music" which the more prosperous already enjoyed. His objective was to provide the "masses" with cultural benefits that, until then, had been reserved for the wealthy. "If Library, Hall, Gallery or Museum be not popular and attract the manual toilers, and benefit them, it will have failed in its mission; for it was chiefly for the wage-earners that it was built by one who was himself a wage-earner, and who has the good of that class greatly at heart."

After "great and prolonged applause," Carnegie was followed to the podium by William N. Frew, the president of the library board of trustees, who announced that Carnegie had established a $1 million endowment for the galleries and museum, thus bringing "the total of Mr. Carnegie's gifts . . . in round numbers, to five million dollars." Then it was the turn of the governor, the mayor, and the local congressman to shower the donor with praise. The governor and mayor were mercifully concise; Congress-man Dalzell, the last speaker, went on forever, recalling in florid language the glories of Pittsburgh, republican institutions, and Andrew Carnegie. "There are unnumbered hearts here and elsewhere, in this, the land of his adoption, and across seas in the land of his birth, that beat to the measure of 'God bless Andrew Carnegie,' and hearts shall continue thus to beat through generations yet unborn and by us unnumbered."

For the moment at least, the ghosts of Edgar Thomson and Home-stead, of the vanquished Knights and the Amalgamated, were put to rest. After three years of virtual silence, much of it spent overseas, Carnegie had come home a hero and would venture forth in triumph. He had, as it were, bought himself absolution—or at least forgetfulness, which amounted to the same.

Pittsburgh was already established as the nation's premier industrial city and Carnegie's name indelibly associated with it. Just as he was not content to be regarded only as a businessman, so too did he not want his American hometown to be known only for its smokestacks. His goal, as he would write William Frew in 1897, was that "not only our own country, but the civilized world will take note of the fact that our Dear Old Smoky Pittsburgh, no longer content to be celebrated only as one of the chief manufacturing centres, has entered upon the path to higher things, and is before long, as we thoroughly believe, also to be noted for her preeminence in the Arts and Sciences."[10]

He would continue to contribute his money—and his ideas—toward this goal for the rest of his life. In 1896, he appointed John Beatty, the sec-retary of the Art Society of Pittsburgh and the director of the Pittsburgh School of Design, to head up the institute's fine arts department. Beatty's first task—and, from this point on perhaps his most important, certainly his most public—was to organize the Pittsburgh art show, the precursor of what would become known as the Carnegie *International*.

Unlike his colleague Henry Frick and the majority of his wealthy con-temporaries, Carnegie had no reverence for the old masters or contempo-rary European artists. He intended, instead, to make his Pittsburgh art gallery the first museum of modern American art. In his "deed of trust," he provided for the establishment of a "Chronological Collection, intended to represent the progress of painting in America, beginning with the year 1896." Prizes would be offered for the two oil paintings by American artists judged "of the highest artistic merit, and worthy to represent the best American art of the year." These works would be purchased for the gallery's permanent collection; runners-up would be exhibited annually in what was, at the time, "the single largest art event in the United States." The first prizewinner—and the first oil painting purchased for the permanent collection—was Winslow Homer's *The Wreck*.[11]

One hundred and fifty-four artists were represented in the 1896 exhibition, but only sixty of them were American, and only thirty from Pennsylvania. This was not what Carnegie had intended, as he made clear to William Frew, the day after the opening. "I cannot but think that [Mr. Beatty] devoted too much attention to the foreign pictures, while the primary object of the Exhibition is to encourage American Art. . . . The absence of the most noted American artists is very marked." Carnegie was also disappointed by the lack of attention his Pittsburgh exhibition had received in the national press. There had not been "the slightest mention in any of the papers here [in New York] this morning. . . . The public sentiment is all right in Pittsburgh, but it now remains to bring the Exhibition before the country."*[12]

THE SECOND, but not less important, component of the Carnegie library complex was the Museum of Natural History. In 1898, Carnegie appointed William J. Holland, a former minister, zoologist, and the chancellor of Western University of Pennsylvania, as director. His initial charge was to "develop collections representative of the Appalachian region," but Holland quickly broadened his mission, with Carnegie's approval. He purchased the collection of the Academy of Science and Art of Pittsburgh and supplemented it with gifts from Carnegie, including two mummies he had brought back from Egypt and a collection of anatomical models from Paris.

If the Museum of Natural History was going to be, as Carnegie intended, a world-class institution, it needed more than mummies, ana-

---

*For the new few years, the annual exhibition would veer back and forth between being a showcase for American artists and an exhibition of the year's best paintings regardless of nationality. Despite Carnegie's wishes, the directors and judges would, in rather short order, open the exhibit to non-American artists. Over the next century and more, the Carnegie *International* would present the best in contemporary paintings, sculpture, and, more recently, video and photographic artists, to Pittsburgh audiences.

tomical models, and Appalachian minerals. It had to have a dinosaur or two. The dinosaur was more than simply a crowd-pleaser. For Carnegie and other devotees of evolutionary science, it was an apt symbol of the unpredictability of a universe in which species and races fell into extinction when they failed to adapt to new environments. For men of slight stature, such as Carnegie, there must have been something quite enthralling about this most vivid demonstration that size and power did not guarantee survival.

In December 1898, William Randolph Hearst's *New York Journal* ran a full-page story on the discovery of the bones of the "Most Colossal Animal Ever on Earth" in Wyoming. Carnegie determined at once to bring them to Pittsburgh. "My Lord—can't you <u>buy</u> this for Pittsburgh—try," he wrote Holland, enclosing the clipping. "Wyoming State University isn't rich—<u>get an offer</u>—hurry."[13]

Holland contacted William Reed, the Wyoming man who claimed to have found the dinosaur bones. He assured Carnegie that he could get the dinosaur for Pittsburgh, but it was going to "cost some time, labor, and money." Excavating the dinosaur would be only the beginning. Carnegie would have to come up with the funds to build a great hall "for the display of such a monster." "See what you can do," Carnegie wrote back. "I should like to do the Colossal [build a new hall] for the Colossal by the Colossal Lord Chancellor [Carnegie had begun to refer jokingly to Chancellor Holland as Lord Chancellor]."[14]

In March 1899, Holland took the train to Wyoming to meet with Reed. He discovered that the land on which the bones had been found was claimed by the University of Wyoming. When he tried to arrange a sale of the claim, the Wyoming officials turned him down flat. So he did what experienced miners—for minerals or dinosaurs—do in such cases; he filed a competing land claim.

With the tenacity of a bulldog and Carnegie's money behind him, William Holland eventually secured the rights to the claim, stole the American Museum of Natural History's top paleontologist, and dispatched a full crew of scientists, assistants, and cowboy-laborers to excavate the Wyoming bone fields. The bones were cleaned, labeled, and photographed; saturated in gum Arabic; wrapped in tissue paper, then wrapped again in plaster-soaked burlap; packed into wooden crates that had been lined with hay; hoisted onto a horse-drawn wagon; and driven to the Union

Pacific siding, where they were loaded onto freight cars for shipment to Pittsburgh.[15]

In mid-October 1899, the first freight car arrived in Pittsburgh. By mid-May of 1900, enough bones had been pried lose of their bandages, cleaned, studied, and assembled to allow the museum's new chief paleontologist to draw a full skeleton, though with the wrong cervical vertebrae attached. The drawing of what was now known as *Diplodocus carnegii* was framed and sent to Scotland for Carnegie to display.

It had become clear to everyone involved that the dinosaur model, when finally assembled, was going to be too large to fit in the space assigned to the natural history museum. The only solution was to enlarge the building, which was fine with Carnegie. Frew, the president of what was now known as the Carnegie Institute, was delegated to oversee the design and construction of the new building. It was no easy assignment. Carnegie, who on these matters professed—rightly—to know more about real estate and construction than Frew did, ridiculed almost every recommendation Frew offered to him. Why, he wanted to know, was Frew even considering building in a new location, instead of adding an extension at the old one? And didn't Frew know that it was impossible to build a hall that was suitable for both orchestral music and grand opera? In the end, the Music Hall would be the only component of the institute that was not enlarged.[16]

Frew persevered and the plans for the new building were, after much give-and-take, approved by Carnegie, who, on selling Carnegie Steel in 1901, donated an additional $5 million for construction. When the building was completed in 1907, Carnegie doubled the endowment of what was now known as the Carnegie Institute from $4 to $8 million.[17]

IF SOMEONE had told Carnegie ten or twenty years earlier that, at age sixty, he would still be tied to his Pittsburgh businesses, he would have scoffed aloud. But Frick's change of title and responsibilities had left a hole in the management of Carnegie Steel. Carnegie had trusted Frick more than he could imagine trusting any successor. Now that Frick had given up the day-to-day management of the firm, Carnegie felt obligated to pay more careful attention.

The business had been designed to run much like the railroad, with department heads reporting to vice presidents who reported to a president who reported to a board. Unlike the railroads, however, Carnegie Steel was a partnership, not a corporation and, because it raised its investment capital internally, beholden not to outside financial interests and directors, but to the senior partner and majority stockholder. The Carnegie board was not, in name or function, a board of directors, but a "board of managers" comprised of the nine men who occupied the most critical management positions in the firm. Every member of the board was a partner, but together they controlled a small minority of the stock. The two largest stockholders, Carnegie and Harry Phipps, were not board members and did not attend board meetings.

The month after Frick stepped down, Carnegie instructed Francis Lovejoy, the board secretary, to rewrite the company's by-laws, in consultation with Philander Knox, the firm's chief counsel. He wanted everything done precisely by the books, so whatever happened next, there would be no legal trouble. The new by-laws should, he instructed Lovejoy, provide Carnegie, as majority stockholder, with veto power over board decisions and full, precise minutes of the proceedings of board meetings. "Some suggestions I made to Mr. Frick are, I think, important: that the votes of each member, pro and con, in the Board shall be recorded; that no new undertakings be gone into except by a two-third majority of the total number of the Board, nor new methods adopted."[18]

Later that year, Carnegie reminded Lovejoy that the minutes should not only record every member's vote on every issue, but "in addition to this . . . any reason or explanation which a member desires to give for his vote. If this were properly done, then any of us looking over the Minutes would be able to judge of the judgment displayed by the voter, which of course, would affect his standing with his colleagues. It would bring responsibility home to him direct, and I do not see any other way that will enable us to judge whether any of our partners has good judgment or not. . . . The minutes cannot err in being too full, the fuller the better. They can err in being too much curtailed."[19]

Carnegie gave the board the right to make decisions, but insisted that it understand he had veto power over those decisions, should he care to exercise it. The minutes, with verbatim reports on what each board member said, were the vehicles through which he kept track of the decision-making process. He went through the minutes of each meeting with pencil in hand, providing "thoughts on the minutes" in the margins and in long memos that he forwarded to Pittsburgh to be distributed to board members.

He kept abreast of recent developments in Pittsburgh through letters from Frick, who, having resigned as president, oversaw long-range projects as chairman of the board of managers. He received as well annual and biannual financial reports from Carnegie Steel and H. C. Frick Coke and monthly statements on profits and loss, disposition of profits, stock of materials on hand, frieght tonnage into and out of the plants, and pig iron production and coke consumption for each furnace.

Carnegie welcomed the give-and-take of long-distance debate and had no problem with partners who disagreed with him, as long as they provided facts, figures, and analyses to back up their conclusions. When, in January 1896, he discovered that the company had bought "two bankrupt furnaces" without his explicit approval, he was outraged. "I leave you to imagine how unsatisfactory it is to have such surprises sprung upon one." In a sharply worded letter to John Leishman, Carnegie protested against what he took to be "an unwarranted stretch of authority upon the part of yourself and the other members of the Board and certainly a violation of every sound principle governing business affairs. I am sorry to have to write this, but I cannot live and have the C.S. Co. degraded to the level of speculators and Jim Cracks, men who pass as manufacturers, but who look to the market and not to manufacturing, and who buy up bankrupt concerns, only to show their incapacity."[20]

Within a year, Leishman had been relieved of his duties. He was replaced by Charlie Schwab, Carnegie's fair-haired boy, who, still only thirty-five years of age, could be molded into the type of executive Carnegie needed to run his companies. The way to Carnegie's heart, Charlie Schwab discovered, was to give him information. On taking office, Schwab arranged to meet weekly with the mill superintendents, detailed minutes of which were dispatched to Carnegie. These meetings, Carnegie wrote Schwab with evident delight, were "one of the best ideas that has ever entered your fertile brain."[21]

It was not easy working for Carnegie. In August 1897, Schwab recommended and the board unanimously approved spending $1 million for improvements at Homestead and Duquesne, the broad outlines of which Carnegie had already agreed to. When Carnegie received the minutes with the decision, he assailed all the board members, but particularly Schwab, for having approved the request without sufficient debate. "A very large question is presented to us which should receive <u>months of study</u> . . . I am not to be considered as deciding that the proposed changes are not desirable; I have had no opportunity to form a judgment upon the subject, but this I do venture to submit to the Board . . . that no such important steps should be taken in haste. There does not seem to be much use in sending copies of Minutes to absent partners, if great questions are to be summarily disposed of." The board members were astounded at Carnegie's overreaction. They had approved the resolution without debate because there was nothing controversial in it—and nothing that had not been gone over in advance and met with Carnegie's approval. Frick spoke for them all when he declared, knowing that his words would be forwarded with the next set of minutes to Scotland, that he feared Mr. Carnegie "did not read very carefully the Resolution covering this matter."[22]

Carnegie would not let go. He conceded that Schwab's proposal was a sound one—and should have been passed by the board—but objected to the way Schwab had presented it. "Even if the President is right, his mode of action was wrong. Any plan involving a serious change in the Works, product, or methods, should be submitted to the Board not for action, but first for study and discussion, and no action taken until all the parties have expressed their views after time taken for study. . . . Would the Secretary kindly refer to the By-laws of the Company, and read to the Board and have entered in the Minutes, that portion regarding important changes in machinery or methods. I think these require a two-thirds vote of the stockholders. This important step was decided with seventy five percent of the shareholders [Carnegie and Phipps] having no chance to express an opinion. . . . These are a few of the points that occur to me as valuable for my partners to consider, and hence they are submitted with all due deference. Hearty congratulations upon August net. Great."[23]

In a private communication to Schwab, Carnegie continued his barrage: "My dear young friend, you say you will answer any list of questions I may ask, but why should a report of a President, recommending an investment, render questions necessary? The report should be full, accurate; fact, not opinions, or impressions: really you do not do yourself justice in the apparent 'slapdash' manner in which you recommend this to the Board."[24]

Schwab, who had been president of Carnegie Steel for less than six months, responded with a thirteen-page letter and report which gave the senior partner the information he needed. Carnegie thanked him, congratulated him on being such a "hustler," and approved the proposal. He did not apologize for the tongue-lashing.[25]

Schwab had erred in presuming that he could judge what Carnegie wanted. He would not make that mistake again.

TWENTY-EIGHT

"An Impregnable Position,"
1896–1898

USINESS does not look well, but what can we expect? Nothing till the Presidential election is over, and the Silver Agitation with it—I hope." So Carnegie wrote Frick on June 27, 1896.[1]

It had become apparent to him that William Jennings Bryan was going to win the Democratic nomination for president on the promise that, if elected, he would move the country off the gold standard. Carnegie was aghast at the prospect. Investors needed both stability and liquidity: gold provided them with both. As long as the United States remained on the gold standard, American manufacturing would remain a safe harbor for domestic and foreign investment. If the nation replaced gold with silver as the basis for its currency, the result would be nothing less than catastrophic. Or so Carnegie believed and had been writing since 1891.

As business slumped in the spring and summer of 1896, Carnegie attributed it to fears that Bryan might be elected on a silver platform. "You see what the Silver Craze is bringing," he wrote Frick from Cluny in late July. "I have, as you know, been anxious about it for years. My belief is, that the canvass [campaign] will weaken Bryan. But it is not enough to beat him to satisfy capital; I am afraid it will be timid for a long time, and therefore, that business will be very dull."[2]

In June and October, Carnegie attacked Bryan, the Democrats, and the "silver craze" in articles in the *North American Review*. He also contributed generously to the McKinley campaign war chest. Carnegie and Frick had done business with Marcus Hanna, the Cleveland iron and coal merchant, who had become McKinley's chief adviser and fund-raiser. Hanna and McKinley were their kind of Republicans: stolidly conservative and

committed to protective tariffs and gold. When J. P. Morgan resisted contributing because he feared McKinley was not enough of a "gold bug,"
Carnegie offered to talk to him. Hanna was delighted. "I am only too glad
to avail myself of your kind offer to put in a good word for us—You will
know how to do it so that it will not appear that I am soliciting influence."[3]

William Jennings Bryan was young, attractive, and dynamic, in sharp
contrast to the dour McKinley. Still, Carnegie was convinced that his popularity would tumble over the next three months, as the Republicans, utilizing their enormous advantage in funds and their control of most of the
nation's newspapers, hammered away at his youth, his radicalism, his inexperience, and his agrarianism. "The political situation in the United States
is sadly mixed," Carnegie confided to Morley on August 1, "still, I do not
believe that the Silver Craze can stand the three months pounding that it
is to receive previous to the vote. I am busy preparing ammunition for the
campaign; short paragraphs for the wage-earners, whose votes are to decide the issue."[4]

On July 22, he published in the *New York Times* and *New York Tribune*
a letter to the editor attacking Bryan on the currency question. Three weeks
later, he expanded on it in the draft of a campaign pamphlet he forwarded
to Hanna. "All that is needed to bring the wage-earners, that is, the masses
of the voters, into line against silver, is to have leaflets printed by the
hundred-thousand, and a copy given to each workingman in every mill,
factory and farm in the doubtful states. I have tried my hand at a leaflet,
and if your literary bureau publishes it . . . I will pay the cost. . . . Do not
be discouraged, the Bryan Boom is bound to burst. It is not founded either
upon fact or reason." Hanna accepted Carnegie's offer. In mid-October, he
reported back that the Republican National Committee had printed and
circulated five million copies of Carnegie's leaflet.[5]

Carnegie was convinced that Bryan would be defeated, but he worried
nonetheless about the long-term effects of the politicization of the currency issue. European capitalists could not help but be frightened by the
possibility that, if not in 1896, then perhaps in 1900 or 1904, a Democrat
would be elected on a silver platform and take the nation off the gold standard. On August 6, he expressed his fears in a letter to the members of the
Carnegie Steel board of managers, who, he feared, were not paying sufficient attention to the looming crisis. Anticipating a fall panic, precipitated
by a flight of capital and followed by plummeting prices, he urged the board

to sell off whatever product the company had on hand and hoard its dollars for the coming crisis. "There is no telling but that our resources may be strained to the utmost, and every dollar will count."[6]

Two weeks later, Carnegie cautioned his Pittsburgh executives again against taking Bryan's defeat for granted. He urged them not to renew the "bonus" that had been given the steelworkers the year before. "The political situation seems to have taken a decided turn for the better; but until McKinley is elected, there is danger of excitement and panic at any time."[7]

By late September, he was sure that Bryan would be defeated. "The majority of the popular vote will be enormous for McKinley, the largest ever obtained by any candidate," he "prophesied" for Henry Yates Thompson, the owner of the *Pall Mall Gazette;* "perhaps, he will have the largest majority in the Electoral College. The Bryan Campaign promises to collapse. Once more virtue triumphs in the Republic."[8]

His predictions were born out on November 3, when William McKinley was elected with 272 electoral college votes to 176 for Bryan. McKinley's margin in the popular vote was 610,000, but Bryan had polled almost 6.5 million votes, more than any other Democratic in history.

The silver menace has been defeated in battle, but the war was still to be definitively won. In a final, post-election attempt to bludgeon Bryan and his pro-silver forces into permanent silence, Carnegie published "Mr. Bryan the Conjurer" in the January 1897 *North American Review.* After twelve pages of accusing Bryan of the usually incompatible crimes of chicanery and stupidity, Carnegie saluted him (and his loyal wife) for being "models of purity in their simple lives"—and then wished them a well-deserved and, he hoped, permanent retirement to their "Sweet, humble, loving home."[9]

THERE WERE many reasons why Carnegie continued to put off retirement: primary among them his love of competition and his commitment to making more money so that he would have more to give away. His Pittsburgh plants were now the marvel of the industry, their productivity higher, their costs much lower than their competitors'. The coke problem had been solved long ago with the purchase of a majority share in H. C. Frick Coke. The major challenge now facing the company was ensuring itself an adequate supply of high-quality, low-cost iron ore.

Carnegie and his partners had declined to join in the "iron rush" that had taken off in the late 1880s with the discovery of soft sandlike iron ore in the Mesabi Range in northeastern Minnesota, about 100 miles from Duluth. Carnegie had no intention of investing in iron-mining ventures hundreds of miles away. All the money earned in Pittsburgh was plowed back into the mills. In 1892, Harry Oliver, who had years before worked with Carnegie at O'Rielly Telegraph, offered him a share in a Mesabi iron mine he had invested in. Carnegie turned him down. He had no use for men like Oliver who, having made and lost fortunes in iron and railroads, were now speculating in mining properties. "Oliver's ore bargain is just like him—nothing in it," he wrote Frick on August 29, 1892. "If there is any department of business which offers no inducement, it is ore. It never has been very profitable, and the Massaba is not the last great deposit that Lake Superior is to reveal."[10]

Like other start-up businesses born in debt and requiring steady infusions of capital to survive, the mining companies and railroads that had been organized during the 1880s Mesabi iron rush were nearly destroyed in the Panic of 1893. John D. Rockefeller, who, according to Ron Chernow, "stumbled, almost by accident, into owning most of the iron ore on the Mesabi Range," stepped into the breach and bailed out the failing companies by loaning them money in return for stock. By the mid-1890s, he controlled "several million tons of iron ore and a railroad to cart it off" to Duluth. To transport the ore the next step of their journey, across the Great Lakes to the nation's steel mills, Rockefeller and his chief financial adviser, Frederick Gates, assembled a fleet of fifty-six oversized lake steamers.[11]

Harry Oliver, who had been steadily expanding his own holdings of mining properties, contacted Frick and Carnegie in the spring of 1894, fearful—and rightly—that Rockefeller would keep on buying Mesabi mines and railroads until he owned them all. Oliver offered Carnegie Steel a 50 percent interest in his Mesabi properties in return for a half-million-dollar loan. From Sorrento, in Italy, where he was vacationing that spring, Carnegie instructed Frick to open negotiations with Oliver "in view of threatened combination. . . . Remember Reckafellow* & Porter [a Rockefeller associate] will own the R.R. [that links the mines with the Duluth ports]

---

*Carnegie would, for the rest of his life, insist on misspelling Rockefeller's name in various ways.

and that's like owning the pipe lines—<u>Producers</u> will not have much of a show. We are big enough, however to take care of ourselves and if <u>forced</u> could make another outlet somehow [to transport the ore to Pittsburgh]. . . . It's a pity we have to go in at all, still I cannot but recognize we are right in flanking the combination as far as possible. . . . I don't think Standard people will succeed in making ore a monopoly like oil, they have failed in every new venture and Rockefeller's reputation now is one of the poorest investors in the world. His railroads are almost worthless."[12]

Within weeks of acquiring his half share in the Oliver Mining Company, Carnegie forced Oliver to give him another third. He did not trust Oliver as a manager and wanted majority ownership of the new mining property. Although now committed to the venture, he still had major misgivings about investing large sums of money in it. "If Massawba ore requires special form of furnaces, it will add force to my instinctive aversion to making investments hundreds of miles away. These, in my opinion, are all wrong. The ore mining business is a business by itself, and ten dollars can be made at home to any one that you can ever make in these outside ventures."[13]

Carnegie, despite his instincts, was being forced into the iron ore business as a defensive measure. He could not allow Rockefeller to continue to buy Mesabi mines, railroads, and lake steamers.

There were two explanations for Rockefeller's oversized investments in Mesabi iron ore. Either he had decided to go into the steel business for himself or he was intent on acquiring a monopoly position in iron ore and then forcing the steel manufacturers to share their profits with him. Either scenario would bring him into conflict with Carnegie.

Though Rockefeller had made his fortune and his reputation earlier than Carnegie, he was in fact four years younger. He looked much older. Tall, gaunt, hairless, and unsmiling, he resembled nothing less than a skeletal ghoul. Carnegie, on the contrary, was beginning to look more like a well-groomed Father Christmas, with a smile to match. By the mid-1890s, both were semiretired. Whereas Rockefeller had virtually retreated from active business affairs, however, leaving more responsibility to Gates, Carnegie still paid close attention to his business empire.

The oil baron and the steelmaker harbored no great affection for one another, but each respected the other's business organizations and commitments to philanthropy. They exchanged Christmas greetings and Carnegie made sure to send Rockefeller copies of his speeches and pamphlets. "I am pleased with the sentiments you give expression to," Rockefeller wrote Carnegie on receiving the address he delivered at the dedication of his Pittsburgh library. "I would that more men of wealth were doing as you are doing with your money; but, be assured, your example will bear fruits, and the time will come when men of wealth will more generally be willing to use it for the good of others. I had intended to call upon you to express my appreciation, or I would have written before."[14]

Rockefeller and Carnegie had achieved dominance in their respective industries by running roughshod over the competition. But they were smart enough to know that they were too evenly matched—in intellectual and financial resources—to enter into combat. It made more sense to combine than compete. Carnegie, having submitted Mesabi ore from Rockefeller's mine for testing in his Homestead open-hearth furnaces, and discovering that it burned cleanly, directed James Gayley, a former furnace superintendent and now a member of his board of managers, to "go and sleep in New York, and do not come home until you bring us a lease of the whole Rockefeller ore." It would be a lengthy negotiation, as neither John Leishman, who represented Carnegie, nor Frederick Gates, who negotiated for Rockefeller, wanted it said that their counterparts had gotten the better of them.[15]

On October 27, Carnegie recommended to Frick, who remained a master dealmaker, that the "Rockafellow negotiation should be hastened and proposition got for our consideration." Three days later, unwilling to let the negotiations drag on any longer, he wrote Rockefeller directly, suggesting that the two men close the deal by themselves. "Our people have been conferring with your Mr. Gates upon an alliance which would give us all the ores we can use from your properties. The differences between the two seems to have been so great as to cause a failure of the negotiations. They came to see me today and explained these differences, which do not seem to me too irreconcilable, if both parties realized as I do, the mutual advantage of such an alliance, and were prepared to meet each other halfway. When Mr. Gates submits the matter to you, as I suppose he will, and you concur in this, I believe you and I could fix it in a few minutes, and I shall be very glad to go and see you if you think it worth while to take the matter up. It is a big operation, and needs to be looked at in a broader light than either Mr. Gates or Mr. Leishman, perhaps, are justified in taking."[16]

By mid-November, Carnegie confided to Cousin Dod that the decision had been made to "align ourselves with Rockafellow—Oliver showed me yesterday a sketch of alliance which is good. Will get Messabi." The final agreement was signed in December 1896. Oliver Mining and Carnegie Steel, its parent company, took a fifty-year lease on the full output of all the Rockefeller mines for a royalty of twenty-five cents per ton, far below the market price. Carnegie Steel guaranteed, in turn, that it would ship all ore from the Lake Superior region, whether it came from the Rockefeller mines or elsewhere, on Rockefeller railroads and steamers. The two titans agreed not to compete with one another in the future: the Carnegie interests promised that they would neither lease nor purchase any new Mesabi mines for the length of the agreement, leaving the field open to Rockefeller to expand his holdings; Rockefeller, for his part, pledged that he would stay out of the steel business.[17]

"I am happy knowing that we are now secure in our ore supply," Carnegie wrote Frick nine months after the deal with Rockefeller. "This was the only element needed to give us an impregnable position. We can now figure cost within a trifle and take contracts ahead without danger." Though he had been hesitant, initially, to divert capital from steelmaking, he was now quite ready to acknowledge the benefits of vertical integration. "It is clear to me," he wrote his cousin Dod on New Year's Day 1898, "that profit is to be made in steel manufacturing only by the concerns which do every step in the process themselves."[18]

Though the deal benefited both men, Carnegie, testifying in 1912 before the congressional committee investigating U.S. Steel, could not help but gloat over the price he had negotiated for the iron ore. "Don't you know, it does my heart good to think I got ahead of John D. Rockefeller on a bargain. . . . This is the only time I really did get ahead of my fellow millionaire." He had, he told the committee, cheerfully digressing from the business at hand, recently visited with Rockefeller, who had given him and Mrs. Carnegie "large photographs" of himself. "Positively, it is a delight to meet the old gentleman. But I did not refer to the ore purchases that I made from him." Carnegie's jest about getting the best of Rockefeller was front-page news across the country the next day, with the cartoonists having a field day picturing the two tycoons locked in combat.[19]

The two men had, in fact, become more friendly with the passage of time, as each moved further away from business and into philanthropy and golf. Carnegie kept sending Rockefeller his publications and books he thought "the old man" would find informative; they also exchanged holiday gifts. In February 1903, Rockefeller, on blue stationery, in tight, almost perfect handwriting with only a hint of a flourish, thanked Carnegie for his latest gift of "the oatmeal of your own manufacture. . . . It is very good and I hope you enjoy the eating of it as much as I do. Be sure to eat it very slowly, and masticate well, (Mrs. Carnegie will explain). You grind oatmeal; I grind apples, and have ordered a bottle of my sweet cider sent you from Pocantico. Keep right on with your grand work of giving away money, regardless of the criticisms of cranks and fools. You have already given away more money than any man living. The good Lord bless you and give you wisdom for your great responsibilities."[20]

"The precious cider has arrived," Carnegie replied,

been drunk and "your good health and all your families" proposed and enthusiastically hailed—verdict rendered by Mrs. Carnegie (whose favorite tipple is cider) best ever tasted. Many thanks. I note what you say about giving as none knows more about that than yourself. "The way of the giver is hard" like that of the transgressor but you and I don't give for applause, nor to please any body of men, or any man but ourselves, what we see to be for good of others, therefore criticism and mean flings don't pierce the skin and we go on—our own reproach alone we fear—that's my talisman. If I please myself I'll have to do much better than ever. Nobody abuses me as keenly as I do myself. I know more faults in myself than all the outsiders do. I played 18 holes St. Andrews [his club in Hastings-on-Hudson] yesterday, Saturday not Sunday. When you return I'll be glad to go and have a round on your links. I wish we could get to see more of each other and our respective wives also become friends not mere acquaintances. Do come and spend two weeks at Skibo, then we should be friends ever after. Your kind [do] not like fashion and smartness, neither do we—Here's my hand, let us be friends. . . . P.S. That's a boy you've got. Took to him first interview. Kind greetings to Mrs. Rockefeller.[21]

CARNEGIE's second major project in the mid-1890s, which he pursued simultaneously with his negotiations with Rockefeller, was the construction of a new railroad that would link his Pittsburgh mills with the Conneaut

Harbor on Lake Erie, the final destination for the Great Lakes steamers with their shipments of Mesabi iron ore.

After twenty years of battling with the Pennsylvania Railroad for lower freight rates for iron ore running south and coke running north, he was ready to invest whatever money it took to provide his own transportation networks. "Railroad Companies simply charge 'what the traffic will bear,'" he wrote Frick in February of 1896. "I do not blame [them] for combining and getting the best rates they can from us. . . . I am sure that you feel with me that if we were in [PR president] Mr. Roberts' place, it is very probable we should do exactly as he does. . . . I would not reduce rates until I thought it was necessary." The only long-term solution was to find an alternate way to move materials into and out of Pittsburgh. Carnegie toyed with the idea of getting the federal government to finance a canal between Lake Erie and Pittsburgh. "If we elect a Republican President, as I think we shall by an immense majority, it is probable that we shall get our bill through for a canal from Pittsburgh to Lake Erie."[22]

The canal idea was, Carnegie knew, rather far-fetched. It would in the long run be simpler, if more costly, to build a railroad linking the Union Railroad, the privately held road that connected the Carnegie Steel plants in Pittsburgh, to Conneaut on Lake Erie, the port of delivery for iron ore shipments, and Connellsville and its coke ovens to the southeast. All that was required was a great deal of capital. Carnegie, having long ago decided that it was best to put all his eggs into one basket, was reluctant to go into the railroad business, but recognized that he might have no choice if he were to gain the leverage he needed to force the Pennsylvania to lower its rates.

In January 1896, he signed a tentative agreement with the president of the small railroad company that owned the ramshackle road from Lake Erie to Butler, Pennsylvania, about thirty miles north of Braddock. The two agreed to enlarge and extend the railroad between Pittsburgh and Conneaut. He simultaneously launched discussions on building a thirty-mile spur to link Connellsville with the Carnegie plants in Pittsburgh.

In February, James McCrea, the Pennsylvania Railroad vice president in charge of roads west of Pittsburgh, wrote to ask Frick to intervene and ask Carnegie to halt construction of the northern link and planning for the southern. "I suggested," Frick wrote Carnegie, that "if he would address a letter to me, stating his position, and what the roads under their control proposed to do [in lowering freight rates], I would see what could be done to prevent its construction. Said he would be glad of an opportunity of doing so."[23]

Carnegie's bluff had paid off. Pennsylvania Railroad officials volunteered to negotiate lower freight rates if Carnegie Steel would pledge to abandon any plans to build new railroads. Frick, as chairman, presented the deal to the Carnegie Steel board of managers and telegraphed Carnegie to suggest that it be approved. When Carnegie refused to approve the deal Frick had negotiated, President Roberts and Vice President Frank Thomson of the Pennsylvania requested an interview with him. Carnegie had by this time obtained information on the rates the Pennsylvania Railroad charged competitors to ship their freight. Armed with these figures—and with plans for his new railroad—Carnegie, as he tells the story in an article he wrote later, strode confidently into the railroad offices in Philadelphia and demanded that Roberts and Thomson lower the rates charged Carnegie Steel to the level his competitors were paying. The railroad officials agreed, but asked, in return, that he drop plans to build competing railroads in the state. Carnegie refused to halt construction of the road north to Lake Erie, but agreed to abandon plans to extend it south to the coke region, in return for reduced freight rates.[24]

It would, in the end, cost Carnegie $2 million—$1 million of it borrowed from the United States Trust Company—to build his Lake Erie railroad. It was worth every penny. The road, renamed the Pittsburgh, Bessemer, & Lake Erie, then the Bessemer & Lake Erie, reduced the costs of shipping iron ore to Carnegie Steel's mills and furnaces. With long-term agreements on cheap iron ore and coke—and transportation costs brought down to what even he now considered a reasonable level—Carnegie saw no limit to the company's future market share and profitability. There was no need, at least for the foreseeable future, for the company to enter into or remain in "pools" that limited its share of the market. "Since we have the ore mines on our shoulders, and coke, and the railroad," Carnegie wrote Frick in October 1897, "we cannot afford to do anything that will restrict us from taking the business of the country and running full."[25]

Carnegie Steel was now ready to take on the world. Carnegie dared his competitors to try to take any of his business, while he prepared to advance into their territories. When Illinois Steel, Carnegie Steel's major rival, put in a bid for an armor contract, Carnegie was outraged. "I never knew a dirtier action in business than that of the Illinois in regard to Armor, it was pure spite—a foul blow, besides, under present management that Company has declared war against us." Instead of trying to arrange a truce, as he had in the past, Carnegie directed Frick to take the battle to the enemy. "Now is the time when we are prosperous and others are not to drive our stakes in everywhere and command the situation."[26]

Its supplies of raw materials assured the future was brighter than ever for Carnegie Steel. "Our organization never was so perfect," Carnegie bragged to Frick in the spring of 1898, "we seem to have reached the secret of moneymaking in iron and steel manufacture." Net profits were not only climbing, they were climbing exponentially, from $3 million in 1893, the first year of the depression, to $7 million in 1897, to $16 million in 1898.[27]

WHILE WE CANNOT discount the effect of the iron mine acquisitions and railroad building ventures on Carnegie Steel's newfound profitability, the foundation for the company's extraordinary growth had been laid a decade earlier with the expulsion of the Knights from E.T., the Amalgamated from Homestead, and potential union organizers from Duquesne. With organized labor banished, Frick and Schwab had been able to cut wages and increase hours with brutal efficiency. In January of 1895, when the 1892 Homestead contract expired, Schwab reduced wages by a further 15 percent. In the spring of that same year, in the midst of a boom in production, Schwab recommended that the pay scale—which he had cut in January—be raised to keep workers from moving to other plants. Carnegie suggested instead that the furnace men and unskilled workers be paid a "bonus," which could be rescinded whenever the company decided it necessary to do so. The bonus was set at 10 percent, well below the 15 percent cut in wages that had preceded it. A little more than a year later, in the midst of a mild downturn in orders, Carnegie proposed that the bonuses be rescinded. "There is a very easy way to stop bonus. When mills stop for a time, as they must [for maintenance], before starting them, let the men be told quietly that the firm regrets it cannot go on paying bonus under present conditions. The men will agree to start without the bonus; if not you can wait. No public notice need be given."[28]

Much of the money that was poured into Homestead—and the other Carnegie plants—was spent on labor-saving equipment. The gangs of men who had lifted, hauled, and shoveled were replaced by huge scooping machinery, automated car dumpers, larger barrows, electric trolleys, traveling cranes, and a variety of other mechanical devices. Between 1892 and 1897, the Homestead workforce decreased by some 25 percent.

Contrary to Carnegie's promises in the 1880s, his workingmen did not share in the firm's remarkable prosperity. On the contrary, there was, through the 1890s, an inverse relationship between the firm's revenues and profits and the amount of money distributed to the workforce as wages. According to figures compiled by the geographer and historian Kenneth Warren, while the value of the goods shipped from the Carnegie mills increased by some 226 percent in the seven years following the strike of 1892, the percentage of revenues paid out in wages *decreased* by 67 percent. The sliding scale, which Carnegie had claimed would serve as the foundation of the employer-employee partnership, was based not on profits, which continued to rise, but on the price of steel, which continued to fall.[29]

CARNEGIE never evinced any guilt at the conditions under which his employees labored, many of them for twelve hours a day, seven days a week, for less than a dollar and a half a day. He was on the contrary proud of his record as an employer. In response to critics of his "Gospel of Wealth" essays, he had declared that "those who insure steady employment to thousands, at wages not lower than others pay, need not be ashamed of their record; for steady employment is, after all, the one indispensable requisite for the welfare and the progress of the people."[30]

Andrew Carnegie was not a cruel or uncaring man. In paying his common laborers $1.35 or $1.50, he was obeying the laws of the marketplace, which established this value for a day's labor. To have paid them or his skilled workers extra would have endangered the viability and profitability of his steelworks. It would also have violated the principles of the Gospel of Wealth which he was determined to live by. Having declared that his role in the larger evolutionary schema was to make as much money as possible so that he would have the maximum amount to give away, he was obligated to squeeze profits out of his enterprises. And that required him to pay his workers as little as possible.

A weaker man, Carnegie implied in his speech at the dedication of his Pittsburgh library in November 1895, might have given in to the entreaties of his workers to raise their wages. But Carnegie would not. Even if it had been possible to share his surplus with his workers without damaging the viability of the enterprise, to do so was neither "justifiable or wise, because there are higher uses for surplus wealth than adding petty sums to the earnings of the masses. Trifling sums given to each every week or month—and the sums would be trifling indeed—would be frittered away, nine times out of ten, in things which pertain to the body and not to the spirit; upon richer food and drink, better clothing, more extravagant living, which are beneficial neither to rich nor poor. These are things external and of the flesh; they do not minister to the higher, the divine, part of man." It was far better, Carnegie insisted, to hold on to the surplus and concentrate it "in one great educative institution, lasting for all time [which] ministers to the divine in man, his reason and his conscience, and thus lifts him higher and higher in the scale of being."[31]

TWENTY-NINE

"We Now Want to Take Root,"
1897–1898

A DECADE AFTER their marriage, any doubts Andrew and Louise may have harbored about their future happiness had evaporated without a trace. Andrew remained as restless as ever; Louise as stable and calm. The combination worked well. As the years passed, the marriage grew stronger. They remained an odd-looking couple—the age and height discrepancy exaggerated as he shrank over time—but they also found more and more to bind them together. Andrew learned to appreciate classical music; Louise, Scottish folk songs and the bagpipes. Louise grew accustomed, though never completely, to having a houseful of guests, her husband always the center of attention; she even came to appreciate the joys of travel. Andrew, for his part, slowly but gradually understood what it meant to have a home to return to when his travels were done.

For the first three years of marriage, Andrew had shared Louise with Mrs. Whitfield; having dedicated years of his own life to caring for his mother, he could not begrudge Louise doing the same. When, in early 1890, Mrs. Whitfield died, Carnegie regained his wife—and her sister Stella, who became a permanent member of the household. "Louise heartily with me since her Mother left us," he wrote Frick, with a mixture of pride and relief in January 1890.[1]

With his father, mother, and brother gone, Carnegie relied on Louise for emotional ballast. There was no one else to whom he unburdened himself, if indeed he did so with Louise. A little man and a majority stockholder in a huge enterprise, he had no choice but to stand tall at all times. His letters were, with rare exceptions, brimming with good cheer. He remained close with several of his boyhood friends, Bobby Pitcairn, Harry

Phipps, Vandy, and Dod among them, and gathered new friends as he grew older; with the exception of John Morley, most of them were also business partners, which added layers of complication to the relationships. Aside from aging relatives in Dunfermline and Cousin Dod, who divided his time between Pittsburgh and Europe, Louise was his family. In a curious passage from his *Autobiography,* he refers to Louise's "guardianship." Like his mother, she worried about his health, tried to slow him down, and made sure he was well fed and clothed.[2]

IN THE WINTER of 1891, after four and half years of marriage, the world Carnegie had built with Louise was put at risk when she took ill with a severe case of typhoid. Louise's illness and the long convalescence that followed were profoundly disturbing. Having married a woman twenty years younger, Carnegie had never anticipated that it was he who might be left alone. Dr. Dennis, who had cared for Carnegie and his mother in Cresson in 1887, was called in at once. For several months Louise was bedridden, in and out of the hospital, with periods of recovery and relapse following unexpectedly one upon another. Carnegie remained at her bedside, moved into the hospital with her, and put off his annual spring trip to Pittsburgh until he was assured that she was out of danger.[3]

In the winter of 1895–96, almost five years to the day she had taken ill, Louise was stricken again. Fearful that the New York winter was delaying her recuperation, Andrew took her south to Palm Beach, and then to his sister-in-law's estate on Cumberland Island. The convalescence took much longer than expected. When Louise's health returned to normal, he brought her north to New York, then traveled with her and Stella to Italy, instead of to England and Scotland, in the hope that warm weather might speed her full recovery.

Louise and Andrew had been married for nine years now. His sixtieth birthday and her thirty-ninth had come and gone and still there was no sign of a child. Louise's authorized biographers, who had access to her diaries and personal correspondence, tell us that "Mr. and Mrs. Carnegie had longed for a child," and that Louise, "with her maternal spirit and her fine gifts for motherhood, was starved for one." Neither they nor Carnegie's biographers provide any explanation as to why that longing had not been satisfied.[4]

The explanation that makes the most sense is the one handed down orally from Louise to the daughter she finally had, Margaret, and from Margaret to her children and grandchildren. According to Linda Hills, one of her great-granddaughters, Louise had always wanted to have children "and certainly more than one. However, because Andrew had a friend who lost his wife in childbirth . . . he was very fearful of losing Louise in the same way and did not want to risk it. She, on the other hand, more than anything, wanted children. In her late thirties she became very ill and was delirious [the time frame corresponds with the 1895–96 illness]. . . . During her delirium, she cradled a pillow and tended to it as if it were a baby. The doctor at the time told Andrew that she was pining away for a child and that if she survived the illness, he must let her have one."[5]

We have no way of verifying the family story, other than to note that it is consistent with the chronology of events. Louise got pregnant in the spring or summer of 1896, probably in Italy; she was very much with child when she returned to the United States in the late fall of 1896. In November, Carnegie wrote his cousin Dod to tell him that Louise had "rented a fine country House 30 miles out [from New York], back of Greenwich Conn.—2½ miles. We are to run out there now and then. Louise gets tired so easily since grippe and I think the experiment well worth trying. She does far too much to please people here, many of them old far away connections who are of all people most exacting, and take offense at refusals to dine & visit etc. Now 'we can be out of town.' Cowardly retreat—but a retreat from them." There was no mention of the pregnancy, though this must have been the reason for their taking the "country House."[6]

All was well in the Carnegie household. Louise was healthy, her sister Stella delighted to be living in the "country," Carnegie as content as he had ever been. The lengthy depression of the mid-1890s was finally lifting; the Republicans were back in the White House, his Pittsburgh library, music hall, art gallery, and natural history museum were a grand success, and his career as a writer had taken off, with regular essays in the *Nineteenth Century* and the *North American Review*.

When in New York, he spent every morning in his library, the grandest room in the Carnegies' home. In the center was a mammoth table, covered with pens, paper, newspapers, and open books. "There are books and books everywhere," wrote one visitor. "They reach from the floor to the ceiling and cover three sides of the room, as well as encroach upon the fourth side, which is the bright spot in the library, with its fireplace." On either side of the mantelpiece, stacked on shelves, were "precious mementos and pleasing reminders of interesting occasions," photos, plaques, and trowels, given as gifts at library groundbreaking ceremonies. There was a large easy chair for reading and a "comfortable lounge" for napping "with the rollicking motto above, 'There's a good time coming, boys.'" Scattered elsewhere in the room were Carnegie's collection of musical instruments, a xylophone-shaped instrument from the Orient, and a set of Japanese bells.[7]

Carnegie entered his library at ten each morning and generally stayed until one in the afternoon. After luncheon, he was likely to take a walk or carriage ride in Central Park. On occasion he would return to his library in the afternoon to read a bit more or give dictation to his secretary. He remained a prodigious correspondent, not only with his partners and managers in Pittsburgh, but with a large and growing assortment of friends, including some of the English-speaking world's most renowned and powerful men.

In one of his letters to Gladstone, he boasted like a small boy of having received in that day's post "three letters, One from you . . . one from Herbert Spencer, One from John Morley. I am quite set up as no other can say this."[8]

He had continued to maintain a steady correspondence with Herbert Spencer, who had, as he aged, become even more sour and ill-tempered. Now seventy-seven, he had written Carnegie at great length explaining why he refused to sit for a portrait to be paid for by donations from his British admirers. Spencer told Carnegie he had no wish to give anything back to the British, who had, by earlier neglecting to subscribe to his works, delayed their publication for several years. The Americans had always been generous and he would sit for a portrait for them, but to his latecomer British admirers, he owed nothing.[9]

Carnegie wrote back at once. Great men, he reminded his old hero, were never appreciated by their contemporaries.

When have the prophets not been stoned, from Christ down to Wagner? . . . Why, my dear friend, what do you mean by complaining of neglect, abuse, scorn; these are the precious rewards of the teachers of mankind. . . . Let me urge you to go carefully over every word you have written which shows other than a spirit of deep gratification at the neglect, scorn, and abuse which you have had to suffer. Your attitude towards ordinary beings should be that of lofty pity and anxiety for their reaching the light by-and-by, which you have discovered and in which you rest. . . . My belief is, that one word showing disappointment, or, may I say resentment, of the treatment you have received from your countrymen, will detract very much from the loftiness of our Guide, Philosopher, and Friend. Do think this over.

If earlier he had worshipped Spencer from a distance, he now acknowledged that he had something in common with his hero—both men were underappreciated for their accomplishments. "I remember you once said to me, that you did not understand how I could [go] forward building Libraries, halls and Museums for the working masses of Pittsburgh, when these had publicly requested City Councils to reject the gifts. If I had entered upon the work with the desire to win popular applause, I should have richly merited the punishment that their action would have inflicted upon my vain nature, but I was sustained by the knowledge that they knew not what they did, and so rendered only more steadfast, if possible, in my determination to give them the precious gifts. The result has been extraordinary. Never, to my knowledge, have Halls, Libraries, Museums, Art Galleries roused the masses of a city to such enthusiasm." Carnegie suggested that Spencer take a lesson from his disciple.[10]

WHILE LOUISE AND STELLA remained in Greenwich through the winter of 1897, Carnegie commuted back and forth to New York. In March, he took the train to Harrisburg for a brief business meeting and, as he wrote Frick, "caught slight cold." The cold developed into pleurisy, a dangerous condition for a man in his sixty-second year. The newspapers having picked up the story, his private secretary was obliged to acknowledge that Carnegie had indeed been struck by "an acute attack of pleurisy," but that there were no complications and reports in the press were "making out his case much worse than it is."[11]

Carnegie insisted, in letters to Frick and Frew, with whom he now consulted regularly on his Pittsburgh library, that he was on the mend, but Louise remained concerned. Handed a note to mail to Frew in Pittsburgh, she added on the bottom that while "Mr. Carnegie is really better as you may see by the above . . . he is very weak and the doctors say he must be exceedingly careful about exposure for some time. That dinner with the subsequent visit to Harrisburg were too much for him. He came home completely fagged, caught a chill and this is the result."[12]

The episode brought dramatically home to Louise the harsh reality that she had married a much older man who was almost certain to die before her. On March 20, from New York, where she was awaiting her confinement, she wrote to John Ross, Carnegie's solicitor in Dunfermline, to inform him that she had now completed paying—out of her own funds—for the property where Andrew had been born, and wished to begin work on erecting "a fitting memorial to Andrew's mother and to himself—of course this cannot be done during either his or my lifetime, but I should like it started." She and Carnegie had "talked a great deal about it this winter and we both cling to the idea of a winter garden or palm house. . . . This palm house should be filled with the choices of palms and exotic plants . . . placed under the care of an educated man who could instruct the people and make their visits interesting. The actual house in which Andrew was born I should like to keep intact—it could be used as a tool house perhaps the superintendent could live on the lower floor, or have his office there. . . . In the center of the Palm House I should like to place a beautiful fountain of the finest marble—really a work of art . . . and if possible to bring the stream where Andrew used to draw water—to flow through the fountain so that it would be a perpetual stream of pure water."[13]

Ten days later, on March 30, 1897, three weeks after her fortieth birthday, Louise Whitfield Carnegie gave birth to a daughter. Carnegie, who had remained behind in Greenwich to convalesce from his pleurisy, returned to New York to visit his wife and daughter. The birth had gone well; the baby was healthy. "As I first gazed upon her," Carnegie recalled in his *Autobiography*, "Mrs. Carnegie said, 'Her name is Margaret after your mother. Now one request I have to make. . . . We must get a summer home since this little one has been given us. We cannot rent one and be obliged to go in and go out at a certain date. It should be our home. . . . I make only one condition. . . . It must be in the Highlands of Scotland.'" Louise had long before fallen in love with Cluny, which had been their summer home for almost a decade. It was here that she wanted to put down roots.[14]

There were, regrettably, more pressing matters at hand than their future Highland home. Carnegie's convalescence was not proceeding smoothly. Having exhausted himself during his trip to New York to meet his daughter, he was driven back to Greenwich to recover his strength. "Every day I find myself better," he wrote his wife on his return. "The trip to New York and excitement of meeting rather upset me and I appeared worse than the normal condition. Wait till you see me here and you will be happy. Now since I have seen you and the Little Saint I seem always with you. Before this all was glamour—like a dream. Now as real as ever Margaret a little 'uncanny' yet—fresh from heaven and not yet just earthly like ourselves. . . . Guess I'll not risk another visit. I do so much wish to be well to welcome you. Only six days more after this. Hurrah! A kiss for Margaret and twenty for her mother. Ever darling, your own Andrew." One tiny cloud lay on the horizon. Carnegie had received "a note from Mr. Macpherson of Cluny" who was engaged to be married and intended, on taking a wife, to take up residence on his estate, instead of leasing or selling it to the Carnegies. "We must remain in that district," Carnegie reassured Louise, "but hopes of our getting Cluny seem faint now, although there's many a slip, etc."[15]

Louise, knowing full well that her husband was overly optimistic, dismissed his cheery reports about his recovery. Worried that he would cut short his convalescence to take the train to Washington on armor business, she asked Stella, who had remained in Greenwich, to "please tell Andrew, the most patriotic duty we can perform to our country—better than the making of armor plate—is the taking care of our wee Margaret so that she in turn may grow up a strong healthy woman and become the mother of men. This duty I cannot perform by myself, nor can he do it alone. We must do it together; therefore please urge him to take good care of his health, not only for our sakes, but for our country."[16]

Carnegie stayed in Greenwich for another two months and received there the congratulations of family and friends on becoming a father. Frick, a devoted father to his own daughter Helen, was among the most enthusiastic well-wishers. On April 30, he wrote Carnegie that he "should like exceedingly to see Mrs. Carnegie, and be introduced to the little daughter, and hope for that pleasure before you go abroad." Carnegie wrote back, as he always did, that he was "gaining daily. . . . Up for breakfast regularly now." He intended to leave for Europe as scheduled on June 2 and invited Frick to bring the whole family to visit at Cluny.[17]

On May 31, just before their departure, he wrote Dod of their plans. "We intend to be quiet for a time at Cluny till all settle down—[the laird of] Cluny's marriage may cause us to lose Cluny and therefore I intend to coach about and see various places. We have decided to own our Highland Home, no more leased houses." He suggested—as he would continue to do for the next ten years—that Dod buy an estate in the Highlands. "Don't you want to invest—buy the adjoining Estate and settle down for summers. I think a nice yacht up there would be worth having. Am improving but not yet fit for the moors. The sea will do it however."[18]

Undeterred by the difficulties of taking a newborn baby on an ocean cruise, Carnegie, Louise, Stella, and Margaret sailed on June 2 with their small army of maids, male servants, and private secretaries, supplemented now by nannies and nurses. "We came via Southampton," Carnegie wrote Gladstone, "only because in the American ship is to be had a complete suite of rooms, including bathetic—our infant traveler only two months old needed all conveniences."[19]

Their first weeks in Britain were not easy ones. "Margaret stood the voyage well," Carnegie wrote Frick from Cluny on June 14,

but a boil or swelling on her neck gave trouble and it had to be lanced in London—poor little tot—she is flourishing here and begins to get her former rosy cheeks. We have had news of the death of Mrs. Carnegie's grandmother, who was more of a mother to Stella and Louise—this coming just after aunt's death has made this for the first time a sad house—Stella has not been out of bed since we received the cable. . . . Louise has Margaret fortunately but the Doctor insists she should have no other cares, for a time. So we are to live quietly and those friends who were coming to see us and Margaret we have had to prevent. Mrs. C. insists upon nursing Margaret entirely. One Doctor suggested a little mixture of our own Cons. [condensed] milk which is fine but no—no use. So as the time approaches for you to sail I feel I must write to say that I have not the heart to suggest to her that we could have the Fricks with us. . . . There are very few lady friends Mrs. C. would welcome so cordially as your wife. . . . But you and Mrs. Frick will understand how we are situated—It would be no pleasure for you anyhow to be in the house with us and so we must just go on ourselves until matters frightened. I am gaining strength daily which is all I lack—can walk around "the Burns" without fatigue which is something.

Of course you could run up or down. . . . See me for a day or two and talk over any business matters. . . . Men need no attention and Mrs. C would not be interfered with in any way.[20]

Frick wrote back at once to say that he not surprised by Carnegie's request. "On my return from New York, Mrs. Frick at once said she did not think Mrs. Carnegie would want even her most intimate friends to visit her this year." He fully understood that the Carnegies were not up for a family visit, but hoped to be able to "run up a day or two to see you. If not on my arrival, will do so before returning home."[21]

Carnegie was exaggerating his daughter's and his wife's condition. They were well enough to take the train from Southampton to London for Queen Victoria's Diamond Jubilee. "Baby Margaret's first trip, nine weeks old. Baby an excellent traveler," Louise wrote in her travel diary. They stayed at the Metropole, from where they watched the Queen's procession from their window.[22]

From London, they traveled directly to Cluny. On arrival, Carnegie set off on a coaching tour of the Highlands, with the faithful Hew Morrison, Edinburgh librarian and general aide de camp, at his side. Their holy grail was a Highland estate for the Carnegie clan, now expanded to include little Margaret.

Louise remained behind at Cluny to care for her daughter and try to talk Macpherson into changing his mind and selling his family's estate to the Carnegies. While she had willingly sent Carnegie off on his journey, Louise worried that he might be enjoying the coaching so much he had taken his eye off the prize. She begged him to focus his considerable talents on this one task. "Am very anxious too for your report by word of mouth. . . . We now want to take root. We haven't time to make mistakes; as many playthings and play places as you like and yachts galore, but a home first please, where we can have the greatest measure of health. . . . But enough—we can talk this over better when we get together, and understand, darling, I want your good first and I'll try to be happy wherever you settle. We shall gang far ere we find anything muckle better than Cluny for baby. Her cheeks are as brown and as fat as possible. She almost talked to me as I was undressing her this evening."[23]

Carnegie, meanwhile, was having a fine time touring. The only property that came close to meeting his requirements was Skibo in the northern Highlands near the ancient town of Dornoch. The estate encompassed tens of thousands of acres of meadows, moors, gently rolling hills, lochs, and streams; a long stately entranceway lined with beech trees and yews planted seven centuries earlier; and a view of the North Sea. An added attraction was its accessibility to several large lochs, the Dornoch Firth, and the North Sea, on which Carnegie could go yachting, his newest passion.[24]

There were unfortunately serious problems with the property. Unlike Cluny, where the main house and out buildings were in fine repair, served by well-maintained roads, and surrounded by finely manicured lawns and gardens, Skibo needed a great deal of work before the Carnegies could consider it their home. The last owner had ripped down what remained of the ancient castle and substituted a faux-Gothic mansion in its place. The house looked grand enough from the outside, but was far too small for the full Carnegie entourage of extended family, servants, and visitors. Worse yet, the grounds, roads, fences, stone walls, and fields were in severe disrepair; the outbuildings, barns, dairies, stables, and the cottages in which the tenants, servants, and day laborers lived were literally coming apart at the seams. The previous owner had gone bankrupt and abandoned the property. The estate had fallen into the hands of court trustees who were willing to sell it relatively cheaply. The real costs would come later: it was going to require vast amounts of time, energy, capital, and on-site supervision to bring Skibo back to its glory.

And then there were the dependents who came with the estate. As the laird of Skibo, Carnegie would become a post-feudal landlord with responsibilities for the hundreds who lived and worked on his land, but had no legal rights to it. Earlier in the century, Scottish landlords had had almost absolute rights to their land; the tenant farmers who lived and worked it almost none. But after a series of revolts in the Highlands and the passage of the Crofters Act of 1886, the laws governing land tenure had been changed to provide tenants with some protection. This almost guaranteed that Skibo, like other Highland estates, was destined to continue leaking money, until and unless Carnegie spent large sums to improve the land, attract new crofters, cottars, and day laborers, and make it possible for the protected tenants to pay their rents.

No one, it appeared, but a rich American would have dared take on such a project. Even Carnegie was daunted. Instead of buying the property outright, he asked permission of the court trustees to lease Skibo for a season. With no other potential bidders in sight, the trustees readily agreed to his terms.

IN THE FALL of 1897, Carnegie, who had that spring suffered through a potentially life-endangering illness *and* become a father, initiated discussions with his partners about purchasing his and Harry Phipps's stock in Carnegie Steel. His fondest wish was that the company remain a closed partnership, with the surviving partners absorbing his and Phipps's shares. To make this possible, he proposed that the payout schedule be extended to give the surviving partners a full fifty years to buy back his stock and sixteen years to pay for Phipps's.[25]

Carnegie's proposal to revise the terms of the "ironclad" agreement had to be approved by all the partners. Phipps, who had balked at the last revision in 1892 but eventually been persuaded to sign, refused to do so this time. Anxious to retire as soon as he could, he did not want to have to wait sixteen years for his payout.[26]

Carnegie was incredulous. "My Dear Pard," he wrote Phipps rather condescendingly, "Surely you are a little 'off.' I know of no reasons why the Iron Clad is not pleasing to you. . . . Is it [the] sixteen years you wish shortened? No doubt every partner will try to meet your wishes in this respect. I know when you consider fully you will never say you will leave your partners in the dark about what they are to meet when you go. If you go before me—and I am well—I think I could meet the occasion [i.e., come up with the money needed to buy Phipps's shares], but it . . . might give serious trouble. Think over this. You have a fine kind nature which will lead you to humane decision. Our partners are next to our family in my opinion."[27]

On October 9, Carnegie wrote Frick to warn him about Phipps, who was also concerned that the company was still offering new partners stock and allowing them to pay for it out of future dividends.

You may find him all awry in regard to Iron Clad Agreement, but if you will have Lovejoy [the Carnegie Steel board secretary] get all the signatures to it promptly, the Squire will be all right. He seems unduly alarmed about matters. Thinks we give new men interests unnecessarily large, favors getting in capital; in other words he would make the firm like [a cor-poration]. . . . The secret of our success has been that we have done just the opposite and I have written him that next to taking care of our own families, I think our young partners have the greatest claim upon us old fellows, for whom they are working, making fortunes. I also suggested that if he wanted enough of cash out of the business to secure his family, if they were not secure, I believed you would buy a part of his interest and could give him satisfactory security and rather prompt payments. He has not been up here; if I had a personal interview with him I could no doubt arrange something satisfactory to him but he sails on the 16th and I shall not see him. You can, no doubt, smooth him down; calm his fears and get his signature to the Iron Clad, which I think it is important to close.[28]

Phipps, having met with Frick, agreed to rethink his position on the ironclad, before declining once again to sign it. Frick, as chairman of the board of managers, declared in October 1897 that with the new ironclad agreement in hiatus—perhaps permanently—because Phipps refused to sign it, the 1892 one would remain "legally operative." The following June, Frick changed his mind. As he wrote Carnegie, he now believed the 1892 agreement was "not binding" on any of the partners, "nor on anybody, and never has been." The agreement to take effect had to have been signed by every partner, but for some reason Vandy, now dead, had never signed it. This meant that the procedures set up in that supposedly "Iron Clad" agreement, including the mandatory purchase of deceased partners' shares at book value, were unenforceable. Where this left the company, Frick did not care to speculate. Nor did he let the rest of the partners know that the ironclad had been pierced. The bottom line was that, if Phipps or Carnegie should die or demand to be bought out, there were no legal procedures in place to determine the price of the shares or the method by which they would be purchased.[29]

THE CARNEGIES decided not to return to the United States in the fall of 1897, as had been their custom. Carnegie, warier than ever of his health—and that of his wife and baby—had decided that they would winter at the Villa Allerton in Cannes, where the climate was gentle, the accommoda-tions luxurious, and the company, including William Gladstone, most hospitable. When the weather turned warm, they would return to Scotland and take up residence at Skibo.

"Off to Cannes Saturday, beautiful Villa Allerton for the season," Carnegie wrote Walter Damrosch in early November, "and I have chartered a yacht—expect to take almost daily excursions with Margaret—Her mother also and Stella no doubt on fine days. All well—I am very well, Louise also except a slight cold last three days, better today . . . I am all right sure, never felt better and the temptation to risk New York this winter was strong. Little Margaret and the Atlantic turned the scale."[30]

The villa turned out to be everything Carnegie had hoped for. It was a relatively new house, built about 1882, with a large garden, a pond, a shooting range, and a caretaker's cottage for the servants. "I'm sitting in my spacious library in shirt sleeves—windows all open," he wrote Hew Morrison in mid-November, soon after arriving. "The blue sea in the distance—all I need now is the coming yacht," which had been chartered from a Glasgow firm and was due to arrive in January.[31]

Margaret was doing brilliantly. She had graduated to porridge, Carnegie proudly reported. Louise was also delighted with the Cannes villa, though she had not gotten over her disappointment that, on leaving Cannes in the spring, they would not be returning to Cluny. "The giving up of Cluny, with all its tender associations," she wrote her friend and former pastor, Charles Eaton, "has affected my sister and me deeply, and we cannot look forward to Skibo with the delight that Mr. Carnegie does, but when we have seen it and have lived there no doubt we shall grow to like it, particularly if it suits Mr. Carnegie and Margaret. We find our home here all we anticipated and more, and we are most delightfully situated. The restful out-of-door life has brought new vigor to Mr. Carnegie and really there is not a trace of his recent illness left. He climbs the hills with the greatest ease and is in the best of spirits."[32]

The Villa Allerton, rented for the winter season, provided everything the Carnegies required except a private secretary. Carnegie had decided to begin work on his memoirs and asked Hew Morrison to find him a discreet, well-organized young man who could take dictation and use the typewriter. "He must be an all round intelligent pleasing young man <u>with brains</u>—one anxious to do everything he can to make himself indispensable to us. Educated of course—typewriter and stenographer—if with some literary ability so much the better. Should like to try him on a special piece of work I have on hand . . . would not engage him beyond three months. If he is just the man I want would engage him permanently £250 per year or even more. . . . It is the exceptionally bright good natured young man I am after but must have good judgment. He may have to see people about Skibo and attend to many little arrangements for me. Don't recommend any ordinary person, give me a young man who can make a future for himself."[33]

Morrison suggested James Bertram, a twenty-five-year old Scotsman who had just returned from South Africa, where he had worked for the railroads. Carnegie was delighted. "You have rendered me a great service anent the secretaryship. Of course you know Mr. Bertram comes of 'good kith and kin' and has a record—We shall expect him as stated. A real treasure of a Secretary is the most important member of the Family, beyond its own members. He ought to become a lifelong friend and companion."[34]

Bertram turned out to be the perfect secretary. The two men would spend their mornings together for the next eighteen years, until Carnegie was too sick to write any more. Bertram found Carnegie to be "the most charming and companionable person" he had ever met. Carnegie's conversation, Bertram would report later to Burton Hendrick, "was brilliant, sizzling with anecdote and epigram, and reaching all fields."[35]

Soon after coming to work for Carnegie, Bertram would take on the task of organizing Carnegie's ever-growing "begging" correspondence, signing his own name to letters he preferred not to bother Mr. Carnegie with, transcribing handwritten scribbles into formally typed letters on the appropriate letterheads, and setting up the application procedure for groups applying for church organs and libraries.

Carnegie, with Bertram at his side, kept very busy at Cannes. He turned over a full complement of business reports from Pittsburgh, started work on his memoirs, and spent increasing time on his philanthropies. As the profits at Carnegie Steel increased annually, so did his disposable income, and the size and number of his gifts. With profits at $3 million in 1893, he had spent less than $1,000 on new philanthropic projects. In 1896, with profits at $6 million, he donated more than $132,000 ($100 million today): $12,500 to the New York Botanical Gardens; $1,000 to the New York Public Library; some $62,000 for his Pittsburgh Institute and Library; $14,000 for a library in Wick Parish in the northern Highlands; $6,300 to Damrosch's Oratorio and Symphony Societies; $4,000 for schools in Homestead and Dunfermline; almost $27,000 for church organs; and $500 to the Old Timers Telegraphers Association.[36]

There would have been more money to spend had Carnegie acceded to the requests of his retired partners, Harry Phipps and Dod, and paid out higher cash dividends. Phipps compared the fate of the senior Carnegie Steel partners with the fabled Philip Nolan, the man without a country, who had wandered the globe, always drawing near land but never landing. "We get in sight of dividends . . . then a new ship, a new voyage—and never land, each time a new and deeper disappointment." Dod was in full agreement. "I have a long communication from Harry on the question of dividends v. improvements—His position seems to me unassailable . . . I cannot see why you do not make dividends." Phipps's and Dod's entreaties fell on deaf ears. With Frick's support, Carnegie maintained that the company had no choice but to reinvest up to 75 percent of its profits in capital improvements, if it were to remain competitive.[37]

For the time being, Carnegie thought it best to continue to concentrate his philanthropic spending on Pittsburgh. He turned down a request for funds for the free library in Wolverhampton, explaining that because he made a practice of not saving any money, he had none on hand to spend on new ventures. "I am depending upon the future to provide the four-hundred thousand pounds which I promised to spend [in Pittsburgh], and therefore I must resolutely confine myself to this department until I have the money. As it will come from Pittsburgh, I think, it is only right that it should be spent there." When Gladstone asked for money for the Bodleian Library at Oxford, Carnegie turned him down as well. He had, he explained to Gladstone, pledged £1 million for his Carnegie Institute in Pittsburgh and "have still about 400,000 to spend there. I am in no position to give any considerable sums for other purposes. All my surplus will be needed to pay for the Pittsburgh additions."[38]

MUCH OF THE NEWS from America, that winter of 1897–98, was of Cuba, the atrocities committed by the Spanish troops, the growing independence movement, and the pressure on the American government to intervene. On taking office, President McKinley had declared himself opposed to intervention, but events were conspiring against him. In February 1898, the Spanish minister in Washington insulted McKinley in a letter published in the Hearst newspapers and the American battleship *Maine* exploded under mysterious circumstances in Havana Harbor. In March, Senator Redfield Proctor, a respected moderate from Vermont, visited Cuba and reported to Congress on the deplorable violations of decency and human rights practiced daily by the occupying Spaniards. "A great pity that Cuba looms up just when the nation was getting financially in splendid shape," Carnegie wrote Frick from Cannes on March 29. "There will be great excitement, but I believe there will be no war. Spain blusters but is too weak."[39]

While leading Republican members of the business community, including Henry Frick, implored the president they had put into office to resist the drumbeat for war, Carnegie kept his silence, if only because he could not believe the Spanish government would be stupid enough to go to war or strong enough, if it did, to hold back immediate defeat. Even after war had been declared in April 1898, Carnegie remained optimistic that it would soon be over. "I am not alarmed, much as I regret war," he wrote Frick on April 23. "Spanish bravado is a proverb—when put to the test the forces of Spain will melt away. My only fear is that we may be induced to linger in Cuba, and become responsible for good government there. This would be more serious than the war. If we restrict ourselves to clearing the Spaniards out, and then clearing out ourselves, the United States will have scored, as showing to the world, a chivalrous act without taint of self."[40]

Twenty years earlier, he had offered up the prayer after traveling through British-held India, "May heaven keep America from the colonizing craze! Cuba! Santo Domingo! Avaunt, and quit our sight!" He had, in the succeeding years, witnessed nothing to convince him that America would benefit from following the British example and becoming an overseas colonial power. Fortunately, he had seen no evidence that McKinley was prepared to embark on such a course.[41]

On June 4, as U.S. troops mobilized in Tampa preparatory to invading Cuba, the *New York Times* published a front-page interview with Carnegie, who was in London on his way to Skibo. He expressed his opinion that General Nelson Miles, the commanding general, was "an ideal warrior who wins victories without fighting," and then went on to "protest energetically against any extension of the Republic." Responding directly to the chatter from home about the emerging American empire, he declared his fondest "hopes that the Americans will justify the sentiment of Mill:

'The Americans often talk as if about to do foolish things; but so far they have never done one.'"*

On June 12, the *New York Tribune* and other newspapers reported that Carnegie had turned down a request from the "Scottish Highlanders of Illinois" that he outfit a regiment "for service in the war with Spain." "I do not believe that the war will last long, or ever reach the dignity of a real war. You will see Spain go all to pieces soon, much sooner than you could get the historical Highland garb provided for the regiment proposed."

THE CARNEGIES arrived at their new Highland home at Skibo in the spring of 1898, almost simultaneously with the American landing in Cuba. While Carnegie was as delighted with the estate as he had been on first sighting, he was still not convinced that he should purchase it, in large part because it was so lacking in the amenities required by a sixty-two-year-old man, his forty-one-year-old wife, and their year-old daughter. Within weeks of settling in, he began making plans—tentative ones—to improve the estate. The overworked but compliant Hew Morrison had already hired a staff, arranged to transport the Carnegies from London—and their fur-nishings from Cluny—and, at Louise's request, found the perfect "organ-ist." He had done so well at all these tasks that Carnegie added a new one: "I understand that 'principal Librarian' means that one has nothing to do but attend to 'odds and end.' Here is one for you. I wish very much to have a Saltwater Swimming Bath (heated). Please ascertain who the man is in Scotland who has distinguished himself building these. I do not wish to get into connection with anyone who has not had great experience, and knows the latest and best. . . . Should like some idea of cost, say 30' x 60'."[42]

Louise found the new estate to her liking, though it would never come close to replacing Cluny in her affections. "We are all very pleased with our new home," she wrote Dr. Eaton that spring. "The surroundings are more of the English type than Scotch. The sweet pastoral scenery is perfect of its kind. A beautiful undulating park with cattle grazing, a stately avenue of fine old beeches, glimpses of the Dornoch Firth, about a mile away, all seen through the picturesque cluster of lime and beech trees. All make such a

---

*Carnegie must have been referring to John Stuart Mill here, though I can find no reference to the statement cited.

peaceful picture that already a restful home feeling has come. . . . To show you the unique range of attractions, yesterday Mr. Carnegie was trout fishing on a wild moorland loch surrounded by heather while I took Margaret to the <u>sea</u> and she had her first experience of rolling upon the soft white sand and digging her little hands in it to her heart's content, while the blue waters of the ocean came rolling in at her feet and the salt sea breeze brought the roses to her cheeks." Louise was especially pleased that her idea to hire an organist for Skibo had worked out so well. She had arranged to surprise Andrew (not told about her plan) by having the organist greet the Carnegies with Beethoven's Fifth "as we stepped on the threshold of our new home. . . . The organist has now become a permanent institution. Every morning we come down to breakfast greeted by swelling tones, beginning with a hymn or chorale, and swelling into selections from the oratorios, etc, In the evening our musician plays for us on our fine Bechstein piano, which we now are really enjoying for the first time. We are all delighted with our musical atmosphere." As important as the organist would be, he would never supplant the piper who, as chief music maker at Skibo, was given the task of waking family and guests by circling the main house before sweeping through the downstairs hall, assuring that all were awake and primed for breakfast, and then returning at dusk to "pipe" the guests in to dinner.[43]

John Morley, to whom Carnegie had confided his misgivings about purchasing Skibo, urged him to think twice before turning it down. "I never put my ballot in, after all. My feel is for it; but you must surely try a little longer? It is of no use to take it for a term by way of experiment, and then to decide before the experiment has been fully made. The only possible drawbacks are (1) distance, and (2) the bother of tenants. The place itself is extremely fine; as pleasant a place as I ever saw." With Morley's vote in favor and Louise's approval, Carnegie purchased Skibo.[44]

IN EARLY AUGUST, Carnegie was startled to receive a densely written letter at Skibo, in a tight, tiny hand, from his former secretary and assistant, James Bridge. Their last communication had not been a pleasant one. Carnegie had donated the copyright and royalties for the first edition of *Triumphant Democracy* to Bridge and John Champlin, who had helped him with the book. Five years later in 1893, Bridge contacted him to request his permission to bring out a second edition. Carnegie rejected the idea, but eighteen months later changed his mind. Instead, however, of commissioning Bridge, he hired new researchers to bring the book up to date. Bridge was understandably angry. He held the copyright and was convinced that he had every right to profit from future editions.[45]

Having heard nothing from Bridge for almost five years, Carnegie was startled to receive what he believed was a thinly disguised blackmail request. Bridge had, he wrote Carnegie, rescued a trunkful of papers from the rubble after his house had burned down. Inside was a bundle which he assumed had to do with *Triumphant Democracy*. When he opened it, "an unaddressed scrap of paper . . . fell out. . . . This unaddressed scrap, signed E, had evidently dropped out of letter written by a Mrs. Seymour. There were other envelopes addressed in the same hand, besides some in the hand of Miss Whitfield—as she was then—and some in another handwriting which I had seen before but did not recognize." Bridge claimed that he had no idea how Carnegie's private letters had ended up in his trunk (a good question), but guessed that when Miss Hood, the maid, "cleaned up your private desk on our leaving Cresson, she dumped the contents on to the pile I had taken out of my desk, which you remember was in the same room." His "first impulse" on finding the letters "was to burn them all; but on reflection I thought that you ought to be told of their discovery." He assured Carnegie he understood how sensitive the letters were and, in order to avoid any embarrassment, had placed them "in a safe place in New York where no one but myself can get them." The scrap from E., the most sensitive note of all, he had locked away in his own safe in San Francisco. He suggested Carnegie should notify him immediately upon his return to New York so that they might arrange for the transfer of the letters—and the scrap from E. "You will understand why I do not wish to have it in my possession any longer than is necessary. It is needless to say that you may confidently rely on my discretion. Your instructions concerning the disposal of these papers will be carried out to the letter, and afterwards I shall try to forget the incident. Of course I have not read anything beyond the note which showed the character of the rest, though as you probably guessed at the time, I know who the Seymours were." Bridge closed his letter by asking for a loan of $10,000 so that he might purchase stock in the *Overland Monthly*, which he currently edited in San Francisco. In return, he would give Carnegie a half interest in the company. "It is a good business proposition as it stands; but I would supplement this by an appeal to auld lang syne when there was a bond of sympathy and mutual trust between us which alone would have justified me in making this request and you grant it."[46]

Carnegie asked Bridge to "mail anything you have of mine," but received nothing. In 1903, when Bridge surfaced once again, Carnegie warned his friend William Stead against him. He told Stead about the blackmail attempt and that he had refused to pay Bridge off. There was no reason why he should have. His relations with E. or Mrs. Seymour, whoever they were and whatever form they may have taken, occurred before he was married. Bridge did not get his loan, but neither did he follow through on his implicit threats.[47]

CARNEGIE followed events in Cuba as closely as he could from Skibo. Never one to put much store in protocol, he took it on himself in mid-July 1898 to cable the ranking officer in Cuba, General Nelson Miles, with his personal advice. (It was a miracle that he got through to Miles, at a time when even William Randolph Hearst, covering the Cuban conflict for his New York newspaper, found it difficult to get an open cable line.) The city of Santiago having fallen to the Americans, Carnegie urged General Miles to proceed at once "full force [to] Porto Rico. . . . Capture Porto Rico; would tell heavily [in] Spain and Europe." Through backchannels, Carnegie had learned that the Spanish had fortified Havana and were prepared for a lengthy siege. The war, he counseled, would be brought to a speedier conclusion should the Americans proceed directly to Puerto Rico. Rather than dismissing this advice, General Miles laid it before McKinley and his cabinet. He was, he tells us in his memoirs, delighted when he was ordered to proceed to Puerto Rico, as the "patriotic philanthropist" had suggested.[48]

The general and his troops landed in Puerto Rico on July 25. By the end of the month, as Carnegie had predicted, the Spanish government, its navy destroyed in Manila Bay and its soldiers defeated in Cuba, opened negotiations for an armistice. On August 12, hostilities were formally suspended. The Spanish agreed to grant Cuba independence and cede Puerto Rico and Guam to the United States. The fate of the Philippines was to be determined at a peace conference to be held in Paris in the fall.

Carnegie wasted no time making his opinions known on how the U.S. government should proceed. In "Distant Possessions: The Parting of the Ways," published in the August 1898 *North American Review,* he presented a strong argument against the annexation of the Philippines, in the process establishing himself as a viable leader for a burgeoning anti-imperialist movement. The American nation, Carnegie argued, had come to a "parting of the ways." Would it remain a republic, governed by the principles of self-determination? Would it continue to prosper as it enjoyed the blessings of Triumphant Democracy? Or would it follow the path of the mother country toward empire and Triumphant Despotism? "The question should be calmly weighed; it is not a matter of party, nor of class. . . . Let us, therefore, reason together, and be well assured. . . . that we are making no plunge into an abyss."[49]

Carnegie had no doubt but that the United States would be best served by withdrawing quickly from Cuba, Puerto Rico, and the Philippine Islands. As a manufacturer, he proclaimed, he had learned that trade did not follow the flag and colonies did not mean new markets. "Even loyal Canada trades more with us than with Britain. She buys her Union Jacks in New York. . . . Possession of colonies or dependencies is not necessary for trade reasons." The annexation of the Philippines would weaken, not strengthen the economy. The nations of Europe were already spending millions to stay abreast of one another in a feverish, escalating, and increasingly threatening race for foreign colonies. "If we are to compete with other nations for foreign possessions, we must have a navy like theirs." France had fifty-one battleships, Britain eighty; the Americans had four, with five more in construction. To secure and protect its future colonies, America would have to spend millions. Arguing directly against his own self-interest as chief stockholder of the nation's leading manufacturer of steel plate and armor, Carnegie argued that monies spent on the military would come out of the funds needed for internal improvements in the Americas: a Nicaragua Canal; a waterway from the Great Lakes to the ocean; new and improved ports, harbors, canals, and railways. "To be more powerful at home is the surest way to be more powerful abroad. And the way to enhanced power and prosperity at home was through investment in internal improvements."[50]

Carnegie's arguments against annexation were, for the most part, economic and political, but there were moral issues at stake as well.

It if be a noble aspiration for the . . . citizen of the United States him-self . . . to have a country to live and, if necessary, to die for, why is not the revolt noble which the man of the Philippines has been making against Spain? Is it possible that the Republic is to be placed in the position of the suppressor of the Philippine struggle for independence. . . . Are we to practice independence and preach subordination, to teach rebellion in our books, yet to stamp it out with our swords? . . . It has hitherto been the glorious mission of the Republic to establish upon secure foundations Tri-umphant Democracy . . . government of the people, for the people, and by the people. Tires the Republic so soon of its mission, that it must, perforce, discard it to undertake the impossible task of establishing Triumphant Despotism, the rule of the foreigner over the people? And must the mil-lions of the Philippines who have been asserting their God-given right to govern themselves be the first victims of Americans, whose proudest boast is that they conquered independence for themselves.[51]

It was a bravura, if uneven performance. In shifting the terms of his argument from the economic to the geopolitical to the moral and then back again, Carnegie diminished the effectiveness of each strand in his loosely woven manifesto. But by extending the range of the anti-imperial-ist argument, he framed the contours of the debate that would follow. The tone of his article was confident, not defensive; he had logic and morality on his side.

There was, in his article, what John Morley would later refer to as "a touch of exaggeration in expression," but Morley excused it as an in-evitable component of Carnegie's "invincible optimism . . . as to the whole world's progressive course." Carnegie had no doubt but that warfare and imperialism belonged to prior eras of world history. The future was to be one of peace through arbitration and the widening of the sphere of "tri-umphant democracy." He was convinced that his arguments against an-nexation would carry the day. His confidence in President McKinley's judgment was bolstered when the president recalled John Hay to Wash-ington to serve as secretary of state. McKinley, Hanna, and Hay were rea-sonable men, who could not possibly disagree with him on the dangers of annexation to the very soul of America.[52]

He could not have been more wrong. He had been a loyal Republican all his life and never veered far from the party line. Even his apostasy on tariffs had been relatively mild and short-lived. It was difficult if not impossible for him to imagine that he would ever be out of step with the leaders of his party, including his friend John Hay. But he was very much out of step—and would remain so for the rest of his life. While the Republicans, timidly under McKinley, more defiantly under Roosevelt, became the party of expansion and imperialism, Carnegie would remain, as he had always been, an opponent of military adventurism and American imperialism.

THIRTY

The Anti-Imperialist, 1898–1899

NDREW CARNEGIE'S VIEWS. A POLICY OF COLONIAL ACQUISITION MEANS DEATH TO BUSINESS PROSPERITY," read the October 21, 1898, *New York Times* headline. Two days earlier, the Carnegie family had returned to New York on the *Kaiser Friedrich* after nearly a year and a half abroad.

Carnegie wasted no time making public his anti-imperialist sentiments. When a *Times* editorial on October 24 questioned his assertion that the Filipinos were capable of governing themselves, he reminded readers that the Europeans had used similar arguments to defend their own colonial acquisitions. "It was the cry against the Spanish Republics that they could not govern themselves; even Mexico not so long ago was thought incapable of self-government. These are all acquiring the art of self-government through the stern but salutary school of experience. So it will be with the Philippines. The people who have organized a large army and beaten their oppressors may be safely trusted eventually to establish stable government." He then proceeded to raise a new set of objections to annexation. Young Americans who had volunteered to fight against the Spanish "oppressor" ought not to be asked now "to shoot down the patriotic [Filipino] soldiers who were fighting against the oppressor for their country's independence long before Admiral Dewey appeared. . . . Let us watch what they say and do, if a President of the United States ever dares so to order."

Carnegie had never, in the past, been much of a team player, but the stakes were too high for him to fight annexation by himself. Just three days after his return to New York, he began making contact with the nation's most outspoken anti-imperialists. "With every word you say as to the gravity of the present situation I am in full accord," he wrote Carl Schurz, the former Republican senator and now a leader of the campaign against annexation of the Philippines. "I have been greatly troubled . . . and have written the President several times from the other side. . . . When can we meet? . . . p.s. I think I have read everything you have said or written upon the subject. If we could have a hundred bold men in public life like yourself, it would be better for the Republic."[1]

Carnegie's efforts were embraced at once by the anti-imperialists. E. L. Godkin, the editor of *The Nation* and the *New York Evening Post,* welcomed him back to the country with a personal note, and congratulated him on his recent articles and interviews. "You are doing the best work of your life. God protect you. . . . Keep it up; we will copy you [in the *Evening Post*] every time."[2]

Mr. Carnegie's reentry into the public arena, after being out of the country for nearly eighteen months, did not go unnoticed by Republican Party stalwarts who were pushing McKinley to annex the Philippine Islands, as he had Hawaii. Republican Chauncey Depew, who would be elected that year to the Senate from New York, attacked Carnegie for believing that "the only thing to do was to 'scuttle and run.'" Depew assured his listeners that he and Teddy Roosevelt, who was running for governor, believed "in assuming the responsibility in the spirit of Bunker Hill" and holding on to the Philippines.[3]

On October 26, a week after Carnegie's return, Secretary of State Hay, acting on President McKinley's orders, instructed the American commissioners to the Paris Peace Conference to demand that Spain cede Philippines to the United States. Carnegie was incensed at the decision and prepared to do whatever he could to get it reversed. On October 31, one day after the commissioners formally presented their demands to the Spanish, he wrote a letter to the editor of the *New York Tribune,* a pro-annexationist Republican newspaper, in which he provocatively, some might say tastelessly, called attention to the stories from the day before on the return of the dead and wounded. "So goes on day by day the weary tale—only the first drippings, these, of the heavy blood tax required to feed imperialism." The following day, the *Tribune* published a second letter from Carnegie, in which he updated the "record of the vampire imperialism, which feeds upon the blood of our volunteers," and asked pointedly "how many lives of American volunteers is occupation of the Philippines worth, I wonder, in the estimation of imperialists? Not one drop of one, I hope, will yet be the reply of the

American people." Two days later, he published his third letter in four days, this one longer and angrier than the preceding two.

In what he promised *Tribune* readers would be his last letter to the editor, Carnegie on November 3 suggested rather bluntly that the men who had volunteered to fight to free Cuba from the Spanish should refuse to take up arms against the Filipinos. "Volunteers cannot be induced to do the work of imperialism. . . . They never expected to be called upon to hold in subjection at Manila insurgents who had risen against the oppressor—Spain. . . . Now, these men can urge with some degree of reason that they have not been fairly treated; that the President has taken advantage of them; that the war being ended, their engagement is also ended." Republicanism and imperialism were essential foes. If McKinley did not retreat from the course he had set, Carnegie was confident that the U.S. Senate would do its duty, reject the Treaty of Paris, and dedicate itself anew "to the policy of the fathers, and keep the Republic solid, compact, impregnable—free from the vortex of European strife."

It is a credit to Carnegie's stature and to President McKinley and his cabinet's commitment to free speech that no legal action was taken against Carnegie for suggesting that American soldiers should refuse to fight in the Philippines.

Carnegie was fully committed now to the anti-annexation campaign, though he knew this would put him at odds with his party, his president, and his friend John Hay. On November 19, he signed on as an honorary vice president of the newly constituted Anti-Imperialist League and sent a check for $1,000. On Sunday, November 20, he attacked the president for vacillation—"I begin to grow doubtful about the President having convictions upon any subject"—in the anti-imperialist, Democratic *New York World.* This change of venue—from the Republican *Tribune* to Joseph Pulitzer's *World*—was a big step away from the political orthodoxy that had marked his public statements to this point. The *World* welcomed him on its front page, with a portrait, all the space he needed, and a huge banner headline: "ANDREW CARNEGIE: 'NO IMPERIALISM.' The Greatest Steel Manufacturer on Earth Writes for The World His Reasons Against Annexation of the Philippines."

On Tuesday, November 22, three days before his seventy-third birthday, Carnegie took the train to Washington to call on the president at the

White House. The meeting was a private one. Carnegie told reporters only that he had left his card "in the White House." He did not say he had returned later to implore the president to take a firm, public stance against annexation. Receiving no hint of any sort that McKinley was going to do anything of the sort, Carnegie stepped up his public attack. On Thursday, he sent Secretary of State Hay a preview of the article he intended to publish that Sunday in the *World*, enclosed with a personal letter—("strictly confidential—I would write this to no one else but you")—imploring him to intervene with the president. McKinley, Carnegie feared, was being ill-advised by "nice courteous gentlemen, the very kind of people the President don't need about him just now." He, Carnegie, did not relish having to contradict the president in private and criticize him in public, but he knew of no other way to get him to reverse his policy. "Some day if the President awakens from the abyss into which he is about to plunge, he will send for me and thank me for being his best friend. If I arraign him it is for his good. . . . My friend I have never had such an unpleasant task to perform in my life." He intimated that McKinley was not listening to reason because he was ill. (Three years earlier, he had suggested the same thing about Frick, the last man to disagree with him.) "I am so sorry for the President— I do not think he is well, and yet I see that if one American Soldier's blood is spilt shooting down insurgents, either in Cuba or the Philippines, he shall be like another Mac[beth], 'he shall sleep no more'; every drop of blood is upon his hands." Carnegie was so used to winning people over to his point of view—through charm, logic, and sheer bullheadedness—that he took it as a personal affront when he failed. "It is a great strain which the President is putting upon the loyalty of his friends and supporters," he confessed to Hay. "Many are bearing it—it has proved too great for me." He signed his letter, "bitterly opposed to you yet always your friend," then added, a P.S.: "How I wish I could stop all this stirring up of the President in the newspapers, but he gave me no hope that he realized how he was drifting to the devil."[4]

Carnegie's self-importance knew no bounds. What, for John Hay and the loyal Republicans who surrounded the president, must have been most infuriating was his cocksure self-confidence combined with a total lack of party loyalty. It was one thing to criticize the president in private, quite another to do so in the Sunday newspapers. On Sunday, November 27, Carnegie published his second anti-imperialist article in the *World*, this one also splashed across several front-page columns. The centerpiece was a monetary accounting of the pros and cons of imperialism. Speaking from his bully pulpit as a successful manufacturer and businessman, Carnegie reckoned the cost of annexing the Philippines to be not less than $100 million per annum; its benefits, zero. Despite the prognostications of Secretary of the Treasury Lyman Gage, who "has never manufactured anything nor exported anything," and President McKinley, who had "no experience of commerce," annexation, Carnegie declared, would yield no tangible rewards for the nation's businessmen, workingmen, wage earners, or farmers. The Philippines were simply too far away to be a viable trading partner. "The claims of the imperialists that foreign acquisitions extend our commerce with the Philippines is groundless. Let us hear no more of it. They must confine themselves to 'Humanity,' with a big H, for business reasons there are none."

Recognizing that he might have exceeded the bounds of propriety in attacking—in a Democratic newspaper—the president's policy, logic, and lack of convictions, Carnegie concluded his onslaught by confessing that he was a personal friend of McKinley who had, just that week, been granted an interview in the White House. "Mutual friends," he claimed, had suggested that he had gone "too far" in questioning whether McKinley "had convictions upon any subject." He declared in his *World* article that he had not been "speaking of the private character of Mr. McKinley" but of his "official acts as President. . . . I have known Mr. McKinley most of my political life. I have always been his friend, but never so much his friend as I am to-day, when I tell him the truth as I see it. Would that he had more such friends." Shamelessly advertising his exalted place within the Republican Party as independent adviser to presidents past and present, he declared that years before he had counseled another friend, former President Ulysses S. Grant, against annexing San Domingo. "I have done with President McKinley just as I did with President Grant—opposed and denounced his policy. Gen. Grant remained my friend notwithstanding to the end, and I his friend."

Carnegie was walking a tightrope now—and he knew it. He had criticized the president and his policy in print, but remained, or so he professed, a Republican who had the best interests of the party and the president in mind. On November 28, he wrote to warn McKinley that "labor" and the nation's chambers of commerce were opposed to his decision to pay Spain for the Philippines. "The true friend," Carnegie assured McKinley, "not only warns a friend of what he sees to be dangers that surround him, but he ventures to counsel him as to what he should do in the crisis. Were I President of the United States I should announce in my message to Congress that I demanded the Philippines from Spain that I might give to them the Independence which every people can claim as a God-given right." He signed this letter, "your friend personally; but the bitterest enemy you have officially, as far as I know."[5]

Secretary of State Hay was beginning to worry for Carnegie's sanity. In a letter to Whitelaw Reid, Hay criticized the "wild and frantic attack now going on in the press against the whole Philippine transaction," and added that he feared that their mutual friend Andrew Carnegie "really seems to be off his head. He writes me frantic letters signing them 'Your Bitterest Opponent.' He threatens the President, not only with the vengeance of the voters, but with practical punishment at the hands of the mob. He says henceforth the entire labor vote of America will be cast against us, and that he will see that it is done. He says the Administration will fall in irretrievable ruin the moment it shoots down one insurgent Filipino. He does not seem to reflect that the Government is in a somewhat robust condition even after shooting down several citizens in his interests at Homestead."[6]

Carnegie would have been aghast to discover that Hay was ridiculing him behind his back. He had indeed thrown caution to the winds in publicly attacking the sitting president he had helped elect. But he could do no less to protest a policy so fraught with danger to his beloved republic. Annexation of the Philippines was wrong, politically, economically, morally; the president had to be made aware of this.

In everything he said or did, Carnegie believed he was acting in the best interests of his nation—and of the Republican Party. He had, it was true, allied himself with the anti-imperialists, many of whom were opponents of core Republican positions, but he had done so as a loyalist who stood with the party 100 percent on the issues of tariff protection and the gold standard. It was incumbent on those in the anti-imperialist camp, whatever their views on other issues, to work together against annexation. He would do his part as a Republican insider; he expected Godkin and other independents and Democrats to do theirs by rallying to the cause as many voices and votes as they could. "Believe me the fight is just begun and we are going to win. [The president] is now getting letters from most important men, both industrially and politically; they are opening his eyes. There is nothing that benefits the cause like such letters from men to whom he is indebted."[7]

CARNEGIE spent most of his waking hours on the anti-annexation campaign. He might have done better to devote some of that time to his steel business. Since Frick's retirement as president almost five years earlier, Carnegie had been trying to redefine his role in the company. He continued to read and comment on the minutes, reports, and accounting statements sent him, and had taken a lead role in negotiating a long-term agreement with Rockefeller for iron ore and in constructing new railroad that linked his mills to Conneaut Harbor on Lake Erie. By the fall of 1898, his company had attained what he had earlier characterized as "an impregnable position" in the steel industry.

This did not mean, of course, that there were not issues that required his full attention. There were.

The steel industry had entered into what Alfred Chandler has called "the nation's first great merger movement." The notion of merging competing firms was not a new one, but it had been sidetracked by a lack of interest in financing industrial consolidations. Only as it became apparent that manufacturing firms had come out of the mid-1890s depression in better shape than the railroads and that the best protection against antitrust legislation was to merge competing companies did capital become available for a new and robust round of industrial mergers. In 1897, there had been six mergers in the manufacturing sector; in 1898, there were sixteen; in 1899, sixty-three.[8]

In September 1898, the Morgan interests organized the Federal Steel Corporation with a capitalization of $200 million by consolidating the Illinois Steel works, the ore mines of the Minnesota Iron Company, the Lorain Steel Company, and two railroads. Judge Elbert Gary, Illinois Steel's general counsel, became Federal Steel's first president. Through 1898, and with accelerating ferocity in 1899 and 1900, the merger movement transformed the steel industry. The Morgans were not the only financiers who understood the magnitude of profits that could be generated by merging former competitors. Speculators like the Moore brothers of Chicago and John "Bet-a-Million" Gates, acting separately and in concert, organized American Can,

American Steel Hoop, National Steel, and American Tin Plate. Judge Gary, with the Morgans' support, merged fourteen different companies into National Tube and another twenty-five into American Bridge.[9]

Carnegie, Frick, and Schwab had at various times during these two frantic years been asked to join the parade, but they had never found an offer to their liking. In January 1898, Judge Gary had broached the idea of having Carnegie Steel merged into the new American Steel & Wire Company he was helping to organize. Four months later, John Gates had suggested that Carnegie might want to purchase Illinois Steel, then in the process of being consolidated into Federal Steel.[10]

In May, with mergers in the air, Frick suggested that Carnegie consolidate Carnegie Steel and H. C. Frick Coke Company, which were still managed as separate companies. "It seems to me time may have arrived when Carnegie Steel Company should own all stock in H. C. Frick Coke Company. . . . One big perfect organization would have many advantages." He didn't add—and didn't have to—that the individual shareholders in the companies would profit enormously from such a merger.[11]

Though Phipps was in favor of the plan, Carnegie's cousin Dod feared that the terms Frick laid out were far too favorable for the coke company shareholders. "How comes it that the coke business has got so very valuable, has increased in much larger rates than the steel works. . . . Let us take a breath anyway, there are a number of different points of view to look at this from." Carnegie agreed with Dod that the issue needed further examination, which he put off until his return to the States in the fall of 1898.[12]

By the time Carnegie returned after eighteen months abroad, the business decisions waiting to be made had mounted, one on top of and often dependent on the other. His partners tried their best to get Carnegie to concentrate on these issues, but he demurred. All through the fall and winter of 1898, while Frick was considering various plans for consolidation, the majority stockholder appeared to be fully absorbed by the anti-imperialist campaign. Phipps, who had been trying to cash out his interest in the company for several years, traveled to Washington to spend time with Carnegie in November and reported to Frick that Carnegie had finally begun considering "the great question of selling out" and contemplating what he would do with the "great sum" he would get. Much of it, he had decided, would be spent on "a fine plum" for Pittsburgh.[13]

Dod, who was in closer communication with Carnegie than anyone else, had no idea whether his cousin was prepared as yet to sell his interest in his companies. "His mind is nothing like made up, sometimes one way and sometimes another," Dod wrote Phipps in late November. "A little circumstance took place during one of our talks which it would be well you should know—Louise came in and sat down, he turned to her and told her what we were talking about, his thoughts were running favorably to the sale at the time—she remarked that when it was done she 'would be the happiest woman in America'—He immediately turned on her quite savagely and went into quite a tirade on men who retired from business dying etc. etc.—that he would be laying down a crown etc. etc., so I judge the matter will make the most progress by being let alone as much as possible—He is in a considerably excited state about the Philippines anyway and this coming on the back of it may have had physical effects I fear."[14]

Carnegie had been talking about selling his steelworks for years, but never very seriously. It was impossible to sell without a buyer—and outside of Messrs. Rockefeller and Morgan, there were few men capable of coming up with the cash or guaranteed 5 percent gold bonds that Carnegie wanted for his share. Still, he knew that he could not hold out forever, that sooner or later he would have to cash in his majority interest in the company that bore his name.

The question was when. In his "Gospel of Wealth" essays, he had stated that it was the duty of the man of wealth to dispose wisely of the "surplus revenues" he had accumulated. Had his fortune been smaller, it would have required less time to dispose of. But it was huge—and growing larger by the day. The sooner he started giving it away, the better. On the other hand, the longer he delayed, the larger that fortune would grow—and the more there would be to give away.

APPROACHING his mid-sixties, Andrew Carnegie had reinvented himself again. The "Star-spangled Scotchman," capitalist, and philanthropist had become the nation's most outspoken anti-imperialist. Almost daily now, new letters, tracts, pamphlets, and articles were sent forth from the library at 5 West Fifty-first Street. He published letters to the editor of the *New York World* on November 30, December 1, December 8, and December 11, then switched to the Republican *New York Times* and published three more on December 12, 17, and 24. The onslaught continued through January 1899 with another five letters to the editor of the *World*.

To make sure that his message reached the widest possible audience, Carnegie hired a press agency to privately "syndicate" his *World* letters to at least five hundred papers in the "agricultural press," as well as to thousands of weeklies and hundreds of the leading dailies in the country. His friend the industrialist Clem Studebaker requested "copies of all the letters that you have written in reference to the Philippine question" to distribute to his own networks. Frank Doubleday approached him with the suggestion that they publish a short book of articles, "Imperial Policy of the United States, which will sell for 25 cents in paper, 50 cents in cloth."[15]

Carnegie also published the speeches and articles of other prominent anti-imperialists. "Print your speech in pamphlet form and distribute it and I will be your banker," he wrote Carl Schurz after receiving an advance copy of a speech Schurz intended to deliver in early January in Chicago. "This is the way in which I can aid the good work. You have brains and I have dollars. I can devote some of my dollars to spreading your brains." Fearing that Schurz, like Godkin, was becoming disillusioned with the mounting drumbeat of support for annexation, Carnegie reassured him as best he could. "Do not lose faith in the Republic or in Triumphant Democracy. It is sound to the core."[16]

As the weeks passed with no sign that McKinley was backing away from his decision to annex the Philippines, Carnegie reached out to Democrat anti-imperialists like Grover Cleveland. In mid-December, another Democrat, William Jennings Bryan, the man whom Carnegie had so caustically referred to two years earlier as a trickster, a charlatan, and a "conjurer," sent him a note asking Carnegie to call at the Hotel Bartholdi in New York. Carnegie replied by asking Bryan to visit him instead at home. "I would go to you, but am sick and unable to leave the house. I believe you to be the only man in the country today who can save us from the twin evils of imperialism and militarism." The newspapers got wind of the meeting—and had a field day with rumors about the canny old Scotsman and the Nebraskan populist plotting an alliance to overthrow McKinley.[17]

Carnegie asked Bryan to abandon his silver campaign and concentrate his energies on the fight against imperialism. He may also have suggested that if Bryan ran for the presidency in 1900 on an anti-imperialist, instead of a pro-silver platform, he might support him. Bryan, of course, had no intention of tying himself to Carnegie politically. "Am informed that you have prepared public statement discussing our interview & suggesting possibility of your supporting me in 1900," Bryan cabled Carnegie on Christmas Eve. "I hope report is untrue. I have not discussed interview publicly and prefer that you do not. I am not a candidate for any office at this time—whether I ever shall be again depends upon circumstances. I not only ask no pledge of support conditional and unconditional but believe a pledge or prophecy likely to injure the cause of constitutional government against imperialism, a cause which is more dear to me than political preferment. I am making this fight in my own way & hope to see the question disposed of before 1900 so that the fight for silver and against trusts and bank notes may be continued. You and I agree in opposing militarism and imperialism but when these questions are settled we may find ourselves upon opposite sides as heretofore. Let us fight together when we can and against each other when we must exercising charity at all times."[18]

The silver issue, Bryan insisted, was far from dead. Still, he agreed that it was important that he and Carnegie join together to fight imperialism and militarism. "Keep after them," Bryan wrote again on December 30. "You will reach republicans and I shall reach silver men. . . . I assure you that I wish you every success in your effort to point out to other people the evils that attend a colonial policy."[19]

Having met the enemy—in his own home—and been spotted doing so, Carnegie had some explaining to do. On December 29, in a note wishing John Hay and his family a Happy New Year, accompanied by a "small lot of whisky from the Queen's vat—i.e. the vat from which she is renewed every year," Carnegie mentioned the "silly reports anent Bryan and your servant" and explained that Bryan had called upon him as well as "upon several Americans (not Imperialists)—I was honored—He's right anent Americanism—but unless he drops silver . . . he has no chance. But he can beat us to death on the right platform." Though Bryan had told him the exact opposite—in no uncertain terms—Carnegie, pulling out all the stops, informed Hay that he now believed that the "democrats will drop silver. Then look out."[20]

Carnegie had become something of a one-note Jeremiah with his dire predictions of gloom and doom should the Republicans become the party of imperialism. Opposition to Republican expansionism, he insisted in another letter to Hay, was mounting across the country. "A large majority of the most intelligent are opposed. As to Labor, that is settled. As to the Farmers I believe they will be ranged alongside of Labor. . . . From the party point of view I see nothing but disaster. If the country should be polled today the majority against Expansion would be something surprising. . . . I believe [President McKinley] stands to-day in grave danger of wrecking the party to which he owes his elevation to the highest political office on earth, and needs today more than ever he did in his life, the counsel of men who will tell him the truth, because they have no favor to seek at his hands."[21]

If McKinley was not going to pull back from the abyss, the Senate could block annexation by refusing to ratify the Treaty of Paris. In January 1899, a month before the Senate was scheduled to vote on the treaty, Carnegie published the first part of "Americanism Versus Imperialism" in the *North American Review*. Having in previous articles dispatched the argument that imperialism promoted commercial expansion, he took aim at the two remaining tenets of the imperialist credo: that America's military might and security would be strengthened by its acquiring a far eastern empire, and that "humanitarian" interests dictated that the Americans benevolently govern the Filipinos who, as an inferior race, were incapable of governing themselves.

Carnegie declared that the annexation of the Philippines would weaken, not strengthen, the nation militarily by providing potential enemies with an easy point of attack. With a tiny navy and almost no regular army, the United States had but two ways to protect its new holdings in the Far East: it could enter into a military alliance with the British and rely on them for protection, or it could embark at once on a twenty-year project of militarization—for it would, he argued, take at least that long to construct a viable navy. In either case, the result would be disastrous.[22]

The Senate vote on ratification of the Treaty of Paris was scheduled for February 6. Carnegie relocated to Washington in late January to lobby against it. Because a two-thirds majority was required for ratification, the Democrats had it in their power to reject the treaty. Bryan, however, already looking ahead to the 1900 presidential election, believed it wise politics to permit the treaty to pass so that he could oppose it and imperialism in the upcoming campaign. He argued as well, and as speciously, that the treaty did not obligate the president to annex the islands. Carnegie and the vast majority of the anti-imperialists did not see it that way. A vote for the treaty was a vote to ratify the sale of the Philippines to the United States, preliminary to formal annexation.

The treaty was ratified by a one-vote margin when Bryan refused to marshal any votes against it. In the years to come, it would be claimed (without proof) that soon after the ratification vote, Carnegie visited with President McKinley and offered to buy the Philippines for $20 million (the amount the Americans had given Spain) and set the islands free. The claim is not credible. Carnegie did not have anywhere near that sum to spend—and would not until he sold Carnegie Steel, an event that was several years in the future. He never mentioned any such offer in his *Autobiography* or any of his letters, but he never denied the rumor either, preferring perhaps to let it stand as testimony to his commitment to peace.[23]

CARNEGIE had now lost every round of his fight against annexation and imperialism. Like a punch-drunk boxer, he staggered forward, refusing to concede defeat. Though the Philippines were now a possession of the United States, McKinley or his successor could, he claimed, with the stroke of a pen grant them independence.

In March 1899, Carnegie published the second part of "Americanism Versus Imperialism." Again, he laid out all the arguments against annexation, but this time around, the article format could no longer contain his anger. The evils of imperialism had assumed human form as American soldiers waged war on the people they had sworn to free from Spanish tyranny. How could this have come to pass? The Filipinos, though an inferior race, were not savages or barbarians who required taming. Carnegie urged his readers to concentrate their attentions not on the differences between the races, but on their similarities. "It is astonishing how much all human beings the world round are alike in their essentials." The Filipinos "love their homes and their country, their wives and children, as we do, and they have their pleasures. . . . They have just the same feelings as we have, not excluding love of country, for which, like ourselves, as we see, they are willing to die. Oh, the pity of it! The pity of it! That Filipino mothers with American mothers equally mourn their lost sons—one fallen, defender of his country; the other, the invader."[24]

. . .

SOMETIME during the fall of 1898, as Carnegie entered deeper and deeper in the battle against the annexation of the Philippines, he made up his mind to sell his shares in Carnegie Steel if a suitable offer were made. He did not advertise the decision or put it in writing, but let Frick and Phipps know that this was his intention.

Frick proposed that Carnegie Steel and H. C. Frick Coke should be consolidated into one holding company and sold to outsiders or to the remaining partners. Carnegie suggested that Frick should "work this up." Frick answered that there was "really nothing to do" but call a meeting of the senior partners "and reach firm agreement." There were, he insisted, several potential investors ready to provide the funds required to buy the new company. "It is surprising the amount of money awaiting investment in this City [Pittsburgh]. On all sides you find people who are looking for investments."[25]

Early in January 1899, Carnegie, Phipps, Frick, Dod Lauder, Charlie Schwab, and the other senior partners met at Carnegie's home in New York. It was agreed to try first to sell the coke and steel companies either to Federal Steel, the new conglomerate organized by the Morgan interests, or to Rockefeller. When neither party consented to bid, Frick, with Carnegie's encouragement, wrote up the alternative plan to consolidate the steel and coke companies into a new company, which the partners would then purchase. Dod, Carnegie, Phipps, and perhaps Frick would be paid for their shares in cash and gold bonds, and retire.

Although there was much to recommend selling now, Carnegie, after initiating talks on selling, hesitated and then declined to move. The latest profit figures for 1898, which he had just received from Frick, convinced him that the business was doing too well to give up just now. It made better sense to wait a few years and then sell out at an even higher price.

On January 24, he cabled Frick that he had decided not to sell his shares or to merge Frick Coke and Carnegie Steel into a new company. He claimed his decision had been made with Frick's best interests in mind. "To be frank I prefer keeping with you in coke. Why should your own concern, biggest of its kind, be merged or changed as long as you 'are to the fore' or willing to look after it, which I know you can't help doing any more than I can Carnegie Steel? These are no Helen [Frick's daughter] or Margaret by a long sight but they are our business creations. I can't get over the feeling that we lose our affection for this baby if ever a change is made. My will gives Carnegie Steel Co. control if I die, and if anything happens to you, which the Fates forbid, of course we should have to do the best we could which I fear wouldn't be very good. Frick Coke Co. is good for a big year, bigger than interest on bonds. Let's let it alone is my vote. I'm not anxious to sell, neither is the Squire. Neither should you be. It's good enough."[26]

Frick did not agree. He wanted out of the partnerships with Carnegie, out of the coke company, out of the steel company. And he believed that that was what Carnegie would, in the end, agree to. He had received too many confused signals from Carnegie to abandon his plans to first consolidate, then sell H. C. Frick Coke and Carnegie Steel. He would, he was convinced, eventually come up with a plan that was too good for Carnegie to refuse.

In March 1899, the next chapter in this extended saga opened when Frick was approached by William Moore, who, with his brother, had made a name for himself by organizing a number of trusts and mergers, including American Tin Plate and National Steel. Moore offered to buy (and then consolidate) Carnegie Steel for $250 million, five times its established book value, and H. C. Frick Coke for the inflated price of $70 million. He intended to raise much of this money by selling shares in the merged company to the public. We don't know if it was Moore's idea or Frick's to keep his name from Carnegie, but it was, in any event, a wise decision. Carnegie had spent a lifetime distinguishing the good he did as a businessman from the evil wrought by stock speculators. He would not have been comfortable handing over the business that bore his name to a man like Moore with a reputation for stock manipulation.[27]

Years later, Carnegie testified under oath that he "did not know it was Mr. Moore that we were dealing with. Mr. Frick told me that the parties had bound him not to reveal who they were." Carnegie claimed that because he did not know who the principal investors were, he required, "as an earnest of good faith," a nonrefundable option of $2 million, of which 58.5 percent or $1.17 million, his share, was to be deposited in his private account. A reputable businessman and investor, he reasoned, would have no trouble coming up with such an amount. Frick agreed that this was a reasonable request. Carnegie then gave "Mr. Frick and my partner, Mr.

Phipps, my power of attorney to act for me in accepting to option, if it were taken."[28]

Frick presented Moore's proposal to the Carnegie Steel board of managers and announced that as the mystery investor was able to put up only $1 million of Carnegie's option money, he and Phipps would contribute the extra $170,000 from their own pockets. He asked the other partners to forego what would have been their share of the $2 million option money—and they agreed.

On May 4, 1899, Frick and Phipps cabled Carnegie in Britain: "option money deposited today. We furnished '$170,000.' . . . Cannot say when [prospectus] will be made public. Will cable frequently." The next day, Frick cabled again, this time with the news that the outline of the prospectus had been "well received although full details not made public. Subscriptions will be received here at First National Bank and like institutions in leading cities in this country. Likely will be oversubscribed." Before five days had passed, Carnegie received another enthusiastic cable from Frick and Phipps. The new company, they announced, was going to be organized in New Jersey, with the current board of managers as directors and "six additional members." The officers would remain the same. Sufficient money had been raised so that there would be "no necessity ask public subscriptions."[29]

Two days later, Frick discovered for himself why Carnegie had wanted nothing to do with speculators like the Moore brothers. On May 12, Roswell P. Flower, the ex-governor of New York, and one of the speculators whom the Moores had enlisted in their syndicate, died suddenly, throwing the whole plan into limbo. Frick confronted William Moore, who confessed that, with Flower out of the picture, he would have a difficult time coming up with the money he had promised. He suggested instead that they raise it by selling 2.5 million shares of stock at $100 each. Before Frick had a chance to notify either Carnegie in Scotland or the board of managers in Pittsburgh, word was leaked in Chicago that Moore was behind the plan to sell stock to the public, infuriating Frick, who directed his chief lieutenant in New York to "say to Mr. Moore if statements of this kind appear in the press I will feel called upon to deny them. The understanding was there was no publicity to be given this matter until we all agreed just how and when it should be done, and I expect that understanding to be strictly lived up to."[30]

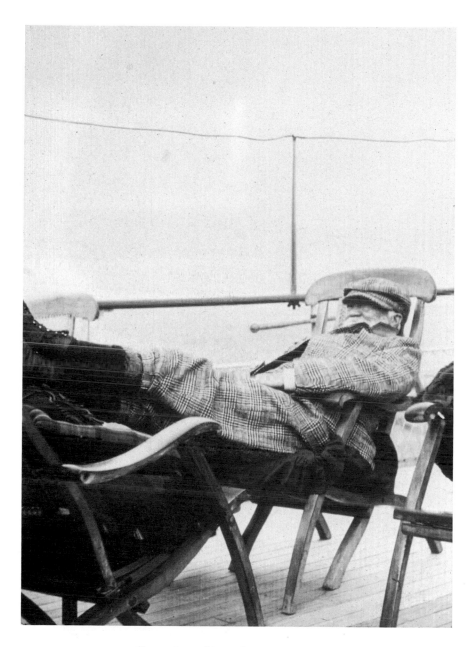

Carnegie on his yacht. (Carnegie Mellon)

A much later photo of Carnegie on his yacht. Sitting on Carnegie's right is John Ross, his Dunfermline solicitor. The other men are the directors of his Dunfermline trust whom he invited to Skibo for a week every summer. *(Anthology)*

Carnegie fishing in one of the Skibo lochs. (Carnegie Mellon)

Carnegie golfing on his links at Skibo. (Carnegie Mellon)

Carnegie would cross Fifth Avenue from his Ninety-first Street mansion, enter Central Park, and go for a turn around the reservoir—sometimes two. Here he is walking with Henry Pritchett, the M.I.T. president who, in 1905, was appointed the first president of the Carnegie Foundation for Advancement of Teaching. This photograph is from 1908. (LC)

In the spring of 1910, Carnegie took his wife and daughter to California. They traveled up and down the coast, Carnegie giving speeches at his libraries while Margaret and Louise went sightseeing. This is a photo of their arrival in Santa Cruz. Their private railway car is in the background. (Santa Cruz Public Library)

Andrew, Louise, Stella Whitfield, and Margaret
in New York City, 1911. (LC)

Carnegie joined the St. Andrew's Golf Club near Hastings-on-Hudson in the late 1890s and had a cottage built for himself on the grounds. Here he is relaxing before the fireplace. The photo is probably from the early 1910s. (Granger Collection)

Carnegie and his best friend, John Morley, at Skibo,
setting out for a long walk. *(Anthology)*

Carnegie and Morley again at Skibo, engaging in their favorite
pastime: extended conversation. *(Anthology)*

Carnegie and Louise together at the opening of one of the many "vacant lot play-grounds" on plots of land Carnegie owned in New York City and loaned to the Parks and Playgrounds Association. Note how Carnegie is standing just behind his wife, on higher ground, so that he will appear taller in the photograph. The photograph is probably from 1911. (Corbis Collection)

Carnegie and Louise at Skibo.
Note Carnegie's plaid suit, his favorite Skibo outfit. (Culver)

Carnegie in his Ninety-first Street library in 1913. He is seventy-eight years old now, but still campaigning for a world court, international arbitration, and naval disarmament. (LC)

In 1913, Carnegie was one of the hosts for the British and Australian peace del-egates who visited New York for a three-day conference. This is one of several photographs taken of him walking with Lord Weardale, the chairman of the British delegation. (Corbis)

Carnegie with his favorite dog, Laddie, in Scotland, probably in 1914. Louise tried her best to transport Laddie to the United States to cheer up her depressed and ailing husband after his "breakdown" in 1915, but ocean travel was restricted because of the war. *(Anthology)*

Carnegie and Louise at the Pittsburgh train station in 1914, bidding good-bye to the city. This was to be Carnegie's last trip to Pittsburgh. (Carnegie Mellon)

Carnegie and Louise, probably after 1915
and his retreat into silence. (Culver)

One of the last formal photographs of Carnegie, Louise, and Margaret, taken on Margaret's twenty-first birthday in March 1918. (ACBM)

Carnegie, in February 1915, during his last public appearance at a hearing before the United States Commission on Industrial Relations. He had been called to testify on the role of public philanthropies created by men of wealth. *(Anthology)*

The cat was out of the bag. On May 20, Frick and Phipps wrote Carnegie about the new plan, which, they explained, would, unlike the first one, capitalize the company at $350 million, exactly what it was worth, with no water added. Mr. Moore, Frick now confessed, had wanted a higher capitalization, but in the new plan, would not get it.[31]

Three days later, Frick cabled Carnegie again, in one final attempt to explain away Moore's failure to live up to the agreement he had made. "Mr. Moore is an honest man, but very sanguine. He led us to believe that the First National Bank and City National Bank would join him in taking charge of this matter. . . . This [new] agreement puts the matter in control of Mr. Phipps and myself, and is on a very conservative basis, in view of what has been agreed to pay you, and on a basis where our employes and friends can safely invest. It is astonishing the demand there is from that source. Notwithstanding the demand, however, amount of money to raise is immense. . . . Believe the public will subscribe [buy common stock] largely. If I should find, however, that it was not all going to be taken, might conclude to sail with my family on 6th of June, and have a conference with you regarding it, in which event would have Mr. Phipps accompany me."[32]

Though he did not reveal it in his letters or cables, Frick was close to panic now. The option was due to expire on August 4, at which point the $1,170,000 paid Carnegie would be forfeited. Frick and Phipps expected that Carnegie would keep Moore's portion of the option money and return the $170,000 they had contributed.

On May 29, Frick wrote to suggest that Moore accompany him and Phipps to Skibo to ask Carnegie for an extension. "If you should decide to go, it would be well to keep it entirely quiet, and not let the newspapers know that you are going abroad to see him. I have grave fears that Mr. Carnegie will decline to extend the option. He will regard it as a cold business transaction, so that the result, so far as you are concerned, would be to lose the money you have paid, and I have serious doubts about Mr. Carnegie's willingness to ever return it. Please think this all over, and let me hear from you." When Moore refused to travel to Scotland, Frick asked if he could, at the very least, organize "an Underwriting Syndicate . . . that would take absolutely, say $50 [million] or $60 [million] of the stock, and pay for it. . . . This, I think, would greatly influence Mr. Carnegie to extend or modify the option. Without this, I fear our effort will be fruitless."[33]

. . .

THE FOUR CARNEGIES—Andrew, Louise, Stella, and Margaret, who had celebrated her second birthday in March—arrived in June to spend their second summer at Skibo, their first as owners. On June 23, they were joined by their tenants and neighbors for the official laying of the foundation stone for the castle they intended to build on the site of the existing house. Construction began at once; the servants were moved to a nearby cottage, the Carnegies settled into their own wing of the old house.[34]

There were fewer guests than usual that summer, though Carnegie did entertain the American ambassador to Britain, Joseph Choate, Choate's wife and daughter, the journalist William Stead, and several Americans who were "shooting" nearby. Carnegie had quickly settled into his new life as a country squire. He was, his friend Stead thought, "like a child with a new toy. For a man of sixty two [sixty-four really], he has succeeded marvelously in preserving unimpaired the delight of youth in all that is new and beautiful. He is as enthusiastic as a boy about Skibo. Heaven itself, he declared, is not nearly so beautiful as Skibo." Carnegie enjoyed fishing for salmon in the Dornoch Firth and trout in the mountain streams that fed it. The *Seabreeze,* his yacht, lay at anchor a short distance from the house. That summer, Carnegie took several trips with his family and one with Rudyard Kipling, who was staying nearby with his father and cousin while recuperating from illness. Carnegie also spent a great deal of time at the golf links, about three quarters of a mile from the main house, down a beautiful winding path. He introduced Ambassador Choate to the game that summer. With Stead as their caddie, he and Choate played three or four holes before a thunderstorm (a frequent Skibo occurrence) sent them scurrying back to the house.[35]

Harry Phipps and Frick arrived at Skibo in the second week of June to petition for an extension of the Moore option. Carnegie's answer was blunt and to the point. "I said not one hour," he reported to Dod, adding that both Frick and Phipps were "delighted, both wished the matter ended." Carnegie then proposed that the company be sold to the partners who, he suggested, could take out a new mortgage on the properties and buy out his share for 4 percent gold bonds. "Pleasant interview at Skibo," Frick and Phipps cabled the board in Pittsburgh. "Will not extend or modify present option. Have advised Chicago [i.e., Moore]."[36]

Carnegie, as always the most gracious of hosts, took the two men on long walks and carriage drives, and proudly showed them the improvements he had made—and planned to make—on his estate. It was, he thought, a very pleasant visit. In July, Carnegie visited Phipps at his estate in England. The partners, who had been friends now for almost half a century, went fishing and "Andrew was made happy by catching two fine salmon—17" to 18" inches long—hooked and landed them unaided," Phipps wrote Frick, who had returned to Pittsburgh. "I landed three the other morning."[37]

The Moore plan had fallen through, but the promise of a huge payout had prompted Carnegie to think again about selling his interests in Carnegie Steel and H. C. Frick Coke. During Stead's visit, Carnegie confided to his old friend that he was going to retire on January 1, 1900. He was not, he insisted, retiring because of health; he was "as active as ever," Stead found. Nor was he retiring because of pressure from his partners who, he told Stead, hoped he would remain active in the business. "But Mr. Carnegie was inexorable. He said it was much better that he should leave and let them run the business themselves." If he held on to the business, it would increase greatly in value. Nonetheless, he had decided to "retire in order that he might spend his life in distributing the money which he had taken so much time to earn." Stead found the prospect of a self-made millionaire embarking on such a venture of giving away his entire fortune "so interesting, and so practical, and so up-to-date," that he chose to devote his upcoming "Annual," the 150–200 page pamphlet he sent in December to his *Review of Reviews* subscribers, to the story of "Mr. Carnegie's Conundrum: £40,000,000: What Shall I Do With It?" On learning of Stead's intention, Carnegie had "rather deprecated my publishing anything about him or his millions until next year. His plans, he said, were not completed." Still, he supplied Stead with the autobiographical materials he needed and tacitly gave him permission to proceed. Stead's pamphlet was published in late November 1899.[38]

Carnegie was busy that summer on his own writing projects. He expanded his anti-annexation articles into the full-length book Frank Doubleday had asked for, then put the manuscript away. It would never be published. Carnegie had reluctantly concluded that summer that there was nothing more to be said on the subject of the Philippine annexation. The Senate had approved the Treaty of Paris, an insurgency had broken out in the islands, American soldiers killed, and a new war declared. No president could dare grant independence to the Filipino insurgents while they were at war with American soldiers.[39]

Carnegie wrote no more articles or letters to the editor or private notes to Secretary of State Hay about the Philippines. He did not give up his commitment to anti-imperialism so much as redirect it from the American annexation of the Philippines to the British invasion of the Transvaal, the northern Boer republic. Britain's conduct in South Africa was, Carnegie insisted in a *North American Review* article written that fall and published in December 1899, "indefensible and her policy foolish. No nation has a right to attack and endeavor to suppress a people so capable of self-government as the Dutch [Boers]."[40]

Carnegie did not feel quite so isolated as an anti-imperialist in Britain as he had in the United States. In the United States, his allies had been apostate Republicans and a few Democrats. In Britain, he was joined in his attack on the Boer War by his friends in the Liberal Party. When Sir William Harcourt, formerly chancellor of the exchequer in Gladstone's government, delivered one of several impassioned speeches against the war, Carnegie congratulated him on his and the Liberal Party's stance.

> Although I have no right to interfere in your politics here in Britain I cannot refrain from writing you a few words having just finished your speech. Never has the question been so clearly, so powerfully placed before the country. It is unanswerable and such is my faith in truth so clearly put that I have new hopes and (barring accident which is always to be feared in such positions as the present) that my nation is to be saved from the indelible disgrace of wrongfully waging war against a weak state, whose internal independence it has itself guaranteed. Yourself and Morley will live in history for your noble defense of the right. Our own branch of the English speaking race is today covered with infamy suppressing allies whom it promised independence—I have tried to imitate you even against my own party. . . . I am going to denounce McKinley and his apostasy to our traditions—wish I could reach our people as I know you have done.[41]

Despite his promise, Carnegie did not, on returning to New York in the fall of 1899, denounce the president. With American troops having returned to battle—this time against Filipino insurgents—he realized that there was now no way of recalling them short of some sort of victory.

THIRTY-ONE

"The Richest Man in the World," 1899–1901

T HE BATTLE was joined in October 1899. This time there would be no reconciliation.

Frick had hoped and expected that Carnegie would refund the $170,000 he and Phipps had put up as option money in the Moore deal. By the end of the summer, it had become clear that Carnegie had no intention of giving it back. He had discovered that Frick and Phipps had, without informing him, written into the agreement with Moore a $5 million bonus for themselves should the deal be consummated. Carnegie had given them power of attorney to act on his behalf in the negotiations. He had never suspected that they were, in fact, copromoters and would profit handsomely if and when Carnegie Steel was sold to Moore's syndicate. The least he could do to show his displeasure was to withhold their $170,000.

Frick did not petition Carnegie for the money he and Phipps were owed. Nor did Carnegie ever raise the issue of the $5 million bonus. Instead, Frick and Carnegie took out their anger by veiled and not so veiled criticisms of one another. Carnegie, who held his temper better, did not mention Frick by name when he criticized several contracts which the board, under Frick's leadership, had recently approved. Frick defended himself by going on the attack. "These contracts have been made, and we must live up to them. If Mr. Carnegie wishes to review past actions," Frick declared at the board meeting of September 11, "we have as much right to review other things. . . . I think we have blundered about in proportion to our interests in our concern." Carnegie, he was suggesting, as the majority stockholder had made the majority of the blunders.[1]

Remarks published in the minutes were intended for Carnegie's consumption and Frick knew this. He had tried to provoke Carnegie but without much success. "The Chairman says that we all have blundered," Carnegie responded blandly on October 16. "True, and always will blunder; no one is infallible, but suggestions of a change do not imply personal reflections. It is simply a business question as to what is best, and experience should teach us to change when thought best."[2]

Frick was not conciliated by what he must have seen as a rather condescending riposte. For more than two decades now, he had bristled as Carnegie exercised his prerogatives as majority stockholder. After resigning as president of Carnegie Steel, Frick had stayed on as chairman of the board of managers and provided the glue that kept the company together. While Carnegie was leading the high life in New York, London, and his Scottish estates, Frick stood at his post in Pittsburgh through fair weather and foul. He had waited patiently for the older man to resign or, failing that, to turn over control of the business to his partners. At the very least, he expected that Carnegie might by now have recognized, as surely everyone else did, that Henry Clay Frick knew as much as he did about the steel business and infinitely more about coke.

Twice before Frick had lost his temper—and his good sense—at Carnegie's hauteur, picked a fight knowing he could not win, and been forced to resign. As long as Carnegie remained the majority stockholder in Carnegie Steel and the controlling stockholder in H. C. Frick Coke, there was no way Frick was going to win a battle with him.

On October 25, nine days after Carnegie's letter acknowledging his blunders was presented at the Carnegie Steel board meeting, the H. C. Frick Coke board met, with Frick in the chair. At the end of the meeting, Thomas Lynch, the president of the company, reported that Carnegie Steel officials had informed him that they had "been advised by Mr. Carnegie that he made a permanent contract with Mr. Frick at a fixed price per ton [$1.35], commencing January 1st last," and that they would pay only that amount, not the higher rates the coke company had been billing them. Lynch insisted that there was "no record of any such contract" for $1.35 a ton coke, and he had "repeatedly so informed the proper officers of the Carnegie Steel Company." There were arguments to be made for and against such an agreement. A year before, Frick, at Carnegie's suggestion, had agreed to fix the price of coke at $1.35 for the next five years, but the oral agreement reached between the two was never finalized. Because the market price of coke was, in 1899, above $1.35 a ton, it was to Carnegie Steel's advantage to enforce the unsigned agreement. It was to H. C. Frick Coke's advantage to deny its existence. Dod Lauder, who represented his cousin and Carnegie Steel on the coke company board, suggested that any questions about such an agreement should not be the subject of board business as they were "between Mr. Frick and Mr. Carnegie." Frick ignored him and asked Lynch if he wished the board to take any action. Lynch recommended a formal resolution rejecting Carnegie Steel's claim that H. C. Frick Coke was bound by prior agreement to deliver coke for $1.35 a ton. Dod Lauder protested again that this was a matter for Frick and Carnegie. Frick overruled him. He had, he insisted, no authority to make any contracts for the coke company. That was the responsibility of the board. He put Lynch's resolution to a vote and it was passed, with Dod the sole dissenter.[3]

On Carnegie's copy of the board minutes is scrawled, in his handwriting: "No Contract. Declaration of War." This had, it appears, been Frick's intention. Rather than attempt to negotiate his differences with Carnegie, he was ready to go to war. Lynch formally notified Schwab at Carnegie Steel that he had been authorized by the H. C. Frick board to cease delivery of coke until the steel firm acknowledged that there was no agreement in place setting the price at $1.35.[4]

Carnegie and Schwab did not respond to the obvious provocation, but instead behaved as if nothing had happened. In early November, Carnegie traveled to Pittsburgh to attend a meeting of the Carnegie Steel board of managers. There was no mention of the coke-pricing dispute at the meeting; the major item of business was a resolution to buy from Frick a parcel of land near Homestead. It was approved unanimously.

While their two companies remained in battle mode over the critical issue of how much the steel company would pay for its coke, Frick and Carnegie continued their long-term correspondence on merging. Carnegie had proposed combining the two companies based on their book values. Frick recommended on November 18 that the merged company be capitalized at $150 million, double the book value for both companies. It was not an unreasonable proposal, as the consolidated steel and coke company would be worth at least that much on the open market.[5]

Carnegie rejected Frick's proposal. That same day, November 20, the board of managers of Carnegie Steel held its regular monthly meeting.

Frick inserted into the minutes an angry, disjointed, frenetic attack on Carnegie. He called the board's attention to the fact that the company had, at Carnegie's insistence, loaded up on advance orders for rails at a full $8 less than the current market price. Then, having accused his senior partner of poor business judgment, he violated Carnegie's cardinal rule of business etiquette and launched an *ad hominem* attack. Frick informed the board that he had learned, from whom he did not say, "that Mr. Carnegie, while here, stated that I showed cowardice in not bringing up [the] question of price of coke between Steel and Coke companies. It was not my business to bring that question up." He insisted that neither he nor Carnegie had the right to determine company policy in regard to coke pricing, then steered off in another direction and accused Carnegie of attempting to destroy the H. C. Frick Coke Company and its directors:

"The value of our coke properties, for over a year, has been, at every opportunity, depreciated by Mr. Carnegie and Mr. Lauder [Cousin Dod], and I submit that it is not unreasonable that I have considerable feeling on this subject. He [Carnegie] also threatened, I am told, while here, that . . . if the minority stockholders [of H. C. Frick Coke] would not give their share of the coke to the Steel Company at about cost, he would, if possible, attempt to ruin them. He also stated, I am told, while here, that . . . he had doubts as to whether I had any right, while Chairman of the Board of Managers of the Carnegie Steel Company" to privately purchase land near Homestead for later resale to the steel company. Why, Frick asked rhetorically, had not Carnegie been "manly enough to say to my face what he said behind my back?" Frick demanded that Carnegie apologize for slandering him and threatened not to sell his land to Carnegie Steel without such an apology. "Harmony is so essential for the success of any organization that I have stood a great many insults from Mr. Carnegie in the past, but I will submit to no further insults in the future. There are many other matters I might refer to, but I have no desire to quarrel with him, or raise trouble in the organization, but, in justice to myself, I could not at this time, say less than I have."[6]

Carnegie wrote Frick at once

to relieve you as promptly as possible from present troublesome thoughts. Never did I say a word other than in praise of your conduct anent the purchase up river [i.e., the property adjoining Homestead which Carnegie

Steel had purchased while Carnegie was in Pittsburgh].... This is just the result sure to come from tale bearers—distortion—words innocent if one hears and knows the conditions and spirit in which they are said become quite another thing when "the informer" injects his venom. Again— I don't remember ever mentioning the coke difference except to those who had said to me you had told them you would fix it with me.... If I have "insulted" you I have known it not—on the contrary I have looked forward until your scheme miscarried to you being in command of all and it has not been a source of anything but a satisfaction to me.... I shall receive your unmerited invective in silence. When you get your usual calm and if you come to me I shall tell you all the circumstances just as they occurred and you will be sorry for your hasty outburst to your partners. I am not guilty and can satisfy you of this—also of the folly of believing tale bearers, a mean lot.[7]

Carnegie had probably gossiped too much about Frick during his most recent trip to Pittsburgh. Discretion had never been one of his virtues. The important point, for Carnegie at least, was that he had acted without malice. Carnegie did not hold grudges. Frick had tried to profit, at his expense, from the Moore deal, but that was past history and Carnegie was always looking forward. The dispute between the two men on the price of coke was about "business" and thus, Carnegie trusted, amenable to settlement.

Cousin Dod, who had never liked or trusted Frick, was not nearly as charitable. By personally attacking Carnegie at the board meeting, Frick had thrown down the gauntlet. Carnegie, Dod insisted, could not now back away. "To my mind the chairman [Frick] seems to have deliberately burned his boats, & the issue is now Carnegie or Frick pure & simple. Should you make any arrangement that leaves him in power everyone will practically look on the settlement as your virtual abdication from the control of the affairs of the firm.... I have considered ever since this controversy about coke began that he is scarcely responsible for many of his sayings and doings and, now that the sting of the failure last summer is added, the less said about his condition of mind the better."[8]

"You voice my views exactly," Carnegie wrote back. He had, he recognized now with a bit of prodding from his cousin, suffered too long from Frick's tantrums. Carnegie had no stomach for personal confrontations—

and never had. He had long ago exiled himself from Pittsburgh because he had no wish to engage in boardroom battles or intrigues with partners. Frick, on the contrary, appeared to enjoy such confrontations. For that reason alone, he had to be sent away. "Frick goes out of chairmanship of board next election or before—that's settled days ago." Carnegie insisted to his cousin that he had, in years past, put up with Frick's outbursts because he needed him. But the time had come to replace Frick with Charlie Schwab, who had demonstrated that he was ready to run the company. "You may show to CMS," he instructed Dod, "and let him lay his plans accordingly— once again we are to be a happy and united family. . . . My birthday—never better nor happier especially since I decided to tell Mr. Frick in kindest manner that I mean divorce under 'Incompatibility of Temper.' I shall tell him never had anything but happy family until he came into it—and I am not going to have anything else—it is divorce between us as far as management of our business is concerned. . . . I believe our best business interests demand an end of quarreling."[9]

Schwab, uncomfortably thrust into the middle of the dispute between his two superiors, tried to effect some sort of reconciliation, but failing, suggested that Carnegie notify Frick himself that he was removing him from office. "Undoubtedly, the best way is for you to come to the offices [in Pittsburgh] and arrange matters with Mr. Frick direct. . . . Believe me, Dear Mr. Carnegie, I am always with you and yours to command. I want to be straightforward toward all. I believe the great majority of important partners feel as I do." Schwab then wrote Frick, advising him that Carnegie was going to depose him as chairman and that there was nothing Schwab could do to protect him.[10]

Carnegie arrived in Pittsburgh a few days later and informed the board members that he was going to request Frick's resignation. Before he had a chance to do so, Frick formally resigned in a letter to the board dated December 5, 1899.[11]

FRICK'S RESIGNATION came at a critical moment in the company's history, as it was being challenged by newly formed conglomerates in finished steel. On December 30, Carnegie outlined his battle plan to the board of managers. If the newest of the giant steel-finishing trusts, in tin plate and wire, decided to produce their own unfinished ingots instead of purchasing them from Carnegie Steel, Carnegie was prepared to fight them to the death. "If they decline to give us what we want, then there must be no bluff. We must accept the situation and prove that if it is fight they want, here we are 'always ready.' Here is a historic situation for the Managers to study—Richelieu's advice:—'First, all means to conciliate; failing that, all means to crush. . . .' We should look with favor upon every combination of every kind upon the part of our competitors; the bigger they grow, the more vulnerable they become. It is with Firms as with Nations, 'Scattered possessions' are not in it with a solid, compact, concentrated force."[12]

Hoping that Frick had cooled down since submitting his letter of resignation, Carnegie wrote him from New York in late December or early January 1900 and took up once the notion of consolidating Frick Coke and Carnegie Steel. At the end of this handwritten letter, he segued into a discussion of the dispute about coke pricing which had precipitated the break between the two partners. "I wish you would fix coke prices. Schwab wrote me about them. My views are as far as I can see now that the price fixed by you $1.35 was right." He suggested that the two companies begin negotiations on a "fixed price for all time and relieve us of friction which has arisen. Surely you and Lauder and Lawrence [Phipps, Harry's son] could figure this out. . . . Do get at a permanent arrangement & greatly oblige— you want to make your pard a Christmas Gift any how—I'll not look for a $40,000 thing. Give me a settlement permanent on Coke & I'll bless you." Below his signature, Carnegie added: "We never had friction before. It annoys me more than dollars even than Philippines."[13]

There is no record of any response from Frick, perhaps because he recognized, belatedly, that he held a losing hand.* Carnegie's position was unassailable. As a majority stockholder in H. C. Frick Coke, he now pushed through a reorganization which gave him five out of seven seats on an enlarged board of directors. He, not Frick, was in complete control now, not only of Carnegie Steel, but of the Frick coke company as well.

On Sunday, January 7, 1900, Carnegie, who had been in Pittsburgh twice in two months, returned once more to ratchet up the pressure on Frick. On Monday, he met again with the Carnegie Steel board and proposed that it

---

*Kenneth Warren, whose account of the breakup is the most compelling we have, concedes that from this point on it is difficult to follow the sequence of events. "There was clearly further tampering with the company records. The evidence now available is not complete"—*Triumphant Capitalism*, 255.

formally withdraw the 1897 ironclad agreement which, because Phipps had refused to sign it, was non-binding. He then asked the partners who had joined the firm in the last ten years to sign the 1892 ironclad. His reasons for adding the signatures of the new partners to the 1892 agreement were transparent. He was making sure that this agreement was legally binding should he choose to invoke it. Like the other versions of the ironclad, the 1892 agreement provided that three quarters of the partners with three quarters of the shares of stock could, at any time, for any reason, expel a sitting partner and demand that he sell his shares back to the company at book value. If Frick did not back down, Carnegie intended to exercise this clause and remove him from the partnership.

On Tuesday, January 9, the reconstituted board of the H. C. Frick Coke Company met and, with Frick and Lynch in a five-to-two minority, approved the $1.35 a ton price agreement. Frick stormed out of the room to confer with his lawyers.

On Wednesday, as Frick worked in the private office at the Carnegie Building in downtown Pittsburgh, he was told that Andrew Carnegie was in the anteroom asking to see him. According to George Harvey, Carnegie announced that "he had dropped in to see if they could not reach a definite and final settlement of the coke dispute between their two companies." He insisted, once again, that Frick had the year before agreed to a permanent price of $1.35. As Frick was uncomfortable with that agreement, Carnegie now proposed that the price stand for two years only. Frick asked if this were a final offer; Carnegie reminded him that he had the votes on the board to do anything he pleased. Frick then inquired if Carnegie would be willing to sell his interest in H. C. Frick Coke "at a price to be fixed by competent and disinterested business men." Carnegie declined to do so. Frick asked if Carnegie would buy Frick's interest in Carnegie Steel "at a price to be fixed in the same way." Again Carnegie refused. Frick wanted to know what would happen if he declined to accept Carnegie's offer to set the price at $1.35 for two years. Carnegie answered that if Frick persisted in causing harm to Carnegie Steel, the partners would have no choice but to buy him out at "book value."[14]

The discussion had gone as far as it could. Frick, realizing he was trapped, lashed out in anger. According to Burton Hendrick, who based his account on a "memorandum" by Carnegie describing the episode, Frick "jumped up and clenched his fist and said, 'Why, I expected that, now you will see what a fighter I am. This is a fight,' and then he began a tirade of personal abuse. I sat very soberly, because there is nothing sobers one man so much as seeing another give way to passion. . . . He became wilder and I was forced to leave."[15]

The next step had already been prepared. Carnegie called into session an emergency meeting of the Carnegie Steel board of managers. A resolution was offered and passed requesting "Henry C. Frick to sell, assign and transfer to The Carnegie Steel Company, Limited, all of his interest in The Carnegie Steel Company." Those signing the resolution represented more than three quarters of the partners and three quarters of the outstanding shares of the company, as per the 1892 ironclad agreement.

On Monday, January 15, the board secretary, Francis Lovejoy, who had been one of the few partners opposed to the resolution, presented Frick with the resolution. Two days later, Lovejoy resigned his position as secretary of the board, in protest against its treatment of Frick.

On Tuesday, Frick delivered his reply to Lovejoy. "Yesterday you served on me a notice, dated January 15, 1900 in which you referred to 'A certain Agreement between The Carnegie Steel Co., Limited, and the partners composing it.' . . . Will you please give me an exact copy of the said alleged agreement, the existence of which I deny?"[16]

On February 1, Charles Schwab, as president of Carnegie Steel, informed Frick that his 6 percent interest had been transferred to the company and that the proceeds from the sale were being held in trust for him. Based on the terms of the ironclad agreement, Frick was to receive $4.9 million, which represented 6 percent of $75.6 million, the "book value" assigned the company. The settlement was ridiculously unfair. Any impartial valuation of the company would have put its worth between $250 and $500 million, 6 percent of which would have yielded Frick some $15 to $30 million.

It was true, as Carnegie and Frick both knew, that on several occasions in the past, the interests of ejected or retired partners or their estates had been formally bought back by the company at book value, but almost always with additional monies added as bonuses or honoraria to bring the sum closer to the market value of the shares. Had Carnegie found a way to do the same for Frick, he might have avoided the trouble that was to follow. But he did not. Frick had turned aside Carnegie's repeated offers of friendship; he had spurned his many attempts at reconciliation; and he had, in the past year alone, betrayed him twice: first in the Moore agreement, then by denying the existence of the $1.35 price agreement he had orally agreed to.

With Carnegie steadfast against any compromise, Frick had no recourse but to turn to the courts. On February 13, 1900, he sued Carnegie Steel in the Court of Common Pleas of Allegheny County, asking the court, among other things, to enjoin the company from interfering in any way with his "interest in said Carnegie Steel Co. (Ltd), and from excluding him from participation in the care and management of the assets and business."[17]

The contents of Frick's complaint exploded across the front pages of the nation's newspapers. It was, to that point, the most spectacular lawsuit in American corporate history, with two flesh-and-blood protagonists, each of whom made for great copy—and better caricature. Frick's complaint and Carnegie's reply were filled with juicy tidbits that provided fodder for the many stories that followed.

Frick charged that Carnegie had been an absentee feudal landlord who, having "conceived a personal animosity [had] without good reason, and actuated by malevolent motives," forced his resignation and concocted a "fraudulent scheme" to defraud him of his rightful share in the company "whilst benefiting himself." There was no properly signed "ironclad" agreement, and had never been one; Carnegie had no legal right to eject him from his leadership role in the company, no right to force him to sell back his 6 percent interest, and certainly no right to fix an arbitrary value on that 6 percent.[18]

Carnegie gave as good as he got. The response to Frick's complaint, filed on behalf of Carnegie Steel and signed by all the board members save Phipps and Lovejoy, declared that Frick was "a man of imperious temper, impatient of opposition, and disposed to make a personal matter of any difference of opinion. . . . At times, moreover, he gives away to violent outbursts of passion, which he is either unable or unwilling to control. He demands absolute power and without it is not satisfied." Frick had been removed from office and from his position as a partner and share owner because he had caused dissent within the board, and had begun to "introduce controversy of a personal character into the business of the association." In demanding Frick's resignation, Andrew Carnegie had not been "actuated by malevolent motives," but rather "by a desire for what he be-

"TAKE THE CRUMBS, LITTLE BOY!"

lieved to be, and what in fact was, for the best interests of the association " Carnegie did not harbor any "personal animosity toward the plaintiff." On the contrary, he had "at all times entertained and exhibited towards the plaintiff the most kindly sentiments [and had always] endeavored at all times to deal with him in the most generous spirit and with the most sincere regard for his interests." As for the ironclad agreement which determined the value of Frick's 6 percent interest, it had been in place for years, was absolutely legal, and had, in fact, been enforced by Frick during his tenure as president. Frick knew from the moment he joined the firm that he would be bound by this agreement and that "the value of his interests is by the terms of said agreement to be ascertained by reference to the books of the company," not by the market value of the company's assets.[19]

The most spectacular revelations to come out of Frick's lawsuit had to do with the outrageous profits Carnegie Steel had been generating as a "tariff-protected" manufacturer. Until Frick's complaint, no one had any idea how profitable Carnegie Steel had become. Carnegie and Frick had kept these numbers secret because they knew they would provide union leaders, Democratic politicians, and antitariff men on both sides of the aisle with vital ammunition against protective tariffs for the steel industry. Now, in an instant, Frick ripped away the curtain, revealing that Carnegie Steel had earned net profits of $21 million in 1899, and that he and Carnegie expected those profits to rise above $40 million for 1900.

The cartoonists had a field day, picturing Frick demanding his share of the loot from Carnegie. The story of the feud was too good to go away. It had everything the newspapers wanted: melodrama, revenge, deceit, and betrayal with political overtones. Democratic politicians and editors were particularly overjoyed. Nineteen hundred was a presidential election year in which a Republican high-tariff man, William McKinley, was running for reelection against a Democratic free trader, William Jennings Bryan. Marcus Hanna, now a U.S. senator and still in charge of Republican Party politicking, insisted that Frick and Carnegie agree to postpone any trial until December, after the election.[20]

Both men were besieged with letters and cables begging them for the good of Carnegie Steel, the steel industry, Pittsburgh, and the Republican Party to settle their differences and avoid the disclosure of embarrassing revelations sure to emerge from a public trial. George Westinghouse, an associate of each, offered his services as mediator. "Will you allow me to say," he wrote Carnegie, "at the risk of being considered officious, that this matter is looked upon by mutual friends, as not only very harmful to your own interests but to Pittsburgh generally."[21]

Among the most poignant letters was one from Samuel Harden Church, the secretary of the board of Carnegie's Pittsburgh Institute. "The sorrow which has fallen upon you has filled my heart with profound pity. Nowhere do I hear any comment except of deepest regret. . . . All look upon it as a very great misfortune for all concerned, including this community. . . . It is a melancholy reflection to those who love you . . . that you should be called back to hard labor, to detail, to drudgery, and, worst of all, to face the friends and partners of a lifetime in the angry controversies of a lawsuit."[22]

Though Carnegie, with his cheery smile and outsized benevolence, was a much more sympathetic character than the tightly laced, perpetually scowling Frick, on legal and moral grounds it was hard to argue with the junior partner, who was being defrauded of tens of millions of dollars. Carnegie could argue that Frick had agreed to the terms of the ironclad when he became a partner. But he could not destroy the evidence that the 1892 ironclad was not binding, as Frick had warned him, because it had not been signed by all the partners in 1892.

Carnegie's resolve not to compromise gave way quickly. Had Harry Phipps been willing to fight on alongside him, Carnegie might have stood his ground; but Phipps was firmly planted in the Frick camp. He believed Frick was entitled not to a share of the book value of the company, but to its market value, which was considerably more.

On March 17, a month after Frick filed his complaint, Carnegie and Schwab met with Phipps and Lovejoy representing Frick at 5 West Fifty-first Street to arrange a settlement. Phipps suggested that, as a first step forward, the proposal that Frick had floated the year before to consolidate the steel and coke companies and increase their "capitalization" or book value be considered. Two days later, again without Frick present, a second meeting was held, this time in Atlantic City, a neutral location a step closer to Pittsburgh and far enough away from New York not to be noticed by the press. The Carnegie Steel board, with wives in tow to fool the press into believing this was a pleasure trip, agreed to organize a new holding company, capitalized at $320 million: $250 for Carnegie Steel, $70 million for H. C. Frick Coke. The existing partners, Frick included, were to receive half their interests in the new company in common stock and half in 5 percent first-mortgage bonds. Under this agreement, Carnegie's share was almost $176 million; Phipps's, $35 million; Frick's $31.6 million. Frick agreed to give up any management role in the new company and withdraw his suit. The base issue of the price of coke was settled quickly and sensibly, with the companies splitting down the middle the price H. C. Frick Coke demanded and the $1.35 Carnegie insisted had been agreed upon.[23]

"Settlement made," Frick telegrammed a friend and former colleague. "I get what is due me. All well. I, of course have not met this man Carnegie and never expect nor want to. It is not my intention to be officially connected with the reorganized concern."[24]

Frick and Carnegie would never meet again. Their final communication came in the form of a nasty telegram from Frick to Carnegie in Skibo, in August 1900. Frick, who remained a stockholder in the new consolidated firm, in his final attempt to convince Carnegie that he, Clay Frick, was the better businessman, caustically criticized the high prices that the

Carnegie Company, as it was now called, was paying for coal and scrap. "Ruinous. . . . Look into these and other matters yourself. Do not let them hide things from you. You cannot trust many by whom you are surrounded to give you facts. You need commercial rather than professional ability to cope with concerns managed by brainy and honest men trained to the business. You are being outgeneraled all along the line, and your management of the Company has already become the subject of jest."[25]

Frick may have had the last word, but as his great-granddaughter and biographer would later write, "though vindicated and victorious," his had been "a hollow victory. All but two of his Carnegie Steel partners had voted against him, reminding him that, in a sense, he had never belonged." Frick severed his ties with the Carnegie Library and the Carnegie Institute in Pittsburgh and withdrew his offer to lend art to the International exhibitions. He would soon leave Pittsburgh altogether to take up residence in New York City.[26]

THE CARNEGIE COMPANY, formed with the merger of Carnegie Steel and H. C. Frick Coke, was formally organized on April 1, 1900, with Charles Schwab as president and chief executive officer. One might have thought this would have been the perfect time for Andrew Carnegie to retire. He was sixty-five years old, and in Charlie Schwab had found a chief executive in whom he had full trust. But reinvigorated by the battle with Frick, Carnegie was not about to let slide one final opportunity to modernize, expand, and extend his market share. Frick had claimed loudly and publicly that he, not Carnegie, had been the genius behind the success of Carnegie Steel. Carnegie appeared determined to prove his former junior partner wrong. With Schwab at his side, he would demonstrate yet again that there was no one, living or dead, who was his equal when it came to the steel business. He would, at the same time, do the larger community a service by amassing yet more profits to be given away when he retired. He had new dragons to slay, new competitors to best, and many more millions to earn before the day arrived when he would turn his attention from accumulation to distribution.

The situation in the steel industry had been transformed in the past two years by the formation of several giant new firms, including American Steel and Wire, Federal Steel, and National Tube. "I have had to take general charge [of] our business for next year," he had written John Morley in mid-December 1899. "Some moves to be made to meet these huge Combinations which are really at our mercy. But my being at helm makes victory easier. So thought my partners, but it is only a short postponement of withdrawal [retirement]. Ashamed to tell you profits these days. Prodigious."[27]

The boom times that the steel industry had enjoyed in 1898 and 1899, with record high prices and profits, encouraged a flow of capital into the industry. Old firms expanded production while new ones were started up. The result was added capacity, which, when the "boom" was over—as it appeared to be by 1900—translated into excessive inventory and a profit crunch. The new conglomerates, which had been organized to produce finished products, like steel hoops, sheets, tubes, tin plate, nails, and wire, were hit hardest. To lower costs and prop up profits, they integrated backwards. Instead of buying steel ingots and billets from Carnegie and his competitors, they constructed their own blast furnaces to produce them, depriving Carnegie of substantial orders. Carnegie's response was to integrate production forward—into finished steel.

With Frick out of the way, Phipps in full retirement, and Tom Carnegie long gone, there was no one left to restrain Andrew's adventurism. "Urge prompt action, essential," he cabled Schwab on July 7 from the telegraph office he had set up at the Skibo lodge house. "Crisis has arrived, only one policy open; start at once hoop, rod, wire, nail mills, no half way about last two. Extend coal and coke roads, announce these; also tubes. Prevent others building. . . . Never been time when more prompt action essential, indeed absolutely necessary to maintain property. . . . Have no fear as to result, victory certain. Spend freely for finishing mills, railroads, boat lines [to transport ore on the Great Lakes]. Continue to advise regularly by cable."[28]

In his communications back and forth across the Atlantic that summer of 1900 Carnegie sounded much as he had twenty-five years earlier urging on his partners to take risks, spend money, keep production up, and prices down. On July 11, he wrote Schwab again: "Confirming my wire upon the situation let me say that all is coming just as expected. There is nothing surprising; a struggle is inevitable, and it is a question of the survival of the fittest. . . . We have a great advantage . . . running non-union, but I do not believe that we shall be allowed to run non-union peaceably unless we give our men steady work; unless we run when others stop as we did for some years previous to the boom." The Carnegie enterprises had survived earlier crises of overproduction by accepting orders at lower prices, keeping their factories running and their men at work. "You have only to rise to the occasion, but no half way measures. If you are not going to cross the stream, do not enter at all and be content to dwindle into second place. Put your trust in the policy of . . . running your mills full regardless of prices. . . . Such is my advice."[29]

Carnegie's competitive juices were flowing again. After Alexander Cassatt, on being named president of the Pennsylvania Railroad in June 1899, declared his intention to eliminate the preferential freight rates his predecessors had negotiated, Carnegie, with Schwab by his side, girded for battle. On his return to the United States in the fall of 1900, he began talks with Jay Gould's son George, who had plans to build a new east-west rail network to compete with the Pennsylvania and the New York Central networks. If the older railroads refused to give him preferential rates, Carnegie would shift his freight to the new Gould lines.

None of this was good news for J. Pierpont Morgan, who had devoted his career to squeezing competition out of American industry. The fact

UNCLE SAM: "GIVE IT TO 'IM, ANDY! GIVE IT TO 'IM!"
Pittsburg, January 6—Andrew Carnegie's decision to engage in the pipe business, as announced yesterday, it was stated here today means a war of millions between Carnegie on one side and J. Pierpont Morgan and the railroad interests of the country on the other.

that Carnegie was threatening the joint sovereignty of the New York Central and Pennsylvania systems was cause enough for alarm. Then, in January 1901, the situation grew more dire still with the announcement that the Carnegie Company intended to spend $12 million to build the world's largest, most technologically advanced tubeworks at Conneaut on Lake Erie to compete with National Tube, the conglomerate the Morgan interests had organized in October 1899. In choosing Conneaut instead of Pittsburgh and pledging to invest millions to build the most modern plant anywhere in the world, Carnegie was signaling that he intended to win this battle, as he had won every other he had fought.

Morgan, like Rockefeller before him, was astute enough to recognize that it made no sense to enter head-to-head competition with Carnegie in steel. If Carnegie followed through with his plan—and he showed every intention and capacity to do so—he would be as invincible in finished steel products as he was in ingots, billets, rails, and structural shapes. No one was to be able to undersell him. Morgan regarded Carnegie as a dangerous adventurer, an old-fashioned businessman who relished competition, eschewed cooperation, and took greater pleasure in breaking agreements than in joining them. A way had to be found to neutralize him.

Carnegie, for his part, had no use for men like Morgan who made their fortunes speculating in and trading paper stocks and bonds. According to Charles Schwab, Carnegie was also appalled at the rumors that Morgan kept mistresses. "Carnegie was always faithful and could not understand Morgan's personal 'freedom.' Carnegie frowned on anything savoring of the flesh and the devil. He was very narrow in some respects, and he had no forgiveness for human weaknesses—because he couldn't understand them. The two men were therefore not on speaking terms—or hardly so."[30]

In the fall of 1900, Pierpont Morgan, determined to head off Carnegie before he built his new tube plant at Conneaut, invited Schwab to call at his Wall and Broad Street office. "When I was in New York last week," Schwab informed the Carnegie Company board of managers at its November 6 meeting, "J. Pierpont Morgan sent word he would like to see me. I did not comply for several reasons . . . but I did meet Mr. Steele, who is his chief assistant, and was informed it was in reference to tubes; that the Morgan people had financed and put through this new tube combination, and were much alarmed about our going into tubes."[31]

On December 12, J. Edward Simmons and Charles Stewart Smith, two of New York's most powerful bankers, held a dinner for Schwab at the new, magnificently luxurious University Club, and invited Carnegie and Morgan to attend. "Schwab's dinner here remarkable," Carnegie wrote Lauder four days before the event. "Mr. Smith tells me that everyone invited has accepted and really the biggest men in New York. [Schwab] is a favorite indeed! This makes him all the more valuable to us. I'm greatly pleased. I am going up for an hour. I must be at the dinner of the Pennsylvania Society to speak on Industrial Pennsylvania."[32]

Pierpont Morgan, as befitted his standing in the financial community, was seated on Schwab's right. At the conclusion of the dinner, long after Carnegie had left, Schwab was called upon to make an after-dinner speech. Instead of offering the usual lighthearted remarks and a toast of thanks, he delivered a lengthy speech on the state of the steel industry, with recommendations for the future. The industry was facing a potentially ruinous crisis of overproduction, he warned, which would lead to lower prices and vanishing profits. The only solution was a massive new consolidation, which would eliminate overproduction and lead to new efficiencies, new products, and an expansion of domestic and foreign markets. Chomping away at his black cigar, Morgan listened intently. When the speech was over and applause had died down, he "took Schwab by the arm and led him to a corner. For half an hour," Burton Hendrick reports, "the two men engaged in intimate conversation." At the end of the evening, Schwab took the overnight train back to Pittsburgh.[33]

Morgan had been won over by Schwab's presentation, which more or less restated his own thinking on the dangers of competition. He asked John W. Gates, the former president of Illinois Steel with whom he still consulted on steel matters, to set up a meeting for him with the Carnegie Company president. Schwab again demurred. He did not want to offend Carnegie by going behind his back to negotiate with Morgan. Gates understood, and suggested that Schwab and Morgan might accidentally run into one another at the Bellevue Hotel in Philadelphia. Schwab consented, but on arriving at the Bellevue at the agreed-upon date and time was told by Gates that Morgan had been taken ill and was unable to travel. Throwing caution to the wind, Schwab took the train to New York, where he had dinner with Morgan and two of his partners. At 3:00 A.M. the next morning, after a solid night of talk, Morgan asked Schwab to prepare a list of the companies that should be included in the grand consolidation he had outlined at the December 12 dinner. The two men met again days later, and Morgan, after reviewing Schwab's list, indicated that he was ready to move forward. "If Andy wants to sell, I'll buy. Go and find his price."[34]

The negotiations had proceeded at almost warp speed and under a veil of silence so that investors in the companies to be acquired—and Carnegie himself—would not have time or opportunity to profit or interfere. Carnegie may have guessed that something was afoot, but if so, he made no mention of it. Schwab, unsure as to how he should approach the old man with Morgan's offer, asked Louise for advice.

Louise had for years been pressing her husband to retire from business and spend more time with her and Margaret. She worried about his health and his age. Although quite active, with no physical complaints, her husband was in his mid-sixties. Louise suggested that Schwab raise the subject of Morgan's offer after a day of golfing at the St. Andrew's Golf Club near Hastings-on-Hudson. Carnegie had a "cottage" there and enjoyed nothing more than spending a day playing golf, followed by a leisurely meal. Schwab took Louise's advice. After their golf game, he and Carnegie retired to the cottage, where Schwab presented Morgan's offer. According to Schwab, Carnegie professed some reluctance at first, but then agreed that it was time to sell. With his blunt, stubby pencil in his hand, he wrote down the price he wanted for his properties. Schwab took the slip of paper directly to Morgan. Carnegie's price was $400 million. Morgan accepted it.[35]

There was, Schwab insisted, no bargaining over price. Only after the negotiations had been concluded did Morgan invite Carnegie on the telephone "to come down to Wall and Broad streets for a little talk." As Hendrick, who interviewed Schwab, tells the story, Carnegie thought the suggestion that he should visit Morgan was "unbecoming." "'Mr. Morgan,' he replied, 'it is just about as far from Wall Street to Fifty-first as it is from Fifty-first to Wall. I shall be delighted to see you here any time.'" Morgan took him up on this invitation and called on Carnegie at home. Carnegie's private secretary, James Bertram, later told Hendrick that he had "kept a watch on the two men to see how long the session lasted. His timepiece showed that the interview took exactly 15 minutes." As he prepared to leave, Morgan grasped Carnegie's hand. "'Mr. Carnegie,' he said, 'I want to congratulate you on being the richest man in the world.'"*[36]

The buyout plan called for the Carnegie Company partners to receive payment in common and preferred stock. Carnegie insisted that he, his cousin Dod, and his sister-in-law Lucy be paid entirely in first-mortgage, 5 percent gold bonds. A stock certificate entailed an ownership right; a first-mortgage bond was evidence of a debt, secured by a first mortgage on the company's assets. Had he accepted stock in U.S. Steel, even preferred stock, he would have been obliged to watch over its progress and profits. As a bondholder, he need do nothing more than watch over his interest as it accumulated. The new company, as he well knew, was not worth the $1.4 billion of stock and bonds that were being issued; its tangible assets, however, were worth more than the $300 million he and his family members were receiving in gold bonds. Even if the company failed, which was unlikely, the first-mortgage bonds would be redeemable at par.

On February 3, Carnegie wrote John Morley with his news: "Have been busy, very—ere this reaches you I may have accomplished my purpose to retire which was frustrated—Morgan, the chief banker, has taken it up & I believe will succeed. He had never failed yet. . . . You'll see. I'll have at least 50 millions [in pounds sterling] all in 5% gold bonds. . . . Ah then, well, I'll tackle it. You'll see—I could as well had 100 millions [sterling] in a few years, but no sir. I'm not going to grow old piling up, but in distributing."[37]

The following day, the board of the Carnegie Company formally approved the offer and thanked Carnegie for all he had done to make them millionaires: "Your sound judgment and profound business sagacity have been the foundation stones on which has been built the fabric of our success."[38]

Samuel Clemens, a friend of Carnegie for many years, was one of the first to learn of the sale, perhaps from Carnegie himself. "Dear Sir and

---

*Years later, according to a story that Schwab told Hendrick, Carnegie and Morgan met on board an ocean liner crossing the Atlantic. Carnegie told Morgan that he realized now he should have asked for an additional $100,000. "'Well,' replied Morgan with a grin, 'you would have got it if you had.'" Carnegie denied the story, and claimed that he had named a price he thought "eminently fair." "I have been told many times since by insiders that I should have asked $100 million more and I could have gotten it easily," he told congressional investigators in 1912. "Once and for all I want to put a stop to all this talk."—Hendrick, II, 142; Hendrick interview with Schwab, vol. 257, ACLC; *U.S. Steel*, 2379.

Friend," he wrote Carnegie on February 6, "You seem to be in prosperity. Could you lend an admirer a dollar & a half to buy a hymn-book with? God will bless you. I feel it, I know it. N.B. If there should be other applications, this one not to count." The note was signed: "Yrs. Mark." Just beneath the signature, Clemens added: "Don't send the hymn-book, send the money; I want to make the selection myself."[39]

On February 26, Carnegie delivered his memorandum of understanding to Morgan. "Morgan has succeeded as I felt he would," he cabled Dod that same day.[40]

On March 3, Morgan formally announced the organization of the United States Steel Corporation, the world's first billion-dollar corporation, capitalized at $1.4 billion—$304 million in 5 percent gold mortgage bonds (for Carnegie, Dod, and Lucy Carnegie), $1.1 billion in preferred and common stock for the other partners. Andrew Carnegie's share came to $226 million, nearly $120 billion today.

"There is nothing new to report," Carnegie cabled his cousin the following day. "Morgan has launched the ship & it will reach port all right. We shall have our Bonds and there an end." To escape New York City taxes on real estate and personal property, Carnegie was scouting property in New Jersey to park his bonds. "Surrogate of New York City assessed Vanderbilt 2½ % on his 4 and 5 per cent Bonds—at present rate half of my 12 M per year [the interest on his bonds] would go to NY City—that is if assessed at value and they can do this any year. We are at mercy Tammany." Carnegie's tentative plan was to organize his own trust company in New Jersey and "acquire a domicile in that state . . . New Jersey taxes nothing."[41]

The next day, he cabled Dod again. There was no need for him to come to New York; he would take care of the transfer of assets and have the new U.S. Steel bonds delivered to the "Hudson Trust Co. Hoboken New Jersey," where, he claimed, Morgan kept his securities. Again, he suggested that Dod "take a house somewhere in New Jersey to be safe—can rent one at a few hundred dollars per year." When, the next week, he wrote Dod again, his ever fertile mind had hatched a plan to set up a Carnegie Steel millionaires' colony in New Jersey, complete with its own bank. "We ought to get in same neighborhood. . . . May build our own Trust Building and get a charter. . . . This frees us all from taxes (outrageous ones) and also ensures freedom from surrogates etc—Cornelius Vanderbilt's fortune levied up fearfully and much trouble caused to Executors. I see it is essential for all of us to get under cover—Lucy, you and I. Also Schwab—maybe HP (no doubt anxious to get in) besides others of Carnegie Steel Co. who will have to remove here—We want a colony—near **Greenw**ood Lake suggested as beautiful belongs to Mr. Hewitt who offers me anything he has. But plenty of time for all this. Pray sleep soundly—all is fixed—your Bonds and mine go as our partners go—into vaults."[42]

THE SALE OF Carnegie Steel to Morgan in early March 1901 and the formation of U.S. Steel was big news everywhere. It was, depending on one's viewpoint, the apogee of American capitalism or the death knell of democracy. The unions were particularly disturbed at the consequences of the great consolidation. The Amalgamated Association recognized, as David Brody has written, that "once firmly established, the Corporation would be impregnable." The first order of business was going to be an attempt to alleviate the crisis of overproduction by closing redundant mills. There was no question but that the first plants closed would be the unionized ones. To protect those plants and its future, the Amalgamated set out to organize every mill in the combine. It began by presenting wage demands at the tin plate, sheet steel, and steel hoop companies. When U.S. Steel refused to negotiate in good faith, a strike was called and quickly broken. The Amalgamated, which had retained considerable strength in the non-Carnegie mills, would never recover from these early defeats.[43]

None of this, of course, concerned Carnegie, who had other matters to contend with. Having discovered that he did not have to move to New Jersey to protect himself from taxes, he was proceeding with plans made earlier to build a New York City mansion for his family. The site had been purchased in November of 1898, at almost the same time Carnegie bought Skibo. The West Fifty-first Street house, large as it was, did not have enough room for the expanded Carnegie family.

Carnegie purchased a plot of land on Fifth Avenue across from the park but well north of the homes of New York's other millionaires. The site he chose, two full block fronts between Ninetieth and Ninety-second Streets, was on the highest point of Fifth Avenue, or, as Carnegie would proudly refer to it, "the highlands of Fifth Avenue."[44]

He and Louise expected to move into the new mansion when they returned from Scotland in the fall. His major concern that spring was that Louise was wearing herself out trying to complete work on the building and grounds. Her health was good, but there had been scares in the recent past. "I feel better get Louise away from this new House," he wrote Dod in February, "architects etc. too troublesome—especially on Furniture & Decorations." He planned to take her and Margaret to the South of France—Antibes and then Aix—to give her a full "six weeks holiday . . . free from House & Housekeeping" before they settled in for the summer at Skibo.[45]

In early March, still worried about "Lou," he wrote Dod again to tell him that he had canceled the family's annual trip to Cumberland Island. "Lou needs a holiday badly—has had none for four years. . . . We shan't get South, wrote Lucy so yesterday—sorry but I saw Lou must have a rest—she works so hard at her new house here."[46]

The following week, accompanied by their full entourage of nannies, nurses, and servants, the Carnegies sailed for Europe. Interviewed by reporters at the pier, Carnegie insisted in a story carried on the front page of the *New York Times* on March 14 that he intended to conduct no business of any sort in Europe. "I anticipate one of the happiest trips of my life, and am anxious to get to work on the golf links. Golf is a great game, and I am very fond of it." Asked if he planned to found any new libraries, he "smilingly replied, 'I have just begun to give away money and if you ask me that question say about ten years from now I may be able to give you an intelligent answer. No. I can't answer that question now; I have only begun, you see, and don't know yet, myself.'"

What he didn't tell the reporters was that he had authorized Robert Franks, his financial secretary and the new president of the Home Trust Company in Hoboken, to transfer $5 million in U.S. Steel gold bonds to the managers of the Carnegie Company in Pittsburgh. One million dollars was to be used to maintain Carnegie libraries at Braddock, Homestead, and Duquesne. The remaining $4 million was for a Carnegie Relief Fund to assist injured employees and the dependents of those killed in service and "to provide small pensions or aids to such employes as, after long and creditable service, through exceptional circumstances, need such help in their old age, and who make a good use of it." The wording of the bequest made it clear that these pensions were not to be given indiscriminately, but only to those workers specifically recommended by the superintendents as "worthy." The $5 million gift to his employees was, he announced, his first bequest since retiring. "I make [it] as an acknowledgement of the deep debt I owe to the workmen who have contributed so greatly to my success." It was a generous offer, though it comprised less than 2 percent of the $226 million he had just received.[47]

Another $5.2 million in U.S. Steel bonds was delivered to John Billings, the director of the New York Public Library, to establish a branch library system for New York. Billings, with whom Carnegie had been in discussion for some time, had estimated the average cost of a branch library at $80,000. Multiplying that figure by 65, the number of libraries Carnegie thought necessary, he had decided to give the libraries $5.2 million (more than $2.7 billion today). "Sixty-five branches strike one at first as a large order, but as other cities have found one necessary for every sixty or seventy thousand of population the number is not excessive."[48]

After a great deal of wrangling, the funds were divided up: $3.36 million went to the New York Public Library for forty-two branches in Manhattan, the Bronx, and Staten Island; $1.6 million to the Brooklyn Public Library for twenty branches; and $240,000 for three libraries in Queens. The agreement that was signed by the New York City government obligated it, in return for Carnegie's money, to provide sites for the libraries and sufficient funding to maintain, repair, staff, and keep them open from at least 9:00 A.M. to 9:00 P.M. every day but Sunday. There was some question about who was responsible for buying the books, but it was agreed in the end that the city should do so.[49]

The building process got under way at once. Between 1902 and 1909, fifty-five libraries were completed; it would take until 1929 to complete the last dozen.* Carnegie was more involved in the planning and building of these libraries than he would be with most of the others he funded. He joined the New York Public Library board in 1902, and though he did not attend meetings or library dedications remained in close touch with Billings. Three prominent New York architectural firms—McKim, Mead & White; Carrère & Hastings, which had built the Central Library on Forty-second Street; and Babb, Cook & Willard, which was building his mansion on Ninety-first Street—were chosen to design the buildings.

---

*Sixty-seven of them would be built, with Queens getting a few extra. When, in 1996, Mary Dierick wrote her book about the New York City Carnegie libraries, she found that fifty-seven of the buildings were still standing, fifty-four of them operating as branch libraries.

A BRAW LADDIE

Andrew Carnegie makes all the other millionaires look like the "thirty cents."

Carnegie protested that more architects should be invited in and the bidding process be made competitive, but Billings convinced him this would slow down the process.

Though no two libraries were exactly alike, they were designed as a collection, with large front windows to let in sunlight, redbrick or limestone facades, and granite or limestone steps leading to a prominent front entrance. Circulation and reference desks and a reading room were located on the ground floor, with a children's room above it, and a general reading room on the quieter third floor, farthest from the street. The Manhattan branches—and a number of the Brooklyn ones—were set in the middle of their blocks and looked rather like elegant town houses. Outside Manhattan, where property was less expensive, the libraries occupied corner lots. Dignified, classical, but not elaborately ornate, the libraries were meant to attract readers—and they did. The branch in Yorkville, the first to be opened to the public, was used by more than 40,000 readers in 1903, almost four times the number of patrons than the year before.[50]

THIRTY-TWO

"The Saddest Days of All," 1901

I T IS DIFFICULT to picture Andrew Carnegie depressed, but there is no other way to describe his state of being in the months following his retirement. Carnegie confessed as much in an early draft of his *Autobiography*, but the editor John Van Dyke, chosen by Mrs. Carnegie after her husband's death, perhaps thinking his melancholic ruminations would displease her, edited them out of the manuscript.

In March 1901, before leaving for Skibo, Carnegie sent a farewell letter to his managers at the Carnegie Company. "But [as] this written and farewell sounded in my heart, there was yet to come the saddest days of all. I had to sail for our customary holiday in Scotland, and where were 'my boys,' several of whom were always sure to see me off on the ship? Who of them were to be our guests the coming summer in Scotland? Alas, alas, here was the keenest pang of all. I realized for the first time that I had lost my boys. I was no longer their business parent. I was alone and oh so lonely as we drove to the pier. . . . All was changed. They had gone from me and were now merely employees of stockholders. We were no longer one family. . . . We were all changed in our relations to each other, all saddened, and oh the difference to me."[1]

Carnegie, as elsewhere in the published and unpublished sections of his *Autobiography,* was exaggerating for effect. The truth was while he professed close ties with his "boys," he was not particularly intimate with any of them, except for Charlie Schwab. Still, he counted them all as his protégés, took great pleasure in their achievements, had dinner with them when they were in New York, and enjoyed nothing more than showing off his Scottish estates and teaching them to fish in his lochs.

The vast difference between life in retirement and as chief stockholder of the Carnegie Company was brought home to him as he prepared to leave for Britain in the early spring of 1901. For close to thirty years, he had scurried about for weeks prior to sailing tying up loose ends. There were documents to be signed, instructions to be left with his partners in Pittsburgh and his private secretary in New York. Retirement brought an end to this round of activities and a strange, inescapable melancholy. The only antidote was activity. He set out at once to refocus his attention, as he had told Morley he would, from "piling up" dollars to "distributing" them. The news that he had given away $10.2 million ($5.4 billion today) for New York libraries and his former Pittsburgh employees was announced after he sailed for Europe. It created quite a stir in the daily newspapers. The Hearst papers supplemented their coverage with a Frederick Opper cartoon, "How It Looks to Some of Mr. Carnegie's Fellow Millionaires," which showed the "close-fisted brigade" of millionaires exclaiming: "Good Gracious. He Must Be Crazy." A St. Paul, Minnesota, newspaper, calling attention to the New York City library bequests, ran a cartoon of Carnegie standing in his hallway hidden behind a pile of letters. In the front yard, a mailman, the sweat pouring off him, unloads by shovel letters from a cart marked "Requests for Libraries." The caption reads: "Speaking of Libraries, How would You Like to be the Mail Man?"[2]

Arriving at Southampton, the *New York Times* reported on March 21, 1901, that Carnegie was greeted "by delegations from various eleemosynary institutions which want checks. . . . The offices of the steam ship company and the American Consulate were crowded yesterday with people inquiring when the *St. Louis* was likely to arrive. The local manager of the American line, who has 160 letters and telegrams from all parts of the Kingdom for the philanthropist, says the envelopes indicate that they are from all sorts and conditions of people, from University Presidents to mendicants." Carnegie, warned of the throngs of reporters and check-hunters awaiting him on shore, "remained on the ship until the last minute," then, just as the train for London left Southampton, "jumped into a reserved compartment." To the correspondent from the *New York Times,* one of the few to reach him, he "expressed surprise that his donation for New York libraries had caused anything of a sensation." Informed that there was movement afoot in New York to run him for mayor, he "pooh-poohed any inspirations in that direction."[3]

Instead of staying in London, as was usual, Carnegie took his family to Antibes on the French Riviera. He was sixty-five years old now, with a four-year-old daughter. "Baba," an adorable-looking child, with a broad face, like her father's, and blue eyes did not, as a young girl, see a lot of her father, who traveled a great deal without her. She claimed to remember the trip to Antibes, one of the first she took with her parents. The night before they were to leave Antibes for the train ride north to Aix-les-Bains, "Daddy stopped the carriage, took me out with him into the night. It was mysterious and wonderful. I had never seen the sky at night, and he pointed to a star and told me it is the star in the Dipper that points to the North sea. . . . We turned in another direction, and he pointed to the bright stars on the constellation of Orion. I am sure I did not understand all he was talking about, but I never forgot the wonder of the experience." Aix-les-Bains, where her parents "rested and took the 'cure' for 3 weeks," had less to offer a four-year-old. "There was not much for me to do, but I loved walking along the country roads, and finding new and lovely wild flowers." J. Pierpont Morgan was, coincidentally or not, staying there at the same time. The *New York Times* correspondent reported that the two men "had several conferences." Though there is no mention elsewhere of any discussions between them, they certainly had a lot to talk about and may have discussed the future of U.S. Steel and Charles Schwab, who was one of the candidates for chief executive officer.[1]

The Carnegies' next stop was Paris, "where Daddy met and talked with men he knew . . . and Mother shopped for evening dresses and especially for the hand-stitched towels, sheets, pillowcases and table cloths for which Paris was famous. A great deal of linen [was needed] for both Skibo and 2 East 91st and she bought lavishly." And then it was off to London for a fortnight at the Langham Hotel on Portland Place. Again Andrew met with his friends, including John Morley; Louise went shopping; Baba was bored. Her mother had her doll's pram shipped from Skibo, and Baba, with Nana alongside, wheeled "my baby doll up to Regent's Park . . . and walked through Regent Crescent," or at least this was what she claimed to have remembered seventy years later, when she sat down to write her journal.[5]

Carnegie was determined to begin at once to give away the $200 million in gold bonds he had just acquired. He had, he wrote Morley, received thousands of newspaper clippings, letters, and cables congratulating him on his retirement and offering suggestions on how he might spend his money. "These nerve me for the long campaign upon which I have just entered. No parade to Pretoria I well know, but one requiring me to clinch my teeth & stand it. I don't see it needs the same principles as acquisition—but it needs some of these. Tenacity and steady sailing to the haven we clear for, a supreme confidence in one's own ideas, or conclusions rather, after thought—and above all placing use above popularity."[6]

Morley had forwarded two clippings from *The Times of London* about a committee that had been established to raise funds to enable the Scottish universities to compete with their English, American, and German counterparts. Morley did not suggest outright that Carnegie contribute to the cause, but the implication was unmistakable.

On arriving in London, Carnegie sent for Lord Shaw of Dunfermline, an MP from Scotland and an old acquaintance. In 1897, Shaw had written an article for the *Nineteenth Century* in which he argued, as he had at the dinner table at Cluny the year before, that university fees should be abolished for worthy Scottish students. Now, several years later, his interest in the Scottish universities having been piqued by Morley's clippings, Carnegie informed Shaw that he was "disposed to realize your idea." Shaw replied that £1 million would do the trick. Carnegie asked Shaw to draw up a proposal and the two put together a list of men they wished to serve on the board of directors of the "trust" that would administer the grant.

Shaw claimed in his memoirs that he left Carnegie soon after, "tumbling there and then into a hansom cab at the Langham Hotel" and was taken directly to Westminster, where he enlisted Sir Henry Campbell-Bannerman, the leader of the Liberals in the House of Commons; Lord Balfour of Burleigh, the current secretary for Scotland; and Lord Reay, all of whom, on being told that Carnegie had committed £1 million, agreed to serve as trustees. Carnegie added several other names to the list of what would become the board of the Carnegie Trust for the Universities of Scotland.[7]

All seemed in order, but several of the lords chosen for the board, Shaw learned, had gone behind his back to suggest to Carnegie that it made no sense to abolish fees altogether and that his money might be better spent on scholarships for the worthy poor. While the Scottish universities—at Aberdeen, Edinburgh, Glasgow, and St. Andrews—were not bastions of upper-class privilege like Oxford and Cambridge, the idea that they would be made free to all was too radical for many, including the editors of the *Scotsman,* a leading Scottish newspaper. Fees were only one part of the cost of sending a student to university, the *Scotsman* explained in a May 20,

1901, editorial. Carnegie's plan would inevitably lead to an increase in university students—which would mean an increase in the costs of university education borne by the state. The *Scotsman* editors insisted they did not want to derail the plan entirely. They asked only that the proposal be revised in a way that would not overburden the Scottish educational system.[8]

Arthur Balfour, at the time chancellor of the exchequer, suggested to Carnegie that his money would have a greater impact if it were spent improving university research facilities and faculties. "According to my view (which I think you share) we ought to regard our Universities not merely as places where the best kind of knowledge already attained is imparted, but as places where the stock of the world's knowledge may be augmented. . . . And yet for sheer want of money our provision both in the department of teaching and that of research is deplorably deficient."[9]

John Morley had yet another perspective to offer. He hoped that "history, philosophy & literature shall have at least an equal place" in the new Carnegie-endowed Scottish universities. "We expect you to show that you have not been the friend of M[atthew] Arnold for nothing—to say nothing of humbler folk [like John Morley]." Carnegie's reply to his friend was rather testy. "Why institute comparisons & thus provoke antagonisms? I have been repelled by such folly. We don't get it in the United States & Harvard & Yale simply could not be commanding Powers today if they ignored, or slighted their scientific Depts. You knew & I knew that for us— yes, even for me, practical as I am—the flavor & philosophy of Poets & wise men is the sweetest of all foods, but for others, not so & these the vast majority who must earn a living."[10]

It was not going to be easy giving away his money, as Carnegie was quickly learning. Fortunately, he had enough to satisfy everyone—almost.

"The main point is settled," he wrote Morley on May 31. "I got Shaw to give way as to abolition fees which I am convinced was unwise, at least impracticable. I increased gift to £2 millions, revenue £104,000 per annum. I believe the total endowment . . . of the 4 universities is now only £72,000. The scheme is made a wide one. . . . It is another proof of the adage, 'The Gods send thread for a web begun.' I began in total ignorance but have had thread supplied by the Gods, you being one." He had decided, he added in another letter to Morley the following week, to donate additional funds for scientific research, because he considered science "the Cinderella of the family of Knowledge in Britain. Her Haughty Sisters, Miss Greek, Miss

Italian & others were not chosen—Now all branches will be equal soon in Scotland I hope—none neglected."[11]

There was one outstanding question. How was he going to prevent well-off families from exploiting his good intentions? Like any British liberal, he opposed government or bureaucratic meddling in private affairs and had no intention of asking prospective students to divulge information about family incomes. His solution was to require them to apply for grants and trust that only students who needed assistance would do so.

"As your Lordship is aware," he wrote the ninth Earl of Elgin, the first chairman of the trust, in a letter that was later distributed to all applicants, "my desire throughout has been that no capable student should be debarred from attending the University on account of the payment of fees. . . . I hope that the honest pride for which my countrymen are distinguished will prevent claims from those who do not require assistance." The Carnegie Trust for the Universities of Scotland would be the only one of his trusts to accept donations. It was Carnegie's hope that those who received assistance as students would later in life repay the trust. "This will enable such students as prefer to do so to consider the payments made on their account merely as advances which they resolve to repay if ever in a position to do so, and that this will protect and foster the spirit of manly independence so dear to the Scot."[12]

It is difficult to overemphasize the impact of Carnegie's £2 million bequest (almost $10 million in 1901; more than $5 billion today). There had never before been a grant for student assistance for this purpose or of this magnitude. By 1910, the Carnegie Scottish Universities Trust was paying the tuition for fully half the students at St. Andrews, Aberdeen, Edinburgh, and Glasgow. Though some claimed that Carnegie had "pauperized" the universities by making it easier for the hordes to attend them, the students and parents who benefited directly, and the people of Scotland in general, applauded—and still applaud—the gift and the good sense with which it has been administered.

BY THE TIME the Carnegies arrived at Skibo, the begging letters from America were on their way. The news of Carnegie's first three gifts—totaling $20.2 million—had spread fast and widely. Frederick Holls, the peace activist and international lawyer, visited Carnegie in August and wrote Andrew White, suggesting that he do the same. "I found my visit to him extremely interesting from a psychological point of view, for the specimen of the genus homo who not only has two hundred and fifty millions to give away, but who has been uncautious enough to say so, is very rare and hence its observation is particularly interesting." Carnegie, Holls wrote White, had always been characterized by his "canniness," but to this had been "added a certain restlessness, tinged with suspicion of the intentions of every person who comes near him, and resulting in the most contradictory states of mind coming in rapid succession—if they do not actually exist at the same time. He wants to speak about his money and what to do with it,—yet, he does not want to speak about it." Carnegie had almost grown wary of conversation, afraid that at any moment, he would be solicited for funds. Yet at the same time, that was precisely what he wanted: proposals on how he should spend his money. "He strongly impressed me . . . with the idea that he is feeling the approach of old age and contemplating the possibility of his early death."[13]

The most disagreeable communication was probably the one from James Bridge, his erstwhile secretary, researcher, collaborator, and, most recently, blackmailer, who resurfaced to demand that he be given the rights to bring out a third edition of *Triumphant Democracy:* "The great prominence which you have attained has greatly enhanced the value of all your books, most of all the one which has always been associated with your name and principles; and I am assured that a new edition of *Triumphant Democracy,* published at once while the whole world is talking about you and your unparalleled benefactions, will sell, if skillfully handed, into the hundreds of thousands. . . . I am unwilling . . . to relinquish placidly and gratuitously my rights in this book, now that they have for the first time attained a high commercial value." When Carnegie ignored Bridge's request, as he had the blackmail threat three years earlier, his former secretary decided to take advantage of his relationship to Carnegie by writing an "Inside History" of Carnegie Steel. Fortunately for both men, *The Inside History of the Carnegie Steel Company,* published two years later, was not nearly as incendiary or defamatory as Carnegie feared it might be.[14]

THE NEWS THAT Andrew Carnegie had given $10 million to Scottish universities must have come as a surprise to American university presidents

who for years had had their requests turned down. But Carnegie had decided long before that America's largest universities "such as Harvard and
Columbia . . . were large enough; that further growth was undesirable;
that the smaller institutions (the colleges especially) were in greater need
of help and that it would be a better use of surplus wealth to aid them." If
he was going to spend money on higher education, it was going to be for
smaller colleges and technical "institutes."[15]

Having learned in November 1900 that the Pittsburgh Board of Education was contemplating the opening of a new technical school, Carnegie
informed the mayor that he would donate $1 million if the city provided
an acceptable site for it. Asked whether Pittsburgh needed another school
when it already had Western University (which would, in 1908, change its
name to the University of Pittsburgh), he answered that the "institute" he
intended to fund was not a university but an institution to provide "technical training" for manual laborers or their sons "in the crafts and scientific
vocations, so as to produce skilled workmen, such as machinists, mechanics, decorators, and so on." The model he had in mind was New York's
Cooper Union, to whose support he had been contributing for several
years.[16]

Simultaneously with setting up the Scottish Universities Trust, Carnegie
had, in fact, been in correspondence with Andrew White and Daniel Coit
Gilman, who was retiring that summer from the presidency of Johns Hopkins after twenty-five years. White had suggested that he donate money
for a national university in Washington, D.C., but Carnegie decided that
rather than establish a university that might compete with Johns Hopkins
in Baltimore, he would give Hopkins funds to set up a new campus in
Washington. "What do you think of the Idea?" he wrote White in April.
"Governor Stanford made a useless rival as you and I saw when in San
Francisco, to the State University [at Berkeley]. I could be no party to such
a thing. Don't care two cents about future 'glory.' I must be satisfied that
I am doing good, beneficial work in my day. Better come to Skibo and
confer." White agreed to join Carnegie and Gilman at Skibo to discuss the
possibility of a national university in Washington. In May, White dispatched a long memo, setting forth the rationale for establishing a large
university in D.C. that looked surprisingly like the one he had been president of in Ithaca, New York.[17]

White had known Carnegie long enough not to be surprised by anything he did. Still, even he was astounded by Skibo. "The attractions of his wonderful domain, forty thousand acres, with every variety of scenery,—ocean, forest, moor, and mountain,—the household with its quaint Scotch usages—the piper in full tartan solemnly going his rounds at dawn, and the music of the organ swelling, morning and evening, through the castle from the great hall—all helped to give me strength." (White was in mourning at the death of his son.) At Skibo that summer, White and Carnegie discarded plans to either establish a university at Washington or a branch of Johns Hopkins. Instead, they came up with the idea for an entirely new type of institution, one without students or a permanent faculty. The Carnegie Institution in Washington, D.C., was to be a research institution, which would supplement the work of established universities by providing financial support to scientists to engage in basic research projects. The objectives were broad and rather vague; the organizational structure undetermined. Carnegie intended to work out the specifics when he returned to the United States in the fall.[18]

By the summer of 1901, the main building at Skibo had been transformed through the efforts of hundreds of local artisans and laborers, directed by teams of architects and contractors, from the Gothic mansion built by the previous owner into a marvelously anachronistic twentieth-century castle, with Gothic Revival battlements and towers, two hundred rooms, four hundred glass windows, electric lighting, modern plumbing, and leaded, stained-glass windows in the front entryway, which, when completed in 1902, would tell the story of the lairds of Skibo, from Surd, the tenth-century Viking chief, to Andrew Carnegie. One of the final touches remaining was the library, which was as yet empty of books. Hew Morrison asked Lord Acton, the owner of the grandest of all private libraries, for advice. "I have been thinking of the books people would like to find at a country house, on a rainy day," Acton replied. "You know Mr. Carnegie's tastes better than I do, and I hope you will warn me where I go wrong, and strike out whatever seems absurd."[19]

The castle had been mostly completed by the spring of 1901, but there remained, as Joseph Wall has written in his history of Skibo, several "even more ambitious projects . . . under way but far from finished: the new lake that Carnegie had ordered to be created to the west of the castle, Loch

Ospisdale, to be stocked with brown trout which one could fish for from the bank; the smaller ponds, Lake Louise and Margaret's Loch, for water lilies and other aquatic plants; the building of a dam at the mouth of the Evelix River to create Loch Evelix with a salmon ladder so that the salmon could still go up the Evelix to spawn and to be caught; the nine hole course . . . and Carnegie's special pride and joy, a great, enclosed swimming pool." There were plans as well for new farm buildings, dairies, barns, stables, coachhouses, cottages for the tenants and laborers, and a baronial-style lodge house for the chief forester and his wife, the gatekeeper.[20]

All that was now lacking from Carnegie's wish list was a waterfall and that would soon be purchased from the duke of Sutherland—with thousands of acres of moor that nearly doubled the size of the new laird's landholdings.

The oversized splendor of Skibo stood in contrast to the restrained elegance of the new mansion he was simultaneously building for his family on Fifth Avenue between Ninetieth and Ninety-first streets. Carnegie felt much more comfortable spending millions on himself in Scotland than he did in the United States. The Old World was used to such display; the New World was not. He had no trouble whatsoever adapting to his role as laird of Skibo. "No man," Bertram later recalled, "ever had a stronger feeling of possession. Those 40,000 acres were his, and he felt it in every fibre. He used to walk over them and survey them, and he found vast satisfaction in adding to them. Nor would he suffer unwarranted trespassing. He was as set against poaching in his lochs as the variest medievalist. He was especially jealous of Loch Migrate, and would not let uninvited people fish it."[21]

Carnegie did not hunt, but as a Scotsman, he understood full well the importance of the "Glorious Twelfth," August 12th, the opening day of the grouse season, which he celebrated by organizing massive hunting parties on his lands. The freshly killed game was plucked, packaged, and sent south to his British friends. "What, more grouse," Herbert Spencer wrote on receiving his package in September. (In June he had been sent a package of trout pulled from Skibo's lakes.) "You will bankrupt me in thanks! I doubt not that these products of the Sutherlandshire moors will be employed, as were the preceding ones, and there will be in the course of the ensuing week (for we leave this day week) time enough to enjoy them. I hope the bracing air of Skibo Castle is working its due effects after the excitements you and Mrs. Carnegie have passed through."[22]

. . .

THAT SUMMER, Carnegie, as he had been since 1898, was preoccupied with an anti-imperialism campaign. He had done all he could to prevent the American annexation of the Philippines, but failing to do so had turned his attention to British adventurism in South Africa, which he considered no less an abomination. That the two branches of "the English-speaking race," the two most civilized nations of earth, had engaged their armed forces in such mindless violence as had occurred in the Philippines and South Africa disturbed him no end.

The immediate problem in Britain was that his friends in government—Morley, Harcourt, Bryce, and Campbell-Bannerman, all of them outspoken anti-imperialists—were in danger of losing the next election and their leadership positions in the Liberal Party to imperialists like Rosebery, who openly supported the war against the Boers. Carnegie, a congenital optimist, could not accept the fact that British voters and political leaders might continue to support irrational imperialist adventures in South Africa. With childlike exuberance he informed Morley and Campbell-Bannerman, in separate letters in the early summer of 1901, that he had told Rosebery (implying that Rosebery had listened) that South Africa was a lost cause and would have to be abandoned. There would never be, he insisted, sufficient British emigrants to make the Transvaal republics truly British. "It can't be done. . . . No Use. Dutch can live out there. Britons can do better elsewhere. . . . As one who wishes my native land well—and would save her from disaster I hope that she will never have to undertake the task of suppressing the Dutch. It can't be done. They are too much like the Scotch."[23]

Carnegie's solution was to offer the Boer republics the opportunity to "federate" with the British Empire for a certain number of years. "After that to be as Canada and Australia are. Free to go."[24]

Campbell-Bannerman mildly questioned Carnegie's rather preposterous suggestion that the Boers might agree to a trial membership in the British Empire. Lord Rosebery dismissed the "federation" idea by reminding Carnegie how the United States, thirty-five years earlier, had dealt with a secessionist movement: "You laid your country waste, spent hundreds of millions, and gave hundreds of thousands of lives to prevent that right. Just now, when we have spent two hundred millions, and will have spent more, in a war to prevent the Boer States being a menace of danger to South Africa, people would not be in a favorable mood to receive your proposition. It would indeed keep up a permanent condition of unrest during the period."[25]

Carnegie did not accept the analogy. No twists of historical logic were going to deter him from his anti-imperialism. As he wrote Sir John St. Loe Strachey, the editor of the *Spectator*, in October 1901, he felt "very keenly for my native land. South Africa is lost but this will not injure Britain. It is the years during which Britain will essay the impossible and waste men and money and incur the bitterest hostility of all nation's including the United States. Truly you are in the greatest danger and all for nothing worth while."[26]

IN LATE SEPTEMBER, as the family prepared to return to New York, Carnegie summed up his summer in one of his strangely disjointed, all-encompassing, newsy letters to his cousin Dod. "Baba continues to amuse and surprise us—Is now grasping management of some departments from her mother. Angus [the organist] gets his list of tunes to be played from her. . . . Nothing like a day at sea for me. . . . Yacht goes into House Oct. 1st—for season. Sorry it's over—very—I am so well and so happy up here away from the maddening crowd."[27]

The family and entourage returned to the United States in October. Carnegie discovered that, even without the demands of business, he had more than enough to occupy his time. One of his first and most welcome tasks that fall was organizing the annual St. Andrews Society dinner. "You will receive a letter from the Secretary of Saint Andrews Society begging you to be one of us on dinner night and speak on what is supposed not to exist, 'Scotch Humour,'" he wrote his friend Sam Clemens in mid-November. "It is my solemn duty, in total disregard of merciful consideration for you, to support the society's prayer. . . . I remember the gods formerly came down and visited mortals, and if your wings are in order you may sail down on the night of the 30th. Let me tell you that many dining-out men have assured me that there is no dinner given in New York equal to St. Andrews for sparkle. I have presided for two years; every ticket is sold long before they are on sale (how's that?); we cannot supply the demand. I think this has come about principally because I made a rule, no mss.; no knowledge or instruction and no boring; 15 minutes is the rule."[28]

Clemens liked nothing more than trading wits with Carnegie—one of the few men who could keep up with him. "Dear friend, St. Andrew," he replied two days later. "I find I am to be there. Mrs. Clemens came in, a minute ago, and furnished the information. If I had had another eighteen hours I could have made up my mind myself. At bottom I am afraid of religious banquet, but now that the matter is settled I am not feeling so worried as I was. To me, the clatter & clash of two or three hundred men rattling dishes & talking is maddening; so you must let me feed at home & take my doze & my smoke and arrive at Delmonico's at 9:20 or :30 . . . 'Scotch Humor.' That will do—let it stand. For lack of ammunition I may possibly apologize & talk about something else, when I get there, but that won't matter. I can't prepare a talk; this is not for a lack of laziness, but lack of time. . . . Put me in the speaker-list about No. 3—can't you? Not earlier, and not more than <u>one</u> later." As promised, Clemens arrived only after Carnegie had offered the obligatory toast to Theodore Roosevelt and Edward VII of England.[29]

Traveling, feasts, and ceremonial dinners accompanied by "the clatter & clash of two or three hundred men rattling dishes & talking" did not, by themselves, fill the vacuum in Carnegie's life. He continued to spend every morning in his library, with his secretary at his side, but instead of going over reports from Pittsburgh, he read begging letters and proposals for funding, and decided how best to distribute his millions. He began by expanding his library-giving. State and city governments had, by the turn of the twentieth century, begun to accept it as their responsibility to build, maintain, and staff hospitals and schools. But they resisted doing the same for libraries. Carnegie intended to change this. Private philanthropy, no matter how generous, could not be expected to substitute its largess for costs that should have been borne by public tax monies. "So," as James Bertram explained to Burton Hendrick, Carnegie "hit upon his scheme to get action out of the public authorities—which in the last resort meant the politicians. This was to offer communities a building, on condition that they would fill it with books and tax themselves for its maintenance. Carnegie himself described this as a 'bribe' to cities and town to establish libraries. . . . His offer would crystallize public sentiment and force the hands of councils and boards of alderman. . . . His real purpose was not to found libraries, himself, but to force the communities to do so."[30]

Since his gift of $5.2 million to New York City for branch libraries had received the widest possible publicity, there was no shortage of requests from other cities and towns. Bertram was given the task of developing a system for responding to these requests. He designed a "Schedule of Questions," which required applicants to supply information on the name, status, and population of the town they represented, whether or not it had a library and, if so, where it was housed, whether it was private or public, and how many books it had. Applicants had to provide assurances, as well, that there was a town-owned site available and a willingness on the part of the population—and the politicians—to raise funds through taxation to support the library.[31]

Carnegie trusted Bertram to make the decisions, though from time to time he would question a particular application to make sure Bertram was paying attention. The communities that were approved were "notified to go ahead with the buildings, and that payments would be made on their order as construction proceeded. The financial office, that is, [Robert] Franks—would be instructed to honor these demands as they occurred, and that ended the matter." The applications poured in; the money poured out—in the form of U.S. Steel bonds. Bertram's record keeping was as meticulous and detailed as that of the accountants and department managers who had worked for Carnegie at his iron and steel companies. Every donation was recorded in a "Daily Register of Donations." Money was never given all at once, but disbursed gradually as the project for which it was given neared completion. Bertram had determined, and Carnegie agreed, that the amount of money allocated for each library should be calculated on the basis of two dollars a person. Bertram relied on census data to verify the population figures the library promoters provided. Some libraries, perhaps a third, carried the Carnegie name, but this was never a requirement. Carnegie was often invited, but seldom attended formal dedications in the United States. When library trustees requested busts, portraits, or life-sized photographs to display at their openings, Bertram forwarded the name of commercial outlets that might supply them, but refused to pay for them.[32]

Carnegie's first libraries had been attached to his steel mills or given to the municipalities of Allegheny City and Pittsburgh. Through 1898, only four Carnegie libraries had been funded outside Pennsylvania—and one of these was for Pittsburgh, Texas. As the profits ballooned at his steelworks in 1899 and 1900, he extended his library-giving to thirty-seven cities, thirty-one of them outside Pennsylvania. What he called the "wholesale" phase of the program began only after his retirement in 1901. In that year alone, he gave 132 library grants, followed by 128 in 1902, and 203 in 1903. One and a half million dollars went to Philadelphia for a public library system like New York's. The librarian from Philadelphia had requested funds for 30 new branch libraries and asked for $20,000–$30,000 for each of them. Carnegie wrote back that he did not think "this sum would be enough. You should have lecture rooms in these Branch Libraries and our experience in Pittsburgh is that we have not spent enough upon them. . . . I think, therefore, it would be well for you to spend Fifty Thousand Dollars for these Branch Library Buildings and it would give me pleasure to provide a Million and a half Dollars," provided that the city agreed to maintain the libraries "at a cost of not less than $150,000 a year."[33]

Speaking at the dedication of the Washington, D.C., library in January 1903, Carnegie whimsically declared that in philanthropy as in manufacturing he had become a "concentrator. . . . 'I have seldom or never known a great success made by a jack of all trades, the board member in twenty companies, the controller of none. I am in the library manufacturing business and beg to be allowed to concentrate my time upon it until it is filled.'"[34]

During his lifetime, Carnegie would give 1,419 grants, at a cost of $41 million, several billion dollars today, for 1,689 public libraries in the continental United States, Hawaii, and Puerto Rico. One hundred sixty library buildings were built in Indiana alone, 142 in California, 106 each in Illinois, Ohio, and New York, 101 in Iowa. From Honolulu, which got its grant in 1909, to Devils Lake, North Dakota, which got its in 1908; from Houlton, 1903, Maine to Santa Rosa, California, 1902, the national cityscape would by 1919 be marked with sturdy Carnegie libraries. An additional $15 million was spent to build 660 libraries in Britain and Ireland, 125 in Canada, 17 in New Zealand, 12 in South Africa, and smaller numbers in the West Indies, Australia and Tasmania, the Seychelles, Mauritius, and Fiji.[35]

James Bertram proved so adept at systematizing library-giving that he was placed in charge of a related program: the donation of organs to churches. This too was a carryover from earlier years. Carnegie donated his first church organ to the Swedenborgian chapel he and his father had attended in Allegheny City and several more to churches in and about the Pittsburgh area. It was in churches that most workingmen and their families were introduced, as he had been, to sacred and classical music. So it was to churches that he gave his organs. As he told his friend William Stead, with a smile, "the organ performance in the morning at Skibo . . . is my substitute for family prayers."[36]

As with the library program, church communities anywhere in the English-speaking world could—and did—apply. The demand for organs was even greater than for libraries. By 1919, some 40,000 applications had been received and processed by Bertram and the administrators who succeeded him after the organization of the Carnegie Corporation. During Carnegie's lifetime, 7,689 organs were given away, costing more than $6.25 million: 4,092 in the United States, over 2,119 in England, 1,005 in Scotland, and hundreds more in other English-speaking nations and colonies.[37]

What was remarkable about the library and organ programs was how little time or energy Carnegie invested in them. He and Bertram had designed their own scientific, corporate system of giving, one that guarded against sentiment and made decisions based on hard data about population, taxation, and site availability. The benefit of such a program was that it did not overwhelm Carnegie with details and small-scale decision making. His staff, knowing clearly what he intended to pay for, followed his instructions as precisely as they could, without bothering him. He had turned his giving into a business—a very efficient one. The "Daily Register of Donations" for 1908 has ten to twenty entries for each day. Amounts vary enormously, from $625 for an organ for North Warren on March 14 to $10,000 for a library in Charlotte the next day. Not a day goes by without some money disbursed to libraries and organs in the United States and Britain.[38]

Carnegie had designed a decentralized and highly efficient bureaucracy for giving away his money. His personal staff of secretaries, assistants, and bookkeepers at East Ninety-first Street looked after library and church organ donations. The trust for his workers was administered by the management of the old Carnegie Steel Company in Pittsburgh. The New York library grant was administered by the New York Public Library. His Scottish Universities Trust was ably managed by Lord Elgin. Only the national university proposal which he and White had worked on at Skibo required his direct attention.

PART OF THE ALLURE of the Washington University project was that it brought him back into contact with the Republican leadership. Nothing delighted him more than visits to the White House and closed-door meetings with party officials; these he had willingly put in jeopardy with his outspoken criticism of President McKinley and his weird, though short-lived, flirtation with William Jennings Bryan. The little Scotsman from Pittsburgh, his Republican friends were beginning to conclude, was a loose cannon, ready to explode in unpredictable directions at any moment. Carnegie was not unaware of these perceptions and tried to soften them, but not to the point of tempering his antiwar, anti-imperialist rhetoric.

His rather studied silence from late spring of 1899 had eased tensions somewhat but not entirely erased the discomfort occasioned in Republican circles by his dalliance with Bryan. In the fall of 1900, the *North American Review* provided him with an opportunity to reaffirm his commitment to the Republican Party by inviting him to contribute to a preelection symposium, "Bryan or McKinley?" Carnegie seized on the occasion to deliver yet another attack on McKinley, but then, in a rapid about-face, endorsed him for reelection. "President McKinley at present stands for war and violence abroad, but Mr. Bryan stands for these scourges at home." The Democrats' reckless critique of the Supreme Court, their proposal for an income tax, and their relentless championing of the silver standard were far more dangerous than the Republicans' missteps overseas. "President McKinley's policy only requires our soldiers to shoot down men abroad guilty of the crime of fighting and dying for their country's independence"; Bryan, as president, would unleash a war at home that would last far longer and pose an infinitely greater danger. "Class once arrayed against class at home, all is lost; restoration of peace and order could only come in a far distant future."[39]

Carnegie's endorsement of the president's reelection was harsh and, because of that, effective. Few men of standing in the nation, Democrats or Republicans, had opposed McKinley's policies in the Philippines as strenuously as he had. For him now to come out in support of the president was a signal to other anti-imperialists to do the same. To ease his way back into the inner sanctums of the Republican Party, Carnegie contributed generously to the reelection campaign, though precisely how much we do not know. McKinley was again elected in 1900 by a plurality of 850,000 popular votes and almost twice as many electoral votes as Bryan.

His second term, officially inaugurated in March, came to an abrupt and bloody end six months later in Buffalo, New York, at the Pan-American Exposition, while he was shaking some hands after an afternoon reception. One of those standing in line to greet him was Leon Czolgosz, a thin, well-groomed man, who, as he approached the president, pulled a revolver out of the handkerchief in his hand and fired twice at point-blank range. One bullet was deflected off a button of McKinley's waistcoat; the second hit him squarely in the abdomen. A week later, he was dead and Theodore Roosevelt had become president of the United States. "President McKinley gone—Isn't it dreadful," Carnegie wrote Dod from Skibo when he

PREPARING TO COLLECT HIS
CAMPAIGN CONTRIBUTIONS.

heard the news. "I was quite depressed by the shock and not very confident about Roosevelt's wisdom, but power may sober him."[40]

In November 1901, Carnegie took the train to Washington to meet with the new president, whom he had only the year before referred to in a letter to Andrew White as a "dangerous man." He was accustomed to visiting Washington regularly to discuss tariff schedules, negotiate armor contracts, and meet with Republican Party officials and colleagues in the steel industry. This time he came in his role as philanthropist to personally apprise Roosevelt of the plans he had formulated that summer with White to build a national scientific research institution in Washington.[41]

Past presidents had carefully cultivated their relationships with the "Star spangled Scotchman," but none with the élan of the cowboy aristocrat who had been so unexpectedly thrust into office. Theodore Roosevelt was a master of seduction. Like Carnegie, he was full of energy, always in motion, and relatively small, though his broad shoulders and puffed-out chest made him appear larger. He welcomed Carnegie to Washington like a long-lost friend. Not unaware of the rumors being spread that he was a trust-busting radical and a danger to businessmen everywhere, Roosevelt could only benefit from having the former Pittsburgh steelmaker on his side. Carnegie was happy to oblige.

On November 28, Thanksgiving Day, 1902, a few days before his meeting with the president, Carnegie sent Roosevelt his plans for a Carnegie Institution in Washington. "Mr. President, believe me that I am made a very happy man this day of thanksgiving by the thought that I have been so favored as to be enabled thus to prove, at least in some degree my gratitude to, and love for, the Republic to which I owe so much."[42]

After his visit to the White House, Carnegie wrote again, this time from the Willard Hotel on Pennsylvania Avenue and Fourteen Street. Thanking Roosevelt for his "cordial reception," he added that he had all along "felt sure you would be captivated by the Scheme." He then rather presumptuously gave the president permission to "pray take your own good time for sending matter to Congress." He closed by reminding him in a postscript that, unlike the corporations Roosevelt had attacked in earlier speeches, "Carnegie Steel Co. was no Trust, but a Limited Partnerships. No Stock for sale—I never bought or sold stock on the Exchange. My Money was all made in making Iron & Steel, no gambling."[43]

Carnegie wanted to give the government $10 million (more than $5 billion today) in gold bonds to establish an institution which would be organized, like the Smithsonian, as a national trust. Roosevelt and his advisers wisely concluded that the government could not accept and retain securities from a private corporation, especially one as controversial as U.S. Steel. Carnegie immediately shifted course and vested control of the $10 million in bonds in the board of trustees of a federally incorporated trust, the Carnegie Institution of Washington. The board was comprised, as the board for the Scottish Universities Trust had been, of the nation's most influential politicians, including Secretary of State John Hay, Secretary of War Elihu Root, Secretary of the Treasury Lyman Gage, former President Grover Cleveland, and, as ex officio members, the president of the United States, the president of the Senate, the speaker of the House, the Smithsonian secretary, and the president of the National Academy of Sciences. Daniel Coit Gilman, who had just retired from Johns Hopkins, was selected as the institution's first president.

The mission of the Carnegie Institution (as opposed the Carnegie Institute in Pittsburgh) was both visionary and vague. Its stated goal was to "encourage investigation, research, and discovery, show the application to the improvement of mankind, provide such buildings, books and instruments as may be needed; and afford instruction of an advanced character." Precisely how any of this was to be accomplished was left to the trustees.[44]

On New Year's Eve 1902, the president sent Carnegie a "personal" note assuring him that he would serve on the new institution's board "with the greatest pleasure. Let me congratulate you upon the very high character—indeed I may say the extraordinary character—of the men who you have secured as trustees; and I congratulate the nation upon your purpose to found such an institution." The deed of trust and the $10 million in U.S. Steel gold bonds were transferred to the trustees in late January.*[45]

---

*The Carnegie Institution began life with a $10 million endowment, to which Carnegie added an additional $2 million in 1909 and $10 million in 1911. Rockefeller's Institute for Medical Research, the precursor to Rockefeller University, was launched with a grant of $200,000; in 1903, Rockefeller donated an additional $660,000 for a tract of land on which to build a permanent home for the institute on York Avenue; in 1907, he responded to a request from his directors for a $6 million endowment by giving $2.6 million; in 1908, he gave another $8 million.—Chernow, *Titan*, 472–78: *NYT*, February 1, 1902, 1.

Carnegie, as might have been expected, was extraordinarily pleased with his new institution, and with himself for having pulled it together so quickly. On January 10, 1902, he wrote Lord Elgin to tell him he had "taken the liberty" of sending Lady Elgin the gift of a "buckboard" (a four-wheeled, horse-drawn wagon). He also enclosed a clipping about the Carnegie Institution. "The enclosed will show you how I am trying to do something for the Republic. . . . We hope ultimately to make this the country that is looked to by the world for the solutions of new problems in Science. Germany is so now at least in some considerable degree, although Britain is not barren by any means."[46]

That same day, he sent Sir Campbell-Bannerman another clipping, this one headlined: "CLEVELAND HEADS CARNEGIE TRUSTEES." "You see from the enclosed what I am about here," he wrote in his accompanying letter. "I believe we shall make the Republic the Country looked to hereafter for the solution of many problems . . . I am very happy in this work—A note from the President with whom I have consulted freely congratulates me 'upon the high—the extraordinarily high character of my Trustees,' but I am used to this quality of trustees [a reference to the Scottish Universities trustees, of whom Campbell-Bannerman was one]."[47]

Despite its rather prosaic name, the Carnegie Institution of Washington was among the most imaginative of the Carnegie gifts. It is difficult to know where Carnegie got the idea for his non-teaching, non-degree-granting university. There were, at the time, medical research centers like the Koch Institute in Berlin, the Pasteur in Paris, and the one Rockefeller was funding in New York City (later to become Rockefeller University). But the Carnegie Institution, with its emphasis on non-medical pure research, was different.

Carnegie was, as Harvard President James Bryant Conant would comment in 1935 on the centenary of his birth, "more than a generation ahead of most business men of this country [in understanding] the importance of science to industry." He recognized far better than his peers how vital basic scientific research was to the applied research that industry fed off. George Ellery Hale, an astronomer and astrophysicist, later to be the chief architect of the National Research Council, was astounded when he learned of Carnegie's commitment to pure research. "The provision of a large endowment solely for scientific research seemed almost too good to be true. . . . Knowing as I did the difficulties of obtaining money for this purpose and devoted as I was to research rather than teaching, I could appreciate some of the possibilities of such an endowment." Hale applied for funds to build an observatory on Mount Wilson in California, and got what he asked for. It would take until 1909 to build and install a 60-inch reflecting telescope in the observatory; in 1917, a second 100-inch telescope, the largest in the world, was added.[48]

The Mount Wilson Observatory—and the work of its astronomers and astrophysicists—was only one of the projects funded in the early years of the new institution. Another, of which Carnegie was equally proud, was the outfitting of the *Carnegie,* an oceangoing yacht with auxiliary engine, built of wood and bronze so that it could collect geophysical data without the errors inflicted on compass readings by iron and steel. The ship was launched in 1909; by 1911, Carnegie could claim that the scientists on board had already been able to correct several significant errors on navigational maps.[49]

In his deed of trust, Carnegie declared that his research institution in Washington should "discover the exceptional man in every department of study whenever and where found . . . and enable him to make the work for which he seems specially designed his life work." That notion would remain the driving philosophy behind the institution over the next century. Some of those "exceptional" scientists, supported by Carnegie money were the astronomer Edwin Hubble, who "revolutionized astronomy with his discovery that the universe is expanding," and Barbara McClintock, whose work on patterns of genetic inheritance in corn won her a Nobel Prize.[50]

Though his Washington institution got less publicity than his other trusts, Carnegie thought enough of it to later add an additional $12 million to his initial gift of $10 million. The institution's endowment now stands at $600 million, which, with government grants, supports an annual budget of $60 million for the work of scientists, fellows, and technical staff in six different departments, two in Washington, one in Baltimore, two in California, and observatories at Mount Wilson, California, and Las Campanas, Chile.*

---

*The Carnegie Institution's administrative headquarters remain in Washington, D.C., where they have always been, though four of its six departments are located elsewhere: the Department of Embryology, founded in 1913, in Baltimore; the Department of Global Ecology, the newest addition, established in 2002, at Stanford University, also the home of the Department of Plant Biology. The departments of Terrestrial Magnetism and the Geophysical Laboratory remain in Washington.

THIRTY-THREE

"A Fine Piece of Friendship," 1902–1905

THE CARNEGIES returned to Britain in the spring of 1902. After their annual sojourn in London—and a speech at Guildhall, where Carnegie was honored by the Worshipful Company of Plumbers—they traveled north to Skibo. With the grand reconstruction of the castle and the outbuildings, Skibo had expanded to the size of a large resort hotel. There was no end of rooms inside the castle and manorhouses, most of them filled all season long by guests. During the summer of 1902, "the Rockefeller boy," John Junior, whom Carnegie had always had a special liking for, arrived with his wife Abby to spend a few days. So did the Polish pianist Ignacy Jan Paderewski, who had made his triumphant Carnegie Hall debut in 1891 and returned many times in the years since then. Paderewski, Carnegie wrote Morley after his Skibo visit, proved to be "a charming man as well as supreme pianist."[1]

The highlight of this—and future—social season was the visit of King Edward VII, who had the year before ascended the throne at the death of his mother, Queen Victoria. "One afternoon in October, 1902," Burton Hendrick writes, with details that could only have been supplied by Louise and Margaret, "a telegram came to Skibo. . . . This conveyed the information that King Edward . . . was on his way to call on Mr. and Mrs. Carnegie. At the moment Carnegie was enjoying his daily siesta and the news, when he was awakened, rather startled him. He jumped up, however, and prepared to give an appropriate welcome. Glancing out the window, the King's motor was visible proceeding up the driveway, and Carnegie, clad in his informal togs, met His Majesty at the doorway. The piper had barely time to get into his Highland garb, and the organist, who had been in the swimming pool, just managed to scramble into his clothes and strike up 'God Save the King' as the royal guest appeared."[2]

The king, who was in the process of remodeling Buckingham Palace, had come to see how Carnegie had managed to incorporate all the modern amenities—including electric lighting and indoor plumbing—into his castle design. He stayed for tea, which he took American-style with lemon, greatly pleasing Louise, who also took her tea without milk or cream. Five-and-a-half-year-old Margaret was presented and, though she forgot to curtsey, triumphed nonetheless. "I had been naughty," Margaret recalled seventy years later, "and as usual on such occasions, after Mother had talked to me, I was sitting alone in the upstairs sitting room to think matters over until I was ready to say I was sorry. Mother never hurried me, but this time she had hardly left the room until she was back. . . . The next thing I knew, I was in the garden picking roses with Nana. . . . Then freshly dressed I was standing . . . in the drawing room with the flowers. A tall bearded man was bending over and asking if I would give him a kiss. I never liked to kiss bearded faces [with the exception, one hopes, of her father]. They had sloppy wet lips, but this face was very different. This man knew how to kiss little girls. I gave the roses to him for the Queen, and a rosebud 'for your ownself', which he put in his buttonhole."[3]

The visit with King Edward, though harrowing, turned out well, Louise wrote Robert Franks in New York. "It was delightfully informal and he seemed to enjoy it as much as we did."[4]

The king, as Carnegie later wrote William Holland, the director of his museum in Pittsburgh, had been attracted during his brief visit to the drawing of *Diplodocus carnegii* on the wall. "He wants one for British Museum badly." Carnegie took the king's offhand request quite seriously and that winter made a formal offer of a duplicate dinosaur to the British Museum. Museums were in the practice of exchanging specimens with one another, but never the size of a dinosaur. On Carnegie's instructions, William Holland got to work constructing a duplicate. He hired two Italian modelers to make molds of each bone, then used the molds to build plaster replicas. As there was no room in the museum for such a task, the work was done at the Western Pennsylvania Exposition Society hall downtown. In December 1904, the duplicate plaster bones were shipped to England, where, after a laborious process of unpacking and assembling, the duplicate *Diplodocus* was displayed in May 1905. The molding process went so smoothly that in the years to come, additional casts would be made and replica dinosaurs dispatched, as gestures of friendship, to Berlin, Paris, Vienna, Bologna, and St. Petersburg.[5]

Carnegie's newfound fame, the result of Morgan's purchase of his company, created new opportunities for him to spread his gospels of wealth, anti-imperialism, and peace. He seized on every one of them. In early 1902, he agreed to Frank Doubleday's recommendation that it was an apt moment to bring out a new collection of his essays. The first of many editions of the book, entitled *The Empire of Business,* was published by Doubleday, Page & Co. in 1902. As Carnegie explained to Lord Avebury, to whom he sent a copy of his book in June, he found himself "in a strange position, the reported publisher of two books, *Gospel of Wealth* [published by *Century* magazine in book form and edited by the daughter of Richard Gilder, the *Century* editor] and this other. I only said to my two friends help yourselves you are welcome to publish anything I have written which I am free to give you. They went to work and selected, I got first copies as presentation copies, that's all."[6]

In that same year, 1902, Bernard Alderson, an English journalist, published the first full-length biography of Carnegie. Frank Doubleday, after checking with Carnegie, bought the American rights and in June wrote Samuel Church, secretary of the Carnegie Institute in Pittsburgh, to ask his assistance in revising the book for an American audience. "Will you be good enough, also, to mark anything which occurs to you as untrue or improper, and to add memoranda of any facts or interesting incidents which occur to you and which have not been touched upon. . . . After this has been done, Mr. C. has expressed his willingness to read the book again and make any suggestions he thinks desirable."[7]

Doubleday was a shrewd enough publisher to know that the public was not going to accept "simply a sort of glorification" of a controversial figure. On the other hand, he had no intention of defaming his subject, whose essays he was bringing out simultaneously with the biography. Although the Homestead strike had occurred a decade earlier, the public had not forgotten it. Doubleday confessed that he felt "hopelessly at sea" as to how to discuss Homestead in the biography. "Could you not send us some material about this strike," he asked Church, "or write or dictate for us a few paragraphs which would help us in this matter? Anything, also, that you could help us to get hold of as to what has been done for Homestead and for the workmen, in the way of information or illustrations, we shall be extremely grateful for. As soon as I can get these things in shape, I am going to set them all in type and we will send it to Mr. Carnegie for his reading."[8]

Church asked William Corey, who still worked for Carnegie Steel in Pittsburgh and had been around at the time of the strike, to write the Homestead paragraphs, but Corey refused to do so. "Mr. Corey thinks that the [Alderson] book is a mass of errors," Church wrote Doubleday, "that it is not written by one who is familiar with what he is describing, and he thinks the point of view is so far away from the truth that the only way to correct it would be to write a new book from beginning to end. This he is not prepared to do and he, therefore, asks me to return the book to you. There is no lack of friendly desire to assist you in the matter either on the part of Mr. Corey or myself, but to those of us who know Mr. Carnegie intimately and who are familiar with the record of his past enterprises in Pittsburgh, this biography seems so far from being a true portraiture of the man that it is simply hopeless for us to give it any real value by any amount of tinkering that we might attempt to do with it."[9]

Doubleday went ahead with the biography without Church's or Corey's assistance. In October, when the American edition of *Andrew Carnegie: The Man and His Work* was published by Doubleday, Page & Co., Alderson wrote a rather plaintive letter to James Bertram, requesting that Carnegie buy copies of the book or, at the very least, acknowledge it in some way. "A word from him would greatly enhance the progress the book is making and I wish that he could see his way to accept the biography."[10]

There is no record of any reply from Bertram or from Carnegie, who apparently agreed with his colleagues in Pittsburgh that the Alderson book was, though laudatory, useless. He was already collaborating with another writer on another biography. We don't know how Joaquin Miller, the California-based writer and poet, got involved in the project, but by July 1902, he wrote Carnegie:

> I have my, or rather your, Biography blocked out, about two hundred pages done. But it is crude, only the skeleton, no soul or heart in it yet; as I must go to Penn. And absorb anecdote and incident. Not that I want Washington's hatchet stories or Franklin's Poor Richard philosophy, but it is the lit-

tle things that show the big man and go to the heart of humanity. And I must have all your books and pictures of your castle and roomy estate, also that of the old-time loom, if possible. In truth, as I go forward, the work, while fascinating, grows almost formidable. I must leave everything else alone, for the time, if I am to do it well. I enclose the preface. Please read it at once. I am sure that the work will do good. But you are so much wiser than I that I shall defer entirely to you and if you do not greatly approve of the plan and purpose of the book I shall regretfully lay it aside. I see that you are busy entertaining Bishops, big men and little children, yet I hope for any early and an encouraging answer"[11]

Miller's biography never saw the light of day. It may have proved too "formidable" a project for him to continue, or perhaps Carnegie, having read the preface, did not encourage him to finish it.

In December, William Stead published yet another profile of Carnegie in *Christian Endeavor World*, in which he remarked, almost in passing, that while Carnegie remained an "inveterate optimist [with an] invincible faith in progress," his faith in the future had taken "one very ugly knock, when his countrymen went crazy for a time over the Philippine conquest."[12]

Although Carnegie had stopped protesting against America's imperialist turn, he had never ceased to mourn it. In the spring of 1902, when asked by the peace activist Frederick Holls to contribute funds for a peace palace at The Hague, he refused. "Please let the idea rest for the present. Let us get our English-speaking race at peace—This forcing ourselves upon unwilling peoples & shooting resisters down is so incongruous with Hague Peace ideas . . . I am not going to think of it at present."[13]

A month later, the "inveterate optimist," had, once again, let his faith in the future get the better of him. In May 1902, Carnegie published a surprisingly hopeful article for the *North American Review*, fittingly entitled "The Opportunity of the United States," calling on the Roosevelt government to grant independence to the Philippine Islands, as if, in that act, it could erase the damage caused by the war.

On April 30, just before he sailed to Britain, he sent a copy of his article to President Roosevelt with a handwritten note: "Will the President of the United States carefully weigh this article from one who wishes him well? . . . Yours for true Americanism." Scrawled across the top of the note Carnegie added: "Don't fear the People. They will rally round you if you once spoke the word."[14]

The president's response was vague but could be interpreted as encouraging, if one sought encouragement as much as Carnegie did. "It was a pleasure to hear from you. As soon as you get back I would like you to come to see me either here at Washington or at Oyster Bay. I am much interested in what you say about Cape affairs [the Boer War], and I want to go over the Philippine business in its present aspect with you."[15]

The cessation of hostilities in the Philippines had not brought an end to the controversy over the war and its legacy. Letters from American soldiers published in newspapers across the country described in almost clinical detail the use of the "water cure" and other tortures to secure information from captured Filipinos. At a meeting in New York at the Plaza Hotel on April 29, chaired by Charles Francis Adams, the Anti-Imperialist League established its own Philippine Investigation Committee, to which it appointed Carnegie in absentia. In July, while Carnegie was at Skibo, the committee delivered its report to President Roosevelt. It began by praising him for his attention to the question of troop "demoralization" and the brutalities that might have resulted from it, but respectfully dissented from his and the U.S. Army's conclusion that instances of torture were isolated. The committee had, on the contrary, found that torture was not only widespread and systematic but often condoned by superior officers. It asked Roosevelt to take action to investigate American atrocities and punish those soldiers and officers found guilty of perpetrating them. The concluding paragraph, to which the signatures of the members were affixed, informed the president that Andrew Carnegie had been a member of the committee, but as he was overseas, it had "been impossible to consult him in preparing this communication or to obtain his signature to it." Instead, a copy of the report had been forwarded to him in Scotland "with a request that he will, after due consideration, communicate with you directly concerning it."[16]

The committee had indeed sent its report to Carnegie at Skibo, but he had never acknowledged receiving it. Only after it was made public did he explain to Adams why he had "not wired to sign my name. . . . President has written asking me to come to him either at Washington or Oyster Bay or wherever he is, upon my return as he wishes 'to confer with me upon present state of Philippines.' . . . I believe I can do more good by abstaining from further action publicly after my outburst in the *North American Review*. That President Roosevelt would not like to see the Filipinos independent and our Republic out of the mess I cannot believe. Now let us see if we cannot help him—What may be our duty next Presidential Election is another matter—Meanwhile I am going to do what I can . . . to get our party right."[17]

Three days later, Carnegie wrote President Roosevelt to explain why he had not signed the "address made to your Excellency in regard to the deplorable excesses which have occurred in the Philippines." His reasons were several. "First—War is Hell! Such hellish things as have occurred in the Philippines occurred in the Chinese War, in South Africa, and will always be the accompaniment of war. In my opinion therefore the responsibility rests with the statesmen whose policy leads to war. . . . Another reason that I did not sign the address to you is because I believe that you have done what the President of the United States was called upon to do." He did not elaborate. A third reason: "I have faith in you," and in Secretary of War Root. "There was a final reason, that I had received your very flattering invitation to call upon you and talk over the Philippines question in its present phase. I believe that one so privileged can exert whatever influence he possesses more wisely and more effectively in friendly consultation with the President than he can possibly do by appealing to the people. It is a privilege which I have enjoyed with three of your predecessors, and in more than one instance I have been assured that I was able to do them some service. If I can be of service to the fourth, it will be one of the most pleasant satisfactions of my life."[18]

Carnegie grossly exaggerated the importance of the president's invitation. The fact that Roosevelt was young and inexperienced in international diplomacy convinced Carnegie that he was being called on to play a major advisory role. This was, of course, far from the truth, as Charles Francis Adams tried to suggest. President Roosevelt, Adams wrote Carnegie in late September, was running for election. He might speak out against the "severities" in the Philippines as he did against the excesses of the trusts, but he would take no action against either.[19]

Carnegie was in no mood to listen. He had all his life been far too trusting of men in power and men whose intelligence he respected. Since James G. Blaine, he had not come across an elected official he admired or wished to befriend as much as he did Teddy Roosevelt. He was not only more powerful and energetic than Blaine had ever been, but more accomplished as an historian and a man of letters, and entirely accessible. "I never enter the presence of the President without awe and reverence," Carnegie wrote Morley in the late summer of 1902. "With friend Roosevelt however this feeling vanished before I knew it—a hearty shake, a slap and hail fellow well met and he was Teddy—A splendid fellow but original. I am writing him today on the Philippines as requested and shall go direct to see him upon my return—It is our duty to obtain influence with those in authority, therefore I always keep in view what effect my action may have there." Carnegie was, indeed, so in awe of the presidency in general, and Roosevelt in particular, that he criticized Nicholas Murray Butler for not bowing to the president before he gave his inaugural speech on being installed as president of Columbia University. "I cannot understand how a man can be in the presence of the President without being awed. I have known three Presidents intimately before they were Presidents, but when I entered their presence, after election, they were surrounded by a halo & I was somewhat of a worshipper." Butler's only response was that he was not guilty of disrespect but had indeed acknowledged the president before he spoke.[20]

Carnegie was entirely captivated by Roosevelt, and had been so kindly treated that he had begun indulging in fantasies of becoming his chief adviser, perhaps even his secretary of state. He wrote Morley that Roosevelt had "asked me to advise him upon British question, Canada . . . troublesome just now, so you see if you cultivate the King and I the President there's no saying what we can do when we get our reward—You Premier don't laugh—<u>character</u> sometimes wins—And I Sec'y State—we'll keep things straight, <u>no war</u>."[21]

NOW IN HIS late sixties, Carnegie, whose appearance had changed little in a quarter century, was beginning to take on the look of an old and rather strange white-haired man. The large head set on the trim body was more gnomelike, his face increasingly puffy. He also shrank in size—or appeared to. Almost every visitor and description noticed his lack of height, but no one wrote about it quite like his friend Sam Clemens who, in an unpublished section of his own *Autobiography,* felt obligated to "dwell for a moment upon Carnegie's stature—if one may call it by that large name—for the sake of the future centuries. The future centuries will be glad to hear about this feature from one who has actually looked upon it. . . . In truth Mr. Carnegie is no smaller than was Napoleon; he is no smaller than were several other men supremely renowned in history but for some reason or other he looks smaller than he really is. He looks incredibly small, almost unthinkably small. I do not know how to account for this; I do not know what the reason of it is, and so I have to leave it unexplained."[22]

As they aged, Louise's height stood out a bit more, though she had learned to compensate for it by slouching a bit and leaning in toward him when they stood together. Her features had softened with age, and, unlike her husband, she had grown more handsome. As her cheeks filled out, her eyes seemed to recede deeper into her face. There was a placidness, a gentleness, almost a world-weary calm to her.

Neither husband nor wife had allowed age to slow them down. Carnegie was, at seventy, as at thirty, incapable of sitting still or remaining in one place for long. While he seldom appeared at the dedication ceremonies for his American libraries, he never turned down a chance to open a British library and to receive the greatest honor a British town could give: its "freedom of the city," a medieval designation that offered the honoree the privileges of the "burgher" enumerated on a parchment scroll encased in an elaborately carved casket-shaped, usually jeweled, box. Every summer, with Louise at his side, Carnegie traveled from town to town collecting his "freedoms" and being fêted with parades, dinners, receptions, and adulatory speeches.*

Carnegie took this aspect of his life very seriously. Every library he opened, every "freedom" he received was another opportunity to preach his gospel. For years now, he had been publishing his speeches in pamphlet form. When James Swank, the former secretary and chief lobbyist for the American Iron and Steel Association, retired in 1904, Carnegie hired him to assemble, publish, and distribute these pamphlets. "With regard to title, etc. Make cover of pamphlet more or less the same as the sample I sent you, heading it, 'More Busy Days,' and below, 'Dr. Carnegie at Dingwall, Tain, etc. etc.' With regard to the paternity, put underneath, 'compiled and edited by Jas. M. Swank, Philadelphia.' No introduction or preface required. Color of cover brown or gray."[23]

---

*Fifty-four caskets and 133 certificates are currently stored at the Birthplace Museum in Dunfermline.

In mid-July 1902, Carnegie traveled to eight different functions, then returned in August to a castle full of visitors. Morley was due to arrive in mid-September. "I am looking forward to five days of pleasant roving rambling talk. Only, I Beseech you, don't ask me to go anywhere or to do anything, for I am as tired as a hound. . . . What a pleasant time we'll have!" A month later, after the visit of Paderewski had "closed the season," Andrew was off again, with Louise in tow, on another round of visits and speeches. "Madam and I this week 'orate' at Perth—Freedom," he wrote Dod on October 1; "Thursday Falkirk [library] opening also evening; Friday Greenoch opening also evening—Saturday Sterling; Monday travel to Liverpool; Tuesday Hawarden Library speech—Wednesday Library Liverpool—Banquet in eve. Twelve speeches . . . is a big contract but I'm in fine fettle & shall no doubt go through all right as usual. Madam has two functions herself.—Hoop la!"[24]

Morley, on being sent a copy of his friend's speaking schedule, warned him to slow down. "Take care of yourself, my friend. This progress of yours will be a strain—and strain has to be paid for in malt or in meal. Don't make so many engagements for a short span: spread them out: or don't make them. Look how well I am. The Oxford people want me to speak at the banquet on the tercentenary of Bodleian next week. No—say I."[25]

Carnegie pushed on through his twelve speeches, then proceeded to St. Andrews for the most important engagement of the summer. The students at St. Andrews, the oldest university in Scotland, founded in 1411, had the year before elected Andrew Carnegie as their rector, no doubt in recognition of his $10 million gift to the Scottish universities. Carnegie had begun planning his inaugural address the summer before by reading through a recently collected volume of addresses delivered by his predecessors. As many of these touched on questions of "religious sentiments," Carnegie decided to explain to the students "how his own had developed and crystallized from year to year." There was, he recognized, "one objection to the choice; it involves a highly personal address; but there is one advantage; it will show you the flesh-and-blood man behind, and I do feel desirous to get in close touch with you. Let us know each other."[26]

Religion was not a new subject for Carnegie. He had been a vocal agnostic since adolescence. His refusal to believe in a personal deity had left such an impression on one old friend, Bobby Pitcairn, that when Pitcairn's wife died, he felt obligated to remind Carnegie that not only she but his dear father had been a believer. "God bless him! Would that you had this consolation."[27]

Carnegie, who had taken such delight in religious disputation and debate as a young man, continued as he grew older to find enormous satisfaction in playing the enlightened man of reason in debate with fossilized, superstitious believers. His Dunfermline friend, Lord Shaw, who helped organize the Scottish Universities Trust, recalled in his memoirs the great gap that stood between him and Carnegie "on the spiritual side. . . . The old rigidity most righteously he despised. But the noble underlying spirit [of Christianity] such things made him impatient; and he would—at least to me, for I declined positively ever to lower my flag to him—he would fling out at you savage tenets of the Old Testament as if they were Religion! . . . Far and wide he voyaged—to Confucius, to Zoroaster, to the world's sages—seeking the truth if haply he might find it. And I do believe that, after all those voyagings, and storms of argufying, and declamatory monologue, into which an uneasiness of mind seemed ever to draw him, that at last his bark landed on the Christian shore."[28]

Despite Shaw's protestations and Pitcairn's hopes, Carnegie never would be reconciled to Christianity, though in time his hostility to the organized religion whose tales of eternal damnation had so frightened him as a child diminished. In his mid-sixties, he even consented to accompany Louise and Margaret to church in Dornoch.

That summer of 1902, in preparation for his "rectorial address" at St. Andrews, he took up again the subject of religion in discussion and correspondence with his British friends. In a letter to Richard Haldane, he proudly recalled that as a young man, he had thrown over "our dogmatic theology of our Bible and our Christ, and all the fables of an ignorant past. . . . Then science brought me back to true Religion."[29]

In the draft of his address, Carnegie denied that science was an enemy of religion. On the contrary, "every discovery of science has exalted and must exalt the Creator of these startling wonders to which science alone keeps the keys." Like Herbert Spencer, he believed in "the truth that there is an Inscrutable Existence . . . an Infinite and Eternal Energy from which all things proceed"; and like him he denied that there was any one preferable way to refer to this "unknown" or worship it.[30]

Carnegie's speech, though charming in parts, was unwieldy. He rambled on, dropping names as he went to show the undergraduates and their professors that, though unschooled, he was not uneducated; that though an opponent of organized theologies, he was a religious man. Principal James Donaldson of St. Andrews, after reading the draft, suggested that Carnegie might choose another topic, as "theology and religion" was at that moment in Scottish history too controversial a subject to be treated so personally. Carnegie, too, apparently had his doubts as to whether this rather informal, autobiographical address was appropriate. He stowed the talk away—it would not be published until after his death.

As a replacement for his address on religion, he took up a subject he knew well: American industrial ascendancy and the economic future of Europe and Britain. This speech, delivered on October 22, 1902, and widely reprinted, charted the decline of British industrial dominance. The present, he declared, belonged to the United States, because of its enormous home market and abundance of natural resources, and to Germany which had become Britain's chief rival in Europe. The German economy had overtaken the British, its population was greater, it was closing the gap in naval armaments, and it was led by a dynamic, ambitious ruler, Kaiser Wilhelm II. Parroting Richelieu's warning to the French king about Cromwell, Carnegie announced to his Scottish audience that "'a great man has arisen in Germany, the Emperor.' It is impossible to follow his doings without feeling that here is a personality, a power potent for good or evil, in the world. . . . He is at once the Emperor and the vital force of the empire."[31]

In his bluff, almost confrontational manner, Carnegie was using the St. Andrews address to alert and reconcile the British to the changing balance of power. Nine years earlier, in the essay that became the concluding chapter of his new edition of *Triumphant Democracy,* he had proclaimed that the only way for the British to retain their exalted place in the world was to join with Canada and the United States in an English-speaking union, with its headquarters in Washington. Now, speaking before an audience of Scottish college students, he declared that the days when such a federation might have rescued the British were gone. Britain was too small "in size and population [to] remain great in material products or material power." "All thought of material ascendancy, even with the empire united, must therefore be abandoned." There was no hope for the British: they would, in the years to come, have but two choices: to assume a subordinate place within Europe, or within an American-led, English-speaking federation.[32]

Having thoroughly depressed his audience by pointing to the inevitable decline of British wealth and power, Carnegie concluded, bizarrely for a successful businessman and capitalist, by suggesting that "material ascendancy" was not all that important. "Gentlemen . . . assembled in Scotland's oldest university, the thought that fills your heart and appeals to mine is what value is material compared with moral and intellectual ascendancy— supremacy not in the things of the body, but in the those of the spirit! . . . What matters what part of the world makes the steel, iron, cloth, or ships, if you produce the highest poets, historians, philosophers, statesmen, inventors, teachers? Let others make more of the food for the body of man, if from you come the best books for the soul, or the highest examples of lives grandly lived. Let more of the millions of the people be clothed by other lands and other hands, as long as you educate and apparel the minds, leading men in the higher paths."[33]

Carnegie's 1902 address at St. Andrews was his way of setting his priorities in order, personally and publicly, as he entered the final decades of his life, of telling the "men of letters" in his audience that he wanted to be thought of as one of them. The St. Andrews students responded, two years later, by electing him to a second term as rector, therefore guaranteeing that he would have one more chance to address them formally.

LOUISE accompanied her husband to St. Andrews, as she did to most of his speeches. She had grown into the role of companion to the great man but she was also, day by day, assuming greater responsibilities of her own. At Skibo, her duties as lady of the manor had increased to the point where they occupied her full time. With the assistance of her personal secretary, Louise planned for the arrival of new guests, decided where to put them, welcomed them personally, and saw to it that they were escorted to their rooms and their bags unpacked. Every morning, she met with the chief butler to determine how many guests might be expected at each of the day's meals and to arrange for the vehicles that would transport them to the golf course or to fish in the Shin River or shop in Dornoch. She also planned the day's musical selections with the organist and met with the housekeeper and cook to discuss the day's menus. In late morning, after her chores were done, and then again after lunch, she consulted with the gardeners, looked after her personal gardens, picked flowers, and joined her guests for a walk, a swim in the pool, a few holes of golf, or a carriage ride. By midafternoon, she was back in the castle to pour tea in the drawing room. After tea, she retreated to her private rooms for a half hour with her daughter and husband, then answered her correspondence, dressed for dinner, heard her daughter's prayers, and, having wished Margaret a good night, went downstairs again, where, escorted by the piper, she led her guests into dinner.

On Sundays, there were "the rounds" to make: visits to the stables, kennels, poultry house, dairy, greenhouses, nurseries; and calls at the cottages of senior staff members; then the carriage ride into Dornoch for church services and hymn-singing. In the afternoon, she and her daughter together gathered blossoms for the ladies' finger bowls.

Louise, though uncomplaining, was exhausted by the strain of the Skibo season. Carnegie, for his part, doted on her, fearful that her health might give way. Their only major disagreements came when she tried to interfere in his grooming and get him to discard well-worn or replace ill-matched articles of clothing. He deferred to her on all household decisions. But, at the same time, as he heaped more responsibilities on her as lady of the manor, he wanted her with him everywhere: when he played golf or yachted or drove into town or took guests on a picnic in the moors or traveled to other towns to receive his honors. He expected her as well to help him welcome and entertain the presidents of the four Scottish universities for principals' week in September and the twenty-five trustees of the Carnegie Dunfermline Trust on their annual visit in July.

In mid-October 1902, after their first guest-filled season at Skibo, Carnegie wrote to tell Morley that he was taking the family to Lake Geneva to "give Madam and Baba two weeks in high air. Madam should have a rest between Houses (Palaces alas, alas). . . . I don't like going so far on continent but Madam needs a rest I think and that settles it." From this point on, upon arriving in Britain in the spring and before departing in the fall, the family would spend at least two or three weeks at grand hotels in London or on the Continent so Louise could enjoy a vacation from housekeeping responsibilities.[34]

In the fall of 1902, the first family vacation in Switzerland was interrupted when all three Carnegies came down with food poisoning. Louise and Baba recovered quickly, but Andrew, either from the food poisoning or some other malady, did not. They returned to London, where Carnegie spent the next ten days recuperating.

The newspapers kept daily watch on his health and celebrated his return to New York on December 11. The *New York Times* reported the next day that although he "said that he never felt better in his life . . . he looked a little pale and shaken and his step had lost some of its accustomed sprightliness." Asked if he was going to present his new Fifth Avenue mansion as a Christmas present to his daughter, he laughed. "I haven't seen the house yet."

At the conclusion of the interview, Carnegie, Louise, and Baba were driven uptown and through Central Park to their new home at 2 East Ninety-first Street. It was quite unlike any other Fifth Avenue mansion—and that was precisely how the Carnegies had planned it. He was reported as having told his architects that he "did not want a palace," but a house that was modest, roomy, and plain. To make sure he got this, he steered clear of the usual society architects and hired Babb, Cook & Willard, who had designed several important buildings but no palaces.*[35]

Harry Phipps had constructed a beautiful, large, but plain marble home for himself on the corner of Eighty-seventh Street. The Carnegies' mansion was larger than Phipps's but less elegant and much more domestic. Instead of being built of marble or granite, it was constructed of redbrick with white stone trim, giving it a Georgian look, like an English city mansion, complicated by a French Beaux-Arts-style canopy of bronze and glass. It did not resemble the monumental structures further south built by the Vanderbilts and Huntingtons in the 1880s, or the massive building that Henry Frick would construct for himself in the 1910s. There was a colorful, lively feel to the property. The front entrance was of yellow brick; large blocks of pink granite faced along the sidewalks. The entire property was surrounded by a black iron fence, but a decorative one that invited passersby to look inside, between the well-spaced pickets.

The property extended the entire block from Ninetieth to Ninety-first Street, but the house appeared to have been pushed back toward Ninety-first Street so that the south side of the property could be given over to

*In 1976, the Carnegie mansion became the home of the Smithsonian Institution's Cooper-Hewitt Museum.

Louise's gardens. As at Skibo, but miniaturized, there would be a central lawn, with paths, and a variety of shrubs and flowers chosen to bloom in the spring and fall while the Carnegies were in residence. Around the edges of the property, full-grown maples, poplars, and elms were planted, though, with the exception of a single poplar, none survived long.

The iron fence did not provide the Carnegies with much privacy. From the moment the family moved in, as Louise remarked in her diary, there were "very troublesome" reporters buzzing about. Everyone in town knew where the richest man in the world lived and what he looked like. Carnegie was not one to hide out. He spent time in his garden, in full view of passersby, and made full use of Central Park just across the avenue. Every afternoon, at 4:00 P.M., he entered the park for his two-mile circular promenade around the reservoir (he sometimes made two circuits), often with a friend or one of the journalists who lay in wait for him along the path.[36]

The ground floor of the house was divided into two wings: one for the family; the other for Carnegie and his assistants. Visitors entered through a small vestibule. If on business, they were directed to the right, through an anteroom, and up a flight of stairs into a waiting room, then into James Bertram's office. Just behind Bertram's office was a wood-paneled lobby that opened onto Carnegie's private library, the largest room in the mansion. Behind the library was Carnegie's study. Carnegie did most of his work in the library at a table so large he looked elflike sitting at it. In front of the table was his soft easy chair with footstool, where he sat to give dictation to Bertram.

Other visitors and friends opened a second set of doors directly in front of the entrance. These led to a foyer and a short stairway into the Great Hall, paneled in Scottish oak. The public and entertainment rooms— parlor, dining room, reception room, breakfast room, conservatory, and gallery—were comfortable, but not large by millionaire standards. There was no ballroom or banquet room, no outrageously expensive paintings or sculpture in the art gallery, no Florentine furniture, oversized medieval tapestries, or ornately gilded ceilings. The private family rooms on the second floor were reached by staircase and an elevator so modern it was featured in newspaper stories. Andrew and Louise had adjoining bedrooms, with a dressing room for Louise. There was a family library and sitting room and a day and night nursery for Margaret. On the third floor was Stella's room, some guestrooms, and storage space. The servant quarters on the fourth floor housed ten female and four male servants. The chauffeurs and some other staff lived on Ninetieth Street at the Carnegies' garage. The basement held the kitchen, laundry, rooms for the steward and chief housekeeper. In the subbasement were state-of-the-art twin boilers that were fueled by coal delivered at the east end of the house and transported over a small railroad track from the bin to the furnace, a quarter ton at a time.

Carnegie's daily routine was much the same as at Skibo, with one slight difference. In Scotland, the household was awakened by the piper. At Ninety-first Street, they rose earlier, at 7:00 A.M., to the sounds of the great organ Carnegie had installed in the lower hallway, played by an organist from the Broadway Tabernacle. After a leisurely breakfast, Carnegie repaired to his private study, where he read through the morning newspapers and the letters Bertram thought he should look after. He dictated answers, memoranda, and instructions, and met personally with those rare petitioners who were granted an interview. His "work" was generally concluded by lunchtime, leaving the rest of the day free for other activities.[37]

Most of the Carnegies' entertaining was done at the mansion, including his annual "literary dinners," held jointly with his friend Richard Gilder of the *Century*. Every year a different man of letters was honored: Sam Clemens, John Morley, Charles Eliot Norton. The tradition was for each of the guests to sign their names on the tablecloth. The names were then embroidered and preserved as a record of the event. Carnegie also held luncheons and smaller dinners at his home for visiting dignitaries and special events for his Carnegie Veterans Association and the various organizations he belonged to and supported.

WITHIN WEEKS of returning to New York and taking up residence in his new home in the fall of 1902, Carnegie took the train to Washington to meet with President Roosevelt and be honored at the dedication of his Washington library. Carnegie, still courting and being courted by the president, returned every compliment. Theodore Roosevelt, he told his audience, was not just the president of the United States but "a prince in the republic of letters . . . I doubt not that of the books taken from this library his will rank high in the list. We hail him to-day, therefore in the dual capacity of President and author, positions unsurpassed in their several spheres, a rare and wonderful combination."[38]

Had they been closer in age, or had Roosevelt had the time or inclination to visit Carnegie at Skibo, they might have become friends. Of Andrew Carnegie's gifts, the one least appreciated was his talent for befriending men he admired. He selected his friends as he chose his dinner companions: for their intellect, their ideas, and their wit. Having chosen those he wanted to befriend, he cultivated them carefully. His letters are replete with invitations to dine, visit, yacht, golf, fish, and travel with him. His warmth, his flattery, his deference—when called for—his loyalty, and his dogged pursuit, usually bore fruit. In the end, even the most restrained, refined Englishmen, like William Gladstone, Matthew Arnold, and Herbert Spencer, were won over by his devotion. "His extraordinary freshness of spirit," John Morley wrote in his *Recollections*, "easily carried Arnold, Herbert Spencer, myself, and afterwards many others, high over an occasional credulity or haste in judgment such as befalls the best of us in ardent hours."[39]

Carnegie gravitated toward those who, like him, had a puckish, self-deprecating sense of humor, could turn a phrase, had published a book or two, and were liberals in the British style, that is, advocates of limited government and opponents of socialist experiment and imperialist adventure. It was perhaps not coincidental that many of his friends—Frick, Morley, Phipps, Hay, among them—were small like he was.

Those chosen to enter the Carnegie circle were showered with gifts, usually from Scotland: grouse, trout, and the finest, smoothest Scotch whiskey available, which he dispensed with good humor and in large quantities. "This is the best as well as the most fashionable medicine of the day," he wrote Richard Gilder in early 1904. "Please take half glass in water Lunch and Dinner as I do and report result—then take good care of yourself and especially take exercise. Come and golf with me for instance. . . . P.S. This Liquor is from the King's Vat which Queen Victoria had for thirty years. Sip reverently, don't gulp it."[40]

Dozens of friends were rewarded with Scotch whiskey, usually from John Dewar, on birthdays, holidays, special occasions, or when they fell ill. At one point, Clemens, having perhaps run out, informed Carnegie by note that he had been "in bed since last Sunday slowly wasting away under an attack of bronchitis complicated with other unnecessary maladies, & I cannot get any Scotch whisky that isn't rank & frank poison. If you will lend me half a bottle I'll be & remain gratefully your friend." Every year, sometimes twice a year, Carnegie would send a new supply and Clemens would find a new way to thank him. "Dear St. Andrew," he wrote in February 1906, "The whisky arrived in due course from over the water; last week one bottle of it was extracted from the wood & inserted into me, on the installment plan, with this result: that I believe it to be the best & smoothest whiskey now on the planet." And again, in January 1908, "That whisky came very handy. I had a very wild & exasperating cold, but a pint of the whisky tamed it in 3 minutes by the watch & I did not wake up again for ten hours. I shall be out of bed tomorrow, I think, & I'll break straightway for Bermuda." Three weeks later, having received yet another batch, he wrote that it had come "at the right time. Of course—for whisky never comes at the wrong time." And a year later, "Many thanks for the whisky. It goes to the right place, & finds a hearty welcome there."[41]

Grover Cleveland, who not only received Scotch whiskey but a personal visit in Princeton during his illness, responded more solemnly to his friend's "thoughtful friendliness. . . . In the midst of your many and large public benefactions, I hope you find an especial gratification in the kind things you do within the sphere of man-to-man relationships."[42]

While Carnegie was extraordinarily generous with his gifts and in paying for his friends' travel and vacations, he wisely stayed away from entering into business deals with them. He turned down Blaine's offers to invest in coal mines, Stead's proposal that he join with him in publishing a partisan, opinionated morning newspaper, and several of Clemens's harebrained business ventures.

Clemens was somewhat of a wild man when it came to investing his own—and his friends'—funds. No sooner had he gotten out of the debts incurred because of disastrous investments in a publishing and printing company than he tried in 1900 to inveigle his friends in new schemes. He urged his financial adviser and savior, Standard Oil vice president Henry Rogers, to share an exclusive option for U.S. rights to an Austrian carpet-weaving machine, and when that failed, attempted to interest Rogers in investing with him in the U.S. and British rights to another Viennese product, Plasmon, a food additive extracted from "the waste milk" of dairies. When Rogers refused, Clemens, tongue in cheek, contacted Carnegie's daughter to invite her to convince her father to invest.

"You are so little that you probably can't remember so large a bulk as I am," he wrote Margaret, at the time aged three, "but that is no matter I remember you very well and this is only a business letter anyway. My scheme is this—a kind of conspiracy, you to be head conspirator, partly on account of your inexperience, and partly on account of your influence with your father which I judge is considerable. Very well. When your mother is not around, give him five or six fingers of Scotch and then talk. This will mellow him up and enlarge his views and before he solidifies again you will have him. That is to say, you will have his cheque for 500 pounds, drawn to order of 'Plasmon Syndicate Ltd,' which you will send to me and you and I will be personally responsible that the money is back in his hands in 6 months and along with it 500 shares in the Plasmon Company, all paid up." There followed a three-page prospectus, written in Clemens's exquisite hand, on the future of Plasmon. Though no doubt amused by his friend's outrageously imaginative pitch, Carnegie declined to invest in this scheme, as he declined to invest in Clemens's publishing company.[43]

Carnegie's reluctance to back his friends' business schemes was no indication of stinginess on his part and was not taken as such. On the contrary, as everyone who knew him recognized, if ever there were a man who contradicted the stereotype of the tightfisted Scotsman, it was he.

"He was the most grateful man in the world and would always reward any kindness done him or his family. . . . He never forgot," Hew Morrison later recalled. His favorite device for helping out his friends in old age was to provide them with private pensions, almost always unsolicited. "For years there was an old lady in Edinburgh who drew a regular pension. Her only claim was that the Carnegies, emigrating to America, slept in her father's house the last night before they sailed."[44]

Hundreds of friends, family members, and former associates were pensioned off with Carnegie funds. In late 1901 or early 1902, he offered Grover Cleveland a private pension, fearful no doubt that the only ex-president still alive might suffer the gruesome fate of Ulysses Grant, who was rescued from poverty when Sam Clemens offered him an advance of $10,000 and an oversized royalty to write his memoirs. Cleveland had no such life story to draw upon. Though a bill was winding its way through Congress to provide ex-presidents with an annuity, its outcome remained uncertain. Not willing to trust to Congress to provide for the former president, Carnegie offered to fund a pension by himself. Cleveland turned him down. "I was so touched and overcome by your last letter that it has taken me some time to get myself to reply to it," he wrote in January 1902. "So far as the present is concerned, I am getting on I think as well as I deserve." Cleveland closed by asking Carnegie's permission to approach him again if "the Fates are so hard with me that I must have a strong friendly hand; and whether I have this permission or not, let me assure you that your kindness and what you have offered to do, will always remain among my most cherished possessions."[45]

Carnegie, knowing how proud Herbert Spencer was, never offered him a pension, but according to Hew Morrison, supported him in his later years by "surreptitiously" supplying money to his housekeeper.[46]

Carnegie's closest friend remained John Morley. The two had been friends for more than twenty years, though they could not have been more dissimilar in temperament, background, and appearance. Carnegie was ebullient, outgoing, optimistic, decisive, white-bearded, and the unschooled son of a Dunfermline weaver. Morley, to the contrary, was dour, depressive, cynical, a procrastinator, clean-shaven, and the Oxford-educated son of an Anglican surgeon. They had met at a London dinner party in 1883, when Morley was forty-five and Carnegie forty-eight. Morley had already made a name for himself in London circles as essayist, editor, and adviser to Gladstone and the Liberal Party hierarchy. In the decades to follow, Morley's output as an author would remain prodigious: philosophical ruminations, history, literary criticism, and biographies of Cobden and Gladstone. But he never permitted his literary career to interfere with his political. He had been first elected to the House of Commons in the early 1880s and had joined Gladstone in fighting for but failing to secure a greater measure of Home Rule for Ireland. His influence within the party grew steadily through the 1890s, as an advocate of Home Rule and an outspoken opponent of the Boer War and imperial adventurism. All this only endeared him further to Carnegie.

Morley did not fish or golf or motor, but he was, like Carnegie, a great reader, with a prodigious memory, and though a bit diffident in the company of others, an enthusiastic conversationalist. The two friends spent their time together walking and talking. "They were frequently disputing . . . Morley was a somewhat ponderous thinker and lethargic talker," according to Hew Morrison, "while Carnegie's chief quality was nimbleness. His mind skipped around rapidly and gaily—it was difficult to drive it into a corner. Morley was more subtle and, of course, much more profound, but in a verbal set-to these characteristics are not the most useful."[47]

In 1902, Carnegie offered Morley the gift of Lord Acton's library, which, with some 60,000 volumes, was believed to be the largest private collection in London. Carnegie had become acquainted with Acton—and his library—in 1890, when he learned from Gladstone that Lord Acton was deeply in debt and going to sell his books. Carnegie offered to pay the interest and principal on a £10,000 (about $1 million today) loan on the condition that his intervention be kept secret. When Acton died in 1902, the library passed into Carnegie's hands. Andrew White, who did not know of Carnegie's connection to the library, wrote to suggest that Carnegie purchase it and donate it to an American institution. "Britain, has, in the British Museum and elsewhere, doubtless, collections as good or nearly as good: America has none. Why not send it there? Of course Cornell would be glad to take it, and I should be proud to see it there; but probably the best place for it would be either the New York Public Library or the Library of Congress."[48]

Morley, to whom Carnegie forwarded White's letter, wrote back at once. "The enclosed does not at all surprise me. If I were an American (which I am heartily glad that I am not) I should say just the same. Only don't overlook the fact that if you do send it over, you will lose a good slice of popularity in this country—I mean England."[49]

Carnegie reassured Morley that he had never had any intention of acceding to White's request. "Now, I sent you White note to show what he, a Scholar thought of Acton Library. I wished to impress upon you its value. I have no idea that it should ever go out of England. My intention has been and is now declared. The Library goes to my friend John Morley. Your refusal of it because you had not room is no bar—You give it as you think best. I pay all expenses but I advise you to throw upon the recipient the labor of attending to it—otherwise you will be troubled with details—you keep your mind upon your present great work—The institution to whom you give it has libraries and a staff, let them see to it."[50]

Morley was overwhelmed. "Your letter, my dear Carnegie moves me deeply. It breathes an air of friendship and true kindness of feeling that refreshes me more than you can suppose. Your gift is the most magnificent compliment that ever was paid to a man of letters. If I were by your side, and I wish I were at Skibo, I should deprecate it with all my might. As you well know, I am not covetous of splendid possessions, and this is indeed a splendid possession. But it would be ungracious and morose if I were to persist in baulking your most gracious purpose. So in short I accept the noble charge you have laid upon me, with the keenest sense of the honour that you do me. . . . I don't think I've written the letter I meant to write: but you will know, my good friend all that I feel."[51]

Though his gifts were both generous and thoughtful, it was in his condolence notes that Carnegie revealed the depths of his regard for his friends. Childhood deaths were more frequent in the late nineteenth and early twentieth centuries, but no less painful to the parents left behind. Carnegie lived through that pain with several of his friends and colleagues, including Henry Clay Frick, James Blaine, Samuel Clemens, and Grover Cleveland, whose daughter Ruth died at age thirteen. "Mrs. Carnegie and I could not write you, Silence, Silence! was the word that came to our mind," read his note to the Clevelands. "What words would not be an intrusion upon you in your grief! . . . Mrs. Carnegie and I think of you at short intervals . . . we feel in our hearts like going to you and asking cannot we do something, is there no avenue for us to pick a thorn out of your pathway? . . . That you may both be able to suffer and not give way entirely is our earnest prayer."[52]

The prose is awkward, even labored; the sentiment a bit strong for our early twenty-first-century sensibilities; but the sincerity is unmistakable. His friends were, especially in his retirement years, dearer to him than anything else save his wife and daughter, and he wanted them to know this.

Carnegie got on best with men with whom he had no business relations. He befriended several of his young partners, only to later turn around and gossip about them or berate them in public. William Abbott, who left Carnegie's employ as a relatively young man, recalled years later that while Carnegie never "treated his associates other than justly," he would also "abuse them, call them fools ('he called me that many times' . . .) and behave in a most outrageous manner." That these outbursts "were purely temperamental, and quickly subsided" did not reduce the pain the young men suffered.[53]

Carnegie was cursed with a loose tongue—and looser pen. He was frighteningly unforgiving when he thought his partners had suffered moral lapses. Charlie Schwab, who had replaced Frick, doubled profits, and then arranged the sale of the Carnegie Company to Morgan, was, according to his biographer, nearly destroyed by Carnegie's criticisms. During the winter of 1902, Schwab, who had moved without a break from Carnegie

Company to U.S. Steel, took a long-awaited and desperately needed vacation in Monte Carlo, where he was spotted by a reporter at the casino tables. The American newspapers took direct aim at the boy wonder who had engineered the largest merger in American corporate history, with elaborately exaggerated stories about his gambling and poker games. Though Schwab was no longer employed by Carnegie, the older man felt personally betrayed by his protégé and suggested that Schwab resign at once. He wrote Morgan directly, apologizing for having recommended Schwab to him. "I feel . . . as if a son had disgraced the family. Never did he show any tendency to gambling when under me, or I should not have recommended him you may be sure. He shows a sad lack of <u>solid</u> qualities—of good sense, and his influence upon the many thousands of young men who naturally look to him will prove pernicious in the extreme. I have had nothing wound me so deeply for many a long day, if ever."[54]

Morgan made light of the matter and rejected Schwab's offer to resign. Carnegie was not, however, prepared to drop the matter. He had spent his lifetime trying to disabuse the public of the notion that capitalists were gamblers, and now, his chief protégé had been caught red-handed. It was his worst nightmare. Carnegie kept at Schwab, with letters and cables, letting him know, over and over, how disappointed he was. In March 1902, he invited Schwab to visit him at Skibo, but Schwab turned him down, saying, "I have not as yet been able to muster up sufficient courage to come to see you. Your very severe letters to me and especially your letter to Mr. Morgan has depressed me more than anything that has ever occurred. I cannot see how you could have so fully condemned me without every giving me a hearing,—no one else did."[55]

Though Morgan accepted his apology, Schwab's days at U.S. Steel were already numbered. From the outset, he had sought the same degree of power at the new company that he and Carnegie had exercised at the old. When he learned that this was not to be, he backed away, defeated. Though he had just turned forty, his health suffered—from overwork, anxiety, stress. In August 1902, he fled to Europe again. Arriving at the Ritz in Paris, he found another letter from Carnegie, filled with new accusations. Someone—we don't know who—had been spreading further stories about Schwab's gambling problem. Schwab could no longer tolerate the old man's meddling: "That you would be willing to listen to, and believe the stories some one has seen fit to tell you was indeed a surprise to me . . . I am no gambler and if the stories published were true, of course I should be condemned. But they are not true. But be what I may, there is no condition of affairs that would make me even listen to a tale of such a character concerning you. I'd defend you or any of my friends until I knew the truth. I admit I have made a serious mistake and one I shall probably never be able to rectify—and I will pay the penalty. I have cabled Mr. Morgan again to-day saying that he <u>must</u> accept my resignation. My chief [pang] is not my loss of position, or loss of public opinion, but the loss of your confidence and friendship. Do not send for me for I should not come."[56]

Like summer storms, Carnegie's bursts of anger soon blew over. When they did, he made believe they had never happened. There were no apologies, no offers of reconciliation, and, except in the Frick case, no excuses or explanations offered. In 1906, learning that Schwab was ill, he sent advice, as he would to any of his old friends. "Have been on the eve of wiring several mornings to ask for the truth about you but desisted fearing reply might reach the Press. Don't like abscess on the thigh—in one so young—Blood out of order. Be a model like me and keep well." His recipe for recovery was a simple one:

Baked apples—Oatmeal—chicken   Breakfast
Fish or chicken—oysters <u>when in season</u>   Lunch
2 spoonfuls Old Scotch—
Soup, oysters—no meats—simple pudding   Dinner
Sago, Tapioca or Rice
2 spoonfuls O.S. [Old Scotch]
Exercise every day, golf often—
Retire about 10 or 10:30
No wine—no liquor between meals
Listen to Madam—she will approve this, I'm sure.[57]

Carnegie enjoyed good health for most of his retirement. But as he aged, so did his friends, and they were not as fortunate as he. Other men might have sought solace in the thought that there was an afterlife where all would meet again. Carnegie did not. "Every year," he wrote Clemens from Skibo in the summer of 1905, when

I return to New York I am mourning the absence of one or more. . . . Why? Why? The everlasting Why. No response, least of all in the realms of present Theology which gives an answer too terrible for credence—My friend we have this only—do our duty here, obey the judge within and bravely meet the fate awaiting us. It is not any future I dread . . . I ask for nothing better, only give us immortality here with one another (I don't want to miss you my friend)—No sir—heaven enough for me with those around me, the loved ones. Well. Well. Press the lips and bear it. It is something that we lived & loved—let us so live that our remaining band of friends repeat Burns' lines over us:

> If there's another world he lives in bliss
> If there be none he made the best of this.[58]

THIRTY-FOUR

"Apostle of Peace," 1903–1904

T HE GREAT EVENT in my life of its kind has happened," Carnegie
wrote Morley in March 1903. "I am Laird of Pittencrieff biggest of all
titles to me—King Edward not in it." Pittencrieff had been the estate of
the Hunt family, relative newcomers to the aristocracy who had extended
their holdings by encroaching on Dunfermline's common lands.
Carnegie's maternal grandfather and uncle had fought back and, as a result, the Hunts had banned all Morrisons and their descendants from
entering the estate on the one day a year it was opened for townsfolk to
visit the ruins of Malcolm Canmore's eleventh-century tower.[1]

As was the fate of so many of the lesser nobility—and a symbol of evolutionary justice for Carnegie—the Hunt family had, by the early twentieth century, fallen into debt, and sought out John Ross, Carnegie's
Dunfermline solicitor, to see if the Scots-American industrialist was interested in buying Pittencrieff. After two years of negotiations, a price was
agreed to and Pittencrieff became the latest jewel in the Carnegie empire.

"This Pittencrieff ownership," Carnegie wrote Henry Campbell-
Bannerman, who had grown up in nearby Glasgow, "is the sweetest event
in my life in the way of material satisfaction. Bailie Morrison my uncle and
all Morrisons were excluded from it by the then owner—He and Uncle
Lauder and my grandfather before them had disputed the Hunts' right to
the Palace ruins and surroundings and finally triumphed in restoring part
to Dunfermline Abbey grounds. Pittencrieff is the world of charm to me
and has been since childhood. No title is precious in all the world as Laird
of Pittencrieff."[2]

Carnegie, who already had a fine estate at Skibo, had no intention of
returning to live at Pittencrieff. "I'm going to make it a public Park and

present to Dunfermline," he informed Morley soon after the purchase. "At least this is my idea, but mum for the present." He toyed with building a house for himself or his family or the Lauder family in the park, but decided against it, after Ross made it clear that such an idea might not be a welcome part of an otherwise magnanimous gift to his home-town.[3]

Dunfermline in 1903 bore little resemblance to the small town Carnegie had been born in. The handloom weavers were gone, long ago displaced by mills and factories. The one constant was the trade with America, which was still the major market for Dunfermline textiles. The population had nearly doubled in a half century to feed the demand for laborers in the power loom factories. As the town grew in population, open spaces like the town green were encroached upon. Dunfermline, in short, had become an industrial town, not as grimy and sooty as Birmingham or Pittsburgh, but not the ideal place in which to raise one's children. Carnegie now sought to change that—and he may have succeeded in doing so. He couldn't cre-ate better jobs or raise the pay of the girls in the factories, but he could bring "sweetness and light" into their lives, or try.

Carnegie's gift to Dunfermline was like no other: to pay the cost of transforming the moldering Pittencrieff estate into a modern people's park—and maintain it and his other Dunfermline benefactions—he do-nated $2.5 million in U.S. Steel bonds to the newly founded Carnegie Dunfermline Trust. (In 1911, he gave the trust an additional $1.25 million.) The money was not to be spent for university fees or a new research insti-tution, or for another library or church organ. It was intended instead, as Carnegie put it in a letter to the trustees, "to bring into the monotonous lives of the toiling masses of Dunfermline more of sweetness and light; to give to them—especially the young—some charm, some happiness, some elevating conditions of life which residence elsewhere would have de-nied. . . . My retirement from business enables me to act in my own life-time, and the fortunate acquisition of Pittencrieff, with its lovely Glen, furnishes the needed foundation upon which you can build, beginning your work by making it a recreation park for the people. . . . Remember you are pioneers, and do not be afraid of making mistakes; those who never make mistakes never make anything. Try many things freely, but discard just as freely."[4]

The trustees did as they were instructed and spent Carnegie's money on 60 acres of beautifully landscaped park close enough to Dunfermline's factories, workshops, and residences to be used on a daily basis. Unlike Central Park, in New York, whose founders had a half century earlier done everything they could to discourage working people from playing games and ruining the pastoral paradise with sweat and noise, the Dunfermline trustees constructed and maintained playing fields for football, hockey, and cricket, and greens for bowling. They built paths for walking, erected swings for the children, added a teahouse, sponsored open-air concerts, and created a Dunfermline Trust band to play for them. Encouraged to range far and wide in their benefactions, the trustees spent part of the endowment to expand and improve the Carnegie baths and gymnasium and the Carnegie library; they paid for medical examinations for the town's schoolchildren and set up separate medical and dental clinics for them; they established Scotland's first College of Hygiene and Physical Education, as well as a craft school and a Women's Institute. Seldom before or since has a town profited so much from the largesse of a native son.[5]

THOUGH CARNEGIE had successfully reinvented himself as a full-time philanthropist, he still took enormous pride in his past accomplishments as businessman, capitalist, and steelmaker. One of the nasty byproducts of the fight with Frick had been his junior partner's allegations that Carnegie had played only a minor role in the making of Carnegie Steel. The summer he became laird of Pittencrieff—these allegations were put before the public once again when Carnegie's former secretary, collaborator, and blackmailer, James Bridge, published *The Inside History of the Carnegie Steel Company: A Romance of Millions.*

In April, Carnegie had been warned by his old friend Tom Miller that Bridge was out to get him. Bridge had called on Miller ostensibly to ask for a photograph and then charmed him into conversing and giving up some documents. "As he was writing up a history, I felt it due to myself to give him such facts as I possessed and now I am sorry I did so, for I am quite sure he is biased, and I fear my statements may be distorted."[6]

Bridge's objective was to write an exposé demonstrating that every success Carnegie had had was due to the genius, perseverance, and diligence of one or another of his partners or associates: his brother Tom, Harry Phipps, and Andrew Kloman in the iron mills; William Coleman, Captain

Jones, and especially Henry Clay Frick in steel. In the course of his research and writing, Bridge had been assisted by Frick, who, Bridge later acknowledged, provided him with the company minutes, "sent me half a dozen fat volumes of newspaper clippings covering the entire period of his connection with the Carnegie interests,"* and arranged for Carnegie Steel lawyer now Attorney General Philander Knox to read the proofs to make sure no illegalities had been incurred by publishing hitherto confidential documents.[7]

In August, *The Inside History of the Carnegie Steel Company* was published in two different American editions: the first, of 50 copies, sold to subscribers for $100; the second, limited to 450 copies, was sold for $25. "Much speculation was indulged in yesterday as to the purpose of the book," the *New York Times* reported on August 9, the day after publication. "By some it is believed that it may be intended as a campaign document to be used by Democrats in the next Presidential campaign, and this belief was strengthened when it became known that the intention is to get out a popular edition at a cheap price."

The same week, Carnegie wrote to Herbert Spencer's private secretary, asking him to inquire of Mr. Spencer "if he remembers writing me a letter putting me on guard against Mr. Bridge, to whom he had given a note of introduction. Mr. Bridge has been trying to levy blackmail upon me for some years and has now vented his spleen upon me for my dropping him completely. . . . He has written a distorted account of the Carnegie Steel Company, which I am told shows great personal spite. What I would like to have is simply a statement that Mr. Spencer recollects having done so, as I do not know where his note is." There was no response from Spencer.[8]

Apparently contemplating action to block publication of an English edition, Carnegie wrote William Stead in September, soliciting his help. Engaging in a bit of character assassination himself, Carnegie claimed that he had dismissed Bridge when he found out that he had married a rich American widow even though he had a wife in England. We have no way of knowing if this was true. We do, however, have evidence that Bridge had tried to blackmail him on several occasions. Carnegie asked Stead to approach Everett & Company, which was planning to bring out a British edition of the Bridge book. "If this house be men of standing would you do

---

*Some of these scrapbooks can now be found at the University of Pittsburgh archives.

me the favor [and] tell them just as much or little of this as you think due to honorable people. I do not wish to become identified with Mr. B. or his book least of all to notice it, that would boom his venomous attack. Be very careful not to get me into public notice in the matter. . . . [Bridge] has tried blackmail upon the wrong kind of a man. He's a bad one sure." As a second P.S., Carnegie added his kicker: "Of course if Everett & Co. publish the book knowing the facts they must be prepared to bear the consequences. It is possible I may have to take action." In the end, the company did not publish the Bridge book, though Limpus, Baker, a London publisher, did.[9]

Carnegie took no action against Bridge or his publishers, other than to ask Harry Phipps to write a letter to the *New York Herald* refuting a few of Bridge's claims. The book, which accused Carnegie of no crime other than being jealous of his more accomplished partners and ruthless in disposing of them, did no real harm. It was not a flattering portrait, but there was certainly nothing libelous in it. It remains today an excellent source and one of the better histories of Carnegie Steel.[10]

FOR ALL HE HAD accomplished, Carnegie remained, at heart, the under-sized outsider with the funny accent who had been uprooted from his home at age thirteen. His reaction to the Bridge book was symptomatic of his need to protect and nurture his standing in the world. In his adopted land, he was the intimate of a president in Washington, an ex-president in Princeton, mayors, congressmen, governors, senators, and cabinet members, as well as Samuel Clemens, America's most famous writer, and Richard Gilder, the editor of the *Century*, its most respected literary journal. In Britain, his circle of acquaintances was, if anything, larger, grander, and more regal still. He had conquered every personal, corporate, political, and ancestral foe, including the Hunts of Pittencrieff. It was not enough. His insecurities about class and status were legion. Now approaching seventy, and if not the richest, then surely one of the richest men in the world, he still sought out and gloried in the approval and recognition of his contemporaries. It was one thing—and quite understandable—for him to worry about his place in history. But what was most remarkable about Carnegie was that he appeared less concerned with the judgment of history or his business peers than with the judgment of those beyond the capitalist classes. Some of his Scottish friends, like Lord Shaw of Dunfermline, mistook his solicitousness toward men above him on the social ladder as a "real weakness towards the aristocrat," but this was not the case. His best friends in England—Gladstone, Spencer, Arnold, and Morley—were not aristocrats (though John Morley would, late in life, become Lord Morley). His first desire, and Shaw got this right, was to be associated "with men of power."[11]

He wanted to be known and honored not simply for what he had accomplished, but for the company he kept. In sections of Clemens's memoirs that were withheld from publication during his and Carnegie's lifetime, he painted a portrait of his friend that was exaggerated and cruel, but captured his egomaniacal side.

"If I were going to describe him in a phrase I think I should call him the Human Being Unconcealed," Clemens wrote in 1907. There was something triumphantly transparent about his friend: "He never has any but one theme, himself. . . . He is himself his one darling subject, the only subject he . . . seems stupendously interested in. I think he would surely talk himself to death upon it if you would stay and listen." Carnegie never bragged and seldom mentioned his achievements as a businessman, steelmaker, or capitalist. Instead, he boasted continually of the company in which he now traveled and of the great men who had paid him compliments. "He talks forever and ever and ever and untiringly of the attentions which have been shown him." Every honor, every appreciation was carefully stored away, none ever forgotten. "He keeps the whole list, keeps it complete; and you must take it all, along with the new additions, if there is time and you survive. It is the deadliest affliction I know of. . . . It is not possible to divert him from his subject; in your weariness and despair you try to do it whenever you think you see a chance, but it always fails; he will use your remark for his occasion and make of it a pretext to get straight back upon his subject again."

It was necessary that everyone he met, old friends and new, knew how important Carnegie was. At Ninety-first Street and at Skibo, he would escort his visitors from room to room, wall to wall, pointing out mementoes, scrolls, presentation books, autographed letters, photographs, "and so on, buzzing over each like a happy hummingbird, for each represented a compliment to Mr. Carnegie." He was shamelessly unaware of the impression he made on others with his constant pursuit of more attention, more praise, more compliments for his good works. He was that rare human animal, possessed of equal portions of modesty and vanity. The problem was that he was modest where he should have been proud and vain where he should have been modest. "He is an astonishing man in his genuine modesty as regards the large things he has done, and in his juvenile delight in trivialities that feed his vanity."

His letters and his conversation were sprinkled, as Clemens knew firsthand, with news that this or that president or great man had "sent for him." "If you let Carnegie tell it, he never seeks the great—the great always seek him." He was incapable, Clemens thought, of reflection or self-knowledge. "Mr. Carnegie is not any better acquainted with himself than if he had met himself for the first time day before yesterday. He thinks he is a rude, bluff, independent spirit, who writes his mind and thinks his mind with an almost extravagant Fourth of July independence, whereas he is really the counterpart of the rest of the human race in that he does not boldly speak his mind except when there isn't any danger in it. He thinks he is a scorner of kings and emperors and dukes, whereas he is like the rest of the human race: a slight attention from one of these can make him drunk for a week and keep his happy tongue wagging for seven years." Fours years before, King Edward had visited Skibo, and "Mr. Carnegie cannot leave the King's visit alone; he has told me about it at least four times, in detail. When he applied that torture the second, third, and fourth times, he certainly knew that it was the second, third, and fourth time, for he has an excellent memory. . . . He has likable qualities and I like him, but I don't believe I can stand the King Edward visit again."

And yet, despite all these qualities, Clemens sought Carnegie out, listened to just about everything he had to say, and when given the opportunity to dine with him, even if the occasion was one of the frightening businessmen's banquets Clemens had come to abhor, grabbed it. Carnegie was, he had to admit, "always a subject of intense interest for me. I like him; I am ashamed of him; and it is a delight to me to be where he is if he has new material on which to work his vanities where they will show him off as with a limelight."[12]

Clemens's portrait, though insightful, was incomplete. Carnegie's conundrum was that while he truly believed he belonged in the company of the world's most powerful men, few of his friends or contemporaries shared this belief. And so he took it upon himself to persuade them that he was indeed the confidant of kings, presidents, and emperors. His enormous success as businessman and capitalist marked him, he was convinced, as a man of destiny—one whose talents were perfectly suited for the era in which he lived. He had demonstrated in the accumulation of millions of dollars that he understood the way the world worked and the directions in which it was moving, two steps forward, one step back, or, as Spencer had described it, citing the French historian and premier François-Pierre Guizot, "progress, and at the same time resistance."[13]

Carnegie had prospered and survived through periods of "progress" and of "resistance" and in so doing had proved himself among the fittest of his generation. His belief that he embodied a new species of modern-day, industrial-era philosopher-king was not pure hubris, but a logical extension of the Spencerian evolutionary philosophy he lived by. Was there anyone living who better understood the workings of the world that industrial capitalism had made? He thought not—and had over $200 million of 5 percent U.S. Steel gold bonds in his safe as evidence. He expected to be called upon for advice and for that advice to be followed.

McKinley's assassination and Roosevelt's ascension had reopened doors in Washington, and Carnegie was ready to march through them into the corridors of power. He was not interested simply in socializing and being seen in their company, as Clemens implied, but in influencing their future actions and setting the world right again after the recent follies in the Philippines and South Africa.

It was, he well knew, fruitless to argue any longer, as he had in years gone by, that America should be satisfied with tending its own garden. As the boundaries of time and space receded, with new advances in transcontinental communications and transportation, Americans had been thrust onto the world stage. Carnegie's self-appointed task was to define the role his nation would play in the developing international drama—not as a competitor in the race for colonies, but as an honest broker, committed to organizing new institutions dedicated to the peaceful settlements of international disputes. The globe was marked by points of tension that might easily escalate into war. Though hostilities had ceased in the Philippines and in South Africa, the British and the French remained at loggerheads in the Sudan; the Austrians and the Russians in the Balkans; the British, the French, and the Germans in Morocco; the Russians and Japanese in the Far East. Had the British been more cognizant of the dangers and more willing to confront them realistically, the threats to world peace might have been diminished. But under Conservative leadership, with Joseph Chamberlain as colonial secretary, the British government was unprepared to compromise or cede its dominant role as the world's leading imperialist power.

It was clear to Carnegie that with the British and Germans at one another's throats and the globe pockmarked by danger zones, only the organization of some sort of international conference, court, or tribunal could prevent war, the inevitable denouement of the race for empire. A "Permanent Court of Arbitration" had been established at The Hague in 1899 to settle disputes between nations, but it remained largely ceremonial and restricted to hearing cases that were voluntarily submitted to it.

As neither the Germans nor the British appeared likely to make any moves toward strengthening the international court, Carnegie hoped to capitalize on his newly renewed entrée to the White House to enlist Theodore Roosevelt to take the initiative. Roosevelt, it was true, had been on the opposite side of Carnegie on every major question of foreign policy since the Venezuela crisis of 1895, but he had flattered the older man by inviting him to the White House, seeking out his opinions, and making a show of reading his articles. It was, ironically, Roosevelt's actions in a second Venezuela crisis, in late 1902–early 1903, that convinced Carnegie that the young president might be the man of destiny he was looking for to assist him in setting the foundations for world peace.

The Germans and the British, in a rather unique display of international cooperation, had joined forces to blockade Venezuela, which, both governments claimed, had refused to pay its debts. The Venezuelan government responded by calling on the United States to arbitrate the dispute. The British appeared to agree to the proposal; the Germans did not. Roosevelt, fearful that Kaiser Wilhelm had declined arbitration because he had designs on Venezuelan territory, threatened the German ambassador with military action to protect Venezuela should the kaiser not stand down. The kaiser agreed to arbitration, and Roosevelt, wisely, instead of arbitrating the matter himself, announced on December 26, 1902, that the issue would be submitted to The Hague tribunal.

"The world took a long step upward yesterday," Carnegie wrote the president on December 27, "and Theodore Roosevelt bounded into the short list of those who will forever be hailed as supreme benefactors of man." Later that week, in a "New Year Greeting" published in the *New York Tribune*, Carnegie repeated the tribute in public. Theodore Roosevelt, in "breathing life into The Hague tribunal, the permanent high court of humanity, for the peaceful settlement of international disputes," had taken action toward the "coming banishment of the earth's most revolting spectacle—human war—*the killing of man by man*. . . . The complete banishment of war draws near. Its death wound dates from the day that President Roosevelt led . . . opposing powers . . . to the Court of Peace, and thus proclaimed it the appointed substitute for that which had hitherto stained the earth—the killing of men by each other."[14]

In his New Year's greetings to his friend John Hay, whom Roosevelt had asked to stay on as secretary of state, Carnegie was exultant. The United States, he declared, was under Roosevelt and Hay's leadership, firmly set on a new path in international relations, as a peacemaker among nations. "I am so happy (& proud excuse me) that I have known you John Hay. You make the Republic what its Founders intended—Something different—Something higher than the governments which preceded its birth."[15]

Teddy Roosevelt's sudden and rather shocking rebirth as a man of peace had proved a godsend for Carnegie. Carnegie had always preferred the company and friendship of practical men of action to dreamers; he moved closer to Roosevelt and Hay because he placed them in the former category. In February 1903, in response to a request for funds for the Anti-Imperialist League, Carnegie wrote a $2,000 check but insisted in a note to Charles Francis Adams that he did not want the money to go toward the work of the committee investigating American atrocities in the Philippines. "I do not believe in that. It is good in its way but I am satisfied it will be an impediment to our obtaining the greater end we have in view. We have only to dub ourselves as blackeners of the American troops to render ourselves impotent for all good to the people of the Philippines. . . . P.S.— I expect men to be beasts when they go out to kill other men. War is hell, as General Grant said."[16]

The year before, in a mood of bitter despondency, he had refused to give money to establish a permanent headquarters for the international court of arbitration that had been established at The Hague. Now, in April 1903, his spirits lifting after the agreement to submit the Venezuela dispute to arbitration, he wrote Baron Gevers, a representative of the Dutch government, committing $1.5 million for the "erection of a Court House and Library (A Temple of Peace)."[17]

Carnegie found himself agreeing with the new president on a number of issues, including the best route for an isthmian canal. There had been talk for decades of the need for a canal across Central American that would provide access for the U.S. Navy and commercial vessels to move from east to west and vice versa without having to circle South America. The routes contemplated were through Nicaragua, and through Panama, which was, at the time, part of Colombia. Roosevelt favored the Panama route, as did Carnegie, who made his opinion known in a series of open letters to Senator Thomas Platt of New York.[18]

In January 1903, Secretary of State Hay negotiated a treaty with the Colombian ambassador, which granted the United States the rights to lease a six-mile-wide "zone" in Panama for ninety-nine years for a payment of $10 million and an annual rent of $250,000. The U.S. Senate approved the treaty in March; the Colombian Senate delayed until August and then unanimously rejected the treaty, demanding more money and more sovereignty over the leased land. Roosevelt was left with two options: renegotiate the treaty with the Colombians or build the canal in Nicaragua. He manufactured a third and let it be known that he would provide naval protection for Panamanian rebels should they declare independence from Colombia.

On November 2, the *Nashville*, an American battleship, arrived at Colón, Panama; on November 3, the nationalist junta secured control of the isthmus and declared independence; on November 6, the Americans recognized the new government of Panama and urged Colombia to do the same. The Colombians, who could not send troops overland through the jungle and were blocked by the U.S. warships from landing them by sea, had no way to reclaim Panama. "A new nation the size of South Carolina was born. . . . The only deaths were a Chinese citizen who had gotten trapped in some desultory shelling, a dog, and according to some reports, a donkey."[19]

The anti-imperialists mercilessly attacked Roosevelt and Hay for their blatant disregard of international law in blockading Panama so that the Colombians could not send troops to put down an illegal secessionist movement. Carnegie held his fire, though he too was dismayed and not a little disgusted. His greatest fear was that the president's action would give the Democrats a weapon with which to dislodge him from the White House the following November. "We are all just a little frightened about our irrepressible President," Carnegie wrote Morley on January 11, 1904. "He's so rapid—Lunched with him recently—His re-election endangered—people afraid to trust him—Panama badly done ... Democrats have a good chance as matters stand at present." On January 18, in his regular Sunday letter to John Morley, he expanded on his fears. Roosevelt's "management of Panama and other impetuosities endanger his election provided Democrats nominate Cleveland—He would probably win, any other not so probably. Still any one of the three others [being discussed as candidates] would make close contest. . . . This Panama folly has hurt many people and alarmed them—so needless—game flying to our hands—patience only required. Now we are in false position with our Southern Republics naturally jealous, or afraid of us—all for nothing. Many friendly to President asking if he does such wild impetuous things now what won't he do if in for four years."[20]

Roosevelt's adventurism in Panama notwithstanding, Carnegie supported him because he believed he was committed to international arbitration and would, with prodding from his friends, agree to negotiate a bilateral treaty with Britain, pledging each nation to arbitrate future disputes. "We shall get an Arbitration Treaty this time," Carnegie wrote Morley on January 11. "President, Secretary of State, Senators, etc. feeling strong for Britain." There was a new buoyancy to Carnegie's political activism, brought to the surface by his sense that he was now working with the White House. Carnegie regarded Roosevelt much as he had Frick and Schwab: as a brilliant young man with the best of intentions who needed his guidance and advice to realize his potential. Roosevelt had convinced him that on essential questions of domestic and foreign policy, they were in full agreement. The president continued to respond promptly to Carnegie's letters, to invite him regularly to the White House, and had arranged for him to meet his friend, conservationist Gifford Pinchot, and his new secretary of war, William Howard Taft, with whom he hoped Carnegie would "have a chance to discuss Philippine matters."[21]

Carnegie was spending more time than ever in Washington, as a peace activist rather than a businessman. In January 1904, he addressed a mass meeting called by the National Arbitration Conference to draw attention to efforts under way to pass an Anglo-American arbitration treaty. "Mr. Carnegie," the *New York Times* reported on January 13, "was introduced as 'the great apostle of arbitration and peace.' He recalled that it was eighteen years ago when he first appeared in Washington to urge arbitration. He said he appeared again to-day to labor in the same cause which had risen phoenix-like, and could not fail. 'We have abolished the duel,' said he. 'Let it be our race that takes the first step to abolish international dueling.'" The following day, Carnegie accompanied a committee of notables from the conference to present President Roosevelt with "resolutions . . . recommending the negotiation of a treaty with Great Britain." The president, the *New York Times* reported on January 14, welcomed the committee and stated "that he was heartily in accord" with its recommendations.

In March, Carnegie signed a petition to the nominating conventions of both political parties "asking them to pledge their constituents to secure to the people of the Philippines independence upon terms similar to those under which Cuban independence was established." The petition drive had been organized by Charles Francis Adams, who had assembled a distinguished list of peace activists, writers, clergymen, and college presidents to sign it.[22]

Taft, the former governor of the Philippines, answered the petition on behalf of the president and the Republican Party. At a dinner of the Ohio Society (to which Carnegie had been invited but was unable to attend), Taft argued that the U.S. government would grant independence as soon as the Filipinos were ready for it—and not a moment before.

Carnegie was disturbed by the tenor and content of Taft's remarks and wrote the president to say so. "Up to the time of the Ohio Dinner, I had reason to believe that Judge Taft could not possibly make a mistake, but he talked two hours after Dinner, so I know he is human and vulnerable. My dear Mr. President, he is like an ostrich, only his head is hid, his whole body exposed." Why, Carnegie wanted to know, was Taft dissembling and disguising Roosevelt's policy, which, he assumed, was to grant independence to the Philippines? He urged Roosevelt to set the matter right by declaring his intentions. "Judge Taft is peculiarly anxious for the Filipinos. Now I confess I am more anxious for the good of the Americans in what I urge. I see grave complications probable in the unfair attempt, as I think it, of enforcing the Monroe Doctrine on our own continent, and yet claiming the right to interfere in other continents. 'America for Americas' implies Europe for Europeans, Asia for Asiatics, etc."

Carnegie thanked Roosevelt for suggesting that he meet with Taft "to talk over Philippines," but regretted that he would have to postpone, as he was about to sail for Europe. He looked forward to Roosevelt's "nomination by acclamation in June," and assured him that he intended to "be here in the Autumn to cast my humble vote for you, offering up in silence and anxious prayers that 'the lesson of the day' will continue to exert its sacred influence over you." He closed with a bit of name-dropping by attaching to his typewritten letter a handwritten postscript, marked "Private," in which he gossiped about British politics—wrongly predicting the fall of the Conservative government and the offer of a high cabinet position to his friend Morley. He also informed the president that he had been invited to "visit German Emperor—Queen Holland—King Belgians," but that he considered all these proposed meetings "poor affairs compared with President in Washington."[23]

THE CARNEGIE FAMILY sailed for Britain on March 20 on the *St. Paul.* For Carnegie, the spring ocean passage to Europe remained one of life's treasures. His beloved Baba, now seven, felt much the same way. On board ship, she had her father to herself in a way that was not possible on land. "Our voyages across the Atlantic," Margaret recalled in her journal, "were full of memories. Many of the family and friends came to the ship to see us off. It was all very hectic until the whistle blew half an hour before sailing and the stewards went along beating on gongs and calling 'all visitors on shore.' Masses of flowers and fruit kept arriving at our staterooms after the ship sailed. It was all very exciting to me and fun to watch." The first thing father and daughter did was to see that the supply of tripe that Koelsh, their butcher, had sent along for the ocean trip was safely stored in the ship's refrigerator. "During the voyage Daddy feasted on this and always included me in the feast." Though she still spent more time with Nana than with her parents, she enjoyed special moments with her father on board ship that were possible nowhere else. They visited the engine room and watched the "huge pistons" and the stokers who kept the engines going. "Daddy always made friends with the chief engineer, who took us around. . . . We stood on the Bridge and watched the sailor who was steering the ship. I was allowed to put my hand on his, and 'feel' how he did it."

The westward voyages in the fall were often quite rough, but Baba appeared to be as fine a sailor as her father: "Daddy took me up to see the waves. . . . We would stand as far forward on the deck as we could get and watch the plunging bow, spray washing our face at times. When the ship steadied down for a bit, Daddy recited Shakespeare [*Henry IV*]. . . . It was wonderful to hear those words spoken so beautifully by Daddy while standing with him on a pitching ship. We always waited for one more big wave. . . . Then Daddy would raise his arm and shout, 'What care these roarers for the name of King.'" Most passages ended with a formal-dress concert "for the Benefit of the Seaman's Charities. My Father was always asked to be Chairman." Baba was immensely proud of her father at these moments: "The audience responded to the remarks he made, warm and friendly, but full of fun and humor, with long and loud clapping."[24]

Carnegie was remarkably fit for someone approaching seventy, though he was more likely now to be sidelined with some minor ailment, each of which, it appeared, was fully reported in the press. Louise had hoped—and expected—that his retirement would mean more time with the family, less running around, and fewer strains on his health. But that was not to be. To Louise's dismay, he pushed himself even harder than before. His campaign for international arbitration entailed regular trips to Washington. He had accepted election to the executive committee of the National Civic Federation, to the rectorship of St. Andrews, and to the presidency of the St. Andrews Society in New York and the Iron and Steel Institute in London. Each position brought with it specific responsibilities, dinners, receptions, speeches. "I am to be busy while in London, three of the old Guilds honor me," he wrote Morley in February 1904, his schedule for the coming spring already beginning to take shape. "Can't decline."[25]

That spring was spent in London, with Carnegie racing from one honorary event and speech to the next. As the weather got warmer, the family moved north to Skibo to enjoy a month alone before the visitors descended. "We are all so happy up here," Andrew wrote Dod in late May. "I'm free of 'Lionizing' which is harder than you can know . . . but having got into harness one has to live up to it. Bertram says one day last week he refused five invitations to perform 'functions.' Just now I'm a drawing card, & like the Trombonist when a fly lighted on his music 'He blayed im'— but I'm cautious now and don't comply. Two electric motors here. George & his men learning fast—They will I think relieve many horses for station work. Trout plenty, salmon not running now—our new organ fine—I say my prayers with more unction—(a good word)."[26]

When, a month later, James Donaldson of St. Andrews asked if he would stand for reelection as rector, he agreed. "Anent Re-election, this is new, had not dreamt of it—I cannot deny I am pleased with my position and think often of it—and do really just love the Dear old Lady University of Saint Andrews, but Madam says she wishes me to give up some things that involve attention. I point out that Rectorship doesn't. . . . She thinks it does, but an address every three years isn't much. We have adjourned the subject."[27]

Louise insisted that Andrew slow down and spend more time with her and Baba. Running what had become a virtual resort hotel at Skibo was becoming too much for her. In years past, Carnegie had given her a month off in London before and after the summer season at Skibo, but that was not enough. He decided to rearrange the Skibo schedule so that the family could spend three weeks by themselves in total retreat—at Auchinduich, a stone lodge on a hilltop about twenty-five miles from Skibo. Even his dearest friend John Morley was asked to reschedule his visit so as not to conflict with Louise's vacation. "Touching July 23—'The Family' go into retreat July 22—to August 10th away up the high moors 'Auchinduich'—Cottage on the Shin [River]. Madam thinks higher air for two weeks best for Baba. She also gets a rest preparatory to shooting season. It is an experiment we are to try—I think a wise one. She wished to postpone it until next year when you wrote you could come but I insisted you could and would come later, or sooner."[28]

Carnegie, who had been invited to write a life of James Watt for a "Famous Scots" book series, seized upon the enforced retreat to get started. As he wrote Morley from the lodge, the "Hilltop Experiment" had proved "a decided success. Lou and Baba and I get a chance to live with each other. We are enjoying our holiday in this delightful cozy lodge. Everything very nice." He was particularly delighted with his new writing project. "It is fascinating. I tell you I have a great mind—a genius to portray. I am in love with my hero and enjoy leisurely penning a few paragraphs of the book." His full-length biography, well researched and written with his usual fluency, was published the following May to good reviews. The book was an old-fashioned hagiography, with a quite lucid description of the science that had gone into the invention of the steam engine. Much of it was composed of long passages imported wholesale from other writers, but such was the style of the day. Richard Gilder asked if he might have permission to serialize the biography in the *Century*.[29]

The stone lodge at Auchinduich, though off the beaten path, was close enough to Skibo for Carnegie to get mail and newspapers. With Roosevelt up for election to a full term in the fall, he kept a careful eye on American politics from his perch on the Shin River. On July 28, he wrote Morley of his fears that Roosevelt might be defeated. "Poor fellow—his path isn't so easy as it promised to be—He failed to keep in touch with our Leaders in the Senate . . . I warned him and one or two of his set that all was not well—Then his extreme militancy, Big Navy, etc. etc.—chill many. Cleveland would have beaten him and [Alton] Parker [the Democratic nominee] may. Odds slightly against this however, I think."[30]

In October, the Carnegies sailed back to New York, accompanied by Morley, whom Roosevelt, after reading his biography of Gladstone, had invited to the White House. Carnegie, who had for years begged his friend to visit America, seized on the opportunity to plan a triumphant national tour, culminating in a visit to Pittsburgh to speak at Founders' Day, the annual tribute to Carnegie put on by the Carnegie Institute. Morley suggested a few possible lecture topics. Carnegie thought "'The Man behind the Book' . . . generally the more interesting," though he warned Morley not to expect too much, or, for that matter, too little of his Pittsburgh audience. "You will have a reading audience not in the main—but an element quite strong. . . . Pittsburgh is the seat of materialism (Birmingham) but it has in the Scotch element a race that reads and is supposed to think after a fashion. The German is also to the fore. Scotch Irish prominent also."[31]

CARNEGIE had, three years into his retirement, succeeded in shifting shape: from ruthless steelmaker to peacemaker and advocate of international arbitration. On Sunday, November 6, two days before Roosevelt was elected to a full four-year term, Carnegie sat down for an artfully illustrated interview with William Griffith of the *New York Times*. The article was headlined "ANDREW CARNEGIE, APOSTLE OF PEACE." Grabbing with both hands the pulpit offered him, Carnegie championed "The Hague

Peace Tribunal as the greatest and most enduring monument of modern civilization. Never has the eminent philanthropist and patron of the Peace Congress," the reporter gushed, "expressed himself more clearly and comprehensively concerning a supreme ambition of his life—to see the dream of international arbitration come true—than in thus throwing the light of his searching and vigorous intellect upon many vital and far-reaching questions of the hour. Since returning from abroad a month ago other interests with him have been subordinated to studying the Peace Congress idea in its many opposing phases. It was from a mind thoroughly saturated with the subject that the great ironmaster and donor of libraries delivered his remarkable prophecy as to the future amalgamation of the power of Europe."

The *Times* interview marked a turning point in the public presentation of Andrew Carnegie. He was now the "apostle of peace." There was no mention of tariffs, Homestead, or strikes. Instead, Carnegie, with the authority of a seasoned statesmen, discoursed on the Russo-Japanese War, the amalgamation of Europe "into one centralized government," and the future of Canadian-American relations. When asked about the "Philippine problem," he prefaced his remarks by reminding the reporter that he had "just returned from Europe and [had] a pretty clear knowledge of European opinion." To bolster this assertion, he had his secretary fetch some "letters and articles," evidence that his views were sought on both sides of the Atlantic. The illustrations that accompanied the article carried forward the theme. One showed Carnegie with head bent and hands touching, as if in prayer. He looked older, wiser, determined, almost stoic. The article ended with Carnegie's taking his leave of the reporter "to spend a brief half hour hearing his favorite tunes [played by his organist]. . . . Perhaps he has taken a chair in front of the fireplace. . . . Perhaps a mist has gathered between the shrewd gray eyes of the great philanthropist and the fire into which they are so intently gazing. Of peace—if not of peace congresses—the bowed figure is perhaps thinking—thinking and dreaming."[32]

As fawning as the portrait was, it was not untrue. Though Carnegie would continue to attract more publicity for his library donations, he was personally invested in the crusade for world peace in a way he had never been in his libraries. For every other philanthropic endeavor he was involved in, he delegated authority to handpicked lieutenants. The peace campaign alone required his personal attention—or so he believed. Money was not going to buy peace in the same way that it might purchase organs or libraries or college fellowships or "sweetness and light" for the working people of Dunfermline. Only the world's leaders could bring peace to the world—and only Andrew Carnegie had access to all of them.

THIRTY-FIVE

"Inveterate Optimist," 1905–1906

A S HE ENTERED his seventieth year, Andrew Carnegie had become something of a national monument. With his distinctive accent, his deep voice, and his seeming joy in letting his opinions fly, he had long before become a favorite of reporters. His words were now frequently illustrated with his likeness. The image of the small, troll-like body, with the full white St. Nicholas beard, and dark, alternately brooding and sparkling eyes, appeared with greater and greater frequency after the turn of the century. He took as much joy in being photographed and having his likeness portrayed as he did in being quoted. Lining the walls of his New York study were dozens of portraits, few of them terribly flattering. During an interview with the *New York Times Sunday Magazine,* published on November 6, 1904, he turned to the man sketching him and "citing a ludicrous caricature on the wall . . . laughingly warned the artist not to omit any lines from his face, lest he pass unrecognized among his friends."

There was little danger of this. His had already become one of the most recognizable visages in the country.

What captivated the press—and the public—was his willingness to speak his mind on so many different issues. He was seldom without a quip or a word of wisdom for the reporters who followed him. In an interview in the *New York Times* published on April 27, 1905, Carnegie, before sailing for Britain, "defied the reporters to ask him a question which he couldn't answer. He seemed to take great delight in the volley of questions fired at him, and when the newspaper men ran out of ammunition Mr. Carnegie supplied them with new subjects." Asked what he thought about his niece Nancy marrying a riding master, he responded that he was delighted that she had not married some worthless duke. That comment, of course, called for a rebuttal,

WHEN MR. CARNEGIE'S
MONEY IS GONE.

quickly forthcoming from the Duke of Manchester, who defended the nobil
ity, thereby giving Carnegie yet another opportunity to make his point.

Articles about him appeared with great regularity. When he came
down with food poisoning in Switzerland, indigestion in Atlanta, and
lumbago in New York, the incidents were fully reported on, with follow-
up stories as his condition improved. Every time he gave a speech, it was
excerpted or summarized in the next day's papers. His views were entirely
unpredictable. In the fall of 1905, he told reporters that he considered
William Randolph Hearst, an independent candidate for mayor for New
York, "extraordinary" and "sincere," and endorsed his call for municipal
ownership of public utilities. The following year, when Hearst ran for governor, this time as a Democrat, Carnegie attacked him fiercely, maintaining that the contest between Charles Evans Hughes, the Republican
candidate, and Hearst was not a simple party contest, but "a contest of the
best people against the worst people." He was willing to support Hearst
when he took on Tammany Hall, but not when he ran against Repub-

licans. Carnegie's attack so rankled Hearst and Clarence Shearn, his campaign manager, that the latter felt obligated to go after "this unlettered laird of Skibo, Scotland," with remarkable venom the next morning, declaring that Carnegie was guilty of all sorts of foul deeds from "stock watering" to manufacturing defective armor to "corrupting Pennsylvania officials" to "defying the laws of the United States by taking millions in secret rebates."[1]

Carnegie's appearances at public meetings were guaranteed to draw attention. In December 1903, he attended the annual meeting of the Educational Alliance, held at Jefferson Street and East Broadway and was accompanied into the hall by a phalanx of reporters. "By what he said formally and informally, Andrew Carnegie added interest," the *New York Times* reported on December 14. "During the reading of the eleventh annual report by the President, Isidor Straus, Mr. Carnegie looked wonderfully like a man who was dozing, but in his speech afterward he showed that he had lost no point in the document." He came out vigorously in opposition to attempts to regulate or restrict immigration, then praised the immigrants' capacity for assimilation. "Ladies and gentlemen, language makes race. Show me the man who speaks English, reads Shakespeare and Bobby Burns, and I'll show you a man who has absorbed the American principles. . . . Let, say, a Russian come here, and he will soon learn that any man's privilege is every man's right. You needn't be afraid that he won't become an American." He continued to perform for the reporters long after the speeches had ended. "Out in the hallway, after the meeting, while a solicitous friend was tying a muffler about his neck, Mr. Carnegie held a little reception . . . 'I think the Scotch a pretty smart people, but I must say I think the Jews are smarter. I think I'm a little afraid of them.' 'You needn't fear, Mr. Carnegie,' replied Mr. Straus promptly and good-naturedly, 'The Jews are not likely to invade Scotland—that is the only country in which they cannot live.'"

By the turn of the twentieth century, the Andrew Carnegie story, told and retold in his own articles, books, and speeches, and paraphrased in dozens of interviews and profiles, had become so well known that an enterprising Cleveland woman, Mrs. Cassie Chadwick, used it to manufacture a sidebar all her own.

In 1902, the year after Carnegie retired with his $226 million in U.S. Steel gold bonds, Chadwick confided to some rather prominent Cleveland lawyers and bankers that she was the illegitimate daughter of Andrew

Carnegie, who, being a forthright, responsible man, wished to establish a $10 million trust to care for her after his death. With these rumors, reinforced by a forged trust agreement and several forged "notes," Mrs. Chadwick borrowed hundreds of thousands of dollars from men who were only too happy to lend Andrew Carnegie's daughter whatever she asked for.

By the fall of 1904, as her debts approached the million-dollar mark, creditors began to call in her loans. Unable to pay back anything, she tried to declare bankruptcy and escape unharmed; but as it became clear that she had defrauded almost every bank in Cleveland, local authorities indicted her for forging Carnegie's name to a series of documents. The newspapers seized on the story with gusto, not because they put any credence in Chadwick's claims, but because she had been so brazen in her larcenies. Day after day, Carnegie's name appeared in news headlines in Cleveland and across the country. Would he or would he not be subpoenaed to verify that the signatures were not his own and that he was not related to Mrs. Cassie Chadwick? Would he comply?

Carnegie, of course, would have preferred to have been left alone in New York. When the first subpoena arrived in December, he claimed that he was too ill to travel to Cleveland and delivered a note from his medical adviser, Dr. Garmany, who confirmed that his patient was suffering "from acute lumbago." By March 1905, he could hold out no longer and made the trip to Cleveland—by private railway car. He arrived in time for jury selection, spent a day in the courtroom, and then left without giving testimony or making any statements to the press. Though the defense attorney tried to make much of Carnegie's disappearance, it did Cassie Chadwick little good. She was sentenced to jail, where she died in late 1907.

Though news of the Cassie Chadwick scandal was splashed across the front pages from November 1903 through the spring of 1904, the story has not been covered in any of his biographies. It is significant, nonetheless, not because there is a scintilla of evidence that Cassie was Carnegie's illegitimate daughter—she most certainly was not—but because the construction of the story and the notice it was given in the daily press tell us a great deal about Carnegie's place in American culture and society at the turn of the century. Cassie Chadwick was no fool. She had chosen Carnegie, not John D. Rockefeller or James J. Hill or Henry Clay Frick, because Carnegie almost alone among the robber barons of his generation was not known as an ascetic. He was instead a man who took his pleasures seriously. He was also extraordinarily generous. Had he fathered a daughter out of wedlock in his twenties, he would have supported her lavishly for the rest of her life, as every one of Cassie's dupes believed.[2]

FROM THE mid-1900s on, Andrew Carnegie began to gather more headlines, though of a quite different nature, by adding his name and dollars to the cause of simplified spelling. He had been persuaded to enter the campaign by two rather distinguished New Yorkers, Melvil Dewey, the inventor of the Dewey decimal system, and Brander Matthews, a Columbia professor and drama critic. Carnegie seized on the idea of simplified spelling as not only a logical evolutionary improvement of the language but as a vehicle for world peace. Simplified spelling would bring English-speaking people closer together by eliminating the inconsistencies between English and American-English spelling and promoting English as a truly global language. (It would also have made life simpler for Carnegie, who was a notoriously poor speller.)

The Simplified Spelling Board, supported in large part by Carnegie funds, recommended that the first steps toward reforming the language include substituting "f" for "ph"; dropping the "u" the English used to spell "honour" and "labour"; and eliminating silent "e's" everywhere. The movement, though endorsed by President Roosevelt, who urged his administration to use simplified spelling in official documents, went nowhere. One by one the distinguished gentlemen who had signed on returned to the old ways. Only Carnegie refused to capitulate. Since his days at the telegraph office, he had employed a form of "telegraphese" in his letterwriting, with incomplete sentences connected by lots of dashes. From about 1906 onward, he insisted on using spellings like "enuf," "delite," "hart," "hav," "offerd" in his personal letters and public communications. The effect was maddening. Even Sam Clemens tried to wean his friend from his new obsession. At a dinner given for Carnegie at the New York Engineers' Club in December 1907, Clemens admitted that while Carnegie's face was "fairly scintillating with fictitious innocence," as if he had "never committed a crime in his life," he was in truth more dangerous than Torquemada. "That old fellow shed some blood in the Inquisition, but Mr. Carnegie has brought destruction to the entire race. I know he didn't mean it to be a crime, but it was just the same. He's got us all so we can't spell anything."[3]

After dutifully forwarding $25,000 a year to the Spelling Board and winning a few victories, "catalog" and "thru," among them, Carnegie abandoned the campaign in 1915. "A more useless body of men never came into association, judging from the effects they produce," he wrote of the Simplified Spelling Board directors. "I think I have been patient long enuf. I have much better use for twenty-five thousand dollars a year."[4]

WHILE THE newspaper-reading public may have been titillated by the Cassie Chadwick scandal and amused by Carnegie's forays into simplified spelling, it could not help but admire the way the "Star-spangled Scotchman" was setting an example for his fellow millionaires. As the *New York Times* reported in a *Sunday Magazine* cover story on June 12, 1904, Carnegie was a major figure in the transformation of "private charity" into "organized business." According to figures supplied by the Charity Organization Society, $80 million had been "expended in philanthropical and charitable donations" over the past twelve months, $40 million of it by individuals residing in New York City. "Giving away money on a large scale," the *Times* reported, "has become a regularly organized business." Leading the way was Andrew Carnegie, who not only disbursed far more funds than any other individual ($95.9 million to Rockefeller's $32.9), but had evolved the most highly developed and "methodical system" for doing so. "Perhaps the general public has the illusion that Andrew Carnegie shelved his business cares and responsibilities when he retired from active commercial life. A glance at his daily life in his Fifth Avenue mansion will dispel this illusion."

Carnegie's most recent endowment had been $5 million for a "hero fund." The impetus for the new trust had been the January 1904 mining accident in Harwick, a town about fifteen miles northeast of Pittsburgh, in which 179 miners, the majority of them boys in their teens, had been killed. In the aftermath of the disaster, there were two more deaths: of "heroes" who descended into the mine to rescue survivors.

Carnegie's first impulse had been to establish a private pension fund to support the families of the deceased. But as he thought more about the disaster—and read Richard Gilder's poem about the "heroes of the land"— he decided instead to establish a new trust to provide for these and other fallen heroes. In March 1904, before sailing for Britain, he signed the deed of trust conveying $5 million in U.S. Steel gold bonds to the Carnegie Hero Fund Commission, which was to be overseen by twenty-one hand-picked commissioners. Included among the men he chose as commissioners were his old Allegheny City friends Bobby Pitcairn and Tom Miller; Thomas Morrison, his distant cousin who had earlier managed the Duquesne and Edgar Thomson plants; Thomas Lynch, who, as president of Frick Coke, had once been his sworn enemy; and William Abbott, whom he had blamed for the 1889 Homestead settlement, but subsequently reconciled with.

The Hero Fund, like Carnegie's other philanthropies, was run as a business operation. Responsibility for oversight was delegated to commissioners who were charged with seeking out "heroes" who deserved honor—and support—for their deeds. The grants were intended for private citizens or those who worked in the "peaceful vocations." No grant was "to be continued unless it is soberly and properly used, and the recipients remain respectable, well-behaved members of the community." Medals would accompany all rewards.

Carnegie was prouder of his Hero Fund than he was of any of his other programs, because it was the only one he had created from whole cloth, without any help from friends or advisers. In a letter to the English writer Frederick Harrison in June, he referred to the "Hero Fund [as] my pet child—Here's worship of Humanity in its highest form—Heroism." "No one suggested it to me," he explained in his *Autobiography*. "As far as I know, it never had been thought of; hence it is emphatically 'my ain bairn.'"[5]

The Hero Fund, Frederick Lynch, one of the original commissioners, insisted, could only have been conceived by Andrew Carnegie. "It grew out of his intense conviction that it took just as much heroism to save life as it did to take it, whereas the man who took it got most of the recognition. How often I have heard him say: 'The more men you can kill the greater hero you are'; and again, 'Most of the monuments in the world are to somebody who has killed a lot of his fellowmen.'"[6]

There was, as Carnegie knew, something both innovative and untimely in his attempt to draw attention from the martial virtues by honoring civilian heroes. As a disciple of Herbert Spencer, Carnegie not only hoped but believed that the age of barbarism, savagery, bloodlust, and war was coming to an end, and would be succeeded by an era of peace in which non-martial values and definitions of true manliness would prevail. "The heroes of barbarism past wounded or killed their fellows; the heroes of our civilized day serve or save theirs. Such the difference between physical and moral courage, between barbarism and civilization."[7]

The first twelve heroes honored included a seventeen-year-old boy from Wilkinsburg, Pennsylvania, who had risked his life rescuing two drowning friends, and a miner from Sherrodsville, Ohio, who had died attempting to save a comrade from suffocation. Recipients of awards—or their heirs—received medals, with the inscription from the New Testament: "Greater Love Hath No Man Than This, That a Man Lay Down His Life for His Friends." In its first one hundred years of operation, the Carnegie Hero Fund Commission, based in Pittsburgh, dispersed $27 million to honor and support over nine thousand Carnegie heroes in the United States and Canada with cash awards, college fellowships, pensions, and medals. Hero Fund commissions remain in operation today in the United Kingdom, the United States, and nine European nations.[8]

CARNEGIE was delighted with Roosevelt's election in 1908. As an un-elected president, Roosevelt had been constrained to follow the mandates of the man whom the people had elected in 1900. Now, after March 1905, he could jettison the legacy of imperialism handed him by McKinley and become the statesman for peace he was meant to be. Carnegie was still not entirely comfortable with Roosevelt—and would never be. The president was too much of a militarist, too committed to building battleships, and too much of an imperialist. "He needs to be watched," Carnegie told a *New York Times* reporter in a front-page interview on October 24, 1904, "but really he is a man of peace."

Unbeknownst to Roosevelt, Carnegie had appointed himself presidential adviser on arbitration treaties. Early in 1905, after Roosevelt's election but before his inauguration, the Senate amended the arbitration agreements with Great Britain, France, Germany, Switzerland, Norway, and Sweden that Secretary of State Hay had negotiated by adding a clause requiring explicit Senate approval before any matter could be submitted to international arbitration. Roosevelt, convinced that the Senate amendments rendered the agreements meaningless, threatened to withdraw them. Carnegie urged him not to do so. "May I venture Mr. President to pray you consider well before withdrawing these treaties. . . . We shall have the substance & this is what you are after—fit additions to your great service rendered peace by sending [the disputing sides in the Venezuela conflict] to The Hague."[9]

Roosevelt, barely containing his anger at Carnegie's presumption in offering him advice on diplomacy and how to deal with the Senate, responded bluntly in two separate letters. "I do not agree with you about the treaties. I am not willing to go into a farce" and approve treaties so weakened by amendments that they were virtually meaningless. In the second letter, marked "Personal," Roosevelt "supplemented" his note to Carnegie by stating that Secretary of State Hay agreed that the treaties should be vetoed. Carnegie let the matter drop.[10]

The president was in no mood to enter into debate with Carnegie on toothless treaties while events in the Far East required his attention. On February 8, 1904, the Japanese fleet had launched a surprise attack and siege on the Russian naval squadron at Port Arthur, Mauchuria. Now, in the second year of the war, Roosevelt was trying to broker an agreement between Russia and Japan. In June 1905, he succeeded, when both nations accepted his invitation to negotiate peace terms in Portsmouth, New Hampshire. On August 30, the newspapers, with banner headlines, announced that agreement had been reached on the terms for a final treaty. The following day, the *New York Times* published on page two a small item headlined "KAISER WILHELM OVERJOYED. Congratulates President, Who Thanks Him for His Co-Operation." Directly underneath, given equal prominence, was a second article: "CARNEGIE AND GUESTS HAPPY. Party at Skibo Castle Send Thankful Congratulations."

Though Carnegie had had nothing to do with the negotiations, not even pretending to offer advice on them, in sending his congratulatory telegram and releasing it to the press, he was signaling to the president that, absent though he might be at Skibo, he was ever present in the campaign for international arbitration. The signatories on his telegram included the Archbishop of Canterbury, Columbia University president Nicholas Murray Butler, Secretary of Agriculture James Wilson, and John Morley, who had left Skibo the day before the telegram was drafted and sent. Carnegie, knowing how much Roosevelt admired Morley, had tacked on his name, expecting that it would add luster to his own.

Morley was not amused. "Between such friends as you and me frankness is best, and I have something to complain of," he telegrammed Carnegie on September 5. "Surely it is rather a strong order to put my name to a message to the President without my leave, and not even to think it worthwhile to tell me that you had done so? Don't you think it is? At any rate, I do. In a very small way I am a sort of public man, and a public man cannot safely allow even his best friend to use his name at large, can he? I daresay I should agree with what you said; still I prefer to put things in my own way. . . . I feel bound to make my humble protest, and then pass on."[11]

Carnegie wrote back the same day offering a rather offhanded apology in the form of a blow-by-blow account of how Morley's name had come to be appended to the telegram. "We celebrate Peace (Madam keeps all flags) and table finely decorated. Walls also. . . . Proposal [is made to] cable Congratulatory Message to President—Carried   Much applause. A voice [adds] we ought to have Mr. Morley's name with some others to cable. . . . I said if he were here he would be among first to sign—He is not entirely outside our party his shade still hovers about us. I'll take responsibility add his name. . . . Had you not been of the party no one would have suggested your name of course, but it did seem you still had some share with us. You expected to be present—called away. While I must expect a stern verdict, let it be please, not guilty but don't do it again. I promise. I was and am still so certain that you would have been glad of the opportunity to sign, that I cannot regret having got you in—I think it was Butler who suggested it but am not quite sure. It was an enthusiastic moment."[12]

If ever the future looked bright for peace, it was now. The British and the French had, the year before, signed the *Entente Cordiale,* an historic treaty of friendship settling, they hoped forever, their disputes over the Sudan and Morocco. In a letter to the editor of the *Echo de Paris,* republished in the *New York Times* on October 9, 1905, Carnegie expressed his hope that America would join the alliance. "It does not seem to me that this should be a chimera. Shall not this be the first achievement realized in the twentieth century? And may we not see in the near future the incorporation in this pacific alliance of the German power, already practically the kinsman of England and the United States. Then never more could the dangers of war be conjured up between Germany and France, America, or England, or between any other two of these powers. . . . Truly the world does move forward."

That same month, Carnegie returned to St. Andrews to deliver his second rectorial address, in which he called upon the students to dedicate themselves to the cause of peace through arbitration. "You will find the world much better than your forefathers did," he began. "There is profound satisfaction in this, that all grows better; but there is still one evil in our day, so far exceeding any other in extent and effect, that I venture to bring it to your notice. . . . There still remains the foulest blot that has ever disgraced the earth, the killing of civilized men by men like wild beasts as a permissible mode of settling disputes." He then proceeded to reproduce citation after citation, in no apparent order—from Rousseau to Homer, Euripides, Buddhists, St. Irenæus, Luther, all stating in their own words that war was hell. After mini-lectures on the history of "reforms in war" and the arbitration movement, he put away the results of his and his assistants' research and returned to the present. Not only was war immoral, uncivilized, ineffective, and contrary to the tenets of all the world's great religions, but preparation for it was sapping the vitality and prosperity of the great nations of Europe. Returning to the notion that had animated the development of his Hero Trust program, he attacked head-on the false and dangerous idea that war "develops the manly virtue of courage." On the contrary, war enhanced only man's capacity for "physical courage, which some animals and the lower order of savage men possess in the highest degree. According to this idea, the more man resembles the bulldog the higher he is developed as man." Carnegie ended this overstuffed, overlong sermon with a direct appeal to the students of St. Andrews to commit themselves to "this holy work and hasten the end of war" by forming their own "Leagues of Peace." "Drop all other public questions, concentrate your efforts upon the one question which carries in its bosom the issue of peace or of war. Lay aside your politics until this war issue is settled. This is the time to be effective. . . . If in every constituency," he concluded, "there were organized an arbitration league . . . it is surprising how soon both parties would accept arbitration as a policy. I know of no work that would prove more fruitful for your country and for the world than this. It is by concentrating upon one issue that great causes are won."[13]

For a man who believed in accomplishing reform by working from the top down, with presidents and prime ministers, Carnegie's suggestion for the students of St. Andrews was rather startling. He was, it appeared, returning to the tactics used by his Chartist and unionist forbears, who had organized local, often secret societies to agitate for reform in Dunfermline. "The way of the reformer is hard," he had written his cousin Dod in March, "but both Lauders and Carnegies were always agitators until present generation." Had any individual or group approached him at St. Andrews to ask for financial support to organize "Leagues of Peace," he would no doubt have granted it. But as no one did, his idea was left to languish when, directly after the speech, he left St. Andrews and Britain to return to the United States.[14]

"JUST HOME, not yet settled," Carnegie wrote Morley from New York City on November 1. "Head whirls a little. Much to take up and finish. Twenty-five Presidents Universities—all day session here & lunch Wednesday—on Ten Million Pension Fund."[15]

Carnegie was referring to the first annual meeting of the board of yet another of his trusts, the Carnegie Foundation for the Advancement of Teaching. He had, as had become his practice, announced the establishment of the trust—endowed with $10 million of U.S. Steel gold bonds—in the spring before sailing to Europe. The foundation's mission was "to provide retiring pensions for the teachers of universities, colleges, and technical schools in our country, Canada, and Newfoundland . . . without regard to race, sex, creed or color." Faculty of public institutions were excluded, because Carnegie believed the states would want complete autonomy in all financial matters.

Because the interest on $10 million was not enough to provide pensions for all professors and because he had no intention of giving money to institutions that were church-affiliated, he empowered his board to determine, within these guidelines, which institutions would be eligible for Carnegie pensions. It is doubtful that he had any idea, in doing so, of the unintended consequences of his action. His board of directors, comprised of the most distinguished presidents of the most distinguished American universities and colleges, did. Carnegie pensions would, in a relatively short time, change the face of higher education in America. Those institutions that were given the right to award Carnegie pensions reaped enormous rewards as potential professors gravitated to them. The most controversial aspect and, in the long run, one of the most important of the provisions in the deed of grant was Carnegie's prohibition on giving pensions to professors at sectarian colleges. Colleges and universities that had once been church connected but were now "free to all men of all creeds or of none" were invited to apply. Those which were "under control of a sect, or require Trustees (or a majority thereof), Officers, Faculty or Students, to belong to any specified sect, or which impose any theological test, are to be excluded." Carnegie was adamant that these rules be followed. Institutions that sought pension support were required to fill out a questionnaire and attach a "memorandum explaining sectarian connection." No exceptions were made, not even for schools like Brown and Northwestern, which considered themselves fully nonsectarian but had provisions in their charter that reserved trustee seats for members of particular dominations.[16]

In the long run, one of the board's most significant decisions, with which Carnegie had little to do, was to restrict eligibility to institutions with endowments of at least $200,000 and to require that students accepted for matriculation must have previously taken a minimum number of academic courses in high school (later defined in terms of "Carnegie Units"). As the biographer Joseph Wall, who served for many years as a college dean, would later remark, "By 1909 . . . the Carnegie Foundation had become the national unofficial accrediting agency for colleges and universities." It would function as such until at least 1949, when the National Commission on Accreditation was organized.[17]

In March 1908, Carnegie gave the foundation an additional $5 million, so that it could begin funding pensions at state universities. In 1913, $1.25 million more was donated. When, by 1918, it became apparent that the foundation would never be able to provide pensions for more than a portion of the nation's ever-expanding supply of college teachers, the trustees devised and funded a new contributory pension plan, known as the Teachers Insurance and Annuity Association.

CARNEGIE had long been in the habit of writing to his friend John Morley on Sundays. When, on November 2, 1905, a Thursday, he sent off his second letter in two weekdays, Morley must have sensed that something was amiss. Carnegie began with his usual chitchat about his business schedule: "I'm going to Boston to deliver address Scots Society 248th anniversary, true." He then segued into the real reason for the letter: Louise had intended on going with him to Boston, but had decided against the trip at the last minute, because she was consumed by anxiety about eight-year-old Baba, who had injured her leg in Scotland, apparently by falling off a swing. It was thought at first that Baba had sprained her ankle and she was given a cast to wear for six weeks. Upon her return to the United States, a "leading specialist" was called in. He removed the ankle cast and replaced it with one which "enveloped entire leg." The prognosis was as uncertain as the diagnosis. The doctors didn't know what was wrong with the leg or whether it would entirely heal. Margaret's cousin Nancy, who was an infant at the time, recalled later that "there was something the matter with her legs and she could not walk. It was said that it came from eating strawberries with the sun on them at Skibo." Margaret herself was told years later that she had suffered from some form of tuberculosis of the limb. Whatever the cause, the illness or injury was, Margaret thought, badly handled.[18]

Carnegie was frightened both for himself and for his wife, who, he feared, would not be able to bear the strain. Nothing in his previous experiences had quite prepared him for this. "We are having the first acute pang of grief," he wrote Morley. "Baba's leg in plaster cast   , She has fixed stilts for it & can hobble about a little—is very patient & cheerful but it does go deep into our hearts, deep, deep—It may only be result of sprain but I fear Edinburgh specialist Prof. Stiles believed it to be more serious—We are so anxious, can't tell for three or four months & naturally fear the worst. It is terrible."[19]

For the next two and a half years, from ages eight and a half to age eleven, Margaret would remain a virtual invalid, her leg encased in plaster casts or splints, supported by an iron brace so that she could hobble along without putting weight on her foot. As she grew taller, the plaster casts were removed and replaced with new ones. "On the whole," Margaret remembered years later, "it was not too bad, but grim at times. The good side was the new and delicious things I was given to eat—juicy broiled lamb chops, fresh lettuce and grapefruit. . . . The grim side was not being able to walk easily and play, and being pretty uncomfortable at times." Her long convalescence was "especially hard for Mother." While Louise refrained from spoiling her daughter with gifts, "she always thought of the right things to do for 'me.' The first Christmas that my splint was on, she gave me a baby doll and all the clothes for day and night, and a bassinet with sheets, pillows and pillowcases." Lu-Lu, the doll, would, in the years to come, provide hour upon hour of pleasure for a little girl who could only play sitting down. Her father was mostly absent during these years, though Margaret seemed to take this in stride. "I did not see so much of Daddy, but when I did, it was always exciting. He believed in Fairies, and made me believe in them too. When he gave me his soft long-drawn out whistle, something for me was dropped in his pocket! At times other lovely mysterious presents were found under my pillow when I went to bed at night—amethyst, rose quartz," and other beautiful polished stones.[20]

During the next three years, though his concentration was at times broken by worries about Baba and the toll her illness was taking on Louise, Carnegie committed himself anew to the struggle for world peace through arbitration. Nothing, it appeared, could dampen the optimism of the new "apostle for peace." When news reached America of the slaughter of the Russian Jews in 1905, Carnegie joined in the relief effort by sending a check for $10,000 to his friend Oscar Straus. "The terrible crimes being committed," he wrote on November 11, "are such as might lead one to lose faith in humanity. . . . Do not be discouraged, however. Under the law of evolution, we must steadily, though slowly, march upward, and finally reach the true conception of the brotherhood of man."[21]

On November 25, 1905, Andrew Carnegie celebrated his seventieth birthday. Ten days later, he received the best of belated birthday presidents when the Liberal Party in Britain won its first election in more than a decade. The cabinet, which was installed in December, was filled with friends and acquaintances. It was, Carnegie would later joke to Morley, "a Skibo-Dunfermline cabinet." Lord Elgin from Dunfermline, who headed up Carnegie's Scottish Universities Trust, was named colonial secretary; Campbell-Bannerman, from nearby Glasgow, became prime minister; John Morley took up the India office; Richard Haldane, James Bryce, and Herbert Asquith, all of whom served with Elgin and Morley on the Scottish Universities board, were appointed secretary for war, chief secretary for Ireland, and chancellor of the exchequer; Gladstone's son, Herbert, was named home secretary.[22]

Carnegie took off at once for Washington to celebrate the news of his friends' ascendancy and make sure that everyone knew how welcome he would now be in the corridors of British power. He had begun to consider himself something of a Washington insider, and indeed he was, with direct access to the president and Elihu Root, who had been called back to Washington as secretary of state on John Hay's death in July. "Saw President & Root, etc.," he wrote Morley on December 17, just after the British elections, and "told them no fear of any discrimination against America from the Government all of whom were well wishers."[23]

What Carnegie did not know was that while Roosevelt afforded him unparalleled access and appeared to take his policy recommendations seriously, he had nothing but contempt for the little Scotsman. The athletic, patrician New York-bred cowboy who had chosen public service over business found little to admire—or respect—in Carnegie's achievements as a businessman and philanthropist or in his single-minded dedication to peace.

In mid-November 1905, having learned of Carnegie's October "rectorial address" at St. Andrews and his insults to the manly, martial virtues, the president confessed to Whitelaw Reid that he had

> tried hard to like Carnegie, but it is pretty difficult. There is no type of man for whom I feel a more contemptuous abhorrence than for the one who makes a God of mere money making and at the same time is always yelling out that kind of utterly stupid condemnation of war which in almost every case springs from a combination of defective physical courage, of unmanly shrinking from pain and effort, and of hopelessly twisted ideals. All the suffering from Spanish war comes far short of the suffering, preventable and non-preventable, among the operators of the Carnegie steel works, and among the small investors, during the time that Carnegie was making his fortune. . . . It is as noxious folly to denounce war per se as it is to denounce business per se. Unrighteous war is a hideous evil; but I am not at all sure that it is worse evil than business unrighteousness.[24]

What rankled Roosevelt most—and one can see how it might—was that the same little capitalist who urged the president to do the right and moral thing in the Philippines, Panama, and international diplomacy had never done the right or moral thing as a businessman. It was a harsh criticism, but not entirely uncalled for.

.   .   .

CARNEGIE, though tormented by Baba's distress, refused to let his anxieties slow down his crusading for peace. "I have numerous engagements," he wrote Morley in mid-December. "Speech in Boston. Three here last week. One at dinner to Mark Twain 70th birthday [Clemens, born on November 30, 1835, was five days younger than Carnegie]—a notable gathering. But I must not forget to report Doctors gratified at Baba's progress—decidedly so although unable to pronounce until March upon its nature. It looks more favorable however and this lessens the throbs that come so suddenly. They are not quite so keen with agony."[25]

Three days after Margaret got her Christmas doll, the family packed up and went south to Cumberland Island. "We are all off tonight for own sister's island off coast Georgia to spend winter because doctors insist upon our little darling escaping New York winter," Carnegie wrote James Bryce. "She has a sprained ankle and sunshine and sea beach demanded. It is quite a change but everything must bend for her sake."[26]

They moved into the "delightful cottage" close to Lucy's house, left vacant when Andrew's nephew, Thomas Morrison Carnegie, moved to New York to work for his uncle's "professor pension program." In a letter to Morley on January 14, 1906, Carnegie sounded a bit more upbeat. "We are happy. Happy because our little darling has improved so much. Our own Doctor came with us for a week & has no doubt the trouble will be outgrown—It is of Gouty nature & not as the Edinburgh specialist feared. This seems decided, a heavy weight is lifted from our hearts. Although we cannot but be anxious—Baba is happy playing on the Smooth Sandy beach quite near, & in driving about. We have everything here. Houses, Boats, Yachts, Autos, etc. Weather sunny & not too warm. The swelling of her legs almost gone. She eats & sleeps well & in short a speedier recovery could not have been made so far."[27]

Every morning, Margaret was pushed down to the beach in a wheelchair and then transferred to a specially constructed low wooden cart, from which she could bend over to pick seashells, as she was pulled along by her nanny. On Sunday mornings, Andrew and Louise accompanied her to the beach, with her father pushing her chair. "There was a bench on the way to sit on. Mother and I stopped there while Daddy went for a walk along the beach."[28]

Carnegie, exiled from New York to Cumberland Island, returned to writing his "Memoirs—am trying to tell the Story for our friends." He found it ironic that while Morley was giving up his literary work to enter the cabinet, he, Carnegie, was again writing. This did not mean that Carnegie had any intention of abandoning his own political work. In mid-January, he wrote Morley to tell him that Prime Minister Campbell-Bannerman's "suggestion of a League of Peace has struck a responsive Chord here" and that he had proposed to Elihu Root that Roosevelt publicly "express his approval." The president was, he added in a "private" parenthetical notation, "studying disarmament . . . just now wondering if that isn't next best step."[29]

In late March, from Hot Springs, Arkansas, where the family stopped off en route north after their three months on Cumberland Island, Carnegie sent off a long, rather rambling, handwritten letter to Roosevelt, with NONOFFICIAL scrawled across the top. Like a garrulous, slightly daft and aging uncle, he saluted Roosevelt's attempts to get Congress to pass legislation regulating railroad "rates," and then proceeded to tell the president the story of his own battles with the Pennsylvania Railroad. He closed with a halfhearted apology: "Sorry to intrude, think of you often as the most oppressed man in the land."[30]

"So far all is well," he wrote Morley at the same time. Margaret was improving, the doctor thought. She and her mother were heading back to New York City, while he planned to stop over in Tuskegee to celebrate its semicentenary with Booker T. Washington, President Eliot of Harvard, and Seth Low, and then on April 24 "I'm off on stumping—tour Canada in Private car, taking Butler (Columbia) & Gilder (Century) with me as chums." On his way north, Carnegie planned to stop over in Washington to lobby President Roosevelt and Secretary of State Root on Campbell-Bannerman's "League of Peace" suggestion.[31]

IN YEARS PAST, the family had departed New York for Liverpool in late March or early April, stopping over for a month in London so as not to arrive at Skibo until the weather turned warm. Baba's illness changed everything. Anticipating that neither she in her splints and brace nor her mother would be comfortable in London, Carnegie delayed sailing until mid-May.

"I should reach London Sunday," he wrote Morley from New York on May 15, three days before they were to depart. Carnegie, who had barely seen wife or daughter since leaving Hot Springs in late March, planned to remain in the London area to give some talks and receive some honors, while Louise took their daughter directly to Skibo. "Baba improving but Doctors say six months more needed before she is free [she had already been in plaster for at least eight months]—Lou & I disappointed. It seemed to us her improvement was so rapid we might have her free from splits sooner, but No, they are certain it is needed—That all goes well however is sure, and that's the Main thing."[32]

Just before sailing for Europe, in yet another sign of the domestic disruptions his daughter's illness had caused, Carnegie took over from Louise the task of hiring a new organist for Skibo. "We are particular about the music," he wrote John Ross, "no fancy pieces, these prostitute the organ. The fine old hymns—Wagner's finest religious pieces Lohengrin—Siegfried March, etc. Played slowly, feelingly—no bounce—no flare."[33]

When Andrew arrived at Skibo in mid-June, after a month in London and traveling through England, he found his daughter looking "very much better" but his wife "thin & worn." He was so concerned that, as he wrote Morley, he decided "we must close Skibo this season to many we should otherwise like to have. Too much of a strain for Madam. Dr. Simpson strongly urges this but it makes the visits of the few intimates more precious, the 'old shoes' we really are intimate with—Madam will be benefited by those so hope Mrs. Morley and you may be able to come—All the Doctors agree that only time is required to ensure recovery."[34]

ALL SUMMER LONG, Carnegie was engaged in a round-robin exchange of letters with President Roosevelt, Secretary of State Root, and John Morley, who as a cabinet member in the Liberal government had become his liaison with Prime Minister Sir Henry Campbell-Bannerman and Foreign Secretary Sir Edward Grey. The international peace conference at The Hague, originally scheduled for 1906, had been postponed for a year, leaving plenty of time for backroom deals among the major powers. In early July, Secretary of State Root sent Carnegie "two printed papers which must still be kept very confidential": one was the U.S. government's instructions to its delegates at the Rio conference on Pan-American affairs; the second, "correspondence . . . relating to the . . . conference at The Hague." Root cautioned Carnegie to "please keep these papers where nobody will get hold of them," but added that he had "no objection to your telling your friends in the British Government what our positions are as you find them exhibited in these papers." Carnegie, of course, did just that, and more. He sent excerpts from Root's memorandum to Morley and asked that he forward them to Sir Edward Grey.[35]

Carnegie's goal was to try to locate the common ground on which Britain and the United States could formulate an agenda for The Hague conference. "Surely nothing could be more popular in Britain," he wrote Morley in mid-July, "than any step which brought into closer co-operation the Race across the Atlantic. Even if we fail to dominate the conference and get some important changes, something would be accomplished by having the Race standing together before the world." In his letters to Roosevelt, he assured him that the British were prepared to follow his lead. "What a relief it must be to you, harassed as Presidents must be under our faulty system with petty political & personal affairs [a reference to Roosevelt's difficulty getting his legislation through Congress], to mount into the high arena of world problems & as in this instance leading mankind to a higher civilization, the only sure passport to enduring fame. . . . Pray don't forget that you are called upon to lead in the world's work."[36]

In early August 1906, Roosevelt wrote Carnegie a long letter in which he did his best to dampen his correspondent's hopes that much would be achieved at The Hague conference. He began by expressing his lack of sympathy with revolutionaries, extremists, and utopians, even those whose stated objective was world peace, a category in which we know he placed Carnegie. He assured Carnegie, nonetheless, that he hoped "to see real progress made at the next Hague Conference. If it is possible in some way to bring about a stop, complete or partial, to the race in adding to armaments, I shall be glad; but I do not yet see my way clear as regards the details of such a plan." He added, almost parenthetically, that the world needed "some system of international police" to bring peace, order, and stability to troubled spots around the globe. Without such a "system" in place—and he saw no hope of one in the foreseeable future—it was sheer folly to believe that half measures would make much of a difference. "The one thing I won't do is to bluff when I can not make good; to bluster and threaten and then fail to take the action if my words needed to be backed up. . . . I believe in peace, but I believe that as things are at present, the cause not only of peace but of what is greater than peace is favored by having those nations which really stand at the head of civilization show, not merely by words but by action, that they ask peace in the name of justice and not from any weakness."[37]

Roosevelt's reference to "weakness" was shorthand for his opposition to American disarmament. He was willing to support stabilization of the naval arms race, but not to withdraw from it.

Carnegie wrote back to suggest that Britain and the United States, short of disarming, might agree not to accelerate naval building. He also proposed a slight alteration in the "League of Peace" plan he had earlier supported. Why couldn't the world's major powers agree to a voluntary arbitration treaty in which they "intimated" that they would "view with disfavor an appeal to force until an offer to arbitrate has been made and rejected?" Roosevelt had in an earlier letter expressed his unhappiness that the "ironclad custom which forbids a President ever to go abroad" precluded him from meeting personally with the leaders of France, England, and Germany to set the groundwork for The Hague conference. Carnegie offered himself as a substitute. He had, he informed the president, been invited twice to meet the kaiser, who claimed that he had "read every word of my first Rectorial Address, dealing with the present and future of nations. Like you I have wished to have a talk with him as being the great power in Europe. I should urge him, as I do you, to take up with each other arbitration of international disputes." He was fishing for the president's approval of such a mission, but none was forthcoming. Carnegie closed this long letter, as he had previous ones, by flattering Roosevelt with the intimations of immortality that would follow should he accept Carnegie's advice: "The man who passes into history as the chief agent in banishing or even lessening war, the great evil of his day, is to stand for all time among the foremost benefactors. . . . Only as strongest apostle of peace of your day you can take permanent rank with the very few immortals whom the tooth of time is not to gnaw into oblivion. I envy you when I think over the destiny you may fulfill."[38]

Carnegie was so convinced that Roosevelt would agree with his suggestions and use him as unofficial plenipotentiary that he asked Morley to arrange "an interview with Secretary Navy . . . and any Cabinet members, so I could report to the President & try to get the two powers to speak as one. . . . I should like to see the Prime Minister & perhaps be bearer of a message to the President who is studying the League of Peace idea. . . . I am certain the President will go hand & hand with Campbell-Bannerman & his band & that he longs to do so. I think Britain should respond. She has no such ally—there is none equal to the one of her race."[39]

Not for the first time, Carnegie had badly misjudged Roosevelt, who promised only that he would "go over with Mr. Root whether it is possible to make somewhat such a proposal about arbitration as you suggest." Roosevelt instead, aware that Carnegie had access to Liberal cabinet members, including the prime minister, let float a trial balloon for Carnegie to convey to his British friends. "I have been thinking more and more that we might at least be able to limit the size of battleships, and I should put the limit below the size of the Dreadnought [the British battleship which, with ten guns rather than usual four, was larger and more invulnerable than anything else in the water]. Let the English have the two or three ships of the Dreadnought stamp that they have already built, but let all nations agree that hereafter no ship to exceed say fifteen thousand tons shall be built."[40]

Carnegie communicated Roosevelt's plan to Morley, who took it to the prime minister and the foreign secretary. Carnegie suggested that Chancellor of the Exchequer Asquith should also be brought into the discussion. "President could & would take strong ground against further increase either in number or size [of new battleships], if he only felt Britain would give it welcome—I should think the Lord Chancellor would be a tower of strength in this. . . . He's surely with us." In a second note to Morley, Carnegie repeated his hope that Campbell-Bannerman "and his shipmates will respond cordially to President's idea. Even if it fail it would be creditable (& I think popular) to attempt United action of the English-speaking race in favor of no increase Naval power . . . I should like to be in position to tell President overture warmly received—can depend upon cooperation in any attempt to limit armaments or size—Truly I feel now is the psychological moment—something may be accomplished."[41]

Roosevelt's halfhearted attempt to open negotiations on a proposal to limit the size of warships, though duly conveyed by Carnegie, met with no response in London. Carnegie's suggestion that the British and Americans formulate some sort of joint proposal or at least pledge to stand together at The Hague was not even discussed. Carnegie, the eternal optimist, was not in the least discouraged. Having opened a channel of communication between the two governments and established himself as a liaison, he had accomplished a great deal for himself—and, he was convinced, for the cause of peace.

THIRTY-SIX

Peace Conferences, 1907

"HAGUE CONFERENCE DRAGS," Carnegie wrote Morley from New York in mid-January 1907, "but I think it will meet. President not disposed to be frustrated." Neither was Carnegie, who had high hopes for the conference and was disposed to do whatever he could to make it a success. He had accepted the presidency of the National Arbitration Conference, which had scheduled its inaugural meeting for April 1907, just before The Hague conference, in an attempt to focus attention on it.

The previous August, Roosevelt had suggested that nothing much would come out of any Hague conference. World courts without an internal police force to back up their decisions were, he argued, meaningless. Roosevelt had intended his disparaging remarks to serve as an excuse for inaction. Carnegie, however, took him at his word and formulated a new proposal for the organization of an "international police force." "Why should we peaceable powers be compelled to increase and maintain great navy fearing attack otherwise," he asked Morley rhetorically. "Let us organize International Police to keep the Peace. War disturbs all Nations and we have a right to say we shall be freed from danger—I am surprised how many hitherto supine warmly support this."[1]

Though he knew that Roosevelt had little sympathy for a "league of peace," much less for an international police force to enforce its decisions, Carnegie continued to press forward. "An 'International Police' that really should be the aim at the next Hague conference," he wrote Roosevelt in February 1907. "If the German Emperor could rise to his destiny & stand with you, favoring this, instead of pegging away, trifling over petty questions—chasing rainbows in form of a colonial empire which he cannot get & which would do Germany no good if he did." Roosevelt did not appreciate being told what to do. But Carnegie ignored this and urged the president to write the kaiser "a private letter & suggest if he take the lead in Europe alongside you in America, between you, war could be banished."[2]

Roosevelt ignored Carnegie's suggestion. He wrote instead to tell Carnegie that he would not be able to accept his invitation to the "Great Peace Society" conference in April, but was delighted that Root had decided to attend. Knowing that his curt reply left much unsaid, he invited Carnegie to lunch with him, "if you are here, on Wednesday, March 27th. If so, I will get one or two of our friends to meet you, especially Root."[3]

Carnegie's arrival in Washington for luncheon with the president, the vice president, the secretary of the Treasury, and other high government officials proved something of a godsend for Roosevelt. In mid-March, the stock market had crashed. While Wall Street blamed Roosevelt's antitrust policy for the crash, Carnegie, on exiting from his meeting with the president, declared that as far as he was concerned, the president was a friend of business and "the best friend the railroads have . . . I mean by that that the president's railroad measures are moderate . . . I indorse the President's position on the railroad question without reservation. His influence on that subject I regard as entirely wholesome and conservative."[4]

The following day, Carnegie did the president another great service by attacking Wall Street gamblers, this time with such colorfully venomous language that the story appeared on the front page of the *New York Times* for March 29. "Let me speak as a plain business man," Carnegie told the reporter. "Wall Street is not America, and even in New York there are other places than Wall Street. Gambling is not business; it is a parasite feeding on values and creating none. It is time for us business men to rise and decline to recognize the men who make money and render no value for it by manufacturing something or giving something in exchange." With his usual self-righteousness on the subject of stock market manipulation, Carnegie proudly declared again that he had never "made a dollar by gambling in stocks."

IN LATE MARCH, after a two-month stay at sister-in-law Lucy's estate on Cumberland Island where he and Louise believed Baba's recovery was sped along by the sun and seashore, Carnegie returned to New York City, via Washington, to preside over the National Arbitration Conference. No sooner had he arrived than he began a round of speaking engagements that would extend over the next four weeks. On March 28, he addressed the reunion of the Civil War telegraphers at the Hotel Manhattan. A few days later, he was at the Hotel Savoy to address five hundred members of the Phi Beta Kappa fraternity. On Friday, April 5, he hosted three hundred members of the National Civic Federation at a dinner at his home. Somewhere in between he composed the "plea for peace" that was published on April 7 in the *New York Times Sunday Magazine*. All month long, his name was on the front pages. Had he been interested in publicity alone, he would have attained nirvana. But he wanted more than the opportunity to stoke his already considerable ego or add to the collection of famous men and statesmen he called his friends. It is easy to poke fun at his egomania, his penchant for self-advertising, his almost intolerable self-confidence. That he was far from selfless in his campaign for world peace does not mean that he was any the less committed to the cause.

In the months preceding the opening of The Hague conference, Carnegie pushed himself to the point where more than once he collapsed in exhaustion and was forced to take to his bed. He had earlier suggested, and it had been agreed, that the National Arbitration Conference would be held in New York one week after the dedication of the Carnegie Institute building in Pittsburgh so that the European guests he had invited to the opening ceremonies in Pittsburgh could also attend the peace conference in New York. When Frederick Lynch, one of the organizers of the arbitration conference, asked gently if Carnegie thought those attending the Pittsburgh dedication, most of whom were professors or museum directors, had "thought much on this particular matter of international peace," Carnegie answered, "'Never mind . . . we will make them speak, and then they will have to think about it.' And then he added, with a twinkle in his eye, 'We'll make them put themselves on record.'"[5]

From April 1, every steamship arriving in New York, including the *Kaiser Wilhelm II*, the *Baltic*, and the *Caronia*, brought several of Carnegie's distinguished guests. They were met at the pier and taken to the Hotel Belmont. Among them were a world-famous astronomer from Cambridge; the master of Jesus College, Oxford; John Ross, Carnegie's Dunfermline solicitor; William Stead; Baron d'Estournelles de Constant of the French government; Baron Descamp, a member of The Hague Court; representatives of the German Reichstag and Kaiser Wilhelm II; the directors of the

Louvre Museum and the Luxembourg Gallery; the principals of the major universities in Scotland; and the editors of several London newspapers and opinion journals. One of the less credentialed visitors, the provost of Dunfermline, explained that he had been invited because "Mr. Carnegie and I are old friends. My father used to play in the streets of Dunfermline with Mr. Carnegie when both of them were barefooted youngsters." Asked how the "old folks" who remembered Andrew as a boy looked on him now, the provost answered: "Why, they look upon him as one of the wonders of the world . . . and they love him dearly. Mr. Carnegie is the most democratic of American millionaires. He remembers the old townspeople, and he talks to them as though he were still one of them."[6]

The demands on Carnegie were extraordinary: he was called upon to play the roles of celebrity, spiritual leader dispensing wisdom to the masses, public relations officer, liaison to Washington, and chief of logistics for a traveling assembly of distinguished statesmen.

Early on the morning of Tuesday, April 9, after a week of receptions, dinners, and meetings in New York, Carnegie, with Louise beside him, secretly left the city in the midst of the season's last snowstorm and boarded a private car for the all-day train trip to Pittsburgh. It had been six years since Carnegie had last visited the city. This time around, there were to be no meetings downtown with his partners, no visits to Homestead or Duquesne or Braddock, no interviews with the newspapers about iron or steel, tariffs or labor contracts.

He was returning as a philanthropist and peacemaker to preside over the opening ceremonies of a vastly expanded Carnegie Institute. The original building had covered 5 acres; the new one took up almost 14. The bizarrely misplaced Venetian towers on either side of the Music Hall had been removed and a sumptuous grand foyer with a gilded ceiling and green marble columns added. The library had expanded outward into the wings that had once housed the museum and art gallery. Around the corner along Forbes Avenue had arisen the new Carnegie Museum and Art Gallery, with separate halls of architecture and sculpture, and a gallery with more than five hundred paintings assembled for the eleventh *International* exhibit. Much of the space in the addition was devoted to the Museum of Natural History, which took its place at once as one of the great museums of the world. It was here that the Carnegie collection of dinosaurs, including *Diplodocus carnegii*, found its final resting place.

Carnegie had left New York with Louise on Tuesday morning so that the two of them could enjoy a full day touring the new building. The following day, his thirty-five European guests, accompanied by 160 pieces of luggage, boarded their train for Pittsburgh. The first day of festivities opened on Thursday morning and concluded with a lengthy evening concert by the Pittsburgh Symphony at the Carnegie Music Hall. Carnegie was so worn out by the travel, the excitement, and the responsibilities in front of him that he stayed in bed the following morning, then skipped the second day's events, recovering only in time to host the banquet dinner at the Hotel Schenley. The following morning, Saturday, he and Louise took their second daylong train ride in five days, this one back to New York.[7]

On Monday afternoon, Carnegie was on the podium of the hall that bore his name as the first session of the National Arbitration Conference was gaveled to order. Carnegie and the organizers had hoped that Roosevelt would open the conference, but when the president declined, Carnegie innocently asked if he might dictate "a short letter to be read . . . expressing your hopes of some decided advances through the coming Hague Conference."[8]

Instead of a short letter, Roosevelt composed a six-and-a-half page memorandum. He was, he insisted, in sympathy with the conference organizers, and it was in that spirit that he sought to "make to you some suggestions as to the practical method for accomplishing the ends we all of us have in view. First and foremost, I beseech you to remember that it is our bounden duty to work for peace, yet it is even more our duty to work for righteousness and justice." He cautioned those who did "not themselves . . . bear the responsibility of upholding the nation's honor" not to insist on the impossible when it came to formulating their peace proposals and not to call for any sort of "general disarmament [which] would do harm and not good if it left the civilized and peace-loving peoples . . . unable to check the other peoples who have no such standards, who acknowledge no such obligations." His administration, he claimed, had sought peace in the Philippines, Panama, Cuba, the Caribbean, Mexico, Santo Domingo, and Central America, but "in a spirit untainted by that silly sentimentality which is often more dangerous to both the subject and the object than downright iniquity." He announced that the American representatives to The Hague Peace Conference would propose discussion on the limitation of armaments and would sign a general arbitration treaty that increased "the classes of cases which it is agreed shall be arbitrated." But he expected little of consequence to happen at The Hague. "It is idle to expect that a task so tremendous can be settled by any one or two conferences and those who demand the impossible from such a conference not only prepare acute disappointment for themselves, but . . . play the game of the very men who wish the conference to accomplish nothing. It is not possible that the conference should go more than a certain distance further in the right direction."[9]

Carnegie disagreed with most everything the president had written but, responding to an advance copy of Roosevelt's letter, referred to "only one point that seems to me weak," the president's assertion that while it was the nation's duty to work for peace, it was "even more our duty to work righteousness and justice." This, Carnegie believed, was sheer nonsense. In every dispute, he reminded the president, each side claimed that it was seeking "righteousness" and "struggling for what is just." The essential question was "who is to decide" where "justice" and "righteousness" lay? "No one, according to you; they must go to war to decide not what is 'right' but who is <u>strong</u>. Pray, reflect. I wish you had time to give a few minutes thought to this. Maybe you would modify the sentence."[10]

Roosevelt released the letter to the press as written.

While the newspapers made much of the fact that the president's "sentiments toward international peace [were] not altogether in accord with those of Andrew Carnegie," Carnegie refused to acknowledge their differences publicly. He opened the arbitration conference by giving his prepared speech, with only a short paragraph interpolated to respond to Roosevelt's letter."[11]

He was omnipresent for the next three days. Frederick Lynch recalled later that Carnegie "was the happiest of men throughout the whole period and was the presiding genius. Nowhere have his amazing versatility and his rare sense of humor been more fully revealed than in his introductions of the various speakers and in his impromptu remarks at the various sessions." When, in the first evening session, Harvard professor Hugo Munsterberg argued that the building of the army had posed no burden on the German people, Carnegie rose from his chair on the podium to answer him directly. "I have heard Professor Munsterberg make the most extraordinary statement that I have heard for a long time: that conscription in

Germany was not regarded as a great burden. I should like to have the gentleman visit our mills in Pittsburg and ask thousands and thousands of Germans what influenced them to leave Germany for this land." Later he interrupted William Stead, who had exceeded his time limit, confiding to the audience in a loud stage whisper, "He is wonderful, and he has been speaking ever since he landed in this country; and some of us, careful of his health are taking care to limit him. . . . Besides we have other speakers. . . . It is now after ten o'clock, and all well regulated families should have the heads of the families at home before eleven o'clock."[12]

The conference came to a close with two grand banquets for one thousand guests each. Former Mayor Seth Low presided at the Waldorf-Astoria, Carnegie at the Hotel Astor, with after-dinner speakers shuttled back and forth from one ballroom to the other. Just before Carnegie adjourned the festivities at the Astor, Baron d'Estournelles, representing the French government, arrived to award him "the rank of a Commander of the Legion of Honor. . . . 'Let me consider now that you are an American, as well as an Englishman, an Englishman as well as a Frenchman, a citizen of the world. You have done great work and we thank you.'" Carnegie, who had not known about the award and had prepared no remarks, spoke extemporaneously of his regard for France, its friendship with Scotland and the United States, and the wisdom of its people, who had in a recent vote, with millions of ballots cast, chosen Louis Pasteur as the hero of French civilization, relegating their greatest soldier, Napoleon, to seventh on the list.[13]

IN MID-MAY, much later than usual, the Carnegie family and servants sailed from New York Harbor for their annual trip to Britain. The sea air cured the "grip" he had been suffering from, Carnegie wrote Morley upon arriving at the Oatlands Hotel near Weybridge in Surrey, where the family was to stay for ten days. "We have our New Argyle Motor. I mean to run about a good deal. Madam has much to do in London not having been there last year—Baba is doing so well—New York Doctors say splint comes off upon our return [it would remain on for almost a year more]. Happy days for us all—Madam is pretty well, rather thin & overworked but she will soon be right—the ten days will give her a rest or at least a change. With our Pittsburgh & New York celebrations etc. & entertaining our

Guests we have all been very busy. Doctors certain my case was one of infection—I was so well & so happy—all at once brought low. But Richard's himself again [a reference to a line from Shakespeare's *Richard III*]."[14]

There was to be no letup in Carnegie's one-man campaign for peace. He intended that summer to visit the peace conference at The Hague and, en route, stop off in Kiel in northern Germany, where Kaiser Wilhelm II was hosting his annual regatta. Carnegie had several times that past year publicly hailed the kaiser as the one man in Europe who could, if he chose, decide whether the coming century would be marked by war or peace. In a note to Morley, marked "private" and signed "The Peace Maker," he insisted that "no other Man has the power to draw a League of Nations competent to keep the peace for an agreed upon period. . . . He has the Cards—May the 'holy spirit' light upon & lead him heavenward. Fortunately he's very devout—very. . . . Never was holy Father more thoroughly convinced of his Mission than I am of mine. I <u>Know</u> I offer H.I.M. [his imperial majesty] the plan that makes him the Greatest Agent known so far in human History."[15]

Morley's response was muted, but to the point. "That you can inflame him with your crusader's zeal I am not sure. But the effort is <u>noble</u>."[16]

The Kiel Regatta, to which the Carnegies had been invited, was heavy with "court functions . . . glittering receptions and ceremonial dinners with heel-clicking generals and administrators, trumpets, brass bands, military marches, and goose-stepping soldiers." It was at Kiel Week that the kaiser hosted foreign dignitaries and statesmen he wanted to meet, showed off the latest addition to his navy, rooted for the German yachts, and met with his ministers, most of whom, according to the historian and biographer Michael Balfour, "spoke to their sovereign only once a year, the occasion, strangely enough, being the Kiel Regatta."[17]

Carnegie was one of hundreds of guests and had little opportunity to engage the kaiser in more than small talk. After his second day of receptions, banquets, balls, naval exercises, and yacht racing, Carnegie took time to write to Margaret, who had been left behind in Britain: "Well Darling, here it is the end of the week and your telegram just came a few minutes ago, and before going to bed I thought I would just write you a note. We have had a busy time here. Warships, yachts, sailing boats, motor boats crowding the bay. I have had one talk with the Emperor, who is very nice indeed. Also I dined with him one evening and he lifted his glass and drank my health and I did drink his. He laughs and talks and you may be sure he tells that he is Scotch. We have great fun."[18]

Though he had no substantive talks with the kaiser about peace or, for that matter, anything else, he came away even more convinced that Wilhelm II was "a Man of Destiny." Six months earlier, Carnegie had confessed as much in a letter to the kaiser in which he declared that in his "reveries you sometimes appear and enter my brain. I then imagine myself 'The Emperor' and soliloquize somewhat as per enclosed." He enclosed an account of how Andrew Carnegie, transformed into the kaiser, "communes with himself."

"God has seen fit to place me [Andrew Carnegie as Kaiser] in command of the greatest military power ever known. For what end? Surely for good and not for evil; surely for peace and not for war. . . . Thank God, my hands, as yet, are guiltless of human blood. What part, then, can I play worthy of my power and position? It must be—shall be—in the direction of Peace on Earth. . . . I become the Peacemaker of the world—the curse of centuries lifted at a single stroke. 'Alone, I did it,' . . . Yes! This is my work! Thank God. Now I see my path and am happy. To this I consecrate my life, and surely, 'The highest Worship of God is service to man.' "[19]

We don't know if the kaiser ever read Carnegie's letter or took anything away from their brief conversations at Kiel.

On June 23, at five in the morning, the Carnegies boarded the special railroad car provided them by the Prussian government for the last leg of their trip to The Hague. Usually such a journey required at least three changes of train, but the Prussian and Dutch governments, the *New York Times* reported on June 24, had arranged for the Carnegies' private railroad car "to go through by the most direct route" with no changes.

The Carnegies arrived at The Hague while the peace conference was in session. They spent two days there, as private citizens, and attended a brief formal ceremony at the site on which Carnegie's peace palace was to be built. In an impromptu press conference reported in the *New York Times* on June 26, 1907, Carnegie expressed his "great satisfaction at his recent meeting with Emperor William at Kiel, adding that he had gained the impression that the Emperor was a most sincere advocate of peace and would do all in his power to prevent conflicts."

He was quite pleased with himself. "Dear Saint Mark," he wrote Clemens from Brown's Hotel in London, on his return from the Continent.

"Madam & I just in from hobnobbing with the Emperor feel the want, (I do, not Madam who is sinless) of my Father Confessor—feel it badly & all over—Hence this call. We are off tonight for Skibo. When are you coming to see us there in your holy capacity, sinner-saint. We hope soon." In the margins of the final page, he squeezed in one final message: "Great character the Emperor. How he might enjoy you—He's <u>bright</u>."[20]

The sad truth was that neither his visit to Kiel nor The Hague Peace Conference had achieved very much. There was no discussion at The Hague of Carnegie's pet projects: compulsory arbitration or an international police force. Ever the optimist, Carnegie took some satisfaction in the fact that Germany, though unwilling to discuss disarmament, had agreed with the Americans—against the British—on a proposal to exempt private property at sea from seizure. "You notice how finely Germany is standing with us at The Hague," he wrote Roosevelt from Skibo at the end of July.[21]

The president responded in a note marked PERSONAL & CONFIDENTIAL that he was less troubled by the failures at The Hague than by increasing tensions with Japan, occasioned by attacks on immigrants in California and Hawaii. "He asked no advice," Carnegie wrote Morley, "but I felt I had the Solution so clearly I wrote him my views fully adding 'no reply desired.'" Carnegie's "solution" was that Roosevelt should continue to pressure the Japanese government to voluntarily limit immigration. There was no other way to stop the violence. "We must recognize that whites everywhere object to them." What was occuring in San Francisco was no different from what was occurring elsewhere in the English-speaking world, in Britain, South Africa, Australia, and Canada.[22]

Carnegie was overjoyed when the president wrote back that though "no answer is required to your letter I must allow myself the pleasure of stating that for downright, condensed, good sense it is one of the most refreshing communications I have had. . . . I hope you will be on this side when I return to Washington as I want to see you at the White House." This was precisely what Carnegie wanted to hear.

> Few responses have equaled that I think & I am really 'set up' to know that
> I have been able to serve my Country. So you must not think me mad in
> seeing the Emperor on a Mission I was impelled to undertake—I hit the
> bulls eye you see with the President & may yet with the other. I know he—

the President—& the Cabinet saw I had the true solution in one case <u>and</u> <u>have adopted it</u> & the President is troubled no more. Why shouldn't the angel of Light choose a dreamer now & then just for a change & not stick always to the combination of Author-Statesman [Morley] for a working miracle?[23]

Carnegie exaggerated the significance of Roosevelt's note. The fact that in this one isolated instance the president had taken Carnegie's advice did not mean that the kaiser of Germany was going to do likewise.

THE CARNEGIES sailed from Liverpool for New York on October 17, after an extraordinarily hectic season abroad. While they were on the high seas, the "Panic" of 1907 hit first New York City, then Washington, and the rest of the country. Prices on the stock market fell, interest rates rose, loans were called in, and the major New York trust companies came close to collapse—if they went down, it was feared, the banks would crumble with them. The day before their ship docked, Carnegie busied himself writing a "statement" to deliver to the reporters he knew would be waiting to interview him. "Cable just rec'd this morning," he wrote Morley on October 25, "asking me say some judicious words upon financial situation. Very serious now but panic was inevitable. . . . Hard times would affect Roosevelt's future but not I think change it—He will be reelected against his real wishes. . . . Am going to Washington for a day or two."[24]

Upon arriving in New York, Carnegie uncharacteristically refused to take reporters' questions. "The present situation," he explained, was "not one to be discussed off-hand." In his prepared statement, which was published in the *New York Times* and other papers on October 27, he assured the public that "nothing unusual or unexpected has occurred," that the panic was in the nature of a temporary readjustment after an extended boom. He concluded by asserting that it was his belief now, and had been for the past two years, "that the interests of our country would require and the Republican Party demand that the President be reelected a second time. He has only been elected once."

Through November and December, Carnegie shuttled back and forth to Washington to meet with Roosevelt and his cabinet members on the financial crisis and to urge a new round of peace initiatives. "I am going to

Washington this week by request, excited times in financial World," he wrote Morley on November 10. "I am going to advise President to invite nations to make treaties [of] arbitration, first asking Britain. . . . I hope to be of some use."[25]

Roosevelt, Carnegie soon learned, had no intention of taking up the question of disarmament. On the contrary, he had decided to recommend an increase in the size of the U.S. Navy. He had hinted as much to Carnegie "at the luncheon table" in mid-November, causing his would-be adviser "deep anxiety." Carnegie warned him that if he reversed his earlier decision and increased the size of the Navy, he would inevitably "appear as either frightened by conditions which you alone know and which are dangerous, or you will render yourself open to the charge of your enemies, exclaiming that here is an impulsive, excitable ruler, who don't know one year what he desires the next. . . . Mr. President, you stand today the foremost ruler for peace and pledged not to increase our navy. Pause and reflect how the world will regard and bemoan your sudden change. . . . Why? Why? Verily, the question needs your most serious attention. I hope my fears are groundless, but cannot refrain from appealing to you to think well before you thus stultify yourself. Great rulers cannot reverse their policies suddenly without their astonished people asking why." At the bottom of the last page of his letter, Carnegie added in his own hand: "Pardon me Mr. President. My main interest & general admiration not unmixed with affection for you prompts this letter." He signed it, "Always Your Friend."[26]

Roosevelt answered the next day in a curt, no-nonsense letter of eight sentences, the first six of which began with his imperious "I." "I shall recommend an increase in the navy. I shall urge it as strongly as I know how. I believe that every farsighted and patriotic man ought to stand by me. I will give sufficient reasons in my message. I can not state <u>all</u> the reasons in my message, and I certainly will not state them in a letter to you or anyone else or state them verbally save in strict confidence. . . . You say the question needs my serious attention. It has had it; and, as I say, I can not imagine how any one, in view of the known conditions of the world and of the absolute refusal of The Hague conference to limit armaments, can fail to back me up."[27]

Roosevelt had thrown down the gauntlet, clearly annoyed by Carnegie's continued attempts to tell him what to do. Years before, Carnegie had felt no compunction about going behind President McKinley's back and lobbying his advisers. He dared not do the same with Theodore Roosevelt who, unlike his predecessor, ran a tight ship and countenanced no hint of mutiny.

After another "fine visit to Washington" in late November, Carnegie confided to Morley that while the president was in "excellent form . . . not a few of his 'judicious friends'" were upset about his plans for new battleships. Carnegie intended to visit him again on December 9. For the moment, the talk in Washington and New York was of the "panic," which was about to ruin several of Carnegie's friends and associates. "Busy these days doing a consulting business, friends in trouble—helping some of them out of course. Strange getting back to business affairs. Glad I'm out."[28]

On November 25, 1907, Carnegie celebrated his seventy-second birthday, though when the *New York Times* referred to it as his seventieth, he did not correct the error. His "birthday message" was reprinted in full on the front page of the *Times* on November 24. "The world is growing better. . . . Men are more kindly disposed, more charitable, more solicitous for others, less selfish. . . . The time is coming, much more rapidly than we dream when war will be a thing of the past. Oh, yes, indeed!" There was, he admitted, much he still did not understand in his eighth decade. "I can't see why a good, omnipotent Power should allow suffering, why He allows poverty, sickness, and sin. It isn't clear to me why He allows men to have still such dreadful delusions as that it is necessary for some of them to kill some others in the savagery of war. . . . In particular, I don't at all understand the mysterious law of evolution, according to which the higher forms of life live upon the lower, rising through slaughter and extinction. That is profoundly, tragically obscure and perplexing, but we must accept and bow our heads and murmur to Universal Law, 'Thy will be done.'" The motto by which he lived his life remained "All is well, since all grows better." Evolution was for him more than "the ruling principle of scientific thought." It had become a "comforting personal creed." He did not worry about the possibility of a "future life. . . . Our duty is to pitch this one high."

THIRTY-SEVEN

Tariffs and Treaties, 1908–1909

A s CARNEGIE AGED into his retirement, he craved the limelight more than ever. A night without a concert, a reception, a dinner, or a speech was an evening wasted. He accepted invitations to speak at a Lotos Club dinner for Sam Clemens and a Delmonico's banquet for the new sheriff of New York County; and sit at the guest of honor's table at a Pilgrims' dinner, again at Delmonico's, to honor Whitelaw Reid. He became a fixture at benefit dinner dances at the Plaza and the Waldorf-Astoria and concerts at Carnegie Hall, at society weddings, and the funerals of notable bankers and railroad executives. His name was in the papers, either in the society listings or the news pages, nearly every day.

In early February 1908, he made bigger than usual headlines by speaking to the Economic Club in the grand banquet room of the Hotel Astor on America's banking system. William Jennings Bryan also spoke, though it was Carnegie who got the most notice when he declared that the American banking system was "the worst in the civilized world," because American currency was not fully protected by and convertible to gold. The response to the speech was so positive that he forwarded a copy of it to Theodore Roosevelt, had it published in *The Outlook*, paid for 70,500 reprints, and sent one to every congressman and as many bankers and industrialists as he could locate. Three days after his banking speech, he was the keynote speaker at the tenth annual dinner of the Society of the Genesee in the Waldorf-Astoria ballroom. By late March, after yet another speech, this one to Pratt University students, he had exhausted himself. "I am in demand as Speaker," he boasted to Morley, "but tired out just now. Have declined all invitations. Never was better however." He had, in truth, declined all but two or three. His final speaking engagement of the season was at the weekly Monday luncheon of the Vagabonds' Club, for writers, composers, poets, and artists, in the grillroom of the National Arts Club, where he "humorously deplored the fact that he was not a vagabond" and had never been able to lead "a bohemian life."[1]

He spent almost as much time in Washington in early 1908 as he did in New York. It was the final spring of the Roosevelt administration and Carnegie intended to savor every moment of it. "I spent two days last week in Washington; lunched with President, Root etc.," he wrote Morley in late March. "The more I see and confer with [Roosevelt], the nobler he becomes."[2]

Carnegie, who had never been shy about expressing his opinions, was only too happy to put his appraisal of Roosevelt into print. His introduction to *The Roosevelt Policy,* a compilation of Roosevelt's speeches, remarks, and public papers, was so sycophantic it would have embarrassed author and subject had they not both been men of overweening ego. "These volumes," Carnegie wrote, "are devoted not to the man but to the Roosevelt policy. The man already stands revealed to all his countrymen to a degree unequalled by any of modern times except Lincoln himself." Carnegie acknowledged that, like Lincoln before him, Roosevelt had his "captious critics." Geniuses, not bound by society's expectations, went their own way and, in so doing, invited criticism from lesser men. (Is there any doubt that Carnegie included himself, with Lincoln and Roosevelt, in this latter category?) "And so we accept Roosevelt for what he is and would not have him different—an able, courageous, honest, democratic man of the people acting himself out just as the spirit leads him without one particle of pretence. . . . The man of destiny comes to nations . . . just when he is most needed."[3]

Roosevelt was pleased with Carnegie's introduction—how could he not have been?—and wrote Carnegie to tell him so. The two men were already scheduled to dine after the governors' conference on conservation, to which Roosevelt had invited Carnegie, but Roosevelt now inquired if it wasn't "possible for you to take lunch with me the day we dedicate the building of the Bureau of American Republics [which housed representatives of the Pan-American League and which Carnegie had funded]. If you care to, I will have Root, too, and you and he and I will drive to the ceremonies together."[4]

On receiving Roosevelt's congratulatory note, Carnegie forwarded it to the kaiser with a copy of the book introduction that had elicited it. He had maintained communications with Wilhelm II, as only he could, by contributing to the Koch Institute in Berlin and by arranging to have a full-sized replica of *Diplodocus carnegii* sent to Germany. In his letter to the kaiser in May, he claimed that he was sharing the president's note because it was "so highly characteristic" of the man. "It never strikes him that a humble citizen like myself might be somewhat abashed driving by his side through the cheering masses to the ceremony, but perhaps he remembers that I've been hobnobbing recently with Your Majesty and King Edward." Unable to restrain himself, Carnegie proceeded to tell the German kaiser how he would, if invited to do so, conclude a similar tribute to him. "Here then we have the evident Man of Destiny. Never has God entrusted to man, since the World began, his chosen prophets not excepted, the power for good or evil that this keen, able, pure, God-fearing Emperor of Germany wields today."[5]

Carnegie put off the family's departure for Britain in 1908 to bask in the president's reflected glory. Roosevelt had invited him not only to speak on "The Conservation of Ores and Related Minerals" at the governors' conference on conservation, but to attend as his guest the formal dinners to welcome the governors and the luncheon to open the conference. As if that were not enough to swell a man's head, the president had been "saying very flattering things" about him. "An article on our disgraceful banking system & and one upon proposed Commission Inter-State Commerce have attracted notice," he wrote Morley. "Notwithstanding all this we sail 14th May per Baltic. [Roosevelt] has agreed I can leave Washington Wednesday P.M.—sail Thursday."[6]

WITH BABA recovering from whatever had ailed her, the Carnegies entered into full entertainment mode in 1908. That August, as one of their guests, President Woodrow Wilson of Princeton, reported to his wife, the Carnegies welcomed "a perfect stream of visitors at Skibo: I should think that a season of it would utterly wear poor Mrs. Carnegie out. The Castle is like a luxurious hotel. Some twenty or twenty-five persons sit down to every meal. Guests are received, for the most part (if—say—of less than Cabinet rank) by the servants; shown to their rooms; and received by the host and hostess when all assemble for the next meal." The guests during

Wilson's stay included John Morley; Whitelaw Reid, now ambassador to England, and his wife and son; a fat (unnamed) Austrian lady, who was introduced as having won the Nobel Prize for a book on peace; Lord Shaw of Dunfermline and his daughter; and Tom Miller. "There was everything to do that you can think of," Wilson wrote in awe,

> hunting, fishing, golfing, sailing, swimming (in the most beautiful swimming pool I ever saw,—the water tempered to about 70 degrees), driving, motoring, billiards, tennis croquet; and there was perfect freedom to do as you pleased. Wednesday afternoon I managed the boat for Mr. Miller and Mr. Carnegie while they fished; Thursday morning and afternoon I was with a party on a small steam yacht; Friday morning I followed the players over the golf course; Friday afternoon I went with a big party in a motor carrying all to inspect the Kitchen gardens of the tenants on the estate who had been competing for a prize. . . . The estate is some twenty miles long and, on an average, about six miles broad, and includes a whole town in its sweep,—or, rather, a large village. The evenings were spent in dining, talking, playing whist or billiards (I naturally chose the latter), or reading,—by those who had nerves steady enough for it.[7]

In addition to entertaining a full complement of guests that summer, Carnegie embarked on a new writing project, a book of essays for Frank Doubleday entitled *PROBLEMS of TO-DAY, Wealth, Labor, Socialism.* The impetus for the project had come three years earlier, Carnegie explained in his preface, dropping a few names along the way. "When President Roosevelt sent his notable message to Congress . . . calling attention to the unequal distribution of wealth, and recommending high, progressive taxes upon estates at the death of the owners, the writer sent him copy of 'The Gospel of Wealth.' The President wrote in reply, that he was 'greatly struck with the fact that seventeen years ago you had it all.' This led the writer to proceed a step further and add another chapter." He was not, he assured his readers, "a recent convert to some of the doctrines which are now promulgated so freely." He had, even before becoming a multimillionaire, "expressed advanced views upon 'Labor' and 'Land,'" views which he intended to enlarge upon in his new essays. That "the unequal distribution of wealth lies at the root of the present Socialistic activity [was of] no surprise to the writer. It was bound to force itself to the front, because, exhibiting extremes unknown before, it was become one of the crying evils of our day."[8]

Carnegie's goal was to critique Socialist doctrine from the inside, as a former workingman and industrial employer who had spent a lifetime among the laboring classes. With a nod to Marx and the so-called revolutionary socialists whom he gave no evidence of ever having read, he focused his attention on the British Labour Party and the Fabian Socialists. There was surprisingly little urgency to his critique, in large part because he did not consider the Socialists much of a danger in Britain and no danger at all in the United States. "Don't trouble yourself about Socialism," he had written Sir John St. Loe Strachey in the summer of 1907. "It cannot do any harm. . . . Here is a story which I am using.—A negro in the South became a Socialist. The following conversation took place one day with a visitor. 'If you had two horses, would you give one to your poor neighbor?' 'Sure's you're born, that's what I would do.' 'And if you had two cows, would you give one to your poor neighbor?' 'Sure's you're living,' that's what I'd do, and mighty glad to do it.' 'And if you had two pigs, would you give one to your poor neighbor?' 'No sir, dere's where I draws de line; I'se got two pigs.'"[9]

Although he did not tell this story in his book, he made much the same point—over and over again. Socialism was a silly utopian theory, espoused by those who had never worked with their hands and knew no one who had. The true reformers were realists like himself, Theodore Roosevelt, and labor leaders Samuel Gompers and John Mitchell, who recognized that social equality was neither attainable nor beneficial, that men prized the differences between them, and that progress was inevitable, but not instantaneous. "We believe that the surest and best way is by continued evolution as in the past, instead of by revolutionary Socialism, which spends its time preaching such changes as are not within measurable distance of attainment, even if they were desirable in themselves." Carnegie did not begrudge the socialists their critique of present-day society; he welcomed it. "Divine discontent is the root of progress, and even our Socialistic friends, with their revolutionary ideas, stir the waters for our good." He feared only that by espousing their utopian solutions, the revolutionary socialists were making it more difficult for bread-and-butter reformers to hasten the pace of evolutionary change. "The extreme Socialists themselves are one of the obstacles to substantial progress today."[10]

Although his Dunfermline relatives had been skilled artisans, not factory workers, and he himself had spent less than a year in the Allegheny City cotton mills, Carnegie continued to present himself as an expert on "workingmen" because, he contended, he was one of them. In early 1904, he had quietly put himself forward to succeed Marcus Hanna as president of the National Civic Federation (NCF), an association of business and labor leaders founded five years earlier by Ralph Easley, a Chicago Republican and journalist, with the support of a number of influential midwestern industrialists. The NCF members—industrialists, union leaders, college presidents, clergymen, and politicians—were united in thinking that the greatest threat to domestic peace and prosperity was labor discontent, and that the only way to curtail strikes and prevent the Socialists from establishing an American beachhead was to bring labor and capital together to peaceably arbitrate their differences. The industrialists who signed on to the NCF pledged to recognize and work with responsible trades unions; the union leaders to do all they could to avoid strikes.

Carnegie was not elected NCF president in 1904, but was instead put on the executive committee, with the support of the labor leaders. This he viewed as proof that he had at long last cleansed his reputation of the stain of Homestead. "I was relieved from the feeling that I was considered responsible by labor generally, for the Homestead riot and the killing of workmen." As the papers reported the morning after Carnegie attended his first NCF meeting, he had been "especially interested in meeting Mr. [William] Weihe, who was one of the leading spirits in the Homestead strike of several years ago. Mr. Carnegie said that if he had been in America at the time the strike would never have taken the course it did."[11]

When, in 1907, Ralph Easley asked him to host a meeting of NCF labor leaders at his home, Carnegie, professing to know what workingmen wanted, agreed to do so, but only if it was arranged not as a "meeting" but as a "reception . . . with a supper after. No wine, but salads, coffee, ices etc. Madam and I receive the guests. I might say a few words of welcome later when supper came, but all should be informal. I see no use in holding a speechifying affair in our home. We wish to receive the labor leaders, only men of position among their fellows, and treat them as we should a party of our intimates whom we were glad to see & welcome to our home. That means a great deal, my friend . . . I like the working man, so does my dear wife, and wish to welcome them to our home, not to talk them to death, but in a friendly way shake hands with them. . . . They could see the gallery, my library, etc. etc. and make themselves at home."[12]

Easley was reluctant to disagree with Carnegie, but warned nonetheless that if the event were billed as a "reception," the labor leaders who attended would be open to criticism by the rank-and-file of their unions for attending a "social function" at a millionaire's mansion. Carnegie accepted Easley's recommendation that the meeting be arranged so that those guests who chose to come early might "spend from 8:15 to 9 o'clock in 'sight seeing' and social converse; then devote from 9 to 10 to a program of short speeches; from 10 to 10:30, or later, supper." August Belmont, the president of the NCF, had been asked by "some of the labor men," Easley wrote Carnegie, "how their wives should dress. . . . We told the ladies to wear high neck dresses and no hats, a room being arranged for checking their wraps."[13]

Easley had ulterior motives in asking Carnegie to host the spring meeting. He hoped that by drawing Carnegie more tightly into the inner circles of the NCF he might be able to elicit more funds. This was fine with Carnegie, who was only too happy to use the National Civic Federation and its labor leaders to validate his credentials as an enlightened expert and to apply the leverage he gained from his contributions to pressure its members into doing his bidding. When, in 1908, Easley requested funds to support the American Federation of Labor's appeal to the Supreme Court of a lower court decision outlawing boycotts, Carnegie agreed to contribute, but only on the condition that the labor leaders pledged in advance not to contest or protest a negative decision. "There is one member of the Civic Federation who will very promptly resign if it gives the slightest countenance to attacks upon the Supreme Court. I am as strong a friend of Labor and I think a wiser one than Mr. Gompers, but if we are to fail to preach and practice implicit obedience to the law as defined by the final tribunals, you can count me out and I mean to watch this point very carefully."[14]

THE CARNEGIES, as was their habit, returned to New York City at the end of October 1908 to vote for the Republican candidates for president of the United States and governor of New York: William Howard Taft and Charles Evans Hughes. Two weeks later, after both of his candidates had won election, Carnegie was on the front pages again. The *New York Times* reported on November 20—with other papers picking up the story immediately—that, in a forthcoming article, the former steelmaker was going to come out against the protective tariff on steel. "If the report is borne out . . . it will undoubtedly create a tremendous stir among the standpatters. . . . Democrats who heard the rumor tonight were in high glee over it." Carnegie was usually evasive when asked by a reporter as he left his mansion if the rumors were true. "'I had a fine game of golf to-day,' he said, 'and I am feeling mighty well as a result. Isn't this motor a smooth one. It's my favorite.'"

Carnegie's article calling for the elimination of the tariff was so politically incendiary that he had asked the *Century* editors to send advance copies to Roosevelt and Taft. When Taft requested that he withhold it for publication until after the election, he agreed to do so.

There should have been no great surprise over Carnegie's break with Republican orthodoxy. He insisted—and rightly—that he had advocated reductions in the tariff in the past and was now taking the next logical step in calling for its elimination "The writer has cooperated in making several reductions as steel manufacturers became able to bear reductions. Today they need no protection, unless perhaps in some new specialties unknown to the writer, because steel is now produced cheaper here than anywhere else. . . . The republic has become the home of steel, and this is the age of steel."[15]

Democratic papers like the *New York World* applauded his conversion; Republicans assailed his apostasy; a *New York Times* editorial declared that "the only thing to do with MR. ANDREW CARNEGIE is to refute him absolutely, to show that if he ever did know anything about the conditions of the steel business he has now forgotten it." The pro-tariff Republican chairman of the House Ways and Means Committee, hoping to discredit the old Scotsman by showing that he was, as the *Times* had asserted, out of touch with business and perhaps a bit daft besides, invited Carnegie to testify at the tariff hearings. When Carnegie demurred, he was issued a subpoena.

He was now right where he wanted to be, in the center of the storm, playing the role he played best: a righteous truth-telling man on a political ship of fools. And yet as much as he enjoyed his reputation as a man who spoke his mind regardless of the consequences, Carnegie knew that he was

"LYNCH HIM!"

taking no great chances in questioning the need for a protective tariff on iron and steel. The nation was moving, albeit in rather slow motion, toward free trade, and so was he. Even President-Elect Taft had endorsed tariff reform.

On November 25, Carnegie celebrated his seventy-third birthday. The *Times* put the birthday story on its front page, though it remained as confused as ever about his age. While the headline read, "SEVENTY-THREE! CARNEGIE," the text declared that "Andrew Carnegie is 71 years old to-day."

"Tomorrow Madam & I go to Washington dine with President," Carnegie wrote John Morley on December 6. "Attend several meetings for three days. You know President appointed me member Conservation National Resources—Also on Waterway Commission. . . . Never had so many duties to perform & as for urgent appeals to visit cities and speak I could be busy every day; I am not going to take one other duty,—Must save myself. . . . I ate a bad oyster or two & had to disappoint the people of Baltimore hence report of illness. Doctor kept me in for a day & all was well—Am in excellent health."[16]

Two weeks later, he was back in Washington to testify before the Ways and Means Committee hearing on tariffs. From the moment he entered the committee room in the morning until he left later that afternoon, he commanded the full attention of the committee, the press, and the spectators. With wit, a ready smile, disarming candor, and a total lack of decorum, he took over the proceedings, answered the questions he wanted to answer, deflected those he felt intrusive, lectured committee members on the steel business, corrected their errors, rephrased their queries, and, as the *New York Times* reported on December 22, "kept the room in a roar of laughter all through the day."

Minutes after the session had been gaveled to order, Carnegie set the tone for the day by interrupting Chairman Sereno Payne, the New York Republican, who had leaned over to whisper something to Congressman John Dalzell, the pro-tariff, pro-steel representative from Pittsburgh.

MR. CARNEGIE. Mr. Chairman, I would like to hear that remark that you just made to my friend Mr. Dalzell. [Great laughter.] That is not fair. Now, just tell us what you told him.

THE CHAIRMAN. I did not make a remark. I said, "We are getting a little more fun than information."

MR. CARNEGIE. I am sorry. I will step out if I am not giving information Mr. Chairman, I can quite understand how you have fun, because the chairman is as full of information as I am; but I am here to tell the truth, I am bound to do it, I have sworn to tell the whole truth, and come what may I am going to do it.

THE CHAIRMAN. Of course I did not mean that as a reflection on you.

MR. CARNEGIE. I have no suspicion that you did. On the contrary, I think you whispered to Dalzell: "The jig is up." [Great laughter.][17]

Carnegie proceeded from this point on to alternately mystify, baffle, bamboozle, and infuriate committee members by ridiculing their attempts to understand the steel industry, disputing the figures they had gathered, and assuring them they were in over their heads when it came to business. "There you are again, gentlemen," he interrupted Dalzell, who was trying to introduce figures to demonstrate that production costs were rising faster than profits. "If you are going to assume that you gentlemen, who know nothing about steel, can in a cursory examination of the case get at the facts of the case, you are deluding yourselves."[18]

When Bourke Cockran, the Democrat from New York who had made a career of criticizing Carnegie and other high-tariff advocates, remarked that Carnegie's smile signaled that he agreed with something Cockran had said, the old man interrupted him: "Mr. Cockran, please do not interpret my smile. I am a born laugher, and I have laughed all through my life, and confronted all the troubles of life with laughter. I have escaped a great many troubles by laughing, and I would not lose that little faculty for anything."[19]

Carnegie's recall of past events was excellent when he wanted to answer a question. When he preferred not to, he claimed loss of memory. "You put a man here who has not been in business for seven years, and naturally, his memory is not so good. Do you imagine that his memory can go back and fix dates? Dates are obliterated in my mind. . . . Because you really must remember I have retired for seven years, and to call upon me unexpectedly to go back thirty or forty years, I am unable to do that."[20]

He showed little respect for anyone on the committee, including Representative Dalzell, to whose campaign coffers he had contributed thousands of dollars and with whom he had consulted in years past in writing the tariff schedules for iron and steel. Brazenly—albeit with good humor—he suggested that the congressmen give up trying to understand the steel business and take the advice of businessmen like himself. The capitalist system was not perfect, but it was, for the most part, self-correcting. It had to be left alone to operate under its own natural laws, not those imposed by politicians. When asked what would happen to steel companies smaller and weaker than U.S. Steel if the tariff were removed, Carnegie professed that he didn't much care. Companies that could not compete deserved to go under. "Do you want the Government to be supporting all these broken concerns that are suffering either from present mismanagement or past mistakes?"[21]

Much like President Theodore Roosevelt, he did not think "bigness" per se was bad; on the contrary, it was good for the economy, as it resulted in lower costs for consumers. The small manufacturer was a relic of the past. "The time has gone past when in this great country the things that are used by the hundreds of thousands of tons, of steel, can be economically produced on a small scale." When Chairman Payne protested that he was "very reluctant indeed to believe that the day of opportunity for the man of fairly modest means and the man who is not even a great genius has gone by, and that he must simply operate under the shadow of the protective wing and care of the big man," Carnegie interrupted him, as one would a naive schoolboy.

MR. CARNEGIE. My dear sir, the enterprising man under the shadow of what you call the big man, the big establishment, has far more opportunity of rising to fortune than he ever had of conducting a small business.

As proof, he cited the example of his forty-two former partners in the steel business—one of whom was Charles Schwab—who had begun their careers as employees of Carnegie Steel and climbed the ranks to become partners. The age of the bootstrap entrepreneur, the self-made, rags-to-riches small businessman, had come to an end. It was high time the politicians understood this and stopped trying to write legislation or set tariff schedules to protect small businesses that were destined for failure. "Those who want to start on their own account without capital betray a lack of judgment that will prevent them from ever being successful men." The millionaires of the future would follow the route taken by Charlie Schwab and hitch their stars to rising corporations.[22]

In the end, neither Carnegie's testimony nor President-elect Taft's commitment to reform were enough to push Congress to effect significant changes in the tariff system. This only confirmed Carnegie in his belief that the politicians would do best to abandon their attempts at regulating the economy. Two months after his appearance before the Ways and Means Committee, Carnegie again suggested in an interview published in the February 13, 1909, *New York Times* that congressmen did not know enough about business to set tariff schedules. He recommended, instead, that some sort of "permanent non-partisan commission of experts" be empowered to set rates. The "industrial world" was, he declared, "about to undergo the most momentous change known in its history, even more far-reaching than was the change from the individual domestic manufacturer, manufacturing at home, to the factory system, and the huge establishments of to-day." Once upon a time, competition had assured "reasonable prices for the consumer," but that was no longer the case. "Some of our most important industries to-day are only nominally competitive and in reality are monopolies so far as an understanding exists as to prices that will prevail.

These virtual monopolies must be controlled in some way or another." Carnegie's rather daring solution was to establish what he called a "supreme industrial court" to regulate prices. That, in interfering with the corporations' right to set their own prices, he was treading on sacred ground did not much concern him. The age of monopoly capitalism was dawning and required bold new solutions to protect the consumer from runaway corporate collusion. His industrial court would, at the very least, protect manufacturers from further interference by elected politicians.

The *Times* responded in a February 14 editorial by ridiculing his "supreme industrial court." Would the court have the power to "mandamus consumers to buy?" Would it be able to "fix wages as well as prices?"

Carnegie gave as good as he got in his response. "This is a serious problem," he wrote the *New York Times* editors on February 16, "and it is to be hoped you will some day, after studying the question, give us some light . . . if any be revealed to you." The courts, he asserted, had in the recent New York Gas Company case directed the company "to refund many millions of dollars because its price was too high. A monopoly could not be permitted [the court had ruled] to make its own price. . . . There is nothing alarming in this: capital is perfectly safe in the gas company, although it is under court control. So will all capital be, although under Government control."

There was no chance that newspaper editors, the president-elect, or Congress was going to take Carnegie's proposals seriously. And he knew this. But he had accomplished what he wanted: to put before the public the notion that the competitive capitalist economy of the nineteenth century, the one in which he had built his fortune, was no more, and no amount of hand-wringing or legislative tinkering was going to bring it back to life.

That he had both criticized Congress for its meddling and called for government control betrayed no contradiction in his thinking. He had, on the contrary, become an advocate of "government control," because he feared congressional meddling. Carnegie's proposal, if effected, would remove the politically volatile questions of trusts, tariffs, prices, and profits from congressional oversight to an appointed "industrial commission of experts."

AS THE DAYS of the Roosevelt presidency wound down, Carnegie positioned himself front and center among the president's closest intimates.

He peppered Roosevelt with letters and gifts; they lunched together, motored together, and attended formal dinners with their wives at their sides. Like the president's other admirers, Carnegie had his own ideas as to what Roosevelt should do once he left the White House. Two years earlier, in response to a letter from Carnegie exhorting him to take on "great problems" like world peace, Roosevelt had mentioned that he "sometimes" wished there was no custom forbidding sitting presidents from leaving the country and meeting overseas with European heads of state.[23]

Carnegie remembered this and prepared to set in motion a series of meetings on world peace between the ex-president and the "responsible authorities" of France, England, and Germany. With no need to stand for reelection and no official responsibilities in Washington, Roosevelt would be able to apply his skills as a diplomat, his unquestioned popularity, and his remarkable personal charm to entice them into joining with him to create a "League of Peace." Carnegie was willing to grant Roosevelt his wish to go big-game hunting and would, in fact, supply much of the funding to pay for it, but "after Africa, then the real 'big game.' Meet the men who rule European nations, then you have a source of power otherwise unobtainable—You promise to become the 'Man of destiny.'" Carnegie's agenda for Roosevelt began with a face-to-face meeting with Kaiser Wilhelm II. Of all the world's leaders, the kaiser appeared, at least in the context of The Hague conferences, to be the least willing to talk peace, but this didn't faze Carnegie. Despite every sign to the contrary, Carnegie was convinced that Wilhelm II was committed to peace. When, in October 1908, the kaiser again put his imperial foot in his mouth by publishing an article in the *Daily Telegraph* criticizing the British press and politicians and insisting that the enlarged German fleet posed no danger to Britain, Carnegie leaped to his defense. "Our impulsive friend the Emperor has made a slip," he admitted in a handwritten note to Roosevelt in mid-November. "He is so deeply hurt at being held up as the enemy of his Mother's country [Wilhelm's mother was the daughter of Queen Victoria]—He is really a fine character. It will all blow over."[24]

By refusing to rule out Carnegie's plans for him, Roosevelt only encouraged him to keep up the pressure. The day before Taft's inaugural, Carnegie sent Roosevelt his and Mrs. Carnegie's greetings "upon your return to your own sweet home, where you will find some respite from public cares—at last. 'Well done' is the verdict. You are to take rank with the foremost who have held the highest office upon Earth." He could not help but remind Roosevelt that he had not yet fulfilled his Carnegie-predicted destiny as peacemaker. "The past is secure; as far as the future, 'The sibyl still remains silent.'" Carnegie hoped that that future would bring the Carnegie and Roosevelt families closer together. "I have known six Presidents more or less intimately but never one to whom I have been so strongly attached. Goodbye to the President and Presidentess [the term "First Lady" had yet to be coined], but Mrs. Carnegie and I earnestly hope that to the man and woman there is to be no good bye while life exists. Maybe you could come & spend a night or two with us some time when visiting New York. We should so like you to do so. We can never get to know people until we visit them at their homes. If you could only come to us at Skibo & spend a week or two?" To sweeten his invitation to Scotland, Carnegie promised to arrange for an honorary degree to be offered by St. Andrews, "the university that gave Franklin his first degree."[25]

There was no response from Roosevelt, who was preparing to leave the country for a yearlong safari in Africa.

CARNEGIE made every effort now to establish a role for himself in the Taft White House. "Have spoken twice at ceremonies following President-Elect & had some talk," he wrote Morley in early January 1909. "A splendid president sure—No mistake." In February, he wrote again, on his way to "stop over in Washington to see the new President. Can hardly expect ever to get upon quite such intimate terms as with our Mutual friend, but we shall see. Mr. Taft is going to secure what Roosevelt rendered securable. He'll prove a good binder of the sheaves."[26]

Like his predecessor, William Howard Taft resented the little Scotsman's meddling in government affairs, but he recognized Carnegie's value—as a campaign contributor and cheerleader for "progressive" economic policies—and tolerated his excesses: his unremitting flattery when he wanted something, his knack for putting himself in the center of a controversy, his oversized ego. As irritating as Carnegie could be, there was something irresistibly amusing about the "Star-spangled Scotchman."

The year after his election, Taft was honored at "an oyster roast" and invited Carnegie to ride with him to Cape Henry, Virginia, on his "special train." Archie Butt, the army officer assigned as Taft's personal assistant, wrote his sister that Carnegie had entertained them both on the ride to the event. He was "more shriveled up than ever, but he is very humorous and at time witty. The President says like all wily Scotchmen [Carnegie] is funniest when he does not mean to be. He loves to talk about giving his money away, and amused and interested the President . . . by giving him some of the plans he had for making himself poor."[27]

THIRTY-EIGHT

"So Be It," 1908–1910

T RY AS HE MIGHT to give it all away, Andrew Carnegie in his seventh year of retirement was still burdened with hundreds of millions of dollars of gold bonds. He had no choice now but to redouble his energies and enlist his friends in his last great task: to wisely give away his fortune.

In January of 1908, six weeks after his seventy-second birthday, he sent out letters to the people he most respected. "Dear Friend," he wrote. "If you have any spare time at your command, will you kindly give me an answer to this question:—If you had say five or ten millions of dollars to put to the best use possible, what would you do with it? Prize given for the best answer." Theodore Roosevelt got such a letter; so did Samuel Church, the secretary of the Carnegie Institute board in Pittsburgh; Secretary of State Elihu Root; ex-President Grover Cleveland; and President Nicholas Murray Butler of Columbia. Butler proposed that $10 million be donated to Columbia University; Grover Cleveland, that funds be given to Princeton; Root, that a sort of "Rhodes fellowships" program be established to bring Latin American students to the United States. When there was no response from President Roosevelt, Carnegie sent him a second letter assuring him that there was "no hurry" in making a proposal. "The fact is that after spending about $50 million on Libraries, the great cities are generally supplied and I am groping for the next field to cultivate. . . . I shall wait for some time and get all the advice I can before taking up the new line." He closed by comparing his responsibilities as a philanthropist to those of the ex-president. "You have a hard task at present but the distribution of money judiciously is not without its difficulties also and involves harder work than ever acquisition of wealth did. I could play with that and laugh."[1]

Bertram and the officers of his various trusts took care of most requests for funds, but Carnegie had to respond himself to petitions from friends, politicians, and assorted notables. The college presidents, of whom he knew dozens, were the most insistent. While his Foundation for the Advancement of Teaching funded faculty pensions, it did not give money for other purposes. Requests for fellowships, buildings, faculty chairs, or endowments were sent directly to Carnegie in New York. Petitions from well-endowed universities, even those run by the men he respected most in the world, like Nicholas Murray Butler of Columbia, Andrew White of Cornell, and David Starr Jordan of Stanford, were invariably denied. "The case of Stanford University fails to arouse the desire on my part to help," he wrote Jordan sometime in 1906. "You tell me it has $16 millions in endowments. The colleges I have been helping for two years, already about two hundred in number, do not average more than $200,000 to $250,000 in endowments, and after deep consideration I decided that it was better to help the small colleges than the large ones."[2]

Instead of supporting the big schools, he had, he explained to Roosevelt in January 1908, been busy "for several years giving aid to small colleges. . . . Mr. Bertram tells me we have assisted about three hundred and fifty colleges and have about fifty under advisement. . . . Contributions to these small colleges aggregate between $19 and $20 million, and the amount is growing."[3]

Many of these small colleges were, in fact, not colleges at all, but technical schools like the one he had established in Pittsburgh. When in the spring of 1909, William McConway, who was charged with overseeing the Carnegie Technical Schools in Pittsburgh, wrote to ask Carnegie for funds to raise the salaries of "certain staff" to the level paid by other institutions, Carnegie reminded him that the technical schools were not like other institutions.

It seems a shame that certain staff should not be paid by us what others are paying. . . . But Yale University, Boston Tech., Colgate University and Hamilton College, might all be considered institutions of higher learning. We are not of that grade and have no intention entering it, being technical schools, in which class, however, we should hope to be at the top. Our field seems to me to be entirely different from that of the Scientific Schools and Universities. We aim to reach the children of poor people, especially those who have to work thru the day and acquire knowledge at night. The richest ore is oftenest found deep down and it is in the low stratum of human life we will find the jewels that will glisten for ages. I was a working boy myself. . . . Naturally I sympathize with this class and I wish my aid to go to this class.[4]

Carnegie was committed to funding schools for the children of the working people, black and white. He explained to Frederick Lynch, who had asked why he didn't fund Atlanta and Fisk universities, that he was not "opposed to the higher education of the Negro," but agreed with Booker T. Washington that black students required specific technical training for the jobs available for them. Washington, who had contacted Carnegie in 1890 to solicit funds for Tuskegee, received his first grant of $20,000 for a library in 1900. In 1906, Washington arranged a special railroad trip to Tuskegee for his most favored donors. "Mr. Carnegie was very happy," Lynch, who accompanied him on the trip, reported in his recollections. "He saw the library which he had given, every brick of which had been made by the students and laid in place by them. He visited all the shops and saw the boys learning trades by making things to be used on the grounds and by building shops and houses, and saw the girls learning dressmaking by making their own clothes. . . . He was greatly impressed and said one day that Mr. Washington was one of the geniuses of the century." Carnegie backed up his praise for Washington's educational practice with dollars: $620,000 for Tuskegee and $441,045 for Hampton.[5]

Carnegie, given to hero worship spoke of Booker T. Washington with the same reverence he used when referring to William Gladstone, Matthew Arnold, Abraham Lincoln, and Herbert Spencer. A 1903 get-well note from Washington was saved among his papers with a penciled notation in Carnegie's handwriting, "Keep for *Auto[biography]*." Washington was not only "the combined Moses and Joshua of his people," he was, Carnegie thought, an educational genius (perhaps because his commitment to technical training most resembled Carnegie's own). Carnegie invited him often to Ninety-first Street, introduced him to his friends, included him among the select few who were privileged to meet John Morley on his tour, and hosted him at Skibo in the summer of 1910. "My friend, Booker Washington, perhaps the most remarkable man living today, taking into account his birth as a slave and his position now as the acknowledged leader of his people, is coming to England," Carnegie wrote a William Archer just before Washington's arrival. "He could be induced to give a lecture in London and one in Edinburgh. I should think he would be a drawing card. He has recently made a triumphal tour through the Southwestern States, being received by white and black,—no hall big enough to hold his audiences. It occurs to me that you might be able to recommend this matter to the proper authorities, whom you know and I do not."[6]

Carnegie believed the cause of Negro education and uplift so vitally important to the future of the nation that when invited to give a lecture to the Edinburgh Philosophical Institution in 1907, he chose as his topic "The Negro in America." Slavery might once have been a blot on the "Triumphant Democracy," he argued, but no more. In its place had arisen a new people who, with the beneficent support of northern whites like himself, would in the course of time prosper and multiply. The Negro population in the South, Carnegie reported, had risen steadily, a sure sign of their "fitness." The portrait Carnegie painted of the position of the African-American in the early twentieth century South was unrecognizably positive. There was no mention of lynching, sharecropping, peonage, Jim Crow, or disenfranchisement. Instead, Carnegie pointed to the progress the southern Negro had made in literacy, land and home ownership, gainful employment, and the literary arts. "All signs are encouraging, never so much so as today. . . . What is to be the final result of the white and black races living together in centuries to come need not concern us. They may remain separate and apart as now or may intermingle. That lies upon the 'lap of the gods.'" While acknowledging that because the black race was younger it was less developed than the white, Carnegie was emphatic that it would become more civilized, more capable, more prosperous in time. His faith in Negro progress enraged southern racists like Tom Watson who, the *New York Times* reported in a front-page article on February 4, 1910, "denounced the iron master as a 'despicable creature,' 'an ass,' and a defamer of the Scotch" for claiming that the "lowest negro of the South is more advanced than were his (Carnegie's) ancestors in Scotland two hundred years ago."[7]

CARNEGIE ran his philanthropic empire much as he had his businesses. He kept in touch with the officers in charge of each, received and studied their reports, and monitored their spending. Having hand-picked them all, he had faith in their judgment and, with a few exceptions, let them run their organizations as they saw fit. Those that did their job well and made a case for more funding got it. In 1909, he increased the $10 million endowment of his Washington-based Carnegie Institution by $2 million, then added another $10 million in 1911. From 1911 to 1915, he added $6.25 million to the $10 million endowment for the Carnegie Foundation for the Advancement of Teaching. The Dunfermline Trust got an additional $1.25 million in 1911. His library and organ programs and the Carnegie Institute and Technical School in Pittsburgh continued to receive regular increases in funding.

The only cause he had yet to generously fund with an endowment was the one that mattered most to him: international peace. He supported a large number of peace and arbitration societies on both sides of the Atlantic, but he did not give any of them more than a few thousand dollars annually.[8]

The peace activists were, as far as he could see, utopian dreamers with no understanding of business or politics. When in April 1905, Edwin Mead, a former editor of *New England Magazine,* solicited funds for an international peace society, Carnegie promised to donate $125,000 if Mead could raise an equal sum elsewhere. He suggested that the word "peace" be excised from its name in favor of "arbitration" and that further thought be given to how the new society would be administered. "If we could only get the effective organization the funds would be forthcoming. So far the path does not seem clear to me but it may be revealed [in] this, the greatest of all causes."[9]

Mead interpreted Carnegie's response as an invitation to continue discussion of his new peace "organization." He badly misjudged the old man's intentions. "One objection that arises to me" in endowing a new organization, Carnegie brusquely informed Mead, "is the copious correspondence that must follow a gift, especially in your case, for you are a most prolific writer." Carnegie already supported several peace societies. He saw no need to fund another. "I never like scattering my shot . . . I wish to feel that I am contributing towards an aboslute necessity."[10]

In January 1909, Nicholas Murray Butler forwarded to Carnegie yet another proposal for an international peace trust, accompanied by letters of support from the men Carnegie most trusted, including among them Andrew White, former Secretary of State John Forster, and Elihu Root.

Carnegie dismissed Butler's proposal, though not without a note of encouragement. "At present I feel that it is too much in the air," he wrote,
"much talk about bringing people together, and all of this sort of thing, and
nothing of a definite character. The avenues of expenditure should be dis-
tinctly stated."[11]

IF EVER A MAN had a gift for savoring life's pleasures, it was Andrew
Carnegie. His major source of worry for the past three years, his daughter's
health, was quickly receding into the past. In March 1908, as the family
prepared to sail for England, Baba's brace was finally removed, and for the
first time in two years, she was able to stand upright and walk on two legs.
Many years later, when Margaret Carnegie was asked by her granddaugh-
ter and namesake, Margaret Thomson, whether Grandpa Naigie believed
in God, she told the story of how when she walked into his room for the
first time without her splints, "he went down on his knees . . . Grandma
felt that he was giving thanks to God for her recovery. . . . Why else would
he have gone down on his knees?"[12]

    With Baba improved, the Carnegies were no longer obliged to winter
on Cumberland Island and were able to spend more of the season in New
York City. Carnegie had become so smitten with golf that he couldn't bear
the thought of giving up the game during the winter. Fortunately, the St.
Andrew's Golf Club in Hastings-on-Hudson was but an hour or so from
Manhattan. The club had been founded in 1888 by two Scotsmen from
Dunfermline. Carnegie was elected to membership in 1896, though he did
not pay his dues and officially become a member until the following year.
In the early 1900s, after personally endorsing the club's new mortgage,
Carnegie built himself a weekend cottage on club property, just north of
the clubhouse. It was here—"in our Golf Cottage, a pretty little gem, cottage furniture throughout, no finery"—that the family spent many quiet
days and nights, including New Year's Day 1908. The cottage was indeed a
gem: wood paneled, rustic-looking, with open beams on the ceiling, and a
large fireplace in the main room. It provided Carnegie with everything he
needed. A photograph taken in the early 1910s shows him with his feet up,
a newspaper in his hand, sitting in front of the fire. Another shows him
formally dressed, with a white handkerchief in his pocket, sitting down to
a meal at the dining-room table.[13]

According to Burton Hendrick, Carnegie had a long list of potential golf partners, including Nicholas Murray Butler, who could be called upon at a moment's notice. "His secretary would call up the favored devotee suggesting his presence at Ninety-first Street at a particular hour. On cold days butlers and friends would bundle the little figure in a heavy coat, with mufflers, huge turned-up collar, and hat drawn well over the ears, until nothing protruded except nose and goggled eyes; the car would emit a honk and off the gay party would whirl to the beautiful Westchester hills." "Weather superb so far," he wrote Morley on December 31, 1907, "& I'll play golf & Motor with Lou & Baba.—Never was better."[14]

By the turn of the century, Carnegie had become so notorious a golfer that he was proposed for the presidency of the United States Golf Association. The charms of golf were many, as he would write in 1911 at age seventy-five. The first was that it was played "under the sky. . . . Every breath seems to drive away weakness and disease, securing for us longer terms of happy days here on hear. . . . No doctor like Doctor Golf." Next in importance was golf's "power to affect the temper and especially the tongue. We have only to remain silent to produce unusual results." Unlike other sports, where the competitors drew farther apart as the game proceeded, in golf "men become dearer friends than ever; the oftener they meet on the green, the fonder they become of each other."[15]

Carnegie was not a particularly good golfer, but this did not detract from his love of the game. He enjoyed the competition, wanted to win, and was said to sulk when he did not. He taught Louise and Baba and played with them whenever they would consent to join him. As proud as he was of Baba's ability to memorize lines of poetry or ask probing questions about theology, he was proudest of all of her golf game. In 1903, he boasted to his cousin Dod that his daughter had finished her nine holes in 91. In July 1906, just before she injured her leg, he wrote Samuel Church in Pittsburgh, that she finished the nine-hole course at Skibo "in 81—her record—pretty good for 6¼ years." That Baba was, in fact, three years older at the time, did not diminish her achievement. (Was Carnegie exaggerating her age to make her score more spectacular or had he forgotten how old she was?) One of the sad byproducts of Baba's years in braces was that Carnegie was deprived of the joy of playing nine holes of golf with his daughter.[16]

Margaret Carnegie emerged whole from her ordeal an attractive young girl with a slight, almost undetectable limp. Her illness was relegated to

A GALLERY OF GOLF ENTHUSIASTS

the distant past, never mentioned, barely remembered in family stories. Andrew could now concentrate his attention on her intellectual growth, her capacity to memorize the passages he gave her from Burns and Shakespeare, her incredulity when it came to Bible stories, and her curiosity about all the things young girls are curious about.

Carnegie prepared a list of poems which he gave Nana to help Baba "learn by heart." She learned other poems from hearing her father recite them. "I must tell you," he wrote Morley in March 1909, the month of her twelfth birthday, "Margaret astonished me the other night by repeating the Seven Ages of Man [and several other poems] . . . All perfect & in fine style—She is developing fast—puzzles her Mother about certain things in Holy Writ; now & then that give Madam some anxiety. . . . She has grown very fast in stature recently." A month later, in another of his Sunday letters, he repeated himself, with evident glee: "She has become absorbed in Shakespeare, as I always told her she would be. . . . She seems to inherit her Father's Knack of absorbing Shakespeare—I repeated pages when not much older & can do it yet, but she grows troublesome on Bible stories, very, her Mother stalled & sometimes appalled at her temerity—

but she has past the Fairytale period." In December of that same year, he confided to Morley, in the few sentences he seemed to reserve in every letter for a report on his daughter, that Margaret continued "to grow & is really the Young Lady, troubling her Mother with questions which you & I would be but poorly prepared to answer. She cannot be put off."[17]

Margaret had never been to school. That fall, at age twelve and a half, she had begun taking formal lessons with a tutor recommended by Miss Clara B. Spence, preparatory to entering Miss Spence's school the next autumn. When the Carnegies asked whether they might interrupt Margaret's schooling and take her with them to the west coast, Miss Spence agreed—it would have been difficult to say no to a Carnegie—but suggested that Margaret's tutor, Anne Brinkerhoff, accompany the party.

The six-week journey, of which Margaret kept a travel diary, began at 7:20 on the morning of February 14, 1910, when the Carnegie party, Miss Brinkerhoff, and Baba's nanny took the Twenty-third Street ferry to New Jersey, where they boarded their private car, "Olivette," for the trip south to Philadelphia, and west across the Alleghenies to Pittsburgh. At Pittsburgh, while the Olivette was parked in the Pennsylvania Railroad shed awaiting the train that would haul it to Chicago, Carnegie invited officials from his institute to meet with him in his railway car. No sooner had they sat down to talk than "Train No. 15," waiting to be taken into Union Station, crashed into the Olivette, shattering vases and hurling ice pitchers, dishes of food, and the diminutive Mr. Carnegie to the floor. The doctor was called for and having pronounced Carnegie fit, though rather pale, the Olivette was coupled to a westbound train.[18]

From the private platform at the back of their car, the Carnegies watched the country recede behind them. Margaret remembered getting off the train and going for walks in the Kansas prairies, in Dodge City, and again in Arizona. Their final destination was Santa Barbara, where they were met at the station by local officials and by the chauffeur driving the Pierce-Arrow Carnegie had leased. "Such a welcome . . . the Scotch society gave Daddy! They had the bagpipes and a band there who played Scotch aires, and then a little girl in a kilt gave Daddy a lovely bunch of roses tied with a tartan ribbon."

Margaret spent most of her time during the six-week vacation in the company of Nana and her tutor. She saw her father in the afternoon when, after her lessons were finished, the family went for a drive in the Pierce-

Arrow. On their second day in Santa Barbara, they visited the Potter Golf Club. "Daddy was delighted with the golf course. Poor Daddy! It was hard for him to see it when he cannot play. I can sympathize with him." Carnegie, now seventy-five, was "not quite well." There was something, we don't know what, the matter with his leg, which left him unable to join his daughter and wife on their walks.

After two weeks in Santa Barbara, the family traveled in their private railway car north to Monterey, where they stayed at the Hotel del Monte and visited "the library Daddy gave at Pacific Grove. We all were delighted with it." At Monterey, they switched to an even more "comfortable" rail-road car, and visited, in succession, Santa Cruz, San Francisco, and Pasadena. Wherever they traveled, the Carnegies were saluted with Scottish flags, foods, fauna, and music. Carnegie was not just a visiting hero, but a foreign exotic as well.

After their final library visit at Pasadena, the Carnegies were packed into motorcars for an excursion to the Mount Wilson Observatory, which was funded by the Carnegie Institution in Washington, D.C.

Margaret thought the observatory, with its "wonderful instruments for making observations and pictures" was interesting, though she was sorry she "could not see something" through the telescopes. Carnegie toured the facilities, peered through the telescopes, chatted with the astronomers, and had several photographs taken with George Ellery Hale, the founding director. Walter Adams, who would succeed Hale, recalled later that Carnegie made sure before each photo was taken that he was standing on "the higher position on a slope since he was somewhat sensitive about his height."[19]

They headed east again and spent three days at the Grand Canyon, where Margaret, with her mother, tutor, and nanny, went on walks, drives, and picnics. There is no mention of Carnegie, who must have been giving more speeches. On March 30, Margaret turned thirteen: "After breakfast I opened my presents of which I had a great many. In fact all the things I most wanted. Daddy gave me a beautiful purple vase made of cloysinnay [cloisonné] which I fell in love with at 'Sing Fat's' in San Francisco. . . . The car was all decorated with paper wisteria, also from 'Sing Fat's.'" With this entry, Margaret's travel book comes to an end. In the front flyleaf she had written that, if lost, "the finder will be awarded $5 in America, £1 in Britain."[20]

"Had stirring times in the West," Carnegie reported to Morley on his return to New York in mid-April, "speechifying almost daily, more or less. Never suspected I was so great a personage out there. Madam and I going to Washington Monday next to Dedicate beautiful building—Temple of peace." A week later, back from Washington, he informed Morley in his Sunday letter that he and Louise had been "feted" there: "2500 handshakes, awful . . . but the President stood it & we were in for it along side."[21]

Carnegie refused to let age slow him down. The only reminder of time passing was the now steady procession of death notices and funerals of friends and loved ones. In the spring of 1909, he got word that Henry Rogers, Sam Clemens's friend—and benefactor—had died. "Gone & only sixty-eight & here you & I are left & both in good health though older men," he wrote Clemens at once. "Pity he did not retire years ago. I tell you my Friend no man is fit to meet business conditions in old age. I have seen too many fail. Fortunately you are clear of troubles & have only to moralize upon life as a looker on, so with me,—never to make another dollar was my resolve & I've kept it. . . . We are en route for Paris & London, Madam & Daughter & myself—the three all very well." The letter was signed: "Good night Saint Mark, Ever your devoted, Andrew Carnegie."[22]

In November, Richard Watson Gilder died. "My greatest loss, a pure white soul," he wrote Morley. "No one of my Circle here can leave such a void."[23]

And then Clemens took sick. Carnegie tried to make light of his friend's illness. "I am just waiting for Saint Mark's return," he wrote Albert Bigelow Paine, Clemens's friend and biographer, who had taken him to Bermuda to recuperate. "It is very hard for me when my confessor is absent so long. I need him. I am in sore straits. He must give me an opportunity to get absolution."[24]

Clemens returned to Connecticut just before Christmas. Carnegie welcomed him back with a postcard, mailed on Christmas Eve: "Hail Saint Mark. Back again to your nest. Merry Christmas and many of them." He signed it: "Ever your devoted discipline and fellow saint in the flesh." It is doubtful that Clemens got the card. On the day it was mailed, his youngest daughter Jean died in the bathtub, after an epileptic seizure. Alone now, with two of his three adult children and his wife dead, Clemens sailed back to Bermuda for the winter. When he returned to Connecticut in April 1910, there was a letter waiting for him from Carnegie: "Dear Saint, So glad you are reported better this morning. Gives one hopes you are to weather this storm and be spared to us a while longer—so be it. . . . When you get real chatty again if you can [and] are not coming down [to New York City] I'd like to make a pilgrimage to your shrine just to get a few sniffs of a real genuine work a day Saint." He added as a postscript: "I have sent you a few bottles of Saintly fluid."[25]

We don't know if Clemens had a chance to read Carnegie's last letter, written on April 16. He died five days later. "A blank in my life is caused by his departure," Carnegie wrote Paine, before departing for Britain and his own last great adventure.[26]

THIRTY-NINE

The Best Laid Schemes, 1909–1911

SINCE 1848, when his family arrived in New York Harbor from Dunfermline, Andrew Carnegie had been a child of two worlds. He had put down roots in America without having to uproot himself from Scotland. If his early allegiance to "the English-speaking race," manifested in his calls for Anglo-American federation, had been narrowly based on cultural and family ties, by the mid-1900s, after a lifetime of travel back and forth between Britain, Europe, and America, he had become a dyed-in-the-wool internationalist. Although as a young man he had indulged in sentimental musings about the "brotherhood of man," his latter-day internationalism was materially based. The nations and peoples of the world were, he now argued, tied together by indissoluble threads of traded goods. "We are coming to understand," he wrote in the *New York Times Sunday Magazine* on April 7, 1907, "that the human race is one. . . . The interest of thousands who depend on the manufacture of agricultural implements or machinery of other sorts is at stake when the farms of Russia are lying untilled or the factories of Germany are closed because men are off to the wars." Every war in the future would be a world war, with consequences felt beyond the battlements and the home fronts. "We may be disinterested in the issues over which the conflict is joined, but we are vitally interested in the conflict. . . . The world is getting to be like a workshop in which it is an impertinence and an outrage for two men to drop their tools and engage in a fisticuff and a scuffle to the destruction of the whole shop and the destruction of machines and of products upon them."

Given these ties, from which there was no escape, it was imperative, Carnegie argued, that the nations of the world establish organizations and

"ALL IS PEACE AND GOOD WILL. THE WORLD MOVES."
—ANDREW CARNEGIE

define processes to defuse crises and arbitrate disputes before they escalated into armed conflicts. At various moments, as the situation suited, he advocated bilateral treaties of arbitration, international disarmament conferences, a permanent world court, and the organization of a league of peace with an active police force. The specific shape of such proposals mattered less to him than that something be put in place before it was too late.

His immediate concern early in the new century was the escalating naval arms race between the British and the Germans. The Liberal government in Britain had, on taking office in late 1905, pledged to slow down its production of new battleships, hoping that the German government would follow suit. It did not. Responding to the British construction of the world's first Dreadnought, a battleship that was larger, faster, and equipped with ten guns instead of the standard four, the Germans set out to build their own monster battleships. The British then stepped up their production. In 1908, the first lord of the Admiralty asked for funding for two Dreadnoughts; in 1909, he requested funds to build six a year for the next three years; a month later, he increased his request to eight new Dreadnoughts. After a fierce debate in the cabinet, Prime Minister Herbert

Asquith agreed to fund four monster battleships in 1909, with an additional four to be added in 1910 "if careful monitoring of the German construction program proved them necessary."[1]

Carnegie's solution to the crisis was ingenious—and unworkable. In a series of letters to the editor and public remarks, he suggested a naval alliance between the Americans and the British. With U.S. battleships protecting the North Atlantic and the Royal Navy the Pacific, neither nation would need new battleships. Such an alliance would preserve the peace by discouraging the Germans from attacking the possessions of either nation, knowing that an attack on one would bring retaliation by the other. Unfortunately, the idea that the British and American governments would ever contemplate coordinating their navies—or entering a formal alliance to do so—was preposterous. It was never going to happen.[2]

In major addresses before a peace rally at Carnegie Hall and at the annual meeting of the New York Peace Society at the Hotel Astor, Carnegie argued that armies and navies did not ensure peace, but rather provoked war. "It is true that every nation regards and proclaims its own armaments as instruments of Peace only . . . but just as naturally every nation regards every other nation's armaments as clearly instruments of war. . . . Thus each nation suspects all the others, and only a spark is needed to set fire to the mass of inflammable material." Men with pistols in their hands were more likely to shoot one another; nations with armies and navies more likely to engage in war. It did not require much imagination to envisage a scenario where a minor incident might lead to world war, perhaps a drunken altercation between British and German marines. "Under the influence of alcohol . . . one is wounded, blood is shed, and the pent up passions of the people of both countries sweep all to the winds."[3]

Carnegie's prescience was remarkable. Only five years hence, an Austrian archduke would be assassinated by a Serbian student terrorist. The European nations would mobilize their armies, each claiming it was doing so for defensive purposes. With no mechanism in place to arbitrate the dispute, the armies remained in place, the dispute unresolved peaceably. Then blood was shed and "the pent up passions of the people [swept] all to the winds," as Carnegie had feared. The result was the Great War, a continent ravaged, and tens of millions of soldiers and civilians left dead, maimed, stateless, destitute.

Carnegie did not in 1909 regard such an outcome as inevitable, but only because he believed that the European leaders would come to understand, as he had, the dangers inherent in spending more and more of their national incomes on armies and navies. "To save the nations from themselves there must sooner or later emerge from the present unparalleled increase of armaments a league of peace embracing the most advanced nations." In his address to the New York Peace Society in late April, which the *New York Times* reported under the headline: "CARNEGIE FEARS WAR; PLEADS FOR PEACE. ONLY A SPARK NEEDED, HE DECLARES, TO PLUNGE ENGLAND AND GERMANY INTO BATTLE," Carnegie suggested that the United States, "at heart friendly toward all the world and lying beyond the vortex of the militarism which engulfs Europe," should take the lead in organizing a League of Peace.[4]

Carnegie had no doubt that his proposals—for a naval alliance and a League of Peace—once effectuated, would bring about world peace. The question was how best to get that notion across to those world leaders whose active involvement was needed. He admitted to Morley in his Sunday letter of April 25 that there was no one in the new Taft administration capable of taking the lead in the peace process. He suggested, rather deviously, that the British government propose holding an international disarmament conference, which Taft would be obliged to agree to. With the Americans and British in favor of such a conference, the pressure on the Germans would be too much to withstand. There was no response from Morley.[5]

His League of Peace proposals having found no champion, Carnegie took it upon himself to organize an international naval disarmament conference. Instead of sailing directly to England from New York in the spring of 1909, he set off with the family on a quasi-diplomatic tour of the Continent to introduce his new peace proposal. The first stop was Naples, where he was met by an Italian senator with a message from King Victor Emmanuel "expressing his desire [to] receive me [at a] private audience." From Naples, Carnegie took his wife and daughter to Florence. Lou and Baba wanted more time for sightseeing, but Carnegie was in a hurry to get to Rome. There, he whisked the family off to the Forum where, with his daughter at his side, he recited "Mark Antony's famous words in *Julius Caesar* beginning, 'Friends, Romans, Countrymen.'"[6]

Though Baba thought her father had hurriedly left Florence because he wanted to take her to the Forum, his more immediate concern was his audience with Victor Emmanuel in the king's residence. The king listened, while Carnegie praised Rome, Italians, the king as a family man, and talked of his plans for peace. Then it was off to Stresa with Baba and Louise for a week on the Italian Lakes, before Carnegie hurled himself back into the diplomatic whirlwind.[7]

In Paris, he sat for an extended interview with Premier Georges Clemenceau, then attended a dinner at the U.S. Embassy, a breakfast at the Sorbonne, a private audience with President Armand Fallières, and a farewell dinner hosted by peace activist Baron d'Estournelles de Constant. He also announced a gift of $1 million for a French Hero Fund. An admiring journalist who had been accompanying Carnegie on his diplomatic tour wrote by "special cable" to the *New York Times* on May 30 that although the donation to the French Hero Fund was receiving a great deal of publicity, it was of secondary importance to Carnegie, who had in mind a "project vaster and more immediate in effect. He proposes an international conference for the purpose of limiting armaments. . . . Mr. Carnegie is now engaged . . . in sounding the rulers of Europe as to what reception such a call would receive. . . . 'I find Europe in a ferment,' he said. 'The nations have gone Dreadnought mad. . . . Our country necessarily is about to be drawn into the vortex.'" Carnegie urged President Taft to issue a call for an international conference. "Here, I say, is probably the way out of the dangers which threaten civilization itself. . . . Never was a holier mission entrusted to a nation than that which devolves on our Republic. Even to fail in the effort to preserve the world's peace would be more glorious than to succeed in smaller issues. May President Taft . . . rise to the occasion and let the world know that there is one nation which stands forth willing even to fail as the champion of peace. Thus shall he, at least, have done his duty and placed our country in its proper position as the leader of the nations for peace on earth and among men good will."

Carnegie's self-imposed diplomatic mission came to a rather abrupt end in Paris. He had hoped to receive an invitation to meet with the kaiser or German government officials to discuss his proposals, but none came. Still he remained upbeat. "Had a very kind note in reply from the Emperor to whom I sent Roosevelt books," he wrote Morley in June 1909. (Either the kaiser had taken more than a year to respond to Carnegie, who had sent him the books in May 1908, or Carnegie was only now bringing up his "note" to remind Morley of his close relations with Wilhelm II.) "He was much impressed by the Introduction—so he tells me,—Glad to see me at Kiel this summer, but I'm not going unless he specially asks me to unfold my ideas or rather Man of destiny idea."[8]

From Paris, Carnegie crossed the Channel and set up shop in London in the hope, unfulfilled, that Morley would be able to arrange an interview for him with the prime minister. He publicized his proposals for an international conference in letters to the editors of *The Times of London* and the *Westminster Gazette*. "I'm having a revised copy printed," he wrote Morley in late June, "& shall send to my August friends, Emperors, Kings, President, Prime Ministers & to every Member Legislatures of Europe & America. Am going to scatter it broadcast. Also get Peace Society here to scatter it in Britain. D'Estournelles is getting it in various languages for Europe. . . . If you talk to Asquith or [Foreign Secretary] Grey wish I knew what they have to say anent Peace on the Seas."[9]

His efforts to bring Germany and Britain to the conference table having failed, Carnegie was more than ever determined to enlist Roosevelt as his surrogate. The ex-president had reestablished contact with Carnegie from Mombasa, off the coast of Kenya, on June 1 after a few months' silence. In duplicate letters sent to Skibo and New York, Roosevelt complained that his expedition was costing much more than he had foreseen. He was prepared to pay his own and his son Kermit's expenses, but required additional funds for the three naturalists and the "immense amount of scientific impedimenta with them. As one item I may mention that there are four tons of salt—which we carried on the backs of porters. . . . We need special skinning tents, special tents for storing the skins, and of course the skins of the big animals have to be carried along by numbers of additional porters. All this will serve simply to show by example why the expedition is necessarily far more expensive than an ordinary hunting trip of the same size." Roosevelt asked Carnegie for $30,000 in the name of scientific research. Suggesting the possibility of a sort of quid pro quo, he inquired "if there [were] any chance of your being in London when I am there next May? Or in Berlin, where I shall be shortly before?"[10]

Carnegie wrote Charles Walcott, the secretary of the Smithsonian Institution, who had organized the safari funding, to suggest that contributors to the project double their original donations. "Tell them I am, Morgan will—they all will if they know T.R. wishes it. . . . We must not fail. . . . We must not let our greatest man suffer, remember." In the end,

Carnegie was almost alone in his willingness to pour more money into the expedition. He pledged another $5,000 in addition to the $2,750 he had already given, and then, when it became apparent no one else was going to make up the difference, he sent Walcott $20,000 more.[11]

The day after he contacted Walcott, Carnegie, sensing that he had Roosevelt in his snares, wrote the big game hunter in Africa to tell him that he was prepared to support his expedition, but expected something in return. "You are supposed to be after big game, my friend. All very well for a holiday, but, of course, unworthy as a pursuit of one who has played and, in my hope and belief, is yet to play a great game in the world. . . . Shall be so glad when you have started upon your return, and hope you will make it a point of meeting the big men of the world. These are the big game, although your present holiday was well-earned."[12]

Roosevelt thanked Carnegie for his contribution. He was, he wrote, looking "forward eagerly to seeing Mrs. Carnegie and you in London next May. There is very much I shall have to talk over with you, and especially what you say of navies and peace. . . . Of course if we could get the principal powers to form a court of arbitral justice with some power of enforcement of its decrees, an immense step in advance would have been taken. You and I & Root must talk the matter over when we get home." In response to Carnegie's suggestion that he should give a lecture at Edinburgh, he admitted that it was "a most attractive invitation," but one he was at the moment unable to accept. "My dear fellow, don't ask me to make a definite engagement at this moment. I shall be a very short time in Europe as I shall be anxious to get back to America. Nevertheless what you wish me to do I shall certainly strive hard to do."[13]

This was precisely what Carnegie had been hoping to hear. Did he recognize that Roosevelt's cooperation in his peace plan had been less than voluntary, that he had bought his assistance by paying for his safari? Perhaps, but it did not matter. Roosevelt was a man of honor. If it took a few thousand dollars to get him moving in the right direction, that was an acceptable price to pay. Sensing that Roosevelt's reluctance to take on the peace mission had much to do with his fear that it might fail, Carnegie tried to reassure him: "If any man can get the [German] Emperor in accord for peace, you are that man. He will go far to act in unison with you, of this I am certain. You are sympathetic souls."[14]

By early fall, Carnegie was planning the details of Roosevelt's peace pilgrimage. After meeting with the kaiser in Berlin, Roosevelt would sit down with the leaders of the British Liberal government—and the opposition Tories—at Ambassador Whitelaw Reid's residence at Wrest Park in Bedforshire. "Am to meet Roosevelt London sure early in May," he wrote Morley on October 7, 1909, "& then that meeting of the right few and none others you are to arrange. I'll write you from New York about it when Roosevelt gives me his dates. I may go to Berlin to meet him & have a meeting there before the London visit. I am hopeful something important may result from Roosevelt's efforts."[15]

Roosevelt and Carnegie remained in communication through the fall, engaged in a round robin of flattery, each convinced he had gotten the best of the other but disguising it. Roosevelt's letters had turned uncharacteristically fawning, almost obsequious. "I have read your two pamphlets* with real interest and with entire agreement as to the general policy—of course could not speak of details. The increase of naval armaments is becoming a well-night intolerable burden. . . . When I see the Kaiser I will go over the matter at length with him, telling him I wish to repeat our whole conversation to you; then I'll tell it all to you when I am in London. I shall be in London about May 1st. I regard the proposed quiet conference [with the British leaders at Wrest Park] as most important. I leave absolutely with you the arrangements to be made through Morley, as you suggest. . . . I only fear, my dear Mr. Carnegie, that you do not realize how unimportant a man I now am, and how little weight I shall have in the matter."[16]

Everything appeared to be going according to plan. In late October, Carnegie wrote Morley from Liverpool on his way back to New York. He was consumed by excitement at the prospect of the next spring's meetings. "Do take care of yourself for believe me you are going to be in position to do great work in May when Roosevelt is with us or I am mistaken. I saw Mr. Balfour [former prime minister and head of the Conservative Party] in Manchester & told him we wanted a meeting & explained—He is responsive to a degree as I expected. He & Lansdowne [the former Tory foreign secretary], Asquith & Grey and You. Maybe Haldane [the secretary for war]—No more. I told you Roosevelt had written me—It is time for Statesmen (not politicians) to understand each other & act in unison re

---

*Carnegie was turning out pamphlets one after another: that spring, he published "Armaments and Their Results" and two open letters to the London papers reprinted as "The Path to Peace."

war. Either Britain or America will bring the subject before the powers unless the Emperor decides to play the part open to him [and calls for a conference]. I'll be in London in good time in May to consult with you. Meanwhile Madam & I accompany Taft and Mrs. President to Hampton [College], & I'll have a free talk."[17]

Through the autumn months, Carnegie continued to funnel money to Roosevelt in Africa. Afraid that the funds he had given through the Smithsonian might not reach Nairobi in time, he instructed Robert Franks to honor any "drafts" Roosevelt presented. Roosevelt, on learning of the arrangement, wrote to thank Carnegie and assure him that he planned to follow through on his post-safari peace mission. He asked only that Carnegie contact former secretary of state and now senator from New York Elihu Root, and ask him to prepare a position paper which Roosevelt could use in approaching the kaiser. "Root's gift of phrasing things is unequaled . . . and his name carries great weight. It would give me just the clear-cut proposition I desire."[18]

Carnegie forwarded Roosevelt's request to Root. Still worried that the ex-president was less than enthusiastic about his peace mission, he indulged in yet more cheerleading for the cause. "I cannot but feel that if you are disposed to cooperate and take the leader's part in conferring with German rulers," he wrote on Christmas Eve 1909, "and especially if you press for a League of Peace, that you would triumph. . . . The only question is whether the idea of promoting World Peace stirs you. It if does, you will not fail, but even failure in such a cause would be noble . . . I am willing to throw aside everything, and I know Root and Butler share this feeling, because we see success with you as the Great Peace Maker."[19]

Understanding full well that it was President Taft, not Roosevelt, who would have to broker any potential international agreement through the U.S. Senate, Carnegie visited Taft in Washington, attended a "Cabinet dinner," and then spent the night of December 16 in the White House. "The President," he wrote Morley, "is advised of our aims & approves. . . . I'll write Mr. Reid & you & he can fix date Meeting at Wrest. Roosevelt says during Second week in May he will be ready." Fearing that Morley, like Roosevelt, might not be sufficiently enthusiastic, he assured him that if Roosevelt thought Britain "favorable" to the idea of a League of Peace, he would "find means to bring the Emperor and his advisers seriously to consider [it]." Even if no League of Peace were immediately forthcoming, the meeting Carnegie had planned at Wrest Park would bring the British leaders and Roosevelt closer together, and that was no small matter. "Remember Roosevelt's career is not yet over. In all probability he will be President again, and it will count for much that he knows your colleagues as he knows you."[20]

In mid-January 1910, responding to an earlier letter in which Roosevelt stressed how anxious he was to get home, Carnegie begged him not to short-change his peace mission. "Please do not hurry away from Berlin until you have made friends with half a dozen men there, because, as sure as you live, that friendship will stand you in good stead some day by enabling you to accomplish a great work. The day must come soon when nations stop this rivalry in armaments."[21]

On February 18, the letter that Carnegie had been expecting—and fearing—was dispatched from Gondokoro on the east bank of the Nile, about 750 miles south of Khartoum. With his year-long adventure coming to its conclusion, Roosevelt had finally taken the time to give Carnegie's plan the consideration it required. He was ready to move forward—and so informed Carnegie—but he wanted his friend and benefactor to fully understand his "reservations."

> Well. Here, I find all your letters, and I guess I shall have to surrender. . . . Now, however for some reservations. First, and least important personal. I want to go home! I am homesick for my own land and my own people! Of course it is Mrs. Roosevelt I most want to see; but I want to see my two youngest boys; I want to see my own house, my own books and trees, the sunset over the Sound from the window in the north room, the people with whom I have worked, who think my thoughts and speak my speech. . . .
>
> Second: as to the policy itself. With *your* policy, as you outline it (of course accepting it generally and not binding myself as to details), I am in hearty sympathy. . . . But you have on your paper certain names Stead and [Benjamin] Trueblood [secretary of the American Peace Society] which inspire me with a most lively distrust. Stead and Trueblood for instance belong to the type that makes a good cause ridiculous. Their proposals are rarely better than silly; and the only reason that the men themselves are not exceedingly mischievous is that they are well-nigh impotent for either good or evil. . . . I cannot conscientiously support, nor could I persuade

any sane and honest ruler or great public servant to support, the fantastic and noxious theories of such extremists as those to whom I have alluded.

Roosevelt, the realist, was laying down the law to Carnegie, the visionary, much as he had done three years earlier on the eve of the New York peace congress. Rather than accuse Carnegie of silliness, mischievousness, or impotence, Roosevelt took aim at his associates in the peace movement. It was one thing to paint pretty pictures in the air, another to formulate a policy that had a reasonable chance of success on earth. On numerous occasions, presidents, to the applause of the peace activists, had sent forward ambitious proposals, only to have them dismissed or amended beyond recognition in the Senate. Fully aware of how seriously the Senate took its responsibilities, Roosevelt tried his best to impress on Carnegie the futility of asking for too much:

> I will do all I can to bring about such a league of, or understanding among, the great powers as will forbid one of them, or any small power, to engage in unrighteous, foolish or needless war; to secure an effective arbitral tribunal, with power to enforce at least certain of its decrees; to secure an agreement to check the waste of money on growing and excessive armaments. If as is probable, so much cannot be secured at once, I will do all I can to help in the movement, rapid or slow, towards the desired end. But I will not be, and you would not wish me to be, put in the attitude of advocating the impossible, or, above all, of seeming to be insincere. . . . I cannot be, or seem to be, an accredited envoy; I cannot work for a policy which I think our country might repudiate; I cannot work for anything that does not represent some real progress; and it is useless to expect to accomplish everything at once. But I will do all in my power, all that is feasible, to help in the effort to secure some substantial advance towards the goal.[22]

Carnegie, dependent on Roosevelt to carry his scheme forward, accepted every caveat attached. He agreed that the organization of world peace would take time and patience. All he wanted now was for the curtain to rise on the drama he had scripted. The key players were in the wings. Taft had signed off on the plan in Washington; American Ambassadors David Hill in Berlin and Whitelaw Reid in London were, with John Morley, awaiting their cues, scripts in hand; Roosevelt was preparing his entrance from off stage (very far off stage). Everything was proceeding according to schedule—or almost.

The tragedy of Carnegie's last years was that no one took him as seriously as he took himself. He was not blameless in this, having long ago abandoned every pretense of moderation in pursuit of his goals. He was an extremist—and proud of it, an optimist who saw only the silver linings, never the storm clouds. It was his task to ask for the impossible and hope that someday it would be granted him. That others might consider him a dotty old fool did not register with him. He was eccentric, that was for sure, but his past achievements demanded that attention be paid.

If Carnegie had a fatal weakness, it was the misplaced faith he put in those he counted as his colleagues in the fight for peace. Roosevelt had written Carnegie that he was in "hearty sympathy" with his general "policy," knowing full well that the crux of any diplomatic agreement was in the details. He had assured him that he "entirely [agreed] with the views you and Root hold," knowing that the two men's views were quite different. In almost every communication he sent, the ex-president tried to dampen the old man's ardor and rein in his expectations. He would accomplish what he could, but it might not be very much.[23]

Carnegie should have read more clearly what the ex-president had to say; he should have remembered how Roosevelt had undercut him in 1907, before The Hague Conference. He preferred not to. The past was not a predictor of the present or the future. No matter how grim today, tomorrow would be brighter. Carnegie's optimism was an essential ingredient of his personality, one that had been confirmed and strengthened by his acceptance of Spencer's evolutionary philosophy. Roosevelt might for the moment appear less than interested in his peace mission, but once swept up in the process, once convinced that he was, with Carnegie, a man of destiny, he would take up the challenge that history—and Andrew Carnegie—had set for him.

Theodore Roosevelt began his victory tour of Europe in early April 1910. Days after he had landed in Italy, the German press was already expressing concern that he might, on his visit to Berlin, take advantage of the kaiser's hospitality to raise subjects that his royal highness wished not to discuss, like naval disarmament. Roosevelt blamed the government-inspired press onslaught on "some inadvertence on Mr. Carnegie's part." Rather than being annoyed, however, he was perversely pleased by the bad publicity as it dampened expectations of future success. "I was really grateful to the Berlin government for taking such public action," he wrote the British historian and politician George Otto Trevelyan a year later. "Not only Mr. Carnegie, but a multitude of well-meaning and ignorant people, had wrought themselves into the belief that if I chose I could do something with the Emperor for peace; and I was glad to be able to point out to them this announcement from the German foreign office in advance of my visit, which saved me the necessity of trying to explain why I could accomplish nothing."[24]

From Paris, Roosevelt wrote Carnegie to tell him of the obstacles that had been placed in his way. "I anticipated, as you of course saw from my letters, that I should have difficulties in accomplishing anything [in Berlin] even along the cautious lines of conduct which Root very properly suggested . . . but if, as I suppose to be the case, you have seen the Berlin papers, you probably already know that even my anticipations of the difficulties came far short of the actual facts." He begged Carnegie to keep quiet in future about the peace mission. Elihu Root "has felt all along, and of course I entirely agree with him, that the correspondence between you, myself and him, on peace matters, should be kept entirely secret, for the very reason that we do not want to arouse the feeling which the Berlin newspapers have shown."[25]

While he anticipated a chilly reception in Berlin, Roosevelt was greeted like a conquering hero in Paris. His ostensible reason for stopping there was to deliver a lecture at the Sorbonne on the duties of republican citizenship. In an almost two-hour speech, he voiced his approval of "righteous wars." Carnegie wrote at once to reprimand him. Perhaps because he was older than Roosevelt or simply because he was Andrew Carnegie, he felt no compunction about treating the ex-president as he might a silly schoolboy. When would Roosevelt, he wanted to know, accept the fact that every nation on earth claimed that its wars were righteous; and every nation that did so was wrong. Just as citizens were obliged to submit their disputes to "the law for redress," so should governments be obligated to do the same. Just as citizens could not take up arms against one another because they believed their cause was righteous, so should governments be prevented from doing so. "Ponder over this. You have a conscience. . . . The whole matter is so simple, my dear Mr. Roosevelt—Germany, Britain and America coming together and agreeing to form a joint police force to maintain peace is all that is needed." There was no response from Roosevelt, who was too busy receiving the European public's accolades to answer Carnegie.[26]

After a non-stop roundelay of speeches, receptions, and dinners in Paris, the Roosevelt entourage—his wife and daughter Ethel had joined the party—moved on to Belgium, the Netherlands, Denmark, and Norway for more of the same. On May 5, Roosevelt belatedly accepted the 1906 Nobel Prize awarded to him for settling the Russo-Japanese War.

The next day, Carnegie's carefully laid plans nearly fell to pieces with the announcement that Edward VII of Britain, Kaiser Wilhelm II's uncle, had died. Until his uncle was officially buried, it was going to be awkward, if not impossible, for the kaiser to entertain a foreign dignitary at his home. Roosevelt, unwilling to cancel the Berlin visit, suggested that he and his family stay at the U.S. Embassy instead of the kaiser's palace. The kaiser agreed and Roosevelt's state visit proceeded, almost as planned.

He remained in Berlin for the full five days that had originally been scheduled and spent a great deal of time alone with the kaiser. "The first day we went out to take lunch. . . . Afterwards he drove us to Potsdam, and showed us over Sans Souci. He also held army maneuvers at which I was present. On this occasion I rode with him for about five hours, and he talked steadily; and on another afternoon we spent three hours together." Roosevelt and the kaiser discussed many topics, including the "relations of Germany and England." The ex-president had every opportunity to present Carnegie's proposals for a League of Peace had he wished to do so. But he did not. As he made clear to Trevelyan, he had no intention—and had never had any—of doing Carnegie's bidding in Berlin.[27]

"Carnegie, personally and through Root . . . had been asking me to try to get the Emperor committed to universal arbitration and disarmament. . . . Root was under obligations to Carnegie for the way that Carnegie had helped him in connection with the Pan-American movement [Carnegie had donated the funds to build a Pan-American headquarters in Washington and the Central American Court of Justice in Costa Rica], and he had also helped the Smithsonian in fitting out the scientific people who went with me on my African trip; and Carnegie's purposes as regards international peace are good, although his methods are often a little absurd; and so I told him that I would see whether I could speak to the Emperor or not, but that I did not believe any good would come of it."[28]

Roosevelt was, in the end, unwilling to present the kaiser with Carnegie's "absurd" methods of achieving international peace. He indirectly raised the question of the naval arms race, but only after assuring Wilhelm II that he was "a practical man and in no sense a peace-at-any-price man." The kaiser replied courteously "that he really had no control over the matter, that it was something which affected the German people, and that the German people, or at least that section of the German people upon whom he relied and in whom he believed, would never consent to Germany's failing to keep herself able to enforce her rights either on land or at sea." Even had he wished to play the role of "man of destiny" Carnegie had scripted for him, Kaiser Wilhelm II had public opinion, the Reichstag, and the military establishment to contend with—and they were, in the aggregate, far stronger than he was.[29]

The ex-president and the kaiser found that they had much in common. Both believed that "war between England and Germany would be an unspeakable calamity." Both were desirous "to see England, Germany and the United States act together in all matters of world policy." And both "agreed in a cordial dislike of shams and of pretense, and therefore in a cordial dislike of the kind of washy movement for international peace with which Carnegie's name has become so closely associated."[30]

Carnegie, of course, was not privy to Roosevelt's private letters and had no idea that his "men of destiny" had bonded together in mutual dislike of and opposition to his peace campaign. He believed, on the contrary, that Roosevelt had acted in good faith in Berlin and had had some success. On May 13, from Torquay where he had stationed himself to await Roosevelt's triumphant return, he welcomed "the Colonel" to London, and warned him to "take care of your throat [the papers had several times mentioned that Roosevelt was hoarse from lecturing too much], dangerous climate this in May and many are the attacks yearly upon those from the South [Africa?; Italy?]—We need you, your work isn't half done yet."[31]

Although it was clear by now that Roosevelt's meeting with the British leaders would have to be postponed until a reasonable period after Edward VII's funeral, Carnegie said nothing about this in his letter. Instead, he interjected—out of nowhere—the thought that he might now try to "see your crony, The Emperor. Shall certainly make the effort. If you and he don't make a team that can drag the cart behind I'm a disappointed man." The next day, Carnegie wrote Roosevelt again, now acknowledging that the meeting at Ambassador Reid's residence at Wrest Park would have to be postponed, but making light of it. Whether or not Roosevelt got a chance to sit down with the British government leaders was, Carnegie hinted, of less importance than the fact that he and Wilhelm II had gotten to know and trust one another. "I . . . doubt not all has passed off well and that you & the Emperor now being friends may some day count for much—The Wrest Park meeting is only to give you a chance to become known to the leaders here and they to know you. It may make all the difference some day that you are friends. Your future is, accidents excepted, likely to excel even your past since you are a born leader of men with the sublime audacity to perform wonders. Pray don't fail to know the Leaders of other lands, no big game equals to this."[32]

Carnegie remained oblivious not only to the failure of Roosevelt's mission to Berlin but to the growing impossibility that a meeting between the ex-president and the British government leaders might ever take place. Roosevelt, believing he had paid his debt to Carnegie by meeting with the kaiser, had no intention of doing anything more. He planned to represent the United States at King Edward's funeral, as President Taft had requested he do, give a speech or two, spend a day bird-watching with Sir Edward Grey, and then sail home, his Carnegie-assigned tasks not only incomplete but forgotten.[33]

Carnegie's British friends, Morley included, had also abandoned him and any plans to hold a naval disarmament congress. Edward VII's death had plunged the nation deeper into the constitutional crisis that had been precipitated when the House of Lords refused to pass the Liberal government's 1909 budget. The assumption was that Edward VII, had he lived, would have created enough new Liberal lords to block the Tories from vetoing another budget. But such assumptions were thrown to the wind with the accession of George V, whom no one quite knew. Preoccupied with a looming constitutional crisis, neither Morley nor his colleagues in the Liberal government had any inclination to focus their attentions on Mr. Carnegie's proposals for international conferences.

Anyone else might have abandoned the chase, but not Andrew

Carnegie. He simply shifted gears and moved forward. There would be no meeting at Wrest Park, no international summit, no Roosevelt diplomatic miracles. But that was all right. Carnegie, always watchful for signs of progress, had found a new one. He had become almost obsessively fixated on a speech President Taft had made in March 1910 to the American Peace and Arbitration League of New York. Taft had rather innocently remarked that, unlike his predecessor, he saw no reason why arbitration treaties should exclude disputes that touched on "questions of national honor. . . . I know that is going further than most men are willing to go. . . . But I do not see why questions of honor may not be submitted to a tribunal supposed to be composed of men of honor."[34]

Upon reading the speech, Carnegie wrote Taft at once, lavishing on him the same outlandish praise he had earlier devoted to Roosevelt: "If you only prove true to your great promise and propose to Germany and Great Britain . . . that they confer confidentially with our country . . . I believe you will succeed . . . and when peace is established, as it finally must be, you would be as clearly the father of Peace on Earth as Washington is father of his country or Lincoln its preserver."[35]

In June 1910, as Roosevelt left Britain, his mission incomplete, Carnegie publicly switched partners for peace. In a speech to the British Peace Society in London's Guildhall, he publicly praised President William Howard Taft's March 22 remarks on arbitration, which, he declared, had "in a flash of inspiration . . . revealed the true path to the realization of peace on earth." Taft's "few words" had elevated him to a "rank among the immortals as one of the foremost benefactors of his race." Using almost the same language he had used to praise Roosevelt in December 1902 for referring the Venezuela dispute to The Hague tribunal, Carnegie now proclaimed that President Taft was "among rulers the leader of the holy crusade against man killing man in war, as Lincoln became the leader in the crusade against the selling of man by man." Gleefully putting behind him the year he had spent prepping Roosevelt for his now-failed peace mission, Carnegie's mood was almost manically upbeat. "Be of good cheer, Brothers," he declared to the Peace Society delegates meeting in London, "the good work goes steadily forward; nothing can prevent its triumph. We are apparently on the eve of a decided step forward, soon the International Judicial Court is to appear and the step from that to a League of Peace follows."[36]

Carnegie was courting the ultimate danger for a public figure: he was very close to becoming a parody of himself—a smiling, wizened, white-bearded fool for peace. Every year, he appeared to come up with a new surefire, guaranteed solution to the world's problems. In the spring of 1909, he had publicly pushed for a three-party naval disarmament conference. Now, in the summer of 1910, he was presenting bilateral arbitration treaties as the path to world peace and substituting Taft for Roosevelt as the agent of progress.

Carnegie was not the only peace activist to have been won over by Taft's conversion. That June, both houses of Congress passed a resolution calling on the president to appoint a five-man commission to explore the possibilities of "utilizing existing international agencies for the purpose of limiting the armaments of the nations of the world" and organizing an international naval police force to preserve "universal peace." Carnegie was delighted. He wrote Taft at once, enthusiastically supporting the new commission. Taft was not nearly as enthusiastic. "I am very hopeful that peace matters may make substantial progress during the coming year. Just what I can make out of the Peace Commission, I am not quite certain as yet."[37]

Carnegie suggested to Roosevelt that he sign on as chairman of the new peace commission. "There never was such a chance for a mortal man to immortalize himself, as is now extended to you." Using the commission chairmanship as his vehicle, Roosevelt could now legitimately "approach Britain with the League of Peace idea. . . . What pleases me is that our country is now leader in the movement to abolish war as a means of settling disputes. . . . When I hear that you have accepted the Chairmanship of that Commission, I shall rejoice."[38]

Roosevelt had no intention of serving on any committee appointed by his successor. Visiting the Tafts at their summer home in Beverly, Massachusetts, he formally declined the chairmanship and then, according to presidential aide Archie Butt, who was present, mischievously volunteered "with a laugh: 'Why not name Carnegie? He would certainly finance the commission, and if you could seal his mouth so that he would not be talking about what we think and so on, he might do fairly well.'"

"'I don't think Mr. Carnegie would do at all,' said Mrs. Taft. It was the first time she had said anything." Senator Lodge, who was also one of the party, agreed. "He would simply get us into world trouble with his officiousness." The president "nodded his approval." As Taft later wrote Philander Knox, who he had appointed as secretary of state, Carnegie "might be a hard man to be responsible for because he talked so much."[39]

Carnegie, of course, had no idea of the contempt Taft and Knox had for him. On the contrary, he was convinced that he had found the perfect junior partner in William Howard Taft, a president who, he expected, would serve as his Frick or Schwab in the pursuit of peace. Carnegie would lay down the guidelines, establish the basic principles, and advise on strategy. Taft, with Knox's assistance, would execute the plan. To cement their new partnership, Carnegie decided to create his own peace trust to provide the president with whatever assistance he might require to write his new treaties and get the Senate to approve them.

Awash in enthusiasm, Carnegie, on returning to New York in October, contacted President Taft with his plans for collaboration. Taft wrote back to invite Carnegie and Louise to Washington for dinner and to stay overnight at the White House. "That will give you and me the opportunity to discuss the matter you mention in your note. If you can come and will name the date by telegram, so much the better."[40]

After several meetings with Taft, Knox, and Root, Carnegie forwarded to the president a copy of the "trust deed" he was going to deliver to the trustees of what would be known as the Carnegie Endowment for International Peace. "You will note that your noble note of leadership among rulers prompted me to create the fund. It is based upon your words. I saw clearly that peace was within our grasp because the other branch of our race (English speaking) was ready to follow you. You have only to push out your hand to secure this & this secured other nations will soon follow."[41]

On December 14, 1910, he signed the final deed of gift, with his wife and daughter as witnesses, formally transferring to the trustees of his as yet unnamed "peace trust," $10 million ($3.5 billion today) of 5 percent U.S. Steel first-mortgage gold bonds. As the *New York Times* reported on December 15, with this grant, Carnegie's bequests had exceeded $200 million, far in excess of Mr. Rockefeller's gifts, which were estimated to be about $120 million.

The "deed" could have been written by no one else. Certainly no one else would have dared to sprinkle through a legal document words like "hav," "giv," "dauter," and other "simplified spellings." Carnegie made the purpose of his new trust eminently accessible to anyone who cared to read his letter: "Although we no longer eat our fellow men nor torture prison-

THE CHECKER PLAYERS

ers, nor sack cities killing their inhabitants, we still kill each other in war like barbarians. Only wild beasts are excusable for doing that in this, the twentieth century of the Christian era, for the crime of war is inherent, since it decides not in favor of the right, but always of the strong. The nation is criminal which refuses arbitration."[42]

Carnegie attended the first meeting of his trustees in Washington on December 14. He wanted them all to know why he had now decided to establish a peace trust. His address, which was taken down verbatim, is quintessential Carnegie, boastful, brash, rambling, and verbose but charming nonetheless. He explained that he had read about Taft's speech on arbitration while visiting

the Grand Canyon of the Colorado ... the grandest spectacle in the world, so far as I know. . . . I then said to myself: "President Taft, foremost among rulers of men, has really bridged the chasm between peace and war." I wrote him an enthusiastic letter which afterwards developed into an article which perhaps some of you may have read in the *Century Magazine,* and every day convinced me more and more, and especially all that I have heard in Britain, for I have the honor of knowing the Cabinet pretty

well, of the possibility and practicability of carrying out this object . . . I
owe you some explanation because I have advised you, please notice, that
you are not required to do anything, that I only hope that you will proceed
in that line. There may be reasons that it is not proper just now, that it
would be better to wait, but there the truth remains that we have it in our
hands, the responsibility is upon this Republic. . . . That is my explanation
and my apology for putting in this deed of trust the hope that you will at
least try to see whether this is not the easiest way to peace.[43]

When Carnegie had finished, Oscar Straus, one of his trustees, suggested that Carnegie be named a trustee. He declined the honor. "Gentlemen, I think such a suggestion as my friend has made is altogether
unnecessary. It is not well in my opinion that the giver of a gift should be
continuously a member of a Board that administers it. It places him in a
very awkward position. I never want to say anything to influence action,
because I would never feel that what I was saying was rated at its proper
value, but that there was danger that it would have an improper value. You
would be under embarrassment."

Senator Root, who chaired the meeting, then spoke and, as he had been
given permission to do, suggested an entirely different path for the endowment than the one Carnegie had laid out:

My feeling about this trust is that if it is to be of value, as I hope and believe it is, it must be something different from many enterprises in behalf
of peace which we have known, in one respect. That is, that it must be
thorough, practical; and it must base its action upon a careful, scientific
and thorough study of the causes of war and the remedies which can be
applied to the causes, rather than merely the treatment of symptoms. I
think the field of general observation upon the subject of war and peace,
general exposition of the wrongfulness of war, and the desirableness of
peace, is already pretty well covered. I think this foundation will be of little use unless it does something further than that, and to do that, to do
something further than that, we must do what the scientific men do, we
must strive to reach some deeper insight into the cause of the diseases, of
which war is a symptom, than can be obtained by casual and occasional
consideration. That deeper insight can be attained only by long and faithful and continuous study and investigation.[44]

Root was intent on establishing a scientific research institution, much like the Carnegie Institution in Washington, one that engaged in funding research and educational activities and abstained from taking a position on political issues. Carnegie's objective, on the contrary, had been to set up an activist organization dedicated to pushing forward his and Taft's agenda.

For the peace activists who had, for decades now, looked forward to getting their hands on the great philanthropist's money, the establishment of the Carnegie Endowment for International Peace was a decidedly mixed blessing. In establishing his new peace trust, Carnegie had taken to heart Roosevelt's and no doubt Root's disdain for the potentially "mischievous" and permanently impotent men who led the nation's peace societies. Only the Quaker Albert Smiley, who had started the Mohonk conferences, and one other of the twenty-eight trustees had been members of peace societies prior to 1905. The majority of trustees were international and/or Wall Street lawyers, college presidents, retired financiers, and businessmen; almost all were Republicans; twelve were already trustees of a Carnegie organization.[45]

On December 15, Carnegie met with President Taft and Secretary of State Knox to discuss his new "peace trust" and the role it might play in the campaign for arbitration treaties. He wrote Taft to suggest that he ask Knox to open discussions with the Senate Foreign Relations Committee on a treaty of arbitration with Britain.[46]

From Cumberland Island, where he had gone in January to visit his ailing sister-in-law Lucy, he bombarded both Taft and Knox with almost weekly letters and telegrams, filled with suggestions, congratulations, and flattery. "Jay's treaty [ending the Revolutionary War] will keep his name in history," he wrote Knox, "but it's a trifle compared to your treaty. . . . What I fear is that if we don't strike while the iron is hot we may fail. We shall deserve to do so, but that only aggravates the offense. . . . There is a tide in the affairs of men, etc. Yours has come—now or never."[47]

Carnegie's strong suit had never been patience—and, at age seventy-five, with the British and the Germans engaged in a headlong race to produce new, faster, stronger, deadlier Dreadnoughts, there was no time to waste. Knowing that it took two sides to negotiate a treaty, he opened his own diplomatic backchannel to his friend James Bryce, who was now the British ambassador to Washington. The question might well have been asked—and surely was by the secretary of state whose prerogatives he was trampling on—what Mr. Carnegie thought he was doing.

"I have a note from President telling me 'Treaty will be pushed just as fast as possible,'" Carnegie wrote Ambassador Bryce on February 15, 1911. A month later—with still no progress—Carnegie explained to Bryce that the delay in drafting the treaty had been caused by Knox's absence from Washington. "Kind soul the President didn't want to shorten Knox's vacation. He assures me he is anxiously awaiting Knox on return to get him and you started—He asks me to Lunch and I'll be down soon—probably next week although I am so busy cannot tell."[48]

Carnegie had no doubt but that treaties of arbitration would be approved by the Senate, then by the French and British governments. "At present I am in the clouds," he wrote fellow peace activist Edwin Ginn, "singing hosannahs, believing that the President's policy will succeed and that we shall have treaties with Britain and France before long, eliminating the possibility of war throughout the boundaries of the English-speaking race and France also. That holy leaven will influence the whole world in the same direction. I am beginning to think that very little of our peace fund will be needed in this country; most of it will be confined to missionary work abroad." He made the same prediction in a letter to James Brown Scott, who had been appointed secretary of his new peace trust. "Assuming the passage of the treaty with Britain and the position our country will thereby occupy as one which is ready and anxious to enter into such treaties with other nations, I cannot but feel that our peace work in our country, so far as propaganda is concerned, will practically cease. We shall not need to preach to the converted. Therefore, a large portion of the fund will necessarily have to be spent in countries less advanced. Germany, Italy, Austria, Russia and others will be the fields left for missionary work."[49]

Assuming that the treaty was on the path to approval in Washington, Carnegie began lobbying his British friends to support it. "It really seems to me treaty is to slide through Senate welcomed by all," he wrote James Bryce in March. "I am uplifted in deed—a new chance comes to me in life here on earth if my native and adopted lands Motherland and wifeland clasp hands and lead the world, Knox and you,—your names to such a treaty ensure immediately a sure passport to every region of bliss even the highest that may be. We must not fail. . . . Everything is subordinated to the one essential that treaty. I know you will do your best."[50]

Unaware of the effect his constant meddling might have had on his relationship with the president, Carnegie kept up the pressure, alternately congratulating Taft on what he had accomplished and pushing him to do more, precisely as he had with his junior partners in the steel business. Worried that Taft might, in the end, not have the good sense or the expertise to do the job himself, he forwarded the precise treaty language he believed was required to satisfy British fears that too broad an agreement would threaten its sovereignty.[51]

It was finally too much for the president. Like Roosevelt before him, Taft had come to dislike the "Star-spangled Scotchman" rather intensely. He could not abide his interference, his constant stream of letters and telegrams, his speeches, interviews, and letters to the editor, all designed to push Taft in directions he was not at all sure he wanted to go. In mid-April, the president confided to Archie Butt that he found it particularly "strange" that the major focus of his presidency had become his arbitration treaties, in large part, he implied, because of Carnegie. He had never intended anything like this. "When I made that speech in New York [in March 1910] advocating the arbitration of questions, even those affecting the honor of a nation, I had no definite policy in view. I was inclined, if I remember rightly, merely to offset the antagonism to the four battleships for which I was then fighting, and I threw that suggestion out merely to draw the sting of old Carnegie and other peace cranks, and now the suggestion threatens to become the main fact of my four years as president."[52]

Taft was particularly irritated by Carnegie's lobbying British government officials to support a treaty that had yet to be approved by the Senate. The president asked Knox to write to Carnegie, which Knox did, suggesting in rather stern terms that "any premature or exaggerated public discussion" of the treaties might be harmful, at this delicate moment in the negotiations.[53]

As much as he disliked Carnegie, Taft, again like his predecessor, dared not alienate an influential Republican contributor and campaigner. In early May, he accompanied Carnegie to the Pan-American Union building in Washington for yet another ceremony honoring him for his contributions to hemispheric peace. "The President groaned and grunted all the way over," Archie Butt recalled, "that he should be called upon so often to attend meetings either called by Carnegie or else in behalf of the canny old Scotchman."[54]

OUR ANGEL OF PEACE

Carnegie remained oblivious to it all, his attention fixed fast on the treaties of arbitration, first with Britain and France, then Germany and the rest of the world. At long last his dreams were to be realized. "What a hit . . . I imagine you," he wrote Knox on May 11, "pen in hand, signing the greatest document [the first arbitration treaty] in its influence upon the world ever signed. Your <u>piloting</u> superb. I am rejoicing that I live in these days." That same day, he wrote the president a similar fawning letter of congratulations. "Consummate statesmanship, Mr. President—France, our Sister Republic, and Britain our fellow of the English speaking race on equal terms with the door wide open for other powers."[55]

The smooth sailing came to a rather abrupt end in the spring of 1911 when Theodore Roosevelt published an article in *Outlook* in which he argued that the nation that pledged to arbitrate its differences would end up dishonored and impotent, like the man who, when his wife was assaulted by a ruffian, took the ruffian to court instead of attacking him on the spot. Roosevelt had never been in favor of open-ended arbitration treaties—as he had made clear to Carnegie on a number of occasions—and he was certainly not predisposed to look kindly on anything that came out of the Taft

White House. In private letters, he insisted that he had no problem with a treaty of arbitration with Britain, but that he would do all he could to make sure that such a treaty was not used as a model for similar arrangements with less honorable and pacific nations, like Germany, Russia, and Japan.[56]

Carnegie was aghast at Roosevelt's intemperate attack on the very principle of arbitration. "Mr. President called yesterday & we both mourned over your article," he wrote Roosevelt, "surprised that you could go so far as to instance a man slapping your wife before your face, her husband. No man ever did so, or could fall so low—the husband would involuntarily attempt to protect his wife, but this done & reason returning he would scorn to touch the brute & let the law direct . . . punishment and condemn the monster to infamy. . . . Forgive me for I esteem you too highly not to tell you how grieved your friends are for a third friend has called this morning & tells me he & his friends are all mourning at this hasty slip, but this is what genuine friendship dares."[57]

Roosevelt was fawning and duplicitous in his reply. Not ready to rule out another run for the presidency, in 1916, if not in 1912, he wanted Carnegie on his side. "You know that one reason why I hesitated long before writing that article was just because I hated to do anything that might seem distasteful to you. I finally came to the conclusion that it would be weakness on my part not to write it."[58]

Carnegie was temporarily mollified. He too was not ready to break off relations with a past and perhaps future president. "So glad to get your note," he wrote on May 24. "Regretted I had 'broken out' upon you. . . . Dined with President last night. He's good humored as ever & said 'Theodore' hadn't quite grasped what we are after. 'He'll come out all right.'" Having apologized, Carnegie returned to the fray, attacking Roosevelt's contention that matters of "honor" might not always be amenable to peaceful arbitration. Correcting Roosevelt as if he were a naughty child, he informed him that "all honor wounds are self-inflicted, my dear friend, that's where you are 'off' sure."[59]

If anything were bound to stiffen Roosevelt's resolve against the treaty, it was Carnegie's condescension. In a letter to the British diplomat Cecil Arthur Spring-Rice, Roosevelt let his anger and contempt burn brightly: "The whole business is tainted by that noxious form of silliness which always accompanies the sentimental refusal to look facts in the face. The sentimentalist, by the way, is by no means always a decent creature to deal with; if Andrew Carnegie had employed his fortune and his time in doing justice to the steelworkers who gave him his fortune, he would have accomplished a thousand times what he has accomplished or ever can accomplish in connection with international peace."[60]

To his comrade in armaments Senator Henry Cabot Lodge, Roosevelt was no less damning of peace activists, in particular the man who had two years before paid for his African safari. "At this moment," he wrote in September 1911, "there is a very grave crisis in Europe [between Germany, France, and England over Morocco], and before the war clouds now gathering, all the peace and arbitration treaties, and all the peace and arbitration societies, and all the male shrieking sisterhood of Carnegies and the like, are utterly powerless."[61]

Carnegie, of course, knew nothing of these letters and would continue his friendly correspondence with the ex-president, who would reply promptly and with courtesy to his "dear Mr. Carnegie." Meanwhile, the damage had been done, though neither Carnegie nor Taft quite realized it yet. Both still basked in the enthusiasm with which the public and the press had initially greeted the idea of treaties of arbitration between the world's great powers.

Carnegie took it on himself to supply Taft with the logistical support he needed to lobby senators on behalf of the treaties. Working directly with Charles Hilles, Taft's secretary and chief political adviser, he set aside $10,000 to pay for clergymen to travel to Washington and lobby their senators. "If any other way of advancing the cause arises," he wrote Hilles in mid-June 1911 from Skibo, "please understand that you have only to apply to Mr. Franks [Carnegie's treasurer] and he has orders to honor your drafts."[62]

That June, as Secretary of State Knox began direct negotiations with Ambassador Bryce on the final form of a treaty of arbitration, Carnegie was almost apoplectic with excitement. "Shake friend Morley, Shake. I am the happiest mortal alive. Couldn't call snakes snake this morning if naming created things." Morley had no idea what his friend was ranting about. "I think my heavy labours must be turning my brain, for I cannot for the life of me satisfactorily interpret the enclosed wire. It was brought to me when I was hailed to the bench of the House of Lords and I've been puzzling ever since to read the words of the oracle. Do tell me. . . . Has it a bearing on some good news from U.S.A.? Anyhow, you would not have sent it if you had not been in tearing good spirits, and thereat I rejoice and will rejoice." Carnegie apologized by return mail. "Sorry my telegram not understood—thought you knew the celebrated American who being elected declared he felt so happy that he couldn't libel snakes by calling them by their real name. I had just heard that the Race—our race had agreed to banish war—the greatest step upward ever taken by any race since history began. . . . Other nations will soon follow."[63]

Carnegie, dismissing Ambassador Bryce's warning that there might be trouble getting the treaty through the U.S. Senate, focused his attention instead on the British cabinet. To Bryce, Alexander Murray, the chief Liberal whip, Morley, and no doubt many others, he spread the rumor that the Germans were prepared to sign an arbitration treaty with the Americans and might do so before the British did. "Impatient for cabinet action re Treaty," he wrote Murray. "Found note on arrival from White House. Germany in earnest, truly it seems we are on the eve of unprecedented advance. German ambassador came over from Washington to attend presentation to me of a book containing signatures of officers of 2600 German societies in America, thanks for Hero Fund of Germany. He dined with us at our own home and told me he was in favor of the treaty. Since then he heard from Berlin. YES, now my fear is that Germany may be first to execute, imagine our race despoiled of its just leadership in abolishing war and yet this is what Cabinet delay endangers."[64]

His message to Sir John St. Loe Strachey of the *Spectator* was even more agitated: "A note from the White House received here upon my arrival yesterday informs me that it is quite true that Germany has applied. A few days before leaving New York the German Ambassador dined with us and I know he was personally in favor of and had no doubt recommended the Treaty to his Government. The greatest step forward ever taken in the history of man is to be taken in our day. I have been optimistic for a year, but never so much as today. You are way behind, my friend, in your forecast in this matter. Wake Up! 'Doubting Thomas' Wake up!"[65]

Carnegie's information was faulty in the extreme. The German government was much appreciative of his Hero Fund—that much was true—but there is no indication that the Foreign Office had any intention of entering into negotiations with the Americans on an arbitration treaty.

On August 3, 1911, President Taft finally signed the first two treaties of arbitration, with Britain and with France. "Treaty pen should be preserved,"

Carnegie cabled the White House. The next day, he cabled Taft again with his congratulations: "You have reached the summit of human glory. Countless ages are to honor and bless your name."[66]

The treaties were now formally submitted to the Senate for ratification. Roosevelt's early assault had left its scars and Taft and Knox had not helped matters by attempting to elude Senate objections with a bit of wordplay. Struggling to find a way to bind the nation to arbitration without antagonizing the Senate, which believed it alone had the constitutional responsibility to determine whether or not an issue should be arbitrated, Knox had used the word "justiciable" to identify those types of disputes that were to be submitted to arbitration. If questions arose as to whether an issue was "justiciable" or not (as they were bound to as the term was undefined in the treaty), a bilateral commission composed of three nationals from each side was empowered to serve as an appeals court. If five of the six commissioners agreed that an issue was "justiciable," it would be submitted to arbitration. One of the problems the Senate faced was attempting to figure out precisely what "justiciable" meant. The word had no standing in international law or diplomacy.

On August 11, the Senate Foreign Relations Committee issued its majority report on the treaties. Only the Senate, it declared, not a bilateral commission, could decide if and when an issue was "justiciable." The majority's decision not to approve the treaty as written hit Carnegie like a thunderbolt. He had convinced himself that the nation was behind the treaties, as evidenced by the positive press coverage, and that the senators, sensing this, would quickly ratify them. His first reaction was to blame Taft and Knox for not appropriately consulting with—and educating—the senators before submitting the treaties. "The result has been a surprise to me," he wrote Bryce, who had anticipated the committee's action. "I had always been assured the Senate Committee would be consulted as the various points touching its prerogatives were formed, and its counsels duly considered. . . . The disappointment is too great to cause annoyance or wrath. It falls like a heavy dull load of disaster which we must slowly surmount. It is a serious struggle to get two thirds majority from a body that changes so slowly. I hope some compromise can be reached. . . . There is so much at stake that we should not stand on forms."[67]

Carnegie was proposing compromise because he could not bear defeat. Taft, recognizing that his treaties were in trouble, asked that Senate action be postponed until December. He planned to take his case to the people in a two-month speaking tour across 15,000 miles and twenty-eight states. "I am going to see," he wrote his son in August, "if I cannot arouse the country. . . . Carnegie and all the peace cranks are interested in this, as well as the church, and I am hopeful that we may set a fire under the senators which may change their views."[68]

Carnegie had from the very beginning expected that his Endowment for International Peace would do all it could to support Taft's treaties. Nicholas Murray Butler, the head of the endowment's division of intercourse and education, had prepared a publicity and educational campaign on behalf of ratification, but was overruled by Elihu Root, who was dead set against the endowment pursuing any program that involved it in partisan advocacy. Admiral A. T. Mahan, with Roosevelt the most outspoken foe of the treaties, had already assailed "subsidized agitation" on behalf of ratification, a pointed reference to Carnegie and the peace societies' campaign. Fearing that the endowment, which was still without a formal congressional charter of incorporation, might lose much of its potential influence if it was perceived as an agency of the Taft administration, Root argued—and Butler and Carnegie reluctantly agreed—that it should not participate in the campaign for treaty ratification.[69]

Carnegie was no doubt disappointed that the "peace trust" he had created to assist Taft would now have to sit out the battle for treaty ratification. But he had long ago decided not to overrule the men he had chosen to run his trusts. Root was the ablest "president" he had—a man committed to peace who understood national politics better than anyone alive. He would not contest his decision that the endowment remain neutral in the upcoming battle. Fortunately, Carnegie had enough money to fund pro-treaty campaigns through other organizations like Nicholas Murray Butler's Citizens' National Committee.

Early in November, Carnegie wrote Charles Hilles, Taft's secretary, to offer his personal assistance in pushing the treaties through the ratification process. In a subtle swipe at Taft's lack of political skills, he confessed that he had "long felt that the President is 'too good for human nature's daily food.' He should be much more careful than he has been." Carnegie knew better how to move a treaty through the Senate. "I should like to have a talk with him and our friends generally over the situation. My feeling is that we should make the best terms possible with the Senate and pass

that treaty." He then offered, unbidden, the language for a new amendment which, he believed, would "meet the objections raised against the
present one."[70]

All through November, Carnegie besieged Taft and Hilles with letters,
telegrams, copies of newspaper editorials, resolutions he had submitted to
the New York Peace Society, and articles he had published in pamphlet
form. On November 22, he took the train to Washington and personally
counseled Taft to swallow his pride and agree to any compromise with the
Senate that might lead to ratification of the treaties. "May I venture to suggest that perhaps the surest way to secure favorable action upon Peace
Treaty will be for you to . . . invite the Foreign Relations Committee to
dinner and <u>after dinner</u> ask their cooperation in the great work. That they
were not invited while Treaty was being formed, as I understood they were
to be, is something I cannot understand, but no doubt there were good reasons therefore."[71]

By late November, Carnegie was confident that the treaties would gain
ratification, his confidence spiked by the belief that Taft would follow his
advice. On November 25, 1911, his seventy-sixth birthday, he invited reporters to Ninety-first Street, as he did every year. "Andrew Carnegie felt
so good today," the *Washington Post* reported the next day in a front-page
story, "that he trotted reporters around his home library and pointed out
the trophies on its walls." The old man was even more voluble than usual:
he gave forth "countless axioms," predicted that Taft would be easily reelected, offered his solutions to the trust problem, and advised "his interviewers to marry young," give up drinking and smoking, and "obey all the
rules," whatever that meant.

"Everywhere I hear most encouraging news about the attitude of the
people toward the arbitration treaties," he declared to a *New York Times*
reporter on December 4. "The public sentiment in their favor has grown
stronger day by day. New York City is to show itself in harmony with the
rest of the country by holding a mass meeting in Carnegie Hall on December 12th to endorse them."

Carnegie's optimism would be sorely tried. The Carnegie Hall rally
that he had hoped would demonstrate New York City's support for the arbitration treaties backfired, as the *New York Times* reported in a front-page
article on December 13. The meeting had barely gotten under way before it
was broken up by German-American hecklers, who insisted that the pro-

posed arbitration treaties with France and Britain were anti-German. "Andrew Carnegie, world leader of the peace movement, under whose immediate direction last night's meeting was attempted, was a sad-faced witness of it all. He was to have been one of the chief speakers. His time never came. When the disturbance began he feebly tried to wave it down, but saw himself powerless. He sank back into his seat, murmuring to himself, and gave the meeting into other hands."

All of Carnegie's efforts had come to naught. He had tried to enlist Democratic senators in favor of his treaty, but as the melee at Carnegie Hall demonstrated only too graphically, the opposition of German- and Irish-Americans to strengthened ties with Britain was impossible to overcome. Another sizable bloc of senators, these mostly Republicans, was siphoned off as it became clear that Roosevelt was running for the presidency and was going to use his opposition to the arbitration treaties as a campaign issue.

Finally, in late December, Taft, who had said nothing to Carnegie about his plans, wrote to tell him that instead of agreeing to any compromise with the Senate, he thought it "wise for us to go for the full treaties as they are. . . . Don't let us give up in advance!"[72]

Senator Lodge, worried that the longer the battle over ratification went on the more serious the split between the anti-treaty Roosevelt and pro-treaty Taft factions would become, proposed an amendment in late January 1912 that gave the Senate the right to cancel any proposed arbitration. Although both sides recognized that the amendment would, in effect, render the treaties toothless, Carnegie pressed Taft to approve it, rather than make arbitration an issue in his fight for the renomination. Taft declined.

The issue of the treaties was now fatally intertwined with the issue of the Republican nomination for president in 1912. The only way to push the treaty—and the arbitration process—forward was to guarantee that Taft was renominated and reelected to a second term.

IN THE MIDST of his campaign on behalf of Taft's arbitration treaties, Carnegie was visited at his home office by Dr. Maria Stopes, an academic paleontologist, whom he had invited to tea. Dr. Stopes hoped to interest Carnegie in funding research on the "scientific paleontological study of coal," which she claimed had practical applications. Carnegie listened to what she had to say, but "nothing," Stopes recalled, "could make him see paleobotany as a matter of importance. 'Hotts lassie' he said, 'we dug coal before you were born, and none of you scientists make any difference to them digging it, or ever will.'" When she asked for a quarter of a million dollars to pursue her research, Carnegie wasted no time in giving his response. "'Not a penny for it! But if ye'd come to me with anything that would help keep the peace of the world I'd give, not a quarter of a million, but a whole million, for you are a bright lassie. World peace is the greatest thing for us all now. I'll give almost anything to ye if ye bring me anything to help with that. . . . After some talk about the aridness of science he said to me with a sigh 'I have often wasted my money' and I replied with the candour of youth, 'Yes, you have, Mr. Carnegie, but you won't waste it if you give it to me.' He said 'You wait and come to me again when you can help the world.'"[73]

FORTY

"Be of Good Cheer,"
1912–1913

THE CHAIRMAN. Mr. Carnegie, you were engaged in the steel business in
  Pennsylvania and all over this country for a great many years?
MR. CARNEGIE. Yes sir; from early youth, you might say.

So opened the proceedings of the Committee of Investigation of the
United States Steel Corporation on Wednesday, January 10, 1912. Augustus O. Stanley, Democrat from Kentucky, chaired the committee. Andrew
Carnegie sat at a small desk across from him. Between them was a stenog
rapher.

In October 1911, the Taft administration had filed suit against U.S.
Steel, charging that it was in violation of the Sherman Antitrust Act. The
House of Representatives organized a special investigating committee,
which called Andrew Carnegie as its first witness.

Carnegie had aged a great deal in the four years since he had last been
before a congressional committee. He looked almost shrunken, with very
little flesh in his cheeks, his eyes sunk deep, his face dominated by the
white beard.

The proceedings began with the congressmen and Carnegie in a rather
jocular mood. When Chairman Stanley apologized for having issued
Carnegie a subpoena, the witness joked that he was "delighted to get that
official document, to hand down to my heirs. [Laughter.] The signature of
Chairman Stanley will count for something. [Laughter]."

THE CHAIRMAN. You honor me overmuch, Mr. Carnegie. There are so
  many people who have received that signature and did not like to see it,
  that it is very gratifying to know that you treasure it.

"STOP YER TICKLIN', JOCK!"

MR. CARNEGIE. Does that mean, Mr. Chairman, you have bills payable
out to an amount of a million or two? [Laughter.] I might offer to help
you out. [Laughter.]

THE CHAIRMAN . . . It is unfortunately true that I am a very poor man,
and am head over heels in debt. [Laughter.]

MR. CARNEGIE. Well, you are not a poor chairman, and that is the main
thing. Would you take a library? [Laughter.]¹

As the hours wore on, the laughter dissipated. Pressed on some point
or other which he was unable or unwilling to answer, Carnegie took to repeating again and again that, as an absentee partner who lived in New
York City and spent up to six months a year in Europe, he had "paid very
little attention to the details in our business." He refused to answer dozens
of questions, claiming that he did not remember or had never been apprised of the financial details of transactions conducted by his younger
partners. When asked about the capitalization of his business concerns in
the 1860s, he dismissed the question with a shrug, "Oh, my dear Mr.
Chairman, I have no more idea of that than you have." Asked if he would
take a guess, he refused to do so. "I do not like to guess. My memory, I am

sorry to say, is not perfect. I have not been thinking about these things for 40 years, and the last 11 years of my life have been busier than any other 11 years, and so much has faded from my memory in regard to these old matters that I do not like to depend upon my memory."[2]

Though the subject of the hearing was U.S. Steel, with which Carnegie had no connection and no stock, he was asked repeatedly about the company's finances, policies, and personnel. He declined to answer any questions about the corporation that had absorbed Carnegie Steel or the men who ran it. When asked about steel rail prices by congressman Augustus Gardner of Massachusetts, Carnegie turned to his attorney for assistance. Congressman Gardner interrupted him,

MR. GARDNER (interposing). You have answered the question. Judge [J. H.] Reed [Carnegie's attorney] could not answer that question for you. . . .

MR. CARNEGIE. Aren't you rather unreasonable about that, Mr. Gardner?

MR. GARDNER. In view of the examination for the last two days, I do not think I am, and I will say that frankly. . . . When I ask you a direct question as to your opinion, you turn around to your counsel and ask him to tell you what your opinion is?

Carnegie, realizing he was running out of wiggle room, confronted the senator directly. "I was in business to make money. I was not a philanthropist at all. When rails were high we got the highest prices we could get."

Asked again if he thought that the rates he had been reported as charging were "unfair," Carnegie responded that he did "not think any profits are unfair. If a man wants my steel rails at $50 a ton, and he is satisfied to buy them and I to sell them, I see nothing unfair in that. Do you?"

When Gardner hemmed and hawed instead of answering Carnegie directly, the witness adroitly called attention to it.

MR. CARNEGIE. I answered you the same way, so we are square. I think, sir, if you were in my position—

MR. GARDNER. I am not in your position. I am examining you, and you are on the stand.

MR. CARNEGIE. That is right, sir. I wish we had the places reversed. Have mercy.[3]

And this was how most of the sixteen hours proceeded, with the congressmen thrusting and Carnegie parrying. The line that brought the most attention—and certainly the biggest headlines—came when he described how he had bested John D. Rockefeller on his deal to lease iron ore mines in the Mesabi.[4]

One of the unintended—and certainly unwanted—consequences of Carnegie's return to the witness stand was the reappearance of James Bridge. In February of 1912, Bridge wrote Horace Harding, a Frick associate, that Carnegie had approached him at the hearings seeking reconciliation. "He has aged greatly and at times his mentality shows such a falling off as to be pathetic. . . . He said to me that he did not bear a grudge against a soul; and his desire to die at peace with his old associates was really pathetic." Carnegie and Bridge later met at one of Carnegie's clubs where, again according to Bridge, Carnegie identified the errors in *Inside History of the Carnegie Steel Company* and offered to treat Bridge "very liberally" and pay the costs for a new edition should Bridge "correct" those errors. Bridge contacted his publishers, as well as Phipps and Schwab, to inform them that, at Carnegie's request, he was going to bring out a new edition.[5]

Carnegie, who despite Bridge's remarks, was as sharp-witted as he had ever been, was furious when the news got back to him. He directed James Bertram to contact Bridge at once. "Mr. Carnegie understood your position is—when you learned the truth you felt impelled to rewrite parts of your book; Mr. Carnegie did not suggest you should do what was manifestly your duty to do, viz., correct mistakes."[6]

Bridge apologized and promised he would no longer claim that Carnegie had anything to do with his new edition, but asked if Carnegie or Bertram would read his page proofs. Carnegie directed Bertram to write Bridge again, this time in a way that could not be misunderstood. "Mr. Carnegie says that he can have nothing whatever to do with the revised edition of your book. He thinks the truth should be told, which, as he understood you, is that you are satisfied you were misled. It is an easy matter for you to tell your readers so frankly without reference to Mr. Carnegie. . . . Mr. Carnegie says he is just home from Hot Springs and finds he will be fully occupied until the date of his sailing, and must beg of you to refrain from introducing the subject of your book."[7]

Bridge did not comply with the request. A month later he wrote Bertram and Carnegie again, this time asking for a new photograph. Bertram replied that neither he nor Carnegie saw anything wrong with the old one.[8]

CARNEGIE had celebrated his seventy-sixth birthday in November 1911. He was in good health, though he complained of a "troublesome cold," the result, he thought, of "too many evening engagements." Louise, who had turned fifty-five in the spring, was herself suffering from "a touch of rheumatism." The Carnegies spent their winter vacation in 1912 at Lucy's estate on Cumberland Island and then motored to Hot Springs, Arkansas, so that Louise could take the baths. Their time in Arkansas was, as Louise wrote a friend, "anything but restful for me." As her husband ascended into his eighth decade, she had become more and more preoccupied with his health. "Everyone laughs when we say we are here for my benefit, on account of my high color, but what with callers for Mr. C's registered letters, Doctor's instructions in regard to the care he needs, etc., it is hopeless for me to try and rest. Home is a perfect haven of rest in comparison."[9]

Though the arbitration treaties had been defeated and the Taft/Roosevelt imbroglio was growing uglier by the moment, Carnegie tried to remain upbeat. Rather than allowing the current state of affairs in the United States to discomfort him, he focused his attention on propping up his friend Morley's spirits. He had often reassured Morley that no matter how sorry the state of the world at the moment, he could take comfort in the fact that tomorrow would be brighter than today.

In the spring of 1912, Morley needed more reassurance than usual. For more than a year, a series of escalating strikes had been ripping through Britain. In March 1912, some 850,000 coal miners had put down their tools, idling over a million workers in industries dependent on coal.

"Sorry to see your troubles are serious but it looks better this morning," Carnegie began his letter of March 23.

> We live in stirring times but all moving in the right direction, progress upward and onward. . . . Madam greatly benefited, so am I, although there isn't much room for betterment in my case except 77 years which cannot be lessened. Roosevelt grieves me deeply but a Niagara will swell and overflow its banks. President Taft behaves as a gentleman should and is rapidly

gaining. I wrote both and have their replies. Roosevelt friendly, very, but wild. Roosevelt's position upon Peace Treaty responsible for failure, so it is said. Until he became a candidate agreement to pass treaty was satisfactory to all—but two thirds majority is always uncertain. . . . Am deluged with telegrams asking me to visit places and deliver my speech, but none of that for me, although in New York I shall do my part. Cheer up. No use looking upon the dark side of things. Time enough to bid the Devil "Good morning" when you must—All's right with the world, or will be later. She's on the upward path—by the law of things can't go backward though it may have a jot or two now and then. The good things of this life should be and will be more evenly divided, all these troubles bound to evolve a higher civilization. Of this I am certain, and so good morning, My Lord and My Lady Morley.[10]

Carnegie and Louise returned to New York in early April for a month's hiatus before leaving for Scotland. Awaiting him at Ninety-first Street was a proposal from John D. Rockefeller, Jr., for a cooperative philanthropic venture. (We regrettably don't know any of the details.) Carnegie turned it down, with consummate grace and good humor. "We find as a rule that we cannot contribute even in a quiet way to a new cause without becoming involved in its operation, more or less. Were we to become equal partners and therefore responsible for the management of a new scheme, we should have to neglect other duties." He then launched into a paragraph in which he described proudly, almost as a new father would, how busy he was kept, night and day, by his "several new movements. The Hero Funds scattered throughout Europe now are bringing us new duties. . . . Library buildings in 2300 communities bring considerable citizens calling here, not a few of them having further suggestions to make. Twenty-one more Library Buildings and fifty-eight church organs given yesterday, accumulated during our short holiday at Hot Springs. Every one of these cases requires preliminary correspondence and believe me, very careful scrutiny. Of course this is done by Mr. Bertram, but many cases have to be discussed by us. The Peace Fund disturbs our peace, etc. etc., and so with the others. Please excuse us and do give us credit for being hardworking, honest people trying to justify a living. If at any time we could trade ages with you and your dear wife, do not fail to apprize us."[11]

. . .

THE SINKING of the *Titanic* in April 1912 had a deep effect on ordinary folk on both sides of the Atlantic, but an especially horrific one on a veteran oceanic traveler like Carnegie. "Can't get the *Titanic* out of mind," he wrote his cousin Dod on April 19. He donated $5,000 to the relief fund set up by Mayor William Gaynor and delivered it with a letter, which was published in the *New York World* on April 19 under the headline "IRONMASTER'S PITHY QUESTION EVOKES PRAISE FROM MAYOR GAYNOR."[12]

"What," Carnegie had asked, "was the *Titanic* doing up among the ice when she had the whole Atlantic Ocean south open and free? This is the root of the matter. Passenger steamships should be compelled to keep far south below the range of icebergs at all seasons. Lifeboats are secondary to this vital requirement." Gaynor thanked Carnegie for his contribution and praised him for "as usual [hitting] the nail exactly on the head."

THOUGH THE arbitration treaties were, by this time, dead in the water, Carnegie refused to give up hope. He had urged Taft to try to get the best compromise he could and then sign whatever the Senate passed. Better a weakened treaty than nothing at all. In late March, President Taft, by personal letter, informed Carnegie that he was not taking his advice, but was going to veto the heavily amended treaties. He preferred to take the issue to the people in the upcoming presidential election. Carnegie thought this unwise. "There is no escape from the general impression that we have not managed the treaties well. . . . The less said in the coming campaign upon this, the better."[13]

The political situation was rapidly deteriorating for the Republicans. The split in the party between those loyal to Roosevelt and those who believed Taft should be given a second term could not be papered over, but grew wider and deeper. Carnegie did his best to save his party from disaster. With blind self-confidence and no understanding of the contempt with which each candidate referred to him behind his back, he attempted to use what he thought were cordial relationships with both to get them to bury their hatchets. The leading culprit in the drama was, in his estimation, Theodore Roosevelt. "Cannot get over Roosevelt's candidacy," he had written Morley in late February. "It isn't fair. Taft should have his second term."[14]

"To see you and your protégé, each struggling for the nomination overwhelms me," he wrote Roosevelt on March 1, "both men to whom I have become deeply attached for their virtues. . . . I am saddened as I have never had cause to be for you as for your successor, both are to be pitied, being the noble men you are the situation for both must be deplorable, I should think unendurable. What a service would that man render who could induce you and the president to meet face to face and just let your hearts speak. It is not too late. You are both big enough to discard mean petty trifles and renew your idyllic relations before history records you as fools, or worse."[15]

Roosevelt's response was suffused with barely repressed anger at the man in the White House and the white-bearded fool who defended him. "You oblige me to speak frankly by what you say about Mr. Taft—I would not say this for publication. I have never been so bitterly disappointed in any man. I care not one whit as to his attitude toward me. But I care immensely as to his attitude toward the people. He has completely reversed the position he held when he was my lieutenant."[16]

Carnegie retreated, momentarily. "Thanks for your kind letter," he replied. "Had I known your quarrel was Political I should not have written you such a note." He had, he explained, assumed that Roosevelt and Taft were friends as well as "patron and pupil" and had tried to call upon that friendship to settle their dispute. He stood corrected now, but disturbed nonetheless at Roosevelt's intransigence. Sensing that he could do no more, he washed his hands of the matter, though not before informing Roosevelt that he had yesterday denied "a report . . . that I was one of your financial supporters [in the presidential primary campaign against Taft for the Republican nomination]." His letter closed on a rather desperate note of strained optimism: "No more of this, it will work out somehow. The Republic is invulnerable."[17]

"I am mourning over the pitiable disagreement of Roosevelt and Taft," Carnegie wrote Morley in mid-May. "Have declared they both should be spanked. Roosevelt wrong in not agreeing second term for President who has done so well. Roosevelt and Niagara quite true—both uncontrollable."[18]

While increasingly angry at Taft's mismanagement of the arbitration treaty in the Senate, Carnegie supported him nonetheless with unsolicited campaign advice and money. "Some time ago I suggested to the President," he wrote Taft's campaign director in mid-May, "that a statement of his triumphs and those of his cabinet could not but impress the thoughtful voter. He agreed, and being asked if he knew the best man to prepare it, he suggested Mr. Leupp [Francis E. Leupp, a political journalist], whose work I send. Now if the President be nominated, perhaps it may be deemed advisable to print and circulate this paper and send it freely through the doubtful states. I have told Franks to send $25,000 to the Treasurer as my contribution to the campaign, provided my candidate is nominated, and you can use part of this to pay for distribution of leaflet. I shall mourn and rage ["and rage" had been penciled into the typewritten letter], indeed, if the President be defrauded of the second term he so richly deserves."[19]

Five days later, on May 22, before sailing for Europe, Carnegie wrote Taft a final letter. "Glad to get away—our country is humiliated by the present canvas [the contest between Taft and Roosevelt supporters] . . . I shall still hope that you control the Convention . . . I am convinced the tide is running strongly in your favor." And indeed, it was. Taft easily won renomination in Chicago. Carnegie, delighted with the outcome, contributed another $75,000 (several million dollars today) for the national campaign.[20]

The Carnegies returned from Skibo in late October so that Carnegie might, as he told the press, "cast a ballot for Mr. Taft." He denied the rumors that he had decided to become a "British subject and retire to the rugged fastness of Skibo castle . . . 'I wouldn't exchange my American citizenship for a pass to paradise, even if the pass was marked "Good for a return trip."'"[21]

Two weeks later, Woodrow Wilson was elected president. Carnegie was neither surprised nor particularly aggrieved. "Having done my best to elect President Taft to the second term I now find myself impelled to congratulate you," he wrote Wilson, wasting no time in trying to enlist him to succeed Roosevelt and Taft as a partner for peace. "My friends for International Peace have not forgotten your reply to my circular letter [during the campaign for Senate approval of Taft's arbitration treaties] addressed to seven leading democrats, yourself among the number all of whom rose above partisanship to statesmanship when a great cause presented itself. Britain, France, <u>Germany</u> stood ready to sign the treaty, but alas it miscarried. Some day I hope to be permitted to tell you why it miscarried. What the fates have in store for you is unknown; perhaps you are destined to succeed in banishing war between the most enlightened nations where President Taft failed. I think I know why." Carnegie's cryptic messages about the inside story of Taft's failure were designed to let the new president know how valuable the white-bearded Scotsman might be as an adviser. He closed his letter, as usual, with some flattery of the man who was now to occupy the White House. "I am sincerely your admirer and cannot help it."[22]

"The election has not surprised many," he wrote Morley on November 7. "Roosevelt's power for mischief unlimited—Taft is as jolly as ever, breakfasted with him last week. Have written Wilson of course, a nice letter. You know he is on board University Professors [Carnegie's Foundation for the Advancement of Teaching] Trust, and has been at Skibo with his wife. He is for Peace and will I think manage better than Taft, who really failed in Treaty thru poor management." He closed his usual chatty, disjointed name-dropping letter by announcing that he was going that morning "to arrange transfer of Bonds to my Executors New York Carnegie Assn—keeping a few to myself for extra calls—shall die poor, according to the Gospel of Wealth."[23]

It had dawned on Carnegie the year before that, try as he might, he was not going to be able to personally dispose of his fortune in his lifetime. He had been defeated in the end by the inexorable logic of compound interest. In the spring of 1911, he had drafted a new will and made provision to put the remainder of his estate in trust. When he showed the document to Elihu Root, Root warned him against trying to be his own lawyer and suggested that instead of establishing a trust to take effect after his death, he create and endow one during his lifetime. This was the genesis of the Carnegie Corporation of New York, the largest Carnegie trust and indeed, the largest philanthropic trust in history, to that point.

The corporation was officially organized in November 10, 1911, with an endowment of $25 million (close to $8 billion today) and considerable fanfare. The *New York Times* and papers across the country hailed the latest Carnegie gift on their front pages. John D. Rockefeller cabled his congratulations. "May your life be spared for many years with health and happiness."

Carnegie graciously replied that Rockefeller's "telegram gave me unusual pleasure. . . . You and I are in the same boat, finding that it is harder to administer, than to make, dollars. But I think I have really found the best possible solution for the future usefulness of what I shall leave behind me."[24]

The new corporation was the only trust he intended to run by himself. "When Mr. Carnegie formed the Carnegie Corporation," Henry Pritchett, an original trustee and later acting president, explained, "he simply incorporated himself." Carnegie named himself the corporation's first president, arranged for all trustee meetings and business to be transacted from Ninety-first Street, and appointed his bookkeeper, Robert Franks, as treasurer, and James Bertram as secretary. Elihu Root, the corporation's first vice president and the only officer not employed by Carnegie, was also named to the eight-member board of trustees; the other trustees were the presidents of Carnegie's U.S. trusts.[25]

Carnegie intended to keep transferring gold bonds from his vault at the Home Trust Company to the corporation, until there were none left. Louise was not going to be left a pauper—she had well over $1 million in assets and would inherit Carnegie's real estate—but neither was she going to inherit the size of fortune that other robber barons bequeathed to their wives. In accepting the gift, the trustees graciously acknowledged that fact by thanking "Mrs. Carnegie and Miss Margaret Carnegie who, with cheerful and active sympathy, have approved and promoted the diversion of a vast fortune from the ordinary channels of family distribution to the benefit of mankind."[26]

Carnegie would live his final years in disappointment that he had not met his lifelong goal of giving away all his money personally. But he had, in leaving it to the corporation, come close. For the first few years, while the corporation was still under the control of Carnegie, Bertram, and Franks, and housed at Ninety-first Street, Carnegie used it to make the kinds of grants that he and Bertram had been handling by themselves, mostly gifts for libraries, church organs, and colleges. Only after Elihu Root became president on Carnegie's death in 1919 did the corporation move into other areas. Carnegie had already anticipated this and given the trustees the broadest possible charter to spend his money "to promote the advancement and diffusion of knowledge and understanding" as they saw fit.

The initial bequest of $25 million made hardly a dent in Carnegie's holdings. On January 14, 1912, the *New York Times,* in a *Sunday Magazine* article entitled "What is Andrew Carnegie Really Worth?", estimated that his fortune was nearly what it had been on his retirement, "over $200,000,000, and probably nearer $250,000,000." The newspaper was not far off. There remained in the vault of the Home Trust Company in Hoboken some $150 million (almost $50 billion today) in U.S. Steel gold bonds. While Carnegie had been giving away between $10 and $20 million a year, he had been earning back between $13 and $20 million in interest.

Two days after the *New York Times* article, Carnegie transferred an additional $75 million in gold bonds from his personal account to the corporation. In October, he gave away another $25 million. Early in 1913, having decided that he needed to set up a comparable organization for the United Kingdom, he asked Root to transfer $10 million from the New York–chartered Carnegie Corporation for this purpose. When Root replied that such a transfer would violate the corporation's charter, Carnegie took $10 million from his private holdings to endow the United Kingdom Trust.[27]

ON NOVEMBER 25, 1912, Andrew Carnegie celebrated his seventy-seventh birthday with a stroll in his garden, after which he repaired to his library to read the hundreds of letters of congratulation that had arrived that day. In the afternoon, he invited the reporters, as had become customary on his birthday, to join him for a conversation.

"'I'm feeling young, indeed,' was his response to their congratulations when he entered his library. 'Why shouldn't I, when I see so much good all about me? The earth becomes more of a Heaven to me every year. Every year I get a higher opinion of the human race, because I know so many more men and women who have attained almost angelic heights.'" In a wide-ranging interview, Carnegie explained that the Hero Fund was his favorite philanthropy because he had thought of it on his own and it had been so successful that he had expanded it to Canada, Great Britain, Germany, Belgium, Holland, Norway, Sweden, and Italy. "The reports that I get from all these countries are the best medicine that can be administered to any man. It keeps me young."[28]

Carnegie's protestations of unalloyed joy—at being alive and having finally succeeded in disposing of his fortune—were his way of whistling away his anxieties. His age was finally beginning to catch up with him. He was noticeably frail, having trouble with his knees, catching colds more often, and no longer nimble on his feet.

His friends and political contacts had aged along with him and no longer occupied important government posts. Campbell-Bannerman had died in 1908. Carnegie had established a correspondence with Herbert Asquith, his successor, but Asquith, born in 1852, had no intention of forging as close a relationship to Carnegie as the previous generation of Liberals had.[29]

The same process was at work in Washington. Woodrow Wilson and his secretary of state, William Jennings Bryan, replied courteously to Carnegie's letters, but they did not invite him to luncheon or dinner or to one-on-one conversations as their predecessors had. He would never again exercise the influence he had enjoyed—or thought he had enjoyed—in Washington and London.

He understood now that with the defeat of Taft's arbitration treaties, the exit of the Republicans from the State Department and the diplomatic corps, and James Bryce's resignation as ambassador to the United States, an opportunity had passed that might not soon return. "I hoped your crowning glory was to be the Treaty," he wrote Bryce in November 1912. "It will come some day. I, like you, have my greatest of all disappointments of my life. What we have lost! When will the Gods give us such a chance again. Well, well, let us hope. Never give up. It will come some day."[30]

He tried his best not to hold Taft responsible for the failure of the treaty, but could not, in the end, help himself. What he refused to recognize was that no matter how carefully the arbitration treaties might have been drafted and no matter how scrupulously the administration might have prepared the groundwork for ratification, the treaties were not going to get the two-thirds vote required in the Senate. As Roosevelt and Hay had discovered a decade earlier, and Woodrow Wilson would learn a few years hence, the U.S. Senate in the first quarter of the twentieth century was not inclined to cede its prerogatives to make treaties and declare war.

This truth was too terrible for Carnegie to look in the face. As usual, he preferred to search for scapegoats—and found them in the persons of Taft and his secretary of state, Philander Knox. On December 12, he and Louise joined the Tafts and the cabinet for a special farewell dinner. Three days later, back in New York on a Sunday, the day he devoted to letter writing, he unburdened himself.

"Why did you fail?" he wrote Taft accusatorily. Then he answered his own question, accusing Taft and Knox of killing the treaties by not consulting in advance with the Senate Committee on Foreign Relations. Lest they bungle another diplomatic initiative, Carnegie urged the president, who would remain in office as a lame duck until March, to begin discussions at once with the Senate over the proposed and highly contentious Panama Canal treaty.[31]

Taft did not answer Carnegie's letter directly, but sent it to Knox, with the note: "Isn't it pleasant to be told how it could have been done?" Knox was even more outraged than the president at Carnegie's presumption that he knew best how to conduct the nation's business. "As an exhibition of ignorance, mendacity and impudence," Knox wrote Taft, "this communication of Mr. Carnegie's is quite up to his well known and well deserved international reputation for these mental and moral failings. It should be appropriately tagged and filed and given no further attention." Knox closed his letter with a sixteenth-century Latin verse, "Mel in ore, verba lactis, Fel in corde, fraus in factis," "A honeyed mouth with milky words hides a heart filled with gall and evil deeds."[32]

CARNEGIE—like the voters—having lost faith in Taft, turned his attention to the president-elect. "Carnegie Now Looks to Wilson for Peace," the *New York Times* reported in a January 25, 1913, article. "Regrets Bad Record of Past Year, but is Strong in Predicting Change." In a speech before a joint meeting of the New York Peace Society and the Civic Forum at Carnegie Hall, "Mr. Carnegie asserted his conviction that the end of war was in sight and expressed the greatest confidence in the attitude which president-elect Wilson would assume on going into office."

He was as intently focused on the threat of war as he had ever been. In the scrapbook of cartoons and Carnegie greeting cards assembled by Margaret Barclay Wilson and donated to the Carnegie Library of Pittsburgh is a painting of a family scene, with a young girl standing on a chair, hugging her father in uniform. The caption reads, "Daddy, are you going to kill some other little girl's father?" Beneath the painting, in Carnegie's handwriting is written, "Merrie Christmas, 1913," and "We pause for a reply."

"DADDY, ARE YOU GOING TO KILL SOME OTHER LITTLE GIRL'S FATHER?"

In April, Carnegie formally welcomed Woodrow Wilson to the presidency (he had been inaugurated the month before) with unsolicited advice on how he might quell the anti-Japanese agitation in California. Like a child seeking to impress his teacher on the first day of a new school year, Carnegie made sure the new president knew that he had been a major adviser to President Roosevelt on this subject. He concluded his letter with a bit of flattery, as was his practice in communicating with the White House: "I watch you progress (for progressing you are) with deep interest, and am sanguine of your success." He then added that he was now a proponent of the progressive income tax. "Citizens should pay taxes in proportion to their ability to do so. Millionaires have undoubted ability to pay. I send you copy of the 'Gospel of Wealth.' Roosevelt's reply to copy sent him when he advocated increased taxation was 'I am much struck with the fact that seventeen years ago you had it all.'"[33]

In early May, Carnegie took the train to St. Louis to give the keynote address at the fourth annual American Peace Congress. Again, he saluted Woodrow Wilson and Secretary of State Bryan, and again, he closed his speech by calling on "Friends of Peace [to] be of good cheer; this savage crime of man killing man is soon to become a crime of the past."[34]

It was almost as if he were stuck in a time warp, continually revisiting the past, still calling for naval disarmament and arbitration treaties, still looking to lead the nations of the world into a League of Peace. Greeting reporters at the pier as he and his family sailed for Europe on May 25, he announced that he planned to make two special trips to the Continent that summer, one to visit the kaiser in Berlin and deliver a "memorial" to him from the American Peace Society, the other to The Hague.[35]

He was, it appeared, returning to the place he had occupied three years earlier when he proclaimed the kaiser a "man of destiny" and dispatched Roosevelt to meet with him. On June 8, he published an article in the *New York Times Sunday Magazine,* headlined, "KAISER WILHELM II, PEACE-MAKER, BY ANDREW CARNEGIE. 'THE CIVILIZED WORLD THIS DAY BOWS REVERENTLY BEFORE YOU,' WRITES THE AMERICAN PEACE ADVOCATE, IN CONGRATULATING THE EMPEROR ON THE OCCASION OF HIS JUBILEE CELE-BRATION." Much of the article recapitulated Carnegie's prior dealings with the kaiser and explained how impressed the kaiser had been with Carnegie's speeches and articles on peace. While tooting his own horn— as he could never refrain from doing on such occasions—Carnegie also re-minded his readers that "for twenty-five years [Wilhelm II] has reigned in unbroken peace over the most powerful military nation of the world, sur-rounded by neighboring less powerful nations. Never has he drawn sword or threatened to draw it; on the contrary, he has labored always to preserve the peace and has triumphed."

The Carnegies arrived in Berlin on June 14. "Everyone wants to see Carnegie," the *Los Angeles Times* reported on June 16; "everyone wants to talk to this Kaiser der Industrie . . . Carnegie, his wife and daughter, occupy the royal suite at the Adlon. They were invited to become the personal guests of the Kaiser . . . but the great American likes to be independent and as he says himself he wants to see everything that is going to happen with the freedom of an American visitor." Two days later, Carnegie attended the official state dinner marking the kaiser's twenty-five-year Jubilee. It was, he remarked the following morning, "the most glittering function of my life." The *New York Times,* reporting on the event on June 19, noted that Carnegie had been the only man in "plain evening clothes." Placed with his back to the tables where the kaiser and his "bejeweled fellow-sovereigns" were seated, "the white-haired little man in somber black was the cynosure of all eyes. Everybody wanted him pointed out. He was taken in tow after the dinner by the Kaiser's chief aide de camp [who] led him to the balcony where the Kaiser's own party was assembled. . . . The Kaiserin as well as the Crown Prince asked to have Mr. Carnegie presented to them, and engaged with him in conversation for several minutes. The Kaiser, too, found time to say several pleasant things to him."

The morning after the state dinner, the Carnegies left for a trip through the Alps along the route Louise Whitfield had traveled with her parents when she was sixteen, Margaret's age in 1913. They stopped in Paris, where, once again, Mr. Carnegie quickly occupied the center of attention. "Andrew Carnegie has been the conspicuous figure in the life of Paris this week," the *New York Times* reported by cable on July 5. "For three days the city talked of nothing but the ironmaster, who was feted by nearly a dozen different organizations, and had receptions given him by a number of leading Frenchmen from president [Raymond] Poincaré downward."

Though Carnegie may have been politic enough not to praise the German kaiser too loudly in Paris, he started all over again in late August, when he visited The Hague for the opening of the Peace Palace built with his funds and unveiled a bust of Sir Randal Cremer, a British peace activist. After reciting a paragraph from a biography of Cremer, Carnegie soared into his stump speech on disarmament and a League of Peace, punctuating it again by reference to the kaiser, whom he implored, as he had Roosevelt before him, to convene an international peace conference.[36]

Carnegie returned to the United States in October almost giddy with optimism. The day on which he had been honored for his contribution to peace at The Hague, Louise would later recall in her diary, had been "perhaps the greatest in Andrew's life." On November 25, the reporters who visited him in his library to celebrate his birthday found him nearly bouncing with joy "at the dawn of his seventy-ninth year. 'How on earth do you expect a youngster like me to know anything about the so-called joys and delights of old age,' asked Mr. Carnegie, 'when I am feeling as young and chipper as any one of you young men? As a matter of fact, I am just exactly 78 years young, and that is all there is to that. But,' added Mr. Carnegie, and he was a bit solemn, 'I have passed another milestone and I am not keen on going ahead too fast. This earth of ours is such a heaven to me that I want to stay here just as long as I can.'"[37]

Carnegie's reveries were interrupted by a question about Mexico. Back in May 1911, rebels had toppled the government of Porfirio Díaz in a nearly bloodless revolution. The new president, Francisco Madero, had barely begun to institute the reforms he had promised before he was assassinated by his chief lieutenant, Victoriano Huerta. Armed resistance to the new government was organized in the south and in the north. The European powers recognized Huerta's government, but the United States put off doing so. As civil war intensified, President Wilson denounced Huerta, outlawed the sale of arms to Mexico, and after an unsuccessful attempt at mediation, pursued what the newspapers referred to as a policy of "watchful waiting." In October 1913, the British affirmed their recognition of the Huerta government, enraging Wilson, who stepped up his criticism of the Mexican president.

While refusing to publicly criticize President Wilson, Carnegie told the reporters that he considered the political turmoil in Mexico "a family affair of the Mexicans and I don't see that we have any right to interfere." Asked to comment on Wilson's increasingly bellicose anti-Huerta rhetoric, Carnegie declined. "Mexico," the reporter concluded, "did not fit in with the well-known peace views of Mr. Carnegie and so at the first opportunity he switched the talk to matters nearer home."[38]

Though he did not comment on it in public, Carnegie had earlier that month sent Wilson a long letter of advice on the Mexican situation. He prefaced his position paper with the same sort of quasi-apologetic statement he had earlier employed in communicating with Presidents Harrison, Cleveland, McKinley, Roosevelt, and Taft. "My ardent wish for your continued success must be my apology for troubling you." After reciting his credentials as an expert on Mexico—his attendance at the first Pan American Conference and his recent award of a gold medal "at the last Pan American Conference by a unanimous vote of representatives of more than 160,000,000 million"—he beseached the president to set aside any thoughts of invading Mexico. "Mexicans . . . will not approve the stranger invading her land, even to right her wrongs. . . . If I were you I'd let Mexico manage her own destiny. . . . When other nations recognized Huerta I would have followed them."[39]

While Wilson threatened Mexico with invasion and war clouds gathered over the Balkans, Carnegie celebrated the imminent arrival of world peace. "We send this New Year Greeting January 1, 1914, strong in the faith that international Peace is soon to prevail."

> *Be of good cheer, kind friend.*
> *It's coming yet for a' That!*
> *When man to man the world o'er*
> *Shall brothers be and a' that.*[40]

FORTY-ONE

1914

I AM NOT A strict vegetarian, nor a great meat eater," Carnegie responded in January 1914 to one of the hundreds of letters sent him, "—just in the middle—neither too much nor too little. I am an abstainer; no liquor except my doctor prescribes a half glass of the <u>very best Scotch whisky,</u> and this I take at lunch and dinner, no wine or beer." He had become an all-purpose expert, willing to dispense advice on just about any topic—to anonymous correspondents, newspaper reporters, politicians, and presidents.[1]

In February 1914, reconciled to the fact that his Endowment for International Peace would never be able to take the advocacy role he had envisioned for it, Carnegie endowed a second peace society, this one dedicated to activism as well as education.

His friend and colleague Frederick Lynch had remarked that clergymen active in the peace campaign never had sufficient funding to pursue their work. Carnegie, intrigued, asked Lynch if he could assemble an ecumenical group of fifty or sixty churchmen, including rabbis. Lynch did so, and Carnegie, after consulting with Louise's pastor, gave the group, which became known as the Church Peace Union,* a $2 million grant from his newly established Carnegie Corporation.

The trustees of the new peace society were invited to lunch with Carnegie on February 10. They approved two peace and disarmament resolutions, which were sent "to each Sovereign, president, Prime Minister, Minister of Foreign relations, President of legislature, and other high offi-

---

*The Church Peace Union is still in existence, but is now known as the Carnegie Council on Ethics and International Affairs.

cial of the World Powers, and to the clergy of Germany, Great Britain and the United States." Lynch, who had worked with Carnegie for many years, recalled later that he had never taken "more delight in any of his gifts than in this child of his later years. After all the [trustees] had gone, he and I went into the library together and he put his arm about my neck and said, 'Hasn't it been a great day! And what a splendid lot of men we've got there! They can do anything.'" Planning began at once for an international conference to be held in Germany the following August.[2]

There was one cloud on the horizon. In February 1914, Carnegie wrote to thank Woodrow Wilson for a recent letter which, he insisted, he was going to put "into my president's drawer—Harrison Cleveland McKinley Roosevelt Taft all there for the future none more valued than yours." He added a p.s. as long as the letter on "Mexico, Mexico, the only danger." Though he fervently hoped the president would take his advice and resist the temptation to invade, if the circumstances should warrant it and intervention became necessary, Carnegie offered his assistance in securing the support of the Latin American republics.[3]

IN MARCH 1914, Carnegie, instead of returning to Cumberland Island and Hot Springs for Margaret's Easter break from Miss Spence's School, spent extra time in Washington, then sailed along the Potomac River to Chesapeake Bay for a few days' visit at Hampton Normal and Agricultural Institute (today Hampton University). "I've been on the go, so many Resolutions presented and Meetings, I could not refuse." Spring was finally, he wrote Morley in his Sunday letter on March 29, poking up its head. "Weather here fine at least, snow drifts all gone thru the city. . . . Our garden alive, roots shooting up everywhere and robins here—now for my morning stroll in it. Madam and Margaret at church—latter 17 tomorrow, a young lady already and a wise one—but bossy—rather but always the Lady like her saintly mother." In April, he and Louise planned to go to Pittsburgh for an event at his Carnegie Institute, "now grown, a gigantic affair, 300 students males, 250 women—and still they come and we keep on building."[4]

In early April, he visited with Woodrow Wilson at the White House. President Wilson, asked at an April 9 press conference what Carnegie "wanted," replied that he "didn't want anything. He is quite removed from want. No; it was entirely a friendly visit. He was passing through and he came in to pay his compliments. He didn't ask a thing or discuss a single public question."[5]

That same day, seven American sailors on shore leave in Tampico, Mexico, were arrested by an officer of the Huerta government. The Wilson government dispatched 7,000 Marines to seize the port city of Vera Cruz. Carnegie, though aghast at Wilson's action and frightened that the landing was but the first step in a full-scale invasion, refrained from publicly criticizing the new president. "Numerous telegrams tell me of proposed meetings to protest against war," he cabled Wilson, "to which I have replied that this is not yet in order, we must wait." Contacted by the *New York World,* Carnegie both praised Wilson as a friend of peace and cautioned him publicly against drawing the nation into a war which would make enemies of every South American republic. "We cannot expect our sister republics to see our giant republic interfering with any one of them without arousing all of them against us."[6]

On April 24, having received no response from the president to his letters, Carnegie wrote Joseph Tumulty, Wilson's personal secretary, to plead again for an end to the military action in Mexico. "I repeat that unless some way is found to obtain an armistice we become the distrusted neighbor of all our southern sister nations." His tone was one of desperation. "Today it is easy to predict that unless the President gets release from some quarter his noble resolve to avoid war will soon pass, and history is to record his failure with years of unexpected humiliating, barbarous and unnecessary war, staining his otherwise noble record. My intense regard and admiration for him as a man of the highest aims is my only excuse for this intrusion, which shall probably be the last, for the sands of time are running down fast."[7]

That same evening, Carnegie received his reply from the White House in the form of a telegram delivered to his first-tier Carnegie Hall box, stage right, where he was listening to the Oratorio Society's last concert of the season. Carnegie read the telegram, then, without a word to his wife, ran downstairs to the orchestra level and made his way to the stage door entrance. The chorus had just completed its final piece before intermission. As the applause died down and the conductor bowed to the audience, a tiny man with a white beard walked onto the stage through an opening in the middle of the risers where the singers were seated. The audience, recogniz-

ing that it was Andrew Carnegie, applauded him generously. Holding the
telegram in his hand and almost out of breath, he bowed.

"'Behold, I bring you good tidings,' he exclaimed excitedly. . . . 'This is
the happiest moment of my life!' . . . 'War has been averted at the last moment. . . . There will be no more hostilities!'" He continued on for a full
fifteen minutes, segueing effortlessly into praise for the Oratorio Society
before turning "to the chorus behind him on the stage. . . . 'This news
about the Mexican situation has put me in such fine spirits that each of you
ladies in the chorus looks like an angel of peace to me.'" Then he shook
hands with the conductor and left the stage. Frederick Lynch, who was in
the audience, made his way to Carnegie's box "and arrived there just before
he did. When he came in he was as happy as a child—all radiant. 'Isn't it
great news?' he said at once. . . . The music began and I went back to my
chair leaving Mr. Carnegie with eyes closed and Mexico and everything
else forgotten."[8]

Carnegie's joy was premature. There would be no imminent war with
Mexico, but Vera Cruz remained occupied by American troops. All
through May, Carnegie bombarded the president and his secretary with
letters urging that American forces be withdrawn from Mexico. "Please
excuse me," he wrote Tumulty on May 7, "but I feel as though I had the
closest and dearest friend on earth in jeopardy. I wish to be candid. . . . It
takes a great man to acknowledge his mistake, but such a man I credit the
President with being."[9]

On May 21, before embarking for Europe, he wrote Wilson one last
time. "I leave for the moors Saturday morning feeling that you are in grave
danger. Your interview in Philadelphia Saturday past, if correctly reported,
commits you to the task of righting Mexico's wrongs. . . . I tremble, seeing
you as it were on the brink of a precipice where one misstep brings such
disaster to our country as the Civil War alone entailed. My hope is that you
will soon see that our departure from Mexico, having tried our best to promote peace by friendly counsel <u>but not by war</u>—is our duty for it is true
that real progress in civilization comes from the abused masses below . . .
not from the rulers of foreign countries. . . . Numerous engagements . . .
call me abroad but my thoughts will be in Washington hoping that the
kind fates will open the path of withdrawal for you, in peace."[10]

That same day, in a second letter, this one formally addressed and type-
written, Carnegie responded to Wilson's request that he donate funds to

Berea College in the Kentucky hills. Wilson had appealed to Carnegie to do for southern whites, "this great mass of people of our own stock and traditions," at least as much as he had done for the southern Negroes. "The South and the Nation would certainly appreciate such action." Carnegie answered that he would be glad to ask the Carnegie Foundation for the Advancement of Teaching to examine the problem and report back to him. The two men had tacitly agreed that their disagreement over Mexico was not going to interfere with possible cooperation in other areas. "You may be sure that your recommendation of the greatness of this cause gives it high importance in my eyes, not only because it is from the President of the United States, but because it comes from one who has an expert knowledge of education."[11]

IN LATE JULY, the three Carnegies prepared to break away from the castle at Skibo and their round of visitors for three weeks at their cottage on the Shin River. Andrew had returned to the autobiography he had been working on in fits and starts since 1889. Six hundred pages of "The Story of a Scotch Lad" had, as Carnegie wrote Gladstone in 1891, been dictated to a "clever stenographer" at Cluny and then laid aside "for some future editor—I trust a discreet one—to condense." In the winter of 1897, Carnegie hired James Bertram in large part to help him with his memoirs. The project was put away for another fourteen years until, prodded by Louise, Carnegie returned to it in the summer of 1911. He hoped to be able to bring his manuscript up to the present and finish it during the family's monthly retreat at Auchinduich in 1914.*[12]

On June 28, 1914, as the Carnegies were leaving the castle for their cottage, Archduke Ferdinand of Austria-Hungary was assassinated during a state visit to Sarajevo. There is no mention of the event in Carnegie's correspondence, no doubt because he, like so many others, could not possibly imagine that this event would lead to world war.

On July 23, as Carnegie worked on the final pages of his *Autobiography*, the Austro-Hungarian government delivered an ultimatum to Serbia, demanding among other things that Austrian police and state officials be

*The *Autobiography* would never be finished by Carnegie. The book that was eventually published was assembled posthumously by an editor chosen by Louise Carnegie.

permitted to enter Serbia to apprehend the assassins and suppress anti-Austrian activities.

On July 25, the Serbian government mobilized its army and declared that it would comply with all demands in the Austrian ultimatum that did not "impair" its independence and sovereignty. The Serbs suggested that disputed items in the ultimatum be submitted to arbitration at The Hague.

On July 28, Austria refused arbitration and declared war on Serbia.

On July 29, the czar ordered the Russian army to mobilize against Austria, in defense of Russia's ally, Serbia.

On August 1, Germany, Austria's ally, declared war on Serbia's ally, Russia. France, an ally of Russia, mobilized its army.

On August 3, Germany declared war on France and poured troops into neutral Belgium. At 11:00 P.M., Britain declared war on Germany.

That day—or perhaps early on the next—the Carnegies received an unexpected visit from the Reverend Robert Ritchie, the local minister and friend of the family. Ritchie wanted Carnegie to hear from him, not from the newspapers, that Britain had gone to war. As Burton Hendrick tells the story, Carnegie received Ritchie's news "with incredulity. As always when the Laird was excited, he began pacing up and down the room. 'It can't be true,' he kept saying. 'Are you sure it is true?' Then he would burst out, 'Can't America do something to stop it?'"[13]

The family returned at once to Skibo, where the next day Carnegie received a letter from John Morley, who was at the time a member of the Liberal cabinet. Morley agreed wholeheartedly that the Germans had no business invading neutral Belgium. But he also believed that this was insufficient *casus belli* to set off a European war of all against all. "My Good Friend, You will tomorrow see in the papers, I expect, that I have left the Government. You may be sure that the strain of the last five days has been severe. I have taken my best pains to come to a right and sensible conclusion, and you will know that I do not leave Asquith, who has been my friend for thirty years, without a mortal pang. As we shall meet on Monday next, I won't go into details now. . . . But what a black panorama! To nobody will it seem blacker than to you. Hell in full blast. This is a sorrowful night for me—probably the last of my public life—but I am in good nerve."[14]

Carnegie's immediate concern may have been his Church Peace Union, which was at the time holding its first annual conference in Germany, with a number of British citizens—including members of Parliament—among the participants. Fortunately for all, the German government offered British and American delegates safe passage to the border. Lynch telegrammed Carnegie from London to ask for funds to provide for the forty Americans.[15]

Morley arrived at Skibo the week after his resignation and the two dear friends tried to make sense of their world gone mad. Carnegie respected and admired Morley's decision to resign, but he himself declined to join the protest against the war. "Protest today useless," he declared in an open letter published in *The Times of London* on August 8. "We advocates of heavenly peace and foes of hellish war must not fail to expose and denounce the guilty originators thereof." The British government, he concluded, "was in honour bound to protect Belgium" and declare war on Germany.

The Carnegies could not remain at Skibo. The British Admiralty had decided to set up a North Sea base at the Duke of Sutherland's residence nearby; horses and men were being requisitioned daily; the war was too close. "We are in perilous times," Carnegie wrote his friend and solicitor John Ross in Dunfermline on August 17. "Our horses, traps etc commandeered—our territorials, ditto. All the household servants included steadily at work, sewing & knitting for the Army. It is all too sad to contemplate but we can indulge the hope that out of this eruption there is to spring the resolve to form an organization among the nations to prevent war hereafter." What must have been especially disheartening for Carnegie was the excitement and enthusiasm with which the British volunteers, including the men of the Highlands, looked forward to crossing the Channel to repel the Boches from Belgium.[16]

Though war had been declared and the troops mobilized, Carnegie clutched at the false hope that somehow the Americans would ride to the rescue and bring the combatants to the bargaining table. John Morley knew better. In late August, he wrote to thank his friend for his hospitality and sympathy. "The only days of peace and refreshment in this Trough of Despair, for me at least, have been my fortnight at Skibo. The company was both genial and understanding. . . . The host and hostess were almost kinder, more considerate, and more sympathetic than usual. . . . There is evidently to be no speedy ray of light upon the European scene; nor will the Devil be chained safely up again in your time and mine. We are seeing evil war at its worst—worst in carnage, worst in its depravation of all moral sense, worst as a murderous gamble. For the moment, there is nothing for people like you and me, but <u>an iron silence</u>. We can keep a vigilant eye upon events—Words are vain or worse than vain."[17]

Carnegie, using every bit of influence he had, arranged an early sailing for the family—on the *Mauritania* from Liverpool in mid-September. Hew Morrison, who had served him faithfully in so many different ways, visited with him for the last time at Skibo. "He was a mental and physical wreck. He had become thin and worn and trembly—he was an aged man. . . . 'All my air castles,' he told Morrison, 'have crashed about me like a house of cards.'"[18]

"The color of the heather and ripening corn is painfully beautiful," Louise wrote James Bryce, as they left Skibo. "We have not had an autumn like it for years and it is one that will never be forgotten for many reasons."[19]

Morley, not knowing when he would see his old friend again, stole away from his home to Liverpool to grab another few hours of conversation before the *Mauritania* sailed. The two old men visited in the hotel sitting room. Though the thought may have entered their minds, neither expected that these would be last moments together. "I low little when we last said goodbye at the Liverpool Station, could we suppose that we were to meet no more, and that the humane hopes that we had lived in, and lived by, were on the very eve of ruin," Morley would write Louise in August 1919. "Our ideas and aims were just the same, but the fire and glow of his spirit was his own, and my debt to him from the year when [Matthew] Arnold made us acquainted, was more than I can find words for."[20]

Carnegie, no doubt, tried to raise his friend's spirits, as he always did. But Morley could not take the bait. He had lost everything, not least the Liberal Party to which he had devoted so much of his life. "What use could I be in the Council of War, into which unhappy circumstances have transformed the Cabinet?" Morley had written Margot Asquith, the prime minister's wife, days after his resignation. "I've run my course and kept the faith. That's enough." No matter if hostilities ceased soon or not or if the death toll reached tens of thousands or tens of millions, the tragic and inescapable truth for Morley was that the Liberal Party had become a war party.[21]

The tragedy for Carnegie was as deeply felt, but of a different sort. It was not the failure of the Liberal government that pained him so much as the failure of the world's leaders and their international institutions to rescue Europe from its suicidal madness. Still, he was not without hope; he never was.

Sometime directly before or after he boarded the *Mauritania,* he sat down with pencil and paper to bring his *Autobiography* up to date: "As I read this [the last passage he had written on his visit to the German kaiser in 1913], what a change! The world convulsed by war as never before! Men slaying each other like wild beasts! I dare not relinquish all hope. In recent days I see another ruler coming forward upon the world stage, who may prove himself the immortal one. . . . He had the indomitable will of genius, and true hope which we are told, 'Kings it makes gods, and meaner creatures kings.' Nothing is impossible to genius! Watch President Wilson! He has Scotch blood in his veins." So ended his manuscript. We do not know whether he intended to return to it at a later date. If so, he never got the chance.[22]

He was trying, with renewed desperation now, to envision a way in which the hostilities might be brought to a speedy conclusion. The British and Germans having surrendered to the gods of war, it was left to President Wilson and the Americans to restore order and good sense. Carnegie suggested, on returning to New York, that Secretary of State William Jennings Bryan, in an effort to establish America's credentials as a possible arbitrator, negotiate with Germany the same sort of toothless but high-minded treaty of conciliation he had earlier signed with the other European powers. To this end he offered to serve as private liaison with the kaiser to ascertain if he would be willing to consider such a treaty. Bryan agreed and approved the draft of the letter Carnegie intended to send to the kaiser. On October 16, Carnegie wrote the kaiser, who responded favorably. But it was too late; no treaty between Germany and the United States was going to end the war in Europe.[23]

Carnegie, recovered from his initial shock, began in the fall of 1914 to speak out in public again, write letters to the editor and articles, grant interviews, and promote a peace agenda in time of war. His first article, "A League of Peace—Not 'Preparation for War,'" was published in the *Independent* and distributed in pamphlet form. He argued that as soon as the war was won, Britain, France, and Russia should invite Germany and Austria to join with them in the establishment of a League of Peace, with a combined naval force to carry out its decisions. For 2,500 years, tribes and nations had "warred with each other, inflicting such barbarities as make the flesh creep . . . and all these years it had been held by many that 'preparation for war' prevents war, yet today we have the greatest outburst of war that this long history recounts. . . . The civilized world has tried 'preparation for war' long enough. We now propose to render war impossible."[24]

Carnegie still held out hope that Wilson would accomplish the impossible and negotiate a settlement. "I shall be disappointed if your valued offer of mediation be not accepted by the Allies," he wrote the president in late November. "Even the German Emperor who was overpowered by the military caste who had resolved upon war during his absence would not be unfavourable to you personally. The present financial and industrial situations are very distressing. I have never known such conditions."[25]

There were few indications that Carnegie had, like his friend John Morley, been overcome by despair at the present and foreboding for the future. On November 25, 1914, he celebrated his seventy-ninth birthday as always by inviting reporters to his library for an extended conversation. He repeated as he had the year before that "the longer I live on this earth the more of a heaven it becomes to me," but he also "admitted that the war had shaken his proverbial optimism about the goodness of this world."[26]

Two weeks later, on December 6, the *New York Times Sunday Magazine* published a long interview with Carnegie, in which he presciently predicted that if a League of Peace were not established at the end of this war, the vanquished would rise up again to renew the cycle of warfare.

FORTY-TWO

Last Days, 1915–1919

CARNEGIE was and had always been an insatiable reader of newspapers and magazines. And it was from them—and his English and Scottish friends—that he followed the war's course through Europe. By the time the family left Skibo in the fall of 1914, 5 million men were at arms, many of them on their way to the eastern and western fronts. The Germans had swept through Belgium into France, but been pushed back at the Marne. At Ypres, in Belgium, in mid-November, more than 5,000 British and 5,000 German soldiers were killed. As winter approached, the armies in the west retreated to either side of a 600-mile line of trenches, which extended from Belgium to Switzerland. In the east, the trench lines extended some 900 miles from East Prussia through Poland. There was no longer any possibility that either side would inflict a knockout blow.

Still, Carnegie refused to give up hope—for the long term. The more deadly the war, the more lasting the peace. In his 1915 New Year's greeting, "War Abolished—Peace Enthroned," and then again in an article published on January 24 in the *Washington Post* and widely distributed, he renewed his call for a League of Peace and a world court. "In these times, when half of our fair world is being blackened by the fire and smoke of shot and shell, when men are at each other's throats and civilization's progress has suffered its most serious setback of centuries, I am asked if I can find any possible prospect for lasting peace. To this I answer an emphatic 'yes.' . . . It is my firm belief and opinion that never at any time in the history of the world did the future hold out such definite promise or permanent peace as it does now. The present war is so appalling and shocking that it in itself is probably doing more to put an end to war than any peace propaganda could have accomplished in half a century. The longer that this war continues and the more terrible its results, the stronger the argument for permanent world peace."

The week before, he had written John Ross that he would not be returning to Scotland for the summer of 1915, not because of the danger posed but because he still had work to do in America. "I am here in constant touch with our President and Secretary of State. . . . I have a part to play here. I know or at least I feel that . . . I may be of use here."[1]

IN FEBRUARY 1915, Andrew Carnegie made his third appearance before a government investigating committee, this time the newly created United States Commission on Industrial Relations, chaired by Kansas City attorney and reformer Frank P. Walsh. The commission had been established in the closing days of the Taft administration. Its mandate was to investigate the larger causes that lay behind industrial violence. The impetus for its creation had been the conviction of the McNamara brothers for the dynamiting of the Los Angeles Times Building in 1910.

On February 5, John D. Rockefeller, Sr., and Andrew Carnegie testified before the commission on the role of philanthropic institutions created by men of wealth. "It was a glorious day for Mr. Carnegie," the New York Sun reported. "He chuckled his way through a carefully prepared statement of his views and then sat down to answer questions. Every rule that Chairman Walsh had made and enforced for the proper conduct of the hearing went by the board within two minutes after Mr. Carnegie went on the stand. . . . Mr. Carnegie appeared in a black frock coat, black bow tie and white stiff bosomed shirt. As he stood to read his statement he looked for all the world like a Scotch preacher high up in his little pulpit on the wall of the church."[2]

Carnegie, older and frailer than when he had last testified and now in his eightieth year, stole the show once again. When asked to state his business, he answered, "My business is to do as much good in the world as I can; I have retired from all other business." "Mr. Carnegie," the New York Times reported on February 5, "was the most remarkable witness that has yet appeared before the commission. Captivating the commission, as well as the audience, by the sheer force of his infectious geniality, he was allowed to tell his story in his own way, and had the crowd in roars of laughter, without any effort being made to restrain him. With an appealing sweep of his arms, as if he wanted to include the whole world in his philosophy of benevolence, the Laird of Skibo beamed as he told how his associates fondly called him 'Andy,' and how he wanted the poor and distressed to share in his happiness." When asked by Chairman Walsh about the possibility that his foundations "might exert undue influence over the beneficiaries" of grants, he replied that he could not "imagine any injury coming from that." He refused to be baited, agreed with the commissioners that government should exercise some control over the foundations, and applauded all efforts to publicize their activities. "Now, I believe in advertising. I would like more men, more people to get interested in my foundation."

That same week, Carnegie appeared again in public, this time at the annual dinner of the Young Men's Bible Class of the Fifth Avenue Baptist Church. With John D. Rockefeller, Jr., at his side—it was his Bible Class—Carnegie told stories of his uncle and of being raised in a Presbyterian nation. "That religion was a little hard for me when I was young, but I got over that," Carnegie told his enthralled audience. The old man, who occasionally leaned on Rockefeller Junior for support, grew more animated as he spoke, sweeping his arms before him and punctuating his points with "short-arm blows with his right fist."[3]

His calendar for February was marked with events and meetings—often two or three a day—but his remarks at Rockefeller's Bible class dinner on Monday, February 8, were the last he would make in public. He was scheduled to preside at William Jennings Bryan's peace lecture at Aeolian Hall on February 25, but did not appear.[4]

On March 21, the *New York Times* published an interview with Carnegie in its *Sunday Magazine*. "It is difficult in printed words," the interviewer wrote, "to give an accurate idea of the feeling in the active, perfectly white-haired, absolutely earnest, world-famous philanthropist's voice." There were no moments of levity, no little jokes this time, only an exhortation to his readers—and no doubt to himself—to keep faith in the peace process and its ultimate victory.

"'Have you lost faith in the peace impulse which centres at The Hague?' I asked.

"'Certainly not,' Carnegie answered. 'I verily believe that in this war exists the most impressive, perhaps the only argument which could induce humanity to abate forever the curse of military preparation and the inevitably resultant woe of conflict. . . . But don't imagine that I underestimate the horror of this conflict. This war staggers the imagination; it goes beyond the bounds of warfare as warfare has been known. I do not underestimate its horror, but I hope, and I believe that this very horrible, newly barbaric excess will so revolt human nature against all things of the kind that the reaction will be great enough to carry us into the realms of reason. And the realms of reason are the realms of peace.'"

Nowhere else did Carnegie so clearly betray his nineteenth-century faith in reason, in progress, in the future. Nowhere else did he so misjudge the dark century of world wars that was to follow.

This was to be his last interview. In May, it was announced that the Carnegies had taken the summer home of the late George W. Vanderbilt in Bar Harbor, Maine, already the watering ground of New York's elites. All summer long, items appeared in the papers about Carnegie's health, which, it was always averred, was satisfactory for a man of eighty. But there were telltale signs, not reported in the press, that indicated otherwise. Carnegie was no longer attending meetings of the board of the Carnegie Corporation, which had moved out of his home into its own offices. Beginning in August 1915, Louise entered into regular correspondence with Robert Franks, the treasurer of the corporation and Carnegie's personal bookkeeper, about individuals, charities, and cultural institutions that required funding. We do not know whether she was acting on her own or communicating her husband's wishes.[5]

The Carnegies returned to New York in mid-October of 1915. The following month, Carnegie celebrated his eightieth birthday, but, for the first time in years, did so without inviting reporters in for a conversation. His new secretary, John Poynton, instead issued a statement, which was carried by the *New York Times* and other dailies on November 26, reporting that Mr. Carnegie "was very much improved in health" but had been "taking life easy." He was, Poynton claimed, playing golf two or three times a week at St. Andrew's and keeping abreast of the news of the world. He had even dictated a short statement on the occasion of his birthday: "Say to the reporters who usually call on my birthday that all goes well with me. Dr. Garmany marvels at the splendid return to health which a Summer on the Maine Coast has wrought. The world grows better and we are soon to see blessed peace restored and a world court established, when, in the words of Burns:

Man to man the world o'er
Shall brothers be for a-that.

For his friends, his extended silence was both baffling and frightening. Not only had he given up public appearances, interviews, visits to Washington, after-dinner speeches, and his letters to the editor, but he had stopped communicating with them as well. John Morley attributed the engulfing silence to the recognition that there was nothing left to say. "It seems a long time since we exchanged letters," he wrote on January 12, 1915. "The reason, I suppose, is the painfully simple one, that the world gives us nothing on which either of us can say to the other a single, new, fresh, cheering instructive world—not one word."[6]

It is impossible from our vantage point to know the cause of Carnegie's silence. He had been, Louise remembered years later in an unpublished interview with Burton Hendrick, "the most vital, exuberant person imaginable—until August 4, 1914. Then he completely changed. He became an old man over night. The war practically destroyed him. Up to that time he had golfed, fished and swam every day,—though he was 78; after that he never did any of these things. He became thin, so that his clothes hung loosely around him; his face became deeply indented; his zest for mere existence had gone."[7]

We cannot diagnose Carnegie's condition. Had he suffered some sort of involuntary breakdown or had he simply retreated into silence because he had nothing more to say?

The answers lie somewhere in between. His campaigns for naval disarmament, treaties of arbitration, and a League of Peace had become more important to him than anything else, more important than his business successes, his philanthropies, maybe even his family. For the past two decades, he had expended every bit of energy and made himself a slightly ridiculous figure in Washington, London, and Berlin in his futile attempt to forestall the horrors of war. He realized now that he had failed. His faith that reason and good sense would ultimately prevail, his Spencerian beliefs that the nations and peoples of the world were becoming more civilized and less barbarous had been spectacularly misplaced.

Had there been the slightest glimmer of hope, any sign at all of sanity, goodwill, or good sense returning, Carnegie might have been moved to comment on it. But there were no signs of peace anywhere on the horizon.

By early 1915, when Carnegie retreated into silence, the trenches had been dug, the soldiers embedded, the supply lines strung out for hundreds of miles in the east and in the west, the blockades established. In January, the war had been widened again as German Zeppelins crossed the North Sea on their first successful bombing raid into Britain. There was no end in sight to the carnage in the fields or the suffering at home. In the five months since war had been declared, the French alone suffered 300,000 military deaths and twice that number wounded, captured, or missing.

In the absence of any word from Carnegie, John Morley began communicating directly with Louise, and she with him. "I had heard one day last week that something was amiss with him, and have been wondering how I should approach you. . . . It is indeed distressing. I cannot bear to think of that pulse of such extraordinary vitality and force going down by a single beat. . . . It is no surprise to me that the strain of the war should be counted among the causes of his illness. I don't believe there is a man in America, or here, to whom this black cloud of misery and horror that has swept over mankind could bring more mortification of heart and soul than to him. This crash of the best ideals of a lifetime may well break us down. I sometimes fall into the impiety of wishing that I had disappeared from a world that can never be the same for some of us again. . . . If there is anything that I can do—in writing to him, or even by crossing the Atlantic for a 'crack' with him—you will command me. He has been my best of friends for more than thirty years."[8]

In sickness as in health, Louise saw to it that her husband remained in his favored state of perpetual motion. No sooner had they returned from the summer in Maine than she arranged for them to winter in Florida. As Lucy Carnegie was gravely ill—she would die in January—there was no possibility of their spending time at Cumberland Island. Instead, knowing how much Andrew loved the sea and yachting, Louise rented two houseboats in Florida for the season, one for the family, the second for staff. Margaret, who was completing her final years at Spence, was left behind in New York City with her aunt Stella and a full complement of servants.

Morley wrote on Christmas Eve 1915, that he had received welcome news from a mutual friend of the Carnegies' "movements," though he remarked, with a rare display of humor, that he was not sure that he "should care for life in a houseboat." On a more somber note, he added that "life is nothing less than hideous in Europe."[9]

Louise, as always, tried to put the best possible face on her and her husband's travails. "We now begin to feel more at home," she wrote Margaret on January 14, 1916, "and I can truly say I like it. . . . After Daddy had his nap, he was willing to take an excursion! I let everybody go ashore and see the town and the Captain took just Daddy and me in the launch up the Miami river. . . . The Captain went ashore and brought us out a delicious kind of drink—and I let Daddy have a little which pleased him greatly. We were gone about an hour and a quarter and Daddy enjoyed every minute of it. He was quite ready for his massage and had a good nap afterwards."

Her favorite moment was in the evenings,

> at sunset . . . on deck just finishing tea, and the beautiful soft colors appearing in the sky. . . . We sit there till dark . . . and then Daddy goes to his massage and I usually go to my writing. . . . We dine at 7:30 and Daddy joins us at the beginning of the meal; he also comes to luncheon but he is so natural there is very little restraint. We only avoid things we know would distress him. . . . I am sure you will have a very happy winter and enjoy all these things which are perfectly right for you to enjoy with a free and happy mind. It is right for you to get all the enjoyment possible out of your life and right for me to be down here helping Daddy to get well and incidentally resting and laying up strength for myself.[10]

Louise's letters to Morley were filled with as much good news as she could gather. Morley tried to take reassurance. "It is a bit of true sunshine," he wrote her on February 16, "that my brave hero of a friend is still progressing. I wonder if he is allowed to read books, or to have them read to him. . . . Tell A.C. that I mean to send him a political epistle when you tell me he will like it. I do not promise that it shall be brilliant."[11]

Louise managed to keep the stories of her husband's breakdown out of the newspapers, but the news spread rapidly through his vast network of friends and admirers. "I hear from Doctor Ross," Lord Grey wrote to Oscar Straus, who forwarded his letter to Louise, "that this war has broken our friend Carnegie's health and his heart; and you tell me that the effort he made in giving testimony before the Federal Commission [on Industrial Relations] broke him down. When you see him tell him that many of us look to him as the great pioneer who has blazed the way to future peace because if his policy of collective responsibility on the part of the signatory nations to The Hague conventions had been adopted, the United States would have been obliged to come into this war at the very beginning and the knowledge that she would come in would have kept Germany quiet. I trust the result of the war may be to make Mr. Carnegie's policy not only a pious aspiration but an international fact."[12]

In March 1916, Morley, unable to tolerate any longer the interminable silences, wrote his friend directly: "This prolonged severance of talk between us two is by no means the least of the troubles of the day. I don't know whether a letter really comes into your hands. . . . I never felt before how much this privation amounted to. 'Tis a year and a half or more since our parting on the Liverpool railway platform. Well, I'm constantly with you in spirit and imagining a ramble with you in the Skibo woods and gardens. We should be bound to hit on different points of view; we have never failed in that, and are never likely to. Yet substantial agreement below the surface of talk would always be there—even about the formidable Curse that now hangs over what absurdly calls itself the civilized world." There was much remorse, but also a touch of anger in Morley now. He could not understand why Carnegie refused to speak or write when his voice was needed more than ever. "Europe is devastated by Plague and the Black Death, but that is no reason why Pasteurs and Listers should not persevere in search of healings." He concluded his letter with a plaintive plea to his long-lost friend: "Send me a little message, will you?"[13]

And so there began, albeit in abbreviated form on Carnegie's part, a renewal of their correspondence. Carnegie managed to write back a note to his friend that March. He was, he confessed, "finding comfort for vacant hours in ancient sages." He proposed that the Morleys come to Miami to spend the next winter.[14]

In the late spring, Louise brought her husband—and their traveling entourage—back to New York City, before moving on to a rented house in Connecticut for the summer. "We lingered in the South until about a month ago," she wrote James Bryce in mid-May. "Our Spring has been unusually fickle but I am thankful to say Mr. Carnegie keeps on improving all the time. He is now allowed to see more of his friends and takes a keen interest in affairs—almost more than is good for him at times, and then the doctor has to be more strict with him, but he is getting along beautifully and we are all so happy. We leave in ten days for Brick House, Noroton, Connecticut right on Long Island Sound where the yacht will be within hailing distance all the time and I expect we shall be on the water as much as on land this summer. Mr. Carnegie and I are very glad to enclose another donation to the fund for the relief of aliens in which you are doing such a noble work. Suffering is so widespread it is difficult to tell where the need is greatest. But there seems to be a feeling of hopefulness abroad in the world just now, which we hope may bear precious fruit."[15]

Carnegie wrote Morley from Connecticut, apologizing for the bareness of his letter. Morley responded that the letter had been a trifle brief, but far from bare. "When people are recovering their health, they are right to be brief." Morley had hoped to travel to Connecticut that fall and had even taken out a passport, but then decided that it was best that he remain in London for the opening of Parliament early in October. He closed with the postscript: "We have been friends for over 35 years!"[16]

In October, Louise, on the advice of the doctors who believed that a higher altitude might be best for her husband, bought "Shadowbrook," a 900-acre estate on the west side of Lake Mahkeenac, two miles west of Lenox, Massachusetts, developed by Anson Phelps Stokes, the New York merchant, banker, and philanthropist, in 1893. It was a property worthy of a Carnegie: a gray stone mansion with a vaguely Scottish look to it, set on a hillside, with more than fifty rooms, two stables, two lodges, six greenhouses, tennis courts, gardens, terraces, and a reservoir fed from mountain streams.

In November 1916, Carnegie celebrated his eighty-first birthday. Again, there was no dictated message to the reporters, no mention in the newspapers.

In December, Margaret Carnegie made her "debut" with a dinner and dance at Ninety-first Street. Her mother formally introduced her to their three hundred guests. It was, the *New York Times* reported on December 9, "a simple entertainment, with a buffet supper at midnight." Carnegie was present early in the evening to greet some of the guests. He was feeling a bit better now, well enough to write President Wilson in January 1917, to congratulate him on his "Peace without victory" address to the Senate. "Yesterday you told the whole world that peace must reign throughout that world, and we all know that the world will have to hearken to those words. This is the greatest service ever rendered by any President, and if your 'Life of

Washington' and 'history of the American People' have not already made you immortal, your address to the Senate yesterday cannot fail to do so."[17]

In the spring of 1917, the family relocated to Shadowbrook. Carnegie had deteriorated noticeably in the months since Margaret's debut. He was now an invalid, under the constant care of nurses. There were occasional visitors: some friends, the heads of the Carnegie trusts, and Charlie Schwab, who had become closer to the old man and an honored guest at Shadowbrook, perhaps because when he visited there was little talk of war or peace, but only of the good old, post-Homestead years in Pittsburgh. One of the visitors, who remained anonymous, confided to a reporter for a May 27 front-page article in the *New York Times* that Carnegie still suffered from disappointment that the world war had come to pass. "The war came, as we all know, as a shock to Mr. Carnegie. The continuation of it over so many months has been even a harder blow to him and to the cause which he had so close at heart."

Despite his steadfast support for Wilson's neutrality policy, Carnegie no longer believed that the German military and government officials would ever agree voluntarily to end the war. "Some time ago, I wrote you 'Germany is beyond reason,'" he cabled President Wilson in February. "She has ever since become more and more so until today she shows herself complete insane. . . . You should proclaim war against her, however reluctantly, and then settlement would soon come." Three months later, when the United States declared war, Carnegie could only applaud the decision. "You have triumphed at last. God bless you. You will give the world peace and rank the greatest hero of all."[18]

Carnegie, blessedly, would not live long enough to see Wilson's dreams for a League of Nations turn to ashes, as his own had done so many times before.

IN NOVEMBER 1917, Louise wrote Morley of her and Carnegie's excitement at the news that Morley had finished the two volumes of *Recollections* he had been working at since his resignation.

> Just a line to say how eagerly we are awaiting the company of the new book!! We are returning to our New York home today and hope soon to welcome its arrival. It will be next best to seeing you and you may be sure

we shall let you know at once and at the same time guard the fact that we are its proud possessors until the proper moment. The five months here [at Shadowbrook] have done Andrew worlds of good and he goes back to town ruddy of hue and with a much stronger step. At the present moment he is sitting out on the sunny verandah all wrapped up, reading this morning papers. The air is mild today although in sheltered woods the heavy snow that fell two days ago, still lingers. Andrew, Margaret and I are just about to plant an oak here each to mark the founding of our new home! . . . Margaret is doing a lot of thinking these days but is coming out all right. There is a lot of her Daddy in her—well dear friends a lot of loving thoughts go out to you both from all of us. We must all keep up good courage.[19]

Ten days later, now safely returned to New York in Charles Schwab's private railroad car, Louise wrote again. They had received *Recollections*, and Andrew, she reported, was sitting beside her as she wrote, totally absorbed in the book. "What rare pleasure he is having, and will have in reading it. It is difficult to get him interested in anything but the newspapers and world events, and your book will do him worlds of good. I expect he will want to write you shortly—He is wonderfully well since coming back to the city—He has abandoned his wheelchair entirely now. He walks a little in the garden and plays a little clock golf with old time vigor and interest. He also motors for an hour every afternoon and sees a few friends at tea time. . . . I wish I could express to you how much your kindness in sending this early copy of your 'Recollections' means to us, and how we value the friendship that prompted you to send it."[20]

Two months later, Morley was astounded to hear directly from Carnegie, who, it appears, had finally finished his friend's two volumes of *Recollections*. "I have read every word of it as if I were again talking these things all over with you face to face on the terrace at Skibo. Your references to me are all too flattering, but I am not altogether displeased, though you know my modest nature! I feel confident that with America's help, the great war cannot last much longer, and Madam and I are talking and thinking of the time when we will return to Skibo and have you with us once more. We intend spending all of this winter in New York for after all our own home is the most comfortable spot we can find at this season."[21]

In April of 1917, Margaret had celebrated her twenty-first birthday. In a photograph taken on the occasion, Carnegie sits stiffly, right arm resting on the side on the chair, his left on his lap. He has a somber, resigned, almost vacant look. Leaning over him, looking directly down on the top of his head, with her hand resting on his back, is an unsmiling almost angelic-looking Margaret. Louise, also unsmiling, sits beside her husband, with her arm also touching his back. There is no joy and little life in any of them. It is a portrait of quiet suffering.

Margaret had graduated from Spence and, according to the papers, had dedicated herself to "uplift work." She had also met a man she adored, the brother of a Spence classmate. Roswell Miller was three years older than she and an ensign in the U.S. Navy. "On the day the First World War ended, November 11, 1918," Margaret noted later in her journals, Roswell "took me out in his open Stutz motor, parked it on the edge of the Palisades with trees all around us and asked me to marry him. It was a very discreet affair. He did not even kiss me, and I didn't say anything except, 'I must tell you I have a stiff right leg.'"[22]

The next week, Roswell arrived at Ninety-first Street to ask Carnegie's consent for his daughter's hand. "He wept," Louise confided to her diary, "but was dear and gave it." The engagement was announced on Carnegie's eighty-third birthday and the wedding planned for April 22, 1919, thirty-two years to the day he and Louise had married.[23]

In November 1918, as it became clear that the war was drawing to a close, Carnegie appeared to come out of his almost four-year trance. On November 10, he wrote a last letter to Woodrow Wilson. "Now that the world war seems practically at an end I cannot refrain from sending you my heartfelt congratulations upon the great share you have had in bringing about its successful conclusion. The Palace of Peace at the Hague would, I think, be the fitting place for dispassionate discussion regarding the destiny of the conquered nations, and I hope your influence may be exerted in that direction." Wilson's response was generous. "I know your heart must rejoice at the dawn of peace after these terrible years of struggle, for I know how long and earnestly you have worked for and desired such conditions as I pray God it may now be possible for us to establish."

While he did not know where the peace talks would be held (they would end up at Versailles, not The Hague), he was sure Carnegie would "be present in spirit."[24]

The next week, Carnegie received his birthday greetings from Morley. "I have no sort of philosophy ready for one of these anniversaries. You don't need that sort of medicine—perhaps less than any other man, past or present known to me. The world has not gone altogether the way that either of us would have chosen. But I feel pretty sure that this mishap has been through no fault of ours. And it may possibly turn out that though the road may have been ill chosen, the end of the cruel stage may not prove an uncompensated mischief for mankind. You and I shall not survive to cast up the great account, for I am four score next Christmas, and you are just over."[25]

Carnegie was not yet ready to go. There was too much left to do and see: a daughter to be married, grandchildren perhaps, and a peace treaty enshrining forever the League of Nations he had dreamed of.

He lived to see his daughter's marriage. "Simplicity marked the wedding," the *New York Times* reported on April 23, 1919. Only one hundred guests were invited to Ninety-first Street for the noon wedding, followed by a reception. Bagpipes welcomed the guests and the pipe organ in the hall played the Wedding March. There were flowers everywhere—"pink peach, apple, and cherry blossoms, white marguerites, and magnolia flowers hung in hundreds of clusters throughout the lower floor." The bridal party, with Carnegie escorting his daughter, walked through "an aisle of flowers" to the "floral bower," where the ceremony was held. It was a "glorious spring day," Louise wrote in her diary. "Our darling's wedding day and our own 32nd anniversary. . . . Andrew so well and alert. He and I gave Baba away and later we walked down the aisle together. After greeting the bride and groom he went upstairs and rested." The entry ended, "Andrew up in the evening. Backgammon."[26]

There had been talk of returning to Skibo—Morley had mentioned it in each of his letters. But Carnegie was too frail and Skibo too forlorn after the war from which so many local men and boys would not return. Louise told Andrew that they would summer in Lenox again. "Well, we must do the best we can, wherever we are," had been his stoic answer. "He had no fuss," Louise wrote her daughter, "he fully understands that it was impossible to go across this year. . . . So the disappointment I dreaded for

Daddy has passed almost without a ripple, and I don't have to put the big ocean between you and me even for a few weeks."[27]

Louise and Andrew, with their huge entourage of servants, doctors, nurses, and secretaries, but without Margaret, returned to Lenox. In years past, Carnegie had paid little attention to his flower gardens. That task was given to Louise, while he concentrated on the big projects: the roads, the dams, the waterfalls. But he took more pleasure from his gardens that summer than ever before, sitting for several hours in his wheelchair admiring the flowers. He was struggling now to stay alive and growing weaker by the day, though he refused to complain to his nurses or doctors or Louise. "He is so dear, tells me not to worry, but it is heartrending," Louise confided to her diary. The end was near. "He was a hollow shell—all the spark had gone," James Bertram recalled on his last visit to Shadowbrook. "The experience was a distressing one. A.C. would sit for an hour at a time and not speak a word—if he did, it was nothing to any point."[28]

On August 5, Louise noted that he had become "so weak and weary." A few days later, as his condition worsened, the doctors, finding his temperature elevated, feared that he had caught pneumonia. "I was called at 6 A.M.," Louise wrote in her diary on August 11, her husband's last day, "and remained with my darling husband, giving him oxygen until he gradually fell asleep, at 7:14. I am left alone. I think he knew me but he did not speak. . . . Everybody so kind, but what is life to me now?"[29]

There was no funeral or memorial in New York City. A brief service for about forty family members and friends, including Charlie Schwab, Elihu Root, the directors of a few of the Carnegie trusts, and the wives of several old friends who had predeceased Carnegie, was held at Shadowbrook. Then Carnegie's coffin was placed in a hearse, and accompanied by Louise, Margaret, Schwab, and a few friends and relatives, driven to Hillsdale, New York, where a special funeral car was attached to a New York Central train for the trip to White Plains. The funeral party was met at White Plains a little after 4:30 and put into limousines for the final trip to the Sleepy Hollow cemetery. Andrew Carnegie was buried amid rolling hills, alongside the Hudson, in a graveyard filled with Americans in a landscape reminiscent of Scotland. The inscription reads only: "Andrew Carnegie born Dunfermline Scotland, 25 November 1835 Died Lenox Massachusetts 11 August 1919."

. . .

ON AUGUST 28, Carnegie's will, which had been written in 1912, with a brief and insignificant codicil added in March 1919, was probated. He had left an estate of about $26 million. He bequeathed to Louise his real estate, his books, works of art, household furniture, horses, carriage, motorcars, and the contents of their several dwellings. No separate bequest was made for Margaret. He did not want to burden her with a fortune of her own and the requests that would have descended upon her. "Having years ago made provision for my wife beyond her desires and ample to enable her to provide for our beloved daughter Margaret; and being unable to judge at present what provision for our daughter will best promote her happiness, I leave to her mother the duty of providing for her as her mother deems best. A mother's love will be the best guide."

In paragraph four he listed the dozens of legatees he had provided for. Robert Franks, his secretary and treasurer, and his cousin Mrs. L. M. Morris, were given the homes they lived in. To his butler and housekeeper, his nurse, and Maggie Anderson, "our oldest servant," he provided a pension for life equal to one half their annual salaries. Special provision of cash awards from $600 to $2,000 (equal to ten times that in today's currency), depending on length of service, was made for every one of his household servants and for the "head of departments at Skibo, including the game-keeper, forester, chauffer, yacht captain, superintendent of his golf links, his piper, gardener." Every laborer at Skibo—and there were hundreds of them—was also left a small sum. To the crofters who resided on his lands, he remitted two years rent.

In addition to these "legacies," which included sizable institutional gifts to the Author's Club, Hampton Institute, Stevens Institute, Cooper Union, Pittsburgh University, and the St. Andrews Society, Carnegie set aside sufficient funds to pay semiannual annuities of thousands of dollars to his nephews and nieces, his Dunfermline cousins, the heads of most of his foundations and trusts, and several friends from Pittsburgh, New York, Dunfermline, and London—including John Morley and David Lloyd George, Dr. Garmany of New York, Walter Damrosch, Mrs. Roosevelt, Mrs. Cleveland, and former president Taft. Almost all of these annuities were for five thousand dollars except for Taft's, David Lloyd George's, and John Morley's, which were set at ten thousand dollars.

Carnegie had struggled mightily to give away his fortune during his life and come very close. According to his treasurer, Robert Franks, at the time of his death, Carnegie had given away more than $350 million (in the tens of billions today). There remained but $20 million of stocks and bonds in the Home Trust Company vaults. In the seventh paragraph of his last will and testament, Carnegie directed that it be bequeathed, in its entirety, to the Carnegie Corporation. And with this he accomplished the final, and to his mind, most important goal he had set himself.[30]

NOTES

ABBREVIATIONS

I. Archive Collections and Depositories

ACAC   Carnegie Autograph Collection, Manuscripts and Archives Division, New York Public Library, New York, NY

ACBM   Andrew Carnegie Birthplace Museum, Dunfermline, Scotland

ACCPL   Andrew Carnegie Correspondence, Oliver Room, Carnegie Public Library, Pittsburgh, PA

ACLC   Andrew Carnegie Papers, 1803–1935, Manuscript Division, Library of Congress, Washington, DC

ACNYPL   Andrew Carnegie, Personal Miscellaneous Papers, Manuscripts and Archives Division, New York Public Library, New York, NY

Adams   Charles Francis Adams Papers, in Adams Family Papers, Manuscript Division, Library of Congress, Washington, DC

Archer   William Archer Papers, Manuscripts Reading Room, British Library, London

Asquith   H. H. Asquith Papers, New Bodleian Library, University of Oxford, Oxford

Avebury   Lord Avebury Papers, Manuscripts Reading Room, British Library, London

Bertram   James Bertram Collection, Carnegie Mellon University Archives, Pittsburgh, PA

BL   British Library, London

Blackwood   Blackwood's (publisher), Manuscript Department, National Library Scotland, Edinburgh

Bryce   James Bryce USA Papers, New Bodleian, University of Oxford, Oxford

Butler   Nicholas Murray Butler Papers, Rare Books and Manuscript Library, Butler Library, Columbia University, New York, NY

Cameron   Simon Cameron Papers, Manuscript Division, Library of Congress, Washington, DC

C-B   Campbell-Bannerman Papers, Manuscripts Reading Room, British Library, London

CCEIA   Carnegie Council on Ethics and International Affairs Papers, Rare Books and Manuscript Library, Butler Library, Columbia University, New York, NY

CCNY   Carnegie Corporation of New York Papers, Rare Books and Manuscript Library, Butler Library, Columbia University, New York, NY

CEIP   Carnegie Endowment for International Peace Papers, Rare Books and Manuscript Library, Butler Library, Columbia University, New York, NY

Century   Century Company Records, Manuscripts and Archives Division, New York Public Library, New York, NY

CFP   Carnegie Family Papers, privately held

Champlin   Andrew Carnegie and John Denison Champlin Letter Collection, Historical Collections and Labor Archives, Special Collections Library, Pennsylvania State University, University Park, PA

CLP   Carnegie Library of Pittsburgh, PA

Cleveland   Grover Cleveland Presidential Papers, Manuscript Division, Library of Congress, Washington, DC

CS   Carnegie Steel Papers, Historical Society of Western Pennsylvania, Library and Archives Division, Pittsburgh, PA

CTUS   Carnegie Trust for the Universities of Scotland, National Archives of Scotland, Edinburgh

D-BLC   Damrosch-Blaine Collection, Music Division, Library of Congress, Washington, DC

D-VTLC   Damrosch–Te Van Collection, Music Division, Library of Congress, Washington, DC

Elgin   Elgin Family Archives, Broomhall, Dunfermline, Scotland

Franks   Correspondence between John and Emma Franks, in box marked "Volumes," Andrew Carnegie Autograph Collection, Manuscripts and Archives Division, New York Public Library, New York, NY

French   Alice French Papers, Roger and Julie Baskes Department of Special Collections, Newberry Library, Chicago, IL

Gladstone   Papers of William Ewart Gladstone, Manuscripts Reading Room, British Library, London

Gladstone Correspondence   County Record Office, Flintshire County Council, The Old Rectory, Hawarden, Wales

Hagley   Hagley Museum and Library, Wilmington, DE

Haldane   Richard Haldane Papers, Manuscript Department, National Library of Scotland, Edinburgh

Harcourt   Richard Harcourt Papers, New Bodleian Library, University of Oxford, Oxford

Harrison   William Henry Harrison Presidential Papers, Manuscript Division, Library of Congress, Washington, DC

Hay   John Hay Papers, Manuscript Division, Library of Congress, Washington, DC

HCFFM   Helen Clay Frick Foundation Archives, Frick Collection, New York, NY

HCFUP   Carnegie Frick Correspondence, Helen Clay Frick Foundation Archives, Archives Service Center, University of Pittsburgh, Pittsburgh, PA

HL   Huntington Library, San Marino, CA

Holley   Alexander Lyman Holley Correspondence, Manuscripts Collection, Connecticut Historical Society, Hartford, CT

Holls   Frederick William Holls Papers, Houghton Library, Harvard University, Cambridge, MA

JMBL   Typescript copies of Morley's correspondence with Andrew Carnegie, Papers of John Morley as Secretary of State for India, India Office Select Materials, British Library, London

JMBL,O   John Morley Papers, New Bodleian Library, University of Oxford, Oxford

Knox   Philander Chase Knox Papers, Manuscript Division, Library of Congress, Washington, DC

Margaret Barclay Wilson Collection   "The Margaret Barclay Wilson Collection of Carnegiana," Oliver Room, Carnegie Library of Pittsburgh, Pittsburgh, PA

Martin   William Martin Papers, Darlington Memorial Library Manuscript Collection, University of Pittsburgh, Pittsburgh, PA

Mead   Papers of Edwin D. Mead and Lucia Ames Mead, Swarthmore College Peace Collection, Swarthmore College, Swarthmore, PA

NA   National Archives, Washington, DC

NCF   National Civic Federation Papers, Manuscripts and Archives Division, New York Public Library, New York, NY

O'Rielly   Papers of Henry O'Rielly, Manuscript Department, New-York Historical Society, New York, NY

Paine   Albert Bigelow Paine Collection, Huntington Library, San Marino, CA

PRR Minute Books   Hagley Museum and Library, Wilmington, DE

PSA   Pennsylvania State Archives, Harrisburg, PA

Reid   Whitelaw Reid Papers, Reid Family Papers, Manuscript Division, Library of Congress, Washington, DC

RG   Record Group

Roebling   Special Collections, Alexander Library, Rutgers University, New Brunswick, NJ

Roosevelt Theodore Roosevelt Presidential Papers, Manuscript Division, Library of Congress, Washington, DC

Rosebery Archibald Primrose, Fifth Earl of Rosebery Papers, Manuscript Department, National Library of Scotland, Edinburgh

St. Andrew's St. Andrew's Golf Club, Hastings-on-Hudson, NY, archives, privately held

Scott Thomas A. Scott Correspondence, Scott Family Papers, privately held

Strachey John St. Loe Strachey Papers, Parliamentary Archives, House of Lords Record Office, London

Taft William Howard Taft Presidential Papers, Manuscript Division, Library of Congress, Washington, DC

Tilden Samuel J. Tilden papers, Manuscripts and Archives Division, New York Public Library, New York, NY

Twain Mark Twain Papers, Bancroft Library, University of California at Berkeley, Berkeley, CA

Vandevort John W. Vandevort Papers, Huntington Library, San Marino, CA

White Andrew Dickson White Papers, Division of Rare and Manuscript Collections, Carl A. Kroch Library, Cornell University, Ithaca, NY

Whitney Henry Payne Whitney Collection of the Papers of William Collins Whitney, Manuscript Division, Library of Congress, Washington, DC

Wilson Woodrow Wilson Presidential Papers, Manuscript Division, Library of Congress, Washington, DC

II. GOVERNMENT DOCUMENTS

Hand-Loom Hand-Loom Inquiry Commission, Great Britain. *Reports of Assistant Commissioners on hand-loom weavers in several districts of England, Scotland, Ireland and Continental Europe, 1839–40,* (1839; Shannon: Irish University Press, 1970)

Tariff U.S. Congress, *Tariff Hearings Before the Committee on Ways and Means of the House of Representatives.* 60th Congress, 1908–09. Washington, DC: Government Printing Office, 1909, vol. 2

U.S. Steel U.S. House of Representatives. *Hearings Before the Committee on Investigation of United States Steel Corporation.* Washington, DC: Government Printing Office, 1912, vol. 3

III. NEWSPAPERS

C&AGW	Commoner and American Glass Worker
NLT	National Labor Tribune
NYH	New York Herald
NYT	New York Times
NYTr	New York Tribune
NYW	New York World
PD	Pittsburgh Dispatch
PP	Pittsburgh Press
PT	Pittsburgh Times

IV. CARNEGIE PUBLICATIONS

AF-I-H *American Four-in-Hand in Britain.* 1883. New York: Charles Scribner's Sons, 1890

EB *Empire of Business.* 1902. Garden City, NY: Doublday, Page & Co., 1913

Andrew Carnegie Reader. *Andrew Carnegie Reader,* ed. Joseph Wall. Pittsburgh: University of Pittsburgh Press, 1992

MW *Miscellaneous Writings of Andrew Carnegie,* ed. Burton Hendrick. 2 vols. Garden City, NY: Doubleday, Doran & Co., 1933

RTW   *Round the World.* 1884. Garden City, NY: Doubleday, Doran & Co., 1933
TD   *Triumphant Democracy, or Fifty Years' March of the Republic.* 1886. New York: Charles Scribner's Sons, 1888

V. INDIVIDUALS

Dod	George Lauder, Jr. (cousin)
EF	Emma Franks
GFMc	Gardiner McCandless (AC's private secretary)
GP	George Pullman
HCF	Henry Clay Frick
JET	J. Edgar Thomson
JF	John Franks
JWV	John Wesley Vandervort
Lauder	George Lauder, Sr. (uncle)
LW	Louise Whitfield
LWC	Louise Whitfield Carnegie
MC	Margaret Carnegie
TAS	Thomas A. Scott
TMC	Thomas Morrison Carnegie
TR	Theodore Roosevelt
WW	Woodrow Wilson

1. CHAPTER ONE: DUNFERMLINE, 1835–1848

1. Burton Hendrick interview with Richard Henderson, August, 1927, vol. 257, ACLC.

2. AC, *Autobiography of Andrew Carnegie* (1920; Boston: Northeastern University Press, 1986), 6–7.

3. Eric Simpson, *The Auld Grey Toun: Dunfermline in the time of Andrew Carnegie, 1835–1919* (Dunfermline: Carnegie Dunfermline Trust, 1987), 9–11.

4. Norman Murray, *The Scottish Hand Loom Weavers, 1790–1850, A Social History* (Edinburgh: John Donald, 1978), 23.

5. Peter Chalmers, *Historical and Statistical Account of Dunfermline* (Edinburgh, 1844), 353–63.

6. "Particular Household Expenses," 1769, Elgin.

7. J. B. Mackie, *Andrew Carnegie: His Dunfermline Ties and Benefactions* (Dunfermline, 1916); Elgin; Duncan McNaughton, "The Families of Carnegie, Morrison, and Lauder connected with Dunfermline," 1979, unpublished memo, ACBM.

8. Hendrick interview with Mrs. Clanachan, September 22, 1927, vol. 256, ACLC.

9. A. Jones, *The revenue book: containing the new tariff of 1846, together with the tariff of 1842 . . .* (New York: Bell & Gould, 1846), 11; E. D. Ogden, *Tariff, or, Rates of duties payable on goods, wares, and merchandise . . .* (New York: Rich & Loutrel, 1840), 14; George Curtiss, *The Industrial Development of Nations . . . ,* vol. II (Binghamton, NY, 1912), 262

10. Chalmers, 373; AC, *Autobiography*, 8.

11. Hendrick interview with Ann Alexander, August 1927, vol. 256, ACLC.

12. Thomas Morrison to Lord Dalmeny, December 3, 1834, vol. 1, ACLC.

13. Hendrick interview with Lauder ladies, August 1927, vol. 257, ACLC; Dominic J. Currie, *The Lauder Legacy, The Life and Times of George Lauder and Lauder College* (Dunfermline: Lauder College, 1999), 20–21.

14. *Hand-Loom*, 200.

15. Murray, 57; Ebenezer Henderson, *Annals of Dunfermline* (Glasgow, 1879), 642.

16. Alexander Wilson, *The Chartist Movement in Scotland* (Manchester: Manchester University Press, 1970), 39.

17. I thank Andrew Campbell for supplying me with copies of these documents.

18. Murray, 7.

19. Engels, 243; E. P. Thompson, *The Making of the English Working Class* (New York: Vintage, 1966), 827–28.

20. AC, *Autobiography,* 10–11.

21. Hendrick interview with Hew Morrison, August 7–8, 1927, vol. 257, ACLC.

22. T. M. Devine, *The Scottish Nation: A History* (New York: Penguin, 1999), 262.

23. A. Aitkin to "My very Dear Sisters & friends," October 7, 1840, vol. 1, ACLC.

24. Hendrick interviews, August, September, 1927, vol. 257, ACLC.

25. Hendrick interviews with Mrs. Charlotte Scott, September 5, 1927, and Macgregor, September 11, 12, 1927, vol. 257, ACLC.

26. AC, *Autobiography,* 12, 14.

27. A. Aitkin to "My very Dear Sisters & friends," April 11, 1842, vol. 1, ACLC.

28. Chalmers, 437.

29. Hendrick interview with Miss Martin, September 13, 1927, vol. 257, ACLC.

30. AC, *Autobiography,* 13–14; Hendrick interview with Mrs. Charlotte Scott, September 5, 1927, vol. 257, ACLC.

31. Hendrick interview with Macgregor, September 4, 11, 12, 1927, vol. 257, ACLC.

32. Thomas Morrison, Sr., *Heddekashun and Handication* (Dunfermline: William Liddell, 1834), 4.

33. A. Aitkin to "My Dear Sister Margaret," May 30, 1844, vol. 1, ACLC.

34. Chalmers, 540.

35. *Poor Law Inquiry Commission for Scotland.* Appendix, Part One, "Minutes of Evidence" (Edinburgh, 1844), 358.

36. *Ibid.,* 357–58.

37. Ian Levitt and Christopher Smout, *The State of the Scottish Working-Class in 1843: A statistical and spatial enquiry based on the data from the Poor Law Commission Report of 1844* (Edinburgh: Scottish Academic Press, 1979), 114–16.

38. Daniel Thomson, *The Weaver's Craft: being a history of the Weavers' incorporation of Dunfermline* (Paisley: A. Gardner, 1903), 336; Simpson, 31.

39. Murray, 22–23.

40. AC, *Autobiography,* 12–13.

41. Henderson, 657.

42. AC, "From Bobbin-Boy to Millionaire," *The Golden Penny,* January 23, 1899, 87.

43. Hendrick interview with Mrs. Finlayson and Miss Anderson, August 30, 1927, vol. 257, ACLC.

44. Hendrick interview with Richard Henderson, August 26, 1927; with Mrs. Finlayson and Miss Anderson, August 30, 1927, vol. 257, ACLC.

CHAPTER TWO: TO AMERICA, 1848–1855

1. William Armstrong Fairburn, *Merchant Sail* V (Center Lovell, Maine: Fairburn Marine Educational Foundation, n.d.), 3349–50.

2. Carl Cutler, *Queens of the Western Ocean* (Annapolis, MD: U.S. Naval Institute, 1961), 223, 259, 509.

3. "Ship Wiscasset" in *Passenger list of vessels arriving at New York, Jan. 7, 1820–June 17, 1897* (microfilm), NA, 1957.

4. AC, *Autobiography,* 27.

5. *NYH,* August 14, 1848.

6. AC, *Autobiography,* 28.

7. Domingo Faustino Sarmiento, *Travels in the United States in 1847,* ed. Michael Aaron Rockland (1847; Princeton: Princeton University Press, 1970), 219–21.

8. Ronald Shaw, *Erie Water West* (Lexington: University of Kentucky Press, 1966), 289; [James Lumsden], *American Memoranda by a Mercantile Man During a Short Tour in the Summer of 1843* (Glasgow: Bell & Bain, 1844), 28.

9. AC, *Autobiography,* 29.

10. Anthony Trollope, *North America* (1862; New York: Knopf, 1951), 369, 371; Alexander Mackay, *The Western World; or, Travels in the United States in 1846–7,* vol. 3 (1849; reprint, New York: Negro Universities Press, 1968), 86.

11. John N. Ingham, *Making Iron and Steel: Independent Mills in Pittsburgh, 1820–1920* (Columbus: Ohio State University Press, 1991), 22–28, 34–37.

12. Burton Hendrick, *The Life of Andrew Carnegie* (Garden City, NY: Doubleday, Doran, 1932), I, 51–52.

13. AC to Lauder, May 30, 1852, vol. 1, ACLC.

14. Joel A. Tarr, "Infrastructure and City-

Building," in Samuel P. Hayes, ed., *City at the Point: Essays on the Social History of Pittsburgh* (Pittsburgh: University of Pittsburgh Press, 1989), 216–28; Leland D. Baldwin, *Pittsburgh: The Story of a City* (Pittsburgh: University of Pittsburgh Press, 1937), 203, 211–12, 241–43.

15. Writers' Program of Works Progress Administration (WPA), *Story of Old Allegheny City* (Pittsburgh: Allegheny Centennial Committee, 1941).

16. Ormsby O. Gregg, Isaac Gregg, and Moses F. Eaton, *Pittsburgh, her advantageous position and great resources, as a manufacturing and commercial city: embraced in a notice of sale of real estate* (Pittsburgh: Johnston & Stockton, 1845).

17. Neville Craig, *History of Pittsburgh* (Pittsburgh: J. H. Mellor, 1851), 311; Monte A. Calvert, "The Allegheny City Cotton Mill Riot of 1848," *Western Pennsylvania Historical Magazine*, 46 (April 1963): 100.

18. AC, *Autobiography*, 29.

19. Calvert, 102–4; 108–14.

20. AC, *Autobiography*, 33.

21. George Henry Thurston, *Pittsburgh As It Is . . .* (Pittsburgh: W. S. Haven, 1857), 164.

22. AC, *Autobiography.*, 34–35.

23. *Ibid.*, 36.

24. AC to Lauder, May 30, 1852, vol. 1, ACLC.

25. AC, *Autobiography*, 36; James D. Reid, *The Telegraph in America* (New York: Derby Brothers, 1879), 177.

26. Erasmus Wilson, ed., *Standard History of Pittsburg, Pennsylvania* (Chicago: H. R. Cornell & Co., 1898), 103; Robert Luther Thompson, *Wiring a Continent: The History of the Telegraph Industry in the United States, 1832–1866* (Princeton: Princeton University Press, 1947), 121–25; Glass to O'Rielly, January 13, 1848, box 7, O'Rielly.

27. AC, "From Bobbin-Boy," 87.

28. AC, *Autobiography*, 41, 46–47.

29. *Ibid.*, 52; Hendrick interview with Macgregor, September 11, 12, 1927, vol. 257. ACLC; David to AC, May 20, 1903, vol. 96, ACLC.

30. *Ibid.*

31. AC, "From Bobbin-Boy," 87.

32. AC, "How I Served My Apprenticeship," in *Andrew Carnegie Reader*, 35; AC,

Autobiography, 57; AC to Dod, June 22, 1851, ACLC.

33. AC to Lauder, May 30, 1852, vol. 1, ACLC.

34. AC, *Autobiography*, 43; Aitkin to My Very Dear . . . , October 7, 1840, vol. 1, ACLC.

35. Wilson, ed., *Standard History of Pittsburg, Pennsylvania*, 901; Sarah Killikelly, *The History of Pittsburgh: Its Rise and Progress* (Pittsburgh: B. C. & Gordon Montgomery, 1906), 549; *Story of Old Allegheny City*, 135.

36. See Hendrick, I, 68–70, for complete correspondence.

37. AC, *Autobiography*, 15, 44.

38. AC to Lauder, May 30, 1852, vol. 1, ACLC.

39. A rather complete set of handwritten letters and transcriptions, 1853–57, between Carnegie and his cousin Dod, is located in box 9, folder 6, 7, CS; others can be found in vol. 1, ACLC.

40. AC to Dod, August 7, 1853, box 9, folder 7, CS.

41. AC to Dod, draft dated September 13, 1854, vol. 1, ACLC.

42. AC to Dod, August 7, 1853, box 9, folder 7, CS.

43. AC to Dod, February 8, 1854, box 9, folder 7, CS.

44. AC to Lauder, May 30, 1852, vol. 1, ACLC.

45. Alexis de Tocqueville, *Democracy in America*, ed. Philip Bradley (New York: Vintage, 1945), I, 314; Trollope, 281.

46. AC, *Autobiography*, 48; Emanuel Swedenborg, excerpts from *Heaven and Its Wonders and Hell*, trans. George F. Dole (West Chester, PA: Swedenborg Foundation, n.d.), chap. 27.

47. Unpublished manuscripts, vol. 250, ACLC.

48. Minutes of board meetings, November 1855, 1856, 1857, folder marked "General," vol. 258, ACLC; *Autobiography*, 49.

49. Miller to AC, April 10, 1903, vol. 95, ACLC.

50. Nathan Hatch, *The Democratization of American Christianity* (New Haven: Yale University Press, 1989), 199; AC to Dod, August 18, 1853, vol. 1, ACLC.

51. AC to Dod, June 22, 1851, vol. 1, ACLC.

52. AC, *Autobiography*, 60–61.

53. AC to Lauder, May 30, 1852, March 14, 1853, vol. 1, ACLC.

54. Hendrick interview with Hew Morrison, August 7–8, 1927, vol. 257, ACLC.

CHAPTER THREE: UPWARD BOUND, 1853–1859

1. Blondheim, 80–83.

2. AC, *Autobiography*, 57–8; AC, "From Bobbin-Boy," 87.

3. Pennsylvania Railroad Company, *Sixth Annual Report to the Stockholders*, January 31, 1853, 32; Thompson, *Wiring a Continent*, 205–6.

4. PRR minute books, vol. 89, April 6, 1853, 327.

5. AC to Lauder, March 14, 1853, vol. 1, ACLC.

6. D. W. Meinig, *The Shaping of America*. Volume 2: *Continental America, 1800–1867* (New Haven: Yale University Press, 1993), 228, 332; Pennsylvania Railroad, "Sixth Annual Report," January 31, 1853, 10; Pennsylvania Railroad, "Twelfth Annual Report," February 7, 1859, 3.

7. AC to Lauder, March 14, 1853, vol. 1, ACLC.

8. AC, *Autobiography*, 62.

9. Pennsylvania Railroad Company, "Organization for Conducting the Business of the Road," 7.

10. Walter Licht, *Working for the Railroads: The Organization of Work in the Nineteenth Century* (Princeton: Princeton University Press, 1983), 84–85, 87.

11. Herbert Gutman, *Work, Culture and Society in Industrializing America* (New York: Vintage, 1977), 296.

12. AC, *Autobiography*, 78.

13. *Ibid.*, 70.

14. AC to Lauder, March 14, 1853, vol. 1, ACLC.

15. PRR minutes books, vol. 90, March 14, 1855, 56.

16. The stock certificates are dated April 11, April 17, 1856; the notes are from May 17, 1856, and November 1, 1857; the mortgage is dated March 27, 1858; vol. 1, ACLC.

17. AC, *Autobiography*, 76; "How I Served My Apprenticeship," 37.

18. R. Taggart to T. Miller, April 4, 1909, vol. 165, ACLC.

19. *Life and reminiscences from birth to manhood of Wm. G. Johnson* (Pittsburgh: Knickerbocker Press, 1902), 217; unpublished ms., vol. 250, ACLC.

20. AC, *TD* (1886), 297–99.

21. Woodruff to AC, June 12, 1886; AC to Woodruff, June 15, 1886, vol. 9, ACLC.

22. *Ibid.*, James A. Ward, *J. Edgar Thomson, Master of the Pennsylvania* (Westport, CT: Greenwood Press, 1980), 183.

23. *Ibid.*, 45–46.

24. Thomas C. Cochran, *Railroad Leaders, 1845–1890* (New York: Russell & Russell, 1965), 124–25.

25. AC, *Autobiography*, 80.

26. *Ibid.*, 86.

27. Tom Miller to AC, April 10, 1903, vol. 95, ACLC.

28. AC, *Autobiography*, 89–90.

29. Alfred D. Chandler, Jr., *The Visible Hand: The Managerial Revolution in American Business* (Cambridge: Harvard University Press, 1977), 109–10.; PRR, 13th annual report, February 6, 1860.

30. AC, *Autobiography*, 87.

CHAPTER FOUR: WAR AND RICHES, 1860–1865

1. AC, *Autobiography*, 89–90.

2. Personal communication from Chris Baer; *Travellers Official Railway Guide*, June 1868.

3. AC, *Autobiography*, 90.

4. *Ibid.*, 93.

5. *Ibid.*, 89.

6. *Ibid.*, 65, 78; AC to Dod, July 15, 1854, box 9, folder 7, CS.

7. AC to Dod, November 12, 1855, box 9, folder 7, CS.

8. Wilson, ed., *Standard History of Pittsburg, Pennsylvania*, 552.

9. Samuel Richey Kamm, *The Civil War Career of Thomas A. Scott* (Philadelphia, 1940), 23; Thomas A. Scott, *NYT*, August 15, 1862; TAS to JET, April 20, 1862, RG 19, box 1, PSA.

10. TAS to AC, AC to TAS, April 19–21, 1861, RG 19, box 1, PSA.

11. Alan Nevins, *The War for the Union*

(New York: Charles Scribner's Sons, 1959), I, 80.

12. United States War Department, *The War of the Rebellion: A Compilation of the Official Records of the Union and Confederate Armies* (Washington, DC: Government Printing Office, 1880, 1901), I, 2, 7.

13. George Edgar Turner, *Victory Rode the Rails* (Westwood, CT: Greenwood Press, 1972), 53; *War of the Rebellion*, I, 2, 10; Benjamin F. Butler, *Butler's Book* (Boston: A. M. Thayer & Co., 1892), 181.

14. AC to TAS, April 20 (two telegrams), 21 (three telegrams), RG 19, box 1, PSA.

15. AC, *Autobiography*, 95–96.

16. Kamm, 34–35; AC to TAS, April 29, 1861, m504, reel 3, NA.

17. Hermon K. Murphey, "The Northern Railroads and the Civil War," *Mississippi Valley Historical Review* 5 (December 1918): 331–32; Thomas Weber, *The Northern Railroads in the Civil War, 1861–1865* (New York: King's Crown Press, 1952), 61–66.

18. Constance McLaughlin Green, *Washington; Village and Capital, 1800–1878* (Princeton, Princeton University Press, 1962), 242.

19. AC to TAC, July 19, m540, reel 3, NA.

20. TMC to AC, July 22, m540, reel 3, NA.

21. John Cowan to AC, "attachment," April 29, 1911, vol. 192, ACLC.

22. AC to W. H. Holmes, July 16, 1861, vol. 1, ACLC.

23. AC to TMC, n.d., m540, reel 3, NA.

24. On Carnegie's return to civilian life, see AC to Enoch Lewis, Altoona, August, 1861, m540, reel 3, NA; AC to Enoch Lewis, October 5, 1861, vol. 1, ACLC; on his stock holdings, see Tom Miller to AC, April 2, 1903, vol. 95, ACLC.

25. Samuel W. Durant, *History of Allegheny Co., Pennsylvania* (Philadelphia: L. H. Everts, 1876), 179–80.

26. AC, *Autobiography*, 132.

27. Andrew Cone, *Petrolia* (New York: D. Appleton, 1870), 259; Paul Henry Giddens, *Early Days of Oil* (Princeton: Princeton University Press, 1948), 26.

28. Tom Miller to AC, April 2, 1903, vol. 95, ACLC; AC to Dod, June 21, 1863, vol. 1, ACLC.

29. AC, *Autobiography*, 111; AC, note on Pittsburgh Division stationery, May 21, 1863, box 25, folder 8, CS; Ward, 177.

30. Tom Miller to AC, April 2, 1903, vol. 95, ACLC.

31. AC to Dod, May 26, 1862, vol. 3, ACLC.

32. Hendrick interview with Eliza Lauder, September 2, 1927, vol. 257, ACLC; AC, *Autobiography*, 106–9.

33. AC to TMC, September 25, 1862, CFP.

34. AC to Dod, June 21, 1863, vol. 3, ACLC.

35. *Ibid.*

36. Weber, 132; Kamm, 135–37.

37. Arthur B. Fox, *Pittsburgh During the American Civil War, 1860–1865* (Chicora, PA: Mechling Bookbindery, 2002), 179–82.

38. AC to Dod, June 21, 1863, vol. 3, ACLC.

39. Receipt, dated June 19, 1864, and "Certificate of Non-Liability," July 19, 1864, Miscellaneous Papers file, CS, cited in Joseph Frazier Wall, *Andrew Carnegie* (1970; Pittsburgh: University of Pittsburgh Press, 1989), 190.

40. Hendrick, I, 120.

41. Fox, 77–78.

42. James Howard Bridge, *The Inside History of the Carnegie Steel Company: A Romance of Millions* (1903; Pittsburgh: University of Pittsburgh Press, 1991), 15.

43. AC, *Autobiography*, 128.

CHAPTER FIVE: BRANCHING OUT, 1865–1866

1. Internal Revenue Assessment lists, 1862–1874, m787, reels 93, 94, NA.

2. AC to TAS, January 1, 1865; TAS to Cameron, n.d., Cameron.

3. AC, *Autobiography*, 137.

4. AC to TMC, MC, May 25, 1865 letters, CFP.

5. AC to TMC, MC, June 15, 1865, CFP.

6. AC to TMC, June 30, 1865; AC to TMC, MC, July 4, 1865, CFP.

7. AC to TMC, MC, various dates, CFP.

8. John Franks (JF) to Emma Franks (EF), November 12, 1865, Franks.

9. AC to TMC, MC, June 23, 1865, CFP.

10. JF to EF, October 18, 29, November 19, December 17, 1865, Franks.

11. AC to MC, June 30, 1865, CFP.

12. AC to TMC, November 2, 1865, CFP.

13. AC to TMC, MC, July 20; AC to TMC, November 2, 1865, CFP.

14. AC to TMC, July 20, August 17, 1865, CFP.

15. JF to EF, November 12, 1865, Franks.

16. Author interviews with Morehead Kennedy, Warwick Scott Wheeler, 2004.

17. AC, "From Bobbin-Boy," 88.

18. AC to MC, June 30, 1865, CFP.

19. AC to TMC, December 14, 1865, November 2; AC to MC, September 2, 1865, CFP.

20. AC to TMC, June 23, 1865, CFP.

21. AC to TMC, n.d., CFP.

22. JF to EF, November 19, 1865, Franks.

23. AC to TMC, July 26, 1865, CFP.

24. AC to TMC, n.d., CFP.

25. AC to MC, TMC, September 2, 1865, CFP.

26. JF to EF, November 12, 1865, Franks.

27. AC to TMC, November 19, 1865, CFP.

28. Chandler, 22; James Henretta, et al., *America's History* (Chicago: Dorsey Press, 1987), 517.

29. Henry Adams, *The Education of Henry Adams: An Autobiography* (Boston: Houghton Mifflin, 1918), 239–40.

30. George H. Burgess and Miles C. Kennedy, *Centennial History of The Pennsylvania Railroad Company, 1846–1946* (Philadelphia: Pennsylvania Railroad Company, 1949), 292–93; Chris Baer, 1865 *PRR Chronology*, June 26, 1865.

31. JET to AC, March 12, 15, 1867, box 44, folder 3, CS.

32. JET to AC, June 6, 1867, March 5, 1868; W. H. Wilson to AC, June 21, 1867, box 44, folder 3, CS.

33. Agreement, February 11, 1865; Biddle to AC, April 6, 1866, box 33, folder 4, CS.

34. Internal Revenue Assessment lists, 1862–1874, m787, reels 94, 96, NA.

35. AC to TAS, March 8, 1869, box 10, folder 6, CS.

36. AC, *Autobiography*, 112.

37. Ward, 177; JET to AC, March 4, 1868,

box 44, folder 3, CS; AC to TAS, May 13, 1869, box 10, folder 6, CS.

38. Washington A. Roebling to John A. Roebling, October 11, 1868, Roebling.

39. David McCullough, *The Great Bridge: The Epic Story of the Building of the Brooklyn Bridge* (New York: Simon & Schuster, 1872), 308, 322.

CHAPTER SIX: A MAN OF ENERGY, 1867–1868

1. Howard Mumford Jones, *The Age of Energy: Varieties of American Experience, 1865–1914* (New York: Viking Press, 1971), 104–5.

2. Ward, 191–92; Meinig, III, 17–18.

3. Noble to AC, December 25, 1866, March 18, 1867, May 28, 1867, box 25, folder 8, CS; City of Ellsworth Web site @http://skyways.lib.ks.us.

4. Draft agreement, September 13, 1867, box 85, folder 3, CS; Reid, 448–50.

5. Memo, March 10, 1871, box 85, folder 5, CS; see letters to and from AC and JET, Thurston, Edmund Smith, and others, dated May, 1873, box 85, folder 1, CS.

6. *NYT,* June 6, 1867, 1.

7. Charles Edgar Ames, *Pioneering the Union Pacific: A Reappraisal of the Builders of the Railroad* (New York: Appleton-Century-Crofts, 1969), 152–54.

8. See letters and memoranda, box 67, folders 6, 7, 8, CS.

9. AC to GP, March 8, 1869, box 67, folder 6, CS.

10. GP to AC, March 19, 1872; AC to JET, March 29, 1872, box 67, folder 8, CS.

11. *Report of the Investigating Committee of the Pennsylvania Railroad Company* (Philadelphia: Allen, Lane & Scott's Printing House, 1874), 125–27; Burgess & Kennedy, 329.

12. Robert W. Jackson, *Rails Across the Mississippi: A History of the St. Louis Bridge* (Urbana: University of Illinois Press, 2001), 18.

13. AC to TAS, January 24, 1870, Scott.

14. AC to TAS, June 25, 1871, box 1, folder 1, CS.

15. AC to JET, December 10, 1868, AC to H. T. Reid, December 10, 1868, box 47, folder 1.

16. AC, "1868," ACAC.

CHAPTER SEVEN: "MR. CARNEGIE IS NOW 35 YEARS OF AGE, AND IS SAID TO BE WORTH ONE MILLION OF DOLLARS," 1870–1872

1. *NYT,* March 9, 1870; Strouse, 138.

2. Strouse, 138–39; AC to J. S. Morgan & Co., March 28, 1870; AC to JET, March 31, 1870, box 51, folder 2, CS.

3. AC to JET, April 2, 6, 1870, box 51, folder 2, CS; AC, *Autobiography,* 151.

4. *Trow's New York City Directory* [for year ending May 1, 1870] (New York: J. F. Trow, 1870).

5. Howard Chudacoff, *The Age of the Bachelor: Creating an American Subculture* (Princeton: Princeton University Press, 1999), 47–48; 98–101.

6. Trollope, 491.

7. *Miller's New York as it is . . .* (New York: J. Miller, 1866); David Dunlap, *On Broadway: A Journey Uptown Over Time* (New York: Rizzoli, 1990), 77–86.

8. Timothy J. Gilfoyle, *City of Eros: New York City, Prostitution, and the Commercialization of Sex, 1790–1920* (New York: W.W. Norton, 1992), 123–24, 197–202, 237–39; Chudacoff, 169–70.

9. Charles Lockwood, *Manhattan Moves Uptown* (Boston: Houghton Mifflin, 1976), 151–58; "Home and Foreign Gossip," *Harper's Weekly,* January 1, 1866; *St. Nicholas Hotel; its plan and arrangements* (New York: Barton & Sons, 1856).

10. *Trow's New York City Directory,* 1870, 1871, 1872; Jackson, 126; H. Phipps, Jr., to AC, Jan. 22, 1872, box 5, folder 3, CS.

11. J. D. Reid, "Andrew Carnegie," *Railroad Gazette* II, November 19, 1870, 171.

12. Baer, PRR chronologies, 1870, 1871.

13. Gerald Berk, *Alternative Tracks: The Constitution of American Industrial Order, 1865–1917* (Baltimore: Johns Hopkins University Press, 1994), 47.

14. Ames, 402, 407.

15. AC to TAS, December 31, 1870, Scott.

16. AC to Schuester, February 21, 1871, box 52, folder 11, CS; Ames, 406; *Report of the Select Committee of the House of Representatives, appointed under the Resolution of January 6, 1873 to make inquiry into the affairs of the Union Pacific Railroad Company . . .* (Washington, DC: Government Printing Office, 1873), 649.

17. "The New Union Pacific Directory," *Railroad Gazette* II, March 11, 1871, 563.

18. GFMc to TMC, May 2, 1871, box 52, folder 11, CS.

19. AC to Linville, July 31, 1871, box 1, folder 1, CS.

20. AC to Linville, August 14, 1871, box 1, folder 1, CS.

21. AC, *Autobiography,* 161–62.

22. Baring Brothers to AC, August 28, 1871, box 33, folder 5, CS.

23. Morton, Rose to Baring Brothers, August 29, 1871, box 35, folder 7, CS.

24. AC to JET, December 8, box 39, folder 7, CS; Baring Brothers to AC, September 13, 1871, box 35, folder 4, CS.

25. AC to Baring Brothers, October 12, 1871; J. S. Morgan to AC, December 30, 1871, box 35, folder 4, CS.

26. AC to TAS, January 10, 1872, box 39, folder 7, CS; AC to JET, December 8, 1871, box 1, folder 2, CS.

27. AC to JET, December 8, 1871, box 39, folder 7, CS; AC to JET, January 19, 1872, box 1, folder 2, CS.

28. Richard White, "Information, Markets, and Corruption: Transcontinental Railroads in the Gilded Age," *Journal of American History* (June 2003), 24; J. D. Reid, "Andrew Carnegie," 171.

29. AC to Baring Brothers, December 8, 1871, box 1, folder 2, CS.

30. AC to J.S. Morgan & Co., November 29, 1871, box 1, folder 2, CS.

31. AC to TAS, July 1, 1872, Scott.

32. White, 30, 31.

33. AC to TAS, August 5, 1871, box 64, folder 4, CS; J. Morgan to AC, December 7, 1871, box 35, folder 4, CS.

34. AC to Hickox, March 18, 25, 1872, box 64, folder 4, CS; Governor of Ohio to "to whom it may concern," March 23, 1872, box 64, folder 3, CS; AC to TAS, JET, John Sherman, March 26, 1872, box 1, folder 3, CS.

35. Memorandum of Agreement, Drexel, Morgan and Andrew Carnegie; Memoran-

dum of Agreement, Drexel & Company and Andrew Carnegie, March 16, 1872, box 58, folder 5, CS.

36. Drexel, Morgan to Sulzbach Brothers, April 1, 1872, box 58, folder 6; J. S. Morgan to AC, June 19, 1872, box 33, folder 5, CS; AC to Messrs Sulzbach Bros., December 16, 1872, box 1, folder 3, CS.

37. Assorted correspondence, box 58, folder 7, CS.

38. AC to H. H. Porter, February 16, 1872, box 1, folder 2, CS.

39. AC to Baring Brothers, February 24, 1872, box 58, folder 1, CS.

40. E. V. McCandless to GFMc, May 12, 1872, box 5, folder 3, CS.

41. AC to GFMc, May 21, 1872, box 35, folder 2, CS.

42. AC, "Pacifism: 'International Arbitration'" (1910), in Andrew Carnegie Reader, 308.

43. See, e.g., AC, memo for Gladstone, July 27, 1893, vol. 21, ACLC.

44. NYT, June 7, 1874, 1; June 15, 1871, 8.

45. Morton, Bliss & Co. to AC, December 9, 1871, 2 letters, box 63, folder 1, CS; AC to Morton, Rose & Co., February 17, 1872, box 63, folder 4; Morton, Bliss & Co. to AC, April 1, 1872, box 63, folder 1, CS.

46. AC to McPherson, October 5, 1870, Union Iron Mills letterbook, February 26, 1870–October 31, 1870, CS.

47. AC to JET, November 27, 1871, box 1, folder 2, CS.

48. AC to J.S. Morgan, September 24, 1872, Book No. 1872–73, CS; J. S. Morgan to AC, May 8, 1873, box 52, folder 9, CS.

49. Jackson, 192–95; NYT, July 2, 1874.

50. Vincent P. Carosso, The Morgans: Private International Bankers, 1854–1913 (Cambridge, MA: Harvard University Press, 1987), 242–45; Jackson, 214–17.

CHAPTER EIGHT: "ALL MY EGGS IN ONE BASKET," 1872–1875

1. TMC to GFMc, September 3, 1872, box 5, folder 3, CS.

2. Carnegie Personal Journal: as of January 1, 1872, series Ic, box 1, CCNY.

3. AC, Autobiography, 129–30.

4. Hendrick interview with Abbott, August 1929, vol. 239, ACLC.

5. AC to Linville, May 6, 1875, box 2, folder 1, CS.

6. AC to J. Lowber Welsh, January 22, 1874, box 1, folder 5, CS.

7. James Dabney McCabe, Illustrated History of the Centennial Exhibition (Philadelphia: National Publishing Co., 1876), 327.

8. NYT, February 11, 1875; McCabe, 334, 509; J. S. Ingram, The Centennial Exposition, Described and Illustrated (Philadelphia: Hubbard Bros., c. 1876), 229, 343.

9. Peter Temin, Iron and Steel in Nineteenth-Century America, an Economic Inquiry (Cambridge, MA: MIT Press, 1964), 173; AC, Autobiography, 140–41; U.S. Steel, III, 2446; Richard Franklin Bensel, The Political Economy of American Industrialization, 1877–1900 (New York: Cambridge University Press, 2000), 8–9.

10. U.S. Steel, 2351.

11. Bridge, 72–73; A. Holley to Coleman, September 18, 1872, box 69, folder 1; TMC to AC, September 24, 1872, box 77, folder 1, CS.

12. Articles of Co-Partnership, November 5, 1872, vol. 4, ACLC.

13. Hendrick, I, 183.

14. AC to F. M. Drake (President of MIK&N), Centreville, September 26, 1872, box 66, folder 7, CS; AC to TAS, February 12, 1873, Scott.

15. G. Sulzbach to AC, January 16, 1873, box 59, folder 4, CS; J. S. Morgan to AC, May 8, 1873, box 52, folder 9, CS.

16. AC to JET, October 30, 1872, box 1, folder 3, CS.

17. JET to AC, November 14, 1872, box 69, folder 1, CS.

18. Shinn to AC, May 15, 1873, box 69, folder 2; AC to Shinn, May 21, 1873, letterbook, 1872–73, CS.

19. Steven W. Usselman, Regulating Railroad Innovation: Business, Technology, and Politics in America, 1840–1920 (New York: Cambridge University Press, 2002), 83–84.

20. U.S. Steel, 2382–83.

21. Sven Beckert, The Monied Metropolis: New York City and the Consolidation of the American Bourgeoisie, 1850–1896 (New York: Cambridge University Press, 2001), 256–57.

22. John Scott to AC, November 22, 1872; D. McCandless to AC, November 22, 1872, box 69, folder 1, CS.

23. Morrell to AC, December 3, 1872, box 77, folder 1, CS.

24. AC, *Autobiography*, 196.

25. AC to Sulzbach Bros., December 16, 1872, box 1, folder 3, CS.

26. AC to Tilden, November 11, 1872, box 7, Tilden.

27. See box 5, folder 4, CS.

28. Sr. Anne Frances Pulling, *Around Cresson and the Alleghenies* (Dover, NH: Arcadia, 1997), 35, 37, 40.

29. Bill from Mountain House, Cresson Springs, September 11, 1873, box 33, folder 6, CS.

30. AC to GFMc, August 7, 1873, box 5, folder 5, CS.

31. AC to GFMc, July 9, 1873, box 5, folder 5, CS.

32. AC to GFMc, September 17, 1873, box 5, folder 5, CS.

33. Harvey O'Connor, *Mellon's Millions* (New York: John Day Co., 1933), 30–31.

34. AC to GFMc, October 24, 1873, box 69, folder 2, CS.

35. AC to GFMc, November 4, 8, 1873, box 5, folder 5, CS.

36. AC to GFMc, n.d.; November 25, 1873, box 5, folder 5, CS.

37. AC, *Autobiography*, 186.

38. AC to J. S. Morgan, December 5, 1873, box 1, folder 5, CS.

39. AC to TAS, February 24, 1872, box 68, folder 3, CS.

40. TAS to AC, May 22, 1872, box 35, folder 1, CS.

41. Ward, 207–08; Baer, 1873 chronology; *NYT*, September 27, 1873, 2.

42. JET to AC, November 3, 1873, AC-NYPL.

43. TAS to AC, January 12, 1874, box 33, folder 7, CS.

44. AC, *Autobiography*, 167.

45. "A Railroad Prince Dead," *NYT*, May 22, 1881, 1; Laura Holloway, *Famous American Fortunes*... (New York: J. A. Hill & Co., 1889), 172.

46. AC to Shinn, December 15, 1874, box 2, folder 1, CS; TAS to AC, May 22, 1876, box 35, folder 1, CS.

47. AC to TAS, January, 1879, Scott.

48. AC, "The Road to Business Success," *EB*, 9–10; AC, *Autobiography*, 168.

49. *NYT*, June 13, 1873, 2.

50. James Howard Bridge, *Millionaires and Grub Street* (New York: Brentano's, 1931), 176–78.

51. AC to GFMc, May 21, 1872, box 35, folder 2, CS; AC to GFMc, [August] 28, 1873, box 5, folder 5, CS.

52. Mrs. E. D. Loomis to AC, April 4, 1874, box 5, folder 6, CS.

53. AC, *Autobiography*, 205; Annette Estess [or Estep] to AC, February 14, 1878, box 6, folder 1; Mary Clark to AC, December 10, 1879, box 6, folder 4; Bella Wilson to AC, October 5, 1880, box 6, folder 6, CS; Robert Waller to AC, December 22, 1881, box 6, folder 8, CS; Mackie to AC, March 30, 1883, box 10, folder 1, CS.

54. See assorted bills in box 21, folder 4, CS.

55. P. Tobin to AC, May 19, 1881, February 18, 1882, box 9, folder 4, CS.

56. C. W. Dickel to AC, November 8, 1880; R. Devereaux to AC, May 13, 1881; James McCrea to GFMc, June 12, 1880, box 9, folder 4, CS.

57. AC, "Memorandum of 1868," ACAC.

58. "Anne C. L. Botta," *Miscellaneous Writings*, I, 152–53.

59. Coleman to AC, March 7, 1874, box 69, folder 3, CS.

60. Holley to AC, March 21, 1874; Shinn to Holley, April 6, 1874; John Scott to AC, April 4, 1874, box 69, folder 3, CS.

61. Alexander Lyman Holley to Alexander Hamilton Holley, August 29, 1874, Holley; AC to Shinn, December 15, 1874, box 2, folder 1, CS.

62. *NYT*, December 11, 1874, 5.

63. *NYT*, February 12, 1875, 4.

64. Paul Krause, *The Battle for Homestead, 1880–1892: Politics, Culture and Steel* (Pittsburgh: University of Pittsburgh Press, 1992), 116.

CHAPTER NINE: DRIVING THE BANDWAGON, 1875–1878

1. George Thurston, *Pittsburgh and Allegheny in the Centennial Year* (Pittsburgh: A. A. Anderson & Son, 1876), 197.

2. A. L. Holley and Lenox Smith, "American Iron and Steel Works. No. XXI. The Works of the Edgar Thomson Steel Company

(Limited)," *Engineering* 25 (April 19, 1878): 295.

3. Upton Sinclair, *The Jungle* (1905; New York: Signet Classics, 1960), 204–05.

4. AC, *Autobiography,* 196–97.

5. *Ibid,* 197.

6. AC, *EB,* 190, 204.

7. *Ibid.,* 208–09.

8. Thomas J. Misa, *A Nation of Steel* (Baltimore: The Johns Hopkins University Press, 1995), 21; Usselman, 82–83.

9. Robert Kennedy to AC, January 20, 1882, box 79, folder 3, CS.

10. AC to Shinn, June 1, 1875, box 77, folder 1, CS.

11. Morrell to Shinn, June 10, 1875, box 77, folder 1, CS.

12. AC to Shinn, April 10, 1876, vol. 4, ACLC.

13. Usselman, 84–87.

14. AC to William Keyser, November 15, 1875, box 2, folder 2, CS.

15. AC to John Garrett, December 8, 1875, box 2, folder 2, CS; Usselman, 89.

16. Bridge, *Inside History,* 110–11.

17. AC to Shinn, December 15, 1874, box 2, folder 1, CS.

18. Bridge, *Inside History,* 112.

19. Bridge, *Millionaires,* 35.

20. *U.S. Steel,* 2419.

21. *Ibid.*

22. AC to J. S. Morgan & Co., August 16, 1875, box 77, folder 2, CS.

23. AC to Gowen, December 24, 1875, box 77, CS.

24. *U.S. Steel,* 2353.

25. AC to Shinn, November 30, 1875, vol. 4, ACLC; Coleman to TMC, n.d.; "Agreement between Coleman and Carnegie," May 1, 1876, box 77, folder 1, CS; "Statement of estate of Wm. Coleman," box 70, folder 2, CS.

26. AC, *Notes of a Trip Round the World* (New York, 1879) 73.

27. Misa, 31; Bridge, *Inside History,* 95–99.

28. AC to Shinn, December 9, 1875, January 15, 1876, letterbook, 1875–76, CS.

29. Shinn to AC, December 13, 1875, box 77, folder 1, CS.

30. AC to Shinn, December 14, 1875, box 77, folder 1, CS.

31. "Agreement signed on May 1, 1877," box 77, folder 5, CS.

32. May 2, 1870 timetable for "Fast Train" in *Travelers' Official Guide of the Railways* (Philadelphia, June 1870).

33. Code books, vol. 259, ACLC.

34. Arthur Pound and Samuel T. Moore, eds., *They Told Barron* (New York: Harper & Bros., 1930), 85.

35. AC, "An Employer's View of the Labor Question," *Forum* (April 1886), in *Andrew Carnegie Reader,* 99.

36. *Tariff,* 1848.

37. Jones to AC, March 28, 1877, box 71, folder 1, CS.

38. Jones to AC, March 24, 1878, box 71, folder 1, CS.

39. *NLT,* December 9, 1876, 1; Krause, 141–44.

40. AC to Pennsylvania RR Engineers, May 29, 1877, box 2, folder 5, CS.

41. Jones to GFMc, July 11, 1877, box 71, folder 1, CS.

42. *Report on the Committee Appointed to Investigate the Railroad Riots in July, 1877* (Harrisburg, 1878); Krause, 126–33.

43. Jones to AC, May 6, 1878, box 71, folder 1, CS.

CHAPTER TEN: ROUND THE WORLD, 1878–1881

1. A. B. Farquhar, in collaboration with Samuel Crowther, *The First Million the Hardest: An Autobiography* (Garden City, NY: Doubleday, Page, 1922), 19.

2. Ron Chernow, *Titan: The Life of John D. Rockefeller, Sr.* (New York: Random House, 1998), 19, 50.

3. All clippings in ACBM.

4. Assorted bills in box 21, folder 8, CS.

5. AC, *RTW,* 2.

6. Richard Gilder to H. Gilder, April 28, 1906, *Letters of Richard Watson Gilder,* ed. Rosamond Gilder (Boston: Houghton Mifflin, 1916), 374.

7. AC, unpublished typescript, 135–36, vol. 247, ACLC.

8. AC to Blackwood, November 25, 1867, Blackwood.

9. Amelia R. Hill to AC, January 22, 1874, box 5, folder 6, CS; JWV to AC, October 7,

1876, box 5, folder 8, CS; JWV to AC, April 24, 28, May 8, 1877, box 5, folder 9, CS.

10. AC to Townsend, October 12, 1878, box 3, folder 1, CS.

11. AC, *RTW*, 1; see also original copy of travel diary in Dunfermline.

12. J. W. Vandevort, notebooks, "Around the World," 1878–79, n.p., Vandevort.

13. AC to GFMc, October 23, 1878, box 6, folder 2, CS.

14. John Steele Gordon, *A Thread Across the Ocean* (New York: Perennial, 2003), 211–12; Bill Glover, *FTL Design: History of the Atlantic Cable and Submarine Telegraphy, Cable Timeline: 1850–1900:* http://www.atlanticcable.com/Cables/CableTimeLine/index1850.htm.

15. Vandevort, notebooks, "Around the World," Vandevort.

16. AC, *Autobiography*, 197, 204; William W. Stowe, *Going Abroad: European Travel in Nineteenth-Century American Culture* (Princeton: Princeton University Press, 1994), 1, 13–15.

17. AC, *RTW*, 91, 149, 197.

18. *Ibid.,* 17–18.

19. *Ibid.,* 76, 80–81.

20. *Ibid.,* 282–83.

21. AC to Lauder, December 10, 1879, box 10, folder 10, CS; *NYT,* February 13, 1880, 2.

22. Champlin to GFMc, July 7, 1879, box 6, folder 3, CS.

23. Assorted letters in vol. 4, 5; "Letters transferred from scrapbook 'Around the World'" in vol. 263, ACLC; AC, *Autobiography*, 198.

24. Lauder to S. E. Moore, April 25, 1878, box 6, folder 1, CS.

25. Torn, untitled, undated clipping, box 17, folder 6, CS.

26. AC to Miss Whitfield [spring 1880], box 3, folder 3, CS.

27. Burton J. Hendrick and Daniel Henderson, *Louise Whitfield Carnegie: The Life of Mrs. Andrew Carnegie* (New York: Hastings House, 1950), 55.

28. *Ibid.,* 57; AC to LW correspondence, CFP.

29. AC, *AF-I-H,* 2, 9–10; AC, *Our Coaching Trip, Brighton to Inverness* (New York: privately printed, 1882); AC to Messrs. Vernon H. Brown & Co., May 24, 1881, box 10, folder 2, CS.

30. Hendrick and Henderson, 58.

31. Hendrick interview with Mrs. Carnegie, August 22, 1927, vol. 256, ACLC.

32. *Ibid.;* Stewart to AC, March 17, 1884, box 7, folder 3, CS; Mary Clark file, series VIA, box 29, CCNY.

33. John O'Hara to AC, April 27, 1881, box 6, folder 7, CS; Hendrick and Henderson, 59.

34. AC to LW, May 31, 1881, CFP; Hendrick and Henderson, 59.

35. AC to LW, June 21, 1881, CFP.

36. AC to Messrs. Vernon H. Brown & Co., May 24, 1881, box 10, folder 2, CS.

37. AC, *AF-I-H,* 18.

38. *Ibid.,* 18–19, 24, 28, 31, 38, 42–43.

39. *Ibid.,* 43–44, 47–50, 53–54.

40. Alice French, "Journal of the Carnegie Tour," 6, 8, French.

41. AC, *AF-I-H,* 42–50.

42. *Ibid.,* 151–2, 182, 323.

43. *Ibid.,* 324.

44. *Ibid.,* 10, 239.

45. French, "Journal," 12; AC, *AF-I-H,* 82, 281–84; AC, *Our Coaching Trip,* 184.

46. AC, *Our Coaching Trip,* 210.

47. AC, *AF-I-H,* 28.

48 *Ibid.,* 103–04.

49. *Ibid.,* 188.

CHAPTER ELEVEN: MAKING A NAME, 1881–1883

1. *NYT,* December 27, 1879, 8; February 13, 1880, 8; March 2, 1880, 1; December 12, 1880, 9; February 6, 1881, 7; December 25, 1881, 9; December 27, 1881, 3.

2. Hendrick and Henderson, 73–74; AC to LW, "calling card," January 1, 1882; February 17, February 18, 1882, CFP; *NYT,* April 13, 1882, 2.

3. AC to Shinn, September 14, 1879, box 76, folder 4, CS.

4. Jones to AC, November 5, 9, 1880; AC to Jones, November 8, 1880, box 71, folder 1, CS.

5. John Stover, *American Railroads,* 2nd ed. (Chicago: University of Chicago Press, 1997), 77, 134–35; Misa, 32.

6. Bridge, *Inside History,* 102.

7. "Statement showing status of each partners interest . . ."; "Statement of Contri-

butions of Partners to the Capital . . . ," vol. 5, ACLC.

8. Kenneth Warren, *Wealth, Waste, and Alienation: Growth and Decline in the Connellsville Coke Industry* (Pittsburgh: University of Pittsburgh Press, 2001), 61–62.

9. Kenneth Warren, *Triumphant Capitalism: Henry Clay Frick and the Industrial Transformation of America* (Pittsburgh: University of Pittsburgh Press, 1996), 27.

10. AC to Robert Garrett, December 28, 1881, box 3, folder 4, CS; Warren, *Triumphant Capitalism*, 29–32.

11. Jones to AC, December 5, 1879, box 71, folder 3, CS.

12. Jones to AC, April 2, 1880, box 71, folder 1, CS.

13. Jones to AC, November 5, 1880; Mackie to Jones, January 20, 1881, box 3, folder 3, CS; George H. Lamb, "The Carnegie Free Library," in *The Unwritten History of Braddock's Field* (Braddock: n.p., 1917), 221.

14. Theodore Jones, *Carnegie Libraries Across America: A Public Legacy* (New York: John Wiley & Sons, 1997), 9–10; Daniel Nelson, *Managers and Workers: Origins of the New Factory System in the United States, 1880–1920* (Madison: University of Wisconsin Press, 1975), 102; Jones to AC, February 20, 1882, box 71, folder 1, CS.

15. AC to Hon. Robert W. Lyon, November 25, 1881, box 3, folder 4, CS.

16. Jones, 9; Lamb, 220; *NLT*, January 26, 1884, 4; *NYT*, October 10, 1885, 2.

17. Krause, 171–92.

18. Jones to AC, February 20, 1882, box 71, folder 1, CS.

19. *NLT*, April 1, 1882, 4.

20. *NLT*, April 29, 1882, 4; April 28, 1888, 4; John A. Fitch, *The Steel Workers* (1910; Pittsburgh: University of Pittsburgh Press, 1989), 88, 88n.

21. *NLT*, June 3, 1882, 4; *NYT*, June 1, 1882, 5.

22. Jones to AC, November 20, 1882, box 71, folder 1, CS.

23. *NLT*, March 31, April 14, 28, 1883, 4.

24. AC to Carnegie Bros., October 30, 1882, box 3, folder 4, CS.

25. AC to Townsend, April 20, 1882, box 70, folder 2, CS.

26. Townsend to AC, April 21, 1882; AC to Townsend, April 22, 1882, box 70, folder 2, CS.

27. Townsend to AC, April 24, 26, 1882; Townsend to R. T. Wilson & Co., May 2, 1882, box 70, folder 2, CS.

28. AC, *TD*, 57–58; "Statement of Expenses incurred in showing Party of Scotch Friends the United States," October 1882, box 21, folder 10, CS; see also box 6, folder 10, CS.

29. AC to LW, January 1, 1883, n.d., CFP.

30. Chudacoff, 50.

31. AC to LW, June 26, 1882, CFP.

32. AC to LW, n.d., CFP.

33. LW to AC, July 23, 1883, CFP.

34. LW to AC, August 2, 1883, CFP.

35. LW to AC, September 13, 1883, CFP.

36. LW to AC, September 22, 1883, CFP.

CHAPTER TWELVE: MR. SPENCER AND MR. ARNOLD, 1882–1884

1. Courtlandt Palmer, "The Nineteenth Century Club of New York: Shall Similar Associations Become General?" April 29, 1887 (London: William Reeves, n.d.): 8.

2. AC, *Autobiography*, 146.

3. "Remarks of Andrew Carnegie before the Nineteenth Century Club upon 'The Aristocracy of the Dollar'" (n.d., n.p.): 4.

4. *Ibid.*, 10–11.

5. AC, "As Others See Us," *Fortnightly Review* (February 1882): 156.

6. J. D. Y. Peel, *Herbert Spencer: The Evolution of a Sociologist* (New York: Basic Books, 1971), 2, 41.

7. Richard Hofstadter, *Social Darwinism in American Thought*, rev. edn. (Boston: Beacon Press, 1955), 33; Henry Adams, *Democracy: An American Novel* (1880; rev. edn., New York: Modern Library, 2003), 3.

8. Bridge, *Millionaires*, 24–27.

9. David Duncan, *Life and Letters of Herbert Spencer*, vol. 1 (New York: D. Appleton & Co., 1908), 289; Spencer to Youmans, March 29, 1882, in Herbert Spencer, *An Autobiography* (New York: D. Appleton & Co., 1904), II, 455.

10. Spencer, *Autobiography*, I, 424; II, 468.

11. Spencer, *Autobiography*, II, 467–72.

12. *Ibid.*, 478.

13. Edward L. Youmans, comp., *Herbert Spencer on the Americans and the Americans on Herbert Spencer* (New York: Appleton, 1883); *NYT,* November 10, 1882, 5.

14. Spencer to AC, January 11, 1883, vol. 6, ACLC.

15. AC to Spencer, April 12, 1884, ACBM.

16. AC, *Autobiography,* 327, AC, "A confession of Religious Faith," undelivered rectorial speech for St. Andrews University, October 22, 1902, in *MW,* II, 297–99.

17. Herbert Spencer, *First Principles,* 5th London edn. (New York: A. L. Burt Co., n.d.), 237, 275, 342.

18. Peel, 100; Herbert Spencer, *Social Statics* (London: John Chapman, 1851), 42, 45.

19. Spencer, *Social Statics,* 42; Herbert Spencer, "Population," cited in Peel, 138–39.

20. Spencer, *Social Statics,* 65.

21. AC, *Autobiography,* 327; Adams, *The Education,* 232.

22. AC, *RTW,* 20.

23. Arnold to AC, July 5 [1883], in Cecil Y. Lang, ed., *The Letters of Matthew Arnold,* vol. 5 (Charlottesville: University Press of Virginia, 2001), 280–81.

24. AC, *Autobiography,* 286.

25. Arnold to Frances Arnold, in Lang, ed., 313; Mackie to Hawk & Wetherbee, October 13, 1883, box 10, folder 1, CS.

26. Mackie to Mrs. Youmans, October 25, 1883, box 10, folder 2, CS.

27. *NYT,* October 28, 1883, 2.

28. Park Honan, *Matthew Arnold: A Life* (New York: McGraw-Hill, 1981), 398–99.

29. AC to Mrs. Annie Adams Fields, October 10, 1888, IIL.

CHAPTER THIRTEEN: "THE STAR-SPANGLED SCOTCHMAN," 1884

1. Mackie to Courtlandt Palmer, April 29, 1884, box 4, folder 1, CS.

2. Mackie to AC, March 30, 1883, box 10, folder 1, CS; Miss Vincent to Mackie, August 14; Mackie to Miss Vincent, August 20, 1883, box 3, folder 5, CS.

3. Hendrick and Henderson, 67; Hendrick, I, 251.

4. "Mr. Carnegie's Tour Through Devon," *Pall Mall Gazette,* in *NYTr,* July 4, 1884, 2.

5. William Black, "A Few Days' More Driving," *Harper's New Monthly Magazine,* 70 (December 1884): 22.

6. AC to Samuel Storey, January 3, 1883, in Hendrick, I, 267.

7. *NYT,* August 23, 1883, 2.

8. See August 1884 clips in scrapbook, vol. 263, ACLC.

9. Arnold to Lucy Charlotte Arnold Whitridge, March 3, 1885, in *Letters of Matthew Arnold,* vol. 6, 17.

10. AC to Rosebery, August 31, 1883, Rosebery.

11. AC to Rosebery, June 19, 1884, Rosebery.

12. AC to "My Dear Sir," January 5, 1885, box 16, folder 5, CS.

13. AC to Gladstone, January 11, 1885, Gladstone correspondence.

14. *NYT,* April 27, 1884; March 10, 1885, 2.

15. AC to LW, July 19, 1884, CFP.

16. AC to LW, marked July 18, 1884, postmarked August 18, CFP.

17. AC to LW, [late 1884], CFP.

18. LW to AC, November 16, 1884, CFP.

19. LW to AC, November 17, 1884, CFP.

20. AC to LW, November 17, 1884, CFP.

21. LW to AC, November 18, 1884, CFP.

22. AC to LW, November 21, 1884, CFP.

23. AC to LW, November 22, 1884, CFP.

24. LW to AC, November 22, 1884, CFP.

25. LW to AC, November 17, 1884, CFP.

CHAPTER FOURTEEN: BOOMS AND BUSTS, 1883–1885

1. Stover, 135; Edward Chase Kirkland, *Industry Comes of Age* (1961; Chicago: Quadrangle, 1967), 30; *NYT,* January 16, 1885, 1.

2. Kenneth Warren, "Charlie: The Businessman as Hero," n.p., ms in author's possession.

3. *NYT,* June 8, 1879, 1; June 1, 1882, 5.

4. *NYTr,* September 24, 1883; Jones to AC, November 2, 1883, box 71, folder 1, CS.

5. AC to Messrs. Carnegie Bros., November 30, 1883, box 3, folder 5, CS.

6. Spencer, *Social Statics,* 323.

7. *Ibid.,* 324–25.

8. AC to Frank Thomson, January 23, 1884, box 4, folder 1, CS.

9. AC to John S. Wilson, January 24, February 22, February 25, 1884, box 4, folder 1, CS.

10. W. C. Whitney to AC, February 8, 1883, box 68, folder 2, CS.

11. AC to Twombly, February 8, 1883, box 68, folder 2, CS.

12. Carosso, 254–57.

13. AC to Roberts, n.d., box 7, folder 4, HCFUP; *NYT,* July 31, 1885, 2; August 8, 1885, 5; August 24, 1885, 5.

14. AC to Roberts, n.d., box 7, folder 4, HCFUP.

Chapter Fifteen: The "Millionaire Socialist," 1885–1886

1. See correspondence in box 17, folder 2, CS; Beckert, 263–65.

2. *NYTr,* January 5, 1885, 1.

3. *NLT,* January 10, 1885, 1.

4. *NLT,* December 20, 1884, 4.

5. Jones to AC, December 3, 1884, box 71, folder 1, CS.

6. Daniel Rogers, *The Work Ethic in Industrial America, 1850–1920* (Chicago: University of Chicago Press, 1978), 159–60.

7. *NLT,* February 14, 1885, 4.

8. Thomas Bell, *Out of This Furnace* (1941; Pittsburgh: University of Pittsburgh Press, 1976), 47.

9. *NYT,* January 4, 1886, 2.

10. *NLT,* January 16, 1886, 4; Fitch, 114.

11. *NLT,* January 3, 1885, 1; *NYT,* October 10, 1885, 2; AC to LW, October 17, 1885, CFP.

12. AC, *Autobiography,* 318.

13. AC, *TD,* 399.

14. Hendrick, I, 266.

15. Series IX, box 1, folder 10, CCNY.

16. AC, *Autobiography,* 318–19.

17. Bridge, *Millionaires,* 159; Mackie to Bridge, October 27, 1884, box 10, folder 2, CS; Champlin to Mackie, December 4, 1884, box 29, folder 4, CS.

18. Bridge, *Millionaires,* 37.

19. George W. Bitner to AC, November 11, 1874, box 5, folder 6, CS.

20. Bridge, *Millionaires,* 37–38.

21. *Ibid.,* 46.

22. *Ibid.,* 54.

23. AC to LW, June 29, 1885, CFP.

24. LW to AC, July 1, 1885, CFP.

25. AC to LW, July 23, 1885, CFP.

26. AC to LW, September 17, 1885, CFP.

27. LW to AC, September 19, 1885, CFP.

28. AC to LW, September 28, 1885, CFP.

29. LW to AC, October 2, 1885, CFP.

30. AC to LW, October 5, 1885, CFP.

31. AC to LW, October 17, 1885, CFP.

32. See, e.g., AC to Blaine, March 13, 1880, box 3, folder 2, CS.

33. American Council of Learned Societies, *Dictionary of American Biography* (1928–37; New York: Scribner, 1946), vol. 1, 325.

34. AC to Morley, October 8, 1884, vol. 27, ACLC.

35. AC to Gladstone, April 27, 1885, vol. 8, ACLC.

36. AC to Gladstone, July 14, 1885, vol. 8, ACLC.

37. AC to Gladstone, January 25, 1886, vol. 8, ACLC.

38. Duncan, 264.

39. AC, *TD,* 484.

40. *Ibid.,* 25, 31.

41. *Ibid.,* 40–41.

42. *Ibid.,* 117, 296, 327, 333, 336, 337, 355, 489–91.

43. *Ibid.,* 500, 237.

44. Bridge, *Millionaires,* 43, 45.

45. Ross to AC, May 16, 1886, vol. 8, ACLC; Morley to AC, May 17, 1886, in Hendrick, I, 278.

46. Spencer to AC, May 18, 1886, vol. 9, ACLC.

47. GP to AC, May 5, 1886; Henry George to AC, May 13, 1886, vol. 9, ACLC.

Chapter Sixteen: Things Fall Apart, 1886–1887

1. AC, "An Employer's View of the Labor Question," 92–93.

2. *Ibid.,* 93, 96.

3. *NYTr,* March 23, 1886, 6; *NYT,* April 2, 1886, 5; *NLT,* April 3, 1886, 4.

4. AC to LWC, March 10, 1886, CFP.

5. Arnold to Frances . . . Arnold, July 26, 1886, in *Letters of Matthew Arnold,* vol. VI, 181.

6. Jeremy Brecher, *Strike!* (Boston: South End Press, 1977), 28, 31.

7. AC, "Results of the Labor Struggle," *Forum,* I (August 1886), in *Andrew Carnegie Reader,* 102–03.

8. *Ibid.,* 112.

9. AC to LW, July 21, 1886, CFP.

10. AC to LW, July 22, 1886, CFP.

11. Hendrick and Henderson, 77.

12. AC to LW, September 23, 27, 1886, CFP.

13. AC to LW, October 3, 1886, CFP.

14. AC to LW, October 16, 1886, CFP.

15. AC, *Autobiography*, 205; *NYT*, October 20, 1886, 3.

16. Bridge, *Millionaires*, 39–40.

17. Hendrick interview with John Walker, Dr. Fred Dennis, vol. 239, ACLC.

18. Bridge, *Millionaires*, 40–41; *NYT*, October 21, 1856, 5; October 22, 1; October 31, 1; Mackie to AC, October 29, 1886, box 10, folder 2, CS.

19. AC to LW, November 24, 1886, CFP.

20. AC to LW, November 29, 1886, CFP.

21. AC to LW, December 2, 1886, CFP.

22. LW to AC, December 4, 1886, CFP.

23. AC to LW, December 4, 1886, CFP.

24. *U.S. Steel*, 2408.

25. Article of Agreement between Carnegie Bros. and Company, Ltd., and Andrew Carnegie, Henry Phipps, Jr., et al., vol. 10, ACLC.

26. AC, *Autobiography*, 204.

27. HCF to AC, August 13, 1883, box 1, folder 1, HCFUP.

28. AC to Carnegie Bros., February 10, 1886; Phipps to Lauder, February 19, 1886; AC to HCF, February 23, 1886, HCFFM.

29. AC to HCF, February 25, [1886], HCFFM.

30. Warren, *Triumphant Capitalism*, 42–43; Article of Agreement between Carnegie Bros. and Company, Ltd., and Henry C. Frick, January 10, 1887, vol. 10, ACLC.

31. Bridge, *Millionaires*, 41–42; Hendrick and Henderson, 81–82; LW to AC, February 9, 1887, CFP.

32. AC to LW, February 22, 1887, CFP.

33. AC to LW, January 21, 1887; LW to AC, January 24, 1887, CFP.

34. LW to AC, March 12, 1887, CFP.

35. LW to AC, assorted letters, March, 1887, CFP.

36. Robert A. M. Stern, et al., *New York 1880* (New York: Monacelli Press, 1999, 578–601; M. Christine Boyer, *Manhattan Manners: Architecture and Style, 1850–1900* (New York: Rizzoli, 1985), 184–87.

37. David Lavender, *The Great Pretender* (Garden City, NY: Doubleday & Co., 1970), 346; LW to AC, March 3, 1887; AC to LW, March 5, 1887, CFP.

38. AC to LW, March 2, 1887, LW to AC, March 7, 1887, CFP.

39. LW to AC, January 23, 26, 1887, CFP.

40. AC to LW, February 10, 1887, CFP.

41. AC to LW, April 1, 1887, CFP.

42. AC to Huntington, April 2, 1887, box 4, folder 4, CS.

43. AC to LW, April 4, 6, 7, CFP.

CHAPTER SEVENTEEN: A WEDDING AND A HONEYMOON, 1887

1. *NYT*, April 23, 1887, 1; *NYTr*, April 23, 1887, 5.

2. *Town Topics*, April 27, 1887, 2.

3. "Indenture of Marriage Agreement between Andrew Carnegie and Louise Whitfield," April 22, 1886, Series VIA, box 8, folder 3, CCNY.

4. AC to LW, April 6, CFP.

5. Hendrick and Henderson, 88–90.

6. *Ibid.*, 91, *NYT*, June 20, 1887, 5.

7. AC to Rosebery, May 24, 1887, vol. 10, ACLC.

8. Hendrick and Henderson, 94; Philip Magnus, *Gladstone* (New York: Dutton, 1964), 357; *The Gladstone Diaries*, ed. H.C.G. Matthews (Oxford: Clarendon Press, 1994), vol. 12, 43.

9. AC to Gladstone, June 29, 1887, vol. 10, ACLC.

10. Gladstone to AC, July 18, 1887; AC to Gladstone, July 21, 1887, vol. 10, ACLC.

11. LWC to Mrs. Gladstone, [1888], Gladstone.

12. LWC to Mrs. Whitfield, n.d., in Hendrick and Henderson, 95.

13. LWC to Mrs. Whitfield, July 10, 1887, in *ibid.*, 99–100.

14. Cited in *ibid.*, 98–99.

15. *NYT*, July 9, 1; July 10, 5; July 12, 1887, 1.

16. Gail Hamilton, *Biography of James G. Blaine* (Norwich, CT: Henry Bill Publishing Co., 1895), 601; LWC to Mrs. Whitfield, n.d., in Hendrick and Henderson, 100.

17. LWC to Mrs. Whitfield, July 17, 1887, in *ibid.*, 103.

18. Arnold to Frances . . . Arnold, Sep-

tember 13, 1887, in *Letters of Matthew Arnold,* vol. VI, 306–07.

19. Mrs. Blaine to Emmons Blaine, July 15, 1887, in *Letters of Mrs. James G. Blaine,* ed. Harriet S. Blaine Beale (New York: Duffield & Co., 1908), vol. II, 156–60.

20. Mrs. Blaine to Miss Dodge, July 18, 1887; Mrs. Blaine to Emmons Blaine, July 15, 1887, in *ibid.,* 156–60.

21. Hay to Adams, July 20, 1887, in William Roscoe Thayer, *The Life and Letters of John Hay* (Boston: Houghton Mifflin, 1915) vol. II, 73–74.

22. Mrs. Blaine to Emmons Blaine, July 15, 1887; Mrs. Blaine to Miss Dodge, July 18, 1887, in *Letters of Mrs. James G. Blaine,* II, 156–60.

23. Walter Damrosch, *My Musical Life* (New York: Charles Scribner's Sons, 1926), 90–92; Walter Damrosch to Frank Damrosch, August 5, 1887, box 2, folder 35, D-BLC.

24. *Ibid.*

25. Walter to Frank Damrosch, August 9, 1887, box 2, folder 35, D-BLC.

26. "Men You Know: Mr. Andrew Carnegie," *The Bailie,* September 14, 1887, in "Biographical Sketches," Margaret Barclay Wilson Collection.

27. LWC to Mrs. Whitfield, July 17, 1887, in Hendrick and Henderson, 101–02.

28. *Three Days Speeches,* reprinted from *Dunfermline Saturday Press,* September 17, 1887, in *Writings, Addresses, Opinions,* vol. 1, Margaret Barclay Wilson Collection.

29. *Town Topics,* December 15, 1887, 8–9.

30. LWC to Mrs. Whitfield, n.d., in Hendrick and Henderson, 104, 107.

31. Uncle Lauder to AC, n.d., in *ibid.,* 111–12.

32. AC to John Vandevort, December 6, 1887, Vandevort.

CHAPTER EIGHTEEN: THE PINKERTONS AND "BRADDOCK'S BATTLEFIELD," 1887–1888

1. HCF to Phipps, Walker, and others, May 13, 1887, box 1, folder 2, HCFUP.

2. AC to HCF, June 1, 1887, HCFFM.

3. HCF to Phipps, Walker, and others, June 7, 1887, box 1, folder 2, HCFUP.

4. AC to HCF, August 2, 1887, September 9, 1887, box 1, folder 2, HCFUP.

5. AC to William Whitney, August 31, 1887, Cleveland.

6. *Triumphant Democracy,* in Margaret Barclay Wilson Collection.

7. *NYT,* December 21, 1887, 2.

8. AC, "An Employer's View of the Labor Question," 96.

9. *PP,* February 25, 1888, 1, March 3, 1888, 1; *NYT,* February 26, 1888, 2.

10. *NYT,* February 28, 1888, 1; *NLT,* March 10, 1888, 2; *PP,* February 29, 1888; March 2, 1888.

11. Kenneth Warren, *The American Steel Industry, 1850–1970, A Geographical Interpretation* (London: Oxford University Press, 1973), 116.

12. *C&AGW,* March 31, 1888, 1.

13. *NYT,* March 26, 29, 1; *PP,* March 24, 1888, 1; *NLT,* March 31, 1888, 1.

14. *C&AGW,* March 31, 1888, 1.

15. *Ibid.*

16. *Ibid.,* March 31, 1; April 13, 1888, 1; *PP,* March, 30 1888, 1; *PT,* April 20, 1888, 1.

17. *C&AGW,* April 7, 1888,1; *PT,* April 4, 6, 1888, 1.

18. *PT,* April 13, 17, 1888, 1.

19. *PP,* April 17, 1888, 1; *PT,* April 16, 18, 1888, 1.

20. *PT,* April 20, 1888, 1.

21. *PP, PT,* April 23, 1888, 1.

22. *PP, PT,* April 23, 1888, 1; *C&AGW,* April 28, 1888, 1; *U.S. Steel,* 2526–31.

23. *NLT,* April 21, 28, 1888, 1.

24. *PT,* April 25, 1888, 1.

25. *NLT,* April 28, 1888, 1; *PP,* April 28, 1888, 1.

26. *PT,* April 28, 1888, 1.

27. *Ibid.,* May 3, 1888.

28. *C&AGW,* May 5, 1888, 1.

29. *Ibid.,* May 12, 1888, 1.

30. *Ibid.,* April 14, 1888, 1.

31. *U.S. Steel,* 2528.

CHAPTER NINETEEN: FRIENDS IN HIGH PLACES, 1888–1889

1. *NYTr,* June 8, 1888, 1; Hendrick and Henderson, 118–19.

2. Walter to Frank Damrosch, June 21, 1888, box 2, folder 35, D-BLC; Mrs. James G. Blaine to James Blaine, June 14, 1888, in *Letters of Mrs. James G. Blaine,* II, 207.

3. Damrosch, 98.

4. AC, *AF-I-H,* 34–35.

5. Mrs. James G. Blaine to Walker Blaine, July 10, 1888, in *Letters of Mrs. James G. Blaine,* xx, 209–10.

6. Walter to Frank Damrosch, July 1, 1888, box 2, folder 35, D-BLC.

7. LCW to Mrs. Whitfield, n.d., in Hendrick and Henderson, 123.

8. Damrosch, 99.

9. Hendrick and Henderson, 126–27; much of the foregoing description of life at Cluny is taken from chap. 6 of their biography of Louise Whitfield Carnegie, 116–31.

10. Walter Damrosch, "Recollections of Andrew Carnegie," *Andrew Carnegie Centenary* (New York: Carnegie Corporation of New York, 1935), 27; Walter to Frank Damrosch, August 4, 1888, box 2, folder 35, D-BLC.

11. AC to Carnegie Brothers, October 18, 1884, box 4, folder 1, CS.

12. *NYT,* October 18, 1887, 5.

13. AC to James Swank, May 16, 1888, in *NYT,* May 18, 1888, 1.

14. *NYT,* September 9, 1888, 2; September 20, 1888, 5; September 25, 1888, 2; *NLT,* October 6, 1888, 3.

15. *NYT,* October 9, 1888, 8; *NYT,* October 9, 1888, 1.

16. *NLT,* October 6, 1888, 2.

17. *NYT,* October 20, 1888, 6.

18. *NYT,* October 25, 1888, 1.

19. Knox & Reed to S. E. Moore, October 31, November 1, 1888, series IX, box 1, folder 10, CCNY.

20. "Duplicate Letter of Intent," series IX, box 1, folder 10, CCNY.

21. AC to Benjamin Harrison, November 7, 1888, Harrison.

22. AC to HCF, September 8, 1888, box 6, folder 13, HCFUP.

23. AC to HCF, February 2, 1889, box 1, folder 3, HCFUP.

24. AC to HCF, February 16, 1889, box 1, folder 3, HCFUP.

25. AC, "Pennsylvania's Industrial and Railroad Policy," address to Pennsylvania legislature, April 8, 1889, in *MW,* I, 290, 297–305.

26. *PT,* March 22, April 11, 18, 19, 1889, 1; *NYT,* April 11, 1889, 5; April 13, 1889, 2; April 15, 1889, 4; May 10, 1889, 4.

27. AC to Gladstone, February 7, 1890, Gladstone.

28. Lamb, 220.

29. AC, "Dedication of the Carnegie Library at the Edgar Thomson Steel Rail Works, Braddock, March 30, 1889, Address to Workingmen," CLP.

CHAPTER TWENTY: THE GOSPELS OF ANDREW CARNEGIE, 1889–1892

1. AC, "Dedication," 15, CLP.

2. AC, "The Bugaboo of Trusts," *North American Review* (February 1889), in *Andrew Carnegie Reader,* 222.

3. John D. Rockefeller, *Random Reminiscences of Men and Events* (New York: Doubleday, Page, 1909), 90–91; Jay Gould testimony, U.S. Congress, Senate Committee on Education and Labor. *Report Upon the Relations Between Labor and Capital* (Washington, DC: Government Printing Office, 1885), 1081.

4. Strouse, 305.

5. AC, "The ABC of Money," *North American Review* (June 1891), in *Andrew Carnegie Reader,* 234, 242–43, 247.

6. *Ibid.,* 256.

7. AC, "Gospel of Wealth II," 1906, in *Problems of To-Day: Wealth, Labor, Socialism* (1908; Garden City, NY: Doubleday, Doran & Co., 1933), 13, 17–21.

8. *NYT,* October 29, 1882, 8; November 19, 1882, 5.

9. AC, "[Gospel of] Wealth," *North American Review,* (June 1889), in *Andrew Carnegie Reader,* 130–31.

10. *Ibid.,* 132–33.

11. *Ibid.,* 134, 138.

12. *Ibid.,* 133–35.

13. *Ibid.,* 134–36.

14. *Ibid.,* 139.

15. *Ibid.,* 139–40.

16. LWC to Gladstone, June 19, 1889, Gladstone.

17. AC, "The Best Fields for Philanthropy," *North American Review* (December 1889), in *Andrew Carnegie Reader,* 153.

18. "[Gospel] of Wealth," 138.

19. AC to Gladstone, November 24, 1890, vol. II, ACLC.

20. W. E. Gladstone, *Nineteenth Century* 28 (November 1890): 683, 692.

21. AC to Gladstone, November 24, 1890, vol. II, ACLC; AC, "The Advantages of

Poverty," *Nineteenth Century,* (March 1891), in *The Gospel of Wealth,* ed. Edward C. Kirkland (Cambridge, MA: Harvard University Press, 1965), 64.

22. Manning, Adler, Hughes, "Irresponsible Wealth," *Nineteenth Century,* 27 (December 1890): 891.

23. AC, "The Advantages of Poverty," 51–55.

24. *Ibid.,* 73.

25. *Ibid.,* 75; Edward Kirkland, *Dream and Thought in the Business Community, 1860–1900* (Ithaca: Cornell University Press, 1956), 154–64.

26. AC to Gladstone, March 28, 1892, vol. 15, ACLC.

27. Rosemary Ruhig DuMont, "The Founding of the Carnegie Library of Pittsburgh," in Robert Sidney Martin, ed., *Carnegie Denied: Communities Rejecting Carnegie Library Construction Grants, 1898–1925* (Westport, CT: Greenwood Press, 1993), 3–4.

28. HCF to AC, February 28, 1890, box 2, folder 6, HCFUP.

29. On opposition to the East End site, see Francis G. Couvares, *The Remaking of Pittsburgh: Class and Culture in an Industrializing City, 1877–1919* (Albany: State University of New York Press, 1884), 35–43.

30. AC to James Scott, July 9, 1890, box 1, ACCLP.

31. Franklin Toker, *Pittsburgh: An Urban Portrait* (Pittsburgh: University of Pittsburgh Press, 1986), 98.

32. AC to James Scott, March 18, 1891, box 1, ACCLP.

33. AC to James Scott, January 25, 1892, box 1, ACCLP.

34. Toker, 98; AC to James Scott, November 3, 1893, box 1, ACCLP.

35. Damrosch, *My Musical Life,* 94–95.

36. Richard Schickel, *The World of Carnegie Hall* (New York: Julian Messner, 1960), 30–34; Ethel Peyser, *The House That Music Built: Carnegie Hall* (New York: Robert M. McBride, 1936), 38–47.

37. Extract from the minutes of the Music Hall Company of New York, Ltd., from meeting of September 29, 1890, vol. 11, ACLC.

38. Peter Tchaikovsky to Eduard Napravnik, May 2, 1891, in Elkhonon Joffe, *Tchaikovsky in America: The Composer's Visit in 1891* (New York: Oxford University Press, 1986), 69; Tchaikovsky to Vladimir Davidov, April 30, 1891, in *ibid.,* 62; Tchaikovsky, diary, April 27, 1891, in *ibid.,* 57.

39. Tchaikovsky, diary, April 29, May 10, 1891, in *ibid.,* 57, 61, 111.

40. Tchaikovsky to Napravnic, May 2, 1891, in *ibid.,* 69.

41. AC to Eliot, December 31, 1904, vol. 110, ACLC.

42. "Schedule of Capital, Stock, Bonds Etc., January 1, 1890," vol. 10, ACLC.

43. AC to Sage, February 3, 1896, vol. 36, ACLC.

CHAPTER TWENTY-ONE: SURRENDER AT HOMESTEAD, 1889–1890

1. AC, "The Advantages of Poverty," 72–73.

2. Krause, 243; Steve Brier, "Technological Change at Homestead, 1881–1892," unpublished paper in author's possession; Mark M. Brown, "Technology and the Homestead Steel Works," *Canal History and Technology Proceedings,* 11 (1992): 186–205; "The Homestead Mill," *NLT,* April 27, 1889, 1.

3. B. Franklin Cooling, *Gray Steel and Blue Water Navy* (Hamden, CT: Archon Books, 1979), 71–72.

4. AC to Whitney, December 8, 1886, box 39, Whitney.

5. AC to LW, March 2, 1887, LW to AC, March 7, 1887, CFP.

6. Krause, 224, 246.

7. Krause, 209.

8. AC to HCF, April 26, 1889, box 1, folder 6, HCFUP.

9. AC to HCF, April 13, 1889, box 1, folder 5, HCFUP.

10. AC to Abbott, Saturday [April] 27 [1889], vol. 10, ACLC.

11. AC to Abbott, n.d., vol. 10, ACLC.

12. AC to "Dear Boys," June 12, 1889, box 1, folder 7, HCFUP.

13. South Fork Fishing Club, notice of board meeting, box 17, folder 2, ACLC; David McCullough, *The Johnstown Flood* (1968; New

York: Touchstone, 1987), 203, 229, 256; AC to HCF, June 15, 1889, box 1, folder 7, HCFUP.

14. Dod to AC, [June] 4, 1889, box 1, folder 11, HCFUP; McCullough, *Johnstown Flood*, 203–29.

15. Jones, *Carnegie Libraries*, 10.

16. AC to HCF, June 15, 1889, box 1, folder 7, HCFUP.

17. AC to HCF, July 18, 1889, box 1, folder 8, HCFUP.

18. Krause, 241–42; *NYT*, May 28, 1889, 4; July 17, 1889, 4.

19. Krause, 212–14, 223, 252–66.

20. *Ibid.*, 246–47.

21. *NLT*, June 15, 1889, 1; AC to "bohoys," July 9, 1889, box 1, folder 8, HCFUP.

22. Krause, 247–48; *NYT*, July 16, 1889, 5; *NLT*, July 13, 1889, 1.

23. Walker to HCF, July 13, 1889, HCFFM.

24. Fitch, 121.

25. AC to Abbott, August 7, 1889, vol. 10, ACLC.

26. AC to HCF, August 7, 1889, box 1, folder 9, HCFUP.

27. HCF to AC, vol. 5, HCFFM.

28. AC to HCF, August 8, 1889, box 1, folder 9, HCFUP.

29. HCF to AC, August 9, 1889, in Warren, *Triumphant Capitalism*, 54.

30. AC to HCF & Boys in General, September 2, 1889, box 1, folder 10, HCFUP.

31. AC to HCF, September 3, 1889, box 1, folder 10, HCFUP.

32. AC to LWC, September 26, 1889, in Hendrick and Henderson, 138.

33. Theodore Dreiser, *Newspaper Days*, ed. T. D. Nostwich (Philadelphia: University of Pennsylvania Press, 1991), 514–15.

34. AC to HCF, October 19, 1889, box 1, folder 10, HCFUP.

35. AC, "Summing Up the Tariff Discussion," *North American Review* (July 1890), in *MW*, I, 306–50.

36. AC to HCF, January 22, 1890 (rec'd), box 2, folder 4, HCFUP.

37. AC to HCF, July 23, 1889, box 1, folder 8, HCFUP.

38. Bensel, 490; HCF to McKinley, October 2, 1891, Special Correspondence, box 3, HCFFM.

39. The stories of these real estate deals were uncovered and described by Paul Krause, 273–83.

40. HCF to AC, January 6, 1890, box 2, folder 3, HCFUP.

41. HCF to AC, January 13, 1890, box 2, folder 3; AC to HCF, January 15, 1890, box 2, folder 4, HCFUP.

42. Lincoln Steffens, *The Shame of the Cities* (1904; New York: Hill & Wang, 1957), 107.

43. HCF to AC, March 19, 1890, box 2, folder 7, HCFUP.

44. HCF to AC, July 28, 1890, box 2, folder 10, HCFUP.

45. Blaine to AC, April 18, 1889, vol. 10, ACLC.

46. *NYT*, March 4, 1890, 3; AC to Duke of Devonshire, December 26, 1895, in Hendrick I, 429.

47. AC to HCF, March 1, 1890, box 2, folder 4, HCFUP; AC to Abbott, n.d., vol. 240, ACLC.

48. Misa, 111–13; AC to Tracy, July 5, 1890, vol. 11, ACLC.

49. Robert Hessen, *Steel Titan: The Life of Charles M. Schwab* (Pittsburgh: University of Pittsburgh, 1975), 91; AC to HCF, July 15, 1890, folder 2, box 8; AC to HCF, August 3, 1890, box 2, folder 10, HCFUP.

50. HCF to AC, July 15, 1890, vol. 5, HCFFM.

51. AC to Tracy, n.d., vol. 11, ACLC.

52. AC to Blaine, May 9, 1891, vol. 12, ACLC.

53. AC to HCF, March 31, 1892, box 3, folder 11, HCFUP; Andrew Dickson White, *Autobiography of Andrew Dickson White* (New York: The Century Co., 1905), vol. 1, 235.

54. AC to HCF, April 2, 1894, box 5, folder 3, HCFUP.

55. AC to HCF, September 21, 1894, box 5, folder 6, HCFUP.

56. AC to Linderman, February 25, 1895, vol. 31, ACLC; Schwab to AC, March 7, 1898, vol. 49, ACLC.

57. AC to HCF, August 14, September 4, 1891, box 3, folder 6; AC to HCF, September 19, 1891, box 3, folder 7, HCFUP.

58. HCF to Schwab, October 24, 1894, Special Correspondence, box 5, HCFFM.

CHAPTER TWENTY-TWO: "THERE WILL NEVER BE A BETTER TIME THAN NOW TO FIGHT IT OUT," 1890-1891

1. AC to HCF, December 9, 1890, box 2, folder 13, HCFUP.

2. HCF to AC, December 30, 1890, Special Correspondence, box 3, HCF to AC, December 30, 1890, vol. 6, HCFFM.

3. David Montgomery, *The Fall of the House of Labor* (New York: Cambridge University Press, 1987), 30.

4. AC to HCF, rec'd December 31, 1890, box 3, folder 1, HCFUP.

5. Fitch, 146; David Brody (New York: Harper & Row, 1969), 96-97.

6. Schwab to HCF, January 1, 1891, in Warren, *Triumphant Capitalism*, 70.

7. Schwab to HCF, January 1, 1891, in Warren, *Triumphant Capitalism*, 71-72; HCF to Schwab, January 1, 1891, Special Correspondence, box 3, vol. 2, HCFFM.

8. HCF to AC, January 1, 1891, Special Correspondence, box 3, HCFFM.

9. Schwab to HCF, January 1, 1891, in Warren, *TC*, 72.

10. *Ibid.*

11. HCF to Gayley, HCF to Schwab, January 2, 1891, Special Correspondence, box 3, HCFFM.

12. HCF to AC, January 22, 31, 1891, vol. 6, HCFFM.

13. AC to HCF, January 26, February 9, 1891, box 3, folder 2, HCFUP.

14. HCF to AC, March 20, 1891, box 3, folder 2, HCFUP.

15. AC to HCF, March 21, 1891, box 3, folder 2, HCFUP.

16. AC to HCF, rec'd April 1, 1891, box 3, folder 4, HCFUP.

17. HCF to AC, April 1, 1891, Special Correspondence, box 3, HCFFM.

18. *NYT,* April 9, 1891, 1.

19. AC to HCF, n.d. , box 3, folder 4, HCFUP.

20. HCF to AC, April 20, 1891, vol. 6, HCFFM.

21. HCF to AC, April 21, 1891, vol. 6, HCFFM.

22. HCF to AC, May 20, 1891, Special Correspondence, box 3, HCFFM.

23. HCF to AC, July 14, 1891, vol. 6, HCFFM.

24. HCF to Morrison, July 3, 1891, Special Correspondence, box 3, HCFFM.

25. HCF to Morrison, July 6, 1891; HCF to Childs, July 3, 1891, Special Correspondence, box 3, HCFFM.

26. HCF to AC, July 14, 1891, vol. 6, HCFFM.

27. AC, *Autobiography,* 243.

28. AC to HCF, rec'd January 22, 1890, box 2, folder 4, HCFUP.

29. HCF to AC, March 26, 1891, vol. 6, HCFFM.

30. AC to HCF, March 29, 1891, box 3, folder 4, HCFUP.

31. AC to HCF, rec'd January 22, 1890, box 2, folder 4, HCFUP.

32. Martha Frick Symington Sanger, *Henry Clay Frick: An Intimate Portrait* (New York: Abbeville Press, 1998), 15.

33. HCF to AC, June 30, 1891, in *ibid.,* 141.

34. HCF to AC, July 9, 1891, vol. 6, HCFFM.

35. AC to HCF, mislabeled July 23, 1889, should be 1891, box 1, folder 8, HCFUP.

36. AC to HCF, July 27, 1891, box 3, folder 6, HCFUP.

37. AC to HCF, September 1, 1891, box 3, folder 6, HCFUP.

38. AC to HCF, September 9, 1891, box 3, folder 6, HCFUP.

39. AC to Champlin, n.d., in Champlin.

40. AC to Champlin, n.d., assorted photographs, in Champlin.

41. AC to Champlin, n.d., in *ibid.*

42. W. T. Hogan, *Economic History of the American Iron and Steel Industry,* (Lexington, KY: Heath, 1971), vol. 1, 184-87.

43. Hogan, I, 220-21; Brody, 17.

44. Hogan, I, 213.

45. AC to HCF, January 9, 1892, box 3, folder 10, HCFUP.

46. *U.S. Steel,* 2388-90.

47. AC to HCF, July 15, 1890, box 2, folder 9, HCFUP.

48. AC to HCF, May 13, 1892, box 3, folder 13, HCFUP.

49. Carnegie Steel Co., "Net profits of the Carnegie Associations," vol. 73, ACLC.

50. AC to HCF, August 21, 1891, box 3, folder 6, HCFUP.

51. *Musical Courier,* May 15, 1891, Magazine articles, vol. 5, in Margaret Barclay Wilson Collection.

52. AC to Halford, September 21, 1891, Benjamin Harrison to AC, October 5, 1891, vol. 12, ACLC.

CHAPTER TWENTY-THREE: THE BATTLE FOR HOMESTEAD, 1892

1. *PT,* June 1, 1892, in Demarest, 13–15.

2. Montgomery, 35.

3. AC to HCF, January 30, 1891, box 3, folder 2, HCFUP.

4. "Questionnaires," Martin; Krause, 290–92.

5. AC to HCF, December 19, 1891, box 3, folder 9, HCFUP.

6. Krause, 300–302, 307. While there is a vast literature on the Homestead strike of 1892, Paul Krause's account stands out from the rest in its interpretive breadth, its uncovering of new sources, and its use of the standard ones. My own narrative owes a great deal to Krause's study. In the story of the strike itself, I have also benefited greatly from Arthur G. Burgoyne's eyewitness account and history of *The Homestead Strike of 1892,* published in 1893, and David P. Demarest, Jr.'s, documentary history, *"The River Ran Red": Homestead 1892* (Pittsburgh: University of Pittsburgh Press, 1992).

7. Bridge, *Inside History,* 204–05.

8. George Harvey, *Henry Clay Frick: The Man* (1928; New York: The Frick Collection, 1936), 165; AC to HCF, April 11, 1892, box 3, folder 12, HCFUP.

9. HCF to AC, April 21, 1892 excerpt, Harvey folder, HCFFM.

10. AC to HCF, May 4, 1892, box 3, folder 13, HCFUP.

11. [AC] to HCF, May 23, 1892 excerpt, Harvey folder, HCFFM.

12. AC to HCF, May 24, 1892, box 3, folder 14, HCFUP.

13. AC to HCF, May 13, 1892 box 3, folder 13, HCFUP.

14. AC to HCF, May 24, 1892, box 3, folder 14, HCFUP.

15. HCF to AC, June 2, 1892, box 3, folder 15, HCFUP.

16. AC to HCF rec'd June 23, 1892, box 3, folder 16, HCFUP.

17. AC to HCF, May 30, 1892, box 3, folder 14, HCFUP.

18. AC to HCF, June 10, 1892, box 3, folder 15, HCFUP.

19. Krause, 303.

20. *PP,* June 4, 1892; Roberts testimony, July 13, 1892, U.S. House of Representatives Report No. 2447, in Demarest, ed., 29.

21. HCF to AC, June 2, 1892, box 3, folder 15, HCFUP.

22. AC to HCF, June 10 and 14, 1892, box 3, folder 15, HCFUP.

23. AC to HCF, June 17, 1892, box 3, folder 16, HCFUP.

24. HCF to AC, June 20, 1892 excerpt, Harvey folder, HCFFM.

25. HCF to AC, June 22, 1892, box 3, folder 16, HCFUP.

26. AC to HCF, rec'd June 23, 1892, box 3, folder 16, HCFUP.

27. Krause 309–10; HCF to AC, June 24, 1892 excerpt, Harvey folder, HCFFM.

28. *PP,* June 28, 1892, in Demarest, ed., 40.

29. *Ibid.*

30. Arthur Burgoyne, *The Homestead Strike of 1892* (1893; Pittsburgh: University of Pittsburgh Press, 1979), 13–14.

31. HCF to Pinkerton, June 25, 1892, in Harvey, 114; Frick testimony, in Harvey, 115.

32. *PP,* July 1, 1892, in Demarest, ed., 44–45.

33. Burgoyne, 37–8.

34. *NYW,* July 3, 1892, in Demarest, ed., 56–57; *NYT, PD,* July 4, 1892, 1.

35. *PD,* July 5, 1892, 1, in Demarest, ed., 60.

36. Krause, 313; HCF to Pinkerton, July 4, 1892, Special Correspondence, box 4, HCFFM.

37. HCF to AC, July 4, 1892, Special Correspondence, box 4, HCFFM.

38. *PD,* July 6, 1892, in Demarest, ed., 66–69; Krause, 313–14.

39. Krause, 18.

40. *PP, NYW,* July 7, 1892, in Demarest, ed., 85–87.

41. *NYW,* July 8, 1892, in *ibid.,* 106–07; *ibid.,* 111.

42. *Pittsburgh Commercial Gazette,* July 8, 1892, in *ibid.,* 114.

43. *PP,* July 8, 1892.

Chapter Twenty-four: Loch Rannoch, the Summer of 1892

1. *St. Louis Post-Dispatch,* July 10, 1892, in Demarest, ed., 119; *NYT,* July 9, 1892, 2; HCF to AC, July 7, 1892, in *ibid.,* 88; AC to HCF, July 7, 1892, in Harvey, 166.

2. *NYH,* July 10, 1892.

3. *NYW,* July 10, 1892.

4. *Pittsburgh Leader,* July 10, 1892, Homestead strike scrapbook, vol. 1, HCFUP.

5. HCF to AC, July 11, 1892, box 4, folder 1, HCFUP.

6. AC to HCF, July 12, 1892, box 4, folder 2, HCFUP.

7. [AC] to HCF, cable, July 12, 1892, Harvey folder, HCFFM.

8. *NYH,* July 10, 1892; *The Times,* July 25, 1892; *The Echo,* July 16, 1892, in Homestead strike scrapbook, vol. 1, HCFUP.

9. AC to HCF, July 14, 1892, box 4, folder 2, HCFUP.

10. AC to Dod, July 17, 1892, vol. 17, ACLC.

11. Burgoyne, 125; Demarest, ed., 22.

12. HCF to AC, July 18, 1892 excerpt, box 4, folder 2, HCFUP.

13. Harvey, 139.

14. AC to Leishman, n.d., in Warren, *Triumphant Capitalism,* 89; AC to HCF, rec'd July 25, 1892, box 4, folder 2, HCFUP.

15. Sanger, 203–07.

16. AC to HCF, rec'd August 6, 1892, box 4, folder 2, HCFUP.

17. *NYW, NYH,* July 27, 1892.

18. Burgoyne, 24–25.

19. *Pittsburgh Leader,* July 9, 1892, in Homestead strike scrapbook, vol. 1, HCFUP; Krause, 343–44.

20. Milholland to AC, July 12, 1904; AC to Milholland, July 16, 1904, vol. 106, ACLC; AC to HCF, July 28, 1892, box 4, folder 2, HCFUP.

21. AC to HCF, July 29, 1892, box 4, folder 2, HCFUP.

22. Harvey, 150–52.

23. HCF to AC, August 23, 1892 excerpt, box 4, folder 3, HCFUP.

24. HCF to AC, August 27, 1892, box 4, folder 3, HCFUP.

25. AC to Reid, in HCF to AC, August 27, 1892, box 4, folder 3, HCFUP.

26. HCF to AC, August 27, 1892, box 4, folder 3, HCFUP.

27. AC to HCF, September 9, 1892, in Harvey, 155.

28. HCF to AC, October 31, 1892, box 4, folder 7, HCFUP.

29. AC to HCF, August 29, 1892, box 4, folder 3, HCFUP.

30. AC to HCF, September 3, 1892, box 4, folder 3, HCFUP.

31. AC to HCF, September 20, 1892, box 4, folder 4, HCFUP.

32. AC to HCF, September 24, 1892, box 4, folder 4, HCFUP.

33. AC to HCF, September 28, 1892, box 4, folder 5, HCFUP.

34. AC to HCF, September 30, 1892, box 4, folder 4, HCFUP.

35. HCF to AC, September 10, 1892 excerpt, box 4, folder 4, HCFUP.

36. AC to HFC, rec'd October 8, 1892, box 4, folder 5, HCFUP.

37. [AC] to HCF, October 1, 1892, Harvey folder, HCFFM.

38. HCF to AC, October 12, 1892 excerpt, box 4, folder 5, HCFUP.

39. AC to HCF, October 21, 1892, box 4, folder 6, HCFUP.

Chapter Twenty-five: Aftermaths, 1892–1894

1. AC to Stead, August 6, 1892, vol. 17, ACLC.

2. Stead to AC, August 9, 1892, vol. 17, ACLC.

3. AC to Stead, August 11, 1892, vol. 17, ACLC.

4. AC and LWC to Gladstone, August 17, 1892; Gladstone to AC, August 19, 1892, Gladstone.

5. AC to Gladstone, September 24, 1892, Gladstone.

6. *NYT,* October 15, 1892, 1.

7. AC, "unpublished 1892 manuscript," ACBM.

8. Charles Scribner to AC, May 4, 1893, vol. 20, ACLC.

9. AC, *TD, rev. edn., Based on the census of 1890* (New York: Charles Scribner's Sons, 1893), 548.

10. AC, *TD*, 1893, 512, 529.

11. Donald Warner, *The Idea of Continental Union* (Lexington, KY: University of Kentucky Press, 1960), 234–34.

12. Burgoyne, 215; AC to HCF, October 28, 31, 1892, box 4, folder 7, HCFUP.

13. HCF to AC, October 31, 1892, box 4, folder 7, HCFUP.

14. AC to HCF, November 9, 1892, box 4, folder 7, HCFUP.

15. Burgoyne, 220–27.

16. AC to HCF, November 19, 1892, box 4, folder 8, HCFUP; AC to HCF, November 20, 1892, Harvey folder, HCFFM.

17. AC to HCF, November 22, 1892, box 4, folder 8, HCFUP; AC to HCF, November 25, 1892, Harvey folder, HCFFM.

18. AC to HCF, December 2, 1892, box 4, folder 9, HCFUP.

19. *PP,* December 9, 1892, in Demarest, ed., 195–96.

20. AC to HCF, December 8, 1892, box 4, folder 9, HCFUP.

21. AC to HCF, December 11, 1892, box 4, folder 10, HCFUP.

22. AC to HCF, December 27, 1892, box 4, folder 10, HCFUP.

23. Leishman to AC, May 4, 1893, vol. 20, ACLC.

24. Hamlin Garland, "Homestead and its Perilous Trades—Impressions of a Visit," *McClure's Magazine* III (June 1894).

25. *Philadelphia Press*, July 9, 1892, in Homestead strike scrapbook, vol. 1, HCFUP.

26. *Pittsburgh Leader,* July 11, 1892, in Homestead strike scrapbook, vol. 1, HCFUP.

27. G. Brooks, "The Typical American Employer," *Blackstone's Edinburgh Magazine* (October 1892): 572.

28. Knox to AC, February 24, 1893, vol. 18; AC to John Robb, Jr., March 7, 1893, vol. 19, ACLC.

29. AC to Alice French, February 9, 1893, French.

30. AC to Reid, March 20, 1893, vol. 19, ACLC.

31. Warren, *Triumphant Capitalism*, 104, 106.

32. Hessen, 45–58; Warren, *Triumphant Capitalism*, 153–58; Hendrick, II, 401–6.

33. HCF to Herbert, December 4, 13, 1893, Special Correspondence, box 5, HCFFM.

34. AC to Cleveland, December 20, 1893, vol. 23, ACLC.

35. AC to HCF, January 14, 1894, Harvey folder, HCFFM.

36. AC to HCF, March 6, 31, 1894, Harvey folder, HCFFM.

37. AC, *Autobiography*, 223; Peacock to AC, April 25, 1912, vol. 205; AC to Peacock, April 30, 1912, vol. 206, ACLC.

38. Montgomery, 41–42.

39. Hogan, I, 87; Warren, *American Steel Industry*, 177; Warren, *Triumphant Capitalism*, 384, table 4; "Net profits of the Carnegie Association," vol. 73, ACLC.

40. Montgomery, 40–42; Brody, 43–45.

41. Dreiser, *Newspaper Days*, 499–502, 524.

42. Bridge, *Inside History*, 81; Brody, 105.

CHAPTER TWENTY-SIX: "BE OF GOOD CHEER—WE WILL BE OVER IT SOON," 1893–1895

1. AC to Cleveland, April 22, 1893, vol. 20, ACLC.

2. Strouse, 320; Steve Fraser, *Every Man a Speculator: A History of Wall Street in American Life* (New York: HarperCollins, 2005), 162.

3. Hogan, I, 184–86.

4. AC to HCF, May 27, 1893, box 4, folder 10, HCFUP.

5. AC to HCF, June 6, 17, 1893; Morris Reno to AC, June 27, 1893, box 4, folder 11, HCFUP; Schickel, 71.

6. AC to HCF, August 1, 1893, box 4, folder 12, HCFUP.

7. HCF to AC, August 7, 1893, box 4, folder 13, HCFUP.

8. AC to HCF, August 8, 1893, box 4, folder 12, HCFUP.

9. Damrosch to AC, n.d.; Caroline Vandevort to AC, n.d..; Lauder to AC, Oct. 11, 1893; C. Scribner to AC, November 1, 1893, vol. 22, ACLC.

10. AC to HCF, Oct. 3, 1893, box 4, folder 14, HCFUP.

11. Hogan, I, 237; The Carnegie Steel

Company, Limited. Accounting Department, "Net Profits of the Carnegie Associations," vol. 73, ACLC; Warren, *Triumphant Capitalism*, table 7, 386.

12. AC to Morley, December 17, 1893, vol. 23, ACLC.

13. AC to HCF, December 26, 1893, box 4, folder 15, HCFUP.

14. AC to HCF, December 26, 28, 1893, box 4, folder 15, HCFUP.

15. AC to HCF, December 29, 1893, box 4, folder 15, HCFUP.

16. HCF to AC, December 28, 1893, box 4, folder 15, HCFUP.

17. AC to HCF, January 1, 1894, box 5, folder 1, HCFUP.

18. AC to HCF, January 1, 1894, box 5, folder 1, HCFUP.

19. AC to HCF, rec'd Jan. 5, 1894, box 5, folder 1, HCFUP.

20. Elizabeth Sanders, *Roots of Reform: Farmers, Workers and the American State, 1877–1917* (Chicago: University of Chicago Press, 1999), 134–35.

21. AC to HCF, December 18, 1892, box 4, folder 10, HCFUP.

22. AC to Dalzell, December 6, 1893; AC to Morley, December 17, 1893, vol. 23, ACLC.

23. AC to Gorman, with attachment, January 2, 1894, vol. 24, ACLC.

24. AC to Reid, January 3, 1894, vol. 24, ACLC.

25. AC to "My Dear Mr. Editor," January 3, 1894, vol. 24, ACLC.

26. Bensel, 480.

27. AC to HCF, February 13, 1894, vol. 24, ACLC.

28. AC to HCF, February 18, 1894, box 5, folder 1; February 28, box 5, folder 2, HCFUP.

29. AC to Hew Morrison, May 10, 1894, vol. 25, ACLC.

30. Hew Morrison to AC, May 31, 1894, vol. 25, ACLC.

31. AC to HCF, May 27, 1894, Harvey folder, HCFFM.

32. AC to HCF, June 2, 1894, box 5, folder 5, HCFUP.

33. Sanger, 224.

34. AC to HCF, July 2, 1894, box 5, folder 6, HCFUP.

35. Hessen, 57–58.

36. AC to HCF, October 23, 1894, box 5, folder 8, HCFUP.

37. AC to HCF, July 16, 1894, box 5, folder 5, HCFUP.

38. AC to HCF, October 11, 1894, box 5, folder 7, HCFUP.

39. HCF to AC, November 30, 1894, Special Correspondence, box 1; HCF to Quay, November 23, 1894, vol. 10, HCFFM.

40. HCF to Stone, October 30, 1894; HCF to Hunsiker, November 8, 1894, Special Correspondence, box 5, HCFFM.

41. HCF to Schwab, November 12, 16, 1894; HCF to Gayley, November 16, 1894; HCF to Thomas Morrison, November 19, 1894; HCF to A. R. Whitney, November 17, 1894, Special Correspondence, box 5, HCFFM.

42. AC to HCF, November 26, 1894, box 5, folder 8, HCFUP.

43. HCF to AC [December 17, 1894], Special Correspondence, box 1, HCFFM.

44. AC to HCF, December 18, 1894 (1), box 5, folder 9, HCFUP.

45. AC to HCF, December 18, 1894 (2), box 5, folder 9, HCFUP.

46. HCF to AC, December 20, 1894 (2 letters), Special Correspondence, box 1, HCFFM.

47. AC to Phipps, December 30, 1894, HCFFM; AC to HCF, December 23, 1894, box 5, folder 10, HCFUP.

48. AC to HCF, December 23, 1894, vol. 10, HCFFM.

49. HCF to Walker, December 26, 1894, vol. 10, HCFFM.

50. HCF to AC, December 28, 1894, Special Correspondence, box 1, HCFFM.

51. HCF to AC, December 30, 1894, Special Correspondence, box 1, HCFFM.

52. AC to Phipps, December 30, 1894, HCFFM.

53. HCF to AC, January 1, 1895, Special Correspondence, box 1, HCFFM.

54. AC to HCF, January 5, 1895, box 5, folder 11, HCFUP.

55. HCF to Morse, January 11, 1895, HCF, vol. 10, HCFFM.

CHAPTER TWENTY-SEVEN: SIXTY YEARS OLD, 1895–1896

1. Warren Zimmerman, *First Great Triumph* (New York: Farrar, Straus & Giroux, 2002), 153; Nathan Miller, *Theodore Roosevelt: A Life* (New York: William Morrow, 1992), 235.

2. Jonathan M. Hansen, *The Lost Promise of Patriotism* (Chicago: University of Chicago Press, 2003), 13–15.

3. AC, letters to editor, *The Times* (London), December 23, 1895; *New York Sun*, n.d., vol. 35, ACLC.

4. AC, "The Venezuelan Question," *North American Review* (February 1896), in *MW*, II, 39–40.

5. *Ibid.*, 44, 46.

6. *Ibid.*, 52–53.

7. See, e.g., AC to Gladstone, Balfour, Chamberlain, etc., July 1896, vol. 38, ACLC.

8. AC to Gladstone, July 25, 1896; AC to Morley, August 1, 1896, vol. 38, ACLC.

9. The following record of the event—and transcript of the speeches given—is taken from "Presentation of the Carnegie Library to the People with a Description of the Dedicatory Exercises, November 5, 1895," reprinted as "The Best Use of Wealth," *MW*, 203–18.

10. AC to Frew, October 1897, vol. 46, ACLC.

11. Pamphlet, n.d. [1896], CLP; Agnes Dodds Kinard, *Celebrating the First 100 Years of The Carnegie in Pittsburgh: 1895–1995* (n.p., 1995), 82, 97.

12. AC to Frew, December 5, 1896, box 1, Carnegie correspondence, CLP.

13. Tom Rea, *Bone Wars: The Excavation and Celebrity of Andrew Carnegie's Dinosaur* (Pittsburgh: University of Pittsburgh Press, 2001), 40–41.

14. *Ibid.*, 42–43.

15. *Ibid.*, 95–97.

16. AC to Frew, October 4, 1900, box 1, ACCLP.

17. AC to Frew, n.d. [April 1907], ACCLP.

18. AC to Lovejoy, February 11, 1895, vol. 30, ACLC.

19. AC to Lovejoy, December 9, 1895, vol. 35, ACLC.

20. AC to Leishman, February 4, 1896, vol. 36, ACLC.

21. AC to Schwab, October 18, 1897, vol. 46, ACLC.

22. "Minutes of September 25," with AC's "Thoughts on Minutes, from September 14, [1897]," vol. 45, ACLC.

23. "Minutes of October 5," with AC's "Further Notes on Minutes of August 31, [1897]," vol. 45, ACLC.

24. AC to Schwab, October 1, 1897, vol. 45, ACLC.

25. Schwab to AC, October 5, 1897, vol. 45, ACLC.

CHAPTER TWENTY-EIGHT: "AN IMPREGNABLE POSITION," 1896–1898

1. AC to HCF, June 27, 1896, vol. 38, ACLC.

2. AC to HCF, July 28, 1896, vol. 38, ACLC.

3. Hanna to AC, n.d., vol. 39, ACLC.

4. AC to Morley, August 1, 1896, vol. 36, ACLC.

5. AC to Hanna, August 12, Hanna to AC, October 17, 1896, vol. 39, ACLC.

6. AC to President and Board of Managers, August 6, 1896, vol. 38, ACLC.

7. AC to Singer, August 21, 1896, vol. 39, ACLC.

8. AC to Thomson, September 26, 1896, vol. 39, ACLC.

9. AC, "Mr. Bryan the Conjurer," *North American Review* (January 1897): 117–18.

10. AC to HCF, August 29, 1892, box 4, folder 3, HCFUP.

11. Chernow, 382–86.

12. AC to HCF, March 16, 1894, in Harvey, 190.

13. AC to HCF, September 4, 1894, vol. 5, folder 6, HCFUP.

14. Rockefeller to AC, January 29, 1896, vol. 36, ACLC.

15. *U.S. Steel*, 2392.

16. AC to HCF, October 27, 1896, box 5, folder 14, HCFUP; AC to Rockefeller, October 30, 1896, vol. 39, ACLC.

17. AC to Dod, November 18, 1896, vol. 39, ACLC; on final negotiations, see box 5, folder 15, HCFUP; Chernow, 387–88.

18. AC to HCF, October 9, 1897, Harvey folder, HCFFM; AC to Dod, January 1, 1898, vol. 48, ACLC.

19. *U. S. Steel*, 2392; *NYT*, January 11, 1912, 1; Cartoon collection, Margaret Barclay Wilson Collection.

20. Rockefeller to AC, February 2, 1903, vol. 94, ACLC.

21. AC to Rockefeller, February 8, 1903, vol. 94, ACLC.

22. AC to HCF, February 7, 1896, HCFFM.

23. HCF to AC, February 22, 1896, box 5, folder 13, HCFUP.

24. AC, "My Experience with, and Views upon, The Tariff," *Century* (March, 1908), reprinted as "Railway Rates and Rebates" in *Andrew Carnegie Reader*, 86; "Copy of Memo," May 11, 1896, vol. 38, ACLC.

25. AC to HCF, October 9, 1897, HCFFM.

26. Carnegie Steel Co., "Net Profits of the Carnegie Association," vol. 73, ACLC; AC to HCF, June 13, 1898, HCFFM.

27. AC to HCF, April 30, 1898, HCFFM.

28. AC to Leishman, August 21, 1896, ACLC.

29. Warren, *Triumphant Capitalism*, 387, Table 8.

30. AC, "The Advantages of Poverty," 75.

31. "Presentation of the Carnegie Library . . ." in *MW*, II, 209.

CHAPTER TWENTY-NINE: "WE NOW WANT TO TAKE ROOT," 1897–1898

1. AC to HCF, rec'd, January 22, 1890, box 2, folder 4, HCFUP.

2. AC, *Autobiography*, 209.

3. AC to HCF, box 3, folder 2, January 26, February 9, 1891, HCFUP.

4. Hendrick and Henderson, 143.

5. Linda Hills, March 2, 2005, private communication, in author's possession.

6. AC to Dod, November 18, 1896, vol. 39, ACLC.

7. Francis Whiting Halsey, *American Authors and Their Homes* (New York: James Pott & Co., 1901), 237–42.

8. AC to Gladstone, February 3, 1897, vol. 41, ACLC.

9. Spencer to AC, December 16, 1896, vol. 40, ACLC.

10. AC to Spencer, January 5, 1897, vol. 41, ACLC.

11. Finegan to Church, March 9, 1897, box 1, ACCLP.

12. AC to HCF, February 15, March 1, 1897, box 5, folder 16, HCFUP; AC to Frew, March 6, 1897, box 1, ACCLP.

13. LWC to Ross, March 20, 1897, vol. 41, ACLC.

14. AC, *Autobiography*, 209.

15. AC to LWC, n.d., in Hendrick and Henderson, 144–45.

16. LCW to Stella Whitfield, n.d., in *ibid.*, 145.

17. HCF to AC, April 30, 1897, box 5, folder 16; AC to HCF, May 8, 1897, box 5, folder 17, HCFUP.

18. AC to Dod, May 31, 1897, vol. 42, ACLC.

19. AC to Gladstone, June 19, 1897, Gladstone.

20. AC to HCF, June 14, 1897, vol. 42, ACLC.

21. HCF to AC, July 6, 1897, box 5, folder 17, HCFUP.

22. Margaret Carnegie Miller, *Margaret Carnegie Miller Her Journals*, ed. Linda Thorell Hills (2000), 1.

23. LWC to AC, n.d., Hendrick and Henderson, 147.

24. Hendrick and Henderson, 147.

25. See Carnegie Steel, board minutes, June–September, 1897, vols. 42–44, ACLC.

26. Phipps to AC, Sept 25, 1897, vol. 45, ACLC.

27. AC to Phipps, September 29, 1897, box 5, folder 17, HCFUP.

28. AC to HCF, October 9, 1897, HCFFM.

29. Carnegie Steel, board minutes, October 19, 1897, vol. 46, ACLC; HCF to AC, June 10, 1898, box 6, folder 5, HCFUP.

30. AC to Walter Damrosch, November 11, 1897, box 2, folder 13, D-BLC.

31. AC to Hew Morrison, November 16, 1897, vol. 46, ACLC.

32. LCW to Eaton, n.d., in Hendricks and Henderson, 147.

33. AC to Hew Morrison, October 22, 1897, vol. 46, ACLC.

34. AC to Hew Morrison, November 16, 1897, vol. 46, ACLC.

35. Hendrick interview with Bertram, September 24–27, 1927, vol. 256, ACLC.

36. "Mr. Carnegie's Gifts," vol. 48, ACLC.

37. Phipps to AC, copy, June 2, 1895; Dod to AC, copy, June 12, 1896, vol. 32, ACLC.

38. AC to Mander, January 16, 1896, vol. 35; Gladstone to AC, January 4, 1897, Gladstone, ACLC; AC to Gladstone, February 3, 1897, vol. 41, ACLC.

39. AC to HCF, March 29, 1898, box 6, folder 3, HCFUP.

40. AC to HCF, April 23, 1898, vol. 51, ACLC.

41. AC, *RTW*, 255.

42. AC to Hew Morrison, June 29, 1898, vol. 53, ACLC.

43. LCW to Eaton, n.d., in Hendrick and Henderson, 152–53; author's interview with Margaret Thomson, June 2004, Clashmore, Scotland.

44. Morley to AC, July 25, 1898, vol. 53, ACLC.

45. Bridge to AC, December 14, 1893, vol. 23, ACLC.

46. Bridge to AC, August 5, 1898, vol. 54, ACLC.

47. AC to Stead, September [1903], vol. 99, ACLC.

48. AC to Miles, n.d., vol. 53, ACLC; Nelson Miles, *Serving the Republic* (New York: Harper & Bros., 1911), 273–74.

49. AC, "Distant Possessions: The Parting of the Ways," *North American Review* (August 1898), in *Andrew Carnegie Reader*, 296.

50. *Ibid.*, 301–2.

51. *Ibid.*, 299–300.

52. John Morley, *Recollections*, vol. II (New York: Macmillan, 1917), 110–11.

CHAPTER THIRTY: THE ANTI-IMPERIALIST, 1898–1899

1. AC to Schurz, October 24, 1898, vol. 55, ACLC.

2. Godkin to AC, November 1, 1898, vol. 56, ACLC.

3. *NYT,* October 26, 1898, 3.

4. AC to Hay, November 24, 1898, Hay.

5. AC to McKinley, November 28, 1896, vol. 57, ACLC.

6. Hay to Reid, November 29, 1898, in Thayer, *John Hay,* II , 188–89.

7. AC to Godkin, November 26, 1898, vol. 57, ACLC.

8. Chandler, 332; Naomi R. Lamoreaux, *The Great Merger Movement in American Business, 1895–1904* (Cambridge: Cambridge University Press, 1985), 1–2.

9. Chandler, 332.

10. Warren, *Triumphant Capitalism,* 225.

11. HCF to AC, May 12, 1898, vol. 51, ACLC.

12. Dod to AC, June 24, 1898, vol. 52, ACLC.

13. Phipps to HCF, November 23, 28, 1898, in Warren, *Triumphant Capitalism,* 227.

14. Dod to Phipps, November 28, 1898, in *ibid.,* 228.

15. Herbert Myrick to AC, December 6, 1898, vol. 58, ACLC; Clem Studebaker to AC, December 17, 1898; Doubleday to AC, December 12, 1898, vol. 59, ACLC.

16. AC to Schurz, December 27, 1898, vol. 59, ACLC.

17. *NYTr,* December 22, 1898.

18. Bryan to AC, December 24, 1898, vol. 59, ACLC.

19. Bryan to AC, December 30, 1898, vol. 59, ACLC.

20. AC to Hay, December 29, 1898, Hay.

21. AC to Hay, December 27, 1898, Hay.

22. AC, "Americanism Versus Imperialism," *North American Review* (January 1899): 1–13.

23. The story first appeared in print in the *New York Times* on May 16, 1902.

24. AC, "Americanism Versus Imperialism—II," *North American Review* (March 1899): 362–72.

25. HCF to AC, December 27, 1898, box 6, folder 5, HCFUP; Warren, *Triumphant Capitalism,* 229; HCF to AC, December 30, 1898, HCFFM.

26. AC to HCF, rec'd January 24, 1899, box 6, folder 6, HCFUP.

27. Warren, *Triumphant Capitalism,* 232–33.

28. *U.S. Steel,* 2343.

29. HCF, Phipps to AC, May 4; HCF, Phipps to AC, May 10, 1899, Special Correspondence, box 2, HCFFM.

30. HCF to Schoonmaker, May 16, 1899, Special Correspondence, box 2, HCFFM.

31. HCF, Phipps to AC, May 20, 1899, Special Correspondence, box 2, HCFFM.

32. HCF to AC, May 23, 1899, Special Correspondence, box 2, HCFFM.

33. HCF to Moore, May 29, June 2, 1899, Special Correspondence, box 2, HCFFM.

34. Hendrick and Henderson, 154–55.

35. The following description of that summer at Skibo comes largely from Stead, *Mr. Carnegie's Conundrum: £40,000,000: What Shall I Do With It?* (London: Review of Reviews, 1900), 54–57.

36. AC to Dod, June 23, 1899; HCF, Phipps to Schwab, June 24, 1899, in Carnegie Steel, board minutes, June 27, 1899, vol. 66, ACLC.

37. Phipps to HCF, July 15, 1899, in Warren, *Triumphant Capitalism,* 238–39.

38. Stead, *Mr. Carnegie's Conundrum,* 58.

39. A copy of the ms can be found in ACBM.

40. AC, "The South African Question," *North American Review* (December 1899): 788–804.

41. AC to Harcourt, September 21, 1899, Harcourt.

CHAPTER THIRTY-ONE: "THE RICHEST MAN IN THE WORLD," 1899–1901

1. Carnegie Steel, board minutes, September 11, 1899, vol. 68, ACLC.

2. Carnegie Steel, board minutes, October 16, 1899, vol. 69, ACLC.

3. H. C. Frick Coke, board minutes, October 25, 1899, vol. 70, ACLC; Warren, *Triumphant Capitalism,* 245–47. I am indebted to Kenneth Warren's discussion of the Frick-Carnegie conflict.

4. Warren, *Triumphant Capitalism,* 245.

5. HCF to AC, November 18, 1899, box 6, folder 7, HCFUP.

6. AC to HCF, November 20, 1899, in Carnegie Steel, board minutes, November 20, 1899, vol. 70, ACLC.

7. AC to HCF, November 21, 1899, box 6, folder 7, HCFUP.

8. Dod to AC, November 24, 1899, vol. 70, ACLC.

9. AC to Dod, November 25, 1899, vol. 70, ACLC.

10. Schwab to AC, November 27, 1899, vol. 70, ACLC, Warren, *Triumphant Capitalism,* 253.

11. *Ibid.,* 253–4.

12. AC to Board of Managers, December 30, 1899, vol. 60, ACLC.

13. AC to HCF, December 1899, box 6, folder 7, HCFUP.

14. Harvey, 227–30.

15. Hendrick, II, 104.

16. HCF to Lovejoy, January 16, 1900, Special Correspondence, box 11, HCFFM.

17. Frick complaint, February 13, 1900, in *U.S. Steel,* 2579–80.

18. *Ibid.,* 2573–81.

19. "Response by The Carnegie Steel Co. (Ltd.)," *U. S. Steel,* 2550–68.

20. AC to Dod, March 4, 1900, vol. 73, ACLC.

21. Westinghouse to AC, February 8, 1900, vol. 73, ACLC.

22. Church to AC, March 13, 1900, box 1, ACCLP.

23. Charter of Carnegie Company, March 22, 1900, vol. 73, ACLC; Bridge, *Inside History,* 348–53.

24. HCF to A. R. Whitney, n.d., in Harvey, 256.

25. HCF to AC, n.d., in *ibid.,* 257.

26. Sanger, 285; Frew to AC, April 7, 1900, box 1, ACCLP.

27. AC to Morley, December 17, 1899, vol. 70, ACLC.

28. AC to Schwab, June 26, July 7, 1900, in Carnegie Company, board minutes, July 9, 1900, vol. 76, ACLC.

29. AC to Schwab, July 11, 1900, in Carnegie Company, board minutes, July 31, 1900, vol. 76, ACLC.

30. Hessen, 121–2.

31. Carnegie Company, board minutes, November 6, 1900, vol. 79, ACLC.

32. AC to Dod, December 8, 1900, vol. 80, ACLC.

33. Hendrick, II, 131.

34. Hendrick interview with Schwab, box 257, ACLC.

35. *Ibid.; U.S. Steel,* 1278–79.

36. Hendrick, II, 139; Hendrick interview with Bertram, vol. 256, ACLC.

37. AC to Morley, February 3, 1901, vol. 81, ACLC.

38. Carnegie Company, board minutes, February 4, 1901, vol. 81, ACLC.

39. Clemens to AC, February 6, 1901, Twain.

40. AC to Messrs. J. P. Morgan & Company, February 26, 1901; AC to Dod, February 26, 1901, vol. 82, ACLC.

41. AC to Dod, March 4, 1901, vol. 82, ACLC.

42. AC to Dod, March 5, 12, 1901, vol. 82, ACLC.

43. Brody, 61–68.

44. Andrew S. Dolkart, *Cooper-Hewitt, National Design Museum* (Washington, DC: Smithsonian Institution, 2002), n.p.

45. AC to Dod, February 26, 1901, vol. 82, ACLC.

46. AC to Dod, March 4, 1901, vol. 82, ACLC.

47. AC to Managers of the Carnegie Company, March 12, 1901, vol. 82, ACLC.

48. AC to Billings, March 12, 1901, AC-NYPL.

49. The following discussion is based on Mary B. Dierickx, *The Architecture of Literacy: The Carnegie Libraries of New York City* (New York: Cooper Union and NYC Department of General Services, 1996), 15–47.

50. Robert A. M. Stern, et al., *New York 1900* (New York: Rizzoli, 1983), 98–101.

Chapter Thirty-two: "The Saddest Days of All," 1901

1. AC, unpublished draft of *Autobiography* [1911], CBMD.

2. AC to Morley, February 3, 1901, vol. 81, ACLC; Jones, 26.

3. *NYT,* March 21, 22, 1901.

4. Miller, 2; *NYT,* May 4, 2001, 2.

5. Miller, 2.

6. AC to Morley, April 9, 1901, vol. 82, ACLC.

7. Lord Shaw [of] Dunfermline, *Letters to Isabel* (New York: George H. Doran Co., n.d.), 151–70.

8. *Scotsman,* May 20, 1901, CTUS.

9. Balfour to AC, May 21, 1901, vol. 83, ACLC.

10. Morley to AC, April 17, 1901; AC to Morley, April 19, 1901, vol. 82, ACLC.

11. AC to Morley, May 31, 1901, June 24, 1901, vol. 83, ACLC.

12. AC to Lord Elgin, June 7, 1901, Carnegie University Trust Papers, Elgin.

13. Holls to White, August 26, 1901, White.

14. Bridge to AC, July 23, 1901, vol. 83, ACLC.

15. AC, *Autobiography,* 263.

16. Frew to AC, December 20, 1900, box 1, ACCLP; Simon Goodenough, *The Greatest Good Fortune* (Edinburgh: Macdonald, 1985), 65, 69.

17. AC to White, April 26, 1901, vol. 82, ACLC.

18. Andrew Dickson White, *Autobiography of Andrew Dickson White* (New York: Century Co., 1905), vol. II, 201.

19. Acton to Hew Morrison, February 5, 1901, vol. 8, ACLC.

20. Joseph Wall, *Skibo* (New York: Oxford University Press, 1984), 70–71.

21. Hendrick interview with Bertram, September 24–28, 1927, vol. 256, ACLC.

22. Stead, *Mr. Carnegie's Conundrum,* 54–55; Spencer to AC, September 2, 1901, vol. 84, ACLC.

23. AC to C-B, June 25, 1901, C-B; AC to Morley, June 24, 1901, vol. 83, ACLC.

24. AC to C-B, November 21, 1901, C-B.

25. Rosebery to AC, December 6, 1901, Rosebery.

26. AC to Strachey, October 21, 1901, Strachey.

27. AC to Dod, September 26, 1901, vol. 84, ACLC.

28. AC to Clemens, November 19, 1901, Twain.

29. Clemens to AC, November 21, 1901, Twain.

30. Hendrick interview with Bertram, box 256, ACLC.

31. George Bobinski, *Carnegie Libraries*

(Chicago: American Library Association, 1969), 203–05.

32. Hendrick interview with Bertram, vol. 256, ACLC; Jones, 25–29; Bobinski, 43, 45, 52–53; "Daily Register of Donations," series IC, box 4, CCNY.

33. Jones, 127–66; AC to James Thomson, January 3, 1903, in Bobinski, 14–15.

34. *NYT,* January 8, 1903.

35. Jones, 127–66; Robert M. Lester, *Forty Years of Carnegie Giving* (New York: Charles Scribner's Sons, 1941), 93.

36. William T. Stead, "Mr. Carnegie As I Know Him," *Christian Endeavor World,* December 18, 1902, in Margaret Barclay Wilson Collection.

37. *A Manual of the Public Benefactions of Andrew Carnegie* (Washington, DC: Carnegie Endowment for International Peace, 1919), 301–3, 320–21.

38. "Daily Register of Donations," series IC, box 1, CCNY.

39. AC, "Bryan or McKinley?: The Presidential Election—Our Duty," *North American Review* (October 1900): 495–507.

40. AC to Dod, September 26, 1901, vol. 84, ACLC.

41. AC to White, June 23, 1900, vol. 76, ACLC.

42. AC to TR, November 28, 1901, Roosevelt.

43. AC to TR, December 2, 1901, Roosevelt.

44. *NYT,* December 10, 15, 1901; *Manual of the Public Benefactions,* 79–80; AC to Hay, December 27, 1901, Hay; AC to TR, December 27, 1901, Roosevelt.

45. TR to AC, December 31, 1901, Roosevelt.

46. AC to Elgin, January 10, 1902, Elgin.

47. AC to C-B, January 10, 1902, C-B.

48. James Bryant Conant, "Andrew Carnegie as Patron of Learning," *Andrew Carnegie Centenary, 1835–1935* (New York: Carnegie Corporation of New York, 1935), 82; Ellen Condliffe Lagemann, *The Politics of Knowledge: The Carnegie Corporation, Philanthropy, and Public Policy* (Chicago: University of Chicago Press, 1989), 37; Goodenough, 103.

49. AC, *Autobiography,* 251.

50. Carnegie Institution, *Year Book, 2003–4* (Washington, DC, 2005).

CHAPTER THIRTY-THREE: "A FINE PIECE OF FRIENDSHIP," 1902–1905
1. Rockefeller, Jr., to AC, August 13, 1902, vol. 90; AC to Morley, October 1, 1902, vol. 91, ACLC.

2. Hendrick, II, 172.

3. Wall, *Skibo,* 176–77; Miller, 2–3.

4. LWC to Franks, September 15, 1902, vol. 92, ACLC.

5. AC to Holland, October 2, 1902, in Rea, 164; Rea, 177, 187.

6. AC to Avebury, June 10, 1902, Avebury.

7. Doubleday to Church, June 9, 1902, box 2, ACCLP.

8. Doubleday to Church, June 16, 1902, box 2, ACCLP.

9. Church to Doubleday, June 16, 24, 1902, box 2, ACCLP.

10. Alderson to Bertram, October 20, 1902, vol. 91, ACLC.

11. Joaquin Miller to AC, July 21, 1902, vol. 90, ACLC.

12. William T. Stead, "Mr. Carnegie as I Know Him," *Christian Endeavor World,* December 18, 1902, in Margaret Barclay Wilson Collection.

13. AC to Holls, April 4, 1902, Holls.

14. AC to TR, April 30, 1902, Roosevelt.

15. TR to AC, June 13, 1902, Roosevelt.

16. *NYT,* July 28, 1902, 1.

17. AC to Adams, August 8, 1902, box 8, Adams.

18. AC to TR, August 11, 1902, vol. 90, ACLC.

19. Adams to AC, September 26, 1902, vol. 91, ACLC.

20. AC to Morley, n.d. [late summer 1902], JMBL,O; AC to Butler, April 26, 1902; Butler to AC, April 28, 1902, box 68, Butler.

21. AC to Morley, n.d. [late summer 1902], JMBL,O.

22. *Mark Twain in Eruption,* ed. Bernard DeVoto (1922; New York: Grosset & Dunlap, 1940), 43–44.

23. AC to Swank, March 3, 1904, vol. 101, ACLC.

24. AC to Morley, September 7, 1902; AC to Dod, October 1, 1902, vol. 91, ACLC.

25. Morley to AC, October 4, 1902, vol. 91, ACLC.

26. AC, "A Confession of Religious Faith," *MW,* II, 293.

27. Pitcairn to AC, May 31, 1898, vol. 52, ACLC.

28. Shaw, 145.

29. AC to Haldane, May 23, 1902, Haldane.

30. AC, "A Confession of Religious Faith," *MW,* II, 296–97, 300, 302–03, 311.

31. AC, "A Rectorial Address . . . 22 October, 1902" in *MW,* I, 87–88, 118–19.

32. *Ibid.,* 122–24.

33. *Ibid.,* 124–25.

34. AC to Morley, October 18, 1902, vol. 91, ACLC.

35. The following discussion owes much to Robert A. M. Stern, et al., *New York 1900,* 342; a good deal of the discussion of the Carnegie residence comes from Dolkart, *Cooper-Hewitt.*

36. Hendrick, II, 267.

37. *NYT,* December 28, 1906, 9; June 12, 1904, [*Sunday Magazine*] 1; October 15, 1905, [*Sunday Magazine*] 4.

38. *NYT,* January 8, 1903.

39. Morley, *Recollections,* II, 110.

40. AC to Gilder, January 18, 1904, vol. 102, ACLC.

41. Clemens to AC, n.d., February 10, 1906, January 22, 1908, April 28, 1908, March 26, 1909, Twain.

42. Cleveland to AC, December 16, 1905, Cleveland.

43. Clemens to Miss Carnegie, May 28, 1900, box 3, ACAC; Fred Kaplan, *The Singular Mark Twain* (New York: Doubleday, 2003), 576–77.

44. Hendrick interview with Hew Morrison, August 7–8, 1927, vol. 257, ACLC.

45. Cleveland to AC, January 13, 1902, Cleveland.

46. Hendrick interview with Hew Morrison, August 7–8, 1927, vol. 257, ACLC.

47. *Ibid.*

48. AC to Gladstone, June 10, 1890, Gladstone; AC to Gladstone, June 13, 1890, in

Hendrick, I, 355–56; White to AC, July 10, 1902, vol. 90, ACLC.

49. Morley to AC, July 17, 1902, vol. 90, ACLC.

50. AC to Morley, July 22, 1902, JMBL,O.

51. Morley to AC, July 27, 1902, JMBL,O.

52. AC to Clevelands, January 11, 1904, Cleveland.

53. Hendrick interview of Abbott, vol. 257, ACLC.

54. AC to Schwab, AC to Morgan, January 14, 1902, in Hessen, 134–35.

55. Schwab to AC, March 19, 1902, vol. 88, ACLC.

56. Schwab to AC, [misdated] July 28, [1902], vol. 90, ACLC.

57. AC to Schwab, March 22, 1906, in Hessen, 176–77.

58. AC to Clemens, August 9, 1905, Twain.

Chapter Thirty-four: "Apostle of Peace," 1903–1904

1. AC to Morley, March 29, 1903, vol. 95, ACLC.

2. AC to C-B, August 10, 1903, C-B.

3. AC to Morley, March 29, 1903, vol. 95, ACLC.

4. AC to Gentlemen of the Commission, August 2, 1903, in *Manual of the Public Benefactions,* 244–45.

5. Goodenough, 118–20.

6. Miller to AC, April 7, 1903, vol. 95, ACLC.

7. Bridge, *Millionaires,* 76–79.

8. AC to private secretary to Mr. Spencer, August 15, 1903, Bertram.

9. AC to Stead, [September] 1903, vol. 99, ACLC.

10. Bridge to Phipps, February 12, 1904, vol. 103, ACLC.

11. Shaw, 163.

12. *Mark Twain in Eruption,* 36–52.

13. Spencer, *Social Statics* (1870), 511.

14. AC to TR, December 26, 1902; "Mr. Carnegie's New Year Greeting," Roosevelt.

15. AC to Hay, December 30, 1902, Hay.

16. AC to Adams, February 7, 1903, Adams.

17. AC to Holls, AC to Baron Gevers, April 22, 1903, Holls.

18. AC to Platt, January 13, February 14, 1902, in *NYTr*, February 17, 1902.

19. Walter LaFeber, *The Panama Canal* (New York: Oxford University Press, 1979), 33.

20. AC to Morley, January 11, 18, 1904, vol. 102, ACLC.

21. AC to Morley, January 11, 1904, vol. 102, ACLC; TR to AC, February 15, 1904, Roosevelt.

22. *NYT*, March 10, 1904.

23. AC to TR, March 11, 1904, Roosevelt.

24. Miller, 8–9.

25. AC to Morley, February 8, 1904, vol. 103, ACLC.

26. AC to Dod, May 29, 1904, vol. 105, ACLC.

27. AC to Donaldson, June 29, 1904, vol. 105, ACLC.

28. AC to Morley, June 29, 1904, vol. 105, ACLC.

29. AC to Morley, July 26, 1904; Gilder to AC, August 2, 1904, vol. 106, ACLC.

30. AC to Morley, July 28, 1904, vol. 105, ACLC.

31. AC to Morley, January 4, 11, 1904, vol. 102, August 28, 1904, vol. 106, ACLC.

32. William Griffith, "Andrew Carnegie, Apostle of Peace," *NYT*, November 6, 1904 [*Sunday Magazine*], 1.

CHAPTER THIRTY-FIVE: "INVETERATE OPTIMIST," 1905–1906

1. *NYT*, November 11, 1905, 9; October 29, 1906, 1; October 30, 1906, 3.

2. *NYT*, December 13, 1904, 2; March 5, 1905, 1; David Loth, *Gold Brick Cassie* (New York: Fawcett Publications, 1954), 57–172.

3. Samuel Clemens, "The Alphabet and Simplified Spelling," *Portable Mark Twain*, ed. Tom Quirk (New York: Penguin, 2004), 552.

4. Goodenough, 223.

5. AC to Frederic Harrison, June 8, 1904, vol. 105, ACLC; AC, *Autobiography*, 253.

6. Frederick Lynch, "Personal Recollections of Andrew Carnegie," (1920) at http://www.xooqi.com.

7. AC, *Autobiography*, 255.

8. *A Century of Heroes*, 3, 36–37, 57, 61; Mary Brignano, "Ordinary People, Extraordi-

nary Courage," *Western Pennsylvania History* (Spring 2004): 16.

9. AC to TR, February 5 [1905], Roosevelt.

10. TR to AC, February 6, 8, 1905, Roosevelt.

11. Morley to AC, September 5, 1905, JMBL.

12. AC to Morley, September 7, 1905, JMBL.

13. AC, "A League of Peace," October 17, 1905, in *MW*, II, 222, 258, 267–70.

14. AC to Dod, March 15, 1905, vol. 112, ACLC; Warren F. Kuehl, *Seeking World Order: The United Sates and International Organization to 1920* (Nashville, TN: Vanderbilt University Press, 1969), 89.

15. AC to Morley, November 1, 1905, JMBL.

16. AC to Trustees of Carnegie Teachers Pension Fund, April 16, 1905, vol. 114, ACLC; AC to White, July 2, 1909, with attachment, White.

17. Joseph Frazier Wall, *Andrew Carnegie* (1970; Pittsburgh: University of Pittsburgh Press, 1989), 877.

18. AC to Morley, November 2, 1905, JMBL; author's conversations with Linda Hills and Margaret Thomson, July 2005; Nancy Carnegie Rockefeller, *The Carnegies & Cumberland Island* (Privately printed, 1993), 27–28.

19. AC to Morley, November 2, 1905, JMBL.

20. Miller, 3–4.

21. *NYTr*, November 11, 1905.

22. AC to Morley, March 21, 1906, JMBL.

23. AC to Morley, December 17, 1905, JMBL.

24. TR to Reid, November 13, 1905, Roosevelt.

25. AC to Morley, December 17, 1905, JMBL.

26. AC to Bryce, December 28, 1905, Bryce.

27. AC to Morley, January 14, 1906, JMBL.

28. Miller, 4.

29. AC to Morley, January 14, 1906, JMBL.

30. AC to TR, March 18, 1906, Roosevelt.

31. AC to Morley, March 21, 1906, JMBL.

32. AC to Morley, May 15, 1906, JMBL.

33. AC to Ross, May 18, 1906, vol. 129, ACLC.

34. AC to Morley, June 14, 1906, JMBL.

35. "Extract from Hon. Elihu Root's letter of July 3, 1906," in AC to Morley, July 16, 1906, JMBL.

36. AC to Morley, July 16, 1906, JMBL; AC to TR, July 27, 1906, Roosevelt.

37. TR to AC, August 6, 1906, Roosevelt.

38. AC to TR, August 27, 1906, Roosevelt.

39. AC to Morley, September 5, 1906, JMBL.

40. TR to AC, September 6, 1906, Roosevelt.

41. AC to Morley, two notes [September 1906]; September 19, 1906, JMBL.

CHAPTER THIRTY-SIX: PEACE CONFERENCES, 1907

1. AC to Morley, January 13, 1907, JMBL.

2. AC to TR, February 14, 1907, Roosevelt.

3. TR to AC, March 11, 1907, Roosevelt.

4. *NYT*, March 28, 1907.

5. Lynch, "Personal Recollections."

6. *NYT*, April 6, 1907, 2.

7. Agnes Dodds Kinard, *Celebrating the First 100 Years of The Carnegie in Pittsburgh* (1905), 29–30; *NYT*, April 14, 1907, 1.

8. AC to TR, April 7, 1907, Roosevelt.

9. TR to AC, April 5, 1907, Roosevelt.

10. AC to TR, April 10, 1907, Roosevelt.

11. *NYT*, April 16, 1907, 1.

12. Lynch, "Personal Recollections."

13. *Ibid.*

14. AC to Morley, May 16, 1907, JMBL.

15. AC to Morley [June 1907], JMBL.

16. Morley to AC, June 14, 1902, vol. 142, ACLC.

17. Robert K. Massie, *Dreadnought: Britain, Germany, and the Coming of the Great War* (New York: Random House, 1991), 157; Michael Balfour, *The Kaiser and His Times* (New York: Norton, 1972), 152.

18. AC to Margaret Carnegie, June 22, 1907, in Hendrick, II, 316.

19. AC to Wilhelm II, January 19, 1907, in *ibid.*, 311–12.

20. AC to Clemens, [June] 28, 1908, Twain.

21. AC to TR, July 31, 1907, Roosevelt.

22. AC to TR, July 31, 1907, Roosevelt; AC to Morley [August 1907], JMBL.

23. AC to Morley [September, 1907], JMBL.

24. AC to Morley, October 25, 1907, JMBL.

25. AC to Morley, November 10, 1907, JMBL.

26. AC to TR, November 18, 1907, Roosevelt.

27. TR to AC, November 19, 1907, Roosevelt.

28. AC to Morley, November 28, 1907, JMBL.

CHAPTER THIRTY-SEVEN: TARIFFS AND TREATIES, 1908–1909

1. AC, "The Worst Banking System in the World," 1908; *NYT*, February 6, 1908, 1; February 9, 1908, 7; March 27, 1908; AC to Morley, March 29, 1908, JMBL; *NYT*, April 28, 1908, 4.

2. AC to Morley, March 29, 1908, JMBL.

3. *The Roosevelt Policy*, Introduction by Andrew Carnegie (New York: Current Literature Publishing Company, 1908), vol. I, ix–x.

4. TR to AC, April 27, 1908, Roosevelt.

5. AC to His Majesty the Emperor, May 4, 1908, Roosevelt.

6. AC to Morley, April 24, 1908, JMBL.

7. Woodrow Wilson to Ellen Axson Wilson, August 16, 1908, in *The Priceless Gift: The Love Letters of Woodrow Wilson and Ellen Axson Wilson*, ed. Eleanor Wilson McAdoo (New York: McGraw-Hill, 1962), 251–53.

8. AC, *Problems of To-day: Wealth, Labor, Socialism*, 1–2.

9. AC to Strachey, August 22, 1907, Strachey.

10. AC, *Problems of To-day*, 153, 155.

11. "Memorandum by Mr. Carnegie," in AC to Easley, May 19, 1911, box 42, folder 4, NCF; *NYT*, March 16, 1904.

12. Easley to AC, March 13, 1907; AC to Easley, March 16, 1907, NCF.

13. Easley to AC, April 3, 1907, NCF.

14. AC to Easley, February 24, 28, 1908, NCF.

15. AC to Johnson, September 22, 1908, *Century*; AC, "My Experience with, and Views upon, the Tariff," *Century* magazine (December 1908), in *MW*, II, 42–44.

16. AC to Morley, December 6, 1908, JMBL.

17. *Tariff*, 1784.

18. *Ibid.*, 1796.

19. *Ibid.*, 1808.

20. *Ibid.*, 1867.

21. *NYT*, December 22, 1908, 1.

22. *Tariff*, 1851–53.

23. TR to AC, August 6, 1906, Roosevelt.

24. AC to TR, November 15, 1908, Roosevelt.

25. AC to TR, March 3, 1909, Roosevelt.

26. AC to Morley, [January] 3, February 24, 1909, JMBL.

27. Archibald Willingham Butt, *Taft and Roosevelt, The Intimate Letters of Archie Butt* (Garden City, NY: Doubleday, Doran, 1930), I, 215.

Chapter Thirty-eight: "So Be It," 1908–1910

1. AC to TR, January 17, 28, 1908, Roosevelt.

2. AC to Jordan, n.d., vol. 136, ACLC.

3. AC to TR, January 28, 1908, Roosevelt.

4. AC to McConway, March 25, 1909, box 3, ACCLP.

5. Lynch, "Personal Recollections"; Booker T. Washington, *Up from Slavery* (1901; New York: Penguin, 1986), 191–92.

6. Washington to AC, February 24, 1903, vol. 94, ACLC; AC to Archer, August 15, 1910, Archer.

7. AC, "The Negro in America," October 16, 1907, in *MW*, II, 88–122.

8. Andrew Carnegie's donations to peace societies, taken over by Endowment, Secretary's Office and Administration, vol. 405, CEIP.

9. AC to Mead, April 2, 1905, box 1, Mead.

10. AC to Mead, April 6, 1905, box 1, Mead.

11. Butler to AC, January 8, 1909; AC to Butler, January 11, 1909, vol. 161, ACLC.

12. Miller, 6; Margaret Thomson to the author, July 18, 2005.

13. Honorary Secretary to AC, December 16, 1896, Hon. Sec'y to Hodgman, March 12, 1897, St. Andrew's; George Peper, "The Apple Tree Gang," *Golf* (July 1988): 74.

14. Hendrick, II, 266–67; AC to Morley, December 31, 1907, JMBL.

15. *NYT*, December 30, 1900, 8; AC, "Doctor Golf" (1911), reprinted in *Carnegie Magazine* (July–August 1996): 18–20.

16. AC to Dod, June 16, 1903, vol. 97, ACLC; AC to Church, July 6, 1906, box 3, ACCLP.

17. Miller, 4; AC to Morley, March, 1909, April 25, December 19, 1909, JMBL.

18. *NYT*, February 15, 1910, 1.

19. Miller, 18–29; Walter Adams, cited in Goodenough, 103.

20. Miller, 29–32.

21. AC to Morley, April 19, 27, 1910, JMBL.

22. AC to Clemens, [May 22], 1909, Twain.

23. AC to Morley, December 19, 1909, JMBL.

24. AC to Paine, December 10, 1909, Paine.

25. AC to Clemens, April 16, 1910, Twain.

26. AC to Paine, April 28, 1910, Paine.

Chapter Thirty-nine: The Best Laid Schemes, 1909–1911

1. Massie, 609–15.

2. *NYTr*, March 14, 1909.

3. *NYT*, March 25, 1909, 1; AC, "Armaments and Their Results" (London: The Peace Society, 1909), 5.

4. *NYT*, April 22, 1909, 6.

5. AC to Morley, April 25, 1909, JMBL.

6. AC to Morley, May 15, 1909, JMBL; Miller, 9–10.

7. *NYT*, May 18, 1909, 1.

8. AC to Morley, June 20, 1909, JMBL.

9. AC to Morley, June 1909, JMBL.

10. TR to AC, June 1, 1909, in Theodore Roosevelt, *Letters*, select. and ed. Elting E. Morison (Cambridge, MA: Harvard University Press, 1951–54), vol. VII, 13–15.

11. AC to Walcott, June 25, 1909, vol. 167, ACLC; Patricia O'Toole, *When Trumpets Call: Theodore Roosevelt After the White House* (New York: Simon & Schuster, 2005), 54, 64.

12. AC to TR, June 26, 1909, vol. 167, ACLC.

13. TR to AC, July 26, 1909, in Morison, VII, 24–26.

14. AC to TR, October 6, 1909, vol. 170, ACLC.

15. AC to Morley, October 7, 1909, JMBL.

16. TR to AC, October 16, 1909, in Morison, VII, 36–37.

17. AC to Morley, October 22, 1909, JMBL.

18. AC to Franks, September 14, 1909, vol. 169, ACLC; TR to AC, December 14, 1909, in Morison, VII, 42.

19. AC to TR, December 24, 1909, vol. 172, ACLC.

20. AC to Morley, December 15, 1909, January 17, 1910, JMBL.

21. AC to TR, January 11, 1910, vol. 173, ACLC.

22. TR to AC, February 18, 1910, vol. 174, ACLC.

23. *Ibid.;* TR to AC, October 16, December 14, 1909, in Morison, VII, 36, 42.

24. TR to Trevelyan, October 1, 1911, in *ibid.*, 377–78.

25. Much of my discussion of Roosevelt's 1910 tour of Europe comes from O'Toole, 72–92; TR to AC, April 22, 1910, in Morison, VII, 75–76.

26. AC to TR, May 11, 1910, vol. 176, ACLC.

27. TR to Trevelyan, October 1, 1911, in Morison, VII, 394–95.

28. *Ibid.,* 377.

29. *Ibid.,* 379.

30. *Ibid,* 395–96.

31. AC to TR, May 13,1910, Roosevelt.

32. AC to TR, May 13, 14, 1910, Roosevelt.

33. O'Toole, 89–90.

34. Larry Fabian, *Andrew Carnegie's Peace Endowment: The Tycoon, The President, and Their Bargain of 1910* (Washington, DC: Carnegie Endowment for International Peace, 1985), 12.

35. AC to Taft, March 26, 1910, vol. 175, ACLC.

36. AC, Speech at the Annual Meeting of the Peace Society in the Guildhall, reprinted as "Honor and International Arbitration," *MW,* II, 279–80, 288.

37. Taft to AC, June 30, 1910, Taft.

38. Kuehl, 130; AC to TR, June 30, 1910, Roosevelt.

39. Butt, I, 423; Taft to Knox, July 7, 1910, Taft.

40. Taft to AC, October 28, 1910, Taft.

41. AC to Taft, December 10, 1910, Taft.

42. "Mr. Carnegie's Letter to the Trustees," December 14, 1910, in *A Manual . . .* 183–84.

43. "Address to Trustees," in *Proceedings of the First Meeting of the Trustees of the Carnegie Endowment, held December 14, 1910,* Secretary's Office and Administration, vol. 402, CEIP.

44. Straus, Carnegie, and Root statements in *ibid.*

45. C. Roland Marchand, *The American Peace Movement and Social Reform, 1895–1918* (Princeton: Princeton University Press, 1972), 120–21.

46. AC to Taft, December 20, 1910, Taft.

47. AC to Knox, March 21, 1911, vol. 189, ACLC.

48. AC to Bryce, February 15, 1911, Bryce.

49. AC to Ginn, March 22, 1911, AC to James Brown Scott, April 15, 1911, Secretary's Office and Administration, vol. 405, CEIP.

50. AC to Bryce, March 25, 1911, Bryce.

51. AC to Taft, March 25, 1911, Taft.

52. Archie Butt, November 1, 1910, II, 553–54; April 30, 1911, *ibid.,* 635.

53. Fabian, 48–49; AC to Taft, with file memo to Knox, March 25, 1911, Taft; Taft to Knox, Knox to AC, March 27, 1911, Knox.

54. Archie Butt, May 6, 1911, II, 640–41.

55. AC to Knox, May 19, 1911, vol. 14, Knox; AC to Taft, May 19, 1911, Taft.

56. John P. Campbell, "Taft, Roosevelt, and the Arbitration Treaties of 1911," *Journal of American History,* 53 (September 1966): 284–85.

57. AC to TR, May 21, 1911, Roosevelt.

58. TR to AC, May 23, 1911, Roosevelt.

59. AC to TR, May 24, 1911, Roosevelt.

60. TR to Spring-Rice, August 22, 1911, in Morison, VII, 334.

61. AC to Lodge, September 12, 1911, in *ibid.,* 343.

62. AC to Franks, May 24, 1911; AC to Hilles, June 13, 1911, Taft.

63. AC to Morley, June 29, 1911; Morley to AC, June 30, 1911; AC to Morley, July 2, 1911, vol. 195, ACLC.

64. AC to Murray, June 19, 1911, Murray.

65. AC to Strachey, June 13, 1911, Strachey.

66. AC to Taft, August 3, 4, 1911, Taft.

67. Campbell, 280–82; AC to Bryce, September 2, 1911, Bryce.

68. Taft to R.A. Taft, August 27, 1911, in Henry F. Pringle, *The Life and Times of William Howard Taft* (Hamden, Connecticut: Archon Books, 1964), II, 747.

69. Fabian, 54–59.

70. AC to Taft, November 7, 1911, Taft.

71. AC to Taft, November 27, 1911, Taft.

72. Taft to AC, December 29, 1911, Taft.

73. AC, "Interview with Dr. Stopes," 1911, BL.

CHAPTER FORTY: "BE OF GOOD CHEER," 1912–1913

1. *U.S. Steel*, 2364.

2. *Ibid.*, 2349–50.

3. *Ibid.*, 2423–24.

4. *Ibid.*, 2392.

5. Bridge to AC, January 17, 1912; Margery Bridge to AC, January 19, 1912, vol. 203, ACLC; Bridge to Harding, February 3, 1912, Miscellaneous Materials [Bridge], box 2, folder 1, HCFUP.

6. Bertram to Bridge, March 12, 1912, vol. 204, ACLC.

7. Bertram to Bridge, April 22, 1912, vol. 205, ACLC.

8. Bridge to Bertram, May 14, 1912; Bertram to Bridge, May 16, 1912, vol. 206, ACLC.

9. Hendrick and Henderson, 197–98.

10. AC to Morley, March 23, 1912, vol. 204, ACLC.

11. AC to Rockefeller, Jr., April 5, 1912, vol. 205, ACLC.

12. AC to Dod, April 19, 1912, vol. 205, ACLC.

13. Taft to AC, March 28, 1912; AC to Taft, April 2, 1912, Taft.

14. AC to Morley, February 29, 1912, vol. 204, ACLC.

15. AC to TR, March 1, 1912, vol. 204, ACLC.

16. TR to AC, March 5, 1912, vol. 204, ACLC.

17. AC to TR, March 10, 1912, vol. 204, ACLC.

18. AC to Morley, May 12, 1912, vol. 206, ACLC.

19. AC to Hilles, May 17, 1912, vol. 206, ACLC.

20. AC to Taft, May 22, 1912, Taft.

21. *NYT*, October 20, 1912, 9.

22. AC to WW, November 6, 1912, vol. 210, ACLC.

23. AC to Morley, November 7, 1912, vol. 210, ACLC.

24. J. D. Rockefeller to AC, November 11, 1911; AC to J. D. Rockefeller, November 13, 1911, series VII, box 3, folder 4, CCNY.

25. Lagemann, 22; *Carnegie Corporation of New York* (New York, 1911).

26. Minutes, November 10, 1911, series I, box 1, CCNY.

27. Report of Executive Committee, November 21, 1912, series 1, box 1, folder 2, CCNY; Lester, 65.

28. *NYT*, November 26, 1912, 11.

29. AC to Asquith, August 16, 1909, Asquith.

30. AC to Bryce, November 12, 1912, vol. 210, ACLC.

31. AC to Taft, December 15, 1912, Taft.

32. Knox to Taft, March 3, 1913, vol. 20, Knox.

33. AC to WW, April 24, 1913, Wilson.

34. AC, *Fourth American Peace Congress. Address by Andrew Carnegie* (New York: Redfield Brothers, 1913), 16.

35. *NYT*, May 25, 1913, 5.

36. AC, "Unveiling of Cremer Bust in the Palace of Peace at the Hague: Address by Andrew Carnegie" (Dunfermline, 1913).

37. Hendrick and Henderson, 181.

38. *NYT*, November 26, 1913, 10.

39. AC to WW, November 3, 1913, Wilson.

40. The passage is from a Burns poem: Greetings card, January 1, 1914, ACBM.

CHAPTER FORTY-ONE: 1914

1. AC to n.p., January 12, 1914, ACBM.

2. "Resolutions Passed by the Church Peace Union, Founded by Andrew Carnegie," February 10, 1914, CCEIA; Lynch, 56–59.

3. AC to WW, February 20, 1914, Wilson.

4. AC to Morley, March 29, 1914, vol. 222, ACLC.

5. Woodrow Wilson, *The Papers of Woodrow Wilson*, ed. Arthur Link (Princeton: Princeton University Press, 1966–94), vol. 29, 417.

6. AC to WW, April 21, 1914, with enclosure of *New York World* article, Wilson.

7. AC to Tumulty, April 24, 1914, Wilson.

8. *NYT*, April 26, 1914, 2; Lynch, 35–36.

9. AC to Tumulty, May 7, 1914, Wilson.

10. AC to WW, May 21, 1914, Wilson.

11. WW to AC, May 18, 1914; AC to WW, May 21, 1914, Wilson.

12. AC to Gladstone, January 12, 1891, vol. 12, ACLC.

13. Hendrick, II, 345.

14. AC to Morley, August 4, 1914, vol. 225, ACLC.

15. Lynch to AC, August 6, 1914, vol. 225, ACLC.

16. AC to Ross, [wrongly marked April, should be August 17, 1914], vol. 223, ACLC.

17. Morley to AC, August 28, 1914, vol. 225, ACLC.

18. Hendrick interview with Hew Morrison, August 7–8, 1927, vol. 257, ACLC.

19. LWC to Bryce, September 4, 1914, vol. 239, Bryce.

20. Morley to LWC, August 20, 1919, vol. 239, ACLC.

21. D. A. Hamer, *John Morley: Liberal Intellectual in Politics* (London: Oxford University Press, 1968), 368.

22. AC, *Autobiography*, 359–60.

23. AC to William II, October 16, 1914, vol. 226, ACLC.

24. *NYT*, October 15, 1914, 5.

25. AC to WW, November 23, 1914, Wilson.

26. *NYT*, November 26, 1914, 7.

CHAPTER FORTY-TWO: LAST DAYS, 1915–1919

1. AC to Ross, January 18, 1915, vol. 228, ACLC.

2. *New York Sun*, [February 6, 1915], in "Scrapbook with newspaper clips," series VII, CCNY.

3. *NYT*, February 9, 1915, 6.

4. February calendar, in pencil, vol. 257, ACLC.

5. Minutes of board meetings, series I, folders 4, 5, CCNY; LWC to Franks, various dates, series VI, box 3, folder 7, CCNY.

6. Morley to AC, January 12, 1915, vol. 228, ACLC.

7. Hendrick interview with Mrs. Andrew Carnegie, August 1927, vol. 256, ACLC.

8. Morley to LWC, May 19, 1915, in Hendrick, II, 1915.

9. Morley to LWC, December 24, 1915, in *ibid.*, 366–67.

10. LWC to Margaret Carnegie, January 14, 1916, in Hendrick and Henderson, 201–02.

11. Morley to LWC, February 16, 1916, in Hendrick, II, 367–68.

12. Oscar Straus to LWC, March 15, 1916, enclosing letter from Earl Gray from February 24, 1916, box 9, ACAC.

13. Morley to AC, March 6, 1916, in Hendrick, II, 368–69.

14. Morley to AC, April 14, 1916, in *ibid.*, 370.

15. LWC to Bryce, May 16, 1916, Bryce.

16. Morley to AC, September 15, 1916, in Hendrick, II, 370–71.

17. Hendrick and Henderson, 208–09; AC to WW, January 23, 1917, Wilson.

18. AC to WW, February 14, April 7, 1917, in Hendrick, II, 379–80.

19. LWC to Morley, November 1, 1917, JMBL,O.

20. LWC to Morley, November 11, 1917, JMBL,O.

21. AC to Morley, January 21, 1918, in Hendrick, II, 373–74.

22. Miller, 15.

23. Hendrick and Henderson, 211.

24. AC to WW, November 10, 1919; WW to AC, November 13, 1919, Wilson.

25. Morley to AC, November 21, 1918, in Hendrick, II, 375–76.

26. Hendrick and Henderson, 212.

27. LWC to Margaret Carnegie, May 2, 1919, in *ibid.*, 212–14.

28. Hendrick interview with Bertram, September 24–28, 1927, vol. 256, ACLC.

29. Henderson and Hendrick, 216.

30. AC, Will and Testament, vol. 257, ACLC.

BIBLIOGRAPHY OF WORKS CITED

ADAMS, HENRY. *The Education of Henry Adams: An Autobiography.* Boston: Houghton Mifflin, 1918.

———. *Democracy: An American Novel.* 1880. Rev. edn. New York: Modern Library, 2003.

ALLEGHENY CENTENNIAL COMMITTEE. Writers' Program of the Works Projects Administration in the State of Pennsylvania. *Story of Old Allegheny City.* Pittsburgh: Allegheny Centennial Committee, 1941.

AMES, CHARLES EDGAR. *Pioneering the Union Pacific: A Reappraisal of the Builders of the Railroad.* New York: Appleton-Century-Crofts, 1969.

BALDWIN, LELAND D. *Pittsburgh: The Story of a City.* Pittsburgh: University of Pittsburgh Press, 1937.

BALFOUR, MICHAEL. *The Kaiser and His Times.* New York: W. W. Norton, 1972.

BEALE, HARRIET S. BLAINE, ed. *Letters of Mrs. James G. Blaine.* Vol. II. New York: Duffield & Co., 1908.

BECKERT, SVEN. *The Monied Metropolis: New York City and the Consolidation of the American Bourgeoisie, 1850–1896.* New York: Cambridge University Press, 2001.

BELL, THOMAS. *Out of This Furnace.* 1941. Pittsburgh: University of Pittsburgh Press, 1976.

BENSEL, RICHARD FRANKLIN. *The Political Economy of American Industrialization, 1877–1900.* New York: Cambridge University Press, 2000.

BERK, GERALD. *Alternative Tracks: The Constitution of American Industrial Order, 1865–1917.* Baltimore: Johns Hopkins University Press, 1994.

BLACK, WILLIAM. "A Few Days' More Driving," *Harper's New Monthly Magazine,* 70 (1884): 22.

BOBINSKI, GEORGE. *Carnegie Libraries.* Chicago: American Library Association, 1969.

BOYER, M. CHRISTINE. *Manhattan Manners: Architecture and Style, 1850–1900.* New York: Rizzoli, 1985.

BRECHER, JEREMY. *Strike!* Boston: South End Press, 1977.

BRIDGE, JAMES HOWARD. *The Inside History of the Carnegie Steel Company: A Romance of Millions.* 1903. Pittsburgh: University of Pittsburgh Press, 1991.

———. *Millionaires and Grub Street.* New York: Brentano's, 1931.

BRIER, STEVE. "Technological Change at Homestead, 1881–1892," unpublished paper in author's possession.

BRIGNANO, MARY. "Ordinary People, Extraordinary Courage," *Western Pennsylvania History* (2004).

BRODY, DAVID. *Steelworkers in America: The Nonunion Era.* 1960. New York: Harper & Row, 1969.

BROOKS, G. "The Typical American Employer," *Blackstone's Edinburgh Magazine* (1892): 572.

BROWN, MARK M. "Technology and the Homestead Steel Works," *Canal History and Technology Proceeding,* II (1992): 186–205.

BURGESS, GEORGE H, and MILES C. KENNEDY. *Centennial History of The Pennsylvania Railroad Company, 1846–1946.* Pennsylvania Railroad Company, 1949.

BURGOYNE, ARTHUR. *The Homestead Strike of 1892.* 1893. Pittsburgh: University of Pittsburgh Press, 1979.

BUTLER, BENJAMIN F. *Butler's Book.* A. M. Thayer & Co., 1892.

BUTT, ARCHIBALD WILLINGHAM. *Taft and Roosevelt, the Intimate Letters of Archie Butt.* Garden City, NY: Doubleday, Doran & Co., 1930.

CALVERT, MONTE A. "The Allegheny City Cotton Mill Riot of 1848," *Western Pennsylvania Historical Magazine* 46 (1963).

CAMPBELL, JOHN P. "Taft, Roosevelt, and the Arbitration Treaties of 1911," *Journal of American History* 53 (1966): 79–98.

CARNEGIE, ANDREW. *Notes of a Trip Round the World.* New York: privately published, 1879.

———. "As Others See Us," *Fortnightly Review* (1882).

———. *Our Coaching Trip, Brighton to Inverness.* New York: privately published, 1882.

———. *An American Four-in-Hand in Britain.* 1883. New York: Charles Scribner's Sons, 1890.

———. "Remarks of Andrew Carnegie Before the Nineteenth-Century Club upon 'The Aristocracy of the Dollar.' My First Speech in New York Somewhere in the Early Eighties" (1883?).

———. *Round the World.* 1884. New York: Doubleday, Doran, 1933.

———. "The Road to Business Success: A Talk to Young Men." (June 1885), in *EB.*

———. *Triumphant Democracy.* 1886. New York: Charles Scribner's Sons, 1888.

———. "An Employer's View of the Labor Question." *Forum* (April 1886), in *Andrew Carnegie Reader.*

———. "Results of the Labor Struggle," *Forum* (August 1886), in *Andrew Carnegie Reader.*

———. "Bugaboo of Trusts," *North American Review* (February 1889), in *Andrew Carnegie Reader.*

———. "Dedication of the Carnegie Library at the Edgar Thomson Steel Rail Works, Braddock, March 30, 1889: Address to Workingmen."

———. "The Industries of Pennsylvania, address delivered before the Legislature of Pennsylvania in Harrisburg." (April 8, 1889), in *MW,* I.

———. "Wealth," *North American Review* (June 1889), in *Andrew Carnegie Reader.*

———. "Best Fields for Philanthropy," *North American Review* (December 1889), in *Andrew Carnegie Reader.*

———. "Summing Up the Tariff Discussion," *North American Review* (July 1890), in *MW,* I.

———. "Advantages of Poverty," *Nineteenth Century* (March 1891), in *Gospel of Wealth.*

———. "ABC of Money," *North American Review* (June 1891), in *Andrew Carnegie Reader.*

———. *Triumphant Democracy. Revised Edition, Based on the Census of 1890.* New York: Charles Scribner's Sons, 1893.

———. "Anne C. L. Botta" (1894), in *MW,* I.

———. "Presentation of the Carnegie Library to the People with a Description of the Dedicatory Exercises" (November 6, 1895). Reprinted as "The Best Use of Wealth" in *MW,* II.

———. "The Venezuelan Question," *North American Review* (February 1896), in *MW,* II.

———. "How I Served My Apprenticeship," *Youth's Companion* (April 23, 1896).

———. "The Ship of State Adrift," *North American Review* (June 1896).

———. "The Ship of State Adrift II," *North American Review* (October 1896).

———. "Mr. Bryan the Conjurer," *North American Review* (January 1897).

———. "Distant Possessions: The Parting of the Ways," *North American Review* (August 1898), in *Andrew Carnegie Reader.*

———. "From Bobbin-Boy to Millionaire," *Golden Penny* (January 1899).

———. "Americanism Versus Imperialism," *North American Review* (January 1899).

———. "Americanism Versus Imperialism, II," *North American Review* (December 1899).

———. "The South African Question," *North American Review* (December 1899).

———. "Bryan or McKinley? The Presidential Election—Our Duty," *North American Review* (October 1900).

———. *The Gospel of Wealth and Other Timely Essays*, 1901, 1906. Reprinted and edited by Edward C. Kirkland. Cambridge, MA: Harvard University Press, 1965.

———. *The Empire of Business*. 1902. Garden City, NY: Doubleday, Page & Company, 1913.

———. "Confession of Religious Faith" (October 11, 1902), in *MW*, II.

———. "A Rectorial Address, Delivered to the Students in the University of St. Andrews 22 October, 1902," New York: Doubleday, Page & Company, 1903, in *MW*, I.

———. *James Watt*. 1905. Garden City, NY: Doubleday, Page & Company, 1913.

———. "The Negro in America: An Address Delivered before the Philosophical Institution of Edinburgh, 16th October, 1907," Inverness: Robt. Carruthers & Sons, 1907, in *MW*, II.

———. *Problems of To-Day: Wealth—Labor—Socialism*. 1908. Garden City, NY: Doubleday, Page & Company, 1933.

———. "Introduction," *The Roosevelt Policy, Vol. I*. New York: Current Literature Publishing Company, 1908.

———. "The Worst Banking System in the World" (February 5, 1908).

———. "My Experience with, and Views upon, The Tariff," *Century* (March 1908). Reprinted as "Railway Rates and Rebates" in *Andrew Carnegie Reader*.

———. "Armaments and Their Results," London: The Peace Society, 1909.

———. "Speech . . . at the Annual Meeting of the Peace Society, in the Guildhall, London," London: The Peace Society, 1910. Reprinted as "Honor and International Arbitration," in *MW*, II.

———. "A League of Peace" (October 17, 1905). New York: New York Peace Society, 1911, in *MW*, II.

———. "Doctor Golf," *Independent* (June 1911).

———. "Address . . . at the Fourth American Peace Congress, St. Louis, May, 1913," New York: Redfield Brothers, Inc., 1913.

———. "Unveiling of Cremer Bust in the Palace of Peace at the Hague," Dunfermline, 1913.

———. *Autobiography of Andrew Carnegie*. 1920. Boston: Northeastern University Press, 1986.

———. *Miscellaneous Writings of Andrew Carnegie*, 2 vols., ed. Burton Hendrick. Garden City, NY: Doubleday, Doran, 1933.

———. *The Andrew Carnegie Reader*, ed. Joseph Wall. Pittsburgh: University of Pittsburgh, 1992.

CARNEGIE INSTITUTION. *Year Book, 2003–04*. Washington, DC, 2005.

CAROSSO, VINCENT. *The Morgans: Private International Bankers, 1854–1913*. Cambridge, MA: Harvard University Press, 1987.

CHALMERS, PETER. *Historical and Statistical Account of Dunfermline*. Edinburgh, 1844.

CHANDLER, ALFRED D. *The Visible Hand: The Managerial Revolution in American Business*. Cambridge, MA: Harvard University Press, 1977.

CHERNOW, RON. *Titan: The Life of John D. Rockefeller, Sr.* New York: Random House, 1998.

CHUDACOFF, HOWARD. *The Age of the Bachelor: Creating an American Subculture*. Princeton: Princeton University Press, 1999.

CLEMENS, SAMUEL. "The Alphabet Simplified," in *Portable Mark Twain*, ed. Tom Quik. New York: Penguin, 2004.

COCHRAN, THOMAS C. *Railroad Leaders, 1845–1890*. New York: Russell & Russell, 1965.

CONANT, JAMES BRYANT. "Andrew Carnegie as Patron of Learning," in *Andrew Carnegie Centenary, 1835–1935*. New York: Carnegie Corporation of New York, 1935.

CONE, ANDREW. *Petrolia*. New York: D. Appleton, 1870.

COOLING, B. FRANKLIN. *Gray Steel and Blue Water Navy*. Hamden, CT: Archon Books, 1979.

COUVARES, FRANCIS G. *The Remaking of Pittsburgh: Class and Culture in an Industrializing City, 1877–1919*. Albany: State University of New York Press, 1984.

CRAIG, NEVILLE. *History of Pittsburgh.* Pittsburgh: J. H. Mellor, 1851.

CURRIE, DOMINIC J. *The Lauder Legacy, the Life and Times of George Lauder and Lauder College.* Dunfermline: Lauder College, 1999.

CURTISS, GEORGE. *The Industrial Development of Nations.* Vol. II. Binghamton, NY, 1912.

CUTLER, CARL. *Queens of the Western Ocean.* Annapolis: U.S. Naval Institute, 1961.

DAMROSCH, WALTER. *My Musical Life.* New York: Charles Scribner's Sons, 1926.

————. "Recollections of Andrew Carnegie," in *Andrew Carnegie Centenary.* New York: Carnegie Corporation of New York, 1935.

DEMAREST, DAVID, ed. *"The River Ran Red": Homestead 1892.* Pittsburgh: University of Pittsburgh Press, 1992.

DEVINE, T.M. *The Scottish Nation: A History.* New York: Penguin, 1999.

DEVOTO, BERNARD, ed. *Mark Twain in Eruption.* New York: Grosset & Dunlap, 1940.

DIERICKX, MARY. *The Architecture of Literacy: The Carnegie Libraries of New York City.* New York: Cooper Union for the Advancement of Science and Art and the New York City Department of General Services, 1996.

DOLKART, ANDREW S. *Cooper-Hewitt, National Design Museum.* Washington, DC: Smithsonian Institution, 2002.

DREISER, THEODORE. *Newspaper Days,* ed. T. D. Nostwich. Philadelphia: University of Pennsylvania Press, 1991.

DuMONT, ROSEMARY RUHIG. "The Founding of the Carnegie Library of Pittsburgh," in *Carnegie Denied: Communities Rejecting Carnegie Library Construction Grants, 1898–1925,* ed. Robert Sidney Martin. Westport, CT: Greenwood Press, 1993.

DUNCAN, DAVID. *Life and Letters of Herbert Spencer.* Vol. 1. New York: D Appleton & Co., 1908.

DUNLAP, DAVID. *On Broadway: A Journey Uptown Over Time.* New York: Rizzoli, 1990.

DURANT, SAMUEL W. *History of Allegheny Co., Pennsylvania.* Philadelphia: L. H. Everts, 1876.

FABIAN, LARRY. *Andrew Carnegie's Peace Endowment: The Tycoon, the President, and Their Bargain of 1910.* Washington, DC: Carnegie Endowment for International Peace, 1985.

FAIRBURN, WILLIAM ARMSTRONG. *Merchant Sail V.* Center Lovell, Maine: Fairburn Marine educational foundation.

FARQUHAR, A. B. *The First Million the Hardest: An Autobiography,* in collab. with Samuel Crowther. Garden City, NY: Doubleday, 1922.

FITCH, JOHN A. *The Steel Workers.* 1910. Pittsburgh: University of Pittsburgh Press, 1989.

FOX, ARTHUR B. *Pittsburgh During the American Civil War, 1860–1865.* Chicora, PA: Mechling Bookbindery, 2002.

FRASER, STEVE. *Every Man a Speculator: A History of Wall Street in American Life.* New York: HarperCollins, 2005.

GARLAND, HAMLIN. "Homestead and Its Perilous Trades—Impressions of a Visit," *McClure's Magazine* III (1894).

GILDER, ROSAMOND, ed. *Letters of Richard Watson Gilder.* Boston: Houghton Mifflin, 1916.

GILFOYLE, TIMOTHY J. *City of Eros: New York City, Prostitution, and the Commercialization of Sex, 1790–1920.* New York: W. W. Norton, 1992.

GLADSTONE, W.E. "Mr. Carnegie's 'Gospel of Wealth': A Review and a Recommendation," *Nineteenth Century* XXVII (1890).

GLOVER, BILL. "FTL Design: History of Atlantic Cable & Submarine Telegraphy, Cable Timeline: 1850–1900," http://www.atlanticcable.com/Cables/CableTimeLine/index1850.htm.

GOODENOUGH, SIMON. *The Greatest Good Fortune.* Edinburgh: MacDonald, 1985.

GORDON, JOHN STEELE. *A Thread Across the Ocean.* New York: Perennial, 2003.

GREEN, CONSTANCE McLAUGHLIN. *Washington: Village and Capital, 1800–1878.* Princeton: Princeton University Press, 1962.

GREGG, ORMSBY O., ISAAC GREGG, and MOSES F. EATON. *Pittsburgh, her advantageous position and great resources, as a manufacturing and commercial city: embraced in a notice of sale of real estate.* Pittsburgh: Johnson & Stockton. 1845.

GUTMAN, HERBERT. *Work, Culture and Society in Industrializing America.* New York: Vintage, 1977.

HALSEY, FRANCIS WHITING. *American Authors and Their Homes.* New York: James Pott & Co., 1901.

HAMILTON, GAIL. *Biography of James G. Blaine.* Norwich, CT: Henry Bill Publishing Co., 1895.

HAMMER, D. A. *John Morley: Liberal Intellectual in Politics.* London: Oxford University Press, 1968.

HAND-LOOM INQUIRY COMMISSION. *Reports of Assistant Commissioners on hand-loom weavers in several districts of England, Scotland, Ireland, and Continental Europe, 1839–40.* 1839. Shannon: Irish University Press, 1970.

HANSEN, JONATHAN M. *The Lost Promise of Patriotism.* Chicago: University of Chicago Press, 2003.

HARVEY, GEORGE. *Henry Clay Frick: The Man.* 1928. New York: The Frick Collection, 1936.

HATCH, NATHAN. *The Democratization of American Christianity.* New Haven: Yale University Press, 1989.

HENDERSON, EBENEZER. *Annals of Dunfermline.* Glasgow, 1879.

HENDRICK, BURTON. *The Life of Andrew Carnegie.* Garden City, NY: Doubleday, Doran & Co., 1932.

————, and DANIEL HENDERSON. *Louise Whitfield Carnegie: The Life of Mrs. Andrew Carnegie.* New York: Hastings House, 1950.

HENRIETTA, JAMES, et al. *America's History.* Chicago: Dorsey Press, 1987.

HESSEN, ROBERT. *Steel Titan: The Life of Charles M. Schwab.* Pittsburgh: University of Pittsburgh Press, 1975.

HOFSTADTER, RICHARD. *Social Darwinism in American Thought.* Rev. edn. Boston: Beacon Press, 1955.

HOGAN, W. T. *Economic History of the American Iron and Steel Industry.* Lexington, KY: Heath, 1971.

HOLLEY, A.L., and LENOX SMITH. "American Iron and Steel Works. No. XXI. The Works of the Edgar Thomson Steel Company (Limited)," *Engineering* 25 (1878): 295.

HOLLOWAY, LAURA. *Famous American Fortunes.* New York: J. A. Hill & Co., 1889.

"Home and Foreign Gossip," *Harper's Weekly* (1866).

HONAN, PARK. *Matthew Arnold: A Life.* New York: McGraw-Hill, 1981.

INGHAM, JOHN N. *Making Iron and Steel: Independent Mills in Pittsburgh, 1820–1920.* Columbus: Ohio State University Press, 1991.

INGRAM, J. S. *The Centennial Exposition, Described and Illustrated.* Philadelphia: Hubbard Bros., 1876.

JACKSON, ROBERT W. *Rails Across the Mississippi: A History of the St. Louis Bridge.* Urbana: University of Illinois Press, 2001.

JOFFE, ELKHONEN. *Tchaikovsky in America: The Composer's Visit in 1891.* New York: Oxford University Press, 1986.

JOHNSON, WILLIAM G. *Life and Reminiscences from Birth to Manhood of Wm. G. Johnson.* Pittsburgh: Knickerbocker Press, 1902.

JONES, A. *The Revenue Book: Containing the New Tariff of 1846, Together with the Tariff of 1842.* New York: Bell & Gould, 1846.

JONES, THEODORE. *Carnegie Libraries Across America: A Public Legacy.* New York: John Wiley & Sons, 1997.

KAMM, SAMUEL RICHEY. *The Civil War Career of Thomas A. Scott.* Philadelphia, 1940.

KAPLAN, FRED. *The Singular Mark Twain.* New York: Doubleday, 2003.

KILLIKELLY, SARAH. *The History of Pittsburgh: Its Rise and Progress.* Pittsburgh: B. C. & Gordon Montegomery, 1906.

KINARD, AGNES DODDS. *Celebrating the First 100 Years of The Carnegie in Pittsburgh: 1895–1995.* Pittsburgh: 1995.

KIRKLAND, EDWARD. *Dream and Thought in the Business Community, 1860–1900.* Ithaca: Cornell University Press, 1956.

———. *Industry Comes of Age.* 1961. Chicago: Quadrangle, 1967.

KLEIN, MURRAY. *The Life and Legend of Jay Gould.* Baltimore: Johns Hopkins University Press, 1986.

KRAUSE, PAUL. *The Battle for Homestead, 1880–1892: Politics, Culture and Steel.* Pittsburgh: University of Pittsburgh Press, 1992.

KUEHL, WARREN F. *Seeking World Order: The United States and International Organization to 1920.* Nashville, TN: Vanderbilt University Press, 1969.

LAFEBER, WALTER. *The Panama Canal.* New York: Oxford University Press, 1979.

LAGEMANN, ELLEN CONDLIFFE. *The Politics of Knowledge: The Carnegie Corporation, Philanthropy, and Public Policy.* Chicago: University of Chicago Press, 1989.

LAMB, GEORGE H. "The Carnegie Free Library," in *The Unwritten History of Braddock's Field.* Braddock, 1917.

LAMOREAUX, NAOMI R. *The Great Merger Movement in American Business, 1895–1904.* Cambridge: Cambridge University Press, 1985.

LANG, CECIL Y., ed. *The Letters of Matthew Arnold.* 6 vols. Charlottesville: University Press of Virginia, 1996–.

LAVENDER, DAVID. *The Great Pretender.* Garden City, NY: Doubleday & Co., 1970.

LESTER, ROBERT M. *Forty Years of Carnegie Giving.* New York: Charles Scribner's Sons, 1941.

LEVITT, IAN, and CHRISTOPHER SMOUT. *The State of the Scottish Working-Class in 1843: A statistical and spatial enquiry based on the data from the Poor Law Commission Report of 1844.* Edinburgh: Scottish Academic Press, 1979.

LICHT, WALTER. *Working for the Railroads: The Organization of Work in the Nineteenth Century.* Princeton: Princeton University Press, 1983.

LOCKWOOD, CHARLES. *Manhattan Moves Uptown.* Boston: Houghton Mifflin, 1976.

LOTH, DAVID. *Gold Brick Cassie.* New York: Fawcett Publications, 1954.

LUMSDEN, JAMES. *American Memoranda by a Mercantile Man During a Short Tour in the Summer of 1843.* Glasgow: Bell & Bain, 1844.

LYNCH, FREDERICK. "Personal Recollections of Andrew Carnegie" (1920), http://www.xooqi.com.

MCADOO, ELEANOR WILSON, ed. *The Priceless Gift: The Love Letters of Woodrow Wilson and Ellen Axson Wilson.* New York: McGraw-Hill, 1962.

MCCABE, JAMES DABNEY. *Illustrated History of the Centennial Exhibition.* Philadelphia: National Publishing Co., 1876.

MCCULLOUGH, DAVID. *The Johnstown Flood.* 1968. New York: Touchstone, 1987.

———, *The Great Bridge: The Epic Story of the Building of the Brooklyn Bridge.* New York: Simon & Schuster, 1972.

MACKAY, ALEXANDER. *The Western World; or Travels in the United States in 1846–47.* 2nd (1849) edn. Vol. III. New York: Negro University Press, 1968.

MACKIE, J.B. *Andrew Carnegie: His Dunfermline Ties and Benefactions.* Dunfermline, 1916.

MAGNUS, PHILIP. *Gladstone.* New York: Dutton, 1964.

MANNING, CARDINAL, HERMANN ADLER, and HUGH PRICE HUGHES. "Irresponsible Wealth," *Nineteenth Century* XXVII (1890).

Manual of the Public Benefactions of Andrew Carnegie. Washington, DC: Carnegie Endowment for International Peace, 1919.

MARCHAND, C. ROLAND. *The American Peace Movement and Social Reform.* Princeton: Princeton University Press, 1972.

MARTIN, ROBERT SIDNEY, ed. *Carnegie Denied: Communities Rejecting Carnegie Library Construction Grants, 1898–1925.* Wesport, CT: Greenwood Press, 1993.

MASSIE, ROBERT K. *Dreadnought: Britain, Germany, and the Coming of the Great War.* New York: Random House, 1991.

MATTHEWS, H.G.C., ed. *The Gladstone Diaries.* Oxford: Clarendon Press, 1994.

MEINIG, D.W. *The Shaping of America. Vol. 2: Continental America, 1800–1867.* New Haven: Yale University Press, 1993.

MILES, NELSON. *Serving the Republic.* New York: Harper & Bros., 1911.

MILLER, MARGARET CARNEGIE. *Margaret Carnegie Miller Her Journals.* Edited by Linda Thorell Hills. 2000.

MILLER, NATHAN. *Theodore Roosevelt: A Life.* New York: William Morrow, 1992.

Miller's New York as It Is. New York: J. Miller, 1866.

MISA, THOMAS J. *A Nation of Steel: The Making of Modern America, 1865–1925.* Baltimore: The Johns Hopkins University Press, 1995.

"Mr. Carnegie's Tour Through Devon," *Pall Mall Gazette,* in *New York-Daily Tribune* (1884).

MONTGOMERY, DAVID. *The Fall of the House of Labor.* New York: Cambridge University Press, 1987.

MORLEY, JOHN. *Recollections.* Vol. II. New York: Harper & Bros., 1917.

MORRISON, THOMAS. *Heddekashun and Handication.* Dunfermline: William Liddell, 1834.

MURPHEY, HERMON K. "The Northern Railroads and the Civil War," *Mississippi Valley Historical Review 5* (1918): 331–32.

MURRAY, NORMAN. *The Scottish Hand Loom Weavers, 1790–1840, a Social History.* Edinburgh: John Donald, 1978.

NELSON, DANIEL. *Managers and Workers: Origins of the New Factory System in the United States, 1880–1920.* Madison: University of Wisconsin Press, 1975.

NEVINS, ALAN. *The War for the Union.* New York: Charles Scribner's Sons, 1959.

"New Union Pacific Directory, The," *Railroad Gazette* II (1871).

O'CONNER, HARVEY. *Mellon's Millions.* New York: John Day Co., 1933.

OGDEN, E.D. *Tariff, or, Rates of Duties Payable on Goods, Wares, and Merchandise.* New York: Rich & Loutrel, 1840.

O'TOOLE, PATRICIA. *When Trumpets Call: Theodore Roosevelt After the White House.* New York: Simon & Schuster, 2005.

PALMER, COURTLANDT. *The Nineteenth Century Club of New York: Shall Similar Associations Become General?* London: William Reeves (1887).

PEEL, J.D.Y. *Herbert Spencer: The Evolution of a Sociologist.* New York: Basic Books, 1971.

PENNSYLVANIA RAILROAD COMPANY. "Sixth Annual Report to the Stockholders," 1853.

———. "Twelfth Annual Report to the Stockholders," 1859.

———. *Report of the Investigating Committee of the Pennsylvania Railroad Company.* Philadelphia: Allen, Lane & Scott Printing House, 1874.

PEPER, GEORGE. "The Apple Tree Gang," *Golf* (1988).

PEYSER, ETHEL. *The House That Music Built: Carnegie Hall.* New York: Robert M. McBride, 1936.

POND, ARTHUR, AND SAMUEL T. MOORE, eds. *They Told Barron.* New York: Harper & Bros., 1930.

Poor Law Inquiry Commission for Scotland. Appendix, Part One, "Minutes of Evidence." Edinburgh, 1844.

PRINGLE, HENRY F. *The Life and Times of William Howard Taft.* 2 vols. Hamden, CT: Archon Books, 1964.

PULLING, SR. ANNE FRANCES. *Around Cresson and the Alleghenies.* Dover, NH: Arcadia, 1997.

REA, TOM. *Bone Wars: The Excavation and Celebrity of Andrew Carnegie's Dinosaur.* Pittsburgh: University of Pittsburgh Press, 2001.

REID, J.D. "Andrew Carnegie," *Railroad Gazette* II (1870).

———. *Telegraph in America. Its Founders, Promoters, and Noted Men, The.* New York: Derby Brothers, 1879.

ROCKEFELLER, JOHN D. *Random Reminiscences of Men and Events.* New York: Doubleday, 1909.

ROCKEFELLER, NANCY CARNEGIE. *The Carnegies and Cumberland Island.* 1993.

ROGERS, DANIEL. *The Work Ethic in Industrial America, 1850–1920.* Chicago: University of Chicago Press, 1978.

Roosevelt Policy. Introduction by Andrew Carnegie. New York: Current Literature Publishing, 1908.

ROOSEVELT, THEODORE. *Letters,* ed. Elting E. Morison. Vol. VII. Cambridge, MA: Harvard University Press, 1951–54.

St. Nicholas Hotel; Its Plan and Arrangements. New York: Barton & Sons (1856).

SANDERS, ELIZABETH. *Roots of Reform: Farmers, Workers and the American State, 1877–1917.* Chicago: University of Chicago Press, 1999.

SANGER, MARTHA FRICK SYMINGTON. *Henry Clay Frick: An Intimate Portrait.* New York: Abbeville Press, 1998.

SARMIENTO, DOMINGO FAUSTINO. *Travels in the United States in 1847,* ed. Michael Aaron Rockland. Princeton: Princeton University Press, 1970.

SCHICKEL, RICHARD. *The World of Carnegie Hall.* New York: Julian Messner, 1960.

SHAW, LORD OF DUNFERMLINE. *Letters to Isabel.* New York: George H. Doran Co., n.d.

SHAW, RONALD. *Erie Water West.* Lexington: University of Kentucky Press, 1966.

SIMPSON, ERIC. *The Auld Grey Toun: Dunfermline in the Time of Andrew Carnegie, 1835–1919.* Dunfermline: Carnegie Dunfermline Trust, 1987.

SINCLAIR, UPTON. *The Jungle.* 1905. New York: Signet Classics. 1960.

SPENCER, HERBERT. *Social Statics.* London: John Chapman, 1851.

———. *An Autobiography.* Vol. II. New York: D. Appleton & Co., 1904.

———. *First Principles.* 5th London edn. New York: A. L. Burt Co., n.d.

STEAD, WILLIAM T. *Mr. Carnegie's Conundrum: £40,000,000: What Shall I Do with It?* London: Review of Reviews, 1900.

———. "Mr. Carnegie as I Knew Him," *Christian Endeavor World* (1902).

STEFFENS, LINCOLN. *The Shane of Cities.* 1904. New York: Hill & Wang, 1957.

STERN, ROBERT A.M., et al. *New York 1880.* New York: Monacelli Press, 1999.

———. *New York 1900.* New York: Rizzoli, 1983.

STOVER, JOHN. *American Railroads.* 2nd edn. Chicago: University of Chicago Press, 1997.

STOWE, WILLIAM W. *Going Abroad: European Travel in Nineteenth-Century American Culture.* Princeton: Princeton University Press, 1994.

STROUSE, JEAN. *Morgan: American Financier.* New York: Random House, 1999.

TARR, JOEL A. "Infrastructure and City-Building," in Samuel P. Hayes, ed., *City at the Point: Essays on the Social History of Pittsburgh.* Pittsburgh: University of Pittsburgh, 1989.

TEMIN, PETER. *Iron and Steel in Nineteenth-Century America, an Economic Inquiry.* Cambridge, MA: MIT Press, 1964.

THAYER, WILLIAM ROSCOE, ed. *The Life and Letters of John Hay.* Vol. II. Boston: Houghton Mifflin, 1915.

THOMPSON, ROBERT LUTHER. *Wiring a Continent: The History of the Telegraph Industry in the United States, 1832–1866.* Princeton: Princeton University Press, 1947.

THOMSON, DANIEL. *The Weaver's Craft: Being a History of the Weaver's Incorporation of Dunfermline.* Paisley: A. Gardner, 1903.

THOMPSON, E.P. *The Making of the English Working Class.* New York: Vintage, 1966.

THURSTON, GEORGE. *Pittsburgh as It Is.* Pittsburgh: W. S. Haven, 1857.

———. *Pittsburgh and Allegheny in the Centennial Year.* Pittsburgh: Anderson & Son, 1876.

TOCQUEVILLE, ALEXIS DE. *Democracy in America,* ed. Philip Bradley. New York: Vintage, 1945.

TOKER, FRANKLIN. *Pittsburgh: An Urban Portrait.* Pittsburgh: University of Pittsburgh Press, 1986.

Traveler's Official Guide of the Railways. Philadelphia, 1870.

TROLLOPE, ANTHONY. *North America.* New York: Knopf, 1951.

Trow's New York City Directory. New York: J. F. Trow, 1870.

TURNER, GEORGE EDGAR. *Victory Rode the Rails.* Westwood, CT: Greenwood Press, 1972.

U.S. HOUSE OF REPRESENTATIVES. *Report of the Select Committee of the House of Representatives, appointed under the Resolution of January 6, 1873 to make inquiry into the affairs of the Union Pacific Railroad Company.* Washington, D.C.: Government Printing Office. 1873.

———. *Report on the Committee Appointed to Investigate the Railroad Riots in July, 1877.* Harrisburg, 1878.

U.S. SENATE COMMITTEE ON EDUCATION AND LABOR, testimony of Jay Gould. *Report upon the Relations between Labor and Capital.* Washington, D.C.: Government Printing Office. 1885.

U.S. WAR DEPARTMENT. *The War of the Rebellion: A Compilation of the Official Records of the Union and Confederate Armies.* Washington, D.C.: Government Printing Office, 1880, 1901.

USSELMAN, STEVEN W. *Regulating Railroad Innovation: Business, Technology, and Politics in America, 1840–1920.* New York: Cambridge University Press, 2002.

WALL, JOSEPH FRAZIER. *Andrew Carnegie.* Pittsburgh: University of Pittsburgh Press, 1989.

———. *Skibo.* New York: Oxford University Press, 1984.

WARD, JAMES A. *J. Edgar Thomson, Master of the Pennsylvania.* Westport, CT: Greenwood Press, 1980.

WARNER, DONALD. *The Idea of Continental Union.* Lexington: University of Kentucky Press, 1960.

WARREN, KENNETH. *The American Steel Industry, 1850–1970, a Geographical Interpretation.* London: Oxford University Press, 1973.

———. *Triumphant Capitalism: Henry Clay Frick and the Industrial Transformation of America.* Pittsburgh: University of Pittsburgh Press, 1996.

———. *Wealth, Waste, and Alienation: Growth and Decline in the Connellsville Coke Industry.* Pittsburgh: University of Pittsburgh Press, 2001.

WASHINGTON, BOOKER T. *Up from Slavery.* 1901. New York: Penguin, 1986.

WEBER, THOMAS. *The Northern Railroads in the Civil War, 1861–1865.* New York: King's Crown Press, 1952.

WHITE, ANDREW DICKSON. *Autobiography of Andrew Dickson White.* Vol. 1. New York: The Century Co., 1905.

WHITE, RICHARD. "Information Markets, and Corruption: Transcontinental Railroads in the Gilded Age," *Journal of American History* (June 2003): 19–43.

WILSON, ALEXANDER. *The Chartist Movement in Scotland.* Manchester: Manchester University Press, 1970.

WILSON, ERASMUS, ed. *Standard History of Pittsburgh, Pennsylvania.* Chicago: H. R. Cornell & Co., 1898.

WILSON, WOODROW. *The Papers of Woodrow Wilson,* ed. Arthur Link. Princeton: Princeton University Press, 1966–94.

YOUMANS, EDWARD L., ed. *Herbert Spencer on the Americans and the Americans on Herbert Spencer.* New York: Appleton, 1883.

ZIMMERMAN, WARREN. *First Great Triumph.* New York: Farrar, Straus & Giroux, 2002.

ACKNOWLEDGMENTS

Members of the Carnegie family generously offered me family stories as well as letters, papers, travel advice, and plain good times. I am especially grateful to Linda T. Hills and her husband Harold, Kenneth Miller, Margaret Thomson, and to William and Katrina Thomson.

One of the first persons I contacted on deciding to write this book was Vartan Gregorian, the president of the Carnegie Corporation of New York. He offered his encouragement then and has continued to do so since. I thank him also for directing me toward the treasure trove of Home Trust Company papers that included Carnegie's prenuptial and citizenship documents and are now part of the Carnegie Corporation of New York archives at Columbia University.

Janny Scott put me in touch with members of her family, including Morehead Kennedy, Warwick Scott Wheeler, and H.D.S. Greenway, who provided me with some hitherto unseen correspondence between Carnegie and Tom A. Scott, his first mentor and business partner.

One of the joys of this project was the opportunity to spend time in Scotland. Nora Rundell, chief executive of the Carnegie Dunfermline and Hero Fund Trusts, not only arranged for my visits to Dunfermline, but also responded to dozens of requests for information over the past years. Lorna Owers, manager of the Carnegie Birthplace Museum in Dunfermline, was a gracious guide to the materials there. Andrew, 11th Earl of Elgin and 14th Earl of Kilmardin, opened his private family archives for me and his insights into Scottish history and the Carnegie family's arrival and early years in Fife. I profited greatly from corresponding with Eric Simpson and A. J. Campbell, historians of Dunfermline and Fife. Angus McLaren showed me around Skibo, Shirley and Ian Somerville through Rannoch Lodge, Alain Angelil through Cluny.

I have been blessed by a number of inventive and diligent research assistants, among them Morgan Arenson, Julia Bell, Kris Burrell, Norma Hamm, Dan Lewis, William Menaker, Daniel Nasaw, Peter Nasaw, Valerie Yoshiye Diane Sakimura, Joseph Sramek, Heather Velez, Martin Woessner. As in the past, my chief research assistant was my mother, Beatrice Nasaw, who was available to find answers to the weirdest questions I could throw at her. When the research phase of the project was finished, she shifted gears and became my final proofreader.

Brendan O'Malley, a gifted editor and graduate student, read the final manuscript, then the galleys, and saved me from committing numerous errors, large and small.

There can be no better environment to work on a project such as this than the CUNY Graduate Center. I thank former president Frances Degen Horowitz for her support and current president Bill Kelly for his encouragement and wise counsel on any number of topics, from Mahlsticks to dinosaurs. I am grateful to Aoibheann Sweeney and Michael Washburn for their good humor and good grammar. As always, I learned a great deal from my graduate students. My colleagues in the Ph.D. program in history have been generous of their time, their libraries, and their opinions. I am specially grateful to Joshua Brown, Martin Burke, Jack Diggins, Joshua Freeman, Thomas Kessner, and James Oakes. Steve Brier read and commented on an early version of the manuscript and saved me from committing some grievous errors of interpretation.

I thank Christopher Baer of the Hagley Museum and Library for sharing with me his inexhaustible knowledge of the Pennsylvania Railroad. Author Richard Gachot provided me with materials on Henry Phipps. Architectural historian Christopher Gray helped me understand how Fifth Avenue was laid out at the turn of the twentieth century. Paul Krause, whose book on Homestead remains a model of research and scholarship, consulted with me on Homestead and the Pittsburgh labor movement. Peter Landau, the historian of St. Andrew's Golf Club at Hastings-on-Hudson, answered my questions and sent me materials on the club. Jeff Madrick helped me convert nineteenth-century dollars into today's currency. Edward Muller of the University of Pittsburgh shared a manuscript on Pittsburgh city planning. Chuck Sabel of Columbia University introduced me to another way of looking at nineteenth-century industrial capitalism. Architectural historian Franklin Toker provided expert advice on Pittsburgh architecture. I am grateful to Steve Fraser and David Rosner for their assistance.

No book of this sort can ever be written without the dogged assistance of the unsung heroes of the scholarly world, its librarians and archivists. I would like to thank Michael Adams and Beth Posner at the CUNY Graduate Center, Jennie Benford at Carnegie-Mellon, Michael Dabrishus at the University of Pittsburgh, Gino Francesconi and Robert Hudson at Carnegie Hall, Jane Gorjevsky at Columbia University, Oliver House at the New Bodleian Library at Oxford University, Julie Ludwig at the Frick Collection in New York City, Greg Priore at the Oliver Room at Carnegie Library of Pittsburgh, Gayle Richardson at The Huntington Library, William Stingone, formerly at Columbia University, now at the New York Public Library, and the staff of the Western Pennsylvania Historical Society in Pittsburgh.

At Penguin Press, Liza Darnton and Alex Lane saw the book through the magnificent final stages of production. Alex, in particular, did a magnificent job in getting me to meet my deadlines.

This book would literally not have been written without Ann Godoff. She suggested the subject, agreed to edit as well as publish it, and with enthusiasm, wisdom, and no small degree of wit, saw it through to completion, improving it every step along the way. I am enormously grateful to her.

I am also appreciative of the support of my agent, Andrew Wylie.

The one person who has been indispensable in this project—from first to last—has been Dinitia Smith. I cannot and will never be able to thank her enough.

INDEX